# THE AMERICAN WAY OF LIFE

# The American Way of Life

## AN INTRODUCTION TO THE STUDY OF CONTEMPORARY SOCIETY

by

**HARRY ELMER BARNES, Ph.D.**

and

**OREEN M. RUEDI, Ph.D.**

Associate Professor of Sociology,
Southwest Missouri State College

## SECOND EDITION

GREENWOOD PRESS, PUBLISHERS
WESTPORT, CONNECTICUT

*Copyright 1942, 1950 by Prentice-Hall, Inc.*

Reprinted with the permission
of Prentice-Hall, Inc., Englewood Cliffs, New Jersey

First Greenwood Reprinting 1971

Library of Congress Catalogue Card Number 72-138200

SBN 8371-5553-3

Printed in the United States of America

*To*
**WILLOUGHBY CYRUS WATERMAN**
*and*
**NORMA PAUL RUEDI**

# Preface

The first edition of *The American Way of Life* was mainly a condensation of the senior author's *Society in Transition, Social Institutions,* and a still unpublished manuscript on leading socio-economic systems. This new edition is not such a book. It has been searchingly revised and drastically rewritten, mainly by the senior author, and considerably expanded throughout. It may be regarded as a book essentially independent of the senior author's previous works and capable of standing on its own merits. At the same time, the cordial reception of the original edition has convinced the publisher and the authors that those teachers who are likely to use this book desire most of all the same general type of subject matter and organization of material brought down to date, not only in factual content, but also in perspective and general frame of reference. This is just what the authors have sought to do.

Broadly speaking, the general content and organization of the earlier book have been retained, but the subject matter and interpretations have been recast in terms of the postwar world instead of the terminal stages of the New Deal era when it was originally planned and written. The world of 1940 is now mainly behind us, for better or worse, and we are entering a new era of human experience.

This edition, as well as the original, was composed on the basic assumption that a useful and interesting introductory textbook in sociology should restrict itself mainly to presenting the various phases of social life and experience, with no more abstract theory than is required to bring out the sociological significance of the facts presented. The authors believe that Part II of this book, together with occasional interpretations interspersed throughout the volume, provide all the theoretical material needed in an introductory text in sociology.

The authors selected the informational social data that constitute the bulk of this book in the belief that contemporary American materials are more cogent and illuminating than those drawn from the social life of the Eskimos, Hottentots, Zulus, or Bushmen. Those who disagree have many manuals at their disposal in the textbooks that seem to prefer to illustrate sociological principles by the life and customs of primitive peoples rather than by those of Americans of the mid-century.

The concept of cultural lag, broadly conceived, remains the guiding principle of the social theory in this book. The authors have par-

vii

ticularly stressed one aspect or phase of cultural lag—the fact that the simple, personal primary groups, which provided most social experience and shaped personality down to recent decades, have been undermined or swept away entirely. The attempt to stagger precipitately from a rural-township perspective to the vision of a United Nations is likely to fail disastrously unless guided by wider experience and a body of social theory as inclusive in concepts and attitudes as the facts of our day. Cultural lag is but one of several organizational themes that might have been employed in preparing this book; its use here by no means precludes the classroom application of other interpretations to the material here presented.

Pedagogical improvements have been provided through topical subheadings in the text, revision of chapter summaries, and the placing of chapter bibliographies immediately after each chapter. The bibliographies have been expanded and brought down to date. Many new and up-to-date pictures have been provided, especially in the chapter dealing with prisons.

Inasmuch as virtually the whole range of contemporary domestic and world problems is dealt with in this book, there are a number of opinions expressed which lack complete documentation. For these, which are stated with customary forthrightness, the senior author takes full responsibility. While such opinions are shared by a number of very eminent historians and social scientists, it is neither expected nor desired that all teachers using the book will share them all. But this fact should encourage dissenters to use the volume.

Nothing could be more dull and intellectually stultifying to both the teaching force and the student body than to use a textbook with which all are in enthusiastic and universal agreement throughout. As that great medieval teacher, Peter Abelard, well put the matter, it is only by raising questions and arousing dissent that we can ever discover truth. The senior author's most stimulating teacher, James Harvey Robinson, used to tell us that the only person really worth listening to or reading is one with whom we disagree: if a statement with which we agree is correct, then we are wasting our time with something we already know, while if it is misleading, agreement only confirms our prejudices and erroneous views. The desirable classroom attitude was perfectly expressed long ago by Cicero when he wrote: "We who search for truths must be prepared both to refute without prejudice and to be refuted without resentment."

In whatever course it is used, the book will be favorably regarded mainly by those who prefer to present to beginners in social science clear and well-organized factual information, adequately supported by basic theoretical principles.

HARRY ELMER BARNES

*Cooperstown, New York*

# Contents

ix

# THE AMERICAN WAY OF LIFE

# PART I

# The Historical Background

## CHAPTER I

## Cultural Lag in the Twentieth Century: Institutional Windmills in an Age of Atomic Energy

### Society in an "Era of Change"

**The contemporary era a period of rapid social change.** The era in which we are now living is variously described as the Power Age, the Empire of Machines, the Age of Speed, the Era of Change, and, more recently, the Atomic Age. All these phrases aptly characterize our age, but one carries more significance, perhaps, than the rest, namely, the Era of Change. Human society is now undergoing the most sweeping transformation in its history. The entire pattern of living is being transformed at an unbelievably rapid rate.

That modern society is challenged by many serious social, economic, and political problems is recognized by everyone. Fewer persons, however, are aware that these problems chiefly reflect the rapid transformation which the material basis of society is undergoing. People commonly believe that social change always comes gradually and that life differs but little from one generation to another. This was true in earlier centuries, but in the past hundred years the material aspects of our culture—the physical basis of civilization—have been revolutionized to such a degree that a contemporary of Abraham Lincoln would be more at home in ancient Rome than in present-day Washington. A healthy society requires that there shall be comparable readjustments in the social basis of human living so that we may make the best possible use of our new mechanical advantages.

1

**Importance of the Industrial Revolution.** The basic reasons for the numerous and far-reaching changes of our time are to be found in man's new methods of earning a living, a result of the Industrial Revolution, which commenced nearly two centuries ago. Before that time, industry and agriculture had changed only slightly for hundreds, indeed thousands, of years. Farming, carried on by simple, time-honored methods, was man's major occupation. There was relatively little manufacturing, and this was done mainly in homes by manual labor, with simple tools. Commerce and trade were not highly developed, for each locality was nearly self-sufficient and required few supplies from outside. Consequently, social life was simple and relatively static, governed mainly by custom and tradition. After about 1750, however, a series of amazing mechanical inventions took place which revolutionized the methods of producing food and goods and, consequently, the entire pattern of human life. These inventions had a long background in the way of improved mechanical ingenuity, beginning in the twelfth century. But their cumulative effect did not become truly revolutionary until after the middle of the eighteenth century.

The epoch-making inventions that we shall describe more fully in the next chapter produced power-driven machinery, self-propelled vehicles, and ocean-going steamships. Farming changed from a simple occupation, undertaken with crude tools like an ox-drawn wooden plow, to a highly intricate enterprise, requiring complicated machinery, swift means of transportation, and a knowledge of chemistry, biology, and related sciences. Manufacturing, once conducted in the home and small shops, moved to gigantic factories with complex and expensive machinery, requiring the supervision of experts versed in chemistry, physics, and engineering. Dwellings changed from simple, one- or two-story frame buildings into many-storied apartment houses of steel, brick, and concrete. Railroads, ocean liners, automobiles, trucks, and airplanes replaced wagons and sailing ships. The telephone, the telegraph, radios, movies, public mails, and modern newspaper presses provided far swifter and more extensive communication than word-of-mouth, hand-printed papers, and a slow, inefficient, semi-private postal system. The Industrial Revolution even penetrated into homes; the vacuum cleaner displaced the broom, electric lights the kerosene lamp, and the washing machine the tub and scrubbing board. Commerce and trade developed on an ever-expanding scale, even between distant corners of the earth, while individuals—once confined mainly to their parishes—became accustomed to traveling thousands of miles each year.

**Cultural lag.** Although mankind has become adapted to the new tempo of living and has accepted and exploited scientific and technological achievements, it has failed to adjust the social structure—economic, political, and social ideas and institutions—to the new pattern of material culture. Indeed, men are trying to manage the

Our cave mind in the Machine Age: the chief cause of cultural lag.

new world of machines with the ideas and institutions of horse-and-buggy days and, in some cases, of the Stone Age. This failure to modernize social ideas and institutions in conformity to our scientific knowledge and mechanical equipment has produced the serious "cultural lag" that confronts our society and causes most of our social problems.

**What we mean by Culture.** By the term *culture,* as we shall use it, for the most part, in this book, is meant the material, social, and intellectual setting in which we live. We may divide our culture into two types: material and non-material. The former consists of such things as factories, railroads, automobiles, paved roads, electric washing machines, brick buildings, and motion pictures. It also includes certain scientific activities, such as medical and surgical practices, synthetic chemistry, and improved methods for growing wheat. In brief, our material culture is composed of our knowledge and tools for coping with the physical environment. Our non-material culture consists of our knowledge and means for living together with our fellows; among its aspects are family life, democratic government, capitalism, property rights, education, art, and religion. Culture in this sense is the social setting and intellectual content of our civilization.

The persistence of the common or popular use of the word *culture* inevitably introduces a confusion of terminology that we cannot avoid wholly in this book. We have just described the sociological meaning of culture, but the popular conception of the term is that it means certain so-called higher aspects of man's life. A "cultured" person is one who possesses a good education and is either talented in, or highly appreciative of, the fine arts, such as painting, music, and literature.

Since we have to deal with these matters occasionally in the course of this book, and because there is no other well-known term to apply to them, we must from time to time lapse into the popular use of the term *culture.* If, however, the student pays attention to the context, it will be apparent when we are referring to culture in its scientific, sociological implications, as the sum total of all our material and social equipment and surroundings, and when we are reverting to the popular use of the word as descriptive of the arts and learning.

**The nature of institutions.** An institution may be defined as an accepted social arrangement for carrying on a particular phase of human life. A public educational system, for example, is an institution which represents a definite arrangement for instructing boys and girls, rather than leaving their instruction haphazardly to their parents, friends, or anyone else with whom they might come in contact. The family is a social institution, accepted by society as the normal way in which a man and his wife and children live together. A state legislature is a political institution, established so that voters of a state may govern themselves through their elected representatives. Capitalism is our primary economic institution to-day—an arrangement whereby private individuals, rather than the government or the workers as a group, own, control, and operate factories, stores, mines, railroads, and the like.

Our non-material culture consists of such institutions or social arrangements as these for guiding and controlling the various phases of human life. The expression *cultural lag*, mentioned above, refers chiefly to the fact that in modern times changes in economic, political, and social relationships have lagged far behind advances in science and technology, but it also includes the fact that some institutions change less rapidly than others, thus promoting institutional maladjustment.

**Historical reasons for institutional inertia.** Why is there such determined opposition to social reform and the readjustment of our institutions? The reasons are numerous and diverse; we can list only a few of them here.

We may first look at the historical reasons for the failure of our institutions to change as rapidly as our material culture. Many believe that our social institutions change more slowly now than ever before. This is not true. Their rate of change is relatively rapid compared to that of ancient and medieval times. The explanation lies in the fact that scientific discoveries and mechanical advances are taking place at an unprecedented speed today. Hence, even though institutions change more rapidly than in olden times, they have not been able to keep pace with the amazing progress in the scientific and mechanical realms.

As a matter of fact, institutions changed more rapidly than ever before in human history from about 1600 to 1800. Feudalism was replaced by the national state. Manorialism and the guild system were ousted by the rise of capitalism and the increased importance of commerce and manufacturing. There were many important changes in law, education, and religion. Most of these changes were produced by the rising business or middle class. By 1800, leaders of this class believed that they had produced an ideal society. Hence, they reversed their previous attitude toward social change and tried to maintain institutions as they were about 1800. But, at the same time, they felt that their prosperity would be increased by encouraging scientific discoveries and mechanical inventions. Therefore, from about 1800 to the present time, the most powerful class in western civilization did all in its power to resist social change and to encourage and assist developments in science and invention.

**Inertia in human nature and social tradition.** In addition to these historical factors in the picture of institutional stagnation, there are a number of elements in the very nature of man and social organization which either resist social change or make for very gradual readjustments in social life, elements which offset the popular enthusiasm for scientific progress and mechanical advances. We may now look into some of these factors.

There is a large heritage of primitive superstition in our mental outlook. While we may no longer believe that the gods will punish us if we alter our customs ever so slightly, many people still have a conviction that customs are sanctified and that harmful results may follow any important changes in our institutional patterns. Social changes still beget nervous apprehension, if not panic.

Persons are often ignorant of the fact that many of our institutions are inadequate to the needs of our day. They have been taught to worship our social institutions and to regard them as beneficent and eternal, like the law of gravitation. Such people may be inadequately educated, or they may have been shielded from any contact with the social sciences, which could have supplied them with information about the workings of our institutions.

Superstition and ignorance are often joined to a natural conservatism in persons of middle and old age. Since the custody of our social institutions is handed over mainly to these age groups, it is not surprising that there is organized and persistent opposition to social readjustment.

The inherent indolence of man is also a factor in opposing social change. What has long been customary becomes habitual to us. We adjust our lives to certain habit patterns, and existence becomes simpler and easier. To alter these patterns would require us to readjust our modes of behavior. All this demands both energy and courage, qualities with which many members of the human race are not richly endowed.

Our family upbringing, the influence of church and school, and many of our daily experiences incline us to worship the past and its ways and to fear and hate the new and untried. The new may seem dangerous, difficult, and even indecent. We naturally recoil from it.

Finally, to all the obstacles to social change growing out of ignorance, superstition, indolence, and habit is added the opposition of those who stand to gain, or who at least think they will benefit, from keeping things as they are. The ruling vested interests of any age, be they priests, warriors, feudal lords, businessmen, or proletarian leaders, vehemently oppose changes which threaten their dominion over the social system.

## Some Effects of Cultural Lag on Society

**Poverty amidst potential plenty.** The nature of cultural lag and the problems to which it has given rise can best be understood by a brief survey of some examples. In succeeding chapters, we shall study more thoroughly the problems mentioned here.

The Industrial Revolution, as we noted, introduced our modern factory system and other great advances in economic life, making it possible to produce a far greater amount of goods than ever before. Indeed, our farms and factories can now produce enough food, clothing, and other articles to provide every person in the United States with a decent standard of living. For the first time in history, it is possible to eliminate poverty and want. Yet, in America today, more than one-half of the families are "ill-fed, ill-housed, ill-clothed." Two-thirds of our children are now being born and reared in the most underprivileged third of our population. At times, tons of food are allowed to rot and hundreds of factories to stand idle while millions of persons are in need of both food and clothing.

Why do we have poverty amidst plenty? The answer is mainly cultural lag. Before the Industrial Revolution, most families and communities were self-sufficient, and there was relatively little commerce and trade. Today, our economic system is a highly complicated organization of factories, stores, railroads, business firms, shipping companies, and the like. No longer is any nation, let alone a family or small community, self-sufficient. Every individual depends upon the labor of thousands of others for the necessities of life. Commerce is complicated and large-scale and extends to the far corners of the earth. Yet, we persist in trying to manage this complex economic structure by economic ideals and social arrangements which were designed for the simple world of two centuries ago. It is little wonder, then, that the economic system functions inefficiently. The presence of cultural lag in our economic thinking is shown by the fact that some of the very businessmen who are eager to introduce new machines in their factories often bitterly oppose improvements in our economic institutions which might enable society to distribute more efficiently the goods and services it can now produce so abundantly.

**Political lag.** In the field of government, examples of cultural lag are so common that it is difficult to choose among them. One often hears political speakers praise the "wisdom of the Founding Fathers" and vow to "stick to the tried and true." These men would be embarrassed if they had to drive along the streets in 1925 automobiles, yet they apply and defend political ideals and practices dating from the days of the stagecoach and pony express.

For example, the founders of our democracy believed that any untrained citizen is capable of holding public office and successfully dealing with the problems of government. This was true to a greater degree when the United States was a small agricultural nation of little importance in world affairs. It is far from true today, however, for our country has developed into a vast industrialized nation, whose internal affairs and relations with foreign countries are highly complex and extremely difficult to understand, let alone administer. Yet we persist in the idea that any honest citizen is fit to hold any office, no matter how complicated its duties. When a man desires to have a bathroom faucet repaired, a sparkplug replaced, or a tooth pulled, he goes to an expert. Yet, in the much more difficult problems of social, economic, and political life he is completely satisfied with the opinions of the man on the street. He wants a "brain trust" to design his automobile but not to plan his government.

**Legal inertia.** Our laws, the rules by which society is supposed to be governed, are so out-of-date in many instances that they are ludicrous. In one southern state, for example, it is still a formal capital offense to miss church three Sundays in a row. Thousands of such laws, some still enforced, clutter up our statute books because we are willing to change our machines but not our social ideas.

Our system of jury trial and many of our ideas of justice date from the Middle Ages or early modern times. Yet, we employ them to handle the problems of twentieth-century civilization. Under our jury system, "twelve good men and true" are given power to judge guilt or innocence in a manner almost as unscientific as the old custom of thrusting the arms of an accused person into boiling water. How, for example, can a jury made up of housewives, mechanics, and gas-station attendants come to an intelligent decision in a case involving such highly complicated matters as the sanity of an accused person or the management of a large corporation?

Our prisons are still operated, despite recent attempts to bring them up to date, on the ancient principle of punishing the criminal to avenge society. Capital punishment, which still exists in most states, is a relic of Old Testament days. Far too little attention is paid to the ways in which criminals may be reformed and enabled to lead a law-abiding existence.

The traditional types of crime, such as robbery and burglary, constitute no more than five or ten per cent of our present enormous crime bill. Yet we go on discussing crime as though these offenses were the core of the crime problem. Not only do we have new and far more serious types of crime, but we also find ourselves all but helpless to deal with modern organized crime and racketeering because we have failed to adapt our laws and police systems to cope with them.

**The lag in education.** The cultural lag in our educational system is strikingly seen in the contrast between the ultra-modern buildings which house our schools and the antiquity of their course of study. Despite impressive advances in our civilization, a large part of our curriculum dates from the Middle Ages and even from ancient Greece and Rome. Emphasis is placed on subjects such as higher mathematics, Latin, foreign languages, and literature, which have little value as training for understanding modern life. Only since the first world war have educators begun to tackle the problem of training youth for careers in the modern industrial world and democratic society, and instruction in crafts and other vocational subjects is still inadequately provided. As a result of this cultural lag in education hundreds of thousands of young people graduate each year from our high schools and colleges unprepared to earn their liveli-hood, while our factories and businesses lack machinists and skilled workers. Equally deplorable is the fact that not enough time and attention are given to the so-called social studies—history, economics, political science, sociology, and the like—to enable those who come out of our school system to understand and cope with the economic, political, and social problems that face the nation.

**The lag in medical care.** Medical science has accomplished miracles in the past century. Improvements in surgical methods, new cures for disease, the introduction of public health programs, and developments in sanitary engineering have saved hundreds of thousands of lives. But, despite this, thousands of persons in the United States still suffer from unnecessary illness, and over 300,000 die each year because they cannot afford good medical care. Private medical practice is the accepted procedure by which we have always sought to bring doctor and patient together, and we seem unwilling to change it. Doctors are enthusiastic about new methods for treat-ing disease, but many oppose new arrangements for making medical care available to more people. In short, medical science is amazingly impressive and up-to-date and is improving rapidly, whereas medical care has not changed in principle since the days of the horse-and-buggy doctor who prepared for practice by reading archaic and un-reliable medical books for a few months in the office of another ill-trained physician.

**Reader interest.** What does the public like to read in newspapers? Does it get excited about honest discussions of current problems or news about important discoveries in science? Unfortunately, it does not. The average person is much more interested in crime, sex, and sports. The communication of information has progressed from the foot messenger and pony express stage to that of the modern newspaper. Radio news comes almost instantly from all over the world. Yet the news we listen to is mainly glorified gossip, expanded from a neighborhood to a national and international scope. Few outstanding discoveries for the betterment of mankind receive the same publicity as scandals, murders, and kidnappings.

**War: The most serious form of cultural lag.** War is probably the outstanding example of cultural lag. Man has taxed his ingenuity to the utmost to make life happier and more secure. Doctors, nurses, and scientists have labored night and day to prevent and cure illness. Yet we have failed utterly to do away with war, which destroys in a few hours thousands of lives and property which took generations to create. War kills or ruins the health of millions of men, women, and children, and leaves in its wake famine, poverty, disease, and hatred. Yet, in recent years, nations have gloried in the creation and use of newer and more deadly instruments of destruction, while devoting little honest effort to the task of building solid foundations for world peace through disarmament, a better distribution of raw materials, international federation, an international police force, and the like.

There are other examples of cultural lag, but enough have already been presented to indicate that most of our social problems—poverty, unemployment, crime, neglected sickness, and war, for example—arise primarily because of the wide gap between our empire of machines and the out-of-date social institutions by which we attempt to manage it.

**Rôle of cultural lag exaggerated?** Some sociologists contend that it is an exaggeration of the rôle of cultural lag in modern society to attribute all, or most, social problems to its effects. Certain problems like excessive population growth, disease and mortal accidents, family discord, divorce, and war would appear at first sight not to be due to cultural lag. A careful analysis, however, will quickly reveal that they are.

Population growth can be controlled and guided by birth-control measures that are well established and fully applicable, but these measures are resisted by ancient folkways and prejudices. Even the decline in population resulting from adverse economic conditions could be checked by efficient economic planning, were such planning not blocked by archaic economic notions. Aside from certain as yet incurable diseases, such as heart disease and cancer, most of the deaths from causes other than old age are a direct product of the cultural lag manifested by current medical practice. The great majority of fatal accidents are due to the fact that we fail to educate people for life in a mechanical age and to train them in adapting their lives to the basic facts of such an era. But for cultural lag, safety education would be one of the most fundamental items in our school curriculum.

Family and divorce problems are often regarded as of such an intimate, personal, and emotional nature that they could not possibly result from cultural lag. Yet, most of the causes of family unhappiness and divorce arise from the fact that we try to operate the family system of our urban, industrial age according to the ideals and economic beliefs of an older, agrarian era. We have not fully applied to the family problems of today the knowledge in biology, psychology, sociology, and psychiatry which is now available, nor have we sought new ideals and controls to replace the religious patriarchism of rural days in holding the family together. In those cases where modern knowledge and economic practices *have* been applied to solve family problems, the divorce rate has been enormously reduced. Though our colleges give only a smattering of the information relevant to family problems, even this works a notable influence, for the divorce rate among families in which the parties are college graduates is far lower than that of the population as a whole. Divorce and unhappiness in families are due mainly to ignorance and poverty, both of which are a direct outgrowth of cultural lag in any such rich and industrially advanced society as that of the United States.

Since wars produce passionate outbursts and emotional violence, it is often held that they are surely not a product of cultural lag. We have already shown, however, that they are. Emotions may be high in wartime, but wars are the product of social and economic maladjustment—overpopulation, maldistribution of raw materials and markets, outworn diplomatic methods, archaic political ideals, and the like.

Hence, aside from such problems as incurable diseases and old age, there are few which are not a product of cultural lag. Even the problems of old age are greatly intensified by the failure to apply to people of this age level the forms of information most relevant to relieving their peculiar disorders—the information now ready to be supplied by the new science of geriatrics.

**Criticisms of cultural lag concept.** Many criticisms of the cultural lag theory clearly reveal that the critics have not mastered the idea. This is particularly true of critics outside the fields of anthropology and sociology, especially philosophers. There is no royal road to learning in the field of cultural lag or any other phase of sociology. It is something that needs to be studied in order to be fully comprehended. It is instructive that the critics of the cultural lag doctrine either have nothing to offer in its place or turn up with what is merely some secondary manifestation of cultural lag or its most important social by-product, namely, social disorganization. Another objection offered to the cultural lag concept is that, since it is now well established, we should abandon it and substitute something else. This idea was embodied in the following kindly comment on the senior author's *Society in Transition* by a leading sociologist:

When this book first appeared, the idea of cultural lag was comparatively new and striking. Since then, largely due to this book, the idea has become commonplace in sociological courses, in the mouths of instructors and students alike. In the revision some of this idea could be taken for granted, or at least played down so that the book could go on from there. Times have changed. It is a testimony to this book that it helped to change them. Its work partly done, it might well lay out and do another job.

The author of this book has been criticized, more than anything else, for his penchant for original and novel ideas, so he would be the last to reject the proposal of innovation. But it so happens that the cultural lag concept is as basic in sociology as the idea of the sphericity of the earth is to geography or the law of universal gravitation is to physics. No one would seriously think of asking geography or physics to abandon such fundamental concepts just because they are now well established. The task of the sociologist in the future is to refine, test, and further apply the cultural lag process in sociological analysis.

The authors of this book do not present cultural lag merely as the simple and elemental concept of the lag of institutions behind scientific knowledge and machinery, vital as this may be. They include in the formula the marked differences in the rate of change among institutions themselves, which results in numerous institutional maladjustments. They also recognize that ideas may change more or less rapidly than institutions, thus producing serious problems. Further, the ideas held by certain groups may lag behind those cherished by other elements in the population, in this way creating intellectual and social conflict. In the important process of social assimilation, certain aspects of culture are accepted more rapidly than others. One could continue to illustrate the complexity of the concept of cultural lag, but this is done throughout the book and need not be anticipated too completely at this point.

Despite all this, the authors fully recognize the right of readers of this book to differ on such matters. The facts about the institutional life and social problems of mid-century American society are set forth in straight-forward fashion, and those who wish to interpret the material in other ways will not find their procedure impeded by the cultural lag frame of reference. They will, indeed, if open-minded, only be challenged to constructive criticism.

## The Prospect for Dealing with Cultural Lag

**Lack of awareness of cultural lag.** Perhaps the chief reason for the existence of cultural lag lies in the simple fact that, to a large degree, most persons have not been aware of the increasing gap between the material and non-material phases of our culture. It is easier to see the need for improving a mechanical contrivance than for altering a social belief or institution. One can touch a piece of machinery, note stresses and strains, and measure its degree of efficiency. An economic, political, or social institution, on the other hand, is not visible to the eye, nor is its efficiency open to easy measurement. Hence, it is more difficult to tell when an institution is becoming outmoded or inefficient. Social institutions are thus allowed to exist long after their usefulness has disappeared; often we are not aware of their inadequacy until they produce some serious disaster.

**Outlook for social improvement.** There is considerable ground for hope that society may awaken to the need for improving its institutions. In the early days of the Industrial Revolution, there was as much opposition to the new machinery as there is now to new social ideas. Until the present century, inventions were often greeted with fear or ridicule. There was general fear of stagecoaches when they first appeared, and later there was opposition to the railroads when they threatened to put the stagecoaches out of business. The electric telegraph and telephone were both ridiculed, and their inventors had a difficult time getting financial support for their "crazy" devices. When the first "horseless carriages" chugged past in a cloud of smoke and dust, onlookers yelled "Get a horse." The Wright brothers, inventors of the airplane, were considered mentally unbalanced by their neighbors.

Today, the banks which once refused money to investors in the telephone and telegraph business conduct much of their activity by means of these instruments. The sons and daughters of those who scoffed at the first automobiles now stare openmouthed at the sight of a horse and buggy on a city street. And the neighbors of the Wright brothers have seen them honored by kings and presidents.

We may hope that men will come to realize that there is even more need for improvement in the economic, social, and political spheres than in scientific and technical knowledge. For, until we apply a scientific attitude to our social thinking, we cannot say that we are truly moderns, living in a scientific world. If we are going to survive, we must exchange outgrown models in social institutions for up-to-date "streamlined" models. Our future welfare lies in the prospect that we shall one day accord to our "social inventors," those who introduce improvements in our social ideas and institutions, the same praise and encouragement we now give those who have produced our scientific knowledge and mechanical marvels.

## Summary

This book will attempt to analyze some of the important economic, political, and social problems that confront modern society. In the case of nearly every problem, we shall find the underlying cause to be cultural lag—the failure to adapt our institutions to new material conditions of living. We shall attempt to trace the historical development of these problems, analyze them in their present state, and offer possible means for their solution. We are living in a period of critical social change. Whether we like it or not, the old order is being swept away and a new one is taking its place. It is our responsibility to determine whether we shall take the initiative and construct a sound new social order that will provide liberty, justice, prosperity, security, peace, and happiness for all, or whether we will shirk our task and allow society to drift into dictatorship, war, misery, and chaos.

### Selected References

*Note:* These chapter bibliographies are designed to be selective and useful rather than exhaustive. The books marked with an asterisk are deemed especially useful to supplement the material contained in the text.

Barnes, H. E., *Can Man Be Civilized?* Brentano, 1932. An elementary and readable introduction to the rational interpretation of our contemporary life and its problems. Stress is laid on the importance of mental hygiene as a guide to modern living.

Barnes, H. E., *Society in Transition,* Prentice-Hall, 1939. A detailed survey and analysis of our modern social problems, based on the underlying theory that these problems are due to the lag between science and technology, on the one hand, and our institutional life, on the other.

Chapin, F. S., *Cultural Change*, Appleton-Century, 1928. Introductory treatment of the main cultural changes since primitive times, ending with a clear theoretical discussion of the nature of cultural transformations and the lag in institutions.

* Fosdick, R. B., *The Old Savage in the New Civilization*, Doubleday, Doran, 1928. A very readable and thoughtful discussion of the manner in which our civilization is menaced by projecting our cave-man mentality into the age of machines and world-wide communication.

Laski, H. J., *Reflections on the Revolution of Our Time*, Viking, 1943. Stimulating and thoughtful discussion of the public implications of the current fourth world revolution produced by cultural lag in our time.

Lee, A. M. and E. B., (Eds.), *Social Problems in America*, Holt, 1949. Valuable collection of readings, with much attention to cultural lag.

* North, C. C., *Social Problems and Social Planning*, McGraw-Hill, 1932. A good discussion of the possibility of bringing our institutions up to date and solving the problem of cultural lag through conscious social planning.

* Ogburn, W. F., *Social Change*, Viking, 1922. A pioneer discussion of the nature of culture as a sociological concept, notable for the introduction into popular usage of the notion of cultural lag. Still the best theoretical introduction to the subject.

Pitkin, W. B., *A Short Introduction to the History of Human Stupidity*, Simon & Schuster, 1932. Really a massive, but vastly entertaining, onslaught on the credulity of mankind. Reveals quite a different Pitkin from the author of his more widely-read books.

* Robinson, J. H., *The Human Comedy*, Harper, 1937. Popular introduction to our contemporary problems, viewed from an historical point of view, by the most thoughtful of all American historians.

Soule, George H., *The Strength of Nations*, Macmillan, 1942. An able statement of the thesis that our social problems are due to cultural lag, growing out of our failure to apply scientific knowledge and rational methods to our institutions. Suggest ways of doing so.

Wells, H. G., *The Salvaging of Civilization*, Macmillan, 1921. Notable appraisal of our social crisis, stressing the "race between education and social catastrophe." The latter appears to have won.

White, L. A., *The Science of Culture*, Farrar and Straus, 1949. The most competent discussion of the cultural interpretation of history and society, and a formulation of a new science of culturology.

# CHAPTER II

# The Industrial Revolution and the Rise
# of an Empire of Machines

## Western Society before the Industrial Revolution

**Historical basis of cultural lag.** As we made clear in the preceding chapter, the serious economic, social, and political problems which beset modern society arise from cultural lag—the gap between the material and non-material phases of our culture. In order to understand how the present manifestations of cultural lag arose, we must briefly survey the sweeping changes of the last two hundred years which brought our present-day industrial society into being.

**Archaic culture of the eighteenth century.** Although extensive changes had occurred in Europe after 1500 as a result of overseas expansion and the Commercial Revolution, life in the middle of the eighteenth century was nevertheless far different from that of today. Material culture, that is, the techniques of manufacturing, trade, and agricultural production, had undergone little change for thousands of years. Most domesticated animals, the chief fruits and cereals, and many aspects of manufacturing then in use had been known since the late Stone Age. In fact, the art of using metals and the development of seaborne navigation represented the chief advances in material culture since prehistoric times.

Industry in the early eighteenth century was conducted either by the gilds, made up of skilled craftsmen, or under the putting-out system. In the small industrial shops, established under the gild system, a master craftsman worked with his few apprentices. Where the gilds had been replaced by the putting-out system, the raw material was taken to the worker's home, to be converted into finished products, and then picked up and transported to distant towns for marketing. Life was still primarily rural, and there were only a few manufacturing and commercial towns.

There was little need for complex financial institutions in the early eighteenth century. The largest bank of the time operated with less capital than the average bank of a second-class American city today. The economic system required few of the modern instruments of credit

15

—bank checks, drafts, and bills of exchange—and these were in the most elementary stage of development.    The problems of modern capitalism and industrialism had only begun to take shape.

**Simplicity and stability of culture.**   The simple economic conditions of the eighteenth century made for cultural stability.   Life went on much as it had done for centuries, with commercial techniques and industrial processes inherited from the Middle Ages and early modern times.   The main social institutions—the family, the church, and the state—followed patterns long set by custom and tradition.

The average man lived a simple existence within the narrow limits

Brown Bros.

Old water wheel.  Primitive method of generating power.

of his parish or town; he therefore knew little of the world outside his circle of family and friends.  The appearance, later on, of daily newspapers, telephones, radios, movies, transcontinental trains, ocean liners, elevated railways, subways, automobiles, and airplanes completely revolutionized living, and greatly widened human interests and perspective.

## The General Nature of the Industrial Revolution

**Phases of the Industrial Revolution.**  There are three main phases of the Industrial Revolution: (1) new inventions which revolutionized industry, transportation, and communication; (2) the rise of the factory system; and (3) the general economic, social, political, and cultural impact of the new machines and the factory system on Western civilization.

**Machinery.**  The invention of power-driven machines had great consequences for human society.  Not only were new machines provided in the textile industry, but cheaper and more effective methods were found to produce metal products.  New kinds of power, such as the steam engine, the internal-combustion engine, and the electric motor, were invented to drive the new machinery and the new vehicles.  Electricity improved our power and transportation facilities and made possible a revolution in our methods of communication.

**The factory.**  The introduction of the factory system proved to be as significant for society as the invention of new machines and the revolution in industrial techniques.  The new machines, too expensive for workmen to purchase and too bulky for the home, required many workers to operate them.  The factory system brought a large number of workers under one roof.  The personal relations between the employer and his employees tended to disappear.  No employer could take as much personal interests in hundreds or thousands of factory hands as in the handful of craftsmen who, under the old gild system, worked in his shop.  The factory system put the laborer at the mercy of his employer, until labor unions arose to improve working conditions and raise the level of wages.  More than any other single force, the factory system brought about the rise of industrial cities and the resulting great revolution in living conditions.

**Stimulus to capitalism.**  The emergence of a machine economy, carried on under the factory system, led to a great increase in the production of goods, stimulated commerce, made a large supply of capital necessary, and forced the laborers into dependence upon the employer class.  Larger banks and better credit institutions were called into being by the need for more capital and credit.  Corporations, trusts, holding companies, and related forms of industrial organization were developed.  The growth of large business combinations, leading to close and powerful monopolies, was stimulated.  Large profits became the chief goal of the new industrial order, and many of the old and worthwhile ideals of craftsmanship, fair dealing, and consideration for others disappeared.  The whole framework of economic operations became an impersonal matter, controlled primarily by monetary patterns and considerations.

**Social changes.**  Social conditions were sweepingly transformed. Civilization shifted from a rural to an urban basis.  The modern city, with its many social problems, was created, and population increased rapidly.  Between 1800 and 1940 the population of Europe nearly tripled.  Vast migrations occurred, mainly from backward countries with their lack of industrial opportunities to more highly mechanized and prosperous areas.

**Intellectual effects.**  The Industrial Revolution transformed intellectual life.  With the new methods of communication, information from all over the world could be secured by the average man.  Free public education was provided in response to the expanding interests and ambitions of workingmen and the growth of democracy.  Illiteracy was greatly decreased or eliminated in the more advanced countries, and the numbers of the educated classes increased rapidly.

Along with the cultural and intellectual advantages of the Industrial Revolution went a number of serious drawbacks.  Urban life imposed greater nervous strains than a simple rural existence.  Culture and behavior patterns became standardized as a result of mass production. People who were subjected to mass education, wore similar factory-made garments, read syndicated news articles, listened to the same radio commentators, saw the same movies, and ate the same foods tended to lose their individuality, and to become deplorably like-minded and unimaginative.

**Political reactions.**  The political life of Europe and the world was greatly modified by the Machine Age.  In every country where the Industrial Revolution made headway, the middle class gained in power and influence, in most cases securing for itself the advantages of constitutional and parliamentary government.  Having achieved dominance through ownership of the machines and tools of production, the middle class was then challenged by the proletariat (working class), whose political program led to universal suffrage and modern democracy.

The development of modern agencies for sending information made a cohesive nationalism possible.  Citizens began to think and feel alike as a result of exposure to similar views and information.  Modern imperialism was inspired by the greater productivity of the Industrial Revolution and the resulting search for colonies, markets, and sources of raw materials and investments.

## The Four Industrial Revolutions

**The first industrial revolution:** *New textile machinery.*  The first important mechanical inventions were developed in the textile industry, in which England then led the world.  The earliest inventions in the textile industry came slowly, over several centuries, and were made in France and what are now Belgium and Holland, as well as in England. But the first great group of rapid textile inventions came in England after about 1750, and England was the pre-eminent leader in the Industrial Revolution until around 1860.

Before cotton or wool can be made into cloth, the fibers must be spun into thread. The medieval spinning wheel, which spun one thread at a time and was operated by foot power, was still in use in the middle of the eighteenth century. In 1764, James Hargreaves, an English weaver, invented a "spinning jenny," the first model of which spun eight threads instead of one. Before his death, Hargreaves developed a machine that would spin eighty threads. Other important inventions followed rapidly. In 1769, Richard Arkwright provided a somewhat cumbersome roller water frame which spun a firmer yarn. The "mule spinner" of Samuel Crompton, invented in 1779, combined the best feature of the water-frame and the spinning jenny. By 1785, Crompton's device had come into general use in England.

More efficient spinning machines demanded better methods of weaving yarn into cloth. A flying shuttle, which facilitated handweaving, had been invented in 1738 by John Kay. Edmund Cartwright devised a power loom in 1785 which soon replaced the hand loom. In 1793, an invention of tremendous significance for the production of cotton goods appeared—Eli Whitney's cotton gin, which removed seeds from raw cotton by mechanical methods. Cotton was thus made available for manufacture in large quantities.

*Steam power.* The development of successful machines for spinning and weaving required new types of power. Water power, which had been used since primitive times, was cheap and adequate where it could be found, but it was not always available in all places where men desired to build factories. A new, fairly inexpensive, easily available source of power was discovered in steam, which had long before been used by a Greek scientist to run mechanical toys. In the early eighteenth century, a steam-operated atmospheric engine was used to pump water out of mines, but it could not be successfully applied to industry. James Watt, a Scottish mechanic, perfected the true steam engine in 1769, thereby providing industry and transportation with a very efficient source of power. Watt's engine has since been supplemented by the steam turbine, the internal-combustion engine, and the electric motor.

*Iron and steel.* To construct the heavy new machines, materials stronger than wood were required. Since iron and steel, as then manufactured, were too expensive, better fuel was sought to smelt iron ore and lower the cost of iron and steel. Early in the eighteenth century, the Englishman Abraham Darby learned how to use coke in his furnaces, and in 1760 John Smeaton invented the air-blast furnace. On the basis of these inventions, a process for making large quantities of malleable iron cheaply was devised by Henry Cort, Peter Onions, and

Joseph Hall between 1780 and 1830.   James Neilson invented the hot-blast furnace and Cort and Purnell the rolling mill.   John Wilkinson and John Roebuck combined factory methods with these new processes for making iron.   In the 1840's William Kelley and Sir Henry Bessemer extended the methods used by Cort and Onions to the manufacture of steel at low cost.   The Bessemer process is still employed for making low-grade steel, but it has been supplemented by the Siemens-Martin open-hearth process, by which far better grades of steel can be produced, and by electric furnaces.

*Roads, canals, railroads, and steamships.*   The more efficient methods of production made it necessary to secure a greater volume and variety of raw materials and a wider market for finished goods.   Hence, improved transportation was imperative.   Early in the nineteenth century, Macadam, Telford, and others devised hard-surfaced roads. A century later, highways of asphalt and concrete were built for automobiles, busses, and trucks.   A great network of canals was constructed following 1760.   Transportation on land and water was revolutionized by the application of steam.   The modern railroad came into being after 1825 through the invention of the locomotive by George Stephenson and others.   Fitch, Symington, Fulton, and others adapted the steam engine to water navigation through the invention of the steamboat.   John Ericsson's screw propeller increased the efficiency of the steamboat, and soon the new methods of manufacturing iron and steel made possible the building of ocean steamships.

**The second industrial revolution.**   The inventions which revolutionized textile manufacturing, iron and steel manufacturing, and transportation are usually regarded as the essence of the Industrial Revolution.   In reality, however, they represent only its first phase; a second followed closely upon its heels.   The first revolution in industry ended about 1860; the second ran roughly from the time of our Civil War into the second decade of the twentieth century; a third dates from the first world war.   Today we are already far advanced in the third and most impressive era of inventions, and stand on the eve of an even more momentous fourth industrial revolution which will be based on electronics and atomic energy.

The second industrial revolution brought into existence bigger and better machinery.   For example, textile, iron, and steel manufacturing became vastly more efficient; railroad trains and steamboats larger and speedier.   The discoveries of Charles Goodyear, about 1840, made possible the development of the rubber industry.   Other new developments of the second revolution had hardly appeared at all in the first, such as the application of chemistry to industrial production, which brought about more efficient methods of making steel and rubber goods. Chemistry further taught us how to refine petroleum and produce the gasoline needed by the internal-combustion engine.   Organic chemistry enabled us to manufacture a great variety of substitute, or synthetic, products and to utilize many by-products which were formerly wasted. For example, several hundred by-products are derived from cottonseed alone, ranging from explosives and camera films to soap and cosmetics.

Power and transportation also underwent tremendous changes during the second industrial revolution. The steam turbine and the internal-combustion engine made their appearance in the last third of the nineteenth century, while in the early twentieth the Diesel engine and the electric motor became common. The automobile and airplane followed. Today, streamlined Diesel trains are competing with fast airplane transport.

A remarkable revolution in communication followed the invention of the telegraph (1844) and the telephone (1876). Marconi invented the wireless telegraph in the late 1890's, and, about twenty years later, during the third industrial revolution, the wireless telephone, or radio, made its appearance. Today, the era of television has arrived. The production of the daily newspaper was transformed through high-speed printing presses, typesetting machines, and stereotyped plates. Radio pictures and the extensive use of cables and wireless have expanded the scope of the news and speeded up its transmission. Newsreels now compete with the newspaper and the radio as sources of information and diversion.

The second industrial revolution also brought a vast increase in the volume of production. Industrial production in the United States grew from less than 2 billion dollars in 1860 to 13 billion in 1900, and to over 25 billion in 1915. Today, in the United States, there are about fifty billion-dollar companies. The administration of these giants presents numerous difficulties. Industrial experts are constantly striving to improve employer-employee relations, eliminate waste, increase efficiency, and expand sales. Commercial advertising and high-pressure salesmanship have been developed to bring to the attention of the public the myriad products of our factories. Newspapers, radios, and billboards repeat, sometimes wearyingly, the virtues of specified brands of every conceivable article.

**The third industrial revolution: Electricity, mass production, and automatic machinery.** Impressive though the achievements of the second industrial revolution may be, we have entered an even more amazing epoch, the third industrial revolution, sometimes called "the Power Age" or "the Electric Age," whose full significance we do not yet completely realize.

One of the most remarkable additions of this new age to manufacturing is the so-called speed-up process which forms the basis of present-day mass production. This has been made possible by the manufacture of interchangeable parts, also invented by Eli Whitney, and by the endless conveyor belt, first introduced into manufacturing on a large scale by Henry Ford in 1913. Under the speed-up process, the machinery is geared to produce at the highest possible efficiency of which the workers are capable.

Even more momentous for industry is the introduction of automatic machinery which reduces the need for human labor. Many complicated mechanical processes can be automatically controlled by the thermostat and the photo-electric cell, or "electric eye." The rise in productive efficiency resulting from automatic machinery is almost unbelievable. The average worker of today, aided by machines, does five times as much work as his ancestor of a hundred years ago, and does it in less time.

*Courtesy of American Gas and Electric Company*

A modern giant turbine: the main device for the generation of power today. Four of the largest turbines can generate as much power as the entire working population of the United States.

Increased use of electricity dominates the third industrial revolution. Formerly generated mainly by water power, electricity is now produced more and more by gigantic steam turbines, located close to the areas of use. Four of the largest turbines in the United States can produce more energy than the entire working population of the country. The location of turbines near the place of use saves the expense of building transmission lines, and eliminates the waste of electric current in transporting power over long distances. Radio, moving pictures, and air transportation attained full development only in the period of the third industrial revolution. Television passed from the experimental stage and was introduced into practical use.

**The fourth industrial revolution: Atomic energy.** While we are staggered by the new inventions and methods of the third industrial revolution, a fourth is already looming on the horizon with the discovery of atomic energy. In August, 1945, scientists predicted the extensive use of atomic energy in industry within ten years, especially in the field of producing power and heat. In December, 1948, David Lilienthal predicted that an experimental atomic plant would be producing electricity within three years from that date. What atomic energy may do to our way of life is too momentous even to forecast with any accuracy. That it will bring great material benefits and force extensive economic readjustments is quite evident.

*Courtesy of Atomic Energy Commission*

The Bevatron: one of the latest complicated machines for generating energy in the approaching Atomic Age.

**Industrial revolutions in agriculture.** The mechanical revolution has not been confined to industry alone. We have had four parallel agricultural revolutions. The first agricultural revolution was brought about in England in the eighteenth century, and is chiefly associated with the names of Jethro Tull, Charles Townshend, Robert Bakewell, and Humphrey Davy. Tull introduced better methods of cultivation; Townshend better food crops; Bakewell scientific stock breeding; and Davy scientific fertilization.   During the second, the iron and steel plow, the mechanical seed drill, the mowing machine, and the reaper were introduced.   In the third, the binder, the tractor, the gang-plow, the steam threshing machine, and the combine appeared; chemistry revolutionized the fertilization of the soil, and engineering was applied to farming by means of great irrigation projects.   A fourth agricultural revolution is on the way, with the electrification of farm areas, intensified scientific production, and the synthetic production of "foods" in chemical laboratories.   Methods of farm production have become so efficient that, according to one expert, if we introduced the most efficient agricultural methods, we could produce on one-fifth of the land now cultivated and with one-fifth the labor now employed all the food needed in the United States to provide a high standard of living.[1]

**Dynamic character of inventions.**   The core of the Industrial Revolution was the series of inventions which appeared after 1750.   Without them, there would have been few of the great changes of the past two centuries.   Gabriel Tarde, a famous French sociologist, once said that inventions are the chief source of change in all cultures.   Only by inventions can material culture be effectively transformed.   A single year now sees the appearance of more inventions than were produced in the thousand years before the Industrial Revolution.   We have become so accustomed to scientific and mechanical advances that only the most striking receive much attention.   Inventions which would have been regarded as miraculous a century ago are scarcely noticed today.   Formerly, the inventor worked alone, and his inventions were the chance product of genius.   Today, inventions are not left to chance; they are becoming the inevitable result of patient research and long experimentation.   Leading industries employ large staffs of experts to devote their time solely to the development of better machinery, more efficient methods of production, and finer products.

**Will inventions swamp us?**   The recent deluge of inventions has created a grave danger for civilization.   If mankind cannot carry out quickly enough the social and economic readjustments that are necessary to handle the new technology, the latter, like a Frankenstein monster, may destroy its creators.   Modern machinery has put at our disposal the means for promoting human welfare to an undreamed-of degree.   But unless we are able to avert future depressions and wars, we face not Utopia, but anarchy and barbarism.

## The Rise of the Factory System

**Machines bring the factory system.**   Many persons believe that the factory system means the same thing as machine production; actually

---

[1] O. W. Willcox, *Reshaping Agriculture*, Norton, 1934; and *Nations Can Live at Home*, Norton, 1935.

the two, though interdependent, are quite distinct.   Machine production refers to our manufacturing methods, the factory system to the method of organizing and using industrial labor.   Fac'ories of a sort existed long before machines were invented, but it was almost impossible to introduce the new machinery without setting up the factory system.

Improvements in transportation so enlarged the manufacturer's market that he could sell a vast number of similar articles.   Each manufacturing process could be broken up into many operations, performed chiefly by machines and demanding only the supervision of workers. Every machine was thus linked up with all the others in the factory in converting the raw material into the finished product—cotton fiber into cloth, for example, or leather into shoes.   Machines had to be installed where power was available.   Before the time of electricity, power was transmitted to machines by belts and shafts directly from the source, so that a factory had to be built close to the river or to engines which supplied the energy.   Other factors, of course, determined the location of factories, such as the existence of natural resources like coal and iron ore, relatively easy transportation, and marketing advantages.   All these considerations made the concentration of industries in certain areas inevitable.

**Nature of the factory.**   The factory system brought together more workmen than had ever before been employed under the same roof. Even the smallest factories were larger than the typical gild or domestic establishment.

In the factory system there existed a greater responsibility for the control and supervision of labor than in any previous system.   It was necessary to devise some form of discipline to prevent inefficiency and confusion among the workers.   The personal contacts of master and workers which existed under the gild system could not meet the situation.   Codes were therefore worked out and enforced, regulating the hours of labor, individual tasks, the worker's responsibility toward his employer, and other details of conduct in the factory.   These codes sought productive efficiency; the first adequate one, devised by Sir Richard Arkwright in England in the late eighteenth century, was widely imitated in Europe.   Leading English pioneers in the factory system, in addition to Arkwright, were Samuel Oldknow and John Wilkinson; the latter was the first to introduce the factory system into the metal industry.

**Gains and losses in the factory system.**   Of late, many experts have come to believe that the traditional codes of factory discipline have had disastrous effects upon the human personality.   They have been criticized for sacrificing the normal impulses of man to order and regimentation.   The recognition that there is something wrong in the picture has led to the development of the sciences of personnel management and industrial psychology, and to an attempt to humanize the factory.

The world's largest factory: the River Rouge plant of the Ford Motor Company at Dearborn, Michigan.

The factory system increased productivity, but its gains were, to some extent, offset by incidental losses. Craftsmanship has declined; quality has become secondary to quantity; the dreary monotony of factory life brings unnecessary fatigue and various occupational disorders. Industrial psychology has tried to get at the exact causes of such human wastage in order to suggest better ways of adapting the factory to human needs.

**Intellectual and social effects of the factory system.** The factory system not only brought a new type of industrial discipline, it uprooted man's intellectual perspective and social attachments. For tens of thousands of years, man had lived close to the soil. The industrial era drove him from the country to the city. Instead of his own small plot of ground, a cottage, and a few animals, the average city laborer lives in a drab tenement that is his only so long as he holds his job and can pay the rent. Stable family habitation has disappeared, the soothing influence of nature has vanished, and the old rural traditions have lost their grip in our restless urban society. The rural personal societies and primary groups which developed the human personality and conditioned human character have been disrupted by urban life, and community planning has not as yet been sufficiently developed to take the place of the primary group services and discipline. The result has been the development of chaotic social conditions which sociologists call "social disorganization."

## The New Capitalistic Ideals and Practices

**Expansion of credit facilities.** As manufacturing and commerce expanded, more capital and elaborate credit institutions were required. Modern commercial banks, underwriting syndicates, stock exchanges, and insurance companies emerged. The use of the now common devices of credit, such as bank checks, drafts, and bills of exchange, gradually was extended, until today the bank check is more important in business transactions than cash. Commercial banks were supplemented by industrial or investment banks. The investment bank not only provides long-term credit for going concerns, but underwrites new enterprises and markets their securities. The development of modern corporations helped promote this extension of banking operations.

**The corporation.** The new industrial techniques required better methods of business organization. The partnership, a combination of two or more persons, and the joint-stock company, which secured its capital through the sale of shares of stock, could not always deal adequately with the new situation. The modern corporation, which dates back to Roman times in its legal aspects, answered the need for a better and safer type of business organization. The corporation not only combines concentration of control with a wide spread of investment, but it possesses special legal advantages, such as legal personality, limited liability, and the capacity to be sued in court without involving its stockholders directly. The corporate form of organization soon led to great business combinations (trusts) with a strong tendency towards monopoly. Trusts were outlawed in the United States by the Sherman Anti-Trust Act of 1890, but they were soon replaced by the even more effective holding companies.

**Return to the tariff system.** The expansion of manufacturing and commerce, together with a revival of nationalism, gradually destroyed the free-trade movement of the mid-nineteenth century. The trend towards high protective tariffs developed in the United States after 1862 and in Europe after 1879. England alone held out against protectionism until after the first world war.

Protective tariffs in many instances help a country to get new industries started. So long as cheap foreign products are not permitted to enter, manufacturing may be stimulated. Protectionism has, however, limited the economic development of nations, and has made it easier for certain industries to raise prices and exercise monopolistic control over their commodities. The endeavor of nations to build high tariff walls, to sell abroad as much as they can, and to buy there as little as possible, has helped to produce modern wars.

**New business ideals.** Business psychology and ethics underwent a radical change in the industrial era. The profit motive became supreme. The idea of profit in business, of course, was not new. It was present in the oriental and classical periods, but it had not developed to anything like its present influence. In the Greek and Roman worlds, high value was placed on craftsmanship, and individual effort was subordinated to the welfare of the state. In medieval industry and trade, there was a deep sense of social responsibility in acquiring and using wealth. Almost every phase of business was regulated by law. The theory of the "just price" prevailed, and there was general opposition to unfair business practices and to charging interest on loans. In other words, the profit motive was subordinated to the merchant's ethical and social responsibilities.

**The profit system.** Centuries before the Industrial Revolution, certain Protestant ministers and writers on economics had declared profit-making to be the goal of economic effort and to accord with sound religious precepts. With the Industrial Revolution, business ideals were made to conform more thoroughly to the price system and the profit motive. Often, high quality of goods was maintained, not primarily because of pride in craftsmanship, but because sales might drop if obviously inferior goods were produced. Thus, it is profits, not workmanship, which dominates the industrial scene today. The chief goal of the average businessman has become the accumulation of maximum wealth in minimum time. Even labor became a commodity, to be bought and sold through a wage system.

## Summary

In reality, there have been three industrial revolutions, with a fourth already on the horizon. The first brought machinery into the manufacture of textiles and of iron and steel. It produced the steam engine for power to run machines and to bring about steam transportation on land and sea. The second industrial revolution was really an extension of the first. Better machinery was introduced, and mass production began; the application of chemistry in manufacturing created many new commodities; better methods of producing and applying power revolutionized transportation and made possible rapid and world-wide communication; powerful business concerns and larger factories appeared. The third industrial revolution, which is by no means complete, is characterized by the speed-up system, mass production, automatic machinery, and a greater use of electricity for power and communication. We are now on the verge of an age of atomic energy which will bring on a fourth industrial revolution, in all probability far more impressive than any of the preceding.

There have been four agricultural revolutions, comparable to those in industry.

These industrial and agricultural revolutions have vastly increased our ability to produce goods and services. Indeed, with our present equipment, we could produce enough to supply every family in the country with the necessities of life. Yet we are not doing this, nor are we taking full advantage of many other possible benefits of the Industrial Revolution. The reason lies in the fact that we have not brought our economic, political, and social institutions up to a point where we can make efficient and wise use of our remarkable technology.

### Selected References

Ashley, R. L., *Our Contemporary Civilization*, Holt, 1935. Lucid and comprehensive survey of the economic, social, and cultural effects of the Industrial Revolution.

Barnes, H. E., *An Economic History of the Western World*, Harcourt, Brace, 1937. Lays special stress on rise of capitalism and social aspects of industrial development.

Bent, Silas, *Slaves by the Billion*, Longmans, Green, 1938. Extremely interesting account of the nature and variety of American machines and gadgets and their social significance and utility.

Burlingame, Roger, *March of the Iron Men*, Scribner, 1938.

————, *Engines of Democracy*, Scribner, 1940. Two extremely readable and suggestive books describing the progress of machines and invention in the United States, and also making clear the social effects of mechanical progress. Brings home the real character of the industrial revolution in our country.

* Dietz, F. C., *The Industrial Revolution*, Holt, 1927. The best brief introduction to the Industrial Revolution in England following 1750. Clear and authoritative.

Giedion, Sigfried, *Mechanization Takes Command*, Oxford University Press, 1948. Probably the best historical and sociological review of the evolution of machinery and mechanical processes since the dawn of history.

Hammond, J. L., and Barbara, *The Town Labourer*, Longmans, 1925. The best book on the rise of the factory system.

Heaton, Herbert, *Economic History of Europe*, Harper, 1948. A clear, elementary introduction to the economic evolution of western European society.

Hecht, Selig, *Explaining the Atom*, Viking Press, 1947. Good introductory book on potentialities and prospects of atomic energy.

Kaempffert, W. B., *A Popular History of American Invention*, Scribner, 1924. Interesting and authoritative introductory survey of the development of mechanization in the United States.

McVey, F. L., *Modern Industrialism*, Appleton-Century, 1932. A readable and reliable introduction to the rise of the machine age and its spread over the modern world.

Mumford, Lewis, *Technics and Civilization*, Harcourt, 1934. An original and suggestive, if somewhat advanced, work on the history of major inventions and mechanical devices, with their social results. Admirably illustrated.

* Rogers, Agnes, *From Man to Machine: A Pictorial History of Invention*, Little, Brown, 1941. One of the most interesting introductions to the Industrial Revolution. Profusely illustrated.

Walker, J. B., *The Epic of American Industry*, Harper, 1949. Interesting survey of industrial development in the United States, stressing the rôle of free enterprise.

# CHAPTER III

# Social and Cultural Results of the Machine Age: An Urban Industrial Society

## The Growth of Industrial Cities

**Social impact of industrialism.** Mechanical production and the factory system not only produced remarkable changes in the economic organization and trade policies of the leading nations, but they also extensively altered social conditions. Perhaps the most important of these social changes was the rise of industrial cities and the development of urban civilization.

**Slow growth of cities.** The metropolis of today is vastly different from the large cities of the past. Athens probably never had more than 150,000 inhabitants, and the population of Rome was perhaps 800,000 in the Augustan era. Alexandria may have had a million inhabitants. In 1800, the cities of the Western world were still comparatively small. London had a population of 864,000, Paris 547,000, and Berlin only 172,000. England, in 1801, had only 15 cities with more than 20,000 inhabitants, their total population being about 1,500,000. By 1891, however, there were 185 cities in England with a population exceeding 20,000, and their combined population totaled 15,500,000. The rapid growth of English cities was characteristic of the changed situation throughout the Western world. The world's greatest "megalopolis" of today, New York City, has a population of over 8,000,000. The whole metropolitan area, including New Jersey cities across the Hudson River, has a population of about 13,500,000. Modern city life thus introduced man to a new social environment, for which he was but poorly prepared by past experiences.

**The new era of industrial cities.** The industrial city was an inevitable product of the factory system, especially of the use of steam power, which had to be applied right on the spot where it was produced, thus concentrating the workers in the immediate location of the factory plant. The gilds could thrive in small towns, and the putting-out system was easily adapted to a population scattered throughout the countryside; but the factory system required the concentration of workers in small areas. This was especially true in the eighteenth century and the first part of the nineteenth. The working day was very long, 16 to 18 hours being not uncommon, and rapid transportation, which now carries the worker to and from his home, was unknown; hence, laborers had to live within walking distance of the place where they earned a livelihood.

The degree to which a country is urbanized depends upon the extent to which modern industry and commerce have been introduced. In the more advanced industrial states, such as England, Belgium, and Germany, most of the population resides in cities—in the case of England, 80 per cent. The United States is rapidly becoming urbanized, especially east of the Mississippi River and on the Pacific Coast. Today, over 60 per cent of our inhabitants live in cities.

*Courtesy U. S. Travel Bureau*

Grand Central Terminal in New York: the modern urban complex of transport, power, and business concentration.

**New social conditions produced by city life.** The remarkable concentration of population in urban areas bred many new social problems. Most of the cities grew in a mushroom fashion. Congestion, bad housing, inadequate public utilities, and epidemics naturally accompanied their appearance. Since the early cities followed no plan of growth, they had few parks or recreational facilities; and because they drew their inhabitants from foreign countries, as well as from surrounding rural areas, increased social, racial, and cultural mixture resulted, thus intensifying the problems of assimilation.

The socialization and discipline formerly provided by simple personal societies and primary groups in rural life were disrupted by urban conditions, and no adequate substitute was provided.

It is no exaggeration to say that the average city dweller may encounter in one month a greater range of experiences than his grandfather saw in a lifetime in the country. Naturally, the strains and stresses imposed upon human beings by the new urban environment have increased enormously. Because man acquired his fundamental physical and mental equipment during life in simple habitats, such as the cave dwellings of the Stone Age, he has found adjustment to urban life difficult. The city has encouraged a spirit of standardization, superficiality, haste, and nervous tension.

The concentration of population in cities has given rise to new problems of transportation and traffic. The development of suburban areas has served only to increase congestion in cities during working and shopping hours.

Health problems assumed a new importance in city life. The concentration of population, the lack of sanitation, and the absence of sufficient medical facilities led to frightful epidemics. These, in turn, stimulated the development of sanitary provisions, public health movements, and urban health centers, so that medical care in the cities, though still inadequate, is today far superior to that in rural areas. Nevertheless, the most important socio-biological effect of the rise of great industrial cities seems to be the fact that the total conditions of city life are the most effective factor in slowing down the rate of population growth in contemporary times.

## Human Migrations and Immigration Problems

**Rise of the immigration problem.** One of the most important results of the Industrial Revolution was the extensive migration of people from backward countries to those which offered greater employment opportunities. We call this international migration the "immigration problem."

Although migration from Europe to America began in the sixteenth century, the number of those who crossed the Atlantic before 1800 was insignificant compared with the number of those who came in the nineteenth century and the early years of the twentieth. In the year 1907 alone, for example, 1,285,349 immigrants entered the United States, a number about equal to the total population of the English colonies in America in 1750. From 1904 to 1914, more than 10 million Europeans entered this country, over three times the population of the United States in 1776. Altogether, over 60 million Europeans migrated overseas between 1600 and 1925.

The chief cause of this tremendous immigration was the new economic opportunities of the industrialized states. The prospect of steady employment at higher wages lured across the ocean millions of poor peasants from the agricultural areas of central and eastern Europe. Many immigrants realized the expected advantages; others, however, were disappointed in the "golden land of opportunity," finding their lot unimproved by the change.

**Internal shifts of population.** In addition to causing international migration, the Industrial Revolution dislocated the population within nations. On the whole, people gravitated to those areas where factories were built, mines opened, or other natural resources quarried or dug, and where the best commercial opportunities were presented.

In the United States, however, the most interesting migration before 1890 was not to the cities but to the unsettled lands of the frontier. The attraction which lured thousands of families, many of them immigrants from Europe, westward to fill up the empty continent was an abundance of cheap and highly fertile land. Not until 1890, when the frontier was closed, did the westward migration cease. Then the movement reversed itself. Westerners drifted back east, and country people moved in great numbers to the city.

The westward migration had an important influence on our social history. The stamp of the frontier may still be seen in our ways of thinking, especially in our belief in rugged individualism, democratic equality, and national unity. The relative absence of class lines may also be traced in part to the influence of frontier life, where all men were regarded as equal. The westward migration also produced our transcontinental railroads, the rise in western land values, greater agricultural production, and the diversification of American culture generally.

## New Population Trends

**Rapid population growth in contemporary society.** Population has increased strikingly in the industrialized countries since 1750. From 700 A.D. to the time of the Industrial Revolution, population growth was slow in western Europe. It is estimated that western Europe had about 35 million inhabitants in the year 1000, 53 million in 1300, and 73 million in 1600. An estimate for all of Europe in 1600 is 100 million, increasing, by 1750, to 140 million. From 1750 to the outbreak of the second world war in 1939, the population of Europe nearly quadrupled, rising from 140 to 540 million. The United States, of course, showed the most remarkable population growth of any industrialized nation, increasing from less than 4 million in 1788 to 151 million in 1950. Explaining this phenomenal increase is the fact that extensive immigration supplemented the natural growth of the American population.

**Causes of rapid population growth.** Several interesting explanations have been offered for the rapid population growth which accompanied the Industrial Revolution. Some persons attribute it to greater prosperity, more goods, and better ways of transporting and preserving food. Probably the most significant factor, however, has been the declining death rate, a result of the development of sanitary engineering and modern medicine. Sanitary engineering introduced better methods of water purification and sewage disposal, which helped to reduce the spread of epidemics. The example of Germany illustrates the effect of sanitary engineering and the rise of modern medicine most graphically. Despite the great increase of the German population during the last seventy-five years, the birth rate showed a marked decrease between 1871 and 1933, indicating that the rise in population may be attributed primarily to a falling death rate. Another important factor in the growth of population was the stimulus given to large families by the demand for child labor in the early factories and mines and on the American frontier, and the relief policies of over a century ago, when the dole was in proportion to the size of the family. Children were then a real economic asset.

**Stabilization of population.** In the twentieth century the rate of population growth among industrial nations has slowed down. There has been a tendency, in fact, to approach a stabilized population. Urban life seems to produce living conditions and attitudes that make for a lowered birth rate. The birth rate has fallen so markedly that even a low death rate does not suffice to maintain the earlier rates of population growth. Today, with the death rate no longer falling rapidly, population growth is almost at a standstill in many countries. The population of France and Germany has already reached a stabilization point, while that of Britain and the United States will probably arrive at a similar point within less than thirty years. The greatly increased death rate in Germany during and after the second world war has markedly hastened the decline of the German population. On the other hand, the still primarily agricultural nations of central and eastern Europe have a rapidly growing population, and this is likely to produce important shifts and readjustments of political, military, and economic power in the future.

The fact that population tends to increase most rapidly among the poorest and least capable groups in society has led certain reformers to advocate a program of eugenics. The eugenicists believe that the quality of the human race would be improved by encouraging the better physical and mental types to reproduce and restricting reproduction among inferior groups, through education and other more positive measures.

## Social Classes and the Problems of Capital and Labor

**Triumph of the bourgeoisie.** The outstanding social change produced by the Industrial Revolution was the triumph of the bourgeoisie (middle class) and the increase in numbers and importance of the industrial workers.

The Industrial Revolution accelerated the growth of the middle class, begun during the Commercial Revolution of the sixteenth century. The capitalistic manufacturers, merchants, and bankers attained economic and political supremacy and, in the United States, secured social leadership as well. In some countries, such as Germany, the old landed aristocracy held its own, and forced the bourgeoisie to compromise. In Russia and Hungary, little affected by the Industrial Revolution before 1900, the land-owning class clung to its superiority until after the first world war. But, in general, in advanced industrial states, the middle class enjoyed supremacy until the working class became sufficiently strong to challenge it.

**Rise of the industrial proletariat.** While the bourgeoisie in many instances was still struggling against the landed aristocracy for control of European governments and industry, it in turn was challenged by the proletariat, whose numbers had swelled as a result of the Industrial Revolution. It was inevitable, as capitalism grew stronger and wealth became concentrated in the hands of relatively few families, that sharp conflicts would arise between capital and labor.

Under the old gild system, the apprentices and journeymen in many crafts expected to become masters as a matter of course. The separation of employers and workers into distinct classes was much more marked under the putting-out system, but the talented worker still had a reasonably good opportunity of becoming a merchant capitalist.

With the development of the factory system, the gap between employers and workers widened. The new industrial organizations required large investments of capital. Only in unusual circumstances could a laborer hope to rise to the position of a rich and powerful manufacturer or merchant. The classes that controlled manufacturing, commerce, and finance became specialized and exclusive. The capitalist or manufacturer, intent on profits, usually showed little concern for the working man, from whose labor, bought at the lowest possible price, he secured the bulk of his wealth.

**The proletariat strives for democracy.** The proletariat made strenuous efforts to improve its situation. It fought for the right to vote, thus stimulating the growth of democracy. Gaining a voice in politics, it sought to pass laws which would protect labor unions, improve working conditions (wage-and-hour laws), and provide for unemployment insurance and old-age pensions. Through its unions, labor strove for collective bargaining and other bulwarks against exploitation by the capitalists. In certain countries, the workers, through political action or revolution, tried to overthrow the capitalist class altogether, and establish themselves in control of industry. Only in Soviet Russia and her satellites has this effort been successful.

## Political Results of the Industrial Revolution: Constitutional Government, Democracy, Nationalism, and Imperialism

**Advantages of constitutional government.**  The Industrial Revolution had important effects on political institutions—among its direct outgrowths are constitutional government, democracy, nationalism, and imperialism.  Most of these developments during the nineteenth and twentieth centuries reflected such economic, social, and political ambitions of the capitalists as protection of property, enforcement of contracts, and freedom from government interference in business and private life.

The development of constitutional government is the result of bourgeois political policies and ideas.  Since 1775, the number of constitutional governments under the republican form has steadily increased.  By means of a constitution which determines the form of government and details the rights and privileges of the citizen, the middle class has been able to safeguard its power and property and enforce contracts.  The constitution has given permanence to the political and legal system, and left the capitalist-owned business relatively free from government interference until recent times.  A constitutional government cannot legally interfere with such personal liberties as are guaranteed in the constitution.

**Popularity of republics.**  In general, the middle class has favored the republican form of constitutional government because monarchy, as it operated in the past, interfered with middle-class business and prosperity.  Therefore, wherever the bourgeoisie gained supremacy a republican form of government and a written constitution followed, except where the tradition of monarchy was too strong for the middle class to overcome, as in England.  However, the purely formal English monarchy has provided a democratic system which, in many ways, has done more for the people than in some countries where the republican form of government prevails.

**Political democracy.**  Down to the time of the Industrial Revolution, the bulk of the working class were agricultural peasants.  Scattered over the countryside, uneducated and docile, the peasants were guided by custom and tradition, and were easily kept in a position of economic, social, and political subordination.  The situation changed, however, with the Industrial Revolution.  The workers went to the city, where they came in contact with large numbers of people like themselves.  It was much easier under these conditions to develop class consciousness and acquire similar views.  Very early the proletariat began to recognize the possible value of the right to vote as a means of influencing public opinion and securing legislation to improve its lot.

The great political aspiration of the nineteenth-century working class, therefore, was to acquire universal suffrage and majority rule, the essentials of democracy. At the beginning of the century, the masses were not allowed to vote in any modern country. Where representative government prevailed, as in the United States, the majority were barred by property and other qualifications. By the close of the century, however, every progressive nation in the Western world had granted universal male suffrage.

**Defects of contemporary democracy.** Though the working class thus won the right to vote, it had reason to be disappointed with the results; for, although the combined rural and urban proletariat had a numerical majority, it could not control the government or policies of any leading modern state until some of the violent overturns following the first world war.

Various methods of political organization and campaign strategy have usually enabled the middle class to prevent actual majority rule. Perhaps its chief instrument in so doing has been the political party. The use of such devices as party names, party programs and catchwords, and propaganda has blinded the masses to the real nature of political issues and induced the working class and farmers in most instances to follow the lead of the middle-class minority.

Many defects in our political system have arisen from the power of the middle-class minority. Perhaps greater corruption and incompetence would have followed actual majority rule, but there is no way of proving this. The fact is that universal suffrage has not brought true political democracy. Moreover, unless economic and social democracy can also be achieved, political democracy has no meaning. The right to vote is of little significance unless it carries with it the right to economic opportunity, at least in proportion to an individual's capacity. So long as the proletariat remains economically insecure and socially inferior, the right to vote in no way guarantees a democratic society.

The working class soon learned that political democracy was only the first step toward economic and social democracy. Except for some gains, notably in the United States, England, France, and Germany, little was accomplished toward improving working-class economic status and social standing down to the first world war.

**Stimulation of nationalism.** Along with constitutional government and political democracy, another leading political effect of the Industrial Revolution was the growth of the national-state system. Before 1750, the masses were usually illiterate and knew little of national politics or achievements. Even great wars attracted little attention, for the armies were chiefly hired professional soldiers, many of them foreigners. The bulk of the population were not disturbed, except when their neighborhood was invaded. There was some mystical loyalty to the reigning monarch and the royal family, but little of modern patriotism and love of country.

The Industrial Revolution changed all this.  The telegraph and the cable made it possible to transmit news rapidly from the remotest parts of the world to the newspaper offices of any country. Daily papers, moving pictures, and radio have brought the citizens of every nation closer together.  With a million people reading at the same time of an insult to some fellow-citizen in a distant land, and feeling the same righteous indignation, statesmen and politicians can readily play on national pride.  The development of free public education has made it possible for an ever larger number of individuals to be influenced by colored and manipulated news.  To make a nation act in accordance with the wishes of a small group of leaders is, therefore, rather easy today.  Under these conditions, nationalism has developed apace, with disastrous results for Western civilization.

**Birth of internationalism.**  The Industrial Revolution has also, of course, introduced influences which have stimulated the growth of an international spirit.  The expansion of world trade, the economic interdependence of nations, and world finance have tended to break down the isolation of nations.  But national spirit prevailed over the international outlook, and has played a major rôle in bringing on two world wars since 1913, and in checking international organization and disarmament.

**Development of imperialism.**  The enormous increase of manufactured goods, resulting in a surplus for export, led to a feverish search for raw materials and wider markets.  As wealth and savings increased, banks piled up greater sums of money, some of which they sought to invest outside their own country.

One of the most striking features of this age, therefore, has been the rise of imperialism since 1870.  By imperialism is meant the control over the territory or resources of less highly developed or less powerful peoples overseas.  As a movement, modern imperialism has varied from mere control over the commerce or finances of an area to complete political absorption.

More overseas territory was occupied, in one way or another, by the leading imperialist nations between 1870 and 1914 than was taken up in the three centuries of the older colonial movement after 1500.  In 1800, only one-fifth of the land area of the world was opened to civilized man through exploration.  As late as 1870, only one-half had been explored.  But, by the beginning of the twentieth century, the whole world, apart from the extreme polar regions, had been explored by the white man.  Resources of the new lands were catalogued, and spheres of influence were established by the European countries and the United States.  During the present generation even the polar areas have been thoroughly explored, mainly through the use of the airplane, which has made it possible to reach hitherto inaccessible areas quickly and easily.  Imperialism helped to cause both world wars and has survived them. Even the United States has been accused by its critics of harboring imperialistic designs under the guise of its program—President Truman's "Fourth Point"—to rehabilitate the backward nations of the earth.

## Liberalism—the Political Religion of the Middle Class

**The middle class favors liberalism.** As we have seen, the political and legal trends of the nineteenth and twentieth centuries reflected the social and economic ambitions of the capitalists. The latter favored legal protection of property, enforcement of contracts, and a large degree of business and commercial freedom. Everywhere, they feared state interference, except where this interference furthered their own interests, as in the case of tariff laws. The capitalists opposed legislation designed to protect the working class because it would interfere with the complete freedom of the employer to treat his employees as he wished. In other words, if working-class legislation was passed, the employer might not be able to enforce long working hours and pay low wages.

The political and economic theory of the middle class took the form of "liberalism." While liberalism has been regarded as one of the fundamental institutions ushered in by the Industrial Revolution, it was really the state of mind which has prevailed among the bourgeoisie during the last several centuries. It was, in its origins, an outgrowth of rationalism and the age of enlightenment. In the nineteenth century it became almost "the political religion of the middle class."

**Main tenets of liberalism.** In the intellectual realm, liberalism stood for tolerance and freedom of thought. The majority of the middle class, being Protestants, many of them dissenting Protestants, persecuted by Catholics on the continent and by Anglicans in England, naturally championed religious toleration. They also realized that free thought, free speech, and a free press were valuable assets in their campaign for political and economic liberty. Liberalism also promoted the battle for civil liberties, which was first won in England in the last half of the seventeenth century. The first ten amendments to our Federal Constitution of 1787 and the civil rights clauses in the constitutions of many other countries are further evidence of the successful battle for the rights of man. The liberals were also early champions of revolution and representative government, and, in the nineteenth century, most of them earnestly supported nationalism and democracy. A few of the more enlightened liberals, such as the mid-nineteenth-century liberals in England led by Richard Cobden and John Bright, repudiated imperialism and favored peace and an international outlook.

In economics, the liberals advocated *laissez-faire,* or free enterprise, and protested vigorously against government interference in business.

Until about 1880, the liberals advocated unlimited free trade, and, during the greater part of the nineteenth century, many of them fought against militarism and imperialism and for world peace.

**Leading liberal writers.** A host of brilliant writers explained the principles of liberalism. An early apostle of economic *laissez-faire* was Adam Smith, author of *The Wealth of Nations* (1776). The theory of evolution was used by Herbert Spencer in his *Social Statics* and *Man Versus the State* to buttress the principle of *laissez-faire* and extreme individualism. Spencer's *laissez-faire* liberalism was brought over into American thought by William Graham Sumner in his *What Social Classes Owe to Each Other* (1883).

One of the most influential liberal treatises was John Stuart Mill's *On Liberty* (1859), which held that the state's only legitimate function is to prevent one citizen from trespassing on the rights of another. According to Mill, the state should never directly promote the public welfare or the good of the individual.

**The "New Liberalism."** Toward the end of the nineteenth century, there were important changes in liberalism, prompted mainly by historical events. The complex social problems in industrialized countries and under city conditions made it necessary for governments to regulate more aspects of human life, a fact which even liberals had to concede. Moreover, many liberals were brought to favor moderate reform legislation out of fear that, if nothing were done, socialism might result. Some of the late nineteenth-century liberals, among them Joseph Chamberlain in England, even began to favor imperialism and protectionism as a way of extending business interests into new areas.

A so-called "New Liberalism" arose, of which Lloyd George and the English Liberal party of 1905–1914 and Theodore Roosevelt's "Square Deal" of 1901–1909 were important examples. Its supporters advocated social and economic reform, so that more extreme doctrines like socialism and communism would not gain ground among the workers. They argued that the more obvious abuses and injustices of the capitalistic system should be done away with, and that gradual and moderate reforms must be carried out by democratic methods if revolution was to be averted. The British reforms of 1905–1914, the so-called "Middle Way" in the Scandinavian countries and Finland, and the New Deal after 1933 in the United States are good examples of this new and more positive liberalism. Those older liberals who, like Herbert Spencer, refused to accept moderate reform legislation joined the ranks of the conservatives, who defended the older liberal ideas of freedom from governmental interference.

**Recent growth of totalitarian liberalism.** The most extreme deviation from the *laissez-faire* tenets of early liberalism has been shown by many younger liberals, especially in the United States since about 1936. They have favored collectivism and far-reaching state activity, verging on extreme state capitalism. They have been the leaders in introducing a managerial régime to replace the earlier elective democracy. They have especially favored executive initiative and presidential independence in foreign relations. They have been dubbed "Totalitarian Liberals" by their critics not only because of their collectivist ideas but also because of their intolerance born of wartime propaganda and pressures.

## Effects of the Industrial Revolution on Women and the Family

**Emancipation of women.** The Industrial Revolution brought about the emancipation of women. Although women, at one time or another in history, had occupied prominent social and economic positions, it was a man's world, for the most part, until the Industrial Revolution. Today, women in many countries have attained economic and legal equality with men.

**Women in industry.** The Industrial Revolution first opened the door to the extensive employment of females. In each industrialized country, the number of women in industry steadily increased after 1800. In Germany, women workers increased from 5,500,000 in 1882 to 11,479,000 in 1933; in France, from 6,400,000 in 1896 to 8,600,000 in 1921; in England, from 3,800,000 in 1881 to 5,600,000 in 1931; in the United States, from 2,647,000 in 1880 to 10,752,000 in 1930 and 17,326,000 in 1949. During the second world war there was a tremendous temporary influx of women into industry in various war plants. Some 19,700,000 women were working in the United States in 1944.

Until the second world war the percentage of women workers in the United States was smaller than in the industrialized countries of Western Europe. In 1931, the ratio of gainfully employed women to the total population in the United States was 18 per cent; it was 37 per cent in France, 34 per cent in Germany, and 27 per cent in England and Wales. The proportion of women workers in the American economy increased after Pearl Harbor and in 1948 they made up 38 per cent of the civilian labor force.

There were many reasons for the entrance of women into industry. Women were often quite as able as men to tend and watch the new machines and, since they would work for lower wages, were more desirable from the employer's point of view. In many American industries, the earnings of women long remained from 20 to 70 per cent below those of men in similar occupations. The Federal Wages and Hours Law of 1938 and the high wages earned by women during the second world war have done something to correct this former disparity between the wages of men and women workers.

Among the reasons why women receive lower wages are: (1) they cannot compete physically with men in the heavy industries, where wages are high; (2) women were long excluded from trade unions and, without organization, had no method of collective bargaining to enforce their demands for higher wages; and (3) many women are willing to accept lower wages than men because they consider employment only temporary until they marry and raise a family.  Despite all this, the position of the working woman is far better than it was fifty years ago.

**Woman suffrage.**  Irked by their subordinate position, women strove for the right to vote, hoping to pass laws that would elevate their economic and social status.  Female suffrage, initiated in the territory of Wyoming in 1869 and in New Zealand in 1893, became general in the twentieth century.  Finland granted the right to vote to women in 1906; Norway in 1913; and Denmark in 1915.  Sweden delayed positive action until 1921.  England introduced limited female suffrage in 1918 and full voting rights in 1928.  American women gained the franchise in 1920.  Many of the European constitutions adopted after the first world war included female suffrage.  Women have not only been given the right to vote, but they have entered public office in legislative, judicial, and executive capacities.

**New legal and social status of women.**  Political emancipation whetted women's appetite for legal and economic equality.  But in this battle they have not been entirely successful.  In the United States, for instance, men usually have superior legal and property rights.  A man has special claims on his wife's property, and he can control her services in the home and, to a great extent, elsewhere.  In some states, a woman cannot engage in an independent business without the consent of her husband; about half the cities discriminate against married school teachers; in a number of states women are at a disadvantage in regard to the guardianship of children and the right to maintain a separate domicile.  In France and some other European countries, women have fewer legal and property rights than in our own country.

Although women do not possess complete economic and legal equality with men, these handicaps are often offset by the fact that women enjoy moral protection and have special advantages which have come down from the age of chivalry.  For instance, a husband is usually forced by law to pay alimony to his divorced wife.  In the United States, women have also attained an enviable position with respect to property rights.  Women are the beneficiaries of most life insurance policies; more than half the country's saving accounts are in women's names; women hold 44 per cent of the country's public utility securities and about 40 per cent of the real estate.  However, many husbands, knowing that the law gives protection to the wife, have merely placed property in her name to prevent mortgage foreclosure, or liability in case of bankruptcy.

**Effects on family life.**  Women's emancipation has had many and extensive effects upon family life.  When women were absolutely dependent on men for their support, the husband was the head of the family. Today, when many wives work, husbands are losing their authority. Often, they are, in an economic sense, no longer actual heads of the family. Many women prefer work to marriage; others work to support relatives until they are too old to marry; and, even if a woman originally chooses marriage instead of employment, she need not stay married but can leave her husband and earn her own living. The working woman is more likely to be discriminating in the choice of a husband. She knows that she does not require a husband to support her and is likely to continue working until she finds one to her liking. In the end, she may not marry at all. In these and other ways, the Industrial Revolution has brought about a great increase in the divorce rate, a decrease in the marriage rate in certain social classes, and a loss of prestige for the family as a social institution.

## Summary

The Industrial Revolution created not only most of our urgent economic problems but also our outstanding social problems. Among the most important social problems are: (1) the adjustment of man, hitherto engaged primarily in agricultural pursuits, to life in complex urban communities; (2) national and international migrations of peoples with their numerous social effects; (3) problems of population growth and stabilization; (4) the rise of new social classes—especially capitalists and laborers—with divergent interests; (5) the chief political problems of the modern era, constitutionalism, liberalism, nationalism, democracy, and imperialism; and (6) the emancipation of women and a new relationship between the sexes, with the resultant decline in the stability of family life. These tendencies and problems have been a direct outgrowth of the sweeping industrial changes in the Western world since the middle of the eighteenth century.

### Selected References

* Barnes, H. E., *Living in the Twentieth Century*, Bobbs-Merrill, 1928. A comprehensive introductory survey of the effects of the rise of modern science and mechanical industry on social life and institutions.

——————, *Society in Transition*, Prentice-Hall, 1939. Comprehensive factual and interpretative survey of the impact of modern industrialism on American society and social problems.

Beard, C. A. (Ed.), *Whither Mankind*, Longmans, Green, 1928.

——————, *Toward Civilization*, Longmans, Green, 1930. Two thoughtful symposiums on the triumph of technology in the present century and on the need for social adjustment to this revolutionary change in the material basis of human life.

Chase, Stuart, *Men and Machines*, Macmillan, 1929. A stimulating and sound analysis of the impact of the machine age on human life and society in the twentieth century.

Coon, Horace, *How to Live in the 20th Century,* Alliance, 1940. A clear, popular introduction to life in the machine age, urban society, and world-wide relations.

Hamilton, Henry, *England: A History of the Homeland,* Norton, 1948. Very informing and interesting account of the reaction of industrialism on modern English society, containing interesting comparisons with American developments and attitudes.

Ogg, F. A., and Sharp, W. R., *Economic Development of Modern Europe,* Macmillan, 1926. A comprehensive and informing presentation of the Industrial Revolution and its economic and social results in Europe through the first world war. Long a standard manual in this field.

* Randall, J. H., *Our Changing Civilization,* Stokes, 1929. A lucid and thoughtful consideration of the manner in which science and machinery are modifying living patterns and our institutional framework. Perhaps the best introduction to the impact of the empire of machines on modern society.

A number of the books mentioned in the bibliographies of Chapters I and II are relevant to this chapter, especially R. L. Ashley, *Our Contemporary Civilization.* Much more detailed references will be found in the bibliographies of Chapters IX, X, XIV, XVI–XVIII, XXIV, XXV.

# PART II

# The Social Framework of Human Life

## CHAPTER IV

## The Role of Social Groups and Classes in Human Experience

### Origin and Nature of Social Groups

**Group life natural and indispensable to mankind.** Men have always lived in groups, and human history is primarily a history of group life. The human being, as Aristotle long ago described him, is a social or political animal who finds association with his fellow-beings pleasant. His physical nature and biological equipment have compelled him to associate with his fellow men to insure his existence, protection, comfort, and progress. It must, of course, always be borne in mind that man did not originally deliberately *choose* to live in groups. The natural sociability of man, together with the elemental facts and problems of existence, led mankind into spontaneous association and group cohesion. As civilization has developed, these early spontaneous forms of group life have been supplemented by many types of association which have been deliberately entered into through conscious choice.

**Human traits require and stimulate group life.** Man is biologically inferior to many other members of the animal kingdom. He lacks the strength of the bear or the elephant, the speed of the leopard or the antelope, the eyesight of the eagle, or the endurance of the ox. In order to make up for this biological weakness, human beings have been compelled to live and co-operate with others. The individual man, unarmed, was no match for a cave bear, but through group organization and co-operation he was able to overcome the strongest and fiercest of the ancient animals. Modern firearms, which are the product of centuries of co-operative human effort, now enable a person singlehanded to vanquish the most powerful beasts.

Although man is inferior physically to most other members of the animal world, he is mentally superior to all of them. He can learn quickly, adapt himself easily, and make decisions readily. These qualities, which separate man from the rest of the animal kingdom, have enabled him to develop a highly organized group life and to create an enduring civilization.

Group life not only was a necessity because of the individual's biological weakness, but it was pleasant and convenient. All through history, men have found it more natural and agreeable to associate with their fellows than to try to "live alone and like it." Although group life and close association have usually required the surrender of some individual freedom, the advantages secured in the way of protection, aid, and progress have more than compensated for the loss of freedom.

**Evolution of group life.** The forms of social organization have differed in size, complexity of relationships, and purpose. In primitive times, mutual dependence and sociability caused men to live together in favorable localities. Groups settled in places that afforded them game, fish, or good grazing lands for their herds and were easy to defend. The first social groups were small, and the relationships between individuals and classes were simple. There was probably little conscious purpose in primitive social organization. The idea that individual, class, and group relationships were a product of the divine will was accepted by early man as an explanation of his social surroundings.

Social development from the simple life of the hordes and local groups of primitive society to the complex urban living conditions and great national states of today has been brought about by means of: (1) the gradual introduction of improved types of group discipline and education as the population increased and the groups became too large to be controlled by informal methods; (2) the invention of tools and machines, which complicated social relationships and made for greater mobility of populations and better control over the physical environment; and (3) the growth of intelligence and culture, which has gradually changed social organization from a spontaneous type of association in simple, local societies to the conscious forms of group life in modern society, which include large-scale economic, educational, political, religious, and social groupings.

**Ever-expanding scope of group life.** The social groupings of modern society are as complicated in nature as they are extensive in geographical scope. It is a long step in history from the first groups of primitive men, working together for food and mutual protection, to the numerous and varied social organizations of modern society, some of them of a national or even an international scope.

Today, a person is not only a member of his local group; he also participates in the life of the state, the nation, and the world.  His economic, political, religious, and cultural activities are influenced by interests which extend far beyond his immediate locality.  For instance, the farmer receives a certain price for his wheat.  This price is not determined wholly by local supply and demand; it is also affected by the supply and demand for wheat in nation-wide and world-wide markets.  In other words, the modern community is not independent and self-sufficient, but is dominated by forces organized on national and, in some cases, world lines, and every person within any community depends in some way on the thought and work of those who live in other communities.  The farmer may own and work his 160 acres, but he is dependent on machinery manufactured in the city to harvest his crop, carry the grain to market, and mill it into flour or feed, as well as to supply him with clothing and other necessities of life.

Economic life has thus advanced from a simple gathering of the fruits of nature, with only the minimum amount of co-operative effort, to the modern machine age, with its extensive factories, its elaborate economic organization, and its world markets.

Political life has passed from control by chiefs or elders of small primitive tribes to the modern national state, which influences almost every field of human endeavor, and controls the individual at almost every step in his life.  The geographical scope of political control has also expanded from small localities of a few square miles to great countries occupying half a continent.  For example, the national government in Washington has jurisdiction over the whole of the United States, and a considerable area overseas.  The dominion of Russia is even more far-flung.  We have even sought to devise some workable form of world government.

Religious life and influences have progressed from the efforts of medicine-men in small primitive groups to ward off evil spirits to world-wide church organizations, whose work includes not merely religious activities in the narrow sense but also various forms of cultural and social life.

Organizations for cultural purposes, such as art, music, recreation, and the like, have become wider and more complex as civilization has advanced.  The widening and speeding-up of transportation and communication have especially aided in promoting inter-group cultural contacts.

All our complex forms of social organization have developed from the simpler types of the past.  No part of man's group life can be viewed as unchanging; we must realize that every effort made by modern man is part of a great social pattern which is constantly moving toward new and more extensive forms of expression.  In other words, society is dynamic, not static.

## Socializing Influences That Create Group Life

**Geographical basis of group life.** It is evident that social life and organization are necessary for the development and welfare of the race, but it is also true that extensive social organization could never have been achieved were it not for powerful socializing forces which have brought and held men together, from primitive times to the present day.

The physical environment has always been an important influence in bringing men together. Good soil, the protection afforded by mountains and rivers, ample resources in fish, game, minerals, and forests, have all caused men to seek favorable spots for settlement, from the primitive days of the flint-bed to the modern oil reserves and rubber plantations. There can be no intelligent study of social groups which does not include a consideration of the geographical factors in human association. Similar geographical influences do not always have the same effect on all groups because human nature and group life are too complex to react invariably in identical ways to the same geographical influences. As civilization develops, man becomes better able to control and master his geographical surroundings.

**Biological impulses to group life.** The biological factor is important in man's social existence. The attraction and mating of the sexes, the relationship of mother and children, the long period of human infancy, and the helplessness of the young child have made the family a permanent institution. Many ancient grazing or farming communities were organized around the authority of the male head of the family—the patriarch. Among the early Hebrews, the patriarchal system not only prevailed in the family, but also dominated the economic, religious, and cultural organization of the time.

Kinsmen, or members of the same clan in primitive society, were usually supposed to be related by blood, but sometimes new members were legally adopted into the group by an elaborate ceremony. These kinship groups were very closely knit. Only kinsmen could function freely and with authority as members of the tribal group.

Racial kinship is another strong social bond. Persons belonging to the same race, such as yellow, white, or black, usually group together whenever possible. In early days, the factor of race was of paramount significance in social grouping, but races have so intermingled through the ages that, in many present-day groups, cultural factors have been a greater determining factor than racial.

**Psychological impulses to group cohesion.** One of the most powerful forces in group life is a psychological attraction, called by Professor Giddings "consciousness of kind." People tend to associate with others in whom they recognize likeness to themselves. We seek the presence of those who resemble us in race and culture and avoid the society of those who do not.

Another strong influence in promoting group life is fear; men have always banded together when they were alarmed about real or imaginary dangers. Groups have been formed to resist the attacks of fire, floods, storms, animals, and men.

Still another psychic factor holding men together has been their choice of the same or similar occupations. From the time of the primitive priests, hunters, fishermen, and shepherds to the present-day labor organizations, men of like vocation have been drawn together.

Common language, common traditions, and similar education and ideals have also been powerful elements in promoting group life and a feeling of social unity among men.

These psychological bonds, which, in the beginning, were almost invariably spontaneous, have led to a conscious attempt by man to improve himself and his social environment through group co-operation. These cohesive forces have been strengthened as civilization has progressed and man has gained more experience in association.

**Economic basis of social groups.** The problems of making a living have, naturally, been extremely vital in creating and conditioning the development of social groups. If there was not enough group co-operation to provide the needed food, clothing, or shelter, the group usually ceased to exist. Since human beings associate spontaneously as a result of biological and psychological impulses, it is hardly true to say that the problems of making a living created social groups. But they did give rise to specialized forms of human association which have become progressively more extensive and impressive as we have moved away from primitive society and toward our own day.

The earliest and most lengthy stage of man's economic experience was the era of the so-called collectors' economy. In this period, mankind lived on nuts, berries, roots, shell-fish, and the like, picked up as nature deposited them. Group economic activity was confined to association in the quest for food, when such association was pleasant or valuable for protective purposes. For example, hunting packs were indispensable because, with only crude weapons available, many primitive men were required to hunt down one large animal.

When settled life began with the development of pastoral and agricultural industry, human groups formed from economic considerations became larger and more permanent in character. This made possible the division of labor and specialization, which encouraged trade and the development of mercantile groups. The development of manufacturing created over the centuries craft groups, the factory system, labor organizations, associations of manufacturers, and various organizations of bankers to provide the credit needed for manufacturing enterprise and expansion. With the development of better methods of transportation and communication, social groups of international scope have been created to deal with tariff problems, cartel arrangements, international trade unions, and the ideological conflicts between free enterprise and collectivism.

**Religion and social groups.** From the very beginnings of society, religion has been a vital factor in creating social groups. It has divided society into groups based on differences in religious beliefs and has had an important disciplinary effect on the whole social order in any given civilization.

**Political factors.** The political tie, while not a natural factor like the biological, is very powerful. It was found necessary in early times to have leaders and laws to control groups and to give unity and purpose to group life. With the progress of civilization, state and government have assumed more and more authority over the affairs of mankind.

These numerous socializing forces have exerted their influence from the beginning of human life to the present. Since men have always lived in groups, those influences growing out of group experiences are the most powerful force in human existence. They give man his outlook on life, his set of values, and his loyalties. Without the group, man would have little or no culture, and would be unable to meet the dangers and difficulties which confront him.

## How the Socializing Factors Operate in Social Groups

**Environmental forces.** Some groups owe their existence chiefly to geographic location. In early days, social groups were, perhaps, more influenced by geographical factors than by any other force. Today, man has overcome the sheer influence of geography to a far greater degree than his primitive ancestors; but it is still true that geographical factors influence the distribution of people over the world. For example, in our own country certain groups settled along the Atlantic coast because they were fishermen; others went west to prospect for gold in California, to raise large herds of cattle in Texas, or to carry on farming in the Mississippi Valley.

In modern civilization, most social groups are no longer isolated as a result of their geographical position. The railroad, the automobile, the airplane, the telephone, the radio, and the newspaper have brought the world to the back door of the hitherto most isolated groups.

Sectional differences remain, however. Certain parts of the United States have definite economic and cultural interests that are a result of geographical factors. For example, the farmers in the Middle West have developed attitudes and ideals that reflect the problems they have faced in land-holding and in raising and marketing their crops. The influence of environment on the farmer will be discussed more fully in a later chapter. Another example of geographical influences on social groups and classes is to be found in the business, professional, and laboring groups of our coastal cities, groups which owe their interests partly to their favorable geographic location.

**Pleasure resorts** such as Miami and health resorts like Saratoga Springs, where people with the same interests come to play or rest, are other instances of the influence of geographical environment in attracting special types of social groups.

The mountaineers of West Virginia, Tennessee, Kentucky, and the Ozark area have developed similar group interests because of their environment. Their lack of contact with other groups made them suspicious of strangers and slow to change their ways of living. The lumber camps of the Northwest, the fishing communities off Puget Sound, and the mining towns of Pennsylvania—all have developed their own particular group forms and cultural patterns partly as a result of their geographical location.

**The biological bond and the family.** The biological bond is one of the most important of social forces because it has produced the family. The family is a universal social group. It is found in some form in all societies and at all stages of development, and is based upon the organic nature of man. Such impulses as mating, reproduction, and love of children, are fundamental in human experience, and have been strengthened by such emotions as racial pride, the urge to perpetuate the family name, affection between men and women, and the desire for the security of a home. Each person is born into a family group, which may include not only parents and children but other blood relatives.

In the intimacy of the family, the child first becomes habituated to group association. He learns the language of his parents, acquires the social attitudes and cultural characteristics of the family, and develops his personality. The family is, therefore, the core, or nucleus, of most other social organizations, and is still the most important primary social group.

Race is another biological influence affecting the creation and activities of social groups. Perhaps the largest of all blocks or aggregates of humanity are the major racial groups of mankind, as distributed in their original habitats. While there has been much migration and mixture of races since the remote period of original racial differentiation, the main races are still distributed in fairly well defined areas of the world—the yellow race mainly in Asia, the black chiefly in Africa, and the white in large part in Europe and the Americas, though there has been a great deal of racial penetration in all continents. Racial minorities which have migrated from their original habitats are often segregated in special areas of their adopted land—usually in urban districts. If persecuted, these minorities may develop an unusually cohesive form of group life in self-defense. A different set of racial policies may favor physical amalgamation and cultural assimilation rather than segregation and conflict. The interaction between racial groups may be friendly and peaceful, or violent, taking such forms as lynching.

**Psychological attraction and mutual interest.** The psychological bond is important in guiding modern life because people with the same traits and interests usually seek each other's society—for instance, in the great variety of economic-interest groups, such as industrial organizations, labor unions, trade associations, and agricultural societies.   Common economic interest has also promoted organizations like the Chamber of Commerce, and the Kiwanis and Rotary clubs.

Vocational and professional groups have also arisen mainly because of mutual interest.   Educational associations, medical societies, fraternities and sororities, women's clubs, and professional and business organizations have as their goal the promotion of the ideals of the particular group in question.   The aesthetic impulse, by producing a similarity in tastes and ideals, has led to organizations to promote recreation, music, the arts, and literature which have been a powerful factor in advancing man's cultural life.   This mutual-interest attraction stands today next to the biological force in power and extent of influence.

The psychological factor is also of primary importance in producing the characteristic temporary groups of modern society—crowds, audiences, and the like.   Psychological forces, depending chiefly on recent and improved means of communication, have created what social psychologists call "the public," which possesses considerable psychic unity and uniformity of information, and often rather similar attitudes and values, despite the variety of elements in its make-up.

**Economic processes in social organization.**   The above reference to groups based on mutual interest and vocational similarity indicates how economic factors influence group development, functions, and motives, at least in so far as the mutual interest rests on an economic foundation.   Economic needs and impulses have, in historic succession, created the groups and the co-operative activities needed to sustain mankind in a collectors' economy, to manage pastoral life, to deal with settled agricultural activities, to execute manufacturing operations, to develop transport and trade, and to provide the capital and credit needed for all types of economic effort.   Indeed, they have, of late, given rise to pressure groups and propaganda activity in behalf of all the leading industrial functions of today.

Within each of the main industrial groups of our day there is an elaborate development of specialization and division of labor, which has given rise to innumerable special-interest and functional groups, each with a duty to perform and an interest to promote.   The farming economy and the laboring world are also highly specialized today; each has its functional groups to carry on special operations and its pressure groups and program designed to enhance its power, prestige, and well-being.   The much discussed "public," in any realistic economic sense, is a conglomeration of a great many diverse economic groups, whose interests seemingly conflict.   About the only common interest of the public is order and survival, so specialized and functional has economic group life become.

**The religious impulse.**   The religious impulse has helped to motivate the most varied groups, from the local religious societies of primitive men to world churches and congregations. It has created such permanent organizations as the churches of the Jews, Christians, and Mohammedans, as well as temporary groupings such as the Crusaders of the Middle Ages. Religious groups vary today from the small, self-governing rural church to the world organization of the Catholic church and the international missionary societies. The religious impulse has also created such welfare organizations as the Young Men's Christian Association, the Federal Council of the Churches of Christ, the Knights of Columbus, the National Catholic Welfare Conference, and a vast number of quasi-religious charitable societies.

**Political organizations.** Political organizations, which have grown out of mutual interest and the need for group protection, range from a simple meeting of the town council in a rural community to the elaborate organization of our national government and the United Nations. The fundamental purpose of political organization is to maintain public order, to promote the general welfare, and to mediate between and adjust the conflicting interests of private groups. Political organization operates under various forms, among them monarchies, representative republics, and democracies. The chief dynamic agency of government in our modern representative democracies is the political party. Political responsibilities are distributed among three departments of government, the executive, the legislative, and the judicial.

## Primary and Secondary Groups

**Primary groups as a socializing influence.** Although man's social life has taken diverse forms, all group association may be divided into primary and secondary social relationships. The primary group is characterized by personal or "face-to-face" contacts between its members who occupy a common locality. Relationships are thus direct and intimate.

The family has already been mentioned as the most important primary group. The play group, usually composed of children whose families live near each other, is also a primary group. In their playful associations children learn how to express their own wishes and adapt them to the desires of the group. Usually the child carries into the play group some of the social attitudes and ideals he has learned at home; the play group is often the first larger social group into which home training is extended.

The neighborhood—a group of families living in the same locality —is also a primary group because it is characterized by direct contact among the members. Socially speaking, the neighborhood is more or less self-sufficing; in its social center, churches, schools, and other organizations are centered the interests of the group.

Within the play and neighborhood groups are found other intimate groupings, such as the congeniality group. The congeniality group consists of persons whom similar interests bring together; for example, the sandlot baseball team or the bridge club. It is usually small and informal, and is most effective when based on direct contact among the members, but it may be extended to include organized recreation and clubs of all types. So extended, the congeniality group usually becomes a secondary group.

These primary groups are the basic forms of human association. They help the individual to become socialized and train him to co-operate with others.

**Origin and nature of secondary groups.** The primary groups are usually spontaneous. When they are extended beyond the personal and local scope through conscious action, and take on some specific function to perform, they become secondary groups. Primitive society had few secondary groups, but, as population increased and life became more complex, the primary groupings did not suffice to meet the diverse needs of society.

Modern life has numerous secondary groups, many of them often called "interest-groups." They represent associations of persons to satisfy a specialized interest or need. One may be a member of numerous secondary groups, such as a political party, a church, a business organization, a trade union, or a school board. The secondary group is usually an extension of the primary group, because attitudes found in the one are carried over into the other. For instance, the social attitudes learned in the family usually influence one's political, economic, and religious affiliations. The play group is extended into the wider secondary groupings of organized leisure-time activities. Both primary and secondary groups are marked by a certain degree of permanence, especially primary groups.

**Increasing importance of secondary groups.** Every individual is, thus, a member of a social group. During his early years his life is centered chiefly in such primary groups as the family and play group, but as he grows older he comes in contact with the church, the school, the government, economic organizations, and other secondary groups. The wider his interests, the more extended his relations with secondary groups become.

After the Industrial Revolution brought about the factory system and the growth of cities, secondary groupings greatly increased, and the contacts of the individual have been correspondingly extended. The city, because of its size, mobility, and diversity of interests, has increased secondary contacts and decreased primary contacts. Few residents of city apartments know their next-door neighbor; a laborer or clerk riding to work on the subway has a brief contact with a large number of people, but he is scarcely affected by the experience. Intimate and continuous relationship with neighbors is not often possible in the varied activities of city life. City play groups are usually rather formal and consciously planned secondary associations.

**The "we-group" and the "others-group."** In all societies, both primitive and modern, there is a division of social groups into the "we-group" and the "others-group," sometimes also known as the "in-group" and the "out-group." The "we-group" is one which has a common kinship, racial, economic, or cultural basis. Every "we-group" has a sense of dislike, fear, or distrust for the "others-group." The feeling of prejudice against those not of the same group is often enlarged into racial prejudice or class hatred. The trade union is often bitter toward employers' associations, and vice versa. Even members of one religious sect often have an aversion for members of another. In ordinary times, relationships of the "we-group" to the "others-group" are passive, though rarely cordial; but when sharp antagonisms arise, the clash of attitudes may bring about active conflict.

## Other Ways of Viewing and Classifying Social Groups

**Giddings' conception of component and constituent groups.** Since group life is so important in the development and operations of mankind, we may well afford to look at some other ways of studying and classifying social groups. Giddings divided social groups into two great types: *component* groups and *constituent* groups. He defined as component groups all spontaneous, self-sustaining, and self-perpetuating groups which have a minimum of conscious deliberation in their formation and participation and are not primarily organized with the aim of achieving any special social purpose. Such are the family, tribes, neighborhoods, villages, towns, and the like. There is a great deal of likeness and similarity, both physically and mentally, in these component groups.

Constituent groups Giddings regarded as those which are consciously organized to carry on particular activities or to achieve a special purpose. They are not naturally self-sustaining or self-perpetuating. Examples of constituent groups are the household, clans, political parties, labor unions, chambers of commerce, corporations, churches, schools, cultural associations, clubs, and, most impressive and powerful of all, the state and government.

**Fairchild's classification of social groups.** A somewhat similar classification of social groups has been proposed by another eminent sociologist, Henry Pratt Fairchild. He divided groups into three types: involuntary, semi-voluntary, and entirely voluntary. We participate in involuntary groups without any deliberation whatever. For example, we involuntarily or spontaneously live with human beings rather than animals. The sex urge impels us into other forms of group life. We normally tend to live within the same racial group in which we are born. Semi-voluntary groups are those in which our participation is brought about in part by natural forces or pressures and in part by some deliberate choice. For example, the natural sex urge impels us to mating, but in all civilized societies the original members of a family exercise some degree of choice in selecting a mate.

Other semi-voluntary groups are the church, political parties, occupational groups, the nation, and the government. Purely voluntary groups are those which we *join* as an act of deliberate preference and conscious interest. Such are professional groups, lodges, fraternities, literary societies, musical organizations, and the like.

**Permanent and temporary groupings.** Kimball Young, who has given special attention to group life and psychology, believes that we should also distinguish between permanent and impermanent or temporary social groups. All primary groups and most secondary groups can be regarded as of a permanent character. Impermanent groups are those which, for the moment, may have a high degree of cohesion and mutual interest, but are likely to fall apart or break up in a relatively short time. Such are crowds, audiences, enthusiastic "fans" of a particular passing hero, and partisans of a temporarily popular public program of economic reform.

**The idea of interest-groups.** One of the most fruitful and illuminating ways of classifying groups is based upon the gravitation of groups around specific human interests. This approach to the analysis of groups and their activities has been developed chiefly by the Austrian sociologist, Gustav Ratzenhofer, his American admirer, Professor Small, and Small's disciple, Arthur F. Bentley. Small held that there are six basic human interests: the Health Interest, divided into the food, sex, and work interests; the Wealth Interest; the Sociability Interest; the Knowledge Interest; the Beauty Interest; and the Rightness Interest.

Groups inevitably arise to advance and defend these basic life interests in the several fields. Such groups we call interest-groups, and they run all the way from the hunting groups of savages to an organization of artists or a philosophical society. What we call the social process, namely, the sum total of human interactions, may be regarded fundamentally as the rise, expansion, conflict, competition, adjustment, and co-operation of these interest-groups. The basic purpose of government is to act as a sort of umpire of this social process, seeking to keep the conflict of interest-groups within orderly bounds without stifling it. Political parties are, in any profound sense, interest-groups or combinations of interest-groups; and the whole political process is, as A. F. Bentley has amply demonstrated, the struggle, adjustment, and accommodation of these conflicting interest-groups. The ideal government, according to Bentley, is the one in which the maximum degree of conflict among interest-groups that is compatible with orderly public life is permitted to exist. This struggle of interest-groups is the most dynamic factor in social evolution; all other things being equal and order being preserved, the greater the volume and variety in this conflict of interest-groups, the more rapid the rate of social evolution.

These classifications of social groups are not mutually exclusive or contradictory, but simply clarify the character of social groupings and drive home the fact of the variety and complexity of group life which forms the raw material of all sociological study.

**Personality and the group.** There has been a traditional effort to set off the person and society as things apart from each other—to contend for a sort of quality or contrast of the personality and the group, as though they were separate entities. There is, of course, often a conflict between individual impulses and group pressures, but the notion that the group and the personality are separate and opposing realities is a fiction. The human personality is invariably developed by group situations and relationships. The eminent sociologist Charles Horton Cooley frequently emphasized the fact that the words *personality* and *group* are largely abstractions unless considered in their natural relation to each other. He held that the individual and the group are inseparable: "The antithesis, society versus the individual, is false and hollow wherever used as a general or philosophical statement of human relations. . . . Individuality is neither prior in time nor lower in moral rank than sociality. The two have always existed side by side as complementary aspects of the same thing."

Without group life and prolonged association there can be no such thing as personality, in the sense in which the latter is understood in social science. The completely isolated human being is only a biological entity, with less personality than an ape that has lived in group situations with other apes. Some physio-psychologists believe that the glandular and other factors in the purely physical equipment of an individual are important in determining his personality; this matter has been ably treated in W. H. Sheldon's *Varieties of Temperament.* However, the experiences of associated life are essential to the creation of personality in any understandable sense of the term.

In a following chapter we shall refer to examples of individuals who have been found more or less devoid of any experience in group life— persons who have grown up without any normal social contacts.[1]  In all cases, such persons are without the normal traits of personality; they are little better than wild animals. Such general differences in personality as exist between the lowest savages and modern civilized men are due entirely to the influence of culture and sociability, and culture itself is a social product that is handed along from generation to generation by social groups. There is no essential difference between the basic physical make-up of a modern Frenchman and one who dwelt in the caves of southern France 30,000 years ago. The striking personality differences between the two are a result of the social experiences and cultural accretions since the Stone Age.

The human personality is built up through a series of social contacts and experiences from the maternity ward to the undertaking parlor. The individual is born with a biological predisposition to a

---

[1] See below, pp. 86–88.

definite personality type—from feeble-mindedness to genius, from sto-lidity to extreme nervous agitation, from extroversion to introversion, and the like.   This biological entity is brought into contact with the cultural heritage of the past through various social experiences from earliest family life to maturity.   As the result of this exposure and the experiences of an ever-expanding social life, the personality is slowly built up from day to day, in a process which ends only with the grave. The same person may exhibit contrasting personality traits at dif-ferent periods in his life.   The process of personality-building begins with the relations of the infant with his mother and other relatives. It is carried on through contacts with neighbors and school associates from the kindergarten to the graduate school, play groups, clubs, occu-pational groups, cultural associations, and the like, whether in the same local environment or with different races on distant continents.

The main point to emphasize here is that personality is the product of group life.   Even solitary reflection and contemplation in isolation is usually little more than passing in review one's reactions to previous group experiences and products.   Yet we should not overlook the fact that there is often a real conflict or antagonism between individual impulses and group pressures.   The ideal society is one which main-tains a proper balance or compromise between these, so as to guarantee progress and yet avert chaos and disorder.   The greatest menace in our present-day trend towards totalitarianism is that dynamic individual impulses may be unduly suppressed.

## The Genesis and Differentiation of Social Classes

**The origin of the traditional hierarchy of social classes.**   The so-cial classes with which we are familiar are a product of the historic experience of mankind and the development of specialization in social operations.   In primitive society, there was rarely any extensively de-veloped hierarchy of social classes—at least in any save the more highly organized primitive groups.   Most social classes in primitive society were of a functional character—military groups, laboring classes (mainly women), religious classes, secret societies, age classes, marriage and relationship classes, and the like.   The hierarchy of social classes which has been fairly persistent during historic times was an outgrowth of the period of feudalism that intervened between primitive, kin-ship society and the dawn of history, which brought in civil or political society, based on territorial residence and property rights.

The successful conquering feudal lords became in time the kings of the city-states which supplanted feudalism.   The war bands of the feudal lords became the royal court and the great landed aristocracy. Below these came the freemen, serfs, and slaves, whose status bore a direct relation to the recency of their conquest.   The freemen were those whose ancestors had been conquered and brought within the conquering group at the most remote period.   The serfs were the product of a later conquest, and the slaves represented those most recently conquered, or their descendants. As soon as a fairly settled life was achieved and manufacturing and trade began to develop, there arose the business class, or bourgeoisie, the first important and outright functional social class. This class differentiation or class hierarchy of king, court, landed aristocracy, bourgeoisie, free peasantry, serfs, and slaves persisted from the dawn of history right down into modern times, when serfdom and slavery were finally abolished (in some regions not until after the middle of the eighteenth century). The class pattern that evolved out of the traditional hierarchy has been made up of the landed aristocracy, the middle class or bourgeoisie, the working proletariat, and the rural peasantry. This class pattern still persists in most parts of the civilized world.

**Functional classes and the future of the class system.** In addition to the traditional or historic hierarchy of social classes, there has been an elaborate development of social classes on a more purely functional basis. There are numerous and diversified economic classes, political classes, religious classes, and social classes, each of which performs some special service in our complicated social system.

Social and cultural progress is most likely to take place when the class system is fairly open and flexible, permitting what is known as vertical mobility—the ability to rise in the social hierarchy on the basis of ability. A caste system, in which one's class status is based on birth and heredity, is likely to arrest progress—at least until stagnation and oppression provoke a revolution.

The question is often raised as to whether the promise of the radicals—Socialists, Anarchists, Syndicalists, and Communists—that their programs will produce a classless society will ever work out in actual practice. Should one of these radical programs succeed and mature, it is quite possible that the hierarchy of social classes based on property and status would be wiped out. But there is every likelihood that class lines would re-establish themselves on a functional basis, as they have already given indications of doing in Soviet Russia.

## Impersonal Relationships and Social Stratification

**Specialization increases impersonal relationships.** In the simple economic life of primitive, ancient, and medieval society, economic relationships were direct and personal. Today, particularly in the city, there is a complex commercial and industrial organization; ownership and control of business are usually separated; and the employer and employee live in different social and economic worlds. This large-scale, impersonal social organization has been brought about in part by increasing industrial specialization and division of labor.

The increase in industrial specialization since the Industrial Revolution has affected almost every phase of economic life The United States Census lists over 25,000 occupations, most of them urban rather than rural. Whenever society becomes complex, new wants and needs develop, and new occupations arise to satisfy these needs. Another factor has been the rapid development of new machines, new tools, and new methods that have subdivided each job many times. Operations once performed by one man are now distributed among tens or hundreds of workers.

The manufacture of shoes will illustrate this point. A century ago, four processes were involved in shoe-making—cutting, fitting, lasting, and soling. A single worker might be employed on all four processes, using only a few simple tools. He was either an owner-operator or employed by the owner of the shop, who worked with him. The modern shoe factory employs hundreds of workers, many of them highly specialized in the use of elaborate machinery. Each process in shoe-making involves many separate jobs; cutting a shoe takes five separate operations and soling twelve. The factory owner, instead of being directly in charge of his business, may have his office thousands of miles away, and have little direct knowledge of the technology of shoe manufacturing.

Not only are occupations specialized, but specialization has entered social, recreational, and political life. All along the line, social groupings tend to become more functional and less personal.

**Contemporary forms of social stratification.** Specialization has also brought about the "stratification" of contemporary social classes. By social stratification we mean a type of social organization in which social contacts, feelings, and controls express themselves chiefly on a horizontal level, as in a well-defined class or caste system. In a rigidly stratified society, persons can move, socially speaking, only in a horizontal fashion. It is difficult or impossible for them to move vertically, i.e., to cut through class lines. As society has become more complex and material culture more elaborate, more numerous lines and levels of stratification have arisen.

Stratification in a democracy may be difficult to understand because class lines are not clearly drawn. Those persons on the same occupational level tend, however, to form a definite social layer. Thus, even in a democratic society there are many social levels, varying from the unskilled workers to the executive and managerial groups. There is some vertical social mobility between groups in the United States; it is possible to move up the social and economic ladder by making money or marrying wealth, but occupation usually remains the index of *economic* and social status. Such terms as capitalist, "white collar" worker, skilled worker, and laborer indicate not only something of the type of work done, but also the social and economic status of the individual.

In modern times, with the growth of industrialization and democracy, social stratification has tended to change from a rigid class and caste basis to a form of stratification based on functions. The main cleavage today is one into capitalists, farmers, and workers. In American society we would find the chief levels of social stratification to be the following: the great investment bankers, the leading commercial bankers, the great industrialists and their legal aids, the lesser bankers and industrialists, the professional classes, merchants, contractors, small business men, civil servants, farmers, skilled workers, semi-skilled workers, unskilled workers, and farm laborers.

Some group relationships are common to all classes. For instance, capitalist, clerk, and laborer may belong to the same political party or church, although there is no personal contact between them.

**Variety and complexity of social groupings in urban society.** Many of the associations in free societies today are a matter of choice; the individuals may select, within certain limitations, those groups which appeal to their interest. Anderson and Lindeman have listed the wide range of social groups to which individuals may belong in our urban, industrial society: [2]

1. Functional groups, organized primarily on behalf of a specific and objective interest, such as trade unions and manufacturers' associations.
2. Occupational groups, organized on behalf of a professional interest, such as medical societies and engineering societies.
3. Philanthropic and reform groups, organized to protect the unfortunate members of society.
4. Religious groups, held together by a common subjective goal.
5. Nationality groups, usually immigrants who cling together because of the same language or traditions.
6. Memory groups, organized to preserve past association for the present and future, such as war veteran societies and alumni associations.
7. Symbolic groups, formed about a set of symbolisms or rituals, such as lodges, fraternal and secret societies.
8. Service-recreational groups, informally organized to meet the desire for recreation and service, such as Rotary, Kiwanis, and Lions clubs.
9. Political groups and clubs, organized for the purpose of perpetuating a set of political principles, such as Tammany Hall, Jefferson clubs, and Lincoln clubs.
10. Feminist groups, composed of women and organized in the interest of cultural, educational, and civic betterment, such as women's clubs and leagues of women voters.
11. Groups such as the bohemian, intellectual, and aesthetic groups and gangs, often called the "atypical" groups of society.

From the above list it is obvious that there is a wide range of interests in contemporary society, that there are a large number of groups which develop to satisfy these interests, and that without cohesive social organization, modern social life could not exist as it does today.

## Social Organization Indispensable to Social Progress

**Man's dependence on social organization.** Social organization is essential to man's progress and security. Unless the rights and achieve-

---

[2] Condensed from Nels Anderson and E. C. Lindeman, *Urban Sociology*, Crofts, 1928, pp. 298–299.

ments of the individual can be protected by some form of social control that prevents disorder and confusion and safeguards the interests of both the individual and the group, there can be no security or progress.

The individual is dependent on the group from birth to death. Only through the social contacts of family and community is he able to develop his personality. Every person is born with a set of hereditary traits or drives, but the way in which these develop depends, to a great extent, on the group in which he lives. The human personality is a product of social organization. The hypothetical "normal" person is one who is completely adjusted to the world about him and is satisfied with the tasks which society has given him.

**Co-operation must guide specialization.** Since individual life can be preserved and continued only through group life, conscious co-operation is necessary to assure social progress. In order that a complicated society may function, there must be a steady flow of activity among all the groups. Every specialized activity must fit logically into a larger whole. The finished pair of shoes depends on the operations of all the workers in the factory, and the more specialized the industry, the more necessary the teamwork. Each activity must have its proper place with respect to related activities. Thus, the need for social organization increases with specialization and the division of labor. Ample evidence that many social activities do not operate smoothly is found in strikes, unemployment, poverty, broken homes, war, crime, and juvenile delinquency.

These social problems result from cultural lag. It is once more apparent, therefore, that if we are to live effectively and happily we must find ways to improve our social organization by bringing our social institutions into better adjustment with material culture and into greater harmony with each other.

## Problems and Mechanisms of Social Control

**Need for social discipline.** All societies recognize that authority is a necessary part of social organization. Even within the family group some form of discipline is required to establish and maintain unity. The decrease of family discipline is apparent in the increase of divorces and illustrates the need for better social organization. In industry, as we have seen, it was necessary to make laws governing wages, hours, and conditions of work so that our complicated economic life would run smoothly. In politics and government, force is extensively relied upon. Instead of the dictates of a monarch, a democracy utilizes the force of public opinion. The dictatorships of Europe have well illustrated the evils of the arbitrary exercise of force.

**Rôle of the state and government.** Society lodges its final use of force in the state. The state, which operates normally and practically through the enforcement of law by the government, is the chief coercive type of social organization. To allow private groups to have the arbitrary right of coercion brings violence. In such instances, the individual loses his freedom, and injustice and exploitation result.

**Custom and public opinion.** The will of the group is enforced not only by the government through law and the fear of punishment but also through custom and public opinion. Custom is the basis of communal life. Each generation receives a cultural heritage from the past which includes knowledge, beliefs, and standards of conduct in every important field of behavior. It is difficult to realize how much individuals depend on the vast body of folkways, traditions, ideals, industrial methods, social beliefs, and religious notions which have been handed down to us from former generations and constitute the basis of the customs and social habits which govern us in our daily life. Our present-day methods of making a living and creating wealth and our family organization, religion, politics, and education are, in part, the products of the past. No individual or community can be wholly freed from the influence of custom and tradition.

Public opinion reflects the customs and traditions of the group. If there are no wide differences of race, cultural traditions, or property, the group usually depends to a large extent upon public opinion to bring about uniformity of conduct and orderly behavior. This was especially true before the Industrial Revolution, when groups were smaller. Recently, however, largely as a result of large-scale shifts of population, these differences in race, culture, and class have come more and more to exist within groups; hence, the growing state enforcement of social order through law and political pressure.

**Rôle of social regulation.** In a complex society, leadership is necessary to promote unity. The workings of a complex system cannot be entrusted entirely to public opinion, custom, or the spontaneous adjustments of a primary group; there must be centralization of authority. Each large-scale organization becomes in a sense an administrative unit. Not only must its own structure be organized, but it must fit into an intricate whole. This adjustment demands established rules, a formal authority with designated powers, and clear-cut responsibilities. Thus, economic and political life, religion, and education, each with its highly complex structure, are drawn together into a unified system by the final source of authority—the state.

**Organization versus freedom.** Many times in the past, groups have rebelled against the excesses or extremes of extensive social organization, but the world of today is essentially a mechanized, impersonal world. Within it, each man has his own small task, which has become more sharply defined as specialization has increased. His work confines him to monotonous routines and techniques, and he occupies a reduced personal rôle in the total social order. Many persons have thought that this imperils the full realization of man's abilities. There is undoubtedly some danger in this restriction of freedom and initiative, but complex social organization has so far brought more gain than loss.  It has made possible wider and more rapid communication between peoples, has extended and improved education, has laid the foundations of a broader culture, and has opened new vistas in the use of leisure time which may free man from his earlier narrow interests.  But we should always be on our guard against totalitarian trends that would extend regimentation beyond the minimum requirements of social security and progress.

## Social Disorganization and Contemporary Social Problems

**Social disorganization creates social problems.**  In the preceding pages we have shown how group life and social organization have made possible the development of civilization and the enjoyment of the security and comforts which we possess today.  But there is another side to the study of group life and social control to which we must give attention, since this book is devoted in considerable part to a study of our social problems in the middle of the twentieth century.  If social organization, when functioning well, produces vast and innumerable benefits, defects in social organization give rise to most of our social problems.  If social organization, operating through the social institutions which we shall study in the next chapter, does not provide the proper guidance and control over living conditions, social life is likely to be chaotic, inefficient, and productive of poverty, misery, crime, family disintegration, and war.  The condition characterized by inadequate social organization has been termed "social disorganization" by an eminent sociologist, W. I. Thomas.  Social disorganization is a concept of great importance in practical sociology.

**Nature of social disorganization.**  Thomas briefly describes social disorganization as any serious "decrease of the influence of existing rules of social behavior upon the individual members of the group." Professor Kimball Young, a student of Thomas, clarifies the idea in the following manner: "Social disorganization refers to the breakdown of the societal order to such an extent that the former controls are dissipated, the former correlation of personality and culture is destroyed, and a certain chaos or disorder arises in which old ways of doing have been lost and new ways not yet developed." [3]

There is nothing difficult about understanding this notion of social disorganization.  Social organization, operating through the ideas and institutions which control group life, is essential for an orderly, secure, and prosperous social existence and a rich individual scheme of life.  Therefore, it is inevitable that, when this social organization breaks down seriously, in other words, degenerates into disorganization, we lose the advantages and guidance of normal group living, and a greater or less degree of social chaos results.  Thus, if the family controls, neighborhood co-operation, and religious guidance that for-

---

[3] Kimball Young, *An Introductory Sociology*, American Book Company, 1934, p. 54.

merly sufficed to discipline life in a rural era no longer function effectively, and no improvements or substitutes are offered, it is quite natural that living conditions in that area will be disorganized and pathological. If effective social organization produces a normal and secure living pattern, a disintegrating social order is doomed to result in abnormal living conditions and social behavior, or what we term social problems.

**Social disorganization produced by cultural lag.** Some may think that there is a discrepancy here between the idea that social disorganization causes social problems and the statement frequently made in this book that social problems are an outgrowth of cultural lag. But there is no contradiction whatever. Cultural lag is precisely what causes social disorganization. The latter arises when social institutions get out of harmony with prevailing intellectual attitudes and material conditions. Archaic and decaying social institutions no longer provide efficient social organization, and the result is that social life goes askew and living conditions become pathological. Social disorganization is only another, and very useful, way of describing the more acute and pathological results of cultural lag.

## Revolutionary Recent Enlargement of Social Groups, Structures, and Interests

**Expansion of social experience.** Among the chief reasons for social disorganization in our day have been the revolutionary changes in the nature and extent of social groups, structures, interests, and controls. These changes are a result of industrialization, the growth of vast urban concentrations of population, and the development of contemporary technology, chiefly the new agencies of transportation and communication which have transferred many of the most important group activities from a local to a national or international basis and have created social structures and interest-groups so vast that neither the social experience nor the social science of the past can cope with their problems.

**Present-day social processes transcend personal and local societies.** The socializing processes of the past, even of the fairly recent past, grew out of human experience in small, personal, and simple societies, chiefly primary and small secondary groups such as the family, neighborhood, and the community. Action and thought were controlled chiefly by relatively stable local custom and the cultural heritage of a limited area. Most sociological thinking about the elementary socializing processes has also been concentrated on what goes on in such small and simple groups. Local group life and the sociological analysis thereof are obviously important, but neither fully prepares the citizen of today to recognize the world he lives in or to deal with its problems effectively.

Many of the most important problems and experiences of the

citizen of the mid-twentieth century have been expanded by our technological revolution to a national or world scope, for which the knowledge and experiences gained in primary and small secondary groups provide no adequate preparation, even in understanding the practices and problems involved, to say nothing of their efficient and rapid solution.

**Examples of broadened social contacts and the problems they create.** There have been vast movements and migrations of peoples, producing extensive racial contrasts and mixtures. Many political and economic problems involve several great racial stocks inhabiting different continents. The socializing experience gained in a small, local society offers little guidance for such relationships and adjustments. The contemporary world has brought about a vast and varied interdependence of groups and peoples, but without having subjected the members to any socializing and educational experience which would fit them to understand each other and co-operate effectively. In a profound social sense, members of these groups are strangers to each other, with all the suspicion and blockage of understanding and action which this relation produces. We have a multiplicity of groups on a national scale, such as business organizations, labor unions, and other interest-groups, made up of millions of persons with a widely diversified racial and cultural background. Even wider in scope and diversity are international organizations, cartels, relief and rehabilitation organizations, and so on. This situation produces struggles for power, prestige, and adjustment which involve conflicts in social philosophies, economic creeds, political ideologies, and moral patterns. In dealing with these conflicts, individual experience gained in the socializing processes of local groups provides little guidance.

**Wider social pressures.** Not only have new and much larger groups and social structures made their appearance, but novel and more extensive forms of social control, social pressure, and channels of information have come into being to supplement or replace family teachings, neighborhood gossip, local public opinion, and stereotyped community customs. We are subjected to a comprehensive, varied, and continuous barrage of consciously framed and deliberately inculcated propaganda that reaches whole nations simultaneously in the effort to shape opinion and control action to preconceived ends. "The Voice of America" speeds in short-wave radio to the Old World with the aim of promoting American policies abroad. All the mammoth interest-groups mentioned above have access to the newspapers and the air and carry on propaganda to advance their several programs. The individual is overwhelmed by pressures thrown at him from every direction.

**Reaction of new experiences and contacts upon the individual.** All this has greatly modified the status and operations of the individual citizen. In the past, the individual was preponderant as the dweller in a small community. He was largely self-controlled, within the confines of local opinion and practice, and exerted a more or less significant influence on the events and activities of his time.   Now he is caught up in the midst of great social structures and movements over which he can exert little influence as a separate individual and the nature of which he often imperfectly understands.   At the very time when individuals are becoming ever more conscious of their basic rights and privileges, they are also constantly getting more dependent on organizations, many of them of wide scope and membership, in order to attain their desired goals and to protect their achievements.   But they are poorly fitted by past experience to function as individuals within such organizations.

**Sociology must reckon with new trends.**   Both society and sociological analysis must reorient themselves in the light of these new and revolutionary trends in social organization; they must re-adapt thought and action to take account of these sweeping changes in the technological and psychological nature of the new era.   Neither social action nor sociological description will have much relation to basic realities if it stems solely from life in, or study of, the simple, personal societies which dominated life down to a generation or so ago.

In this book we shall endeavor to present social processes and problems in the light of these new trends, though always remaining conscious that many individuals still live out their lives in small groups and are in part controlled by local codes of opinion, definitions, and moral patterns.

## Summary

The group is the social basis of human life.   Primitive man was naturally social, and he soon learned that he could get more enjoyment out of life and better achieve his desires if he joined forces with his fellow men.   Although he lost individual freedom in the discipline of group life, he gained more by working with others than in trying to make his way alone.

As the primitive group enlarged, men found it necessary to have leaders and make laws for the welfare of the group.   Man broadened his horizons by coming in contact with other groups.   This gradual expansion of social experience led to the social groupings of modern society, which are based on social, economic, political, educational, cultural, and religious interests.   Man has developed a multitude of different forms of association.

No community or member of a community is self-sufficient.   Everyone depends in some way on the help of others, some of whom may live in remote parts of the world.   Most group life in our day has a definite, conscious aim, in contrast with primitive group life, which was natural and spontaneous.

Certain bonds or forces, have brought men together since primitive times.   Out of these have grown the leading forms of social groups. Geographical forces usually determine the areas in which social groups will settle. The most elementary social force—the biological—has produced the family, a leading primary group. Next to the biological in power and influence stands the mutual-interest bond, which is psychological and economic in nature. Mutual interest draws men together in the organization of agriculture, business, and the professions. Most of these are secondary groups.

Each of these associations has a definite object, whether it be as temporary as the common interest of the crowd at a football game or as permanent as the family, the church, and the state. In modern times, forms of group life have become diverse and more interdependent over wide geographical areas. This situation is shown by the rapid and extensive growth of secondary forms of association.

The individual must learn to fit into the group and to uphold its standards. While the individual might theoretically live a freer life independent of group control, he has learned that it is to his advantage to remain a part of the social organism. No person deprived of the assistance of social organization and group life could enjoy the fruits of contemporary civilization.

The breakdown of the institutions which guide group life produces what is known as social disorganization—the more acute and pathological aspect of cultural lag.

The extensive development of new methods of transportation and communication and the rise of vast urban centers of population have tended to break down the old moorings of life and disrupt the social patterns of the simpler, personal societies of the past—the primary and smaller secondary social groups. As a result, man has been forced to meet new and more difficult problems of adjustment and control, for which he has been little prepared by either social experience or social science. One of the great responsibilities of social science in our time is to explore and clarify these new social situations and to supply means of coping with the difficulties they present.

## Selected References

Burgess, E. W., *Personality and the Social Group*, University of Chicago Press, 1926. Symposium that makes clear how personality is developed through social contacts.

Bushee, F. A., *Social Organization*, Holt, 1930. A reliable and mature discussion of the forces, mechanisms, and institutions which create group life and produce and maintain coherent social organization.

* Carter, C. C., and Brentnall, H. C., *Man the World Over*, Appleton-Century, 1939. A brilliantly written and profusely illustrated survey of the geographical background of human life in all lands. Descriptive rather than theoretical.

Centers, Richard, *The Psychology of Social Classes*, Princeton University, 1949. Valuable analysis of the nature and effects of class structure and consciousness in American life.

* Cooley, C. H., *Social Organization,* Scribner, 1909. The classic account of primary groups and their impact on all social institutions, especially the democratic way of life.

Faris, R. E. L., *Social Disorganization,* Ronald, 1948. Latest sociological study of the important concept and process of social disorganization.

* Groves, E. R., *Personality and Social Adjustment,* Longmans, Green, 1923. A good elementary account of the socializing of the personality in group life, being especially strong in its discussion of psychological forces.

Hiller, E. T., *Social Relations and Structures,* Harper, 1947. One of the most up-to-date and useful books on the social basis of culture and institutions.

* Keith, Sir Arthur, *A New Theory of Human Evolution,* Philosophical Library, 1949. Most comprehensive exposition of the doctrine that group life has been chiefly responsible for the physical types, anatomical evolution, and socio-mental traits of the human race, by the dean of living physical anthropologists.

Kluckhohn, Clyde, and Murray, H. A. (Eds.), *Personality in Nature, Society, and Culture,* Knopf, 1948. Recent symposium on the social and cultural basis of personality.

Lowie, R. H., *Social Organization,* Rinehart, 1948. Able book on forms and types of social organization, with emphasis on anthropological problems and primitive social organization.

* Marshall, L. C., *The Story of Human Progress,* Macmillan, 1925. A deservedly popular introduction to man's conquest of nature and the modes of group organization and co-operation. The best introduction to the theme of this chapter.

McConnell, John W., *The Evolution of Social Classes,* American Council on Public Affairs, 1942. Important introductory historical survey.

Moore, W. E., *Industrial Relations and the Social Order,* Macmillan, 1946. Discusses the bearing of occupations and industrial relations on social stratification and mobility.

Müller-Lyer, Franz, *The History of Social Development,* Knopf, 1921. A classic European survey of many phases of social evolution, being especially strong on the evolution of labor and forms of producing wealth.

North, C. C., *Social Differentiation,* University of North Carolina, 1927. Pioneer work on social differentiation and the rise of social classes.

————, and Hatt, P. K., *A Study in Occupational Ratings and Prestige.* Important forthcoming work.

Queen, S. A., Bodenhafer, W. B., and Harper, E. B., *Social Organization and Disorganization,* Crowell, 1935. Good treatment of both social organization, and the disorganization resulting from institutional changes and cultural lag.

Sears, P. B., *This Is Our World,* University of Oklahoma Press, 1935. An extremely readable and interesting survey of the relation between nature and human life. Very important for perspective on modern culture and social life.

Sorokin, P. A., *Social Mobility,* Harper, 1927.   The most complete discussion of the process of social mobility.

Stern, B. J. (Ed.), *The Family: Past and Present,* Appleton-Century, 1938. One of the best books on the history and social rôle of the family.

Warner, W. L., Meeker, M., and Eells, K. W., *Social Class in America,* Social Research Associates, 1948.   Comprehensive study of social classes and class status in the United States.

Woods, R. A., *The Neighborhood in Nation Building,* Houghton Mifflin, 1923. A thoughtful and illuminating study of the social influence of one of the major primary institutions.

# CHAPTER V

# The Institutional Framework of Social Life

## The Basic Drives to Human Activity

**Institutions supply the framework of group life.** In the preceding chapter we saw that social organization is necessary if the individual is to be protected and society is to function efficiently. The structure required for the successful control and direction of group activities is supplied by our social institutions.

**The basic human drives.** All human activity grows out of the basic drives which are inherent in man's physical nature. These drives give rise to certain needs and stimulate the appropriate activities to satisfy them. Our social institutions have been created to satisfy individual needs.

The most powerful human drive is that of self-preservation. Every normal person has a strong will to live; he tries to protect himself against exposure, hunger, sickness, assault, and accident. Another primary drive is for self-perpetuation—the continuance of the human race. This gives rise to man's sexual desires, which lead him to love, marriage, and raising children. The third important drive is for self-expression, the urge "to do something" rather than sit idly around.

These basic drives arise in all human beings regardless of the group in which they live. Even if a normal person were completely isolated from any contact with a group, he would have the will to live, an urge for sexual activity, and a desire for self-expression. Under normal circumstances, however, these human drives are intensified, conditioned, and regulated by the fact that man is a social being and lives in a group consisting of other individuals with the same basic impulses.

**The drives conditioned by their social setting.** It was noted in the preceding chapter that man, because of his physical weaknesses, found it easier to survive in a group. It follows that the basic human drives are profoundly affected by their social setting. The drive for self-perpetuation is conditioned to a great extent by group life; the sex impulses can be fully gratified only in a group consisting of both men and women. Organized society attempts to regulate the sexual relations of individuals by sanctioning marriage for the purpose of bearing and rearing children. The drive for self-expression, also, can only be fully stimulated and realized in group life. While the isolated individual might be able to indulge in plenty of physical action, other forms of self-expression require group association for their fullest development.

We may thus conclude that, while the basic human drives are inherent in the individual's physical nature, their expression takes place within social surroundings and is controlled by the rules of the group. Indeed, these basic human drives may be looked upon as the primary forces which lead to social organization and create institutions.

**Self-preservation.** The basic drives express themselves in definite needs. Out of the drive for self-preservation arise the needs for food, clothing, shelter, and health. These needs may vary with the conditions under which an individual lives. For example, the need for clothing and shelter is less in warm climates than in cold. Nevertheless, self-preservation depends upon the satisfaction of some such needs under any circumstances. Other needs brought forth by the drive for self-preservation are of a social character. Group customs and tastes determine the extent and type of demand for food, clothing, shelter, and medical treatment. Our modern system for producing these things is the result of many centuries of co-operative social effort.

**Self-perpetuation.** Love, marriage, affection for children, and the desire to provide comforts for one's family grow out of the drive for self-perpetuation. From this drive also are derived such complicated social needs as population policies, designed to regulate the rate of population growth and improve the quality of the population.

**Self-expression.** The drive for self-expression takes many forms; fighting, working, play, and creative work in the arts are among the more basic. While fighting and working are usually necessary for self-preservation, many persons engage in these activities merely for self-expression. Many rich business men, for example, continue to work for prestige or because they enjoy working, even though their fortunes could support them in idleness the rest of their lives.

Primitive man expressed his artistic impulses by painting on the walls of caves and making crude musical instruments. From the informal play groups of early times to the highly organized recreation centers of today, man has played in his leisure time. Curiosity also seems to be an outgrowth of the desire for self-expression. Very early in his existence, man began to show curiosity about his existence and physical surroundings and attempted to explain personal emotions, the sun, moon, and stars, the seasons, and other mysteries of nature. He first found an answer in religion, which regarded every natural phenomenon as an expression of divine will. This quest for knowledge later led mankind to seek a more satisfactory explanation in science. Much of our intellectual life has been stimulated and guided by curiosity.

Thus, out of the fundamental drives, self-preservation, self-perpetuation, and self-expression, have grown varied human needs. To satisfy them a wide variety of activities have been developed. In primitive groups, these activities were simple, because the needs were few; but, as civilization has progressed and population increased, the range of human and social activities has steadily widened.

## Human Needs and Drives Produce and
## Diversify Social Activities

**Efforts to master the physical environment.** To a great extent, man's needs and activities are regulated by the climate, natural resources, and other physical factors.

At first, human beings made little attempt to change their environment, but conformed their activities and their mode of life to their surroundings. As civilization progressed, groups were able to make nature work to satisfy their needs. They learned how to domesticate animals, clear the ground and plant cereals, dig for minerals, and fashion tools. Later on, machines were devised to provide clothing, shelter, and other goods in greater volume. The search for ways to adapt the environment to human needs led to the development of steam power and electricity. These advances not only supplied man's needs but increased his activities as well; he was able to travel and communicate with other men in different places. Ocean and air, once barriers to human movements, became agencies of transportation and communication.

The manifestations of nature have stimulated other forms of activity. Man's curiosity concerning nature, life, and death led to the earliest forms of religion, based on the divinity of natural phenomena, which were worshiped because they were not understood. In the same way, earthquakes, tidal waves, and hurricanes were interpreted in a supernatural manner.

**The struggle for health and physical well-being.** Man's need for health and physical well-being has brought forth many activities. From the days of the magical rites and potions of the primitive medicine-man to the rise of modern medicine, the search for good health has been constant. Not only has scientific medical care been developed, but there has been much activity along the lines of public health and sanitation, making it possible for mankind to live together and carry on modern industry.

**Earning a living.** The task of earning a living has produced more activity than any other basic need. Attempts to secure food, clothing, and shelter have been constant and ever expanding. The problem of getting men to work effectively has extended from the days of ancient slave labor to the modern factory system. The need for training laborers has brought forth family training, gild and trade union apprenticeship, and advanced technical education. The problem of supervising industry, trade, and banking has created some of the chief activities of government.  The many persons who are unable to make a living because of physical or mental handicaps have made it necessary for society to provide means of caring for them.  The accumulation, protection, and transfer of property, which are part of the activity of making a living, have led to the development of banks, trust companies, legal firms, insurance agencies, and other related activities.

**Transportation.**  More effective means of transportation have been developed in answer to human needs.  Modern industry depends on wide areas for the supply of raw materials and markets for finished products.  War, also, has stimulated better transportation, as troops were compelled to move rapidly over greater distances.  Government has promoted the growth of transportation; the creation of large states with strong central governments would have been impossible without some means of speedy communication and transportation.  Travel, recreation, and curiosity have also encouraged the development of more efficient means of transportation.  Routes of travel have progressed from pathways through forests and marshes to six-lane concrete highways, four-track railroads, ship canals, and world-wide airplane routes.

**Communication.**  In order to make group life easier, man needed some workable means of communicating his ideas.  He developed first a spoken language and then an alphabet, by which to put down his ideas in written form.  Written language made possible books, periodicals, and newspapers, which in turn led to the establishment of libraries.  These facilities for communication enabled man to create one of his outstanding achievements, a cultural heritage, which could be handed down from generation to generation.

Railroads made possible the rapid transmission of written communications.  The postal service on railroads helped to conquer distances; newspapers provided for rapid collection and distribution of news.  The effects of electricity were even more revolutionary.  The telegraph transmitted words almost instantaneously.  The telephone and the radio made it possible to hear, as well as read about, what the rest of the world was doing.  Television projected the doings of the world visually into the home.  Space and time have almost been eliminated today because of man's efforts to meet the need for rapid communication.

**Sex and the family.**  The needs connected with sex, the family, and the home have given rise to a wide variety of activities.  Love and courtship occupy much of the attention of youth.  The institution of marriage involves also the activity of those connected with religion and the law.  Homes create a problem of architecture and housing.  Earning a living for the family and rearing children call forth innumerable forms of activity of an industrial, educational, religious, and cultural character.

**Government and public life.**  Next to making a living and rearing a family, the most extensive human activities are associated with government. These range from the direction of a rural township to the administration of a vast empire. There are town, city, county, state, national, and colonial governments. As civilization becomes more complex, government is forced to enter more fully into social activities, engaging ever greater numbers of persons. The elaborate development of business, banking, and labor problems, for example, has required an ever more extensive intervention of government in economic affairs.

An important sector of government is devoted to law and order and the prevention of crime. Arresting, convicting, and imprisoning criminals cost huge sums of money and require the services of many agencies. War is another government activity which engages the attention of large numbers and requires vast expenditures. Millions of persons have been employed in fighting and making munitions. A trillion and a quarter dollars were spent on military materials and activities during the second world war.

**Play and recreation.** Out of man's need for self-expression a wide range of activities has developed. Organized play and recreation have been important since the days of the Greeks and the Romans. Large numbers of persons are engaged not only in direct participation in play but also in teaching, supervising, constructing buildings and equipment, manufacturing pleasure vehicles, and conducting the moving picture, radio, and television industries, night clubs, skating rinks, and countless other amusements.

**Literature and the arts.** More refined forms of self-expression are found in literature, music, and the arts. Art, once a luxury of the wealthy few, is now cultivated by the many. In recent years, the dictator governments have promoted art and music for the purpose of building up strong national unity. In this country under the New Deal some money was spent by the government on artistic projects. Community activities, such as singing, dancing, and art classes, have made the arts more popular. The movies have also helped, and the radio has brought the great music of the world to its listeners. Art and music are encouraged by education, and there has been a great increase in the number of art museums.

**Religion and scientific research.** Human curiosity, as a form of self-expression, has led to the search for religious and scientific knowledge. The church, around which much social life centers, has extended its services into such fields as foreign missions, community service, recreation, and art. Science occupies a great deal of our attention today. Scientific and technical research have become major activities. Applied science is one of the basic foundations of modern industrial life, for, without inventions, the machine era would have been impossible.

Our complex social life, with its innumerable activities, has thus grown out of the efforts to satisfy the human needs arising from the fundamental drives of self-preservation, self-perpetuation, and self-expression. Our civilization is based on this heritage of social activities and habits which has been handed on from one generation to another.

## The Origin and Nature of Social Institutions

**Emergence of social institutions.** The social institutions, through which man's activities are organized, directed, and carried out, have been in a process of development since man's earliest association in group life. The basic drives have always been present, because man has not changed biologically for tens of thousands of years. The same human needs have developed from the fundamental drives, although their nature and variety and the manner of satisfying them have changed as culture has advanced. Social institutions are the habits and customs which have been sanctioned, regulated, and established by group authority and have developed into formal social structures.

**The folkways.** In the beginning, man did not deliberately plan how he would satisfy his needs. His methods were mostly those of trial and error. If one method seemed to prove fairly satisfactory, it was repeated, taken up by others in the group, and eventually became a group habit. As time went on, these habits became folkways, or group customs. Folkways, long repeated in the same way, usually received conscious group sanction. Whatever was thus approved became the right type of conduct for the group and was enforced by group authority. Professor Sumner, in his famous book, *Folkways,* showed the manner in which folkways develop into institutions.

**The mores.** The folkways thus became ways of right living for the primitive group. When the elements of assumed truth and right in the folkways were developed into conscious doctrines of group welfare, the folkways took on new significance. They gradually extended their influence over man and society and became mores. The mores are folkways which have come to be the social standards set by the group. They determine such basic social usages as sex behavior, industry, government, worship, dress, and manners. Each individual, from childhood onward, learns the standards set by the group in which he lives. If he wishes to be accepted by the group, he must conform to its mores.

**The primary institutions.** When certain mores become so important to group welfare that rules, regulations, and procedures are set up to enforce their observance, they become social institutions. The family, property, government, war, industry, communication, religion, and education are primary or fundamental institutions.

At any given time in history, we find that about the same primary institutions exist among all peoples. This uniformity arises from the fact that all men have the same fundamental drives. The needs that arise out of these basic drives are correspondingly similar. Therefore, the elementary or primary institutions, which develop by trial-and-error methods out of these fundamental needs, will naturally be much the same also, although the specific forms and detailed expressions of such institutions may show considerable diversity.

**Secondary institutions.** As civilization develops, we find secondary institutions arising within the field of the primary institutions. For instance, government is a primary institution which spontaneously arose from the general need for public order and group protection; but a republic or a monarchy is a special form of government which has been consciously decided upon by the group and, therefore, is a secondary institution. Primary institutions are far more important than secondary institutions, because they are basic and fundamental, and have grown directly out of human needs.

**Industry.** Industry is a primary institution, since a person must make a living. As we have seen, there are many types of industrial activities. Various forms of secondary industrial institutions have arisen, from time to time, as patterns acceptable to the group. The family provided the earliest type of industrial operation; slavery supplied a leading form of industrial organization in ancient times. The gilds of the Middle Ages, the putting-out system of the seventeenth and eighteenth centuries, and the capitalism of today are all forms of secondary industrial institutions.

**Property.** Property is another primary institution. Although at first most property belonged to the social group, private property became increasingly important and now has long been protected by law. Ways of holding and transmitting property were developed, and property became such an important institution that other institutions, notably law, are now mainly concerned with its protection.

**The family.** The family is one of the leading primary institutions. Growing out of the drive for self-perpetuation, the family has taken various forms throughout the history of man. The "monogamous" family, the pairing of one man and one woman, has been most usual, but "polyandry," the marriage of one woman to several men, and "polygyny," the marriage of one man to several women, have existed from time to time. The family exists chiefly for the purpose of bearing and raising children, but it contributes to other types of institutional activities, especially those associated with industry, religion, and education.

**The state and government.** The state, together with its operating agent the government, is the most powerful of all primary institutions today. It exerts the fundamental authority in modern life. It can, and often does, determine the character of all the other primary institutions, and forces them to conform to the legislation it enacts.

**War, diplomacy, and world trade.** The relations between nations have given rise to various institutions. War—a primary institution —is the most important of these, and today the most disastrous. In the beginning, war was a personal or private affair between small social groups, but today war has become so much a part of the social pattern that definite laws and accepted usages connected with it have been developed and have become secondary institutions. Peacetime relations between nations are conducted through diplomatic negotiations, which have become a leading public institution. Attempts are made to avert war through such institutions as arbitration. Efforts to control and extend trade between nations have become institutionalized, and there are many institutions associated with international exchange, such as tariffs, trade laws, and the like.

**Travel and communication.** The need to travel and the many activities connected with it have brought about certain rules and devices, such as the passport, which are accepted between civilized states. There are rules and practices which regulate almost every phase of land and sea travel.

Communication between men and groups has created many institutions in which language and other symbols are the fundamental tools. All human learning may be regarded as an accumulation of the results of human communication since the origin of language.

**Religion and science.** The activities growing out of man's curiosity, such as religion and science, have been encouraged and protected by institutions. Religion is one of the leading primary institutions. It has a wide sphere of influence beyond the field of worship. There are several world religions, each one of which has established special rituals and standards of ethical behavior.

Science is a secondary institution that has become a primary institution in our own day. Modern society has now learned the value of scientific research in the furthering of human knowledge; it has protected mechanical inventions and scientific discoveries, and has developed means of applying them to the welfare of the group.

**Recreation.** Sports have developed into an institution of major importance. The supervised playground has become one of the leading secondary institutions in urban life today. Commercialized sports have provided a great variety of secondary institutions of both recreational and economic significance. The vast development of spectator sports has provided new and significant economic patterns.

**Education.** The primary institution of education, which transmits the social heritage from one generation to another, has existed since primitive times. Education has become more complex in the modern era, because of the immense amount of knowledge which must be transmitted. Some educators are now suggesting that education should not try to pass on the whole of human knowledge, but should criticize and select from it only those things which are useful in modern life. However, these suggestions have met with little favor; education, today, is filled with much relatively useless learning, while a great deal of highly relevant social information is neglected or receives very scanty attention.

**Multiplicity of secondary and tertiary institutions.** The secondary and tertiary institutions which have grown out of the primary institutions are, as we have already implied, almost without number. In the beginning, the simple activities of men did not make specialization necessary, and the primary institutions were sufficient to regulate group life.

The primary institution of government offers an example of the complexity of the secondary and tertiary institutions of modern times. Even in modern times, there are three forms of government—monarchy, aristocracy, and democracy. Within democracy there are three branches—executive, judicial, and legislative—each of which has become an institution where it exists. Democracies are usually run by parties, but either a two-party or a group system may be used. Candidates for political office may be nominated in one of several ways and may be elected either directly or indirectly. The legislature may have one or two houses. Some democracies may be conservative, others radical. All these numerous forms and techniques of democratic government are deliberate attempts by society to meet the needs of man. Monarchy and aristocracy have produced nearly as many secondary institutions as democracy. Each of the other primary institutions has, like government, developed secondary and tertiary divisions.

**Culture, the superorganic, and human nurture.** Institutions thus develop out of human nature. The whole body of human institutions comprises what is called the superorganic realm (that is, beyond the biological or organic). This is only another term for culture as used by the sociologists. Human nature is organic and has been unchanged for thousands of years, but institutions, or "human nurture," have evolved from those of simple primitive society to those of our modern industrial civilization. Many different forms of the family, industry, social groups, religion, and education have appeared from time to time.

It is often said that, unless we change human nature, we can never have a better social order. We have, however, moved from a simple tribal culture to modern civilization without changing man's biological or "human" nature. Hence, there is no reason to believe that extensive changes cannot be made today in political, economic, and social life without changing human nature. So far, we have made little effort to discover and establish institutions that accord with the best in human nature. Our primary institutions are a result of the trial-and-error methods of primitive times rather than of deliberate attempts to choose a political, economic, or social system which would be most satisfactory to man's needs.

**Need for constant development and readjustment of institutions.** Social institutions are vital to any advanced form of human life. Without them, there could be no social progress and no orderly complex civilization. Our institutions could, however, be made much more efficient. The greatest turning-point in man's history will come when human beings are capable of examining their institutions and deliberately readjusting them to the needs of the time. Until then we shall only toy, spar, and shadow-box with our social problems.   We will not solve them.

## Summary

Man can exist and prosper only as a member of a social group.   If the activities of group life are to be maintained, there must be a basic social structure.   This social structure is supplied by social institutions.   Social institutions have developed out of the fundamental human drives, the basic needs of human beings which are produced by these drives, and the activities in which mankind engages to satisfy these needs.

There are three important drives, inherent in human nature: self-preservation, self-perpetuation, and self-expression.   While they form part of man's biological nature and exist apart from his social surroundings, they are strongly influenced by the fact that man is a social being.   The basic drives tend to give rise to certain important needs. The drive for self-preservation, for example, gives rise to the need for food, clothing, shelter, and the like; that for self-perpetuation to love, marriage, and family life; and that for self-expression to literature, art, music, religion, science, and so forth.   Each need, in turn, gives rise to certain human activities for its satisfaction.   Thus, for example, man's quest for food gives rise to hunting, fishing, and farming.

Social institutions represent methods of satisfying human needs that society has found reasonably successful and has stamped with its approval.   Certain institutions, classed as primary, arise naturally and without conscious planning.   Such, for example, are the family, industry, property, government, war, religion, and education.   Other institutions, classed as secondary, arise mainly as the result of conscious planning.   Schools, labor unions, and political parties are examples of such institutions.   While institutions arise as methods of satisfying man's basic drives, we must be willing to recognize that institutions may change, even if man's biological nature does not.   Although man's physical nature has not altered in thousands of years, our institutions have greatly changed since in primitive times.

It should be noted that each individual is born into a complex of institutions.   They are the framework within which his needs and personality are cultivated, directed, and stabilized.   In this way, institutions mold human beings as they grow up in their groups.

Most changes in human institutions have been made unconsciously, often only by the operation of the selective process, rather than by deliberate planning.   For, while man is intelligent and progressive in regard to his tools and machinery, he seldom thinks in an intelligent and progressive manner about his institutions.   By refusing to take steps to correct his institutional thinking, man has brought civilization face to face with disaster.

## Selected References

Ballard, L. V., *Social Institutions*, Appleton-Century, 1936. A somewhat academic and traditional, but sane and informing, survey of our institutional life and its social functions.

Barnes, H. E., *Social Institutions*, Prentice-Hall, 1942. The most comprehensive historical and descriptive survey of social institutions, with emphasis on the current American scene.

Chapin, F. S., *Contemporary American Institutions*, Harper, 1935. A competent description and criticism of American institutions in the light of modern knowledge and experience. The book is especially strong on politics and business.

Faris, Ellworth, *The Nature of Human Nature*, McGraw-Hill, 1937. An anthropological and sociological analysis of the interrelation of human nature and social institutions.

* Hertzler, J. O., *Social Institutions*, McGraw-Hill, 1946. Able and scholarly brief introduction to the nature and evolution of social institutions.

Hiller, E. T., *Social Relations and Structures*, Harper, 1947. Excellent treatment of the social background of institutions.

Keller, A. G., *Man's Rough Road*, Stokes, 1932. A survey of the origin and development of our institutions, with many data drawn from anthropology and primitive life. Less competent on modern developments.

Mitchell, W. C. *et al.*, *Recent Social Trends*, 2 vols., McGraw-Hill, 1933. The most comprehensive survey of American institutions before the New Deal and the second world war.

Panunzio, Constantine, *Major Social Institutions*, Macmillan, 1939. Good general textbook treatment of the origin and nature of our basic institutions and of how they fare under twentieth century conditions.

* Sumner, W. G., *Folkways*, Ginn, 1907. A classic work in the origin of and the control exerted by customs, folkways, and mores. It has rightly been called "the most civilizing book ever written."

Thorndike, E. L., *Human Nature and the Social Order*, Macmillan, 1940. A massive and authoritative book on the relation of human nature and its biopsychic impulses to human institutions and social processes. The culmination of the life work of America's leading functional psychologist.

* Woodworth, R. S., *Dynamic Psychology*, Columbia University Press, 1918. An authoritative and readable summary of the original nature of man and the basic drives lying back of human activity.

# CHAPTER VI

# Leading Factors and Mechanisms in the Social Process

## Isolation: The Frustration of Socialization

**The meaning of social isolation.** In the two preceding chapters we have dealt with the rise, development, and social significance of group life and the manner in which individual and social activities produced by the basic human drives have come to be controlled by social institutions. In this manner, we demonstrated the social basis of human life and achievement. In the present chapter we shall discuss briefly some of the leading mechanisms involved in the social process and the activities of associated life. But, before we take up the social process in its various manifestations, we can fruitfully examine the situation involved in that blockage or stoppage of normal social relations and experiences which the sociologists designate as the phenomenon of isolation.

By isolation is meant the lack of normal communication with other members of society. Individual isolation takes place when a single person, voluntarily or involuntarily, breaks away from the group and lives in solitude; group isolation, when a community is cut off from contact with the rest of the world by geographic or other barriers that sever communication with outside areas and communities. In short, isolation is the absence of those social factors which have tamed and civilized the race and made possible such progress as it has thus far attained. Since the members of the human race are inherently inclined to social relations, isolation is usually involuntary, the product of accident, coercion, or other factors frustrating to normal human inclinations.

**Leading causes of isolation.** There are a number of types of isolation. Groups may be cut off from adequate contact with other communities by mountains, deserts, or vast expanses of water. Individuals also may be isolated in this manner, by shipwreck or by voluntarily retirement to remote fastnesses of forests and mountains. Biological factors may work for isolation, as in the case of race prejudice and segregation. In their most extreme form, biological considerations

84

lead to the segregation of low-grade feeble-minded types in institutions and to the isolation of those suffering from incurable contagious diseases, such as leprosy.

Psychological forces also promote isolation. Since human beings are brought together by consciousness of kind or a recognition of similarities, whatever makes a person or a minority group strange or unlike the majority tends to work for isolation. The "out-group" is a prominent case of social isolation. Socio-psychological exclusiveness, such as arises from conceptions and practices associated with caste and rigid social classes, tends to breed isolation. The so-called upper and lower classes are isolated from each other, an extreme manifestation being the "untouchables" of India. The attitude of exclusiveness which separates the upper classes from the lower in the social scale is known among sociologists as "social distance." It still persists, with the gulf between members of the "Social Register" in metropolitan society and the residents of the slum areas easily as great as that which existed between nobles and slaves in the ancient civilizations.

Economic attitudes and interests play their part in fostering isolation of various kinds. Those who possess great wealth isolate themselves from the poor and build up a whole pattern of ostentatious exclusiveness, a pattern that has been ironically dissected by Thorstein Veblen in his classic work, *The Theory of the Leisure Class.* Capital and labor are mutually exclusive organizations. Special cliques, or groups within each, tend to isolate themselves from the majority. Until the recent revolutionary developments in transportation and communication, rural economic operators and interests were usually isolated to a considerable extent from urban life and wider social interests.

There are all sorts of social impulses to isolation, some already mentioned as being primarily psychological—for example, the Social Register complex. Modern city life has brought about a good deal of personal isolation and loneliness; oddly enough, it is far easier to be isolated, voluntarily or otherwise, in cities than in rural areas. In the country, one always seems to know his neighbors, but in city apartments one may have little or no personal relationship with those who live for years on the opposite side of the corridor or hallway. It is in the city, also, that we find immigrant groups segregated into "Little Italys," Chinatowns, and the like.

Though religion is supposed to be a universalizing force, before which all men are equal, it has actually produced a considerable amount of isolation. In primitive times, religious leaders, the shamans and priests, were prone to isolate themselves for protracted periods from the mass of tribesmen. The great world religions have tended to segregate their believers into major religious camps, separated from others by hostility, suspicion, and lack of mutual understanding. Even within single religious beliefs there are often numerous sects separated from each other by as much bitterness and hatred as divides the several main religious groups of the world.    Finally, the religious and the non-religious, or anti-religious, groups are psychically isolated from each other.

Political and legal institutions and practices may work for isolation. National pride may at times take on such extreme manifestations as virtually to isolate the nation from world intercourse. This is less possible today with our modern transportation and communication, but Japan persisted in isolation until the middle of the nineteenth century. The Boxer Revolt of 1900 in China was an effort to restore China to nationalistic isolation. Strong and closely-knit party organizations tend to isolate their members from contact with, and insight into, the ideals and goals of opposition parties. Governments may banish or exile both groups and individuals. They may segregate others in concentration camps or sentence them to penal servitude—even to solitary confinement.

Ideological factors have produced a great deal of isolation. Conservatives separate themselves from radicals, and vice versa. Democrats and totalitarians look askance at each other, and different sects of totalitarians have been divided on the basis of hostility and suspicion perhaps greater than that existing between libertarians and totalitarians. The separation and hostility of capital and labor have been based in part on ideological grounds. Relatively fanatical conservative or reform groups may often develop such intensity of conviction and intolerance that they essentially isolate themselves from the majority of the community and thus reduce the effectiveness of their campaign. The development of contemporary propaganda has tended to intensify the ideological convictions that make for psychic isolation. The smear technique of current propaganda aims primarily to isolate the victims of smearing from the society and esteem of the community and to produce psychic and moral exile.

Certain cultural factors have favored isolation. One of the more common is linguistic difficulty, the inability of one group to master the language, and thus to understand the culture, of another. Minority national groups in our urban populations are segregated quite as much for cultural and linguistic reasons as on account of race.

Sexual isolation exists in certain religious orders, which prescribe celibacy for the elect of both sexes and provide institutions for those of one sex only. Another type of sexual isolation occurs in our penal and correctional institutions, where the sexes are sharply separated and prevented from having contact of any sort whatsoever.

**Effects of isolation on the individual.** We may now consider briefly some of the more obvious results of isolation, both individual and social. There are a few authentic cases of more or less complete isolation of individuals from birth or very early years. Some of the best known of these are assembled and described by Professor Frederick E. Lumley in his *Principles of Sociology*.[1]   Such individuals present the

---

[1] McGraw-Hill, 1928, pp. 108 ff.

best possible proof of the social basis of culture and human achievement. More or less completely isolated human beings possess essentially animal and bestial traits; they possess no culture, not even the gift of language. They can only cry and grunt like other animals. They show no traces of adjustment to normal social relations. In short, complete isolation of an individual means a reversion to the lowest stages of savagery.

There are many more cases of persons who have been brought up in the midst of normal social relationships and have later deliberately, or through the vicissitudes of fate, been subjected to a life of solitude and social isolation. If sufficiently prolonged, such experiences usually lead to differing degrees and manifestations of personal degeneration or disability. Isolated individuals develop sentiments of hostility and suspicion and, often, delusions of persecution. A compensatory fanaticism and intolerance may arise. Many of these traits developed by a life of prolonged isolation bear a remarkable similarity to the classic symptoms of neuroses and psychoses among the mentally diseased. Hermits are notorious for their air of suspicion, "queer" ideas and behavior, and hallucinations.

Excessive personal solitude may lead to insanity and suicide. Solitary confinement in the famous Eastern Penitentiary of Pennsylvania and in the State Prison at Auburn, New York, brought about "epidemics" of insanity and had to be abandoned. A number of prisoners in the Auburn institution committed suicide. The great French sociologist Émile Durkheim contended that a main cause of suicide is the psychic isolation of individuals who have been driven out of, or have broken away from, normal group association and controls. Sexual isolation usually leads to all manner of sexual aberrations and abnormalities, having in common only their unhealthy nature.

Only one advantage has ever been persistently alleged to arise from personal isolation; this is the supposed stimulus to inspiration. The main examples cited to support this view have been the great religious leaders who subjected themselves to more or less protracted periods of isolation and soul-searching, among them Buddha, Christ, St. Paul, and Mohammed. Arnold J. Toynbee, in his popular book *A Study of History*, has extended this concept to include great political geniuses, such as Caesar, who isolated himself for a time in Gaul, and Peter the Great, who left Russia to study new economic and political developments in Western Europe. The literary accomplishments of Henry David Thoreau are often cited to prove the value of isolation from social distractions and the resulting ability to concentrate and contemplate. The alleged profundity of philosophical geniuses, such as Immanuel Kant, has been attributed by many to their personal isolation. Toynbee contends that most great leaders owed their inspirational powers and visions to a process of withdrawing from society and becoming inspired during a period of contemplation.

There may be some truth in this hypothesis of the inspirational contributions of isolation, but it has certainly been greatly exaggerated; the resulting inspiration has often led to the formulation and promulgation of grossly misleading ideas and fanatical social programs. There is much to be said for such moderate isolation as will temporarily assure freedom from distracting trivialities; beyond this point, however, isolation is more likely to result in personal deterioration and ideological fantasies than in true inspiration.

**Results of the isolation of social groups.** The effects of isolation on social groups are as clear and diversified as on individuals. Communities which are isolated by natural features or other barriers to intercourse and communication are likely to develop what are called arrested civilizations—cultural intertia and backwardness, owing to the lack of stimulation and information from other cultures. Such isolation frustrates the diffusion of culture, which is one of the more important factors in cultural progress. Isolated nations may develop the same feelings of suspicion and hostility as do individuals separated from normal contacts. Backwoods Kentucky is a popular example of regional isolation, and ancient Sparta is a classic example of national isolation.

The psychic isolation of capital and labor leads to industrial warfare, strikes, lockouts, and the like, which are detrimental to capital, labor, and the public alike. The whole process of antagonism reduces the possibility of fully co-operative endeavor in the production of goods. Racial segregation and isolation encourage prejudice and persecution on the part of the dominant race and lead to resentment and bitterness in the case of the repressed racial minorities. Racial and cultural segregation has delayed and partially frustrated the assimilation of immigrant groups into American culture. Religious isolation has led to all sorts of misunderstanding, hostility, suspicion, and persecution, and even to numerous and bloody religious wars. Political isolation, especially as between parties, has promoted a passionate partisanship which all too often blinds party members to the great realities and problems of the age. It may also produce intolerance and persecution; witness the policies of the totalitarian states which have arisen since the first world war.

About the only type of group isolation that can be said to have any great virtue is the deliberate isolation of a nation from foreign quarrels and squabbles. By so isolating itself, a nation may develop the detachment and powers of contemplation which are required to work out practical plans for world understanding and peace. This is as essential for international peace as is individual isolation from petty local distractions for the production of works of personal genius. But excessive national isolation can lead to the same pathological results in world affairs as extreme personal isolation produces in individual experience.

## The Development and Range of Social Contacts

**Increasing scope of social contacts.**  It is obvious that contact is the reverse or opposite phase of isolation.  Since we have already discussed in Chapter IV those forces which bring persons and groups into contact, we need take no great amount of space to deal with the developments of social contacts.

It is obvious that the number and scope of social contacts have enormously increased in the course of human and social evolution. In the earliest days, social contacts were rudimentary and limited to the relations between members of a family or a small local group dwelling in a very restricted area.  Today, social contacts are worldwide and cover a vast range of interests and activities.  Indeed, any person who can provide the modest funds necessary to purchase a radio with a short-wave band can quickly put himself in contact with thoughts and activities in nearly any portion of the globe.  Modern transportation and communication have revolutionized many phases of social life, but none more completely than that of social contacts.

**Causes and means of social contacts.**  Geographical factors are responsible for many social contacts.  They force or invite peoples to come together in specific areas for purposes of subsistence, protection, or both.  The more fertile the area, the greater the possible density of the population which can be supported; and the greater the density of population, the more social contacts which result.  A fertile area and a prosperous population may invite invasion, thus providing another increase in social contacts.  Biological forces promote some of the more vital contacts, such as those between the sexes, between members of a family, between members of quasi-biological groups such as clans, and between members of the same race.  We find in race war violent contacts encouraged by biological factors.  Psychological forces which produce social contacts revolve mainly about consciousness of kind.  If the "out-group" complex leads to aversion and group isolation, the "in-group" complex promotes close intra-group contacts.

The economic impulses increasing social contacts center mainly around mutual aid, co-operation, and the division of labor; these contacts become ever more complex and comprehensive, from a hunting party of primitive men to contemporary international cartels and plans for world economic rehabilitation.  In the course of social evolution, and especially in the last few generations, social contacts have tended to become less spontaneous and intimate and more deliberate, impersonal, functional, and selective.

Cultural interests and activities bring about a great variety of social contacts.  The cultural heritage performs a special function in the realm of social contacts, in that it effects at least a mental contact between the living generation and all generations from the past. Religious activities bring persons together out of a mutual interest in the supernatural world or because of common membership in a particular religious group or cult. Political forces in society promote those social contacts incident to the provision of leadership, public order, and group protection. These contacts include those with government agencies, those involved in the operations of political parties, and those between the various organs and departments of government.

**The enlargement of social contacts.** In an earlier chapter we emphasized the fact that the most striking social phenomenon of our day has been the vast enlargement and extension of social contacts as a result of the development of contemporary transportation and communication. With people able to move about more readily and rapidly, their contacts show a corresponding increase in number. Further, even when there is no physical contact, there can be mental contact on a world-wide scale at all times, owing to the transmission of information by the newspapers, movies, radio, and television. As a result, economic, cultural, religious, and political contacts are taking on a world scope and responsibility.

With the progress of industrialization and urbanization, the contacts arising out of personal, primary-group situations have tended to shrink in number and influence, while those associated with secondary-group activities have increased correspondingly in scope and importance. In city life, the more purely personal contacts are limited mainly to clubs and congeniality groups. The great majority of contacts in other fields are chiefly functional, professional, and selective. Personal associations and reactions enter but slightly into the routine daily life of city dwellers. There is little that is personal in one's relations with grocers, doctors, lawyers, tailors, landlords, pharmacists, subway conductors, and taxi drivers. Even in those congeniality groups where personal interests predominate, membership is deliberate and selective, rather than a spontaneous product of personal contacts in a local neighborhood or some other personal, primary society. The implications of all this for the future operations of human society have not been fully considered and elucidated even by professional sociologists, but a great revolution in human relations and social psychology is surely involved.

## The Nature and Extent of Social Interaction

**Importance and types of social interaction.** It is obvious that social interaction is the very essence of society and the basis and content of all social relations. Everything put down in Part II of this volume on "The Social Framework of Human Life" is directly related to social interaction. Indeed, in its broadest sense, social interaction provides the complete scope of the subject-matter of sociology. All group life is made possible and continuous as a result of social interaction. In treating the topic here, we must limit ourselves to a few essentials; most of the remaining items of the social process to be described in this chapter are really phases or aspects of social interaction.

Social interaction falls into two main fields: (1) the interaction between individuals in the process of socialization and group-building; and (2) the interaction between social groups. Of the two, the first is the more important in the realm of sociological analysis. The interaction between individuals may be involuntary and unconscious, as in the case of the spontaneous reaction to likeness or strangeness in others, sex attraction, and the protective impulses in the mother-child relationship, or it may be conscious and deliberative, as in our occupational, prefessional, and recreational relationships.

The interaction between individuals begins with biosocial relations between the infant and his parents, and then moves on to those between the child and his family and playmates. These interactions are gradually extended to the school group, and finally to occupational and professional relationships. They include also the interaction between the individual and those whom he meets in the enjoyment of his leisure-time activities, the members of his sports group, club, lodge, discussion group, or musical society. The earliest interactions are spontaneous and personal, but, as life goes on, interactions become more deliberate, functional, and selective.

**Struggle between individuality and socialization.** In studying the process of social interaction we find that it aims at a resolution or satisfactory compromise of two persistent opposing forces. On the one hand, we have the ego impulses, which are inherent in every individual and arise out of the basic drives discussed in the preceding chapter. The ego impulses constitute the dynamic factors in the social process; yet, if not controlled, they would lead to chaos, anarchy, criminality, and exploitation, which would make orderly social relations quite impossible. Therefore, the ego impulses must be brought under such limitations as will make a coherent and stable society possible without, at the same time, stamping out human initiative. Our ego impulses are natural and spontaneous; the socializing restraints are reluctantly accepted at the outset, but ultimately become habitual and cherished. Human life is, as the philosopher Kant emphasized, a constant struggle between these two opposing forces of individuality and socialization, and the ideal society and government are those which provide for the most perfect balance and adjustment of these forces.

**Interaction between individuals.** The interactions between individuals may be positive or negative. The positive interactions are pleasant; they are usually based on consciousness of kind, help to socialize the individuals involved, and are the main group-building factors in human experience. Negative interactions are unpleasant;

they are often based upon the recognition of strangeness, lead to various forms of antagonism and conflict, and act to frustrate efforts at group formation.

Another classification of individual interactions is into the primary and the secondary. Primary interactions are those which arise in small personal groups. They are usually the product of face-to-face contacts and are spontaneous and personal. Secondary interactions include the reaction of a clerk to his employer and the interaction between members of the Assembly of the United Nations. Secondary interactions are formal, selective, and functional, and only to an incidental degree personal. They have become increasingly numerous and important with the progress of urbanization.

The causes of interaction between individuals are mainly of three types: (1) natural and involuntary, such as birth in a given family, sex attraction, and numerous accidental situations in the course of life; (2) psychological, based mainly on the attraction of like for like; and (3) functional, which are conscious and deliberate and involve those interactions associated with our occupational and professional life and the selection of social services essential to comfort, health, safety, and pleasure.

The means of individual interaction extend from animal-like gestures to a broadcast of the exchange of information in an international scientific congress. While some human interaction operates at a purely animal level, the most marked contrast between human and animal interaction is that human beings can interact by means of symbols, which are unknown to animals. Language is the most elaborate and well-developed form of symbolic communication. The levels of interaction rise from those of mere sense, such as smell, sight, and the like, through the emotional, based on reactions of joy, anger, passion, congeniality, hatred, and the like, to the intellectual level, where interactions are founded on professional interests, occupational needs, informed debate, scientific knowledge, and so on. Intellectual interactions tend to take on institutionalized forms of expression and often result in the creation of secondary groups to carry them out.

Individual interactions in society result in either the creation of socialized and disciplined members of orderly society or the development of anti-social types, dominated by hostility and antagonism to society and given to criminal acts, overt exploitation, and the like. Unmitigated extremes are unlikely in either case. Few persons are so completely disciplined in the process of social interaction that they lose all their non-social ego drives, and few are so unreservedly given over to anti-social activity as to exclude all social restraints and impulses. The criminal is usually as much restrained by the folkways of the underworld as is the law-abiding citizen by the mores of normal society. In any event, whatever we have in the way of orderly social life and permanent group organization is the outcome of social interaction.    As a result of social selection, those groups which could not develop a degree of socialization sufficient to produce concerted group action have been eliminated during the struggle for existence among societies.

**Group interaction.**    Group interaction has developed from simple to complex along the lines of individual interaction.    The level of group interaction is usually on the intellectual plane.    There is obviously no group interaction on the sense level and even most emotional interaction between groups is based on intellectual affinity or antagonism.    The interaction between groups may be peaceful, harmonious, and co-operative, or it may be hostile, competitive, and antagonistic. The eminent English sociologist Leonard T. Hobhouse laid great stress upon the assertion that the extent of social perfection in any nation is to be measured by the degree to which the interaction between the groups within a nation is harmonious, well-co-ordinated, and devoid of frustrating and wasteful antagonisms and cross-purposes. In great periods of social change, like our own era, there is likely to be a maximum of ideological hostility and strong functional antagonism among social groups.

## The Existence and Function of Competition in Society

**Nature and forms of competition.**    As a form of human activity, competition ranges all the way from a ruthless struggle for the sheer necessities of existence to rivalry between different philanthropic foundations in conferring the greatest possible benefits upon the recipients of their awards.    Competition may take the form of rivalry between individuals within a group, of competitive efforts of social groups to gain their objectives, of racial rivalries, or of a contest of cultures and institutions for pre-eminence.    Competitive effort may be expended to achieve sheer existence and survival, or it may be devoted to a struggle for prestige.    Sociologists usually differentiate competition from conflict by limiting competition to what are normally non-violent types of rivalry.    They also hold that competition is less personal and emotional than conflict.    We may first consider what are primarily personal or individual types of competition.

**Causes of competition.**    Men have to compete with the physical environment to gain the material means of existence and to protect themselves against natural phenomena such as cold, heat, storms, and floods.    Toynbee has described this competition of mankind with the physical environment as "challenge and response," and holds that the greatest success is found when enough of a struggle is demanded to bring forth man's greatest efforts, without such overwhelming obstacles as to paralyze or discourage human action.    Primitive man had also to compete with other members of the animal world, but, with the improvement of man's material culture and social organization, animals are no longer a threat. Some insect pests have, however, been able to defy human efforts, at least until recent discoveries in the way of chemical insecticides.

The most important forms of personal competition are, however, those between members of the human race. Strength and intelligence have been the main basis of personal success in such competition, though the institutions which control human effort have played a large part in competitive struggles, especially in recent times. The more advanced the technology and the more efficient the institutions, the greater the prospect of survival and triumph in the competitive process.

**Human drives and competitive efforts.** Individual competitive efforts are, in considerable part, a by-product of the three basic drives of self-preservation, self-perpetuation, and self-expression. The drive to self-preservation impels men to compete for the best food, clothing, and shelter. The drive to self-perpetuation leads men to compete for mates, to seek the more beautiful women, and to struggle to give their families more comforts and higher standards of living. Women, perhaps more coyly and covertly, compete for the more handsome, talented, and opulent men; they, too, usually strive to gain the best possible existence for their children. The drive for self-expression carries man beyond the competitive struggle for material necessities into the non-material realm; for example, scientific research and literary accomplishments. But, even here, there may often be economic or financial concomitants and objectives. When and where wealth is a main basis for status and prestige, the drive for self-expression takes on a preponderantly material motivation and expression, such as Veblen describes in his *Theory of the Leisure Class.*

**Main forms of competition.** Economic, political, religious, and racial competition may manifest themselves in both individual and group forms of rivalry. The individual may strive to better his economic lot, or such groups as capital and labor may compete to secure an ever larger share of the total social income. Individuals may strive to obtain political office or organizational leadership within a party, or political parties may carry on rivalry for domination and the capture of political patronage. Persons may struggle to maintain their own religious beliefs or disbeliefs against opposing cults, or great religious organizations may seek domination by proselyting, missionary effort, or persecution. In the racial realm, individual members of either dominant or minority races may struggle for superiority or for mere tolerance and fair play. Or, large segments of rival races may compete for primacy through political tactics, imperialism, or a differential birth rate. The same is true in sports; individuals compete for success and prestige in special fields of sport, or in single games, while different types of sports compete against each for popular esteem, support, and financial profit.

Since institutions are a phase of culture, institutional competition is a form of cultural competition.  Institutional competition may be seen in such struggles as those between church and state in the medieval period, between the state and private business in the last few generations, between democracy and totalitarianism, and between Capitalism and Socialism.  It is generally maintained by sociologists that, all other things being equal, institutional competition leads to the triumph of the superior institution.

The competition between social groups runs the whole gamut of human drives and interests.  The largest-scale group competition is the rivalry of national states or of alliances of national states.  It is maintained that group competition produces improvements in group organization, strategy, leadership, and efficiency; in case the competition is too one-sided, however, it may lead to the complete disruption or extinction of the weaker groups.

**Competition and social progress.**  The spirit of competition has been vigorously extolled by writers on social science, especially by economists of the classical school who followed the ideas of David Ricardo and his associates.  Such economists contended that free competition and a free market—in short, the economic complex we know of as free enterprise—are the main foundations of material prosperity and human progress.  It is difficult to pass any final judgment on such contentions, since the degree of freedom assumed by such writers has never actually existed.

It may safely be contended that, under favorable conditions, competition is a very powerful stimulus to the best efforts on the part of both individuals and groups and will produce the greatest personal success and the most rapid advances in different fields of culture and institutional life.  It may at times even lead to greater mutual understanding and tolerance among rival persons and institutions, since greater knowledge of a field of action is attained in the process of rivalry.  But competition may just as frequently bring about personal dishonesty and shameless disregard of natural resources and national well-being. The ruthless competitive spirit was mainly responsible for the criminal waste of our natural resources and for the disastrous maldistribution of the national income which has led to the serious contemporary crisis in the capitalistic system.  In the realm of personal competitive ruthlessness, the lowest depths here have been reached in very recent times in the smearing techniques utilized by certain newspaper columnists and radio commentators, who murder with relative safety the personal reputations of their defenseless victims.

In conclusion, one may say that the social effects of competitive effort are largely determined by the rules under which competition takes place.  If a spirit of fairness, tolerance, and public weal prevails, competition may be a powerful agent of social progress.  If competition is dominated by a ruthless drive for success at whatever cost, it is likely to be more destructive than conducive to social benefits. The more extreme forms of competition are embraced in the social process known as conflict.

## The Rôle of Social Conflict

**Forms of personal conflict.** It is obvious that conflict, like competition, is manifested among individuals and among all kinds of groups, social classes, races, political organizations, economic interests, and religions. Personal conflicts range all the way from psychic antipathy to mayhem and murder. As civilization has advanced, there has been a tendency to substitute litigation for physical conflict in settling disputes. An important type of personal conflict stressed by some writers is the struggle within the individual mind produced by conflicting ideologies and interests and the impact of social changes on the individual psyche. Toynbee has called this type of personal conflict a "schism in the soul." Graham Wallas called it a "balked disposition." Psychiatrists call it a "complex."

**Group conflicts.** Virtually every type of social group is at times involved in conflict. The most prevalent and bitter type of group conflict, short of war, today is that between economic groups, but in the Middle Ages and early modern times the struggles of religious groups were the most numerous and violent. Group conflict may also take the form of the clash of interests and classes within a group—what we call intra-group conflict. Racial conflict may be the attempt of a dominant race to persecute minority races or it may represent the efforts of minority races to achieve equal rights or ascendency. The bitterest racial struggles may rest on fanciful foundations, as in the case of the Aryan-Jewish conflict in Hitler's Germany—there being neither an Aryan nor a Jewish race.

Class conflicts have existed throughout the course of human history. Pastoral nomads fought against settled agricultural aristocrats; the rising bourgeoisie battled against feudal lords; since the Industrial Revolution the industrial proletariat has opposed the bourgeoisie or middle class in the so-called class struggle, immortalized in radical economic literature by the writings of Karl Marx.

**Social results of conflict.** What has been said about the results of competition also holds true for the results of conflict: intra-group conflicts usually weaken group structure and invite anarchy and disintegration, while inter-group conflict results in strengthening the contending groups, at least until one of them is overcome or destroyed. An impressive example of this strengthening was the vast increase in national unity and material production in the United States during the second world war, an increase that would not have been deemed possible in the preceding decade.

In the case of class conflict in the economic field, the result has been the predominance of one great economic class after another. First the tribal chieftains ruled; then we had the domination of the feudal lords in the transitional period between tribal and civil society. Next came the era of the great landed aristocrats, who were, in turn, unseated by the bourgeoisie. Now, many predict that the bourgeoisie will be overthrown by the industrial proletariat, as they have been in Russia, along with the landed aristocracy. Whether this means social progress is a matter of opinion, but it surely represents social and economic change.

The phase or type of conflict which has received the greatest amount of attention in sociological analysis is political conflict. One aspect of this is what is roughly known as Social Darwinism, namely the idea that war plays the same rôle in social evolution that the biological struggle for existence does in the organic realm. On the basis of this doctrine, an eminent Austrian sociologist, Ludwig Gumplowicz, and his followers, showed how the physical conflict of social groups gradually built up the folk-state or nation, while the struggle of groups within this growing state brought about racial amalgamation and cultural assimilation and produced workable unity within the state. Other sociologists, among them Gustav Ratzenhofer and Albion W. Small, regarded the struggle of interest-groups within the state as the most dynamic factor in social evolution. They looked upon the government as the umpire in this conflict of interests, keeping conflict within those limits which point toward progress and away from chaos, tyranny, or stagnation.

In the past, war performed an important social function by welding small groups into large political entities and thus produced order and security, the essential foundations of further cultural progress. This being true, some writers today hold that further political evolution and world government must be achieved through more wars. Today, however, war is an unmitigated social calamity. Atomic and bacterial warfare threaten to write an end, not only to orderly social life and enlightened government, but to all civilized existence.

**Novicow's theory of the evolution of conflict.** A suggestive appraisal of the rôle and destiny of social conflict was presented by the famous Russian sociologist, Jacques Novicow. He held that there have been four main stages in the development of conflict—physiological, economic, political, and intellectual—the highest type being the intellectual. There is no doubt, says Novicow, that conflict is a constructive factor in social evolution, but to secure its greatest benefits and avert it worst disasters, we must reduce conflict in its lower and more rudimentary forms, such as war and exploitation, and increase it in its higher or non-violent forms, notably the political and the intellectual. In this way, we may secure whatever dynamic impulses reside in conflict and eliminate its more destructive manifestations.

## How Accommodation Lessens or Resolves Conflict

**Nature of social accommodation.** Conflict is often reduced or brought to an end for the time being, usually by the social mechanism known as accommodation. The latter denotes a more or less habitual acceptance of the existing folkways and social organization. It is usually preceded by a conscious effort to adjust to existing relations, customs, social arrangements, political systems, legal controls, and the like. The main difference between adjustment and accommodation is the larger element of conscious effort in the former and of habitual acceptance in the latter. Since there is never any complete or perfect accommodation which eliminates all conflict, most accommodation is preceded by or based on compromise. Any given social order or cultural heritage is the net product and current manifestation of accommodation, even though it may hold within itself the seeds of new conflicts and later adjustments and accommodations.

**Personal accommodation.** Like all other important social processes, accommodation has both personal and group manifestations. Personal accommodation involves the progress of adjustment to the point where an individual habitually adapts himself to the folkways of the group, the social requirements of marriage, the obligations of family life, the occupational set-up and his place therein, the existing political system, the legal codes of the society, and the religion, if any, which he espouses. Accommodation may be imposed upon the individual by sheer force of one kind or another or it may be completely voluntary. The most extreme manifestation of voluntary accommodation is what we call conversion. Though popularly limited to a religious act, conversion in its sociological use means a complete acceptance of or transfer of allegiance to any system or program, religious, economic, or political.

**Group accommodation.** Group accommodation implies a routine acceptance of the prevalent group organization and folkways and of the status and rôle of any given group in the whole social framework of the population. Racial accommodation may express itself in acceptance of a dominant race and discrimination against minority races, or in complete acceptance of the theory and practice of full racial equality. The "fair economic practices" agitation in this country is the product of gradual transition in our policy of racial accommodation. We have sexual accommodation in the prevailing rights, and spheres of the sexes, particularly the so-called "position of women." Class accommodation may extend all the way from a rigid social hierarchy in class arrangements to a classless society, such as exists, at least in ideological rhetoric, in Soviet Russia. A caste society represents the most extreme example of stereotyped class accommodation. The existing social ideology is usually an attempt to rationalize and justify the social hierarchy which exists—or the absence of such a hierarchy.

**Immigrant accommodation.** The processes connected with whole-sale immigration present probably the most illuminating case study of accommodation. Immigrants must first consciously accept or adjust themselves to the new culture into which they have moved, if they plan to remain. They must also immediately accommodate themselves to the political and legal system, if they hope to remain free and out of jail. In order to make any economic or social headway, they must acquire many of the cultural traits of the adopted country, along with its language. In due time, most immigrants formalize and legalize their more or less complete accommodation to the new order by the mechanism of naturalization. Often, however, immigrant accommodation is achieved by segregation rather than by cultural assimilation; the Chinese, for example, live apart in their Chinatowns.

**Chief mechanisms of accommodation.** Sociologists have differentiated and elucidated a number of leading forms or mechanism of accommodation; they are coercion, compromise, toleration, and conversion. Most of these are self-explanatory. A social order based on coercive accommodation can only exist in a tyrannical or totalitarian state. The most extreme and imposing example of this today is Soviet Russia. As we have indicated earlier, compromise is the usual device for transforming conflict into adjustment and accommodation, unless there is a complete victory in social conflict and no two or more parties remain to compromise. The compromise may be one involving ideological principles, economic interests, or political and legal equity; it may arise out of voluntary gestures on the part of one or more of the parties involved, or it may be encouraged or imposed by the public authorities. Toleration is both a mental state and a social practice which is highly favorable to accommodation. A tolerant frame of mind hastens that habitual acceptance of new reactions which constitutes accommodation. We have already briefly described the mechanism of conversion and have shown that it applies not merely to religious accommodation but manifests itself in the complete and enthusiastic acceptance of any aspect of the cultural complex.

## The Social Rôle of Assimilation

**Differences between accommodation, assimilation, and amalgamation.** If conflict usually terminates in accommodation, so accommodation normally leads to assimilation, which is the process of reducing dissimilar individuals, groups, and cultures to relative similarity of type, interests, attitudes, and behavior. Assimilation may be regarded as a relatively mature and complete stage of accommodation, no longer merely a matter of adjusting to or accepting patterns of behavior and types of culture, but of merging and fusing the culture of individuals and groups. For all practical purposes, assimilation is limited today to the relations between the culture of any given country and the cultures of immigrants who come to its shores. The process of assimilation is especially important in American civilization, which has been built upon the basis of successive waves of immigration representing widely diversified types of culture. Assimilation is at times confused with amalgamation, but in sociological usage the latter term is reserved to describe the physical fusion (intermarriage) of different racial types, while assimilation is employed to cover the purely social process of cultural fusion.

**Limits of assimilation.** The fusion of cultures through assimilation is never complete or perfect, partly because of the tenacity with which cultural traits endure despite centuries of competition with new traits, and partly because new immigrants and cultural traits appear to create further problems of assimilation. Nor is assimilation entirely one-sided, even in cases where immigrant groups constitute a decided minority of the population. There is always at least some interchange of cultural traits. American civilization of today is a composite product of the assimilation of divers and widely different cultures which have come in between the arrival of the first Indians from Asia in the Stone Age and the recent immigration of peoples from central, eastern, and southern Europe.

**Attitudes favoring assimilation.** Certain attitudes and policies are most favorable to relatively rapid assimilation. Such are tolerance of new cultures, a sympathetic attitude towards immigrants and their ways of life, ideals of racial equality and free intermarriage with immigrants of any and all races, equality of economic opportunity for all, and the absence of barriers to free and extensive contacts between the native culture and that of immigrants.

In the interchange of cultural traits, material culture is most quickly and readily adopted, primarily because it is today less vested with sanctity than institutions and folkways and because the advantages of superior tools, machines, and weapons are most readily apparent and demonstrable. There is much more resistance to accepting new social institutions; among social institutions, the greatest resistance to change is found in those associated with religion and sex, which are most completely enmeshed in tradition, myth, and emotion. Finally, the forms and rhetoric of new institutions and cultural traits are adopted far more speedily than the vital content. Immigrants take over the forms of native culture long before they really understand their meaning or the opportunities and responsibilities they involve.

**Imitation as a mechanism of assimilation.** Imitation plays so large a part in the process of assimilation that it may be worth while briefly to describe its nature and operations. Imitation means the conscious or unconscious repetition of the actions, practices, usages, and ideas of others. Some sociologists would include within the concept of imitation our repetition of our own previous acts, but most writers regard the latter as habitual rather than imitative action.

The sociologist who devoted the greatest amount of attention to imitation was the Frenchman Gabriel Tarde, who wrote a famous book entitled *The Laws of Imitation*. Tarde believed that the social process is made up primarily of four main activities: invention, repetition of the invention, opposition to the invention, and an ultimate adaptation of the invention to the competing items in the culture. This adaptation serves as a new invention, and the process is repeated indefinitely. By repetition, Tarde meant imitation and he gave much more attention to this social activity than to the others he named. He set forth a number of generalizations as to the ways in which imitation takes place: Those of an inferior status in society tend to imitate their social superiors; imitation spreads in a geometrical progression, thus exerting a wide influence; imitations are influenced and altered in different degrees and ways by the imitators; and imitations are vigorous and influential in proportion to the prestige of the person or act imitated. There are three main types of imitation: fashion, or the imitation of the novel items in culture; convention, or the imitation of formal rites and ceremonials; and custom, or the imitation of old, established, and respected usages and institutions.

**Personal and group assimilation.** Assimilation applies to both personal and group experience. Personal assimilation in the case of an immigrant usually takes the following form: He adjusts to the new situation in the basic essentials of living, then accommodates himself to leading usages and social institutions; much more slowly, he adopts the native culture, first taking over material culture and then language, folkways, social institutions, and ideals, roughly in the order named. The rapidity with which this cultural assimilation proceeds will depend upon factors to be discussed shortly, but it is rare that any immigrant is completely assimilated. The most dangerous period is the one intermediate between rather complete retention of the immigrant's native culture and fairly thorough assimilation to the culture of the adopted land. It is this fact of hovering between two cultures that accounts for the relatively great proclivity of the second-generation immigrants—children of immigrants—to crime and vice.

Group assimilation of immigrants follows the same pattern as personal assimilation. Less extreme problems of assimilation are faced by a group moving to another portion of their native country, even though the new manners, customs, and dialect be different from those of the migrants.

**Rapidity of assimilation.** The speed and thoroughness with which assimilation will proceed depends upon a number of considerations. One is the relative impressiveness, unity, and coherence of the native culture to that of the immigrants. If the native culture is far superior to that of the immigrants, the latter are more likely to take over the native culture fairly rapidly. If the reverse is true, then the assimilative process will proceed more slowly. In extreme cases, as in the instance of the Chinese, there will be little assimilation. In less extreme cases of greater antiquity and integration of the alien culture, the process will be slowed down and incomplete; this has been true of French immigrants in America.

A tolerant and friendly attitude on the part of natives towards alien cultures, accompanied by many contacts and opportunities for cultural interchange, will speed up assimilation, while the segregation, isolation, or persecution of alien cultures will greatly retard the process. Overzealousness on the part of native groups relative to the assimilation of alien cultures arouses resentment on the part of the immigrants and encourages them to resist assimilative policies. If marked differences in race accompany cultural contrasts, the assimilative process will be rendered more difficult and gradual because of the additional obstacle of race prejudice.

**Agencies and institutions assisting assimilation.** Among the social agencies and institutions that seek to promote the assimilation of alien cultures to that of the native country are schools, churches, social settlements, and political parties. Compulsory education laws force the children of immigrants to attend school and thus learn the language and culture of their adopted land. Membership in a church is one important cultural trait which the immigrants are likely to share with the native population; where this is so, immigrants can attend churches along with natives. Social settlements have as one of their main purposes the sympathetic introduction of immigrants into native folkways and institutions. Political parties, especially city political machines, court immigrants in the hope of speeding up their naturalization and getting their political support. Economic groups are somewhat less sympathetic and eager to take in immigrants on terms of equality, though some labor unions have in recent years opened their ranks enthusiastically to immigrant workers and have promoted assimilation. Professional groups are usually the least eager to welcome the entrance of immigrants.

**Cultural integration.** When assimilation has become relatively complete, sociologists call the result cultural integration. Some nations, like England and France, which have had little immigration for centuries, have attained a high degree of cultural integration. This is conspicuously not the case with the United States. There was no native culture here, save for the relatively primitive culture of the original Indian population. What passes for American culture has been the product of more or less continuous immigration from the early seventeenth century to the present time. There has been little unity or maturity in American culture at any time. With the marked decline in immigration since 1914 and the development of more effective agencies of communication, American culture may attain some approximation to integration by the close of the present century, but surely not even then to the extent now enjoyed by Britain and France. No small part of the political inefficiency and corruption, the waste of our natural resources, and our relative inability to work out an efficient social and economic order may be attributed to our lack of adequate cultural assimilation.

## Co-operation and Mutual Aid

**Nature and function of co-operation.** Co-operation stands at the opposite pole from active social conflict. Its social importance has been advanced with as much assurance as was the social significance of group conflict. Co-operation both promotes accommodation and assimilation and is rendered more feasible by them. Kimball Young defines co-operation in a simple and straightforward fashion as "a form of interaction of two or more persons directed towards some goal, the result of whose common action, mutual helpfulness, will benefit them." Co-operation may be partly unconscious, as in the routine of daily social life, or it may be the execution of very deliberate action and the outcome of a definite social and economic ideology. The latter is well represented by the world-wide co-operative movement, which has many millions of members. Co-operative efforts and organizations vary from temporary neighborhood co-operation, in such emergencies as harvesting, threshing, and illness, to international co-operation and division of labor.

**Causes of co-operation.** Human co-operative endeavor has grown by necessity out of the elemental problems of life. Some co-operative effort was necessary to exploit physical nature sufficiently to provide for subsistence in primitive times. Men had to co-operate in the primitive hunt because of the number and ferocity of wild animals and the crudity of the weapons available at that time. Co-operation was also necessary in warding off human enemies, as well as in organizing groups to attack others. The natural play impulses of mankind also helped to promote co-operative activities. Likemindedness and sympathy are indispensable to the creation of any permanent group life, so in human groups these attitudes which are indispensable to co-operative effort were early present. Social organization itself implies the existence of a considerable amount of co-operative activity, both conscious and unconscious. Some sociologists, such as R. M. MacIver, regard social organization as virtually another term for social co-operation. The cultural heritage hands on ideas and practices of co-operation from the past. The steady improvement of communication has enlarged and encouraged the field of co-operative activity. The demonstrably greater efficiency of co-operation and mutual aid, as compared with unaided individual efforts, has helped to promote co-operative endeavor and organization.

**Main types of co-operation.** Social organization offers the typical example of social forms of co-operation. Charitable organizations are particularly devoted to co-operative efforts. There have been many examples of economic co-operation in historic times. The medieval manor, which dominated economic life during the Middle Ages, was a rather thorough case of co-operative economic endeavor on the part of the semi-servile peasantry. The elaborate development of the division of labor and economic specialization in modern times is a good example of more or less unconscious and indirect co-operative activity. Deliberately planned economic co-operation is well exemplified in our day by the international co-operative movement. There are several types of co-operatives: producers' co-operatives, marketing co-operatives, consumer co-operatives, credit unions, and service co-operatives. We shall describe them in more detail later on in this volume.[2]  Many regard the co-operative movement as the only possible way to gain all the advantages of our present potential technological efficiency without being subjected to totalitarian controls. World-wide economic co-operation was aimed at by the Bretton Woods Agreement and the Marshall Plan.

Political co-operation is represented in a way by all public measures and activities which are supposed to serve the nation as a whole. More especially, one might select various national service activities, such as the social security legislation and administration, public health measures and activities, and public health insurance. International political co-operation is illustrated by arbitration tribunals, political federations, leagues of nations, and international alliances. Co-operative religious activities may be discerned in such organizations as the late Interchurch World Movement, the Federal Council of Churches, and the National Catholic Welfare Council. One of the most far-flung types of co-operative endeavor is scientific and technical research and scholarship generally, through which the intellectual activity and talents of all mankind are pooled and made available to every civilized land, except during times of war or political stress. No form of co-operative endeavor has done more to change the face of civilization in contemporary times.

**Co-operation aids socialization.** Co-operation exerts no little influence on the processes of socialization. It promotes unity of purpose on the part of the co-operators. It encourages sympathetic collaboration in concerted activity. It co-ordinates and integrates social action, intensifies group solidarity, and helps to restrain selfish impulses, all without stifling the dynamic impulses arising from constructive forms of competition. The co-operative movement actually encourages and stimulates all forms of competition which will increase public prosperity and well-being.

## The Division of Labor and Specialization

**Sociological implication of division of labor.** Much of the total co-operative effort in society rests upon an elaborate social and economic division of labor. In a broad sociological sense, the division

---

2 See below, pp. 344–346, 591–592.

of labor embraces all differentiation and specialization of social functions, the labors of all the professions and occupational groups, the
operations of interest-groups, the activities of most social classes, and
the execution of individual rôles in various forms of social organization. In fact, the whole institutional framework of human effort
constitutes social division of labor. This conception may be narrowed,
for our purposes, to include only the socio-economic division of labor
involved in the separation of economic functions and the specialization of economic activities.

**Economic advantages of the division of labor.** The division of
labor leads to far greater industrial skill and efficiency than would
otherwise be possible. If applied on a world scale, through the operation of universal free trade, the resulting increase of efficiency would
be even greater, since each nation could specialize in the forms of
economic activity best suited to its people and resources. Specialization encourages and facilitates mechanical production and the constant
improvement of machinery. This has one incidental bad social effect:
the breaking down of the industrial process into many small operations produces the serious boredom and fatigue that result from the
rapid and endless repetition of a single slight manual operation in connection with a machine. This ever greater efficiency of mechanical
production, together with the development of more and more automatic machinery, may end up in a tremendous volume of technological
unemployment unless we are willing to spread employment through
constantly shortening the working day and week.

**Division of labor and social solidarity.** The most important socio-
economic aspect of the division of labor is the ever greater co-ordination and integration of economic life. All phases of our economic
order are interdependent; if any one large sector breaks down badly,
the whole economic system is likely to collapse, at least temporarily.
In short, our economic order is dependent upon the efficiency and full
co-operation of its parts.

## Expanded Scope of Social Processes

**Revolution in scope and complexity of social processes.** We have
now examined the main processes involved in socialization and social
interaction. As in previous discussions of social processes and group
life, we need here to emphasize again the necessity of readapting our
perspectives to the revolutionary changes which have taken place in
social processes in most parts of the civilized world as a result of the
rise of modern industrialism, urbanization, and rapid, world-wide
social processes in most parts of the civilized world as a result of the
classic books on the social process were written back in the early days
of the automobile or before, and based their analysis on the small,
simple, personal societies characteristic of a primarily rural society.

Ever larger numbers of our population no longer live under rural conditions. Many of the personal groups have passed away in an urban setting, and those that do persist in cities, such as the family, have been profoundly modified by their new surroundings and stimuli. Fifty years ago, persons responded in their social relations primarily to stimuli arising out of local conditions and pressures. Their children and grandchildren of today are affected daily by information and pressures of national or global scope and derivation. Our sociological analysis of social processes must reckon with this change—perhaps the most profound social transformation since the dawn of history.

**Examples of widened scope of social processes.** This great transformation has been pointed up constantly in the course of our brief review of the main factors in the processes of socialization. We have seen that many of the daily contacts of the individual are global; and, while most of these are mental rather than physical, there are more and more globe-trotting diplomats and pleasure seekers providing global physical contacts on a scale never before known. Social interaction is daily affected by ideas and activities on the opposite side of the world, as in the case of vigorous American reaction to developments in Korea, China, and Indonesia since 1945. We have reacted sharply to the policies of the Soviet Union for several years, though fifty years ago we paid little attention to even more distinctly "un-American" doings on the part of the Tsarist régime. Persons and interests from all over the world interact in the Assembly of the United Nations.

Competition has become world-wide, all the way from Olympic games to the competition of great global ideologies. Soviet totalitarianism competes with American capitalistic democracy. European nations compete for American financial aid, and all nations for a greater share of world trade. Today, we accommodate not merely to local pressures and institutions but to world issues and developments, as when the United States wrote off Chiang Kai-shek's régime after many years of expensive and bloody support, or when we accepted the rise of a socialistic state in Britain, despite bitter hostility to a rather similar economy in Soviet Russia. Assimilation has, for decades now, been limited mainly to adapting to our civilization the products of trans-oceanic migrations. Co-operation is no longer limited to threshing bees in a rural community, but has been extended to world co-operative societies, the Marshall Plan and the Economic Co-operation Administration, the International Monetary Fund, the Bank for Reconstruction and Rehabilitation, and the like. An international division of labor has been long maintained through world trade and other agencies.

**Dangers in undisciplined globaloney.** All this does not mean that we should ignore local or national processes and problems. Indeed, the better our house is put in order at home the greater the prospect of our reacting successfully to issues on a larger scale. But, at the same time, we cannot overlook the vast changes which have taken place in the scope and character of social processes in the twentieth century.

## Summary

Social interaction is the core of sociological study and is usually dealt with as the social process.   Studies of personal and social isolation have shown how the lack of contacts frustrates or disintegrates the personality and produces arrested civilizations.   A well-rounded personality and a dynamic culture require ample and stimulating contacts. The latter are produced by many forces—geographical pressures and opportunities; biological factors such as mating, marriage, and the family; economic efforts; and similarity of cultural interests.   Social contacts have been greatly enlarged in the last century as the result of revolutionary developments in transportation and communication, having grown from a local and neighborhood basis to the international contacts of our own day.

Social contacts produce social interaction and set in operation the main mechanisms of the social process—competition, conflict, adjustment, accommodation, assimilation, social integration, co-operation, and the division of labor.

Social interaction takes many forms, from the relations of infant and mother to the deliberations of the Assembly of the United Nations.   It socializes the individual and gives rise to the main social structures. It is chiefly limited to mankind, since men alone can make use of symbols, especially of language, the main tool of social interaction.

Competition is a type of social interaction that stimulates and encourages social achievement if conducted in a fair and constructive fashion, but it can be ruthless and disastrous, as it has been in many forms of contemporary economic life.   Conflict, the most extreme degree of competition, may even take the form of physical violence and war; it has made many important contributions in the past to the creation and solidification of social structures, but in our day, in the shape of war and gross economic conflict, it threatens the social order and personal security.

In the course of normal social development, competition and conflict are mitigated by social adjustment and accommodation, in which both individuals and social groups accept the basic essentials of the culture and social order of which they are a part.   They usually accept material culture first and most readily, religious and moral traits most slowly and reluctantly.   If accommodation is successful, the individuals and social groups usually merge themselves with the surrounding culture through the process of assimilation.   In this, imitation, studied by the great French sociologist Gabriel Tarde, is the most potent factor.

Well-assimilated cultures promote co-operative efforts, which run all the way from aid in rural neighborhood emergencies to the efforts of functional bodies of the United Nations.   The division of labor and specialization have made co-operation more effective and habitual.

The social process has now outgrown local and personal societies and taken on world-wide aspects and implications; these place new responsibilities on individuals, social groups, and nations and create many

THE SOCIAL PROCESS

novel social problems. There is always a danger that extreme absorption in extra-national activities may reduce the effectiveness of national co-operation and reduce the security and prosperity of the citizens of any country.

## Selected References

The idea of the Social Process was first well developed by E. C. Hayes in his *Sociological Construction Lines* (1905) and A. W. Small in his *General Sociology* (1905). It was further extended by Hayes in his *Introduction to the Study of Sociology* (1915). But it was first made the core of sociology texts through the example and influence of Robert E. Park and Ernest W. Burgess in their *Introduction to the Science of Sociology* (1924). Since that time the concept has been, perhaps, overworked, until it has become almost identical with the whole field of sociology in most of the sociology textbooks written since 1925. Hence, any good recent text provides ample reading in this field. The most comprehensive panorama of the social process has been provided by E. A. Ross in his *Principles of Sociology* (1930) and *New Age Sociology* (1947). But the Park and Burgess volume still remains the best textbook treatment of the subject.

Anderson, Nels, *Men on the Move,* University of Chicago Press, 1940. Good study of the social contacts of American migratory workers.

* Angell, R. C., *The Integration of American Society,* McGraw-Hill, 1941. Comprehensive survey of accommodation and adaptation through the development of American institutions.

* Bristol, L. M., *Social Adaptation,* Harvard University, 1915. Review of the leading doctrines of sociologists with respect to conflict, adaptation, and co-operation.

Burns, A. R., *The Decline of Competition,* McGraw-Hill, 1936. Restrained critical analysis of the recent modification of the competitive process.

Cooley, C. H., *Personal Competition,* American Economic Association (Economic Studies, v. 4, no. 2), 1899. Pioneer study of personal aspects of the competitive process.

* Cox, O. C., *Class, Caste and Race,* Doubleday, 1948. Detailed study of social interaction and differentiation involving race contacts, class building, and caste relationships.

Durkheim, Émile, *On the Division of Labor in Society* (Trans. by George Simpson), Macmillan, 1933. A classic work by a leading French sociologist.

Eddy, A. J., *The New Competition,* McClurg, 1915. Criticism of the competitive process and argument for co-operation.

Gumplowicz, Ludwig, *Outlines of Sociology,* Stechert, 1899. Contains the essential doctrines of the leading writer who stresses social conflict, amalgamation, and assimilation as the leading social processes.

* Hartman, E. G., *The Movement to Americanize the Immigrant,* Columbia University, 1948. Best study of the melting-pot technique in American assimilation.

Jennings, H. H., *Leadership and Isolation,* Longmans, Green, 1943. Good study of the isolation produced by the separation of the leader from the masses.

Kropotkin, Peter, *Mutual Aid: A Factor of Evolution,* Knopf, 1925. The classic book portraying co-operation as the essence of the social process.

Kulischer, E. M., *Europe on the Move,* Columbia University, 1948. Recent study of social contacts produced by internal movements of European peoples and their emigration from 1917 to 1947.

Locke, Alain, and Stern, B. J., *When Peoples Meet; A Study in Race and Culture Contacts,* American Education Fellowship, 1946. An able discussion of the problems of assimilation.

* May, M. A., and Doob, L. W., *Competition and Cooperation,* Social Science Research Council, 1937. Perhaps the best socio-psychological introduction to the processes of competition and co-operation.

Miller, H. A., *Races, Nations and Classes,* Lippincott, 1924. Stimulating pioneer work on conflict and assimilation.

Morley, John, *On Compromise,* Macmillan, 1896. Classic exposition of the intellectual basis of accommodation.

Page, C. H., *Class and American Sociology,* Dial Press, 1940. Review of the leading notions of American systematic sociologists relative to social classes.

* Reuter, E. B. (Ed.), *Race and Culture Contacts,* McGraw-Hill, 1934. Detailed analysis of contacts, interaction, accommodation, and assimilation in American society.

Rose, Arnold and Caroline, *America Divided,* Knopf, 1948. Recent discussion of racial, ethnic, and social conflict in contemporary United States.

Snyder, Carl, *Capitalism the Creator,* Macmillan, 1940. Outstanding defense of competitive capitalism as the most dynamic force in modern society.

Tarde, Gabriel, *Social Laws,* Macmillan, 1899. Summary of the social process as conceived by one of the leading French sociologists. Stresses invention, imitation, opposition, and adaptation.

Tawney, R. H., *The Acquisitive Society,* Harcourt, Brace, 1920. The most brilliant critique of the competitive economic order.

Veblen, T. B., *The Theory of the Leisure Class,* Vanguard, 1926. The classic work on the attitudes and practices of contemporary capitalist society.

Vincent, M. J., *The Accommodation Process in Industry,* University of Southern California Press, 1930. Best book on the economic aspects of accommodation.

Watson, Goodwin, *Youth after Conflict,* Association Press, 1947. Analyzes the effects of the two world wars on American youth.

Wood, M. M., *The Stranger; A Study in Social Relationships,* Columbia University Press, 1934. Analysis of isolation and incipient social contacts.

Woofter, T. J., *Races and Ethnic Groups in American Life,* McGraw-Hill, 1933. Good treatment of accommodation, amalgamation, and assimilation in American civilization.

Young, Donald R., *American Minority Peoples,* Harper, 1932. A study of conflict and assimilation.

# PART III

# The Physical Basis of Social Problems

## CHAPTER VII

# How We Have Wasted Our Natural and Human Endowment

## Some Influences Exerted by Nature and Geography on Human Society

**Geographic basis of the great civilizations.** Historians and geographers have pointed out that there seems to be a rather specific geographical setting for each great stage in the development of civilization. Human culture appears to have become established first in river valleys: the earliest notable civilizations were located in the valleys of the Nile, the Tigris and Euphrates, and the great rivers of China and India. This early stage of civilization we call the fluvial or river-basin stage. Next, cultures developed along seacoasts, notably the Mediterranean and the shores of Western Europe. Such were the Greek city-states, the Roman Empire, medieval monarchies like France and Britain, and the great Moslem centers of civilization during the Middle Ages. This era is known as the thalassic or seacoast era. Then, after 1500, new methods of navigation and better ships enabled men to conquer the seas and oceans and strike out boldly all over the world. This created the oceanic or world stage of civilization in which we are living today.

**Environmental factors favoring the rise of civilizations.** It is the opinion of historians and sociologists that geographical factors played a leading rôle in determining where men made the first transitions from a bestial form of life to the beginnings of orderly civilization. Such regions usually combined the bounties of nature with reasonable security. Food was available in sufficient quantity through fishing, hunting, or the products of good pastures and fertile land; but adequate protection from more barbarous intruders was needed if the beginnings of culture were not to be shattered. Some writers have maintained that the bounties of nature should not be too great or life too easy, lest there not be enough of a challenge to creative activity. Others have held that a bountiful habitat, by attracting a dense population, would facilitate the division of labor and industrial specialization, thus making for greater efficiency and social progress.

**Contacts and isolation.** Social contacts and the mutual sharing of different cultures have always been a potent element in promoting change and social advances. Populations that are too isolated by mountains, deserts, or water tend to stagnate and produce arrested civilizations.

**Natural bounties.** Rich natural resources have always encouraged the rise and growth of civilization. But those resources which are desirable for progress vary with the development of civilization and technology. In early days, good hunting and fishing grounds, good pastures, and fertile lands were of greatest importance. Since the Industrial Revolution, the presence of plenty of coal, oil, and vital minerals has come to have increasing importance, and countries which have only good agricultural resources have tended to fall behind in the social procession.

**The climatic factor.** Climatic factors have played a large rôle in the history of human society. They have helped to determine the physical traits of races. It is generally agreed that temperate climates are most conducive to social progress. Historians have pointed to "the northward course of progress" during historic times. Changes in climate affect the destiny and location of civilizations. What were once fertile areas have dried up as a result of climatic changes, and the inhabitants have been forced to migrate afar in search of better pastures and more fertile soil. The great invasion of Europe by the Huns in the early Christian Era may have been caused by the drying up of their former habitat in Western Asia. The tropical climate has kept out white men, save in the rôle of conquerors and minority rulers.

**The ideal environment.** Sociologists and geographers hold that the ideal geographical situation for social prosperity and progress is one which combines a temperate climate, adequate moisture, rich soil, plenty of lumber, a good supply of coal, oil and minerals, natural routes of travel for ingress and egress, and good harbors.

We shall now proceed to make clear how the United States was originally endowed with all these natural advantages, how these helped to make us a great nation, and how, through needless waste over more than two centuries, we have now reached a critical stage, in which waste must be eliminated if we are to maintain and utilize what still remain of our natural assets.

## The Importance of Natural Resources
## for Human Well-Being

**Natural resources the basis of our economic life.** How many of us have ever stopped to consider what is the real work of the farmer, the miner, the manufacturer, or the merchant? Vaguely, we realize that these people are engaged in making and selling things we need— bread, clothing, automobiles, building materials, vacuum cleaners, drugs—without which we would find it impossible to carry on our daily lives. And there, for most of us, our thinking ends. Yet, have we really answered our question? What does "making bread" or "making autos" mean? Perhaps we can find the answer in looking, briefly, at what goes into the making of an ordinary loaf of bread.

Bread is made from flour, and flour, in turn, from wheat. So, first of all, there must be farm land with fertile soil, situated in a locality with good rainfall and favorable temperature. To plan and cultivate wheat, the farmer must have tools—tractors, seed drills, plows, harrows, binders or combines, threshing machines, and so forth. And he and his family must have a house in which to live.

Think, for a moment, of what must go into the making of this machinery and the house. Coal, iron ore, and limestone must be mined and manufactured into steel and iron for the machinery, timber cut and sawed into lumber for the house. Many other materials are needed, among them glass, copper, nickel, tin, zinc, and lead. Thousands of hours of labor are required to convert the coal, limestone, iron, and lumber into buildings, tools, and machinery. Gasoline and oil are needed to run the tractors, and these must be pumped from the earth and shipped thousands of miles to the farm. After the wheat is cut and threshed, it must be shipped by truck or train to a flour mill. Consider the labor, machinery, and materials necessary to make the trucks and railroad trains. The flour mill requires buildings and machinery. From the mill, the flour goes to the baker, who also needs buildings and machines. The baker sends the finished bread to the grocer, into the making of whose store, counters, scales, cash registers, and so forth, have gone vast quantities of labor and materials. When one considers all the human effort and the vast amounts of materials necessary for the manufacture of a mere loaf of bread, one's imagination is staggered.

**The natural basis of prosperity.** This sketch of the origin of a loaf of bread will suggest, perhaps, the fundamental task of the farmer, manufacturer, and merchant—to take the things found in the earth, convert them into articles of use to human beings, and then put them in the hands of consumers. Soil, water, and sunlight are turned into wheat; coal, iron ore, and limestone into steel, thence into machinery. Since this is the real function of agriculture and industry, it follows that the prosperity of a nation depends to a great extent upon the supplies of raw materials provided it by nature. Forests, fertile soil, minerals, water, oil, gas, and wild life are among such natural resources.

Since our country's prosperity depends in large measure upon its supply of natural resources, it is worth while to take an inventory of our original stock of raw materials. In the process of building our nation, we have used up vast quantities of the lumber, minerals, and soil with which nature bountifully provided us. If we are to continue to be prosperous, we shall need even greater supplies of natural resources. Unfortunately, we shall find from our inventory that we have been very wasteful and that, unless we are more careful in the future, we may lack many of those raw materials which are needed to supply us with food, buildings, machinery, and other essentials of life.

## What We Started With

**Our remarkable original endowment.** When our country was first explored by the white man, it possessed an amazing abundance and variety of natural resources. This rich natural endowment enabled the United States to become one of the most prosperous and powerful nations in the world. Our fertile soil furnished food for millions of people, while our timber and minerals provided the materials out of which we built up our impressive material civilization.

**Our vast forests.** When the first colonists settled in America in the early seventeenth century, over half the United States was covered by unbroken forests, one billion acres in area, stretching from Maine to Florida and westward well beyond the Mississippi River. In the northern forest belt, the trees were chiefly poplars, pines, and spruces. The white pine and spruce were the most valuable timber in the East. The central part of the country was covered by various hardwoods—sugar and red maples, beech, birch, ash, elm, oak, hickory, walnut, and chestnut. In the South, there was the short-needle pine, from which tar, turpentine, and pitch, as well as lumber, were derived. In the Far West, there were mainly softwoods, some of which grew to enormous size; the most important of the western trees was the red, or Douglas, fir.

**Soil resources.** At the beginning of the seventeenth century, we had at least 500 million acres of fertile soil, much of it created by a great glacial ice sheet which covered a large part of the country in prehistoric times. The ice sheet extended over the northeastern part of the continent as far south as the Ohio River and west to the Great Plains. As the ice sheet melted, it deposited glacial drift, a fertile type of soil, on the surface of the ground. We also owe to the glaciation most of the beautiful lakes and convenient watercourses of the Northeast.

**Mineral deposits.** The country was almost as fortunate in its endowment of minerals as in its supplies of timber and fertile soil. Coal deposits underlie about one-sixth of the total area of the United States. In fact, some kind of usable coal is found within a short distance of every well-inhabited part of the country. Engineers estimate that, originally, there were about 7 billion tons of iron ore in the various deposits of the United States. Many other forms of minerals existed in profusion—gold, silver, copper, lead, zinc, aluminum, and quicksilver. In our oil sands there were over 40 billion barrels of crude petroleum.

**Bountiful wild life.** The early settlers, more interested in animals for food and skins than in mineral resources, found wild life abundant; no other country in the world had more species of wild animals. Buffalo, now almost extinct, roamed the land by the millions. Moose, bighorn sheep, grizzly and black bears, elk, and deer were common, along with fur-bearing animals of all sorts. Migrating birds darkened the skies every spring and autumn, and fish abounded, particularly in the North Atlantic, the Great Lakes, and the waters of the Northwest.

This, then, was our natural heritage. We had a bountiful supply of nearly all the resources needed to supply the home, the farm, and the factory. How much of our natural resources remains today? Have we a sufficient volume and variety to insure our prosperity in the future?

## The Picture after Three Centuries of Exploitation

**Fruits of ruthless exploitation.** The story of what has happened to our natural resources can be briefly told. Only about 100 million acres of uncut virgin forest remain out of the original 1,000 million. About three-fifths of our fertile soil has been ruined or made at least temporarily unfit for farming. A considerable portion of our rich deposits of minerals and petroleum has been exhausted; in several cases we face the prospect of serious shortages. We have ruthlessly destroyed our wild life and fish. In brief, we have paid a high price for our impressive industrialization and urbanization.

**Causes of exploitation and waste.** What has caused this alarming reduction of the abundant supply of natural resources we once possessed? In the task of building our civilization, it was only natural that we should use up considerable amounts. But was it necessary to consume as much as we did? The answer, plainly, is that it was not necessary. Many of our resources have not gone into the building of homes, tools, machinery, and factories but have been wasted. Ignorance, carelessness, and greed have taken a tremendous toll of our natural heritage.

**Destruction of our forests.** When the early settlers came to this country, they cleared the land in order to build homes and plant crops. The magnificent hardwood forests which extended from the Atlantic Ocean to beyond the Mississippi were chopped down and burned off to make way for farms and villages. Some of this woodland, of course, had to be cleared away, but far more timber than necessary was cut. At least half the forests in this region could have been retained and there still would have been enough land for agriculture.

*Farm Security Administration, photo by Rothstein.*
**This picture shows vividly the stark devastation caused by the 175,000 fires that sweep our forests annually.**

The destruction of our forests was further encouraged by Congressional legislation favored by private interests, such as the Timber Cutting Act of 1878, which gave private interests permission to cut timber free of cost, so long as it was on mineral lands belonging to the government. This law was intended to clear the land for mining and to furnish wood for fuel and building. But not one acre out of 5,000 that was defined as "mineral land" by the Timber Act contained ore that was worth mining. The law merely put our western forests at the mercy of private lumbermen.

Another law, known as the Timber and Stone Act, also passed by Congress in 1878, provided that, since land with trees and stones on it was unfit for farming, it could be sold in 160 acre lots for $2.50 an acre. Originally applying only to far western states, the law was extended in 1892 to all states where there was public land. Land that was worth up to $500 an acre was thus sold for $2.50. The law did not intend that one person should buy more than 160 acres, but a large California lumber company, for example, took 100,000 acres of the choicest timberland at this low price. Over 12 million acres of forest were bought by lumber firms under the Timber and Stone Act. Worth at least 300 million dollars, they brought the government about one-tenth of that amount.

Although the private lumber business helped to build up our country, it has caused great destruction in our forests. Partly because huge quantities of white pine and spruce had been shipped to England in colonial times, most of the New England forests were unproductive after 1850. This marked the first stage in the destruction of our valuable forest domain. The lumber men then turned to the forests around the Great Lakes, where there was white pine in abundance. In about sixty years the large forests in that part of the country were stripped by industry and fire, and desolation remained. Around 1890, the lumber men moved in on the pines and other evergreen forests of the South. By 1910, the best trees had been carted away, and the lumber industry had moved on to the dense forests of the Pacific Northwest. Lumbering methods have been incredibly wasteful. As late as 1949, it was estimated that we totally wasted 35 per cent of the lumber cut; another 22 per cent was used for fuel, most of it very inefficiently.

A large amount of forest exploitation today is carried on for pulp wood to provide newsprint. Over 300 acres of forest are required to furnish enough pulp wood to print one Sunday issue (about one million copies) of *The New York Times*. Ten million young trees each year are wasted by those who require an annual Christmas tree.

Around 175,000 forest fires annually devastate our forests. The embers of a camp-fire, or a cigarette carelessly tossed from an automobile, may start a fire that will rage for days, destroying millions of dollars worth of trees. In the five years following 1910, 7,000 out of every million acres in our national forests were devastated by fire. In 1933, more standing timber was burned in the Pacific Northwest alone than was cut in the whole United States. Fire protection, however, has been improved in our national forests; as a result, most of the timber burned in the last few years has been located on privately-owned land. Insects destroy even more lumber than fire—about 625 million cubic feet each year to 450 million cubic feet destroyed by fire.

**Soil wastage: erosion.** Our waste of soil resources has been as tragic as the destruction of our forest reserves. An estimated two-fifths of our 500 million acres of fertile land has been destroyed and another fifth seriously injured. Even the best land has only a few inches of fertile topsoil; if this layer is removed, the remaining soil becomes unproductive. The process that wears away the fertile topsoil is called "erosion." Trees, with their network of roots beneath the surface, hold back the moisture, which filters down into the earth and gradually finds its way to the streams. Where there are no tree roots, the rains quickly wash away the fertile topsoil; heavy rainfall may cause a dangerous flood, as the water flows swiftly and unchecked down the treeless slopes. The great floods of the Ohio, Mississippi, and Missouri rivers in recent years were mainly a result of the destruction of the forests in those regions.

Other causes of erosion are the failure to check and fill gullies when they have started; one-crop agriculture, which leaves the soil exposed to eroding influences during most of the year; the removal of protective grasses; the insufficient application of fertilizer; and the unskilled plowing of sloping lands.

Millions of acres of fertile land have been destroyed by unscientific farming methods. A single crop, like wheat or cotton, planted on the same land year after year, wears out the soil. Formerly, when a plot of ground was exhausted, that is, when the crops had extracted all the richness from the soil, the farmer began the same operations on an adjoining plot, leaving the original to erode or grow up to brush and waste. The soil exhaustion resulting from intensive cultivation of cotton in the South was the chief reason why the southern planters were always hungry for more land. Only after millions of acres were wasted by these methods was it discovered that some crops—corn, wheat, cotton, and tobacco, for example—take vital elements from the soil, while others, like clover and alfalfa, increase its fertility. Today the wise farmer follows a plan of crop rotation—planting such soil-building crops as clover between plantings of soil-exhausting crops.

**The dust bowl.** Unwise opening of grassland to farming has caused wind erosion, particularly on the plains occupying the plateau east

*Farm Security Administration, photo by Rothstein.*

Grim picture of poverty and desolation on submarginal farm, ruined by erosion, drought, and dust.

of the foothills of the Rockies. This area was once covered with a thick growth of buffalo grass; so long as the grass remained, the soil did not blow away. But the tractor, the combine, and other power machinery entered the picture after 1910. The first world war increased the demand for, and price of, wheat. A farmer could plant

*Courtesy of J. W. McManigal.*

**Contrast with the opposite picture this scene on a rich, fertile, and scientifically cultivated farm.**

and harvest more grain than ever before, and sell it at a high price. Thousands of acres of western grassland that should never have been put into cultivation were plowed under and sowed to wheat.

The profits from the wheat were short-lived. With the end of the war, European countries curtailed their purchases of American grain. Moreover, Australian and Argentine wheat began to compete more sharply with the American output. But the western farmers did not stop plowing up the grasslands and, soon, trouble began. A serious drought occurred. The dried-up soil, without protective grass roots, was attacked by strong winds, and millions of cubic feet of dirt were blown away. These dust storms ruined millions of acres of farmland and left thousands of families homeless and poverty-stricken. The hardships of the discouraged farmers of the Great

Plains, forced to load their possessions into cars and trucks and wander in search of new homes, have been immortalized by John Steinbeck in his novel, *The Grapes of Wrath.*

Three billion tons of fertile soil were washed and blown from crop and pasture land in 1932. If this were loaded on freight cars, the train would reach nineteen times around the earth. In 1933–34 dust storms ruined 4 million acres of western land and injured some 60 million more. The great dust storm of May, 1934, which was probably the most terrifying, whisked away some 300 million tons of fertile topsoil.

Unfortunately, farmers learned no permanent lesson from the "dustbowl" catastrophe. With the unprecedentedly high prices of grain during and after the second world war encouraging further plowing up of grassland, another great dust-bowl calamity is now in the making.

Heealessness and ignorance have thus jeopardized our agricultural future. It is estimated that about 100 million acres have already been ruined by erosion, and that serious erosion is under way on another 200 million acres. In all, there are not more than 200 million acres of land still fit for good farming. Unless education in reforestation and the best methods of preventing soil erosion is stepped up, it is estimated that, in another fifty years, the United States will have less than 150 million acres of good farming land.

**Ravages of insects and blight.** Both our crops and our forests have suffered severely from insect pests and blight. The chestnut blight killed off many of our chestnut trees, and our elms are now being seriously attacked. Boll weevils, locusts, grasshoppers, moths, worms, caterpillars, and countless other insects, as well as parasitic growths, devour the farmer's produce and profits. It has been estimated that crop destruction by various insects totals at least one billion dollars a year in the United States. Between 1925 and 1934, the damage wrought by grasshoppers alone amounted to about 250 million dollars. Currently, one of the greatest menaces to our crops and trees is the Japanese beetle. Experts estimate that insects destroy or devour ten per cent of all our crops.

**Waste of mineral resources.** No part of our natural resources has been wasted more heedlessly than our once vast mineral deposits. Our coal supplies present an outstanding example. Government coal lands were opened to the public in 1864, selling at that time for $25 an acre; this price was dropped to $15 in 1873. By the end of the nineteenth century, more than 600,000 acres had been sold for a trivial fraction of their real value. Such cheap prices encouraged careless and greedy methods of mining, which in turn resulted in the loss of over 35 per cent of the coal in our soft coal fields. Although we have enough soft coal to last a long time, the end of the best reserves is in sight. Since hard coal has been mined longer than soft and with almost equally wasteful methods, and the original reserves were far less, our hard coal supplies are even closer to exhaustion.

While the coal reserves are not seriously threatened today, the coal industry is. Railroads are rapidly converting to oil-burning diesel locomotives. All but 60 of the 1,800 locomotives built in 1949 were diesels; in the the same year steam locomotives were used on only 26 per cent of passenger and 49 per cent of freight mileage. Electric power and other industries are also converting to oil and other fuels —their use of coal dropped off by 36 million tons in 1949. Oil heating is growing by leaps and bounds. Over 550 thousand oil heating plants were installed in 1949—twice the number for 1948. The main outlook for any expansion of coal consumption seems to be in synthetic chemical industries for the production of such things as oil, rubber, plastic, nylon, and dyes.

Wasteful mining methods and the exigencies of two world wars have wreaked havoc with our supply of other vital minerals. A recent government investigation revealed the following startling facts: Even if used only at the 1935–39 rate, the supply of iron ore will be exhausted in 79 years (the high-grade Minnesota ore in 17); zinc in 20 years; copper in 19 years; lead in 10 years; bauxite, from which aluminum is made, in 9 years; vanadium in 7 years; antimony in 4 years; tungsten in 4 years; asbestos in 3 years; and manganese in 2 years. If we go on making vast quantities of munitions in preparation for a third world war and continue the vast export of our metal goods and mineral products abroad, the supply will be even more rapidly exhausted.

**Rapid exhaustion of petroleum.** One of the most serious dangers is the possible exhaustion of our petroleum supplies, upon which modern transportation and industry are dependent. It is not possible to estimate exactly how much of this precious liquid remains in our soil, but it is known that the reserves are definitely limited—estimated to be about 21 billion barrels—and, at the present rate of consumption, may well be exhausted by 1975. This would create a serious crisis, which could be met only in part by importing petroleum from abroad, where war may rapidly deplete the supply, or, by producing it synthetically from oil shale and coal.

An extensive search for new oil reserves conducted by government agencies and private interests in 1948 and 1949 revealed the existence of more than a billion barrels in new fields. But it is likely that any additions to our oil reserves will be offset by the vastly greater use of oil in power, transportation, industry, and heating.

Our petroleum supply has been reduced partly because of inadequate drilling methods. For every barrel of oil taken out of the ground, four have been wasted through drilling methods that prevent their being pumped out successfully. Much oil was also lost on the surface, by leaks in storage tanks, evaporation, or fire. But, of course, the greatest waste of our petroleum has been in war and rehearsal for war.

## THE WASTE OF NATURAL RESOURCES
## IN THE PRODUCTION OF GOODS

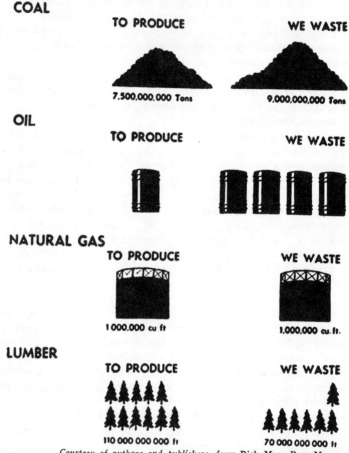

**COAL**

TO PRODUCE        WE WASTE

7,500,000,000 Tons        9,000,000,000 Tons

**OIL**

TO PRODUCE        WE WASTE

**NATURAL GAS**

TO PRODUCE        WE WASTE

1 000,000 cu ft        1,000,000 cu. ft.

**LUMBER**

TO PRODUCE        WE WASTE

110 000 000 000 ft        70 000 000 000 ft

*Courtesy of authors and publishers, from* Rich Man, Poor Man,
*by* R. A. *and* O. P. Goslin, Harper & Bros.

**Loss of natural gas.** The waste of our natural gas is even more disheartening. The people of Oklahoma suffered severely during the cold weather of January, 1940, because the supply of natural gas upon which many depended for heat was limited. Schools were closed and people went to bed to keep warm, because the gas pressure was too low to supply the demand. Yet we once had plenty of this natural resource. The people in Oklahoma shivered because we have blown a billion feet of natural gas a day into the air, completely wasting an amount sufficient to supply the daily needs of all those using either natural or manufactured gas in the entire United States. The annual Texas gas waste has been equivalent to about 60 million barrels of petroleum or 24 million tons of soft coal—enough to supply all the Texas consumers of gas for at least seventeen years. Even as late as 1949, we were wasting natural gas enough to produce two-thirds as much electrical energy as all our water power sources combined. The marked increase in the use of natural gas for fuel in the last few years underlines the need for curbing the atrocious wastes of the past.

**Floods and erosion.** Good climate is an extremely essential natural resource. While man, as Mark Twain observed, can do nothing about the weather, he can and has done much to increase its devastating effects. Drought has become more destructive since the protective grasses have been removed from the topsoil of the western plateau. The winds have blown this soil eastward, where it has covered and ruined valuable farmland. Rains that might have been a blessing, if held back by forest and sod, have become powerful agents of erosion, and have turned the waters of once placid rivers into soil-laden torrents, ruining both countryside and cities and bringing death or misery to every living thing in their path. The average annual loss from floods since 1918 has been in excess of 100 million dollars.

**Water wastage and pollution.** We have failed, in many areas, to use our abundant water power to generate cheap electricity. Instead, we have consumed valuable coal and petroleum.

Water power contributed only 4 per cent of our total energy in 1947. The total installed water power of the country is only 17 million kilowatts. There are 77 million kilowatts which remain to be developed, but at the present rate of construction it would take 150 years to de velop this potential water power now at our disposal. The full development of our hydroelectric power would be a great step ahead in conservation. It would save vast quantities of oil and coal each year. In some areas, we have gone to the opposite extreme and drained rivers dry through excessive power development.

One very vital aspect of water wastage was brought forcibly to public attention due to the acute water shortage in New York City in the autumn and winter of 1949–1950. This was believed by many to be a very temporary and abnormal situation, due to lack of normal rainfall. But in a striking article entitled "Turn Off That Faucet" in the *Atlantic Monthly,* February, 1950, a veteran conservationist, Arthur H. Carhart, made it clear that the enormous use and waste of water by our increasingly large population, especially the city population, is lowering the water level all over the country and may ultimately produce tragic results.

At the present time, the average daily use of water per person, irrespective of that used in hydroelectric plants and for any and all recreational purposes, is 700 gallons. Through leaking plumbing equipment alone, New York City wastes 100 million gallons of water daily. Air conditioning has recently vastly increased the use of water in urban areas. In Brooklyn, such use of water seriously lowered the water level as far as 12 miles away and over an area of 150 square miles. Heedless use of water from artesian wells has almost fatally lowered the water level in some states of the southwest and the Pacific coast.

Deforestation, breaking up of water-retaining sod land, draining swamps and bogs, and excessive grazing have led to a scandalous waste of water; these operations cause water to run off in floods, leaving parched land later on in the season. No amount of dam construction can solve this problem unless the water is retained on the upper slopes of the watershed. Unless water conservation is developed in systematic fashion, water shortages will restrict industry, reduce millions of acres of farm land to deserts, and result in calamitous deprivation in personal consumption needs.

The pollution of rivers and lakes represents yet another abuse of our water resources. Sewage, refuse, and chemicals have been emptied into the waters, making them unfit for drinking, swimming, or fishing. Pollution has also contributed extensively to water shortage for personal consumption requirements.

**Our disappearing fish and wild life.** Stream pollution and greed of "fish pirates" have helped to destroy the fish with which our rivers, lakes, and coasts once abounded. Americans have been equally ruthless in wiping out our once plentiful wild animals, principally through destroying their homes by cutting down the forests and building cities, villages, and farms. Other wild life was destroyed ruthlessly by hunters; over 5,500,000 buffalo were slaughtered on the western plains in the ten years following 1871.

Equal sufferers have been our once abundant wild fowl. Today, only a tiny fraction remains of the countless millions of birds of a century ago. The draining of 20 million acres of swamps and marshes since 1914 to provide more unneeded farm land dealt a severe blow to the migratory water fowl; the guns of "game hogs," before the passage of Federal protective legislation in 1913, also played their part.

## Economic and Social Factors in Human Wastage

**Economic basis of human wastage.** The tragedy of waste, unhappily, has not been confined to our natural resources alone. Equally great losses occur in the production, distribution, and consumption of goods. But even more serious and tragic is the waste of human life and energy through sickness, death, and war.

**Unnecessary sickness and deprivation.** Few of us realize, perhaps, the tremendous loss to the nation from unnecessary sickness and death. Here is a waste of incalculable human energy and labor power which might be devoted to producing goods and other tasks. The lack of proper food, clothing, and housing are factors of primary importance in causing sickness and disease. Yet, a large share of our people have not been able to provide themselves adequately with these essentials. Though an income of $2,000 a year was considered necessary to support a family on a minimum scale of health and decency, about one-half of all American families had a yearly income of less than $1,500 on the eve of the depression in 1929. This meant, of course, insufficient food and clothing, overcrowded and unsanitary housing, and little or no money for medical care.

Each year over 300,000 persons die from preventable illnesses. On an average day in the United States some 7,000,000 persons are out of work or school because of sickness; more than half of these do not get adequate or competent medical care. The annual losses from preventable illnesses, accidents, and deaths in the United States amount to about 38 billion dollars—over 3 times as much as the largest New Deal Federal budget before Pearl Harbor. We lose 4,300,000 man-years of labor each year through bad health, much of which is preventable.

**Inefficient production and distribution.** If our industries were conducted efficiently, we could produce far more food, goods, and services each year. During the second world war we increased our physical production fourfold over that of 1932. Waste in distribution is apparent on every side; for every dollar we pay to farmers and manufacturers for producing food and goods, we have had to spend around twice that amount to get them from the farm or factory to the consumer.

**Consumption wastes.** In the field of consumption, the public taste may be blamed for many wastes. For example, oats are far richer in food value than wheat, yet the average American eats wheat cereal instead of oats and wheat bread rather than oat cakes. Ignorance also accounts for the spending of great sums on worthless or actually harmful patent medicines, food substitutes, or debased food products. Americans buy many billion dollars worth of perfumes, cosmetics, jewelry, fur coats, and other expensive and often unnecessary items each year. We spend over 13 billion dollars annually on alcohol and tobacco, while gambling involves 15 to 18 billion dollars each year.

An itemized list of such relatively non-essential expenditures for 1947 reveals that we spent $9,600,000,000 for alcoholic beverages; $9,400,000,000 for recreation; $3,900,000,000 for tobacco products; $2,300,000,000 for toilet articles, cosmetics, perfumes, beauty parlor treatment, and the like; and $1,500,000,000 for jewelry. Over against this were expenditures of only about $6,500,000,000 for medical services and a little over $3,000,000,000 for all public education.

Of course, no sensible person would regard all the above expenditures as completely non-essential or wasteful; it is a matter of degree. Recreational expenditures are probably the most essential in the above list, but even here the millions spent in expensive night clubs and gambling "joints" can fairly be regarded as completely non-essential.

**War: the great destroyer.** Of all forms of present-day waste, war is by far the most destructive and the least defensible.

The Civil War cost 620,000 lives, and probably three times that number were wounded. The direct monetary cost was over 4 billion dollars. In 1950, Gordon Gray, Secretary of the Army, estimated that the ultimate cost of modern wars is about four times the initial direct cost—the Civil War monetary costs to date have been 15.3 billion. The direct initial monetary cost of the first world war, to all nations involved, was about 331 billion dollars, so its ultimate cost may be reckoned at about $1,324,000,000,000. About 10 million persons were killed in that conflict and over 20 million wounded, along with several more million listed as missing. The total direct monetary cost of this war to the United States was 27 billion dollars, and the ultimate cost has been estimated as in excess of 100 billion. Some 126,000 American soldiers were killed or died in the war, and 234,000 were wounded. It is estimated that we used as many of our natural resources as we would have in a decade of peace.

Some 3 million persons were killed in war between the signing of the Kellogg Pact, supposed to outlaw all war, in 1928, and the outbreak of the second world war in 1939. The best estimate of the human losses in the second world war puts the military and civilian dead at 40 million and the wounded at about 35 million. The direct monetary cost of all military activities and losses, including physical destruction, was at least 4 trillion dollars. This means that the ultimate monetary cost will be around 16 trillion dollars—an utterly astronomical sum. A usual estimate for the direct monetary cost of the second world war to the United States is 351 billion, but Lend-Lease and other costs surely bring the direct outlay to more than 400 billion. The ultimate monetary cost of the war to the United States will be in the neighborhood of 1.5 trillion dollars. American casualties amounted to nearly 400,000 who were killed or died, and over 700,000 wounded and missing. We used up as many of our natural resources as we would have in a quarter of a century of normal peacetime production. Nor did V-J Day bring an end to armament expenditures and the excessive exploitation of our natural resources. In 1950, we were spending far more for armament than in either year of the first world war, and relief and war rehearsal continued the abnormal utilization of our natural resources. In 1950, for example, we were using more petroleum than at the height of the war effort. All authorities agree that, if a third world war comes, the monetary and human losses will dwarf those of the second.

## Summary

In building our impressive material civilization, we have used far more than was necessary of our heritage of natural resources. We began our national existence with almost a billion acres of forests, 500 million acres of fertile soil, rich deposits of minerals, and an abundance of wild life and fish. To build our cities and farms, we had to use up a part of these resources, but ignorance, carelessness, and greed have caused us to destroy far more than was necessary. So wasteful have we been that only 100 million acres of uncut forest remain in the United States, our fertile soil is three-fifths gone, our rich mineral resources are seriously depleted, and our wild animals, birds, and fish are rapidly disappearing.

Nor has our waste been confined to natural resources. We have been equally careless with human resources, allowing sickness and death to take a tremendous toll of energy and life. Inexcusable waste has marked our production, distribution, and consumption of goods and services, while hundreds of billions of dollars and a million and a half lives have been lost on the battlefield.

## Selected References

* Beals, Carleton, *American Earth,* Lippincott, 1939. Brilliant and readable account of the resources, settlement, and physical exploitation of the United States.

Bernard, Frank, and Netboy, Anthony, *Water, Land, and People,* Knopf, 1950. A very readable but authoritative survey of the increasingly serious water problems of the United States, the inadequate solutions currently in vogue, and the program required for success.

* Coyle, D. C., *Waste; The Right to Save America,* Bobbs-Merrill, 1936. A brilliant little book on the waste of both natural and human resources. The "must" primer on the subject.

Chase, Stuart, *The Tragedy of Waste,* Macmillan, 1925. The pioneer work in the recent study of waste in American life. Lays main stress on the waste incident to competitive capitalistic enterprise.

Jacks, G. V., and Whyte, R. O., *Vanishing Lands,* Doubleday, 1939. One of the best discussions of the economic and social importance of soil erosion.

Johnson, Vance, *Heaven's Tableland,* Farrar, Straus, 1947. A very readable and intelligent portrayal of the nature and problems of the dust bowl of the Rocky Mountain plateau.

Loth, David G., *Public Plunder: A History of Graft in America,* Carrick and Evans, 1938. A vivid and devastating account of the manner in which the politicians have promoted the looting of the North American continent.

* Muelder, H. R. and Delo, D. M., *Years of this Land,* Appleton-Century, 1943. A brief and interesting geographical history of the United States, stressing the extent and exploitation of our natural resources.

Osborn, Fairfield, *Our Plundered Planet,* Little, Brown, 1948. Widely read and startling presentation of the waste of the various natural resources of the world and its social and international implications.

Pearson, F. A., and Harper, F. A., *The World's Hunger,* Cornell University, 1945. Concise effort to attribute famine and inadequate food supply to the pressure of population on land resources.

Sears, P. B., *Deserts on the March,* University of Oklahoma Press, 1935. A timely warning of the impending destruction of our natural resources and the fertility of our soil, showing that our country is repeating the natural history of the great deserts of the world.

Vogt, William, *Road to Survival,* Sloane, 1948. A highly controversial and widely discussed book on the social and economic aspects of the world-wide waste of natural resources from virtually all causes. Exaggerates effect of overpopulation and has given rise to unfortunate and unjustifiable revival of Malthusianism. Very valuable for its dramatic description of waste. The false Malthusian argument is best answered by O. W. Willcox, *Reshaping Agriculture,* Norton, 1934; and *Nations Can Live at Home,* Norton, 1935; and K. F. Mather, *Enough and to Spare,* Harper, 1944.

Note: Most of the books listed in the bibliography of the next chapter are also valuable on the subject of waste.

# CHAPTER VIII

# Belated Efforts to Conserve and Replace Our Wasted Natural Resources

## We Begin to Awaken to the Ravages of Waste: 1870-1901

**Long-continued public indifference to exploitation and waste.** Although the exploitation of our natural resources began with the arrival of the earliest colonists in the seventeenth century, little thought was given to their protection or replacement for over two hundred years. The nation drifted blissfully along, content in the belief that there would always be an abundance of raw materials. The realization that we were using up our natural resources far too rapidly did not occur until nearly the close of the nineteenth century, when a few far-sighted citizens and public officials initiated what has come to be known as the "conservation movement."

**Purposes of conservation.** Conservation, as applied to natural resources, has two basic functions: to protect resources against further waste and to replace, so far as possible, those resources which have been destroyed. Many of our vital resources, like minerals, coal, and petroleum, cannot be replaced; hence, they must be guarded against further waste. Other resources, however, such as timber, soil, and wild life can be renewed and replenished, although the process takes many years.

**Stages in the conservation movement.** It was 1870, before the earliest timid movements toward conservation began. The period from 1870 to the administration of President Theodore Roosevelt (1901-1909) is often regarded as the first stage of the conservation movement. In this era, little actual conservation work was undertaken, but several governmental scientific bureaus were established to gather information about our natural resources.

When Roosevelt became president in 1901, he undertook to educate the general public to the need for conservation, and he and his successors were able to secure laws reducing the further exploitation of public lands. A systematic, well-planned program of conservation and replacement was not undertaken, however, until President Franklin D. Roosevelt's New Deal administration took office in 1933. The New

129

Deal marked the beginning of the third stage in the American conservation movement.

**Gradual development of early conservation policies and measures.** Earliest among the sundry scientific bureaus created by the Federal government in the first period of the conservation movement was the office of Commissioner of Fish and Fisheries, set up in 1871. The office was given little power to check stream pollution or the destruction of our fish supply, but it did gather valuable information for later use. In 1903, this office, with extended powers, became the Bureau of Fisheries in the Department of Commerce.

A Federal Forest Bûreau was created in the Department of Agriculture in 1876. Here, the first forestry experts in the United States took up their work. Like the fish and game bureaus, however, the Forestry Bureau could do little except to gather facts. The forests themselves remained under the control of the Public Lands Office of the Department of the Interior until 1905, when they were transferred to the Department of Agriculture.

**Pioneers of conservation.** The first prominent public official to become interested in conservation was Carl Schurz, Secretary of the Interior from 1877 to 1881. Aroused by the shocking waste of our forests and minerals, Schurz succeeded in having a Federal commission appointed in 1879 to investigate the situation. The commission suggested a number of reforms to protect our public mineral and forest lands against further exploitation. However, Congress, which had passed the notorious Timber Cutting and Timber and Stone Acts only the year before, was more interested in aiding the powerful private mining and lumber interests in their pilferings than it was in furthering the public welfare. Hence, no remedial legislation was passed.

In 1879, the United States Geological Survey was created. Its chief duty was the exploration and surveying of the public lands. In 1888, the irrigation division of the Geological Survey was brought into being, with Major J. W. Powell at its head. He was authorized to survey the water-power sites of the country and determine the irrigation needs of the West. Powell, a colorful personality, brought many abuses and dangers to public attention and even predicted the dust bowl calamity of the 1930's.

**Closing of the frontier.** The United States had, until about 1890, always possessed a frontier, that is, a wild, unsettled region, rich in timber, fertile land, minerals, and wild life. But, as the frontier was pushed further towards the Pacific, desirable unsettled land became less available. Finally, in 1890, the frontier was officially closed. This was a boon to the conservation movement, for it forcefully brought to public attention the fact that the days when limitless natural resources were available for exploitation had come to an end. The nation slowly came to realize that it would have to carry on its industrial and commercial development with the resources it already possessed, and that it might not be wise to continue to throw these resources away too carelessly.

**Creation of our national forest reserves.**   Congress, spurred to action at last, passed a law in 1891 which created the first forest reserve and empowered the President to add new areas to be withdrawn from public lands which had been available for sale to individuals under earlier laws, such as the timber acts of 1878.   Acting under this law, President Cleveland (1893–1897) added about 25 million acres to the forest reserves, and President McKinley (1897–1901) about 7 million acres.   Little else was done, however, in the first stage of the conservation movement, except to gather and publish the facts regarding the wasteful exploitation of our natural resources by private companies, and their purloining of our land, forests, minerals, and water power.

## Theodore Roosevelt Launches an Active Conservation Movement

**Theodore Roosevelt's interest in conservation.**   The conservation movement entered its second stage with the presidency of Theodore Roosevelt.   Roosevelt was an enthusiastic sportsman and nature lover. He had personally observed the wasteful exploitation of the beautiful western country.   Moreover, he was no friend of those whom he called "the malefactors of great wealth," who had taken the lead in seizing and exploiting our natural resources.

**The country aroused to the needs.**   Roosevelt got thoroughly excited over conservation and succeeded in arousing the country as well. This he did in a number of ways.   He strongly advocated the passage of the Newlands Act in 1902, which provided Federal support for irrigation projects.   In 1903, the President appointed a commission to report on means to avoid waste in the nation's remaining public lands.   In 1907, he sent a strong message to Congress exposing and condemning the pillage and destruction of our natural resources.   In the same year, he appointed the Inland Waterways Commission to study our unused water transportation routes and water-power sites.

The crowning effort of President Roosevelt's campaign to educate the public to the need of conservation was the calling of a national conference of governors in May, 1908.   The conference lasted three days, provoked much discussion, and received extensive publicity in the newspapers.   For the first time in our history, conservation became a major public issue.

**The National Conservation Commission.**   Following the governors' conference, President Roosevelt appointed a National Conservation Commission, made up of forty experts from various walks of life.   The preliminary report of these investigators, which was presented in another national conference, made for more publicity.   In January, 1909, the final report of the commission was received by the President, who presented it to Congress with a forceful message.

**Congress tries to balk conservation.**  Congress, however, refused to support President Roosevelt's conservation efforts.  Many members, especially in the Senate, were friends and allies of the greedy private interests which had benefited from the exploitation of our resources. Even the small sum of $25,000 requested for the expenses of the Conservation Commission was refused, and efforts were made to prevent cabinet departments from furnishing facts for the commission to use. This attitude may well be contrasted with the different state of affairs under the administration of Franklin D. Roosevelt, when money was lavishly appropriated for conservation.  Theodore Roosevelt, nevertheless, succeeded in making conservation a national issue and was able, through executive acts (orders which may be signed by the President without the approval of Congress), to carry out some important conservation measures.  Some historians consider Roosevelt's contributions to conservation as the most outstanding achievement of his administration.  In the administration of his successor, President William Howard Taft (1909–1913), many important laws were passed to extend the conservation program, partly as a result of the impetus given to the movement by Roosevelt's energy and enthusiasm.

**The achievements of the Roosevelt administration in conservation.**  Though meeting strong opposition in Congress, Roosevelt was able to put through some effective conservation measures during his two terms in office.  Partly as a result of Major Powell's work, the Newlands Act was passed in 1902, providing 20 million dollars for the construction of irrigation dams.  This laid the basis for the Federal Reclamation Service.  By 1928, the Federal government had spent some 178 million dollars on irrigation projects, and two million acres of hitherto useless land had been made suitable for farming. Under the New Deal, tremendous sums were spent on irrigation projects.

Roosevelt's efforts to improve and enlarge the national forests rank among his major achievements.  He created the United States Public Forest Service in 1905, transferring control of the forests from the Department of the Interior to the Department of Agriculture.  As he pointed out, before this time the trained foresters in the Department of Agriculture had nothing officially to do with the forests.  This move resulted in greatly improving the supervision and care of the public timber lands.  Acting under the law of 1891, Roosevelt added 148 million acres to the forest reserves, bringing the total up to some 180 million acres.  Only a little over 5 million acres were added between 1909 and 1933.

The creation of the national forest reserves, now covering some 207 million acres and containing over 35 per cent of our remaining timber, has been of great benefit to the American people.  The national parks and forests furnish valuable places of recreation, public camping grounds and fishing streams, and refuge for many vanishing species of wild life.  The major advantage of this policy is that the national forest reserves are not being wasted or exhausted but are subject to a careful program of conservation and restoration.

By an act of 1907, President Roosevelt withdrew from access to private owners millions of acres of coal lands, phosphate lands, and water-power sites. He also tried to regain for the public domain land containing petroleum and natural gas, but Congress blocked this move until 1920.

## The Conservation Movement from Roosevelt to Roosevelt

**Taft continues the conservation program.** President Taft (1909–1913) carried on the conservation program begun by his predecessor, despite his unfortunate quarrel with Gifford Pinchot, who had been Roosevelt's chief aide in the struggle for conservation. Further restrictions were placed on the sale of public lands. In 1909, Congress passed a law to check the sale of coal and other mineral lands as "agricultural land." In 1910, the Bureau of Mines was created to survey our mineral resources. The following year, Congress passed the Weeks Act, which permitted the government to buy forest land from private owners. Before this time, the President was permitted only to withdraw public timber lands from sale to private owners. The great Roosevelt Dam on the Salt River of Arizona was completed in 1911, making possible the irrigation of 700,000 acres of very fertile land. This was but one of several important irrigation projects completed during the Taft administration.

**Slump in the conservation movement: 1913–1933.** No other important conservation measures were taken until after the first world war. In 1920, an effort was made to save our remaining mineral resources by the passage of the Mineral Leasing Act, which put the government coal, oil, gas, and phosphate lands under strict Federal control. Theodore Roosevelt had recommended such a law in 1908. In 1920, Congress also passed the Federal Water Power Act, which extended the control of the Federal government over water-power development. The main defect in these laws was that they were passed too late. Our most valuable forest, mineral, and water-power resources had, unfortunately, already passed into the hands of private owners.

In summarizing these earlier stages of the conservation movement, it is evident that little was accomplished in checking the wholesale waste of our natural heritage or repairing the damage already done, except on the rather limited government reserves set up by belated legislation.

A setback was given to the conservation movement by the scandals of the Harding administration (1920–1923). Important oil reserves—Elk Hills in California and Teapot Dome in Wyoming—were transferred from the Navy Department to the Department of Interior. The Secretary of Interior, Albert B. Fall, then proceeded to lease them to two leading oil barons, E. M. Doheny and Harry F. Sinclair. The oil reserves were recovered by the government in 1927, and Fall was sentenced to prison in 1929.

President Hoover (1929–1933) added about three million acres to the forest reserves, started the construction of Boulder Dam, and undertook some important irrigation and reclamation projects. But he vigorously opposed the development of electric power under public auspices at Muscle Shoals or elsewhere. After 1933, the conservation movement entered a new era.

*Courtesy of Bureau of Reclamation.*

The great Hoover Dam across the Colorado River in Boulder Canyon. Located near Las Vegas, Nevada, it provides irrigation and electric power for several neighboring states.

## How the New Deal Extended the Program of Conservation and Restoration: 1933–1940

**Reasons for New Deal concern with conservation.** While other nations have been struggling to acquire new lands which contain oil and valuable minerals, our country, between 1933 and 1940, under the leadership of Franklin D. Roosevelt, began work on a conservation program which, at the time, gave promise of restoring to the country some portion of what had been used up. This program necessarily emphasized not only a policy of conservation but one of replacement as well. Considerable credit for the promotion of conservation and replacement after 1933 should be given to President Roosevelt. Although his personal interest in conservation was less than that of Theodore Roosevelt, a series of events preceding his inauguration stimulated him to undertake the huge New Deal program of conservation and restoration.

The business depression, which began in 1929, had reached a desperate stage by March, 1933, when nearly 17 million men and women were unemployed. The new President saw in conservation a type of public-works activity, which, coupled with agricultural reforms, would open the way for large-scale employment. The public, whom the administration naturally wanted to please, liked the idea of conserving natural resources and of giving jobs to the needy. The President was fortunate in selecting two enthusiastic conservationists as cabinet members, Secretary of the Interior Harold L. Ickes and Secretary of Agriculture Henry A. Wallace. These departments were those most directly concerned with the conservation program. Finally, a series of disasters, in the early days of the New Deal, such as dust storms, floods, and droughts, dramatically aroused the general public to realization of the need for conservation.

The conservation stage was thus very favorably set, with an interested President, two co-operative cabinet members, an economic crisis creating a dire need for employment, and a public aroused to conservation and willing to try anything that might bring some relief to the critical economic situation. It is small wonder that conservation ceased to be merely a policy of "locking the barn door after the horse was stolen," and temporarily, at least, became an active program for the restoration and replacement of natural resources.

**New Deal conservation agencies.** Congress, formerly slow in providing money to support conservation, lost its reluctance under President Roosevelt's leadership. Beginning in 1933, congressional acts and executive orders launched the greatest conservation movement in our history. New Federal agencies were created to put the legislation into operation. The most important were the National Resources Planning Board, the Tennessee Valley Authority, the Soil Conservation Service, the Rural Resettlement Administration, the Civilian Conservation Corps, and the Rural Electrification Administration. Along with the new agencies, the older bureaus, such as the Forest Service, the Biological Survey, the Geological Survey, and the Reclamation Service, continued to expand their work.

**National Resources Committee.** Theodore Roosevelt had set up a National Conservation Commission to study the problem of waste, but his Congress had refused to appropriate the small sum of $25,000 for its expenses. In June, 1934, President Roosevelt created a National Resources Planning Board, for which he had no difficulty in securing ample funds from Congress. The National Resources Planning Board made a careful and extensive study of both resources and waste which furnished an excellent basis for planning a comprehensive conservation program.

**The Tennessee Valley Authority.** The outstanding conservation achievement of the New Deal was probably the Tennessee Valley Authority, a project which aimed to recast the physical surroundings of the region and to rehabilitate the economic and social life of the people dwelling in the Tennessee Valley. It represented the most thorough and systematic effort at conservation ever attempted in the United States, and may furnish a pattern for similar projects in the future.

The need for the rehabilitation of this area may be judged from the fact that the average dweller in the Tennessee Valley, in 1934, had an income of only $259, as against an average of $486 for the whole nation. The Tennessee Valley covers an area of over 40,000 square miles and has 2,500,000 inhabitants, while 6,000,000 more are affected directly by economic and social conditions within the valley. When the project was started, two-thirds of the land in the region was owned by farmers who were struggling to make a bare living on soil whose fertile top layer had been seriously damaged or destroyed by erosion.

The act of May, 1933, that created the Tennessee Valley Authority outlined as its main purposes: (1) the development of the Tennessee River for navigation: (2) flood control; (3) generation of electric power; (4) study of the proper use of farm land; (5) plans for reforestation; and (6) recommendations for the economic and social well-being of the people living in the valley. Navigation was placed first on the program because the administration feared that the Supreme Court would object to the government's openly undertaking the generation of electric power. This stratagem proved wise because the Supreme Court, in the first test case, ruled that the government may generate power only as an incidental sideline to the improvement of navigation on interstate rivers. Actually, however, the generation of electric power and the rebuilding of the social and economic life of the valley were the main purposes of the act.

The Tennessee Valley Authority has already accomplished a great amount of valuable work, but the full development of the project will take a generation or more. Since 1934, the Tennessee River has been made navigable from Knoxville, Tennessee, to Paducah, Kentucky; seventeen huge dams have been completed and others are in process of construction. The electric power generated by the dams is sold at low rates to cities, villages, and individuals, and is also used in the huge atomic energy project at Oak Ridge, Tennessee, and for the manufacture of plant fertilizers and of aluminum and nitrates. An elaborate program of soil control and conservation is enabling the farmers of the area once more to earn a decent living. Much work has been done in reforestation, more than 75 million trees having been set out. The large lakes created by the dams already contain many game fish.

Model towns have been built, better schools opened, and a well-planned educational program started. Community centers have been created, where people may gather for music, plays, and games. In-

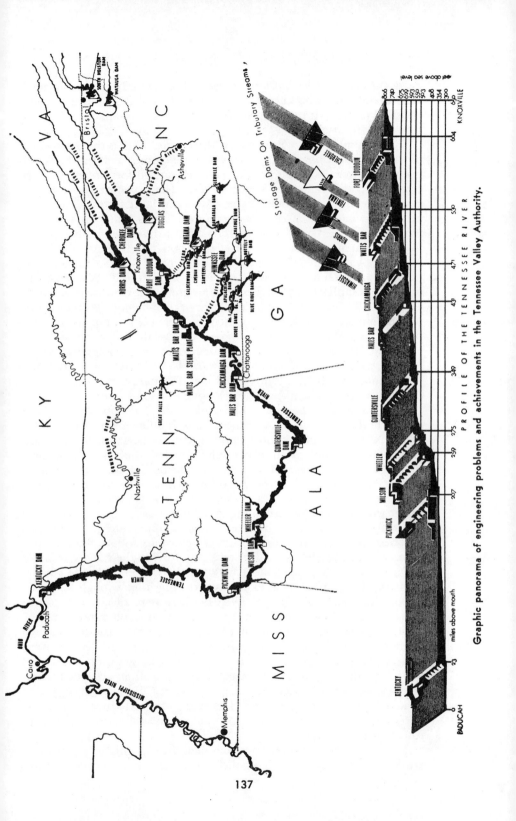

Graphic panorama of engineering problems and achievements in the Tennessee Valley Authority.

137

deed, the entire valley has undergone such a marked change in a short time that people who knew the region in the old days and have since revisited it feel that they are entering a new region—almost a different type of civilization.

**The Columbia River Project.** Although the TVA is the best known of the New Deal power projects, even more ambitious from the standpoint of power development was the work carried forward by the government in the Columbia River Valley. Here, two great dams, the Bonneville and the Grand Coulee, have been built for the purpose of improving navigation, developing power, and storing up water for irrigation. The Grand Coulee Dam, the largest ever built by man, will generate nearly six times the electric power to be generated in the entire TVA region. The Bonneville project will generate about three-quarters as much power as will be turned out by the TVA when all its dams are completed. Many lesser dams are under construction on the Columbia River. The Columbia River development is less thoroughly worked out as a complete social enterprise than TVA, but its ultimate possibilities may even exceed those of the latter. In April, 1949, President Truman requested Congress to create a Columbia Valley Administration comparable to the TVA. Considerable opposition was voiced, not only by powerful vested private interests but even by liberal political leaders, like Senator Wayne Morse of Oregon.

**Soil Conservation Service.** The work of the Soil Conservation Servive of the Department of Agriculture was another major achievement of the New Deal, and possibly ranks next in importance to the TVA. Its activities fell mainly into two related fields: the teaching of more scientific methods of agriculture, and the installation of various policies and practices designed to check erosion and to restore ruined land.

The government set up a co-operative arrangement with farmers under which it supplied technical advice and assistance and such labor and materials as the farmers were unable to contribute. The farmers enrolled in soil conservation districts agreed to follow the scientific plans laid out by the government and to provide their share of labor and materials. The agreement between the farmers and the government was for a five-year period, thus providing time enough for really permanent accomplishments. By 1949, there were 2,033 soil conservation districts. About three-fourths of the farms and ranches in the nation, containing two-thirds of all farm land, were included in these districts. Conservation plans had been prepared for 158,000,000 acres, and about half of these were in operation. In addition, work was carried on in restoring and protecting some 7 million acres of Federal land. The Soil Conservation Service has set up many projects to demonstrate scientific methods of farming and soil conservation. It also operates 28 large nurseries to supply trees and shrubs to the soil conservation districts.

The Soil Conservation Service compiled the first complete report on erosion, on the basis of which policies were suggested to check erosion and restore partially ruined land.  The government has devised economical ways of filling up gullies produced by erosion, and has developed and demonstrated methods of scientific contour plowing to prevent formation of new gullies on sloping land.  Scientific rotation of crops has been introduced to do away with the necessity of leaving land unplanted for long periods of time to restore its fertility; land thus exposed is subject to erosion by wind and water.  Other work carried on by the Soil Conservation Service included the building of ponds and reservoirs for storing water; the draining of swamps and marshes; and the planting of protective belts of trees to check erosion.

*Federal Reclamation Service.*

How irrigation transforms a desert area into fertile farming land.

**Rural Resettlement Administration.**    Another important agency in the Department of Agriculture was the Rural Resettlement Administration.  Like the Soil Conservation Service, the Resettlement Administration was designed to aid the farmer, but, under the latter agency, the families were moved from worn-out farming regions, where they could not possibly support themselves, to better agricultural areas.

By 1937, while some 160 resettlement projects had been laid out, only about 5 million acres of better land had been purchased and about 4,500 families moved.  In that year the Resettlement Administration was replaced by the Farm Security Administration, which tried to carry on the work.  About 9 million acres of submarginal land were removed from cultivation, and 15,000 families were resettled on about a million acres at a cost of 138 million dollars.  But the project was soon liquidated and it turned out to be little more than an instructive demonstration project.

**The Civilian Conservation Corps.**    During the depression, many boys who had graduated from high school were unable to find jobs, and it was with these in mind that a new agency—the Civilian Conservation Corps—was created in March, 1933. The CCC contributed valuable work in the conservation of human as well as natural resources. Camps were established in areas requiring reforestation, soil conservation, and state park construction. The CCC camps not only gave employment to over 2 million persons in a time of emergency, but the CCC workers provided the shock troops for the New Deal conservation program.

Much work was done by the CCC in soil conservation. Its reforestation activities were equally impressive. The National Resources Board had recommended that abandoned crop and pasture land in the East and South should be planted with trees and made into a new forest reserve. It had also been suggested that protective belts of trees should be set out in the Great Plains country to check erosion. The CCC planted about a billion and a half trees altogether, and the total value of its conservation work has been estimated at around a billion dollars. Most of the reforestation work begun by the CCC was later taken over by other public relief agencies, among them the Works Progress Administration (WPA).

**Rural Electrification Administration.** We have noted how the government is generating electricity in the Tennessee Valley and the Columbia River projects. This is only the beginning of an electrification program which is lighting up the rural regions of the whole United States. Today, in many farm homes the old kerosene lamps are placed on high shelves for emergency use in time of storms, and the farm housewife proudly turns on a switch in kitchen, dairy, and barn. She has her electric iron, her power cream separator; the chicken house is lighted at night to produce more eggs, and the cows are milked by electric machines. Rural electrification, stimulated by the government since 1935, has given farm life new meaning. Boys and girls, who formerly hoped to escape to the city to enjoy modern comforts, may henceforth prefer the rural home where they can now be comfortable and less crowded and confined than in urban centers.

Rural electrification is a very recent development. In 1933, comparatively few farm homes were equipped with electric service, although some prosperous farmers had home lighting systems operated by batteries. The Rural Electrification Administration was set up in 1935 as a part of the program of supplying work to the unemployed. By 1943, the number of farm homes supplied with electricity—some 2,500,000—was four times that of 1935. Rural electrification work got under way vigorously shortly after V-J Day, directed by former Secretary of Agriculture, Claude R. Wickard. In January, 1949, Mr. Wickard reported that some 70 per cent of all the nation's farms now have electrical service, as compared with 11 per cent in 1935. The REA is carrying on numerous projects to complete the electrification of all accessible farms.

The rural electrification program has been doubly beneficial. Not only has it done valuable work itself, but the threat of government electrification has forced private power companies to extend their service in country areas where they had earlier refused to operate.

**The Great Plains Committee and the dust bowl.** Nowhere have the farmers more desperately needed help than in the dust bowl of the Great Plains. In December, 1936, a Great Plains Committee was created to submit plans for restoring the land in the dust bowl. This body advocated more adequate irrigation and facilities for storing water and the planting of protective belts of trees and shrubs for windbreaks; it also suggested that the states involved limit the amount of land used for farming. Secretary Wallace set up a new agency in the Department of Agriculture to unify all the agencies which could be used in rehabilitating the dust bowl. An elaborate co-operative program between the Federal government and the states was worked out, but only later years will tell how much it will accomplish. Unfortunately, the high price of wheat during and after the second world war has encouraged further plowing of land that should be kept covered with grass, and the expansion of the dust bowl into adjacent areas seems all too likely.

**The WPA and the PWA.** When President Roosevelt first guided the New Deal into conservation channels, his chief thought, as we have seen, was to find some means to solve the unemployment problem. To meet the economic crisis created by a scarcity of jobs, public-works programs and agencies such as the Public Works Administration and the Works Progress Administration were created, and huge sums of money were appropriated by Congress. These government programs furnished jobs to millions of men and women and carried on important conservation and building projects. The PWA built dams, water supply systems, and more adequate power resources, planned and built drainage works, and constructed new sewage plants, thereby helping to do away with serious stream pollution. Much of this kind of work was also carried on with WPA labor.

**Flood control.** Floods, as we have seen, are one of the chief causes of soil erosion. To combat this menace, a Catastrophe Relief Act was passed in 1934, which appropriated 5 million dollars for the relief of sufferers from floods and other disasters. The floods of 1936 led to the passage of a much more complete Flood Control Act in June, 1936, based upon Federal-state co-operation.

It has come to be recognized that floods cannot be controlled unless we have a comprehensive national program that will include upstream control to prevent mud and silt from filling our streams and high water from rising in the upper reaches of the country's drainage system. A flood which begins in Pennsylvania or the Dakotas may do its greatest damage in Kentucky, Arkansas, or Louisiana. Though a sound program of flood control thus calls for close co-operation between Federal and state authorities, the governors of several states have attempted to block the Federal plan. Even great

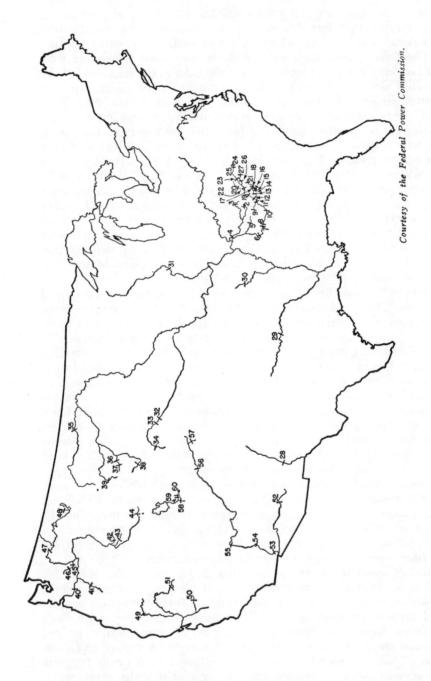

142

| Name of Plant | River | | Name of Plant | River |
|---|---|---|---|---|
| 1. Dalecarlia | Potomac | | 31. Rock Island | Mississippi |
| 2. Great Falls | Caney Fork | | 32. Lingle | No. Platte |
| 3. Dale Hollow | Obey | | 33. Guernsey | No. Platte |
| 4. Kentucky | Tennessee | | 34. Seminoe | No. Platte |
| 5. Columbia | Duck | | 35. Fort Peck | Missouri |
| 6. Pickwick Landing | Tennessee | | 36. Heart Mountain | Shoshone |
| 7. Wilson | Tennessee | | 37. Shoshone | Shoshone |
| 8. Wheeler | Tennessee | | 38. Pilot Butte | Wind |
| 9. Estill Springs | Elk | | 39. Mammoth | Gardiner |
| 10. Guntersville | Tennessee | | 40. Bonneville | Columbia |
| 11. Hales Bar | Tennessee | | 41. Cove # 2 | Deschutes |
| 12. Chickamauga | Tennessee | | 42. Black Canyon | Payette |
| 13. Ocoee # 1 | Ocoee | | 43. Boise River | Boise |
| 14. Ocoee # 2 | Ocoee | | 44. Minidoka | Snake |
| 15. Ocoee # 3 | Ocoee | | 45. Prosser | Yakima |
| 16. Blue Ridge | Toccoa | | 46. Rocky Ford | Rocky Ford Canal |
| 17. Apalachia | Hiwassee | | 47. Grand Coulee | Columbia |
| 18. Hiwassee | Hiwassee | | 48. Big Creek | Big Creek |
| 19. Watts Bar | Tennessee | | 49. Shasta | Sacramento |
| 20. Norris | Clinch | | 50. Yosemite | Merced |
| 21. Fontana | Little Tennessee | | 51. Lahontan | Carson |
| 22. Fort Loudoun | Tennessee | | 52. Coolidge | Gila |
| 23. Cherokee | Holston | | 53. Siphon Drop | Yuma Canal |
| 24. Wilbur | Watauga | | 54. Parker | Colorado |
| 25. Watauga | Watauga | | 55. Hoover | Colorado |
| 26. Douglas | French Broad | | 56. Grand Valley | Colorado |
| 27. Nolichucky | Nolichucky | | 57. Green Mountain | Blue |
| 28. Elephant Butte | Rio Grande | | 58. Payson | Petneetneck Creek |
| 29. Denison | Red | | 59. Lower | Spanish Fork |
| 30. Norfork | No. Fk. White | | 60. Upper | Spanish Fork |

**Location of the chief Federal hydroelectric plants.**

143

disasters are not always enough to terminate local jealousies and states-rights prejudices, it would seem.

Disastrous floods in the upper Missouri Valley in 1948 showed all too plainly that the flood problem is still with us. It re-emphasized the fact that we need a Missouri Valley Authority to do for that great area what the TVA has accomplished for Tennessee and adjacent regions.[1] On March 2, 1949, Senator Murray of Montana, introduced a bill in the Senate to create a comprehensive Missouri Valley Administration, but state and private interests vigorously opposed it.

Little has been done to curb the serious water wastage described in the preceding chapter. Even the extensive dam construction projects launched since the second world war will accomplish little until reforestation and the reversion of marginal farming land to sod land holds the water in the upper reaches of watersheds.

**Conservation a good public investment.** In this chapter we have presented some of the highlights of America's new conservation program, which must be put on a permanent basis if the country's natural resources are to be restored. The swing to conservation indicates that the American public has finally realized the mistakes of the past and has taken a new and more sensible attitude toward the husbanding of our natural endowment. Expenditures for conservation should be regarded as paying investments, because, if our physical resources are further depleted, our economic situation will become far worse instead of better.

**Failure to check economic and social waste.** The New Deal accomplished a great deal in conserving and replenishing our natural resources, but did very little to eliminate waste in consumption and distribution. Before the institution of the rearmament program in 1940, there were at least 10 million persons unemployed. A large part of the working population was underpaid, and could not buy what it needed of the goods, services, and food made available by industry and agriculture. We continue to buy adulterated food, worthless or harmful patent medicines, and dubious luxuries in the same wasteful manner as before the New Deal. In 1947 we spent three times as much for alcoholic beverages as for all public education. The human wastage due to unnecessary disease, accidents, and death continued unabated. Finally, the second world war consumed our human and material resources at a fantastic rate.

## Decline of Conservation Program since Pearl Harbor

**Cost in resources of second world war.** Experts have estimated that, between Pearl Harbor and V-J Day, we used up an amount of oil equal to one-fourth of all our known oil reserves, more than

---

[1] See *The Big Missouri: the Hope of the West.* Washington, Public Affairs Institute, 1948.

one-fourth of our lead reserves, nearly one-fourth of our zinc reserves, one-fifth of our copper reserves, and seven per cent of our iron ore reserves. We mined so much of our best iron ore that the matchless Mesabi deposits in Minnesota may be exhausted in less than a decade. Most serious, perhaps, were the wartime ravages on our forests and timber reserves, despite which we continued to send vast quantities of lumber abroad after V-J Day. The coming of peace did not lessen the enormous demand on many of our natural resources. In July, 1949, we were using petroleum at a rate of 600,-000 barrels a day more than at the peak of the wartime demand.

In the light of the above facts, it is obvious that any conservation and replacement activities of the New Deal were trivial compared with the wastes later brought about by President Roosevelt's foreign policy and the second world war. All of which goes to show the precarious, if not futile, nature of domestic reform policies if we cannot keep free from devastating foreign wars.

**Conservation after the second world war.** Despite the fact that President Truman vowed his intention to carry on the New Deal policies, relatively little has been accomplished since 1945 in conservation and replacement. The passing of the WPA, the CCC, and other emergency agencies virtually brought to a standstill for the time being the remarkable work accomplished in the conservation of our soil resources. Land conservation and forestation agencies are now lagging far behind, without adequate political or financial support.

The main trend in the conservation field since the second world war has been the launching of a program for the construction of many spectacular dams, at a cost of billions of dollars. Unfortunately, these dams are not integrated into a program of national flood control, soil rehabilitation, and social achievement such as that of the TVA.

## Summary

The conservation movement in the United States originated only after 1870, although the waste of our natural resources began with the arrival of the earliest settlers. In its first stage, the conservation movement was confined to little more than setting up fact-finding bureaus whose investigations revealed the grievous waste of our natural resources.

It was President Theodore Roosevelt who gave the first great impetus to conservation. Between 1901 and 1909, he carried on an extensive educational program to acquaint the public with the need for conservation. Roosevelt did not have the support of Congress, however, and the practical conservation achievements in his administration were limited. Chief among his accomplishments were the improvement of the forest service, the addition of 148 million acres to the forest preserves, and the passage of the Newlands Act, which gave encouragement to irrigation developments.

Following Theodore Roosevelt's administration and its aftermath in that of Taft, little was accomplished towards conservation except the passage of some laws designed to protect remaining public mineral lands from exploitation. Not until the New Deal of President Franklin D. Roosevelt was there any systematic government program for replacement of those natural resources which had been destroyed.

The economic crisis of 1933 stimulated President Roosevelt to make use of conservation as a means of meeting the problem of unemployment. Under the New Deal, a thoroughgoing program of conservation and replacement was begun at last. Among its most notable features were the projects undertaken by the Tennessee Valley Authority, the Columbia River developments, and the diversified projects of the Soil Conservation Service, the Civilian Conservation Corps, the PWA, WPA, and other agencies. Much was temporarily accomplished toward restoring and protecting our soil, forests, wild life, water power, and mineral resources.

The New Deal program represented, however, only the merest beginning towards the systematic and thorough conservation that will be necessary if we are truly to restore our wasted natural heritage. The waste of our resources by the second world war far more than wiped out any conservation and replacement savings accomplished during the Roosevelt administrations.

Little of substantial importance has been accomplished by the Truman administrations in conservation or replacement.

### Selected References

Bennett, H. H., *Soil Conservation*, McGraw-Hill, 1939. Monumental book of reference by leading world authority on soil conservation; treats waste as well as conservation of soils.

* Chase, Stuart, *Rich Land, Poor Land*, McGraw-Hill, 1936. In this work Mr. Chase continues his study of waste, shifting mainly to the subject of the waste of natural resources and the conservation program of the New Deal.

Coyle, D. C., *Brass Tacks*, National Home Library, 1935.

————, *Our Forests*, National Home Library, 1940.

————, *Roads to a New America*, Little, Brown, 1938. Three books by an industrial engineer supporting the conservation policy of the New Deal on a wide scale. The books cover a broader field than conservation.

De Kruif, Paul H., *Health Is Wealth*, Harcourt, Brace, 1940. Brief and lively discussion of human erosion and the remedies therefor, especially in a bigger and better public health movement.

Franklin, Jay, *Remaking America*, Houghton Mifflin, 1942. Spirited description and defense of New Deal conservation policies.

Gabrielson, I. N., *Wildlife Conservation,* Macmillan, 1941. The only comprehensive and readable account of this important subject.

\* Glover, Katherine, *America Begins Again,* McGraw-Hill, 1939. A competent and readable book. Probably the best introduction to the waste of our natural resources and the recent conservation policies.

Lilienthal, D. E., *TVA: Democracy on the March,* Harper, 1944. Official and authoritative exposition of the achievements of the Tennessee Valley Authority.

Lord, R. R., *Behold Our Land,* Houghton Mifflin, 1938. One of the better books on waste and conservation.

Mitchell, Lucy S.; Bowman, Eleanor P.; and Phelps, Mary, *My Country 'Tis of Thee,* Macmillan, 1940. Comprehensive and interesting treatment of our natural resources and their conservation and replacement.

Neuberger, R. L., *Our Promised Land,* Macmillan, 1938. Appreciative description of New Deal conservation policies in our great Northwest.

Pinchot, Gifford, *Breaking New Ground,* Harcourt, Brace, 1947. Interesting autobiographical material by a pioneer conservationist.

Pritchett, C. H., *The Tennessee Valley Authority,* University of North Carolina, 1943. Good presentation of the work of the TVA, with special emphasis on political problems and administrative techniques.

Selznick, Philip, *TVA and the Grass Roots,* University of California Press, 1949. The best analysis of the social motives and accomplishments of the TVA.

Terral, Rufus, *The Missouri Valley,* Yale University, 1947. Survey of basis and need for Missouri Valley Authority, indicating necessary modifications of TVA to fit this larger and more complex area.

# CHAPTER IX

# Population Growth as a Social Problem

## The Nature of Population Problems

**Size and quality of population.** "What's the population of this town?" This is one of the first questions a stranger asks when entering a new community. For the number of a community's inhabitants is a key to its economic and social life. In a village of 500 people there will be little more than a post office, one or two churches, a few small stores, and a single school. A city of 30,000 to 50,000, on the other hand, will contain a dozen or more churches, a number of factories, numerous stores, three or four movie theaters, and a modern school system. Obviously, life in the city will be considerably different from that in the village, though not necessarily more pleasant.

The inquiring stranger, if he plans to settle in the new urban community, will, however, be interested in more than the size of the population. Equally important to him will be its quality. Quality refers to the relative presence or absence of such things as feeble-mindedness, insanity, vice, crime, and sickness. A community where these are prevalent will have many more serious social problems than one in which they are infrequent, and will be a less desirable place to live.

It is thus evident that there are two distinct population problems. One concerns the size of population and its rate of increase; the other centers around its quality, as determined by its physical and mental characteristics.

**Age-old interest in population problems.** Population problems have held the attention of men from a very early period. For instance, we are told that David was tempted to count the heads of the Israelites (I Chronicles 21). In the fourth century before Christ, the Greek philosopher Plato suggested in his *Republic* a systematic plan for improving the quality of the population. Even before Plato's time, Theognis, a Greek poet writing in the sixth century B.C., recommended that the practice of selective breeding be extended from domestic animals to the human race. Both Theognis and Plato were forerunners of the modern eugenics movement.

148

In this chapter we shall discuss the historic trends of population growth, mainly in western Europe and in the United States, the causes and consequences of increases and decreases in birth and death rates, the population problems facing us at the present time, and some ideas that have been put forth for improving population quality.

## Population Trends in the Western World in Modern Times

**Slow growth of population until modern times.** Today, there are two and a quarter billion persons on the earth, of whom about 550 million live in Europe. Yet, in the year 700 A.D., the earliest period for which we have much information, the population of western Europe was only around 30 million, increasing slowly to about 35 million three centuries later. More settled conditions and the rise of urban communities accelerated the growth somewhat, until, by 1300, the estimated population of western Europe was 53 million.

Despite the ravages of the Black Death (an epidemic of the deadly bubonic plague that swept Europe in the mid-fourteenth century), population continued to grow steadily, because governments preserved order, doctors saved more lives, and more food was produced. A modern scholar, Karl Julius Beloch, estimated the population of western Europe in 1600 at 73,500,000, and that of all Europe at 100,000,000. Devastating wars (like the Thirty Years' War, 1618–1648) and epidemics (such as the London plague of 1664–1665) temporarily slowed down population growth, for, at the end of the seventeenth century, the estimates of contemporaries were still only a little over 100 million. The total population of the world in 1643 is estimated to have been about 450 million.

**Effect of the Commercial Revolution.** The expansion of Europe after 1500, the Commercial Revolution, a marked increase in urban life, the greater prosperity of at least the middle class, and some improvements in medical science, favored population growth, so that by 1750 Europe had an estimated 140 million inhabitants. In the next half century, owing to the industrial and agricultural revolutions, there came the first major boom in population. Industry changed from hand labor to machine labor, the factory system was developed, former agricultural workers settled in large numbers in the new urban areas, and new ways of farming produced more food. Trade and commerce also expanded, thus bringing the increased amount of food to the growing city populations. More people could make a decent living. Medical science began to cut down the death rate. From 140 million in 1750, the population of Europe increased to 187 million by 1800.

After 1800, population multiplied much more rapidly. By 1850, Europe had 266 million; by 1914, 463 million; and by 1940, about 540 million. In 1940, Europeans and persons of European descent scattered over the earth numbered nearly 800 million.

**Rapid growth of United States population since 1800.** The population of the United States grew even faster than that of Europe, from less than 4 million white persons in 1789 to more than 155 million persons of all races in 1952. This remarkable growth was brought about not only by natural population increase, that is, more births than deaths, but also by the most extensive immigration that has ever occurred in human history.[1] Between 1820 and 1936, over 38 million persons left their homes in foreign countries to come to the United States.

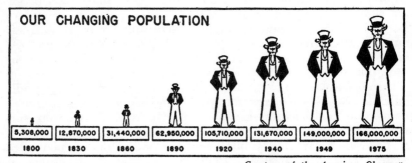

**OUR CHANGING POPULATION**

| 5,308,000 | 12,870,000 | 31,440,000 | 62,950,000 | 105,710,000 | 131,670,000 | 149,000,000 | 166,000,000 |
|---|---|---|---|---|---|---|---|
| 1800 | 1830 | 1860 | 1890 | 1920 | 1940 | 1949 | 1975 |

*Courtesy of the American Observer.*

Chart shows remarkable growth of population of the United States. Immigration was an important factor in population growth before 1920.

**Facts of world population.** The population of the entire world increased from 660,000,000 in 1750 to 2,264,000,000 in 1950. If the 1900–1940 rate of growth were to continue, it is estimated that the world would have more than 15 billion inhabitants by the year 2200, a condition that might bring wholesale starvation. But, scientists do not believe that such over-rapid growth will actually occur. Indeed, the social effects of urban life, as noted in a previous chapter, are slowing down the rate of population growth in all industrialized areas of the world.

We often regard the United States as the strongest nation in the world, and perhaps it is. But from the standpoint of manpower we rank rather low. The population of Soviet Russia is over 50 million greater than that of the United States today and is growing much more rapidly. The following table gives the approximate populations of the several continents in 1950:

Asia ..................................... 1,223,000,000
Europe .................................. 547,730,000
Africa .................................. 175,870,000

---

[1] See below, 172 ff.

North America (including Mexico and Central
America) ............................  192,650,000
South America .........................  101,400,000
Oceania (including Australia and New Zea-
land) ...............................  23,795,000

## Explanation of Rapid Population Growth

**Causes of rapid population growth.** When there are more births
than deaths, population naturally increases. This fact has misled
many persons into believing that the enormous growth of the European
and American population in the second half of the nineteenth century
and the first half of the twentieth has been due to a marked increase
in the birth rate. Actually, the birth rate, almost without exception,
was falling markedly during this period. For example, in England,
the birth rate for the years 1838–1842 was 31.6 per 1,000 persons,
while in 1938 it had dropped to 14.9. In France, the birth rate
dropped from an average of 29.9 in the 1838–1842 period to 14.7 in
1937; in Germany from 36.1 in 1848–1852 to 14.7 in 1933; and in Italy
from 36.9 in 1868–1872 to 23.4 in 1934. Even in Russia there was a
decline from 48.9 in 1868 to 38.3 in 1938. Although we lack complete
data for the United States, such facts as we have demonstrate that our
country has shared in this decline of the birth rate. In 1800, our birth
rate was about 55; in 1880, 35; and in 1940, 17.9. There have been
many reasons for the declining birth rate but the most important factor
again has been the net effect of urban living conditions.

Population increase has resulted from the fact that, although the
birth rate has fallen, the death rate has declined much more rapidly.
For example, there were over 22 deaths per 1,000 persons in 1840 in
England, but only 10.8 per 1,000 in 1948. In the United States, the
death rate fell from 19.8 in 1880 to 9.6 in 1950. In Sweden, on
which we have statistics for 150 years, the death rate dropped from
27.9 in 1790 to 9.8 in 1948. The most sensational drop was to be
observed in Germany—from 28 in 1872 to 10.8 in 1932.

**Reasons for a declining death rate.** Two main reasons for this
striking decrease in the death rate, particularly within the last seventy-
five years, were the development of sanitary engineering and improvements in medical science, especially in preventive medicine.

Living conditions in London from 1700 to 1750 were so unhealthy
that the excess of deaths over births averaged about 10,000 annually,
and the growth of the city in this period was due to the influx of
persons from country and other urban areas. Sanitary engineering
has made it possible for people to live in cities better constructed
and equipped for healthful living. Water supplies have been improved and freed from germs, sewage disposal plants have been installed, and streets have been cleaned of dirt and refuse. These

sanitary advances have notably lessened the ravages of epidemic diseases.

Preventive medicine, concerned with efforts to combat disease before it starts, has made especially great progress in the last century. Diseases which formerly caused many deaths, such as smallpox, diphtheria, yellow fever, pneumonia, and tuberculosis, have been brought under control. Schools now offer courses in hygiene and physical education, designed to safeguard the health of growing boys and girls. Inoculation and quarantine are well-known developments designed to combat contagious diseases.

Another factor in the decline of the death rate is the reduction of infant mortality. Although fewer babies are born now than formerly, fewer mothers and children die at childbirth, especially since the discovery of the sulfa drugs and penicillin. Mothers are taught improved methods of feeding and caring for children. With fewer children in the average family, each child can have better care and more medical attention. In England only 703 out of every 1,000 children born in 1838–1854 lived to be ten years old. By 1920–1922 the number of children surviving ten years had increased to 868 per thousand. A similar increase may be found in most civilized countries over the same period. In the United States, during the 35 years between 1911 and 1946, the death rate of children between the ages of 1 and 14 was reduced by over 79 per cent, and that from the chief communicable diseases of childhood—measles, scarlet fever, whooping cough, and diphtheria—by more than 90 per cent.

Moreover, the average length of human life—what we call life expectancy—in civilized countries has been notably increased. One hundred years ago, the average length of life for a man in England was about 40 years, and for a woman about 42 years. By 1936 these figures had advanced to 61.8 and 65.8 respectively. The average life expectancy of whites of both sexes in the United States in 1947 was 67.9 years, an increase of almost 18 years over 1901. The life expectancy for the total United States population in 1947 was 66.8, an increase of two years since 1939.

**Death rate becoming static.** The greater part of this progress in reducing the death rate was made before 1920. In the last thirty years the decrease in the death rate has not been as rapid as it was from 1850 to 1920. In the United States it only declined from 13.0 per cent in 1920 to 10.7 in 1940 and 9.6 in 1950. By the end of the first world war, medical science and sanitary engineering had already won the major victories so far achieved in reducing the death rate. Today, doctors tell us that the maladies of middle and old age, such as high blood pressure, heart trouble, chronic kidney disorders, and cancer, are on the increase; these chronic, degenerative diseases now account for about three-fourths of all deaths in the United States. They are also the diseases which medical science still finds it most difficult to cure. Students of population believe we may be nearing the end of any spectacular decrease in the death rate. Any further progress in conquering disease will be offset by the higher death rate among the ever increasing number of persons in the population over 60 or 65 years of age.

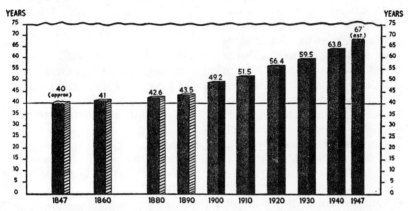

*Bureau of Medical Economic Research, American Medical Association.*

1. BEGINNING WITH 1900 COLORED POPULATION IN REGISTRATION AREAS IS INCLUDED.
2. AVERAGE LIFE EXPECTANCY AT BIRTH FOR 1947 ESTIMATED BY THE BUREAU. WHITE FEMALE LIFE EXPECTANCY AT BIRTH IS ALREADY OVER 70 YEARS. THE BUREAU ESTIMATES THAT THE AVERAGE FOR ALL WILL RISE TO 70 YEARS BEFORE 1955.

**Chart showing how life expectancy has increased as a result of improved medical science.**

**Minor causes of population growth.** Minor social and economic factors have operated to check the decline in the birth rate. England, in the latter part of the eighteenth century, enacted laws which provided allowances for the poor in proportion to the size of their families. Before the second world war, certain countries like Italy paid a bonus to parents for every child born. Germany, under Hitler, even encouraged the begetting of healthy illegitimate children. Soviet Russia today gives material rewards for large families, among them a bounty for all children born after the first child.

The high value formerly placed on child labor also stimulated the birth rate. In the early days of the Industrial Revolution, employers preferred to hire children because they would work for very low wages. Parents were eager to have many children because they added to the family income. Children were invaluable for performing the endless chores of the frontier family in our country.

These social and economic factors, which made for a higher birth rate in earlier days, have become less important today. Child labor laws restrict the exploitation of youth, machinery has replaced many small hands both in city and country, and the frontier days are over.

## Recent Trend toward the Stabilization of Populations

**Rate of population growth slowing down.** This startling news story appeared in a metropolitan paper only a few years ago. Is there actually a possibility that we shall have a world without babies? From 1900 to 1940, the rate of population growth decreased in western Europe and in the United States. From 1790 to 1860 the population of our country rose at a rate of about 35 per cent a decade. Since 1870, the rate of growth fell off until 1940. From 1870 to 1890, the rate was 27.8 per cent; from 1890 to 1910, 20.8 per cent; from 1910 to 1930, 15.5 per cent; and from 1930 to 1940, 7.3 per cent (a striking decline). The national average of persons per family was 4.9 in 1890, but only 3.8 in 1940. In all major countries except France the population was still growing but the rate of growth was declining in most parts of the Western world.

> ### NO BABIES IN 1961
> ### IS DREAD OUTLOOK
> ### FOR BARREN GOTHAM
>
> *By International News Service*
>
> New York, Jan. 30—If New York's falling birth rate continues its decline, it's possible that no children will be born in the city in 1961.
>
> This hypothetical possibility was contained in the annual report of the health commissioner. In 1900, the birth rate was 35.7 babies for each 1000 population, but last year the rate had fallen to 13.5 babies per 1000.

The slowing down of the rate of population growth in our country may further be illustrated by the relative decrease of the number of children under five in the United States population. In 1930, there were 11,444,390 children under five, but in 1940 only 10,541,524. This decline took place despite the fact that the number of women in the child-bearing ages of 14 to 44 rose from 30,418,336 in 1930 to 33,184,085 in 1940. Indeed, the census of 1940 indicated that the current generation of women of child-bearing age was failing by 4 per cent to reproduce itself. The breakdown of this figure by social areas gave a reproduction rate of only 76 per cent for urban regions, as compared with 116 for rural non-farm groups, and 136 for farmers. As a result of the wave of wartime, post-war, and "cold war" marriages, a record of nearly 23 million children were added to our population. This trend delaying stabilization may continue if the conditions stimulating a high birth rate become rather permanent.

**City life cuts down birth rate.** The birth rate tends to be lower in industrialized urban nations than in predominantly agricultural countries. Since the United States is rapidly becoming a nation of cities, we can better understand the decrease in the number of babies born here each year.

One of the most important reasons why city dwellers have fewer children than rural families is social ambition. As a French writer on population, Arsène Dumont, once put it, "People who are climbing the social ladder do not want too many children clinging to their skirts." To improve their social and economic status, people move from the country to the city. In order to enjoy luxuries and to have a greater degree of financial security and higher social position, many urban dwellers, particularly of the middle and upper classes, prefer to limit the size of their families. Social and economic ambition, in normal times, also leads young persons to postpone marriage. A working wife sometimes wants to keep her job instead of remaining at home and raising a family. The larger the city, the more marked are these tendencies and the lower the birth rate. Also, because birth-control devices are better known to urban than to rural dwellers, the former are more able to carry out their desire to restrict family growth.

Finally, the greater living costs, tensions, and distractions of city existence use up energy and divert attention which, under simpler rural living conditions, have in the past been devoted to reproductive activities. Students of population problems now believe that urban living conditions are more effective in reducing sexual activity and procreation than any deliberate, ambition-inspired effort to prevent conception—indeed, that they are the most important single cause of the falling birth rate and the trend towards population stabilization.

**Relative birth rates.** Within the city, there are marked differences in the birth rate between the various economic classes. In the higher income groups, the desire to succeed financially and socially and to be personally free from too much family responsibility has reduced the size of the family. The professional people, such as doctors, lawyers, dentists, and teachers, either absorbed in their work or with modest incomes, also tend to have small families. The skilled workers rank higher in the size of their families. The unskilled workers and the very poor from other groups have the largest number of children of any urban class. The desire to improve social and economic status can be noticed in the country as well as the city, even though the rural birth rate remains high. Machinery has made children less essential for farm work. Many a farmer, in the hard times after 1921, reasoned that, if there were fewer children, there would be more comforts for the whole family.

**Effect of wars on the population.** The world war of 1914–1918, used as an example because its total results are more easily assessible than those of the second world war, had an important effect in checking the rate of population growth. As a result of this conflict, nearly 12 million soldiers lost their lives and an equal number of civilians were killed or died of starvation and disease. Almost 20 million men were wounded, and 24 million persons were made widows, orphans, and refugees.

Many of those who were killed at the front would probably have had more children if they had lived; others, who returned wounded and maimed, were not able to carry on normal lives, and their families often suffered severely. The influenza epidemic of 1918, produced and spread by wartime conditions, killed almost as many persons as the famous Black Death of 1349. The British blockade for six months after the Armistice of 1918 starved to death some 800,000 men, women, and children in central Europe.

No complete and accurate estimate of the extensive and diverse effects of the first world war and of the epidemic on population problems has yet been made. But the figures do show that the rate of population growth in all belligerent countries was far less in the decade of 1911–1920 than in the previous decade, and that some countries showed a net population loss for 1911–1920. The losses were especially severe in Jugoslavia, Poland and the Baltic states. In the most authoritative study yet made, Dudley Kirk estimates the net population loss to Europe to have been in excess of 30 million.

Professor W. F. Ogburn has shown that the first world war cut the birth rate in half in France and Germany; there were 1,500,000 fewer babies born in France during the war years than would have been born in time of peace. The British birth rate was cut about one-fourth during the war. The war increased the death rate among the participants by about 25 per cent. The quality of the population was also reduced because the best physical types were in the army and sustained the most casualties.

The second world war caused greater population losses than any other single episode in human history. The military dead amounted to at least 10 million and the civilian dead to three times that number. Russian losses are estimated as 7,000,000, Polish as 4,620,000, German as 3,620,000, and Jugoslav as 1,680,000. The net population loss will, of course, be far greater than the total dead. Germany well illustrates the impact of war in reducing the birth rate and leaving an excess of females over males. In Berlin, the birth rate dropped from 15.7 in 1939 to 4.9 in 1946. In the country as a whole, in 1946, there were 36,597,000 females and 29,319,000 males, and 8 per cent of the population was over 65 years of age.

**Post-war population spurt may be relatively permanent.** There has been a remarkable spurt in the birth rate since 1937 in the United States. In 1937, it was 17.1, in 1947 25.9, and in 1952 approximately the same as in 1947. The population of the United States increased from 131,670,000 in 1940 to 155,800,000 at the beginning of 1952. Unusual increases in population have taken place in some European countries during this same period.

It was thought in the late 1940's that this was a temporary situation due to the various factors stimulating marriages and a high birth rate during the war and the immediate post-war years. Population statistics seemed to support this view at the time. But they did not reckon with the revival of quasi-wartime conditions with the "cold war," the

Korean War, and the resumption of selective service. As a result of these new conditions, the birth rate rose again until in 1952 it was approximately equal to the record rate of 1947. Nearly 23 million children were added to the population between 1946 and 1952. Some 3.9 million babies were born in 1951 and an equal number were predicted for 1952.

Another new trend which accounted for the marked increase in population after the war was the increase in the size of families which reversed the movement towards smaller families. In the year 1946, some 2,291,000 marriages took place. This had fallen to 1,600,-000 in 1951, but 24,000 more babies were born in 1951 than in 1947.

**Population stabilization likely to be postponed.** On the basis of trends in the late 1940's, population experts predicted the stabilization of the American population about 1980 with a figure of between 160,000,000 and 185,000,000. The revival of population growth since 1949 has upset all such predictions for the time being. The Bureau of the Census estimated in January, 1952, that the population of the United States would grow to between 162,000,000 and 180,000,000 even as early as 1960.

World conditions are so fluid today that no precise predictions as to population figures can be valid. But stabilization is likely to take place sooner or later. The present rapid population growth is likely to continue as long as quasi-wartime conditions exist. But, if these go on, they are likely to lead to a third world war which may greatly reduce the population during and after the conflict. In a third world war, the population of the United States would not be likely to escape serious decimation and post-war conditions would probably be discouraging to rapid population growth.

## Probable Effects of Population Stabilization

**Some social and economic effects of a stable population.** Although unforeseen future changes may upset all predictions, it is worth while to contemplate the possible effects of a stable population upon the American economic and social situation.

We cannot hope that foreign trade and European relief will continue for long to absorb our surplus supply of goods and foodstuffs. The highly industrialized nations of Europe, with their own declining rates of population growth, will, after the reconstruction period following the second world war, face the same situation of over-production.

As population growth falls off, there will be a smaller market for farm products. This may be especially serious, since we already produce more food than people can buy with their present incomes. Increasing unemployment and poverty may result for the rural population, whose rate of increase is greatest today.

The only solution of our future economic problems in a period of population decline may be to shorten the working day to provide steadier employment and to raise wages and salaries, so that, even if there are fewer buyers, each will have more money to purchase the goods and food which our factories and farms can produce.

**False alarm over population stabilization.**  Many persons predict "race suicide" and the extinction of humanity as they observe the falling birth rate.  Their fears arise from the fact that the unusually rapid population growth of the nineteenth century accustomed men to find large population increases normal and desirable.  Actually, the tremendous population growth in the nineteenth century was unique.  A stationary, rather than a rapidly growing, population is the normal law of nature.  The alarm over "race suicide" stemmed largely from the totalitarian warmongers in Europe who were concerned lest they would not have enough men for their armies.  Even if this were a worthy reason for alarm, it should not cause great concern, for the second world war showed that machines can, to some extent, replace men, even in military combat.

The decline in population growth has, indeed, a more cheerful side.  It would be highly disastrous if the rapid rate of population increase of former years were to continue indefinitely.  New land has been pretty well exhausted, the Industrial Revolution has passed through many stages, and medical science has done its major work, for the time being, in reducing the death rate.  Should the abnormal rate of population growth of the last century continue indefinitely, there might not be enough food and other necessities to give men a decent existence.

## Social, Economic, and Political Problems Arising from Overpopulation and the Differences in the Rate of Population Growth

**Relative population density in world regions.**  The relative pressure of population differs greatly among the various countries of the world, thus creating an unstable equilibrium in world society.  The following table presents relative and typical contrasts in population pressure, as measured by number of inhabitants per square mile:

| | |
|---|---|
| Great Britain | 504.7 |
| Japan | 469.0 |
| India | 176.3 |
| China | 145.6 |
| United States | 44.2 |
| Brazil | 14.0 |
| Argentina | 12.2 |

This situation has made for international tension and war in the present economic and political order.  Britain could only support its population by the receipts from a great colonial empire; hence, she fought to maintain this empire.  Japan thought she must expand in order to relieve population pressure and get income from colonies. In this way, Britain and Japan clashed. The United States refused to acquiesce in Japan's expansion; hence, we tangled with Japan, and so on.

While in the Western world, as we have seen, population growth has slowed up markedly and may well decline in the future, this condition is not universally true, even in parts of Europe. In predominantly rural countries, such as Russia, population growth remains relatively high. This is due, as we have pointed out, to the fact that the ambitions and living conditions of city life, which discourage large families, do not operate so effectively in rural areas.

**Population prospects in the Far East.** P. K. Whelpton, a leading population expert, predicts an increase of 250 millions in world population in the next twenty years, with 135 million of this increase taking place on the continent of Asia. The justification for this estimate can be seen in the case of Japan, where the birth rate has increased nearly 10 births per 1,000 persons since 1880 and the death rate has decreased by about the same amount since 1925. China, at its present rate of population growth, will double its 450 million population in less than 90 years. Industry, city life, and birth control may stabilize Oriental populations, but probably not before Asia becomes an overcrowded "danger spot" in the world population picture. It was thought by many that the disastrous results of the second world war would drastically reduce the Japanese birth rate, but they failed to do so. The Japanese birth rate in 1948 was 33.8, about what it had been in the 1921–1925 period.

**Population trends and world politics.** The differences in gross population growth in the various continents are, as we noted above, an unsettling factor in world relations and the world economy. The population of Asia, despite wars and devastating epidemics and famines, grew from about 600,000,000 in 1800 to about 1,223,000,000 in 1950. The total increase of population in Asia since 1800 is thus much more than the total population of Europe today, and over four times the population of the United States.

Notable military and political consequences have resulted from the fact that the Oriental countries had a rapid population growth in the twentieth century while most of the West grew very slowly. Japan began to seek more "living room" early in the twentieth century, when it annexed Korea after wars with China and Russia. In 1931, Japan invaded and conquered Manchuria and in 1937 invaded China proper. At the height of her successes in the second world war Japan had occupied much of eastern China, had captured the American bases in the Philippines, had driven the English back from Malaya and Hong Kong, had ousted the French from Indo-China and had overrun Thailand and much of the East Indies. The defeat of Japan has not produced any permanent political or international equilibrium in the Far East. Japanese population pressure is greater than in 1940.

Emigration, even if freely allowed, would not take care of the excess population in Asia. Japan's net annual increase in population before the war, 900,000 people, would be unable to settle in other areas without profound economic and political disturbances. Moreover, even if such emigration were possible and peaceful, it would not greatly lessen the rate of population increase at home. If the United States were to take in only those suffering from famine in China (5 to 10 million in average years and 20 million in bad famine years), these immigrants would utterly swamp us without greatly reducing the frequency or severity of famines in China.[2]

Important and devastating as the effects of population growth in the Far East may have been already, in helping to produce such international clashes as the wars between Japan and Russia and Japan and China, and the Far Eastern aspects of the second world war, it is evident that this is only the mild beginning. By the time that industrialization and medical science have brought their full influence to bear in the Far East, it is possible that China will have a population of a billion and a half, India a population of a billion, and Indonesia a population of at least quarter of a billion. In the meantime, the white population of the Western world will have stabilized and declined and will not be larger than it is today. The Russian population will possibly have reached a half-billion by this time, and Russia seems inclined to veer toward Asia in its political interests and alliances. It will have the atom bomb in profusion long before the Asiatic populations have reached their maximum—and the Asiatic nations will also probably have the bomb by this time.

It is obvious that, by the time all this happens, the white hegemony in the world will have passed, and in the process the whites will probably have been expelled from all of Asia, either by political pressure or by further world wars. Whether or not Spengler was right in predicting that white civilization is doomed and that the next great culture will arise in the Far East, it is evident that the overpopulation that looms ahead in the Far East is bound to have political and military repercussions far exceeding anything hitherto known in that area and probably in the whole world.

Europe has already been swept by two wars as overpopulated countries have sought to gain needed territory, raw materials, and markets at the expense of their neighbors. Germany was a highly industrialized state, demanding *Lebensraum* (living space) as well as food, raw materials, and better foreign markets for her goods. Italy demanded colonies as an outlet for her large population and also required raw materials and markets. Together, these nations risked the most devastating war in history in 1939–1945 to achieve their aims.

**Implications of rapid population growth in Soviet Russia.** One of the most remarkable aspects of differential population growth in

---

[2] See H. P. Fairchild, "Land Hunger and Peace," *Common Sense*, February, 1942.

relation to world politics today is to be found in contrasting the situation in Russia and southern Europe to that in western Europe. Countries in the latter region are already approaching a stable population, while the prospect is for an enormous increase of population in the next thirty years in Russia and southern Europe. Our ablest students of population believe that Russia, even within its 1937 boundaries, will have an increase in population of some 77,000,000 from 1940 to 1970, and will have a total population at the latter date of some 250,-000,000. In 1970, Russia will have more males of working age than all the countries of western Europe combined. She will have 32,-000,000 men of prime military age, between 20 and 34, more than the next seven largest European countries combined. The United States in 1970 will have only about 18,000,000 men in the 20–34 age-group. In addition to all this, Russia has annexed territory since 1937 containing at least 25,000,000 inhabitants, a figure which will probably grow to 40,000,000 by 1970. In southern and eastern Europe, outside Russia but under Russian hegemony, it is estimated that the population will gain by some 27,000,000 between 1940 and 1970.

Moreover, there will be a relatively larger number of young men in Russia in 1970, which means that the Russian population will go on increasing rapidly long after that of western Europe has become stabilized. Such differences in population will inevitably mean a shift in relative political prestige and military power, as well as in economic strength. These facts are among those which alarm leaders in western Europe and the United States who fear Russian plans for expansion.

**Results of differential rates of population growth in the United States.** The differences in the rate of population growth among the various economic groups and classes in our own country may also produce important social consequences. Where the birth rate is high, we find that it is, unfortunately, among those with low incomes and a low standard of living. It was estimated that, just before the second world war, more than one-third of the two million births each year in the United States occurred in families receiving help from welfare agencies or in those families with total incomes of less than $750 per year. One of our leading social economists has pointed out that two-thirds of our children are growing up in families which do not have an income sufficient to provide even the physical necessities which constitute a decent standard of life.

Many unfortunate economic and social results may develop from this differential rate of population growth. The excessive birth rate among the agricultural population and the poorer urban groups may lead to lowered standards of rural and urban life. The increase of unskilled workers in the city may produce a large group of laborers who cannot find employment and will be forced to go on relief or become migratory workers without decent homes. The growth in the number of unskilled workers is especially alarming in this era of automatic machinery. The lower-income groups have fewer educational and cultural advantages, and intellectual standards may be undermined if the increase in our population continues to come mainly from those without adequate economic support and cultural opportunities.

**Shifts in age groups in the population.**  Our population trends will also profoundly affect the distribution of age-groups in society.  In 1820, the average age of the total American population was 16.7 years; in 1880, 20.9 years; and in 1940, 29.0 years.  Sociologists say that, in the "world of tomorrow," there will be nearly as many persons over forty as under forty.  It has been predicted that by 1975 there will be over 40 million persons between 45 and 64, and more than 20 million 65 or over.  The number 65 or over increased by 37 per cent between 1940 and 1950.

In 1860, only 2.7 per cent of the population, or 860,000, were 65. In 1952, 8 per cent, or 12,400,000 were 65 or over.  If this trend continues, there will be 16,000,000, or about 10 per cent, over 65 in 1970, and 21,000,000, or more than 12 per cent, over 65 in 1980.  With a longer life expectancy, these older persons will go on to a riper old age.

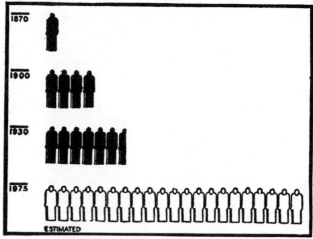

*Courtesy of the Committee on Economic Security.*

How the declining birth rate and increased life expectancy are increasing the number of older people in the population. Each figure represents one million persons 65 years and over.

This "aging" of the population may cause a noticeable change in tastes and ways of living.  More money will be spent on the interests, demands, and amusements of maturity, and less on those of youth. There will, for example, be more money spent on books, lectures, spectacles, pipes, and wheel chairs, and less spent on milk, baby-carriages, toys, bicycles, and jazz records.  Since old age is more cautious than youth, the future may tend toward conservatism in business and politics.

Important changes may also take place in education. With schoolrooms less crowded, teachers may be able to give more time to improving the quality of education through individual instruction. This situation will, of course, be temporarily checked by the great increase in the number of children born in the 1940's and early 1950's, to which we shall call attention shortly. There will be more classes in adult education for the increasing number of mature persons who may wish to adjust themselves to changes in world conditions and modes of earning a livelihood.

As the population grows older, there will also be more aged persons in need of aid from welfare agencies, the Federal social security program, and old-age pensions. Child-welfare programs may well become less important than old-age pensions.

## Some Probable Results of the Spurt in Population Growth in the 1940's and 1950's

**Spurt of birth rate in the 1940's and 1950's.** While the marked spurt in the birth rate in the 1940's and 1950's may be a temporary matter, it is bound to affect social conditions in this country for a generation, and, hence, needs some comment. Let us look at some of the facts.

The birth rate in the United States increased from 17.9 in 1940 to 25.8 in 1947, and was about as high in 1952 as in 1947. There were only 2,312,000 babies born in 1933, but some 3,910,000 were born in 1947 and about an equal number in 1951 and 1952. About 23,000,000 children were added to the population between 1946 and 1952. Though the marriage rate has fallen off markedly since 1946, there were 24,000 more babies born in 1951 than in 1947.

**Results of recent gains in the birth rate.** What are some of the probable results of this striking temporary variation in normal population trends? In the first place, by 1950 children under 15 were the largest single age-group in the population. This will temporarily reduce the disproportionate growth of the sector over 65, mentioned earlier, and briefly restore a better balance between youth and old age in the population. Second, it will postpone by a decade or more the time when the total population growth of the nation may be expected to level off, and will make the population figure at which the leveling off occurs larger (perhaps 200,000,000 as against an earlier estimate of around 170,000,000). Third, unless more teachers are induced to enter and remain in the profession, there will be a real crisis in our public schools. Where some 32,500,000 were enrolled in our public schools in 1952, there may be 40,000,000 enrolled by 1957. Yet, owing to inadequate pay, higher taxes, and other unattractive features of the teaching profession, the number of teachers is decreasing, rather than increasing to assume the additional teaching load. Some 400,-000 teachers have left the profession since 1940. About 125,000 of these have never been replaced, and many of the replacements have been of inferior quality. Finally, there is bound to be a boom in industries which furnish food and supplies to babies and youth, and a further intensification of the already menacing housing shortage.

**Rapid population increase may continue.** As we have noted earlier, it was believed in the late 1940's that the spurt in the birth rate from 1941 to 1948 might be a temporary matter and that a decline would set in. This has not proved to be the case because the "cold war," the Korean War, the revival of selective service, and quasi-wartime prosperity have revived the very conditions which stimulated the birth rate from 1941 to 1948. It is likely that the rapid increase in population will continue as long as this situation persists.

## The Malthusian Theory of Population

**The Malthusian law of population growth.** Population problems have been discussed by writers for thousands of years. Of modern works on the subject, the *Essay on Population,* first published in 1798 by an English scholar, Thomas Robert Malthus, has been perhaps most influential. Malthus contended that population tends to increase faster than the food supply. Population, he claimed, tends to increase at a geometrical ratio (1, 2, 4, 8, 16) while food tends to increase only in an arithmetic ratio (1, 2, 3, 4, 5). In time, population will tend to outrun the available food supply unless certain checks, such as war, pestilence, famine, and starvation, cut down the population growth. Malthus urged postponement of marriage as the best way to restrict population growth and make its reduction by wars and pestilences unnecessary.

Malthus was chiefly concerned over the situation in the England of his time, for he believed that, unless the growth of population was checked, a large percentage of the English people would be forced to live in poverty and misery. Many who have not carefully examined the theory of Malthus have criticized his conclusions harshly, forgetting that he wrote before an adequate food supply had been guaranteed by the changes following the great nineteenth-century revolutions in industry and agriculture. For his own day and country, his ideas were generally sound. It is also very important to remember that Malthus wrote when population was increasing rapidly and before industrialization and urbanization had brought about those living conditions and personal reactions which have tended to produce population stabilization in city districts in more recent times. The specter of rapid population growth was much more vivid in 1800 than in 1950.

**Malthusianism no longer valid.** Although Malthus was justified in presenting such a viewpoint in England at the end of the eighteenth century, scientific agriculture and modern methods of transporting, canning, and preserving food have generally invalidated the Malthusian theory. Moreover, Malthus considered mainly a given population within a definite boundary. When these boundaries are changed, as they have been in Russia, the United States, and the British Empire since 1800, it takes a certain length of time for the population to absorb the newly available food supply drawn from additional lands. Countries can now also more easily import food to supplement their own resources.

Malthusianism is, thus, an intellectual curiosity in normal times today, since the industrial and agricultural revolutions have made a sufficient food supply potentially available to all industrialized states in peacetime. The great problem now is to get enough income into the pockets of the masses, so that they can buy as much as they need of the abundant food that our farms can produce and our transportation agencies can ship.

**Recent revival of Malthusianism.** The severe postwar famine in central Europe, Japan, China, and India, and the publication of two striking books in 1948, William Vogt's *Road to Survival* and Fairfield Osborn's *Our Plundered Planet,* have recently tended to give a new vogue to Malthusianism among superficial thinkers.

Vogt and Osborn, however, stressed the great waste of land and resources owing to erosion, floods, soil exhaustion, and war devastation. Any attempt to link up these facts with Malthusianism is quite beside the main point in the matter. Malthus held that the products of human nature must inevitably outrun those of physical nature—that the products of procreation are bound to exceed those of cultivation. History has proved this to be signally untrue. The rate of population growth has fallen off rapidly in every industrialized and urbanized country at the very time when science and technology have enabled us vastly to increase the food supply, as well as the supply of all other material needs of mankind. We now know that world population can reach its limits without seriously diminishing the food supply per capita if full use is made of our knowledge and equipment.

**Causes of present-day starvation and famines.** What causes famine and starvation today is not the alleged fact that population must invariably outrun the food supply unless checked by war and famine, but the social, economic, and political stupidity of mankind, which prevents us from increasing the food supply as rapidly as science and technology permit. In short, famine and starvation today are caused by cultural rather than natural factors.

Wars, both foreign and civil, have absorbed or diverted the scientific and technical ability that should have been put into scientific agricultural research aimed at better methods of agricultural production. Wars, and their aftermath of political stupidities, have greatly reduced the potential output of crops and other material necessities. Civil strife and foreign wars, far from cutting down population to where its food supply is adequate, are in large part responsible for the starvation in central Europe, Japan, China, and India, as well as for the economic waste and soil exhaustion that Vogt and Osborn so wisely deplore. Of course, in addition to the diversion of money into armament and war instead of agricultural research and improvements, we must always remember that inadequate income for the masses prevents the majority of citizens from procuring as much as they need of the food that is produced even by existing methods.

**Bullets instead of bread.** The answer to all revivals of Malthusianism in our day is contained in O. W. Willcox's *Reshaping Agriculture* (1934), and *Nations Can Live at Home* (1935). Using a thorough mastery of agricultural science as the basis for his analysis, Willcox shows that even the least well-endowed of the so-called "have-not" nations, such as Great Britain (exclusive of her empire), Italy, Germany, and Japan, could, if they adopted the best agricultural science of our day, not only exist but be able "to supply their every essential need for food and clothing in overflowing abundance from their own land."

Even China and India, the classic lands of famine, could provide enough food to eliminate all famine if they would curb civil strife and adopt modernized methods of production. The Chinese civil wars have had much more to do with Chinese famines of today than Malthus and his principles, though of course the real responsibility goes back to the whole archaic and exploitative character of Chinese agrarian feudalism and the Chinese failure to attain political unity and economic modernity. The vital fact is that, if the countries that now have acute food shortages had put even a fraction of what they have spent on armament and war into introducing the best agricultural methods, there would have been no such shortages. Moreover, there are some 1,300,000,000 acres of good farm land in the world that are still entirely uncultivated. Much of this land is located in the tropics and possesses almost unbelievable fertility and productivity.

The books of Vogt and Osborn are to be commended for their call to action to reduce the wicked and needless waste of our natural heritage, but they afford no basis whatever for reviving Malthusianism today. There is no rational basis for seeking to obscure or deny our current political and economic stupidity by "passing the buck" to Malthus. Measures to limit population growth may be commendable, but they are no substitute for statecraft in the economic and political field.

## The Eugenics Program: Improving the Quality of the Population

**Danger of lowering the quality of the population.** As we have remarked before, the highest birth rate occurs among the poor and uneducated, who lack the money and ability to give their children adequate care and proper educational opportunities. While it is true that many poor and uneducated persons are of average, or even superior, intelligence, as a rule the lower-income classes do not possess as high a level of intelligence and ability as the wealthier and better educated elements of the population. Even when the lower classes are physically and mentally equal to the more prosperous elements, they cannot, owing to economic handicaps, provide decent living standards and good educational opportunities for their children. Thus, the fact that the largest population increase occurs in those groups which are in the lowest levels of income and culture is unfortunate. It means that the general level of intelligence and culture in the population is being progressively lowered.

**Sir Francis Galton and the rise of the eugenics movement.** Concern over the quality of population is not new, but widespread interest in this subject did not arise until the end of the nineteenth century. At that time, certain scientists began to recognize the unfortunate consequences that might result if the less fit elements in the population produced most of the children. Under the leadership of a great English biologist, Sir Francis Galton (1822–1911), the eugenics movement began. Galton's first book on the subject, *Hereditary Talent and Character,* appeared as early as 1865, but his first important work was *Hereditary Genius,* which was published four years later. It was in a later book, *Inquiry into Human Faculty* (1883) that he coined the term "eugenics."

The fundamental goal of the eugenicists is to improve the quality of the population by increasing the number of desirable elements and correspondingly reducing the undesirable. Galton was convinced that society can only be improved if those persons who are mentally and physically superior are encouraged to have large families, and the weaklings in mind or body are discouraged from having children. Galton wrote extensively on this subject and his books attracted much attention. His work was carried on in England by his disciple, Karl Pearson. In the United States, the eugenics movement was espoused by a leading biologist, Charles B. Davenport, and given financial support by Alexander Graham Bell, the inventor of the telephone.

**The goals of eugenics.** There are two major eugenic proposals: positive eugenics, which aims to encourage the abler types in the population to have more children; and negative eugenics, which hopes to end reproduction by feeble-minded and insane persons, habitual criminals, degenerates, and those suffering from serious diseases which may be hereditary. The methods advocated for negative eugenics are the sterilization or the segregation of the unfit.

The leaders of the eugenics movement have an excellent goal. There is no doubt that the quality of the population would be greatly improved if only the superior types had children. But often those persons who are intellectually superior do not have sufficiently large incomes to enable them to raise large families. There would also be social and cultural difficulties today in carrying out the methods of positive eugenics. It would be difficult to agree on who are the "superior types" or how to restrict further breeding among the "unfit." The excesses of the Hitler régime in Germany in enforcing a drastic eugenics program have tended, at least temporarily, to discredit the eugenics movement.

**Sterilization programs.** There is a more immediate prospect of the adoption of negative eugenic measures. That the feeble-minded should not be allowed to have children is generally agreed, and for this reason some thirty-two states have passed sterilization laws which provide for performing a simple sterilization operation to prevent the feeble-minded from reproducing. Few of these laws have, however, been enforced. California has done far better than any other state in executing its sterilization law, but even there its practical application has been slight. To make even an effective start at least two million Americans would need to be sterilized at once. Ten states now require a doctor's certificate signifying physical fitness for marriage before a license to marry is issued. Twenty-four states require a waiting period between the license and the marriage ceremony, so that marriage will not be hasty or illegal. These laws, even if enforced, are only a slight step in the right direction. Raising the physical and mental level of a population requires a long, slow process of education, and it might well take over a century to put into effective operation a complete eugenics program.

Our modern problem is both how to improve the race in future generations and how to provide more ample opportunities for everybody today. If families had an adequate and steady income, sufficient to take care of their children, many of our important economic and social problems would be solved. Even though a eugenics program may be desirable, the social and economic barriers to individual opportunity, hindering those who are now alive, should be tackled first.

**A sound population policy.** The essentials of a sound national population policy, taking into consideration both population quantity and quality, have been thus summarized by Lorimer, Winston, and Kiser, in their *Foundations of American Population Policy:* [3]

1. Promote economic well-being on an all-out scale, to give the citizens we have a better and more secure life.
2. Give some economic encouragement for larger families. Develop the plan slowly after experimenting with methods.
3. Distribute universally sound information to improve the quality of children and to reduce class inequalities.
4. Provide good education and medical care for every citizen.
5. Modify, after careful study, the conditions of employment for women, so that more women can become mothers if they wish to.
6. Finally, undertake a general program of education to obtain wide cooperation from the public for the measures recommended.

## Summary

From the middle of the eighteenth century down to the world war of 1914–1918 there were rapid increases in population in the indus-

[3] Harper, 1940.

trialized portions of the Western world. Among the major causes of this population increase were the reduction of the death rate by medical science and the effects of the industrial and agricultural revolutions in making available more goods and food.

Contrary to the assumption of many persons, an increased birth rate has not been the cause of population increase. Instead of increasing, the birth rate in most of the civilized world has decreased markedly since 1850. The tendency of city dwellers to try to improve their social status by having smaller families is considered to be among the more important causes of the declining birth rate. The general conditions of city life also operate powerfully to keep the birth rate down.

The decline of the death rate has been mainly responsible for population growth in the last hundred years; though the birth rate has fallen, the death rate has declined more rapidly than the birth rate. Owing to the steady decline in the birth rate and the slowing down of the decline in the death rate in recent years, the populations of the Western nations are increasing much less rapidly, and population growth is approaching a standstill in many countries.

There is a marked difference between the main social and economic groups in rate of population growth; the poorer classes in both country and city tend to have the largest families, but they are not able to rear their children under advantageous conditions. Along with inducing the well-to-do to have more children, one of the most important social problems is that of providing an adequate and stable income for workers in both city and country, so that their standard of living may be higher and their care of children improved.

The contrasts in population pressure and the rate of population growth in different parts of the world, especially between the Western world, on the one hand, and Russia and the Far East, on the other, have helped to bring about devastating wars and internal disturbances and threaten to create further wars in the future.

The eugenics program, which would encourage "superior" types to have children, has an ideal goal, but it will require a long period of education before superior mental and physical types will supply the main increases in the population. In the meantime, it will be well to restrict reproduction among the defective and degenerate types.

### Selected References

Burlingame, L. L., *Heredity and Social Problems,* McGraw-Hill, 1940. Population and other socio-biological problems discussed within the framework of the concepts of hereditary forces and influences.

Carr-Saunders, A. M., *World Population: Past Growth and Present Trends,* Oxford: Clarendon, 1936. A good general historical treatment of population tendencies in modern times, including a survey of the situation before the second world war.

Dublin, L. I., and Lotka, A. J., *Length of Life,* Ronald Press, 1936. Able general and statistical study of the increase in life expectancy and related population trends.

Glass, D. V., *Population Policies and Movements in Europe,* Oxford: Clarendon, 1940. Survey of the prewar European population situation, with special emphasis on efforts to increase the rate of population growth.

Holmes, S. J., *The Eugenic Predicament,* Harcourt, Brace, 1933. A restrained and thoughtful discussion of the province, goals, and prospects of eugenics.

Kirk, Dudley, *Europe's Population in the Interwar Years,* League of Nations Publications, 1946. Best discussion in English of the impact of the first world war on population trends, and of developments between the two world wars. Ample tables and statistical data.

* Landis, P. H., *Population Problems,* American Book Co., 1943. One of the more recent manuals on population problems. Especially valuable for emphasis on social and cultural aspects of population growth.

Lorimer, Frank, *The Population of the Soviet Union: History and Prospects,* Columbia University: League of Nations, 1946. Comprehensive analysis of current population trends in Russia, with predictions of remarkable future growth in next half century.

* Lorimer, Frank; Winston, Ellen E. B.; and Kiser, L. K., *Foundations of American Population Policy,* Harper, 1940. An excellent book on prewar population trends in the United States and their social implications.

Mather, K. F., *Enough and To Spare,* Harper, 1944. A counter-argument to the views of Vogt and Osborn. Contends that the world still has plenty of natural resources if wars and waste are curbed.

Myrdal, Gunnar, *Population: A Problem for Democracy,* Harvard, 1940. Able discussion of public and political problems of population trends.

National Resources Committee, *Problems of a Changing Population,* Government Printing Office, 1938. The official summary of prewar population tendencies in the United States and predictions of future trends. Stresses the slowing down of population growth and the increasing number of old people.

* Notestein, F. W., *et al., Future Population of Europe and the Soviet Union,* Columbia University: League of Nations, 1944. Best analysis of the extent and implications of the differential rate of population growth in eastern and western Europe.

* Osborn, Frederick, *Preface to Eugenics,* Harper, 1940. The best book on eugenics in the present state of the development of this important science. Authoritative but modest in its claims for eugenics.

Smith, T. L., *Population Analysis,* McGraw-Hill, 1948. Extensive descriptive demographical material dealing with the population situation in the United States today.

Thompson, W. S., *Population Problems,* McGraw-Hill, 1935. The standard book on population problems. It deals with many related social problems, such as the growth and redistribution of city populations.

* —————, *Plenty of People,* Ronald, 1948. Supplements the previous book by bringing it down to date in light of subsequent population trends.

* —————, *Population and Peace in the Pacific,* University of Chicago, 1946. Thoughtful discussion of local and international implications of future population prospects in Asia. Essentially supplants author's previous book on *Danger Spots in World Population.*

Whelpton, P. K., *et al., Forecasts of the Population of the United States: 1945–1975,* Government Printing Office, 1947. Probably the most expert and authoritative prediction of population trends in the United States.

# CHAPTER X

# Human Migrations and the American Immigration Problem

## The Nature, Causes, and Effects of Human Migrations

**Historic course of human migrations.** From prehistoric times to the present era, men have often gathered together their possessions and set out to find better places to live. These large-scale movements across the face of the globe are termed "migrations." In ancient and medieval times, whole tribes were accustomed to migrate periodically in search of new homes or in the hope of despoiling the rich lands of more prosperous peoples. More recent migrations, usually limited to individuals and small groups, have ultimately involved greater numbers than the ancient movements of whole tribes and peoples.

**Migration, emigration, and immigration.** *Migration* is the term used to describe any general movement of people; people moving from one country or region to another, are referred to as *migrants*. The word *immigration* means entrance into a country for permanent residence; people who enter that country are called *immigrants*. *Emigration* means leaving a country; an *emigrant* is one who moves from his homeland to another region. Therefore, any person settling in a new country is both an emigrant (as viewed by those remaining in the old homeland) and an immigrant (as regarded by the citizens of his adopted country).

**The American immigration problem.** There has been an immigration problem in the United States for nearly four centuries. No other migration in human history compares in numbers with this one. Between the founding of St. Augustine in 1565 and the second world war, over 40 million persons came to live in what is now known as the United States. The intermingling of these different peoples and their cultures has created what we call our American civilization.

**Main causes of migrations.** What causes men to leave established homes and risk the dangers of an unknown land? Three main reasons underlie such migratory movements: economic, political, and religious.

The economic motive has been the principal cause of most of the great migrations. Peoples in early times, lacking hunting grounds,

172

food, or pasture lands, sought more productive regions. Tribes that increased rapidly in population were forced to expand beyond the confines of their original habitat. Much of the colonization of America from 1600 to 1765 was economically motivated; even those who, like the Pilgrims, fled political and religious persecution were not indifferent to the possibility of a better economic prospect in the new lands overseas. After the Industrial Revolution, men moved from rural areas to the new factory towns, both at home and across the Atlantic, hoping to secure better economic opportunities.

The political motive for migration was often mixed with the economic. Migrations sometimes took the form of armed invasions. Warlike groups, greedy for more territory and power, invaded lands occupied by other tribes. It will be recalled how Cortez and his Spaniards, in their desire for gold, conquered Mexico. Often, the vanquished groups were forced to move on to less desirable land that was unoccupied or undefended. The American Indian, for example, was pushed farther and farther from his original hunting grounds as the white man filled up the wide spaces of North America. Oppressed people in Old World despotisms often fled to new lands in search of political freedom until after the European revolutions of 1848, and again after the totalitarian oppressions of a century later. Thousands of refugees—so-called displaced persons—sought entry into the United States after the second world war.

Religious persecution has also been a motive for numerous migrations. The Huguenots, at the end of the seventeenth century, were driven out of France because their Protestant beliefs conflicted with those of the Catholic French king. Numerous German Protestant dissenters left western Germany because of persecution and came to colonial America. The Pilgrim Fathers, familiar characters in colonial history, are an example of a group that sought freedom from religious, as well as political, oppression.

**Migrations produce new cultures.** The history of every nation includes migrations of both social and cultural significance. The Spaniards spent many years driving the Moors out of their country, but they could not erase the effects of the Moorish conquest on their architecture, their language, and their customs. The development of American civilization since 1600 is, perhaps, the most impressive illustration of the important contributions of migrations to the building of a nation's culture. The fusion of the Norman and Anglo-Saxon cultures in England and that of Mongol, Byzantine, and western European elements in Russia are other examples of the cultural effect of migrations.

**Migrations as the key to the history of civilization.** According to Andrew Reid Cowan, a stimulating English writer on history and politics, the main reason for the fall of civilizations in the past has been the invasion of mature, rich, and settled cultures by warlike and more barbarous nomads. Culture and prosperity appear to reduce warlike capacities and military prowess. Hence, as soon as a civilization was able to produce prosperity and display, it offered itself as an invitation to attack and spoliation by envious nomads. Cowan points to such historic episodes as the Kassite invasion of Mesopotamia, the invasion of the Egypt by the Hyksos, the Median and Persian conquest of Babylonia, the Macedonian conquest of Hellas and the Near East, the Germanic and Hunnish invasions of the Roman Empire, and the Mongol invasions of western Asia and eastern Europe as examples.

The settled and mature civilizations rarely seemed to be able to hold off the marauding nomads by hand-to-hand fighting with spears, swords, battle-axes, bows and arrows, and the like, which the nomads could also procure. But the invention of gunpowder changed all this. This provided the settled civilizations with implements of warfare which they could procure in greater profusion and better quality than the poorer nomadic peoples. From this time onward, civilized groups could more than hold their own against nomadic invaders, and established civilizations had a greater prospect of permanent existence. As an explanation of many leading trends in history down to modern times, this view possesses much merit. But Cowan failed to reckon with the fact that improved military technology would also provide mature civilizations with the means for their own destruction.

Another very important idea in regard to the effect of migrations on the course of civilization has been offered by Professor Frederick J. Teggart in his book, *The Processes of History.* According to Professor Teggart, the most dynamic factor in the rise and spread of civilization has been human migrations. If a civilization is cut off from external contacts, it tends to become stagnant; migrations must bring in new ideas and impulses if civilization is to thrive. These influences stimulate the conflict of social ideas, create new cultural patterns, and hasten the abandonment of outworn practices. New vistas of thought and behavior are thus opened and the way is cleared for social innovations and the further progress of civilization.

An important qualification in regard to the notion of human migrations has been set forth by the eminent English physical anthropologist, Sir Arthur Keith. He holds that, while migrations have been very important in shaping history in the last ten thousand years or so, they began very late in human experience, which runs back well over a million years. In his *New Theory of Human Evolution,* Keith holds that it was the fixity of the habitat and the isolation of social groups for tens of thousands of years that led to the inbreeding which he regards as the explanation of the origin of the various types of prehistoric men and the main races of mankind today.

## Some Major Historic Migrations

**Prehistoric migrations.** The earliest migrations, so far as we can trace them, began on the continent of Asia, which many regard as the "cradle of the human race." From this area, prehistoric groups seem to have moved out in all directions. One outstanding migration in primitive times was the first invasion of America. The earliest settlement in the Western world was made from ten to twenty thousand years ago by Mongolians (peoples of the yellow race) who came from Asia in successive migrations through the Bering Straits area and then moved down the continent as far as South America. The American Indian traces his ancestry to these early Mongoloid migrants, distantly related to the present-day Chinese.

Only a few of the migratory movements in Europe and Asia can be mentioned here. Beginning in prehistoric times, Europe has been settled by peoples who came from Africa and Asia. It is widely believed that the ancestors of the two long-headed European racial types, Nordics and Mediterraneans, came in from Africa across the land bridges which then connected the two continents. Hence they are known as the "Eurafrican" race. The Mediterranean race spread around the entire shore of the Mediterranean Sea. Others believe that the Nordic types came from the neighborhood of the Caspian Sea. In either case, they came from outside of Europe.

The ancestors of the round-headed peoples (called Alpines) who now live in Europe, probably came from Asia in the late Stone Age and settled along the highland area from the Balkans to France. They were, in part at least, the ancestors of the present Celtic and Slavic types. Alpine peoples, first the Achaeans and then the Dorians, moved down into the Greek peninsula between 2500 and 1100 B.C. They pushed over into Crete and destroyed the high native culture there during the fourteenth century B.C. In the early fourth century B.C., the round-headed Gauls (an Alpine group) began their great migrations. They crossed the Channel into Britain and Ireland, swept down over Italy, and overran most of Germany and the Balkans.

**Medieval migrations.** Beginning in the first century B.C., the Germanic tribes made devastating raids into the Roman Empire. These later developed into a series of migrations which lasted until well into the Middle Ages. It is thought that the German tribes had been forced out of their homes around what is now the Ukraine by the warlike Mongoloid Huns, who moved into Europe when their western Asiatic pasture lands dried up. Beginning in the seventh century, the Moslems—originally the Arab followers of Mohammed—spread over western Asia, northern Africa, and Spain. They threatened to occupy all of western Europe, but were turned back by Charles Martel at the battle of Tours in 732.

A wave of Mongols, or Tartars, swept over Asia in the thirteenth century and menaced eastern Europe. As late as the fifteenth century, the Mohammedan Turks captured Constantinople and ended the existence of the Byzantine, or Eastern Roman Empire. These warlike Turks moved on and, for a time, seemed likely to overcome Western

Europe. But the Christian army of John Sobieski, king of Poland, turned back the infidels from the gates of Vienna in 1683.

**Modern migrations.** The most impressive migrations in history, however, have been those of Europeans to our own country, to the Far East, and to Africa. These began at the close of the fifteenth century, when Columbus and Vasco da Gama discovered sea routes to America and the East Indies, respectively. This expansion of Europe was the chief factor in the creation of modern civilization. It launched the great movement of world colonization which has not yet entirely run its course. Over 60 million Europeans have left Europe since the days of Columbus to seek new homes in foreign regions.

## Immigration to the United States

**Causes of migrations to the United States.** Immigration to the United States differed from earlier migrations in that it was, for the most part, peaceful. Moreover, it was a movement not of an entire race or people, but of families, individuals, and small groups who broke away from the associations of their homelands.

The standard motives, economic, political, and religious, that brought immigrants to North America during the colonial period have already been discussed. Many were so eager to migrate to America that they sold their labor for a period of time to anyone who would pay their passage across the Atlantic. These people were called redemptioners and indentured servants. After they had "worked out" their passage money, they were free to do as they pleased. In some of the colonies redemptioners and indentured servants numbered half or more of the early settlers.

Not all immigrants, however, came voluntarily. Some were transported from Europe to America by force. England saw in America a profitable and convenient place to get rid of her undesirables, and transported some 50,000 criminals to this country. Paupers were also sent here in large numbers. Kidnapping in England and on the continent also helped to supply the demand for labor in the colonies. The colonists welcomed all able-bodied comers, for extensive manpower was needed to develop the country.

**Encouragement of migration to the United States.** There was little or no opposition to immigration into America until about 1850. In fact, even in the period during and following the Civil War, immigrants, for a time, were encouraged to come here by both the national government and private industry. Congress, wishing to settle the West, passed the Homestead Act in 1862, offering 160 acres of land free to those who declared their intention of becoming citizens. After 1865, many workers were needed in the new factories and mills, and for railroad construction and farm work. The cities required immigrant labor to erect new buildings and public works. Employers even sent representatives to Europe to contract for workers, holding out the bait of high wages and improved living conditions. Newly-arrived immigrants often wrote back home of the wonders of the new land. America was pictured as the immigrant's dream, a Utopia, where anyone, regardless of his nationality, could achieve economic, political, and religious freedom.

**Immigrants to the United States before 1870.** The history of immigration into the United States may be divided into two main periods. The first, sometimes called early immigration, extended from colonial times to 1870; the second, or mass immigration, covered the period from 1870 to 1914, especially from 1890 to 1914.

The majority of immigrants in the colonial period were of English and Scotch-Irish stock. About 500,000 came from the British Isles in the seventeenth century and approximately 1,500,000 in the eighteenth. The Scotch-Irish contingent from Ulster in Northern Ireland is estimated to have amounted to at least 500,000; they came mainly in the middle of the eighteenth century, impelled chiefly by the great Ulster famine of 1740. Paupers and criminals, as we have seen, comprised a considerable element of the English migration in colonial times. The English were also mainly responsible for the importation of over two million Negroes from Africa, to work as slaves on the plantations of the South and the West Indies.

A considerable number of persecuted German Protestants were encouraged to migrate to America by the British, who paid part of their expenses. Many of them settled in Pennsylvania and have come to be known as the "Pennsylvania Dutch." The Germans had suffered from rulers who swung back and forth between Lutheranism, Calvinism, and Roman Catholicism, and tried to impose their beliefs on the people. Added to this religious persecution was the misery caused in Germany by the wars of religion and the wars of Louis XIV in the seventeenth century.

Small groups came to the colonies from other nations, among them Spain, France, the Netherlands, and Sweden. Except for some settlements in Louisiana, Florida, the Southwest, and California, few French and Spanish migrated to what is now the United States. Louisiana was settled by the French, New York by the Dutch, and Delaware by Swedes and Finns.

After the Napoleonic wars and their attendant misery, there was a great increase of migration from Europe to the United States. The growth of the textile industry in New England after 1789 provided an economic attraction to those seeking employment in new lands. The opening of the American West, where both freedom and land were guaranteed, was a further inducement to the poor and oppressed Europeans. Some of the newcomers settled in the rising industrial towns of the East, others in the newly-opened farming areas west of the Alleghenies. The completion of the Erie Canal in 1825 facilitated the westward migration.

All through the first half of the nineteenth century, political oppression and unrest continued in Europe, and millions came here in the hope of securing economic and political freedom. Before 1860, Irish and German immigrants predominated. The potato famine of 1846–1847 greatly swelled Irish immigration; in two decades, 1840–1860, approximately 1,700,000 Irish came to this country. They were the first to settle to any great extent in the new urban centers, where they exercised a deep influence on political, economic, and religious developments. Though the Germans were attracted by cheap land or by growing industrialization, a chief cause of their migration in this period was political. When the revolutions of 1830 and 1848 failed, thousands of German republicans and liberals fled to the United States. About 1,380,000 Germans entered this country from 1840 to 1860. Many settled in the Midwest and were an important element in the Union army during the Civil War.

Scandinavian lands supplied large numbers of substantial and hard-working immigrants in the latter half of the nineteenth century. They settled mainly in North and South Dakota, Iowa, Nebraska, and Minnesota, and made their living by farming, lumbering, and dairying.

**Mass migration and new types of immigrants after 1870.** Improved ocean transportation, as well as European population growth, greatly stimulated immigration from Europe after 1870. About 25 million persons entered the United States between 1870 and 1914, or over half the total migration since the discovery of America in 1492. The major causes of this great transatlantic movement were economic: the rapidly multiplying industries sought cheap labor, while free western land, provided by the Homestead Act, beckoned to the land-hungry European peasants.

Just as significant as the increased volume of immigration were the changes in the racial composition and nationality of the majority of the immigrants. In the early immigration, most of the newcomers had been Teutonic types from northwestern Europe. After 1870, however, the English, Germans, and Scandinavians were far outnumbered by peoples who came from central and southern Europe; between 1890 and 1914, two-thirds of our immigrants came from these areas, with those from Italy and Austria-Hungary heading the list in the 1890's. Russia and Poland supplied the largest number between 1900 and 1914. Many of these were Jews, who had fled from fierce political and religious persecution and settled in the cities of the East and Middle West, where a large number entered mercantile and professional occupations.

**Rise of restrictive legislation.** Large-scale immigration continued until the outbreak of the first world war in 1914, after which it was checked by restrictive legislation, which we shall discuss later. Many persons felt that those who came after 1870 were undesirable, because they were less literate than earlier immigrants, were willing to work for low wages, had low living standards, and came from countries where autocracy, not democracy, was the form of government. They contended that the southern and central Europeans could not be absorbed so readily into the American way of life as the Teutonic types and would lower our standards of living. Those opposed to the new

# TRENDS OF IMMIGRATION

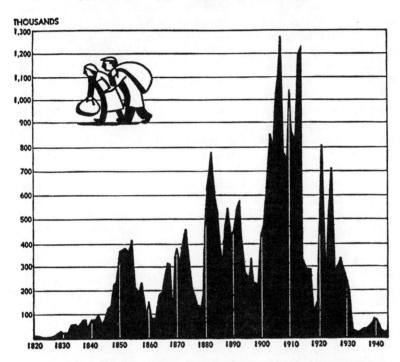

GRAPHIC ASSOCIATES FOR PUBLIC AFFAIRS COMMITTEE, INC.

Graph showing the great influx of immigrants from 1900 to 1914, and the remarkable decline since the restrictive legislation of the 1920's.

immigration were successful in 1921 and 1924 in blocking further large-scale immigration. Immigration problems now involve mainly the task of adapting those already here to the pattern of American life, though there has been a considerable temporary revival of immigration since 1945.

**Immigrants from the Far East.** Any discussion of immigration must include an account of the Chinese and Japanese, who, for the most part, settled in the Pacific Coast area, where their presence created serious economic and social problems.

Chinese immigration began about the time that gold was discovered in California (1848), but the Chinese had a more urgent reason for leaving his homeland than to prospect for gold. The Opium War with England in 1840–1842 and the later Taiping rebellion caused such misery and destruction in southeastern China that large numbers of Chinese sought to emigrate. About 25,000 poured into California in the three years following 1848. They were welcomed at first as laborers in the mines, in lumber camps, and on the railroads. But the completion of the first period of railroad construction in the 1870's left thousands of Chinese stranded and unemployed in the West.

Animosity towards the Chinese soon arose. Fantastic stories of their wicked heathen practices began to spread. Sober citizens decided that something must be done to prevent California from being overrun with "yellow foreigners." As a result, Congress passed a law in 1882 which barred the entry of Chinese laborers for ten years. More drastic legislation was passed in 1904, excluding all Chinese, except students and visiting professional persons. A considerable number, however, have been smuggled in since that time. In 1940, there were 77,504 Chinese in the United States. The rigors of our Chinese exclusion policy were slightly relaxed after Pearl Harbor, and resident Chinese were authorized to become American citizens on July 4, 1946.

Most of the stories circulated about the wicked practices of the Chinese were, of course, false. Opposition to the Chinese had an economic basis. They were able to live on a pittance and, hence, to accept very low ("coolie") wages. American laborers felt that their presence constituted a serious threat to our wage levels and standards of living. Moreover, the great contrast in ideas, habits, and culture between the Orientals and the whites made real understanding and warm friendship between them exceedingly difficult.

Japanese immigration did not begin until after the passage of the Chinese Exclusion Act in 1882. The Japanese also settled, for the most part, on the west coast, whose inhabitants soon developed intense hostility to them because they were not docile, like the Chinese, but ambitious to get ahead in the world. They became successful farmers, worked hard and long, and lived simply. In the early twentieth century, Japanese farmers produced 90 per cent of the asparagus of California, about half the green vegetables and sugar beets, and much of the fruit and berries. In 1940, there were 127,000 Japanese in the continental United States; 87 per cent of them lived in California, Washington, and Oregon. The number of Japanese in the country had declined by over 10,000 between 1930 and 1940.

California passed laws to prevent the Japanese from owning land. Because the laws were often evaded, the whites were resentful. Finally, antagonism led to the negotiation of a "Gentleman's Agreement" between Japan and the United States in 1907, by the terms of which Japan promised to prohibit further emigration of laborers to our country. The Japanese government carried out the agreement honorably and Japanese immigration ceased. We gratuitously offended the Japanese in 1924 by a law that specifically excluded the Japanese from entry and settlement, though there was no need whatever for such legislation at the time.

## Economic, Social, and Political Problems
## Produced by Immigration

**Criticism of mass immigration.** It was mainly after 1890 that immigration became an acute social problem. Nearly every ship brought its cargo of immigrants; the large amount of free homestead land had been occupied; and, in the crowded cities, the native-born workers complained that aliens were taking their jobs.

**Immigration, the wage level, and working conditions.** The immigrant was criticized because he was allegedly willing to work for lower wages than the native. But let us consider his side of the question. He needed a job to keep from starving, was unfamiliar with American wage rates, and the pay offered seemed large compared with the pittance he formerly received in his overcrowded homeland. Who was at fault—the foreigner who worked for low wages, thus lowering the wage-scale of all workers, or the American employer who deliberately kept the immigrant on a lower standard of living by underpaying him? One must not forget that many employers actually encouraged immigrants to come here because they provided a supply of cheap labor; as late as 1910 the Immigration Commission asserted that the income of foreign labor was still below that of native labor.

It has been claimed that foreign labor was often employed to break strikes, thus weakening the strength of the American labor movement. It is true that, in our early industrial history, the employer whose native-born employees refused to work unless he granted their demands would often hire immigrants to keep his factory in operation. However, it was not long before the foreigners, eager for more money and shorter hours, joined the unions when they could. Today, the foreign-born workers and their descendants are often among the most enthusiastic union members.

**Immigration and unemployment.** The relation of immigration to unemployment is frequently overlooked, since most of our unemployment problems are blamed on business slumps and the displacement of workers by machines. A considerable part of the responsibility, however, rests with those who permitted the tremendous mass movement into this country between 1900 and 1914.

Thirteen million aliens came to the United States during this period, the great majority of them settling in the cities and the mining areas. At the same time, a considerable migration of native Americans from country areas to cities also took place. The result was a great massing of the working population in our cities, where they depended entirely on their jobs and lost all other means of subsistence. Whereas nearly every country family had a vegetable plot to depend on for some of its food, the city family depended entirely on wages. When jobs were lost during the depression of the early 1930's, the average city man had to go on relief, or seek work on the WPA or some kindred relief agency.

Urban concentration was aggravated by the war of 1914–1918, when factories were working overtime, and men and women were needed to take the place of those in the armed services. After the war, business boomed for about a decade. The building industry revived on a grand scale, the automobile industry expanded, and new industries such as radio appeared.

The year 1929 is generally considered as the beginning of the depression; yet, before this time, there was considerable unemployment in the United States, with often as many as 5 million out of work. During the depths of the depression in the early 1930's between 15 and 17 million persons were unable to find jobs. The excess supply of labor produced by immigration became evident as machines and the depression lessened the number of jobs available in industry. The children of the great mass of 1900–1914 immigrants were ready by the late 1920's to take up employment in factories which were already beginning to curtail employment or close down. When our economy ceased to expand in 1929, and, instead, began to contract, the hordes of immigrants and their large families were among the first to suffer.

**Social problems created by immigration.** This is the negative side of immigration. There are positive aspects as well. Immigrants have provided not only manpower for industry, but also a vast army of consumers and a large market for goods which could not otherwise have been sold. But we must note that the immigrant, who long earned less money than the native-born worker, generally had lower living standards. Moreover, certain types of immigrants, especially the Italians, tended to save a good deal of their money, and send some of it back to the old country. A great number also returned to their native land after accumulating a modest fortune. From 1902 to 1924, the number of Italians who returned to Italy equaled 62.8 per cent of those who entered the United States in this period.

Wretched living conditions have provided one of the chief social problems arising from immigration. Immigrants have been criticized because, unable to afford homes in better residential districts, they have herded together in city slums, forming huge colonies of fellow-countrymen—"Little Italys," "Little Polands," "Little Russias," and the like. Because many were unable to speak our language and understand our ways, they clung to the customs of the fatherland.

It is, to be sure, very unfair to blame the immigrants for concentrating in wretched slum areas; they would have been only too glad to live in better homes had they been able to earn enough to pay a substantial rent.

**Immigration and crime.** Most studies have shown that the most markedly criminal element in the population, at least in our larger cities, are the children of foreign-born parents.

We must remember, however, that this situation arises mainly because of social and cultural maladjustments rather than from racial influences. Slum children grow up under conditions of deprivation and misery. Having few or no public places such as parks, play-grounds, and club rooms, to spend their leisure hours, they have often resorted to association with evil companions. The children of immigrants may turn to crime not because they are of an inferior race or nationality, but because they have not assimilated American customs and culture, and have little opportunity for healthy play and self-expression.

The adjustment of the immigrants to the American pattern of living has been difficult because of the great numbers involved and the many and diverse cultural groups represented. The immigrant has often been slow to learn our ways because he lives among his kind. His children go to American schools and often come to resent the Old World ways of their parents. It is this maladjustment of the children of immigrants that is partly responsible for their criminal and other unfortunate tendencies. They have broken away, in part, from the controls formerly exerted by their native culture, but have not become effectively adjusted to the discipline imposed by American customs.

**Assimilation problems.** Immigrants who came here after 1890 were less literate (that is, less able to read or write) than those who came in the earlier period. The total illiteracy or unfamiliarity with English of many immigrants proved a severe handicap to their children in school.

Some persons have thought that the immigrant should be encouraged to isolate himself and retain his native culture, so far as possible. But this brings unfortunate results, because it makes for too many divergences in American life. Others would force the immigrant rapidly to blend his traditions and beliefs with the basic American culture. This latter or "melting pot" technique has been used in the public schools, where the children of immigrants learn the English language and follow courses of study laid out by Americans.

But there are disadvantages and dangers in brusquely depriving the immigrant child of most of his Old World heritage. Many an American-educated immigrant youth, his home life upset by strife between the older generation and the new, has left home and drifted into crime.

The social settlement, perhaps, has done the most to help the immigrant to adjust to American ways. The settlement workers have realized the necessity of proceeding slowly in breaking down cultural barriers and imposing new standards and beliefs. But the settlements, with their citizenship classes and their clubs and play groups, can only reach a small percentage of the alien population of a large city. Other agencies have assisted in the process of assimilation. Some large business concerns, for example, have supported English classes, because they realize that the foreigner who speaks English well learns efficient methods of work more readily.

**Acquiring citizenship.** Not all immigrants can become American citizens. Orientals were totally barred until 1946, when the Chinese were allowed to become citizens. The qualifications for other groups are essentially the following: One must be a member of either the white or African race, twenty-one years of age, of good moral character, able to speak English, and devoted to the principles of the Constitution; he must have entered the country legally, renounced his former allegiance, and taken the oath of allegiance to the United States; and he must prove he is neither an anarchist nor a polygamist.

Today, most judges are trying to impress upon the new American the honor of citizenship. In the past he was, too often, "run through the mill," and received his naturalization papers without fully realizing the responsibilities they entailed.

Certain requirements still keep some aliens from going through the long process of naturalization. The Alien Registration Act of 1940 revealed that there were in the United States 4,900,000 unnaturalized aliens; it seems likely that many of these were avoiding naturalization because of the fixed and incidental expenses it entails, in many cases as high as $50. It was estimated that there were about 3 million aliens in 1945.

**Immigration and the American party system.** Hearty welcome has usually been given to immigrants by our political parties. In the early days, delegates of politicians met the boats, sometimes rushing the immigrants illegally to the voting booths even before they found places to live. Though the alien was welcomed so joyously mainly for his vote, yet he did receive something in return. Active participation in the political group made him feel that he had a real place in American democratic life.

Down to about 1933, the Irish probably exerted greater influence on American politics in proportion to their numbers than any other alien group. They usually remained faithful to the Democratic party. In many cities, like New York, the Irish controlled city government and the party machine for generations. The Germans who came to the United States after 1848 generally accepted the then liberal views of the new Republican party, and to this same political party most of the Scandinavians, who later settled in North and South Dakota, Minnesota, Iowa, and Nebraska, also adhered.

The Slavs, especially the Poles, have recently become an important element in American politics. Settling in the cities, they have often contested Irish supremacy. At first, the Slavs joined the Republican party because this was the organization favored by most of their employers. But many did not like Prohibition, enforced under Republican auspices, and turned to the Democrats. Now, they form a significant group in the Democratic ranks of Illinois, Michigan, Pennsylvania, and New York.

The Italians also tended to join the Republican party to please their employers, but they also were unhappy about Prohibition and many deserted to the Democrats. After the first world war, and especially after 1933, increasing numbers of naturalized immigrants became politically more alert and active.

The most deplorable effect of immigration on American politics has been the close connection of immigrant groups with the corrupt political machines, although the latter by no means found a lack of native citizens to support them. We should not entirely blame the immigrant, therefore, for our own failure to educate a large portion of our foreign-born to the real opportunities and duties of democracy.

**Immigrant contributions to American culture.** Whatever the social, economic, and political problems which the immigrants have created, they have liberally imparted to us some of their rich and varied cultural heritage. In the last three decades, especially, America has attracted many of the best minds and finest personalities of Europe. As intolerance and persecution engulfed one European country after another, numerous sensitive and oppressed spirits fled to what is still the "land of the free." Here came great scientists like Albert Einstein, literary masters like Thomas Mann, composers like Arnold Schoenberg, statesmen like Count Carlo Sforza, dramatists like Henri Bernstein and Ferenc Molnar, and painters like George Grosz, not to mention hosts of less known savants, actors, cinema producers, writers, artists, musicians, and statesmen. Since 1933, an increasing portion of the most cultivated European types have migrated to the United States. There are a large number of refugee professors in American colleges and universities. Many refugees have become American citizens.

In the words of Louis Untermeyer, "America may be the last frontier of culture." If the civilizations of Europe are destroyed by war or rendered culturally sterile by totalitarianism, the United States may be, perhaps, the last bastion of a free culture, assimilating and protecting the priceless learning and wisdom for which men have struggled since the Dark Ages. This will be true, however, only if the United States can welcome these contributions, not refusing them because they are "foreign."

The cultural benefits of recent immigration, however, should not blind us to one of its less promising aspects. The refugees from the Old World often carry their former quarrels and hatreds to the New. Eager to rescue their native lands from the barbarism which has overtaken them, many have helped to arouse an unnecessary belligerency in our countrymen. The European immigrant, throughout our national history, has given us an opportunity to learn the international point of view. But he has also helped to drag us into the bloody wars of the unhappy continent on which he was born.

## Immigration Policies of the United States

**Main periods of our immigration policy.** American immigration policies have passed through four phases: (1) encouragement, up to

1882; (2) regulation, from 1882 to 1921; (3) severe restriction, from 1921 to 1941; and (4) some modification of restrictions in the 1940's.

**Early encouragement of immigration.** In the colonial era, immigrants were not only welcomed but were compelled to come through kidnapping, forced labor, and the like. After the Revolutionary War, there was no opposition to foreigners. The rising factory system needed laborers. The nation was expanding geographically and industrially. Settlers were induced to take up land beyond the Alleghenies. The only laws relating to immigration were designed to encourage newcomers and to promote their welfare.

Immigration was encouraged in every way possible until about 1830, at which time native-born laborers began to fear the competition of foreign workers. They were sometimes joined by social reformers, who dreaded the influx of paupers and criminals. During the so-called Protestant Crusade of the 1840's and 1850's, many vigorously demanded the exclusion of Roman Catholic immigrants, especially Irish Catholics.

Despite the agitation for anti-immigration legislation, however, none was passed. During the Civil War, opinion changed in favor of immigration, for laborers were needed to replace men who had joined the armies. Some laws were passed which encouraged immigration, like the Homestead Act of 1862.

**Restriction of immigration.** The Immigration Law of 1882, which excluded criminals, paupers, the insane, and the disabled, marked the beginning of positive Federal control of immigration. Also in 1882, as we noted, Chinese laborers were excluded. A famous law of 1885 forbade the entry of contract laborers and strikebreakers. The Bureau of Immigration was created in 1906, to keep careful records of immigration. The next year, the famous "Gentleman's Agreement" was made with Japan.

An Immigration Commission was appointed by Congress in 1907. Its full report, submitted in 1910, deeply affected the later immigration policy of our country. It recommended that immigration be restricted by means of a literacy test; that unmarried and unskilled workers be excluded; that no country or race be permitted excessive immigration; that the amount of money which immigrants must possess on landing be increased; and that the head tax be raised.

A law was passed in 1917 which required the immigrant to be able to read and write some language. The head tax, which was only fifty cents in 1882, $1 in 1894, and $2 in 1903, jumped to $8 in 1917.

**Trend toward exclusion of immigrants.** This legislation of 1917 was but a prelude to the famous quota system introduced in 1921. The annual entry of foreigners was limited by the Act of 1921 to three per cent of those of each nationality who were living in the United States in 1910. For instance, if the Finns living here had numbered 15,000 in 1910, only 450 would be allowed to enter annually after

1921. Not more than one-fifth of the yearly quota could be admitted in any one month.

The opponents of immigration were not even satisfied with this drastic law. In 1924, the quota was reduced to two per cent of the population of each nationality, this time estimated on the basis of the 1890 census. The 1924 law thus not only reduced the total immigration from Europe, but also favored certain nationalities, the year 1890 being chosen as the basis for estimating the quota because the migration from the southern and central European countries had not then reached the tremendous proportions it had by 1910. The new quota favored Germany, the British Isles, the Netherlands, the Scandinavian countries, and France. Beginning with 1927, no more than 150,000 persons could be admitted in any year. The policy established by the laws of 1921 and 1924, called the "National Origins Plan," is still in force.

The restrictive legislation, together with the depression, all but terminated immigration from the Old World for more than a decade. The net population gain from immigration in the 1930's was only 68,693; between 1930 and 1935, some 103,654 more emigrants left the country than came in as immigrants. The foreign-born population dropped from 13,172,754 in 1920 to 11,419,138 in 1940.

**New spurt in immigration.** As a result of devastation and misery during and after the second world war, immigration to the United States began, once more, to move upward, especially after 1945—from 38,119 in 1945 to 170,570 in 1948. There was a great influx of aliens in addition to the immigrants under the quota system. In the three years 1946–1948, some 1,472,000 aliens were admitted, only 326,000 of these as immigrants. Owing to our sympathy for oppressed persons, a good deal of illegal immigration was winked at. How many came in illegally is not known, but they probably numbered at least as many as the legal entrants.

Immigration from Latin America was not restricted by the act of 1924. Therefore, there has been an influx of immigrants from South America, Central America, and Mexico.[1]

**Our present immigration policy unscientific.** Has our immigration policy merely swayed from one unwise extreme to another? Some critics say that we have not based our legislation on a scientific study of either our own needs or those of the immigrant. It would have been wiser if immigration had been moderately restricted by 1890, instead of allowing an avalanche of foreigners to descend on us until the first world war and then suddenly shutting the doors to them in 1921 and 1924. Moreover, the whole quota system is jaundiced and unscientific. There is no proof that one national group is better than any other. Our restrictive policy should be based upon a more

---

[1] See below, p. 211.

rigorous examination of each immigrant, in order to get the best physical and mental types, whatever their nationality.

## Forced Migration during Second World War and the Problem of Displaced Persons

**Forced migrations during and after the second world war.** Because the matter directly touches American public problems, with respect both to our appropriations for relief abroad and to our policies about temporarily relaxing our immigration restrictions, we should say a word about the movement of peoples during and after the second world war. In the course of the second world war, both the Nazis and the Russians moved millions of persons about, as labor battalions and the like. Other millions fled before the advances of German and Russian troops. It is estimated that about seven million had returned to their home countries or had been repatriated by the end of 1947. But, at the outset of the year 1950, it was believed that at least one million were still what we call Displaced Persons, scattered from Great Britain to China and living on a veritable subsistence level under the most distressing conditions. As late as 1948, about 850,000 were living in crude and crowded camps in Europe, mainly in Germany and Austria. By 1950, they had been reduced to about 400,000.

**Main groups of displaced persons.** These displaced persons fell into some four main groups in Europe: (1) the survivors of the Nazi labor battalions of the war period, mainly Slavs and Rumanians; (2) anti-Communist refugees from the Baltic states who fled before the Russian invasion, as the Soviet armies closed in on Hitler; (3) slave laborers, mostly Germans, held by Russia, Czechoslovakia, and France; and (4) Jews, mainly refugees from the postwar anti-Semitism in Poland.

These displaced persons have provided the basis for serious international crises. The Jews sought entry into Palestine, but the British objected; violence flared up and resulted in the British withdrawal from Palestine, the Israeli-Arab War, and general confusion in this region. The retention of many German slave laborers by Russia, Czechoslovakia, and France has increased and perpetuated the ill-feeling and bitterness in Central Europe. Efforts have been made to permit 500,000 displaced persons to enter the United States. In 1948, Congress passed a law permitting the entry of 205,000 displaced persons during the next two years. In 1950, a new law was passed increasing the number who could be admitted to 344,000.

**Expelled Germans and Japanese.** Much more numerous than the groups usually classified as displaced persons are the Germans who have been expelled with incredible brutality from Czechoslovakia, Hungary, the Balkans, Poland, and those portions of eastern Germany handed over to Poland. The number is estimated as between ten and fifteen millions. They have been forced to crowd into a Germany which has lost its main food-producing areas and is able to provide even near-starvation rations only through extensive foreign relief.[2]

In addition to the displaced persons in Europe and Siberia, three millions of Japanese were forcibly brought back from Korea, Manchuria, and China, to intensify the struggle for existence in an already overcrowded Japan whose economy and capacity for self-support had been shattered by the war. The Germans and Japanese torn from their previous places of residence are usually classified as "expellees" rather than as displaced persons.

## Migrations within the United States

**Settling the frontier.** The story of the frontier movement is dramatically told in books like Francis Parkman's *The Oregon Trail*, Emerson Hough's *The Covered Wagon*, and several volumes by Hamlin Garland. Travel was slow and perilous before the building of the transcontinental railroads. Many persons died on their way to the West. But enough determined people overcame the hardships to settle the entire central and western part of the country. Thousands of immigrants, in the decade before the Civil War, fired with the zeal of Abolition and Free Soil politics, and helped by the treasury of the Emigrant Aid Society, crossed the plains to set up free communities in Kansas and Nebraska. Railroads were built and the frontier was pushed ever westward. By 1890, most of the desirable farming land had been taken up under the Homestead Act, and the historic frontier era came to an end.

**Traits of the frontiersman.** The westward migration strengthened some of the best American traits. Frontier society was intensely nationalistic and patriotic. The frontiersman was loyal to the national government and had little sympathy for the state-rights movement. The struggle to make a living and to subdue nature developed a respect for individual industry and thrift. Democracy was fostered. Optimism and idealism flourished. Every pioneer felt that he had an opportunity to carve his own future. The "American dream"— the hope of universal freedom and prosperity—gained in popularity. The frontier was responsible for the rise of many programs of social and economic reform, among them the Greenback, Granger, and Populist movements. None of these was successful in winning decisive national victories, but each nourished the spirit of reform and social justice, so necessary to democracy.

**The Mormons.** A number of special migrations contributed to this westward movement. An important one was the Mormon trek to Utah. The Mormons were founded in central New York, in 1823, by a religious dreamer, Joseph Smith. Smith and his followers soon

---

[2] See Roger N. Baldwin, John Haynes Holmes, John Dewey, *et al.*, *The Land of the Dead.* Committee against Mass Expulsion, New York, 1947.

moved to Missouri, where they were not welcome. They then went to Nauvoo, Illinois; again the natives were hostile. Smith was killed by a mob in 1844. Led by Brigham Young, the Mormons sought a new home in the West. In 1847, they settled in what is now Salt Lake City, Utah, a desert inhabited by the warlike Ute Indians. The Mormons placated the Indians, and, by energy and hard work, irrigated the region and made it productive.

The Mormons profited from trade with the pioneers on their way to California. The followers of Brigham Young believed in polygyny (having more than one wife), but this practice was abolished in 1890, in order that Utah might be admitted to the Union. The Mormons have built up a powerful and closely-knit political machine and a prosperous economic community.

**The Gold Rush.** Gold was the magic word which started a great migration to California in 1848 and 1849. A journey to California today means a quick trip in an airplane or train, or a scenic motor drive over smooth highways; but, in 1848, it was a long and hazardous journey. In long stretches of the West there were no roads or bridges, and the trails led through the territory of hostile Indians. Some travelers took the long sea voyage around Cape Horn to California. Others took a ship to Panama, then rode across the isthmus on horseback and waited until passage could be obtained on a boat for San Francisco. Thousands died of yellow fever in Central America. Yet, despite the large numbers of adventurers who perished on the way, more than 80,000 had reached the "golden land" by 1850.

**Negro and Mexican migration.** In the United States itself, there have been two important recent racial migrations. Some 2,300,000 Negroes in the years 1916–1919, 1921–1924, and 1941–1945, left southern farms and cities and headed for the northern industrial centers. Here they found work mainly in the factories and packing houses. The whites of the North objected to this sudden influx of Negroes, and serious race riots often resulted. The Negro migrations will be discussed more fully in the next chapter. Many Mexican laborers have drifted into the southwestern states, especially since 1921. While the census of 1940 listed only a little over a million Mexicans or persons of Mexican descent in the United States, the best students of the subject estimate that there are between 2,500,000 and 3,000,000 persons of mixed Mexican-Spanish-Indian blood or descent now resident in this country.

**Migratory workers.** In the last three decades, a serious social problem has developed in seasonal or migratory laborers who go from place to place to harvest grain and pick fruit. The United States Department of Labor estimates that there are between 750,000 and 1,500,000 of these migratory workers—"Harvest Nomads"—depending on the seasons and the general agricultural and business conditions. They follow the fruit and harvest line from Florida and California to the Middle West and Far West. Florida needs men in the winter and

# FLOW OF SEASONAL MIGRATORY FARM LABOR IN THE U.S.

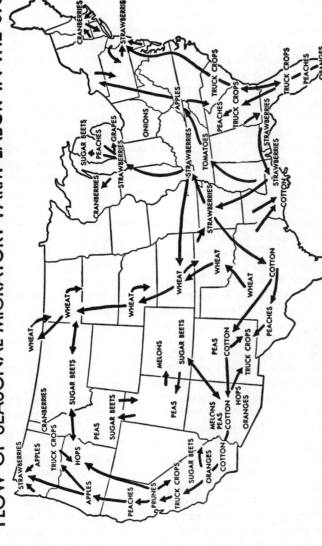

The chart indicates only direction, not volume.
The number of migratory farm workers in the different areas varies considerably from year to year.

*Courtesy of the Public Affairs Committee.*

spring to gather the citrus and berry crops. Georgia draws them for the peach crop; and, from there, they move northward for the straw-berry, potato, and vegetable seasons along the Atlantic seaboard. Some of the berry pickers follow the season all the way from the Gulf states to Lake Michigan. The Southwest calls for workers in the cotton fields. The beet fields of Utah and Colorado take care of many migrants until cold weather comes. The western states need laborers for the grain harvest. California and the Pacific Coast states are a mecca for seasonal workers. Over 150,000 men and women find work in the cotton, citrus fruit, hops, and vegetable harvests of this region from early spring until late fall.

Living conditions of migratory laborers are not satisfactory in any part of the country. Hobo jungles and dismal, unsanitary automobile camps often serve as settlements. Because of their excess numbers, they have been easily exploited by unscrupulous employers, who have paid wages too low to maintain a decent standard of living. Migratory workers have little recourse to labor unions because of the seasonal nature of their jobs. Educational conditions and child care are especially bad among the migratory workers. In 1949, the National Education Association estimated that there were a million children of migratory workers who were without any systematic or formal educational opportunities.

**"Grapes of Wrath" nomads.** It is estimated that, by 1935, mechanization had reduced the need for farm laborers by more than 350,000. Better seed, breeding stock, and farm practices cut the need by over 600,000 more by 1939. Hundreds of thousands of farm families were driven from their homes by drought in the 1930's. Erosion ousted others. As a result, the highways of the 1930's were filled with migrants, who, like nomads of early historic times, assembled their meager worldly possessions and sought better living conditions. Probably over a million and a half such Americans took to the road in the 1930's in old automobiles—"jalopies"—or in buses.

Refugees from the dust bowl of the western states poured into California during the depression at such a rapid rate that the taxpayers of the state were aroused and organized an attempt to keep out poverty-stricken migrants. The Supreme Court declared this effort at exclusion unconstitutional. As a matter of fact, however, more outsiders moved into California in the 1920's than in the 1930's— two million as against 1,100,000 in the latter decade. It was mainly "hard times" which aroused Californian opposition in the 1930's.

**Movement from backward areas to industrial centers.** Since the decade of the first world war, there has been a large migration of mountain folk from Kentucky, Tennessee, and other southern regions to Detroit and other northern industrial centers. This has been, in the main, a voluntary search for employment in the automobile and other industries, but it was also encouraged by open-shop employers who believed that it would prove more difficult to force these new-comers into organized labor movements.

**Persistent inter-regional migration of Americans.** Owing to the pop-ularity of John Steinbeck's *Grapes of Wrath* and to newspaper pub-licity, there is a common misapprehension that our continental or interstate migration is sporadic, made up mainly of poverty-stricken farmers fleeing the dust bowl. There has, actually, been a wide-spread and gradual movement in the last three decades from the whole central section of the country (from the Appalachians to the Rockies and from the Canadian to the Mexican border) to the Pacific Coast states, and, to a lesser extent, to the northeastern states. Proof that those who went to California were not all dust-bowl refugees is amply shown by the figures: less than one-fourth of those who settled in the state in the 1930's were former farmers or farm laborers. The magni-tude of interstate migration in recent times is shown by the careful estimate that there were at least four million migrants in each year from 1930 to 1940, and in 1937 there were over five million. The causes are "not only climatic reverses and soil depletion but also a large number of other situations—factors such as seasonal jobs, fluctu-ations in wages, the depletion of mineral and other natural resources, rise and decline of industries, technological displacements, population pressures, fluctuations in market conditions, migratory industries, and special demands for labor (such as New Deal construction projects and war and defense industries)." [3]

**Wartime migrations.** Interstate migration was greatly increased by the employment offered in war industries during the second world war. The new migrants drifted mainly towards manufacturing cen-ters, which had a great expansion as a result of war orders. It has been estimated that at least 15 million civilians voluntarily left their homes between 1940 and the end of the war to move into other counties and states, mainly to secure employment. There are no reliable figures as yet on what proportion returned to their homes after the war, but the Census Bureau reported in August, 1948, that some 12,338,000 persons had changed their state of residence between 1940 and 1947. Some 19,500,000 persons were living in a different county in 1946 from the one in which they were living in 1940.

**Forcible movement of Japanese in wartime.** One important case of wartime migration was the forcible evacuation of the Japanese from the western states. At the time of Pearl Harbor, there were about 127,000 Japanese in the country, some 113,000 of whom lived in California, Washington, Oregon, and Arizona. On the ground that these Japanese would be a military risk if allowed to remain in their homes, some 110,000 persons of Japanese ancestry were evacuated by

[3] "Schools and the 1940 Census," National Education Association Bulletin, No-vember, 1941, p. 216.

order of the War Department from their homes in these western states and moved to relatively isolated assembly centers and relocation projects, enclosed within barbed wire. Where work was provided, wages were low, and living conditions were bad. In retrospect, this action now appears to have been a needlessly harsh and undiscriminating product of wartime hysteria. The best authorities on the subject estimate that about 60 per cent of the evacuated Japanese had returned to their homes by 1950.

## Summary

In this chapter we have followed the migrations of people from prehistoric days to the modern era. We have noted the important part played by migrations in the distribution of population over the face of the earth, and in the development of the civilizations of the world. We have noted that, so far as numbers are concerned, the outstanding migration in the history of mankind has been the movement of about 40 million persons, mainly from Europe, into what is now the United States.

Immigration into the United States is divided into two periods: (1) early immigration, through the colonial period to 1870, when the people who drifted in came mainly from northwestern Europe; and (2) later immigration, since 1870, when the exodus from the northwestern countries decreased, and a tidal wave of immigrants came from southern and central Europe.

Many social, economic, and cultural problems have been produced by this excessive immigration and the diverse racial groups represented. Especially serious was the oversupply of laborers from 1929 to 1941.

Through the colonial period and down to about 1880, immigrants were welcomed to hasten the industrialization of the new country, but, later on, laws were passed to restrict the number of entrants. The United States immigration policy may be divided into three main phases: encouragement, regulation, and restriction, the latter amounting almost to exclusion from 1924 to 1940. There has been a considerable revival of immigration since 1940.

Our immigration problem today is mainly one of how to provide for the most successful assimilation of the large numbers who came in during the period from 1890 to 1914, and to find employment for their offspring.

During and after the second world war, forced migrations of peoples produced incredible hardships, created the pressing problem of displaced persons, and precipitated serious international crises.

There are also migrations within our borders which have produced special problems: (1) the two racial movements, Negro and Mexican, and (2) the westward trek of large numbers of seasonal laborers and dust-bowl refugees.

During the second world war there was an unprecedented shift of our population, especially from rural areas to urban armament centers.

## Selected References

Adamic, Louis, *From Many Lands,* Harper, 1940. Interesting propaganda for immigration and immigrants.

\* Anderson, Nels, *Men on the Move,* University of Chicago, 1940. The best book on hoboes and migratory workers.

\* Baldwin, R. N.; Holmes, J. H.; and Dewey, John, *The Land of the Dead.* New York: Committee against Mass Expulsion, 1947. A vivid, brief survey of the forcible expulsion of Germans, Jews, and others from their homelands after 1945. A narrative of incredible brutality, showing that the postwar action of the victors was in many ways more harsh than Hitler's treatment of conquered peoples.

Bernard, W. S. *et al., American Immigration Policy: A Reappraisal,* Harper, 1950. Critical history of the period since 1921, and a moderate argument for a more liberal policy.

Bloom, Leonard, and Riemer, Ruth, *The Socio-Economic Effects of the War on Japanese-Americans,* University of California Press, 1949. Best account of the impact of wartime evacuation experiences upon the Japanese.

\* Boudreau, F. G., and Kiser, C. V. (Eds.), *Postwar Problems of Migration.* New York: Milbank Memorial Fund, 1947. A very valuable symposium on postwar migrations, including several useful chapters on civilian migation in the United States during the period since 1939.

Davie, M. R., *World Immigration,* Macmillan, 1936. General study of migrations, with special reference to the United States.

Dees, J. W., *Flophouse,* Marshall Jones, 1948. Valuable sociological study of the life and attitudes of the homeless man.

Fairchild, H. P., *Immigration,* Macmillan, 1928. The standard and classic textbook on the immigration problem. Judicious in its appraisal of the effects of immigration.

——————, *The Melting Pot Mistake,* Little Brown, 1926. Criticism of the melting-pot procedure in the assimilation of immigrants by the leading American authority on immigration.

Gold, Michael, *Jews without Money,* Liveright, 1930. A graphic account of the life of the poorer Jewish immigrants to America.

Hansen, M. L., *The Atlantic Migration, 1607–1870,* Harvard University, 1940.

——————, *The Immigrant in American History,* Harvard University, 1940. Two very valuable historical studies of immigration to America.

\* Hartman, E. G., *The Movement to Americanize the Immigrant,* Columbia University Press, 1948. An excellent historical and sociological study of the American melting-pot technique in dealing with the immigrants.

Isaac, Julius, *The Economics of Migration,* Oxford University, 1947. Best study of economic forces encouraging human migration.

Kirkpatrick, Clifford, *Intelligence and Immigration,* Williams and Wilkins, 1926. The most scientific and objective study of the intellectual level of our immigrant population.

Konvitz, M. R., *The Alien and the Asiatic in American Law,* Cornell University, 1947. This is probably the best volume on the legal aspects of the rights of aliens and Asiatics in American society and the problems of naturalization.

Kulischer, E. M., *Europe on the Move,* Columbia University, 1948. Excellent review of European population movements from 1917 to 1947, including migrations overseas.

Ross, E. A., *The Old World in the New,* Century, 1914. A great sociologist's brief, critical analysis of the social effects of unrestricted immigration to America.

Seabrook, William B., *These Foreigners,* Harcourt, Brace, 1938. A highly favorable view of the contributions of immigration to American life.

Smith, Bradford, *Americans from Japan,* Lippincott, 1949. Authoritative study of Japanese immigration.

Stephenson, G. M., *A History of American Immigration,* Ginn, 1926. The standard treatment of the history of immigration to this country prior to the "national origins" legislation.

* Taft, D. R., *Human Migration,* Ronald, 1936. A careful work, well fortified with statistics, correcting many common prejudices about the immigration problem.

Thomas, D. S., and Hishimoto, Richard, *The Spoilage,* University of California Press, 1946. The definitive account of forced Japanese evacuation during the second world war.

* Utley, Freda, *The High Cost of Vengeance,* Regnery, 1949. Most reliable survey of postwar Europe. Fully reveals the horrors of the policies of the victorious United Nations since July, 1945.

* Wittke, Carl F., *We Who Built America,* Prentice-Hall, 1939. An appreciative interpretation of immigration, especially of that before 1890.

# CHAPTER XI

# The Race Problem and Race Contacts in the United States

## Racial Traits and Differences

**Race and American history.** The United States was settled as a result of the migration of peoples from every corner of the earth. To its shores have come men and women from England, Poland, Germany, Italy, Russia, Sweden, Norway, Switzerland, Japan, China, Africa, and many other countries and regions. As a result, the American population is a mixture of numerous races and nationalities. In the preceding chapter, we discussed some of the difficulties involved in adjusting so many different peoples to American ways of life; difficulties which have arisen, in large part, because of popular misunderstanding and ignorance. On few subjects are people more dogmatic and prejudiced than on race; yet, on few are they more woefully misinformed.

**Basic facts about races.** If one should ask a random group, "What is race?" one would receive about as many different answers as there were individuals in the group. Some would define race as a particular nation, like the "British race." Others would confuse "race" with an imaginary physical type, such as Arab or Jewish, or use the word to describe those speaking a certain type of language, as the "Latin race," lumping together the Spanish, French, and Italians. Some persons like to talk about an imaginary "pure" race, which existed in the dim past but has been "tainted" by mixture with other races. None of these conceptions of race is correct.

So far as we have any reliable characteristics and criteria of race, they are all physical. Several different forms of classification of the races of mankind have been proposed. Among the most common bases of classification are: (1) cranial formation, that is, the shape of the skull and the structure of the nose; (2) texture of the hair; and (3) the color of the skin.

On the basis of the shape of the skull, mankind has been divided into three types: longheaded, broadheaded, and intermediate between those; on the basis of the hair, we have the straight-haired, wooly-

197

haired, and an intermediate group of wavy-haired; on the basis of color of the skin, there are three main races—white, yellow, and black. Properly defined, the term *race* means a definite physical type, descended from a specific group of ancestors and, in that way, distinct from other peoples.

One of the oldest classification of mankind and one still in popular use is that based on the color of the skin. But the yellow (Mongolian), the black (Negro), and white (Caucasian) race each has other definite physical traits, in addition to the basic skin coloration. We may now roughly characterize the physical traits of each of these three traditional racial types.

Members of the yellow, or Mongolian, race have yellow skins and straight, black hair, slanting eyes, wide faces, and round skulls. Their stature shows great variations. The yellow race includes the Chinese, Tibetans, and Eskimos. The American Indians, usually called the "red men," are a branch of the yellow race. Because the Indian's skin is of a slightly different hue, many persons do not realize that he is related to the Chinese. The Japanese are a mixture of Mongolians and Malayans.

Members of the black (Negro) race have dark skin, wooly or kinky black hair, very long heads, and flat noses. Their stature varies all the way from very tall and stalwart types to pygmies.

The white race includes three main groups: the Nordic, the Mediterranean, and the Alpine. Though we refer to longheaded and roundheaded white men, the heads of all members of the white race are intermediate between the extreme longheadedness of the Negroes and the extreme roundheadedness of the Mongolians.

The tall, blonde blue-eyed, longheaded white type is called Nordic, that is, of the north European group. The short, stocky type, with dark hair, dark eyes, and long head, constitutes the Mediterranean group, found in southern Europe. Between these two extremes of tall blondes and short brunettes, there is the Alpine group, dwelling mainly in central France, Switzerland, southern Germany, the Balkans, and parts of Russia. The Alpine type is, however, found in every country, from Ireland to Russia. Members of this group are of medium height, and intermediate in color between blondes and brunettes. Their heads are relatively round, if compared with the longheaded Nordic and Mediterranean types, but not as round as those of the Chinese.

While the major races of mankind have these general physical traits, we should be on our guard against too precise and dogmatic statements about the physical characteristics of races.

We would have to go far back into the past to find a race that might be considered physically "pure." All existing races are mixtures of several racial stocks. Historical evidence would seem to indicate that race mixture has aided cultural achievement, since most of the great civilizations have been produced by highly mixed types. European civilization, for the most part, was created during the period of the blending of the three types of the white race. The United States is one of the best examples of race mixture.

**Origin and distribution of human races.** There have been two main theories about the origin of human races: (1) the monogenist; and (2) the polygenist. According to the first theory, the transition from lower forms of simian life to man was made at one time and in one place. From this original place of origin, which was believed to be around the island of Java, perhaps a part of the mainland at that remote period, the primordial human race moved into various parts of the Old World and later took on the special traits of the three main races as a result of environmental influences, inbreeding, or both. Those who uphold the polygenist doctrine contend that the transition from our anthropoid ancestors to man was made in a number of places —from China, Java, and Australia to western Europe and South Africa. The polygenists hold that the several racial types of the prehistoric period derived their traits primarily from the original stocks which arose out of the transition from anthropoid to man, with subsequent modification by environmental factors and inbreeding.

While many anthropologists and sociologists, especially the Polish-Austrian sociologist, Ludwig Gumplowicz, held to the polygenist theory, the trend for many years has been to support the monogenist theory as most compatible with logic and the known facts. Very recent discoveries of transitional types and primitive races in widely distributed portions of the Old World have tended to give new plausibility to the polygenist interpretation. In the most recent book on the subject, *A New Theory of Human Evolution,* the dean of living physical anthropologists, Sir Arthur Keith, holds that the origin and diversity of human races have been due to the fact that the close group life of man for a million or more years has promoted the development of the specific physical characteristics that we attribute to the different races. Therefore, according to this theory, whether there were one or many transitions from anthropoid to man, the various races arose in several isolated areas and were a product of inbreeding, and their dispersion through migrations occurred very late in man's experience.

**Race and culture.** We have said that race is primarily a matter of physical traits. But, among the many peoples of the world, different patterns of living have been adopted. There are, thus, cultural as well as physical characteristics of the several races. Every individual belongs not only to a racial but to a cultural group. That we may better understand the meaning of cultural traits and differences, let us say that man, in adjusting himself to his environment, has developed definite habits and ways of doing things: he has made tools to subdue nature and devised laws to regulate group life.

Each generation receives what the last has built, thought, and achieved. Along with his physical racial heritage, every individual has a cultural heritage made up of material things, like buildings, automobiles, machinery, shoes, and typewriters. He also has a non-material heritage, consisting of such matters as belief in God, ideas of right and wrong, economic convictions and traditions, and all the other customs and folkways of any particular group. Man must adapt himself to both the material and the non-material culture.

Each racial group thus has its own cultural environment, which plays the major rôle in its life. It is common for persons to confuse the cultural heritage of a people with their racial traits. This leads to all sorts of misunderstandings.

**The problem of race superiority.** Because some races have accomplished more in certain ways than other races, there arises the question of racial superiority. But what do we mean by "superiority"? Superior adaptation to the physical environment, superior size or weight, or superior mentality? Even though we could show that one race is superior in intelligence, it would not necessarily follow that it must be superior in all other ways.

The race that is best able to make a living and develop a creditable culture in its natural environment should be considered superior for that region. The white man has always considered himself superior to the Negro, yet West Africa, the home of the Negro, has been called the "white man's graveyard," because the white man has never been able to adapt himself successfully to its climate and living conditions. Even the advances of medical science have been of little aid to the white man in Africa; he cannot stand the intense, damp heat as well as the native Negro. If he does not die from some tropical disease, the climate saps his energy. The Negro, however, with his simple food and crude living conditions, can work hard and stay healthy in hottest Africa.

The Eskimo is another example of a racial group that manages to live successfully in a harsh natural environment. If the Eskimos had not been able to adjust themselves to their stern climate, they would have died out long ago. White men find it wise to follow the Eskimo's way of living when they are in his country. Thus, the Negro and the Eskimo are both capable of adjusting themselves to their native environments and, hence, can be called superior in this respect.

**Racial differences.** Racial groups, doubtless, show some differences in mental traits and patterns, as well as in physical characteristics. But do these arise wholly from the physical fact of race, or are they associated primarily with the cultural heritage? So far, no adequate tests have been devised to determine the actual mental capacity of races. The tests that have been given fail to reckon fully with the fact that the customs and habits of one group may be of little use or have little meaning to another. Until an intelligence test is devised which measures "pure intelligence," irrespective of the cultural heritage, we cannot demonstrate that one race is mentally superior to another.

Since we have no accurate means of precisely testing the comparative innate abilities of different races, our popular attitudes towards race are based mainly on prejudice and lack scientific objectivity. Dislike of strange races seems to stem chiefly from consciousness of kind, which causes people to admire and enjoy the familiar and to fear and hate the strange.

**Race prejudice.** In many parts of the world, racial hatred is still very bitter and real. Such hatred seems to exist primarily between the white and yellow races and between the white and black races. Much of it has arisen because the white race, considering itself superior, has assumed the duty—the "white man's burden"—of ruling the world, and in so doing has naturally caused extreme resentment on the part of the black and yellow peoples. The white man may have to pay a heavy price, within the next few decades, for his arrogant assumption of racial superiority. In the Orient, India, Africa, and other parts of the world, the supposedly inferior black and yellow races are trying, with much success recently, to overthrow white rule and assert their independence. Some of our ablest students of international affairs and racial contacts fear that wars between the races, more terrible than anything man has ever experienced, may occur within the next century. With the preponderance of population, and ultimately of economic, political, and military power, likely to pass to the yellow and black races within less than a century, we may very well be treated later on to "Mongolian" and "Ethiopian" myths of race superiority.

The United States, as we have noted, presents an outstanding example of the contact and mixture of races. It also offers, unfortunately, an extended example of the harmful results of racial prejudice. For, while the diversity of the races has benefited the country's development in many ways, it has also produced serious social problems.

Race prejudice can be overcome only through adequate education. People must be educated to the realization that no one race is universally superior or inferior to another, and that all are entitled to an equal opportunity in the world. Attention must be paid to spreading accurate information about other races, for this will lessen the feeling of strangeness and, therefore, may reduce fear and hatred.

## Racial Contacts in the United States: Whites, Indians, Mongolians, and Mexicans

**The American Indians.** The American Indians have lived on our continent for thousands of years. Some were probably here as early as 20,000 or 15,000 B.C.[1] At the time Columbus discovered America,

---

[1] Recent discoveries indicate that the first Indians may have come as early as 40,000 years ago.

anthropologists estimate that there were between 600,000 and 850,000 pure blood Indians occupying what is now the continental United States. When the white man first trespassed on his land, the Indian remained indifferent; but when the whites demanded ever more territory, the Indian tribes were roused to savage opposition. But, even while the two races were in conflict, the white man was learning Indian customs which he needed to know before he could adjust himself successfully to the New World. If the whites had not adopted Indian methods of getting food, preparing shelter, and making clothes, they would have suffered even more than they did from starvation and cold. Colonists became skilled in paddling canoes, an Indian method of transportation. Indian dress was comfortable and practical. Pictures of frontiersmen show them in skins and wearing soft-soled Indian moccasins. Our language has been enriched with such commonplace Indian words as skunk, hickory, squash, pecan, toboggan, tomahawk, and squaw.

Not all white settlers, of course, treated the Indians in the same way. The French adopted many Indian customs and lived much like the red men in the backwoods. French trappers often married Indian women. The Spanish and Portuguese attempted to raise the Indian's standard of living to something like the European level. The remains of ancient missions throughout the Southwest are memorials to the Spaniards' attempt to convert the Indians to Christianity. Other colonial nations, the English and Dutch, refused to mingle with the "savages." Following the Revolutionary War and the adoption of the Constitution, the Indian problem fell into the lap of the newly constituted government of the United States.

**The treaty system.** From 1804 until 1871, the relations of the government with the Indians during rare times of peace were governed mainly by specific treaties, many of which early involved the settlement of Indians on reservations. The treatment of those Indians who were put on reservations and were regarded as wards of the nation was careless and demoralizing. The Indians were fed, clothed, and housed at government expense, but were given little incentive to develop a self-sufficing economy or independent self-respect. Private individuals and corporations were permitted to absorb much of their lands. With the settlement of the Far West after the Civil War, a series of new Indian wars broke out, one of the most dramatic incidents being the annihilation of General George Custer's command at the battle of the Little Big Horn (1876) by the Sioux chief Sitting Bull. The inefficient and corrupt treatment of the Indians inspired Helen Hunt Jackson to publish her *A Century of Dishonor* in 1881, which did much to arouse public interest in the plight of the Indians. The result of this and other influences was the passage of legislation that has gradually improved the lot of the Indians.

**Administrative machinery for handling Indian affairs.** The first official action of the Federal government in dealing with the Indian problem was the passage of a law in 1793 authorizing the president to appoint temporary agents who were to "reside among the Indians." In 1796, a law was passed creating trading posts in Indian areas, and in 1798 a Superintendent of Indian Trade was appointed.

The trading-post system was ended in 1822, and in 1824 Secretary of War John C. Calhoun organized the Bureau (now Office) of Indian Affairs. In 1832, a Commissioner of Indian Affairs was appointed; and this office has continued as head of the administrative machinery dealing with the Indians. In 1834, a law known as the "Indian Intercourse Act" was passed. This law, providing for 12 field agents to handle Indian matters, was long the organic law regulating the administration of Indian affairs. In 1849, the Bureau of Indian Affairs was transferred from the War Department to the newly-created Department of the Interior. This action was sharply resented by the War Department and the army, and the friction and bickerings between military and civilian officials over Indian problems seriously impaired a scientific and fair handling of the Indian situation for many years. In 1869, an unpaid Board of Indian Commissioners was created to advise the Commissioner.

The reservation system. The utterly inadequate nature of the treaty system was so apparent that, in 1871, it was abandoned in favor of congressional legislation on Indian matters, and the reservation system became completely dominant in our public Indian policy.

A typical Indian reservation is a tax-exempt tract of land owned by the tribe and held in trust for the Indian inhabitants by the government. In theory at least, it cannot be levied upon or alienated, and the Indians are free to go and come as they wish.

The first important reform legislation was the Dawes Act of 1887, which provided for the division of tribal lands among individual Indians, under certain limitations, particularly a government trusteeship of 25 years. The land allotment system was liberalized by the Burke Act of 1906, which eliminated the 25-year waiting period before full ownership could be conferred.

Among the chief defects of this legislation were that the land included in the reservation was usually not sufficient to support the Indian inhabitants and was of inferior quality, and that no adequate provision was made to prepare the Indians to own and cultivate land. But probably the greatest weaknesses in the administration of Indian affairs was the failure to protect the Indians from the alienation of their land by greedy private interests. Between 1887 and 1933, the land belonging to Indians under Government grants shrank from 130,000,000 acres to 49,000,000 acres.

The right of citizenship was conferred on the Indians in 1924, but in Arizona and New Mexico they were not permitted to vote at all or only under severe limitations for over 20 years after this date. As we shall point out later on, many Indians refused to exercise the right of suffrage.

**Belated development of Indian education.** One of the main reasons for the unsatisfactory nature of Indian affairs has been the failure of the Federal government to provide adequate educational facilities for Indian children.

The origins of Federal interest in the education of Indian children came in the passage of a law in 1819 appropriating $10,000 annually for this purpose, but no government schools were established. Rather, the money was paid over to missionary organizations operating among the Indians, and this system prevailed until 1873, when the law of 1819 was repealed, and an educational division was established in the Bureau of Indian Affairs.

The next step was the provision of a small number of inferior non-reservation boarding schools, which were later supplemented by reservation boarding schools and, later still, by reservation day schools. In 1926, out of 24,591 Indian pupils enrolled in government schools, 20,092 were in boarding schools and only 4,499 in day schools. The program of supplanting boarding schools by day schools did not really get under way until 1934; ten years later, in 1944, more than a third of all Indian children in government schools were still attending boarding schools.

One of the main defects in the boarding-school system was the prevalence of harsh military discipline. The education provided was of an inferior sort, the teaching force was numerically inadequate and often ill-prepared, and insufficient attention was paid to vocational education.

The Meriam Report of 1928 revealed that, at the end of the first quarter of the present century, only about 65,000 out of 77,577 Indian children of school age were getting any education. About 34,500 were in public schools, with the Federal government paying tuition for most of them, and the rest were in government boarding and day schools and in mission schools. The appropriation for an Indian child in boarding schools was usually only about $225 a year, as against $700 a year for low-cost white boarding schools.

When Charles J. Rhoads was appointed Commissioner of Indian Affairs, in 1929, he began to improve the education of Indian children. Many new school buildings were built, military discipline was abolished, better vocational instruction was provided for, more reservation day schools were created, and the per capita allowance for children was increased to $375 a year. When Rhoads was succeeded by John Collier in 1933, these reforms were continued, special stress being laid on the creation of more government community day schools on the reservations. Perhaps the most important law of the time affecting Indian education was the Johnson-O'Malley Act, passed in 1934, which authorized the Bureau of Indian Affairs to make contracts with the states to educate Indian children with the aid of Federal funds. Indian education is, however, still inferior to that provided for whites. Many children are not in school at all, the educational force remains inferior to that provided for white children, not enough good vocational courses have been introduced, and there are still not enough community day schools. Indian children are frequently discriminated against in public schools, and are entirely excluded in some instances.

But the fault is not all that of the government. Many Indians do not wish to send their children to school—at least for a whole school year. Compulsory education laws have been on the books since 1892, and they were made more rigid in the 1920's, but this has not assured anything like full attendance by Indian children, even where good schools are available. Indians often like to keep their children home to help until the year's work is over. Moreover, the memory of the harsh military discipline of earlier times has not been blotted out.

The present status of Indian education may be summarized on the basis of 1945 figures, the latest available. The Federal government operates 238 schools for Indian children in the United States, ranging all the way from rural schools with one room and a dozen pupils to consolidated or centralized schools with from 400 to over 500 pupils. Some 155 of these schools are reservation day schools; 66 are reservation boarding schools; and 17 are non-reservation boarding schools. The Federal government encourages Indian children to attend public schools wherever they are available, and more Indian children now attend public schools than Federal schools. For the most part, the Federal day schools are maintained only in areas where public schools do not exist or are inaccessible to Indian children. In 1945, of 92,296 Indian children between 6 and 18, some 31,927 were attending public day schools; 27,252 were enrolled in Federal boarding or day schools; 7,813 were attending mission boarding or day schools; 19,375 were not in any school (some 15,000 of these being children on the Navajo Reservation); and 5,929 were unaccounted for in the educational picture. In 1948, some 7,204 children were attending reservation boarding schools, and 6,269 non-reservation boarding schools. In Alaska, the Federal government operates 78 elementary day schools, with 3,750 pupils, while 2,852 attend the territorial public schools. About 1,500 Indian children in Alaska are without any educational facilities. Federal education for Indian children ends with high school, there being no Indian colleges, but several Indian high schools offer two years of post-graduate vocational training.

**Serious medical and health problems among the Indians.** Medical care for Indians, like educational opportunities, has lagged behind that provided for whites. The medical and health problems among Indians have been complicated and intensified by a number of special factors, such as the necessity of readjustment to a sedentary life on reservations, bad economic conditions making for inadequate food, clothing, and shelter, the special susceptibility of Indians to such diseases as tuberculosis and trachoma, and the lethal effect of alcoholic excesses on Indians. But the sickness and mortality could have been greatly reduced had adequate and competent medical care been provided.

The first casual effort to provide medical care for Indians was embodied in the Indian Appropriation Act of 1856, which allotted pay for doctors in Indian agencies. But not much was accomplished since, even as late as 1873, only half of the agencies had any doctor at all. In 1873, a medical division was set up in the Bureau of Indian Affairs. In 1878, the Commissioner of Indian Affairs ordered that all doctors on Indian reservations had to be graduates of an approved medical college. The first hospital for Indians was opened in 1882. The paucity of medical care at the turn of the century, however, is shown by the fact that in 1900 there were only 86 doctors in the entire Indian service and only 5 Indian hospitals, though the number of Indians in 1900 was 237,196.

A number of improvements took place in the next quarter of a century. The medical division was revived in the Bureau of Indian Affairs in 1909, a medical supervisor was appointed, and $12,000 was appropriated to study and treat trachoma. In 1912, President Taft earnestly recommended better medical care for the Indians. Indian medical appropriations increased from $60,000 in 1912 to $700,000 in 1926. In the latter year, the medical service in the Bureau of Indian Affairs was reorganized in co-operation with the Public Health Service. Four medical districts were created for the country and a medical director was provided for each. The Meriam Report of 1928 stressed the fact that medical care for Indians still remained far below the standards maintained by the Public Health Service and the Veteran's Bureau. Commissioners Rhoads and Collier strove to improve the service, adding more medical districts, doctors, and hospitals. Primarily owing to their efforts, medical appropriations rose from $700,-000 in 1926 to a little over $4,000,000 in 1936, at which time there were in the Indian service some 160 full-time and 78 part-time doctors and 500 nurses. At the present time, the Indian Service operates some 64 hospitals and sanatoriums with approximately 4,000 beds in the United States, and 8 hospitals with over 400 beds in Alaska. In addition, the Indian Service makes contracts with a number of public and private hospitals to render hospital care to Indians where the Service does not maintain its own facilities. Over 50,000 Indians receive hospital care each year. In 1950, the total appropriations for medical care were $11,833,917, and some 150 full-time and 119 part-time doctors and 833 nurses were employed by the Indian Service.

But medical care for Indians still lags behind that for whites in most areas. A number of doctors left the Indian service during the war, and not all of them have returned or been replaced. Doctors are more poorly paid, hospitals have to operate on a much lower appropriation than Public Health hospitals, and the number of doctors and hospitals per capita is far less than among whites. There is a high prevalence of tuberculosis and trachoma, particularly among some of the more economically unfortunate Indians of the Southwest, especially the Navajos. Nevertheless, the improvement of medical care in the last half century is reflected in the fact that the Indians are now increasing in number more rapidly than any other racial minority in the country. The use of sulfa drugs and the antibiotics has greatly cut down the prevalence of trachoma, and the more scientific methods of treating tuberculosis are being introduced in Indian hospitals.

**The famous Meriam Report of 1928 and subsequent improvements in the Indian service.** We have already mentioned several times the Meriam Report, which was published in 1928. This gave the greatest impetus to the study and improvement of Indian conditions since *A Century of Dishonor,* half a century before.

Various organizations interested in Indian affairs seriously criticized the Indian service during the years following the first world war. They asserted that there was little to show for the increased expenditures on the Indian service, that the Indians were being cheated out of their lands, that poverty was widespread among the Indians, and that health and educational conditions were scandalous. Mr. Herbert Work, Secretary of the Interior, was impressed by these charges and determined to learn the truth about Indian affairs. He requested the Institute for Government Research to make a survey of the Indian situation and of the government service to the Indians. The survey was conducted under the direction of Dr. Lewis Meriam, and the Report was published by the Brookings Institution in 1928 under the title *The Problem of Indian Administration.*

Among the recommendations made were the following: that a Division of Planning and Development be set up in the Bureau of Indian Affairs to carry on studies of the Indian situation and reorganize the Indian service; that 5 million dollars be appropriated at once to rehabilitate the Indian service; that the Civil Service Commission should set about to provide the number of qualified employees needed in the service; that $75,000 be appropriated to strengthen the medical research staff; and that the educational system should be reorganized, strengthened, and liberalized.

The educational and medical reforms of Charles J. Rhoads and John Collier have already been discussed. Collier, appointed by President Roosevelt in 1933, was especially active. He set up a relief system, established an Indian unit of the Civilian Conservation Corps, cancelled some of the Indian debts to the government, checked the alienation of Indian lands, and bought land for the Indians. He sought to educate the public on Indian matters by publishing a Bureau magazine known as *Indians at Work.*

Especially important was the passage of the Wheeler-Howard Indian Reorganization Act of 1934. This repealed the earlier land allotment acts, put an end to the alienation of Indian lands and other physical resources, established an indefinite government trust period for Indian lands, returned to tribal ownership the surplus reservation lands, enabled the Commissioner to buy more land for the Indians up to an expenditure of 2 million dollars a year, and created a revolving credit fund of 12 million dollars for the Indians. Perhaps the most important phase of the act in the political field was the effort to revive Indian self-government. The Indian tribes were authorized to draw up constitutions and by-laws and to elect officers to handle tribal matters and negotiate with the Federal, state, and local governments. The Indian Service has been much expanded and strengthened since 1934. In 1948, there were 7,496 full time civil service employees, and 3,563 part time workers.

**Economic difficulties of the Indians.** Except for some valuable Indian reservation holdings in forest and mineral lands, the Indian economy has revolved chiefly around agriculture and stock raising. Here the Indians have been handicapped by poor land, lack of irrigation, and primitive farming technique. At the present time, some 60,000 Indian families own about 56,000,000 acres of land, with some 40,000,000 acres owned tribally. About 13,000,000 acres are semidesert and unfitted for any kind of economical operation. Only about 12,000,000 acres have enough rainfall to make possible dry farming, and only 3,000,000 acres are classified as good farm crop land. Until recently, Indian farmers used only rather primitive farming methods, which still further reduced their income.

As a result of the progress in the Indian Service since 1928, and especially since 1934, the situation has been somewhat improved. Better farming methods have been introduced. Government grants and loans to Indians have increased, and some progress has been made in irrigating Indian lands. About 600,000 acres are now irrigated, and plans have been made to irrigate another 700,000 acres. Partly as a result of these improvements and partly as a result of improved farming conditions and prices generally since 1939, the income from Indian agricultural operations, exclusive of stock raising, grew from around a million dollars in 1932 to $25,000,000 in 1948. The improvement in the livestock industry has been comparable. The number of livestock owned by Indians increased from 171,000 head in 1932 to over 400,000 in 1948, and the income from livestock grew from $1,224,000 to $31,000,000. An important source of Indian income is from wage work. This increased from 12 million dollars in 1933 to about 25 million dollars in 1945, the increase being due in part to the extensive entry of Indians into war munitions factories. Despite all this improvement in the Indian economic situation, there has been an increasingly critical period since the end of the second world war.

**Indian problems after the second world war.** The progress made by Rhoads and Collier, and by William Brophy, who succeeded Collier in 1945, has led many to conclude that the Indian problem is settled. The special problems affecting Indians during and after the second world war have, however, created a new crisis in Indian affairs. For one thing, the administrative and humanitarian work of the Bureau of Indian Affairs was seriously restricted by the diversion of Federal interest, personnel, and resources to the war effort after Pearl Harbor. For another, some 65,000 Indians who served in the armed forces or worked in war industries acquired new perspective and new ambitions.

An important factor contributing to problems of postwar readjustment has been the recent spurt in the Indian population growth. There were 244,437 Indians in the country in 1920, and 392,000 in 1950. Counting those in Alaska, there were over 450,000 Indians under our jurisdiction in 1950, and the rate of Indian population growth is still rising.

Since it has become increasingly difficult for this larger number of Indians to support themselves on reservations, they must be helped to get employment in non-reservation industrial centers. Veterans' loans to Indians for business purposes have been inadequate. Arizona and New Mexico even denied the Indians Social Security aid.

While the Indians as a minority group still constitute a national problem, some are in especially acute distress. This is notably the case with the 60,000 Navajos, the largest Indian tribe. They are "cooped up" on a desert reservation in the Southwest that could not support half that number of Indians on any decent standard of living. The current median income of a Navajo family is about $500 a year. Moreover, they have scandalously inferior educational and medical service.

Educational problems have been increased because in many areas prejudice against Indian children has kept them out of the public schools off the reservations. While, in legal theory, Indians formally enjoy all the civil rights of whites, in practice they have failed to get them in many regions.

An important victory came in July, 1948, when the Arizona Supreme Court granted the right of suffrage to the reservation Indians who could meet the educational qualifications laid down in the state constitution. In August, 1948, a Federal court decision removed the barriers to Indian voting in New Mexico. For the first time, all qualified Indians in the United States were legally entitled to vote in a presidential election. A majority of the Indians do not vote, however, even when they are legally entitled to do so. In some cases not over two to five per cent even bother to register as voters. One reason for this is that the Indians have a somewhat unfounded fear that, if they vote and otherwise behave like ordinary citizens, they will lose their special rights and benefits as Indians.

A number of voluntary organizations are assisting the Indians in securing their rights and in improving their economic and educational status. Such are The Indian Defense Association, The Indian Rights Association, The Association on American Indian Affairs, The National Congress of American Indians, and the American Civil Liberties Union. They have plenty of work ahead. And it is obvious that the

American Indians are far from a "disappearing race," as is commonly believed. The Indian population of the area now occupied by the United States is estimated to have been between 600,000 and 850,000 at the time of the landing of Columbus. Of course, most of the approximately 450,000 Indians now under American jurisdiction are no longer "pure-blood" Indians, since Indians have mixed extensively for many years with whites and Mexicans. There is less white prejudice against race mixture with Indians than with Negroes, Chinese, and Japanese.

**Deceptive emancipation program of Indian relief.** The main "trick," or subterfuge, employed by those who still wish to exploit the Indians is to urge the ending of the reservation system and the complete "emancipation" of the Indians. Until the Indians are fully prepared by education and economic aid to fare for themselves on an equal basis with white citizens, nothing could be more fatal to their cause than to remove the protection they derive from the reservation system and Federal wardship. As the eminent authority on the Indian problem, Oliver La Farge, has well said, this proposed emancipation would actually "emancipate the Indians out of everything they have."

**Development of Chinese immigration.** The contacts of the American white man with other groups of Mongolian ancestry have been less extensive than our contacts with the Indians. The first wave of Chinese came in the decade 1840–1850. In Chapter X it was pointed out that the Chinese continued to migrate until the whites protested against their willingness to work for low wages. Another objection was their use of opium. Although an act of 1882 barred Chinese labor from our country, the Chinese element is slowly increasing because of the excess of births over deaths. There were 77,500 Chinese in the country in 1940.

**Relations with Chinese immigrants.** In large cities the Chinese usually live by themselves in crowded sections called "Chinatown." Here, they operate businesses in which they do not compete extensively with the whites. The Chinese and the whites respect each other; neither race desires intimate social contact with the other, and, thus, intermarriage is rare. Americans have a traditional respect for Chinese culture. For this reason, and because there are so few of them, prejudice has not developed against the Chinese so much as against the Japanese. As we noted in the preceding chapter, the Chinese residents in this country were given the right to become American citizens on July 4, 1946.

**Our treatment of the Japanese.** Many Americans, especially those dwelling on the Pacific Coast, have frequently brought forward two main reasons for objecting to Japanese immigration: (1) Japanese competition in agriculture; and (2) the Japanese loyalty to Japan.

The Japanese were forbidden to own real estate in California, and were deprived of the right to become citizens. The famous Gentle-

man's Agreement (1907) and the Japanese Exclusion Act of 1924 shut
off all Japanese immigration. Many people felt that the law of 1924
was unfair to Japan, which had faithfully kept the Gentleman's Agreement prohibiting its laborers from coming here. There is little intermarriage between Japanese and whites. There were 127,000 Japanese
in the country in 1940, as compared with 138,834 in 1930. The second
world war intensified feeling against the Japanese. In January, 1942,
it was announced that the Japanese would be forced to move from
Pacific coastal areas vital to our defense. In the preceding chapter,
we discussed this evacuation process. Less than two-thirds of those
removed have thus far been restored to their homes after the war.

**Mexican immigrants.** Mexicans, coming from an independent nation in the Western hemisphere, were not restricted by the immigration acts of 1921 and 1924. They have migrated across the border in
large numbers since 1921. It is estimated that there are between
2,500,000 and 3,000,000 persons of Spanish-Mexican-Indian descent in
the United States today.

Many Mexicans in the United States are illiterate and their standards of living are low. They usually crowd together in shabby city
areas, living an essentially segregated racial and cultural existence.
As workers, they have found employment in agricultural regions, or
on the railroads of the Southwest. Some have gone into mining and
into the steel and automotive industries of the East. Many moved
into the armament and munitions manufacturing areas of the Middle
West and Pacific Coast during the second world war.

The Mexican does not often settle where he is not wanted, and
those who resent his presence usually find that he moves out of their
way. Teachers claim that the Mexican children are quick to learn
and that, if given a chance, they will readily adopt cleaner and better
ways of living. There is little logical ground for racial prejudice
against the Mexican, since he is descended from the Spaniard and the
Indian. Devoted to music and art, the Mexican can contribute to
American life, if only he is permitted to develop his native talents.

## The American Negro Problem

**Origins of the Negro problem.** The most difficult race problem in
the United States has been that of the Negro. The Civil War ended
in 1865; legal slavery has "gone with the wind"; but the Negro has
not yet been accorded economic, political, or social equality. Race
riots in recent years have shown that the attempt of the black man to
rise economically and socially breeds resentment in the white. The
struggle for Negro civil rights since Pearl Harbor has created a nationwide political crisis.

The Negro problem has developed in two main stages: (1) from
the introduction of slavery into the United States (1619) to the Emancipation Proclamation (1863) and the Thirteenth Amendment (1865);
and (2) from 1865 to the present day.

The germs of the Civil War were brought with the first shiploads of Negroes in 1619. The slavers (importers of Negroes) soon developed a good business supplying the markets of the New World. By 1770, one-half the population of Virginia was colored, and, even in the northern colony of New York, one-seventh was black. At this time, one-fifth of the total population of the colonies were Negroes. It is estimated that the British brought over, altogether, some two million Negroes to their settlements in the West Indies, Bermuda, the Bahamas, and the mainland in the colonial period.

**Negro slavery.** Slavery flourished in the South, but did not prove so successful in the North. On the plantations of the South the slaves were profitably and, in many cases, happily employed. The black workers were not so well suited to the farms or factories of the North. Conscientious Yankees often objected to the importation of slaves for moral reasons as well as from economic jealousy. The dispute was first fought out in the Constitutional Convention of 1787, and a compromise was reached whereby the slave trade was allowed to continue for twenty years. In 1808, the importation of slaves became illegal, but down to the time of the Civil War smugglers carried on a considerable trade in Negroes.

The invention of the cotton gin by Eli Whitney in 1793 stimulated the demand for Negro slave labor. Whitney's machine, which mechanically separated the seed from the fiber of the cotton, greatly increased the supply of cheap raw cotton.

Since most Southerners were convinced that large-scale cotton production would be difficult, if not impossible, without Negro slaves, slavery was regarded as the very basis of southern prosperity. The plantation owners argued that slavery was good from every point of view. The Negroes benefited because they had been rescued from savagery, and, unlike free laborers, were assured of care in sickness and old age. The masters, it was argued, benefited because they could more easily manage slaves than free laborers. Moreover, the plantation owners, relieved of manual labor, were free to devote themselves to politics, government, and intellectual tasks. Finally, America as a whole benefited because there was no labor unrest or real poverty among the slaves, such as existed in the northern factories; and the extensive production of cotton supplied the world with an essential article.

The Northerners, however, offered some vigorous arguments against slavery. Slave labor, they held, was inefficient, ignorant, and wasteful. Plantation owners were slowing down the progress of the South by sticking to one crop which wore out the land. Much land was abandoned as the planters moved to more fertile ground. Slavery had injurious economic and social effects on both whites and blacks. Since only one white man in twenty could afford to own slaves, the poor whites were forced to till either marginal lands or the tracts of worn-out land which great plantation owners had deserted. The planters, and even many Negroes, looked down on what they called the "poor white trash."

Feeling against slavery grew between 1800 and 1850 in the North, and loud demands were made for its abolition. The anti-slavery movement was fanned by Northern abolitionists and gradually split Congress and the country. Opposition to the extension of slavery in the new western states culminated in the Civil War of 1861–1865. But even this terrible conflict did not settle the Negro problem.

**Results of emancipation.** Four and a half million Negroes were set free by the Thirteenth Amendment to the Constitution in 1865. The famous Emancipation Proclamation of 1863 had freed only slaves in states which had seceded. Since 1865, the Negro has striven to obtain an economic and political foothold in this "land of the free." His problem is not restricted to the South, although his rights are more curtailed there, in most respects, than in the North.

For the most part, the ex-slaves remained in the South working in the fields. Over 60 per cent of Negro workers were employed as farm laborers as late as 1890. A few became farm owners. The picture changed in the years after 1890. More Negroes became small farmers. The new industries also attracted the Negro, and he left the rural areas of the South, where wages were low, to seek the markedly higher wages in both southern and northern factories. The failure of the cotton crop for several seasons in parts of the South, the ravages of the boll weevil, and the depression of agriculture throughout the country after the first world war seriously affected the Negro farmers. As a result of this and new employment opportunities in the North, a mass migration from southern farms to northern industrial cities took place.

**Growth of Negro population.** The Negro population of the United States has trebled since emancipation. In 1860, there were 4,441,830 Negroes in the country; in 1940, the number had increased to 12,-865,518; and by 1950 there were well over 15,000,000. But the proportion of Negroes to the total population has fallen off considerably over the same period. In 1860, the Negroes constituted 14.1 per cent of the population; in 1940, only 9.8 per cent; and in 1950, about 10.0 per cent. The Negro birth rate has been consistently higher than the white since 1860; in 1943 it was 24.1 as against 21.2 for whites. But the rate of population growth among the Negroes has been lower than that of the whites because of the higher Negro death rate. The death rate for Negroes of all ages in 1943 was 12.8, compared with 10.7 for whites; the death rate for Negro infants is 63 per cent higher than that of white infants. Such serious forms of illness as tuberculosis, venereal diseases, kidney diseases, and pneumonia are especially frequent among Negroes. The life expectancy of Negroes in 1947 was 59.8 years, compared to 67.9 for whites.

**Negro health problems.** The high death rate and incidence of sickness among Negroes is due in part to the increased concentration of the Negro population in congested, substandard areas of northern cities, with their bad living conditions, and in part to the notorious inferiority of medical care for Negroes. In 1948, there were only 3,800 Negro physicians in the United States, or one for every 3,777 Negroes, as contrasted with one doctor for every 750 persons in the total population. The hospital situation is even more backward and deplorable. There are only 124 Negro hospitals, many of them substandard, with a total of only 20,800 beds, out of the total of 1,500,000 beds in hospitals of the country. The outlook for any rapid improvement in Negro medical care is not good because of barriers to Negro medical education and interne training, and the increasing rigors and expense of medical education.

**Negro population shifts.** The location of the Negro population has undergone considerable change since emancipation, most notably a movement from the rural South to the industrial North and South. In 1860, 92.2 per cent of the Negroes lived in the South, 7.7 per cent in the North, and 0.1 in the West. In 1940, only 77 per cent lived in the South, 21.7 per cent lived in the North, and 1.3 per cent in the West. The reasons for this shift of the Negro population have been the increasing difficulty of the growing Negro population in making a living on the farms of the South and the supposedly better economic opportunities in the industrial cities of the North and West. While there was a gradual drifting of Negroes northward from 1865 to 1916, the great Negro movement to the North has come since 1916, and in three major waves of migration: (1) in the years from 1916 to 1919, between 200,000 and 400,000 Negroes came North; (2) between 1921 and 1924, over 500,000 moved North; and (3) in the second world war, about 1,500,000 migrated to the North and West. In the first wave of migration, they were attracted mainly by war industry; in the second they were impelled by the bad farming conditions in the South and the revival of industry in the North; and in the third by the higher wages paid in the northern armament industries.

**Increasing urban concentration of Negroes.** Since the Negroes who have come to the North and West have settled in cities, this northward migration has also produced a great dislocation of the Negro population in respect to rural and urban distribution. In 1860, not over 10 per cent of the Negroes lived in cities; by 1949, well over 50 per cent were city dwellers. In 1940, 44.7 per cent of the Negroes who lived in the South still dwelt on farms, but over 90 per cent of those in the North and West lived in cities.

Almost invariably, the Negroes have fared worse than the whites in regard to housing conditions and sanitation in both southern and northern cities, with results reflected in the greater amount of Negro sickness and the higher Negro death rate just discussed. Further, the marked growth in the number of Negroes in cities inevitably increased the moral, cultural, economic, and political problems connected with city living in general, intensified in the case of the Negroes by the adverse living conditions forced upon them.

**The Negroes in agriculture.** In the economic life of the Negroes since emancipation, the most notable development has been the relative decline in the number engaged in agriculture and increase in the number employed in various industrial pursuits. In 1860, the overwhelming majority of the Negroes in the South were farm laborers under the slavery system. In 1940, only 33.2 per cent of all the employed Negroes were engaged in agriculture. But the preponderance of agricultural laborers among the Negroes who are engaged in farming pursuits has continued to our own day. In 1890, there were 1,105,728 Negro farm laborers, or some 64 per cent of all Negroes employed in agriculture. In 1940, the number of Negro farm laborers in the South had dropped to 468,126, but they still greatly outnumbered any other Negro agricultural group: owners and managers, 173,628; cash tenants, 64,684; other tenants (except sharecroppers), 142,836; and sharecroppers, 299,118. The pay of Negro agricultural laborers has remained relatively low; in 1945, the average weekly income of an employed Negro farm laborer was $8.60, and his average annual income, $224.

Between 1890 and 1910, the level of Negro prosperity in southern agriculture—95 per cent of all Negro agriculture is carried on in 16 southern states—improved somewhat, and by 1910 there were 218,972 Negro farm owners, who owned some 12,847,348 acres of land, valued at $620,587,241. After 1910, this development of Negro farm ownership was checked, chiefly by ravages of the boll weevil, the depression of southern agriculture, and the general depression of the country after 1929. The depression of Negro agriculture, reflected in the decrease in Negro farm owners after 1910, and especially after 1920, tended to put a larger proportion of the Negro farmers in the tenant group, especially the sharecropper class. In 1910, Negro cash tenants had constituted about one-half of the total tenant group; by 1940, they made up only a little over one-sixth of the tenants. In 1940, 74.5 per cent of all Negro farmers, exclusive of farm laborers, were tenant farmers. The lowest of these Negro farm tenants in income and economic well-being, as well as by far the largest element in the tenant group, are the some 300,000 sharecroppers (in 1940), who live on a level of bare subsistence.

While the New Deal farm legislation provided some benefits to Negro farmers, and while the increased demand and prices for farm products since Pearl Harbor also helped them out, neither or both sufficed to check the decline in Negro agriculture; it is estimated that over a million Negroes left southern farms between 1940 and 1948.

Even the comparatively well-off Negro farm owners operate under distinct disadvantages. The Negro farm units are usually of inferior fertility and too small in acreage to permit use of the most efficient agricultural methods. There is too much concentration on a limited number of crops, sometimes on one crop. And few Negroes are able to purchase the best and latest farm equipment. The obstacles to efficient farming by the poorer farm owners and farm tenants are, naturally, greater, and the efficiency of these groups is lower. With the increased mechanization of southern farming, the outlook for the Negro farmers is even less promising than their past experience. The main group of Negro farmers who have improved their condition recently are the handful—some 37,763 families in 1944—who have been aided by the Rural Rehabilitation Program of the Federal Farm Administration. A sampling of these Negro farmers showed that they had an average annual farm income of $1,006; small indeed, but a great gain over their previous near-destitute condition.

**The Negroes enter American manufacturing industry.** As the Negroes, slowly at first, turned from farms to other forms of industrial employment, they began, chiefly after 1890, to find employment in southern labor camps, cotton factories, tobacco factories, and steel mills. They were mainly employed at heavy labor and unskilled tasks, receiving very low wages, usually not over 75¢ to $1.50 a day, even in steel mills around 1900. In the tobacco factories, their wages ran from 50¢ to $1 per day. It was difficult for the Negroes to compete for employment and wages with the numerous southern poor whites in the rising cotton factories of the new South. After 1914, with the increased demand for labor in the North, Negroes were able to make their way more generally into many forms of factory employment and other types of industrial occupations. The fact that many Negroes have shifted from farming to industry and from the South to the industrial and urban North has modified the economic picture of Negro life. But a disproportionate number of Negroes still remain laborers and domestic servants. The following table gives the distribution of Negro workers, according to the industrial groups in which they were employed in 1940:[2]

MAJOR INDUSTRY GROUP OF EMPLOYED NEGROES 14 YEARS OLD AND OVER (EXCEPT ON PUBLIC EMERGENCY WORK) BY SEX, FOR THE UNITED STATES, 1940

| Employment Status and Major Industry | Total | Male | Female | PER CENT DISTRIBUTION | | |
|---|---|---|---|---|---|---|
| | | | | Total | Male | Female |
| Employed (except on emergency work) ............. | 4,479,068 | 2,936,795 | 1,542,273 | 100.0 | 100.0 | 100.0 |
| Agriculture, forestry and fishery * .................. | 1,484,914 | 1,238,301 | 246,613 | 33.2 | 42.2 | 16.0 |
| Mining ................... | 52,981 | 52,754 | 227 | 1.2 | 1.8 | — |
| Construction .............. | 142,419 | 141,261 | 1,158 | 3.2 | 4.8 | 0.1 |
| Manufacturing ............. | 515,514 | 467,286 | 48,228 | 11.5 | 15.9 | 3.1 |

* Only about one per cent of all Negro workers is engaged in forestry and fishing.

2 *Negro Year Book, 1941–1948,* edited by Jessie Parkhurst Guzman, Tuskegee Institute, 1947, p. 14.

Major Industry Group of Employed Negroes 14 Years Old and Over (Except on Public Emergency Work) By Sex, for the United States, 1940 (*Continued*)

| Employment Status and Major Industry | Total | Male | Female | PER CENT DISTRIBUTION | | |
|---|---|---|---|---|---|---|
| | | | | Total | Male | Female |
| Transportation, communication and other public utilities | 200,191 | 196,762 | 3,429 | 4.5 | 6.7 | 0.2 |
| Wholesale and retail trade .. | 348,760 | 286,930 | 61,830 | 7.8 | 9.8 | 4.0 |
| Finance, insurance, and real estate | 68,117 | 56,309 | 11,808 | 1.5 | 1.9 | 0.8 |
| Business and repair services.. | 48,863 | 47,783 | 1,080 | 1.1 | 1.6 | 0.1 |
| Personal services | 1,292,524 | 243,700 | 1,048,824 | 28.9 | 8.3 | 68.0 |
| Amusement, recreation, and related services | 32,187 | 27,516 | 4,671 | 0.7 | 0.9 | 0.3 |
| Professional and related services | 176,685 | 84,014 | 92,671 | 3.9 | 2.9 | 6.0 |
| Government | 56,921 | 48,632 | 8,289 | 1.3 | 1.7 | 0.5 |
| Industry not reported | 58,992 | 45,547 | 13,445 | 1.3 | 1.6 | 0.9 |

Despite the greater diversification of Negro industrial employment, the great majority of Negro workers have remained unskilled laborers. In 1940, while 15.6 per cent of all employed white men were skilled laborers, only 4.4 per cent of employed Negroes were so rated. Some 30 per cent of employed white men were engaged in professional, proprietary, managerial, clerical, and sales occupations that employed only 5 per cent of working Negroes.

The wages and salaries of Negro workers have always, with only the few exceptions that prove the rule, been lower than those received by employed whites. This has been true even when Negroes and whites have performed the same tasks, requiring the same skills. In a Chicago foundry, in 1927, the average weekly wage of white laborers was $37 per week, that of Negroes $29. In the clothing industry in Chicago at the same period, white workers were paid $37.40 per week, and Negroes $18 to $25 for the same type of work. A study of the median wages of Negro women in 1929 in fifteen states showed that in only two of the states were the median weekly earnings as high as $9, while in four states they were below $6. These examples could be multiplied, but they sufficiently reveal the general situation before the Federal legislation of the late 1930's.

Since Negroes had to have work, discriminatory wage policies were easy to enforce; one reason why Negroes could not obtain higher wages was that they found it difficult to get into labor unions and secure the prevailing union wages. The American Federation of Labor, the only strong labor organization until the Congress of Industrial Organization was formed in 1935, was long opposed to admitting Negroes to membership. Moreover, the A.F. of L. is a craft organization made up mainly of skilled workers, and there were few Negro skilled laborers, even if the A.F. of L. had been willing to admit them. The new CIO by admitting unskilled laborers, including Negroes, compelled the A.F. of L. to liberalize its policies.

This new development, along with the growth in the number of Negro industrial laborers, has led to a great increase in the unionization of Negro workers. By the year 1946, the number of gainfully employed Negroes reached 5,500,000 and the Negroes in labor unions numbered about 750,000, as compared with only about 100,000 in 1930. Perhaps the most successful Negro union has been the Brotherhood of Sleeping Car Porters, organized by A. Philip Randolph. This was recognized by the Pullman Company in 1937, hours of labor were reduced, and pay increases totaling $1,250,000 per year were granted at the outset.

Other factors that have helped to raise the wage level of Negro city workers have been the Wage-Hour Law of 1938, which reduced discrimination against Negro workers in industries engaged in interstate commerce, and the Fair Employment Practices Laws, outlawing wage discrimination because of race, which have been passed in Connecticut, Massachusetts, New Jersey, New Mexico, New York, Oregon, Rhode Island, and Washington. Similar laws have been proposed in other states, and a weak Federal law passed the House of Representatives in February, 1950.

Despite all these improvements since the turn of the century, the Negroes have a long way to go in gaining economic equality with whites; they will require more complete unionization, and they will have to be protected by a greater number of state laws—or a Federal law—prohibiting wage discrimination solely on the basis of race. Establishing anything like economic equality with whites will also involve increasing the number of Negroes in the skilled trades and in professional and clerical work. The chief gain here in recent years has been the growth of the relative number of Negro employees in the Federal government. A careful check made in 1943 revealed the fact that Negroes made up about 12 per cent of all Federal employees in that year, as compared with 9.8 per cent in 1938.

**Negroes in American business.** The Negroes have made considerable headway in insurance, banking, and retail business. In 1945, it was reported that there were 205 Negro insurance companies doing business, 46 of them members of the National Negro Insurance Association. These 46 had $57,000,000 in assets; 3,695,000 policy holders; $630,000,000 worth of insurance in force; and $33,000,000 in annual income from premiums. There were 11 Negro banks in 1943, with combined resources of $15,176,000, most of it in government war securities. Deposits amounted to about $14,000,000. There were 91 Negro credit unions in 1945, and they were doing as well as comparable white organizations. In 1939, there were 29,827 Negro retail stores, with combined sales of $71,466,000. This was a marked gain over the figure for 1935. But the blow dealt to Negro business by the depression is evident from the fact that the sales of Negro stores in 1929 amounted to $98,603,000, some 27.5 per cent greater than the 1939 sales.

**Negro living conditions.** The living conditions and habitations of the great majority of American Negroes are substandard. Only the better class of Negro farm owners in the South, the more prosperous Negro business and professional men live under desirable physical conditions. Often, not even the relatively highly-paid Negro skilled laborers can secure decent habitations, though they may have the money to pay the high rentals required. The Negroes who live under the worst conditions are the sharecroppers in the shacks of the South, and the unskilled Negro workers, herded in tenements in slum areas of the industrial cities of both the North and the South.

Since a Federal report before the second world war showed that about 60 per cent of all urban dwellings are substandard, and since the Negroes usually get the worst of these substandard habitations, the conditions under which they live in the cities can easily be pictured. Listed as overcrowded in 1940 were only 8 per cent of urban dwellings for whites, as against 25 per cent of those occupied by Negroes. This was a very modest estimate. Negro tenements are notoriously in a state of disrepair and lacking in conveniences, especially anything like modern plumbing. But, save when curtailed by rent ceilings, the so-called rent-hogs among the landlords unmercifully gouge the Negroes by charging them high rents for their miserable living quarters. Such substandard living quarters naturally breed disease and are one of the causes of the high sickness and death rate among Negroes; they also increase immorality and delinquency. There are relatively few home owners among urban Negroes, less than one-third as many as among whites, though the number increased in the 1940's—from about 24 per cent in 1940 to about 34 per cent in 1948.

These conditions existed before Pearl Harbor, and the bad situation was greatly intensified by the crowding of many more Negroes into urban centers to take part in war industries. The acute housing shortage for all urban dwellers during and since the war has afflicted the Negroes with special severity. The whole matter of urban Negro housing has been well summarized in the *Negro Year Book* (1947):

Informed observation and available facts indicate that the vast majority of Negroes and other non-whites live in substandard housing and in slum or blighted areas, and that they are bound to such housing and neighborhoods by reason of their income limitations, resulting from racially restricted job opportunities, and imposed residential segregation reinforced by racial restrictive covenants, traditions, or law.

There is little prospect for any great immediate improvement in Negro living conditions. Negro agriculture in the South is depressed and likely to become more so. The new urban housing program for both whites and Negroes is pathetically inadequate, and improvement will come most slowly in Negro quarters. Only 19 per cent of the low-rent units of the Federal Public Housing Authority, or some 145,584 units, were occupied by or planned for Negroes in 1945. This is a mere drop in the bucket. The struggle to break down restrictive covenants, if successful, may minister to Negro pride, but it will do little for a long time to provide better habitations for Negroes.

**The Negro in American politics.** Bitterly disputed also is the right of the Negro to vote. It is now rather generally admitted by students of the problem that it was a mistake to have given the Negroes the right to vote immediately after emancipation, without any preparation for the duties of citizenship. At any rate, the Negroes not only exercised the right to vote after 1865, but participated in the government of the South for a time under the direction of northern carpetbaggers and the protection of northern armies. White southerners, determined to prevent the recurrence of the abuses of this period, have since made every effort to keep Negroes from the polls.

When the whites regained control in the South, they enacted very high and diversified qualifications for all voters, both white and black. This device, however, also excluded many southern whites. The dilemma was solved by the so-called "grandfather clause," invented by Louisiana in 1898, which provided that those who were excluded by existing qualifications could, nevertheless, vote if their male ancestors had been able to vote before 1867. This ruse continued the exclusion of Negroes but removed the barriers to most white voting.

When the Supreme Court declared the grandfather clause unconstitutional in 1913, other devices were found to keep the Negroes away from the polls. One such device is to set up such elaborate tests and qualifications for registering voters as will operate to the disadvantage of Negroes. Another much debated method of preventing or discouraging the Negroes from voting is the poll tax or head tax, which Negroes are often unable to pay. Many efforts have been made to pass Federal legislation outlawing the poll tax, but they have all been blocked by filibustering southern Congressmen. Interestingly enough, it has been estimated that the poll tax legally disqualifies more than twice as many whites as Negroes—about 7 million whites to 3 million Negroes. But the fact that whites have not paid their poll tax is often overlooked at the polls.

Another way of nullifying the political power of southern Negroes has been to keep them away from the primaries, since the primaries are far more important than the election in most southern states, which are usually safely in the Democrat column. Though the Negroes make up about 47 per cent of all persons of voting age in Mississippi, it is estimated that only between 1,000 and 3,000 Negroes voted in the primary elections in that state in July 1942. Some states, including Texas, made the primaries a sort of "association" or "club" and denied the Negroes membership. The United States Supreme Court, in the Louisiana primary case in 1941 and the Texas primary case of 1944, ruled that primaries are an integral part of the election procedure and declared the club ruse unconstitutional. Following this decision, some other southern states dropped their restrictions on Negroes at primaries. South Carolina has been able to take care of the matter of Negro exclusion or intimidation by refusing to adopt the secret ballot. There has been a notable increase in the number of qualified Negro voters in the South since 1940; for example, between 1940 and 1947, the number rose from 4,000 to 47,000 in Arkansas, from 20,000 to 125,000 in Georgia, from 20,000 to 80,000 in Tennessee, and from 30,000 to 100,000 in Texas. There has been a considerable increase since 1947.

Despite these legal gains in clearing the way for Negro suffrage, Negro leaders still contend that the great majority of southern Negroes are denied the right to vote. It is worth remembering, however, that the non-southern portions of the country have violated the Constitution as well as the South. The South has defied the Fifteenth Amendment, outlawing discrimination, but the non-southern majority in Congress has ignored the mandate of the Fourteenth Amendment to penalize such discrimination by reducing the congressional representation of offending states.

Since the Republican party was the party that carried through Negro emancipation, the Negroes long remained primarily loyal to the Republicans, even if they could not cast many votes for Republican candidates. Incidentally, this led to some abuses in connection with the selection of Republican delegates from the South to the Republican national nominating conventions. In the last twenty-five years, following the migration of so many Negroes to northern industrial cities, there has been a slackening of the bonds attaching the Negroes to the Republican party. Especially during the New Deal era did the Negroes turn to the Democrats, who passed much legislation favorable to their race.

At present, the Negroes tend to pursue a program of political expediency in party support, backing in any election the party most likely to promote Negro interests. The Negroes of voting age number approximately 7,500,000, with about 3,000,000 of these eligible to vote. About half of the eligibles are found in northern states. The Negro vote is now powerful out of all proportion to its numerical strength because the eligible Negro vote is concentrated in close states with a large electoral vote. The Negroes hold a potential balance of power in 17 states with some 281 electoral votes. Indeed, some expert political observers have contended that Mr. Truman owed his election victory in 1948 to the Negro vote. They point out that he won because he carried Ohio, Illinois, and California. In these states most of the Negro vote went for Truman and was considerably larger in each state than the Truman majority. The Negro voting population in New York State today is 950,000; in Pennsylvania, 470,000; in Ohio, 330,000; in California, 310,000; in Michigan, 230,000; and in Missouri, 205,000.

Many southern Negroes, perhaps less socially and economically alert than those in the North, may still cling rather generally to Republican leadership, but the Negroes in the northern cities incline to be bipartisan, giving their support to whichever party promises the most in the way of legislation favoring Negro interests. The Negro question at least temporarily split the Democrat party in 1948, the Truman following in the party sponsoring a civil rights program which flew right in the teeth of the traditional southern policies of State rights and the subordination of the Negro.

**Civil rights for Negroes.** The question of conferring full civil rights on Negroes and all other racial minorities is now vigorously before the country and has precipitated a national crisis. Civil rights problems are intimately related to the issue of the Negro in politics, for the right to vote is a major civil right. The civil rights controversy has now come to a head, primarily for four reasons: (1) the favorable attitude of the Roosevelt New Deal administration to increased civil rights for Negroes, and the personal encouragement given by Mrs. Roosevelt, especially, to the Negroes to battle for their civil liberties; (2) the important part taken by Negroes in the second world war, some 700,000 Negroes being in the Army on V-J Day, and 167,000 in the Navy, while more than two million Negroes took some part in wartime industry; (3) the appeal of the Truman administration for the political support of racial minorities, and its proposal that Federal legislation enforce full civil rights for Negroes and other racial minorities; and (4) the growth of a more liberal attitude on racial matters among some southern white leaders.

We have already referred to the abuses which arose under the Negro-carpetbagger rule in the South right after the Civil War. This provoked a white defense-reaction in the form of the Ku Klux Klan, and the passage of the so-called Black Codes by southern states which rigorously restricted the Negroes in their civil liberties and social relations. Congress responded in 1875 with the Civil Rights Act, designed to guarantee the Negroes equal privileges in hotels, theaters, and public conveyances, but this law was set aside by the Supreme Court in 1883. Today, restrictive laws and ordinances in the South, commonly known as "Jim Crow" regulations, compel Negroes to use a separate portion of railroad stations, to occupy special coaches on railroad trains and separate sections of street cars and busses, to live in segregated areas of cities, to have separate schools for Negro children, and the like.

The National Association for the Advancement of Colored People was formed under the directorship of Dr. William E. B. DuBois, and has devoted itself particularly to the struggle to obtain civil equality for Negroes, but not much progress was made until late New Deal days. There have been a number of legal victories in the courts in recent years which have at least extended the legal basis of Negro civil liberties, whatever the failure to realize them in practice as yet.

In the Mitchell case, in 1941, the Supreme Court ruled that railroads must provide accomodation for Negro passengers equal to those supplied for whites.    In 1946, a Supreme Court ruling that it is illegal to segregate Negro passengers in busses crossing state lines affected state laws in some ten states requiring such segregation.    In several cases in state and lower Federal courts, it has been ruled that Negroes must be served in regular order in railroad dining cars.

Equal rights for Negroes in state-supported universities have been upheld by the Supreme Court.    In the Gaines case in Missouri, in 1938, the Supreme Court held that students could not legally be barred from admission because of race and color, and ordered that equal educational facilities must be provided for Negroes.    In the Sipuel case in Oklahoma, in 1947, the Supreme Court ordered the state of Oklahoma to provide legal education for a Negro girl equal to that given white law students.    A law was passed in New York State, in 1948, outlawing discrimination in university admissions on the basis of race, color, or creed.    In the Alston case, the Supreme Court upheld an earlier (1940) decision by a lower Federal court ordering that Negro teachers must be paid the same as white teachers for comparable work.    A number of cases in which Negro pupils were denied admission to northern public schools have been carried to the courts, and, in some instances, the Negroes have won.    Pressure has been put on the upholders of Negro segregation by such disinterested groups as the Actors' Equity Association, which voted to refuse to put on plays in cities which segregated or excluded Negroes.

Some gains were made by the Negroes in the armed services.    On July 8, 1944, the Army was ordered to abolish segregation of Negroes in Army recreational and transportation facilities.    Some limited experimentation was carried on in 1945 in mixing Negroes and whites in replacement units in combat.    When the peacetime draft was being debated in 1948, Negro leaders demanded the abolition of all racial segregation in the armed forces, but the Army has not acquiesced in this, pending Congressional legislation supporting the demand.

Efforts to give Negroes equal rights in regard to urban residence have centered of late mainly on the attempt to outlaw restrictive covenants, namely, agreements by property owners in urban neighborhoods to refuse to sell, lease, or rent their property to Negroes or to permit any Negro occupancy thereof.    Several state and lesser Federal courts have ruled that such covenants are illegal, but the final settlement of the matter depends on working out a recent (1948) ruling by the Supreme Court that, while restrictive covenants are not unconstitutional, neither Federal nor state courts have any right to enforce them.    Efforts have been made to secure Negro admission to northern hotels, and, in the Bowman case in New York City, in 1944, the state court upheld the Negro complaint.

As we have already stated, the whole civil rights issue for Negroes and all other racial minorities has been brought actively to the fore by

the proposal of the Truman administration to extend full civil rights
to racial minorities by Federal legislation. This has provoked heated
resistance from southern leaders because it not only threatens white
supremacy in the South but also challenges State rights in handling
such problems as racial controls. At the Democrat National Con-

# AMERICA'S MINORITIES

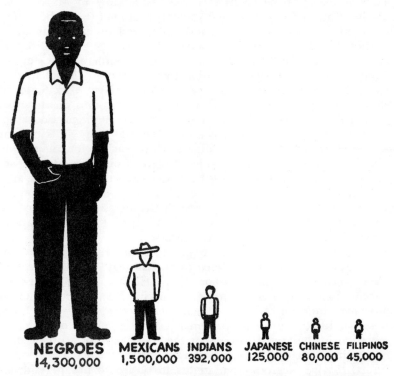

| NEGROES | MEXICANS | INDIANS | JAPANESE | CHINESE | FILIPINOS |
|---------|----------|---------|----------|---------|-----------|
| 14,300,000 | 1,500,000 | 392,000 | 125,000 | 80,000 | 45,000 |

GRAPHIC ASSOCIATES FOR PUBLIC AFFAIRS COMMITTEE, INC.

vention in Philadelphia in 1948, the civil rights clause in the platform,
inserted by pressure of the Truman following, provoked an active
revolt on the part of southern Democrats and a threat to desert the
Democrat party in the coming election. The threat was made good
in South Carolina, Alabama, Mississippi, and Louisiana, where the
state rights Democrats nominated Gov. J Strom Thurmond of South
Carolina for President. Thurmond received a popular vote of 1,006,-
363 and 38 electoral votes.

In the 81st Congress, the Truman forces sought to amend the Senate
debate rules so that the civil rights program could be pushed through
Congress. This met with a determined filibuster by southern Demo-

crats in the Senate in February and March, 1949, and President Truman had to beat an ignominious retreat. The civil rights program may be indefinitely postponed, so far as Federal legislation is concerned. What the final outcome will be remains to be seen; it can only be said that the matter of civil rights for racial minorities is now, more than ever, before the country.

**Reduction of lynchings.** An important gain in a matter closely related to Negro political and civil rights has been the reduction in the number of Negro lynchings in recent years. Lynching has been widely used in the past as a phase of vigilante justice in our frontier society. Before the Civil War it was far more usual in other parts of the country than in the South and was more frequently used on whites than Negroes. As late as 1884, 160 whites were lynched and only 51 Negroes. After this time an ever greater proportion of lynchings were of Negroes and took place in the South, primarily for the alleged purpose of discouraging sex crimes on the part of Negroes. Between 1882 and 1939, some 4,689 persons were lynched, of whom 3,400 were Negroes. In the decade of 1920–1929, no less than 95.5 per cent of lynchings took place in the South.

Owing to the leadership of both enlightened southern whites and Negro crusaders for civil rights, the number of lynchings has now been reduced almost to a nullity. The movement against lynching was primarily directed by the National Association for the Advancement of Colored People, founded in 1909, and the Commission on Inter-racial Coöperation, organized in Atlanta, Georgia, in 1918, and made up of 100 white and Negro leaders drawn from the whole South. The number of recorded lynchings has been reduced from 83 in 1919 to 6 in 1946, 1 in 1947 and 1 in 1948.

**Negro education.** The outstanding facts about Negro education today are: (1) a vast improvement since 1900; and (2) still a marked inferiority to the education of white children. It is estimated that about 97 per cent of Negroes were illiterate in 1860. In 1940, only about 10 per cent were so rated, as compared with 1.3 per cent for native whites and 12.2 per cent for foreign-born Americans.

The number and proportion of Negro children in schools have greatly increased since 1900. In that year, 1,083,516 Negro children, or 31 per cent of all those between 5 and 20 years of age, were attending school. In 1940, 2,698,901 out of a total of 4,188,500, or 64.4 per cent, were in school. For the age-group of 5–17 years, the figures were even more impressive. In 1940, about 86 percent of all Negro children between 5 and 17 were enrolled in public schools.

Moreover, Negro public school education is no longer so markedly concentrated in the lower elementary grades. More pupils get into higher grades and more go on to high schools, though the ratio is still far below that for white children. The length of the school term for Negroes is beginning to catch up with that for white children. In 1945–1946 in 17 southern states and the District of Columbia, the average school term for Negroes was 170.1 days, as compared with 174.9 for whites. The average number of days attended by pupils in 1945–1946 was 139 for Negroes and 149 for whites. The teacher-pupil ratio has also improved; in 1945–1946 it was 35 for Negroes and 28 for whites.

All this is encouraging, but other figures bring out additional facts about the lag between educational facilities for Negroes and those available for white children. The median percentage of Negro teach-

F. S. A., photo by Rothstein.

Courtesy of General Education Board.

The top picture shows one of the older and dilapidated Negro schools. The bottom picture is of the admirable new Negro centralized rural school at Piney Woods, near Jackson, Mississippi.

ers who had four years or more of college education in 1940 was 28.9 as against 52.7 for white teachers, and, as a rule, the Negro colleges offered poorer instruction than the white. The school buildings for Negro children are inferior to those for whites in most cases in the South, though there are some notable exceptions and the situation in this respect is improving. In 1940 the median expenditure for a standard classroom-unit in southern states was $476 for Negroes and $1,160 for whites. The spread of such equipment cost for Negroes was great, running from $154 in Mississippi to $1,250 in West Virginia.

The pay of teachers in Negro schools remains lower than that of white teachers. In 14 southern states, in 1941–1942, the average annual salary of Negro teachers ran from $226 in Mississippi to $1,593 in Maryland; the pay of white teachers varied from $712 in Mississippi to $1,796 in Delaware. The United States Supreme Court has upheld a Federal court decision of 1940 ordering Negro teachers to be paid the same salary as white teachers for comparable work, but the salary situation has not been equalized thus far. In 1945–1946, the average salary of Negro teachers was $1,134, as compared with $1,640 for white teachers. In 1945–1946, the annual expenditure for Negro pupils in 17 southern states and the District of Columbia was $57.57 per pupil, as against $104.66 for white pupils.

The general picture of Negro public school education is, thus, one of steady and gratifying improvement, but much additional progress must be made to bring Negro education up to anything like a parity with white education in southern states. Negro education in urban northern areas is better than in the South, but even in the North the level is often below that for white children, with respect to both the educational plant and the quality of instruction.

Despite these handicaps more and more Negroes are getting a college education. In 1940, 1.1 per cent of Negroes had one or more years of college education; this figure was far below that for whites, which stood at 5.4 per cent. In 1945–1946, there were 117 Negro institutions of higher learning, with 57,500 enrolled, as compared with 43,000 in 1940. Some fourteen of these institutions offer instruction on the graduate level, and, in 1944–1945, some 576 graduate students were enrolled. Among the best of these Negro colleges and universities are Atlanta University, Fisk University, Florida A & M College, Hampton Institute, Howard University, Knoxville College, Langston University, Lincoln University, North Carolina A & T College, Tuskegee Institute, Virginia State College for Negroes, West Virginia State College, and Wilberforce University. There are now over 45,000 Negroes who have college degrees. It is an interesting fact that large numbers of students in Negro colleges and universities, which are concentrated mainly in southern states, come from the North.

The legal struggle for Negro admission to state-supported colleges and universities has taken on a new impetus after the Supreme Court victories in the Gaines and Sipuel cases mentioned above. If states admit Negroes to the regular state universities or open comparable institutions for Negroes, the situation will be markedly improved. Northern states may follow the example of New York which, as we noted, has passed a law barring discrimination against Negroes in college and university admissions.

Special aid for Negroes. A number of foundations have given special assistance to the improvement of Negro education, especially in the South. Such are the Julius Rosenwald Fund, the Rockefeller General Education Board, the Peabody Fund, the Slater Fund, and the Phelps-Stokes Fund. There is much agitation for Federal aid to Negro education, but the South has not been very cordial to this movement because it challenges State rights and white supremacy and because it is feared that Federal aid may be contingent on the abolition of racial segregation in the school system.

**Negroes in scholarship, journalism, the arts, and sports.** The number of Negroes who have distinguished themselves in various fields of scholarship is so extensive that they cannot be completely listed here. Some of the best known are the great Negro chemist, George Washington Carver; the historians, William E. B. DuBois, and Carter G. Woodson; the economist, Abram L. Harris; and the philosopher, Alain L. Locke.

Negro education outside the schools has been promoted by the increasing number and improved nature of Negro newspapers. In 1943, there were 164 active Negro newspapers, of which the circulation of 106 increased by 27 per cent between 1943 and 1945. There are 15 Negro newsgathering agencies which serve these papers. Some of the Negro newspapers, such as the *Pittsburgh Courier,* are of high quality. George Schuyler, columnist for the *Courier,* is regarded by other commentators as one of the best in American journalism, and he does not stand alone. The Negro newspapers are abandoning their former more or less exclusive concern with Negro problems and interests and are giving more coverage to public affairs and world events. Important newspaper awards and prizes have recently been won by Negroes.

Even those who are skeptical about the Negro intellect have to admit the success of the black race in literature, music, and art. There are the novelists, Walter F. White, Jessie Fauset, and Claude McKay; the poets, Paul Laurence Dunbar, James Weldon Johnson, Langston Hughes, and Countee Cullen. Samuel Coleridge-Taylor, W. C. Handy, William Grant Still, and H. Lawrence Freeman are outstanding Negro composers. Negro singers can be counted by the dozen, the outstanding being Paul Robeson, Roland Hayes, and Marian Anderson. Other important Negro artists are the conductors, Dean Dixon and Duke Ellington; the pianists, Hazel Harrison and Roy Tibbs; the violinist, Baughan Jones; the composer and pianist prodigy, Philippa Schuyler; the painter, Henry Farmer; the sculptor, Richmond Barthe; and the architect, Paul R. Williams.

The Negro has competed successfully with whites in sports. Among pugilists, Joe Gans, Jack Johnson, Henry Armstrong, and Joe Louis head the Negro list. Jesse Owens is one of the greatest of modern athletes. A great gain, recently, for Negroes in the world of sports has been their admission to membership on major league baseball teams. Jackie Robinson of the Brooklyn Dodgers was voted the most valuable player in the National League in 1949.

Although some mental tests claim to have shown the Negro to be inferior to the white man with respect to sheer intelligence, there is absolutely no scientific evidence to support the view that the Negro belongs to an inferior race. The brief survey of distinguished Negroes should remove any doubt that the Negro is capable of achieving greatness in a chosen field if given the opportunity.

**Negro religion.** The church has been one of the main cultural factors in the Negro's life, for there he feels no color or racial inferiority. He is one of "God's own chillun." Negro church membership increased from 5,203,487 in 1926 to 5,660,618 in 1936, an increase of 8.6 per cent in the decade, while the percentage of increase in total church membership during this period was only 2.4 per cent.

*Courtesy of Howard University.*

**Pictured in front of the School of Engineering & Architecture at Howard University is a group of students doing a surveying job for one of their courses.**

The majority of Negro church members are highly orthodox and Fundamentalist in their religious beliefs. Contrary to the general opinion, however, Negroes are not overwhelmingly and universally religious. The above figures indicate that over one-half of the American Negroes do not attend any church.

The most recent dramatic demonstration of Negro religious enthusiasm has been the work of Father Divine in New York City. The Father has attracted thousands of Negroes into his religious establishments, or "heavens," as he calls them. More realistic has been the religious leadership of Adam Clayton Powell, Jr., minister of the great Negro church in Harlem, New York City. Powell carried his leadership from religion into politics when he was elected to Congress in 1945.

**Programs for improving Negro-white relations.** Negro leaders have sought for ways of improving the condition of their race. One of the most frequently advocated schemes is "interracial conciliation," or the education of both Negroes and whites so that they may become less race-conscious and realize the advantages of mutual respect and co-operation. The outstanding advocate of interracial conciliation was Booker T. Washington (1856–1915), founder in 1881 of the famous Tuskegee Institute in Alabama. Washington appealed to the self-interest of the whites by contending that it would be impossible for the South to rise so long as it imposed legal and social handicaps on the blacks. The program of interracial conciliation may promote peace and good will between the two races, but it has done little, as yet, to improve the social and economic position of the Negro.

A more forthright plan for solving the Negro problem is advocated by William E. B. DuBois, who demands full social and political equality. In 1909 DuBois helped to found the National Association for the Advancement of Colored People, currently the most effective organization in promoting social equality and civil liberties for Negroes. The NAACP, now led by Walter White, lays great stress upon education as a means of equipping Negroes for worth-while positions in American life.

Another useful program, stressing the practical improvement of economic well-being and living conditions among Negroes in industrial cities, has been carried on by the National Urban League, established in 1910. The League lays primary stress on finding employment for Negroes, promoting industrial training for them, improving employer-worker relationships, providing civic education for Negroes, and developing programs for better social adjustment in urban living.

Somewhat different from these plans for Negro betterment on a national scale are the programs which concentrate on improving interracial relations in local urban areas. These usually seek to bring Negroes and other racial minorities together with native whites, and, by various educational, cultural, and recreational activities, to promote better interracial understanding and tolerance. The idea is that interracial understanding, like charity, should begin at home to be most effective. An example of such local movements is the Fellowship House established at Philadelphia.

**The outlook for Negro-white relations.** The problem of racial adjustments and conflicts in the United States is in too fluid a condition to justify any dogmatic predictions. Not since the slavery controversies before the Civil War has the issue of civil rights for racial minorities been so forcibly before the American public or the matter of racial equality and race relations been so warmly debated. The fact that the forces supporting race equality are more powerful and better organized than at any earlier time has simply provoked correspondingly stronger reactions on the part of those who wish to continue white superiority. The developments in the future will depend not only on public education and debate on the race issue, but also on the general economic and social situation in the country. Continued prosperity will be likely to restrain interracial violence, while prolonged depression may encourage various elements to find a scape-goat in a racial minority. Moreover, economic and social chaos are a natural breeding ground for intolerance and violence.

It was natural that the increased prominence and movements of Negroes during the second world war and the readjustments immediately thereafter would tend to promote clashes between whites and Negroes. The most important of these race riots were the Mobile (Alabama) Riot of May, 1943; the Beaumont (Texas) Riot of June, 1943; the Detroit Riot of June, 1943 (the most bloody of all); the Harlem Riot of July, 1943; the Columbia (Tennessee) Riot of February, 1946; and the Athens (Alabama) Riot of August, 1946. While these incidents were unfortunate, they were not as numerous as might have been anticipated nor as bloody as several earlier race riots following the first world war.

The main interest in interracial relations has recently tended to shift from the prevention of sporadic race riots to the promotion of a comprehensive movement for civil rights for all racial minorities. In this movement, the leaders have been drawn from all racial minorities as well as from native whites who believe in racial equality and interracial toleration.

While the material in the preceding pages on the Negro problem demonstrates marked progress in the education, alertness, and public power of the Negro element, this does not mean that the problem of racial prejudice and conflict has been solved or even reduced. Indeed, the opposite may be the case. The greater the advances made by Negroes, the more impatient they become over their remaining handicaps and the more determined to remove them. This, in turn, encourages the champions of white superiority to take stronger steps to keep the Negroes under control. Further, the idea that all prejudice against the Negro is a monopoly of the South is a gross misconception. The South has been in greater contact with more Negroes for a longer period of time. When Negroes have seemed to threaten vested white interests in the North, there has been no dearth of anti-Negro sentiment and action. Some of the worst race riots have taken place in northern cities. In fact, many southerners probably have less actual prejudice against the Negro than some northerners. The southerners are mainly interested in perpetuating white supremacy.

Undoubtedly, the most important single factor in promoting greater Negro strength in public affairs and more success in securing Negro civil rights has been the migration of large numbers of Negroes to northern cities located in states where the vote is fairly evenly divided between the two major parties. Here, the Negroes can hold something like a balance of power, especially if they join forces with other racial minorities. This new situation has led northern politicians of both parties to pay more attention to Negro demands. Politically speaking, the Negroes can no longer be ignored as a voteless minority, segregated in a group of southern states. This, again, does not necessarily promote either political or racial harmony. It has stimulated southern political leaders to resist proposed Federal legislation which would better the lot of the Negroes. Another factor in winning more civil rights for Negroes was the fact that President Roosevelt remade the United States Supreme Court in his own image, or at least in New Deal image, which was unusually friendly to the idea of racial equality.

These concluding considerations are offered mainly to make it clear that, although there are plenty of rocks ahead in the race problem in the United States, sporadic recent gains may point to the eventual triumph of racial tolerance and ideas of racial equality.

## Summary

In any strictly scientific conception of the term, race is wholly a physical fact or condition, the differences among races being based upon such things as color of the skin, head form, physiognomy, stature, texture of the hair, and the like. Racial traits are often confused with cultural traits, which are far more a product of the natural and social environment than of race, strictly speaking. Race prejudice, itself, is chiefly a cultural manifestation.

There are no literally "pure" races today. Even the three main races of mankind, the white, yellow, and black, are all shot through with race mixture. There is no proof that any one main race is comprehensively superior to any other race. Superiority is primarily a matter of the most successful adjustment to the environment. It is even doubtful if any one race is superior to another in sheer intelligence, if the latter is viewed in any broad sense.

The United States has experienced a wide variety of racial contacts, though the white race has been dominant here since the days of discovery and exploration. Our contacts with the Mongolian race have involved relations with Indians, Chinese, and Japanese, in which it must be confessed that the record of the white majority is not conspicuous for sympathy, insight, tolerance, or statecraft.

The Negro problem has been our most serious racial issue, primarily because of the greater number of Negroes and their relative concentration in a few southern states. The Negroes have made much and varied progress since slavery days in regard to numbers, economic well-being, political power, civil liberties, educational achievements, literary and artistic accomplishments, and the like. But Negroes still lag far behind the native whites in most facilities and opportunities for advancement and prosperity.

The most unsettling item in recent Negro history has been the migration of large numbers of Negroes to northern industrial cities. This has vitally reshaped the status and prestige of the Negro in American politics and given him more power in battling for his civil rights. The Negro has made many gains in most aspects of life since 1933. Whether this is the first great step in the achievement of virtual racial emancipation or will only serve to provoke a resurgence of various programs to perpetuate white supremacy cannot be said with dogmatic assurance today. The greatest hope for tolerance lies in continued economic prosperity and the avoidance of another devastating world war. Chaos and crises tend to breed scapegoats in the form of racial minorities.

## Selected References

Allen, J. S., *The Negro Question in the United States,* International Publishers, 1936. Lays special emphasis on the relation of the Negro situation to industrialization and the labor problem. One of the most searching studies of the economics of the Negro question.

Benedict, Ruth, *Race: Science and Politics,* Viking, 1940. A spirited attack on race myths and prejudices and their exploitation in political policies, especially in Europe in recent times.

Bond, H. M., *The Education of the Negro in the American Social Order,* Prentice-Hall, 1934. A standard account of the education of the Negro.

Collier, John, *The Indians of the Americas,* Norton, 1947. Comprehensive historical and sociological treatment of the Indian problem by the former Commissioner of Indian Affairs.

Cox, O. C., *Caste, Class and Race,* Doubleday, 1948. An extended critique of doctrines and practices based on the ideas of social aristocracy and race prejudice.

Dale, E. E., *The Indians of the Southwest: A Century of Development under the United States,* University of Oklahoma Press, 1949. An unusually intelligent, interesting, and expert account of the sector of Indian life most important in our time.

* Davie, M. R., *Negroes in American Society,* McGraw-Hill, 1949. A sociological study of Negro life and Negro-white relations from the African background to the current struggle for FEPC laws. The outstanding recent book on the Negro problem.

* Davis, Allison, and Dollard, John, *Children of Bondage,* American Council on Education, 1940. Competent and interesting analysis of the efforts of Negroes, especially Negro youth, to adjust their life to city conditions and mechanical industry in the South.

DuBois, W. E. B., *The World and Africa,* Viking, 1947. An able book on the historical African background of Negro culture and social experience. Fills an important gap in the literature on the Negro problem.

* Fairchild, H. P., *Race and Nationality, as Factors in American Life,* Ronald, 1947. Realistic book by the leading American authority on immigration. Good supplement to the Hankins volume noted below.

Franklin, J. H., *From Slavery to Freedom,* Knopf, 1947. Comprehensive historical survey of American Negroes, from their African background to the gains in race equality since the second world war.

Frazier, E. F., *The Negro in the United States,* Macmillan, 1949. Regarded by many as the most competent and important single volume on the Negro problem. A professional sociological analysis.

Graeber, Isacque, and Britt, S. H. (Eds.), *Jews in a Gentile World,* Macmillan, 1942. Symposium on Jewish life and anti-Semitism in the United States.

Grant, Madison, *The Passing of the Great Race,* Scribner, 1916. An influential statement of the theory of race superiority. Deals particularly with the Nordic race.

* Hankins, F. H., *The Racial Basis of Civilization,* Knopf, 1926. The best single volume on the race problem. Debunks the more vulgar theories of race superiority without surrendering a scientific attitude toward racial problems and eugenics.

Herskovits, M. J., *The American Negro,* Knopf, 1928. A useful little book, presenting the main facts about the origins and physical traits of the Negro in the United States.

* Klineberg, Otto, *Race Differences,* Harper, 1935. Competent analysis of the problem of race superiority and racial abilities.

* La Farge, Oliver, *As Long as the Grass Shall Grow,* Longmans, Green, 1940. Sympathetic treatment of the Indian peoples and cultures, and of the relations of the Indians with the government.

————— (Ed.), *The Changing Indian,* University of Oklahoma Press, 1942. General symposium on Indian life, social conditions, and public treatment.

Lee, G. W., *River George,* Macaulay, 1937. A social novel portraying the difficulties of educated Negroes in the South after the first world war. Gives information which does not get into textbooks and throws light on Negro folkways.

MacLeod, W. C., *The American Indian Frontier,* Knopf, 1928. Best single book on Indian life and culture prior to white domination.

McWilliams, Carey, *Prejudice; Japanese-Americans: Symbol of Racial Intolerance,* Little, Brown, 1944. Critical analysis of racial contacts between Americans and Japanese in this country.

—————, *North From Mexico,* Lippincott, 1949. Best book on American racial contacts with Mexicans and Spanish-speaking Americans.

Myrdal, Gunnar, *An American Dilemma,* 2 vols., Harper, 1944. The most elaborate study ever made of the American Negro problem.

Ottley, Roi, *Black Odyssey,* Scribner, 1948. Intensely interesting journalistic history of the Negroes in the United States.

Park, R. E., *Race and Culture,* The Free Press, 1949. Important collection of essays by a leading American expert on race problems. Stresses cultural aspects of race problem.

Pinson, K. S. (Ed.), *Essays on Antisemitism.* New York: Jewish Social Studies, Inc., 1946. Able symposium on American Jewish problems.

\* Powdermaker, Hortense, *After Freedom,* Viking, 1939. Probably the best case-study ever made of contemporary Negro life in the Deep South. It is an account of life in a Negro community in a cotton-growing section of Mississippi. An indispensable book on the Negro problem.

\* Rose, A. M., *The Negro's Morale,* University of Minnesota Press, 1950. Important treatment of Negro reaction to race discrimination and the effect of this on Negro relations with whites.

Sandmeyer, E. C., *The Anti-Chinese Movement in California,* University of Illinois Press, 1939. A study of Chinese-American racial conflicts in California.

Schermerhorn, R. A., *These Our People,* Heath, 1949. Able descriptive panorama of American minority groups and their problems.

Snyder, L. L., *Race: A History of Modern Ethnic Theories,* Longmans, Green, 1939. A readable and reliable account of the origins and spread of the dogma of racial superiority.

Spero, S. D., and Harris, A. L., *The Black Worker,* Columbia University Press, 1931. An authoritative account of the relation of the Negro to problems of employment and unionization. Written before the CIO, it needs to be supplemented by H. R. Cayton and G. S. Mitchell's *Black Workers and the New Unions,* University of North Carolina Press, 1939.

\* Tannenbaum, Frank, *Slave and Citizen,* Knopf, 1947. Authoritative brief study of various historic policies relative to treatment of Negroes by whites.

*The Negro Year Book,* edited by J. P. Guzman, V. C. Foster, and W. H. Hughes, Tuskegee, 1947. Most comprehensive compendium of facts on Negroes. Especially valuable for description of Negro achievements in scholarship, science, literature, arts, and sports.

Weaver, R. C., *The Negro Ghetto,* Harcourt, Brace, 1948. Comprehensive study of racial segregation of Negroes in Northern cities and the Negro struggle to get decent housing.

White, W. F., *Man Called White,* Viking, 1948. Autobiography of Walter F. White of NAACP, the most active proponent of Negro emancipation from civil disabilities. Contains much interesting and cogent information on race relations.

# CHAPTER XII

## Improving the Nation's Health

### Health and Disease as a Social Problem

**The medical revolution.** In few fields of human endeavor has greater progress been made in the past hundred years than in medical science. The brilliant work of doctors and research scientists has revealed the causes and cures of many once incurable diseases. Impressive advances have been made in surgery and medical practice. Ultra-modern hospitals, with the newest and finest equipment, stand on the sites of the dingy "nursing homes" of a century ago. Indeed, if we speak of an Industrial Revolution as having occurred within the past century, we must also acknowledge a "medical revolution."

**Persistence of bad health.** Yet, medical examinations of selectees for the United States army during the second world war revealed a startling percentage of poor health, among the very group who should be physically most fit. Some 5,000,000 out of 15,000,000 men called up by the draft boards were rejected because of physical and mental defects which made them unfit for military service. The results of these examinations have led medical authorities to declare that the health of the American population is definitely below par. This opinion is confirmed by examination of our annual statistics of sickness and death. Competent medical authorities have stated that only about one person in a hundred in the United States today can be regarded as in truly perfect health. In 1945, some 1,401,719 persons died from all causes. It is estimated that some 325,000, or 23 per cent, of these deaths could have been prevented by timely and sufficient medical care.

This paradox of great advances in medical science along with a high sickness and death rate demands explanation, for it presents a serious challenge to the United States. Since our birth rate is falling in normal times, population growth depends upon our ability to lower the death rate. Furthermore, the quality as well as the quantity of population is affected by health. Sick men and women cannot think clearly or do a normal amount of work. Sickness causes an appalling loss of working time, wages, and profits. It has been reliably estimated that the total direct and indirect monetary cost of illness, pre-

236

ventable deaths, and accidents amounted to 38 billion dollars in 1947 [1]. Bodily illness also produces a vast amount of misery and worry, which increases mental disease.

The total losses from illness, accidents, and preventable deaths equal nearly 15 per cent of our national income; our total public and private outlay for all types of medical care and health services amounts to about $8,500,000,000, or only about 3 per cent of our national income. In short, the ravages of disease and accidents cost us more than four times as much as we are willing to spend to check them.

## The History of Disease

**Ancient origin of diseases.** Sickness and disease have always been mankind's lot. Skeletons of early man indicate that many diseases known today were common in prehistoric times. Lesions (scars and distortions) in these skeletons suggest that primitive men suffered from tuberculosis. The primitive practice of cutting open the skull may be an indication that early peoples suffered from headaches, brain tumors, and related disorders.

Cholera, smallpox, and leprosy are known to have existed in the ancient Orient. The Old Testament, the records of the Egyptian tombs, and Greek medical literature reveal many other present-day afflictions. During the Middle Ages, there was a series of deadly epidemics, among which the Black Death, or bubonic plague, of the fourteenth century was the most serious. Although our present ways of living have given rise to few new diseases, they have made certain long-existent diseases more prevalent and serious. The strains of modern life increase high blood pressure, serious heart disorders, and mental diseases. Richer and softer foods and nervous tension help to cause dental and digestive troubles.

## Causes of Disease

**Main causes of diseases.** Before men could find cures, they needed to know how diseases started and how they were "caught." Modern medicine is based on the theory that most sickness is started by germs, which spread from one person to another. This is called the "germ theory" of disease; diseases which spread in this manner are regarded as "contagious." The most important non-contagious diseases are the chronic ailments of old age and mental and nervous disorders.

**The germ theory.** Early peoples realized that diseases spread, but they did not know how or why. The modern theory that diseases are carried by microscopic organisms, called microbes or "germs," was first set forth by Dr. Jacob Henle, about 1840. Some diseases, like typhoid fever, cholera, and dysentery, are carried by germs contained

---

[1] For the items and calculations on which this remarkable estimate is based, see O. R. Ewing, *The Nation's Health*, Federal Security Agency, 1948, pp. 26–29.

in bodily discharges which infect the soil and water. Insects also spread disease: certain types of mosquitoes carry malaria and yellow fever; the deadly spotted fever is caused by a tick bite, and African sleeping sickness by a fly bite. Another group of contagious diseases is transmitted mainly by direct contact with other infected human beings. Measles, diphtheria, and venereal diseases are examples. Certain diseases, like colds, influenza, smallpox, and infantile paralysis, are what are known as virus diseases, that is, they are caused by ultramicroscopic bodies that lie on the borderline between the organic and the inorganic worlds and are so small that they can only be seen with the recently invented electron microscope.

Bacteriologists (scientists who study bacteria or germs) have been able to discover most of the germs responsible for contagious diseases, but the specific germs or viruses of influenza, typhus, smallpox, and rabies have not yet been completely isolated. Ignorance of the germs has not, however, prevented science from taking effective measures to prevent the contraction and spread of these diseases.

**Chronic and degenerative diseases.** Today, in most civilized countries, the deadliest diseases are not the contagious maladies, but the chronic, degenerative illnesses of middle life or old age. Nearly 25 million persons in the United States are suffering from these chronic or degenerative diseases. Seventy-five years ago, these diseases accounted for only one-fifteenth of the deaths; today, they account for over three-fourths of the deaths.[2] Although such diseases are especially numerous among older people, at least half of those suffering from them in the United States today are under 45 years of age. Chronic diseases also greatly increase the problem of medical care and hospitalization because their victims usually live many years and require prolonged treatment. The most serious of these chronic and degenerative diseases are heart maladies, cancer, brain lesions, and kidney disorders.

## Extent of Disease and Accidents in the United States

**Amazing extent of illness.** In the autumn and winter of 1935–1936, the United States Public Health Service, aided by grants from the Works Progress Administration, made a house-to-house canvass of illness in 740,000 urban families in 19 states and 36,000 rural families in 3 states.

On the basis of this survey it was estimated that, in the United States, 6 million persons are not able to work on any average day during the winter months because of illness resulting from disease or injury caused by accident. This figure is higher than it would have been for the summer months, since in winter there are more cases of influenza,

---

[2] In April, 1949, it was reported that death from heart disease among all ordinary life insurance policy holders had climbed to a new record high of 327.9 per 100,000 of the population.

pneumonia, and colds.   An official estimate in 1948 held that at least 7 million persons are laid up every day by illness.

"**The great killers.**"   The most serious diseases are the "great killers," those which are most likely to produce death and do actually bring about the greatest number of deaths.   Heart disease heads the

## CHANGING CAUSES OF DEATH*

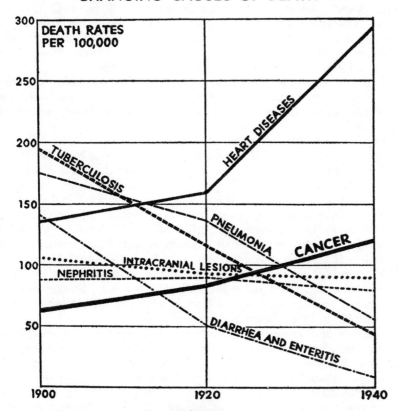

GRAPHIC ASSOCIATES FOR PUBLIC AFFAIRS COMMITTEE, INC.

*In the United States.*

The graph above makes clear the decline of the more mortal diseases of 1900 and the alarming increase of such chronic diseases as heart troubles and cancer.

list.   An estimated 60 million persons now alive in the United States will die of heart disease and circulatory troubles unless treatment is radically improved and applied in the immediate future.   It is highly amazing that, in the light of these appalling figures, only about 200 out of some 150,000 practicing physicians in the United States limit themselves solely in their practice to the specialized treatment of heart disorders, and less than 450 others are even part-time specialists in this field.   The amount of money spent for research and the study of heart disease is also distressingly low.   In 1948 the per-death expenditure for these purposes was $525 for infantile paralysis, $2.13 for cancer, but only 17 cents for heart disease.   Despite all the money spent on infantile paralysis research, the epidemic of 1949—about 40,000 cases—was the worst in our history.

Cancer ranks next to heart and circulatory diseases as a killer today.   Some 500,000 persons died from cancer from 1942 through 1944, or nearly twice as many as were killed in battle among the American armed forces in the second world war.   No less than 188,-000 persons died of cancer in 1947.   Around 20 million persons now alive will die of cancer unless a cure is speedily found.

Medical statistics indicate that third in order as a menace to health and life come the various brain lesions, and fourth, the chronic, degenerative kidney diseases, sometimes lumped together under the name of nephritis.

As we have indicated above, the money we spend to fight the more deadly diseases has been illogically apportioned.   The National Foundation for Infantile Paralysis collected 22 million dollars in 1948, and had a reserve of over 10 million.   The National Tuberculosis Association collected about 20 million, and the American Cancer Society over 13 million.   But the American Heart Association, which has to combat the greatest "killer" of all, collected only $1,600,000.   The most important achievement in the campaign against heart diseases came in 1948.   The federal government passed the National Heart Act, which provided for the establishment of the National Heart Institute as a unit in the United States Public Health Service.   Some 3 million dollars was appropriated for this work in 1949 and over 15 million will be available in 1950 to carry forward the program.

**Arthritis and rheumatic disorders a leading cause of disability.** Not a chief cause of death but the most serious chronic ailment and the second largest cause of disability today is arthritis, along with allied rheumatic ills.   While arthritis is a peculiarly stubborn disorder, the causes of which are little understood even by specialists, and for which there is no specific remedy, its serious ravages are due mainly to ignorance and neglect.   One of the leading medical specialists in the field, Dr. LeMoyne C. Kelley, has recently estimated that "more than 75 per cent of all arthritis cases can be benefited or cured if adequate treatment is begun during the first year.   Even more advanced cases can be helped."   And the treatment and remedies thus far found most effective are relatively cheap.

**Industrial diseases.**   Any discussion of the nature and incidence of disease would be incomplete if mention were not made of industrial diseases.   One of the great penalties that we have had to pay for our machine age is the harmful effect of factory work upon human health.

Occupational diseases may take many forms, from the general undermining of the health of miners and office workers, who fail to get

enough fresh air and sunshine, to such specific ailments as lead poisoning contracted by painters and silicosis contracted by stone cutters
from stone dust.    It would be difficult to estimate the amount of ill
health for which modern working conditions are responsible.

There is also little doubt that the fatigue associated with many jobs,
especially in mass-production factories has a serious effect upon health.
The sheer boredom of factory work produces nervous reactions which
keep many people from work.    An English medical journal, *The
Lancet*, stated in 1931 that boredom caused industrial workers in
England to lose more time from their jobs than all the recognized industrial diseases combined.

Fortunately, increasing attention has been paid to industrial fatigue
and occupational diseases within the past fifty years.    Many employers now take elaborate precautions to safeguard their workers, and
some state laws provide compensation for those suffering from occupational diseases.    The application of the principles of scientific management has helped to remedy the situation somewhat, and perhaps
even more beneficial has been the introduction of industrial and clinical psychology by some enlightened employers.    But, as yet, only
the surface of this major economic and medical problem has been
scratched.

**Prevalence of accidents.**    Disease is not the only leading cause of
death.    There are over 30,000 accidents every day and over 10 million
a year serious enough to keep a person home from work for a day or
longer.    Fatal accidents have decreased from a high of 110,000 in
1936 but the figure is still far too high.    Some 275,338 Americans lost
their lives in the armed forces during the second world war, but during this same period the deaths from accidents numbered over 355,000.
Some 670,584 Americans were wounded during the war, but during
the same years those injured in accidents numbered 36,000,000.

In 1940, accidents produced a loss of man-days in industry some 20
times greater than the loss of work time due to strikes.    It has been
pointed out that the loss of 340 million man-days through accidents
in the first nine months of 1941 might have built 20 battleships, 200
destroyers, and 1,000 heavy bombers.    The total cost of caring for all
the physically handicapped—deaf, dumb, blind, and crippled—many
of them maimed by accidents, is over 250 million dollars annually.
Only a few of these afflicted men and women are employed.

**Chief causes of accidents.**    The causes of accidents are an over-
powering desire for profit, which keeps employers from installing
safety devices on dangerous machines; the mania of motorists for speed
on the highways and on city streets; and carelessness in factories and
mines, on the streets, and, above all, in the home.    In a normal peacetime year, about one-third of all accidents causing death take place in
the home.    Nearly 20 per cent of the 100,000 deaths from accident in
1947 occurred on farms.

In the last few years there has been a decline in industrial acci-

dents, for workmen's compensation laws have forced employers to provide better safety devices: for example, goggles to shield the eyes of
the metal or stone worker, steel covering for dangerous machinery,
and emergency levers to stop a machine before it crushes a man's
hands. Pressure by John L. Lewis and his United Mine Workers and
enlightened self-interest on the part of some mine operators have

## UNLESS WE ACT · · ·
## CANCER DEATHS WILL RISE

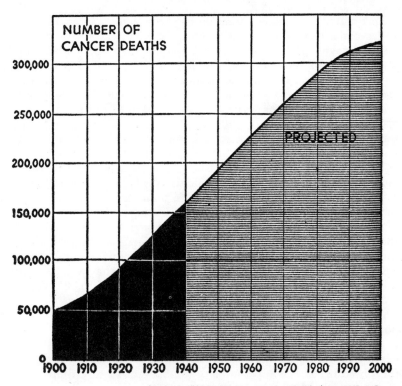

GRAPHIC ASSOCIATES FOR PUBLIC AFFAIRS COMMITTEE, INC.

markedly reduced the accidents in mining in recent years. Beginning
in 1912, the vast steel industry of the United States has given special
attention to accident prevention. In 1949, its accident record was
about half that of the average for all industries. Safety measures have
also reduced railroad accidents. In 1937, the safest year on record,
there were only 18 passenger fatalities, a rate of 0.073 per hundred
million passenger miles. Lack of repair and replacement on road beds
and equipment, as well as greater speeds and traffic, led to a considerable increase of accidents after Pearl Harbor, but they were even then

far fewer than thirty years ago, and new equipment is now bringing the accident fatality rate down to prewar levels—0.074 per hundred million passenger miles in 1949.

**Rise of the safety movement.** The accident menace has been countered by the rise of the safety movement.[3] Safety campaigns in large cities are waging war on the careless motorist who does not "Stop! Look! and Listen!" Special educational movies have been prepared showing the dangers of drunken driving and carelessness at home. The striking and shocking educational pamphlet, *And Sudden Death*, on automobile accidents, by J. C. Furnas, made many persons more careful on the roads.

**Handicapped persons.** An important item in the health and medical problem is the matter of handicapped persons. There are at least 28 million handicapped children and adults in the country, distributed, according to the estimate for August, 1948, as follows: deaf and hard of hearing, 9 million; orthopedically handicapped, 8 million; dumb and lesser speech defects, 6 million; cardiac troubles, 4 million; epileptic, 800,000; and blind and defective vision, 250,000. That this estimate is moderate can be seen from the fact that a special survey of those suffering from hearing ailments in 1949 put the number at 15 million. It was estimated that, of this number, 3 million were children, the great majority of whom could be cured if they received adequate treatment in time.

The cost of caring for the handicapped runs to well over a quarter of a billion dollars a year. When one also considers the cost of the loss of labor and of professional and industrial skill involved, the economic cost of handicapped persons is astronomical, presumably running into several billion dollars a year. Since many of these handicaps result from preventable diseases and accidents, the problem is directly linked with that of medical care and safety precautions to prevent accidents.

## Economic and Social Aspects of Illness

**Close interrelation of illness and poverty.** There is a direct relationship between poverty and the amount of disease, and between poverty and inadequate medical care. While there are many in the population whose income is so low that they could not provide themselves with medical care under any scheme of co-operative medicine or health insurance, all except those in a state of poverty could get fairly adequate medical care if they were able to budget medical care through some group or public insurance scheme. It is the combination of low income and the absence of insurance plans which deprives millions of proper medical care. About 70 per cent of the population would have to borrow money to pay the cost of any serious illness.

---

[3] See below, pp. 697–698.

We may present some figures illustrating the high prevalence of disease among the poor.  The Federal health survey of 1935–1936 showed that serious illness was 57 per cent higher among families on relief than among families with an annual income of $3,000 or over.  Chronic illness ran 87 per cent higher among relief families.  Nonrelief families with an income of less than $1,000 had twice as much

## ACCIDENTAL DEATHS BY PRINCIPAL TYPES – 1948

each symbol ✝ represents 4000 deaths

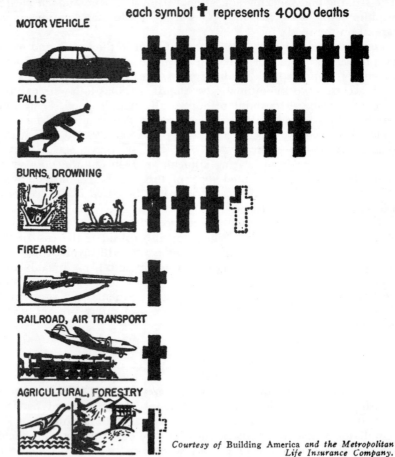

MOTOR VEHICLE

FALLS

BURNS, DROWNING

FIREARMS

RAILROAD, AIR TRANSPORT

AGRICULTURAL, FORESTRY

*Courtesy of* Building America *and the Metropolitan Life Insurance Company.*

illness as families with an income of more than $1,000.  As Professor Bernhard J. Stern puts it: "It is clear that ill health and high mortality are products of poverty and low income and do not arise from any postulated organic inferiority of those belonging to the lower income groups."[4]

---

[4] "Income and Health," *Science and Society,* Summer, 1941, p. 206.

It is taken for granted that health conditions among the poor in city slums are bad, but we assume that even the poor in country districts are robust and healthy. This illusion was shattered by a health survey of low-income farm families conducted by the Farm Security Administration in 1941. The findings have been summarized as follows:

Farm security officials were shocked to find that only four per cent were in good health while the number of physical defects averaged three and a half per person. An appalling rate of defective teeth, vision, and hearing is disclosed in the report, and clinical diagnoses revealed that one child out of every 12 under 15 years of age suffered from malnutrition and one out of 17 from rickets.[5]

**Higher death rate among the poor.** The death rate is higher among the poor for three main reasons: (1) crowded and unsanitary living conditions expose them to greater danger of infection; (2) low incomes deny them sufficient money for good medical care; and (3) improper or insufficient food and bad housing lower resistance to disease, so that even when poor people get medical care, they may die from lack of proper diet and shelter.

**Social impact of illness.** The United States may well be concerned with the social cost of illness. Avoidable illness and deaths reduce the rate of population growth. Unnecessary sickness lowers the vitality and prosperity of the nation. Loss of time from school, due to illness, creates educational problems. Money spent on sickness subtracts from the amount which can be spent by a family on goods and food. Where there is sickness, there is misery. Unhappy people cause others to become discontented, and a quarrelsome and nagging social environment can become the breeding place for more mental and nervous diseases.

## How Medical Science Has Sought To Conquer and Prevent Disease

**Isolating contagious diseases.** In ancient times, long before men knew anything of the scientific theory of disease, people had learned that, if the sick were kept away from the village well and communal gatherings, many illnesses would not spread. Quarantine (isolation) of lepers was practiced as early as Biblical times. But the adoption of quarantine as a deliberate medical practice did not come until 1348–1349, the time of the Black Death. The term *quarantine* is derived from the words *quaranta giorni,* or forty days, the period of time set for the isolation of those suffering from the Black Death.

**Discovery of disease germs.** Medicine had no answer to the question of how diseases start until the science of bacteriology was developed. Not long after the origination of the germ theory with

---

[5] *The Progressive,* December 13, 1941, p. 12.

Jacob Henle, Louis Pasteur found that germs can cause ferment and decay. Then, in 1870, Robert Koch discovered that infections in wounds are caused by germs, and in 1882, he made the sensational discovery of the germ which causes tuberculosis. With Koch's demonstration that tuberculosis is produced by a specific germ, bacteriologists sought the germs that produce other diseases. Between 1880 and 1905 many were found—the germs of Asiatic cholera, leprosy, malaria, tetanus, diphtheria, pneumonia, typhoid and Malta fever, gonorrhea, and syphilis. A revolution in health conditions in the South became possible when Charles W. Stiles, in 1902, discovered the parasite causing hookworm.

Other physicians and laboratory specialists ascertained the existence and nature of the virus diseases, though they were never able to see any virus until the recent invention of the electron microscope. Further study of viruses, some of which are not more than a millionth of an inch in diameter, seems to have proved that viruses are definitely living organisms, capable of independent movement.

**The medical war on disease.** Once germs or the viruses were understood, medical science was able to make war on them. Epidemics of plague, smallpox, typhoid, diphtheria, and scarlet fever were eventually brought under control. The death rate from disease among white children was cut down remarkably in tł e first forty years of the present century—from 116 per 1,000 in 1901–1910 to 50 in 1937. The death rate from the main communicable diseases of childhood—measles, scarlet fever, whooping cough, and diphtheria—has been reduced by 90 per cent during this period. Between 1898 and 1948, the infant death rate in New York City was cut from 140.9 per 1,000 to 30.4.

**Preventing the breeding and spreading of disease germs.** Medical science found that certain unhealthy surroundings and conditions of living breed disease germs. When it was suggested that swamps bred the mosquitoes which carried some tropical diseases, and it was later proved (1898) that the bite of a mosquito causes malaria, a new interest was taken in cleaning up the swamp lands. Walter Reed, an American doctor, was the central figure in the conquest of the deadly yellow fever, which is carried by a certain type of female mosquito. Under his guidance, engineers drained or sterilized swamps and stagnant pools, breeding places of the mosquito carriers of yellow fever and malaria. Knowledge that typhoid fever usually comes from a polluted water supply led to measures designed to purify water.

**Antiseptics.** Chemistry, in conjunction with medical science, has enabled us to wage the most successful battle against disease germs. We give the general name of antiseptics to chemicals that kill disease germs by direct application. These chemicals were first applied to wounds to prevent further infection and to promote healing. They were also soon used in connection with surgery to prevent infections arising out of surgical incisions.

The man who was chiefly responsible for launching the use of antiseptics in surgery was the famous English surgeon, Lord Lister (1827–1912). In order to keep the incisions made in surgery free from infection, he advocated careful cleansing of the hands and instruments of the surgeon and the application of strong, germ-killing solutions to incisions. In this way, he founded what is known as aseptic surgery, which has saved countless thousands of human lives. The earlier antiseptics or germicides were such simple and crude chemicals as carbolic acid and iodine. During the first world war, such improved chemicals as Dakin's solution (commercially known as Zonite) were introduced. In recent years much more effective germicides have been found. Sulfa preparations, penicillin, streptomycin, tyrothricin, and gramicidin have been introduced to supplement the older germicides.

**The sulfa drugs.** The greatest contribution ever made by chemistry to the struggle against disease has been the discovery and introduction, since about 1935, of the sulfa drugs and, a little later on, of the various so-called antibiotics.

The first of the sulfa drugs was sulfanilamide, derived from a dye product and first brought out in Germany in 1935. A large number of improved sulfa drugs have since been discovered and made available, such as sulfapyridine, sulfathiazole, sulfadiazine, sulfasuxidine, sulfamerizine, and sulfaguanidine. These later improvements are, generally speaking, more effective against germs and less toxic (that is less harmful to the system) than the original sulfanilamide.

The sulfa drugs do not kill germs but they paralyze them until the white corpuscles in the blood can destroy them. The sulfa drugs have not only been very valuable in reducing infections arising from surgery and childbirth, but have been unprecedentedly effective in treating meningitis, serious streptococcic infections, kidney infections, gonorrhea, certain types of pneumonia, erysipelas, and several other maladies. In 1948, a new sulfa derivative, known as thalamyd, was reported to be effective against ulcerative colitis, bacillary dysentery and even cholera. Derivatives of sulfanilamide, the so-called sulfone drugs, have proved the only effective agencies in treating leprosy.

Unfortunately, certain persons cannot use sulfa drugs safely. In some cases the application of sulfa drugs appears to reduce the number of red corpuscles in the blood and, more rarely, to kill off the white corpuscles and result in death.

**The new antibiotics.** It is, thus, very fortunate that, about the time the sulfa drugs were beginning to work their wonders on those who could use them safely, a whole new range of so-called antibiotic substances were discovered, most of which can be used without any disastrous results to patients. Antibiotics are microbes which are able to cluster or clump together disease germs in the body so that the white corpuscles can quickly and easily dispose of them. Most of these antibiotics are derived from various molds or from soil bacteria.

The most famous and useful of these antibiotics is penicillin, derived from a blue-green mold like that which forms on bread and cheese. It was first discovered by Dr. Alexander Fleming in London, in 1929, and was made available for general medical use during the second world war. Penicillin is non-toxic and can, therefore, be given in very powerful doses. It is probably the greatest single discovery in the whole history of medical science and has checked and cured more infections and diseases than any other single drug ever known. Further research has provided ever more powerful types of penicillin, such as the one known as penicillin X. Penicillin is invaluable in destroying infections in ordinary wounds and in surgical incisions. It is potent against nearly all the diseases which have yielded to the sulfa drugs and is more effective, since it can be used in unlimited doses. Penicillin has completely revolutionized the treatment of venereal diseases: one large injection of a special penicillin preparation called duracillin will cure gonorrhea nine times out of ten.

There are, however, a number of disease germs, called gram-negative microbes, which do not yield to penicillin. To overcome these, Dr. Selman Waksman of Rutgers University discovered in 1943 another remarkable antibiotic known as streptomycin. It appears to be the first antibiotic that is fairly effective against tuberculosis and the hitherto almost fatal tubercular meningitis. Other powerful antibiotics, derived from soil bacteria, are highly toxic and cannot be injected into the system, but they are very effective in curing hitherto refractory surface infections.

The latest important additions to the antibiotic arsenal are chloromycetin, discovered by Dr. P. R. Burkholder in 1947, and aureomycin, discovered by Dr. B. M. Duggar in 1945. Chloromycetin has been found to be extremely effective against typhoid fever, and scrub typhus. Aureomycin works rapidly in the treatment of virus pneumonia, Rocky Mountain spotted fever, and undulant fever, the latter of which has previously proved an extremely stubborn disorder. No important toxic after-effects have yet been discovered in the use of either of these drugs, but it may be some time before they are in mass-production and relatively inexpensive.

Dr. Waksman, the discoverer of streptomycin, announced the discovery of a new antibiotic, neomycin, in 1949. It promises to be effective against paratyphoid fever, tuberculosis, and boils and abscesses. A great revolution in the future provision of antibiotics came in 1949, when Dr. Mildred Rebstock learned how to produce chloromycetin synthetically by chemical methods. If this technique can be applied to other antibiotics it will greatly increase production and lessen costs.

**Resistance of germs to new drugs.** It might be thought that, with the discovery of the sulfa drugs and the antibiotics, many dread diseases and serious infections are now fully conquered. But there is a joker in the picture: there seems to be a struggle for existence and the survival of the fittest in the realm of disease germs, and new strains of these germs appear which are highly resistant to both the sulfa drugs and the antibiotics. However, chemical and medical researchers are making these remedies more powerful all the time and are discovering new antibiotics to conquer the newer and more resistant strains of disease germs. It now seems that the chemists and doctors can always keep one step ahead of new and more resistant strains of germs.

An interesting juncture of the old and new in medical history came on the 600th anniversary of the famous and devastating Black Death (bubonic plague) of the later Middle Ages (1349). Several cases broke out in the United States in the summer of 1949. They were promptly treated and quickly and easily cured by use of the sulfa drugs and the new antibiotics. Some cases were cured by a combination of sulfadiazine and streptomycin, and others by combining penicillin and aureomycin. This experience demonstrated impressively how modern medical science can readily conquer one of the most fatal and dreaded diseases of all recorded medical history.

**Other contributions of chemistry to the war on disease.** Chemists have discovered a number of other useful new drugs. One is thiouricil, which is effective against the worst form of goiter. Then, there is the new group of anti-histamine drugs, which are useful in treating the great range of allergic diseases from asthma and hay fever to skin diseases and serum sicknesses. Chemistry has also been very important in developing our ideas of increasing human vitality and resistance to disease. Especially important here has been the discovery of vitamins.

Those chemists and physiologists who study nutrition have found that certain foods have elements vital to health while others lack such nourishing qualities. Dr. Joseph Goldberger of the United States Health Service discovered that the poor whites in the South who were afflicted with pellagra lived mainly on an unbalanced diet of corn bread and molasses. Dr. Goldberger pointed out that the pellagra sufferers lacked proper diet for body needs. When these people were fed green vegetables, rich in vitamins, pellagra all but disappeared. Knowledge of vitamins is causing many people to eat more sanely. For example, fat women who yearn for slender figures are warned to keep plenty of vitamins in their diet. This discussion leads us logically to the next topic, resistance to disease, because vitamins and other essential items found in milk, eggs, butter, green vegetables, and citrus fruits help to build up bodily resistance to illness.

**Building up resistance and immunity to disease.** Doctors learned from their study of tuberculosis that certain diseases apparently could not be cured by drugs alone. The only way to check them was to adopt healthier diets and habits, thus enabling the body to become strong enough to throw off disease. This was demonstrated by Dr. E. L. Trudeau, who established a famous sanatorium for tuberculosis patients at Saranac Lake, New York, in 1884. This pioneer work in treating tuberculosis was the inspiration for the Public Health Service in much of its experimentation with preventive medicine. It now seems possible that in streptomycin, neomycin and viomycin we have at last found antibiotics that will check tuberculosis, which claimed 48,000 lives in 1947.

**Progress in anaesthesia.** Chemistry has also been responsible for the discovery of anaesthetics, or drugs which eliminate pain from surgery. The most important of these are gas, ether, and chloroform, as general anaesthetics, and novocaine for local anaesthesia.

The famous English chemist, Sir Humphrey Davy, discovered, in 1799, that inhaling nitrous oxide gas deadened pain; it was not until 1844 that it was first used in medical practice by Henry Wells, a Hartford, Connecticut, dentist. As early as 1842, Dr. Crawford Long of Georgia had already used ether to remove a tumor. The use of ether was introduced into northern surgery by Dr. William T. G. Morton of Boston, in 1846. Chloroform was first used in operations by Dr. James Y. Simpson in Edinburgh, Scotland, in 1847. In the last hundred years much progress has been made in more adroit use of anaesthetics, especially in combining various types and in extending the use of local anaesthetics.

**Physics aids the battle against disease.** The science of physics has also been of great value to the improvement of medical science. X-rays, discovered by Wilhelm von Roentgen in Germany, in 1895, and radium, discovered by the Curies in France, about 1900, are the two main contributions of physics to medicine. X-rays are a great aid in guiding surgeons in ascertaining the need for operations and in locating tumors, fractures, and the like. Both X-rays and radium are valuable in treating numerous disorders, especially cancer. Diathermy has proved very useful in relieving many forms of pain. The most recent discovery in physics which may be of great utility in medicine has been a product of the research in intra-atomic energy. Here, radioactive isotopes have been discovered which may have opened a whole new and promising type of treatment for cancer. The many important recent applications of electro-physics in psychiatry will be described in a later chapter.

**Psychology and psychosomatic medicine.** Biology, physiology, chemistry and physics are not the only sciences enlisted to battle disease. Recently, psychology has been called in to aid, especially in the new field which is called psychosomatic medicine. This lays great stress upon the effect of bad mental states and hypochondria in causing medical cases. It has been estimated that as high as 4 out of ten persons who consult physicians are suffering more from mental symptoms than from physical disorders. This is aside from all who are victims of obvious nervous and mental diseases. Psychosomatic medicine stresses the importance of using sound psychology and psychiatry to deal successfully with such cases. It also emphasizes the fact that the mental attitude of physicians may be quite as important in bringing about cures as their use of drugs. Some regard psychosomatic medicine as, next to the discovery of the sulfa drugs and the antibiotics, the greatest medical advance of the twentieth century. Advances in psychiatry will be treated in a later chapter.

**Vaccination, immunity, and serums.** "An ounce of prevention is worth a pound of cure"; so thought the men who laid the groundwork for modern preventive medicine. Almost every school child today can display his smallpox vaccination. Inoculation and vaccination are not new. Inoculation was used in Turkey about 1675, injections being made of a serum derived from those suffering from light cases of smallpox. In 1798, an Englishman, Dr. Edward Jenner, improved protection against smallpox with his discovery of vaccination. Vaccination is a special form of inoculation, using virus taken from cows suffering from cowpox; the Latin word *vaccina,* or cowpox, gives us the term. Vaccination has become an important item in the public health program. Inoculation and vaccination are employed today to ward off many other diseases, in addition to smallpox.

This attempt to build up immunity against diseases, along with efforts to prevent the spread of disease, to clean up insect-infested swamps, ponds and jungles, to provide better sanitation and water supplies, and to establish public health programs, constitutes what is generally known as preventive medicine. Important as it is, the money allotted to preventive medicine is only about one-twenty-fifth of the total expended for all forms of medical care and research.

Even if one has contracted a disease, there may be ways to check it before it gets a good hold. Serums now hasten the cure. A diphtheria serum proved successful as early as 1891. Now there are serums to treat infantile paralysis, tick fever, certain types of meningitis, and some kinds of pneumonia. The most remarkable recent development in serums has been the discovery of a serum by the noted Russian biochemist, Dr. Alexander A. Bogomolets, which is alleged to check the chemical changes in body cells which produce senescence (old age) and may increase the normal life span to 100 years or more.

**Recent advances in dealing with chronic diseases.** While we are as yet only in initial stages in this field, important advances have been made in checking or curing the more important chronic diseases. Antibiotics are coming into use to prevent rheumatic fever, one of the great killers in the heart disease field, and sulfa drugs have been found effective in preventing its recurrence. Drugs are effective in reducing high blood pressure and coronary occlusion. Remarkable advances in heart surgery, touching such matters as abnormalities and congenital defects of the heart and acute heart infections, have been made since the second world war. Especially notable is the operation on "blue babies." But most cases still have to be handled through reducing the strain on damaged hearts and lessening fear and anxiety.

While there is as yet no specific to cure cancer, even here mortality has been reduced through prompt diagnosis and immediate treatment by surgery and by the use of radium and X-rays. The greatest hope, so far, resides in speedy diagnosis and treatment.

Dramatic new medical discoveries in the late 1940's give much promise of soon producing revolutionary gains in the treatment of arthritis and allied disorders. Thus far, four new drugs—cortisone, ACTH (adreno-cortico-tropic hormone), pregnenolone, and percorten —are the outstanding recent discoveries which promise to check or cure most arthritic troubles.

**Persistence of quacks and nostrums.** Although medical science has made great advances, there are regions where home remedies like those of a hundred years ago are still used. Old women brew teas for fever cures and apply poultices for assorted aches and pains. Even in cities, where people can have the services of up-to-date physicians and hospitals, they still go to "quack" doctors and buy worthless drugs and patent medicine cure-alls. Laws against "quack" doctors and harmful drugs seem to be ineffective, for, as a nation, we spend 600 million dollars each year on such items. This is about ten per cent of our total expenditures for all competent medical care.

**Improved training of physicians and surgeons.** We have more trained doctors in proportion to the population than any other country: one to every 750 persons, as compared with 870 in Great Britain, 1,300 in France, 2,400 in the Union of South Africa, and 25,000 in China. The better medical schools now have at their disposal the medical lore and knowledge of the whole world. They have fine laboratories and excellent clinics. They usually require a college degree for admission, and demand special pre-medical training in this college work. Four years of work are required in medical college, with several years of internship thereafter. Young physicians must follow their internship with several years of an all but unpaid medical or surgical residency in a hospital to obtain additional training and experience if they wish to specialize. This means that the young doctor who has the best medical training today will have spent from ten to sixteen years after graduation from high school in getting his medical training before he starts remunerative practice. This is a strenuous and expensive process, and the average reward is pitifully low—an average of about $5,000 a year in 1940 and $10,000 in 1949. But, whatever the exactions imposed on the incipient physicians, the public is the gainer in the way of the vastly increased competence of the medical profession.

**Need for more trained physicians.** Though the inadequacy of medical treatment today is due more to the defective system of medical practice than to shortage of doctors, it has been estimated that we could well use 20 per cent more well-trained physicians than we have, and we shall soon need even more, for the population is currently growing more rapidly than the supply of newly admitted practitioners. There are only 77 good medical schools in the country, and their output of graduates each year is only about 6,000—6,389 in 1947.  There should be twice that many graduates if we are to have the 250,000 doctors we shall need by 1960.  We had only some 201,278 licensed physicians and surgeons in 1950, and only about 150,000 of these were in active practice.  There are fewer doctors today per capita than there were forty years ago—one to 750 today and one to 671 in 1909.  There were in 1950 only 100,000 general practitioners—one to 1,500 persons.  Some 25,000 qualified young men applied for entrance to medical schools in the autumn of 1949, but less than 7,000 could be admitted.

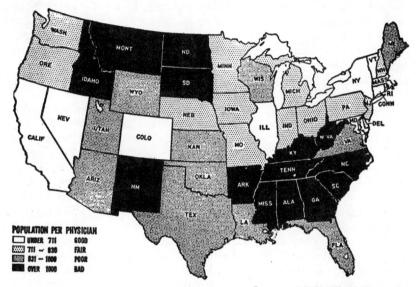

POPULATION PER PHYSICIAN
UNDER 711     GOOD
711 ~ 830     FAIR
831 — 1000    POOR
OVER 1000     BAD

*Courtesy of Wide World Photos, Inc.*

This graphic map reveals the very uneven distribution of physicians and medical care in the United States.

In some branches of medicine, such as psychiatry, there is a desperate shortage of trained physicians.  There are only about 4,500 psychiatrists in the country, while we need at least 20,000.  One of the reasons for the shortage of psychiatrists is the absurd attempt of physicians to monopolize this field, even though clinical psychologists have a much better professional training in psychotherapy than the average M.D., especially for treating functional mental and nervous diseases.

The shortage of dentists, good nurses, medical technicians, and trained hospital personnel is even greater than that of doctors.  Federal and State aid will be needed to enable more capable young men to undertake the arduous and costly task of preparing for the practice of medicine.  Today, only a young man of independent means can afford the time and expense required to prepare for the practice of surgery on the staff of a good hospital, or for most other medical specialization.

**Attitude of many older physicians and surgeons.** One of the reasons for the shortage of good medical and surgical service in many cities and towns is the attempt of older and intrenched physicians and surgeons to monopolize the practice in these areas, on the wholly fictitious ground of their superior training and ability.

The average physician and surgeon now past 50 years of age usually entered medical college directly from high school or after only two years of college training. After completing his four years of work in medical college, he usually took a year of internship in medicine or surgery and immediately started to practice, in most cases with no residency training at all, or training of one or two years at the most in special instances. Today, in order to specialize, a young man takes four years of pre-medical work in college, four years of medical college instruction, two years of internship, and from two or three to as many as eight years of residency training, before being allowed to practice.

During his residency the young physician or surgeon does most of the routine work in hospital medical treatment and surgery, the older and intrenched doctors limiting themselves chiefly to the more lucrative cases, except for an occasional charity operation. Hence, much of our medical and surgical care is provided by men who are well trained but get virtually no pay. Even after such abuses, when a doctor has finished his long residency he finds his progress blocked by the intrenched staffs of the urban and community hospitals who refuse to admit him on terms of equality and limit his possibilities in practice. This deplorable situation was aired by J. D. Ratcliff in an article in the *Woman's Home Companion* of October, 1948, which was prefaced by a statement from no less an authority than Dr. Allen O. Whipple, former president of the American Surgical Association, to the effect that: "There is no question that [younger] well-trained physicians and surgeons . . . are far better qualified and more competent than many of the older practitioners in the smaller cities of this country. There is no doubt that these younger qualified doctors are prevented from demonstrating their ability in a good number of communities by the failure of the local physicians to give these younger men an opportunity to practice in the hospital or hospitals of the community."

**Urgent need for more hospital facilities.** Though we already need more well-trained physicians, technicians, and nurses, the shortage of hospital facilities is even greater. We do not have half the number of acceptable hospital beds we need. Including the Federally owned and operated hospitals, we have a total of 6,280 registered hospitals and about 1,500,000 hospital beds in the country. Of the 1,020,000 hospital beds outside the Federal system, some 150,000 are obsolete and sub-standard. This means that we have less than 900,000 hospital beds which are acceptable for use. Of these there are only about 470,000 beds in general hospitals which care for most of the ordinary medical and surgical cases. The others are for mental, tubercular, and chronic cases. In some 40 per cent of the counties of our country, with a total population of 15,000,000, there is no hospital whatever. It is conservatively estimated that we need an additional 900,000 hospital beds.

## The Development of Sanitary Engineering

**Importance of sanitary engineering.** In the struggle against disease, the doctor has often enlisted the aid of the engineer. Dirt, refuse, and garbage breed germs. Engineers are needed to plan sewers for the disposal of city refuse, to clean insect-breeding ponds and drain swamps, and to build water systems capable of furnishing pure drinking water.

**Origins of sanitary engineering.** The Greek cities, even Athens, were notoriously filthy and lacking in sanitation, though there apparently was some improvement in the better sections of Alexandria. The ancient Romans built some excellent aqueducts and sewers, but even this slight beginning in sanitary engineering disappeared during the Middle Ages. Covering the pomp and glory of the age of medieval kings, queens, knights, and ladies was a thick layer of dirt, which we do not see in film versions of medieval life. More knights probably fell victim to diseases contracted in their unsanitary castles than perished in battle.

The situation did not improve notably with the coming of modern times. In New York City, as late as the close of the Revolutionary War, sewage and garbage were thrown out of windows into the street below as a matter of course. Streets were seldom, if ever, cleaned, and the refuse was left until blown or worn away. Drinking water was obtained from wells and streams into which all manner of filth had been thrown.

**Disposing of sewage.** Down to modern times, sewers were used chiefly to drain excess water off streets. When Sir John Harrington, an unheralded benefactor of the human race, invented the indoor toilet in 1596, there arose for the first time a real and widespread need for sanitary sewers. The earliest of these sewers came in the late seventeenth and early eighteenth centuries. At first, they were open ditches, but eventually were covered over. Until 1850, however, cesspools were the chief means of disposing of human waste in cities, while privies served this purpose in the country, and, all too often, in cities, as well. The fact that cesspools drained into wells and streams, polluting the water, was the main reason for the systematic construction of sewers.

Soon after 1850 most cities began to build sewer systems. When, in some areas, such drainage polluted the water supply, plants were constructed to destroy sewage by chemical treatment. The first important city disposal plant in the United States was set up in Worcester,

Massachusetts, in 1890. Although such plants are now very common, our sewage systems nevertheless need improvement. It is estimated that 90 per cent of our city dwellers live in cities with inferior or inadequate disposal systems.

**Garbage collection and street cleaning.** In the modern city, garbage is usually collected in trucks. Some of it is used to feed hogs, but the most popular method of disposal is burning. Street cleaning has been revolutionized by the introduction of mechanical sweepers and water flushers. Modern cities have made such progress in cleanliness that the Greeks, or even our colonial forefathers, would be amazed at the lack of filth. This is true, of course, only of the better sections of modern cities. Slum areas are still notoriously unsanitary and filthy.

**A supply of pure water.** A very important phase of sanitary engineering has been the provision of an adequate water supply for cities. The Romans were the first people to provide themselves with an abundant water supply. Throughout their empire, they erected an impressive system of aqueducts, which brought them fresh water from mountain streams. In the Middle Ages, however, men turned back to the use of wells. These were often infected by drainage.

Although crude mechanical water pumps were in common use by the sixteenth century, many European and American cities lacked an adequate water supply for centuries. London, for example, had no decent public water supply until after 1900. A main reason for the construction of sanitary water systems was the discovery that polluted water carries typhoid germs. Water in modern cities is now carefully inspected, filtered, and purified before being pumped to homes.

**Inadequacy of current sanitary engineering.** Although we take justifiable pride in our achievements in sanitary engineering, they are today about as inadequate as other forms of health provisions. To bring them up to our requirements would involve an outlay immediately of 7.7 billion dollars—3.7 billion for sewage disposal systems, 2.2 billion for water works, 1.6 billion for rural sanitation facilities, and 166 million for garbage disposal facilities.

## The Public Health Movement in the United States

**Origins of interest in public health.** Development of a public health movement in the United States followed directly on the heels of a similar movement in England. Some local health boards were established between 1800 and 1840. The American Public Health Association was founded in 1872 and began to promote research and public information on public health problems. A Federal public health service, based on a law of 1798, was gradually built up in the latter part of the nineteenth century and was administered by the Treasury Department until 1939. A National Board of Health was created in 1879. The United States Public Health Service was formally established in 1912. It was transferred from the Treasury Department to the Federal Security Agency in 1939.

Active support has been given to the public health movement by the states, especially since the Civil War. The first state health board was that set up in Massachusetts in 1869. The first state law providing for the medical inspection of school children was that passed in Connecticut in 1899. There are now health departments in nearly every state, county, and city. Government owned and operated hospitals provide about three-fourths of the hospital beds and hospital service in the United States. Yet, the money that all governmental agencies spend for public health measures and services is pathetically inadequate. It does not equal that spent on the most absurd details and wastes in armament and the military services.

**The public health program.** Among the measures sponsored by the public health movement in its earlier days were sanitary water supply, adequate sewage disposal, and quarantine regulations. As the science of bacteriology revealed the causes of diseases, the public health movement turned its efforts to preventive medicine by removing sources of infection, enforcing vaccination, setting up public clinics, passing pure food and drugs acts, and the like. In the present century, the health movement has also taken account of the social and economic factors affecting health, such as working conditions, accidents, unemployment, and poverty. Education is one of the most important interests of the public health movement today.

The activities of public health organizations at the present time are varied. They provide free educational lectures, movies, and literature. Clinics are maintained for treating disease among the poor. Visiting nurses aid the sick, while social settlements care for many who need medical help in the cities. Efforts are directed toward removing conditions which create poor health, such as slums, low wages, and poverty.

## Medical Care Lags Behind Medical Science

**Medical care and sample of cultural lag.** At the beginning of this chapter it was stated that medical authorities consider our national health to be definitely "below par." Yet, we have sketched a story of remarkable progress in modern medicine. Why, one may well ask, should there be so much illness and disease when medical science has made such brilliant advances? The answer is simple. We have not developed the means of making medical care available to the mass of people. The fault lies with the way medicine is put into practice. As we pointed out early in this book, medical practice presents one of the most obvious, extensive, and tragic examples of cultural lag in our social pattern today. Medical science represents the best that science and technology can produce, but medical practice still jogs along much as it did in the days of the horse-and-buggy doctor. Its basic principles have not changed in a hundred years.

Inadequacy of medical care today.   The inadequacy of medical care in the United States was demonstrated by the number of men rejected for the United States army under the Selective Service Act of 1940.   Despite all the progress in medical science since 1917, a greater proportion of recruits were turned down because of physical defects in 1941 than in 1917—less than 33 per cent in 1917 and over 43 per cent in 1941.   While the examinations and standards were more rigorous in 1941 than in 1917, it is clear from these figures, after making all due allowances, that the nation at large has not been able to benefit sufficiently from the progress of medical science.   That it has not been able to do so is due mainly to the expense of medical care under the prevailing system of private practice and to the failure to educate communities about the great advantages and economies of co-operative medicine and health insurance.   As General Hershey summed up the situation:   "The fact remains that while we may not be worse now than 24 years ago we seem certainly to be no better . . . . We are physically in a condition of which nationally we should be thoroughly ashamed."

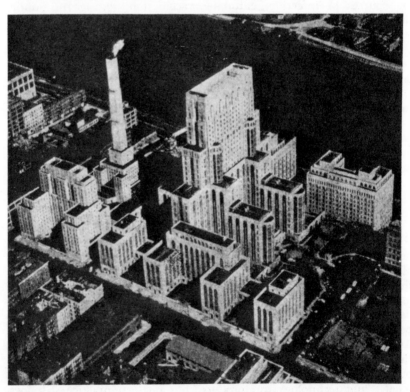

*Courtesy of the New York Hospital—Cornell Medical Center.*

This picture of the New York Hospital–Cornell University Medical Center in New York City illustrates the impressive development of the physical plant devoted to medical care in our larger cities.

**Financial obstacles to adequate care under the present system.** Under our present system of medical practice, where the doctor furnishes his services on a personal business or fee basis, the very rich and the very poor fare the best. The rich can afford to pay high fees for good medical care; the poor can get free, though far inferior, service in clinics and charity wards. On the great mass of people, in between the extremes of wealth and poverty, the cost of medical care falls as a heavy burden.

The average man can personally plan to lay out a definite sum for rent, food, and clothing, but he does not know how to budget for illness. Who can estimate how many will be sick in the family during the coming year? Most family incomes are not large enough suddenly to afford large sums for hospital care and physicians' fees. Sickness causes families to do without many necessities in order to pay their medical bills; often, it is necessary to borrow money. As we pointed out earlier in the chapter, it has been estimated that five-sevenths of the population would have to borrow money to pay promptly for medical care in the case of any serious or protracted illness. The upshot of the matter is that many families do not call in the doctor until too late; they hope to "get by" without medical care. Treatments may be cut short before the patient is cured. Necessary physical examinations are neglected. Poor eyesight and abdominal pains are borne in silence. In every way efforts are made to cut down on doctor bills.

A few statistics will clarify the situation. The Federal health survey of 1935–1936, already discussed, showed that 30 per cent of the families on relief had no medical help at all. Another expert estimate states that four out of ten Americans who are ill normally receive no attention from a doctor. Oscar R. Ewing has pointed out that about half of our American families, those with incomes of $3,000 or less, "find it hard, if not impossible, to pay for even routine medical care." It is said that death takes 325,000 persons every year in the United States who would live if given proper medical care.[6]

**Doctors are poorly paid.** Yet, the doctors, on the whole, are very poorly paid for their services. In 1936, the median net income of doctors in the United States was only $3,234; in 1938, $3,027; and in 1940, $3,245. The average net income in 1940 was $5,047. The only authoritative recent estimate of the income of physicians and surgeons was published in *Medical Economics*, September, 1948. This placed the average net income of physicians and surgeons in independent or private practice at $11,300. Because the questionnaire excluded doctors over 65 years of age and because of the mail questionnaire technique employed, experts regard this estimate as too high. Even if correct, the doctors would be little better off than in 1940, since their living costs and other expenses have also doubled. There is a

---

[6] It is estimated that at least 40 per cent of the American population cannot pay for medical care under our present system without sacrificing the bare necessities of life. Another 20 per cent can pay for medical service only with great hardship.

common illusion that specialists, whose training is particularly long, arduous, and expensive, are at least rewarded by a lavish income. This is not true. In 1949, it was estimated that the average income of general practitioners was $9,000 a year, and of specialists, $14,000.

Only in a few cases do doctors receive large incomes. Nearly two-thirds of the patients receiving treatment are on the free or partly free list. Most of these go to free clinics, but a large number of private patients do not pay their doctor bills. Yet, despite all this, it is claimed that the total cost of medical care is too high and could be reduced by an improved system of medical practice which would average medical costs to the individual patient, give everybody adequate care, and pay the doctors far better than they are paid today.

**The problem of socialized medicine.** Here, indeed, is a paradoxical situation. Large numbers of people cannot afford any medical attention, medical care is far too expensive for the majority of patients, and yet many good doctors are poorly paid. What is the answer to the riddle? Leading experts have suggested the introduction of a new system of administering medical care, designed to reduce costs as far as possible, and to place financial arrangements on an insurance basis. Toward this end, many plans have been devised.

The more extreme would have the government take over the provision of medical care, hiring the doctors, and running the hospitals. But this would require costly governmental machinery and considerable appropriations of money, though relatively slight compared to the sums spent on even the completely needless phases of the military machine. Other plans, however, are not so drastic.

The nearest we have come to state or government medicine in the United States, thus far, is in the army and navy hospitals, the Federal hospitals for war veterans, state hospitals for the insane, the state and county clinics, and the public health services. Out of a total of about $8,500,000,000 spent in 1947 for all medical care and health service in the United States, the Federal, state and local governments contributed $1,962,000,000, or nearly one-fourth of the total. About three-fourths of the hospital beds in the country are in publicly owned and operated hospitals, though many of the physicians and surgeons who make up the staffs supply treatment on the basis of private practice.

The time is not yet ripe, according to the late Dr. Kingsley Roberts, formerly Director of the Bureau of Coöperative Medicine, for the domination of all health activities by the government. We would have to pass much drastic legislation to meet the needs of the sick in this country by such extreme methods. The best way to prevent complete state medicine is to make available adequate medical care by some more moderate form of socialized medicine.

We may think of socialized medicine as based on averages, just like any other insurance plan. If people could budget payments for medical insurance, as they do payments for life insurance, the costs would not seem so great, especially if payments were arranged on the basis of the worker's income.

**Benefits of a health insurance system.** Though we spend only about one-fifth as much to check and treat disease and accidents as they cost us each year, it is believed that, if the money were expended efficiently through a system of health insurance and socialized medicine, the $8,500,000,000 we pay for all forms of medical care and health service would provide first-class medical care for all. At any rate, it is evident that the American people could readily pay this amount and more, despite the disproportionate number of persons in the low income brackets, if their payments were handled through an efficient type of health insurance.

Look, for example, at our annual bill for alcoholic beverages, which amounts to about 10 billion dollars and to which even the very poor contribute their quota. The reason the poor and the moderately well-to-do can buy their liquor is that they usually make small purchases at frequent intervals. They are not suddenly or unexpectedly called upon to pay a liquor bill which may be ten times what they normally spend for liquor in a whole year—which is comparable to what they are faced with in connection with a prolonged illness or a serious operation. If a poor family spent only $1 to $1.50 per week for liquor, this sum diverted to medical care through a health insurance system would be ample to take care of all the expenses involved in complete medical care for the whole family. In fact, Henry Kaiser, in the scheme of industrial group medicine which he set up for his workers during the second world war, made good medical care available to his employees for about seven cents a day each. Indeed, it is probable that the sum spent each week by the average poor family on tobacco alone would, if put into a good plan of health insurance or co-operative medicine, amply provide for all needed medical care.

**Group clinics and hospitals.** Let us first consider some of the less sweeping plans by which the doctors and patients try to budget medical care. There are doctors who divide expenses by employing the same office help and renting a suite of offices together. This reduces costs. Each doctor collects his own fees. Then, there are the famous medical and surgical clinics, like the Mayo establishment at Rochester, Minnesota, where the poor man pays what he can and the rich pays what he is charged. Such devices are, of course, only highly efficient private medical practice. They do not even approximate socialized medicine or health insurance. But group clinics can, if they choose, supply a fairly satisfactory form of co-operative, socialized medicine. One of the best examples is the Ross-Loos Medical Group in Los Angeles where a large staff of physicians and surgeons serve over 75,000 members for a specified yearly sum, determined by contract in advance.

**Fraternal health insurance.** Another way of budgeting medical care is by voluntary health insurance. One of the oldest forms of this procedure is fraternal insurance, where a fixed sum is collected monthly from members, and doctors are employed to treat them. But this scheme is too limited and inefficient to be of any general use. Employees' mutual benefit associations and trade union medical benefit plans have proved more satisfactory, but they are no answer to the problem of providing for adequate medical care on a group basis.

**Industrial prepayment health insurance plans.** Employers like the Endicott-Johnson Shoe Company near Binghamton, New York, have successfully used an industrial group-insurance plan. The employer deducts a small amount out of the employee's wages for medical and hospital care and the costs are averaged, as in any insurance plan. One of the most successful of these industrial group insurance plans is that maintained by the Standard Oil Company in Baton Rouge, Louisiana, in which excellent medical attention has been provided for about $42 a year. This includes hospital service. About 1,500,000 persons were covered by industrial plans in 1945.

Colleges use similar group-insurance plans in which the students pay a small yearly sum for the infirmary services of doctors and nurses.

**Commercial insurance company service.** Life insurance companies are entering into the field of health insurance. They both issue policies to individuals and offer group insurance to the employees of industrial concerns. In the latter case, the employer deducts the premium to be paid from the wages of the workers. Cash payments of specified sums are made in the case of somewhat restricted types of medical care and hospitalization. The adequacy of this form of health insurance depends mainly upon the terms of the contract, the reliability of the company, and the size of the group covered.

**The Blue Cross-Blue Shield plan.** More persons have some form of protection against hospital, medical and surgical costs through the Blue Cross-Blue Shield service than by any other type of coverage or organization. The Blue Cross Plan originated in 1937 and it is "a non-profit corporation organized under community and professional sponsorship and approved by the American Hospital Association for the purpose of enabling the public to defray the cost of hospital care on a prepayment, group basis." All of the 90 Blue Cross plans are sponsored by local hospitals, doctors and surgeons, and by members of the public who wish coverage. Usually the initiative in setting up such a plan in any community is taken by the state or county hospital association.

Blue Cross plans provide only for hospital care, but in this field most of the 90 plans now in operation cover room and board, nursing care, operating room, laboratory service, routine medication, and use of the delivery service. A majority of the plans also provide for special services, such as special diets, emergency room, anesthesia, basal metabolism tests, oxygen therapy, X-ray, and electro cardiograms. These benefits are available to subscribers for 21 to 30 days, and most of the plans pay about half the costs for an additional 90 days. The plans and rates are determined locally to meet the particular community need. While rates vary from locality to locality, the national average monthly rates are $1.25 for one person, $2.00 for husband and wife, and $2.75 for an entire family. More than 36,000,000 persons are now protected under some Blue Cross plan, and subscribers have access to some 4,000 hospitals containing 85 per cent of all general hospital beds. The total income from the 90 Blue Cross hospital plans in 1948 was $317,473,030, of which $270,928,123 was paid to hospitals for the care of subscribers.

The Blue Cross plans have been satisfactory for hospital care, but they do not provide for medical and surgical treatment. To meet this need, the Associated Medical Care Plans, Incorporated (now known as the Blue Shield) was founded in 1946, under the auspices of the American Medical Association. This is also a non-profit, prepayment plan, and has three main types of contracts: (1) the service-benefit contract in which all fees due physicians and surgeons are paid by the Blue Shield organization; (2) a indemnity contract by which the subscriber receives credit towards the fees; and (3) a combination of the two. The latter is the best and most common contract. Out of the 90 Blue Cross plans, some 79 are also combined with a non-profit plan to provide medical and surgical care; of these 79, some 64 are Blue Shield and have a combined membership of about 14,000,000. The average Blue Shield coverage costs $1.17 per month for an individual, $2.26 for husband and wife, and $2.75 for a family.

There is little doubt that the Blue Cross-Blue Shield combination affords the most extensive facilities for budgeting and prepaying for medical, surgical, and hospital care in the United States. But, large and rapidly growing as is the list of subscribers, not enough of the population is as yet covered, many take the cheaper and less adequate contracts for coverage, and there is a large turnover of subscribers. Pending, however, some general public health insurance plan, the Blue Cross-Blue Shield plans are the most adequate protection which the American public has against the disasters that result from sudden, protracted and serious illness.

Medical Society Coverage. Prior to the second world war, several city medical societies, such as the Cleveland Academy of Medicine, worked out economical plans for hospitalization insurance. But, since the rise of the Blue Cross and Blue Shield Plans, the tendency has been to abandon these and provide coverage through the Blue Cross and Blue Shield. Some state medical societies have provided plans for health insurance. The state of California has such a plan under which a person can receive fairly complete medical and surgical care for a payment of about $5 monthly.

Rural community medicine. Some towns in the Canadian Northwest hire the local doctor at a fixed salary, to which each family contributes a part. This is a small-scale example of the plan known as rural group medicine. The Federal Farm Security Administration has aided such plans here through co-operation with local associations of farmers.

Community co-operative medicine. One of the most discussed plans of voluntary socialized medicine is called community co-operative medicine, such as the Farmers' Union Co-operative Association of Elk City, Oklahoma. Under this program, the community, through a selected committee, hires the physicians and surgeons and builds or leases a hospital. The members who subscribe pay a fixed annual insurance fee and receive complete medical and hospital care. The community then pays the doctors. If there is any money left over, it is returned to members or spent for additional medical equipment. No one person can predict his illness, but the cost of medical care for an entire community can be accurately estimated.

This co-operative plan has advantages for both patients and doctors. The doctors do not have to wait for patients; they can spend their spare time in working to reduce illness. The less the illness, the less the doctors have to do. The people of the community are guaranteed prompt and competent medical care at low cost. Perhaps the most famous of these community co-operative medical plans is the Group Health Association of Washington, D. C., made up of government employees. When it was attacked by the American Medical Association, Thurmond Arnold sued the latter under the anti-trust laws and won his case.

Full yearly medical and hospital care under the system of co-operative community medicine can be provided for a maximum of $30 per person, and the physicians can be far better paid than the average doctor is today. This system is adequate where it exists, and, it avoids the bureaucracy and red tape of state medicine. The main argument against the community system, and for compulsory health insurance, is that not enough communities install co-operative programs to meet the needs of more than a handful of the total population.

Extent of insurance coverage. Limited though the coverage still is, there has been a marked increase in some sort and degree of insurance protection against medical, surgical and hospital costs. In 1950, about 40 per cent of the population has some type of coverage, mainly through the Blue Cross-Blue Shield system and commercial insurance plans. Some 61 million have some form of hospital insurance, about 57 per cent of this through the Blue Cross system, and 43 per cent through commercial insurance companies. About 34 million also have some degree of insurance against at least a part of surgical costs. Some 13 million have partial insurance against physicians' charges. Only about 3½ million have fairly full insurance coverage against nearly all medical, surgical and hospital expenses.

The new English system of state medicine. Prior to 1948, England had a rather comprehensive system of compulsory health insurance for the low-paid workers.   But the Labour Party Government broadened this into what is virtually a complete system of state medicine. Under this scheme, each physician is paid a basic salary of $1,200 annually, and is allotted an additional $3 for each patient under his care.   The cost of the new plan is paid for almost entirely by taxation. There is complete free medical and hospital service and dental and optical care for every man, woman, and child in England who wishes to register under the plan and make the required contribution. Physicians are allowed to engage in private practice in their spare time, and anybody who wishes can get private medical care if he can pay for it.   The majority of English doctors vigorously opposed this plan; some 89 per cent of them voted against it in February, 1948, but the Labour Government, led by Aneurin Bevan, Minister of Health, persisted and the doctors gave way.   The new system was put into operation in July, 1948.   Critical judgment of the merits of the plan will need to be applied cautiously in the light of the obvious fact that many of the doctors may seek to prove it a failure.   Nevertheless, after two years' experience with the new system, it had proved so popular that even the British "Tories" did not dare to attack it directly.   It has produced the lowest English death rate in history.

**State medicine in Russia.**   Russia has placed all medical care in the hands of the state.   All doctors are public officials, paid by the state. All citizens are entitled to complete medical treatment without charge.   All hospitals and sanatoriums are state-controlled and are free to all citizens.   Unlike the new English system, the Russian system does not permit doctors to engage in private practice.

**Better medical care is indispensable.**   We have now outlined the leading plans of socialized medicine and state medicine.   Whether or not we approve of any of them, we must think in terms of community well-being and the future of medicine.   John P. Peters, in the *Virginia Quarterly Review,* remarks, "Today, the scientific practice of medicine demands knowledge, expert technical training, diagnostic and therapeutic facilities undreamed of ten years ago; the armamentarium which it will require in another ten years is beyond prediction.   If the world is to reap the benefits of these scientific discoveries, they must be made available to the public."

Will we continue to advance in our fight against disease, and lag behind in our administration of medical care?   Why should we learn how to cure ailments if people generally do not benefit from the knowledge?   Is co-operative medicine the answer, or should we allow the government to assume complete control of the medical world?   Most doctors in our country disapprove of state medicine. Regardless of the plan chosen, we should hasten the day when people will receive adequate medical service.   The greater the current opposition of the vested medical interests to such moderate plans as those of President Truman, the greater the probability that we shall later adopt some such drastic program as that of Britain or Russia.

**The movement for public health insurance in the United States.**
In 1945, the Wagner-Murray-Dingell Bill was brought forward in
Congress. It provided for compulsory health insurance, supported
by Federal and State aid, to the annual amount of some 4 billion
dollars, about the cost of our carrying on the second world war for a
week in 1945. It was a very mild measure, since persons able to get
private medical care would remain perfectly free to do so. Extensive
government aid for building and operating hospitals and training
doctors was included in the provisions of the bill. On November 19,
1945, President Truman sent a strong message to Congress in favor of
it, but certain conservative members of Congress, like Senator Robert
A. Taft, thought the measure too "Socialistic" and demanded a more
moderate bill.

Mr. Taft introduced such a bill, which was an improvement over the
slight Federal aid to health that now exists, but its proposals were
inadequate and difficult to enforce. Even the timid Taft bill was
not brought to a vote by the time of the adjournment of Congress
in October, 1949, nor was it brought up in the next session.

In his address on the state of the nation at the opening of the 81st
Congress, President Truman reiterated his support of national health
insurance and state-supported medical care. The American Medical
Association girded for the battle, assessing members $25 each to raise
a giant fund of three million dollars to fight the President's program.
Faced by such opposition on the part of the AMA and many other
conservative forces, all stressing the alleged failure of the British state
medical plan, the Truman medical program was not even brought
up for serious debate and was unceremoniously shelved. Indeed, the
creation of a Federal Department of Welfare, recommended by Mr.
Hoover's committee on governmental reorganization, was rejected
mainly because it was feared that Mr. Oscar R. Ewing, head of the
Federal Security Agency and the chief government proponent of the
Truman medical plan, might be appointed Secretary of Welfare.

## Summary

The story of modern medicine presents an amazing paradox. On
the one hand, the progress in medical science in the past century has
been startling; on the other, over 300,000 persons die every year
in the United States who might be saved, and millions suffer from
unnecessary illness and disease. Our system of medical care constitutes one of the most striking and tragic examples of cultural lag.

The discovery of the bacteria responsible for diseases has led to
preventive and curative measures, such as inoculation, vaccination, the
use of a wide variety of serums, the employment of many new and
powerful germicides and antibiotics, aseptic surgery, and sanitary
engineering, all designed to prevent the spread of disease and help the

afflicted. The public health movement has tried to improve and safeguard the nation's health and educate people in ways of living that will strengthen their resistance to disease. Despite such progress, the fight against disease is not yet won. For, our present system of bringing medical care to the people of the United States is inadequate. Four out of every ten Americans who need medical attention do not receive it.

To remedy this situation, several plans for the reorganization of medical treatment have been proposed. Such are fraternal health insurance, hospitalization insurance, employers' group health insurance, co-operative community medicine, compulsory health insurance, and thoroughgoing state medicine.

None has yet been adopted on a wide scale in this country, except for the Blue Cross hospitalization plan. But, whichever plan is chosen, the United States must speedily take steps to safeguard the health of its citizens by assuring adequate medical care to all who need it.

### Selected References

Armstrong, B. N., *The Health Insurance Doctor*, Princeton University Press, 1939. Excellent account of public health insurance in England (prior to the 1948 system), Denmark, and France. Shows how this method of averaging medical costs works in practice.

Blake, R. P., *Industrial Safety*, Prentice-Hall, 1943. Standard work on safety campaigns and methods, especially in industrial operations.

Clark, Evans, *How to Budget Health*, Harper, 1933. One of the pioneer books on plans to average the costs of medical care.

Davis, M. M., *America Organizes Medicine*, Harper, 1941. Important work by an expert on medical care, dealing with development of trends towards community and socialized medicine and public health insurance.

De Kruif, P. H., *Microbe Hunters*, Harcourt, Brace, 1926.

——————, *Men Against Death*, Harcourt, Brace, 1932.

——————, *The Fight for Life*, Harcourt, Brace, 1938.

——————, and Rhea, *Why Keep Them Alive?* Harcourt, Brace, 1936. Four lively books by the chief popularizer of the war on disease by medical science. Entrancing and generally reliable. The last book is a powerful statement of the relation of poverty to disease and problems of medical care.

* Dietz, David, *Medical Magic,* Dodd, Mead, 1938. One of the better popular treatments of the present status of the more deadly diseases and the triumphs of medical science in the last generation.

Dunbar, Flanders, *Mind and Body: Psychosomatic Medicine*, Random House, 1947. Pioneer work on new field of medicine which stresses mental influence on bodily disorders and their treatment.

\* Ewing, O. R., *The Nation's Health,* Federal Security Agency, 1948. Official argument and cogent data supporting the Wagner-Murray-Dingell bill and President Truman's program of national health insurance.

Gray, G. W., *The Advancing Front of Medicine,* Whittlesey House, 1941. Good review of progress in American medical science and treatment.

Heiser, V. G., *Toughen Up, America!* Whittlesey House, 1941. Vigorous argument for better medical care for the mass of Americans.

Kingsbury, J. A., *Health Security for the Nation,* League for Industrial Democracy, 1938. The best introductory treatment of the principles of socialized medicine and the averaging of the costs of medical care.

Mott, F. D. and Roemer, M. I., *Rural Health and Medical Care,* McGraw-Hill, 1948. The most comprehensive and competent treatment of rural medical problems.

Newsholme, Sir Arthur, *The Story of Modern Preventive Medicine,* Williams & Wilkins, 1929. Excellent survey by a leading British authority on medical problems.

Reed, L. S., *Health Insurance: the Next Step in Social Security,* Harper, 1937. A sane and authoritative presentation of health insurance as a medical and social problem.

\* Rorty, James, *American Medicine Mobilizes,* Norton, 1939. A slashing attack on professional greed and reaction in the medical profession and a graphic account of the steps taken by progressive physicians to socialize medical practice.

Shyrock, R. H., *Development of Modern Medicine,* Knopf, 1947. Admirable book for the lay reader on the origins and development of contemporary medical science.

Sigerist, H. E., *Socialized Medicine in the Soviet Union,* Norton, 1937. Authoritative description by the leading world authority on medical history.

Stern, B. J., *Society and Medical Progress,* Princeton University, 1941. An able and progressive study of the social factors which have affected, and often retarded, medical progress and medical treatment.

Wilson, C. M., *Ambassadors in White,* Holt, 1942. Readable professional account of tropical medicine dealing with such things as the conquest of malaria, yellow fever, and other tropical diseases.

# PART IV

# The Economic Foundations of Society

## CHAPTER XIII

# The Evolution of Industry

### Stages and Types of Industrial Evolution

**Inclusive character of human industry.** Industry, in the broadest sense, includes all the ways mankind has tried to provide the necessities of life and produce a surplus of wealth. Today, we use the term most frequently to describe the various phases of manufacturing, but gathering herbs, hunting, fishing, agriculture, mining, trading, and banking are all forms of industry.

**Some leading efforts to classify the stages of industrial development.** There have been many attempts to arrange man's economic activities through the ages into so-called "stages of evolution," but it is difficult to formulate a uniform pattern of industrial development. One group of economic historians bases its analysis on trends in man's search for food and clothing. Thus economic activity has been divided into eras of collecting, hunting and fishing, pastoral industry, agriculture, commercial expansion, and machine industry and finance.

Other economists have classified industry according to its organization: the home, the small shop, the gild, the putting-out system, the factory, and the super-factory. All such classifications assume that man has gone through definite stages in his economic life, that these were universal, and that they have followed each other in a uniform way all over the world.

**Value of the stage concept.** Such attempts to formulate economic development are useful, because they provide historical perspective and a framework for study. In any culture, there will be much overlapping. In our own civilization, for example, manufacturing is dominant; yet agriculture remains important, and we still attach significance to the pastoral industries.

## The Development of Agriculture

**An economy of collectors.** A million years ago, man probably lived by picking up fruits, herbs, berries, and nuts and by eating those animals or fish which he killed with a stick or stone or caught with his hands. Unable to kindle fire, he ate his food raw. This period is often called the collecting stage, or the economy of collectors.

In the Old Stone Age, man continued to gather berries, herbs, and nuts, but by then he had learned how to make stone and bone weapons for hunting and fishing. His food was more palatable, because he had mastered the art of making fire. The dog was domesticated in this period and probably aided in hunting. But not until the New Stone Age, which began about 20,000 years ago, did man domesticate cattle, swine, and sheep and begin to till the soil. In some areas, rudimentary agriculture seems to have come about prior to the domestication of animals.

**Origins of pastoral life and agriculture.** The domestication of cattle, sheep, swine and goats brought about a definite advance toward civilization. Man probably did not begin to raise animals on a large scale until he had a fairly permanent home, though nomads had their flocks and continued to drive them about for many centuries. By the end of the New Stone Age, man had learned that animals were valuable as a reserve supply of food, as well as for their skins and milk. It was not until later, when man had invented the wheeled vehicle and learned to use metals, that animals were employed to draw plows and carts.

The beginnings of agriculture are shrouded in mystery. We do know, however, that toward the close of the New Stone Age, barley, wheat, millet, peas, beans, certain fruits, and flax were planted by man. Since there were no plows, the ground was not systematically cultivated; a pointed stick was used to make depressions in the soil for the seeds. It seems likely that lack of implements caused man to seek very fertile soil to make his work easier. The Nile valley, and the valley of the Tigris and Euphrates, both rich in fertile land and blessed with favorable natural conditions, may have been the first areas in which cereals were cultivated.

**Agricultural advances in the ancient Near East.** In the ancient oriental cultures of Egypt, Babylonia, and Assyria, pastoral and agricultural industries made important advances. The donkey was first used in Egypt, and the domesticated horse appeared in western Asia around 2200 B.C.; camels came into use in the late Assyrian period in western Asia, and about 500 B.C. in Egypt. The ancient peoples knew how to breed some domesticated animals for specialized purposes.

A crude wooden plow was developed to take the place of the wooden hoe, and the wheeled vehicle, destined to play such an important part in the history of mankind, was invented by the Sumerians about 4000 B.C. Agriculture was revolutionized not only by the plow but by other improvements, such as the discovery of more and better cereals and the invention of a crude seed-drill. The seed-drill, invented hundreds of years before the birth of Christ, did not enter western European agriculture until two centuries ago. The Egyptians and the Babylonians learned how to irrigate the soil to get a better crop and how to store up water for use in the dry seasons.

**Ancient agriculture as illustrated by Egyptian practice.** We may illustrate the character of oriental agriculture by describing its operations in ancient Egypt. The plow used by the Egyptians was a crude instrument. Two men were required to operate it; one controlled the plow, the other drove the oxen. Frequently, the men themselves drew the plow. Once the soil had been sufficiently plowed, the seed was scattered over it, and then trodden in by herds of sheep. Wheat, barley, and millet were the most common grains cultivated in Egypt. Onions, cucumbers, peas, beans, lettuce, leeks, radishes, and melons were raised; the olive was cultivated in certain parts of the country, and vineyards were generally plentiful. Flax and cotton were grown for weaving cloth.

The Egyptians used sickles, made of metal or wood, with a cutting edge of flint. Wheat and barley were cut just above the middle of the stalk to make threshing easier, and what was left standing in the fields was later used in making bricks. Both men and women worked in the fields—the men usually did the reaping, and the women followed them to garner the grain. When the grain had been gathered, it was threshed on the ground by flails or by oxen and donkeys. Winnowing—generally the task of women—was done by throwing the grain and chaff together up into the wind, so that the chaff might be blown away. Then the grain was stored in granaries, and a suitable harvest celebration was held.

Horses were not brought into Egypt until after 1750 B.C., and never assumed the importance of oxen and donkeys in agriculture. Sheep, goats, and some varieties of poultry were raised. The chicken, unknown in Egypt, was later introduced to the West from India.

Agriculture provided much of the wealth and prosperity of ancient Egypt. It was by far the most vital occupation. The lives and activities of farmers were completely controlled by the Pharaohs and the priests. The Pharaoh, through his officials, decided what crops were to be grown, how they were to be cultivated, and what percentage of the yield was to be handed over to the government. In return, the Pharaohs undertook irrigation and reclamation projects and gave police and military protection. Egypt was a true patriarchal economy as well as a political empire.

**Greek agriculture.** In ancient Greece, agriculture was the basic occupation. Although handicraft manufacture and trade were fairly well developed, most of the citizens lived on their land, or at least on its products. Few possessed large holdings, and only crude methods of cultivation were then known. Since artificial fertilization was almost unheard of before the fourth century B.C., each plot of ground had to lie fallow every other year in order to produce good crops. Most of the soil was poor, and cereals could not be grown in sufficient quantities to supply the needs of the people. In order to meet the demand for grain, the Greek mainland had to import cereals from Sicily, Egypt, and the Black Sea region. Fruits and vegetables were grown in large quantities, and flax was extensively cultivated to make linen for clothing and household use. Goats, sheep, donkeys, and mules were abundant, but there were few horses or cows. As the Greek city populations grew, they became more and more dependent on imports.

**The development of agriculture among the Romans.** Roman agriculture underwent great changes between the days of the early Republic and the decline of the Empire. In the early Republic, small-farm agriculture was the chief form of industry. By the time of the Roman Empire, however, the small farms had been largely taken over by wealthy men, who combined them into great estates, *latifundia*, cultivated by slaves.

In the late Republic and the early Empire, the Roman farmer grew wheat, barley, and millet, and raised many vegetables. His vineyards provided him with grapes, raisins, and wine, and he usually had fig orchards. During the Imperial period, olive orchards became of great importance; olive oil was used as food or burned in lamps. Farm implements were rudimentary, and much of the work was done by hand, as in ancient Egypt. Stone mills, operated by hand or water power, ground the grain into flour and feed. Crude presses were used to make wine and olive oil.

Horses were used for travel, war, and races more than for farm work. Cattle were common for working in the fields and dairying, but beef was not eaten except by the wealthy. Hogs were grown, pork being the chief meat eaten by the middle class and by those of the lower classes who were fortunate enough to get any meat whatever. Sheep were raised for wool and mutton, and goats for milk and cheese. The bee industry was of great importance, since sugar was unknown in ancient times and honey was highly valued for sweetening purposes.

**Medieval agriculture under the manorial system.** During the Middle Ages, agriculture came to be carried on under a communal or manorial system. The village, with its cottages, church, parish house, and cemetery, was the center of the manor. If the manor was large, the village might nestle against the thick outer walls of the lord's castle; otherwise, the manor house, with its barns and stables, would be located on a choice site not far from the village. Surrounding the village was the manorial land, separated usually into three main sections. Each was in turn further divided into small strips of varying lengths. Near the manor house lay the *demesne*—the land cultivated by the peasants or serfs for the special use of the lord, usually the best farm land on the manor. The peasants gave about half their time to cultivating the demesne in return for the privilege of holding and cultivating their own strips and for the protection the lord gave them.

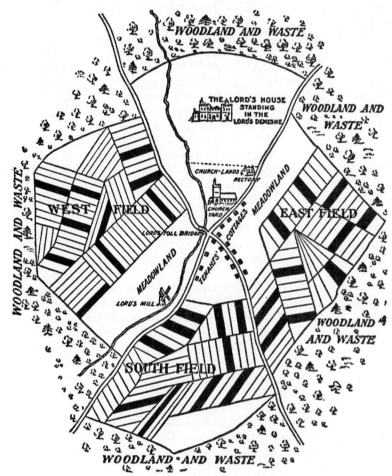

Graphic Map illustrating the layout of the medieval manorial system. (From Henry Allsop, *Introduction to English Industrial History*, George Bell & Sons.)

Part of the manorial land was rented to free cultivators, but most of it was worked by the quasi-servile villagers, whose shares were scattered among the strips which ran through the three large fields. The meadow, woodland, and waste land were shared in common by the lord and the serfs. The parish priest also had land, which might lie in one single area or in strips scattered throughout the fields.

The land worked by the peasants was arranged in such a way that none held two adjoining strips. This scattering of the strips was done to assure a fair distribution of holdings among the most fertile and the least productive parts of the manor. Each strip was separated by unplowed land. Several strips were held by each household. The peasant did not own his land; he had only the right of cultivation. The crop harvested from the strips was his, but the land itself belonged to the lord.

The arable land was divided into three sections—one was planted in the spring, the second in the fall, and the third was left idle to recover its fertility. The strips on the idle field became part of the common land after the harvest. When the next planting occurred, the strips were again divided among the peasants. In most instances, each household kept the same strips, but periodically they were redistributed, so that every family might have its chance at the better sections.

This three-field system was the one great innovation in agriculture during the Middle Ages. The early Germans and the Romans had used the two-field system; that is, they cultivated half of the ground and let the other half lie idle for a season to restore its fertility. But the discovery that wheat or rye could be planted in the fall, as well as in the spring, made it possible to work two-thirds of the land each year. The three-field system permitted two crops to be produced annually, and also kept more land under cultivation, with actually less plowing.

Since few peasants owned many tools, most of them pooled their tools and their labor and carried on agriculture under a co-operative system. The plow, somewhat improved by the Germans, was drawn by six to twelve oxen, and required as many as four men to operate it. The farm work was back-breaking and tedious, because thorn trees, weighed down with logs, were far from adequate as harrows, and the large lumps of soil thrown up by the plow had to be broken with crude mattocks. Since there were no grain drills, the seed was sown broadcast by hand, and birds often got much of it. Weeding had to be done mostly by hand or with forked sticks, and the sickle and scythe were the main implements for cutting the ripened grain. The methods employed by the Egyptians in threshing and winnowing were still in use.

Oxen were generally utilized for farm work, because they were stronger and less expensive to keep and could be slaughtered and eaten when old. While horses were raised on the manor, especially for military purposes, they were not usually employed in farm work. Since the peasantry did not understand selective breeding, their cattle, sheep, and hogs were of poor quality, and of less value than today. For example, a cow which produced enough butter fat to make one pound of butter a week was considered a good cow; today, with selective breeding, a cow may produce 10 to 15 pounds of butter a week. The poor quality of the stock was also due to the fact that good fodder was rarely available. Sheep were valuable because of their wool, but they were so poorly cared for that many died every year. Both cattle and sheep were watched over by the village shepherd, who took them out to pasture in the morning and went after them in the evenings. Hogs were an important meat supply, but they were half-wild creatures that usually ranged the woods.

The peasants raised many fowls: chickens, geese, ducks, and pigeons. Beekeeping also occupied a prominent place, for both beeswax and honey were in great demand.

In addition to working half their time for the lord, the medieval peasants also owed him other services. Carefully stipulated amounts of manufactured articles and farm products, such as shoes, wool, grain, eggs, were turned over to the lord. In return for labor and goods, the lord offered protection to the peasants; gave food in times of famine; constructed bridges, mills, and ovens for general use; and sometimes kept superior stock which was occasionally offered to the peasants for breeding purposes. There is no doubt that the lord received more than he gave, but he did offer the peasants important aid and security.

**The Agricultural Revolution.** The next striking change in agriculture came in early modern times, the so-called Agricultural Revolution, which occurred first in England in the seventeenth and eighteenth centuries and later spread to continental Europe and the United States.

By the seventeenth century, the manorial system, so far as methods of landholding were concerned, had been pretty well wiped out in England. But the technique of agriculture had changed little since the thirteenth century. Although legally the manor no longer existed, the agricultural village, strip ownership of land, co-operative cultivation, and the common pasture were still the rule until about 1700. The eighteenth century brought a series of remarkable changes, among which the introduction of new implements, successful experimentation with new crops, improvements in stock breeding, drainage of waste land, the introduction of scientific methods of fertilization, the organization of scientific societies to promote agricultural improvements, and the growth of large estates were outstanding.

**The contributions of Tull, Townshend, and Bakewell.** The work of four men helped to bring about these remarkable changes in agriculture—Jethro Tull (1674–1740), Lord Charles Townshend (1674–1738), Robert Bakewell (1725–1795), and Arthur Young (1741–1820).

Jethro Tull introduced the first successful modern seed-drill. He also stimulated the practice of working up the soil about crop roots and eliminating weeds. It has been said that Tull left to his successors the basic farming principles of "clean farming, economy in seedings, drilling, and the maxim that the more irons are among the roots the better for the crop."

Lord Townshend was mainly responsible for the introduction of new crops, notably new winter crops, which eliminated the necessity of leaving land idle to restore fertility. Townshend promoted the cultivation of crops like clover to restore nitrogen to the soil and provide feed for cattle; he introduced crop rotation by showing how land might be put into different crops in successive years and thus not lose its fertility; and he recommended turnips as food for cattle in both summer and winter. Townshend was so enthusiastic about turnips that he was called "Turnip Townshend."

The experiments of Robert Bakewell in selective stock-breeding brought about important improvements. The improvements introduced by Tull and Townshend soon made it possible to support a greater number of livestock than ever before. Stock-raising for profit now became a definite possibility. Although some progress in stock-breeding had been made in the Netherlands, the manorial system of the Middle Ages had paid little attention to breeding specialized types of animals for different purposes. The same animal was used for both food and work or for beef and milk. Bakewell understood that no one animal can be suitable for all purposes. A beef cow might not be a good milk cow, and a sheep that produced heavy wool was often not so suitable for mutton. Bakewell successfully bred specialized animals —draft, carriage, and hunting horses; beef and milk cows; wool and mutton sheep. His work was carried on by the Duke of Bedford and Lord Somerville.

The enclosure movement and the growth of great estates. Arthur Young made a contribution of a different sort. He spent much of his life spreading knowledge of the above-described reforms in agriculture. He realized that England could not adopt the innovations of Tull, Townshend, and Bakewell unless the traditional and inefficient methods of small-scale farming were abandoned and farmers had enough capital to operate their farms along scientific lines. He urged the consolidation of small holdings into large farms. Modern capitalistic farming arose in England between 1760 and 1830, displacing the small farmer and bringing many social evils, as well as more efficient farming. Similar in nature to that of Young was the work of William Marshall and Sir John Sinclair.

Further advances were made by draining land, mixing soil, and improving fertilization. Lord Townshend had suggested the desirability of mixing soils to produce better yields, and the idea was carried on by Thomas Coke and other early capitalistic farmers. Advances in chemistry in the eighteenth and nineteenth centuries made possible scientific fertilization. Sir Humphrey Davy, early in the nineteenth century, was the first chemist to devote serious attention to soil fertilization. Through the work of Davy and others like Justus Liebig in Germany, experts became able to tell what elements the soil lacked and to add the needed chemicals cheaply and speedily. Agricultural societies were organized to promote scientific farming methods. Such were the famous Smithfield Club in London and the Highland Society in Scotland.

These agricultural improvements were carried on rapidly because of the effects of the Commercial Revolution. Many successful merchants invested their money in great estates, not only for added social prestige, but also because of the possibility of large profits. Coke was one of the more prominent and successful of those who applied the newer agricultural techniques on large estates built up through the enclosure of former small peasant holdings.

Although the creation of large estates increased agricultural efficiency and production, it brought ruin to many small farmers, who lost not only their land, but also their livestock and the common pasture and waste land. Under the manorial system, the peasants worked hard, but they at least had some security. With the enclosure system (the enclosing of small farms into great estates), they became dependent on the wages paid by the owners of large estates. The Industrial Revolution after 1750 helped to lessen the insecurity and distress of the dispossessed farmers, because many found work in the new factories, though usually at low wages and under poor working conditions.

**Recent developments in mechanization and applied chemistry.** The most important recent changes in agriculture are those associated with the coming of farm machinery and the application of chemistry to agriculture. The most striking transformation has occurred in the United States. In Chapter II we discussed the chief agricultural inventions, such as the seed-drill, better types of iron and steel plows, and the mower, reaper, and binder, which appeared in the nineteenth century. In the twentieth century, came the farm tractor, the automobile truck, the gang plow, the multiple disc harrow, the harvesting combine, and the mechanical cotton picker. The use of larger and better grain drills, and even of airplanes, for sowing crops, has revolutionized American farming methods. Chemistry has made important contributions to agriculture, and we are on the eve of remarkable achievements in the chemical production of artificial foods.

The extent to which mechanical and chemical inventions have increased the possible production of food is almost unbelievable. Dr. O. W. Willcox has shown that, if we were to employ the best known methods of agricultural production, we could produce all the food needed for a liberal diet for every American citizen on one-fifth the land now cultivated in this country and with one-fifth the farmers now engaged in cultivation. Even greater marvels can be produced by hydro-chemical cultivation, known as hydroponics. By such methods, for example, the potato yield per acre can be increased from 125 bushels to 2,500 bushels. New methods of transporting, canning, and refrigerating food have also helped to create an agricultural surplus that is becoming a major problem of our era.

Paradoxically enough, while the rise of machinery has had its impact upon agriculture and has enormously increased the production of food per capita, the general process of mechanization has relentlessly pushed agriculture into a secondary position in the economy of every industrialized state. Mechanization has produced the great cities of our era, and an ever smaller number of the gainfully employed are engaged in agricultural pursuits. More than two-thirds of the working population in the age of Jackson were occupied in agricultural and allied operations; by the time of the second world war only about one-fifth were so engaged.

Effects of two world wars upon agriculture. The first world war brought about important changes in agriculture; England, for example, concentrated on food production when her possibilities of importing foodstuffs were limited by German submarine warfare. Land which had formerly lain idle, or had been used for pasture or hunting, was brought under cultivation. After the war, there were sweeping land reforms throughout Europe, consisting mainly in breaking up the great estates and giving them to the people. The most striking reforms were those of Soviet Russia, where all private land was taken over by the state, and agriculture was speedily mechanized.

The second world war once more created a food crisis. Because Germany, in 1941, controlled much of continental Europe and could not get food from overseas on account of the British blockade, she attempted to secure food through intensive cultivation. By forcing the people of the conquered countries to work the land, the Nazis temporarily nationalized agriculture in these countries as the Soviet régime had done in Russia. By tearing most of the agricultural areas of Germany away from that country and giving them to Poland and Russia, we created a serious agricultural and food crisis in central Europe after the second world war.

The United States produces far more food than its people can afford to buy. Only about 10 per cent of Americans could afford enough food to maintain a liberal standard of diet even in the relatively prosperous years of 1928–1929. Between 1920 and 1933, the condition of the farmer grew steadily worse. The attempts of the New Deal after 1933 to solve the farm problem have been touched on in the chapter on conservation and will also be described in a later chapter on rural life. The great demand for American farm products during the second world war and, later, to feed the starving peoples of postwar Europe gave the farmers of this country a marked increase in income after 1940, but much of this was absorbed in the greater costs of everything the farmer had to buy. Moreover, it was evident that the increased income and improved prosperity of the farmers rested on very abnormal and temporary conditions.

## The Evolution of Manufacturing

Origin of tools and weapons. The foundations of manufacturing like those of agriculture, were laid in man's remote past, long before records were kept. One of the most important contributions to civilization was the discovery of tools to aid man in his search for food, clothing, and shelter.   While wood, bone, shell, skin, and stone were used for tools by early man, stone implements are the ones which best enable us to measure cultural development in primitive times.

At first, man used his tools as he found them but, during the Old Stone Age, he began to make scrapers, knives, awls, and bone needles. He was thus able to cut and sew the skins of animals into rude garments.   His weapons were fashioned, for the most part, of stone; but, by the end of the Old Stone Age, he had begun to make a variety of bone and wooden tools and weapons.   Far and away the most important and widely-used weapon and implement of man in the Old Stone Age was the *coup de poing* or fist hatchet, a chipped stone weapon, with a large, rounded base, held in the palm of the hand, and a long, sharp point.   With this man could do everything from killing an animal or human enemy to boring a hole in a stick or piece of hide. The fist hatchets were used for an ax, hammer, knife, scraper, dagger, and awl.   So popular and important were they that no less than 20,000 of them have been picked up in one single Old Stone Age site in France.   In this period, man also discovered how to make a fire, perhaps by rubbing two pieces of wood or stone together.   The discovery was probably accidental, but it was an enormous step forward in man's development.   For early man, fire meant light, heat, protection, and cooked food.   By the end of the Old Stone Age, many of the fundamental elements of material culture had been provided.

In the New Stone Age remarkable progress was made.   Earlier tools and weapons were improved and new ones invented.   The bow, arrow, and stone ax made their appearance.   By the end of the period, the ax had been polished, ground, and perforated, and a handle inserted. Another significant tool was devised in the New Stone Age—a stone mill for grinding corn.   Devices for spinning and weaving cloth were also invented.

**The dawn of history and the invention of metals.**   The stone ages were followed by the metal ages in which, as their name implies, man learned to use copper, iron, gold, silver, bronze, and most of the other well-known metals except aluminum.   Copper was the first metal to be worked.   We find copper needles in the Egyptian tombs dating from before 4000 B.C., and copper chisels in graves of around 3500 B.C. Bronze, a mixture of tin and copper, came into use in the Near East about 2500 B.C.   During the fourteenth century B.C., the Hittites of Asia Minor learned how to manufacture iron implements and weapons. Excellent steel was manufactured in Syria and elsewhere before the close of the pre-Christian era, and gold- and silver-working was well developed by the ancient oriental peoples.

**Increasing importance of the textile industry.**   The textile industry expanded rapidly with the growth of civilization.   Spinning and weaving began in the New Stone Age.   The earliest spinning was done by twisting the flax fibers by hand; later, a weight was attached to one end of a stick, and the so-called spindle-whorl was invented and became the basic spinning device until the spinning-wheel was invented during the Middle Ages. By the end of the New Stone Age, weavers were using a hand loom, which endured with few changes until the eighteenth century of the Christian era. The weaving of tapestry began in the ancient Near East.

*U. S. Department of Agriculture.*

**A Southern family making cloth, illustrating handicraft methods of manufacture which dominated industry from the Stone Age to the Industrial Revolution of the eighteenth century.**

The improved methods of manufacture increased the number of articles that could be sold and stimulated trade. Better transportation was made possible by the domestication of the donkey, horse, and camel. Improved roads made it easier to travel further for raw materials and to dispose of the finished articles. Sea trade was first developed on a large scale by the Cretans, Egyptians, and Phoenicians.

**Industrial life in Greece.** Among the Greeks, little distinction was made between the crafts and the professions; physicians were regarded as craftsmen just as much as metal workers. For vocational training the apprentice system was in general use, and there was a great deal of specialization in industry. Not only did particular crafts make different articles, but there was a division of labor within each craft. For instance, in the making of sandals, one craftsman cut the leather and another sewed the pieces together. The Greeks had no large factories, and most craftsmen worked in their homes or in small shops. The chief reasons for the absence of large-scale factories were the large amount of work done in the home and the cheapness of slave labor.

The Greeks were notable for their pride in fine workmanship—many workers were not only artisans but virtually artists.

**Roman industry.** Although agriculture was more important than manufacturing industry, there was no lack of industrial enterprise in ancient Rome. The growth of population in the city of Rome and other urban communities made it necessary to increase the production of goods. Within the urban centers, specialization progressed rapidly, but in the rural areas family workshops still prevailed. On the large estates, the slaves provided much of the labor in the shops. The large supply of cheap slave labor for Roman industry discouraged attempts to invent labor-saving tools or machines. In the Roman imperial era the most highly skilled craftsmen and builders were those of Syria and Egypt.

Most Roman factories were small and used simple machinery. Only in pottery and brick-making was anything like large-scale organization to be found. Some large workshops were established by wealthy Romans in which slaves were usually employed under the management of a freedman or a slave. The free craftsman, working at home with his family and one or two slaves, and the small shops, were the most common types of Roman industrial organization.

**Industrial life in the early Middle Ages.** Throughout the early Middle Ages there were three main forms of industrial production—domestic, manorial, and monastic. In the domestic or home industry, the family produced, so far as possible, all the necessities of life. In manorial industry, manufactured goods were produced by quasi-servile craftsmen on the manors. Their position was almost identical with that of the serfs, and they rendered payment to the lord of the manor in manufactured articles instead of agricultural products. Most of the manufactured goods produced in the manorial system were intended for local use. A part of the regimen in the monasteries was devotion to hard work. Many monks became skilled craftsmen, turning out materials all the way from heavy hardware to fine wines and liquors. Monastic industry had an important advantage in that no wages had to be paid. It tended to thrive and, in the later Middle Ages, was a considerable competitor with the gild manufacturing in the medieval towns.

**Industry under the gild system.** After the eleventh century a new stimulus to manufacturing industry was provided by the revival of commerce. Larger markets, more raw materials, and new capital stimulated industrial activity. New articles and more advanced industrial techniques were introduced in western Europe as a result of contact with the Byzantines and Moslems of the East. Soon, the Europeans learned how to make many of the articles brought from the East and, in some instances, to improve on them.

In the cities, industry was carried on by the gilds, or organizations of craftsmen. The gild industrial establishments were usually small shops presided over by a master craftsman. He was assisted by his family, by skilled workmen known as journeymen, and by young boys learning the trade, called apprentices. Only one type of article was usually produced by a given craft. The master owned his tools and generally provided his raw materials, although occasionally his customers furnished their own materials to be made into goods. After the articles were completed, the master craftsman sold them in his workshop or in the market. He seldom produced for a "blind" market, or for that matter, manufactured more than he could sell. He made goods on order, or for the town market, and in this way ran little risk of overproduction. Although his profits were small, he enjoyed the fruits of his labor, and pride in his work made him eager to produce articles of high quality.

To maintain a uniform standard of excellence, the craft gilds regulated hours and conditions of labor. The working day was long during the spring and summer, but night work was forbidden, since poor artificial light made it difficult to supervise or inspect the products. The gilds regulated competition, as well as the wages of journeymen and the prices of commodities. But, despite all the precautions taken by the gilds to maintain good workmanship, there was some fraud. Material supplied by customers was sometimes stolen, cloth was stretched, and inferior goods were substituted for those of better quality after the sale had been made. Fraud, if detected, was punishable by a fine, and repeated offenses meant expulsion from the gild. To maintain the quality and regulate the production of goods, changes in manufacturing methods were usually prohibited; the gild thus acted as somewhat of a brake on the development of industrial processes. Yet innovations did creep in, and complete uniformity in the quality of goods could never be maintained. When new techniques arose, the gilds could no longer control prices so rigidly.

While most medieval industry was carried on by the craft gilds, the monasteries accounted for a good deal of manufacturing. Much of the work at monasteries was done by serfs in the later Middle Ages. Since the labor of serfs cost little, the monasteries could compete unfairly with the gildsmen who employed journeymen at regular wages. The gilds, therefore, became highly antagonistic to the industrial activities of the monasteries, and tried to protect themselves by getting anti-clerical legislation passed by the town governments. The monasteries continued, however, until about the thirteenth century, to do a flourishing business, especially in clothing, leather goods, and beverages, particularly wine and beer.

**Industrial impact of the Commercial Revolution.** The Commercial Revolution, which began in the sixteenth century, produced greater changes in manufacturing than any development that had taken place since the days of the ancient Egyptians and Babylonians. The discovery of new trade routes to India, China, and Japan and the opening up of the New World brought Europe into contact with other old civilizations and large new markets. The expansion of commerce and the creation of colonies made it necessary to increase manufacturing, especially in England and Holland, in order to supply the growing markets. The governments encouraged the importation of raw materials from the New World, to be made into finished products, and then resold to their colonies at a good profit. This led to trading monopoly in some instances, but production was notably increased.

The textile industry was the first to be affected by the expansion of markets. The manufacture of woolens after the fourteenth century in England, and the making of silk, especially by the French and Italians, became two major industries. In the seventeenth century, England produced coarse cotton cloth, known as fustian, for export. By the beginning of the Industrial Revolution around 1750, the cotton industry dominated the English textile scene.

The demand for all kinds of goods increased after 1500. Pottery, hardware, glass, and upholstered furniture, introduced from the East, began to be manufactured in large quantities in England. There was a large market in the colonies for various types of hardware, especially muskets, swords, hoes, nails, tools, pewter, and tinware. The development of the hardware industry in turn stimulated the mining of iron, lead, and tin.

Shipbuilding was immediately affected by the new commerce. Ships were made larger, stronger, and more adaptable to the demands of ocean travel. Figures showing the growth of English shipping give an indication of the expansion of commercial activity during the sixteenth and seventeenth centuries. In 1560, the total tonnage of English merchant ships was 7,600; by 1607, it was 23,000; a century later, it was over 120,000 tons.

Much of the new industry was carried on by the putting-out system, which had replaced the gilds of the Middle Ages in England. The merchants supplied raw materials to workmen who worked them up at their homes, scattered about the countryside. The finished products were then collected and marketed by the merchants.

**The technology of abundance and the economy of scarcity.** The industrial changes before the seventeenth century were insignificant, however, compared with the transformation produced by the Industrial Revolution and the rise of machinery and the factory system, discussed in Chapters II and III. In the twentieth century, the further mechanization of industry, the application of electrical power, the introduction of automatic machinery, the endless conveyor-belt, and the speed-up system all combined to make possible a far greater production of goods than had ever been known in previous human history. In 1850, men and horses supplied 94 per cent of our power and machines only 6 per cent. By 1950, the situation was exactly reversed —machines produced 94 per cent of our power.

The potential productivity of our machine age has, however, been reduced by modern capitalistic business and financial practices, and by the separation of ownership from control and management. These matters will be discussed in the following chapters, but it might be pointed out that, except in wartime, we have rarely reached anything like the limits of our productive capacity.   The heavy production record in the years immediately following 1945 was due mainly to the efforts to supply the backlog of demands unfilled during wartime, to maintain a quasi-war economy after V-J Day in rehabilitating Europe and Japan, and to prepare armaments for a possible third world war. Our economic system is based on a "scarcity economy," which often limits production to keep prices high and profits large.   Until our economic order is adjusted to the concept of abundance, we shall never reap the full benefits of our tremendous present-day capacity to produce goods and services.

*R. I. Nesmith.*

A modern cotton mill, illustrating contemporary mechanical production and the factory system.

**State-dominated industry.**   In recent times, some European states, especially Soviet Russia and Nazi Germany, have taken over control of industry, in order to expand the production of goods.

Russia has introduced a fully-planned state economy.   The government completely dominates industrial life, and production is planned in accordance with governmental policy to reach the highest possible efficiency in industrial methods.   Although the Russians have not been able as yet to establish the mechanical expertness characteristic of industry in Germany and the United States, they have succeeded in vastly increasing their productivity.

In Nazi Germany, there was at first a less sweeping effort to set up a planned economy.   The Nazi government did not assume the ownership of factories, as Russia did, but, rather, regulated and controlled industrial operations. The result was an increase in industrial efficiency and the wiping out of unemployment, but the advantages thereof were lost through Hitler's idiotic war policy.

**Archaic economic ideas and war perpetuate poverty.** Today, we have all the technological equipment we need to provide a high standard of living and plenty of material comforts for all; but, so long as our ideals demand restricted production and permit monopoly, and so long as wars destroy hundreds of billions of dollars worth of goods at frequent intervals, there is little prospect that the masses will fully benefit from our impressive facilities for production. It is estimated that the total economic cost of the second world war was four trillion dollars, enough, if wisely expended, to have created an economic paradise throughout the civilized world. In the most strikingly prophetic book of the mid-century, *Nineteen Eighty-four*, George Orwell fears that governments may come to use cold and lukewarm wars as the means of perpetually depriving the masses of the benefits of our ever more efficient technology.

## The Development of World Trade

**Development of trade in the ancient Near East.** Systematic and large-scale trade first began in ancient Egypt and Babylonia. Egypt carried on trade overland across the desert, down the Nile to Nubia and the Sudan, and eastward into Syria and Arabia. The Egyptians carried on their land commerce at first by donkey caravans, later by camels. The Egyptians also seem to have been the first people to conquer the sea. The Babylonians built up a large trade along the Tigris and Euphrates rivers through the mountain passes to the Syrian coast. The Babylonian government sent part cf its army to police the trade routes and thus gave security to commerce.

The foremost land traders of the ancient Near East were the Arameans of Syria; the first people to develop a culture mainly on the basis of sea trade were the ancient Cretans. By 2500 B.C., the Cretans had created a prosperous maritime civilization, which lasted until about 1500 B.C. Then, the Phoenicians became the great sea traders of the ancient world.

**Trade from Pericles to Columbus.** By the fifth century B.C., Athens had become the leading commercial state; it continued to dominate Mediterranean commerce until the loss of its political independence. Rome developed a large external trade to import luxuries and to bring in grain to feed her people. The Romans used conquered peoples, such as Athenian and Alexandrian sailors, to assist in their carrying trade. The lands around the eastern Mediterranean and Gaul in the west were the chief sources of Roman imports.

In the early Middle Ages, there was a sharp commercial rivalry between the merchants of the Greek or Byzantine Empire at Constantinople and the Moslem traders. The Moslems were undoubtedly the leading merchants of medieval times, ranging with their ships from India and China to Africa and Spain.

# MACHINE POWER The Secret of Productivity

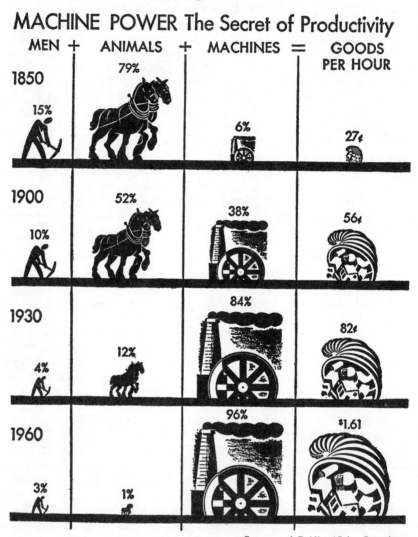

Courtesy of Public Affairs Committee.

This chart shows the striking substitution of mechanical for horse and other animal power, and the resulting vast increase in productivity.

After the Crusades had brought western Europe into contact with the Near East, trade began to expand rapidly. The Italian cities dominated western European foreign commerce, bringing the products from the East to the cities of western Europe, where they were disposed of at national or local fairs. Trading operations in the towns and at the national fairs were controlled by the merchant gilds. Travel overland was still extremely difficult because of poor roads, inferior vehicles, and robbers who assaulted the merchant caravans. Much of the commerce in northern Europe was sea trade, controlled by great organizations like the Hanseatic League, made up mainly of merchants in the north German cities.

**Growth of trade following the Commercial Revolution.** Down to the time of Columbus, the trade of the world had been conducted by land, or on rivers and inland seas, but with the expansion of Europe and the Commercial Revolution, trade became oceanic. In an attempt to reach China and Japan by sea instead of the customary overland routes, Christopher Columbus discovered America in 1492. In 1498, Vasco da Gama sailed around the Cape of Good Hope and reached India. These discoveries led to a period of exploration and brought about the Commercial Revolution, which created early modern civilization.

Between 1500 and 1800, the building of larger and more seaworthy ships made possible the expansion of commercial activities. New commodities and raw materials were brought to Europe from both East and West, and finished goods were sold in the colonies of the New World. By the close of the eighteenth century, Holland, France, and England had become the leading trading and naval countries.

**Expansion of trade after the Industrial Revolution.** New types of power, introduced after the Industrial Revolution, produced the modern steamship and made travel and exchange between foreign countries still easier and more voluminous. In 1800, the gross world commerce was $1,400,000,000; by 1870, it had increased to 10 billion dollars. The second phase of the Industrial Revolution brought about concentration and increased efficiency of industry, through the building of giant factories; and foreign trade increased rapidly, until, in 1913, the gross commerce of the world was valued at over 40 billion dollars, and in 1929 at nearly 70 billion.

The depression reduced world trade to 24 billion dollars in 1934. Improved economic conditions and the importation of materials needed for armaments brought the total volume of world trade up to 28 billion in 1938.

The devastation and impoverishment of the European and Asiatic countries by the second world war cut down their trade in drastic fashion. But there was a vast increase in American exports abroad, primarily for relief and rehabilitation. This served a worthy humane cause, but most of the goods were not sold but given away to needy peoples and ultimately paid for by American taxpayers. For this reason, the American foreign trade system since V-J Day has been cogently described as "deficit mercantilism."

**Crucial nature of international trade today.** While certain schools of economic and political thought have greatly exaggerated the im-

A Medieval Fair at which merchants and money-changers gathered from many parts of Europe.

portance of international commerce, as compared with domestic trade there can be no doubt that international trade is today of crucial importance to many countries, especially those of western Europe. The improvement of technology in recent years has made possible the production of an ever larger volume of goods. At the same time, the vast debt created by two world wars, the war losses and dislocations, tradition, and ideological inertia have prevented these countries from raising wages and salaries enough to provide an adequate home market for this increased volume of goods produced.

Hence, international trade and foreign markets are indispensable for the time being to many nations, especially those of western Europe, not merely for prosperity but for survival. At the same time, a complex combination of circumstances, mainly due to unfortunate foreign policies, makes it all but impossible for these countries to secure the needed markets. The German and central European economy, one of the great markets of western Europe, was destroyed as a result of the Casablanca unconditional surrender program and the Morgenthau Plan, adopted at Quebec and applied with few modifications through the Potsdam Conference of July, 1945. The other western European nations can buy little from each other; since they all produce more than they can consume under the present economic order. The United States and Canada refuse to take many European goods and have erected a high tariff wall against others. The natural market for western European goods would be the great undeveloped, agricultural areas of eastern Europe, Soviet Russia, and China. But the "cold war" and ideological strife have blocked these great potential markets from trading in any natural manner with western Europe. About all that remains for the latter is a fading dribble of colonial trade and some barter trade with the agricultural countries of Latin America—a procedure which evokes sharp criticism and resistance on the part of the United States. The United States program of maintaining its own prosperity on the basis of armament expenditures and making gifts of money and goods to the economically wobbly western European countries has proved no solution of the world economic problem.

The European Recovery Program, which has been hailed as the way of salvation for western Europe, actually only hurries these countries onward to ultimate disaster by making it possible to produce more goods while providing few additional markets in which to dispose of them. Moreover, it does not provide for the restoration of the German and central European economy to anything like the level needed to revive the market there. At the outset of 1950, the British were still dismantling German plants. The alarming British financial and commercial slump of 1949 was only the harbinger of what may become the fate of all western European nations under the present pattern of economic behavior. The dollar shortage, so bewailed in England, seems rather a minor symptom than a main cause of the crisis. Not even the drastic devaluation of the British pound in the autumn of 1949 seemed to accomplish much in the way of providing the needed foreign markets for Britain. In 1949, the United States exported 12.5 billion dollars worth of goods and imported but 6.5 billion dollars worth. The excess of our exports over imports was as great as when the ERP was initiated.

## Development of Local Trade

**Local trade in the ancient world.** So long as everyone in primitive society made the same things, there was little need for exchange; but, as different groups began to specialize, the impulse to exchange arose. Local trade on a large scale originated in ancient Egypt, where, by the end of the imperial period, a distinct merchant class had arisen. In Babylonia and Assyria, where a similar class developed, many of the retail merchants set up their wares close to the temples, which were centers of both industry and trade, while in Athens most of the booths and stalls were in the public markets. Rome had less retail trade per capita than Athens, since many commodities used by the rich landlords were made on their estates by slave labor. Roman trade was divided between craftsmen manufacturing directly for their customers and merchants offering their wares for sale in the public market place.

**Medieval local markets.** In the Middle Ages, local trade was centered chiefly in the public markets situated just outside of a town or adjoining a monastery or castle. Here, merchants and craftsmen displayed their wares, traded products for food, and sold articles to the peasantry. Regional or national fairs, held periodically, lasted for many days and drew customers from distant places. Special laws and courts governed the operations of these fairs in order to insure just treatment for those who attended. During much of the Middle Ages, both the town markets and the fairs were controlled by the merchant gilds, though in the later Middle Ages a good deal of the control of local trade was taken over by the craft gilds.

Medieval trade was sharply limited by the ethical ideals of the church. Only a "just price"—the cost of raw materials plus a fair charge for manufacture—could be demanded. Cornering the market and monopoly were forbidden. Interest was regarded as usury, and money-lending was usually limited to Jews and infidels.

**Local trade in contemporary times.** When the gild system disappeared, local and domestic trade fell into the hands of the merchant capitalists, who conducted the putting-out system, and the small shop owners, who handled retail trade through private stores. The greatest development in local trade since the Industrial Revolution took place when mid-nineteenth-century increases in production and improvements in transportation made possible growth of chain stores, which have greatly increased the efficiency of retail trade, have improved the appearance and quality of stores, and have made it possible for customers to secure better goods at lower prices.

*Courtesy Chain Store Age.*

A self-service Winn Store, San Antonio, Texas, illustrating the interior of a modern chain store, which represents the chief twentieth-century improvement in local trade.

## Control over Agriculture, Manufacturing, and Trade

**Methods of controlling agriculture in modern times.** We have already described in detail the manorial system of landholding in the Middle Ages. In England, after the break-up of the manors, there were many medium-sized farms cultivated by hired workers; agriculture was dominated by the squires or free farmers. This was the era of so-called yeoman farming. After the middle of the eighteenth century, however, English agriculture came under the control of the great landlords, who, as we have seen, created vast estates worked by hired peasants.

Since the first world war, some European countries have entered upon a system of state control of agriculture. In Soviet Russia, for example, the state owns and controls farming as well as industry; in fascist countries, the state controlled agriculture, but private ownership of land was allowed to continue.

In the United States, private control of agriculture has continued from colonial times to the present. The farm crisis after the first world war, however, compelled the government to intervene on behalf of the farmers, and the New Deal farm policies indicated for the future an increasing degree of governmental control of agriculture.

**Development of manufacturing control.**   Manufacturing industries in primitive times were carried on in homes and were usually in charge of women, so that the men might be free for hunting and fighting. In the Middle Ages, as we have seen, the craft gilds controlled industrial operations.   The gild system was followed by the putting-out system, to which we have already referred.   The disadvantages of the putting-out system led some merchants to build large central shops, even then called factories.   These were restricted to a few industries and their growth was slow.

**The factory system.**   The most striking development in factory production in recent times is the speed-up system which depends on the endless conveyor belt, on which the interchangeable parts that are to be assembled are kept moving at a speed set by the employers. The idea of interchangeable parts was first suggested by Eli Whitney in making muskets for the government in 1807; the endless conveyor belt was first used in great meat-packing plants to carry carcasses along before the butchers.   In 1913, Henry Ford and his production manager, Charles Sorensen, joined the conveyor belt and interchangeable parts to create the speed-up system.   In 1914, only about 700 cars a day were turned out in the Ford plant; ten years later, production was 7,500 cars daily.   Despite its drawbacks, the speed-up system has made mass production possible, and the system has spread to virtually all large-scale industries.

**Scientific management.**   A more humane method of attaining industrial efficiency is associated with scientific management.   The foremost figure in this field was the American industrial engineer, Frederick W. Taylor (1856–1915).   A desire to eliminate unnecessary waste and fatigue and to introduce more efficient standards of production, based on a careful study of factory methods and improvements in technology, has led to a scientific-management movement.   Its supporters seek to adjust the speed-up system to reasonable human capacities.

The fundamental features of Taylor's system of scientific management are the following:   (1) the attempt to make business management a true science through applying all known scientific principles and methods;   (2) the use of industrial psychology in a scientific selection of managers and the adaptation of workers to their tasks, according to their abilities and aptitudes;   (3) the scientific education of workers; and   (4) the development of a friendly co-operative relationship between managers and workers.

**State control of industry.**   Since the first world war, there has been a marked tendency for the state to enter more fully into the control of industry.   Even in democratic countries, depression and war have brought industrial operations firmly under the control of government. The co-operative management of economic life seems to many to offer the best prospect of combining efficiency with liberty and democratic methods.

**Development of trade control: mercantilism.** When the gild system broke down in early modern times and commerce expanded enormously as a result of the Commercial Revolution, there developed an extreme form of government control of trade, generally known as mercantilism. Under this system, the government attempted to regulate foreign commerce closely, especially that of its colonies, in order to increase national wealth and accumulate a large supply of precious metals in the mother country.

**Free trade followed by high tariffs.** After the Industrial Revolution, manufacturers and merchants were, for a time, chiefly from 1830 to 1870, able to reduce governmental interference and encourage free trade. But, after 1870, the system of protective tariffs, which is the modern form of governmental control of foreign trade, became ever more prevalent. England was the only important country to hold out for free trade in the twentieth century, and even England surrendered gradually to the tariff system between 1921 and 1932. United States Secretary of State Cordell Hull worked valiantly for freer trade during the New Deal administrations, but he accomplished little in any practical way in reducing tariffs.

**Autarchy.** In totalitarian states, the government assumes complete control over both domestic and foreign trade, though it may allow a certain amount of freedom in domestic trade when governmental regulations are respected. In the 1930's, the totalitarian policy was to work for national self-sufficiency and controlled foreign trade, a condition known as autarchy. The great export trade developed by the United States after 1945 to feed and rehabilitate the stricken countries of Europe and Asia was extensively controlled by the government. With increasing government regulation the ideological keynote of the times, there seems little prospect that free trade will be revived for many years to come, if ever.

**International cartels.** During the twentieth century, international cartels developed, especially in the oil, chemical, optical, and electrical industries. These drew up private international agreements as to production, prices, and distribution. Many critics regarded them as a greater force in keeping up high prices than the protective tariff system. The destruction of German industry during and after the second world war tended temporarily to halt the development and operation of cartels, but the system still endures.

## Summary

Industry comprises the ways in which man has tried to provide himself with the necessities of life and produce a surplus of wealth. The history of agriculture, manufacturing, trade, and commerce goes back to the beginning of man's group life. Gradually man learned to till the soil, domesticate animals, make tools, engage in specialized labor, manufacture needed articles, and carry on trade and commerce.

Agriculture has evolved from the simple scratching of the soil with sticks to the complicated mechanical farming of today. All ancient peoples engaged in agriculture. For the Egyptians, Assyrians, Greeks, and Romans, agriculture was, for the most part, the basis of their economic life.

The Middle Ages introduced a communal system of producing agricultural and pastoral products. The lands of the manor were worked mainly by serfs; the latter enjoyed certain rights, especially that of tilling strips of land for their own use, in return for goods and services rendered to the lord.

The Agricultural Revolution of the seventeenth and eighteenth centuries wiped out the remains of the manorial system. New implements and scientific methods of fertilizing the soil were introduced; extensive experiments were carried on in stock-breeding; and much waste land was reclaimed. Small farms and holdings were consolidated, and the era of large-scale capitalistic farming appeared. These innovations were especially notable in England. Many English merchants, who had become wealthy as a result of the Commercial Revolution, invested their money in large estates in order to gain social and political prestige.

Modern farming techniques make it possible to produce almost unlimited quantities of food, so that today our agricultural problem is not how to produce food, but how to get the fruits of the soil to the greatest number of needy consumers.

All ancient peoples engaged in some kind of manufacturing. Handicraft methods of production prevailed well into the eighteenth century and dominated most countries until the middle of the nineteenth. The Industrial Revolution, beginning about 1750, created modern mechanical industry, substituting the factory system for the gild and putting-out systems of the Middle Ages and early modern times. Today, industry is thoroughly mechanized in the more advanced countries. New types of power and the introduction of automatic machinery and the speed-up system have combined to make possible a far greater production of goods than has ever before been known in human history. But the possibilities of full production have been restrained by waste and by the restrictions imposed on production by private business to keep prices high.

Trade and commerce have evolved from the barter of primitive peoples to the vast domestic and foreign trade of today. The progress of trade has depended on advances in manufacturing, transportation and communication, as well as upon various national commercial policies.

Control of industry has developed from that of the family in primitive society to the complicated system of finance capitalism, in which ownership is separated from management. In chronological order, the main types of control over industry have been by the family, the gilds, the putting-out system, and the factory system. The state closely regulates industry and commerce in totalitarian countries, and even the democracies have been forced to move in this direction by depression and wartime conditions.

The future of industry and commerce is uncertain. Unless some additional economic incentive can be found to supplement the profit motive, mankind is faced with the prospect of scarcity, misery, economic crises, and devastating wars. But there are dangers to liberty and initiative in the attempt to supplant the system of private profit by completely state-controlled economic life. The most serious threat to prosperity and security is the diversion of production into armament, the economic chaos produced by the second world war, and the threat of a devastatingly destructive third world war.

## Selected References

Barnes, H. E., *Economic History of the Western World,* Harcourt, Brace, 1937. Survey of industrial evolution in all phases from the earliest times. Includes an account of the successive modes of controlling industry. Can be supplemented by Heaton's *Economic History of Europe,* listed in bibliography of Chapter II.

Barnes, J. A., *The Wealth of the American People,* Prentice-Hall, 1949. Comprehensive and up-to-date survey of American economic history.

Beckman, T. N., and Nolen, H. C., *The Chain Store Problem,* McGraw-Hill, 1938. Appraisal of the rise and operations of chain stores.

Buchanan, N. S. and Lutz, F. A., *Rebuilding the World Economy: America's Role in Foreign Trade and Investment,* Twentieth Century Fund, 1947. Enthusiastic argument for the revival and development of world trade.

* Carskadon, T. R., and Modley, Rudolf, *U. S. A.: Measure of a Nation,* Macmillan, 1949. Useful popularization of the Dewhurst study mentioned below.

Day, Clive, *History of Commerce,* Longmans, Green, 1922. The standard introduction to the subject in English.

Dewhurst, J. F., *et al., America's Needs and Resources,* Twentieth Century Fund, 1945. Monumental symposium giving a comprehensive panorama of American economic development and its social relationships. Far and away the most ample and impressive summation of American economic and social conditions in a single volume.

Dobb, Maurice, *Soviet Economic Development since 1917,* International Publishers, 1948. Probably best single volume on Soviet industrialization under state socialism. Sympathetic in tone.

Emmet, Boris and Jeuck, J. E., *Catalogues and Counters,* University of Chicago Press, 1950. Elaborate account of the development of Sears, Roebuck and Company, presenting the main facts about the development of mail order houses and chain stores.

Ezekiel, Mordecai (Ed.), *Towards World Prosperity*, Harper, 1947. Authoritative and optimistic symposium on possibilities of greater economic prosperity and security through planned systems of industrial and agricultural expansion.

Faulkner, H. U., *American Economic History*, Harper, 1943. The standard manual on American economic history.

Gras, N. S. B., *A History of Agriculture in Europe and America*, Crofts, 1925. The best introductory survey.

* Huberman, Leo, *Man's Worldly Goods*, Harper, 1936. A brilliant elementary account of economic history since the Middle Ages. The best book with which to begin a study of this subject.

Loeb, Harold, *Full Employment without War*, Princeton University Press, 1946. Able exposition of a program for American economic planning which might give us sustained prosperity without recourse to war.

————, *Life in a Technocracy*, Viking, 1933. Interesting picture of economic life in a system run by engineers engaged in producing goods for human use rather than private profit.

Orwell, George, *Nineteen Eighty-four*, Harcourt, Brace, 1949. The most important book of social prophecy since Edward Bellamy's *Looking Backward* (1889) which it largely supplants. The main thesis is that nations are now slipping into a pattern where they use phony war to deprive the populace of the benefits of an advancing technology. It is an equally cogent reference to the chapters on capitalism, property, democracy and liberty, international relations, propaganda, and censorship.

Stocking, G. W., and Watkins, M. W., *Cartels or Competition?*, Twentieth Century Fund, 1948. Good description of the operation of international cartels and their frustration of competitive enterprise.

Usher, A. P., *A History of Mechanical Inventions*, McGraw-Hill, 1929. A competent history of the evolution of mechanical industry by a leading economic historian.

# CHAPTER XIV

# Leading Economic Problems of American Society

## The Nature of Capitalism

**Private profit the mainspring of capitalism.** The Industrial Revolution enormously increased the volume and efficiency of man's equipment for producing goods and services. Before the introduction of power-driven machinery, factories, and scientific agriculture, it was physically impossible to produce enough food. clothing, buildings, and other goods to maintain everybody in a large population at a relatively high standard of living. Today, however, any failure to provide the required goods to those who need them is due to the defects of the economic system in which our potentially hyper-efficient technology operates.

The task of providing essential goods and services in the United States is left mainly in the hands of private individuals and associations under a system of "capitalism," which derives its name from the fact that the control of business enterprises lies, in theory at least, in the hands of those who have invested money, or "capital," in them. The mainspring of our economic system, still based chiefly on private ownership and control of business, is the perfectly natural desire of businessmen for a monetary profit.

**Essential traits of capitalism.** Summary and abstract definitions of private capitalism are not likely to be especially helpful. We can get a clearer idea of what capitalism is like and how it operates from a listing of its main traits, attitudes, and methods. The most essential features of the capitalist pattern of economic organization are the following: (1) the desire for private profit in economic life, with service to the community secondary and incidental to the personal quest for profit; (2) a money economy and the determination of the social status and prestige of the individual in terms of monetary possessions; (3) the accumulation by individuals and associations of large monetary reserves available for investment in business ventures; (4) the existence of a relatively free, competitive market for the sale of goods; (5) the evaluation of goods and services in terms of prices set by bargaining in the market rather than by considerations of intrinsic worth or utility; (6) the presence of a sufficient supply of paid labor

297

to assure the needed personnel for the production and distribution of goods; (7) the development of a system of exchange and credit adequate to the needs of the economic system at any given time; (8) a reasonably mature development of commercial and industrial life; (9) the saving and reinvestment of a sufficient portion of the profits from business to assure expansion; (10) the depersonalization of business relationships as the result of a money economy and a monetary nexus in business life; and (11) concentration of attention on short-time gains and losses, a result of the development of double-entry bookkeeping.

Viewed in a broad sense, then, capitalism has as its purpose private profit; as its method free competition in production and exchange; and as its spirit private initiative.

## Main Stages in the Evolution of Capitalism

The essential spirit and practices of capitalism, the primary concern with private profit and the accumulation of capital for reinvestment to produce more profit, were weak before early modern times. The civilized Greeks were more concerned with art, philosophy and rhetoric than with business and profits, and the Romans gave more attention to politics than to economic life. In the Middle Ages, the ideals of the canon law of the church, as applied to business through mercantile law, outlawed such essentials of present-day capitalism as cornering the market, monopoly, selling goods at a high profit, and interest-taking.

**Mercantile capitalism.** Modern times brought about new conditions that favored the birth of capitalism. Protestantism, especially Calvinism, praised the practice of money-making and blessed hard work. The acquisition of large fortunes was regarded as proof of God's grace. The expansion of Europe and the Commercial Revolution created new business opportunities and new fortunes. This period marked the first stage of capitalism, usually known as mercantile capitalism. Business was controlled mainly by the merchants and by the merchant-capitalists who operated the new putting-out system of production. Its heyday was, roughly, from about 1600 to the coming of the Industrial Revolution a century and a half later.

**Early and expanding industrial capitalism.** The Industrial Revolution, the invention of machines, and the rise of the factory system produced a new type of capitalism, which we call early industrial capitalism. The fortunes made in trade in the previous centuries produced more capital for the building and expansion of factories. The early industrial capitalists owned and operated their plants, usually as personal enterprises or as partnerships. As this period developed into a later era of expanding industrial capitalism, joint-stock companies became popular and corporations began to appear. Throughout both periods, the financial assistance rendered by banks was less important than the initiative and resources of the industrialists themselves.

**Monopoly industrial capitalism.** In the latter half of the nineteenth century, factories grew still larger, industrial mergers became more common, and industry tended to become a large-scale affair. Efforts were made to secure a monopoly over the production and sale of many types of natural resources and manufactured goods. Hence, economic historians have designated this stage of capitalism as monopoly industrial capitalism. Partnerships still persisted, but corporations and trusts became the more usual form of business organization because they were better suited to the needs of the larger industrial concerns. Investment banks became very useful in selling securities and providing the loans needed by new concerns and expanding businesses. The owners of industrial enterprises often controlled their business, but the financiers were becoming more important. Interest in craftsmanship tended to fade, and desire for profits to become dominant.

**Finance capitalism.** At the beginning of the twentieth century, with the rise of the giant corporations and holding companies and the steady expansion of the scope of industries, the control of business by the financiers grew apace. The great investment banks not only supplied the money for new enterprises and the expansion of existing plants, but also placed their representatives on the board of directors of many a corporation. As a result of the capture of big business by the financiers, we call this last stage of capitalism finance capitalism.

The monopolistic tendencies of the previous period continued, usually with more success. Though the trusts, which were the earliest form of monopoly, had been outlawed in the United States by the Sherman Act of 1890, holding companies proved far more efficient in securing a monopoly over production and sale in many fields. Through super-corporations and holding companies, ownership was separated from control, and control from daily management. The nominal owners were the stockholders of the great corporations, but they had little to do with the actual policies followed by the corporations; these were determined by the officers and boards of directors, chosen by favored insiders who rarely owned more than 5 per cent of the securities. The actual day-by-day management of business was usually handed over to specialists trained in schools of business administration.

**State capitalism.** It is believed by many students of economic history that the next stage in capitalism will be state capitalism, an economy in which industry and finance will be mainly controlled or managed by the state. Fascism and the second world war hastened this trend abroad. "Middle-way" countries, like England and Sweden, introduced a good deal of state capitalism. Some steps were taken in this direction under the New Deal in the United States. The outbreak of the second world war and the postwar crisis speeded up the

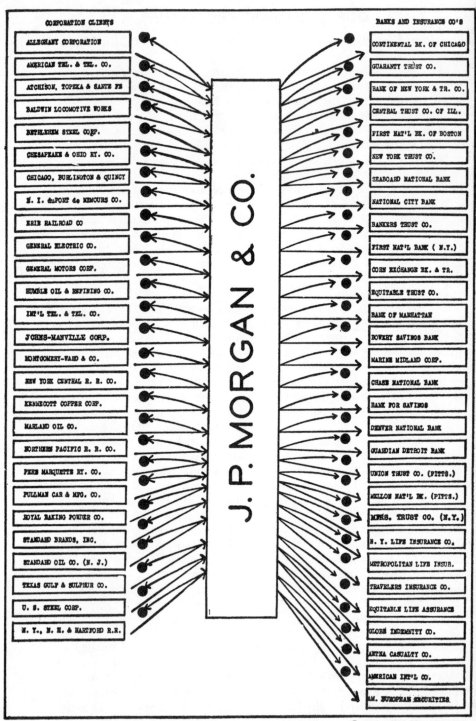

*Courtesy* The New Republic.

**The system of Finance Capitalism as dominated by the House of Morgan.**

progress of state capitalism. The economy of every major country involved, except Soviet Russia, already a state-socialistic economy, moved in the direction of state capitalism, perhaps never to return completely to the pattern of private capitalism. Through the victory of the Labour Party in July, 1945, Britain seemed definitely committed to state socialism, albeit of a more moderate type than that in Russia.

**Evolution of capitalism in the United States.** If we apply these stages of capitalism to the history of American business, we find that our period of mercantile capitalism came during colonial times. The early industrial capitalism of this country was mainly associated with the cotton textile industry in New England. Expanding industrial capitalism (roughly 1830–1870) included not only the textile industry, but also the iron and steel industry, early railroad building, and meat packing. New methods of making steel led to increased manufacturing, particularly of agricultural machinery.

Monopoly industrial capitalism developed after the Civil War, owing to the efforts of such men as Andrew Carnegie and H. C. Frick in steel making, John D. Rockefeller in oil, and Commodore Vanderbilt in railroads and shipping. Carnegie (1835–1919) was probably the most important figure in this stage of American capitalism, though Rockefeller (1839–1937) better illustrated the monopolistic urge.

Finance capitalism forged ahead at the turn of the twentieth century when the United States Steel Corporation, the first billion dollar holding company, was formed by J. P. Morgan, the elder. This latest era of capitalism has been dominated by the House of Morgan, along with other great investment bankers like Kuhn, Loeb; Dillon, Read; J. & W. Seligman; Lehman Brothers; Lee Higginson Corporation; Drexel and Company; and the Giannini interests in California. By the close of the first world war, the ten leading banks and three leading insurance companies—the latter were under banking control—dominated nearly all the great business enterprises of the country; the Ford Motor Company was probably the only important exception. Henry Ford, who survived a vain effort by the financiers to put him out of business in the early twenties, was an anomaly, a man with the ideals of expanding industrial capitalism, born to do business in the era of finance capitalism. At the present time, Lehman Brothers have supplanted the House of Morgan as the dominant investment banking firm in the country.

The New Deal headed the United States at least mildly in the direction of state capitalism, and our entry into the second world war placed us temporarily in a system of extensive state capitalism. That private capitalism will fully regain the position it held before Pearl Harbor is doubtful, although no valid predictions can yet be made. The fact that President Truman campaigned and was elected in 1948 on a rather advanced state-capitalistic platform would seem to indicate that we are destined to move still further in the direction of state capitalism, even though we avoid a third world war.

## Main Types of Business Organization and Financial Institutions

**Early and simple forms of business organization.** The simplest form of business organization is that owned and managed by a single person who bears all the risks and responsibilities and likewise receives all the profits. It is also the oldest form of business enterprise, for it appeared as soon as individuals began to produce or buy commodities to sell for a profit.

Another form of early business organization is the partnership, a business undertaking owned and controlled by two or more persons. Their respective powers and rights in control, ownership, and profits usually depend upon the amount of money each has invested in the firm. Where partnerships could not raise enough money, joint-stock companies were formed to which a number of persons belonged, sharing in the profits according to their investment. Unfortunately, the partnership and joint-stock companies exposed their members to unlimited liability for the debts of the business. If members proved dishonest, or the company failed, the honest and solvent partners or investors had to make up the losses.

**Origin of the corporation.** Until the nineteenth century, individually-owned firms, partnerships, and joint-stock companies were the principal types of business organizations. But, as the effects of the Industrial Revolution began to be felt, there arose a need for more capital than could be provided by these earlier forms. Huge sums of money were needed for building factories, buying expensive machinery and raw materials, and hiring workers. Further, the operation of large business enterprises often required more managerial direction than one individual or a few partners could provide. To remedy this difficulty, there arose a new form of business organization —the "corporation."

A corporation is an association that is regarded by law as a legal "person," having an existence apart from that of its members. Possessing many of the rights and privileges of persons, the corporation may own property, carry on business, and enter into lawsuits. The corporation has a marked advantage over the individually-owned firm or a partnership, in that the death of its original owners has no effect upon its legal existence.

**Nature of a corporation.** The ownership of a corporation is divided among stockholders—those who have invested money in it. Each stockholder receives stock certificates, representing his share of the property, profits, and obligations of the corporation. The stockholders ordinarily have the right to vote for a board of directors, to whom is delegated the power of controlling the corporation. The directors, in turn, usually elect the officers, who are directly responsible for the conduct of the business and the management of the corporation's affairs.

**Advantages of the corporate form of business organization.** The outstanding advantage of the corporation is the limited liability of the stockholder. The stockholder has no obligation for the debts of a corporation beyond the proportion of his investment to the total capital. This attracts many investors who would otherwise be afraid to risk their money in an enterprise. The courts have endowed the corporation with legal personality, thus enabling the corporation to be sued in court without personally involving the stockholders. Furthermore, ownership in a corporation may be divided into many small shares, which may be freely bought and sold, thus permitting the resources of many persons to be combined in a great business venture under a single management. In addition to selling shares of stock, the corporation may obtain money by issuing bonds which represent long-term loans to the corporation from investors. Finally, the corporate form of business organization makes it possible for investors to buy shares in several companies, thus spreading their risks.

All these favorable features of the corporation have made it possible to raise vast sums of money for business undertakings. Some 50 corporations in the United States now have resources of over a billion dollars each, while many others possess wealth running into hundreds of millions of dollars. The corporation has proved to be an effective economic institution. Its ability to raise vast sums of money has facilitated the impressive and rapid expansion of industry and trade during the past hundred years. Had it been necessary to finance business by means of individually-owned firms or partnerships, economic expansion would have been much slower and on a smaller scale. Furthermore, the corporate form of organization has made possible concentrated management of large-scale business undertakings.

Corporation securities are owned by millions of stockholders and bondholders; corporations employ millions of workers; and corporations' products are purchased by millions of consumers throughout the country. The government, perceiving this increasing public character and significance of corporations, has begun setting up controls in the interest of the public welfare. Although corporations have assisted our economic development, their mismanagement has also frequently undermined sound business practices.

**Rise and outlawing of trusts.** Another business organization is the trust, a combination of corporations, usually organized for the purpose of gaining control over the production and sale of a particular commodity so that it may set its own prices, or, in other words, enjoy a monopoly. In forming a trust, the new company would absorb other smaller corporations and then issue to their stockholders trust certificates entitling them to a share of the profits of the trust. The share was supposed to be proportionate to the amount of their original corporation holdings. Smaller companies had little prospect of competing successfully with a trust. If they fought the trust, they were usually driven into bankruptcy and forced to go out of business.

The trust form of business organization was outlawed by the Sherman Anti-Trust Act of 1890, but mergers and monopolies were secured and perpetuated by other means, notably by holding companies and consolidations. The courts have ruled that business concentration or consolidation does not violate the anti-trust laws if this is accomplished through buying up the physical assets rather than the securities of the companies which are merged and consolidated. The concentration of business and financial power through these mergers has been going on more rapidly than ever since 1939.

**Appearance of holding companies.** During the last half of the nineteenth century, the new developments in business—larger factories, the corporation, and the extension of credit institutions—were all designed to aid and further industry. But in the twentieth century, the motivation and control of business activities have changed. Large-scale industry has come to be controlled by financiers; ownership, control, and management have been separated in great business concerns.

The holding company, which replaced the trusts after 1890, has become common and powerful. The holding company is a super-corporation which obtains control of a number of corporations through buying enough of the stock in each to dominate the board of directors. Sometimes, it is possible for a holding company to gain control by purchasing only a small proportion of stock—even one per cent—because the shares have been spread very widely among thousands of stockholders, who cannot unite for action.

Unlike the industrial corporation, the holding company is not usually directly interested in production. The holding company is mainly concerned with "milking" the productive corporations which it controls by skimming off the profits made by these corporations and diverting them to the coffers of the holding company. The latter, through its control, compels the controlled corporations to pay unearned dividends on holding-company securities out of corporate earnings. The holding company rarely renders any important service to the corporations it controls, though it may provide them with common directors and common legal services. Particularly is this true when the controlled companies are engaged in a similar enterprise, as in the New England Electric System. The holding company may also provide management of a quality higher than that which would be available to the individual companies. It is possible for a super-holding company to secure the controlling interest in other holding companies. This complicated legal structure is known as a financial or paper pyramid.

**Types of banks.** Accompanying and aiding in the evolution of business organizations came the growth and diversification of banking.

The expansion of business required more elaborate credit institutions. The industrial or investment bank and the stock exchange emerged or were extended to meet the modern businessman's needs for more capital. Much of our big business enterprise would have been impossible without the aid of the modern banking system. The bank is not only a place to deposit money for safekeeping and interest, but also an agency from which businessmen may secure loans to conduct current operations or launch new enterprises.

There are four main types of banks. The "commercial bank" accepts money for deposit and lends it to business firms for short periods. It is here that many companies secure funds for buying raw materials, paying workers, and meeting other current expenses. "Savings banks" accept deposits and pay interest upon them, investing their funds in mortgages, bonds, and other relatively safe investments. "Trust companies" often operate in much the same manner as commercial banks, but have other duties as well. They act as trustees for estates, taking care of property for widows and children who lack the ability to handle their business matters. The fourth type of bank is the "investment bank," primarily concerned with securing funds for big business enterprises. Unlike commercial banks, the investment bank does not make short-term loans and usually does not receive deposits. It is sometimes known as an industrial bank.

**The investment bank in finance capitalism.** The investment bank has achieved greater power in directing our economic life than other financial institutions. This power has arisen out of the nature of its work. A corporation, desiring funds to start or expand its operations, goes to an investment bank. For a fee or commission the bank agrees to guarantee and handle the sale of the corporation's stocks and bonds. These securities are sold to banks and personal investors. It would be difficult for a large corporation to market its securities without the aid of an investment bank. This means that the investment bank can dictate terms to the corporation; these often include the privilege of placing one or more officers of the bank on the corporate board of directors. Thus, without investing any considerable amount of money, the investment bank secures a voice in managing the corporation. In this and other ways, investment banks have built up "empires" of corporations under their control. Interested more in immediate financial profits than in producing goods or serving consumers, these few powerful banking interests have often caused corporations to be mismanaged, with serious losses to stockholders, workers, and the public. Very seldom have the investment bankers made good use of their power to stabilize American business and render it more efficient.

**Power of the investment bank may be reduced.** The rôle of investment banks may decrease as time goes on. The government, through the Securities and Exchange Commission and other agencies, created under the New Deal, has exerted control and restraint over the issuance of new securities. Moreover, the great corporations are becoming less dependent on banks in raising funds. Much of the money needed for repairs and expansion is now derived from a replacement fund set up by the corporation itself. Moreover, corporations prefer to borrow from a great insurance company, rather than from the investment bank, which, in turn, gets its money from the insurance companies. During and after the second world war, corporations working on government orders could obtain capital directly from the Federal government through the Reconstruction Finance Corporation. The investment bank has not, however, declined as much as some progressive economists, led by wishful thinking, have imagined.

## The Depression and Other Problems of the Thirties

**How the depression of 1929 shattered the hope of permanent prosperity.** During the 1920's it was not only popularly believed, but also asserted by leading economists, that our nation would enjoy permanent prosperity. This dream was rudely shattered in 1929 with the beginning of an economic depression that lasted over ten years and was brought to an end only by the development of armament and war industry. The depression forced thousands of factories and stores to close; others operated on a reduced scale; millions of persons lost their jobs. In brief, our economic system failed in its task of producing and distributing the goods and services our mechanical equipment is capable of providing.

This breakdown was due to faults in the operation of our economic institutions—the social arrangements for providing our daily needs. The basic causes of the depression may be conveniently listed as follows: (1) abuses of the corporate form of business organization; (2) wastes in production; (3) the lack of adequate mass purchasing power by farmers, wage earners, and salaried groups; (4) failure to provide through fair taxation the revenue for essential state activities in industry and social welfare; (5) the high cost of war and armaments; and (6) the increasing burden of debt.

**Corporate abuses.** The corporation can provide an excellent system of business organization. It has often been used, however, as we have already noted, to serve the avarice or speculative purposes of officers and directors in such a way as to harm the interests of society. The stock of most corporations is spread among a large number of investors, so that it is hard for them to get together and have much voice in the selection of officers and directors. Furthermore, many stockholders fail to exercise their formal privilege of voting for directors. The result is that a small, coherent group of "insiders" may manage to become corporation directors and officers and to shape corporate policies to their own ends.

The danger of this type of control lies in the fact that the speculative interests of "insiders" frequently differ from those of the stockholders, workers, and customers. If the managing group of a large corporation owns 5 per cent of the stock, hard work and good management will bring them 5 per cent of the dividends. Yet, in the past, if they manipulated the corporation from the inside, they could get a far larger percentage of the profits. This situation naturally encouraged the looting of corporate financial resources—particularly before 1929.

By granting themselves unreasonably large salaries and bonuses, and through other wasteful devices, unscrupulous directors and officers have sometimes ruined corporations, causing stockholders to lose their investments, workers their jobs, and consumers their supplies of necessary goods. In other instances, men have purposely mismanaged and ruined a corporation and then proceeded to buy up its property at a fraction of its real value. Occasionally, groups of men have organized mythical corporations, sold stock in them, and then run off with the money, instead of employing it for genuine business purposes. A frequent evil of corporate business is that large corporations and holding companies have developed monopolistic control over important commodities, thus enabling them to curtail production and raise prices. The consumer is, therefore, forced to pay more than he should, and the total volume of goods which could be produced, distributed, and consumed is reduced. Many corporations, however, through efficient management have operated for the benefit of stockholders, workers, consumers, and society in general.

**Waste in the production and distribution of goods.** An important factor in reducing the supply of available goods and services is inefficient and wasteful production and distribution. Each year, for example, large quantities of inferior or unnecessary goods are put on the market. When these remain unsold, the labor and material put into them is wasted. Another wasteful practice is that employed in the automobile, clothing, and other industries, where annual changes of style render millions of still useful commodities "unfashionable," and thus cause them to be discarded. Excessive advertising also constitutes serious economic waste. Two and a half billion dollars were so spent in 1946 in the effort to increase the competitive sales of various brands of products. Actually, there may be no vital difference in quality between the various products advertised, but the consumer has to foot the bill in the form of higher prices.

Furthermore, the methods of production have frequently been wasteful. Engineers in the 1930's estimated that, if our factories were operated in a truly efficient manner, it would be possible to turn out from 50 to 100 per cent more goods than were then produced. Production records during the second world war and immediately thereafter proved that they were right. Taking the average production from 1935–1939 as 100, the index of production of durable goods rose to 258 in 1943 and the index of non-durable goods to 176. Pre-war inefficiency in production often arose from the fact that factories were under the control of corporate directors and officers who were more interested in making immediate financial profits for themselves through manipulating securities than in operating the corporation at the level of maximum production.

There has been an enormous increase in the costs and wastes in the distribution of goods; that is, in getting goods and food from the factory and farms to the consumers. Before the first world war, it cost less than one dollar to get a dollar's worth of goods or food from the factory or farmer to the user. By the mid-1930's it cost about $2 to move a dollar's worth of goods or food from the factory or farm to the consumer. This increased cost was due to many factors, but chiefly to wastes in sales processes and advertising.

**Lack of mass purchasing power.** One of the most important reasons for the failure of our economic system to provide society with an abundant flow of goods and services is the lack of purchasing power by the great mass of farmers, workers, and clerks. There is little advantage in the fact that our farms and factories can create an abundance of food and goods if the majority of the people do not have sufficient incomes to purchase them.

Evidence of the lack of mass purchasing power as a cause of the depression of 1929 and thereafter has been shown by a number of studies, especially the Brookings Institution publication, *America's Capacity to Consume*. For example, in 1929, supposedly a year of great prosperity, 6 million families, or 21 per cent of the total, had an income of less than $1,000; 12 million families, or 42 per cent of the total, had an income of less than $1,500; while 20 million families, or about 71 per cent of the total, had an income of less than $2,500. Only about 2 million families, or less than 8 per cent of the total, had an income of over $5,000. The 0.1 per cent of the families at the top of the ladder, each with an income in excess of $75,000, received almost as much of the total national income as the 42 per cent of the families at the bottom. Nor was the situation improved greatly under the New Deal. In 1935–1936 the average income for an American family was $1,070 a year. The 195,000 families with largest incomes received as much as the 13 million lowest-income families. Despite the boom provided by the armament industry, there were millions of families on the eve of Pearl Harbor who did not have income enough to provide for bare subsistence. The government estimated at that time that a family of four needed $29 a week to subsist. Yet, the Treasury Department revealed that 3,324,000 workers were earning only $5 to $10 a week; 4,975,000 were earning $10 to $15; and 10,747,000 from $20 to $30.

Much has been made of the increased monetary income of families between 1940 and 1950: the number of families with an income of less than $2,000 dropped from 61 per cent to 26 per cent of the total; those with an income of $2,000 to $3,000 decreased from 21 to 20 per cent; those with an income of $3,000 to $4,000 increased from 9 to 20 per cent; those with an income of $4,000 to $5,000 increased from 4 per cent to 12 per cent; and those with an income of more than $5,000 from 5 per cent to 22 per cent.   Impressive as these figures may appear at first sight, they show that 66 per cent of our families have an income of $4,000 or less, which, in terms of purchasing power, puts them just about where the families with an income of $2,000 or less were in 1940 —the 1950 dollar is worth only about 54 cents in terms of the 1940 purchasing power of a dollar.   One may, perhaps, best sum it all by saying that it costs more to be poor in 1950 than in 1940.

**Inadequate mass purchasing power means glutted inventories and depressions.**   This inequitable distribution of the national income meant that billions of dollars worth of goods remained unsold, for the mass of consumers lacked sufficient money to buy them.   The volume of goods produced between 1923 and 1929 increased by ten billion dollars, but the purchasing power of workers, clerks, and farmers increased by only $600,000,000.   The relatively few ʿamilies who received such a disproportionately large share of the national income could not buy and use—or even waste—more than a small fraction of the goods produced.   Indeed, they often continued to invest their surplus funds in still more factories and machinery, thus stimulating the production of additional unsalable goods.

We need not consider whether it is morally right or wrong for a few persons to receive such a large share of the national income.   All that concerns us here is the stark fact that food and manufactured goods cannot be sold unless people are provided with sufficient income to purchase them.   Business depressions are bound to result when huge quantities of unsold goods pile up.   Everyone, including the high-income group, would be better off if the mass of workers, cˡerks, and farmers received a larger income and could thus be able to purchase all the goods produced.   While businessmen may make ¡arge profits in the short run through high prices and low wages, they lose out in the long run because unsold goods pile up, operations have to be reduced, unemployment mounts, and depressions set in.   It should be clear that our economic system must provide full employment and higher wages and salaries if all the goods and services produced are to be sold in normal times.

**The ledger psychosis.**   Many have wondered why our captains of industry have not realized that we must have sufficient mass purchasing power to keep capitalism in a healthy condition and why they have not been able to take a long-range view of the needs of a prosperous capitalism.   This question has been answered by a great economic historian, Werner Sombart.   He lays the blame on what may be called "the ledger psychosis."   This grew up out of double-entry bookkeeping which computes daily, weekly, monthly and yearly gains and losses, thus concentrating attention on immediate profits, which can be temporarily increased by high prices and low wages and salaries—policies that mean the impoverishment, and, perhaps, the ruin, of business in the long run.   So far, however, the ledger psychosis has usually triumphed over economic statesmanship, with a few exceptions such as Henry Ford's high-wage policy of 1914.

THERE'S YOUR PURCHASE POWER!

*Scripps Howard.*

The only way to revive capitalism.

A cartoon emphasizing the importance of adequate mass purchasing power in maintaining prosperity under capitalism.

**Capitalism can thrive if mass purchasing power is provided.** There are numerous examples to prove that capitalism can thrive if mass purchasing power is provided. Between 1914 and 1941, Henry Ford paid his employees approximately a billion dollars more than they would have received elsewhere. Yet, he became the first American billionaire. The Lincoln Electric Company of Cleveland, Ohio, furnishes a more recent example. Between 1929 and 1947, the average annual wage of a worker in this plant increased from $2,100 to $5,800. The production per man-hour increased 700 per cent. The selling price of the product was reduced from $1,500 to $200.   Yet, dividends increased by over 300 per cent.

**Taxation as an aid to mass purchasing power.**  The most urgent economic reform is, thus, to put increased purchasing power into the hands of the mass of consumers.   In case employers will not take adequate steps to do so, one alternative, suggested by the famous English economist, Lord Keynes, is heavy taxation during periods of prosperity and government spending of the receipts on public works during periods of depression.   So far, this has been attempted only to a limited extent, under the New Deal from 1933 to 1940, and by the Truman administration since 1945.   Under the latter, the proceeds of extremely high taxes have been used chiefly to pay for wars, past, present, and future, rather than for public works.   The tax burden has, however, usually fallen heavily upon the lower economic groups —those least able to pay—thus further decreasing the amount of their purchasing power.   This is especially true of the sales tax.   Many students of economic problems feel that sales taxes of various sorts should be reduced or eliminated since they tax the necessities of life and constitute an unfair burden upon the mass of people with low incomes.

Taxes have not only been levied unfairly, but also have displayed loopholes by means of which many rich persons escaped paying their just portion of taxes.   One of the principal loopholes was investment in government bonds, the income from which was long free from taxation.   Another loophole permitted investors to subtract the amount of their "paper" losses in the stock market or other deals from their actual earned income.   In this manner, some persons with large incomes in the United States escaped paying income taxes altogether between 1929 and 1933, when this type of loophole was partially closed. But the maximum tax on capital gains today is only 25 per cent, while the highest earned incomes may be taxed as much as 90 per cent. Many of the wealthy now prefer to leave their money in undistributed corporate profits where the tax is only 38 per cent rather than pay the higher personal income tax.

**War menaces prosperity.**   All through the course of history, the costs of war have taken a tremendous toll from society.   A scandalously large portion of governmental expenditures is devoted to paying for wars.   In the 131 years following 1789, about 78.5 per cent of the expenditures of our Federal government went for war purposes, and the relative proportion of expenditures for war has enormously increased since 1930.   President Coolidge conservatively estimated that the total cost of our participation in the first world war would ultimately amount to 100 billion dollars.   We spent about 400 billion dollars, directly and indirectly, on the second world war.   It will ultimately cost us 1.5 trillion dollars.   We are now spending another 20–25 billion dollars annually on the cold war, and on armament in getting ready for a third world war.   We spent over 25 billion dollars for European, Chinese, and Japanese aid in the four years after August, 1945, and have allocated another 22 billion for the first stages of the European Recovery Program.

Expenditures for war, of course, mean that so much less can be spent on socially useful services, such as education, medical care, social insurance, conservation, and public works. In January, 1949, President Truman proposed a Federal budget of 42 billion dollars for 1950. Of this total, no less than 76 per cent was allotted directly to war purposes, past, present and future. Altogether, over 80 per cent of budget was designed to go into one or another type of war expenditure. Only six per cent of the total was allotted to all health and welfare projects, and, so far, only about half of Mr. Truman's welfare projects have been approved by Congress.

**The debt burden.** The last outstanding weakness of the capitalistic system that we shall mention is the staggering burden of debt which has been piled up through the construction of unnecessary plants, the encouragement of installment buying, financial speculation, the mortgaging of farms, excessive government spending, vast war expenditures, and the like.

A careful study of our debt structure showed that, even in 1937, before the second world war had shot our national debt up to astronomical figures, the total public and private debts of the country amounted to at least 250 billion dollars, a sum almost equal to the total national wealth of the United States. The main items in the breakdown of this vast debt structure were: (1) government debts, 53 billions; corporate debts, 50 billions; mortgages, 35 billions; short-term debts, 30 billions; deposits of commercial banks, 40 billions; deposits of mutual savings banks, 10 billions; cash value of life insurance policies, 20 billions; and withdrawable shares of building and loan associations, 5 billions.

At the end of 1948, the national debt alone stood at approximately 217 billion dollars, or nearly $1,500 per capita. In 1916, before we had entered any world wars, the per capita national debt was less than $12. In addition to the formal national debt, the Federal government has other extensive obligations known as "contingent liabilities." Such are insured housing loans, other guaranteed loans, Federal insurance in force, social security obligations, and funds due postal savings depositors. These are estimated to total over 300 billion dollars. State and local debts in 1948 amounted to over 16 billion dollars. These state and local debts made up a total public debt of about 233 billion dollars. The total private debt was approximately 197 billion dollars. This made the total private and public debt of the country in 1948 about 430 billion dollars, not reckoning with the contingent liabilities of the Federal government mentioned above. These public debt figures for 1948 are "net public debt." The gross public debt in 1948 was in excess of 280 billion.

Debt endangers the capitalistic system. This great debt structure is a millstone around the neck of capitalism and greatly hampers any effort to reorganize our economic system. The interest on the vast debt principal takes up too large a share of the national income, and reduces the amount that may be spent for socially useful purposes. The interest alone on our national debt is far larger than any total peacetime Federal budget before New Deal days. As has been frequently pointed out, our present and future are mortgaged to the past. Our whole national wealth would not pay off the public debt and other obligations of the Federal, state, and local governments. Bassett Jones and Stuart Chase hold that our productive capacity cannot safely carry under a capitalistic system more than a fraction of the debt claims which have been piling up against it in the last generation.

## The Outlook for Private Capitalism after the Second World War

Temporary restoration of prosperity by second world war. In an earlier section of this chapter we described how the critical condition of private capitalism in the United States led to the depression of 1929 and thereafter. Before considering in detail the new situation that has developed since 1940, it will be well to remember that we never got out of the depression by any normal readjustment of our economy to maximum production in peacetime, or by any redistribution of the national income that would assure mass purchasing power on a scale large enough to keep our capitalistic economy in a healthy state of prosperity.

Despite all the New Deal reforms and public spending, production was at a relatively low ebb in 1938 on the eve of the launching of the new rearmament program. The production index was 89, as compared with 91 in 1930. Somewhere between 8 and 10 million potential workers were unemployed by industry. In short, the New Deal, however much more daring and enlightened than the preceding régime, did not solve the problem of assuring prosperity and security under capitalism in a period of peace. Full employment and large personal incomes were brought about only gradually by first setting up a vast rearmament industry and then entering a full-scale war economy.

Superficial evidence of increased national well-being. As a result of the war economy and its aftermath, there was an enormous increase in the volume of production. Taking the production average of 1935–1939 as 100, the index of industrial production rose to about 194 in 1948 in terms of money values. Even the physical volume of production in 1948 was about 60 per cent higher than in 1939. At the beginning of the year 1949, there were over 61 million persons employed in civilian occupations, as compared with a little over 55 million in 1940, after considerable new employment had been found in the rearmament program. Only about 4,500,000 were unemployed in March, 1950. The total personal income in 1949 was 211 billion dollars, as compared with 78 billion in 1940. Even after taxes, the total personal income in 1947 was 179 billion as compared with a little over 75 billion in 1940. It was estimated that the average family buying power in 1948 was 35 per cent higher than in 1940.

Other very cogent figures bring out perhaps more strikingly the apparent vast increase in national well-being between the collapsing New Deal and the middle of the century. National income increased from 72.5 billion dollars in 1939 to 233.2 billion in 1949—an increase of 207.8 per cent. Corporate profits after taxes grew from 5 billion to 17 billion—a gain of 240 per cent. Dividend payments rose from 3.8 billion to 8.4 billion—an increase of 121 per cent. Undistributed profits advanced from 1.2 billion to 8.6 billion—an increment of 600 per cent. Rental income rose from 14.7 billion to 45.7 billion—a growth of 210.9 per cent. Total compensation of employees (both public and private) increased from 47.8 billion to 142.2 billion—a jump of 197.5 per cent.

**The specters of war and collectivism menace capitalism.** In the light of such figures as these, and many others of similar import which might be cited, many will raise the question as to why we can sensibly talk of any crisis in American capitalism today. But any careful analysis of both the world situation and our national economy will quickly reveal the fact that the basic crisis still remains and that the conditions which have developed since 1939 have only shifted and delayed any normal and lasting solution, and have served to make the realities of the depression, when it comes, all the more ominous and devastating.

In the first place, our foreign policies, which have grown in part out of pressures from our domestic economic situation, have put us in grave danger of a third world war. This war would inevitably put an end to what little remains of private capitalism in the Old World. The expense and regimentation involved in a long war could not well avoid severely curtailing private capitalism and fastening extensive state capitalism more or less permanently on this country, even in the case of an American victory. Private capitalism is already all but finished throughout the Old World, save in a few small countries; all the countries that benefited by the Marshall Plan were committed to a collectivist economy of one sort or another. Our intimate association with collectivist countries, notably England under the Labour Government, may inevitably encourage a greater trend toward collectivism in our own country.

**Semantic obfuscation in "prosperity" statistics.** All gross figures relative to economic improvement since 1939 are, of course, extremely misleading unless properly qualified. This is a second main reason for discounting appropriately the optimism based on such statistics.

The above statements about impressively increased income are made in dollars, and 1949 dollars are worth only a little over 50 cents in purchasing power in terms of the 1939 dollar, due to the spectacular rise in prices. Wholesale prices rose from 78.6 in 1940 to 154.9 in 1949 on the index. In such dollar terms, a doubling of the national income would not necessarily mean any actual gain whatever. The trebling of the national income could be accomplished, fictitiously, just by trebling prices. When Germany was virtually ruined by inflation in 1923–1924, the German national income was so astronomical that it could hardly be stated in Marks—only mathematical symbols could encompass it. Most of the above "prosperity" figures would need to be cut about in half to give any realistic view of the changed economic status of the country since 1939. The boasts of optimists based on them are only an example of our "newspeak" and "doublethink," as such semantic ruses are designated in Mr. Orwell's *Nineteen Eighty-four*.

**Conditions favoring prosperity temporary.** It is obvious that the current prosperity and full employment are based on conditions that cannot endure for long without endangering our national financial solvency. The bases of our postwar prosperity are the printing and circulation of a vast quantity of irredeemable paper money, the war employment situation in 1940–1945, and the perpetuation of a quasi-war economy since V-J Day.

The great current demand for goods that has brought about full employment is in part a result of delayed wartime orders. Another source of this demand is the fact that we have shipped a vast volume of food and goods to Europe since the war, largely without compensation, thus creating a trade situation called "deficit mercantilism." Some 20 billion dollars worth of loans, food, goods, and services were sent to the Old World between V-J Day and the 1948 launching of the Economic Recovery Program in accordance with the Marshall Plan. The latter calls for approximately 22 billion dollars more in its first phases and much more will be required to bring about any complete European recovery. The third main reason for full employment and high production is the launching of a great new armament program which, directly and indirectly, calls for an expenditure of between 20 and 25 billion dollars in the 1949 budget and an equal amount in the 1950 budget. The fourth basis of temporary prosperity is the greatly increased farm income, a result of shipments of food abroad and the increased income of city workers who can now buy more food. This boost in the farm income has enabled the farming group to buy more factory-made products.

The increasing costs of deficit mercantilism and vast expenditures for wars in the shape of pensions, veteran's aid, the "cold war," and armament will increase our already topheavy national debt and contingent liabilities, will keep our national budget somewhere around the astronomical figure of 40 billion dollars, and will insure the perpetuation of our present high tax levels which take so large a portion of personal income today. When the artificial boom of today fades out, the debt structure, the vast amount of money in circulation with its inflationary threat, technological unemployment, and other unhealthy aspects of the present economic set-up will threaten us not only with a depression but with national financial insolvency.

**Main causes of depression of 1929 still persist.** Even a brief review of the economic scene in our country today also reveals the fact that the basic evils which brought on the depression in 1929 still remain, even if obscured by a feverish temporary prosperity.

**Inequalities of income still limit mass purchasing power.** The steady concentration of business power in the hands of a few mammoth corporations, which alarmed many even in the 1930's, has continued apace since the onset of the second world war; the mergers were greater in 1947 than in any year since 1930, with the exception of 1945. This creates a growing danger of monopoly and price-fixing, as well as a threat to small business and free business enterprise.

While the total national income has markedly increased since 1939, there is the same tendency towards concentration of income in the higher brackets which undermined mass purchasing power in the 1920's and led to the depression of 1929. In 1945, according to the Federal Reserve Board, the top 10 per cent of asset holders held 60 per cent of all liquid assets and the top 30 per cent held 87 per cent of the liquid assets; moreover, the top 10 per cent received 29 per cent of the total money income. In 1946 the top 20 per cent received nearly half of the total national income, while the bottom 20 per cent received only one-twenty-fifth of the total national income. In 1946, the last year of available statistics on the subject, out of a total population of about 145 million some 6,373 persons—those with incomes over $100,000—received about 10 per cent of all corporate dividends paid in that year.

Another government report presented the average money income of American families in 1946, before taxes: lowest fifth, $825; second fifth, $2,023; third fifth, $3,050; fourth fifth, $4,201; and highest fifth, $8,291. In March, 1949, the Treasury Department reported that 4.23 per cent of the taxpayers paid 51.27 per cent of total income taxes for 1948. Income statistics for 1949 showed that about 85 per cent of American families had an income of $6,000 or less—about equal to $3,000 or less in terms of 1939 purchasing power. Some 10 million families, about 22 per cent, had an income of less than $2,000; 7,900,-000, or 20.6 per cent, had an income of $2,000 to $3,000; 8 million families, or 20.7 per cent, had an income of $3,000 to $4,000; 5 million families, or about 11 per cent, had an income of $4,000 to $5,000; 3,100,000 families, or about 7 per cent, had an income of $5,000 to $6,000. Some 1,100,000 families, or 2.9 per cent had an income of over $10,000.

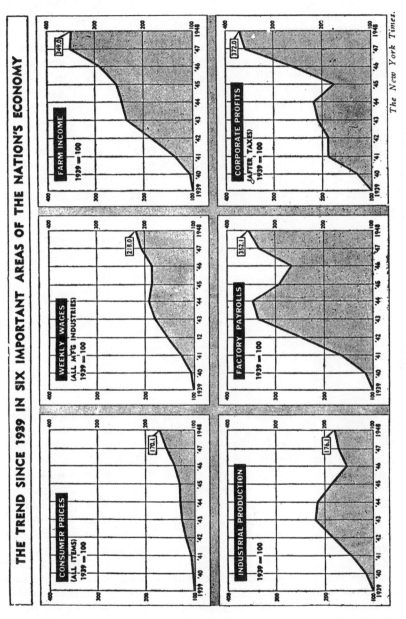

# THE TREND SINCE 1939 IN SIX IMPORTANT AREAS OF THE NATION'S ECONOMY

**CONSUMER PRICES**
(ALL ITEMS)
1939 = 100

170.1

**WEEKLY WAGES**
(ALL MFG INDUSTRIES)
1939 = 100

218.0

**FARM INCOME**
1939 = 100

349.0

**INDUSTRIAL PRODUCTION**
1939 = 100

176.1

**FACTORY PAYROLLS**
1939 = 100

352.1

**CORPORATE PROFITS**
(AFTER TAXES)
1939 = 100

372.0

*The New York Times.*

These graphs reveal the chief economic trends during and after the second world war.

While the situation revealed by all these figures is not quite as inequitable as that of 1928–1929, it is striking enough to reveal that there is nothing in the picture to support the idea that we have found how to provide the mass purchasing power required for a healthy capitalism, even in a period of maximum temporary prosperity. Indeed, members of the lower-income groups had to withdraw some 10 billion dollars from their savings to meet their increased living expenses for the year 1946.

It is also interesting to note that corporate profits, even after taxes, have grown in spectacular fashion since the war, as compared with the relatively gradual increase in wages since 1945. The net income of 3,000 of the largest corporations, after taxes, was 37 per cent greater in 1947 than in 1946. Corporation profits after taxes in 1948 were about 5 times as large as in 1939. The following table from Department of Labor statistics reveals the comparative gains in wages and corporate profits during the last decade.

| YEAR | WAGES AND SALARIES (PRIVATE) | CORPORATE PROFITS AFTER TAXES AND INVENTORY ADJUSTMENT |
|---|---|---|
| | (In Billions of Dollars) | |
| 1939 | 37.5 | 4.3 |
| 1940 | 41.1 | 6.3 |
| 1941 | 51.5 | 6.8 |
| 1942 | 65.6 | 8.1 |
| 1943 | 78.7 | 9.6 |
| 1944 | 83.3 | 9.5 |
| 1945 | 82.1 | 8.4 |
| 1946 | 91.0 | 12.8 |
| 1947 | 104.7 | 18.1 |
| 1948 | 115.6 | 21.7 |

**Who is better off today?** Despite the large gross increase in formal wage and salary payments—from about 49 billion dollars in 1940 to nearly 135 billion in 1949—the rise in prices during this same period has more than absorbed the wage and salary gains in the case of millions of workers. Indeed, although the gross total of wage and salary payments in 1948 was much higher than in 1939, a smaller percentage of the total national income was going into employee compensation than in 1939. In 1939, employee compensation amounted to 66 per cent of the national income; in 1949 it constituted about 63.7 per cent. The statement given above that the average buying power of the American family was 35 per cent higher in 1948 than in 1940 is deceptive. It does not mean that the buying power of every family was 35 per cent above the 1940 figure. Because of the above described concentration of income in the upper or more prosperous group of families, the buying power of millions of families in the lower income groups was less than in 1940.

One careful estimate held that, in 1948, while about 41,800,000 workers were somewhat better off in buying power than in 1939, no less than 19,500,000 were distinctly worse off. Among the groups whose real wages and salaries were lower than in 1939 were automobile workers, those employed in trade, finance and insurance, government employees, school teachers, and service employees. The greatest gains were made by the bituminous coal miners, whose take-home pay after taxes was 75 per cent higher in 1948 than in 1939, thus proving that the policies of John L. Lewis were good for his miners, whatever their effect on public welfare. The farming class has, of course, gained because of greater demand and higher prices for farm products, while the farmers have not been quite so seriously affected by high rents and other living costs as the city population. The total cash income of American farmers increased from $8,685,000,000 in 1939 to $31,018,-703,000 in 1948. It dropped to about $28,100,000,000 in 1949. The net farm income in 1948 was 18 billion dollars, and in 1949, 15 billion.

Even many of those usually in upper income brackets—those living on fixed incomes, such as bondholders—are much worse off than in 1939. In 1939, net interest payments were 4.2 billion dollars; in 1949 they were only 4.3 billion—an increase of only 2.4 per cent. Hence, in terms of purchasing power, many living on fixed incomes were only about half as well off in 1949 as in 1939.

**Precarious nature of all gains since 1939.** Even in the case of those workers and farmers whose actual buying power was greater in 1948 than in 1939 or 1940, their gains rested on such precarious foundations and were so menaced by inflation and the threat of war that, substantially, their situation could hardly be regarded as more favorable than in 1939. The main improvement over 1939, undoubtedly a temporary one, lay in the fact that more persons—nearly the total able-bodied working population—were employed than in 1939 and that unemployment was less of an immediate specter. It seems probable, however, that when the next recession and depression come, as they must if we avoid a third world war, the unemployment problem will be more serious than in 1929–1933. Social security legislation cannot take care of mass unemployment for long. The technological advances since 1933 will enable us to meet normal needs with far less man power per unit of production than before 1933.

**Balance sheet of economic trends in the last decade.** In conclusion, one may appraise the present situation fairly in something like the following manner: If we go ahead as we are at present oriented and enter another world war, that means the end of private capitalism both at home and abroad. Even though we avoid involvement in a third world war, the outlook is not conducive to optimism. If, after we reduce or cease deficit mercantilism, supply the delayed wartime and postwar orders, cease lavish armament expenditures, and return to an economy which must be readjusted chiefly on the basis of the normal peacetime home market, we shall find that we are confronted by virtually the same situation that faced us in 1933, save for Social Security legislation and some curbs on the ravages of finance capitalism.

The day of reckoning is only being postponed by current trends, and the longer they continue the more extensive and serious will be the problems to be reckoned with.

If, as many now contend, our economic future is directly linked with the destiny of nations across the water, then the outlook is far less happy for American capitalism than in 1933. We will have to associate closely with moderate collectivist régimes as our friends, and must face not only their competition but that of the totalitarian states like Soviet Russia and her satellites, which do not need to make profit on private investments or on world trade. Hence, it is an optimist, indeed, who can contend today that the crisis of private capitalism has passed.

Perhaps the greatest threat to what remains of private capitalism is the danger that we may use war scares, cold wars, lukewarm and phony wars—even hot wars—to maintain full employment and high production levels. If this is the case, state capitalism will inevitably be fastened upon us, and that will be only one of the lesser evils that will result from the continuance of this policy.

Of course, it is probably true that we could avoid a depression if we took steps at once to abandon the colossal armament program and launched out on a great housing program, set up a half-dozen new valley authorities, spent tens of billions on new and better roads, recreation and other service facilities, gave adequate Federal support to education and medical care, and the like—in other words, set up a real welfare state. But there are no signs of such a policy. President Truman's welfare-state budget of 1950 allotted only six per cent of the total budget to welfare purposes, and he received from Congress only about half of what he requested.

## The Labor Problem and Collective Bargaining

**Historic basis of the labor problem.** No problem faced by the capitalistic system is more serious than the relations between capital and labor. Ever since the rise of the factory system, society has been agitated by growing friction between workers and their employers. This has arisen principally because of the separation of contacts and interests between the two groups.

Until the coming of the factory system, the relations between workers and their employers were personal and fairly simple and direct. In the small shops of the handicraft system and on the farms, employer and workers labored side by side, usually at the same tasks. Each had a personal interest in the affairs and welfare of the other. Any difficulties which arose between them could usually be settled in a friendly, or at least in a personal, manner. Furthermore, they stood on somewhat the same level, so far as their relative bargaining strength was concerned. The employer needed the worker's skilled labor as much as the worker needed a job. Also, if the worker disliked laboring for an employer, he could usually set up his own business without too much difficulty. He could also fall back upon farming, hunting, or fishing as a means of support.

The growth of cities, the development of the factory system, and the expansion of urban industry brought a marked change in the relationship between employer and worker. The adjustment of difficulties could no longer take place upon a personal, informal basis. The increasing use of machinery reduced the need for skilled labor. With a few weeks' training, almost anyone could successfully tend a machine. Thus, the skill of the worker no longer counted for much in bargaining over wages and other matters. Furthermore, the urban worker was now entirely dependent upon his job for a livelihood. No longer could he turn to agriculture or set up his own small shop, if he disliked his conditions of employment.

Factory owners adopted an impersonal approach, often regarding their employees almost as pieces of productive equipment rather than human beings and judging them solely by their efficiency as producers. The development of such an impersonal relationship meant that the old informal teamwork tended to disappear. The worker's chief aim became to secure as high wages as he could obtain for as little work as possible. The employer's goal was to get a maximum of work done at the lowest possible wages.

**Collective bargaining and the rise of labor unionism.** The labor situation thus tended to develop into a struggle between employer and employees over wages and working conditions. At the outset, the advantage lay mainly with the employer, for one workman came to mean little or nothing to him. With thousands of persons seeking jobs, the employer could always find somebody to replace the workers who demanded wages higher than he was willing to pay. On the other hand, the job meant everything to the individual worker, for he was threatened with starvation if he lost it.

The workers came to realize that their only hope of bargaining successfully with the employer was through collective action. If they banded together and collectively presented their demands, employers would not be able to refuse them so lightheartedly, for it was not easy for an employer to replace his entire labor force all at once. Also, a group of workers, by pooling their resources, could provide strikers with food and other necessities while they were out of work. Thus organizations of workers, or labor unions, arose. The unions took over the task of bargaining collectively with employers concerning wages, hours of work, and other matters of interest to the workers.

Labor unions possessed a number of advantages as bargaining agencies. Each union could appoint a committee of its members to deal with employers. As a result, such negotiators became skilled in this capacity. Then, too, if protesting workers were discharged, the union could support them until they found other jobs. Most important of all, the union could threaten the employer by sheer force of numbers.  If the employer refused to grant its demands, the union could call a strike and perhaps leave the employer powerless to continue operations.  If the union were large enough to include all the skilled workers in a particular trade, the employer would find it impossible to secure replacements.

**Development of labor unions in the United States.**  The first labor unions in the United States appeared early in the nineteenth century.  For a long time, however, they were relatively small and powerless; not until after the Civil War did they achieve much strength.  Until very recently, most unions consisted of skilled workers.  The unskilled, who most needed the aid of unions, remained unorganized for the most part from the decline of Knights of Labor in 1887 until the 1930's.

Few in number and members, the earliest labor unions in the United States were confined mainly to the larger cities.  Their strength gradually increased, however, so that after the Civil War several national organizations were established.  At this time, numerous efforts were made to establish labor unions having both unskilled and skilled workers in their ranks.  The most successful of these was the Knights of Labor, which flourished in the 1870's and 1880's, and at one time seemed destined permanently to lead the American labor movement.  It met misfortune, however, in a series of disastrous strikes and had virtually disappeared by the 1890's.

In the meantime, the unions of skilled workers, such as carpenters, masons, machinists, printers, plumbers, and so on, were growing.  In 1886, they formed a central organization, known as the American Federation of Labor—a craft or horizontal union—which, led by Samuel Gompers, dominated the American labor movement for many years.  The unions belonging to the Federation achieved considerable strength and commanded respect from employers, but they failed to organize more than a fraction of the unskilled laborers, who were steadily increasing in numbers and importance.

In 1935, a group of powerful unions broke away from the Federation and, under the leadership of John L. Lewis, formed the Congress of Industrial Organizations (CIO)—an industrial or vertical union.  This body has devoted itself to the task of organizing unskilled as well as skilled workers, with the result that millions have joined the ranks of organized labor in recent years.

**Craft unions incompletely protect workers.**  Unionism was long confined to the skilled workers for special reasons.  It requires time and training to become a skilled craftsman like a carpenter or stone mason; hence, the numbers of skilled craftsmen were limited and it was possible for the unions to make nearly all of them union members.  On the other hand, since anyone may become an unskilled laborer, it was difficult for unskilled workers to organize and include in their ranks all those who might compete for jobs.  This meant that, in the event of a strike, the employer could easily replace the unskilled striking workers by non-union men. The skilled workers also received higher wages and thus had more money than the unskilled workers to finance strikes and union activities.

As we have noted above, the Congress of Industrial Organizations was organized from the beginning as a vertical or industrial union which took in unskilled as well as skilled workers. The CIO offered the first great opportunity for American unskilled workers to join the ranks of union labor. The need for the protection of unskilled labor greatly increased during the second world war when the labor force grew in numbers by some 10,600,000 persons, mainly recruited from males under 20 and married women between 35 and 64 years of age.

**Employers against union labor.** From the first, labor unions were bitterly opposed by employers, who naturally disliked to see the workers gain more power to secure higher wages. In their battle against the unions, the employers used all the weapons at their command, among them private militia, strikebreakers, and lockouts. The history of American industry is filled with bitter struggles to break up the unions and drive them out of existence. For many years, the employers were aided by the legislatures and courts, which long denied vital legal rights to the unions, and readily granted injunctions against strikers.

**Company unions.** One of the prominent ways in which employers more recently tried to combat the organization of workers into strong unions was to form "company unions." The late Professor R. F. Hoxie accurately defined company unions as "unions instigated and practically dominated by the employers, organized and conducted for the purpose of combating or displacing independent unionism."

The main weaknesses of the company union were: (1) In order to negotiate effectively with an employer, a union must control a large portion of the labor market in its industry. A company union at best only controlled the laborers in a given factory. Hence, it was only a step ahead of the solitary individual in dealing with the corporate employer. The latter could bring in outsiders to take the place of striking employees. Workers in company unions in other plants were in no position to co-operate in restricting the flow of strikebreakers. (2) The company union could be dominated by employers. Union meetings were almost invariably held in the plant and permitted easy spying on the workers. Employees who were aggressive in the union and attempted to build it up were easily identified and discharged. (3) Limited by the resources of a single plant, the company union could not formulate such effective policies as a national trade union. (4) Company unions could not readily produce trained negotiators, capable of coping with employers and their attorneys.

In 1933 some form of company union existed in about 1,000 plants involving about 1,500,000 workers. The Wagner Labor Relations Act of 1935 made it illegal for employers to organize company unions.

**Use of the strike and picketing.** The labor unions have found their main weapon in the strike—the stoppage of work by all union members until their demands have been granted. The strike, as we have pointed out, is a powerful weapon, for it is usually impossible for the employer to replace his entire labor force. In conducting a strike, the union usually resorts to a device known as picketing. This consists of surrounding the plant where the strike is going on with guards or "pickets" to dissuade or prevent any workers from entering it. The purpose of picketing is to force the employer to deal with the union or close his plant. Strikes and picketing were long considered illegal by the courts. Gradually, however, the right of labor to strike and to carry on peaceful picketing was legally recognized.

Naturally, employers have vigorously opposed or combated strikes, frequently calling upon police or state militia to disperse strikers. In the course of American industrial history, thousands of persons have been wounded or killed in labor disputes. Often, the strikers have been responsible, becoming unruly and stoning or shooting police and damaging property. But, in far too many cases, the violence has been started by the police or by thugs hired by the employers.

A novel type of strike, the so-called sit-down strike, was widely used in 1936 and 1937, especially to unionize the motor industry. While later outlawed by the Supreme Court, it did more than any other strike stratagem to break the opposition of employers to unionization.

**Employer violence.** That employers have frequently encouraged violence in dealing with striking workers has been proved by many investigations by the Federal government and other agencies. For example, a Senate investigating committee (the LaFollette Committee) in 1936 found that enormous sums of money were paid by some employers to private detective agencies to spy upon labor unions, to break strikes, and to stir up violence in strikes, in order to make it appear that the unions were threatening to destroy life and property. In 1935, one large corporation alone paid $168,000 to detective agencies for such services. Perhaps the most amazing fact to be revealed by this investigation was that employers, between 1933 and 1936, purchased large quantities of tear gas, machine guns, and other weapons for the purpose of fighting strikers. During some strikes, factories bristled with barbed wire, machine guns, and armed guards, as though they were fortresses under attack.

During the early 1930's, employers also developed a very clever propaganda program, known as the Mohawk Valley Formula, by which they sought to stir up local public opinion against striking unionists by making it appear that the union was wholly responsible for the strike and for all violence attending it. The Wagner Act of 1935 outlawed this procedure as an "unfair labor practice."

**Labor racketeering.** One cannot, however, fairly place all responsibility for labor troubles upon the employers. Many long and expensive strikes have little or nothing to do with the relations between employers and workers or with improving the status of workers. A notable example are the often silly and stubborn jurisdictional strikes.

In all too many cases, the labor unions and their officials have far from honorable records. Racketeers and criminals have succeeded in forcing their way to power in many labor unions. In the depression years of the 1930's, when many workers were unemployed or working for very low wages, racketeers heading labor unions were drawing down huge salaries. The president of one local union in New York City received $21,800 a year. This same man received "gifts" over a period of five years which amounted, on the average, to $11,000 annually. This money came from the dues of union members earning, at the most, not more than $1,000 to $2,000 a year. Often, crooked labor leaders acquire control over large union funds. One union had $7,500,000 of its funds stolen by dishonest officials.

Furthermore, criminals and racketeers who have become union leaders often carry on their activities outside the unions and force employers to pay large sums for "protection" against strikes and labor troubles. Several such prominent labor racketeers have been convicted and punished for such extortion.[1] Dishonest union officials also frequently "sell out" their own followers. Although collecting large dues from union members, they enter into agreements with employers, promising the latter protection from union demands for higher wages and the like. They have even been known to furnish strikebreakers to the employers.

**The Wagner Act of 1935.** The right of labor unions to exist and to carry on collective bargaining with employers has been recognized by the Federal government. Their right to carry on strikes and peaceful picketing has also been recognized by the courts. Various laws and court decisions during the nineteenth and twentieth centuries honored and extended these rights, but they were not made a part of our national law until 1935, when the National Labor Relations Act (the Wagner Act) was passed, specifically recognizing the legality of labor unions and the right of collective bargaining. The Wagner Act not only provided that employers must deal with labor unions when the latter have a majority representation in their factories, but forbade employers to attempt to break up labor unions or discharge workers for belonging to unions. The closed shop, which makes prior union membership a condition of employment, was permitted, as well as the automatic check-off of union dues by the paymaster of the employer. Further, while union leaders were permitted to speak their mind freely about employers, any public criticism of labor unionism by the latter was regarded as an "unfair" labor practice. Finally, the National Labor Relations Board was virtually administrator, prosecutor, and judge in labor cases.

---

[1] See below, pp. 830–831, 836.

**Growth of union membership since the Wagner Act.** As a result of the protection and encouragement given to unionization by the Wagner Act, especially when supplemented by defense and wartime legislation, and of the vast increase of employment during the war, the number of organized laborers virtually doubled between 1939 and 1949. At the latter date, labor union membership in the United States was estimated at about 15,600,000, of which 7,200,000 were claimed by the American Federation of Labor (which had only 3,000,000 members in 1935), and 6,000,000 by the Congress of Industrial Organizations. The rest of the membership, about 2,400,000, was distributed among independent and unaffiliated unions, chiefly the International Association of Machinists, the United Mine Workers, and the railroad brotherhoods. Despite these gains in union membership, the fact remained that about 48,000,000 workers out of the

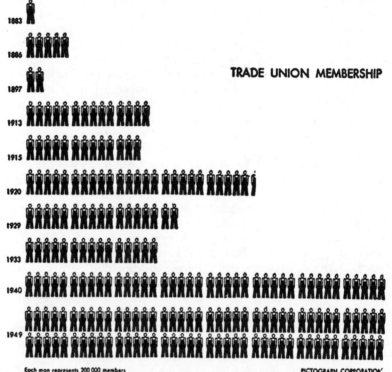

TRADE UNION MEMBERSHIP

Each man represents 200,000 members      PICTOGRAPH CORPORATION

Graph showing impressive growth of trade union organization as a result of the Wagner Act and the second world war.

total labor force of some 63,815,000 in 1949 remained outside of union circles.

**Postwar labor troubles.** After the second world war there was an epidemic of strikes, especially in the automobile, steel, coal, and transport industries. Labor desired to retain its high wartime wages and other wartime advantages, whereas employers sought to cut down expenses by lowering wages. Production of needed commodities in the postwar period was for a time notably slowed down by strikes, though labor was by no means entirely to blame in all cases. Some 116 million man-days were lost in strikes in 1946; 34.6 million in 1947; 34.1 million in 1948; and 53 million in 1949.

In the soft coal industry, the owners would not come to terms with John L. Lewis and his United Mine Workers. On May 1, 1943, therefore, the Federal government seized the mines and made a contract with Mr. Lewis. In November of 1946, Lewis, prevented from terminating this contract by the courts, called a strike as a result of which he and his union were heavily fined by the Federal courts. Lewis was cited for contempt in the Federal courts again in 1947 and in 1948, and heavier fines were levied. In 1949, a notable slowdown in coal production was ordered by Mr. Lewis, and by February, 1950, the nation's coal reserves were reduced to an alarmingly low point. President Truman asked Congress for authority to seize the mines. At this point, the coal operators agreed to negotiate seriously, and Mr. Lewis won most of his demands, though having to make some concessions. A CIO strike in the steel industry in 1949 was notable for winning a non-contributory pension plan from the employers, the latter paying for the pensions out of industrial earnings.

**The Taft-Hartley Act supplants the Wagner Act.** The Wagner Act was one of the New Deal laws most bitterly criticized by conservatives, especially conservative employers. So, when a Republican Congress was elected in November, 1946, it was inevitable that some change would be made in the law. This new labor legislation was embodied in the Taft-Hartley Act of June, 1947. The new law, which sought to remedy alleged abuses in the drafting and operation of the Wagner Act, was more favorable than the latter to the employers, although not as drastically so as some unionists had feared.

The Taft-Hartley Act abolished the closed shop, but permitted, under certain limitations, the union shop, which requires the employee to join a union after being employed. It made the National Labor Relations Board a judicial body and created a General Counsel to handle the execution of the administrative aspects of the law. It provided for a 60-day notice—"cooling-off period"—before terminating a labor contract and going out on strike. The employer was permitted to express his opinion of labor unions and their practices without being guilty of an unfair labor practice. Industry-wide bargaining was restricted. The individual member of a union was given more legal protection against the possible tyranny of his union. Injunctions to end secondary boycotts and jurisdictional disputes and to prevent strikes threatening national security were facilitated. All political contributions by both unions and corporations were banned and union officials were compelled to take an oath that they were not members of the Communist party, if they wished access to the services of the NLRB. The most dubious clause in the law was one which compelled employers to deal with all the small craft unions involved in the operations of a factory rather than with one large vertical union. This provision seemed to invite, if not industrial anarchy, at least more frequent disturbances and strikes.

The law was bitterly opposed by most labor organizations, but how it would operate and to what extent it would be upheld or undermined by the courts only time could tell. It was obvious, even to fair-minded men as far to the "left" as Norman Thomas, that much of the storm of abuse and protest heaped upon the Taft-Hartley Act by labor was mere ballyhoo and propaganda. Further, nothing in the act appeared to be such a threat to labor unionism as President Truman's own request for authorization to draft strikers into the army and make them work under threat of court-martial—a demand which was frustrated chiefly through the efforts of Senator Taft. The victory of the Democrats in 1948, partly attributable to the opposition of organized labor to the Taft-Hartley Act, indicated that the bill might be either repealed or greatly modified by the 81st Congress. Despite successive rebuffs from Congress, even from a considerable contingent of Democrats, President Truman demanded the outright repeal of the Taft-Hartley law and the revival of the old Wagner Act. His program was weakened by what seemed to some the insincerity of his devotion to the cause of union labor. These opponents claimed that, when it seemed to suit his political interest, Truman had been willing to go further than any other American president in the twentieth century to intimidate organized labor. The first session of the 81st Congress failed to modify the Taft-Hartley law.

The Taft-Hartley Act seemed to many to have broken down in the long coal strike of 1949–1950. Operators refused to negotiate effectively, for they expected to have an injunction granted which would weaken the power of Mr. Lewis and his union. The latter delayed coming to an agreement in the hope of a threat of government seizure of the mines which, they believed, would give them more favorable bargaining power. In this they were right. Upholders of the Taft-Hartley Act contended that the reason it failed was President Truman's delay in invoking its powers, despite his dislike of Mr. Lewis.

## The Problem of Unemployment in the United States

**Causes of unemployment.** Broadly speaking, unemployment is mainly the result of cultural lag. Few persons possess all the goods and services they desire; most need far more in the way of food, clothing, housing, and other essentials than they can now obtain. Hence, there exists plenty of work for men to do even in peacetime. Furthermore, we possess ample farms, factories, railroads, machinery, and other equipment with which to work. But our economic institutions and our social arrangements for putting men to work in supplying needed goods and services have proved unequal to their task.  We have failed to supply the mass purchasing power needed to provide a sufficiently large body of solvent customers to buy the volume of goods required to keep our factories going at full speed and employing all available workers.

More specifically, unemployment is due to four main causes: (1) business depressions; (2) displacement of workers by machines; (3) the "seasonal" character of some occupations; and (4) old age.  The first two are by far the most important.

**Unemployment as a social problem.**  From 1929 to 1940, unemployment was one of our major economic and social problems.  In 1933, between 15 and 17 million persons of working age were unemployed. The unemployment census of 1937 indicated that, even after four years of New Deal "pump-priming," nearly 10 million were still unable to find jobs in private industry.  The expense of furnishing relief to these people weighed heavily on public and private agencies as well as on generous relatives and friends of the needy.

The armament industry of 1939 to 1942, the second world war, delayed wartime orders, the "cold war" after March, 1947, and the vast new armament program which followed all helped to reduce unemployment to a minimum.  There were over 61 million employed in civilian industries in 1949, with only about 2,500,000 unemployed at the outset of the year.  By March, 1950, some 4,684,000 were unemployed, the largest number since Pearl Harbor.  This was not due so much to a decrease of jobs as it was to the increase of the labor force as young persons entered it for the first time.  It indicated that jobs had not kept pace with population increase.

**Serious nature of unemployment.**  Nothing is more disastrous to the average person than to be out of work, for it is hardly possible to exist in our urban society without a money income.  Poverty-stricken farmers may raise enough food to keep their families alive, but this is not possible for the unemployed in a city, where the only source to which they may turn for support is public or private charity. This means of support can furnish the unemployed only a few of the necessities of life.  Furthermore, the necessity of accepting charity is a severe blow to the pride and morale of most Americans.

**Mythical charge that all unemployed are "bums."**  We often hear the statement that any man can work, if he wants to, and that the only people on relief are the "bums" and loafers, who would not take a job if it were offered to them.  Investigations show that this is not true.  For example, it was found by *Fortune* magazine that, of those on relief in 1935, more than two-thirds had held jobs for more than five years at a time.  One-third had held the same job for 20 years before the slump.  Other evidence that the unemployed were not loafers is seen in the fact that over 60 per cent of those on relief in 1935 had been rehired by private industry by 1939.  A great many

# UNEMPLOYMENT

## A. F. OF L. ESTIMATES

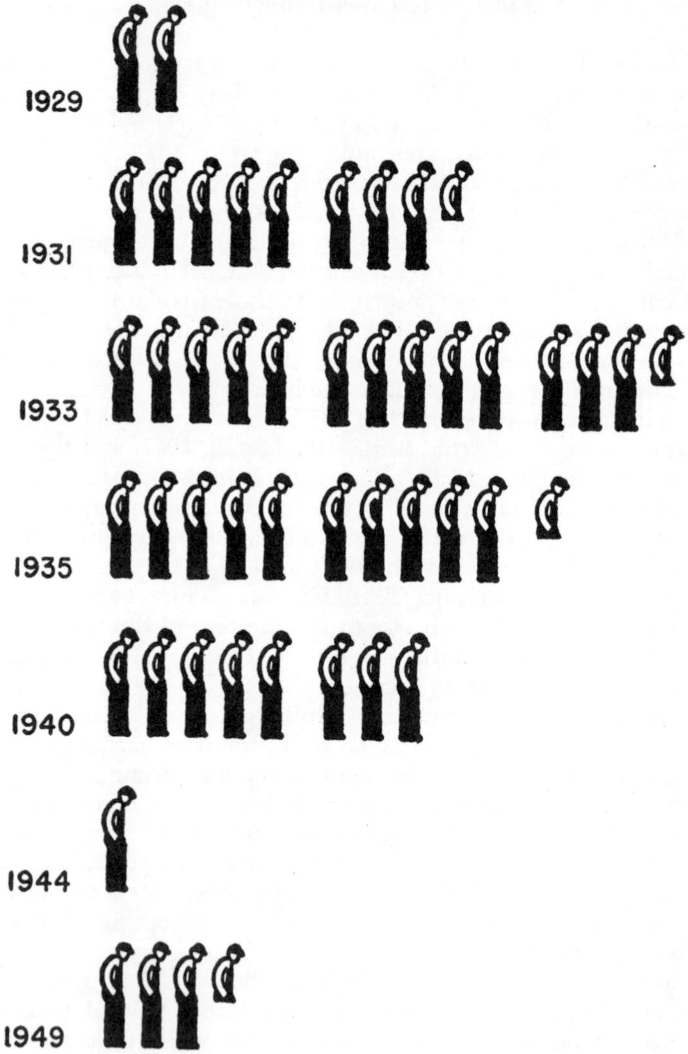

**1929**

**1931**

**1933**

**1935**

**1940**

**1944**

**1949**

Each symbol represents 1 million unemployed

*Courtesy of the Public Affairs Committee.*

This chart shows how unemployment was reduced by industrial demands of
the second world war and the cold war that followed.

men on relief would have gladly accepted jobs, if they had been available. Some were unskilled workers, not trained for the type of work available. Others had been turned down because of their age, which generally ran between 35 and 55 years.

The "business cycle," unemployment, and depressions. The capitalist system has experienced alternating periods of prosperity and depression; lean years follow the fat. Periods of minimum unemployment, high wages, and expanding business activity have alternated with years of unemployment, low wages, and declining business. This so-called business cycle is regarded by many economists as a normal and inevitable feature of the capitalist system. Forrest Davis, however, in his *What Price Wall Street?* (1932) offered rather conclusive evidence that the major examples of what economists have regarded as normal business cycles were primarily the product of excessive financial speculation, rather than of inevitable trends. There is good reason to regard business cycles as a myth of the traditional economists, which they have supported with a statistical morass. Whatever its cause, the depression of 1929 was unusually severe.

Many factors contribute to depressions. A major cause, as pointed out earlier, is the lack of mass purchasing power. In the years preceding depressions, more goods are produced than the mass of the people can afford to buy. Hence, unsold goods tend to pile up and business falls off, forcing many companies to reduce their labor force. Extensive curtailment of operations starts a wave of large-scale unemployment. Business stagnates until something happens—like government "pump-priming" (extensive government spending)—to restore prosperity.

Technological unemployment. Technological unemployment—the displacement of human labor by efficient machines—is a major cause of unemployment in our day. This type of unemployment dates back to prehistoric times, when the invention of the first crude stone weapons and tools enabled a single person to do tasks which formerly required the efforts of several, and the labor of domesticated animals replaced that of innumerable human beings. In fact, throughout the course of man's history, new methods and new tools have usually reduced the need for human labor. New occupations have often arisen to take up the slack, but usually not until after a period of hardship on the part of the unemployed.

The Industrial Revolution brought the greatest of all changes in methods of production. It then became possible to produce by machinery vastly more than by the earlier handicraft methods. But neither the Industrial Revolution nor earlier improvements in methods of production created long periods of widespread unemployment. The new methods and machines lowered the prices of goods so that much greater quantities could be sold. Hence, more men were put to work to produce them. The rapid growth of population at the time produced more customers for the greater volume of goods produced. Furthermore, until recently, new lines of industrial activity were continually opening up and absorbing those displaced from older industries by the introduction of machinery. For example, while thousands of hand weavers were displaced by the power looms, many found work in the new factories.

About the time of the first world war, a new development appeared, the automatic, continuous-process machine, capable of turning out unbelievable quantities of everything from cigarettes to pre-fabricated houses. Formerly, laborers were required to watch and tend machines. Now we have machines, such as the thermostat and the photoelectric eye, to watch and operate other machines. Hence, increased production no longer requires a larger number of workers in many lines of industry. Furthermore, very few important new lines of economic activity have appeared in recent years.

A few statistics will illustrate the amazing growth of efficient machinery. According to the National Resources Committee, the available mechanical power in the United States rose from 70 million horsepower in 1900 to about 1,231 million horsepower in 1935. With this, and the new machinery, 88 workers in 1936 produced 7 per cent more goods than 100 workers could in 1923–1925. Between 1919 and 1928, the man-hours of labor required to manufacture a long ton of pig iron fell from 5 to 2. From 1921 to 1929, the man-hours needed to produce a metric ton of copper fell from 128 to 48; in zinc, the man-hours declined from 108 to 55 between 1919 and 1929; and in lead they dropped from 48 to 17 between 1919 and 1931. In all manufacturing industry, the index of production (physical output) went up from 28 in 1899 to 135.2 in 1940, and there has been a notable gain since 1940. As a whole, it has been estimated that man-hour output in American industry has more than trebled since 1900 as a result of improved mechanical facilities and the speed-up system; it increased by 18 per cent between 1940 and 1946 alone.

The mechanical progress in agriculture has also been striking. In 1880, the average farm worker harvested 23.1 acres; in 1900, 28.4 acres; in 1920, 33.2 acres, and in 1930, 35.5 acres. In 1787, 19 farmers in the United States fed one city person. In recent years, 19 persons living on farms have produced enough food for 56 non-farm persons, plus 10 living abroad. It has been estimated that the mechanical inventions of the nineteenth century brought a saving of 79 per cent in farm labor, and those of the twentieth century have been even more striking. Morrow Mayo tells us that it required three hours of labor in 1900 to produce a bushel of wheat; today a bushel of wheat can be produced in three minutes of machine time. The output per man-hour in agriculture increased by nearly 30 per cent between 1940 and 1946. Other estimates confirm the above data: between 1800 and 1940 the number of man-hours needed to produce 100 bushels of wheat dropped from 373 to 47; in 1820, one farmer supported $4\frac{1}{2}$ other persons, and in 1946, $14\frac{1}{2}$. No wonder Dr. Willcox estimates that we could produce all the food we need on one-fifth the land now cultivated and with one-fifth of the farmers now employed.

The technological basis for unemployment is now increasing by leaps and bounds. The fact that the remarkable technological improvements of the war years did not result in widespread unemployment for some years after 1945 was due mainly to the frenzied demand for goods to supply orders that could not be filled in wartime, to the shipping of many billions of dollars worth of goods abroad for relief and rehabilitation, to the perpetuation of a vast armament industry after the war—actually surpassing that in the war years of 1917 and 1918—and to the fact that the increased income of farmers enabled them to buy more factory-made products. As we have pointed out, however, these factors are temporary in nature and serve only to postpone the evil day. When the present abnormal demand for goods falls off, we face unprecedented technological employment—probably within a few years, or a decade at the most.

**ONE MAN – ONE HOUR**
INCREASE OF OUTPUT PER MAN-HOUR
(IN 1947 PRICES)

27¢  56¢  $1.21  $1.40  $1.74

1850   1900   1940   1944   1960

HARRY A. HERZOG FOR THE PUBLIC AFFAIRS COMMITTEE, INC.

This chart indicates how mechanical power has enormously increased output per man-hour in the last hundred years.

**Seasonal unemployment.** Another cause of unemployment is the seasonal nature of certain industries and occupations. Most summer hotels and beach resorts, for example, close down when the season ends. Toy manufacturers employ more people in certain months before Christmas than at any other time. Wheat growers need laborers mostly at harvest time. Hence, many workers in such industries are unemployed part of the year. Indeed, few industries in normal times are entirely unaffected by seasonal unemployment. The workers who, perhaps, most perfectly reflect seasonal employment are the migratory farm laborers whom we discussed in an earlier chapter.

**Age restrictions on employment.** A deplorable factor in our unemployment problem is the refusal, in normal times, of many employers to hire men over forty, or even over thirty-five. In this manner, millions of able-bodied persons have been denied the right to earn a living. Many employers believe that men have outlived their usefulness in a factory when they have reached thirty-five or forty, but actually this policy is one of the most wasteful and unjust in modern industry.

The tendency to refuse employment to those over 65 is increasing. In 1890, some 70 per cent of men over 65 were employed. In 1950, the figure had dropped to 35 per cent, and it is expertly estimated that by 1960 only 30 per cent of those over 65 will be employed. Dr. Thomas Parran estimates that this policy loses the potential labor of at least 1,500,000 persons who could earn some $4,500,000,000 yearly.

**Declining menace of child labor.** Another cause of unemployment, now much less important than in former years, is the tendency of some employers to hire children in place of adults. Employment of children began on a large scale in the early days of the Industrial Revolution, when employers found that children were almost as capable of tending machines as adults and would work for much lower wages. In early English and American factories thousands of children, many under ten years of age, toiled from 10 to 16 hours a day in the early nineteenth century. Gradually, the more enlightened and humane employers realized the harm they were doing and replaced their child workers with adults. Many states passed laws regulating, and in some instances forbidding, the employment of children. The number of children under eighteen now employed in manufacturing and other industries is only a fraction of what it once was. In 1938, the labor of children under 16 in manufacturing goods sold in interstate commerce was banned by Federal law. The census of 1940 revealed that there were about one million employed children between the ages of 14 and 17, about 250,000 of these under sixteen. Wartime conditions enticed more children into employment and it was estimated that about three million between 14 and 17 were employed in 1944. While it is certain that this number has been substantially reduced since 1945, it is worth noting that an amendment to the Federal Constitution abolishing all child labor has been before the country for more than 25 years without securing the approval of the required number of states.

**Employed children take jobs away from adults.** Further, work in ill-ventilated factories, stores, and mines tends seriously to injure their health and stunt their growth. They grow up without the happy childhood and educational opportunities that are the right of all young people.

**Solutions for the problem of unemployment.** Unemployment can be dealt with in only two ways: by the initiative of private industry, and by the state, through unemployment insurance, public works, and the like.

Private industry can usually, if it so wishes, deal satisfactorily with the unemployment caused by the seasonal character of industry, old age, and child labor. Many companies with business of a seasonal nature have managed to spread work throughout the entire year, instead of concentrating all their activities in a few months. Some manufacturers of toys, for example, plan to spread their operations over the year, instead of rushing to manufacture their entire output in a few months. Many coal companies also sell ice to give their employees work in the summer as well as winter.

There exists little excuse for discharging or refusing to hire workers over forty. It is doubtful whether older men and women are always less efficient than younger workers. Even if they are, it is the duty of industry to supply older workers with jobs in return for their services during the best years of their lives. For child labor there is no excuse whatever.

Technological unemployment can be dealt with by spreading work among more people through shorter hours for each. Unemployment could be kept at a minimum if sufficient wages were paid for the shorter working period to provide adequate mass purchasing power. This would avoid the piling up of unsold goods, the main cause of business depressions.

When private industry does not take care of the unemployed, the government is forced to do so. The government may undertake more and more work projects, until finally it will surpass private industry as a producer and employer. The way would thus be opened to state control of our economic system. It would seem that only by taking active steps to deal with unemployment can private industry prevent more extensive state intervention in the economic field.

The government has tried to aid the worker substantially in solving some of his economic problems. In a later chapter we shall examine the ways in which the government has endeavored to alleviate poverty by means of direct relief, public works projects, and unemployment insurance.

## Is State Capitalism the Next Step?

**Increasing extent of state capitalism.** The amazing growth of state capitalism in the United States already was brought out in a striking article in the *United States News*, March 17, 1950. Here it was pointed out that in some 21 states individuals get more cash from federal, state, and local governments than they receive from factory payrolls. In 15 other states, government payments are more than half as large as manufacturing payrolls. In no state do government payments amount to less than one-fourth of manufacturing payrolls. In 10 states, government payments are more than twice the amount derived from manufacturing payrolls; in North Dakota, they are six times as great. In only the thoroughly industrialized states do factory payrolls provide

### HOW THE UNITED STATES EMPLOYMENT SERVICE WORKS

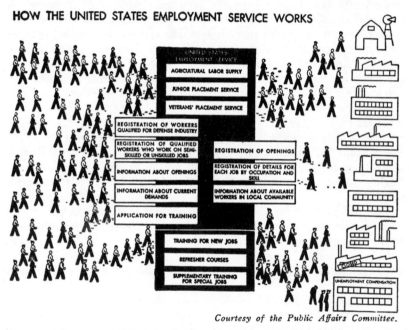

*Courtesy of the Public Affairs Committee.*

**This graph shows one of the important ways in which the Federal government seeks to lessen the burden of unemployment.**

as much personal income as government payments. But even in California government payments to individuals are greater than factory wages and salaries; and in New York they are 60 per cent as large. Some 6 million civilian workers, or about 10 per cent of all employed, depend for their livelihood on income from government units. Government payments to individuals amount to about 28 billion dollars a year, as compared with a 46 billion dollar payroll in manufacturing. These payments equal the gross income of the whole farming population, and account for 14 per cent of all income received by individuals in the country. Federal subsidies since 1934 have amounted to 17 billion dollars.

The above figures and implications only cover actual government entry into some kind of industrial or cultural business. They reveal only indirectly the extensive government controls over business in sectors of our economic life where private business still meets the payrolls.  Many regard such controls as an even greater symptom and evidence of growing state capitalism than the above-described government payments to individuals.

**Economic reforms necessary to avoid state capitalism.**  Government efforts, however, have not thus far solved our outstanding economic problems.  At best, aside from war, government measures have thus far provided only temporary and inadequate aid to millions of hard-pressed Americans.  The complete solution of such problems as unemployment, business depressions, and low living standards will come only when we thoroughly overhaul our economic institutions and adapt them to present-day conditions.  Most essential is the adoption by both businessmen and workers of a spirit of co-operation and responsibility.  Especially must employers become more interested in the welfare of their workers.  They must be willing to pay higher wages for shorter hours of work, and, at the same time, guarantee steady employment.  Workers are also the main customers of industry, and they can purchase goods only if they receive adequate incomes.

In the United States, we possess both the mechanical equipment and the workers that are required to produce an ample supply of goods and services for all.  Our task is to put both to work at top speed, in time of peace as well as war.  There is little prospect that the economic pump-priming based on war scares and armament expenditures can assure prosperity, and they always run the risk of provoking war.

We have an ample opportunity to base a long-range prosperity program on the combination of a high standard of living for American citizens and needed welfare industries to supplement activities growing out of private enterprise.  There is need for more than 250 billion dollars worth of welfare enterprises, many of which would be self-liquidating and all of which would be beneficial to Americans.  The Federal Works Agency in 1949 estimated the following 100 billion dollars worth of items in needed state and local public works: highways, 60 billions; schools, 10½ billions; sewers and water systems, 9½ billions; hospitals, 8½ billions; airports, 3½ billions; public buildings, 3½ billions; public service plants, 2½ billions; recreational facilities, 2 billions.  In addition to this, there are Federal works projects of even greater moment.  It would require at least 150 billion dollars to rehouse Americans decently.  We could profitably expend 25–50 billion dollars on additional valley authorities and other conservation and replacement enterprises.  Ten billions annually in Federal aid to education and public health—less than half of what we spent on armaments and the "cold war" in the period following the second world war—would not be unreasonably high.  The main difficulty is that the populace can be readily frightened into foreign boondoggling and armament but it is very loath to spend money for constructive purposes at home.

## Alleged Weaknesses of American Capitalism Today

**The suicidal methods of finance capitalism.** It is evident from the foregoing material in this and other chapters that, despite great natural resources, a large labor force, and unprecedentedly efficient technology, American capitalism has not thus far been able to develop and maintain a healthy and prosperous economy or to give security and plenty to the mass of the American people. Whether a different economic system would have done better or worse is an academic question, since capitalism has been the dominant American system since the landing of the first white settlers. We may fruitfully close this chapter with a consideration of some of the leading explanations of the weaknesses of American private capitalism, mainly those offered by able economists who favor the capitalistic system, and of leading reforms suggested as a means of rehabilitating capitalism.

One important group of writers emphasizes the devastating effect of the rise of finance capitalism, which has replaced the industrial capitalism that dominated the nineteenth-century American economy. As we have made clear earlier, finance capitalism separated ownership from control and management in the large corporations which control much of American industrial and business life. A small group of insiders, controlled by the great investment banks, has been able to gain control of the policies and management of many of these corporations on the basis of the ownership of a very small block of stock, usually less than five per cent of the total. Their situation has enabled them to loot the corporation, by means of holding companies or other financial devices. The result is that great businesses have been ruined and that, as Professor W. Z. Ripley put it, the stockholders have had little to show for their often hard-earned investments save "ashes and aloes." [2]

**The trend toward monopoly and the scarcity economy.** Another type of criticism of American private capitalism today has been that which finds the main evil in monopolistic control of business, the limitation of output, the resulting high prices, and the maintenance of a scarcity economy in the face of the potential economy of abundance that our remarkably efficient technology could produce. This attitude and procedure hold back production, keep prices high, pile up inventories, and lead to unemployment and depressions. In the long run, such a policy is disastrous to capitalism, however much monopoly and high prices may lead temporarily to greater profits. The failure of capitalists to understand that monopoly, limitation of production,

---

[2] This criticism of American private capitalism was first stated in effective fashion by Ripley in his *Main Street and Wall Street*, published in 1926, and was more elaborately documented in the monumental books of A. A. Berle and Gardiner Means on *The Modern Corporation and Private Property*, and James C. Bonbright and Gardiner Means on *The Holding Company*. Other important contributors to this line of criticism have been John T. Flynn, I. M. Wormser, Max Lowenthal and P. M. O'Leary.

scarcity, and high prices undermine the capitalist system in the long run is probably attributable, as the great German economic historian Werner Sombart claims, to the "ledger psychosis" discussed earlier.

This criticism of capitalism gained headway under the lead of the early so-called "trust busters," the supporters of the Sherman Act of 1890. Theodore Roosevelt was in sympathy with this point of view, and it was vigorously supported by Senator Robert M. LaFollette, Sr. and the Republican Progressives following the Roosevelt era.[3]

**Wastes in production and distribution.** Another line of criticism of American private capitalism is based on the allegation that monopoly, the scarcity economy, and inefficient management, the latter stemming in part from the indifference of finance capitalism to the efficient operation of business, have produced production wastes that have prevented us from reaching our potential technological efficiency. As a rule, we have in peacetime operated at about 50 per cent efficiency, as our production record during the second world war shows. This inefficient attitude toward production has held back the introduction of the most efficient known machinery, thus further retarding potential productive capacity. The restriction of output by labor plays its part in this waste of production potential, but even the Hoover Committee of capitalistically-inclined engineers, away back in 1921, admitted that the wastes attributable to management were twice as great as those traceable to labor practices. Many have held that we produce too much, in any event, and have called attention to the fact that overproduction is often regarded as a main cause of depressions. The chief responsibility here, however, is underconsumption. The mass of Americans have never had the material necessities and conveniences, clothing, or housing that they need. We have never even begun to produce enough to give Americans a high standard of living.

Moreover, the wastes in our economy have not been entirely limited to production. Those in distribution have been, perhaps, even worse; these have been due to ever-increasing overhead costs, including advertising. Before 1914, it cost less than a dollar to get a dollar's worth of food or goods from the farm or factory to the consumer; by 1935, it cost $2.00.[4]

**Inadequate mass purchasing power.** We have already called attention to the fact that a major weakness of capitalism has been the inequitable distribution of national income, with the result that the very

---

3 The case against monopoly has been revived and most effectively expounded in more recent times by Thurmond Arnold in such books as *The Bottlenecks of Business* and *Democracy and Free Enterprise.*

4 A considerable number of important economists and industrial engineers have exposed the wastes of productive power in our economy, but Stuart Chase, and the abler and more restrained technocratic authors, such as Harold Loeb, have produced the most important critical literature in this field, the classic work being Chase's pioneer treatise, *The Tragedy of Waste;* his later *Rich Land, Poor Land* was devoted mainly to the waste of natural resources and inefficient agriculture. An eminent industrial engineer, Walter Rautenstrauch, has written the best book on the wastes of distribution, *Who Gets the Money?*

rich have much more than they can spend for food, goods, and housing, while the very poor cannot get enough to buy the sheer necessities of life. We have quoted many statistics on this point, but no figures are more conclusive than the income figures for 1928–1929,[5] when the richest 0.1 per cent of the families received as much of the total national income as the bottom 42 per cent. Entirely irrespective of moral or humanitarian considerations, this situation is fatal to any healthy capitalism. The underpaid or unemployed masses simply cannot buy enough food and goods to keep the economy healthy or prosperous. The value of goods produced increased by 10 billion dollars between 1923 and 1929, but mass purchasing power increased by only 600 million dollars. Ten billion dollars worth of goods are not sold for 600 million dollars. Inadequate mass purchasing power means glutted inventories, unemployment, and depressions. Had the 70 per cent of American families with an income of less than $2,500 each had their income raised to $2,500 each, an entirely practicable matter under a reasonable distribution of the national income, there can be little doubt that they would have been able to purchase enough additional food, goods, and housing to have averted the depression of 1929. A similar adjustment today would go a long way toward avoiding the coming depression. There seems to be no possibility of perpetuating private capitalism unless the system can assure steady employment at high wages, and labor in return assumes the responsibility for turning out a greater volume of goods.[6]

**Failure of capitalism to reinvest enough profits in plant and business expansion.** A highly popular critical approach to private capitalism in recent years is one that claims that a fundamental tenet of private capitalism is not being carried out in practice. One of the basic assumptions of capitalism, as we have seen, is that enough of the profits obtained from business will be reinvested—"ploughed back"—into the business to assure needed plant expansion and increased production and employment. It was assumed that this would assure a dynamic and expanding capitalism and would take up any slack in employment. The school of criticism that lays stress mainly upon this particular alleged weakness of capitalism insists that business has not ploughed back enough profits into plant expansion to provide the needed employment and mass purchasing power, that too much money has been either saved or absorbed in riotous living by the rich.

This line of attack on traditional private capitalism has been pur-

---

[5] Although later figures are available and have on occasion been used in this chapter, those of 1923–1929 have been chosen because they are from the period of our past most resembling in nature the decade to come.

[6] The most important treatises on the inequitable distribution of national wealth and income and its effects in the way of reducing mass purchasing-power and undermining prosperity have been the various Brookings Institution studies, notably that of Maurice Leven, H. G. Moulton, and C. A. Warburton on *America's Capacity to Consume,* and the important work of R. R. Doane on *The Measurement of American Wealth.*

sued most effectively by the distinguished English economist, John Maynard Keynes, in books which suffocated much clear and logical reasoning in reams of complicated and largely irrelevant statistics and obscure equations. The most famous of Keynes' books was *The General Theory of Employment, Interest and Money.* His ideas gained great popularity and he is rather generally regarded as the most influential English economist since Adam Smith and Ricardo. Keynesian economics have been most enthusiastically expounded in the United States by Professor Alvin H. Hansen of Harvard University. They were transferred from statistical obfuscation to a clear blueprint of policy and program by another eminent English economist, Sir William Beveridge, in his *Full Employment in a Free Society.*

**A predatory capitalism versus an expanding technology.** Many European and American economists have stressed the acquisitive nature of capitalism, but a very influential American economist, Thorstein Veblen, went even further and maintained that capitalism is basically predatory. He traced the origins of the capitalist businessman back to the buccaneers of the Elizabethan era, if not to the medieval robber barons. Veblen contended that there is an inevitable and insoluble conflict between the capitalist, who prefers profits based on scarcity to abundance founded on technological efficiency, and the technician and industrial engineer, who are primarily concerned with improving and expanding the industrial equipment—hence, that capitalism opposes efficiency and progress. In his later works, Veblen also laid much stress on absentee ownership and the separation of ownership from management and control as a main stimulus to predatory activities on the part of capitalists in twentieth-century America. Veblen thus substituted for the Marxian thesis of an inevitable and eternal class struggle between employer and laborer the notion of a somewhat comparable conflict of interests between the profit-seeking capitalist and the efficiency-seeking technician and industrial engineer. This made his books the inspiration of the most extreme version of this line of reasoning, what has come to be known as technocracy.[7]

**The Marxian critique of capitalism.** The most important attack on capitalism by those who hold that capitalism is inherently doomed, whatever reforms are undertaken, is that made by Marxian Socialism. These Socialists hold that capitalism is fatally weakened by inherent and internal contradictions of doctrine and practice, and that there is an eternal class struggle between the capitalist employers and the laboring proletariat which can never be solved under capitalism. It can only be overcome by a proletarian revolution which will put a working-class state in charge of the production and distribution of wealth. Hence, the Marxian Socialists reject any possibility of reforming capitalism by legislation.

---

7 Veblen's most important books for this type of criticism were his *Theory of the Leisure Class, The Theory of Business Enterprise, The Engineers and the Price System,* and *Absentee Ownership.*

**Fabian Socialism.** Less extreme are the Fabian or Revisionist Socialists, whose ideology governs the British Labour party today. These Socialists reject some Marxian dogmas, especially the Marxian objection to social-reform legislation. They believe in getting as much alleviation of social and economic ills as is possible rather than waiting passively for the inevitable economic revolution. But their final goal of a working-class state is essentially the same as that of the Marxians.

## Plans for Rehabilitating, Reforming, and Stabilizing Capitalism

**Moderate reform plans designed to eliminate the abuses of private capitalism.** The proposals for improving capitalism most acceptable to Americans are those which, envisaging the continuation of a basically capitalistic form of American economic life, seek only to remove the more flagrant abuses of capitalism and assure its effective operation. They desire to remove the defects that have been set forth by the various critical schools of thought whose notions we have just reviewed.

**Curbing finance capitalism.** Those who find in the devices of finance capitalism the main defect of capitalism today recommend measures all the way from protective legislation designed to eliminate the main abuses to outright abolition of non-owning management and its financial devices. A beginning along the lines of protective legislation occurred in the New Deal acts covering security and exchange operations and outlawing holding companies in the electric utility field. In England, most predatory practices of finance capitalism have long been unlawful.

**Enforcing laws against monopoly.** We already have laws designed to curb monopolistic abuses, prevent price-fixing, and reduce the possibility of maintaining a scarcity economy. But it is difficult to enforce them in the face of powerful vested economic interests, pliant politicians, and the devious legal skill of highly-paid corporation lawyers. Thurmond Arnold, as Assistant Attorney-General in New Deal days, made the most vigorous effort to enforce the anti-trust laws, only to give up the attempt as hopeless, even though executed under the auspices of an administration formally favorable to such an enterprise. It would certainly be possible, however, to enact adequate legislation and enforce it without impairing either the fabric or theory of capitalism. Failure to do so will surely further endanger the capitalist system.

**Curbing waste and inefficiency.** The best means of forcing capitalism to avoid unnecessary waste is that adopted by Sweden, namely, to set up some public yardstick by which to measure the efficiency of private capitalism and force it to conform under penalty of being replaced by public capitalism or a co-operative arrangement. We made a faint step in that direction in the Tennessee Valley Authority. There is every reason to keep private capitalism in existence so long as it operates efficiently, but there is no reason why it should not be forced to operate as efficiently as the given state of technology will permit. It is well to bear in mind, however, that curbing waste involves workers as well as owners; neither must be permitted to limit output. The restrictions on output maintained by some unions, especially in the building trades, is as flagrant as any wasteful device of capitalist employers.

**Assuring mass purchasing power.** Various forms of legislation can encourage capitalism to provide adequate mass purchasing power; minimum-wage laws are one of the most direct. Unemployment insurance, Social Security legislation, public-works projects, and the like are other powerful aids in such a program. As a last resort, excessive profits can be taken over by taxation and returned to the masses, either in expanded employment opportunities or in welfare projects.

The solution of the defects stressed by Keynes and his school is much the same as that needed to deal with inadequate mass purchasing power. The proposal of the Keynesians is that the state take over through taxation excess profits which are not ploughed back into industrial expansion and spend this new revenue in public-works and service-industry projects that will supply the needed employment and mass purchasing power. This will entail a certain amount of state capitalism, and the great Keynesian blueprint, the Beveridge Plan, envisages a rather complete program of state capitalism in which the government will plan and control much of the economy and will handle the solution of conflicts between capital and labor.

**Technocracy and engineering managerialism.** While Veblen did not openly advocate such a program, the only solution for the impasse he portrayed in capitalism would be a technocracy in which the engineers handle the operation of economic affairs—a sort of engineering managerialism.

It is obvious that no reforms that could be carried out within the capitalistic framework would meet the criticisms of Socialism, either Marxian or Fabian, though the latter will accept ameliorative social legislation pending the social revolution.

## Great Economic Systems of Today and Tomorrow

**Reformed and chastened private capitalism.** There are many who believe, perhaps rightly, that private capitalism can survive and be made to work if its main abuses are eliminated by wise remedial legislation, including such measures as drastic minimum-wage laws, comprehensive social insurance programs, incentives to workers, further development of the science of industrial relations to improve employer-labor relations, and the enforcement of anti-trust laws to insure

competition and prevent price-fixing. Such legislation, promptly enacted, might give capitalism a long lease on life but the resistance to
needed social legislation is so great that it threatens to bring on a
crisis from which we can be extricated only by state capitalism or state
socialism.

**State capitalism.** All interference of the government with business
constitutes some degree of state capitalism, but any thoroughgoing
form of state capitalism means complete control of economic affairs
by the government, though it rarely involves any extensive government ownership or operation of business enterprises. State capitalism
in any extreme form usually comes into being when private capitalism
is breaking down and the government has to take over control to avert
chaos or a socialist revolution. About as thorough a form of state
capitalism as is compatible with civil liberties is that embodied in the
Beveridge Plan, according to which the state would plan and direct
the production and distribution of wealth and the chief financial operations. The most extreme form of state capitalism was found in
Italian Fascism and German National Socialism and still lingers in
Spanish Falangism. Here, not only economic but civil liberty is for-
feited, and the state assumes the right to control all phases of life in
a tight totalitarian régime.

Though state control may be complete in state capitalism, the latter
should not be confused with state socialism, which is the earlier stage
of Marxian Socialism in operation. In state capitalism, the government intervention rarely goes beyond state control and direction of
economic life; in state socialism the government not only controls but
also owns the economy. The most important distinction, however,
lies in the motives and goals of the two systems. State capitalism is
devoted to patching up and preserving capitalism and preventing a
socialist revolution. State socialism has as its primary purpose the
uprooting of capitalism, the execution of an economic revolution, and
the establishment of permanent government ownership of the means
of producing and distributing wealth under a working-class state. It
may be noted that everywhere in the world today, outside socialist
states, the trend seems to lie in the direction of moderate or extreme
state capitalism.

**Co-operation and co-operatives.** Many sociologists and economists
believe that a co-operative commonwealth offers the main hope of
combining economic and civil liberty with the complete economic efficiency our advanced technology makes possible. Under a co-operative system, there is every incentive to produce as efficiently as possible, since the total product or income goes to the members of the
co-operatives. There is no possibility of great concentration of economic power, since each member has only one vote, whatever the
relative extent of his investment. There can be no separation of
ownership and control, for the co-operatives hire their own management and can dismiss the managers whenever they prove dishonest or

inefficient.    The advantages of political democracy are assured because the methods of operating co-operatives are based on economic democracy.

Co-operative enterprise can operate in all needed phases of economic life: production, marketing, distribution and consumer activities, credit, and all kinds of service operations.    Co-operatives have been tried out in all these fields and have functioned very efficiently.    There is a large amount of co-operative business in England, the Scandinavian countries, Finland, and Switzerland.    While successful so far as ex-

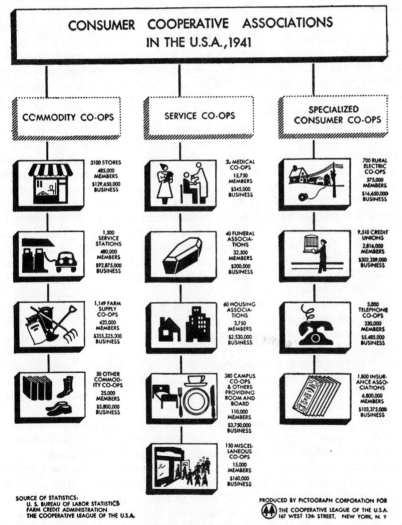

CONSUMER COOPERATIVE ASSOCIATIONS
IN THE U.S.A., 1941

COMMODITY CO-OPS | SERVICE CO-OPS | SPECIALIZED CONSUMER CO-OPS

3100 STORES
485,000 MEMBERS
$129,650,000 BUSINESS

3, MEDICAL CO-OPS
15,750 MEMBERS
$345,000 BUSINESS

700 RURAL ELECTRIC CO-OPS
575,000 MEMBERS
$16,650,000 BUSINESS

1,500 SERVICE STATIONS
480,000 MEMBERS
$92,875,000 BUSINESS

40 FUNERAL ASSOCIATIONS
32,500 MEMBERS
$200,000 BUSINESS

9,510 CREDIT UNIONS
2,816,000 MEMBERS
$302,339,000 BUSINESS

1,149 FARM SUPPLY CO-OPS
420,000 MEMBERS
$355,325,000 BUSINESS

60 HOUSING ASSOCIATIONS
3,750 MEMBERS
$2,530,000 BUSINESS

5,000 TELEPHONE CO-OPS
330,000 MEMBERS
$5,485,000 BUSINESS

50 OTHER COMMODITY CO-OPS
25,000 MEMBERS
$5,800,000 BUSINESS

380 CAMPUS CO-OPS & OTHERS PROVIDING ROOM AND BOARD
110,000 MEMBERS
$3,750,000 BUSINESS

1,800 INSURANCE ASSOCIATIONS
6,800,000 MEMBERS
$103,375,000 BUSINESS

150 MISCELLANEOUS CO-OPS
15,000 MEMBERS
$160,000 BUSINESS

SOURCE OF STATISTICS:
    U. S. BUREAU OF LABOR STATISTICS
    FARM CREDIT ADMINISTRATION
    THE COOPERATIVE LEAGUE OF THE U.S.A.

PRODUCED BY PICTOGRAPH CORPORATION FOR
THE COOPERATIVE LEAGUE OF THE U.S.A.
167 WEST 12th STREET,  NEW YORK, N. Y

This chart shows the development and diversification of consumer co-operative enterprises in the United States on the eve of the second world war.

perimented with here, it has as yet made little headway in the United States.

**The mixed system or middle way in Sweden.** Many observers believe that Sweden has hit upon the best method of combining efficiency with democracy and liberty in the economic field. Sweden combines private capitalism, state capitalism, and co-operation. The Swedes have the sensible conviction that private capitalism should be allowed to continue wherever its operates well. But they do not rely upon capitalist propaganda to tell them whether it is operating successfully or not; rather, they test its results against those of state capitalism and co-operation. If private capitalism falls down badly compared with the achievements of either of these, then it is supplanted by one or the other. The Swedes have found that state capitalism works best in regard to state lands and forests, mining, public utilities, and the like, while the co-operatives seem to be most satisfactory in dealing with consumer needs and housing. All three economic systems are thus operated in a society in which democracy and liberty prevail to a greater degree than in either the United States or Great Britain.

**Soviet state socialism.** Soviet Russia has abandoned capitalism entirely and has gone over to a state socialistic economy and society. The state owns virtually everything except such portable personal property as tools and clothing. Little or no private economic enterprise is allowed to exist. Owing in part to fear of counter-revolution and in part to fear of war or to actual war and invasion, the Soviet system has developed into a harsh totalitarianism in which liberty is crushed out as thoroughly as in any Fascist state. But the Russians give some lip-service to democracy and liberty, promising to introduce them when internal conditions and foreign relations will permit this to be done safely. Whether and when these promises will be carried out, only time will tell.

There is as yet no "Communism" in Russia. Communism is the socialist heaven on earth—a propertyless and classless society, operated as a co-operative commonwealth in which everybody loves his neighbor more than himself and there is no need for police. Prosperity, security, and liberty are the birthright of all. One who is familiar with the harsh totalitarianism of Soviet Russia today can well realize how far the Russians are from any true Communism. If they achieve it in two centuries they will be very fortunate.

**British Socialism.** This is less extreme than Russian Marxism, partly because England has had a long heritage of civil liberty and partly because English economic conditions have not been as critical as those in Russia. Further, the English socialists in the Labour Government favor the gradual legislative achievement of a socialist society over revolutionary violence. But all this should not deceive any Anglophile Americans into imagining that the British socialists are any less devoted to the ideal of a working-class state than are the Rus-

sian Marxians.  The British Labour Government has already nationalized the Bank of England, all cable and wireless communication
agencies, the coal industry, the transportation system (except for shipping), the electrical utility industry, the gas industry, and housing construction.  It has proposed a program to nationalize the heavy
industries—iron and steel.  In addition, it has set up a "cradle-to-
grave" social insurance program, and a free and complete national
health program, which gives medical, dental, and optical care to all
Englishmen who apply for it and pays for such care out of general
taxation.

## Summary

The economic system under which we live, capitalism, came into
being after 1500.  Its chief characteristics are private property, individual enterprise, a free market, the selling of goods for profit, a
money economy, and the unlimited acquisition of wealth.

The Industrial Revolution was responsible for the rapid development of capitalism.  The magnitude of the typical commercial and
industrial enterprises under capitalism and the increased cost of
factories and machines required huge amounts of capital which generally could not be supplied by individuals.  Partnerships, joint-stock
companies, and corporations therefore arose to undertake business
ventures.  As the latter became more elaborate and complex, trusts
and holding companies appeared.  The rise of trusts and holding
companies brought into prominence the rôle of investment bankers
and financiers.  After the Civil War, industrial capitalism tended to
give way to monopoly capitalism, which in turn was superseded after
1900 by finance capitalism, the last and perhaps most disastrous form
capitalism has taken.

Modern financial institutions arose in response to the demand of
industry for capital funds and commercial loans.  There are four
types of modern banks: commercial banks, savings banks, trust companies, and investment banks.  The investment banks have become
the dominant force in finance capitalism.

Under finance capitalism, the ownership, control, and management
of industry are usually separated.  The ownership of great commercial
and industrial enterprises is spread among hundreds or thousands of
stockholders; control passes into the hands of a few insiders who
dominate the boards of directors and officers and rule the companies.
Usually, the financiers who help to launch the company's stock issues
obtain seats on the board of directors, and thus capture a strategic
position.  Day-by-day management of industries is delegated to hired
experts.  The industries themselves are operated mainly in the
interest of the few insiders, often to the detriment and loss of the
investors.

Next to the chicanery and mismanagement of corporate business by officers and directors who own but a small fraction of the securities of corporations, the most serious weakness of the capitalist system is its failure to provide the great mass of people with incomes sufficient to purchase the goods and services our factories are capable of producing in such great abundance. This lack of mass purchasing power is a major cause of the depressions which periodically rend the structure of capitalistic society.

The relations between employers and employees since the rise of the factory system have been marked by increasing strife. Labor unions were organized to give workers bargaining power more nearly equal to that of employers. After many years, unions have been recognized as legal and desirable by our government and the courts. Nevertheless, employers have fought them bitterly, often resorting to violence in their attempts to break up unions and combat strikes.

Unemployment, although temporarily reduced to a minimum by abnormal postwar policies and economic activities, represents one of the most serious economic problems in modern society. Perhaps the most fundamental cause of unemployment is the lack of enough mass purchasing power to keep the factories running and the workers employed. More recently, unemployment has arisen as the result of the introduction of automatic machinery, which displaces thousands of workers in production. Another factor in unemployment is the fact that men over forty are not desired in factories because employers hold the mistaken idea that younger men are always more efficient.

Unemployment is so important a problem in modern industrialism that it threatens the very future of capitalism and private enterprise. If capitalism does not "feed its sheep," then the government must provide relief through employment on public works or in vast armament booms, which generally lead to war. If this development is allowed to go far enough, it will mean a gradual triumph of state capitalism; private business will then take a secondary position in our economy.

The plans offered to overcome the weaknesses of capitalism range all the way from reform legislation aimed at eliminating the more obvious defects of capitalism to Socialism, which would eliminate capitalism and private business entirely. Extreme state capitalism might be almost as ruinous to private business. More moderate plans that seem compatible with the American spirit of democracy and liberty are a co-operative commonwealth and the Swedish middle-way program, which sagaciously combines private capitalism, state capitalism, and co-operation.

## Selected References

Baker, R. J. (Ed.), *Report of the Inquiry on Coöperative Enterprise in Europe, 1937,* Government Printing Office, 1937.

————————, *American Coöperatives*, Vanguard, 1939. These two books give the best account of the state of prewar co-operative activity in Europe and America.

Beard, Miriam, *A History of the Business Man*, Macmillan, 1938. An entrancing story of the motives and methods of the masters of business from ancient times to the present day.

Beveridge, Sir William, *Full Employment in a Free Society*, Macmillan, 1945. A landmark in economic literature, which reduced Keynesian economics to a blueprint for practical procedure.

* Blair, John M., *The Seeds of Destruction*, Covici, Friede, 1938. The ablest critique of capitalism from the economic point of view. Clear and factual.

* Cochran, T. C., and Miller, William, *The Age of Enterprise*, Macmillan, 1943. The best book on the rise, nature, and exploits of American finance capitalism. A brilliant performance.

Cole, Margaret, and Smith, Charles (Eds.), *Democratic Sweden*, Greystone Press, 1939. Symposium by experts on most phases of Swedish economic and social life. Best single volume of Sweden's middle-way system.

Daugherty, Carroll, *Labor Problems in American Industry*, Houghton Mifflin, 1941. A standard and enlightened treatment of American labor problems.

* Davis, Jerome, *Capitalism and Its Culture*, Farrar & Rinehart, 1935. A searching account of capitalist civilization from the sociological point of view.

Doane, R. R., *The Anatomy of American Wealth*, Harper, 1940. Able analysis of American national wealth and the jeopardy in which it may have been placed by war, debt, speculation, and governmental extravagance.

Flynn, J. T., *Graft in Business*, Vanguard, 1931. The most devastating picture of graft and incompetence in business under the dominion of finance capitalism.

Gill, Corrington, *Wasted Manpower*, Norton, 1939. The best introduction to the problem of unemployment under capitalism.

Gras, N. S. B., *Business and Capitalism*, Crofts, 1939. An able eulogy of finance capitalism by a leading economic historian, formerly of liberal leanings.

Hacker, L. M., *The Triumph of American Capitalism*, Simon and Schuster, 1940. The best history of American capitalism to 1900.

Hansen, A. H., *Economic Policy and Full Employment*, Whittlesey House, 1947. A clear statement of Keynesian-Beveridge economics by the leading American disciple of Keynes.

Hutchinson, Keith, *The Decline and Fall of British Capitalism*, Scribner, 1950. Able study of the retreat of British capitalism before the growth of the labor movement and socialism.

Laski, H. J., *Where Do We Go From Here?*, Viking, 1940. Good statement of the economic and political philosophy of the British Labour Party.

Lieberman, Elias, *Unions before the Bar*, Harper, 1950. Indispensable book on evolution of legal rights of labor, as illustrated by chief historic labor trials and cases.

Loeb, Harold, *Life in a Technocracy*, Viking, 1933. Best introduction to the nature of a technocratic society and economy.

* Loucks, W. N., and Hoot, J. W., *Comparative Economic Systems*, Harper, 1948. The best comparative study of capitalism, Fascism, and Communism.

McDonald, Lois, *Labor Problems and the American Scene*, Harper, 1938. An admirable treatment of the problems of capital and labor down to the eve of the second world war.

Mills, C. W., and Schneider, Helen, *The New Men of Power: America's Labor Leaders*, Harcourt, Brace, 1948. A sympathetic study of the personalities, policies, and tactics of the outstanding American labor leaders of our day.

* Mitchell, Broadus, *Depression Decade*, Rinehart, 1947. Best study of the causes and course of the depression of 1929 to 1941.

Moulton, H. G., *Controlling Factors in Economic Development*, Brookings Institution, 1949. Argument for controlled capitalism as the desirable economic system of the future. Lays special stress upon saner distribution of income and greater mass purchasing power if capitalism is to survive.

* O'Leary, P. M., *Corporate Enterprise in Modern Economic Life*, Harper, 1933. A competent introduction to the rôle of the corporation in contemporary American economic enterprise under finance capitalism.

Rauch, Basil, *The History of the New Deal, 1933-1938*, Creative Age, 1944. The best account of the New Deal and moderate reform measures down to the period of interventionism and the war program after 1938.

Roberts, Stephen H., *The House that Hitler Built*, Harper, 1938. Probably the best single volume on Nazi Germany and its leaders, by an Australian professor.

Schneider, H. W., *The Fascist Government of Italy*, D. Van Nostrand, 1936. The best introductory treatment of Fascist Italy, by the leading American authority.

Snyder, Carl, *Capitalism the Creator*, Macmillan, 1940. An elaborate statistical effort to vindicate capitalism and the profit system as the bulwarks of business prosperity. Snyder and Gras should be read in connection with Blair, Flynn, and Davis.

Veblen, Thorstein, *The Engineers and the Price System*, Viking, 1921. Best statement of Veblen's thesis of the conflict between technology and the profit system of capitalism.

* Warbasse, J. P., *The Coöperative Way*, Barnes & Noble, 1946. Best brief introduction to the co-operative economic and social program in the postwar period.

Webb, Sidney and Beatrice, *The Decay of Capitalist Civilization*, Harcourt, Brace, 1923. The ablest English critique of capitalism.

——————, *Soviet Communism*, 2 vols., Longmans, Green, 1941. Far and away the best book in English on Soviet Russia before the second world war.

Wecter, Dixon, *The Age of the Great Depression, 1929–1941*, Macmillan, 1948. Best single volume on the impact of the depression and New Deal on American economic and social life.

Williams, Francis, *Socialist Britain: Its Background, Its Present, and an Estimate of Its Future*, Viking, 1949. The best book on the policies and achievement of the Labour Government in Britain. A sympathetic treatment.

# CHAPTER XV

# The Problem of Private Property

## What We Mean by Private Property

**Basic concepts of property: ownership and possession.** The average person regards ownership and possession as the same thing. The terms, however, have different legal meanings. *Ownership* means that a person has legal rights to the object; *possession* means that not only does he have legal rights, but the object is within his keeping, to do with as he pleases. Stated otherwise, possession is ownership plus a direct physical relationship, while ownership is only the legal right to possess.

**Types of property.** Tangible property consists of visible items, such as livestock, buildings, tools, land, and jewelry. Intangible property is ownership of rights that are not physical entities like land or automobiles but are nevertheless of true value. For example, the right to a name, the copyright on a book, or a patent on an invention are intangible but valuable possessions. Such intangible property as a copyright or a patent is an important source of income; other intangible property is valuable mainly because it gives personal satisfaction or prestige to the owner.

Property may also be divided into real and personal. Real property consists chiefly of immovable objects, such as land and buildings, while personal property consists of goods and money, which can be moved wherever the owner wants to go. There is also private and group property. Private property is owned outright by individuals. Group property is property owned in common by the group, such as a school, a church building, a public power plant, or a city street.

**Legal definitions and protection of property.** Elaborate legal codes have arisen to define and protect property rights; in fact, many persons think that property is a product of law. Property laws, however, have grown out of the usages and practices surrounding property. They serve as a means of sanctioning and protecting the use of property, according to the social customs of the time.

The development of the institution of property and its legal safeguards has been an important element in man's social life. Egyptian laws very early defined and protected property rights, especially the extensive property claims of the patriarchal Pharaohs.   In the ancient code of Hammurabi, drawn up about 1700 b.c., there was extensive legal regulation of various kinds of property and special protection of contracts.   The Greeks and Romans had elaborate codes which governed the acquisition and disposal of property.   Throughout medieval times, feudal law, the mercantile codes, and religious precepts regulated the possession of property.

The property law of modern times is based upon both traditional property concepts and the social and political ideas of present-day society, and covers every phase of the possession, ownership and transmission of property.   Modern property law is very thorough and complex because of the high esteem which has been placed on property following the rise of capitalism and great fortunes and because of the highly complicated nature of contemporary property.   John Locke, the most famous of the early apologists for bourgeois society, held that the main purpose of government and law is to protect property. Modern property law has been developed in accordance with Locke's attitude.

## The Property Complex

**Why we desire property.**   There seems to be no convincing reason to believe, as some psychologists have maintained, that the desire to possess property is an instinct.   Rather, it is an outcome or by-product of the basic drives of self-preservation, self-perpetuation, and self-expression discussed in Chapter V.   Of these, the last is especially important in regard to property.

**Culture determines property values.**   The desire for property is complicated in origin, depending on human vanity, group approval and the social values present in the culture of the time.   Customs determine the values and ratings given to various forms of property. The individual, striving to secure the attention of his fellows, wants to possess those objects that the group most esteems.

Certain possessions may be highly desirable in one group and useless to another.   The Eskimo will trade fine furs, valuable to the white man, for trinkets or a bright tin pan, which are of slight worth to the trader.   Possession of the trinkets gratifies the vanity of the Eskimo and improves his status within his group, which places high value on trinkets and little on furs.

The culture of a group controls property values in another way. Articles valuable at one stage of social development may become valueless in another.   The early settlers in America placed high value on spinning wheels and hand looms.   As modern inventions replaced the old methods of spinning and weaving, spinning wheels and looms lost their value, until today we prize them, if at all, only as antiques and museum pieces.

**Psychological factors in the property complex.** The possession of property on which most members of any group place a high value gratifies, as we have noted, the vanity of the individual. Vanity, then, is an important element in the desire to accumulate possessions. In early historic society, the man who had accumulated large flocks or rich lands or could afford to keep a number of wives was esteemed by the group. Today, the woman who wears an expensive diamond ring values it not only for its worth in money, but also because other women will admire or envy it. The husband who gives his wife expensive jewelry also satisfies his vanity by proving to the group that he can afford such luxuries.

Often more property is accumulated than is actually needed, in order to give the owner a sense of power or superiority. Primitive hunters at times accumulated more food than they were able to eat and piled it up in front of their huts to impress less fortunate members of their group. The same tendency to accumulate for display is present among people today who flaunt their showy and expensive material possessions in a conspicuous manner.

**Religious influences on property.** Other elements have entered into the creation of property values at different times. The influence of religion is a good example. In primitive days, belief in magic was very strong. Certain personal possessions were thought to possess magic and to share in the owner's personality; no primitive man who held this belief wanted to steal or use things belonging to another, because the magic power in them might harm him. The dead were often buried with their personal possessions lest the latter harm any of the living who might later try to use them. In the Middle Ages, wealthy persons gave large sums of money to the Church, because they believed that such gifts would assure them a satisfactory existence in the world to come.

The influences of religion on property have been diversified and often contrasting or contradictory. Medieval Christianity encouraged the accumulation of wealth by legitimate means so that the wealthy could give freely to the Church. Protestantism, especially Calvinism, blessed the acquisition of wealth and regarded conspicuous success therein as special evidence of divine grace and approval. Powerful clergymen have blessed most of the great fortunes of our day. On the other hand, St. Francis and other medieval friars praised poverty and warned against the evil influence and contamination of property and riches.

There are innumerable illustrations of the way in which social and cultural factors influence property values and usages, but the main point is that the desire to possess property is complex, going far beyond the use of property for the satisfaction of basic human needs and changing with every alteration of the cultural values of the group.

## The Historical Evolution of Property Concepts and Practices

**Property in primitive times.** In primitive society, there was both group and private ownership of property. There was usually private or family ownership of tools and weapons, while the hunting and fishing grounds might be owned in common by the group. As human culture developed beyond the hunting and fishing stages and agriculture came to predominate, the amount of private property increased —probably because, after the hard work of clearing the ground, tilling the soil, and harvesting the grain, the individual desired to keep the products of his labor.

In primitive times, magic, utility, and convenience all encouraged the desire for privately-owned tools and livestock. Primitive peoples even recognized intangible property rights in personal names, songs, magic formulas, local legends, and ceremonial privileges. But, although private or family property increased, communal ownership of land did not disappear. Waste and forest land usually remained under group ownership.

**Development and protection of property rights in the ancient Near East.** As civilization progressed, property rights were reduced to written laws. The ancient Near East was ruled by kings who often claimed ownership of all lands within their realm but gave it out to their followers in the form of gifts or leases. In this way, gift or leased land came to resemble private property, except that it could not be disposed of without permission of the king.

During the more than 4,000 years of Egyptian civilization, there were many changes in property ideas and practices. Before the rise of strong kings in Egypt, the primitive pattern of group ownership of land and private ownership of flocks and tools prevailed. As the kings grew more powerful they took over the land and gave it out through leases to nobles, who could dispose of it only with the permission of the Pharaoh. Later on, the priesthood acquired possession of vast areas of the best land. The priests became the largest slave owners in Egypt, and were usually able to resist royal interference.

The civilization of Babylonia and Assyria took on a more commercial cast than that of Egypt. Here we find the first high development of the application of property laws to trade rights and practices, and to commercial papers and credit instruments. Deeds and other legal devices were provided to guarantee and protect landed property.

**The property system in Ancient Greece.** Homeric times in Greece represented a transition from primitive to historic culture during which there was a definite tendency toward the increase of private ownership of land. At this time, collective ownership of land often existed side by side with personal ownership. Large estates were surrounded by medium-sized farms and small plots.

In early Attica, a family system of land ownership predominated, but individual ownership was already making strong headway. By the time of Pericles (fifth century b.c.), private ownership of landed property was the rule, although such property was under the general control and supervision of the state. The state owned most of the mines and quarries, though they were frequently leased to private concerns. There was some private capitalism, but it bore little resemblance to that of modern times.

Sparta was, perhaps, the first outstanding totalitarian state. It was run under a system of military socialism, in which the state theoretically controlled all property, mainly landed estates, and distributed it equally among the free Spartan citizens. But this system was often upset in practice; inequality of landholding frequently existed and there were many rich landlords. Sparta is interesting as one of the first examples of thoroughgoing state control of property in political and legal theory, whatever the abuses in the actual operation of the system.

**Property in the Roman economy and law.** In early Rome, landed property was regarded as sacred, because Roman religious life at that time centered around agriculture. In the earliest days, the Romans followed the primitive custom of group ownership of land and private ownership of tools, weapons, and herds. In the days of the kings and the early Republic, private ownership had progressed to the point where each family possessed a little plot of ground, known as an *heredium* or homestead, usually a little less than two acres. When the Romans conquered Italy, some of the land was sold to individuals, some was rented or sold to the conquered population, and the rest was kept as public land, which the state rented or sold to Roman citizens for private cultivation.

The Roman conquest of the Mediterranean world brought the era of the small landholder to an end. Many small farmers were killed in the wars. Vast estates appeared and were cultivated mainly by slaves. The disappearance of small landholders was one of the leading causes of the decline of the Roman Republic.

Capitalism and monetary property developed much further in Rome than in Greece. Certain individuals, like tax collectors and public works officials, amassed large fortunes and exerted great power and influence. A considerable portion of the famous and voluminous Roman law was devoted to the elaboration of property rights, the protection of private property, and a statement of the extent to which the state could control property. The growth of large estates and the heavy taxes imposed by the Empire brought misery to the mass of Roman citizens. The cities were filled with poor people who flocked there from rural districts and lived on public donations. Crushing taxation gradually wiped out the business class in the cities, while in the rural areas, the former small land owners became virtually serfs, bound to the great estates. Few of the urban or rural masses could afford to own property.

**Landed property in the Middle Ages.** Medieval civilization, like that of early Rome, was based on agriculture. Feudalism dominated the landholding system. The only person who had actual possession of land was the lord, who held his property under a complicated system of "investiture." The land held by the feudal lord was known as a fief and could usually only be inherited by the eldest male heir in the family under the system known as primogeniture. The king or overlord exacted payment from the holder of the fief in the form of military service, money, or labor; and, if the fief-holder did not meet these obligations, he could be put off the land. The church owned vast estates under the feudal system, and bishops and abbots were often among the most powerful feudal lords.

The medieval agricultural system revolved around the manor, which might be regarded as the fief from an economic point of view. A part of the manor, the demesne, was cultivated for the lord by the serfs, who gave half their time to the lord. The lord received all its produce; the rest of the land was under communal cultivation. No serf could own land, but he had the customary right to cultivate certain strips and claim the produce as his own. A rare serf might own his own animals and tools, but group ownership of these essentials was the usual arrangement.

**The property patterns in medieval towns.** In the few medieval towns property was held chiefly by the master craftsmen and merchants. The shops and tools were usually owned by the masters; sometimes journeymen, who were skilled craftsmen, had their own tools; apprentices usually possessed no tools. In most towns, the town buildings, fortifications, and military equipment were owned by the municipalities rather than private individuals. The gildsmen also owned property in common, such as the gild hall. The most impressive example of communal control of property in medieval towns was the Hanseatic League, which maintained a merchant marine, trading stations, and an army and navy.

**Property concepts of the medieval Church.** The medieval Catholic Church exerted a deep influence on property conceptions and rights during the Middle Ages. The Church not only permitted the accumulation of large individual fortunes in property, but was itself far and away the greatest single holder of property in the medieval period. But it always maintained, in theory, that property is inferior to spiritual interests and never should assume such importance in the mind of the individual as to distort his sense of values or impede the workings of religion in his bosom. The Church particularly opposed, and sponsored laws to prevent, the accumulation of property in an unfair manner. It held that property should be accumulated and administered in the interest of the community. Those who had large fortunes should be grateful to God and therefore contribute generously to the Church.

**Transition to modern civilization alters property concepts.** The Middle Ages thus provided a partial return to a group-owned or group-controlled property system. Between the fifteenth and seventeenth centuries, medieval culture gradually gave way to modern civilization, as a result of the growth of town life, the increase of commerce, the expansion of wealth, the rise of the national states, and the break-up of feudalism. These changes encouraged the rise of individualism and made the private property system supreme. The feudal landlord was supplanted by the private landholder, who owned his property outright and was under no obligations to an overlord. Many monasteries were confiscated, and their holdings handed over to private owners. Serfs, once bound to the land under the feudal system, became wage workers on farms.

**Effects of Commercial Revolution on property.** The Commercial Revolution, which followed the expansion of Europe overseas, brought about the rise of capitalism, glorified private property, and marked the end of communal ownership. In countries like England and the Netherlands, which were most affected by the Commercial Revolution, the change to private ownership was most rapid. In some parts of Europe, especially in eastern and central Europe, the gild and manorial systems held on for centuries. In the early American settlements, much of the land was owned by great proprietors under royal grants. In the later colonial period, private ownership of small plots or farms became more usual; and, after the American Revolution, private landed property and individual farming enterprise were firmly established and elaborately protected by law.

Private ownership was fully extended to industry and commerce after the Commercial Revolution. The gild system was replaced by the putting-out system, operated by private capitalists. The expansion of commerce created a need for more capital, and businessmen pooled their resources and divided ownership through joint-stock companies in order to engage in large-scale activities. One of the most revolutionary changes in the history of property was the rise of capitalism and a money economy and the complete triumph of the freedom to use money and property for private profit. The growth of great fortunes brought about an increased esteem for property. Private property assumed so much importance that, by the latter part of the seventeenth century, it came to be considered one of the natural rights of man. John Locke, the most influential political philosopher of modern times, held that the chief function of government and law is to protect private property. Laws were passed to protect private property; fire insurance and maritime insurance arose to protect merchants against loss of ships and cargoes. Finally, both the Catholic and the Protestant church continued to give private property religious sanction. John Calvin regarded the successful accumulation of property a sure sign of the indwelling of the grace of God. This emphasis on, and sanction of, private property and personal profits created a new business incentive.

**Effects of the Industrial Revolution on property concepts.** The Industrial Revolution extended the scope and power of property. The factories were small at first and personally owned; but, as production methods improved, increasing amounts of raw materials became available, and larger factories and more machinery were needed. Joint-stock companies and corporations arose to meet the demand for more capital, and ownership of factories became separated from management. While much property was accumulated to buy up vast landed estates and otherwise to display wealth and meet the demands of vanity, the chief incentive for the acquisition of property at this period was to reinvest it in business in order to expand operations and make greater profits.

While the Industrial Revolution and the factory system brought large profits to the factory owners, the condition of factory laborers sometimes became worse than under medieval serfdom. Laborers no longer owned their tools, shops, or homes; they worked for their living, becoming wholly dependent on the wages paid by capitalists for the necessities of life.

**Reforms in landed property practices in modern times.** Modern times also brought about numerous changes in the ownership of land. The manorial system disappeared in England between 1400 and 1550 and was replaced for a considerable time by yeoman farming, that is, by farming on fairly small estates owned by country squires. But, when many merchants became rich as a result of the Commercial Revolution, they began to buy up land and to create vast estates worked by hired farm laborers. This system of great estates, at its height between 1760 and 1830, continued, with some slight reforms, down to the first world war, when some of the estates were broken up to produce more food.

In France, the reforms of the French Revolution and the Napoleonic period set up a system of small farms under private ownership, and this system spread to Italy and western Germany where, however, many large estates endured. In eastern Germany, in central and Balkan Europe, and in Tsarist Russia great estates under private ownership were the rule until 1918. They even persisted in eastern Germany and Hungary until 1945.

**Revolutionary changes in landed property in the twentieth century.** After the first world war, many of the great estates of central Europe were divided among peasant farmers on small farms. The most striking change was the abolition of all private landowning in Soviet Russia after the Revolution of 1917 and the gradual but complete substitution of state ownership of all Russian land. Fascist countries, like Italy and Germany, took over control of national agricultural policies and practices, but allowed private ownership of land to continue.

The second world war greatly increased the domain and influence of Soviet Russia and extended its system of state ownership of landed property into the very stronghold of previous peasant proprietorship— Balkan Europe and the Baltic states. Russian influence also permeated much of eastern Germany, which was put under formal Polish dominion. The long period of Anglo-American-French occupation of western Germany after 1945 introduced state control of agriculture there under alien domination. The Labour Government in England assumed complete control over all British land in July, 1948, though it did not take over complete formal ownership, as in Soviet Russia. The Government announced its intention of breaking up the great estates and devoting all arable land to the production of crops. Unrestricted private ownership of land thus disappeared in England.

These developments since 1918, and especially since 1939, have been described by Henry Beston as marking "the end of the peasant civilization of Europe." At least, we can say that the developments since 1918 have constituted an enormous restriction of the private ownership of land in Europe and may indicate its eventual extinction before the rapid advance of economic collectivism.

**Private land tenure and tenancy in the United States.** In the United States, private ownership of land has endured as a system with few changes in legal principles since Revolutionary days. But there has been a marked increase in tenant farming, especially after the depression in farming which set in following the first world war. In 1890, only 28 per cent of all farm occupants were tenants, but by 1940 about 39 per cent were tenants, even after all the New Deal aid to farmers. A large number of farmers were forced to mortgage their farms and many of these mortgages were foreclosed. The great demand for food for soldiers and munition workers during the second world war and for the relief of Europe after the war brought temporary good times for farmers in the United States and checked for the moment the growth of farm tenancy. In 1945, only 32 per cent of farm occupants were listed as tenants. Yet, because there have been no sweeping reforms in American farming methods, there seems every prospect that hard times will return when the abnormal demand for American farm products ceases.

**Legal extensions and abuses of the property concept.** Though the growth of corporations and finance capitalism has transformed the ideas and control of property, the legal concept of property has been extended to unreasonable lengths in order to protect corporations and big business.

The Fourteenth Amendment to the Constitution of the United States, originally adopted to protect the civil rights of Negroes, directs that no state shall deprive any person of life, liberty, or property "without due process of law." In the 1880's, corporation lawyers induced the Supreme Court to regard corporations as legal persons entitled to protection under the Fourteenth Amendment. The amendment has been exploited to extend the concept of property to protect almost every type of vested economic interests. Lawyers have been able to induce the courts to declare unconstitutional many laws which attacked powerful corporate interests or were opposed by the latter. On many occasions, the Supreme Court has sustained the opinions of the lower courts. Such policies and practices as the right to maintain whatever working conditions businessmen saw fit to impose upon their employees, the right to exclude union labor, the right to employ child labor, and the right of business to evade government control of its practices, have been upheld by the Supreme Court as property rights, protected by the Fourteenth Amendment.

One of the most interesting phases of the legalistic battle to protect property rights is this enormous extension of the concept of property. Any interest or practice that the wealthy and powerful wished the courts to protect was called "property." As a famous law professor has accurately observed, the courts did not really protect property, strictly regarded, but designated as property whatever they wished to protect. This policy has been a standing abuse of property concepts in our time and has helped to discredit property rights in the minds of many who would otherwise have supported all reasonable property claims. It has also delayed, perhaps fatally, social progress through reform legislation and helped to create that cultural lag today which threatens not only all property but civilization itself.

**Complex character of property and property claims today.** Property holding and claims have now become far more complex than they were in the days when property consisted mainly in direct ownership and use of lands, weapons, tools, and livestock. The twentieth-century types of property vary all the way from simple ownership of personal articles to complicated legal claims on monetary rewards. For example, there is property in payments made for personal service; in personal possessions necessary to health and comfort; in land and tools used by their owners; in copyright and patent rights owned by authors and inventors; in monopoly and holding-company profits; in urban ground rents; in royalties; and also in the profits of good fortune.

## Inroads on Private Property in the Twentieth Century

**Wars and resulting high taxes ravage property.** The officers and directors of great corporations, with their batteries of legal servants, have been mainly responsible for the great legal extension of the concept of property; through the devices of finance capitalism they have also, as we pointed out in the preceding chapter, deprived the owners of corporate securities of all control over the handling of their property.

But wars, which have been heartily supported, for the most part, by property owners and corporate executives alike, have done far more than anything else to destroy private property in recent years. Wars have destroyed hundreds of billions of dollars worth of property outright and have cost hundreds of billions more in taxes. It is probable that finance capitalism and wars have done more to date in the way of bringing about debt, high taxation, and state intervention than the outright challenge to private property in Russian State Socialism or Fascist interference with property rights.

**Most contemporary property a legal fiction in the face of debt.** Debt and the resulting taxation, both mainly a product of war, are the most overwhelming challenge to private property in the middle of the twentieth century. Except for Soviet Russia, which has wiped out most private property by other methods, there is hardly a country in the modern world, save perhaps Sweden, Denmark, and Switzerland, that would not be plunged into utter bankruptcy if compelled abruptly to pay off its debts.

The total public and private debt of the United States today, about 430 billion dollars, is far more than our formal national wealth. This can be broken down into our national debt of about 217 billions; state and local debts of around 16 billions; and a private debt of 197 billions, constituted mainly of corporate debt and mortgage obligations. On top of all this are the contingent liabilities of the Federal government, which amount to at least 300 billion dollars and would have to be met by any government making serious claims to solvency. In 1916, before we entered the first world war, our total public debt was only $1,225,000,000.

The British debt is far greater in proportion to population and resources than that of the United States, and other countries are still worse off; the national debt of France, for example, stood, in 1947, at the astronomical figure of 2,574,643,000,000 francs. These countries could pay off their debts only by following the drastic inflationary methods utilized by Germany in 1923–1924, which wiped out most of the property of the middle class. Such inflation destroys not only the value of all money property and bank deposits, but also that of all long-term investments, such as bonds, insurance, and annuities.

## The Inheritance of Property

**Inheritance practices in primitive society.** The problem of inheritance has not always been as important as in modern times. Primitive peoples paid less attention to the inheritance of private property, since most of the land was owned by the group or family. In tribes believing that personal possessions retained the magical powers of their owner, no survivor wanted to claim them; where inheritance was in favor, its practice depended a good deal upon the type of kinship rules which prevailed in the group. Sometimes, property went to the surviving brothers of the deceased, sometimes to his sons or to one of them, not necessarily the eldest.

**Inheritance in ancient times.** In ancient Egypt, nobles could transmit, with the consent of the Pharaoh, the lands and goods given to them on lease or as a gift by the Pharaoh. Tools and implements were handed down from father to son, but the right of inheritance of land was always limited by the power of the monarch. This was also true in Mesopotamia. In Greek society, kinship ties determined inheritance. A man's property went to his sons, and no legitimate son could be disinherited. If a dying man had no sons, he might adopt one and will him his property, if he agreed to marry an unmarried daughter of the family.

In early Rome, inheritance of property was controlled by family relationships. Both male and female children had equal rights according to Roman law; and a grandchild had the same inheritance rights as a child if his own father was dead. Since the early Roman farms were small, they were usually owned in common by the beneficiaries of the will. The claims of the family continued to be protected in later Roman times. In the year 9 A.D., a law was passed that prevented distant relatives from inheriting the complete estate of the deceased and resticted married couples without children in the amount of property which they could will to each other.

**Medieval inheritance: Primogeniture.** Under the feudal system, inheritance of property by the eldest son (primogeniture) was customary. By this device, the fief was kept intact. The serfs had no rights of transmission of property because they possessed no land and their tools were usually communally shared. Those who owned tools or other personal possessions handed them on through the family. The masters of the gilds usually transmitted their property to their wives and children, as did the journeymen.

**Inheritance practices of today.** In England and the United States, there is today wide freedom of inheritance, but even here there are some restrictions. The male usually has an advantage over the female in his claims to inherited property. If a man disinherits any or all of his legitimate children and gives his money to charity, legal action can be taken by the heirs. The court, in that case, may set aside or modify the will in favor of the legal heirs. When there is no legal heir, the general rule is that the closest relatives inherit the estate, subject to the conditions of the will, if there is one.

The legal freedom of private inheritance in England is today largely a fiction. England's tremendous industrial and commercial losses from the second world war have resulted in taxation so crushing that it is difficult for any Englishman to accumulate much property to bequeath; moreover, the inheritance taxes there are virtually confiscatory.  Inheritance taxes are also becoming ever higher in the United States; the Federal inheritance tax alone on large estates may amount to about 80 per cent, to which are added often drastic state inheritance taxes.

In most other countries there is less freedom of inheritance.  In countries still dominated by Roman law, such as France, Spain, Italy, and Latin American countries, the widow and children have a definite legal claim on the property of the husband or father under the so-called right of *legitim*.  In peasant countries, the land is often regarded as a family affair and is transmitted accordingly.

In totalitarian states, the rights of property inheritance, like other economic and political policies, are closely controlled by the state. At first, all inheritance rights were wiped out in Russia; later on, some slight freedom of inheritance was restored.  Since most private property has been taken over by the state, there is little to bequeath except personal possessions.  In the Fascist states of Germany and Italy, heavy inheritance taxes and confiscation of property extensively limited inheritance.  The enormous destruction of property in central Europe during and after the second world war has all but eliminated any property to be passed on, even in countries which maintain the legal fiction of freedom of inheritance.

**Merits and defects of the inheritance system.**  Those who approve of unlimited private inheritance argue that it provides a strong economic incentive to a man to accumulate wealth, and that it is the only way in which enough capital may be amassed to conduct modern business enterprises.  Another argument for the inheritance system is that it promotes great bequests to charitable organizations.

Others maintain that little or no property should be transmitted to the family of the deceased.  These persons claim that, through inheritance, great fortunes are passed on from one generation to another, thus perpetuating the unequal distribution of wealth.  The rich seek to acquire wealth for themselves, as well as their children, and hold on to their estates until their death, despite the high taxes to be levied on those who inherit what remains of their property.  There is already too much concentration of wealth among relatively few families, and more goods are produced than the masses, on low income, can afford to purchase.

Finally, it is contended that charitable bequests by the wealthy are insignificant.  After a careful study, Abraham Epstein concluded that "the vast bulk of the wealthy" make no contributions whatever to charity.  In the years before the second world war, only about one per cent of those filing income-tax returns in New York City contributed anything to either of the two main organizations in the city for the alleviation of the poverty-stricken.  Over 75 per cent of the contributions to charity in the United States come from those with incomes of less than $5,000 a year.  Certainly, charitable bequests are unimportant when compared with the evil economic effects of the unequal distribution of property and income.   The same is true of bequests for great cultural and humane foundations.   The bequests of Andrew Carnegie and of the Rockefeller and Ford families account for three-fourths of the billion and a half dollars in such foundation funds today.

Even our near-confiscatory inheritance taxes today are not able to induce the wealthy either to give liberally to philanthropic purposes during their lives or to leave any large part of their estates to non-taxable philanthropic foundations at death.   This has been pointed out in a striking article by John Pearson entitled "Death and Taxes," in the *Atlantic Monthly*, May, 1949.   He quotes an expert on inheritance and trust funds on this strange state of affairs: "Your wonderment as to why more people of means do not make more bequests to charity, and avoid taxes thereby, is understandable.   I really don't have an answer for you, as it is hard to explain human behavior."

## The Social Justification of Property

**Property rights a social problem.**   We have made it clear that there is no natural right to property.   Property, especially private property, is a social institution that appeared at a relatively late period in the history of mankind.   If private property has made contributions to the well-being of society, it is worth protecting.   If it has done more harm than good, it should be modified.

**Private property not essential.**   There is no inherent argument for private property; it is clearly not necessary to provide for man's bare needs, nor is it the object of an innate, irreplaceable human craving. Early in this chapter the point was made that the individual values what the group esteems.   If private property is an object of marked group esteem, the individual exerts himself to secure as much of it as he can.   But if group standards should shift, then some other set of values might offer as much incentive as the desire to accumulate property.   There have been many instances of this substitution; for example, in the medieval period, the high value placed by some leading churchmen on the ideal of poverty became the chief incentive for some groups, especially the friars, who renounced the desire to accumulate wordly goods and concentrated on doing good.

**Ownership, combined with control, may stimulate industrial effort.** There is no doubt that, during the Commercial Revolution and the earlier days of the Industrial Revolution, private property stimulated industrial expansion and increased production.   When a man owned and operated his own fleet of commercial ships or his own factory, he had a powerful incentive to increase his profits, so that he might reinvest them in his trade or plant and make larger profits.   Thus, until recent times, the accumulation of capital promoted industrial expansion and prosperity.

After the establishment of finance capitalism in the twentieth century, however, the tide turned.  The non-owning managers of great corporations had less interest in efficient operation of business than in making speculative profits for themselves.  The non-managing owners had no opportunity to insist upon sound business practices.  Wages and salaries of workers and clerks remained low.  The laborer whose income was too low to maintain himself and his family on a decent standard of living could not buy many of the products of industry; and, consequently, there was underconsumption, usually called over-production.  This led to industrial stagnation and depressions.

**Property under the system of absentee ownership no stimulus to production.**  Under the present system of finance capitalism and absentee ownership, the possession and accumulation of corporate property does not directly lead to increased productive effort.  We have seen how ownership is usually separated from control and management in large corporations and how those who own most of the securities do not take a direct part in running the business.

Large property holdings today seem to be valuable mainly for the social prestige they confer.  Much of our "conspicuous consumption" or waste is the result of the urge to display property.  The rich stockholder who owns an expensive yacht, several flashy automobiles, a town house, and a villa on the seashore, does not require all these to satisfy his needs, nor do they contribute notably to increased production.  The owner wants them because they all call attention to his great wealth and thus give him social prestige.

Today, private ownership of wealth does not always contribute to the public welfare; often it leads to the exploitation of the masses.  Surely, private property does little to stimulate productive energy and activity today, since the main property-owning class, stockholders and bondholders, have little or nothing to do with the management and operation of large business enterprises.  Their wealth and the economic setup in the corporate era condemn them to indolence, lassitude, and waste.

**Some historic evils of the property system.**  Property may have offered a real stimulus to human effort in the past, but it has also produced many evils.  Slavery in ancient times, serfdom in the Middle Ages, the exploitation of the workers in the factories of the Industrial Revolution, and the unequal distribution of wealth today are only a few examples of the evil results of man's desire to accumulate more property than he needs, or than his business needs to run at its best.

## The Future of Private Property

**Growth of collectivism and state control menaces private property.** The future of property is deeply and inseparably involved in the contemporary crisis in private enterprise and capitalism all over the world. The present tendency is in the direction of increasing state control over property, even toward overt state assumption of ownership of much that has been previously regarded as private property. We may first look at the status of property in two countries that have been strongholds of private property in the past, the United States and England.

**Increasing jeopardy of private property in the United States.** In the United States, state control over private property, already considerable before 1933, was greatly extended during the New Deal and the second world war, and these controls were only slowly and incompletely relaxed or surrendered after the war. President Truman repeatedly requested the restoration of many of these wartime controls in peacetime.

Taxes, especially income taxes, were enormously increased by the second world war, thus depriving the individual of much of the income from his property. The number of those who had to pay income taxes was greatly increased, from 4,000,000, in 1939, to 47,000,000, in 1948. The percentage of income taken in taxes shot up sharply. In 1929, a man with an income of $250,000 retained 80 per cent of his income after paying taxes; in 1945, he had 17 per cent of his income left after taxes.

Inheritance taxes grew higher, both state and Federal. In 1948, the

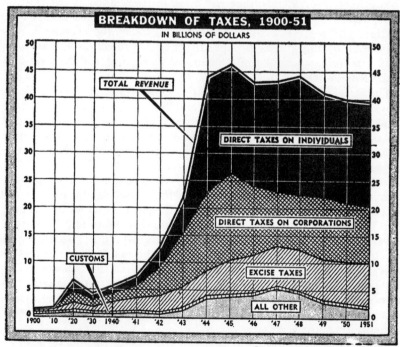

*Courtesy of* The New York Times.

This graph indicates the source and increase of taxation which is the chief menace to private property today.

estate of Mrs. Henry White of New York City was assessed at $9,748,-
000 and the taxes levied were $7,036,000. The Federal and state in-
heritance taxes on the 35-million-dollar estate of W. K. Vanderbilt
amounted to 30 million dollars. Thomas W. Lamont observed that,
in the light of heavy inheritance taxes, a gift of 500 million dollars
by him while living would cost his heirs only 23 million dollars.

The reversal of the attitude of the Supreme Court toward taxation
of property and income in the last half-century has opened the way to
unlimited taxation. Formerly, the Court went to unwarranted extremes in protecting property and income against taxation. Since
1932, however, the Court has made the sky the limit on the type and
extent of taxation legally permissible. It has ruled that no tax can
be regarded as illegal on the ground that it is too high or that it is a
duplication of taxation. The same personal income is taxed by both
the Federal and the state governments; if the state of residence and
the state in which income is earned are different, both states may tax
the same income. Corporate earnings are, literally, legally liable to
seven distinct and duplicate forms of taxation. Especially flagrant is
the double taxation of corporate profits. On profits of $50,000 or
more, the corporations pay a tax of 38 per cent before any of the profits
are distributed to stockholders as dividends. Then, when the stockholders receive dividends, they pay a tax of from 20 to 91 per cent on
these, depending on the amount of the dividends received and the de-
ductions allowed. It is quite evident that, today, the average American citizen has no greater probability of legal protection against arbitrary taxation than had the Roman citizen against the depredations
of the Roman taxgatherer.

**The withholding tax.** In olden times, tax collection was a harsh,
brutal, and disagreeable procedure and the methods employed made
taxpaying an obnoxious matter, irrespective of the money paid out
in taxation. This opposition of the populace acted as a brake upon
onerous government taxation, but the hatred of tax collectors nevertheless resulted in many an assassination.

In the United States, in recent years, we have gone to the opposite
extreme and developed a clever device for collecting the income tax
which actually makes the person taxed all but unconscious of the fact,
even though the taxes may amount to a third or more of his total income. This is the so-called withholding tax procedure, according to
which the employer automatically deducts the tax from the wages or
salary of the person taxed and gives the employee the balance. The
employee, after a brief period, regards the balance after taxation as
his actual wage or salary, and virtually forgets that he is being taxed.
As a result, there is little popular support even for the most valid tax-
reduction proposals.

In the same way that contemporary anaesthesia has made possible
painless surgery, so the withholding tax has brought about painless
taxation and has made property in income a safe prey for any irre-

sponsible government.   Some experts find it disquieting that the refusal of some employers to collect the withholding tax has been
speedily and sharply outlawed by the Supreme Court and penalized
by the tax-gathering authorities.

Excise and other allied Federal taxes also usually escape personal
scrutiny.   Examples of the vast amount paid in such taxes are the
following figures: liquor taxes, $2,475,000,000; tobacco taxes, $1,238,-
000,000; taxes on common carrier services, $520,000,000; gasoline taxes,
$434,000,000; telephone and telegraph taxes, $253,000,000; and jewelry
taxes, $237,000,000.

Hence, though private property is still more adequately safeguarded
and more stable in the United States than in any other major country
of the world, the situation is far from what it was at the turn of the
century when state control of business and property was abhorred
even by the leading liberals, when owners still usually managed their
property and business, when there was no income tax, when the Federal budget was trivial compared to that of today, and when there was
virtually no public debt.

**Growing tax burden the chief menace to property and income in the
United States.**   Aside from war, with which it is so inevitably and directly associated, it is probable that excessive taxation is the chief
menace to property and income in the United States today.   And the
tax menace is virtually free to mount without limit because of the
absence of any effective criticism or opposition.   The business classes
can be quieted and neutralized by raising radical bogies, or, if necessary, by launching a cold and then a hot war.   The wealthy, who were
in almost open revolt against the relatively moderate taxation of New
Deal days, have whimpered but slightly over the near-confiscatory taxation of wartime and the cold war aftermath.   And, as we have noted,
the masses have been benumbed and conditioned to acquiescence by
the withholding-tax stratagem.

**Sabotage of the New Deal undermined American property.**   Despite
the sad state of affairs today, the vast public debt, crushingly high
income taxes, near-confiscatory estate taxes at death, astronomical
Federal budgets, and the jeopardy of the whole capitalist system, there
is little ground for dolorous or tearful sympathy for the wealthy.   Had
the wealthy co-operated with President Roosevelt's New Deal efforts
to rehabilitate capitalism, the nation might not have had to wait for
the second world war to end the depression.   If the wealthy had, in
1938, warmly espoused Mr. Roosevelt's proposal of a 100-billion-dollar
housing program, we could have halted the depression on the basis of
a vastly stimulated domestic industrial program rather than by the
armament and war economy that eventually ended the depression by
a remedy worse than the disease.   Moreover, the cost would have been
less than a quarter of our war expenditures, and the money would have
gone into socially valuable and largely self-liquidating projects instead
of being wasted.

**Severe limitations on private property in England under an economy of austerity.** England remained relatively free from the ravages of finance capitalism, which has divorced ownership from control in the United States, though the Bank of England has exerted a great influence over the government. But England's participation in two world wars so weakened its economic position that private property lies in great jeopardy in that country today.

While taxation was far higher in England than in the United States before 1939, even in that year there were 7,000 persons in England with a net income after taxation of over $24,000. In 1948, only 45 persons retained an income of over $24,000 after taxes. It has been estimated that the million or more dollars paid to Mr. Churchill for his memoirs will net him only about $25,000 after taxes. A capital levy on income was decreed for the year 1949, and, for at least 12,000 Englishmen, this levy exceeded their income. Inheritance taxes in England are pretty close to confiscatory.

We have already pointed out that, in July, 1948, the Labour Government asserted complete control over all landed property. Banking has been nationalized in England, as have been transportation, public utilities, and mines, and the nationalization of heavy industries was envisaged. State control over property uses is stringent under the system of national planning and the economy of "austerity." No Englishman can take more than $300 out of the country, even if he plans to spend a year or more abroad. The English national debt is far greater in proportion to the national wealth than that of the United States. England has ceased to be a creditor in relation to the rest of the Empire and is a debtor to the sterling bloc nations to the tune of nearly 15 billion dollars.

Despite desperate and highly intelligent efforts at recovery since 1945, the outlook for a return to even prewar standards of living is not bright, and the ablest commentators agree that the best that is in prospect for Britain is adjustment to a generally lower standard of living, accompanied by a much larger rate of emigration. The Labour party is definitely committed to state socialism. Moreover, the alternative program of the British Conservatives admittedly envisages a great amount of collectivism—about as much as was provided for in the Beveridge Plan.

**War the chief reason for disintegration of private property.** The property damage in the first world war was conservatively estimated at around 35 billion dollars. What with the promiscuous and extensive bombing of non-military objectives, the deliberate destruction of cities, the dynamiting of plants, the parched earth policy of Russia in retreat in 1941–42, and the foolhardy dismantling of German plants after V-E Day, it has been estimated that the property damage from the second world war, entirely aside from monetary costs, amounted to at least two and a quarter trillion dollars. The property damage to Russia alone was far in excess of the cost of the three Five-Year Plans from 1928 to 1941. It has been estimated that the United States used up more of its natural resources in the four years of the second world war than it uses in a quarter of a century of peacetime operations.

After the war, the policies of occupation in central Europe, Italy, and Japan carried out by the victorious nations subjected private property to alien state control of the most drastic type. There was no opportunity whatever for private ownership to function independently in a spirit of free enterprise. In Germany, at least, such postwar economic programs as the slightly modified Morgenthau Plan may have done as much damage to property as the war. The later policies of rehabilitation, like the Marshall Plan or the European Recovery Program, actually promote collectivism and state control of property and business abroad, even though support of this program has been justified on the ground that it will save private enterprise in western Europe. All the countries that have been aided are committed to a planned and state-controlled economy in greater or less degree, and at one stage even they complained that the Marshall Plan would lead them towards collectivism more rapidly than they wished to proceed.

Relief and rehabilitation to check Communism have not worked very well. We poured over a billion dollars into Italy between V-E Day and the onset of the Marshall Plan and, during this period, the Italian Communist Party increased by leaps and bounds, until it became second only to that in Soviet Russia in numbers. Though we gave Chiang Kai-Shek four billion dollars the net result was the Communist conquest of China.

**Virtual extinction of private property under Soviet State Socialism.** While wars, almost invariably warmly supported by the property owners of the countries involved, have done more than any form of socialism or Fascism to destroy private property, there is no wisdom in denying the challenge that Russian State Socialism offers to private property. Though private property in personal possessions may still persist in Russia, there is no private property in the means of production and distribution, in utilities, in trade or banking, or in anything else of a business nature.

The second world war left Russia the dominant power in the Old World. The Russian system gained correspondingly in prestige and was imposed by force, persuasion, or intrigue on a great protective cordon of neighboring states in Europe. The destruction of Japan laid China, India, and Indonesia wide open to Communist penetration. Russia gained temporary control of Manchuria, the past and future workshop of China, and stripped it of all machinery. The Chinese Communists have now taken over control of China. It is not likely that the expansion of Russian influence can be checked short of a third world war, and such a war would mean the end of most private property outside of Russia, even if Russia's opponents were victorious in the war. The expense involved in prolonged occupation of the vast spaces of Russia and Asia would wreck what remained elsewhere of the capitalist system, private enterprise, and the institution of private property.

## Summary

The value of property is determined by the standards of the social group; the individual desires property not only to satisfy his needs but also because it is highly valued by the group. The culture of the group, rather than any acquisitive instinct, creates and shapes the desire for property.

The concept of property is a product of human culture. There is no such thing as a natural right to property, even though the philosophers of the seventeenth and eighteenth centuries spent a great deal of time trying to prove that property is a natural right of man.

The concept of property has undergone considerable evolution during the course of human history. In all ages, social groups have had definite ideas about property holdings and relationships and appropriate laws to uphold them.

Individual property rights became increasingly important after 1500, as a result of the Commercial Revolution and the rise of modern capitalism. Private ownership of property was vastly extended, eulogized by philosophers, and protected by the laws and the courts. The Industrial Revolution and the factory system not only multiplied the wealth of individuals, but added greatly to the number of property owners. The rights of private property became ever more sacred, and were consistently protected by the courts.

The rise of the modern corporation, however, complicated property relationships, and resulted in a separation of ownership from the control and management of corporate property. At the same time, the legal rights of corporations and property were extended to an unreasonable degree by the courts. As a result of the huge expenditures connected with war and social services, the democratic states, as well as the totalitarian governments, now impose severe restrictions on private property in the effort to preserve a stable economic order.

Although the desire for property stimulates economic effort, it has also made for considerable human misery, because private wealth is not fairly distributed. If some other supreme group value were substituted for private property, perhaps the desire to accumulate wealth would decrease, and another stimulus to economic endeavor might be found.

Whatever the virtues and value of private property, it is in great jeopardy today, owing to: (1) the weakening of private enterprise; (2) the impact of two world wars that have increased state control over property, brought about crushing taxation depriving the individual of much of the income from his property, piled up an overwhelming debt burden, and actually destroyed an astronomical amount of private property; and (3) the growth of state socialism, notably in

Soviet Russia, but also, on a lesser scale, in Great Britain and other countries.

## Selected References

Beaglehole, Ernest, *Property: A Study in Social Psychology*, Macmillan, 1932. The best single book on property, from the psychological viewpoint. Destroys the illusion of an instinct of property in man or animals.

Berle, A. A., and Means, G. C., *The Modern Corporation and Private Property*, Commerce Clearing House, 1932. The classic work on the relation of the separation of ownership from control under finance capitalism to the system of private property.

Clay, Henry, *Property and Inheritance*, The Daily News Co. (London), 1923. A leading English economist depicts on a broad canvas the outstanding problems of property and its transmission.

Coker, F. W. (Ed.), *Democracy, Liberty, and Property*, Macmillan, 1942. Important collection of readings and source-material on the history of liberalism and property.

* Coon, Horace, *Money to Burn*, Longmans, Green, 1939. The best study of the motives and results of benefactions by the rich, with special attention to endowments and foundations.

Ely, R. T., *Property and Contract in Their Relations to the Distribution of Wealth*, 2 vols., Macmillan, 1914. Monumental defense of property, especially real property.

Gore, Charles (Ed.), *Property, Its Duties and Rights*, Macmillan, 1922. A symposium edited by a prominent English churchman treating historically and sociologically the main ethical and economic aspects of the property complex.

Haxey, Simon, *England's Money Lords*, Harrison-Hilton, 1939. Vivid and authoritative study of the main property-holding class in England and its influence over English life and politics.

Helton, Roy, *Sold Out to the Future*, Harper, 1932. Vigorous attack on the dangers of public and private indebtedness incurred through installment buying and excessive government spending.

Jones, Bassett, *Debt and Production*, Day, 1933. Heavily documented argument that our economic system has been rendered bankrupt by excessive public and private debt. Author's position would be far stronger since the additions to our debt produced by second world war.

Lindeman, E. C., *Wealth and Culture*, Harcourt, Brace, 1936. Comprehensive and scholarly statistical investigation and exposition of the contributions of foundations and community trusts to charitable and cultural causes. Conclusion is that such contributions are not at all in proportion to the great fortunes of the rich.

Lundberg, Ferdinand, *America's 60 Families*, Vanguard, 1937. A startling and absorbing account of the domination of American politics, economics, and society by a few very wealthy families.

\* Ratner, Sidney, *American Taxation*, Norton, 1942. An excellent historical and economic analysis of the development of the American system of taxation and its social effects on American life.

Taussig, F. W., *Inventors and Money-Makers*, Macmillan, 1915. Interesting discussion by a leading American economist of the relative rôle of technicians and businessmen in economic enterprise. Seriously challenges the idea that private profit and property have been primarily responsible for modern mechanical industry.

\* Tawney, R. H., *The Acquisitive Society*, Harcourt, Brace, 1920. A searching analysis of capitalist society, containing a brilliant chapter on property.

—————, *Religion and the Rise of Capitalism*, Harcourt, Brace, 1926. A classic work on the attitude of the medieval church and early Protestanism toward property and business enterprise.

Tilden, Freeman, *A World in Debt*, Funk & Wagnalls, 1936. Popular but reliable account of the debt complex throughout history.

Utley, Freda, *The High Cost of Vengeance*, Regnery, 1949. Reveals the incredible destruction of property in central Europe during and after the second world war.

\* Veblen, Thorstein, *Absentee Ownership*, Viking, 1923. Brief, pioneer work on the separation of ownership from control and management under finance capitalism.

Winthrop, Alden, *Are You a Stockholder?* Covici Friede, 1937. Able and spirited account of the relative economic helplessness of stockholders under a system of finance capitalism. Invaluable for understanding the property situation of stockholders.

# PART V

# Public Problems of the Contemporary Age

# CHAPTER XVI

# The Political Framework of Modern Life: The National State, Representative Government, and the Party System

## Some Preliminary Definitions

**Conflict between popular and technical use of political terms.** Those who seek to deal with political problems without previous training are often confused by the marked differences between the use of political terms in popular parlance and in the technical phraseology of political science. For example, when we ordinarily talk about a "state," we mean one of the states of our Federal Union—New York, for example, or Colorado. But the political scientist never uses the term in this meaning, save in a descriptive sense to mention one of the 48 administrative units in our Federal system. Likewise, the terms *state* and *government* are popularly used interchangeably with little understanding of the distinction between them. *Nation* and *country* are commonly used interchangeably, often synonymously with state or government.

**The state.** In formal political science, the word *state* is used to demote the fundamental and omnipotent political organization of any independent community. The "people of the United States of America," as politically organized, constitute a state in political science. But the only time when the state as such actually operates in any country is when it makes or amends the constitution. Otherwise, the people function politically only through the government, which is the active and efficient servant or agent of the state. The state possesses sovereign power, according to political scientists; that is, the

375

original, absolute, unlimited, and universal power of the political community over any subject or groups of subjects.

**The government.** Through its making and amending of the constitution, the state determines upon and establishes the government, which in turn carries out the routine functions of political control and applies, subject to constitutional restrictions, the sovereign power of the state to maintain public order. Though the government is, theoretically, no more than the errand-boy of the state, virtually all the political activities of the community are carried out by the government. Political science recognizes the states in our Federal Union only as local governmental agencies. No state, in this sense, possesses an iota of sovereign power or any other attribute of a state, as understood by political science.

**The nation.** The nation is primarily a psycho-social entity—a group of persons united by a well-diffused sentiment of affinity and unity, which is usually based on some degree of racial unity, cultural homogeneity, a common historical tradition, a common language, and the like. Sometimes, for example in France, the nation may be identical in make-up with the state, in that all or most members of a given nation are included within the borders of the political community we call the state. Very often, however, members of a given nationality are scattered throughout several states; this has been a leading cause of divided loyalties and of political friction and war. At the other extreme, as in the case of Austria-Hungary before 1918, a single state may include members of a number of national groups.

**The country.** The term country, in so far as it has any precise meaning, has no political connotation whatever, but is a geographical concept which refers to the physical content and natural features of the territory inhabited by any political community or state. In popular use, however, it is often used to include not only the physical basis of any state, but also its inhabitants. It is even used at times as more or less identical with the nation.

## The Origin of Political Institutions

**The patriarchal theory.** The origins of the political experience and machinery of mankind must be sought in the institutions and practices of primitive society. The first modern attempt to trace the historical development of political origins during the period of tribal society brought forth a theory—which was supposed to be of biblical origin and sanction and had been confirmed by the generalizations of Aristotle, Bodin, Pufendorf, Locke, and Blackstone—namely, that a patriarchal organization was the earliest form of family, social, and political life. This thesis received its ablest synthesis and defense in the *Ancient Law* (1861) and other monumental contributions to comparative jurisprudence and politics from the pen of the great English jurist, Sir Henry Maine (1822–1888). Yet, as Robert H. Lowie has done well to point out, Maine was no fanatical partisan of patriarchalism. Indeed, he denied that the patriarchal family had been universal in primitive society. He stressed patriarchalism because his work dealt mainly with early Indo-Germanic society, which had been organized on a patriarchal basis.

**The matriarchal doctrine and early evolutionary theories of primitive organization.** The patriarchal thesis was attacked by Johann Jacob Bachofen (1815–1887) in his *Das Mutterrecht* (Mother Right), published in 1861. He argued that promiscuity had dominated early human sexual relations. Later, there developed a matriarchate, or a social and political system controlled by females. Bachofen based his generalizations upon data drawn from a study of classical mythology and tradition. This rather archaic line of investigation was soon abandoned for what has come to be known as the "evolutionary" approach to historical sociology. A group of distinguished scholars brought evolutionary principles and Darwinian biology to bear upon the reconstruction of the early history of human society and reached results that appeared to be disruptive of the patriarchal position of Maine.

These social evolutionists arrived at the following definite conclusions. The monogamous family shows a slow but distinct development from original promiscuity, and the family of any permanent type is a late product, developing within the kinship or gentile organization of society. In the development of tribal or kinship society, certain successive stages can be isolated and their sequence correlated with the development of material culture. The earliest traceable primitive groups permitted members to intermarry; there were neither fixed family arrangements nor other wider social relations. This stage was followed by the appearance of well-defined kinship or tribal society, which outlawed intermarriage within the group. The earliest form of gentile society was the maternal clan, which was in time succeeded by the paternal clan, with an accompanying advance in material culture. The paternal clan or gens was gradually converted into a patriarchal organization of society. The latter, as a result of the development of property and the infiltration of foreigners, was in time superseded. Kinship relations were abolished and civil society, based on territorial residence and legalized property rights, was established with the rise of the city-state in the ancient Near East. This orderly synthesis of primitive social and political evolution was most effectively set forth in the famous work on *Ancient Society* by Lewis Henry Morgan, published in 1877.

**Later scientific ideas of primitive social and political institutions.** Since Morgan's day new methods of anthropological investigation and more thorough studies of existing primitive society have disproved many of the conclusions reached by the older methods. The application of this more scientific method to the study of primitive society has been nothing short of revolutionary. The complete universality of gentile or kinship society cannot be proved; many groups have developed to a relatively high stage of culture without any relationship system wider than the family and the local group or village. Where gentile society exists there is no general tendency for relationships to change from a maternal to a paternal basis; in fact, there has probably never been a deliberate change in kinship from a maternal to a paternal basis in the whole range of primitive society. Further, there is no evidence that maternal kinship is correlated with lower material culture or paternal with more advanced economic life.

**The sociological theory of the origin of the state and government.** The next problem in the sociological theory of political evolution centers around tracing the origin of civil society—the territorial state. Older views, following Aristotle, regarded it as a natural expansion of social groupings from tribal to civil society. Morgan and the evolutionary school accounted for political origins on the basis of the rise of property and the need for a more advanced type of political and legal institutions to cope with these more complex economic problems. Gradually, however, the doctrine has gained ground that the territorial state has usually been the product of the forcible amalgamation of smaller groups through long-continued warfare. Today, this may be said to be *the* sociological theory of political origins.

Though this view of political origins has received general assent, some authorities have criticized it as minimizing the element of cooperation and other peaceful agencies, such as industry and trade, in the history of the state. Among the better known of such writers have been Alexander Sutherland, in his *Origin and Growth of the Moral Instinct;* Prince Peter Kropotkin, in his *Mutual Aid: a Factor in Evolution,* and Jacques Novicow, in his *Criticism of Social Darwinism.* Eclectic writers have tried to work out a synthesis to show that, while conflict played the dominant rôle in political origins, co-operative activities have not been without great influence in the past and will probably be even more powerful in the future.

## The Evolution of Political Institutions

**Political institutions in primitive times.** First, as we noted above, humanity was organized, for the most part, in what has been called kinship or tribal society, in which the individual's position and the power of the rulers were founded upon blood relationship, real or assumed. One did not have rights or prestige because he resided in a certain place or because he was protected by some overlord. He owed his status and privileges mainly to the fact that he was a member of a quasi-biological clan or gens that was believed to be composed of blood brethren, irrespective of whether the relationship was traced through the male or the female line. An interloper had no rights or privileges. Those who ruled were elected by and from the blood brethren. Even such elaborate primitive political organizations as the

Iroquois tribes rested fundamentally on clan units that were made up of alleged kinsmen. The same was true of even the early Germanic tribes when they appeared on the historical horizon in the first century B.C.

Real or fictitious blood relationship, then, was the usual foundation of primitive political organization, though simple family relations and a common local habitat served occasionally to hold men together and secure public order. The tribe was usually the dominant political organization in primitive society, and generally the tribal council was elected by clansmen and the chief of the tribe by the council. As a rule, the clan had charge of most of the routine legal affairs in primitive days, enforced justice through the blood feud and other concepts and practices, and controlled primitive economic life.

**Feudalism the transitional period between kinship society and civil society.** As a result of the frequent and numerous wars that took place during the long interval of several thousand years between primitive times and the rise of historic civil society in Egypt and Mesopotamia, many kinship groups were conquered and subjected to the rule of the victors. Blood relationship was thus gradually obscured and broken down. During this age of conquest, personal loyalty to dominant leaders became more and more important. The basis for public control was the loyal support of the leader by his followers and the protection of his subordinates by the leader, who divided the spoils of conquest with his followers. In short, personal relationships, founded on superiority and subordination, on loyalty and protection, supplanted the kinship basis of primitive society. The resulting political and social order was what we know as feudalism.

This rudimentary feudal system seems to have existed as the background of most early historical political societies, intervening between primitive tribal organization and the more highly developed political state, grounded in territorial residence and property rights. Early city-states and monarchies appear to have arisen almost invariably out of feudal origins. This feudal order reappeared again in western civilization when the Greek and Roman social structure collapsed and the Germanic barbarians gained control of public affairs. This medieval feudalism is the best-known example of the feudal system.

**Civil society brought in by the city-state.** The earliest type of truly political organization was the city-state that appeared first in Egypt and Mesopotamia some 60 centuries before Christ. The city-state was created as a result of the conquest of several feudal groups by a victorious feudal lord or kinglet. During the centuries when feudalism was the prevailing type of political and social organization, property tended to play an ever greater rôle in public affairs and successful conquering feudal lords became more accustomed to settling down permanently on the lands they had acquired.

The city-state was the first example of what we call civil or political

society.  It rested mainly, as Morgan did well to emphasize, on territorial residence, the recognition of private property rights, and the development of laws and institutions to protect property.  It persisted in
various forms and areas down to the rise of imperial Rome, though
earlier empires had sporadically blotted it out in wide sections of the
ancient Near East.  Indeed, city-state culture was revived in late
medieval Italy, Germany, and Holland.  The Greek city-state was
perhaps the highest development attained by this form of politico-
social organization.

Antiquity produced not only city-states but also patriarchal empires,
the latter welded together by the conquest of several kingdoms.  But
neither city-state, kingdom, nor empire brought about a truly national
psychology or political organization.  The city-state was too small
and provincial.  The empires were too vast, embraced too many
different peoples and cultures, or were of too brief duration to weld
their divergent cultures into a national unit.  Even the Roman
Empire did not attain a national, self-conscious character.

**Medieval feudalism.**   The political, social, economic, and cultural
conditions of the Middle Ages were no better adapted to the creation of
the national state than were those of imperial antiquity.  Just as in
the period before the dawn of history in the ancient Near East, a
period of feudalism followed on the heels of the breakdown of Germanic tribal or kinship society after about 200 A.D.  The unit of
political organization and administration was the *fief*—the domain
of the feudal lord.  This varied greatly in area, but rarely was it
coexistensive with any cultural or national entity.  Usually, a single
feudal domain was only a small isolated item in the feudal hierarchy,
and it made for political decentralization and local immunity rather
than for national unity.

Only the most tenuous authority inhered in the average feudal
monarch.  Such power as he did have was primarily derived from his
own position as a strong feudal lord and from the aid given him by his
subordinate feudal lords.  The stronger kings of the feudal period
owed their power chiefly to the creation of some sort of royal army.
Each feudal lord was supreme in his own domain, and he was immune
from higher control after he had met his duties and obligations to his
overlords and king.   Feudalism was an institutional testimonial to the
relative unimportance of the universal and impersonal aspects of life
at this period.

Medieval social life was centered in the large number of rural
medieval manors and in the few small and scattered medieval towns.
The units of agrarian and urban industry, the manors and the towns
respectively, were relatively isolated, nearly self-sufficient, and narrowly
provincial.  They were thoroughly unadapted to providing any firm
economic foundations for national unity.  The pivotal points in
medieval culture were the royal palaces, the towns, and the monasteries.
The feudal kingdoms were too weak, too poorly united by means of

communication, and too much governed by the spirit of localism and jealous isolation to be able to bring into being that general cultural homogeneity so all-essential to the existence of national unity. Nor was the international ecclesiastical system of the Middle Ages any better suited to promote national spirit.

**Modern times produce the national state.** With the origin of modern times humanity arrived at the point where a new political entity of great import for the future of humanity emerged, namely, the national state. Political power became centralized, first in monarchs and later in elective rulers. The state, in both cases, became absolute, and all too often it crushed out at will the immunities and privileges of individuals, whether lords or common men. The authority and administration radiated from the center of the realm, instead of being scattered about in outlying feudal regions. The kings hired their own army and administrators, instead of relying on levies of feudal troops and the administration of justice by feudal lords. Order was preserved by the monarch; his will had to be respected by all under his dominion. National sovereignty supplanted local immunity. Order gradually grew out of chaos.

During the decline of feudalism at the close of the medieval period, the stronger feudal monarchs, such as Henry II of England and Philip Augustus and St. Louis of France, were beginning to assert their power at the expense of the feudal lords and to lay the foundations of the national monarchy. This movement was hastened by the expansion of Europe and the Commercial Revolution, which brought into play forces that served to extinguish the political aspects of feudalism and to create a system of nationalism. The Commercial Revolution supplied the kings with more money to hire loyal armies and administrators. The revived ascendancy of the infantry made it cheaper and easier to hire efficient mercenary armies. The middle-class lawyers and other functionaries provided the kings with the administrative bureaucracy that the new centralized governments required. Strong monarchs, the Tudors in England, the Bourbons in France, the Romanovs in Russia, and the Hohenzollerns in Prussia, created well-knit national states governed under the absolutist pattern. Later, absolutism was tempered slightly by the benevolent despotism of eighteenth-century rulers like Frederick the Great of Prussia, Catherine the Great of Russia, Joseph II of Austria, and Charles III of Spain.

**Representative government and democracy.** Later on, absolutism was undermined by the growth of revolutionary doctrines and the rise of representative republican government. Republics proved, however, no less nationalistic than the earlier monarchies. Political liberalism has not yet consistently produced cosmopolitanism or internationalism. Progressive democracies in the twentieth century remained as nationalistic as seventeenth-century monarchies. The greatest of all the wars of the nations were fought in the second and fifth decades of our own century, and democratic states entered them with as much nationalistic ardor as the most reactionary empires or the most ruthless totalitarian states. Even the great socialist state of Soviet Russia, originally consecrated to internationalism, has now become the most intensely nationalistic country in the Old World, thus refuting the traditional socialist contention that the end of capitalism would mean the end of nationalism.

The outstanding event in political evolution since the Middle Ages, was, thus, the rise of the national state. It was at first monarchical and tyrannical, then it was slowly adapted to representative government, mainly as a result of the series of revolutions conducted by the middle-class merchants and lawyers—the English Revolution of 1688, the American Revolution of 1776, the French Revolution of 1789, and the European revolutions of 1830 and 1848. Finally, in the nineteenth and twentieth centuries, government became democratic in most countries in the Western World, largely as a result of the increased numbers and power of the industrial workers.

**The crisis in nationalism.** In our day, nationalism has proved quite inadequate to deal successfully with the institutional conditions brought into being by the urban, industrial world-civilization that has been created by three industrial revolutions. The national state now threatens mankind with devastating bellicosity, and has created a centralized political unity in juxtaposition with public problems that may be too vast and complex to be solved through democracy and party government.

**The program of regional federation.** The experience of mankind since 1914 has made realists aware that, whatever virtues nationalism may have, they certainly do not warrant the perpetuation of any system which invites successive world wars and the imperiling of all civilization. The problem has arisen of providing some form of political organization more rational than the national state, at the same time protecting those traits and manifestations of nationalism that are of permanent value to mankind. The most popular programs of political readjustment involving the control, though not necessarily the total suppression, of nationalism take the form of what is called regionalism. Regionalism, loosely comprising all movements designed to unify or co-ordinate an area on a political or economic basis, ranges in scope from plans for local commercial unions to proposals of continent-wide federations.

**New ideas of representative government.** Representative government produced political parties as the agency to provide the representatives, but traditional party government is breaking down in our day. Political corruption has paralyzed the conventional party system. Political blocs bring anarchy to party government. The other extreme, the one-party system, is the formula of totalitarian systems. The reform of representative government has become an outstanding problem of our era.

One suggestion is to abandon the principle of representation by territorial districts and population and found political representation upon the basic occupational and professional groups in modern society. Vocational representation of this type has been tried to some extent in Europe, but it has rarely been introduced except as the result of revolution or war.

## The Origin of Representative Government, Constitutions, Republics, and Democracy

**Direct and representative democracy.** If the average American were asked: "What form of government do you have?" he would unhesitatingly reply: "A democracy." Our democracy was once described by Abraham Lincoln as "government of the people, by the people, and for the people." A pure democracy, however, means direct management of the government by the people. How can the will of 150 million Americans be directly expressed and put to work?

The only way the will of large numbers of persons can be expressed is by means of representative government, namely, through delegates elected by the people. Direct democratic government is only possible when the population is small enough, as in the forest cantons of Switzerland or a New England town, for the people to vote and govern directly without choosing representatives.

**Essentials of American representative democracy.** Representative government by majority rule is the American form of democracy. Our type of representative government is a republic, as are most other governments in our era. But we may have representative government in a monarchy, as in England today and in Germany before the first world war. The American system of representative government is based upon a written constitution, adopted in 1789, and now supplemented by 21 amendments, binding the 48 states in a strong Federal union. All the states have kept some of their local independence, but there has been a steady tendency to centralize the powers of government in Washington, and to encroach on state rights. This process has been encouraged by industrialization and the increasing number of problems of nationwide significance, including two world wars.

There are three branches or divisions in our Federal government. Each is supposed to act as a check upon the other. The legislative branch, the Senate and the House of Representatives, makes our laws; the executive branch, headed by the president, carries out the laws; and the judicial branch, the Supreme Court and lesser Federal courts, interprets the laws.

Each of the 48 states has a similar plan of government. The state legislature, the governor, and the state supreme court are the state counterparts of Congress, the president, and the Supreme Court. States make their own laws, but these must be in accord with the limitations on state action laid down in the supreme law of the land, the Constitution of the United States.

**Origins of representative government.** A constitution or charter of government specifies and enforces the type of government that will prevail under its authority and usually guarantees certain rights—life, freedom for business enterprise, sanctity of contracts, the protection of property, and the basic civil liberties—against violation or change, except through a formal expression of the public will in an amendment to, or a revision of, the constitution. Constitutional government is thus the fundamental basis of our representative democracy.

According to the Declaration of Independence, the government derives its powers from the consent of the governed. Since the powers of the Federal government are determined by the will of the people, it is apparent that the ultimate responsibility for good or bad government rests with the people and those whom they elect to represent them.

There were brief periods in ancient and medieval times in which some of the people were allowed a voice in the government. Indeed, true representative government actually arose in medieval towns, especially those of Spain. But it was not until after 1500, when Europe began to expand and trade and commerce increased, that any strong and widespread movement for representative government appeared.

The era of exploration and the rise of world trade increased the numbers and power of middle-class merchants and shopkeepers. As the merchants became more powerful, they were eager to join with the monarchs to crush their age-old enemies the feudal lords. But, soon, the merchants found that strong monarchs also interfered with their trade, levied heavy taxes, and arbitrarily took away their property. The middle-class merchants and businessmen therefore turned against the kings and, as they grew ever more powerful, were able, by a series of revolutions, to overthrow the tyrannical rulers.

In the place of royal absolutism, they established parliamentary government in which the middle class could have a powerful representation. At first, representative government meant mainly representation of the landed and merchant classes, but this laid the basis later on for the representation of all classes in the government. In order to safeguard their interests, the middle class drafted new constitutions embodying their ideals—freedom for business enterprise, the protection of property, the enforcement of contracts, and the guarantee of other civil liberties, such as freedom of assembly, speech, press, and religion.

**Nature of constitutional government.** The fundamental principles in these constitutions assured representative government at the time and made democratic government possible later on. First among these principles was the concept of an absolute law to which all rulers are subordinate; second, the inalienable rights of individuals to life, liberty, and property; and third, the notion of a written charter to catalogue and protect these rights. A constitution may be a written document, drafted by a constitutional convention, as was our Federal Constitution in 1787, or it may be a collection of documents and unwritten precedents accumulated over many centuries, like the English Constitution of today.

The main pressure for constitutions in early modern times, as noted above, came from the bourgeoisie or middle class merchants and businessmen. Constitutions that established representative government tended to limit the power of absolute monarchs to confiscate property and levy arbitrary taxes. The creation of constitutional government also made it more difficult to change governmental systems and legal codes arbitrarily and thus gave greater protection and stability to trade and business, as well as to government and law. All constitutions previous to the American Constitution of 1789 were designed to protect property and business from depredations at the hands of the kings and nobility. The makers of our constitution, frightened by Shays' Rebellion and other evidences of popular discontent, drafted the Constitution of 1789 primarily for the purpose of protecting property and business against the masses and popular radicalism.

While constitutions were brought into being mainly to protect private property and free enterprise and exerted this function down to the twentieth century, they can be used for the opposite purpose. The constitutions of 1918 and following years in Soviet Russia have been based upon the idea of expropriating private property and setting up a state-owned and operated economy.

**Rise of republics.** Since 1688, and especially since 1800, every civilized country in the Western world has adopted constitutional government. Because absolute monarchies had been associated in the past with the oppression and exploitation of the middle class, most of the new constitutional governments set up were republics or limited monarchies. The development of representative, republican government was furthered by: (1) extending the right to vote; (2) increasing the importance of the legislative branch of government and limiting the executive power; (3) specifying and defining the functions of government; and (4) drafting written constitutions that acknowledged and guaranteed these achievements.

**Problems of representative democracy intensified by nationalism and industrialism.** Democracy arose out of the impact of the Industrial Revolution and the new social and economic conditions, but the problems of democracy were increased and complicated by the previous or parallel growth of large national states. So long as the majority of the people were rural dwellers, the problems of government were relatively simple. Although rulers soon became nationally minded, and were eager to extend their boundaries and bring large areas under their control, the governing of large rural populations presented no insuperable difficulties. But, today, the majority of the population live in congested urban industrial centers, and serious new political problems have resulted. Mass movements of population and international migrations, for example, have required some definite governmental policy of control and selection. Problems of industry and transportation have called for public regulation; the financial and commercial policies of nations have become ever more complicated; poverty, dependency, and other social problems have arisen. The old idea that the state should never interfere extensively in social problems slowly but surely gave way to the notion that state intervention is not only desirable but necessary.

It is evident that the complex social and economic problems created in the last 150 years can no longer be solved as the founders of our republic imagined that they might be. So long as the United States was sparsely settled and a primarily agricultural nation, problems of government were relatively simple. The people were not so easily misled in political campaigns as they are today. The isolation of communities and the lack of efficient methods of transportation and communication made machine rule in anything beyond local politics very difficult. It is interesting to note that Thomas Jefferson foresaw the threat of industrialization and urbanization to liberal and republican government and declared that we could not remain free and democratic if we became a country of factories and great cities.

## Political Parties in the United States

**Political parties the indispensable instrument of democracy.** Democracy and representative government require some practical way to assure and carry out majority rule. The only means, thus far discovered, of effectively attaining and executing representative government in large areas is party government. Although not all people think alike on political issues, there will usually be enough persons agreeing on fundamental objectives to form a political organization or party for concerted action, and to nominate for election men who best represent the party ideals.

A political party is a public group, drawn together by similar interests, economic, social, or cultural. It exists and carries on primarily to further these interests through political activity. In short, a political party is a public "interest-group."

**The party system in the United States.** There have almost invariably been two major political parties in the United States—today they are the Republicans and Democrats. From time to time, third-party movements have arisen, when enough persons became dissatisfied with the general policies of the major parties to revolt and form a new group. Such were the anti-slavery, anti-foreign, and anti-Catholic parties before the Civil War; and the Greenback, Granger, and Populist parties after 1870. Among the urban workers, radical parties have gained some sway; the most prominent of these are the Socialist party, the Socialist-Labor party, and the Communist party. These third-party movements have had an important effect upon American political life by forcing the major parties to accept some of their progressive policies. We have never had a strong and permanent labor or farmer party in the United States because of the influence of the so-called American Dream. Neither laborers nor farmers have liked to think of themselves as remaining permanently such, but have hoped to rise in the social and economic world.

**Party behavior.** The loyalty of people to parties rests on a number of factors and differs with individuals. Some people vote "Republican" or "Democrat," regardless of the candidates, simply because their fathers or grandfathers voted that ticket. Political propaganda is designed to perpetuate these traditional partisan loyalties as well as to gain new support by attracting voters from other parties. Some vote the straight ticket—that is, they vote for every party candidate on the ballot—because it is the line of least resistance. Many persons use their membership in a political party to advance their own personal or class interests. They will vote for any candidate put up by the party, regardless of his fitness for office. In return for their votes, they secure favors, jobs, or even money. Party leaders often promise favors to special groups of voters during a campaign in order to secure their support.

**Party machines and methods.** Political parties are strengthened through a close-knit party organization. This organization, which operates to keep all its members in line and gain control of the offices and spoils of victory in city, state, and national governments, is known as a political machine. In some of our large cities, the political machine controls all municipal offices. Political parties vie with each other to elect their candidates in city, county, state, and national elections. Supposedly, the political campaign is carried out to acquaint the voters with the party platform and the relative merits of the candidates; but, in many cases, campaigns are largely emotional wars of empty words and planned deception. Propaganda on both sides confuses the voters and obscures the issues at stake. Emotion takes the place of rational thought.

The system of rival political parties has been called the only effective way to bring public issues before the people. If only one point of view or policy were presented, the voters would have no choice. The advocates of our two-party system contend that a one-party system would make for corrupt or dictatorial government, while a large number of parties would produce political instability, as in France.

**Our Federal system of government encourages political parties.** The system of government created by our Federal Constitution strongly encouraged the origin and development of a party system. Although the fathers of our country regarded party government as detrimental to patriotic and unselfish public life and tried to guard against it by the creation of a non-partisan Electoral College to select our presidents, they were unable to prevent the rise of parties.

The Constitution called for a popularly elected House of Representatives and there had to be some means of choosing these representatives. Moreover, the fact that the Constitution divided political authority between the Federal and state governments and separated the executive, legislative, and judicial departments in the Federal government made it necessary to have some sort of organization with a unified policy to provide for coherence of action in the executive and legislative branches of the Federal government and to integrate Federal and state policies. The national political party was the agency which grew up to achieve this unification.

**Origins of American political parties.** Although there was no widespread organization of parties until after the adoption of the Constitution in 1789, political factions had existed since the early colonial days. Soon after the adoption of the Constitution in 1789, our traditional two-party system arose, and the non-partisan scheme that the framers of the Constitution thought they had safeguarded by means of the Electoral College was speedily discarded. George Washington, our first president, sought to prevent the rise of any faction opposing the Federalists, the group that had placed him in office. The Federalists were so called because they supported a strong Federal union and, under the leadership of Alexander Hamilton, planned to carry through constructive legislation to restore order and prosperity in the country. They also hoped to establish a sound system of public finance.

The Federalists were backed by the monied groups in the East, but they aroused the opposition of the farming interests in the South and West. The farmers cared little about reviving city business and strengthening Federal finance. They feared lest, in order to carry out their plans, the Federalists might place heavy taxes on the people. Some of the southern states, like Virginia, that had already paid off their own state debts and did not want to help pay off the debts of other states, resented Hamilton's proposal to have the Federal government pay off the state debts and contended that the Constitution conferred no such power of Federal interference in state affairs. This group opposing the Federalists found a leader in Thomas Jefferson, who took the position that the government should interfere as little as possible either in private business or in the affairs of the states. They formed the Republican party (the present-day Democratic party), which drew much of its strength from southern and western farmers, aided somewhat by the slowly growing class of laborers in the industrial towns of the Atlantic seaboard.

In 1800, the Republican party won the election and Jefferson became our third President. During his administration, many of the constructive national policies of Hamilton were adopted, usually with democratic modifications. Jefferson believed in special political training, high intelligence, and expert direction of government. He believed, with Aristotle, that some persons are born to lead and others to follow, and that the mass of people can be trusted to choose the wisest men to lead them. Jefferson's followers became so strong that they were almost unopposed from 1816 to 1824, and we had virtually a one-party system for those years.

As other governmental problems arose, new factions sprang up in the mid-1820's to put forth their ideas and defend their interests. The remnants of the old Federalists, and the more conservative Republicans who did not agree with Jefferson, formed the National-Republican party, which later developed into the Whig party. Henry Clay and Daniel Webster were its spokesmen. They represented the commercial business and financial interests of the East and the nationalistic element in the West. The Whigs adopted for their program national improvements, such as the building of canals and railroads, the fostering of industry, the maintenance of a United States Bank, and the granting of loans to the West to encourage its development.

**Rise of Jacksonian democracy.** As was to be expected, the Whigs encountered strong opposition. The more radical members of the old Republican party, the eastern factory workers, and some frontiersmen, together with many of the slaveholding elements of the South, formed a new party, called the Democratic party, and chose for its leader Andrew Jackson. Jackson and his followers did not agree with Jefferson that special preparation was necessary for political office. They stressed the theory that all men are actually equal, and that any good man elected to office can competently represent and execute the will of the people.

The Jacksonian Democrats resented the power of the eastern bankers. They desired state banks, so that they might supply their own credit and be free from the economic control of the East. In line with their belief in democracy, the new party demanded that the right to vote be extended to all males and that imprisonment for debt be done away with. The Democrats elected Jackson to the presidency in 1828, drove their opponents from office, and instituted the spoils system, based on the theory that "to the victors belong the spoils." We shall discuss the defects and abuses of the spoils system in a later section.

**The slavery controversy and our party system.** The struggle over slavery caused a split and fatal disunity in the ranks of the Whigs, and the party finally broke up. The Democrats gradually came to be dominated by the pro-slavery group and the Jeffersonian philosophy of freedom for all lost its hold. The Democrats became the party of the slaveholders in the South and of those former Whigs who favored slavery.

Out of the anti-slavery element in the disintegrating Whig party, and numerous minor radical and anti-slavery groups, a new party, the Republican, was formed in 1856. It was, at first, a somewhat radical party, with its chief support drawn from eastern laborers and western frontiersmen. It elected Abraham Lincoln in 1860 and led the North to victory in the Civil War. The Republican party however, soon lost its early radical tone, and after 1865 it supported severe treatment of the southern states which had seceded, the new banking plans, railroad expansion, land grants, a high tariff, the growth of large corporations, and elimination of government interference in business. In other words, the Republicans become identified with conservative, capitalistic groups. The Democratic party, once the question of slavery was settled, supported political reform and a more liberal policy in the reconstruction of the South.

**Unreality of Republican-Democratic antagonism today.** Since about 1876, however, neither the Republican nor the Democratic party has been consistently liberal or conservative. While the Republicans have been more uniformly conservative than the Democrats, and have favored big business and high protective tariffs to protect American industry, they have at times been liberal, as under Theodore Roosevelt. There have always been liberal, almost radical, factions in Republican ranks, which have gone under names such as the Liberal-Republicans, the Mugwumps, and the Progressives. The Democratic party has varied from marked liberalism, as under William Jennings Bryan in 1896, Woodrow Wilson in 1912, and Franklin D. Roosevelt in 1932, to extreme conservatism, as in the campaigns of 1904 and 1924, but it has usually inclined towards the moderately conservative point of view, as evidenced, for example, during Grover Cleveland's administration. In 1948, there was a notable split in the Democratic party over civil liberties, racial minorities, and state rights, and some of the southern wing bolted the party. Four southern states nominated a States' Rights candidate in opposition to President Truman.

Today, as implied above, the differences between the policies of the two major parties are not clear-cut. The two major parties now exist chiefly to compete for office and the political spoils and economic power that go with it. Within each major party we find conservatives and liberals, and it is not uncommon for members of either party to break away and join the ranks of the other. A prominent example of this was the desertion of prominent Democrats like Alfred E. Smith to support the Republicans in 1936 as a gesture of disapproval of the New Deal administration under Franklin D. Roosevelt. In 1940, the Democrats "loaned" Wendell Willkie to the Republicans as their candidate for the presidency. After 1941, both parties joined heartily in prosecuting the war. In 1949, many Republicans joined with southern Democrats—the so-called Dixiecrats—to block President Truman's civil rights program.

It is well to emphasize the fact, however, that while our two-party experience has not recently presented the voters with any sharp or definite choice of political attitudes and policies, it has at least preserved the two-party system and saved us thus far from one-party dictatorship or the anarchy resulting from political blocs.

**Effect of third-party movements.** As we mentioned earlier, there have been progressive and radical groups which, skeptical of gaining their ends in the major parties, have organized third parties. Although not sufficiently strong to elect many candidates, the third parties have had a powerful effect upon the policies of the major parties. The restriction of the activities of trusts and monopolies, the development of more liberal currency and taxation policies, and government regulation of railroads and other public utilities, are examples of reform directly due to the influence of the third-party groups.[1]

## Defects and Abuses in Party Government

**Party oligarchy.** Although political parties appear to be an indispensable instrument of representative government, the party system inevitably produces certain grave abuses and defects as a mechanism of democracy. Political parties have made for non-democratic practices in government and have produced oligarchy (machine control), corruption, and graft.

Political control by the party machine in power has been mentioned earlier in this chapter. Party leaders formulate the policies of the party and, through efficient organization, put them into operation. The people are supposed to decide in a rational and deliberate manner on the candidates and public issues set before them by the party. Yet, in reality, the people are often misled by glittering phrases, catchwords, party names, and symbols; and they are so intoxicated by fantastic promises of better times to come that they will vote for irresponsible candidates.

The power of the political machine has become ever stronger and more menacing with the increase of large cities. Machines can operate more effectively in cities, where large populations are concentrated in a small area. It is easier to weld the people of a city into a loyal organization than to organize the scattered rural dwellers. The political bosses can more readily check on the activities of their party workers in the city. Racial and national differences in cities also aid the machine. Finally, there are far more political spoils in the city than in the country.

**Leading political machines.** The most widely known political machines in recent years have been the Pendergast machine in Kansas City, Tammany Hall in New York, the Kelly-Nash machine in Chicago, the Crump machine in Memphis, the Hague machine in Jersey city, and the Curley machine in Boston.[2]

In Kansas City, the Democratic party was long controlled by the Pendergast machine, which was so influential that a Pendergast-opposed candidate in the state of Missouri had little chance of election. It was the Pendergast machine which launched President Truman on his political career. The power of the Pendergast machine was tempo-

---

1 See below, pp. 579–580.
2 See below, pp. 616–617.

rarily broken as a result of the investigations officially launched in 1938 by Governor Lloyd Stark of Missouri, who was himself put into office by Pendergast.

This episode illustrates how even the more cynical party methods may, at times, bring party reform. District Attorney Thomas E. Dewey had developed a great reputation as a gang-buster in New York City and loomed as a Republican rival of President Roosevelt. Therefore, the Roosevelt administration decided that it must have an equal reputation for sleuthing and housecleaning. So Attorney-General Frank Murphy and J. Edgar Hoover, head of the F.B.I., were turned loose on the Pendergast gang, whose political support the Roosevelt régime had previously warmly welcomed.

**Election abuses.** There are many defects in the ballot system itself. Although the Australian, or secret, ballot is used, there have been many instances when the ballot box was stuffed by persons paid by the machine to vote several times or to cast votes in the names of persons who did not even exist. Instances of crooked election clerks have been all too common. The charge of destroying or tampering with ballots to assure victory for the machine candidate was made against both the Pendergast machine in Kansas City and the Hague machine in Jersey City. Corrupt political machines have even made up rolls of voters from names taken off tombstones.

**The "interests" control parties.** In the last seventy-five years, the major political parties have usually been dominated by powerful economic groups that spend large sums to elect the candidates most favorable to their interests and most certain to take orders from them. Government thus controlled by special interests becomes the servant of the few instead of the many. Men of high ability and intelligence, who are independent thinkers and doers, are not wanted in political offices by the great economic interests.

Conflicting desires have, however, often made for confusion within the parties. A banking group may desire free trade, so that foreign debtors can pay their debts in goods shipped to us; a manufacturing group may favor high tariffs, so that foreign goods will not compete with them. Each group is willing to use either fair or corrupt means to elect its servants.

**The evils of the lobby.** Powerful interests may succeed in controlling a whole political administration, but even in such cases there are other interests that carry their quest for favorable political action and legislation into the centers of government, chiefly into the legislative halls. Usually, no one interest or closely integrated group of interests completely controls an administration either in Washington or in any state capital. All interests—capital, labor, religious groups, professional organizations, reform associations, exporters, importers, publishers, and even organized criminal groups—seek special favors from politicians. Since they cannot elect representatives who publicly and openly represent them, they hire special and extra-legal representatives to go to Washington and the state capitals and seek to secure these favors.

These hired and extra-legal representatives make up what is called the "lobby." The lobby is often the most influential factor in representative government and legislation, but it possesses no official standing. It is not subject to effective scrutiny or control; its powers may be very great, and the abuses therefrom many and varied. E. Pendleton Herring, our chief expert on the lobby, has called it "the third house of Congress," claiming that it is frequently more powerful than either the Senate or the House of Representatives.

While the actions of lobbying interests may at times produce beneficial public results, such government by private interests is always potentially dangerous, since it is not directly subject to public control. Further, government by lobby is likely to be undemocratic, since wealthy and powerful interests are disproportionately represented. Wealth however, is, not everything. Votes count with elected politicians, and groups which can sway a large or vital number of voters possess special power in lobbying for their objectives. This accounts for the very great power of the labor lobby, and the frantic efforts of the Truman administration to secure the repeal of the Taft-Hartley Law.

A law of 1946, required the lobbyists to register and give an accounting of money spent. It was estimated that about 8 million dollars were so spent in 1949. Many escape registration by contending that their activities do not constitute lobbying in the sense described by the 1946 act. Congress recognized the need for further control of the lobby and a thorough congressional investigation was launched in March, 1950.

There seems to be no immediate remedy for the lobby nuisance, at least pending a rational reorganization of our major political parties in such a manner that each will represent distinct, well-integrated interests—for, as we have seen, both major parties have long represented similar interests, so that alignment with one or the other party offers little special advantage for any powerful interest. The direct public representation of vocations or interest-groups has been proposed, but while this has logical merit it runs afoul of the democratic dogma of numerical representation and majority rule.[3] Since the essence of representative government is the representation of interests, these interests will get their representation through the lobby if they cannot secure it through the public party system.

**Loss of interest in voting.** Another defect of our party system is that the candidates are not truly "the people's choice," because often half or more of the people who are legally entitled to vote do not go to the polls to nominate candidates in the primaries or to choose or reject them at election time. The struggle for the right to vote was

---

3 See below, p. 402.

long and hard.   It was believed that, as soon as the masses received the vote, they would flock to the polls.   Yet, even in presidential elections, which usually create the most excitement, only about half the qualified voters turn out to cast their ballots.   Statistics show that, on the whole, a smaller percentage of legal voters now cast their ballots on election days than they did in 1856.   In 1856, 83 per cent went to the polls; in 1920, 43.6 per cent; in 1932, 52.8 per cent; in 1944, 53.8 per cent; and in 1948, 51.9 per cent.   Woman suffrage, expected to bring about an increase in the percentage of votes, did no such thing.

Part of the loss of interest in voting has been produced by the complicated nature of modern politics.   Formerly, in the local neighborhood, there was keen interest in elections because the candidates were personally known to the voters and the issues at stake directly touched their daily lives.   Today, few persons know the candidates, especially in cities, or understand the public issues involved in the campaign.   The realization that there is .corruption in political life, and that incompetent and dishonest candidates are often put up by the machines, has also kept many persons from casting their votes.   They feel that they can only choose between two incompetent or dishonest candidates, or that their vote will not count for much, even though they go to the polls to cast it.

**Our two-party system unreal.**   The unreality of our two-party system for several generations has also tended to undermine party government in the United States.   As we pointed out earlier, our parties are not sharply divided on any great issues as they were in 1856 or 1896.   This has become increasingly true since the adoption of the so-called bipartisan foreign policy after 1945.   The transparent sham of our political campaigns, with their obvious concern for the spoils of office rather than for high principles of government, has generated a feeling of indifference among intelligent voters.   Any sound two-party system should reflect conservative versus progressive attitudes.   Then, the voters could choose between two fundamental attitudes concerning society and government.   The fact that our two major parties reflect much the same social background and represent the same economic interests destroys the reality and logic of the two-party system.

**Is our two-party system doomed?**   Many feared that the sixteen-year Democratic tenure of power, and the inertia, ineptitude, and lack of aggressiveness and imagination on the part of the Republican party during these years might mean the end of the two-party system in this country.   This fear was intensified by the Democratic victory in 1948.   It is doubtful if conditions can ever again be more favorable to a Republican victory than they were in 1948, had the party been willing to appeal to the people on the basis of the vital issues of the day.

**Democracy, party government, and the growth of bureaucracy.**   Since one of the most popular ways of rewarding a faithful party worker is by giving him some government job, political parties and democracy have greatly enlarged the number of jobholders and thus increased the cost of government.

## GROWTH OF FEDERAL BUREAUCRACY

**EACH FIGURE REPRESENTS 250,000 FEDERAL EMPLOYEES**

This chart shows the remarkable increase in the number of federal workers from New Deal days to the mid-century.

While the growth of the Federal bureaucracy was well under way at the turn of the century and had reached impressive proportions before the depression of 1929, the most remarkable increase in Federal employees and payroll came after 1932. In 1929, there were 596,492 persons on the Federal payroll and their salaries and wages came to $1,079,940,000. In 1932, there were 621,580 on the Federal payroll and their income amounted to $1,059,138,000. The extension of government activities under the New Deal and our entrance into the second world war led to a really mushroom growth of the Federal bureaucracy. In 1941, there were 1,431,961 Federal employees, with a payroll of $2,701,694,000. By 1945, the number of civilians on the Federal payroll had risen to 3,569,092, and their income to $8,153,-686,000. There was a decline after 1945, but it was by no means spectacular or back to the 1941 level. On January 1, 1949, there were 2,375,000 civilian Federal employees and the 1948 payroll was $6,209,-369,000. Including the armed services, the total Federal payroll in 1949 was about 10 billion dollars, and 6 out of every 100 employees were directly in the pay of the Federal government.

Government employees were, of course, only a small percentage of those receiving payments from the government. In addition to the 2,375,000 government workers, there were, at the end of 1948, 125,000 retired civil service employees, 1,412,000 members of the armed forces, 2,900,000 veterans or their dependents on pension, 2,538,000 veterans attending school or college, 546,000 veterans receiving on-the-job training, 3,205,000 farmers getting soil conservation and parity payments, and 2,471,000 receiving benefit payments under the Social Security system. This made some 16,000,000 persons getting Federal payments, or about one out of every six adults in the country. The total income of those receiving some form of payment from the Federal government in 1949 was close to 20 billion dollars.

It was found desirable in 1947 to create a commission, headed by former president Herbert Hoover, to make a study of the Federal bureaucracy and to suggest ways of consolidating it and reducing it. The Hoover Commission discovered a vast complexity and overlapping in the Federal bureaucracy. For example, there were 75 separate bureaus with authority in the field of transportation, 93 in the business of public lending, 37 engaged in foreign trade activities, 64 dealing with relations with business, 22 handling insurance, and 44 involved in agriculture. How much reduction in the bureaucracy the work of the Hoover Commission will be able to achieve remains to be seen. Its report was not followed by any evident intention of Congress to act immediately and decisively on its recommendations. Those adopted in the session of 1949 related to details rather than to any general reorganization.

Since most public criticism is directed at the Federal bureaucracy and its costs, we tend to lose sight of the fact that there is a state and local government bureaucracy which is larger and even more expensive. In 1932, the state and local governments had 2,667,000 employees with an income of $3,504,000,000. In 1945, there were 3,181,000 such employees and their income stood at $5,600,000,000. This state and local bureaucracy did not fall off after the war, but actually increased. In January, 1949, there were 3,975,000 on the state and local government payrolls, which amounted to $9,560,000,000. The growth of the state and local bureaucracy and the expenditures thereby are reflected in the rise of the state and local debt from $4,400,000,000 in 1912 to $16,200,000,000 in 1948.

Commerce Department statistics showed that in 1949 some 7,685,000 persons were on some type of government payroll, Federal, state or local. This number included those in the armed services, and constituted one out of about every eight employees in the country. The total payroll for such persons was approximately 22 billion dollars, accounting for about one dollar out of every six paid for wages and salaries in the whole country in 1949.

Of course, this great increase of the bureaucracy, Federal, state, and local, is not to be attributed solely to political graft and corruption under the party system. A considerable portion of the growth has been due to the inevitable extension of government activity as our mode of life under an industrial and urban civilization has become more complex. But no small part of it is due to the methods of partisan politics, strikingly summarized in the remark attributed to Harry Hopkins: "We must tax and tax and tax, and spend and spend and spend, and elect and elect and elect."

**Political graft.** Also to be noted is the stimulation of graft by party government and democracy—graft not only in jobs, but also in special favors, phony contracts, and the like. Federal graft has been notorious in the so-called pork-barrel legislation in Congress, through which large sums have been wasted or partially wasted as special favors given to constituents of congressmen in the way of Federal buildings, lavish public works, pensions, and the like. Political graft in states has taken the form of wasteful construction of public buildings, roads, and other public works, and of padding the public payrolls. City graft under such machines as those of Thompson and Kelly in Chicago, Walker and Tammany Hall in New York, and Pendergast in Kansas City has been especially notorious. Padded payrolls, bogus or especially favored contracts, tax-rebates, kick-backs, and protection of gambling and vice have been comomn forms of urban political graft. They were flagrant at the beginning of the present century, when Lincoln Steffens wrote his famous book *The Shame of the Cities,* and little has been done to remedy the abuses since that time.

**Minority pressure groups place majority rule in jeopardy.** There have been two recent developments in party government in this country which menace both the two-party system and efficient democratic government. One is the development of powerful pressure groups which endeavor to influence elections. They are drawn from both conservative and radical elements. The conservative Liberty League opposed President Roosevelt and the New Deal, while the radical Political Action Committee (PAC) favored New Deal policies and candidates, especially those who supported Mr. Roosevelt's war program. These pressure groups were unintentionally encouraged by the Hatch Acts of 1939 and 1940 which limited contributions to the formal political parties. There is no such limitation placed on contributions to the pressure groups. The pressure groups have sometimes formed special political parties in states where the vote is close, such as the American Labor party and the Liberal party in New York, but more usually they concentrate on the support or defeat of a candidate of one of the main parties. In the former case, they threaten the rise of a bloc system in this country, and in both cases they place political control of millions of voters in the hands of a small minority.

**The menace of party government by emergency.** The other disturbing innovation has been the rise of "government by emergency," especially the emergencies created by foreign crises, real or imaginary. This creates a pseudo-patriotic appeal for both parties to unite in a situation of implied national emergency and danger. Since 1945, there has been a bi-partisan foreign policy uniting Republicans and Democrats on foreign issues, one field where there might be a legitimate and logical division of party policies. This trend has made for one-party government in a very important range of public policy. Moreover, since emergencies produce strong emotions, this government by emergency has tended to introduce into normal governmental procedure the highly emotional atmosphere which was previously limited to campaigns or wartime politics. This state of mind tends to obstruct the application of common sense and rationality to governmental problems, both domestic and foreign.

The most serious danger in such a policy is that these emergency situations, usually based on war scares, have already produced a worldwide "cold war" and may precipitate a "hot war." If persistently pursued, this procedure is bound to hamper, if it does not actually terminate, representative government and democracy.

## Attempts to Reform Representative Government and Party Politics

The false hope of direct primaries. Attempts, so far rather unsuccessful, have been made to reform party politics, in order to improve the democratic system. Among the more important reforms have been the direct primary, the initiative and referendum, the recall, civil service, and attempts to curb campaign expenditures. The main idea behind the direct primary, the initiative and referendum, and the recall was that the best cure for the defects of democracy is more democracy.

The direct primary is an attempt to lessen the influence of political bosses and party leaders and eliminate the bribery and corruption that often goes with caucuses and nominating conventions. The convention nominates candidates by a vote of the majority of delegates, who have usually been selected by the bosses. The slate of candidates under the traditional convention system is almost always selected in advance by the bosses and usually accepted in perfunctory fashion by the delegates. The convention system thus provides many opportunities to facilitate machine control. So, it was hoped that the direct primary, which puts the matter of selecting delegates, candidates, or both, directly up to the voters, would aid the people in naming the candidates of their choice.

Primary elections are held a few months before the regular elections. A person desiring to run for office files a petition signed by the required number of voters. Several candidates from one party may run for the same office in the primary. The one receiving the highest vote obtains the nomination, which is usually formally confirmed by a nominating convention. Unfortunately, even fewer persons usually turn out for the primaries than for regular elections; and the party leaders and bosses, with ample funds at their disposal, have found ways to control the primaries, so that, as a reform measure, the direct primary system has not been very successful. It merely provides a more expensive method of ultimate boss control of nominations. It is not as warmly supported today as it was a generation ago. By the time of the presidential campaign of 1948, only 14 states used the direct primary, choosing only 496 out of the total of 1,094 delegates to the national convention. Of these 496 delegates only 153 were directly obligated to vote for a particular candidate at the convention.

**Initiative, referendum. and recall.** Direct legislation, or the initiative and referendum, constitutes another attempt to reform partisan politics and the democratic system. The use of the initiative means that a proposed law is formulated by its sponsors and submitted to the legislature or the voters. A group of citizens desiring to obtain its passage must submit a petition to the election officials signed by a certain percentage of voters. The initiative has not proved satisfactory because of the lack of interest and activity on the part of the voters. The referendum is the submission to the voters of a measure which has been either proposed by the people or passed by the legislature. The referendum is based on the theory that it is the people who ought to decide whether or not a law should go into effect. This attempted reform has also failed to accomplish its purpose because voters refused to take advantage of this opportunity to control legislation.

The recall, like the initiative and referendum, is based on the theory that the people must have a direct and determining control over political issues and officials. In theory, the recall is intended to do away with graft and corruption by according the people an opportunity to recall an official whom they believe to be inefficient or dishonest. But the recall is often used by bosses as a weapon against a worthy official who has incurred the resentment of the party machine. In such cases, instead of being a weapon of democracy, it becomes an additional tool of the machine.

**Proportional representation.** Another proposal to improve democracy is that of proportional representation. Under our present system of absolute majority rule, one voter can theoretically determine the election in a state having millions of voters. In New York State, in which five and a half million persons normally vote, a single vote could determine whether the Democrats or the Republicans would carry the state, and the defeated party would be unrepresented, even though it turned out a vast vote. Under a system of proportional representation, all parties would be represented in proportion to their voting strength.

There is no doubt about the logical soundness of this system or of its potential contribution to improving the fairness and efficiency of representative government and democratic methods. But the system of voting and counting the votes is so complicated that it requires more interest and application than the average voter or election officials are inclined to display. Hence, it has been no more successful in gaining general approval than direct primaries, the initiative and referendum, and the recall, which likewise demand special interest and alertness on the part of the electorate.

**Civil service attacks the spoils system.** Civil service, or the merit system, was designed to curb the evils of the "spoils system." Civil service is a system of political selection whereby appointments to office are based on the fitness of the candidate, as determined by examinations. The civil service system in our country was launched in the 1870's and has made impressive headway since.

Although most Federal and many state offices are now filled through civil service, political "pull," exercised by public officials, is often responsible for the choice of civil service appointees from a list of those who have passed the examination. Usually a certain number of persons who stand at the head of the list are "certified" as eligible for the post. But the actual appointments from this certified list are often determined by the degree of political influence the eligible persons can command.

There is also the danger that officials appointed through civil service may, because of their long experience and permanent tenure, exercise too great an influence over officials who are elected to office. In England, for instance, permanent civil service officials have become a powerful bureaucracy, and the elected officials are often powerless to change the administrative machinery or put through desirable new legislation.

**Increased nomination and campaign expenditures.** The growing expenditures for nomination and election to public office—often running into millions of dollars—have encouraged attempts to curb these abuses. Large amounts of money have been spent on nominations since the introduction of the direct primary system. In fact, the direct primary was partly responsible for the huge increases in campaign expenditures. It has cost more to entice the votes of the large number going to the primaries than it did to control the few who used to vote in conventions and caucuses. The nominating expenditures, particularly for the presidency, have been excessive. Theodore Roosevelt's campaign for nomination in 1912 cost $750,000; in the period preceding the Republican convention of 1920, so much money was spent by candidates in the struggle for delegates that two of the most prominent contenders were virtually disqualified. The campaign of one, Leonard Wood, cost $1,775,000. The candidates for United States Senator in Pennsylvania spent some $1,500,000 in the primary elections of 1938.

Election expenditures have also become very lavish. A good example is the list of official expenditures during the presidential campaign of 1936, when approximately $24,000,000 were spent publicly and officially, all but about $300,000 by the Republicans and Democrats. These official campaign expenditures were broken down as follows:

| | |
|---|---:|
| Republican National Committee | $8,892,971 |
| Democrat National Committee | 5,651,118 |
| Communist Party | 162,040 |
| Union Party | 65,296 |
| Socialist Labor Party | 31,659 |
| Socialist Party | 24,962 |
| Prohibition Party | 13,081 |
| State Republican and Democrat Committees | 7,876,533 |
| Miscellaneous Political Organizations | 1,255,266 |

Unofficial and informal expenditures during this campaign cannot be stated precisely, but authorities have estimated that they may have equaled the official public outlay. It was these figures and those for the congressional campaigns of 1938 that led to more drastic efforts to curb primary and election expenditures.

**Failure of efforts to curb party expenditures.** Laws such as the Corrupt Practices Acts from 1911 to 1925 and the Hatch Acts of 1939 and 1940 were designed to prevent elections from being controlled by those who could buy the greatest number of votes. These laws have outlawed contributions from employees of the Federal government, ordered Federal employees to refrain from campaigning, forbidden contributions from national banks and public corporations, limited the amount of money to be spent in campaigns for Federal offices, made it illegal to promise jobs in return for political support, forbidden bribery in voting, and required that campaign expenditures be made public.

The poor man is still handicapped, however, in running for office. The laws do not cover money spent for personal expenses, stationery, postage, printing, telephone or telegraph charges, and the like. Friends may privately spend almost unlimited amounts for their candidates. Large sums may be spent before the campaign begins, or debts may be piled up to be paid after the expense account is published. In other words, the laws have not effectively curbed campaign expenditures. Despite the Hatch Acts, it was charged that more money was spent in the presidential campaign of 1940 than ever before in our history. The Republicans spent, altogether, about 15 million dollars, and, while the Democrats did not spend as much directly, they are said to have made adroit indirect use of the vast defense appropriations for campaign purposes.

**Serious crisis in representative government.** Representative government has not, so far, provided an efficient democracy. The voice of the people, even when it exists, is often too weak to be heard. The people have been unwilling to take advantage of such suggested reforms as the initiative, referendum, and recall. These more direct democratic programs have, thus, proved a failure for the same reasons which produced a need for them—public ignorance and apathy.

Since 1940, our efforts to reform our own democracy have been checked or minimized because we have concentrated our primary effort on forcibly imposing a sham democratic system on foreign countries before we had made a real success of democracy at home. Further, American democracy has suffered in the last twenty years or so from the increasing use of unscrupulous propaganda, and especially from the so-called "smearing technique," which has concentrated more on discrediting rival candidates and platforms than on honestly informing the voters on political issues. This greatly intensified use of ever more conscienceless propaganda has been forwarded by the public capitulation to the spellbinding tactics of irresponsible newspaper columnists and radio commentators.

An able student of democracy, the late Dean William E. Mosher, has remarked: "Our citizenry which customarily leaves politics to the politicians is paying a staggering price for its apathy. Occasionally it grumbles at the high tax bills, but only rarely . . . does it bestir itself and make itself heard in the political arena. . . . The parties as at present constituted and conducted are, in my opinion, unequal to the task of keeping democracy afloat."

**Occupational or vocational representation.** The proponents of vocational representation claim that, since each territorial district is inhabited by persons who represent many interests, even the most conflicting interests, no elected representative under such a system can logically or competently represent his whole district in a legislature. If, however, the leading interest-groups or vocations elected their own representatives directly, those thus elected could competently, even expertly, represent those who had selected them. It is further argued that such a system of vocational representation would assure superior representatives, since no interest-group or vocation would risk the chance of being represented by a venal, ignorant, or incompetent man. And this method would eliminate the evil of the lobby, since all interests would be openly and directly represented.

There is much to support the force and logic of this proposition, but it runs counter to the venerable democratic dogma that representative government must be based on territorial districts, numerical representation, and majority decisions—a doctrine we inherit from the French political philosopher, Jean Jacques Rousseau. Confusion and controversy would arise concerning the distribution of power and numerical representation among the various vocational groups—the bankers might demand more representatives than the barbers, and the teachers more than either. Vocational representation has been tried in different degrees in various states of Europe, but it has rarely been installed except as the result of revolution or war.

## Summary

The main stages in the evolution of the state and government have been the elective bodies of kinship society, feudalism based on personal relations and loyalties, patriarchal city states, kingdoms, and empires and, in modern times, the national state. It is thought by some leading students of political evolution that the next stage will be that of regional federations and that, ultimately, we may have a world federation. The national state was at first absolutist and tyrannical, but with the development of the middle class after 1500 it became constitutional, representative, and republican.

Our form of democracy is representative government in a republic. The people do not rule directly; such a system is impossible in a large national state. Instead, they elect men to represent them and to carry out their wishes. The responsibility for good government however, does lie with the people, for they have the power and responsibility of selecting officeholders.

The Industrial Revolution helped promote democratic government, for the workers in the factory towns demanded the right to be represented, so that they could improve their social and economic conditions. By the end of the nineteenth century, most industrialized European countries had granted universal male suffrage. The United States established political democracy over a hundred years ago, in the era of Andrew Jackson. Here frontier farmers joined with factory workers to help on democracy.

So long as the people lived chiefly in rural areas, the problems of democracy were not too complex. But, as the nation became urbanized, people could no longer know their candidates personally, or understand the issues at stake. Political parties were created for the purpose of making known the qualifications and platforms of certain candidates.

Because it is both logical and usual for opinions and political interests to vary, more than one party arose. The United States has always had two major parties; for about a century they have been the Republicans and Democrats. In earlier days, these two parties disagreed on many issues. Now, however, discerning people see little difference between the Republican and Democratic platforms. Our political system has many faults, the chief of which, machine control of parties, breeds corruption and graft in office.

Big business often controls party government by putting into office men who will take orders from the great economic interests of the country. Men of high intelligence and integrity are not usually nominated or elected, for they may at times refuse to follow the dictates of the economic powers. The conflicting desires of the larger business groups have often made for confusion in party platforms.

Improved means of communication have enhanced the power of party propaganda in election campaigns. Instead of telling the voters the truth about the issues and candidates involved, too often the campaign only serves to confuse them. Only about half of the citizens vote, because many are bewildered and confused and feel that their vote is meaningless, what with so much graft and corruption in the political system and such minute differences in the principles and policies of the major parties.

There have been attempts to reform politics, but the failure of the public to take an active interest in making the reform measures a success has all too often rendered them useless. The best known reform measures are the direct primary, the initiative and referendum, the recall, and civil service.

Because the people have taken so little interest in supporting reform, democracy is now faced with a severe crisis. The will of the people has been too weak or confused to create an effective democracy. Unless the public becomes alert and determined and brings about the necessary reforms to make democracy work in the coming generation, there is grave danger that it will be overthrown and supplanted by some form of dictatorship.

## Selected References

Adams, S. H., *The Incredible Era*, Houghton Mifflin, 1939. Absorbing exposure of the corruption of the Harding régime by the leading journalistic authority on the period.

Anderson, F. M., *Constitutions and Other Select Documents Illustrative of the History of France, 1789–1907*, University of Minnesota Press, 1908. Valuable collection of source material on French constitutional evolution.

* Beard, C. A., *The Economic Basis of Politics*, Knopf, 1922. A stimulating book on economic factors in politics by the dean of American political scientists.

Bentley, A. F., *The Process of Government*, University of Chicago Press, 1908. Development of the idea of democratic and party government as a struggle of interest-groups. Probably most profound American book on government written in the twentieth century.

Billington, R. A., *Westward Expansion*, Macmillan, 1949. The latest and best book on the relation of the American frontier to democratic trends in this country.

* Brant, Irving, *Storm over the Constitution*, Bobbs-Merrill, 1936. Probably the best of the many books precipitated by the struggle over the Supreme Court and constitutional reform under the New Deal.

Burns, J. M., *Congress on Trial*, Harper, 1949. Searching study of the adequacy of congressional government in our critical postwar years. Warns against obstructionist nature of congressional tactics.

Endicott, Stephen, *Mayor Harding of New York*, Mohawk Press, 1931. A vivid account in quasi-fictional form of the Tammany Hall-Walker administration in New York City.

* Fisher, H. A. L., *The Republican Tradition in Europe*, Putnam, 1911. Brilliant account of the rise of republican government.

Flynn, J. T., *The Roosevelt Myth*, Devin-Adair, 1948. Vigorous exposure of the alleged corruption and inefficiency of the New Deal administrations.

* Ford, H. J., *Representative Government*, Holt, 1924. An authoritative history of the theory and practice of representative government.

Gosnell, H. F., *Democracy*, Ronald Press, 1949. Important study of the problems of suffrage, voting, and representative government.

Hayes, C. J. H., *Essays on Nationalism*, Macmillan, 1926.

* ————, *The Historical Evolution of Modern Nationalism*, R. R. Smith, 1931. Two interesting books by the foremost American student of nationalism.

Herring, E. P., *Group Representation before Congress*, Brookings Institution, 1929. The classic work on the lobby in American politics.

* Jenks, Edward, *The State and The Nation*, Dutton, 1919. Perhaps the most useful introduction to the history of government, by a leading English legal historian.

* Key, V. O., *Politics, Parties, and Pressure Groups*, Crowell, 1942. Probably the best single book on party and campaign methods in the United States today.

MacLeod, W. C., *The Origin and History of Politics*, Wiley, 1931. The best introduction to the history of the successive forms of the state and government.

McIlwain, C. H., *Constitutionalism, Ancient and Modern*, Cornell University Press, 1940. Scholarly account of origins of constitutional government.

McKean, D. D., *Boss: The Hague Machine in Action*, Houghton Mifflin, 1940. A forthright study of the powerful Hague machine in Jersey City.

* Merriam, C. E., *The American Party System*, Macmillan, 1940. Authoritative presentation of the essential characteristics and methods of American party government.

Michels, Robert, *Political Parties*, Hearst International Library, 1915. The leading sociological study of political parties. Stresses oligarchical trends.

* Michelson, Charles, *The Ghost Talks*, Putnam, 1944. Restrained autobiography of the director of publicity for the Democratic party from 1929 to 1944 and the cleverest and most unscrupulous political propagandist in American history.

Myers, Gustavus, *A History of Tammany Hall*, Boni and Liveright, 1917. A vivid and candid account of the history and operations of the most powerful political machine in the United States.

Salter, J. T., *Boss Rule*, Whittlesey House, 1935. A study of party politics and city machines, especially in Philadelphia.

Swisher, C. B., *American Constitutional Development*, Houghton Mifflin, 1943. The origins and development of our American Federal constitutional system.

Walker, Harvey, *The Legislative Process*, Ronald, 1949. Probably the best book on the lawmaking process under congressional government in a democracy.

Wallas, Graham, *Human Nature in Politics*, Houghton Mifflin, 1909. The first thorough discrediting of the Benthamite doctrine of the rational character of political life under the democratic and party system.

* Wallis, J. H., *The Politician*, Stokes, 1935. Perhaps the best single volume ever written on the character, methods, and activities of party politicians of all ranks and classes.

————, *The Pattern of Politics*, Macmillan, 1940. An able socio-psychological interpretation of party government in our democracy.

Wormuth, F. D., *The Origins of Modern Constitutionalism*, Harper, 1949. Brief but scholarly account of the origins of constitutional government in England, including some attention to the Greek and Roman background.

# CHAPTER XVII

# The Crisis in Democracy and Civil Liberties

## The Fathers of the Constitution Created a Republic Rather than a Democracy

**Our country founded by political aristocrats.** It will give us a much better historical perspective for understanding the evolution of the American political system if we recognize that our Federal government did not start out as a democracy. Very few men who helped to make the Constitution in 1787 and set up the new government in 1789 actually believed in democracy. They deliberately created an aristocratic republican form of government which excluded the majority of the people from any direct participation in government. Moreover, they set up an Electoral College to assure the selection of the ablest men for president on a non-partisan basis. Republics may be either aristocratic or democratic. Our republic did not become democratic until the Jacksonian era.

**The American Revolution based on middle-class ideals.** The American Revolution was conceived and fought on the basis of the same middle-class revolutionary theories that inspired the English commercial classes in the seventeenth century. England did not set up a fully democratic government until 1918, though considerable democratization of the English system came about through the reform legislation passed in 1832, 1864, and 1884. The United States provided at least the legal basis for democracy nearly a century before England did, but our government was not democratic at the outset.

**Aristocratic political philosophy of the fathers.** Benjamin Franklin, George Washington, Alexander Hamilton, John Adams, and most of their associates were devoted believers in aristocracy in government and were fearful of the results of mass rule. Even Thomas Jefferson, who is usually regarded as the father of American democracy, was moderately aristocratic in his political theory. Although he differed from men like Washington and Hamilton in holding that the people could be trusted to select able men to rule them, he meant by the "people" only that superior minority who were allowed to vote in his time.

407

The Federal Constitution made and adopted by republican aristocrats. Our Federal Constitution was made by men who held these aristocratic views of politics, and it was adopted by the vote of a minority of the people, the majority being disqualified from voting because of religious beliefs or the failure to own property. Historians are pretty generally agreed that, if there had been universal suffrage in 1787, the Constitution would have been rejected by popular vote.

The transition to a democratic republic. Great changes took place in political philosophy between 1787 and 1829, when Jackson was inaugurated as president. These were based in part upon the rise of industrialism, especially in New England, which produced a growing body of factory workers who desired a direct share in government; in part upon the development of the western frontier, which produced strong convictions concerning the literal equality of all men and the right of all to participate personally in public affairs.

As a result of the agitation of workers and frontiersmen and the vigorous leadership of the Jacksonian group, our republic was transformed from an aristocratic system to a democratic régime. A slogan of the Jacksonian era, attributed to George Bancroft, declared that "the voice of the people is the voice of God." This was a far cry from the views of even Thomas Jefferson, to say nothing of those of Alexander Hamilton, who once declared that "the people are a great beast."

## Leading Principles of the Democratic Ideal

The fundamental meaning of democracy. There have been many notions of democracy in the history of the struggle for human rights. Democracy, from a political point of view, has meant government by a majority of the people. This majority rule has been achieved by means of universal suffrage and representative government. We have shown in the previous chapter how representative government has operated by means of political parties.

Democracy, as an ideal, is, however, more than a mere form of government. It not only means the participation of the people in public affairs, directly or through their representatives, but also implies that there will emerge out of popular sovereignty a beneficial type of social organization. Democracy thus places responsibility upon the people to control public policy and to produce a social organization that will give every member of society an opportunity to develop his personal capabilities to the fullest extent. Today, as we have already seen, democracy faces a serious crisis. Nearly all the European democracies have been undermined or menaced by Fascism, Communism, and war. American democracy not only faced a serious international situation in the second world war, but continued after the war to be challenged by complicated problems both abroad and at home.

The assumptions underlying American democracy. In order to understand the crisis of American democracy, we must look at the fundamental ideas on which our democracy is based. The more important original assumptions of our American democracy about 1830 were: (1) that the country would remain predominantly agricultural; (2) that the government should not interfere in business; (3) that all men are literally equal in ability and are qualified to hold any office; (4) that the majority of the people would certainly make use of their long-desired and eagerly fought-for right to vote; (5) that the masses would take a deep interest in political issues and carefully consider platforms and candidates before voting; (6) that the judgment of the masses can be trusted in facing and solving great public issues; (7) that political problems are almost exclusively of a domestic or national character, and foreign affairs need not be a matter of deep concern to political leaders; and (8) that a democracy can be established and made to work irrespective of the national traditions or social background of its constituents. This last idea has been revived in ambitious and highly expensive fashion in our occupation policies in Germany and Japan since V-J Day.

**Jeffersonian notions of agrarianism and laissez faire.** The fathers of our country based their theory of government on the belief that the United States would remain primarily a nation of farmers. Thomas Jefferson, for example, declared that republican government could exist only so long as there was a frontier and the population was relatively scattered in rural areas.

Another fundamental belief of the founders of our country was that the best government is that which governs least; in other words, that government should leave private enterprise alone. This is known as the laissez-faire theory of government. Jefferson once declared that a free press is worth more than any government.

Between Jefferson's presidency (1801–1809) and that of Andrew Jackson (1829–1837), there was a period in which the opposition party, the National Republicans, favored increased government aid to roads and canals, a higher tariff, a national bank, and larger Federal loans to states. But, under Jackson, the tariff was lowered, the United States Bank was abolished, and Federal grants for public improvements were reduced or withdrawn. During the entire period of Democratic ascendancy, from 1829 until the Civil War, the democratic system of government was developed along the lines of state rights and non-interference in business.

**Jacksonian ideas of the equality of man.** The Jacksonians held that a man needs no special training to hold any political office. They believed that, if a general system of education were made available to all citizens, there would be almost complete cultural and intellectual equality in a democratic society. The democratic movement was, thus, an important force in spreading the idea of popular education.

This theory of the equality of all men and the fitness of everybody to hold any office was not so absurd then as it is now. In Jackson's day, life was hard, and only strong men could endure the rigors of the frontier, build homes in the wilderness, clear the land, and fight the Indians. The weaklings died off; and the survivors, who were the fit, had relatively uniform ability and could handle the comparatively simple problems of government. Moreover, in those days there were no psychological tests to demonstrate that persons are not equal in mental ability.

**Assumed eagerness to vote.** Those who believed in the democratic ideal contended that not only were all people competent to vote and govern, but that, once given the right to vote, all would take an active interest in political matters. They had full confidence that, universal suffrage would solve all political problems. This assumption, too, was more logical a century or so ago, when government was more definitely related to local needs and seemed to touch people's daily life more closely than it does today, and when voters knew many candidates for city and state officers personally.

**Political campaigns as adult education.** The Jacksonians believed that all voters would carefully examine the candidates and political platforms, size up the situation shrewdly, and then make a deliberate intellectual choice. Political campaigns were expected to be periods of intensive adult education in public affairs.

Another related belief was that, if the masses became aware of injustices in government and wrongs in society, they would speedily and intelligently exercise their rights and powers to overcome them.

**Democracy and splendid isolation.** Further, there was a belief that our democracy could develop without our reckoning too much with world affairs. This seemed entirely logical at the time of the Monroe Doctrine of 1823, before the development of rapid overseas communication. Only a decade before, we had entered a war (that of 1812) after the British had removed our chief reason for declaring war, and won the main American victory of that war (the Battle of New Orleans) after the treaty of peace had been signed. We failed to learn of either of these events in time because of the lack of an Atlantic cable.

**Democracy as a fiat of pure reason.** Finally, there was the idea in early days that democracy could be installed by a decree of the human will—by the application of the dictates of pure reason. If a people passed legislation legalizing democracy, this was essentially all that was needed. Not much concern needed to be given to the question of whether the traditions, ideals, culture, and social background of the people were favorable to the reception and success of the democratic experiment.

## Putting Democratic Assumptions to the Test

**Great cultural changes since the Age of Jackson.** The basic principles on which our democratic government was established may have been sound and workable for the social, economic, and cultural life of 125 years ago, but conditions have now been completely changed.

In the place of the simple agricultural and frontier society of Andrew Jackson's time, we have a complex, urban, industrial world-civilization, which presents an increasing volume and variety of problems that must be regulated in some degree by political action.   No longer are political communities small rural social units.   Over 60 per cent of Americans now live in cities and another 25 per cent are more influenced by urban conditions than by rural life.   The United States is today a land of cities, factories, and machines.   Rapid transit and communication have broken down the isolation of former days.   Large-scale industry and the interdependence of producer and consumer have taken the place of the former self-sufficient farmer.   Free land is no longer available for settlement, and the rugged individualist of the frontier has gone forever.

**Development of state interference in economic life.**   In our complicated industrial society, there is relatively little free competition, and unemployment, arising from various causes, has made it difficult for millions of workers to get jobs in "normal" times.   There is no such equality of opportunity as our forefathers knew.   Government has been forced to interfere in the activities of society and individuals to an extent that would have horrified Jacksonians.   The whole trend of political life is toward greater centralization of power in the hands of government.

Our public utilities, transportation and communication agencies, economic planning, public works, and relief are matters that require centralized supervision, control, or administration by Federal and state governments.   Such New Deal and wartime measures as the National Industrial Recovery Act, the Agricultural Adjustment Act, Works Progress Administration, the Social Security Act, the Office of Price Administration, rationing boards, and government aid to housing, medical care, and education are instances of the growing government intervention in the economic affairs of the country.   There are countless other examples of increasing governmental regulation.   Those who oppose government intervention in business in behalf of the masses are usually passionately in favor of government intervention in behalf of the classes, through such obvious and extensive government interference as our extremely high protective tariff system.

**Are all men equal in ability?**   No longer can we support the doctrine that all men are equal in ability.   Modern biology and psychology have revealed striking innate or hereditary differences between individuals.   Very reliable mental tests have shown that only about one-sixth of the population can be described as superior types, capable of leadership, and that 45 per cent of the people in the United States have a mental age of twelve years or under.[1]

While this does not mean that majority rule is always the rule of the stupid, since even in a democracy the leaders may guide the masses,

---

[1] See below, pp. 810–812.

still it does amply prove that we cannot always expect to get the benefit of political wisdom merely by depending on sheer majority rule.

Political offices in our day can no longer safely be filled with untrained persons. Obviously, no living man is fully equipped by ability and knowledge to be President of the United States, and few are qualified to be a United States senator or governor of an important state. What we can and must aim for in such cases is relative or approximate competence. Most of the problems which must receive governmental attention today are complex and technical. A legislator, to be qualified for his office, needs professional knowledge as great as that possessed by an economist, engineer, physician, or college professor. We insist on special training for a physician, a lawyer, or a druggist before we consider him capable of handling even our minor personal problems. Yet, despite the improvements of civil service, we allow many an unprepared person—and no few ignorant bunglers— to occupy responsible political positions.

**The problem of non-voting.** The old belief that all citizens would show an absorbing interest in public matters and, given the right to vote, would flock to the polls has been disproved by voting statistics. Only about half or less of the authorized voters get out to the polls,

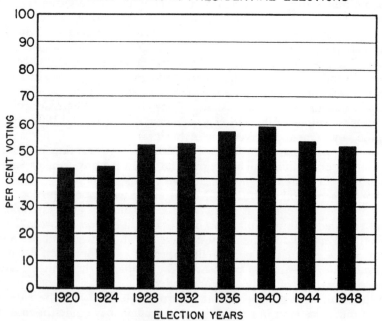

PER CENT VOTING IN PRESIDENTIAL ELECTIONS

This chart indicates the extent to which qualified American voters fail to use the right of suffrage.

even in presidential campaigns.   In 1920, 43.6 per cent of the eligible voters went to the polls; in 1924, 44.2 per cent; in 1928, 52.2 per cent; in 1932, 52.8 per cent; in 1936, 57.1 per cent; in 1940, 59.1 per cent; in 1944, 53.8 per cent; and in 1948, 51.9 per cent.

The voting in state and local elections and in congressional elections in "off years" is far smaller than in the presidential contests. For example, of the 49,500,000 voting in the presidential election of 1940 only about 27,000,000 voted in the congressional election of 1942. The popular vote in direct primaries has been so small that the primary as a democratic reform measure has often been abandoned. Issues submitted to the people in the form of a referendum create less interest than party elections, apparently because the latter involve personalities.

**Political irrationality and incapacity of masses.**   In the preceding chapter, we showed how the rise of the party system and our newer propaganda techniques for stirring up violent emotions during campaigns have completely upset the earlier hope that political campaigns would be periods of serious adult education for the masses on public issues.   Modern psychology has shown that man is not a cool, calculating being, carefully considering his every act, but is dominated by tradition, habit, emotion, and crowd psychology.   The successful party, therefore, is usually the one that develops the best propaganda techniques to exploit successfully these springs of human behavior.   As a result, campaigns frequently degenerate into emotional orgies rather than being periods of clear and lucid thinking on public affairs.   They becloud such rationality as we are able to muster in normal times.

Moral problems are becoming so complex that only well-informed persons can solve them successfully.   They can hardly be trusted to uninformed mass impulses and movements.   Our two great mass movements of a moral nature, the Abolitionist Movement and Prohibition, are thought by many to have been great mistakes.   It is held that Abolitionism, by precipitating the Civil War, ruled out a sane and peaceful solution of the slavery question, and that Prohibition set back by many years the cause of reasonable and effective temperance.

On the other hand, the majority of our citizens are usually indifferent to obvious public moral wrongs and abuses.   The corruption of the Harding administration, for example, did not lead to the repudiation of the Republicans in 1924; instead, the Republican candidate, though associated with the corruption and lacking in personal appeal, was given an unprecedented majority of the votes.

**International implications of democracy today.**   Democratic leaders cannot safely ignore international trends and problems today.   Even the first world war showed that the most successful democratic governments may be undermined or destroyed by ignoring foreign affairs, or by adopting unwise foreign policies that involve them in wars that the majority of people do not desire.   An excellent democratic government, like that of England in 1905–1914, may be fatally weakened or destroyed by a quite needless foreign war. Our own two most promising democratic experiments, Wilson's New Freedom and Roosevelt's New Deal, were disrupted and ruined by our entry into wars. Democracy can never function well if disturbed by frequent and expensive wars or burdened by heavy armament expenditures.

## THE BUDGET DOLLAR

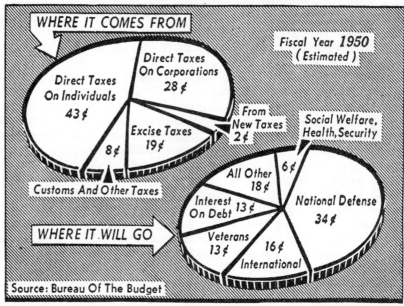

WHERE IT COMES FROM

Fiscal Year *1950* (Estimated)

Direct Taxes On Corporations 28 ¢

Direct Taxes On Individuals 43 ¢

Excise Taxes 19 ¢

8 ¢

Customs And Other Taxes

From New Taxes 2 ¢

Social Welfare, Health, Security 6 ¢

All Other 18 ¢

Interest On Debt 13 ¢

National Defense 34 ¢

WHERE IT WILL GO

Veterans 13 ¢

16 ¢ International

Source: Bureau Of The Budget

*Courtesy of Wide World Photos, Inc.*

The above diagram indicates the heavy proportion of federal revenue from direct personal taxation; the overwhelming financial burden of wars, past, present, and future; and the trivial portion of the budget assigned to welfare in the so-called welfare state or "Fair Deal" program.

Moreover, the twentieth century has proved that democracy is, in itself, no safeguard against war. Democratic leaders have frequently proved more deliberately bellicose than powerful monarchs and dictators. There is not the slightest evidence that democratic politicians are more loath to make war than dictators. President Poincaré of democratic France was far more eager for war in 1914 than was the Tsar of Russia or the German Kaiser. If, however, democracy does not cure war, war tends to "cure" democracy, by obliterating it.

**Social conditions should be favorable to democracy.** Political and social science have shown that it is foolish arbitrarily to establish a form of government and then expect it to create and mold a favorable social system. Democracy can develop only where the historical tradition of the nation and social conditions are well adapted to encourage

democratic institutions.   The conditions that once promoted democracy, and under which the original form of democracy might have
functioned with success—a simple agrarian society and a stable civilization—have now disappeared.   The assumptions of the fathers of
democracy have, as indicated, been disproved or greatly revised.   The
sensible procedure in the future would be to accept the fact that we are
expecting too much of the older democratic beliefs and practices in the
twentieth century.   We then might proceed to make the changes necessary to create an up-to-date or streamlined democracy, suited to our
new and complex social era.   In this way, democracy might safely
weather the political crisis.

## Important Aspects of the Current Democratic Crisis

**Efficiency in public service.**   Our most important problem in democratic government is that of getting trained, efficient, and socially-
minded persons into positions of authority.   Suggestions have been
made that only persons of at least normal intelligence be allowed to
vote, that expert knowledge be required of officeholders, and that
schools of politics and public administration be established to train
all government officials, for both domestic and foreign service.   Our
public schools and colleges should provide far more extensive and
realistic education in civics and political matters.

Inasmuch as a great deal of our information about public life and
problems comes from newspaper editorials, newspaper columnists, and
radio commentators, some method must be provided to assure that this
information will be more reliable and responsible.   We insist that an
instructor in political or social science shall spend some seven years in
college and graduate work before we will permit him to face a class
of a dozen freshmen.   But we permit men to write for millions of
readers and to go on the air before millions of listeners without even
the rudiments of education in the subjects they discuss.

**Men of ability often unavailable for public office.**   During the last
seventy-five years, the great economic interests have virtually taken
over the conduct of our government.   Men of great personal ability,
real dignity, broad education, and independence of character have not
been wanted in political offices because they would not always meekly
take orders from the powerful economic interests.   This explains why
Dr. Nicholas Murray Butler, independent and outspoken conservative
scholar, was not regarded favorably by the business interests as presidential material.   It also explains why, in the election of 1924, great
bankers deserted John W. Davis, the chief attorney of J. P. Morgan
and an outstandingly able conservative, and enthusiastically supported
Calvin Coolidge.

Moreover, men of dignity, integrity, and outstanding ability are not
likely to be attracted by, or to excel in, the somewhat vulgar, rough-
and-tumble methods required for political success under the party

system. Men with deep understanding of public problems are not usually enthusiastic adepts at baby-kissing or political banter.

One important and needless obstacle to the availability of able men for the presidency is the obsolete Electoral College. If a man comes from a state with a small number of electoral votes, he has virtually no chance whatever of being nominated for the presidency. A candidate must come from a state like New York, Pennsylvania, or Illinois, with a large electoral vote that the "favorite son" is likely to carry in an election. A man of great ability, like Senator George Aiken of Vermont, which has only four electoral votes, is about as ineligible for nomination as though he hailed from New Zealand.

**Democracy produces more politicians than statesmen.** Our democratic government and party system are admirably suited to producing skilled politicians—that is, men who are extremely adroit in getting elected to office. The same system is somehow deficient in providing us with statesmen, namely, men who know what to do after they get into political office—what to do, that is, beyond planning to get re-elected.

There is a vast difference between a politician and a statesman; indeed, very few superb politicians have ever shown much capacity for statecraft. Jefferson and Lincoln were two notable exceptions to the rule. It is one thing to be able to intrigue and manipulate the voters, but quite another to understand how best to deal with major public problems. Unless the present party system can give us a higher percentage of statesmen, as compared with politicians, than it has in the past, it is likely that democracy will be supplanted by a political system that will provide more expert leadership.

**Civil service helps to provide trained public officials.** There are some bright spots in this gloomy picture however. The civil service system, despite the drawbacks pointed out in the last chapter, has made a good start in getting competent persons to handle the details of governmental problems.

The origins of civil service came as a phase of the general revolt against the political corruption that raged unchecked during the administration of President Grant (1869–1877). After considerable debate in Congress, a civil service commission was created in 1871. In 1883 President Arthur signed the Pendleton Act which greatly strengthened the civil service movement, and with the appointment of Theodore Roosevelt in 1889 as civil service commissioner civil service came into its own. Cleveland, in his second term, and Presidents Theodore Roosevelt and Taft did far better than McKinley, Wilson, and Harding in checking the raids of the spoilsmen on the public service. Under the New Deal, great progress was made in bringing competent persons into government service and in extending the civil service system to many classes of Federal employees who had not previously benefited from it. An important measure was the placing of first-, second-, and third-class postmasters under the civil service.

The number of posts subject to competitive civil service examinations increased from 15,590 in 1885 to 1,751,000 in 1948, out of a total average Federal employee list of 2,090,000 for 1948. In the continental United States, some 1,714,487 out of a total of 1,859,807 Federal employees were in the civil service group—about 92 per cent.

**The spoils system promotes civil service.** It should be made clear that, while the civil service system is ostensibly designed to curb partisan politics and political graft, partisanship and graft have really been primarily responsible for the extension of the civil service system. They have actually accomplished more than the agitation of reformers. One party would get into power and appoint a great many of its followers to public offices. Then it would extend the civil service system to cover these government posts, so that the party appointees could not be thrown out after the next party defeat. When the opposing party got into power it repeated the process with other positions. The classified service has thus been extended until it covers nearly every administrative post in the Federal government. Graft and partisanship are likely to be much more limited in this field in the future.

**Need for extension of civil service to legislators and judges.** The Federal civil service, brought into existence and extended by the spoils system, has thus become a formidable bulwark against the spoils system. What we need is equal progress in state and municipal government, although here, too, much has been accomplished in the last decades. If democracy is to thrive, however, we should require rigorous civil service qualifications for legislators and judges, as well as administrative officials. There is no logical reason why the "merit system" should be limited to the executive branch of governments. There is little sense in subjecting a petty employee in the Bureau of Standards to severe information and proficiency tests and allowing United States senators to be chosen without any such qualifications whatever.

If there was once a day when government could be efficiently conducted in a hit-or-miss or rule-of-thumb fashion, and issues decided by the spicy repartee of rhetoric-loving politicians, that day is over, and legislation should be revised accordingly. The spread of the civil service system is a long step in the right direction.

**Streamlining Congress.** Among the other suggested steps is the proposal of ex-Senator Robert M. LaFollette, Jr. that Congress be streamlined. LaFollette's plan would involve the reduction and simplification of congressional committees, the removal of the seniority rule in determining committee chairmanships,[2] and the furnishing of congressional committees with competent research staffs. Ironically enough, Senator LaFollette, a supremely able senator, was defeated in

---

[2] This rule, an outmoded holdover from the nineteenth century, often results in the placing of a senile or uninformed congressman in charge of a vitally important committee.

a bid for re-election at the very time a badly emasculated version of his bill was being passed. Nevertheless, if his suggestion were fully heeded, this reform, along with those recommended by the Hoover Committee concerning the streamlining of the executive branch, would do much to revamp democracy and save us from the danger of seeking managerial efficiency in totalitarianism.

**Technocracy and democracy.** To preserve democracy, we must comprehend that our government, more than ever, requires honest and expert guidance. One of the most interesting suggestions along this line has been that of Technocracy—economic government by expert engineers. A corps of trained industrial engineers could easily determine the material needs of the American population and lay out an effective plan for building and maintaining future prosperity. This plan would necessarily require the public regulation of our economic life to an extent undreamed of in the philosophies of Jefferson and Jackson. Outside the economic realm, however, Technocracy would impose no limits on our freedom.

**Managerialism.** More comprehensive is the managerial system, which would combine political control by experts trained in public administration with the guidance of our economic life by industrial engineers, who would create a planned economy, producing mainly for human service rather than private profit. The New Deal régime under President Roosevelt was a sort of rudimentary managerialism. The British Labour Government, Italian Fascism, German National Socialism, and Soviet State Socialism are recent examples of more thoroughgoing managerial systems.

According to managerial theory, the future solution of our political problems lies in government by expert planners who, by relieving the public of economic worries, will make it easier to maintain true democracy in the cultural and social realms. We may anticipate a great deal of economic planning in any successful democracy in the mid-twentieth century.

Whatever the advantages, it is no substitute for forthright reforms in our democratic system. If we allow democracy to continue to decay and make up for its deficiencies by relying on the extension of managerialism, we may wake up some day to find that democracy is defunct and totalitarianism has taken over in its place.

**Social and economic democracy.** The perfecting of our system of political democracy would amount to little without concomitant advances toward social justice and economic security for all. It is of little significance to be able to go to the polls on an empty stomach, to campaign for a candidate while half-clothed, or to vent one's opinions freely from a broken-down tenement. Our potentially rich country is scarcely a real democracy when, in even the most prosperous periods, only 10 per cent of our families can buy what the government itself regards as enough to eat, when government reports announce that over 70 per cent of our families live in substandard dwellings, and when millions of people without enough clothing stand by while government-subsidized farmers plow under thousands of acres of cotton.

A great sociologist, Albion W. Small, once said that our present system is really "a combination of lottery and famine," and that we can never accurately call the United States a true democracy until we give security and plenty to the masses.

**Foreign meddling and war scares a threat to democracy.** While there are important domestic problems and tendencies which have created a crisis in democracy, excessive concern with foreign governments and attitudes, and the war scares which have resulted, are the chief menace to democracy in our time. They distract attention from improving our own democracy while there is yet time, and they threaten the onset of emergency and wartime controls and dictatorship, which are fatal to democratic society.

## Our Civil Liberties

**Democracy and liberty.** One of the most important issues of the present day is the problem of civil liberties.[3] By civil liberties we mean primarily the right to "life, liberty, and the pursuit of happiness"; the right to fair trial; freedom of speech, press, and assembly; and freedom to worship according to the dictates of our conscience. These civil liberties, long regarded as "natural rights," have been guaranteed to every citizen by the first ten amendments to the Constitution of the United States.

The question of civil liberty is closely linked with democracy, since the chief advantage of democracy is the fact that it is supposed to give us more liberty than other forms of government. Dictatorships may be more efficient, at times, than democracy, but they do not provide the blessings of liberty. Hence, if democracy does not carry with it the above-mentioned civil liberties, it denies its own right to exist; moreover, we are likely to suffer doubly from it, having to endure both inefficiency and tyranny.

**Civil liberties a social product.** We usually take our civil rights for granted and rarely inquire how we have come to enjoy them. In the first place, these liberties are not "natural rights." They are social conquests, which have been slowly won by human effort through the ages, often at the cost of blood and suffering. We have no "natural right" to anything, not even to life, but courageous persons and groups in the past have fought, and often died, that later generations might enjoy a larger share of freedom.

**The establishment of our traditional civil liberties.** Our civil liberties were chiefly a contribution of the English middle class. In order to carry on a propaganda war against the monarchs who threatened their personal safety and class interests, the middle class de-

---

[3] On the history and stages of Liberalism, see above, pp. 40–42.

manded and eventually secured freedom of speech, press, and assembly. Gaining added wealth from the new commerce, they ardently defended the sanctity of private property. To protect themselves from the danger of rotting in jail at the pleasure of the monarch, they demanded trial by jury and the right of *habeas corpus*. Since most of the mercantile and business class were dissenters in religion, the right to worship as they pleased would protect them against persecution by orthodox rulers. These tenets, so essential to the promotion of middle-class interests, became the battle cry of the merchants and businessmen who opposed Charles I and James II in the English revolutions of the seventeenth century.

The first decisive battle for civil liberties was won in England in the "Glorious Revolution" of 1688–1689. The Bill of Rights of 1689, embodying what the middle class considered to be its rights at the time, came over to America with the colonists. It was adopted in some colonial charters and, later, in the Declaration of Independence and in the early state constitutions after 1776. It found a permanent place in the first ten amendments to our Constitution. The rights and liberties enumerated in the English Bill of Rights were also embodied in the Declaration of the Rights of Man of 1789, the chief libertarian product of the French Revolution, and went on to play a part in the slogans of the continental revolutionaries during the nineteenth century.

**Civil liberties in the United States.** The citizens of the United States are guaranteed, under the Constitution, the rights to personal security, liberty, equality before the law, trial by jury, "due process of law," and freedom of worship, press, speech, and assembly. These rights involve restrictions placed upon the Federal government and, in some instances, the states. They can be legally taken away only by changing the Constitution.

Although all citizens are given these civil liberties under the Constitution, in many instances powerful economic interests have used them against the well-being of the working class. For example, the freedom most prized today by those who dominate our society has been the unrestricted right to hold property and to carry on private business unhampered by restrictive legislation. Large companies, in proclaiming their own right to hold property and do business as they wish, do not concern themselves with upholding the comparable rights of their workers. The working class most cherishes its freedom to organize labor unions and urge legislation to raise wages, improve working conditions, and promote old-age security. But these liberties often oppose the interests of the dominant economic groups. The latter have often induced the courts to set aside reform legislation as contrary to due process of law, an infringement of property rights, and the like.

Though the United States has protected civil liberties better than most countries, we have not been free from intolerance, persecutions, and denials of civil rights. Racial intolerance has not disappeared.

THE BILL OF RIGHTS

① FREEDOM OF RELIGION, PRESS, SPEECH, ASSEMBLY AND PETITION

② RIGHT TO BEAR ARMS

③ NO QUARTERING OF SOLDIERS WITHOUT CONSENT

④ NO UNREASONABLE SEARCHES AND SEIZURES

⑤ LIFE, LIBERTY, PROPERTY, MAY NOT BE TAKEN WITHOUT DUE PROCESS OF LAW

⑥ RIGHT TO TRIAL BY JURY ETC.

⑦ CITIZEN MAY NOT BE TRIED AGAIN ONCE ACQUITTED OF AN OFFENSE

⑧ NO EXCESSIVE BAIL & FINES - NO CRUEL AND UNUSUAL PUNISHMENTS

⑨ RIGHTS NOT MENTIONED TO BE RETAINED BY PEOPLE

⑩ POWERS NOT DELEGATED TO FED. GOV'T, BELONG TO STATES OR PEOPLE

HARRY HERZOG, FOR THE PUBLIC AFFAIRS COMMITTEE, INC.

Graphic portrayal of our basic civil liberties.

421

The Ku Klux Klan intimidated the Negro after the Civil War. Even today the Negro is discriminated against politically, economically, and socially. Persons who hold economic beliefs contrary to the ideals of big business have been persecuted; on the other hand, in the more radical years of the New Deal, the persecution worked the other way. The main forms of intolerance today grow out of economic issues; an excellent example of economic intolerance is the Communist witch-hunting that began early in 1947.

**Invasions of our civil liberties by the Federal government.** Although most of our civil liberties have remained intact in peacetime, some have been destroyed or restricted by laws and court decisions. Examples of actions taken by the Supreme Court, the Labor Department, the Post Office Department, Customs officials, the Federal Communication Commission, and state courts will illustrate this point. The United States Supreme Court has upheld the right of Congress to penalize expressions of opinion; sustained the right of the Post Office to bar publications from the mails; denied citizenship to alien pacifists (decision later reversed); and permitted the tapping of telephone wires to secure evidence. The Smith Act of 1940 made it a crime to advocate the violent overthrow of the Federal government. Most astonishing of all, even the present liberalized Supreme Court has legalized the search of a man's house without a search warrant, a practice which was vigorously fought centuries ago and had come to be regarded as reprehensible in any civilized nation.

The Labor Department, with the authority of Congress, has forbidden the entry of aliens holding moral or political views deemed not to be in harmony with our economic and social system, and has deported aliens holding such unorthodox views. The Customs officials have been vested with authority to seize imported literature or art which they hold to be obscene or dangerous. The Federal Communications Commission controls the establishment and re-licensing of radio stations, and has at times threatened and censored them. Federal and state courts can still issue injunctions to prevent laborers from striking and picketing, and are empowered to imprison for contempt of court those who publish criticism of a judge's action on issues which are pending (restricted by later decisions of the Supreme Court).

**State and local infringement of liberty.** State governments have, in many instances, denied the civil rights of citizens. Negroes are prohibited in 10 states from voting freely; 17 states separate Negroes from whites in the schools and public conveyances; seven censor movies. As we noted earlier, in dealing with the Negro problem, recent court decisions have modified some of these restrictions against Negroes. Some states have denied jury trial to accused persons, and sheriffs, in some states, have been given power to suspend all civil liberties in emergencies. City governments have passed permanent ordinances requiring permits for meetings in public halls.

Suppression of civil liberties by state and local governments is espepecially serious, since, for the most part, the Federal Constitution protects our liberties only against arbitrary action by Federal authorities, and only in specific instances against arbitrary action by state and local officials. Of course, state constitutions may afford some degree of protection in this respect; many of them contain a state bill of rights.

**Recent Federal policy on civil liberties.** Beginning with the Fourteenth Amendment of 1868, there has been a growing tendency on the part of the Federal government to protect our civil liberties against state and other local interference. The Fourteenth Amendment held that no state could abridge the privileges and immunities of citizens of the United States, or deprive any person of life, liberty, or property without due process of law. But it took a long time to make this protection effective, even in part, against state action.

An important start came when Justice Holmes, in a free speech and sedition case in 1919, enunciated the famous "clear and present danger" doctrine in the following words: "The question in every case is whether the words are used in circumstances and are of such a nature as to create a clear and present danger that they will bring about the substantive evils that Congress has a right to prevent." But it was not until the 1940's that the Supreme Court systematically adopted this doctrine in setting aside state laws that challenged the principle.

An important victory for the rights of a free press against state intervention came earlier in the Minnesota case of 1931, in which Justice Hughes issued the Supreme Court decision setting aside the press-gag (padlocking) Minnesota statute. Religious and racial rights have also been extensively protected against state invasion in the 1940's. A Civil Rights Section was set up in the Department of Justice in 1938, with the special aim of scrutinizing state infringement of civil liberties. President Truman appointed a Civil Rights Committee in 1946, which reported the following year and strongly protested against state violations of civil liberties. The embodiment of the spirit of its recommendations in the Democratic platform of 1948 led to a temporary bolt of some southern states. These states combined to defeat the Truman civil rights program by a senatorial filibuster in the early days of the 81st Congress.

At the same time, the Federal government has recently seemed to place in jeopardy some civil liberties in the co-ordination of United States domestic policy with our stand in the "cold war."

**Recent restrictions of liberty in the United States.** The twentieth century has seen many economic, social, religious, and military restrictions on our civil liberties. Court injunctions helped to paralyze labor unionism. Employers were permitted to keep private police who have defied the law and intimidated workers, particularly in Pennsylvania, where industrial and mining districts were long dominated by the notorious "Coal and Iron Police." Some of these excesses were removed by New Deal labor legislation, but the recent practice of Federal courts in imposing heavy fines on labor unions for the threat to strike, a practice upheld by the Supreme Court, has set an ominous precedent. Employers have also had their liberties curtailed in dealing with labor, especially by the Wagner Act of 1935, whereby employers were not permitted to criticize unions and union policies or to hire non-union workers in a unionized shop.

The United States once prided itself upon the fact that it gave refuge to all those who sought asylum here. Since the first world war, however, we have feared contamination by persons with progressive ideas. Count Karolyi, a cultured Hungarian nobleman, was excluded from our shores for years because he favored land reform in feudal Hungary. John Strachey, the distinguished English writer, had to cut short his lecture trip and return to England because he was thought to have radical views, though most of the ideas he expressed had been expounded long before by Thomas Jefferson and Abraham Lincoln. English labor leaders and eminent Anglican churchmen have been prevented from landing in this country because they had a friendly attitude towards Soviet Russia. A distinguished German pianist, alleged to have performed in the Hitler era, arrived in the United States for a series of concerts only to find his engagements canceled and himself labeled for deportation. Leftist scholars and artists seeking permission to attend a New York peace rally in the spring of 1949 were denied visas.

In 1941, the state of New York banned a birth-control exhibit at the state fair in Syracuse. Books, sometimes classics, have been suppressed by the Post Office authorities and the Customs officials. Theatres have been padlocked, in violation of the right of jury trial. The right to bear arms has been curtailed in a number of states.

Religious liberty is far from complete. A number of states make reading of the Bible compulsory in public schools; not until 1948, in the McCollum case, did the Supreme Court declare this practice illegal. The testimony of those who do not believe in God is not valid on the witness stand in six states. In some states, children have been excluded from the schools because their religion would not permit them to salute the flag.

**Eternal vigilance the price of liberty.** Many of the laws curbing civil liberties are deemed necessary to "protect" the people. But the American Revolution was fought to make secure the rights of a free people, and the Constitution was enacted to protect our civil liberties. The price of our liberty is eternal vigilance. Freedom is something that must be alertly and bravely protected at all times by all citizens of a democracy. A self-constituted and self-supporting organization, the American Civil Liberties Union, was brought into existence after the first world war to prevent Americans from being deprived of the liberties for which our forefathers fought.

Many American citizens are lax and indifferent with respect to their historic rights. They refuse to admit that their liberty is in danger, even though in the past thirty years the crisis has grown more acute. In Germany, Italy, and other Fascist states, liberty was suppressed. Religious beliefs or democratic ideals meant nothing in those countries; there was no freedom of association, thought, or movement; the law was not the will of the people but the will of the dictator and his

*From a cartoon by Art Young.*

"What's he been doin'?"
"Overthrowin' the guvment."

**Cartoon emphasizing the exaggerated fear of unpopular ideas in a witch-hunting era.**

associates. In place of belief in God and the rights of man, there was substituted the worship of an omnipotent state. Russia has also suppressed civil liberties, though the Soviet government promises to introduce and protect them when it is no longer threatened by war and counter-revolution.

**Need of supplementing our traditional civil liberties.** We have added to our Federal Constitution few, if any, basic civil liberties since we took over those worked out in the seventeenth century by the English middle class. In a few state constitutions, the right of labor to organize is a guaranteed civil liberty, but even this has not been made a part of explicit Federal constitutional law, though the 1935 Federal statute on this subject has been upheld by the Supreme Court.

The fact that the middle class, the main bulwark of civil liberties in the past, is now being weakened or wiped out in much of the civilized world is ominous for the future of civil liberty. No other social class has shown any such enthusiasm for the promotion of liberty. The working class has been chiefly concerned with complete freedom for labor union tactics. This has been a gain for liberty in many respects, but it has done little to promote liberty for all classes, whatever their economic convictions and practices.

**Civil liberty and the war.** Certain temporary wartime restrictions of civil liberties were unquestionably justifiable, but it will avail little for us to have won the war abroad if, in the process, we crush civil liberty at home. It is significant that, in the same week, our government both celebrated the 150th anniversary of our Bill of Rights and imposed upon the press and other agencies of communication the most extensive censorship in our national history. While there was more witch-hunting in the first world war than in the second, the latter did occasion the first mass sedition trial in our history, a trial regarded by many as a travesty on justice and an ominous threat to our civil liberties.

Some of the worst abuses of liberty in recent years have come in connection with the purging of allegedly disloyal incumbents of Federal posts. Manifestly, all actually disloyal employees should be discharged, but unnecessary harshness and abuses have crept in. In the Dorothy Bailey case, a young woman was dismissed on entirely anonymous information, which even the Federal Bureau of Investigation was unable to identify or confirm, and the Federal district court and court of appeals upheld the action.[4]

If we enter a long and devastating third war there is little probability that our system of civil liberties will survive the ordeal.

**Government by emergency a threat to liberty.** One unfortunate heritage of the war period has been the trend toward "government by emergency" in peacetime, which we have mentioned earlier as threatening our two-party system and rational democratic government. It is also a menace to our civil liberties, since emergency situations, whether real or fictitious, invariably are used to justify high-handed measures that would not otherwise be tolerated. This has been especially true of our Federal government since the close of the second world war. Most of the witch-hunting and other inroads on our liberties in the last few years have been based on alleged emergency situations. The danger in all this was well stated by an eminent lawyer, Mr. Frank E. Holman, on the occasion of his election as President of the American Bar Association:

Our country has endured much through government by crisis in recent years. Public officials have too easily fallen into the habit of asserting that some crisis exists which justifies extraordinary and extra-legal procedures. Almost invariably, these "temporary" expedients tend to become permanent. We often permit our rights and liberties to be whittled away in this manner. We have taken free government for granted and in doing so have already lost some considerable measure of our independence and dignity as individuals.

---

[4] For a most admirable description of the attitudes and techniques in this latest witch-hunting and smearing episode, see Daniel Lang, "The Days of Suspicion," *New Yorker*, May 21, 1949, pp. 37–54. For the Dorothy Bailey case, see, *Ibid.*, October 9, 1949, pp. 86 ff.; and for the Adler-Draper case, *Ibid.*, April 15, 1950, pp. 86–98.

Trial of Communist leaders in 1949.  What many, even of vehement anti-Communist convictions, regarded as the most serious recent
invasion of civil liberties was the trial and conviction of eleven top
Communist leaders between January and October, 1949.  They were
tried and convicted under the Smith Act of 1940 which made it a

## "You Read Books, Eh?"

*Courtesy of the* Washington Post.

Cartoon humorously stressing the absurdities to which witch-hunting often leads.

crime to teach or advocate the violent overthrow of the government
of the United States.  Some anti-Communist critics regarded this as
a violation of American tradition, recalling that even the conservative
"fathers" of the constitution-making period, such as Alexander Hamilton and John Adams, enthusiastically endorsed such teaching, as well
as put it into active practice, and that Abraham Lincoln had endorsed

such ideas.   Others felt that it was dangerous to set the precedent of
prosecuting any group, however much hated, for their ideas and teachings, lest this later on open the way for proceeding against *any* unpopular group, even of the most conservative type.   More legally-
minded critics regarded the conviction as a repudiation of Justice
Holmes' sensible "clear and present danger" doctrine.   Those who
upheld the trial and conviction, on grounds other than hysteria, believed that the defendants had exceeded the boundaries of teaching
and action protected by the First Amendment.   The case was appealed
to the Supreme Court, which had never handed down an opinion on
the constitutionality of the Smith Act.   Whatever the legal and
libertarian aspects of the case, there was little ground for sympathy
with the Community party, which had been one of the main pressure
groups prompting the government to institute the mass sedition trial
of 1944–1945.

Cultural lag and civil liberties.   We have often mentioned cultural
lag throughout this book.   It is well here to point out that our traditional system of civil liberties, precious as they may be, are a striking
example of cultural lag.   These liberties were fought for and achieved
nearly three centuries ago and were those which the middle class felt
to be necessary in a simple, agrarian era, before the rise of modern industrial society.   They need to be supplemented by a new Bill of
Rights reflecting the needs and rights of all classes in the urban and
industrialized society of the middle of the twentieth century.   Such
a list of up-to-date rights were formulated by the National Resources
Planning Board in 1942:

1. The right to work usefully and creatively through the productive years.
2. The right to fair pay, adequate to command the necessities and amenities
of life in exchange for work, ideas, thrift and other socially valuable services.
3. The right to adequate food, clothing, shelter and medical care.
4. The right to security, with freedom from fear of old age, want, dependency, sickness, unemployment and accident.
5. The right to live in a system of free enterprise, free from compulsory
labor, irresponsible private power, arbitrary public authority and unregulated
monopolies.
6. The right to come and go, to speak or be silent, free from the spyings
of secret political police.
7. The right to equality before the law with equal access to justice in fact.
8. The right to education for work, for citizenship, and for personal growth
and happiness.
9. The right to rest, recreation and adventure, and the opportunity to
enjoy life and take part in an advancing civilization.

## Summary

Our democracy was founded on the belief that the United States
would remain primarily agricultural; that government would not need
to interfere with private enterprise; that all men are equal; that the
masses would take an interest in politics once they had the right to

vote; that the voters would always carefully consider political platforms and the fitness of candidates for office; that the sound judgment of the masses could be trusted on public moral issues; that we could live within our own boundaries, preserving our own democracy without bothering too much about the rest of the world; and that democracy can thrive whether or not social and economic conditions are favorable.

Many of these fundamental assumptions have been undermined during the last century. For this reason, democracy today faces an acute crisis. The United States is no longer a predominantly agricultural country; there is need for more government intervention in social and economic matters; all men are not equal in ability; the public, by failing to take an interest in intelligent voting, has allowed many evils to develop in our party government; and unintelligent attitudes toward world affairs have involved nations in war and destroyed promising democratic experiments.

If we will make the necessary changes and improvements in our democracy, we may still be able to save it. One of the most essential reforms is to get honest and efficient men into office. We need fewer politicians and more statesmen. We need not turn from democracy to any other form of government if we adapt democracy to the conditions of present-day life. It is only if democracy fails that we are in danger of Fascism and Communism.

We must have a planned democracy. It has been suggested that a corps of trained industrial engineers might determine and supply the material needs of the population. The supporters of this program say that, if we let such experts take care of our economic problems and assure us plenty and security, then democracy can function successfully in the social and cultural realms. Such managerial programs may insure greater efficiency, but they contain the seeds of totalitarianism.

One of the most important aspects of the crisis in democracy is the danger of losing our civil liberties. Men struggled for centuries to secure these liberties, which colonists brought to the New World and we incorporated in the first ten amendments to our Federal Constitution. Our civil liberties are our personal rights, such as freedom of assembly, speech, press, and religion.

Sometimes great economic interests, in maintaining their right to hold property, deny civil liberties to the workers, who should have their own right of freedom of action and expression. Civil liberties represented the outcome of a fight against intolerance; yet, we have permitted intolerance in religion, politics, and economic life to persist in this country. The average citizen has been indifferent to the liberties granted him by the Constitution. If democracy is to survive the current international crisis, the civil liberties of all citizens must be preserved at all costs. The price of liberty is eternal vigilance; liberty is not automatically protected or preserved.

Our traditional civil liberties are an invaluable safeguard of democracy, but they must be supplemented by a more modernized category of rights and liberties which conform to the needs of man in our modern industrialized age.

### Selected References

* Agar, Herbert, *The People's Choice*, Houghton Mifflin, 1933. Pulitzer Prize historical work maintaining the thesis that American democracy rarely puts an able man in the White House.

Andrews, Bert, *Washington Witch Hunt*, Random House, 1948. Good journalistic account of loyalty tests and red-baiting since 1946.

* Bates, E. S., *This Land of Liberty*, Harper, 1930. A brilliant survey of the invasions of liberty in the United States. The best book on the subject at the time of publication.

Burnham, James, *The Managerial Revolution*, Day, 1941. Prediction that the political future lies with technicians and trained bureaucrats who will streamline traditional capitalism and democracy.

Carr, R. K., *Federal Protection of Civil Liberties*, Cornell University Press, 1949. Good summary of recent trends in Federal solicitude to protect the civil liberties of citizens.

* Counts, G. S., *The Prospects of American Democracy*, Day, 1938. Perhaps the ablest defense of democracy, by a leading liberal professor.

Dennis, Lawrence, *The Coming American Fascism*, Harper, 1936.

————, *The Dynamics of War and Revolution*, Harper, 1940. These two books contain the most vigorous warning that domestic fumbling and foreign meddling will produce Fascism, however the trend is semantically disguised.

Dreher, Carl, *The Coming Showdown*, Little, Brown, 1942. Able industrial engineer supports same general point of view as Burnham.

Forman, S. E., *A Good Word for Democracy*, Appleton-Century, 1937. A spirited defense of democracy. A brief but trenchant book.

Friedrich, C. J., *The New Belief in the Common Man*, Little, Brown, 1942. Eloquent but somewhat naïve effort to rehabilitate the Jacksonian apotheosis of the political acumen of the masses.

* Gilbert, R. V., et al., *An Economic Program for American Democracy*, Vanguard, 1938. A brief symposium by seven Harvard and Tufts professors setting forth the economic reforms essential to the preservation of American democracy. A brilliant and realistic little book.

Hallgren, M. A., *Landscape of Freedom*, Howell, Soskin, 1941. Splendid account of the history of civil liberties in the United States, with much attention to the social and economic forces involved.

Hays, A. G., *Democracy Works*, Random House, 1939. An able book by a leading liberal lawyer. The title is misleading, for the book is valuable mainly for its emphasis on the reforms necessary to make democracy work.

* Holcombe, A. N., *Government in a Planned Democracy*, Norton, 1935. A progressive political scientist outlines a program for a dynamic and efficient form of democratic government.

Kingsley, J. D., *Bureaucracy in Britain*, Antioch Press, 1942.

—————, and Petegorsky, D. W., *Strategy for Democracy*, Longmans, Green, 1942. The first of these books is a good study of bureaucracy in a democracy. The second is a program for realistic democracy in the United States.

* Laski, H. J., *The American Democracy*, Viking, 1948. The ablest description and appraisal of American democratic society since the publication of James Bryce's *American Commonwealth* in the 1880's.

Loeb, Harold, *Life in a Technocracy*, Viking, 1933. Best description of what a technocratic society would be like.

Loper, H. J., *The American Democracy*, Viking, 1948. One of the most recent discriminating defenses of democratic government in the United States.

* MacIver, R. M., *The Ramparts We Guard*, Macmillan, 1950. Good brief appraisal of the state of American democracy today. Warns against the dangers of censorship and witch-hunting.

Maverick, Maury, *In Blood and Ink*, Modern Age, 1939. An animated history and defense of American civil liberties.

Mencken, H. L., *Notes on Democracy*, Knopf, 1926. A vigorous attack on the whole notion of democracy by the ablest American opponent of democracy and party government.

Morstein Marx, Fritz; Hobbing, E. R.; and Radway, L. I. (Eds.), *Public Management in the New Democracy*, Harper, 1940. Symposium suggesting ways of introducing managerialism and efficiency without endangering democracy.

Mosher, W. E. (Ed.), *Introduction to Responsible Citizenship*, Holt, 1941. One of the most comprehensive and stimulating co-operative books on the problems of democratic citizenship.

Myers, Gustavus, *History of Bigotry in the United States*, Random House, 1941. Interesting history of persecutions, crusades, and invasions of civil liberties since colonial times.

* Pink, M. A., *A Realist Looks at Democracy*, Stokes, 1931. The ablest English criticism of democracy.

Rogers, Cleveland, *American Planning: Past, Present and Future*, Harper, 1946. Supports idea that planning is a basic tradition in American capitalistic democracy.

Rogge, O. J., *Our Vanishing Civil Liberties*, Gaer Associates, 1949. Vigorous criticism of recent governmental crackdown on Communists and radicals by the man who was a leader in the wartime governmental crusade against conservatives.

* Rossiter, C. L., *Constitutional Dictatorship*, Princeton University Press, 1948. Important and timely book stressing the dangers to democracy from the great extension of executive powers in emergencies, real and alleged, and in the managerial "end run" around democracy which has been taking place in the United States since 1933.

Seldes, George, *You Can't Do That*, Modern Age, 1938. A trenchant study of violations of civil liberty in the United States. Contains remarkably good and complete bibliography on civil liberty.

Shalloo, J. P., *Private Police, with Special Reference to Pennsylvania*, Annals of the American Academy of Political and Social Science, 1933. A scholarly and readable book; the most adequate account of the methods of industrial private police.

St. George, M. J., and Dennis, Lawrence, *A Trial on Trial*, National Civil Rights Committee, 1946. A masterly indictment of the mass-sedition trial of 1944–1945 by one of the leading attorneys and the chief defendant.

Tead, Ordway, *The Case for Democracy*, Association Press, 1938. A brief, elementary defense of democracy. Contains an excellent bibliography.

Ward, H. F., *Democracy and Social Change*, Modern Age, 1940. Able and vigorous plea for social and economic democracy.

Watkins, Frederick, *The Political Tradition of the West: A Study in the Development of Modern Liberalism*, Harvard University Press, 1948. Scholarly history of the rise and evolution of liberalism in modern times.

Whipple, Leon, *Our Ancient Liberties*, Wilson, 1927.

* —————, *The Story of Civil Liberty in the United States*, Vanguard, 1927. Two brief books which give us the best history of civil liberty in the United States. They trace the origin, development, and attacks on our Bill of Rights.

# CHAPTER XVIII

## International Relations: Problems of War and Peace

### War as a National Social Problem

**Need for a realistic approach to the war problem.** From 1941 to 1945 we were involved in the most expensive and desperate war in all human history. We claimed we were fighting because our nation hates war and because our participation in the struggle would best promote the cause of freedom and international organization. Although both the United States and other nations through the ages have advanced similar reasons for going to war, wars have persisted.

**Development of total war.** The chief wars of early modern times were fought mainly by small armies of mercenaries and other professional soldiers. Relatively few were killed. For example, in 1704, the year of the famous battle of Blenheim, only 5,000 were killed in battle. The introduction of the draft during the French Revolution produced the first immense armies. With the introduction of mass warfare, mortality in battle became far greater; Napoleon lost 32,000 men and the Russians 42,000 at the Battle of Borodino in 1812. By the time of the first world war, armies had become larger, and it is estimated that in the battle of Verdun in 1916 the French and Germans lost over 500,000 men. The slaughter in the Neville-Mangin offensive in 1917 was so great that it brought about a mutiny in the French army, and the British losses in the Passchendale offensive in the same year were about as heavy. The first world war produced what is known as "total war," for it involved not only armies but the total reserves of manpower and munitions.

The second world war was even more "total," for it launched the indiscriminate bombing and massacre of civilians. Some 200,000 or more were killed in one night in the Anglo-American bombing of Dresden, a non-military objective. A vast number of homes and factories were wiped out by bombing and other modes of destruction. That the very destiny of civilization is involved in the struggle to prevent a third world war is evident; not only are mechanisms of unprecedented destructive power ready or in the process of development,

433

but also the leaders of the warring nations would not hesitate to use the very worst of them, since they know defeat means another Nuremberg.

**War intensifies cultural lag.** During times of peace a country has numerous and difficult problems to solve. The quest for economic justice and efficient government baffles men even when they are not faced with the gigantic task of defending themselves against foreign enemies. Our social thinking is slow enough in catching up with the progress of our machine equipment without complicating the situation with warfare and its resulting confusion. During wartime all the issues that party government and democracy have failed to solve swell to gigantic proportions. The preparations for war take hundreds of billions of dollars which might be used to promote economic and social security; the public debt is enormously increased; prices usually rise, and our whole economic life is seriously disrupted.

War tends to upset social reforms and to destroy the results of years of constructive statesmanship. The reforms carried through in England from 1905 to 1914 by the Liberal-Labour coalition government were probably the most extensive and impressive ever wrought by any major democratic state. The Asquith-Lloyd George Cabinet was the outstanding ornament of democratic society and politics. But, owing to Tory warmongering, the Germanophobia of Sir Erye Crowe, permanent undersecretary of state, and the pontifical weakness of Sir Edward Grey, England was needlessly thrown into world war. The result was the termination of reforms, the destruction of the Liberal party, the alternation for over 20 years between Tory senility and Labour inexperience, involvement in a second world war, and the descent of Britain to the rank of a second-rate and near-bankrupt country.

From April, 1917, to November, 1918, when the United States was involved in the first world war, domestic reforms almost completely ceased. Conservatives and reactionaries, who had persistently opposed the constructive measures of President Wilson's "New Freedom" for four years, were brought to Washington to assist in the war effort, and their continuing influence effectively prevented social reforms for fifteen years after the Armistice.

The domestic reform program of the New Deal was immediately suspended after Pearl Harbor and its previous achievements were seriously undermined by the second world war. Men whom President Roosevelt had previously bitterly denounced as "economic royalists" were given the leading cabinet posts. There was little New Deal crusading after 1945. Even the moderate "Fair Deal" program of President Truman was rejected in 1949 by a Congress in which the Democratic party had a majority in both houses.

Observers believe that if the second world war had continued for many more years it would have fatally undermined capitalism, democracy, and liberty throughout the civilized world. The technical advances of the Machine Age, which constitute our chief claim to a superior civilization, cannot promote human happiness unless they are used for the benefit rather than the destruction of mankind. Today, in the atomic age, men face a more uncertain and danger-laden future than at any time in human history.

*Courtesy of Federal Public Housing Authority.*

Uplifting the underprivileged might begin at home. While we spend billions on armament to combat evils in other countries, and propose to spend more billions under President Truman's "Point Four" program to uplift the Hottentots and others, slums like those in the above picture are allowed to exist virtually within a stone's throw of the National Capitol.

Although the total cost of the second world war has not been exactly computed yet, a committee of economists estimated that the total monetary expenditures amounted to a trillion and a quarter dollars ($1,250,000,000,000). The property damage was unquestionably twice as great as the monetary cost. The most competent student of the problem, C. Hartley Grattan, has estimated the total economic cost of the second world war, including the cost of property damage, to be at least four trillion dollars. The ever increasing cost of wars can be illustrated by the fact that it cost 75 cents to kill a man in Caesar's time; $3,000 in the Napoleonic period; $21,000 in the first world war; and $50,000 in the second world war.

Not even the United States, whose war expenditures came to 400 billion dollars or over 30 per cent of the world total, can stand a third world war entailing such a drain on its resources. Even were we to win such a war in short order, the expenses of the subsequent occupation alone would bankrupt us.

As we noted in an earlier chapter, the costs of wars do not end with the astronomical expenditures of war time. During the last hundred years, the ultimate cost of wars have tended to be about four times the wartime expenditures. This means that the final cost of the second world war will be around 15 trillion dollars. What such a sum of money could do in the way of raising living standards staggers the imagination.

Until the vast destruction due to air bombing, the main cost of the aftermath of recent wars has been the pension bill. Some pension facts are almost unbelievable. It was not until 1911 that the United States paid its last pension check for the Revolutionary War. The final pension payment for the War of 1812 was made in 1946. In 1948, there were 36 persons still receiving pensions from the Mexican War. Civil War pensions have already amounted to over 8 billion dollars; there are over 16,000 still receiving Civil War pensions, and the bill in 1948 was nearly 20 million dollars. About 195,000 are receiving pensions from the Spanish-American War, and the pension bill from that war to date has been about 3 billion dollars. Pensions growing out of the first world war have amounted to over 6 billion dollars, to say nothing of the cost of taking care of disabled veterans in federal institutions. Expert students of veterans' affairs estimate the total pension bill for the second world war at 50 billion dollars.

Strategic and indiscriminate bombing has made the cost of rebuilding devastated areas far greater than pension bills. Property damage in the second world war was in excess of 2 trillion dollars—that in Russia alone was more than double the cost of all the Five Year Plans prior to 1941.

## Some of the More Disastrous Effects of Wars

The biological impact of war. The coming together of men from divers areas helps to spread diseases; a prominent instance was the influenza epidemic of 1918–1919. In the first world war, seven million days of service were lost to the United States army as a result of venereal infection; 338,746 men, the equivalent of 23 divisions, received treatment. In the second world war, about 500,000 were infected with syphilis, and several times as many with gonorrhea, despite vigorous prophylaxis propaganda. The lessening of physical resistance to disease because of wartime hardships increases the volume and mortality of disease among those at home. The birth rate decreases and the death rate rises, and further population losses are added to those of the battlefield. The quality of the population is also lowered by war because many of the best physical specimens are killed off in combat and the poorer physical types are left at home to procreate during the war period.

**Industrial dislocations and disasters.**   A sharp industrial dislocation accompanies war.   The manufacture of consumers' goods falls off. Price Administrator Leon Henderson announced in February, 1942, that the nation's standard of living in 1942 would be the lowest since 1932, despite the fact that nearly all the employable persons were employed at high wages and the depression had finally been conquered, at least for the war period.   The full employment and high-geared production that the nation could not accomplish in time of peace it accomplished in time of war.   But this did not bring society many added benefits, for the bulk of production, as Henderson said, was for death not for life.   This fact offers a striking indictment of war and the war system.

Furthermore, many hardships arise as a nation geared for peace-time production is asked to produce swiftly for war.   Industries that cannot be converted to wartime uses close down, and temporary unemployment results until industry can be fully shifted, if this is possible, to a war basis.   Much small business is driven to the wall, and the giants gain in wealth and power.   Both capital and labor are regimented under government control.   Strikes and lockouts are forbidden.   Prices and living costs tend to rise and it is difficult to make salaries and wages keep pace with prices.   Thus the standard of living falls; in addition, many commodities cannot be obtained because factories formerly producing consumers' goods are producing guns, shells, and other instruments of destruction.   Moreover, taxes rise astonishingly, taking away a considerable part of nearly everybody's income.

**Humanity brutalized.**   The military experiences, hatreds, and sorrows of war inevitably brutalize human nature, as the first world war amply proved.   After the war we were able to contemplate with relative calm atrocities that would have aroused the utmost indignation before 1914.   By 1945, the peoples of the world had all but lost any sense of horror over the most brutal massacres, particularly those carried out by their own forces.   A war generation tends to become hard-boiled.   The intense propaganda and the war psychology make for intolerance and persecution.   Calm thinking and social insight tend to disappear.   Moral standards are lowered in the strains of war and evils are overlooked or condoned in the struggle for victory.

**Effect on social institutions.**   Our leading social institutions are deeply affected by war.   Families are broken up as men join the army or obtain employment in war industries, some never to return.   The absence of former breadwinners reduces the family income and lowers the standard of living.   Students in the schools are distracted as interest is concentrated on war matters.   Many teachers are drawn off to war and war services.   About 350,000 American teachers left the profession between 1939 and 1946.   School appropriations are cut. Educational institutions become centers of war propaganda, and honest regard for facts and respect for clear thinking are abandoned.   The church ceases to be a spokesman of the "Prince of Peace" and throws the weight of its influence behind the war effort. Ministers who remain true to their former support of peace are often dismissed and persecuted. Artistic life is degraded by war; leading artists turn their talents to caricaturing and slandering the enemy, engendering hatreds that endure long after active warfare has ceased. Now that indiscriminate bombing has become the normal pattern of warfare, there is great destruction of historical and artistic treasures. Ordinary community efforts in behalf of the miserable and downtrodden are tapered off in the interest of war exertions. Property rights are jeopardized by wartime regimentation, taxation, and confiscation.

**Wars and revolutions.** Wars are likely to promote extensive social changes—often revolutions—if they last long enough. This is especially true of wars at the end of a great epoch of civilization; for example, the wars of the later Roman Empire, those at the close of the Middle Ages, and the great middle-class revolutions of modern times. The first world war brought revolution to Russia (1917), Italy (1922), and Germany (1933); the second world war brought to power a socialist government in England, and a Communist régime took over control of China.

**Wars produce vindictive treaties.** The hatreds of war make it difficult to negotiate a generous and constructive peace. Peace treaties are usually vindictive and oppressive; such treaties naturally make the loser sulk and plan for an opportunity to avenge his defeat. The unfortunate Treaty of Versailles, for example, and the other treaties which followed the first world war unquestionably led to the rise of Mussolini and Hitler. That it is hard, for this reason, to wage a war to end war Woodrow Wilson saw clearly when he urged a "peace without victory"; and he lived to see his peace *with* victory lay the foundations for an even worse war.

Apparently, the Allied nations learned nothing from the Versailles failure. The policies of the victors after 1945 were far more vicious and vindictive than those which produced the Treaty of Versailles. The Morgenthau Plan, adopted by Roosevelt and Churchill at Quebec, was originally designed to starve tens of millions of Germans and to reduce Germany to a pastoral and agricultural country. This was slightly modified, but even five years after V-E Day Germany had not returned to more than 50 per cent of 1939 production levels. German industrial plants were being dismantled by the British at the very time the United States was pouring in vast sums to rebuild German industry.

If the Treaty of Versailles was a bad treaty, at least it was a treaty. Five years after V-J Day, no treaty had yet been made with either Germany or Japan, nor did any such treaty seem nearer completion in 1950 than in the summer of 1945. There was even reason to fear that the third world war might break out before the more important treaties which would normally follow the second world war had been seriously considered.

## Why War Persists in a Civilized World

**Biological causes of war.** The causes of war may be classified as biological, psychological, economic, and political. Perhaps the leading biological cause of war is the tendency of population to increase more rapidly than the food supply—a fact noted by Malthus at the end of the eighteenth century.[1] As we pointed out in the chapter on Population, if nations would spend even a fraction of what they spend on war in improving agricultural techniques, any important country in the world today could readily support its population.

Until about the time of the first world war, there were many areas to which people living in the more densely populated countries might emigrate. But nations did not wish to lose their citizens nor citizens their nationality; hence the search for colonies to which surplus populations might move and yet remain politically attached to the mother country. This search naturally led to conflicting claims, and thence to wars; the desire of Germany, Italy, and Japan for colonies, for example, played an important rôle in bringing on the war of 1914. While need for "living space" has been exaggerated as an alibi for war, yet there is much truth in the allegation that the international problems of the last fifty years have been due, in part, to the division of the world into "have" and "have not" nations.

Another important biosocial cause of war is the fact that man has, during most of his existence on the planet, obtained part of his livelihood and much of his prestige by engaging in war. It was because of his fighting ability that man was able to conquer other animals and rule the earth. War and fighting have undoubtedly left their imprint upon man's biological nature in many ways. It would be foolish to claim that man is inherently a fighting animal; but it is not natural for him to be completely peaceful. In reality, man is adapted by nature for either war or peace. Any sensible program for peace must include an educational and social system that will promote man's peaceful tendencies and suppress his warlike desires. Any scheme for peace that ignores man's natural capacity for blind rage and anger toward his enemies is likely to be wrecked on the rocks of reality.

Among the most powerful causes of war is the doctrine that war is a necessary and desirable part of the struggle for existence. It holds that only the most fit will survive in war, and hence a more orderly and higher type of society will result. This may have been true in early historic society, to a limited extent, but for modern society the reverse is true. Only the best physical specimens are chosen to engage in modern warfare and to face its many hazards. The physically and mentally unfit are left at home to become fathers of the next generation. Added to this factor, and often tending to lower the quality of

---

[1] See above, pp. 164–166.

the population, are the ravages of disease, suffering, starvation, and mutilation, which war always brings in its train.

**Psychological factors encouraging war.** The second main group of causes of war are psychological. One example is the doctrine of the "war cult," which maintains that military activities are the most noble form of human endeavor, and that war brings forth the highest and most unselfish of human sentiments.

How false this assumption is can easily be shown. Widespread increases in lust, cruelty, corruption, profiteering and sexual laxity are part of any war; there is abundant evidence that the great conflicts of recent times have had a debasing rather than an ennobling effect on Western civilization. In his important book, *Advance to Barbarism,* the eminent English lawyer, F. J. P. Veale, gives evidence to show that the second world war produced barbarities worse than those attributed to Sennacherib or to the wars described in the Book of Judges. The second world war was the most barbarous and brutal war in all recorded history.

Akin to the glorification of war is the sentiment of false patriotism. There are two distinct types of "patriotism." One is the high ideal of devotion to the public community, putting the welfare of one's group ahead of personal and selfish interests. This is perhaps the noblest expression of man's social nature. But there is another type of "patriotism," founded upon arrogance, prejudice, and selfishness, which upholds the belief that the established order in one's country is perfect, and that the homeland is fully justified in anything it may do, even in seizing the land of another nation.

Such narrow patriotism is extremely dangerous to peaceful international relations. It results in lack of understanding and blind hatred of other peoples and thus leads to war. It prevents the peaceful settlement of disputes, because, in such settlements, each nation usually has to make some concessions and sacrifices; bellicose patriots will usually want to fight before "giving an inch." Because war rarely benefits anybody today, even the victors, patriotism that unnecessarily stirs up warlike feelings is really harmful to the nation it is supposed to aid.

The development of modern means of transit and communication has greatly fostered the spread of warlike national sentiments. When news traveled slowly, people knew little of events outside their own neighborhood. As late as the seventeenth century, when wars were still fought by small mercenary armies, many of the population did not know that any war was being fought unless their local territory was invaded. Today, one may pick up his morning paper or turn on the radio and be roused by the speech of a warmonger denouncing some supposed insult to our national honor in Peiping or in Timbuktu. The possible power of the press, radio, movies, and television as a means of spreading fanatical patriotism almost surpasses the imagination.

Another strong influence in stirring up warlike sentiments has been the overemphasis of history and literature on national military achievements. History books, at least until comparatively recent years, were chiefly filled with records of battles and military and naval exploits. A country's prestige is, for some people, based chiefly on its military victories. The activities of scientists, inventors, business leaders, and others, who have been the real builders of civilization, receive little notice. Children are taught that their country has always been right in international disputes, and all wars are portrayed as glorious struggles for justice. In this way, arrogance and intolerance are put into the minds of the young. In later years, these sentiments are fostered by propaganda in newspapers, in the moving pictures, and over the radio. When minds are thus poisoned in youth, there is little hope that they will later develop a sensible attitude toward international affairs.

**Economic forces making for war.** The economic causes of war are, perhaps, the most powerful of all. As noted in Chapter II, the Industrial Revolution produced an enormous increase in the supply of goods. Nations in which home markets, hampered by inadequate mass purchasing power, could not absorb the entire product of the factories found it necessary to secure overseas outlets. Some goods could be sold to other civilized nations; but the industrial countries tried to develop colonies as important customers for their surplus products, as dependable sources of raw materials, and as areas for profitable investments. This policy has been termed "economic imperialism." Efforts to obtain raw materials, such as oil, rubber, and vital minerals, created the severest trade wars of the last generation. The scramble for overseas territory was also one of the leading causes of international disputes in the fifty years before 1914.

Not only has there been a struggle for overseas markets and raw materials, but businessmen have invested in foreign countries some of the profits brought to them by the Industrial Revolution. In itself, this would be proper enough, but the investors often sought special protection and rights, even though these conflicted with the laws and customs of the country where the investments were made. When the exploited country was weak enough, investors persuaded their home governments to obtain for them special economic advantages and legal rights. Thus, Germany, England, and France forced China and Turkey in the nineteenth century to admit their goods at very low tariff rates and to give them special trading advantages. This pattern of behavior has even been carried to the point where merchants persuaded their home governments to send troops or warships to a foreign country to keep order and protect their investments.

Such government intervention has led to a tremendous amount of international ill will and hatred. Nothing else, for example, so aroused the enmity of the yellow race toward the white as the harsh treatment of China by Europeans and Americans between 1840 and

1941. In China, under a system of extra-territoriality, the Chinese government could not even enforce its own laws against lawless foreigners. Foreign governments insisted that their nationals be tried in their own courts and under their own laws. Further, the customs rates were regulated by foreign governments in a way oppressive to China and favorable to foreign traders.

Another economic menace to international peace is the present world-wide system of protective tariffs. A protective tariff is a tax imposed by a nation upon goods coming to it from other countries. Its purpose is to prevent foreign producers from selling their merchandise in the home country and thus injuring the profits and sales of home producers. For example, European shoes are taxed heavily when they enter the United States, lest they sell for less than American-made shoes and take sales away from American manufacturers and jobs from American labor.

Although nations try to keep out foreign goods, they devote every effort to selling their own commodities abroad. Protective tariffs thus become a kind of economic warfare—battles without bullets. Among modern nations, there is a constant struggle to sell as much as possible to foreign customers and to buy as little as possible abroad. Of course, this sort of struggle defeats itself, for a nation cannot find sufficient customers when every country is seeking to sell a great volume of goods abroad and to buy no more foreign goods than absolutely necessary. The menace of protective tariffs to peace lies in the fact that many nations cannot exist at present without buying and selling abroad; as a result, if they are unable to get the necessities they require through peaceful trade, they are all too likely to go to war.

Germany is a good example. Primarily a manufacturing nation, she had to import food to feed her people. The only way Germany could get money to pay for this food was by selling her manufactured goods abroad. But other countries had high tariffs which made German goods so expensive that people in foreign countries could not afford to buy enough of them. Consequently, Germany did not have the money to pay for adequate supplies of food and raw materials. As a result, she set out to gain control over food-producing countries, such as Rumania, Hungary, Denmark, and the Russian Ukraine, so that she could force them to buy her manufactured goods and sell her the needed food supplies. Italy and Japan have also engaged in wars partly for this reason. Once more, however, it is desirable to call attention to the fact that, if the German leaders had devoted to agriculture what they spent for armament, Germany could have supplied most of her important needs from home production. The same was true of both Italy and Japan.

A leading economic cause of war is the activity of those who find in vast armaments and war an opportunity for profit. To these "merchants of death," especially the manufacturers of guns, explosives, battleships, airplanes, and other instruments of warfare, war is the means of reaping huge profits; some devote strenuous efforts in times of peace to promoting huge armies and navies. They support every type of organization that issues propaganda in favor of military preparedness and war. Agents of munitions manufacturers have been known to wreck disarmament conferences, lest the nations cease using arms to settle their disputes. In Europe, it was not uncommon for munitions merchants to bribe newspapers to create war scares in order to frighten nations into arming themselves more heavily.

Modern methods of transportation and communication have tended to make the world an economic unit, in which there is need for cooperation and freer exchange of goods. Imperialism and protective tariffs serve only to bring disunity and trouble. No war today can be profitable, even to the victors. If peace is to be furthered, an educational program must be developed to reveal the dangers of imperialism and protective tariffs. Light must also be thrown on the pernicious activities of munitions makers.

**Political causes of war.** Most important of the political causes of war is the existence of a large number of independent, sovereign national states. Each considers itself absolutely sovereign—that is, each nation is omnipotent within its own boundaries and it cannot endure the thought of surrendering any iota of its omnipotent power in any international agreement. Actually, every state's sovereignty is limited in practice by treaties and international arrangements and by the actual power of the state relative to its neighbors. For example, a small nation cannot disregard the wishes of a much larger and more powerful neighbor. Yet, statesmen strive to maintain the fiction of complete independence and absolute sovereignty, and oppose plans for leagues or federations of nations, which might help greatly to bring about world peace. The situation is especially tragic when we realize that the only way to guarantee small nations safety from conquest by more powerful neighbors is through such federations. Americans realize that there would be nothing but perpetual confusion and warfare if each of our 48 states were an independent power. But proposals to form a "United States of Europe" have been blocked persistently by European nations, large and small. In fact, such proposals were less enthusiastically supported in 1948 than in 1848. Such stubbornness has contributed to wars in which some small nations have lost their prized independence completely.

The final solution of the problem of war will not come until individual nations realize that none is truly omnipotent or independent and that each forms part of a world family. For all to live peacefully and happily, each must be ready to.make sacrifices and co-operate with others. Formation of a "United States of Europe" would be an epoch-making step in this direction. The final goal should be a "United States of the World."

**Ethical and religious causes of wars.** Ethical and religious impulses, however ill founded, also help to stimulate and perpetuate wars.

It has been generally believed that dying in war is the noblest form of personal devotion and sacrifice. Wars are assumed to bring forth the most lofty ideals and sentiments of the human race. It is taken for granted that God is aligned with the forces of any warring nation. Even the supposedly wholly secular wars of our time take on a quasi-religious cast and motivation. Capitalism, plutocracy, Fascism, and Communism are regarded as "sin" by their opponents, and combating them is held to be a sort of religious compulsion and necessity. This helps to perpetuate wars in our day, when all persons of sense and information realize that there can be no ultimate material benefits from them.

## Eliminating the Basic Causes of War

**Need for a comprehensive peace program.** The elimination of war is necessarily the first step in creating a decent world order and assuring the continuation of civilization. The only way to end war is to face squarely the causes of war and attempt to eliminate them as rapidly and thoroughly as possible. Attacking one or another of the symptoms of war, as they appear, does little good. The only effective procedure is to seek the fundamental causes and then uproot them. No one factor, by itself, is responsible for war.

**Essentials of a rational program for peace.** Men and nations must be taught to co-operate by peaceful means instead of resorting to war. Intellectual and cultural conflict must be substituted for physical combat; civic obligation and sacrifice for hysterical patriotism. People should be taught that wars tend to leave a population biologically and economically worse off than before. There should be an international economic organization to control the supply of raw materials and natural resources, so that no nation need go to war to protect its reasonable economic interests. It should be emphasized that willingness to settle disputes peacefully is really a far better proof of national honor than eagerness to fight. It should also be easy to show that war, far from stimulating our more heroic virtues, tragically debases man, and that God does not put the stamp of divine approval on every nation engaged in war.

Because all nations are never at the same stage of cultural development at the same time, it is probable that some nations will express a desire for sane peaceful dealings in international affairs before others. Or, nations like England, which have conquered and seized vast territories in the past, may now be strong for peace in order to preserve their conquests, while branding current programs of conquest by other nations as criminal bellicosity. Some states, misguided by their leaders and lagging in cultural development, may continue to cling to the idea of war after others have given it up. This would make necessary some form of international organization among the peaceful nations to curb the activities of more backward countries; in other words, an international police force.  Some form of international organization would also be necessary, of course, to handle by peaceful means the numerous minor disputes that naturally arise between countries.  Had the powerful nations of the world been willing to set up an adequate international peace organization between 1919 and 1933 and give genuine aid to countries that found themselves in economic and political difficulties, the second world war might never have broken out.

Any program of world peace may take generations to accomplish. Only through a long educational process and patient co-operation of those who have the interests of mankind at heart will it be possible, perhaps, to outlaw war and turn the attention of nations wholly to the task of making life worth living within their own boundaries.

With the arrival of the atom bomb and deadly bacterial warfare it has become evident that there is no time to waste in launching this peace program.  Nevertheless, the nations of the world still seem bent on doing all possible to intensify present disputes, and to line up allies and arm to the hilt for war.

## Efforts to Promote Peace and International Organization

Early plans for international organization.  Though mankind has so far failed to rid the world of the horrors of war, organized peace programs date far back in history.  The Italian poet-philosopher, Dante, suggested in the thirteenth century that the Christian nations unite to end the struggle between the Holy Roman Empire and the Italian city-states.  The terrible Thirty Years' War (1618–1648) gave birth to a number of peace plans.  One, set forth by Emeric Crucé in 1623, involved a permanent council of ambassadors to settle international disputes; another, conceived by the great French statesman, Sully in 1638, urged the formation of a Christian republic of 15 states, managed by a council with power to enforce its decisions if necessary. About 1715, the French savant and humanitarian, the Abbé de Saint Pierre, proposed a real and effective European federation.

And so, down through the years, men have proposed plans to unite the nations in some manner to prevent war.  Usually, these schemes took one of three forms: establishment of an international court to settle international conflicts through arbitration; provision of international legal codes to settle disputes; or the institution of a federation, or union, of nations.  Not until the early nineteenth century, however, was any organized peace program really put into operation.

The "Concert of Europe" represented the first practical large-scale effort to settle international disputes by peaceful methods.  It grew out of the famous Quadruple Alliance of Russia, Prussia, Austria, and England, established in 1815.  It provided at first for periodic conferences of the major European states to take common action against the threat to peace believed to come from the revolutionary movements in France.

The Concert of Europe remained in more or less active force from 1815 until the Congress of London in 1913. It aided in the settlement of disputes between Russia and Turkey in 1856, of Near Eastern problems in 1878, of African problems in 1906, and of Balkan problems in 1913. An attempt was made to use the Concert to prevent the first world war, but national grievances were too deep and national feeling too high to accept conference methods or arbitration.

**Development of the peace movement.** After the Napoleonic Wars, there also arose a number of private peace movements. The New York Peace Society appeared in 1815 and was followed by the American Peace Society in 1828. A similar organization was founded in England in 1816. At the outbreak of the world war in 1914 there were about 150 peace societies in existence, each with many branches. Elihu Burritt, a self-educated American blacksmith, became a world figure by promoting five great international peace congresses, held in Europe between 1842 and 1851. Peace congresses met almost annually from 1889 to 1914; their delegates were influential in bringing the Hague conferences into existence.

In addition to the peace efforts of private groups, important attempts were made by individuals to promote the cause of peace. In 1896, Alfred Nobel, a Swede who made a huge fortune out of the invention and sale of dynamite and other high explosives, established an annual prize of about $40,000 for the person who made the greatest contribution toward world peace in any given year. The Nobel peace prizes have often been fantastically awarded, sometimes to persons who have been notorious warmongers, sometimes to men responsible for diplomatic developments leading directly to war. Edwin Ginn, a book publisher, founded the World Peace Foundation in Boston, in 1910, with an endowment of one million dollars. In 1911, Andrew Carnegie, the steel manufacturer, established the Carnegie Endowment for International Peace. This is the richest and most powerful private peace society in the world. Unfortunately, the official spokesmen of the Endowment were strong advocates of our entering both world wars, and the Endowment seemingly works for peace mainly when there is no likelihood of our being involved in war. In addition to his peace endowment, Carnegie built the Peace Palace at The Hague, Holland, seat of the World Court. He also donated the building occupied by the Pan-American Union in Washington, and the edifice used by the Central American Court in Costa Rica.

The Hague is famous in the history of the peace movement. Here met two imposing conferences in 1899 and 1907. At the first, provision was made for the establishment of a Permanent Court of Arbitration, which opened in April, 1901. While both conferences and the Court were in the long run unsuccessful, they helped somewhat to promote the idea of a peaceful settlement of international disputes.

An outgrowth of the Hague conferences, and the last important development in the peace movement before 1914, was a series of arbitration treaties with foreign nations negotiated by William Jennings Bryan, Secretary of State from 1913 to 1915. Bryan was one of our last resolute public exponents of neutrality and pacific diplomacy. Whatever the fantasies of his free silver program and his views on Prohibition and evolution, history will record him as one of our great statesmen in the cause of peace. The Bryan treaties provided that, in case of disputes, the nations involved would not go to war for at least a year; meanwhile, an international commission of inquiry would investigate the problem. After its report was made, the nations would be free to act as they saw fit. The main check on their actions then would lie in the critical opinion of the world, which might condemn action by the state that the commission believed to be in the wrong. Some 21 treaties of this sort were actually signed. If Germany had signed such a treaty, our entry into the first world war might have been avoided.

The peace movements were never stronger than in the years just before the first world war, nor were the hopes of those devoted to the cause of peace ever higher. But the war rudely destroyed all the peace plans. Many pacifists in all warring countries surrendered their ideals and enthusiastically took part in the war propaganda. Nevertheless, after the war the peace movement was temporarily revived with increasing vigor.

**The rise and fall of the League of Nations.** During the first world war a number of influential persons, both in the United States and Europe, came to the conclusion that some sort of international organization must be established after the war to insure the peace of the world. Inspired by this idea, President Wilson submitted a plan for a League of Nations to the Peace Conference in 1919. It was embodied in the Treaty of Versailles, which followed the war. Despite his eloquent pleas, Wilson was unable to get the United States to sign the peace treaty or to join the League. Nevertheless, the League began operations in 1920 with a membership of about 60 nations.

As a forward-looking gesture, the League of Nations was the most important development that grew out of the war. The League might have been able to curb war, if it had not suffered from certain fatal weaknesses. It was able to deal successfully with many minor disputes, especially those between small and weak nations, and provided a world-wide organization for many valuable social services. But it could not settle any major dispute between the strong powers.

The chief weakness of the League was the fact that its basic spirit was entirely contrary to international co-operation and good will. It was a creature of the harsh and unjust Treaty of Versailles and seemed determined to maintain the faults of the Treaty rather than to correct them. Moreover, Germany and Russia were kept out of the League until it was too late to gain any important benefits by admitting them. Furthermore, the nations which belonged to the League all retained the same political and diplomatic system that had brought on the war in 1914—that is, supernationalism, big armaments, secret diplomacy, and the like. It was hardly to be expected that, in their League operations, they would vigorously follow a policy opposed to the one they were carrying on at home.

Japan openly defied the League by invading China in 1931. It is typical of the League that some of the important nations which formally condemned this action in the League meetings were secretly encouraging Japan. Italy successfully seized Ethiopia in 1935 against the protests of the League. These rebuffs, together with its failure to stop foreign governments from taking part in the Spanish Civil War in 1936–1938 virtually doomed the League as an international force. With the coming of the second world war, the League became a hollow shell, the grave of forlorn and betrayed hopes. On April 18, 1946, the League formally voted itself out of existence and proceeded to liquidate its affairs and property.

The World Court—the Permanent Court of International Justice—was founded by the League of Nations to deal with international legal disputes. It handled successfully a number of minor disputes, but had little importance in maintaining peace, since it did not deal with the basic causes of war. Like the League, the World Court was obliterated by the second world war.

**The sham Kellogg Pact.** The Kellogg Peace Pact, signed by 64 nations by July, 1929, renounced war as a means of settling international disputes. It proved an even worse failure than the League of Nations. From the beginning, the pact was a sham, for it did not apply to any probable type of war. The British and French reservations excepted from its provisions wars of national defense, wars to fulfill treaty obligations, wars in defense of special interests, and wars to enforce the sanctions of the League of Nations. All likely types of war could be put under one of these headings. Indeed, as Professor Edwin M. Borchard pointed out, by implying that the excepted wars were good wars, it put the moral force of the world behind all probable types of war and was, in fact, the first international war pact. Furthermore, the Kellogg Pact provided no punishment for violators; it contained no real provision for disarmament; and it did not attack the basic causes of war. Therefore, it need surprise nobody to learn that, in the ten years after the Kellogg Pact was signed (1928–1938), some 3,500,-000 persons lost their lives in war—more than in any previous decade in human history prior to 1914.

Several world disarmament conferences held in the 1920's and 1930's failed utterly to prevent the mad armament race that helped on the second world war. The disarmament effort came to an inglorious end with the failure of the general disarmament conference in 1934 and of the final naval conference in 1936.

**The current crisis in the peace movement.** In the light of existing world conditions, the weaknesses of all past attempts to establish lasting peace are clearly revealed. It has become the fashion in some circles to regard all efforts at international organization as foolish and doomed to failure. Yet, we shall see the end of war only when the dreams of those few who sincerely supported the League, the World Court, the United Nations, and similar organizations are realized. War will disappear only when those who hate war outnumber or overpower those who desire to preserve it as a means of national policy.

The second world war came because the nations were not willing to pay the price of peace, even though it is much less than the costs of war. It is easy to suggest policies which would promote peace. We might provide for mental disarmament by a realistic system of education, which would tell the truth about international affairs. All nations might be permitted easier access to supplies of raw materials, thus removing a great deal of the economic pressure for war. Arrangements might be made between nations for easier migration of surplus populations. Free trade might well be encouraged, thereby removing the evil effects of tariff walls and tariff wars. Finally, international organizations, such as the recently established United Nations and the Atomic Energy Commission, might be encouraged to provide intelligent and peaceful settlement of disputes.

It will not be possible to establish lasting peace until the causes of war are attacked with vigor. The failure of past efforts to achieve peace was largely due to the fact that they concentrated on only a few of the many basic reasons for war. Most of them tried to prevent war simply by recommending agreements among nations without providing the mental and material basis for such agreements. We must realize that a long and thorough education of the peoples of the world with regard to international issues is essential to the successful elimination of war.

Finally, it is evident to all thoughtful persons that war cannot be ended until we recognize that all modern nations have had their share of responsibility in producing and waging wars. Trying to find a scapegoat or to shift the blame for all wars to one nation, be it Germany, England, or Russia, will only blur and retard the movement toward peace and world unity. The world has never moved more rapidly toward needless and fatal war than since 1945, when Germany had already been reduced to complete military impotence for an indefinite period.

## New Trends in American Foreign Relations

**United States helps to make and then joins the United Nations.** Our intervention in two world wars, in 1917 and 1941, showed that, whether wisely or unwisely, for better or worse, the United States has definitely abandoned the advice of Washington and Jefferson to avoid entangling alliances and foreign quarrels. After the first world war, we refused to join the League of Nations because it was linked to a nefarious peace treaty. During the second world war Presidents Roosevelt and Truman took steps to prevent a repetition of such negative action and helped to create a new world organization, the United Nations, which the United States joined before any peace treaties were made or even proposed. The United Nations has had several meetings and, in December, 1946, decided to locate its permanent headquarters on the east side of New York City.

The United Nations has a legislative body in the Assembly, in which each nation has one member and vote. It has an executive body in the Security Council of eleven members, five representing the five so-called big powers and six elected by the assembly. A permanent executive organization to handle routine business is provided for in the Secretariat, the head of which is elected by the Assembly. A judicial branch was created in the International Court of Justice. Each of the big powers has a veto power over any action taken by the Security Council.

**The Truman Doctrine and the end of the Monroe Doctrine.** After the second world war, there were many signs of the contraction of the British Empire. Britain withdrew from Egypt, gave India independence in 1947, and surrendered the Palestine mandate in 1948. In February, 1947, she announced her inability to continue assistance to war-impoverished Greece. Whereupon, on March 12, 1947, President Truman went before Congress to recommend that we finance a loan to Greece and Turkey. Congress approved this measure for sending money, supplies, and military and civilian personnel to support anti-Communist elements in these regions and to aid reconstruction of these countries.

This was a complete repudiation of the Monroe Doctrine, which very clearly and explicitly declared that the United States would never interfere in the domestic policies or international quarrels of European peoples. Further, with the precedent for taking over such international responsibilities set, there is no logical place to stop. Perhaps, too, by implying that the United Nations is not capable of dealing with such a problem of international interest as the Greek-Turkish situation, a serious blow was delivered to the prestige of that organization before it had got fairly under way. The signing of the North Atlantic Pact in July, 1949, sealed the doom of the Monroe Doctrine and the traditional American policy of neutrality, for better or worse.

**The development of the cold war.** The Truman doctrine and its implementation set in motion vigorous friction between the Anglo-American bloc of nations and Soviet Russia and its satellites. The Republicans, led by the former isolationist, Arthur Vandenburg, warmly supported the so-called Truman doctrine and the excitement and tension grew apace. The Russians were exasperating in their diplomacy and in their conduct in the United Nations and the various international conferences of 1946 to 1949.  But they actually did little more than to claim and consolidate the gains that President Roosevelt had needlessly presented to them at Casablanca, Teheran, Quebec, and Yalta, and which had been confirmed at Potsdam in the summer of 1945.

The struggle over the Russian blockade of Berlin and the Berlin air lift intensified the cold war.  It helped the Truman administration to obtain appropriations for a vast new armament program, and was a major factor in producing the North Atlantic Pact of July, 1949, and the proposal for the United States to finance the arming of the Atlantic Pact nations.  The air lift lasted from June 26, 1948, to May 11, 1949.  It cost the United States nearly 174 million dollars and a vast amount of gasoline.  Some 27 American airmen and 28 American planes were lost.  The British expenditure was about 23 million dollars, paid indirectly by the United States.  Over a million and a half tons of goods and food were carried, and 180,000 flights were made.

The institution of the Marshall Plan helped divide the Anglo-American bloc and the Soviet-dominated group of nations, while our vacillating intervention in Palestine and the Chinese crisis late in 1948 further intensified international friction.

The emergence of the hydrogen bomb menace early in 1950 stepped up the momentum of the cold war.  The proposal of Senator Brien McMahon that, instead of pushing the cold war and the arms race to an inevitable and devastating conclusion, we spend 5 billion dollars a year to improve world relations and promote peace was statesmanlike, but it went unheeded.

**Early impotence and disintegration of the United Nations.**  All these developments served to intensify nationalism and national pride at the critical moment when true friends of peace were seeking to stimulate internationalism and create a stable and effective international organization through the United Nations.  An impasse developed between the United States and its allies and Soviet Russia and its satellites, chiefly concerning matters in Germany and Austria, and the frequent Russian use of the veto, whether justified or not, showed that the veto power of the great powers could nullify any decisive action proposed by the Security Council, the only organ in the United Nations that possessed even theoretical power to use force.  The utter impotence of the United Nations in checking the aggressive action of Holland in Indonesia in the winter of 1948–1949 seemed to indicate that the new organization was a sham in preserving world peace.  If a small and weak nation like Holland could not be checked by an organization which included in its membership powerful states like the United States, Russia, Britain, and France, there appeared little prospect that the United Nations could intervene effectively in quarrels between the major states of the world.  The development of the North Atlantic Alliance in 1949 divided the world into two armed camps, and at least temporarily destroyed any possibility of there being any United Nations long before the cornerstone was laid for the world capitol in New York City. The crisis in the United Nations has been intensified by the communist conquest of China, since another communist nation with the veto power may be added to the "Big Five" on the Security Council.

**War may become an instrument of domestic political and economic strategy.** In the past, most wars have been a product of emotional rage, national arrogance and ambition, or plans to conquer territory. Warfare has rarely been accepted as the normal pattern of domestic political strategy. There is disconcerting evidence, however, that in our time nations may use war, or at least continuous war scares, as the main agency of domestic political and economic policy.

Far from rejecting and suppressing war, it may be that we are entering a period in which rulers will gamble with war as an effective means of assuring political domination and economic "prosperity" in domestic affairs. The experience with a cold war in recent years has shown how such a stratagem works wonders in maintaining political unity, assuring tenure for the party in power, bringing at least temporary economic "prosperity," allaying economic strife, and guaranteeing the stability of whatever economic system prevails in a country. Any threat to political ascendancy, any symptom of economic strife can be stifled by fomenting a war scare. An impending depression may be warded off by the feverish manufacturing of arms designed to meet the alleged war threat.

## Cultural Lag and the War Problem

**Cultural lag in diplomacy.** No phase of human relations better illustrates cultural lag than the current handling of international affairs in the atomic age. Right down into the twentieth century diplomacy was still dominated by Machiavellian tenets. As Walter Weyl wrote after the first world war, it was still controlled by "the approved diplomatic type, the aged, bemedalled, chilly, narrow, and conservative Excellency, very gentlemanly, very astute, fundamentally stupid." By the time of the close of the second world war, the situation had grown worse. An early English diplomat, Sir Henry Wotton (1568–1639), defined a diplomat as "an honest man sent abroad to lie for the good of his country." After 1945, realists came to view many a diplomat as a dishonest man sent abroad to lie in the interest of a foreign country.

**Open diplomacy actually increases international tension.** After the first world war, there was much criticism of secret diplomacy. This was virtually abandoned for some years after 1945, and full publicity was given to most of the international negotiations from 1945 to 1949. This seemed to make matters worse; international tension was increased by provocative speeches made primarily for home consumption and given exaggerated publicity in the papers and over the air. Secret diplomacy at least had the merit of keeping the public opinion of the world fairly well quieted down during negotiations, however much of an explosion might later arise when the nefarious results were revealed.   Even the explosion was usually kept at a minimum because the fruits of secret diplomacy were generally made known piecemeal and after the more acute tension had passed.   Open diplomacy only served to fan the existing tension.

This is a picture of an explosion of an atom bomb. Its destructive power, and the potentially greater destructive power of the proposed hydrogen bomb, point up the necessity of bringing war under control if civilization is to survive.

**The atom bomb brings cultural lag to a head.**   The persistence of the war system and the coming of the atom bomb and other technological advances in mass murder have brought the question of war and cultural lag to a head.   When it comes to devising and manufacturing bigger and better machinery for the destruction of humanity, we are unsurpassed—there seems to be no limit to the intelligence we apply to the technical problem of war.   We pool every intellectual resource of university laboratories, scientific foundations, and industrial research to discover how we may wage war more effectively.

On the other hand, we approach the whole social and cultural problem of war with attitudes dating back to the period of bows and arrows and the battle-axe, if not to the first hatchet.   We do not apply even sixth-grade intelligence to studying the problem of how we might rid the world of the menace of war.

Whatever social services war may have rendered in early days, it has now become a fatal anachronism and the chief threat to the preservation of contemporary civilization. It does not require even grammar-school intelligence to see that the institution of war is a stupid monstrosity. Yet the very best brains of the world are still being employed to facilitate and extend its deadly ravages. As matters now stand, our failure to bridge the gulf between devastating war machinery and our archaic institutional approach to the problem of war and peace may ultimately wipe out human civilization with atom bombs and atom rockets, poisonous chemicals, and deadly disease germs. We were protected from the use of the more barbarous new scientific methods of destruction in the second world war mainly through fear of retaliation and condemnation by world opinion. The Nuremberg Trials made it certain that this protection will be removed in the third world war. Since the losers will be hanged in any event, they will withhold no destructive measures which may avert their defeat, or make it as costly as possible.

**The threatened extinction of civilization.** This discussion of war as an example of cultural lag brings us to the very heart of the whole matter. For a long time, the issue of cultural lag has been of great practical importance. The failure to modernize our institutions has been responsible for nearly all of the public problems and social evils of our age. Cultural lag has produced our economic problems of waste, underconsumption, low standards of living, poverty, unemployment, and the like. It accounts for our inadequate housing and our insufficient medical care. It is what has produced most of the wars in contemporary times and prevented really adequate and constructive plans for peace.

Despite all the handicaps and evils produced by cultural lag, humanity could survive in the past. But the arrival of intra-atomic energy, the atom bomb, bacterial warfare, chemical warfare, and the like, have introduced an altogether new and more alarming prospect. This time, and from now onward, the problems of cultural lag involve the very survival of the human race. Unless we are able to bring up to date the institutions most directly concerned with the causes and prevention of war, it will not be long before humanity will be partly extinguished and the remainder consigned to barbarism. Nothing short of an institutional readjustment sufficient to hold all wars in check—and that without barbarizing fears and preparations—will suffice to preserve anything deserving the name of civilization. Otherwise, cultural lag will exact its final penalty in the destruction of human civilization, just as physiological maladjustments once doomed the dinosaurs.

It will avail nothing to retreat from this challenge into the fog of mysticism so popular with those who lack the courage to face the issues and consequences produced by our scientific laboratories and empire of machines. Dodging the issue through metaphysical and mystical befogging of our thought has been a main reason for the alarming growth of cultural lag, until it now threatens us with racial extinction. Less than nothing will be gained by seeking refuge in dogmatic cults or in the mystical writings of Toynbee or Sorokin. We must face the problems with the resolute courage of men like the late H. G. Wells, who saw that scientific and mechanical marvels can bring untold benefits to mankind if we will but learn how to use them for the advantage of the race and are able to face social problems with the clarity, directness, and honesty of science.

## Summary

War is by far the greatest threat to our civilization. The perplexing problems of peace are doubled and trebled in wartime. War obstructs social and economic progress; it increases the national debt; money that should be spent on constructive work is wasted in destructive efforts; liberal reforms are neglected; and the benefits of the Machine Age are used to produce weapons of death and destruction.

War persists in the civilized world for many reasons, biological, social, psychological, economic, and political. The biological causes of war arise chiefly out of man's nature which makes him both a peace-loving and a fighting animal, depending upon his social experience and conditioning. The psychological causes of war center around such things as false patriotism and extreme nationalism, which place the individual's country, right or wrong, above all else, including the welfare of humanity. Social factors in war are found in the struggle of various groups and vested interests and races for political and economic supremacy. Imperialism, tariffs, and the like are important economic factors producing war. The principal political influence is the theory that every nation is sovereign and should enjoy complete independence in the field of international affairs, with little regard for the interests, rights, or well-being of other nations.

Numerous efforts have been made to settle international conflicts by peaceful methods. All have failed, for they depended upon ending war by political declarations and legal gestures rather than by attacking and removing its basic causes. Peace societies, international peace and disarmament conferences, treaties, "world courts," and international leagues have all been used unsuccessfully. The most important of these was the League of Nations, established by the Versailles Treaty. Though it formally functioned down to the time of the second world war, the League was not able to prevent a single major act of war during the period of its existence. Great hopes were placed in the United Nations, created in 1945, but the international impasse between the United States and the North Atlantic Pact nations and Soviet Russia and its satellites split the world down the middle and at least temporarily made the United Nations a hollow sham.

The way to permanent international peace lies in a thoroughgoing attack upon the real causes of war. This will involve, as its most important elements, education on a world-wide scale to eliminate attitudes favoring war, better distribution of raw materials and markets, the creation of an international organization to promote peaceful relations among nations, and generous treatment of the less fortunate nations by prosperous states.

War, which can today be waged with greater devastation than ever before, since we are now equipped with jet and rocket planes, atom bombs, giant and speedy rockets, deadly methods of bacterial warfare, and the like, has finally brought the issue of cultural lag to a head. Either we must bring our international institutions up to date in time to prevent future devastating world wars, or the prospect is that warfare will destroy what remains of our present era of civilization.

## Selected References

* Allen, Devere, *The Fight for Peace*, Macmillan, 1930. The best and most thorough history and analysis of the movement for world peace.

Barnes, H. E., *The Genesis of the World War*, Knopf, 1927. A disillusioning critique of the myths surrounding the origins of the first world war.

* Beard, C. A., *President Roosevelt and the Coming of the War, 1941*, Yale University Press, 1948. A masterly and definitive analysis of the foreign policy of the Roosevelt administration which led to Pearl Harbor.

Bernard, L. L., *War and Its Causes*, Holt, 1944. Erudite and objective sociological analysis of the institutional causes and aspects of war. Stresses economic factors. Far and away the best sociological treatment of war in English.

Carr, E. H., *International Relations between the Two World Wars*, Macmillan, 1947.

——————, *Conditions of Peace*, Macmillan, 1947.

——————, *The Soviet Impact on the Western World*, Macmillan, 1947. Three able books by a brilliant English scholar. The first deals with the manner in which the vindictive peace treaties following the first world war helped to produce the second. The second volume is probably the best summary of the essentials of a program of permanent peace. The final book is a sane appraisal of Soviet Russia's rôle in world affairs.

Clarkson, J. D., and Cochran, T. C., *War as a Social Institution*, Columbia University Press, 1941. Historical analysis of the institutional basis of war and military society.

Cottrell, L. S., and Eberhart, Sylvia, *American Opinion on World Affairs*, Princeton University Press, 1948. Valuable survey of American attitudes on world affairs from the internationalist point of view.

Curti, M. E., *Peace or War—The American Struggle*, 1636–1936, Norton, 1936. A scholarly and interesting study of three centuries of the peace movement in the United States.

Darby, W. E. (Ed.), *International Tribunals*, American Peace Society, 1925. A collection of the texts of the main plans for international organization and peace down to the first world war.

Davie, M. R., *The Evolution of War*, Yale University Press, 1931. A socioanthropological study of the development of warfare and its social agencies.

Eaton, H. O., *et al.*, *Federation: the Coming Structure of World Government*, University of Oklahoma Press, 1944. Symposium by experts arguing the case for world federation.

Engelbrecht, H. C., *Revolt against War*, Dodd, Mead, 1937. An authoritative discussion of the social effects of warfare.

——————, and Hanighen, F. C., *Merchants of Death*, Dodd, Mead, 1934. The best exposure of the armament manufacturers.

Evatt, H. V., *The United Nations*, Harvard University Press, 1948. Brief and sympathetic official exposition.

Friedrich, C. J., *Inevitable Peace*, Harvard University Press, 1948. Able argument for peace under international law.

Gross, Feliks (Ed), *European Ideologies*, Philosophical Library, 1949. Comprehensive symposium dealing with economic and political philosophies which dominate the current world scene.

* Hamlin, C. H., *The War Myth in United States History*, Vanguard, 1927. A revelation of the distortions of war in American historical writings and a realistic account of our war record.

* Jennings, W. I., *A Federation for Western Europe*, Macmillan, 1940. Thoughtful and thorough program for substituting international federation for the national-state system in Europe west of Russia.

* Johnsen, J. E. (Ed.), *United Nations; or, World Government*, H. W. Wilson, 1947. Valuable collection of materials on United Nations.

Knight, B. W., *How to Run a War*, Knopf, 1936. An ironical guide to the efficient conduct of war, which has been amply vindicated and confirmed by the course of the second world war.

* Lippmann, Walter, *The Cold War*, Harper, 1947. A devastating criticism of American foreign policy under the Truman doctrine.

Major, R. H., *Fatal Partners: War and Disease*, Doubleday, Doran, 1941. Accurate and readable book on ways in which wars spread disease and increase mortality.

Morgenstern, George, *Pearl Harbor: The Story of the Secret War*, Devin-Adair, 1947. The pioneer study of the devious diplomacy that led us into the second world war. See review by G. A. Lundberg, *Social Forces*, May, 1948.

\* Morley, Felix, *The Society of Nations*, Brookings Institution, 1932. Probably the best single book on the late League of Nations.

Mowrer, E. A., *The Nightmare of American Foreign Policy*, Knopf, 1949. Vigorous criticism of the Truman foreign policy and of earlier American neutrality. Argues for world federation. Book is characterized by fanatical hatred of Germany.

Muralt, Leonard, *From Versailles to Potsdam*, Regnery, 1949. Distinguished Swiss publicist shows how the unwise peace treaties of 1919 led to the second world war and the current world crisis.

Murray, Gilbert, *From the League to UN*, Oxford University Press, 1948. Account of the development of the United Nations by a distinguished English scholar and publicist.

Neumann, W. L., *Making the Peace, 1941–1945*, Foundation for Foreign Affairs, 1950. A concise and objective review of the manner in which the Allied Powers lost the peace after winning the war.

Nickerson, Hoffman, *The Armed Horde, 1793–1939*, Putnam, 1940. Able historical demonstration of the manner in which republicanism, democracy, and universal military service have contributed to mass murder and the greater mortality in war.

Ogburn, W. F. (Ed.), *Technology and International Relations*, University of Chicago Press, 1949. Symposium dealing with the effects of mechanization and modern methods of communication and transport upon world affairs and the war pattern.

Orwell, George, *Nineteen Eighty-four*, Harcourt Brace, 1949. This book presents in strikingly prophetic fashion the main motive for perpetuating war in the twentieth century.

\* Porritt, Arthur (Ed.), *The Causes of War*, Macmillan, 1932. A symposium which constitutes the best one-volume account of the many causes of modern wars. A very valuable book.

Reves, Emery, *The Anatomy of Peace*, Harper, 1946. Extended argument that national sovereignty is the chief cause of war and the main obstacle to world peace.

Seldes, George, *Iron, Blood, and Profits*, Harper, 1934. Another competent critique of the armament industry, by a veteran journalist.

Spiegel, H. W., *The Economics of Total War*, Appleton-Century, 1942. Expert summary and analysis of the impact of contemporary warfare on the economic system.

Steiner, H. A., *Principles and Problems of International Relations*, Harper, 1940. An excellent and comprehensive survey of international relations and diplomacy on the eve of the second World War.

Stolper, Gustav, *German Realities*, Reynal and Hitchcock, 1948. Realistic book by eminent German refugee economist debunking much of the wartime mythology in regard to Germany and the war system. Good answer to Vansittartism.

Utley, Freda, *The High Cost of Vengeance*, Regnery, 1949. Frank and competent statement of the idiocy, waste, and barbarism involved in the Potsdam-Morgenthau program applied to Central Europe since 1945.

Waller, Willard (Ed.), *War in the Twentieth Century*, Random House, 1940. A symposium providing the best background for understanding the second world war.

\* Warburg, J. P., *Germany, Bridge or Battleground*, Harcourt, Brace, 1947. Restrained criticism of Allied bungling and vindictiveness in Germany since V-E Day.

—————, *Last Call for Common Sense*, Harcourt, Brace, 1949. Collection of able papers by the author seeking to halt the mad race for a third world war. Highly critical of Truman policy and the Atlantic Pact.

Wright, Quincy, *et. al.*, *A Study of War*, 2 vols., University of Chicago Press, 1942. A monumental, factual study of the causes, frequency, impact, techniques, and prospects of war, and of the institutional factors therein.

# CHAPTER XIX

# Law, Justice, and the Crisis in Legal Practice

## Law and Society

**Importance of legal problems in society.** Our laws provide the formal regulation of human conduct; as social conditions change, laws must change or injustice, crime, and confusion will result. Since laws force members of society to follow certain specific patterns of conduct, they should be carefully and wisely drafted. They must also be competently and fairly administered, or human life, freedom, and happiness will be jeopardized. Unfortunately, there are defects in our laws and in the administration of justice. Many of our laws, especially our state laws, are antiquated, many are poorly drafted, and many are unnecessary. The administration of justice is impeded by unnecessary delays, legal technicalities, and abuses of power, and by weaknesses in the jury system. If we are to expedite social progress, we must reform our laws and legal procedures.

**Hesitation in criticizing the law.** Many persons hesitate to examine our laws and legal system critically; they have been taught that the law is a sacred institution, above human reproach. This is paradoxical, for these same persons do not hesitate to point out deficiencies in our other social institutions. Laws are made by men, administered by men, and designed for the welfare of men. Like all other institutions, laws should be altered if they fail to promote human welfare.

There are numerous definitions of law. Law is regarded as "the publicly enforceable rules of human conduct and social behavior which prevail in any country at any given time." Some of our folkways and mores govern our conduct through the force of public opinion; others have the power of the state behind them. The latter are known as laws.

## The Main Theories of Law and Jurisprudence

**Theories of law.** Some persons believe law to be the product of divine wisdom, others an expression of inherent natural principles, and still others the outcome of human legislation. Although the last theory is the only rational and defensible notion, a glance at the earlier ideas of law will be helpful in illustrating how legislation is the product of social custom and public opinion.

**Primitive law.** Primitive peoples possessed no written law. Their laws were the customs of the tribes, passed on by word of mouth from one generation to the next and enforced by group pressure. They believed that their customs were established by the gods and represented divine will; to break a group custom meant offending not only the group but also the gods. As a result, primitive codes were expected to be obeyed without any questioning and punishment was swift and severe. Punishment demonstrated to the gods that the group as a whole did not sanction the acts of the guilty, who had dared to threaten the safety of the group by incurring divine displeasure.

**Idea of natural law.** The theory of natural law was an early historic idea, based for the most part on the philosophy of Socrates and other Greek thinkers. Those who accepted this theory believed that law existed as a spontaneous manifestation of nature before the rise of human society and is unchanging through the ages. Man's various legal codes are imperfect attempts to grasp and interpret the principles of the natural order, that is, to understand and adopt the perfect law that reflects nature's norms.

Scientifically, there are several ways in which law may be approached. Legal codes and procedure may be interpreted from four points of view —analytical, historical, comparative, and sociological.

**The analytical school of jurisprudence.** The analytical school includes philosophers such as Thomas Hobbes, Jeremy Bentham, and John Austin, who analyzed law as it actually existed in legislation at a given time without giving much consideration to the social background out of which law is formulated. The analytical approach to law is useful for the judge and the attorney, who are primarily interested in knowing what the law *is* at a given time rather than in exploring its historical or social background or its ultimate outcome.

**The historical school of law.** The historical school includes those who regard law as the product of the various social and cultural forces that have operated throughout the history of a nation. They thus consider legislation, at any given period in a nation's history, to be the result of the past events that have shaped the nation's institutions. Writers such as Adam Ferguson, Edmund Burke, and Friedrich Savigny were among the first to interpret legal procedure historically.

**Comparative jurisprudence.** The comparative school extends the historical concept of law. Its followers, among them Joseph Kohler and Sir Paul Vinogradoff, argue that, since nations do not live within themselves but have contacts with and borrow from other nations, all the great national legal systems of the past must be studied and compared in order to understand the legal procedure of any community and to discover the complete basis of any given system of national law.

**Sociological jurisprudence.** The historical and comparative schools helped to explain the origins of law but made little attempt to show whether the law fitted the needs of those to whom it applied. The sociological approach, represented by men like Léon Duguit, Oliver Wendell Holmes, and Roscoe Pound, is concerned mainly with the effectiveness of law as an instrument of social control—a technique of social engineering—and divorces it from any idea of divine will or a natural, unchanging force. The sociological school regards law as man-made—a means for guiding social change and a leading agency in maintaining social order and stability. This theory of law is the most useful as a basis for legal efforts to improve society.

## The Organization of Legal Practice Today

**Purpose of legal practice.** Human beings generally recognize the fundamental need of law and are inclined to obey it, but actual legal practice today has tended to undermine the respect of many for existing law and legal procedure. There is a vast difference between jurisprudence, or the science of law, and legal practice, the law in operation.

Among the leading purposes of law today we may list three: (1) to establish rules that will apply uniformly and permit our complicated society to function in an orderly manner; (2) to protect the life and liberty of individuals and the property of the public, individuals, and corporate owners; (3) to keep up with the changes in a dynamic society as rapidly as the various sectors of our society can absorb them.

Although we like to think that courts and lawyers are concerned only with carrying out justice impartially, in practice this ideal is not always achieved. Some courts and lawyers seem overly interested in protecting the vested interests in society; many lawyers are interested merely in winning cases and in making a living or fortune for themselves. As Newman Levy, a distinguished New York attorney, has said: "We hear much talk about justice. In the abstract, it is a beautiful and desirable concept. But justice *per se* [for itself] plays a small part in the daily activities of the busy practitioner." We shall deal with the defects of legal practice later on.

In fairness to the people in the legal profession today, however, it must be pointed out that in all times, in all countries, and under all systems of law there have been complaints against lawyers and dissatisfaction with the administration of justice. Also, in all professions, trades, and businesses there are people who are exceptionally high-minded and ethical, and those who are conscienceless and selfish. In the legal profession, more than in most others, men have given unstintingly of their time and service, frequently at great sacrifice of income, for the public good. Also, the legal profession has not failed to establish ethical canons beyond reproach. Perhaps if they enforced them more strictly, there would be less room for complaint against lawyers and judicial administration.

**Types of law firms.** There are three main types of lawyers in the United States today: the top-ranking firms, the intermediate firms, and the mass of individuals who practice law. A recent survey [1] showed that 88 per cent of all law firms have only one member, and that 9 per cent have two members. Thus, only 3 per cent of all law firms have more than two members, and in this 3 per cent are the top-ranking firms in the country.

**The great legal partnerships and corporation law.** At the top of the legal profession are a few great legal partnerships with their offices in New York, Chicago, Philadelphia, and other large cities. There may be as many as 27 partners in such a firm,[2] together with as many as 80 associated attorneys, and 150 other employees. Such a firm may do millions of dollars of business each year. Much of the hard work is done by recent law school graduates who receive small salaries.[3] The eminent lawyers at the top of the firm appear in court only if court appearances happen to be their specialty. Otherwise they rarely do, preferring to devote their time to bringing business to the firm. One critical lawyer has remarked that, if the small-fry lawyers specializing in negligence cases can be called "ambulance chasers," we may equally well call the social lions at the top of our great legal partnerships "banquet chasers." By attending social functions at which wealthy individuals and corporation executives and their wives are present, some socially famous lawyers have been able to extend and perpetuate their contacts with members of society whose legal business they find desirable and profitable.

The activities of these great legal concerns are not primarily connected with actual courtroom practice. In fact, they try to advise their clients in such a way as to keep them from having to appear frequently in court. Most of the activities of the big legal organizations are associated with corporation and commercial law, namely, advice to investment bankers, holding companies, and corporations, and the drafting of various types of technical, legal, and financial papers.

The more prominent members of these great legal aggregations have been active in the bar associations of the country and have tried to keep our legal philosophy in harmony with the policies of big business. On the whole, although some of them have made contributions to legal literature, few of them are known for their scholarly works;

---

[1] "Income of Lawyers, 1929–48," by William Weinfeld, *Survey of Current Business,* U.S. Department of Commerce.

[2] The report referred to in footnote 1 states: "Although survey returns were received from lawyers practicing in firms with as many as 23 partners (and although there may even be a few larger firms in existence), the proportion of lawyers practicing in firms of five or more members was less than 5 per cent."

[3] In 1947, the median net income of all lawyers with fewer than five years of practice, 10 per cent of the entire group, was $3,354 ("Income of Lawyers, 1929–48" cited in footnote 1). In 1950, the average salary at which the leading law firms employed graduates with good grades from the leading law schools was $3,000 in New York City and $2,400 in Boston.

some have been interested in politics and have gone on to the Senate and Supreme Court of the United States.

**The intermediate group of legal firms.** Below the large legal concerns are smaller firms with 3 or more partners; these are the firms that usually lead the profession in the actual courtroom practice of our larger cities. For the most part, their practice is limited to civil cases, in which there is the greatest opportunity to make money. Lawyers in this group make the greatest contribution to legal thought and scholarship of any class of lawyers outside the law schools; also, they frequently take a prominent part in municipal politics. Many of the leading criminal lawyers are recruited from this class.

**The mass of lesser lawyers.** At the bottom of the legal profession are the great mass of ordinary lawyers, who practice either alone or in small partnerships and whose activities are devoted chiefly to negligence cases, defense of petty offenders, small business affairs, domestic relations, and probate matters. Many types are found among them, from the honest, hard-working lawyers who are interested in their fellow men to the dishonest "shysters" who are engaged in near-criminal, shady practices.

## Types and Methods of Legal Practice

**Legal practice and legal rackets.** Although much of the following material will be critical in tone, since it deals with problems and defects in legal procedure, the criticisms offered are drawn wholly from writings by distinguished members of the legal profession, in some cases eminent judges. Many of these writings have awakened the public and the legal profession to the need for reform, and some progress has been made in dealing with the defects; they have not, however, by any means been eliminated. This section merely tells what many capable lawyers consider to be some of the more serious defects of their profession.[4] Some of the reforms that have been made will be mentioned here; others will be discussed in the last section of this chapter.

Two fields of legal practice have evoked the censure of critical lawyers given to self-examination if not to self-reproach. One of these is the respectable and remunerative field of corporation law practice, involving mainly constitutional law and the legal knowledge required for organizing, financing, and managing corporations. The other is the field of negligence practice, which occupies far more lawyers, although it brings in much less revenue.

---

[4] For critical discussions of the abuses in the law and legal practice by able lawyers and scholars, see Roscoe Pound, *Causes of Popular Dissatisfaction with the Administration of Justice* (1906); Jerome Frank, *Law and the Modern Mind*, Brentano, 1930; Elihu Root, *The Layman's Criticism of the Lawyer* (1916); Morris Gisnet, *A Lawyer Tells the Truth*, Concord, 1931; Max Radin (Univ. of California), *Lawyers Should Be Abolished*, 1938; Fred Rodell, *Woe Unto You, Lawyers!* Reynal and Hitchcock, 1939; P. E. Jackson, *Look at the Law*, Dutton, 1940; Maynard E. Pirsig (Univ. of Minnesota Law School), *Criticisms of the Legal Profession*, 1946.

Some observers have contended that the practice of criminal law by the intermediate group of lawyers mentioned above is pretty much of a racket. It surely was such as practiced by several prosperous New York City criminal lawyers of the latter part of the nineteenth century. They relied upon extortion, blackmail, and all kinds of shady practices to get business and win cases. Some criminal lawyers may still follow such patterns of action, but they are much more rare today. The main criticism of the highly-paid criminal law practice today is the readiness of some lawyers to aid, advise, and defend powerful racketeers and organized criminals. Men like Al Capone seem to have had little difficulty in getting able and respectable legal firms to represent and defend them. Of course, under our guarantees of individual rights, everyone is entitled to be represented by counsel, and under our judicial system everyone is innocent until he is proved guilty. But how much more fitting it would be if criminals of the Capone type had to be defended by an attorney appointed by the court because of failure to find a lawyer who would be willing to associate himself with the case.

The corporation law practice. By adroit efforts the corporation lawyers have aided their clients to keep within the law and yet avoid some of its effects. An extremely important method has consisted in showing the large corporations how they can continue their gigantic operations without running afoul of the anti-trust laws and other restrictive legislation. It was these lawyers who advised the promoters and financiers of holding companies in the public utility field, for example, how to carry out their plans for creating gigantic electric utility systems. It is they who are now helping the holding companies unscramble their interlocking directorates and complicated corporate structures under the Public Utility Holding Company Act of 1935.

Although financing in the twenties brought about a crisis in the capitalistic system (see Chapter XIV), the practices of the investment bankers were made legally possible chiefly by the services of highly paid corporation lawyers. With these lawyers helping them keep their operations within the law, the exploiters of corporations made huge profits, investors lost their money, and many lawyers grew wealthier from the large fees received for their services. There has been considerable discussion concerning crime in the United States, but little attempt has been made to estimate the losses to the American people through the ruin of corporations and the decline of stock values, or to attribute any of the blame to the corporate legal maneuvering that helped create the fiasco.

With the advice of lawyers, a failing corporation can reorganize under our recently reformed bankruptcy laws and survive. The volume of legal work involved in bringing about the reorganization may be prodigious. In one large but not unique proceeding of this kind, lawyers of the insolvent company alone (not including the lawyers for the creditors) put in the equivalent of more than a hundred years of legal work.[5] The sums eaten up in lawyers' fees can be imagined. On the other hand, the savings to creditors and securityholders because of the reorganization cannot be overlooked.

The corporation lawyers render an important service to their clients by preparing and arguing cases involving the constitutionality of legislation designed to curb the activities of big business and bring them under legal control. These men occasionally supplement their legal knowledge and acumen by drawing upon their political contacts and their association with members of the bench to win a favorable decision.

Through the operation of such laws as the Securities Act, the Securities Exchange Act, the Public Utility Holding Company Act, and the Investment Company Act, the directors and officers of the large corporations can no longer freely exploit their stockholders and the public. The power of the large corporations, therefore, has been reduced. Such trends as competitive bidding, registration rules, supervision of underwriting and legal fees, restrictions on corporations, and more favorable action by courts in protecting stockholders are making investment bankers lose out in the control of business. Since the large corporations and the investment bankers are the clients of the giant law firms, it can be said that the power of the latter too is now waning, though they remain dominant and prosperous in the legal profession.

**The practice of the intermediate legal firms.** The smaller, but nevertheless highly reputable, legal firms handle some corporation cases, inheritance and estate tax practice, the administration of trusts, and the like. They often specialize in arguing appeals before the higher state courts and the Federal courts. They also usually furnish the outstanding and most highly paid criminal lawyers.

In acting as attorneys for trust companies, they have undoubtedly passed upon the legal aspects of many of the practices that resulted in losses to beneficiaries of trust funds.[6] Some of these practices are now prohibited by statute. For example, in some of the states it is no longer legal for a trust company acting as a trustee to sell the property of a securities affiliate to a trust that it is administering.

**Desperate competition at the foot of the legal profession.** There are now about 170,000 practicing lawyers in the United States. The law schools of New York City alone have over 7,000 students. Today, all lawyers must have professional training, and the better law schools are graduate schools, admitting only students who have previously received a bachelor's degree. In spite of these obstacles, however, and in spite of the fact that the bar examinations are becoming more difficult, more lawyers are practicing today than ever before. The sharp competition resulting from the increase in the number of practicing at-

---

[5] "The Lawyer and Business," *Fortune,* October 1948, p. 180.

[6] Former abuses in the trust company field are well described in Fred O. Kelly's concise book, *How to Lose Your Money Prudently,* Swain, 1933.

torneys has been a chief cause of the evils that prevail in the lower ranks of the profession today.

**Recent invasions of the field of legal practice.** The competition for clients has been made worse by the fact that, although new tax laws and a multitude of Federal and state regulatory laws have provided new opportunities for lawyers, there is less work for them to do. Laymen such as accountants and tax specialists practice before the administrative boards. Agencies such as title companies, trust companies, tax bureaus, and collection agencies sometimes perform duties that lawyers say are an unauthorized practice of law. For example, such activities as searching titles, transferring properties, and drawing up mortgages are sometimes part of the work of title companies. Credit and collection agencies do much of the business of collecting overdue accounts. Casualty companies handle a great many negligence cases, especially in the field of accidents. Although the agencies that perform the legal activities mentioned do employ trained lawyers, they turn over a good deal of the routine details to clerical assistants, thus reducing the need for lawyers. In the juvenile courts lawyers are being displaced by psychiatrists and social workers.

**The unsavory aspects of negligence practice.** Many lawyers, in their attempts to earn a living from their profession, have entered the field of negligence cases. These comprise suits for damages resulting from various kinds of accidents, especially automobile accidents. Some unsavory methods have been used by lawyers to "drum up" work in the negligence field. In the practice known as "ambulance chasing," the lawyer employs "runners" to follow ambulances leaving the scene of an accident and then report the names of the persons involved to their lawyer employers. The lawyer then immediately visits or writes to the persons involved in the accident. Ambulance drivers, reporters, policemen, hospital attendants, doctors, and nurses have been known to tip off ambulance chasers about accidents soon after their occurrence, in return for a fee paid by the lawyer. This fee is sometimes a "cut" of the lawyer's compensation. Usually the ambulance-chasing lawyer makes a proposal to the injured person on the basis of what is known as the "contingent fee" principle. The lawyer agrees to bring suit for damages if he is promised a fixed proportion— usually half—of the sum awarded the victim by the court if the lawyer wins the case.

Most injured persons need a lawyer to represent them because the insurance companies, who are frequently defendants in negligence suits, invariably have competent attorneys to represent them. Prosperous attorneys look with scorn upon the lawyer who thus secures clients; but so long as middle-class and working-class families ignore help from legal and other agencies, many persons would not secure legal assistance if it were not for the ambulance chasers. Even though damages awarded must be shared with the lawyer, half the damages is better than nothing. Following up accidents has thus helped both poor lawyers and people who ordinarily do not use the services of lawyers.

Ambulance-chasing lawyers have, however, abused the system of contingent fees. The passage of compulsory automobile insurance laws in several states has increased this abuse, for it is known that all automobile owners are insured and that the insurance companies have funds to cover damage suits and awards. The abusers of the practice often take the cases of guilty persons in automobile accidents and actually urge them to bring a suit for damages. In one instance known to the authors, a drunken driver pulled out of the line of traffic and smashed into the car of a motorist who was driving carefully on his own side of the highway. Although there were witnesses to testify to the criminal negligence of the drunken driver, a conscienceless lawyer took the case of the guilty driver, filed suit, and persuaded the jury to award damages to a person who should have been sent to prison. Many such atrocious cases undoubtedly occur each year.

Insurance adjusters and casualty companies are also guilty of abusing justice. Frequently, an insurance adjuster hurries to the bedside of the accident victim, sometimes racing against the ambulance-chasing lawyer. The adjuster then offers a sum of money to the victim if the latter will sign a release from court action; or, if he cannot obtain a release, the adjuster may try to get the injured person to make a written or oral statement of the way the accident occurred. Such statements, often given while the victim is in pain or in a serious nervous condition, do not furnish a true picture of the situation. But they may later be used against the unfortunate person in court.

**Abuses in criminal law practice.** In a class with the ambulance-chasing lawyer is the one who seeks criminal cases by employing persons to hang around the magistrates' and criminal courts looking for possible cases. Bondsmen, court attendants, and policemen also call criminal cases to the attention of favored lawyers. A lawyer too poor to employ a "snooper" might hang around the courtroom himself. Often, he is a regular daily caller who "drums up" trade by chatting with the attendants, with the bondsmen, and even with the indicted men. Some of these lawyers have been guilty of exploiting the persons whose cases have been entrusted to them by agreeing to charge only a small fee, paid in advance, for pleading a case and then, a short time before the trial or even on the day of the trial, demanding more money. In some instances, such a lawyer continues to demand money for services rendered even after the case is closed. On the other hand, there are many public-spirited attorneys who have generously given their time and talents in behalf of poor persons involved in criminal actions. The late Clarence Darrow was such a lawyer. Nevertheless, the number of able attorneys who can afford the time to take the cases of poor but worthy persons with little or no pay is so slight that the provision of justice for the poor will require a greater development of legal aid societies and the Public Defender movement, which we shall discuss later on.

## Defects in Legislation and Legal Procedure

**Cultural lag in legal practice.** Waste, expense, and unfairness are to be found in our legal procedure. Our courts in most states will not tell us until after a law is passed and has been put into operation whether it is constitutional or not. Political influence can cause long delays in trials. The simplest story told in court can be interrupted and chopped into pieces until both the witness and the jury are confused. Our judges and lawyers cling to precedent, trying cases in some states by rules of legal procedure that were used in the Middle Ages or early modern times.

In no other profession, perhaps, is there as much cultural lag as in law. A surgeon of 1750 would be absolutely at sea in a present-day operating room, but a good lawyer of 1750 would be reasonably familiar with the atmosphere and jargon of one of our courtrooms. We would not tolerate in the medical profession practices such as we see daily in the courtroom. No surgeon would delay an operation merely because some minor instrument had been misplaced or an attendant had not arrived. Perfect parallels of this situation happen frequently in the courtroom. No doctor would make a diagnosis of a patient according to the medical concepts of the seventeenth century, yet lawyers must sometimes follow rules laid down in that period, or even earlier. No doctor would employ a procedure that had frequently proved fatal to patients, yet lawyers must sometimes follow precedents that posterity has found unjust.

**Reverence for constitutional law.** Aside from the important principles embodied in the common law, our body of law may be divided into two parts—constitutional and statutory. Constitutional law is that laid down in our Federal and state constitutions. Statutory law is legislation passed by Congress, the states, or municipalities.

The prevailing reverential attitude toward the Federal Constitution, due no doubt in part to the fact that the Constitution is designed to protect minority rights, makes it all but impossible to put through worth-while constitutional amendments. To many persons, the Constitution is a sacred document, one that should not be altered in any way. They fail to realize that the Constitution was designed to serve us and not to be worshiped. The framers of the Constitution regarded it as an instrument that should be modified as the need arose. Jefferson thought the Constitution should be amended or replaced by a new one about every twenty years.

Reverence toward constitutional law and the right of the Supreme Court to set aside statutory law as unconstitutional create a serious social problem. It makes it difficult to adjust law to social realities. We have had relatively few amendments to the Constitution since the days of Thomas Jefferson. From Jefferson to Lincoln, the Constitution was not amended. Then, after the three Reconstruction Amendments, there was no new amendment until the Sixteenth Amendment, legalizing the income tax, was ratified in 1913. A child labor amendment has been before the country for over twenty-five years without ratification.

It is difficult to estimate how much social damage arises from the failure to keep the Constitution and court decisions in harmony with the pace of American civilization. It is frequently said that we do not need to amend the Constitution because the courts can interpret the Constitution to harmonize with social progress. But courts also can interpret—and have often interpreted—our constitutional law in such a way as to block much needed social legislation.

**Levity in regard to statutory law.** When we turn to statutory law, we find a very different attitude—sanctity is replaced by levity. Our legislatures, both Federal and state, pass so many laws, such needless laws, and such trivial laws that the populace finds it difficult to know what the law is or to respect it. Whereas it takes almost a revolution to produce a constitutional amendment, about the easiest thing a government does is to pass another law.

Much of our legislation is trivial. William Seagle has dealt with this triviality in an interesting little book, *There Ought to Be a Law*,[7] from which the following examples are taken, as an indication of the absurdity of some of the laws now on the books. In Kentucky, all persons are forbidden to appear on the streets in bathing suits unless there are police to run them in. An Oregon law stipulates that all beds in hotels and lodging houses shall be provided with sheets not less than 9 feet long. Iowa says that no persons "shall have, erect, or use, while fishing on or through ice, any house, shed, or other protection against the weather, or have or use any stove for creating artificial heat." Kansas makes it a crime to eat, or seem to eat, a snake in a public exhibition; South Carolina compels railroads to carry free all baby carriages belonging to passengers; and so on through a whole book of such ludicrous legislation. Our laws on sex practices are notoriously absurd and petty. The famous book of Professor Kinsey on *The Sexual Life of the Human Male*[8] showed that many of the ordinary sex practices of respectable married couples are legally felonious.

**Excessive laws encourage excessive lawlessness.** It has been observed that America has more laws and more lawlessness than any other nation in the world. At the present time, there are over 2,500,000 Federal, state, and municipal statutes on the books. It is not unusual for 10,000 bills to be introduced by a single Congress, although fewer than 500 public laws are passed at each session. About 22,000 state laws are passed every two years, or an average of 230 new laws in each

---

[7] Macaulay, 1933.
[8] Philadelphia: W. P. Saunders, 1948.

state annually. Many states pass similar laws, duplicating each other's efforts in framing the legislation. Few new criminal statutes are passed in any year. Many laws deal with appropriations, the powers, and judisdictions of government, charters of private and public corporations, and building and health codes. Much of the legislation has little effect upon the individual. Yet, there are a mass of laws on the books that do affect our behavior. Many of these are necessary, but others are foolish and are often disregarded. Once a person disregards a foolish law, it becomes easier to have less respect for good laws.

There are many laws of which the average person knows nothing. Any law-abiding citizen may unconsciously break in the course of 24 hours enough laws to put him in prison for several years and require payment of fines running into thousands of dollars. This is more serious than it may seem. An average well-to-do citizen, if picked up for a minor infraction, can usually get out of it; but a poor, friendless person may be tried, convicted, and sent to prison, to become associated with criminals and degenerates and placed on the road to habitual criminality.

**Obsolete laws.** Not only are we plagued with new foolish laws to which we pay little attention, but there are many obsolete laws that should be repealed. Twelve states can still imprison persons for debt. Most of the criminal codes still include some Old Testament ideas— for example, punishment for heresy, blasphemy, swearing, and cursing. Delaware has a law making it a misdemeanor to practice witchcraft. An atheist cannot take an oath in several states. Under ordinary conditions, the dying declaration of a murdered or injured person is treated as valid testimony, but the dying declaration of an atheist is disregarded in a number of states. In some states, even the dying declarations of a religious believer are disqualified if he uses profanity under the stress of pain or excitement.[9] Unenforced laws regulating the observance of Sunday, laws that date back to Colonial times, are common on the statute books.

**The verbosity of laws.** Thomas Jefferson once asserted that laws seem to be drawn in such a way as to be incomprehensible or ambiguous, even to lawyers. They are still usually drawn in a verbose and technical jargon that even lawyers cannot understand clearly. Prominent students of law, like Professor Fred Rodell of Yale University Law School, charge that "the law" is a vast verbal racket that would lose its force and prestige if laws and the legal language were reduced to plain and lucid English. The following excerpt from Section 504 of the Internal Revenue Code, which should be intelligible if any law can be expected to be, well illustrates the prolix and confused nature of conventional legal jargon:

---

[9] On the nature and extent of archaic religious legislation and its relation to the administration of justice, see Frank Swancara, *The Obstruction of Justice by Religion*, Courtright, 1936.

For the purposes of this subchapter the term "undistributed subchapter A net income" means the subchapter A net income (as defined in Section 505) minus—

(a) The amount of the dividends paid credit provided in Section 27(a) without the benefit of paragraphs (3) and (4) thereof (computed without its reduction under section 27(b)(1), by the amount of the credit provided in Section 26(a), relating to interest on certain obligations of the United States and Government corporations); but, in the computation of the dividends paid credit for the purposes of this subchapter, the amount allowed under subsection (c) of this section or of section 405 of the Revenue Act of 1938 in the computation of the tax under this subchapter or under Title IA of the Revenue Act of 1938 for any preceding taxable year beginning after December 31, 1937, shall be considered as a dividend paid in such preceding taxable year and not in the year of distribution. . . .

To make some of the new and important Federal laws that regulate business comprehensible to the businessmen who must obey them, some of the administrative agencies have distributed simple questions and answers concerning the laws. This practice, however, has not been carried very far. Also, some of the states have created Law Revision Commissions to eliminate outmoded and defective rules and statutes and to simplify, clarify, and organize the entire body of law, but so far there has been little progress in improving legal language.

The written decisions of judges are frequently as verbose and incomprehensible as the laws themselves. A 1948 questionnaire asking of 115 judges how judicial opinions could be improved, brought forth the opinion generally that they should be shorter than they are and that their quality should be improved. However, there were few concrete suggestions concerning how these objectives could be accomplished. Most of the judges felt the solution must be left to the individual judge.[10]

**Delays in legal cases.** Legal theorists believe that justice should be prompt. But, actually, there are many delays, particularly in the lower courts. In most instances, these delays occur because there are not enough judges; in other instances they arise because the judges are lazy, careless, or indifferent. Since many judges are beyond the reach of public opinion because of long-term appointments, little can be done to remedy this situation. Some of the delays are necessary, but others are brought about through arrangements with the judge by influential attorneys. There are instances of cases having been postponed for as long as a decade after they were entered on the court calendar. For the poor client, postponement ordinarily means greater cost and hardship; for the wealthy client, indefinite postponements may mean winning the case or getting a favorable compromise.

Some reforms have been made to speed up justice. In civil actions

---

10 Mary K. Wall, "What the Courts Are Doing to Improve Judicial Opinions," *The Journal of the American Judicature Society*, February, 1949. This survey was made by Associate Justice Gordon Simpson of the Supreme Court of Texas for a session of the American Bar Association's meeting in September, 1948, which was devoted to the subject of improving judicial opinions.

the number of pleadings has been limited and declaratory judgments have been permitted.   But many reforms must still be made to reduce delays, such as shortening the time for appeals and restricting the number of continuances in any case.   Equally as important is the need for increasing administrative efficiency on the part of the judges, clerks, and prosecuting attorneys.

**Legal technicalities obstruct justice.**   We customarily accept the idea that law has a primary regard for facts.   Yet the courts are hampered by legal technicalities in considering the facts.   There must, to be sure, be some regard for form and consistent legal practice, but our present court procedure has more regard for form and precedent than for fact and reality.   The rules regarding the nature and admission of legal evidence are based upon a body of ancient precedents. The rules of evidence can be manipulated by a clever lawyer or a biased judge in such a way that important evidence is excluded.   Often the most important item in the case is the previous criminal record of the defendant.   It is virtually impossible to bring this into a case unless the defendant takes the witness stand.   Even then, there is always a danger that this will cause a mistrial or constitute a reversible error. In criminology and penology, the previous record of the criminal is regarded as perhaps more important than the commission of the crime in question.   Cases in which the fact of guilt has been clearly proved have been thrown out of court merely because some trivial error occurred in the indictment or procedure.   For example, a conviction was set aside because the indictment described the weapon involved as a "Smith and Weston" revolver, when it should have been a "Smith and Wesson."

Criticism in the late twenties and early thirties of the way in which justice was allowed to miscarry for trivial technical reasons was followed by a wave of reform.   Some states passed laws forbidding appeals or reversals based merely on stenographic and similar errors that had nothing to do with the matter in dispute.

**Difficulties and defects in magistrates' courts.**   In the magistrates' courts—the lower courts of our larger cities—we find the worst offenses against justice.   This situation is due in part to the congestion of the calendar.   On the bench usually sit third- and fourth-rate lawyers, often party-machine appointees with low ethical standards.   Sometimes they are not even lawyers.

It is not surprising, therefore, that many magistrates' courts are a blot on American justice.   Because of crowding and haste, it is frequently impossible to give proper attention to cases.   The judges in most of these courts are not prepared for the labors demanded of them. Also, they are, for the most part, under obligations to render favors to politicians and political "fixers."   Another abuse associated with the inferior courts is the frequency with which innocent persons are jailed because they cannot furnish cash for bail.   The poor and friendless individuals who frequently appear in the magistrates' courts are particularly subject to this handicap. Not only is the poor man put at a disadvantage by his inability to furnish bail, but it is difficult for him to pay the ordinary court fees, hire a competent lawyer, and meet other necessary expenses of a courtroom procedure. The poor man is also at a disadvantage with some judges who are oversympathetic toward the well-to-do. It is no wonder that there is widespread belief that justice for the rich man is different from justice for the poor man.[11]

**Defects in criminal law practice.** In criminal law there are probably more obvious defects than in any other branch of legal procedure. We shall discuss these defects of criminal law in later chapters, but to mention some of the outstanding evils here will serve to emphasize the point.

We still impose punishment for a crime, instead of attempting to find the right treatment to fit the individual criminal and convert him into a decent citizen. We still use the brutal third degree to force a confession of guilt from suspects. Our jury trials often depart from the dignity and earnestness of the law, so that our courtrooms frequently become the scenes of every type of horseplay, cunning, and ingenuity that can be devised by lawyers to win cases. Facts are often obscured, evidence is sometimes excluded or twisted, and perjury or lying under oath is common. Wealthy defendants, who can afford to employ good counsel, private detectives, handwriting experts, accountants, and other assistance in the preparation of their cases, have the advantage over poor clients. The clever and experienced criminal also has a decided advantage in our court system, because he has already had contact with the law and knows how to get around it.

**Weakness of the jury trial as a means of ascertaining guilt.** Among the legal institutions of our day, the jury trial is, perhaps, the chief obstacle to swift and certain justice.[12] No single legal practice contributes more to the miscarriage of justice. The jury is chosen from a panel selected by lot and is made up of twelve men, though the number varies, who often may not measure up to the average in honesty, intelligence, and education. On occasion, an unscrupulous jury commissioner, for monetary or political reasons, will favor one of the parties in the selection of a panel of prospective jurors. Even when a panel is honestly drawn, there is no way of assuring its competence. The professional classes, for example, are automatically excused from jury service. Those literate enough to have read and formed an opinion about a case and honest enough to admit it are disqualified from

---

[11] For an oft-cited study of the difficulty of the poor man in getting justice, see R. H. Smith, *Justice and the Poor*, Carnegie Foundation, 1919, a survey warmly praised by Elihu Root and Charles Evans Hughes. See also footnote 18.

[12] See below, p. 852. For criticisms of the jury trial, see Irvin Stalmaster, *What Price Jury Trials?* Stratford, 1931; Jerome Frank, *Law and the Modern Mind,* Brentano, 1930; Leon Green, *Judge and Jury,* Vernon Law Book Co., 1930; H. W. Taft, *Witnesses in Court,* Macmillan, 1934; Jerome Frank, *Courts on Trial; Myth and Reality in American Justice,* Princeton University Press, 1949; Edgar Lustgarten, *Verdict in Dispute,* Charles Scribner's Sons, 1950.

jury service. The system of challenges further serves to eliminate competent and intelligent persons from the "twelve good men and true" who are actually chosen to serve as the jury.

Distortion of evidence, manufacturing of testimony, overt perjury, overworking of circumstantial evidence, frequent objections, rhetorical and passionate speeches, maudlin appeals to sentimentality, attempts to stir prejudice or pity, distraction of attention from important evidence, and the like are among the methods used by counsel to influence juries. As Dorothy Bromley pointed out in an article on "Perjury Rampant," [13] perjury is so universal in courtrooms that much testi-

*From the Warner Bros. picture* Alcatraz Island.

Typical American courtroom scene: an attorney summing up before the jury.

mony and evidence presented are worthless or worse. The charge of the judge may be worded or expressed in such a way as to leave little doubt in the minds of the jury about the verdict he desires. On the other hand, when a jury returns an ordinary general verdict, it usually "has the power utterly to ignore what the judge instructs it concerning the substantive legal rules." [14] All these courtroom practices frequently make a travesty of criminal justice.

One of the flagrant examples of the burlesque and abuses of the jury trial occurred at the close of the first trial of Alger Hiss for perjury in the summer of 1949. The jury was polled after the verdict, and it was ascertained which jurors had voted for an acquittal and which for conviction. The latter denounced the former as being prejudiced and influenced rather than being guided by the facts. The names of the

---

13 *Harpers Magazine,* June, 1931.
14 For a "dissertation" on special verdicts in which the above statement is made about the general verdict, see Judge Jerome Frank's opinion in Skidmore v. Baltimore and Ohio R. Co., 167 F. 2d. 54–8–, decided March 15, 1948.

jurors and their attitude toward the defendant and the verdict were given the fullest publicity in the newspapers, and some of the jurors who voted for acquittal received threatening letters. All this not only held the jury up to implicit ridicule but made it less likely that dignified and competent persons would welcome jury service.

That innocent people are often convicted in jury trials is apparent from the able book of Professor E. M. Borchard, *Convicting the Innocent*,[15] in which he cites many cases of men who were apparently guilty beyond the shadow of a doubt but were later clearly proved to be innocent. The innocent are, obviously, much more likely to be convicted in cases involving reasonable doubt. On the other side of the picture are the cases in which unscrupulous lawyers have aided veteran criminals in gaining acquittals.

## Reforms in Law and Legal Procedure

**The outlook for reform.** There are promising signs on the horizon that the none too happy picture presented in the preceding pages will be brighter in time. Reference has already been made to some of the reforms made in our laws and legal practices. Other improvements that have been made will be mentioned in this section. It is significant that the legal profession, which has been principally responsible for the improvements made in the present century in the administration of justice, has undertaken, through a Survey of the Legal Profession, to gather facts for an objective appraisal of lawyers as they function today.

A brief review is given here of the most important suggestions for improving American law and legal practice. They include socializing law and legal practice, establishing an office of Public Defender, extending the activities of the legal aid societies, developing the Lawyer Reference Plan, and improving legislation and legal procedure.

**Proposed socialization of law.** The most drastic proposal is that which recommends socialization of the law and legal practice. In such a plan, the lawyers representing both the prosecution and the defense would be paid by the state, which would also defray the costs of lawsuits and trials. The argument for this plan is based on the fact that the state makes the laws and therefore should assume responsibility for carrying them out. The adoption of socialized legal practice, it is claimed, would help the poor man to receive the same treatment as the rich; costly delays and postponements would no longer add to the personal expense of securing justice; and justice would be within the reach of every citizen.

**The Public Defender.** Less ambitious and drastic than the socialization of law and legal practice is the proposal that the office of Public

---

[15] New Haven: Yale University Press, 1932.

Defender be established, so that all persons charged with crimes may receive free defense. Of course, those who are able or prefer to hire lawyers would be permitted to do so, but the Public Defender, a competent lawyer, would be available to the poor. The Public Defender is highly recommended by many who are interested in the reform of our legal procedure. Their opinion is well summarized by Charles Mishkin in an article in the *Journal of Criminal Law and Criminology*.[16]

Mr. Mishkin contends that "rich and poor should be on an equal plane before the bar of justice, but in practice they are not equal." The rich man can employ a brilliant, high-priced attorney and pay large fees to investigators to secure witnesses and to prepare an adequate defense; but the poor man is helpless. He often has little understanding of legal proceedings and is forced to rely upon a lawyer who has been assigned by the court to represent him. Although excellent services have been rendered by counsel assigned to indigent persons, and without fee, sometimes the assigned attorney is inexperienced and relatively incompetent, though well-meaning. Since it is still orthodox practice for the court to assign an attorney who happens to be in the courtroom on other business, some lawyers hover around the courtroom eager for such assignments. Such a person is likely to try to get as much as he can from the desperate accused person and his relatives and do as little as possible in return. These conditions lead many high-grade attorneys who might otherwise be willing to defend poor persons to avoid the responsibility.

The state, which should be as interested in proving a man innocent as in demonstrating his guilt, maintains a prosecuting attorney, but leaves the accused to defend himself as best he may. Since the function of the state is to seek the truth, this function is not fully performed unless there is a Public Defender, as well as a public prosecutor, both equally honorable and equally well paid. Although the Public Defender has usually been recommended chiefly for criminal cases, an eminent New York lawyer, Eustace Seligman, has logically argued that the function and service should also be extended to civil cases.

The Public Defender is not a new institution. The office was created in Spain over five hundred years ago. Hungary, Norway, and Argentina have adopted it, and Argentina has developed the practice to a high degree. There is a strong public-defender movement in England. Some of the states, including California, Connecticut, Mississippi, Nebraska, and Virginia have legally established public defenders; and several cities, Chicago, Columbus, Memphis, Omaha, Providence, St. Paul, San Francisco, and Tulsa,[17] have tried out the experiment with success.

The advantages of the Public Defender, from the standpoint of both

---

16 November, 1931.

17 J. E. Lumbard, Jr., "For Equal Justice—a Public Defender," *New York Times Magazine*, Nov. 2, 1947.

justice and economy, are the following: Obviously guilty offenders are urged to plead guilty, thus saving unnecessary trials; adequate defense is provided for all valid cases; jury trial is often dispensed with; cases are tried promptly and in a more expert fashion; great economies result from the avoidance of delays and postponements; trial judges will often heed the Public Defender's advice about sentencing; and there is a great reduction in the probability that a poor and innocent man will be convicted.

**Valuable work of legal aid societies.** In many cities, legal aid societies have had definite value in improving legal practice. Those societies give competent, free advice to those who cannot afford to pay for legal aid. Most important of all, they save poor persons from expensive and often useless suits. The New York City Legal Aid Society obtains settlements out of court in nine out of ten cases. The movement now has a national basis in the National Association of Legal Aid Organizations, which came into being in 1923. The legal aid societies have in many instances protected the rights of the poor by increasing their understanding of such rights. Fair-minded legal aid lawyers have, in some cases, changed the attitudes of employers toward employees. An efficient legal aid society in a city helps the prestige of the legal profession. It gives an opportunity to young lawyers to secure training and often does more than any other legal organization to combat the evils prevailing in petty legal practice. One of the most important contributions of the legal aid movement has been the support of legal reform.

**Lawyer reference plans.** A rich person has always been able to get good legal advice. The indigent person can turn to the legal aid society. The needs of the great middle class who are neither well-to-do nor desirous of charity may some day be met through the Lawyer Reference Plan, when that system becomes better established.[18] The large group of middle-class people run into many problems on which legal advice is essential; for example, leases of dwellings, installment sales, unpaid wages, money owed them, separations, divorces, and crimes. Through a combination of fear and ignorance these people keep away from lawyers.[19] They thus harm their own interests and in addition

---

[18] The development of legal aid societies was immensely stimulated by the survey called "Justice and the Poor" by Reginald Heber Smith (see footnote 11). Mr. Smith, Director of the Survey of the Legal Profession, which is examining various aspects of the legal profession and its relationships to the public, social, and economic life of the United States, is credited with promoting the lawyer reference plans. For an explanation of the creation and operation of lawyer reference plans, see *Lawyer Reference Plans—a Manual for Local Bar Associations,* by Charles O. Porter, Survey of the Legal Profession, Boston, 1949.

[19] A study entitled *The Family and the Law,* a report of a study of family needs as related to legal service, made for the Survey of the Legal Profession by Earl Loomis Koos, 1948, states: "Recent researches have shown that both middle-class and working-class families often resist help from legal and other agencies which are designed for the sole purpose of bringing aid to the family. Among working-class families this resistance may be due to ignorance of the true purpose of the agency, to a resentment of 'charity,' or to one or more other factors. Among middle-class

deprive low-income lawyers, who would be willing and competent to render them legal service at reasonable fees, of opportunities to provide such aid.

The Lawyer Reference Plan is designed to overcome both of these conditions. It is "an agency through which a member of the general public can be referred to a competent and reliable lawyer who for a fixed, moderate fee will be willing to give a consultation on a legal problem and then render additional legal service for a moderate fee if further legal service seems desirable and necessary." [20]

The movement toward the creation of lawyer reference plans is young and has not yet been well publicized. Although bar associations of the larger cities have been experimenting with these plans since 1937, by 1949 they existed in only twenty-odd cities. More local plans will undoubtedly be set up as greater publicity is given to the movement in the future. Its potentialities for good in the field of law are recognized.

**Improvements in legislation and legal procedure.** Some progress is being made in the way of reducing the number of archaic laws and limiting the deference paid to paralyzing legal technicalities. Some of the states, New York and Louisiana, for example, are engaged in revising the laws and improving court procedure. A considerable number of states have an agency charged with statute revision in the sense of editing and compiling the statutes. A good many states—including Illinois—have types of law revision under which commonly consulted compilations of statutes are kept reasonably up to date. However, in most states no agency has been set up officially to call attention to the fact that a statute has outlived its usefulness or is probably unconstitutional and should therefore be rewritten or removed from the statute books.[21]

The Judicial Conference of the United States, established in 1922, has since 1946 dealt with such questions as appointment and compensation of referees in bankruptcy, selection of juries and increase in their compensation, habeas corpus procedures, pre-trial techniques, and other matters. The new Federal Rules for Civil and Criminal Procedure, prepared with the help of the bar, embody the fruits of many years of professorial research and recommendations. They are kept up to date by Judicial Conferences in which practicing attorneys participate. The establishment of the Administrative Office of the United States in 1939 has helped to make Federal judicial administration more businesslike. A legal investigator, under the supervision of the Federal

---

families the resistance arises mainly from the need in our society for the 'respectable' family to stand upon its own feet, to solve its own problems (or at least to hide them), and to prove the rightness of the every-tub-stands-upon-its-own-bottom philosophy which permeates American middle-class family life."

20 William Dean Embree, "A Comparative Analysis of Lawyer Reference Systems," *Bar Bulletin,* New York County Lawyers Association, November, 1946, p. 6.

21 "Law Revision Agencies," Illinois Legislative Council, Research Memorandum File 845, January, 1949.

courts, is now charged with the duty of making a constant survey of the practical operations of our courts and recommending needed changes in procedure.

The American Law Institute has worked out and is promoting a new code of legal evidence, prepared by two of the foremost authorities on the law of evidence. The Institute has also drafted a model procedure in criminal law, the Youth Correction Authority Act, which introduced the principle of reformative treatment of criminals under a liberal indeterminate sentence pattern. An increasing number of lawyers and judges are criticizing the conventional jury trial. Reform in judicial administration in the states, which began in 1937, has, however, been slow to develop, principally because of a lack of complete detailed knowledge of what should be done in each state to give it a reasonably effective procedural system. The information was recently made available, and progress in the struggle for seriously needed reform should now be able to move forward.[22]

**Eliminating abuses in the third-degree procedure.** It is especially necessary, if reforms are to be made, to eliminate the evil of the third degree in criminal cases. The Federal rules of criminal procedure adopted in 1946 may help, since they provide that confessions must be obtained "without unnecessary delay" for them to be admissible as evidence. Some American cities, such as Philadelphia and Cincinnati, do not employ the third degree and have proved that good results can be obtained without it. Since most of the police brutality comes between the arrest and the arraignment of the accused, attention must be concentrated on cutting down the time beween arrest and arraignment, and on giving proper publicity to the action taken during this interval. It is the opinion of legal scholars that we do not need any more laws against the third degree; we have enough laws to give formal legal protection to the accused.[23] The difficulty arises in the fact that it is hard to enforce the laws we have. Reform, to be effective, must be gradual. Changes drastic enough to disrupt our present police system would be temporarily disastrous.

The following measures have been suggested to promote prompt arraignment after arrest: [24] compulsory records of the time of arrest and time of arraignment; improvement in the quality of the police; and the creation of an independent and fearless public authority that can hear complaints of third-degree practices and make prompt investigation. The Public Defender might well be used in this way to investigate and give publicity to abuses.

---

[22] *Minimum Standards of Judicial Administration,* edited by Arthur T. Vanderbilt and published by The Law Center of New York University for the National Conference of Judicial Councils, 1949, contains an analysis of the extent to which each state in the union measures up to the minimum standards recommended by the American Bar Association.

[23] Though not recent, the article by Zechariah Chafee, Jr., "Remedies for the Third Degree," *Atlantic Monthly,* November, 1931, is still in point.

[24] Ibid.

**How to reduce courtroom tyranny.** It has been said that public prosecutors, with their power to determine who shall be brought to trial and who shall not, have "the scope for tyranny of a Venetian Doge." [25] The prosecutor's varied functions make for abuse of power. By the nature of his office he acts as investigator, as magistrate (in that he can decide when and whether to prosecute), as solicitor (in that he prepares cases for trial), and as advocate (when he is trying the case). His bias can be attributed to many factors. In both rural and urban communities he is almost always elected and is therefore eager to show results. He can see the work of organized gangs, the frequent "fixes," and the freeing of notorious offenders through the machinations of clever attorneys. These observations fan his zealousness. The most basic recommendation for reform is to have prosecutors appointed, perhaps by the governor, with some legislative power of confirmation. Other reforms, such as increasing the salary and term of office and setting up age and experience qualifications, will help to attract more capable and intelligent men to the office and tend to reduce bias.

Effective action must also be taken to curb the dictatorial authority that some judges with long-term appointments exercise, and to eliminate favoritism toward certain lawyers and clients.[26] If a system were introduced whereby judges and judicial decisions could be recalled, and if impeachment of judges who deliberately intimidate juries or misinterpret a statute were instituted, there would be less likelihood of arbitrary action on the part of judges. It has been suggested that legislative commissions should be established to hear complaints against judges, so that attention may be promptly called to charges that should be pressed. It is difficult today to bring charges against judges. Lawyers, no matter how prominent they may be, hesitate to proceed against judges. They fear the hostility of judges before whom they must practice. This makes it difficult to launch proceedings or to obtain an impartial hearing against a judge who has acted lawlessly.

It has also been suggested that the sentencing power be taken away from judges. After an accused person is found guilty, he should be turned over to the proper authorities for study and treatment. This would help to end many abuses connected with both the severity of sentencing and the wide variations in the use of the sentencing power. Many prominent persons support this scheme. The late Alfred E. Smith, while Governor of New York, made such a suggestion. What we need above everything else is a broader and more humane view of the law. In the following paragraph, Professor Raymond Moley clearly emphasizes this point:

---

[25] "Prosecutor's Bias, an Occupational Disease," by Sam Earle Hobbs, 2 Alabama Law Review, pp. 40–60, Fall 1949.

[26] For an extremely illuminating and informing account of the qualifications, attitudes and methods of some judges in our courts, see Howard Whitman, "Behind the Black Robe," *Ladies Home Companion*, February, 1948.

LAW AND JUSTICE

What is wanted really is a doctor of human relations, a new kind of lawyer. As Judge Seabury has recently pointed out, we need in the criminal courts something closely akin to what has been developed in the medical profession in provisions for public clinics where science and public service develop side by side; where able young lawyers may learn and apply a wider range of wisdom than they find in their law books; and where the victims of a complex and exacting social order may find enlisted in their service genuinely interested and adequately endowed friends in court.[27]

**A better break for labor.** The Wagner Act of 1935 opened a new era for organized labor. Under the leadership of men like Supreme Court Justices Douglas, Black, and Rutledge, Judge Jerome Frank, and Dean Leon Green, there has been a real effort to remold the law to square with the new concepts of the rights of labor and to be less sensitive to conflicting property rights. The courts upheld a large majority of the decisions of the National Labor Relations Board. Some observers believe, however, that labor recently received a serious setback in the Federal courts when Judge Alan Goldsborough imposed a tremendous fine on John L. Lewis and the United Mine Workers in an action upheld by the Supreme Court, though the fine was somewhat reduced. This was offset, at least in part, by Judge Richmond Keech's more favorable decision in the United Mine Workers' case in March, 1950. There is less of a tendency to set aside progressive labor legislation as unconstitutional since the Supreme Court has been reorganized.

**Caution against easy optimism.** The developments described are promising, and we may logically expect many desirable reforms in the years that lie ahead. But we should avoid easy optimism; over a hundred and twenty years ago, Thomas Jefferson was criticizing the same legal abuses that confront us today in language almost identical to that used in our day by men like Justice Black, Fred Rodell, Jerome Frank, and Leon Green.

## Summary

We face grave legal problems that have grown out of defects in the law and weaknesses in current legal procedure.

Corporation lawyers have given big business advice on how to get around restrictive legislation and have led the constitutional law battles in court to void such legislation and laws promoting the rights of labor.

Despite the fact that educational requirements are higher, the number of lawyers has increased. There are about 170,000 practicing lawyers in the United States today. The work available to them, however, has decreased as other agencies such as title companies, trust companies, collection agencies and others have entered the field. It is no wonder that some lawyers use any means to find cases, including "ambulance chasing."

There are many outstanding defects in legal practice arising not only

---

[27] *New York Times*, May 3, 1931.

from the methods of practicing lawyers, but also from our attitude toward the law. We have a feeling of reverence for constitutional law and not enough respect for laws passed by Congress or the states. Respect for statutory law might be increased if our laws were fewer, better drafted, and more sensible.

There is too much delay in courtroom procedure, and more regard for precedent than for justice. A clever lawyer or biased judge can twist the rules of evidence in such a way that justice is denied and facts ignored. The poor man is at a disadvantage in getting justice because it takes money to carry a case to court, hire a good lawyer, and pay the fees demanded.

Criminal law has, perhaps, more defects than civil law. We still punish the criminal to avenge society, instead of trying to find a treatment that may make him a decent citizen. We still use the third degree to force confessions from suspects, and the jury trial is all too often an obstacle to ascertaining fact and administering justice.

Certain reforms have been proposed to bring law and legal procedure up to date. Socialization of legal practice is the most drastic proposal. This scheme is based on the fact that the state makes the laws and should assume responsibility for carrying them out. Another proposal is that, since the state provides a prosecutor to try the accused, it should also provide a Public Defender for him. In many cities, legal aid societies have been established to give free legal aid to those who cannot pay for it. This is a worth-while reform and should be made universal. A system known as the Lawyer Reference Plan is getting under way to bring competent legal service at moderate rates to middle-class families.

The third degree should be eliminated and there should be a shorter period between arrest and arraignment. Relentless publicity on the activities of the police during the time elapsing between arrest and arraignment would do much to curb the evils of the third degree.

There should be an improved program of legal education, so that law would be made more humane and better related to the needs of present-day society. We should encourage a new type of lawyer, one who would be interested in the needs of his fellows rather than in the letter of the law, and in justice as much as in making money.

Although the law still all too frequently delays social progress and defeats justice, more progress has been made in legal reform and legal thought in the last twenty-five years than in any comparable period in our history. There is also reason to believe that drastic reforms in the rules of legal evidence and court procedure may be expected before too many years elapse.

### Selected References

Frank, Jerome, *Law and the Modern Mind*, Coward-McCann, 1930. A valuable and thoughtful analysis of the rôle of law in modern life, written from a critical and enlightened viewpoint.

\* —————, *Courts on Trial; Myth and Reality in American Justice,* Princeton University Press, 1949. This excellent and delightfully written book presents the arguments against the jury system and shows how the legal profession can improve its means of honest inquiry.

Freund, P. A., *On Understanding the Supreme Court,* Little, Brown, 1950. A very interesting analysis and description of the operations of the Supreme Court, the background of its decisions, and the practice of constitutional law.

Gisnet, Morris, *A Lawyer Tells the Truth,* Concord, 1931. The pioneer book in the tidal wave of self-examination by members of the legal profession. A sincere and earnest little book, with no effort at sensationalism.

Goldberg, L. P., and Levenson, Eleanore, *Lawless Judges,* Rand School Press, 1935. Best book on judicial arbitrariness and irresponsibility.

\* Jackson, Percival, *Look at the Law,* Dutton, 1940. The ablest criticism of the American legal system, by a very distinguished member of the American bar.

Parker, J. R., *Attorneys-at-Law,* Doubleday, Doran, 1941. An objective description of corporation law practice in a prosperous metropolitan legal firm at the present time.

Pritchett, C. H., *The Roosevelt Court,* Macmillan, 1948. A survey of the manner in which President Roosevelt revamped the Supreme Court and its decisions by appointment rather than reorganization.

Radin, Max, *The Law and Mr. Smith,* Bobbs-Merrill, 1940. An account of the law and the common man by a leading American legal scholar. Frankly faces defects in the law, without any effort at muckraking.

\* Rodell, Fred, *Woe Unto You, Lawyers!* Reynal and Hitchcock, 1939. Slashing criticism of the whole "legal racket" by a famous professor in the Yale Law School.

Rovere, Richard, *Howe and Hummel, Their True and Scandalous History,* Farrar, Straus, 1947. An amazing but authentic tale of the legal morals and practices of the most famous American criminal law firm at the turn of the century. An eye-opener for those who share the pious and "polyanna" notions of legal practice. But the "take" of Howe and Hummel was slight compared to that of the "banquet-chasing" corporation lawyers.

Schlosser, A. L., *Lawyers Must Eat,* Vanguard, 1933. An exposure of shady legal practices and an indication of how the pressure for business corrupts the law.

Seagle, William, *There Ought To Be a Law,* Macaulay, 1933. A sprightly and entertaining little book exposing the trivial character of much law-making.

—————, *The Quest for Law,* Knopf, 1941. A scholarly history of law and legal ideals written in excellent style.

Smith, R. H., *Justice and the Poor,* Scribner, 1919. The classic account of the difficulties and handicaps which beset the poor man in getting justice from our courts.

Stalmaster, Irving, *What Price Jury Trials?* Stratford, 1931. Devastating critique of jury trials by an able lawyer.

Stone, Irving, *Clarence Darrow for the Defense,* Doubleday, Doran, 1941. A brilliantly written account of the great defense lawyer most prominently associated with the aid of the underdog.

Wellman, F. L. (Ed.), *Success in Court,* Macmillan, 1941. Symposium by great lawyers expounding their methods of attaining success in the horseplay of conventional courtroom procedure.

* Zane, J. M., *The Story of Law,* Washburn, 1927. The best popular history of law. Readable and generally reliable.

CHAPTER XX

New Agencies of Transportation

and Communication:

The Conquest of Time and Space

## Transportation as a Social Force

**Dynamic and unsettling effects of modern transportation and communication.** Nothing has done more to unsettle our former mode of life, to reshape our social attitudes, and to create difficult problems of institutional readjustment than the development of improved methods of transportation and communication. The progress of civilization has been directly dependent upon those inventions which have conquered time and space. The results can be seen historically in the expansion of trade over wider areas and its increasing volume, the migration of peoples, and the unification of small local groups and territories into great nations and empires. Equally important, though less apparent, have been the indirect effects: the rapid spread of new ideas and customs from one group to another, the growing tendency toward unification of thought among citizens, the speeding up of technological progress through the spread of knowledge of new and better tools and machines, and the revolutionary expansion of group contacts, experiences, and social pressures. These latter developments, as we made clear in earlier chapters, have both revolutionized social experience in our generation and created new problems in sociological description and analysis.

**Rôle of transportation and communication in human history.** The social importance of transportation and communication finds abundant illustration in history. The great Persian Empire of ancient times was made possible because transportation had developed to the point where people could travel on horseback over wide areas and some good roads had become available. The Greek and Roman Empires were dependent upon land and sea communication. One reason for the decline of the Roman Empire was inadequate transportation and communication facilities for the policing, administration, and defense of so vast an area. Medieval civilization was handicapped by the isolation of people in most parts of Europe as roads were neglected and travel became difficult and dangerous. It was the development of improved methods of water transportation and such inventions as the compass that helped to bring the Middle Ages to an end by making possible the conquest of the oceans, the expansion of Europe, and the Commercial Revolution. These, in turn, as we saw in Chapter II led

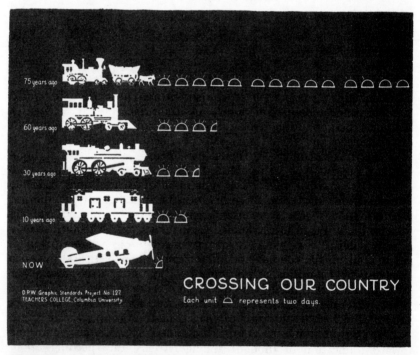

CROSSING OUR COUNTRY

Each unit △ represents two days.

D.P.W Graphic Standards Project No. 127
TEACHERS COLLEGE, Columbia University

Graphic presentation of remarkable conquest of time and space in travel since "Covered Wagon" days. It is even more impressive than the chart indicates, for in 1949 a plane flew across the United States in about four hours.

to the Industrial Revolution and the rise of contemporary civilization. Today, of course, our industrial and urbanized civilization is vitally dependent on rapid and efficient means of transportation and communication.

## Improvement of Highways

**Highways in modern transportation.** While the Romans built magnificent roads that stood up under heavy traffic for centuries, it was not until the beginning of the nineteenth century that scientific road building was revived by Telford and Macadam, who experimented successfully with hard-surfaced roads. These developments were followed by asphalt and concrete roads in the twentieth century.

Early in the history of the United States, it was recognized by Washington and other statesmen that men and products must be able to travel more easily between the eastern seaboard and the territory west of the Appalachians if the country was to develop rapidly. In 1811, the national government took over the building of a road from Cumberland, Maryland,[1] to Wheeling, West Virginia, and from there to what is now Columbus, Ohio, and on into Indiana. This was called the National Road, the best long road in America at that time.

After the introduction of the automobile, good roads became indispensable. At the beginning of the twentieth century, there were few hard-surfaced roads in America, with the exception of paved city streets. Today, there is a vast network of surfaced highways, and roads are no longer a local project. The Federal government and

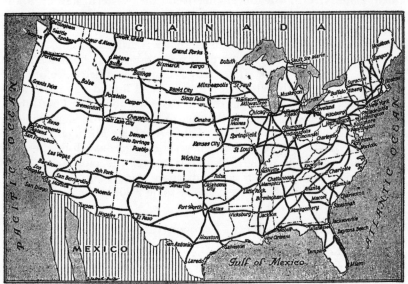

*Courtesy of* The New York Times.

Map showing how the proposed 37,681 mile interstate road system would link the main cities of the nation, including nearly all the state capitals.

---

[1] Originally, the state of Maryland had built the road from Baltimore along the Potomac River to Cumberland.

the states take an active interest in the construction and improvement of highways. In 1942, Federal, state, and local units spent $1,374,000,-000 on highway construction, and in 1947, $1,154,000,000. Costs are covered by general taxation and by fees from fines, bridge tolls, gasoline taxes, motor vehicle registration and the like.

The total rural road mileage in the United States today is about 3,250,000. Of this total road mileage, over 1,500,000 miles are surfaced roads, and of the total of surfaced roads some 200,000 miles are those with a high type of first-class surface. Mechanical snow plows have been invented to clear the roads for traffic in the winter, so that most roads are open even under unfavorable climatic conditions. Summing up the history of road building since the Industrial Revolution, we may say that Telford and Macadam made good roads possible and that the automobile made them an absolute necessity.

**Inland waterways.** Rivers and lakes have long been favored as transportation routes, wherever possible, and the cheapness of water transportation made the digging of canals desirable. After 1800, great interest was shown in the construction of canals, both in Europe and America. The incentive had been given by two Englishmen, the Duke of Bridgewater and James Brindley, some decades before. The Erie Canal across New York State, begun in 1817 and finished in 1825, aided materially in the development of the western states. Many canals were built during the first half of the nineteenth century and, while some have become useless, canal transportation was an important factor in facilitating American westward expansion. It was a convenient and cheap means of transportation for both men and freight. The New York State Barge Canal, completed before the first world war, greatly extended and facilitated inland water transportation between the Great Lakes and the eastern seaboard. The Illinois River and Waterway, a barge channel of some 328 miles, provides a vital connection between the Great Lakes (via Lake Michigan) and the Mississippi River system. After ten years of vigorous effort, the Panama Canal was opened in 1914. It is one of the most remarkable engineering triumphs of our age, shortening the distance by water between New York and San Francisco by some 8,000 miles.

## Railway Transportation

**Rise of the railroad era.** Speedier inland transportation by road and water represented an important advance, but the coming of the steam locomotive and the railroads brought even greater changes in industry and culture. Most business depends, to a large extent, on the services of rail transportation. Railroads slowly came into general use after 1830. The first important railroad in the United States was the Baltimore and Ohio, begun in 1828. By 1860, some 30,000 miles of railroad had been built, and there was through service from the Atlantic seaboard to Chicago and the Mississippi Valley.

Steel rails, mainly introduced after the Civil War, gave an added impetus to the expansion of railroads, for their greater strength meant that larger cars and engines could be used, greater speed and safety attained, lower rates introduced, and a vastly extended volume of business handled. The Union Pacific and the Central Pacific railroads were joined in 1869, thus providing the first transcontinental

Courtesy U. S. Travel Bureau.

An early American passenger train. The "Atlantic" locomotive was built in 1832 for the Baltimore & Ohio Railroad by Phineas Davis, a watchmaker of York, Pa. It has a remarkable service record of sixty years and is still capable of running under its own steam.

service from New York to San Francisco. After 1870, railway service was rapidly expanded. Between 1880 and 1890, the growth of the railroads was phenomenal. In this decade, about 70,000 miles were built, bringing the total mileage in the United States to over 160,000.

By 1900, our main railroad systems, as they now exist, had been completed. The total railroad mileage in 1946 was 226,300. In 1947, the gross investment in all railroad property used in transportation was about 30 billion dollars. The net operating income of American railroads was 781 million dollars in 1947, 1,022 million in 1948, and 686 million in 1949. Net income after fixed charges were deducted was 700 million in 1948, and 438 million in 1949.

**Competition with motor traffic brings great improvements in railroad service.** An outstanding event in our inland transportation history during the twentieth century has been the rise of serious competition for the railroads in the form of automobiles, motor buses, and trucks. For some years, the railroads seemed unable to compete successfully with motorized vehicles. Passenger travel and freight shipments declined, and railroads were forced to take vigorous steps to make train travel more attractive. Passenger rates, which had been high, were reduced in some cases to two cents a mile or less in coaches, in order to compete with the low bus rates. Not only were fares lowered, but in the last twenty years there has been a great improvement in the speed and equipment of trains. Steam locomotives have been built for faster travel and heavier loads. Some rail lines have been electrified. Today, clean, smooth, swift, streamlined Diesel-electric trains, with chromium cars, running between New York and the Pacific coast and from New York and Middle Western cities to Florida, are competing with the airplane as a means of speedy transportation. Diesel locomotives are now being widely introduced in freight service. Of the 1,800 locomotives built in 1949, all but 60 were Diesels. But, already, powerful new electric locomotives are replacing the Diesels, and the turbine locomotive is in an advanced experimental stage.

*Courtesy New York Central System.*

The Empire State Express "999" of 1893. Its speed record of 112.5 miles per hour, made in 1893, has never been equaled by another steam-propelled train.

The railroads, in order to meet the competition of buses and airplanes, have installed many conveniences and luxuries on trains, such as telephones and stock tickers to enable businessmen to keep informed on their affairs while traveling; radios are common in trains, and some have shower baths, beauty parlors, luxurious lounging cars with suitable attendants, and even moving-pictures. Glass dome cars have greatly increased the scenic advantages and opportunities of railroad travel. The Twentieth Century Limited, operated by the New York Central Railroad, would have seemed a miracle to Theodore Roosevelt.

Travel by coach has also been revolutionized on most of the better railroad systems. Cleaner, more convenient coaches with "snack bars' have been installed. The railroads themselves regard the improved coach service as the most striking innovation in present-day railroading. To quote an authoritative statement by a railroad executive: "The greatest revolution in the design and equipment of new trains is found in the new low-fare, lightweight luxury coaches. Diesel-powered, these luxurious coach trains are a symbol of the new day in railroading."

Summer travel has been made more pleasant by the introduction of air conditioning. Transcontinental travel has been encouraged by re- duced rates for round trips, and by the courteous and helpful service available in company travel bureaus. One of the latest induce- ments to travel by train is the sale of tickets for tourist trips on the installment or credit plan. This credit plan has been particularly attractive to teachers, who have steady winter jobs but receive no salaries during the summer months. Robert R. Young of the Chesapeake and Ohio Railroad has been the leader in working for improved railroad passenger service in the way of better Pullman cars, direct transit from the Atlantic to the Pacific coast without chang- ing in Chicago or St. Louis, and more rapid Pullman reservation service.

Railroad travel became increasingly safer until the second world war. At a time when automobile accidents are frequent, the safety of travel by train cannot be overlooked. There are relatively few passenger accidents on the railroads. The year 1937 was the safest on record for railroad travel, with a fatality rate of only 0.073 per hundred million passenger-miles. Inability to replace or adequately repair rolling-stock and trackage in the war years, as well as greater traffic and higher speeds, led to an increase of accidents. By 1949, however, rail- roads had almost equaled their prewar record for safe travel, with a fatality rate of only 0.074 per hundred million passenger miles. The increased safety of railroad travel is due chiefly to such inventions as steel coaches, improved automatic signal systems, and new devices for automatically stopping trains that have entered danger zones.

Mr. Young believes that great improvements lie ahead in the design and operation of railroad passenger service. He predicts a "train of tomorrow" that will be much lighter than present trains but will be both safer and stronger. A wheel arrangement, much like that now used on roller coasters, will allow trains to round curves at 80 miles an hour and to reach a speed of 150 miles an hour on the straightaway without danger of derailment. A new type of locomotive may even use jet power.

An even more drastic method of meeting the competition of motor buses has been the growing tendency of railroad companies to pur- chase bus lines and operate them in connection with the railroads.

## Growth of Motor Traffic

**Rapid development of the automobile and motor traffic.** The auto- mobile has become a universal method of travel in the United States. Although the scientific and mechanical inventions upon which the automobile is based originated in the nineteenth century, the last forty years are those which have brought about mass production of low-priced, efficient, and attractive cars. The great popularity of the automobile dates from after the first world war. Henry Ford had brought out the unattractive but serviceable "Model T" about 1912, and in 1928 he produced his first modernized four cylinder car, the durable "Model A." Other companies adopted Ford's methods and

*Courtesy of General Motors.*

The latest development in railroad speed and comfort. The train is drawn by a Diesel engine, and its cars are equipped with glass domes that afford passengers an unusual opportunity for viewing the scenery.

soon the era of the speedy, dependable, low-priced automobile transformed American travel. In 1929, over 5,500,000 cars and trucks were produced in the United States and Canada. After 1929, because of the depression, fewer cars were made, but by 1936 car sales had almost reached the 1929 level. In 1940, over 31 million motor vehicles were registered in the United States, or about 70 per cent of the world's total. In February, 1942, the manufacture of automobiles for personal civilian use was abandoned. When it was resumed after the war, car prices soared to more than double prewar prices, but still the producers could not begin to supply the demand. Good secondhand cars frequently sold for much more than the list price of a new car of the same model. Some 5,285,425 motor vehicles were produced in 1948, and over 6 million in 1949. In 1950, it was estimated that there were over 42 million motor vehicles in the United

States. The most striking recent technical development in the automobile realm came in 1950, when two English inventors produced a practicable jet-propelled car which they expected to put into mass production within a year. The British have also just invented a gas-turbine automobile engine that burns kerosene and is expected to reduce fuel costs greatly.

With the development of the automobile we have become travel conscious. Trips are taken frequently and on short notice. In 1900, the average American traveled only about 200 miles per year. By 1940, his average annual travel amounted to over 2,500 miles, and the automobile accounted for much of this impressive increase. Formerly a journey of even fifty miles by horse and buggy required much planning and discussion. Today, a 500-mile pleasure or business jaunt in a single day occasions little comment. Transcontinental automobile trips are a commonplace today. Touring has become a basic pattern of the American psychology. As a recreational and educational agency, the automobile has become increasingly important.

**Social impact of motor travel.** This extensive automobile travel has brought new social problems and habits. Resort hotels that formerly catered to season guests have been forced to change their facilities in order to take care of tourists. Tourist homes and cabins, usually located along the main highways, have become a paying business. It has become usual to license and inspect tourist cabins, and they are now rated by automobile associations or other organizations according to standards of cleanliness and suitability for tourist trade. Tourist camps or courts have also become an important business. Their income was 36 million dollars in 1941. Today, tourist camps are generally licensed and inspected in order to attract the patronage of legitimate tourists.

A recent development in automobile travel is the trailer. Today, many American homes are on wheels, drawn behind the family car. The trailers range in price from $500 to $10,000 or more. The average trailer answers the demands for cheap and comfortable travel. It eliminates the overnight stop in a hotel or tourist home. The traveler can avoid the congested areas and park his trailer in a field or a trailer camp for a small sum. By as early as 1936, about 50,000 trailers had been built, and each year the demand increases. As a result of the shortage of housing during and after the second world war, trailers came to be widely used as semi-permanent homes for war workers and others. Many college students under the GI system were compelled to live in trailers, as, indeed, were some faculty members.

**Extension of motor bus traffic.** Motor buses have become very popular. By 1948, the total investment in motor bus equipment was about 900 million dollars. Although less comfortable than train transportation for long trips, bus travel appeals to travelers because it is cheap; although increasingly safeguarded, however, it is still not as safe as train travel. The motor bus was in use in cities even before the first world war, but its use for interurban travel did not become widespread until after 1918. By 1948, interurban motor buses were carrying 1,065,000,000 passengers annually and covering 1,800,000,000 bus-miles. In 1941, only 434 million interurban passengers were carried. Over 8,300,000,000 passengers were carried on city buses in 1948.

In the last ten years, the bus has almost displaced the electric trolley in cities and suburban areas. Centralized school districts, with better equipment, teachers, and curriculum, have been made possible because buses carry the children from outlying districts to and from school each day. About 5,000,000 pupils are today dependent on school buses for their transportation. Some 900 million school children passengers were transported in buses in 1948.

**Increasing importance of motor trucks.** Motor trucks, providing transportation facilities never before known by farmers, have cut deeply into the express and freight business formerly handled by railroads. There are well over 5 million motor trucks now in operation. About one million of these are owned by farmers; 66 per cent of all live-stock and 71 per cent of all poultry are taken to market by motor trucks. Fleet operators, commercial trucking lines, railroads, and express companies use most of the other 4 million. In short, commercial trucking has become a major item in our transportation system.

## Bigger, Better, and Faster Ships

**Progress in water transportation.** While transport by water is not as important in American life as land transportation by railroads, buses, and trucks, its significance and services cannot be ignored. In the chapter dealing with the industrial revolutions we touched on the origins of steam navigation, and earlier in this chapter we mentioned the growth of inland water transportation.

Great improvements have been made in the last century. Wooden boats have been replaced by iron and steel vessels. Turbines, Diesel engines, and electric motors have been introduced. The size of ships has increased markedly. The *Great Western,* which made the first transatlantic trip under steam power in 1838, had a tonnage of only 1,340 and was 236 feet in length. The largest ship afloat today, the *Queen Elizabeth,* has a tonnage of 86,673 and is 1,129 feet in length. The engines of the *Great Western* generated 450 horsepower, while those of the *Queen Elizabeth* generate about 200,000 horsepower. It took the *Great Western* some 15 days to make its first trip across the Atlantic, while the *Queen Mary,* the fastest contemporary ship, crossed the Atlantic in 1938 in 3 days, 20 hours, and 42 minutes, a record that still stands. The convenience, accommodations, comforts, and safety of ocean vessels have correspondingly increased, along with their greater size and speed. The United States now leads in the size of mercantile marine, with over 35 million gross tons, nearly twice that of our nearest competitor, Great Britain.

The inland waterways of the United States are, as we have noted, an important item in our transportation system. The principal inland waterways are the Great Lakes system, the Mississippi River system, the Illinois Waterway, the New York State Barge Canal, and the Columbia River system. The channels connecting the Great Lakes have been deepened to accommodate deep-draft ships. Commerce on the Great Lakes system increased from 171 million tons in 1938 to 357 million tons in 1945. There has been a plan long under way to construct a waterway from the St. Lawrence River to Chicago which will accommodate ocean-going vessels, but it has been held up by the opposition of eastern seaboard and Gulf states.

## The Rise and Development of Aviation

**The conquest of the air.** Since 1920, the conquest of the air has has been the most spectacular improvement in the field of transportation. The first successful flight by air was made in 1903 at Kitty Hawk, North Carolina, by the Wright brothers. Three years later, they made a non-stop flight of 40 miles. The first world war brought a number of technical improvements in airplanes, but commercial air travel did not begin on a large scale in the United States until about 1925. Since that time, there has been a remarkable expansion. In the year 1948, the commercial air lines carried 13,168,105 passengers in the United States, as against 5,782 passengers in 1926; in 1948, American air lines flew 7.76 billion passenger-miles.

The carrying of air mail started soon after the first world war, and air express service was instituted in 1927. After the second world war, air freight service began. In 1948, our domestic air lines transported over 101 million ton-miles of air express and freight. Some 38 million ton-miles of mail were flown in 1948. The impressive speed of airplane travel makes it attractive to those who want to get some place in a hurry. It is possible to leave New York in the evening and breakfast next morning in Los Angeles. The most striking and dramatic event in the conquest of the air came on March 2, 1949, when a B-50 bomber, the "Lucky Lady II," made the first non-stop flight around the world in just 94 hours. This was a far cry from the transport situation a generation ago, when Jules Verne's project for circumnavigating the world in 80 days was regarded as utterly fantastic.

**Relative safety of air travel.** The main drawback to air transportation for a time was its comparative lack of safety, which has, however, been exaggerated. Airplane design and the training of pilots have reached the stage of relative perfection and security. The leading expert on airplane insurance risks recently declared that: "The human factor remains the most important factor in underwriting aviation risks. Crashes on scheduled airlines have resulted chiefly from disregard of known safety rules and regulations." Air lines are sometimes unwilling to lose passengers by canceling scheduled flights in bad weather, and many passengers are so eager for speedy transportation they are insistent on taking unnecessary risks.

In reality, air accidents are few when compared to automobile accidents. We are inclined to notice plane crashes because they are headlined in the news. Only 98 persons were killed in civil aviation in the United States in 1948, but during the New Year's weekend of 1949 alone 207 persons were killed in automobile traffic accidents, while some 301 were killed in traffic accidents on the previous Christmas weekend. The following statistics will demonstrate the relative safety of air traffic on well-established commercial lines. In 1937, the number of deaths per 100 million passenger-miles flown was 8.39; in 1940, 3.05; in 1944, 2.12; and in 1948, 1.41. In June, 1948, it was shown that some 23 airlines, combined, had flown 7 billion passenger-miles, or 280 thousand times around the earth, without a single passenger fatality. Planes of the Northwest Airlines had flown 1,229,000,000 passenger-miles since the last fatality in May, 1942.

The British have had considerable success in operating huge flying boats or seaplanes, which already travel from England to various European port cities, from England to South Africa, and from the East Indies to Hong Kong. Their greater ability to land safely in an emergency makes them safer than land planes as a means of air travel.

**Increasing speed of air travel.** The advances in the speed, size, and convenience of airplanes during and after the second world war have been extremely impressive. Not many years ago, it was believed that no airplane could reach 500 miles per hour, to say nothing of attaining or surpassing the speed of sound, which is 761 miles per hour at sea level and 663 miles per hour at altitudes of from 40,000 to 100,000 feet. In September, 1948, a British De Havilland DH-108 engine-driven plane attained a speed of 700 miles per hour in a power dive. Some American engine-driven military planes have equaled this speed in dives, and there is every prospect that future engine-driven planes will exceed the speed of sound in continuous level flight.

The most revolutionary progress in plane speeds was made by the Germans during the war with jet planes and rocket missiles. Jet planes have become common in military equipment and rocket planes have been built for experimental uses. Both dispense with the propeller of the conventional airplane. Early in 1948, it was announced that an American military rocket plane, the X-1, built by Bell Aircraft, had exceeded the speed of sound. A year later, a speed of 1,700 miles per hour was announced for this plane. In February, 1949, Bell Aircraft announced that it was building a new rocket plane expected to reach a speed of 2,400 miles an hour. Once the so-called sonic wall —the speed of sound—is broken through, the resistance is notably reduced.[2]

---

[2] See *Time*, April 18, 1949.

The enormous fuel consumption by rocket and jet planes has led to further experimentation, and the British have combined jet and propeller propulsion into what are known as "turbo-prop" planes. These planes have two jets, one behind the other, the rear jet takes up the hot gases exhausted by the front jet and uses this power to

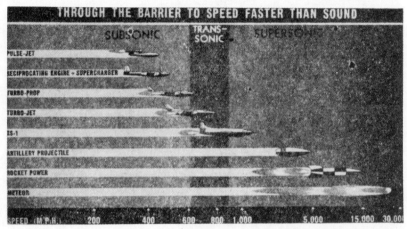

Prepared for The New York Times by James Lewicki.

Man-carrying craft are pressing hard on the speed of projectiles.

turn a conventional propeller. In this way, high speed can be maintained with a considerable reduction of fuel consumption. But much more will have to be accomplished along this line before the great speeds of the jet and rocket planes can be profitably used for commercial air travel. The X-1 uses so much fuel that it can only fly for two and a half minutes at full power. Indeed, it is always accelerating when it runs out of fuel. The British have already mastered some of these engineering problems, and put jet-propelled planes into operation in commercial aviation in 1950.

**Greater conveniences in commercial aviation.** Almost as amazing as the increase in airplane speeds has been the improvement in the size, beauty, convenience, and flying range of the largest commercial airliners, of which the most impressive today is the Boeing Stratocruiser, which was put into operation on six major airlines late in 1948. It was developed from the giant B-29 bomber, also built by Boeing. It is 110 feet long and has a wing-spread of 141 feet and a gross weight of 135,000 pounds. It is powered by 4 Pratt-Whitney Wasp engines of 3,500 hp. each. Its normal speed is about 320 miles per hour, with a maximum speed of 375 miles. The cruising range without refueling is 4,200 miles, thus making possible a non-stop flight from New York to London, or any other western European city. It can carry from 60 to 114 passengers, depending on whether it is used for day or night flying. It has a cargo capacity of 9,000 pounds. The main cabin is 74 feet long, with a lounge deck below. There is great convenience, even luxury, in the appointments; no luxury train provides greater comfort for passengers. There is a complex system of air-conditioning and heating, making allowance not only for temperature but also for altitude. Despite all this, the direct cost of operation is only one cent per passenger-mile.

**Air express and freight.** The Boeing Company has also built a Stratofreighter, capable of carrying 41,000 pounds of freight. Experience in the air transport of freight was greatly extended in the task of flying supplies to Berlin during the blockade of 1948–1949. Airlines have a distinct advantage over railroads in carrying express and freight, entirely aside from the matter of greater speed; their terminal costs and many other incidental costs are borne in part by the taxpayers who provide landing fields and related facilities. Out of a total of 6,414 airports in 1948, some 2,050 were municipally owned, and the Federal and state governments had helped to pay for many others.

**More and better airports.** The most acute need in the airplane picture in the United States today is for more, better, and larger airports, because airport construction has not kept pace with the increase in air travel. Airplane manufacturing companies are equipped to turn out many more planes than can be used. The shortage of good airports led to the passage of the Federal Airport Act in 1946, which authorized Federal expenditures of 500 million dollars on building and extending airport facilities. It is now planned to deal with 4,835 airport locations. Of these, 2,745 will be new airports and 2,090 involve the repair and extension of existing airports. The total cost

*Courtesy of Boeing Airplane Company.*

**The Boeing Stratocruiser: the largest and finest commercial airplane at the mid-century.**

will be in excess of a billion dollars, with private sponsors supplementing Federal appropriations. More than half of the money expended will go into the provision of large airports.

**Commercial aviation operates at a loss.** Despite the enormous increase in passenger and other traffic, the commercial airlines of the country as a whole have recently been operating at a loss. For the year ending September 30, 1948, the total operating revenue of the 16 leading American airlines was 385 million dollars, and the operating expenses were 404 millions, making a loss of 19 million dollars for the year. The loss had been over 20 million dollars for the year ending September 30, 1947. Of the 385-million-dollar operating revenue, 324 millions came from passenger fares, 32 millions from mail, and the remainder from express, freight, and incidental earnings. A small minority of the 16 domestic trunk airlines made a slight profit. Early in 1949, a congressional investigation was proposed to examine into the causes of this critical financial condition of the airlines. Liberal mail payment awards late in 1948 and early in 1949, amounting to about 8 million dollars, improved the financial situation of the airlines somewhat.

Recently, some of the more hard-pressed airlines have sought to increase their income by installing so-called coach service at a fare equal to railroad coach service. This has proved financially successful where it has been tried. But most of the great airlines kept air travel as a luxury service down to 1949, and resisted the general introduction of coach air service. Fares averaged about 6 cents a mile, and it was estimated that two-thirds of those who traveled by air were persons with an income in excess of $6,000 a year. Government economists assailed airlines for their failure to boost air travel and airline income by a wide installation of air coach service. Because of this pressure and because of financial losses in operation, the airlines began to cut fares in 1949 and to institute more coach service. By 1950, airplane passenger rates had been brought into line with railroad traffic charges for both first-class and coach fares.

## The Revolution in Communication

**Dramatic reduction of time element in transportation and communication.** From the standpoint of travel time, distance has been strikingly conquered within the past century by the development of the railroad, automobile, and airplane. Even more dramatic, however, is the fact that distance has been virtually overcome in the communication of information. The startling new agencies of communication have shrunk men's ideas of distance, created new mental attitudes, altered old ones, and brought about many new social, political, and cultural problems.

Only a little more than a century ago, it took almost a week to carry news on horseback from New York to Boston. The time depended on the weather and the condition of the roads. In the 1840's it required five months of desperate effort for Marcus Whitman to make the trip from the state of Washington to the city of Washington. Today, the fastest jet planes can cross the entire continent in less than as many hours. On February 8, 1949, a six-engine B-47 jet bomber flew across the continent in 3 hours and 46 minutes, at an average speed of 607.2 miles per hour.

Faster still were the new methods of communication. Even as late as 1909, when Admiral Peary reached the North Pole, it took months before he could come out of the polar regions to tell of his discovery. When Admiral Byrd arrived at the South Pole, in 1926, the fact was known in New York City by radio at almost the instant his airplane passed over the Pole. *The New York Times* radio station picked up the news as it was sent by wireless from Byrd's airplane to his own base camp.

It requires less than 16 seconds to telegraph a message from New York to London. From the standpoint of the time element involved in communication, the problem of distance has been almost eliminated. Not only has the time needed to communicate messages been shortened, but the new methods of communicating information are so cheap that all except the very poor and underprivileged can enjoy them. The telephone and the radio have brought the world's news to the door of even the most isolated village.

## The Development of Our Postal System

**Rise of the postal system.** One of the most important examples of the efficiency of modern communication is the speedy distribution of mail. The postal service is overlooked in many discussions of communication. But its importance is shown by the fact that, in 1945, about 38 billion pieces of mail were handled by the post offices of the United States. This is an average of over 260 pieces per person. Our modern business and financial system would be virtually paralyzed if it had to depend on the mail service of 1830, when postal systems were either unknown or privately owned, and letters were carried by coach or on horseback.

About 1840, Rowland Hill worked out a new plan for cheap mail distribution in England by establishing uniform country-wide postage rates. The plan has been imitated in most civilized countries of the modern world. As a result, the rates for the transmission of letters have been greatly lowered and standardized. The extension of the rural free delivery service in the United States after 1899 has been of great value to the rural population, and has helped to break down their cultural isolation. Over 32,000 rural mail carriers serve some 30,000,000 persons daily, and cover routes totaling more than 1,400,000 miles. Rural free delivery would have been less successful with out good roads and the automobile. In many instances, the rural postal service has encouraged the improvement of rural roads.

**Recent improvements in our postal service.** The cheap rates and rural free delivery have made the postal service available to both rich and poor, in the country as well as city. Today, the rural dweller can send a letter to the most remote parts of the earth for a small fee and feel sure—at least in peacetime—of its speedy delivery. Parcel post, established in the United States in 1913, has not only been a real boon to rural dwellers, but has also greatly stimulated the mail order business. In 1946, over 134 million insured parcels were handled, and probably the number of uninsured parcels was even greater.

There has also been a marked improvement in the methods of transporting and distributing mail. By close co-operation with the railroads, the mail service has been speeded up. Such devices as mechanical stamp-canceling machines, pre-sorting of mail in railroad mail cars, and the use of automobile trucks and pneumatic tubes for distributing mail have made for remarkable postal efficiency. The insistence on speed has greatly increased the use of special delivery service and air mail.

## Telegraph and Telephone Service

**Origins of the electric telegraph.** Most of our recent improvements in rapid communication have depended on progress in the knowledge and use of electricity. The telegraph, the telephone, moving pictures, television, and the radio—our most important new mediums of communication—are based on electricity.

Although the electric telegraph was demonstrated to be practicable in the United States between 1826 and 1831, in Germany between 1833 and 1836, and in England in 1837, it was not until May 24, 1844, that Samuel F. B. Morse successfully transmitted a formal telegraph message in the United States. Since then, there have been numerous improvements, all designed to eliminate the time element and to produce more speedy and efficient service. Putting telegraph and telephone wires underground in cables not only reduced installation costs but vastly lessened possible damage from wind and ice storms and other natural hazards. The multiplex system, invented in 1915, enabled operators to send eight messages simultaneously over one wire.

**Recent technical improvements in wire telegraphy.** Recent remarkable inventions, of which the multiplex system is only one, have enormously increased the number of messages that can be sent over a given transmission conductor, as well as the speed with which they can be transmitted. Transmission by the traditional Morse code has now been supplanted by the teleprinter, which types the messages both in transmission and reception. It was introduced in the 1920's, at first for short circuits with light traffic. In 1910, 90 per cent of messages were sent by Morse code; now 95 per cent are sent by the tele-printer. More amazing is the telefax which, by the use of the photo-electric eye, automatically transmits a message, drawing, or picture. The most spectacular innovation in rapid electrical transmission is the so-called ultrafax, by means of which photographed material can be transmitted with incredible speed. When demonstrated in the autumn of 1948, in Washington, it transmitted the 1,047 pages of *Gone With the Wind* in a little over two minutes. Recently, the desk-fax has been invented, which makes possible the sending and recep-tion of telegraph messages in private business offices.

The carrier circuit system has impressively increased the number of messages that can be sent over any given set of transmission facilities. As many as 288 messages can now be sent simultaneously over a single pair of wires. Radio-beam telegraphy is now an established fact. Messages are transmitted by radio, using radio towers set from 30 to 50 miles apart, thus dispensing with wires. Such a system now con-nects New York, Philadelphia, Washington, and Pittsburgh. Radio-beam telegraphy will enormously increase the possible speed and vol-ume of telegraph business. Whereas the maximum number of mes-sages that can be sent simultaneously over a pair of wires is 288, no less than 2,000 messages can be sent simultaneously on one radio beam.

The push-button system of automatic switching has greatly facili-tated and speeded up the transmission of messages. The most im-pressive development along this line has been the establishment of automatic selective switching centers (electric brains). These were first installed in 1946 at St. Louis, Oakland, Richmond, Atlanta, and Dallas. Eleven had been set up by the end of 1948, and the complete mechanization of the whole national service, with 15 centers, was achieved by the end of 1949. These switching centers each serve a group of states. The switching center automatically receives and routes all non-local telegrams received in the area. Telecars have been introduced which cruise in suburban areas, pick up messages from the central office by radio, deliver them at once, and pick up and transmit the return message if one is sent.

**The Western Union Telegraph Company.** Most of the telegraph business of the United States is in the hands of the Western Union Telegraph Company, which was founded by Hiram Sibley, Ezra Cor-nell, and others, in 1856. Cornell established Cornell University from his earnings. In 1943, Western Union acquired the facilities of the Postal Telegraph Company. Today, Western Union has 128,000 miles of pole line, 4,500 miles of land line cable, 30,000 miles of ocean cable, 30,000 telegraph offices, 59,000 employees, and a payroll of $141,000,-000. Improved techniques have reduced the labor force required; for example, the number of employees in 1929 was 94,500. About 220 million revenue messages are sent annually. The "non-revenue" mes-sages, such as those of railroads, stock reports, and commercial news, are probably about as numerous. Rates have been reduced; special rates have been set for night messages, long messages, and tourist messages. Advertising slogans like "Don't Write, Telegraph" have popularized the telegraph. The great commercial merit and utility of the telegraph today is, of course, its service in transmitting long-distance messages quickly and at low cost.

**Main uses of the telegraph.** The average American does not use the telegraph as much as the telephone and mail service, but the telegraph has become vital to business. It has also made possible the efficient development of safe railroad transportation. Train movements are still based primarily upon communication by telegraph, although the telephone has assumed an increasing importance in this field in the last few years. It is already evident that telegraphy will also play a large rôle in the transmission of television programs. The telegraph has become more widely employed in public life during the last fifteen years; senators and representatives have been deluged with telegrams asking them to support or to oppose various measures.

**Sub-oceanic cables.** The scope of telegraph service was greatly widened when the first workable Atlantic cable was laid by Cyrus W. Field in 1866. By 1931, there were 20 cable lines connecting North America with Europe. As the land telegraph system has been improved, so has the cable system by increasing the speed and number of messages that can be sent over any cable. The invention of the permalloy cable, in 1924, enormously increased the number of messages which could be sent over the same cable wire. Some 2,400 letters per minute can now be sent over the same cable from New York to London. The wireless telegraph, however, has increasingly competed with cable messages.

**Development of wireless telegraphy.** In 1901, Marconi sent his first message by wireless telegraphy across the Atlantic Ocean, and regular trans-Atlantic service by wireless telegraph began in 1910. In 1927, nearly 4 million wireless messages were transmitted by Americans. By 1946, the figure had grown to over 12.5 million. In the same way that wire telegraphy made possible safe and efficient land transportation on railroads, so wireless telegraphy has brought about more scientific control over ocean navigation. With the introduction of radio-beam telegraphy, it is probable that wireless will become ever more important in the transmission of messages over land areas.

**Origins and technical improvements in the telephone.** The telephone is a far more popular means of mass communication than the telegraph. In 1900, there were only 1,355,000 telephones in the United States; in 1950, there were over 40 million, or about 60 per cent of the world total. Considerably over 10 million telephones were installed between 1945 and 1950; nevertheless, although two-thirds of the American families now have telephone service, there is still a long waiting list. Telephone service is still very deficient in country areas, however, with only about 45 per cent of American farm homes having telephone service in 1949.

The telephone system has about 132 million miles of wire, of which over 64 per cent is now in underground cable. This renders the equipment less at the mercy of weather conditions, such as severe ice storms, violent winds, and the like. The new coaxial underground cable is also far cheaper to manufacture and lay than poles and wires that would carry a comparable volume of messages.

The first successful telephonic message was sent on March 10, 1876, by Alexander Graham Bell. A large number of improvements have been made on Bell's device, such as better instruments, the construction of multiple and automatic switchboards, the increased number of wires on the same pole line, the introduction of underground cables, and automatic repeaters and toll-switching devices, the latter of which have made possible the swift handling of long-distance calls. Perhaps the most striking innovation is the dialing system and the automatic switchboard, which have greatly reduced the number of operators.

There has been an almost incredible increase in the number of messages that can be sent simultaneously over one medium. Especially important here is the coaxial cable; it is possible to transmit as many as 600 simultaneous telephone conversations over one pair of coaxial tubes. A coaxial cable containing six of these tubes will permit 1,800 simultaneous conversations over a tube $2\frac{1}{2}$ inches in diameter. At the turn of the century, to carry on as many conversations would have required 15 open air pole lines with 90 foot poles, each having 25 cross arms with 10 wires per arm. Of course, no pole line of such size and capacity was ever constructed. The coaxial cable has proved invaluable also in making possible the most efficient transmission of television programs.

The telephone system has attempted to make its service more popular by giving special rates for long-distance calls on Sunday and during early morning and evening hours. The cost of the average long-distance call in the United States has been cut from $6 to $1.60 since 1920. The increasing accessibility of the telephone has developed what may be called "the telephone habit." In 1950, there were over 160 million telephone conversations, on the average, each day.

The telephone is indispensable to radio and television broadcasting service. All network radio and television programs must be sent over telephone lines from their point of origin to the stations broadcasting them locally. There are about 150,000 miles of program transmission circuits now in operation. A new teletypewriter exchange service, known as TWX, makes it possible to use the telephone system, as well as the telegraph wires, to transmit typewritten messages.

**The telephone industry.** The telephone industry is one of the largest in the country. In 1948, the total investment in telephone plant and equipment was nearly nine billion dollars, or about $258 per telephone. The gross operating revenue was about three billion dollars. Only steam and electric transportation, and electric and gas power and light, exceed the telephone industry in size among public utility industries. The telephone was first developed by small private organizations, and there still are a number of small companies, particularly in the rural districts. Most of the telephone business today is, however, in the hands of the American Telephone and Telegraph Company and associated companies.

**The telephone in American life today.** The telephone has extended the facilities for rapid personal communication to an almost incredible degree. It is now possible, by means of wireless telephony, to talk directly to almost any part of the world. So important is the telephone in modern life that its disappearance would paralyze many daily operations of modern cvilization. The telephone is vital in transacting business. It also facilitates the location of executive offices far from factories. Railroads, ocean vessels, and airplanes depend in many vital ways on the telephone and telegraph.

The increasing popularity of the telephone in rural areas has helped a great deal to break down the former isolation of the farmer, has extended the facilities for gathering and exchanging our gossip, and has all but destroyed privacy. The listening in on the "party lines" of rural communities has often made it impossible to transact business and personal affairs without the knowledge of the entire neighborhood. The telephone has, of course, been of much practical value to the farmer. Orders for supplies and calls for the physician or veterinarian are now made by telephone and save much time and energy.

## Radio and Television

**The wireless telephone or radio.** Development of the wireless telephone, which we ordinarily call the radio, has gone far toward revolutionizing the transmission of information. The radio was invented between about 1910 and 1920 by De Forest, Fessenden, Poulsen, Colpitts, and others. Since 1920, there have been many revolutionary improvements.

**Development and promise of the Frequency Modulation radio.** For about two decades these technical advances in radio consisted mainly in improving the conventional Amplitude Modulation (AM) broadcasting technique and reception sets. Then, on the eve of the second world war, a new type of broadcasting and reception was introduced, mainly as a result of the ingenuity of Major Edwin H. Armstrong. This is what is known as Frequency Modulation (FM) broadcasting. It has notable advantages over AM broadcasting and reception: the elimination of all static and other interference, the absence of station and background noise, greater range and higher fidelity of tone, and the possibility of having a vastly greater number of transmission channels.

The introduction of FM broadcasting began in earnest right after the war. There were about 750 FM stations operating in 1949, over

400 construction permits had been issued, and about 450 applications for new stations were on file. It is predicted by experts that FM broadcasting will ultimately supplant all AM radio activity, but the investment in the older technique and facilities will slow down the transition. It has been predicted that television will challenge any kind of sound radio within a few years. But FM broadcasting will probably dominate in television service.

**Use of the wireless telephone.** While we usually think of the radio —wireless telephony—in connection with broadcasting, it is also used to transact business speedily between people on different continents. Today, we can communicate by wireless telephone with about 60 foreign countries. Extensive ship-to-shore telephone service is made possible by radio. Our wire telephone service, however, is so efficient that we need not use the wireless system within our own country, except for such things as the control and guidance of airplanes and aid to police in crime detection. Both the wireless and the wire telephones are used in radio broadcasting, for the wire telephone is still needed to transmit broadcasts to distant stations on a national hook-up.

**The radio industry.** Radio has developed an enormous popularity. Over 120 million radio sets were manufactured between 1930 and 1949. It was estimated that over 81 million of them were in operation in 1949. Some 42 million families, virtually all of them, had radio sets in 1949.

The chief economic result of this has been that radio has developed into an enormous industry. For the year 1949, the total investment of the 1,100 radio manufacturers, the radio distributors and dealers, and the 1,800 broadcasting stations stood at 555 million dollars. There were 275,000 employees and the payroll was 775 million dollars. The personal investment in the 81 million listeners' sets then in use was about four billion dollars.

The second world war slowed down the radio manufacturing industry, for, in March, 1942, the manufacture of private sets was ordered to cease. But it picked up rapidly after the war, and in 1947 some 17 million sets were manufactured, compared to 13 million in 1941, the largest volume in any pre-war year. In 1948, the American people purchased about 14 million new radio sets—an all-time high. The war actually stimulated the broadcasting and advertising business, owing primarily to the income tax laws affecting excess profits in the higher brackets. Advertising costs could be deducted from taxable income. In 1949, the time sales revenue of radio climbed to an unprecedented peak of about 430 million dollars. Despite this, the impact of television on radio had become ominous by the end of 1948. One-fourth of the standard radio stations and some 58 per cent of all new stations which first came on the air in 1948 lost money. Chairman Wayne Coy of the Federal Communications Commission predicted in 1949 a grim future for sound radio and said that television would become "the dominant medium of broadcasting in the future." This was reflected in the fact that only 8,500,000 radio sets were manufactured in 1949, compared with 17 million in 1947, while television production doubled in 1949.

A serious blow to the future popularity of radio came on August 19, 1949, when the FCC virtually ruled the increasingly popular "give-away" programs off the air. The FCC announced that, after October 1, 1949, it would not renew the license of any radio station operating a give-away program, on the ground that such programs are lotteries.

**Large income from radio advertising.** The income from radio advertising is tremendous. As early as 1937, Procter and Gamble, the largest radio advertiser, spent $4,500,000 in advertising their soap products. In 1938, Chrysler spent $45,000 for each program of Major Bowes' Amateur Hour, and the Charlie McCarthy program cost Chase and Sanborn $35,000 every Sunday night. In 1948, the Columbia Broadcasting System paid $2,500,000 for the "Amos 'n' Andy" program, which it sold to Lever Brothers, and it paid an unrevealed sum in excess of two million dollars for the Jack Benny program, which was retained by the American Tobacco Company. In 1949, the total net income from time sales in the broadcasting field was about 430 million dollars. In 1927, it had been less than 5 million.

**Concentration of radio control.** The radio industry is concentrated in the hands of a few large companies. The Radio Corporation of America, backed by the General Electric Company, the Westinghouse Electric Company, and the American Telephone and Telegraph Company, is the largest. Great investment banks, controlled mainly by the Morgan and Rockefeller interests, stand behind General Electric, Westinghouse, and A.T.&T. The broadcasting facilities and activities are also highly concentrated. The leading companies are the National Broadcasting Company, a branch of the Radio Corporation, the Columbia Broadcasting System, the Mutual Broadcasting System, and the American Broadcasting Company. These major networks control not only much of the business and financial resources of broadcasting, but also the more important broadcasting stations. NBC and CBS are said to be controlled by common investment banking interests. This concentration of radio control makes for better programs and more efficiency, but it also gives great—almost monopolistic—power to the major companies in controlling the policies and facilities of radio broadcasting.

In 1941, Chairman James L. Fly of the Federal Communications Commission made a drastic effort to break up this concentration of radio control, especially the near-monopoly of broadcasting by the National Broadcasting Company and the Columbia Broadcasting System, but he was compelled to modify his plan, and even the modified plan has not been put into operation thoroughly. The Mutual Broadcasting System had brought suit against NBC, alleging monopolistic practices.

**Appraisal of the social significance of radio.** The importance of radio as a means of communication can be understood from the estimate that somewhere between 50 and 80 million persons listen daily to various programs. There were nearly 80 million radio sets available for use in the United States at the close of 1949, and it has been estimated that radio sets are on at some time during the day in 3 out of every 4 homes. The most popular hours on the radio are between 7 and 10 P.M.

The social and intellectual significance of radio can hardly be overestimated. Its cultural impact is highly varied. Radio has meant an enormous increase in public education, mass entertainment, propaganda, and misinformation. By radio, the events, thoughts, emotions, and music of the world are brought into nearly every household in the land.

Since radio, like journalism, has become a sector of big business and depends for its income mainly upon advertising, it is little given to social criticism or crusading for social justice. Great care is taken not to offend powerful interests. Indeed, radio is more cautious than newspapers, on the ground that everybody in the house may have to listen to a radio when it is on, while people only read newspapers of their own volition. Radio commentators usually slant their interpretation of the news to suit conventional and conservative opinion. During the second world war a considerable number of radical commentators got on the air, but, after the war, and especially after the "Red hunt" began in 1947, such commentators were pretty thoroughly dropped. Some news programs are straight reporting; such news commentators as Lowell Thomas do as good a job of reporting as the average newspaper. But the usual commentator has his special group of fans because they like his particular brand of editorializing and bias. Clever broadcasting networks provide a fictitious semblance of fairness and objectivity by very infrequently inviting some dignified and cultivated radical like Norman Thomas to use the air.

The effect of the radio on youthful and adult minds is both good and bad. The radio provides attractive "stay-at-home" recreation, it informs children on many important subjects, and it develops their musical appreciation. It also tries to teach the virtues of honesty, obedience, sympathy, good sportsmanship, and good manners. But the radio is also charged with influencing youngsters to follow criminal activities, for they enjoy listening to programs that feature violence. Banality and stupidity are also featured on the air, especially in the daily serials, the "soap operas" and the like. Whether the radio produces more evil than good in its influence on private and public morals would be hard to say. But there can be no doubt that radio has enormously increased the information and broadened the mental experience of mankind.

While the greater proportion of radio programs are intended to provide entertainment and amusement and to appeal to the masses, the radio offers a real opportunity for education to those who are interested. Great minds, once known to most people only through books, magazines, or newspapers, are brought within the hearing of millions in their own home. The poor man can enjoy an opera, a lecture, or a symphony concert by turning the dial of his radio. A mental and cultural bond may be formed among different classes and races, and among peoples living in widely separated localities, by listening to the same program, whether it be opera, a mystery story, or the news from Europe. Some sponsors have attempted to combine entertainment and information. In the famous Philharmonic Orchestra program on Sunday afternoons, the intermission has been used for lectures by eminent scholars on science, history, literature, and public affairs. Professional students of radio, such as Paul F. Lazarsfeld, contend that since the second world war there is evidence of popular demand for less banality and for a higher order of radio program.

Most of the radio programs which provide any educational benefits are what are known as "sustaining programs." These are programs which are financed mainly by the broadcasting companies themselves rather than by advertising sponsors. Such programs give a better balance to radio broadcasting and provide programs that advertisers would not be likely to support. The Federal Communications Commission has tried to encourage more of these programs. But, after a study of the situation, Jerome H. Spingarn concludes that: "Broadcasters have tended to drop sustaining programs whenever they could sell the time and the networks have failed to provide nationwide distribution for even outstanding network sustaining programs."

The influence of the radio on public opinion is tremendous and has not yet been fully recognized. It is probably more powerful than the printed page, because the human voice often has far greater power to sway emotions than printed material. President Franklin D. Roosevelt owed some of his wide popularity to his clever radio addresses and his pleasant voice and manner. Under proper conditions, the radio can make the whole country think alike on a national issue. Even the modern newspaper depends to a considerable extent on the radio for its news-gathering services.

Radio has greatly facilitated the smearing technique and extended its influence. Two or three of the more irresponsible commentators are able to intimidate even courageous and independent writers and speakers, because the latter fear that they may be smeared in a nationwide broadcast without having a comparable opportunity to answer the smear. Even a successful damage suit cannot begin to undo the harm done by a nationwide smear before millions of listeners.

Radio in public life enormously increases the significance and influence of the accidental and episodic. Winston Churchill gained world renown in 1940 with his "blood, sweat and tears" speech. But he was cast out as a national leader because of a political speech in

1945 in which he smeared the Labour Party as a totalitarian agency, As Viscount Samuel has well observed, in commenting on the Churchill case: "A single speech may found a national reputation, but one mistake may also be magnified into a catastrophe. A succession of eloquent and moving broadcasts during the war helped Mr. Churchill to win fame and influence . . . The war over, a single broadcast, out of tune with the spirit and mood of the people, brought disaster."

**Remarkable recent development of television.** An important addition to radio is television. Invented mainly by E. F. W. Alexanderson following 1926, it was introduced on a commercial basis when the World's Fair opened in 1939. By means of television, the listener can see as well as hear a symphony orchestra, a drama, a great public meeting, or a leading sporting event.

Like FM broadcasting, television has come in by leaps and bounds since the war, and its growth has far exceeded that of FM. There were 50,000 television sets in use at the end of 1946, and the growth since has been spectacular. No less than 7,400,000 television sets were manufactured in 1950 and 5,250,000 in 1951, the drop being due to overproduction in 1950. By 1952 there were some 15,000,000 set owners and the television audience was estimated to be at least 40,-000,000.

The increased popularity of television has been due in large part to the improvements in technique, especially in the greater clarity and fidelity of the pictures produced. The revolutionary innovation of color television was introduced commercially in June, 1951, but its development has been held up because of legal tangles and government restrictions due to the scarcity of critical materials needed for war and armament.

The distance over which television programs can be transmitted is constantly being increased. Much of the seaboard area could see and hear the national nominating conventions in Philadelphia in 1948. David Sarnoff predicted then that, when the nominating conventions of 1952 came along, they could be "televised" from coast to coast. This was borne out, and the conventions of 1952 were witnessed from coast to coast by millions in those parts of the country reached by television. Government restrictions on new stations, not technical problems, were all that prevented the entire nation from viewing these conventions.

The following facts will serve to emphasize the remarkable expansion of television since 1947. We have already pointed out that the number of set owners increased from about 50,000 in 1946 to 15,000,000 by 1952. There were six television stations at the beginning of 1947. Today, there are 108 stations in some 63 metropolitan centers, with some 420 applications for stations awaiting the lifting of the government "freeze" on new stations at the end of 1952. The "freeze" was imposed in September, 1948, by the FCC, with the result that about half the country cannot receive television service. If the "freeze" is lifted, it is estimated that, by 1954, there will be over 500 stations with 35,000,000 television sets in operation. The American Telephone and Telegraph Company completed a $40,000,000 coast-to-coast relay system carried by steel towers just in time to transmit baseball World Series in the autumn of 1951. The total investment in television today is estimated to be close to 3 billion dollars.

**Early commercial aspects of television.** At first, television broadcasting was compelled to operate at a big loss because radio advertising brought a product before an incomparably larger group of potential purchasers. After 1948, there was a great increase in the earnings of the television broadcasting industry as a result of the greater number of sets and the larger audience. The total gross income in 1950 was $85,000,000, and it rose spectacularly to $275,000,000 in 1952. When the government "freeze" is lifted, the earnings may treble or quadruple.

**Probable social and intellectual impact of television.** The intellectual significance and social problems of television will be much the same as those connected with radio. Programs will become increasingly commercial-minded, will be designed to provide mass appeal, and will be keyed to a low mental level. Sporting events and other emotion-provoking scenes will naturally take precedence over conferences devoted to science and learning. The propaganda power of television will be much greater than that of radio, since visual appeal can be exploited with great effect. There is no doubt that the entertainment appeal and facilities of television will vastly exceed those of radio; it is already apparent that television will make serious inroads into the popularity of moving pictures and the theater.

Sociologists believe that one of the beneficial results of television will be to give greater cohesiveness and integrity to the urban family, which has been falling apart alarmingly in the last generation or so. The automobile and the moving pictures took most entertainment out of the home; television is bringing it back. It is certain that television will have more influence on children than any other agency of communication. Recent surveys have shown that children give about as much time to television programs as they do to school activities. Some believe that this vivid interest and attention will decline to some extent as television becomes more common.

Television has been very useful in education, notably in medical and surgical education. The televising of government investigations and conventions has increased public interest in politics, at the same time raising serious questions as to the invasion of individual liberty and civil rights.

**Possibility of a radio newspaper.** It is believed that we may soon have radio newspapers. A device has already been invented, which can be attached to an ordinary radio, that picks news and pictures out of the air and puts them down in black and white. This machine prints without type through a complicated series of electrical opera-

tions. The radio newspaper may become one of the most revolutionary inventions in the history of communication.

## The Development of Modern Commercial Journalism

**Nature of the contemporary newspaper.** The daily newspaper is
not an instrument of personal communication, like the postal service,
the telephone, and the telegraph. It is, nevertheless, one of our leading devices for communicating information. It gathers news from all
parts of the world by means of the telegraph, telephone, cable, and
radio, puts it into print, and makes it available to the reading public.
It also presents the opinion of columnists and other special writers
on important topics of the day. Most daily papers even maintain a
limited type of personal communication through their correspondence
columns.

The invention of the printing press made newspapers possible. We
find references to newspapers in the Netherlands at the close of the
sixteenth century. The first American newspapers were established
in the English colonies at the close of the seventeenth century.

The development of the American newspaper has closely followed
the cultural and economic trends in American life. In the last seventy
years, the metropolitan daily paper has undergone many changes from
the standpoint of both the mechanics of printing and the editorial and
newsroom policy. The speedier methods of printing include new
and more efficient types of printing presses and typesetting machines
and more rapid methods of making stereotyped plates. News gathering has been speeded up by use of the telegraph, telephone, cable, and
radio. The former policy of printing mainly what the editor personally believed should be published has changed; today, newspapers
print the news that will most directly appeal to the great mass of
people.

All the agencies of contemporary communication are combined to
make our modern newspaper. Great international news services, like
the Associated Press and the United Press, have built up a world-wide
coverage. Even small newspapers can afford to get news from all over
the world by joining or subscribing to these news services. Since the
service can be used at the same time by many papers, the cost to each
member or subscriber is greatly reduced.

**Stages in the evolution of American journalism.** In the early days,
newspapers were small sheets, airing personal spites and grievances.
There was little news printed, and slight prospect of getting even this
quickly. About the time of the Civil War, the newspapers became
larger and printed more news, but people still bought papers primarily
because of their vigorous editorial comments. These were the days
of influential editors, like Horace Greeley of the New York *Tribune,*
Charles Dana of the New York *Sun*, and William Cullen Bryant of the

New York *Evening Post;* this period, from about 1860 to 1890, was the heyday of the editorial newspaper.

In the last two decades of the nineteenth century, the true commercial newspaper, the kind we know today, made its appearance, mainly owing to the efforts of James Gordon Bennett, William Randolph Hearst, Joseph Pulitzer, E. W. Scripps, and some. others. Cheaper paper and more efficient methods of printing enabled publishers to print larger papers with more news, and the news-gathering organizations supplied them with a larger volume of news to print. More stress was laid on the *news* element. News became more colorful and dramatic, heavily charged with emotion, in order to attract readers. Circulation grew, and advertisers were willing to spend vast sums to bring their products to the attention of a larger potential buying public. The commercial newspaper of our day was thus developed.

Evening papers are more popular than morning papers in most cities, because more persons have the leisure time to read in the evening. In January, 1948, evening papers had a total circulation of over 30 million and morning papers about 20 million. In the early 1930's, newspaper circulation fell off, but the second world war stimulated newspaper reading, and an all-time high down to that date was attained by dailies in 1946, with an average circulation of 51,410,089 each day. Newspaper circulation continued to grow in 1947 and 1948. At the end of the latter year, the total daily newspaper circulation was 52,285,297, and Sunday circulation, 50,311,509. These figures allayed the fear that movies, radio, and television might drive newspapers out of existence.

The trend in journalistic organization and operation in the last half-century has been decidedly in the direction of fewer, larger, and more powerful newspapers. The number of daily newspapers per million of our population dropped from 29.3 in 1900 to 12.3 in 1947.

**Chain newspapers.** A phase of concentration and the growth of big business in the newspaper world has been the rise of newspaper chains. Chain newspapers offer considerable advantages and economies in operation and administration and make possible greater concentration of control. Chain-newspaper circulation today accounts for about 40 per cent of the 52 million newspapers sold daily and for more than 50 per cent of the Sunday circulation. The six main newspaper chains are the Hearst, Scripps-Howard, Gannett, Patterson-McCormick, Paul Block, and Ridder organizations. They publish 81 dailies with a combined circulation of about 11 million. Scripps-Howard also owns the great United Press news service and Hearst the International News Service.

**Importance of advertising in present-day journalism.** Sensational news and feature material are printed in order to attract a large number of readers. The large circulation that results enables newspapers to charge and receive high prices for advertising space. Revenue from advertising is sufficient to keep the price of the daily newspaper low and thus further increase the circulation. The daily newspaper makes its money mainly through its advertising. No newspaper could break even today merely through circulation revenue, no matter how large the circulation; less than a third of the total newspaper income is derived from circulation revenue. The total income from the sale of all newspaper space for advertising in 1949 was $1,697,000,000, an all-time high at that time.

**Decline of editorial crusades and influence.** The desire of the newspaper publisher to express his own ideas is usually less important today than his ambition to make a fortune, so the newspaper is more a vendor of news, entertainment, and advertising than a means of airing vigorous editorial views. The reading public apparently pays far less attention than formerly to the editorial page. This fact was well illustrated in the presidential campaigns of 1936 and 1940, when President Roosevelt was overwhelmingly re-elected, despite the fact that the majority of papers campaigned against him vigorously in their editorial pages. It was even more thoroughly confirmed in 1948, when 65 per cent of our newspapers supported Dewey and only 15 per cent favored Truman.

The decline in the integrity and moral earnestness of editorial writing can be well illustrated by the fact that at least one writer of first-rate newspaper editorials also writes editorials for a prominent magazine in support of diametrically opposite positions and attitudes.

Because of the desire to make money, the modern newspaper is seldom vitally interested in crusading. The publisher does not want to alarm or offend his reading public or lose his advertisers. A crusade, unless it is directed against community elements everyone dislikes, such as criminals or vicious persons, or our enemies in a foreign war, may not be commercially profitable. Hence, the newspaper has declined as a progressive social force in the community.

It has been frequently charged by Upton Sinclair, George Seldes, and others, that newspapers are intimidated into relative silence on many abuses and into editorial impotence or innocuousness by big business advertisers. There is some truth in this allegation, but the main reason for the decline in crusading zeal and editorial fire is that newspapers have themselves become a part of big business and have no more inclination to crusade for progressive causes than the rest of the big business world.

**Rise of the tabloid.** In keeping with the speed of the times is the streamlined tabloid, or picture newspaper. The reader of a tabloid can get his news at a glance and it is more convenient to read in crowded subways and buses. Unfortunately, the tabloid has a reputation for gross unreliability and for being composed mainly of scandal stories. There are, however, tabloid newspapers with high standards. There is no reason why a newspaper printed in tabloid form may not be dignified in tone and reliable in news content; the editorial pages of some metropolitan tabloids are excellent. The growing popularity of tabloids may be seen in the fact that two of them have the largest circulation of any daily papers: the New York *Daily News* (2,287,337), and the New York *Mirror* (1,079,978).

**Newspapers buy into radio.** There was a time when it was thought that the radio might replace the daily paper, but that possibility now seems remote, for publishers have found that the people who listen to the condensed radio news still like to read the full account in their daily paper. In fact, many radio stations are owned by great publishing concerns. They broadcast the news with the announcement that further details may be obtained in their morning or evening papers. What the radio has done is to kill the old "flash extra," which announced the occurrence of some spectacular event. Such information is now mainly given out over the air. The extent to which the newspapers have bought into the radio industry can be seen from the fact that newspapers own or control 44 of the 53 largest radio stations in the country, own outright 238 broadcasting stations and control 270 others, and have received 60 per cent of the FM franchises already granted.

**Periodical journalism.** Periodical publications are an important item in the American communication system. In 1947, some 18,500 periodicals were published in this country. About 3,500 of these were monthly magazines, and 1,400 weeklies. Some had an enormous circulation—*The Ladies Home Journal,* 4,611,462; *The Saturday Evening Post,* 3,961,510; *McCall's,* 3,750,000; *The Woman's Home Companion,* 3,708,286; *Collier's,* 2,846,582; *American Magazine,* 2,440,-553; *True Story,* 2,127,940; and *Liberty,* 1,570,469. The figures for *Reader's Digest* are in excess of 15,000,000; carrying no advertising, it is now published in a number of languages, and its circulation has thus been extended to non-English-speaking countries in Latin America and the Old World. In 1947, the advertising revenue of magazines amounted to $442,000,000.

With the declining influence of the editorial policy and editorial page of newspapers, intellectual leadership in American journalism has passed to the magazines. Pre-eminent here are the *Atlantic Monthly, Harper's, The Nation, New Republic,* the *Christian Century,* and some others. The *Progressive* was notable and almost unique for maintaining some semblance of realism and integrity before and during the second world war, but it paid the penalty usually exacted for such a policy by going on the rocks financially.

The public is also coming to depend more and more on weekly magazines that digest the news in clever fashion. The most notable of these are *Time, Newsweek,* and the *United States News. Time* has developed an enormous circulation for this type of magazine, some 1,612,587 in 1949. Its total income increased from 74 million dollars in 1945 to 130 million in 1948.

Visual appeal in presenting the news has been exploited by *Life,*

*Look,* and many lesser imitators. *Life* had a circulation of 5,500,000 in 1948. Sumptuous "class magazines" have appeared, notably *Fortune, Esquire,* and *Holiday.* The first is an earnest, well-illustrated journal devoted chiefly to business matters; the second is a leisure-class publication, made up chiefly of clever short articles and stories, and lavishly embellished with pictures not devoid of quasi-aesthetic sex appeal; and the last is a beautifully illustrated publication devoted chiefly to the natural beauties of the country and its main recreation spots and facilities. Another class magazine, *The New Yorker,* is the best example of urbane satire and criticism in our day. The tireless critic of our newspaper press, George Seldes, gets out a small weekly, *In Fact,* devoted almost entirely to important news that is allegedly distorted or suppressed by newspapers.

An important sector of magazine publication usually overlooked in discussions of the press are the so-called House Organs, or publications maintained by corporations and labor organizations. In 1947, there were 5,348 of these publications: 2,430 being internal house organs mainly for management and employees; 1,770 external house organs, designed chiefly to influence potential customers and the public; and 1,148 a combination of both types. The total circulation of all house organs in 1947 was 50 million, or twice the total combined circulation of *Time, Life, Reader's Digest, Saturday Evening Post,* and *Collier's.* These house organs exert no inconsiderable influence upon the opinions of management, labor, and the consuming public. Whether they make for greater enlightenment, better understanding, and more tolerant attitudes is another matter.

## The Motion-Picture Industry

**Origin of moving pictures.** Moving pictures are another important instrument of communication and entertainment. The industry was founded on the development of scientific photography and certain mechanical inventions by Thomas Edison and others. At the close of the nineteenth century, motion pictures were produced by means of the rapid shifting of still pictures. By 1900, crude movies of animated scenes, among them a train passing and a Negro boy eating a watermelon, were produced. The first movie story, consisting of a reel of film of 1,000 feet, was turned out in 1905.

**Evolution of movie technique and industry.** "The Birth of a Nation," produced in 1915 by D. W. Griffith, revolutionized the movies. This was the first great full-dress moving picture. Since then, there have been numerous improvements in the technique of movie-making, and the mass appeal of the art has grown steadily. The sound picture (talkie), introduced in 1928, has greatly expanded the scope of the films, as well as improved their artistic qualities. The average weekly attendance at the movies, which now show technicolor as well as black and white films, is estimated to have been 80 million in 1946; 78 million in 1947; 67 million in 1948; and 62 million in 1949.

The decline is attributed mainly to the rise of television. There are 18,750 motion picture theaters in the country, seating over 11 million persons.

**The economics of the moving picture industry.** The total investment of capital in the film industry in the United States is $2,750,000,-000, some $2,475,000,000 of it in the theaters. The total income from moving pictures in 1947 was $1,855,000,000. The industry employed 255,000 persons, with an annual payroll of 533 million dollars, in 1947. Many pictures are produced at a lavish cost. "Gone With the Wind" is reputed to have cost $4,500,000, but it paid a handsome profit, with a gross revenue of over 20 million dollars. "The Birth of a Nation" had cost only $100,000 to produce, but it grossed more than any other picture ever made and is still being shown. Television is proving a serious threat to the prosperity of the moving picture industry.

**D. W. Griffith and Adolph Zukor.** The leading figures in the development of motion pictures were D. W. Griffith, who really created modern movie production by his use of the "close-up," "cut-back," and "fade-out," and his clever handling of massed actors, and Adolph Zukor, who introduced the "star" system, and linked moving-picture production with producers' control of the distribution and showing of films.

The latter practice led to abuses, particularly block booking and the ownership of motion-picture theaters by producers. On June 11, 1946, a Federal court decision banned monopoly practices in film distribution. The court ruled that, in the future, moving pictures must be distributed by a system of free bidding for individual films, and it outlawed the system of block booking, under which exhibitors had to agree to take a number of films in advance of release and to show them at minimum admission prices. The court refused to oust moving-picture producers from ownership of theaters, pointing out that only 2,500 of the 18,000 theaters in the country were producer-owned and holding that the free-bidding system would eliminate the former monopolistic abuses.

**Social and intellectual impact of moving pictures.** From the standpoint of communication, the most important contributions of the movies have been the newsreels, travel films, and educational films. Of these, the newsreels are the most numerous and significant. Even if the average American does not turn on his radio or read his newspaper faithfully every day, he can keep up with events to some extent at the movies. He is likely to be even more impressed by what he sees than by what he hears or reads.

There is no doubt that the movies exert a large influence in shaping the ideas of the American people. Their greatest popular appeal arises from the fact that they enable us to escape from the monotony or drabness of everyday life and enter vicariously into the more exciting and glamorous experiences of imaginary characters or of the "stars" themselves. Through the movies, the small town or rural housewife gets a glimpse of the fascinating world of fashion and high society. Those who live a drab life at home can share in the exotic loves and high adventures of film characters. The movies have also probably done more than anything else in recent times to acquaint the masses with landscapes, natural features, flora, fauna, and manners and customs of their own country and distant lands. The movies thus help to break down the isolation of formerly backward areas.

The moral and social effects of the movies, like those of radio, are both good and bad. The film producers have been charged with showing exciting and exotic forms of life, scenes of criminal activity, and the like, which may have a bad effect on young people. The importance of fine clothes and plenty of money, which is stressed in pictures of high society, may cause dissatisfaction and family discord among those who must live more simply. Yet, as we shall see later on, the movie censors try to see to it that virtue and honesty are always rewarded in the long run, while sin and crime inevitably bring fitting punishment.

On the whole, probably the chief criticism of the movies from an intellectual and social point of view is the general triviality and banality which inevitably arises from the necessity of constantly pandering to emotionalism and mass appeal. But, occasionally, a movie with some social significance does get produced and is able to slip through the censors. Also, at times, moving pictures exert considerable influence on technological and business trends. For example, Samuel Hopkins Adams' movie "It Happened One Night" gave publicity to bus travel and enormously stimulated the use of buses.

## Social and Sociological Significance of the Development of Contemporary Transportation and Communication

**Outstanding social importance of transportation and communication.** While a familiarity with the main facts about the revolutionary developments in transportation and communication summarized in the preceding pages constitutes an indispensable item in the intellectual equipment of the beginning student of sociology, one should not get so absorbed in the drama of the facts themselves as to lose sight of their fundamental social significance. This we have at least briefly discussed in connection with each major type of progress in the fields of transportation and communication, as well as in earlier chapters dealing with the increasing scope of group contacts and social interactions. It will be useful, however, to bring matters together at this point by stressing some leading and representative effects of the innovations described in this chapter upon various aspects and processes of social life.

**Some obvious effects of contemporary transportation.** Modern transportation methods have broken down the isolation and provincialism that dominated human life and social organization well down into the nineteenth century. They have made human society a mobile and dynamic entity, with correspondingly wider and more varied stimulation. Economic life has become ever more dependent upon rapid transit, both within a nation's boundaries and over world-wide areas. Many new public problems have been created, especially those connected with war and peace, since every portion of the world is now vulnerable to those deadly new methods of warfare which modern aviation can transport and deliver. The development of the atom bomb and bacterial and chemical warfare, in conjunction with airplane and rocket warfare, may reverse the most notable social trend of the last hundred years, the increasing size and importance of urban units. Great cities may be broken up and all centers of population moved or redistributed to lessen the danger of their being bombed or gassed.

**Enlargement of personal and social horizons.** Contemporary transport and communication have played a dominant part in producing the cultural lag and social disorganization that have brought about most of our current social problems. Institutions that developed out of family and local situations in small, personal societies now have to operate in conjunction with a technological system which has brought the world to nearly every door. Every home has, in one way or another, become a part of a world community, even in the case of those global influences which encourage and increase conflicts and prejudices. The basic primary groups (the family, neighborhood, play group, and the like) still persist and have a vital influence in socializing the individual, but today local habits, gossip, and exhortations are mingled with world news and pressures in bringing about socialization and social control. The child held on his grandfather's knee in our time may also be listening to information and influences originating on the opposite side of the planet. Such global stimuli and pressures may be too vast and diversified for the average individual fully to understand and assimilate.

**Economic and political impact of contemporary communication.** In the economic realm today, world economic problems and trends impinge upon our ears and bank accounts, along with price fluctuations in the local grocery store. A nation may rely on abnormal and temporary foreign economic situations rather than a healthy home economy to maintain prosperity. Our intellect and our emotions may be stirred up by global economic revolutions and ideologies, as well as by local strikes and wage disputes.

Our political life is as much affected by news and pressures from all over the country and the globe as it is by local issues and the pleas of local candidates. During political campaigns everyone with a radio in his home can listen to the leading candidates in comfort, and he can hear with greater clarity than those who sat in the front row of an auditorium to listen to William Jennings Bryan in 1896. Every voter is subjected to constant, and frequently contradictory, stimulation. The result is, all too often, sheer mental confusion; there is little sane analysis or impartial information provided by contemporary communication agencies—mainly because a sane and informative approach to personal and public problems possesses little mass appeal and sales value. Hence, the average citizen is comprehensively stimulated but rarely reliably guided in his thinking. Those who control communication today also control political life and public policies to a considerable extent. This fact poses ominous problems for democracy. The influence of the superficial sensationalist or the ignorant spellbinder was limited in former times; today, he may reach many millions. Walter Winchell has a thousand-fold more public influence than a great statesman like Robert Moses.

**Communication and international relations.** In no other public field has the impact of modern transportation and communication been so revolutionary as in the international realm. Our modern facilities, if sagaciously and discreetly used, can enable us to reduce the prospect of war, but, if utilized to promote aggressive meddling abroad, they can constitute an unprecedentedly potent means of provoking friction and conflict.

The situation today has produced two equally extreme and unfounded views of world affairs. On the one hand, we have those who look upon global matters in terms of the splendid isolation of the Monroe Doctrine of 1823; at the other extreme, we find the equally naïve proponents of the idea that, just because we can fly or telephone around the world with great rapidity, it will be equally easy to govern the world from a common capital. We are no longer isolated, as we were in 1823, but the very factors which have made possible the radio telephone and the jet plane have also enormously increased the complexity of governing a national state, to say nothing of ruling the world. Those who today ignore the extent and diversity of world contacts may suddenly awaken, perhaps too late, to formidable global threats. Those who suffer from the Globaloney complex may fatally ignore indispensable domestic reforms through hysterical absorption with trends abroad that lie beyond their control.

**Moral conditioning and personal conflict.** Modern transportation and communication have exerted a strong influence on moral and personal problems. Family and neighborhood influences now have to compete with national and world-wide stimuli and experiences in shaping our moral concepts and practices. Psychologists and psychiatrists have called attention to the fact that a leading cause of mental instability today is the clash between horse-and-buggy institutions and aviation technology, so to speak. Our personalities have been shaped by institutions that grew out of a simple technology and small, personal societies. Yet, we now have to live in a social environment that has been created by a complex technology and is today characterized by a growing diversification of social groups. This situation produces mental blocks and conflicts that may result in neurotic and psychotic manifestations of mental instability and disease—in what Graham Wallas has called "balked dispositions," and Arnold J. Toynbee describes as "schisms in the soul." We shall have more to say about such matters in a later chapter on mental disease and mental hygiene.

**Need of new emphasis and orientation in sociology.** The main sociological significance of all this lies in the fact that the great majority of all past sociological analysis of personality-building, group life, and social interaction has been based upon rural personal and social experience in primary and small secondary groups with limited contacts. Such analysis, however shrewd and penetrating, can provide only very imperfect understanding and guidance in the world we inhabit in the middle of the twentieth century. The professional sociologist, as well as the citizen, must come to grips with the new world of mental contacts and social experiences created by contemporary technology in the realms of transportation and communication.

## Summary

Modern civilization rests to a great extent upon improved methods of transportation and communication.

Good roads and canals, as a means of assembling raw materials and carrying the products of the Industrial Revolution to market, were vital to the factory system. Speedier transportation, by means of the steam locomotive, the railroad, and larger and faster steam vessels, brought even greater changes in industry. The railroad has been a great boon to industry, but, in recent years, the automobile, bus, and airplane have forced the railroads to make many improvements in order to compete with them. The automobile has completely changed the travel habits of Americans; the tourist era has put the American home on wheels. Telford and Macadam made good roads possible, but the automobile made them an absolute necessity. The airplane has become a popular means of speedy travel. Although not yet as safe as some other forms of transportation, the airplane is an increasingly important addition to human transportation.

The chief improvements in the field of communication have been the extension of the postal service, the invention of the telegraph, the telephone, radio, and television, the development of the daily newspaper, and the appearance of the moving picture.

Today, the world is being brought closer together, from the standpoint of both the conquest of distance and the exchange of cultural ideas and developments. Time has been virtually annihilated and space vastly shrunk. The telephone, radio, and movies have broken down the isolation of the rural communities, the postal service has introduced cheap and speedy delivery of mail, the radio has brought entertainment and educational opportunities to rural as well as urban areas, and the daily newspaper carries the news of the world to our doorsteps. Moving pictures have helped to spread ideas and information. The newsreels, travel films, and educational shorts are of real value to persons who prefer to see events rather than hear or read about them. But most movie production provides only entertainment, some of it excellent and some of it banal and trivial. Rarely do the movies present anything of great social significance.

The revolution in communication has to some extent broadened people's outlook and interests because even the most remote parts of the world can now be reached by our modern methods of communication, and foreign thoughts, ways, and manners can be revealed to Americans, thus making it possible to promote the understanding and tolerance which are necessary if we are to make any progress toward world government and peace.

## Selected References

Anderson, R. E., *The Story of the American Automobile,* Public Affairs Press, 1950. An interesting account of the development of the motor car and its effects on American life and culture.

Baus, H. M., *Publicity: How to Plan, Produce and Place It,* Harper, 1942. A very comprehensive, if not too critical, panorama of all types and media of publicity.

Bent, Silas, *Newspaper Crusaders,* McGraw-Hill, 1939. Interesting account of the now fading practice of editorial crusading, as represented by men like Pulitzer, Scripps, Older, and the like.

Blumer, Herbert, *Movies and Conduct,* University of Chicago Press, 1933.

————, and Hauser, P. M., *Movies, Delinquency and Crime,* University of Chicago Press, 1933. These two books are the best sociological appraisal of the effects of moving pictures on social behavior, morals and crime.

Brucker, Herbert, *Freedom of Information,* Macmillan, 1949. Valuable and up-to-date survey of newspaper data, journalistic methods, and freedom of the press.

* Chase, Stuart, *The Tyranny of Words,* Harcourt, Brace, 1938. A stimulating introduction to semantics, or the science of meaning as expressed through words. It lays stress on the difficulties in ascertaining the real meaning of words and in communicating our sense of their meaning to others. Also shows the fatal tendency to identify words with things.

Dilts, M. M., *The Telephone in a Changing World,* Longmans, Green, 1940. An excellent popular history of the telephone and an account of its influence on the modern world.

Faris, R. E. L., *Social Disorganization,* Ronald Press, 1949. Latest work dealing with manner in which technology has undermined primary institutions of the past rural culture.

Forman, H. J., *Our Movie Made Children,* Macmillan, 1933. The author summarizes the results of an elaborate study of the effects of the moving picture upon the minds and mental images of children. He concludes that this effect is extensive and in some ways detrimental.

Gauvreau, Emile, *My Last Million Readers*, Dutton, 1941. A veteran newspaper editor, both of conventional newspapers and of tabloids, frankly reveals the sensationalism and venality of the contemporary press. An illuminating and appalling tale.

* Howe, Quincy, *The News and How to Understand It*, Simon and Schuster, 1940. A popular and authoritative account of the dissemination of the news by the radio and newspapers, and of the biases of the leading columnists and radio commentators.

Hutchins, R. M., *et al.*, *A Free and Responsible Press*, University of Chicago Press, 1947. Perhaps the most searching inquiry into contemporary American journalism, and constructive suggestions concerning its possible improvement.

Johnston, S. P., *Horizons Unlimited*, Duell, Sloan, and Pearce, 1941. Perhaps the best introduction to the history and development of aviation, including its early use in the second world war.

* Laine, Elizabeth, *Motion Pictures and Radio*, McGraw-Hill, 1938. A good introduction to these important new avenues of communication, with considerable attention to their social effects.

* Lazarsfeld, P. F., and Field, Henry, *The People Look at Radio*, University of North Carolina Press, 1946.

* Lazarsfeld, P. F., and Kendall, P. L., *Radio Listening in America*, Prentice-Hall, 1948. The most recent and authoritative presentation of facts and interpretations relative to radio as a social force and the response patterns of radio listeners.

* Lee, A. M., *The Daily Newspaper in America*, Macmillan, 1937. The best analysis of the commercial journalism of our day.

Lee, J. M., *History of American Journalism*, Houghton Mifflin, 1923. A standard history of the American newspaper to the commercial stage.

McKelvey, St. Clair, *Gossip: the Life and Times of Walter Winchell*, Viking, 1940. A keen description and appraisal of the background, ideals, and methods of a popular columnist.

Moody, John, *The Railroad Builders*, Yale University Press, 1921. Probably the best brief history of American railroading.

* Morris, Lloyd, *Not So Long Ago*, Random House, 1950. An absorbing account of the rise and social effects of the automobile, moving-picture, and radio industries.

Ogburn, W. F., (Ed.), *Technology and International Relations*, University of Chicago Press, 1949. Most recent and important work on relation of contemporary communication and transportation to world affairs.

Robinson, Howard, *The British Post Office: A History*, Princeton University Press, 1948. A monumental and exhaustive study of the origin and growth of the British postal service.

Rolo, C. J., *Radio Goes to War*, Putnam, 1942. A preliminary account of the effect of the second world war on radio communication.

Rosewater, Victor, *History of Coöperative News-gathering in the United States*, Appleton-Century, 1930. Standard account of the rise and methods of the Associated Press, United Press, International News Service, et cetera.

\* Rosten, L. C., *Hollywood—the Movie Colony, the Movie Makers*, Harcourt, Brace, 1941. The most vivid and competent account in print of movie ideals, production, and management.

Seldes, George, *Lords of the Press*, Messner, 1939. A highly critical discussion of the modern American newspapers and their management, by a veteran newspaper man.

Smith, H. L., *Airways*, Knopf, 1942. Perhaps the best book on the status and activities of aviation.

Starr, J. W., *One Hundred Years of American Railroading*, Dodd, Mead, 1928. Interesting popular history of railroad transportation.

Thompson, R. L., *Wiring a Continent*, Princeton University Press, 1947. A competent, scholarly, and interesting history of the American telegraph industry in its relation to the evolution of the American economy.

Waples, Douglas, Berelson, B. R., and Bradshaw, F. R., *What Reading Does to People*, University of Chicago Press, 1940. Important book on social effects of the reading habits of Americans—chiefly reading of magazines and newspapers.

\* Webster, H. H., *Travel by Air, Land, and Sea*, Houghton Mifflin, 1934. The best general introduction to the history of transportation. A clear and brief survey.

# CHAPTER XXI

# Prejudice and Propaganda as Social Forces

## Nature and Origins of Our Prejudices

**Improved communication has not eliminated prejudice.** The peoples of the world have been brought into closer contact by improved methods of communication, but the ideas and actions of the majority of persons are still deeply affected by their personal prejudices derived from their local social surroundings.

While it is true that modern transportation and communication, by bringing us into contact with hitherto strange races, cultural groups, ideas, and manners and customs, may ultimately increase understanding and tolerance, yet these very processes and tendencies do hold within themselves the seeds of prejudice. This is the case because we have an automatic liking for the peoples, things, ways of life, and conventions with which we are familiar, and are spontaneously sceptical or hostile toward the strange and unknown in the social world. We naturally incline towards the whole cultural heritage of our "in-group" or "we-group" and react unfavorably toward whatever diverges notably from it.

**What we mean by prejudice.** By a prejudice we mean an essentially automatic bias or pre-judgment, toward a given person, race, thing, idea, type of conduct, and the like. This bias may be favorable or unfavorable; we may be prejudiced for or against anything. In this chapter, we shall be considering prejudice mainly as an unfavorable bias. On the whole, as noted above, we usually dislike persons, ideas, and experiences that are unfamiliar. These differences may lie in race, dress, tastes, beliefs, or economic interests. In other words, we are prejudiced against certain people because they do not possess the physical traits, social ideas, and behavior patterns of our group. They usually belong to an "out-group" or "others-group."

**The genesis of prejudice.** We saw in an earlier chapter how group life has been essential to human progress. Every social group, desirous of assuring its own safety, develops rules of conduct and modes of thought that unify the community. This was true of primitive and ancient communities; it is still true today. Our conduct reflects the ideas and behavior of our group. The group in which we live is the source of our ideas of right and wrong. Our customs seem right to us, and we are prejudiced against other customs. Our social attitudes do not have a scientific basis but develop naturally out of human experience in group life.[1]

Custom and habit incline us to accept, esteem, and defend the familiar, whether it be our own race, our national customs, or the accepted convictions of our social group. We feel safe in adopting and following the traditional ideas of our group, for if we do we will not be unpopular or punished. It is also easier to think and act in the habitual ways we have learned earlier in life. Any new idea or course of action spontaneously arouses in the average person a dislike or prejudice, and he clings with determination to his familiar ideas and conduct, unwilling to have them challenged, even though there may be no logical or scientific support for them. Prejudice is thus firmly intrenched in our personal conditioning by group life from infancy onward.

One of the most conspicuous facts about the origin of our prejudices is that they are picked up automatically and unconsciously, as our personalities develop. They inevitably furnish a large part of the mental equipment of each individual. Most prejudices are acquired in childhood, before we possess enough knowledge to recognize that certain of them have no substantial basis in fact. Children learn much from their parents, their teachers in school, and their daily companions. Then, as they grow older, they learn, in addition, from books, newspapers, magazines, movies, and the radio. The ideas imprinted on a child's mind in the formative years of his life become the most important item in creating and fixing his beliefs, convictions, and standards of behavior.

## Causes and Types of Prejudice

**Superficiality a cause of prejudice.** One reason for the existence and persistence of prejudice is that we do not analyze adequately what superficially seem to be sound reasons for prejudice. This has been well explained by Professor James W. Woodard:

Races probably do differ in innate ability, though how is not yet clear. Those at the upper levels of socio-economic status have higher abilities on the average than those at lower levels. As of this moment, the repressed minorities, religions, classes, and races do have in fact many of the shortcomings they are charged with having: e.g., mediocre ability, shiftlessness, bitterness, compensatory aggressiveness, clannishness, etc.

Further facts however, yield further precision: Group differences are always differences of degree, never of kind. The differences are slight on the average. The overlappings far outweigh the differences in significance. The traits are less significant than they are made out to be. Some individuals do

---

[1] See above, pp. 47 ff; 73 ff.

not show them at all.  Some even develop compensatory virtues.  Many of the traits are not innate as such.  Prejudice itself has caused many of them.[2]

**Ignorance, mental weakness, insecurity, and isolation as causes of prejudice.**  While persons of superior mental capacity and good education possess and retain all too many prejudices, it is also true that prejudice is much more prevalent among those of inferior ability and inadequate education.  As Woodard puts it:

> For the untutored, as for the feeble-minded, most of life is necessarily screened through a few simple preconceptions.  For them, most adjustments, too, are necessarily processed out emotionally rather than intellectually.  This, too, is the way of prejudice.  It is no accident that prejudice most abounds in those regions of the country where educational facilities are most neglected, and among those socio-economic levels which have least access to education.

One cause for the persistence of prejudice in our day, despite the extension of educational facilities, is insecurity.  Since our age is one of rapid social change, it is also one in which uncertainty and insecurity are, at least temporarily, on the gain.  As Woodard says:

> Historically, prejudice had increased proportionately to the insecurities and unpredictabilities of status. . . . The whole process of social adjustment and social change is thus set in the climate of prejudice and counter-prejudice, propaganda and crude counter-propaganda.

Sometimes, prejudice is caused by cultural isolation.  If a group is cut off from contact with other groups, it is likely to be unaware that other people may think and act differently.  Hence, cultural conceit and smug self-satisfaction with group customs and personal convictions may continue unchallenged.  Yet, if isolation were the only source of prejudice, the revolution in transportation and communication just described would have greatly lessened prejudice as a problem in modern life.

**Class and group basis of prejudice.**  Often, prejudices arise from differences between social classes.  The landed nobility may look down upon the businessman, and both of them may be prejudiced against the laborer.  On the other hand, the laborer and farmer may be prejudiced against the upper classes, because they envy the superior wealth and pleasures and resent the snobbish behavior of the rich.  The very nature of our present-day urbanized and industrial society inevitably breaks it up into specialized groups, each of which possesses a body of strong prejudices.  Turning once again to Professor Woodard's study:

> The Great Society of the present fractures into sub-groups—races, nations, classes, regions, religions, and ideological and economic blocs.  Each of these is equipped with a battery of rationalizations, loyalties and prejudices.

---

2 Unpublished paper on "Some Implications of Our Present Knowledge Concerning Prejudices."

They support the morale of the in-group, give it solidarity, and provide a justification for its strategic offensive and defensive tactics.

**Race prejudice.** Prejudice against those of a different race has been marked and persistent. Usually, the prejudice of one race against another is founded on fear and mistrust of any person who looks "different" or strange. This basis of prejudice is supplemented by the differences in manners, customs, and beliefs, which often go with real physical differences between races. Many racial prejudices are not based on the actual physical differences between races, but on related cultural factors. Race prejudice has been the source of many serious social problems and, both directly and indirectly, has helped on world wars.

**Rural-urban prejudices.** The social customs of one class or region may prejudice it against those of another group or area. The city man often regards the rural dweller as a "hick," "rube," or "hayseed." The country dweller, on the other hand, may regard the city man with suspicion and hostility, as a "dude" or a "city slicker." Fortunately, new transportation and communication facilities have helped to lessen this type of prejudice to some extent.

**Political prejudices.** Political prejudice is rampant; one of its chief expressions, as we have seen in a previous chapter, is associated with extreme nationalism. Glorifying one's own country and looking with contempt on another is a common form of political prejudice. Nationalism has been gaining force, rather than declining, since the first world war. Fascism elevated nationalism almost to the status of a religion. The hatreds engendered by the second world war and by the cold war that followed have greatly encouraged the growth of national feeling and arrogance. Intense nationalism makes it difficult to respect the culture and conduct of other nations, for it teaches that devotion to country, whether the latter be right or wrong, is the only desirable attitude for a patriot to entertain. Nationalism is included in the educational tradition of most countries and is thus formally strengthened and perpetuated. Ardent nationalism makes it difficult, if not impossible, to preserve a reasonable and tolerant attitude with respect to foreign affairs and international relations.

There are also many prejudices associated with political parties. With many persons, loyalty to their party almost exceeds loyalty to the nation. Members of other political parties are looked upon as inferior beings or as the natural enemies of society. Party names, symbols, catchwords, and songs serve to keep these prejudices alive. This type of prejudice has been particularly noticeable in the United States for the last hundred years. We have already pointed out that there are no striking differences between the Republican and Democrat parties. Both represent the same general economic interests and support the same capitalistic system. The differences between them are of a minor nature—almost wholly prejudices. Yet, party prejudice has been able to stir up deep bitterness even between friends, neighbors, and families, especially during the last twenty years.

**Economic prejudices.** Many prejudices are created by economic conditions. Farmers are often prejudiced against businessmen, and both are frequently hostile toward unionized factory workers. Even within the laboring classes, there are bitter prejudices. For instance, the two major labor groups, the American Federation of Labor and the Congress of Industrial Organizations, have bitterly opposed each other.

Moderate Socialists hate Communists, who are only another group of more radical Socialists, and this hatred is cordially returned by the Communists. Property interests give rise to many prejudices, as Thorstein Veblen pointed out. Those possessed of little property develop hostility to the display of wealth by the more fortunate, while the rich snub or patronize the poor, and fear and detest any plans for a more equitable distribution of wealth.

A mounting prejudice against radicals is now developing in this country, owing in part to our temporarily excessive fondness for Communist exponents of war after June 22, 1941. Now we have gone to the opposite extreme and have started a witch hunt that has exposed to actual or potential persecution many who have no Communist leanings whatever.

**Law as a basis and support of prejudice.** The law expresses and enforces both political and economic prejudices. The courts and judges are held in great awe, even when venal and incompetent. Lawyers have their own special prejudices. Rich corporation lawyers, engaged in the manhandling of law to the advantage of their wealthy clients, hold in contempt the poverty-stricken attorney who chases ambulances to get clients. It is realized by many that trial by jury is not reliable as a means of ascertaining guilt but so strong is our prejudice against discarding the traditional system that jury trial not only persists but is still sanctified. Both prosecutors and defense attorneys rely chiefly on provoking prejudices in jurors to win any case in court.

The law has, in many cases, stood in the way of social progress, by declaring reform legislation unconstitutional. Child labor laws were declared unconstitutional on two different occasions. Law has also been used at times to exclude those without property from voting and to bar women from the right to participate in political life. Law has often been used on behalf of religious and racial prejudices. Religious observances in the schools have been frequently prescribed by law. Race discrimination exists in the laws against the immigration of orientals and against the equality of Negroes in the South. The use of law to support special interests has led to hostility toward law on the part of those who suffer at its hands.

**Religious prejudices.** Many religious persons are prejudiced against unbelievers, who, in turn, look with contempt on the faithful. Jews are often prejudiced against Christians; Protestants and Catholics are frequently suspicious of each other and of Jews. The different

Protestant denominations hold many prejudices against one another, even on such minor points as the ritual of baptism and communion.

**Moral prejudice.** We all have moral prejudices that reflect our home training, community associations, and beliefs. Deep convictions on such subjects as card-playing, dancing, gambling, drinking, sex behavior, and the like are examples of moral prejudices. We usually regard those who have different opinions from ours on such matters with disfavor and show them little tolerance. We think they are either wicked or foolish.

**Prejudice against Jews.** The persecution of Jews in European countries is an example of a prejudice, based not on real differences in race, but on conduct and ideas mistakenly associated with race. The prejudice against Jews is as definite as though there were a Jewish race. Anthropologically speaking, there is no such thing today as a Jewish race. Many Gentiles are prejudiced against the religious practices of the Jews, their social customs, and their reluctance to marry outside of their faith. The Jews have been compelled to live in ghettos and other segregated areas in Europe. In turn, the Jews, who have been treated as inferiors, have in self-defense developed an assertiveness and aggressiveness which non-Jews often mistake for a racial characteristic. Some Jews even contend that there is a Jewish race or hold to a racial view of Jewish culture.

**Educational prejudice.** Formal education helps to create, confirm, and store up prejudices in many other fields. The educated are prejudiced against the uneducated; one school of educational theory is biased against another; some uphold the value of discipline in training, while others upport the idea of freedom for personal development. The traditional educators who teach the classics look with increased alarm on the new courses in vocational education, progressive education, and the social sciences. Since education transmits our whole cultural heritage, it inevitably transmits our prejudices. It hands on through the schools the respectable prejudices about race, nationality, religion, economic classes, morality, and the like.

## Possible Ways of Reducing Prejudice

**How not to attack prejudice.** The fundamental fact about prejudice is that it can only be eliminated by removing its causes. It cannot be dealt with successfully by striking wildly here and there at symptoms. Merely to denounce and scold prejudice will do little good; indeed, it is likely to increase it. As Professor Woodard observes:

> Anything so integral as prejudice will not be removed by scolding it. Prejudice being seen as due to wrong attitudes, the solution is too often seen as a simple matter of changing attitudes. But we do not really have such free-will choices about our own attitudes. Denunciation is often enough only attacking symptoms. The prejudice resists reason, builds up its defenses the

more elaborately it is under attack, and may actually increase in strength under our moral indictment of it. There was never a time when so many sermons, editorials, and other direct attacks on prejudice were being made as at present. Yet prejudice is rising steadily. . . . Too direct an attack sometimes only aggravates prejudice. That is why both individuals and peoples, when cornered in the illogic and injustice of their prejudices, do not then acquiesce and alter them. They lose their tempers. They fight back with the grim hate warranted by the fact that their very integrity and way of life are jeopardized.

How to attack prejudice. The only sane and effective manner to attack the problem of prejudice is to undermine its causes as rapidly as possible. Since some of the main causes of prejudice are cultural isolation and provincialism, ignorance and inferiority, economic insecurity, and class and international strife, whatever tends to reduce such factors in social life will inevitably help to reduce prejudice.

Wider contacts may reduce prejudice. An effective way to lessen prejudice is through travel and observation. Contacts with different groups and their customs may lead to a comprehension of the fact that there are many different viewpoints and ways of living, all of which are cherished and supported by the groups that have adopted them. Other lands, strange though their customs may be, have qualities which, if understood, can be appreciated and respected.

Social science can undermine prejudice. Increasing our knowledge of history, anthropology, and sociology is an effective way to undermine prejudice. History makes clear the origins of our current prejudices and shows that the most confirmed prejudices of the past have often been proved wrong and foolish with the passage of time. We find through the study of anthropology and sociology that others feel much the same about the superiority of their customs as we do about ours. As Professor Sumner showed in his *Folkways*, the mores make everything right or wrong for us. The study of sociology can thus do a great deal to overcome prejudice.

Educational attacks on prejudice. In any type of educational attack on prejudice it is of great importance to start with children at their very entry into school life. They already have a large body of prejudices when they first reach the schoolroom. These should be skillfully undermined as the process of education continues. Prejudices can be unlearned, but this unlearning is likely to be most effective if started early. If education ignores or intensifies prejudices during the elementary and secondary school period, no amount of enlightened higher education is likely to be wholly successful in eliminating them. Of course, if prejudice is to be undermined in the elementary schools, the teachers must themselves be free of prejudices and eager to undermine them in pupils—rarely the case in our schools. Most teachers have the same prejudices as their pupils and are more interested in perpetuating such prejudices than in destroying them.

Importance of economic security. Economic and social reforms which provide for a better distribution of income, assure more steady employment, give higher wages and salaries, and set up adequate systems of social insurance would tend to reduce those prejudices which grow out of a sense of economic insecurity and uncertainty. Emphasis on the fact that national prosperity depends upon a unified effort of all classes and groups in the efficient production and distribution of goods would help to lessen the prejudices developing from the class struggle in the economic field.

**Value of a world perspective.** The cultivation of a world-wide point of view in approaching cultural and public problems would also help to overcome prejudices that grow out of national arrogance. We would find that no nation has been able to develop its civilization without many cultural contributions from others. In particular, we could clearly discern that our American civilization has resulted, in considerable part, from the cultural contributions of the immigrants who came here from Europe.

## Outlook for the Reduction or Elimination of Prejudice

**Social change favorable to prejudice.** Prejudice has been one of the major and most persistent evils of society since the dawn of history. What are the prospects of reducing its ravages in our day? Unfortunately, the outlook is not promising, despite all our knowledge and our recognition of the evils of prejudice. Nearly all the major factors that make for prejudice are now operating to an unusual extent, with every apparent probability that most, if not all, of them will become more active and potent in the predictable future.

Most important of all is the fact that we are now in the midst of the fourth great world revolution, comparable to the dawn of history, the break-up of the Roman Empire, and the dissolution of medieval society. On account of this fact, we are in a period of maximum personal insecurity and social uncertainty. This state of affairs, as we noted earlier, is uniquely favorable to the development and continuation of fears and prejudices.

Some recent progress in reducing race prejudice in the United States has given many persons an unjustified optimism concerning the future of race prejudice. It is probable that the most extended and bitter race prejudice is yet to come, with the increasing importance of the yellow and black races in world affairs.

**Wars perpetuate prejudice.** The fierce hatreds generated by the second world war had not even begun to abate before a cold war was instituted between Soviet Russia and her satellites and the Anglo-American bloc of nations. A cold war, deemed indispensable to the fortunes of both sides, can only be prolonged by evoking violent hatreds, deep fears, and strong prejudices.

The ideological struggle which lies at the roots of the cold war is the most intense and crucial since the days of the great bourgeois revolutions of the seventeenth, eighteenth, and nineteenth centuries, when quasi-medieval autocracy was assailed by revolution and republicanism. Democracy and capitalism are now being challenged by managerialism and Socialism (Communism), and the struggle is likely to go on until one or the other triumphs. Each will provide the most intense propaganda possible and thus intensify and continue the inherent prejudices. Russia has long since instituted and executed purges and witch hunts, and we seem on the way to duplicating her example.

Race prejudice is likely to be added to political and economic prejudice in the cold war, as Russia turns eastward in her interests and activities. Already, the opponents of Soviet Russia are beginning to denounce the European Russians as orientals and Asiatics. This trend has been intensified by the Communist conquest of China.

If the cold war and the ideological struggle ultimately bring about the third world war, the war and the postwar occupation period will last from 25 to 50 years and will call for vast privations and sacrifices. These can only be sustained on the basis of violent passions and equally strong prejudices.

**Depression and prejudice.** In case peace can be maintained, we are likely to run into an economic depression of unprecedented seriousness and duration because of our failure to carry out the needed economic reforms and reconstruction at an earlier and appropriate time. Such a state of affairs will increase economic insecurity and intensify prejudice. There will be an attempt to find a scapegoat, and such efforts invariably lead to persecution and intolerance, as in the case of Hitler's treatment of the Jews.

The greater the extent of prejudice, the more its victims react against it; as a result, the original prejudice and intolerance are often increased. As Professor Woodard pointed out, our current scolding of prejudice has mainly had the effect of increasing it.

**Will education eliminate prejudice?** Our main resource in combating this dolorous outlook seemingly lies in education. But, as of this writing, formal education is shot through with prejudices, and even when it honestly seeks to divorce itself from prejudice the result is usually only the adoption of a new pattern of prejudice. Moreover, as the ideological battle gains in intensity, it is likely that the groups in control of society will insist that the educational system be an instrument of their ideas and will ruthlessly purge those educators who seek to check panic, recklessness, propaganda, and prejudice. This tendency is already well under way in the United States.

We may hope that some miracle will intervene to alter the apparent outlook, but it is obvious to any informed and clear-thinking observer that only a miracle will suffice to turn the trick and check the growth of prejudice.

Prejudice is kept alive and intensified by appealing to public opinion through the new methods of communication. We may turn now to a discussion of propaganda and the new and varied ways in which prejudices are built up, spread, and perpetuated in our day.

## The Development and Techniques of Propaganda

**Meaning of propaganda.** No factor in contemporary life is more powerful than propaganda, which has been defined as "the attempt to influence others to some predetermined end by appealing to their thought and feeling." Propaganda is a more powerful force today than ever before, because it is possible to reach a larger number of persons at the same time by means of motion pictures and printed or spoken words.

**Historical development of propaganda.** Propaganda is nothing new in history; it is as old as human speech itself. Primitive tradition handed on by word of mouth was propaganda, for it spread the beliefs and customs of the social group from one person to another; the group was kept together through its belief in the rightness of its own folkways. From primitive times to the present day, propaganda has been used in every phase of living. Even in our age of elaborately studied and planned propaganda we have never had greater masters of propaganda than Demosthenes and Cicero. The "glittering generalities" technique of propaganda reached its highest development in the rhetoric and oratory of Greece and Rome. The Christian religion was promoted, unified, and later split up by propaganda. Virtually all medieval political philosophy was propaganda for the Church or the State. In medieval and early modern times, kings and revolutionists both developed propaganda to support their conflicting interests. Later on, the bourgeoisie and the proletariat hurled all manner of propaganda into the most bitter social conflict of all history.

In the history of our own country, there have been innumerable instances of propaganda. For example, the American Revolution was launched and won by propaganda against England and the Loyalists. Our Constitution would probably not have been adopted save for the able propaganda carried on by the authors of *The Federalist*. The struggle over slavery produced a great wave of propaganda. William Lloyd Garrison's abolitionist pamphlets and Harriet Beecher Stowe's *Uncle Tom's Cabin* on the one side were met with A. T. Bledsoe's *An Essay on Liberty and Slavery,* and George Fitz-Hugh's *Sociology for the South* on the other. The period of reconstruction produced harsh propaganda against the Southerners. The answer was the rise of the Ku Klux Klan in the South and the bitter hatred of southern Democrats for northern Republicans. Labor and capital have fought with vigorous propaganda for the last seventy-five years. We entered the Spanish-American War mainly as the result of the most extensive program of journalistic propaganda organized and executed down to that time. Political propaganda was especially prominent in the campaigns of 1896 and 1912.

Propaganda during the first world war was more vigorous than in the Spanish-American War. Following the war, there was brisk propaganda for and against our entry into the League of Nations. It was also in this period that propaganda was developed into a "science," and that public relations agencies began to spring up. The New Deal provoked the most violent propaganda ever known in this country in peacetime, at least before the cold war that began in 1947.

**New facilities and enthusiasm for propaganda.** Today, the facilities for using propaganda successfully have been tremendously increased by the new devices and instruments of communication. In the summer of 1948, the prominent British publisher Lord Beaverbrook frankly declared: "I run my papers purely for the purpose of making propaganda, and with no other object." It is safe to assume that the only thing unique about Beaverbrook is his candor. Further, the sciences of psychology and sociology have given much new information on how to sway public opinion and shape private convictions. This new knowledge has promoted the rise of public relations agencies which have elevated propaganda to a profession and made it commercially available to those able and eager to purchase its potent services. The most varied groups have recognized the value of propaganda; today, in the United States, we have several thousand organizations which have been founded primarily for the purpose of molding public opinion through propaganda.

**The main devices of propaganda.** One of the leading authorities on propaganda, Clyde R. Miller, formerly director of the Institute for Propaganda Analysis, has listed what he considers the seven most common devices of propaganda. They are:

1. Name-calling
2. Glittering generalities
3. Transfer
4. Testimonial
5. Plain folks
6. Card-stacking
7. Band wagon

These devices are all designed to appeal to the emotions, rather than to the intellect. They endeavor to make us believe in a cause or product or take some definite action without pondering and weighing the issues carefully. Most propaganda devices are designed to appeal to our prejudices in matters of religion, race, politics, economics, and moral and social ideals. People whose prejudices are thus aroused may be swayed into making decisions without realizing that they are being manipulated.

**Name-calling.** The name-calling device is no more than a modern application of the old adage of "giving a good dog a bad name." If we dislike a person, we may prejudice others against him by calling him names associated with something considered loathsome or unworthy. For instance, to call a person a Communist, a fifth columnist, a Fascist sympathizer, an isolationist, a "Pink," a warmonger, or an Economic Royalist, although he may be nothing of the sort, will make many others dislike and distrust him. Name-calling is widely used in political campaigns. One of its most extensive recent uses was by

President Truman during the campaign of 1948 in attacking the 80th Congress, certain Republican leaders, and "plutocrats."

**Glittering generalities.** A glittering generality is a sweeping statement or slogan that is superficially agreeable and plausible. A person representing his program as a worthy cause by associating it with such noble sentiments as love, truth, honor, and patriotism is usually dealing in glittering generalities. The cause may not be actually worthy, but if the propagandist leads people into thinking it is by associating it with things they hold dear, he can usually win his point.

"Making the world safe for democracy" and "the war to end all war" were glittering generalities of the first world war, which obscured the true facts of why America entered the conflict. Republican slogans in the 1928 campaign—"the end of poverty" and "a chicken in every pot" —are other glittering generalities. President Roosevelt launched his "New Deal" administration with the especially appealing glittering generality that "we have nothing to fear except fear itself"; and as his slogan for the second world war, he invented perhaps the most influential glittering generality of all time—the "Four Freedoms."

That such propaganda may be justifiable or beneficial does not lessen the fact that it is still propaganda. Statements based not on scientific analysis but on emotional appeal, such as the advertisements for various complexion creams—"The skin you love to touch"—are glittering generalities of a simpler sort.

**Transfer.** When a policy or an idea is associated or identified with a symbol revered by the people of a country, such as God, the Cross, the Swastika, the Star of David, the Hammer and Sickle, the flag, or the family, then the device of propaganda is known as transfer. Newspaper cartoonists frequently make use of this device by employing the figure of Uncle Sam, the American Eagle, or the American Flag to imply that the mass of Americans favor the policy illustrated by the cartoonist.

**Guilt by association.** A very important and menacing utilization of the transfer device has been the development of the practice of conferring "guilt by association." According to this use of the transfer device, those who happen to hold the same views on a given action or policy are lumped together and held equally culpable, however different their general ideological attitudes or their political, social, and economic backgrounds. Accordingly, all those who opposed our entry into the second world war were identified with the Nazis and accused of pro-Nazism, whether they were Communists (before June 22, 1941), arch-conservatives, or patriotic liberals of international reputation. This notion of guilt by association was the basis of the government case in the mass-sedition trial of 1944, when the most conglomerate group was assembled for trial. After the second world war, all who opposed the cold war and the manipulation of the United States into the third world war were lumped together as communist sympathizers, whether they were members of the Communist party, reactionary Republicans, liberal pacifists, or responsible scholars and publicists whose views were based on honest and substantial convictions.   Ironically, many of the Communists and fellow-travelers, who had earlier been most eager partisans of the guilt-by-association technique, were themselves trapped by their own previous strategy when the Red hunt began in 1947.

**Testimonial.**   The testimonial device is a popular method of gaining public support by using the statement of a well-known person in behalf of a given article or cause.   It is most commonly used in newspaper, magazine, or radio advertising.   A good example is provided by a whiskey manufacturer's advertising device of associating numerous "men of distinction" with his product.   Endorsement by a President's wife or a movie star of a soap, a beauty preparation, a hair dressing, or a cigarette, will presumably help to sell the article.   Sometimes, the testimonial technique is used in connection with public issues.   A well-known individual condemns or approves a social issue; then, because he is believed and respected, many persons are induced to share his expressed opinions.   A program endorsed by the president of the American Federation of Labor or the CIO will influence large numbers of labor unionists.   The pronouncements of officials of the United States Chamber of Commerce or the National Association of Manufacturers will have great weight with businessmen.

**Plain folks.**   The plain-folks device is calculated to appeal to the great mass of Americans, who still like homely virtues.   It is most frequently used in political campaigns.   A candidate, photographed with a rake in his hand, working with the threshers, or kissing a baby, will get many votes from people who think he is one of them.   A candidate often appeals to sentiments of family affection by having his picture taken with his whole family.   If he has grandchildren to hold on his knee, so much the better—he will probably get more votes from grandparents.   Front porch campaigns give a common, homely touch.   If a candidate goes to country picnics and clambakes, or on fishing trips, his chances of election may be improved.   Senator O'Daniel of Texas, self-styled "Pass the Biscuits, Pappy," owed his election, both as governor and senator, in great part to the plain-folks "gag."   Senators Albert B. ("Happy") Chandler and Glen H. Taylor both gained their initial political popularity through their talents as crooners.   President Truman utilized the plain-folks appeal widely in 1948 by taking his family with him on his campaign train, exhibiting them on every plausible occasion, and referring to Mrs. Truman as "the Boss."   Despite all his efforts to pose as a farmer, Governor Dewey was lacking in the plain-folks appeal.

**Card-stacking.**   Card-stacking means rigging the game so that the real facts will be obscured.   Claims and statements are made on the basis of assumptions that are mostly fallacious, in the hope that the assertions will be taken for granted without any factual analysis.   The build-up of movie stars is a good example.

Confusing and misleading the public by card-stacking is a common policy of political candidates, big business, and labor interests. For instance, big business and financiers claimed that the sharp setback of business in the late summer and fall of 1937 occurred because the budget was not balanced. The business critics of the administration carefully avoided mention of the fact that one reason for the 1937 recession was that the President actually did try in that year to balance the budget. Another interesting case of card-stacking was afforded by the president of a rich and powerful university, who denounced labor for seeking a 40-hour week; he stated that he would like a 40-hour day. What he did not make clear was that most of his days (and nights) were spent in pleasant conversation, club life, and other leisure pursuits, and not in heavy manual labor in a foundry. Most coal miners would like a 40-hour day if it could be spent in convivial relaxation in exotic surroundings. President Truman stacked the cards in his violent attacks on the Republican Congress in 1948, for he concealed the fact that many Democrats in Congress also failed to vote for his policies, and that the preceding Democratic Congress had failed to pass much liberal legislation.

**The band wagon.** The band-wagon device is based on the old adage that "nothing succeeds like success." It appeals to the average person who wants to follow the crowd. If a person can be made to think that a cause will win, or is winning, he, not wishing to be left out, will get on the band wagon; that is, he will follow the crowd in joining and praising that particular cause. Many candidates for public office have used the band-wagon device. Governor Dewey exploited the band-wagon device in 1948, by his constant assumption that the Republicans were bound to win and that his election was a foregone conclusion from the moment of his nomination. The polls of public opinion in campaigns help along this propaganda device.

The public opinion polls have exerted much influence outside the field of politics. They have greatly affected the shaping of public opinion with respect to all forms of taste, style, manners, morals, economic trends, and the like. Many felt that they were in danger of reducing us to a "band-wagon civilization." Even the bad guessing of the pollsters in the election of 1948 only temporarily lessened their prestige. It failed to be ruinous to them as it did in the case of the ludicrous poll of the *Literary Digest* in 1936.

In all these seven methods, there is one fundamental appeal, namely, to emotion. If this emotional appeal were removed, any propaganda device would be all but useless, for logical reasoning by any informed person subjected to propaganda would rob the device of its magical power.

## Examples of Political Propaganda

**American political propaganda.** In order to understand what a powerful force propaganda is in American life today, let us look at some fields where it operates. Propaganda in politics, foreign affairs, business, religion, and education is the most important, but it permeates all phases of American life.

Politicians have made use of all the devices mentioned in the preceding paragraphs. The opponents of the New Deal vigorously attacked its policies by name-calling. Speaking for the conservative Liberty League, Alfred E. Smith implied that those who followed the New Deal were following Moscow rather than American traditions. The leaders of the New Deal used such propaganda devices as testimonial, transfer, the band wagon, and card-stacking to sell its policies to the American people. President Roosevelt made effective use of the transfer device when he linked up the New Deal with universal freedom and national defense, and of card-stacking when he said he had been drafted for a third term. Because, in part, of the bitter attacks made on it, the New Deal administration made wider use than ever before of governmental propaganda. The use of propaganda was greatly increased and intensified during the second world war and was vigorously continued in the postwar years.

Our political campaigns have made use of nearly all the propaganda devices in a variety of ways, of which we have already described some. Generally speaking, the use of propaganda has made political campaigns all but useless as efforts to enlighten the public about candidates and policies. As we noted in earlier chapters dealing with political problems, there has been a vast increase in the propaganda carried on by quasi-political private pressure groups since the Hatch Acts of 1939 and 1940 severely limited the use of funds by public party organizations.

The radio and telegraph have been used in novel ways in carrying on political propaganda. Father Coughlin persuaded thousands of his radio audience to flood Congress with telegrams, urging them to vote against the entrance of the United States into the World Court; the response is generally credited with having influenced enough Senators to defeat the proposal. The electric utilities later used this same device, and showered Congress with telegrams at the time when the Wheeler-Rayburn bill to curb utility holding companies was under consideration. In this case, the propaganda was especially unscrupulous, because many names were picked from telephone directories at random and were signed to the telegrams without the knowledge of the persons whose names were used. During the drive against the Supreme Court reorganization bill in 1937, newspaper publishers and editors exhorted their readers to put pressure on Congress to defeat the measure. Congressmen were so deluged with letters and telegrams that the New Deal administration was once described by Secretary Harold Ickes as "mail-order government."

The political propaganda in the United States during and after the New Deal has not been exclusively a matter of pelting Washington lawmakers and officials with propaganda from without the Capitol.

Government bureaus and departments have developed a vast counter-propaganda activity, particularly through their public information services. In the year 1946, these bureau and department services spent no less than 75 million dollars directly on information and propaganda, and indirect expenditures may have been as large. Much of the material sent out was designed to extol the work and defend the programs of the bureaus and departments involved and to check any efforts made in Congress or elsewhere to curtail their staffs or activities. Those who suggested reforms or retrenchment were often denounced as seeking to endanger our national safety.

**Nazi propaganda.** But political propaganda has gone far beyond supporting or opposing laws, candidates, or parties. Whole systems of government have been founded upon and supported by propaganda. The government of Nazi Germany was one of the best examples. In Germany, there was a Ministry for Propaganda, headed by Dr. Joseph Goebbels. Goebbels openly expressed his contempt for mass intelligence and proved himself able to rule the mass mind by propaganda. Goebbels was the first great propagandist openly to exploit the fact that the human race is of simian heritage and descent. He frankly based his propaganda techniques on "monkey appeal." The methods used by the Nazis were ably summarized by the Institute of Propaganda Analysis in its bulletin of May, 1938.

The Nazis made great use of vague and high-sounding slogans—glittering generalities—such as honor, sacrifice, leadership, comradeship, and racial purity. They stressed the fact that they worked only for the common good and to rescue German national honor from the disgrace of the first world war and the Versailles treaty. The transfer device was used to give Hitler and his associates great prestige. An effort was made to confer on Hitler the quality of a god; in fact, the prestige and authority of God, race, and nation were freely used to bolster up the policies of the Nazis. Whatever Hitler sanctioned had to be right.

The elaborate propaganda and censorship system maintained by the Ministry for Propaganda enabled the Nazis to make good use of the card-stacking device. Only what the government approved could be said in newspapers, books, or magazines, on the air, or in the films. Even personal conversations were subject to censorship. The cards were so well stacked that scarcely any opposition to the beliefs and practices of the Nazis was ever heard. Offenders were subject to drastic punishment. The band-wagon device was used in the great patriotic demonstrations, the Nazi congresses, and the occasions when Hitler spoke to "his people." Those affairs gave the impression that everyone in Germany was behind Hitler and his policies. Nazi propaganda destroyed all traces of democracy and built up a strong state based on an appeal to the emotions instead of the intelligence of the German people.

**Soviet propaganda.** The totalitarian government of Soviet Russia makes as extensive use of propaganda as did Nazi Germany, though Russia has never produced a master of propaganda technique of Goebbels' caliber or ruthless cleverness. The Russian authorities carry on a ceaseless propaganda in behalf of the Marxist ideology of the Soviet system. This defends and eulogizes the Soviet achievements and leaders by all the standard methods of adroit propaganda and smears the opponents of the Russian system. Stalin is sanctified, as Hitler was in Nazi propaganda. During and since the second world war, Russia has sloughed off much of its former internationalism and become more nationalistic. Hence, the government has revived and glorified the national military heroes from Russia's tsarist past, like Alexander Nevsky, conqueror of the Teutonic Knights, Alexander Suvorov, the greatest Russian military genius of the eighteenth century, and General Kutusov and Prince Bagration, opponents of Napoleon at Borodino. During the cold war with the United States following 1947, Soviet Russia has developed an elaborate propaganda asserting the warlike intentions of the United States and the Anglo-American bloc generally.

**Propaganda in the second world war.** Mussolini carried on expansionist propaganda in his Ethiopian foray. Hitler maintained constant propaganda against the Treaty of Versailles and the Soviet Union and in favor of German commercial expansion and so-called Aryan supremacy.

The propaganda before hostilities was nearly as rampant in the United States. For example, there were: Roosevelt's emphasis on Axis plans for literal world domination, his assertion of a Nazi plan to invade the United States—the notorious Hitler "timetable to invade Iowa" via Dakar, Brazil, and Mexico—and his declaration that the war aims of the United States were to extend the Four Freedoms to the world and build up a world organization to curb aggressors and preserve peace. Roosevelt used name-calling effectively, for example, by designating the Nazis as "rattlesnakes," and American peace leaders as twentieth-century Benedict Arnolds. The attack on Pearl Harbor automatically became a propaganda event of the first magnitude for it provided the basis for President Roosevelt's famous speech of December 8, 1941, and his "day of infamy" indictment served to win over many people reluctant heretofore to the idea of war.

When the second world war broke out, propaganda naturally became more extensive and vehement. Hitler redoubled his propaganda against Jews and international capitalists, whom he accused of starting the war. After June 22, 1941, Nazi propaganda against Russia became more fierce and voluminous than ever, and Russia responded in kind. The name-calling device, which appeals to the emotions of hate and fear, was used by Goebbels to attack everything which could be called a liberal, democratic institution. "Liberals" were denounced by the

Nazis as insipid, decadent, and unprincipled. To be a liberal or believe in the "stupid" doctrine of equality was, for Goebbels, to be a "lily-livered Red."

In the United States, after Pearl Harbor, Japan and the "Yellow Peril" added fuel to the propaganda flames, and the Japanese were declared to be still in the ape stage of biological evolution. The Italians were branded a decayed and dying race; the Germans were portrayed as incurably depraved and deserving of extermination. The devastation wrought by Nazi bombing and the destruction of whole cities or towns like Coventry and Lidice were luridly played up, as were the alleged bombings of hospitals, schools, and Red Cross stations.

**Postwar Propaganda.** After the war, propaganda was continued in the interests of international organization and for the alleged purpose of making war less acceptable in the future. The Nuremberg and Tokyo trials were based on the essentially propagandic issue of "aggressive war" as a crime.[3]

The most elaborate development of propaganda after the war accompanied the cold war between the United States and Russia. The Russians accused the Americans of lining up the rest of the world against the Soviet Union and of provocative and warlike intentions. The United States charged Russia with bad faith, with the violation of wartime and postwar agreements, with aggressive designs, with absorbing satellite nations, with a program of world conquest, with fifth-column activities, and the like. The United States organized a radio program called "The Voice of America" to bombard Europe with propaganda designed to give a favorable impression of this country and its policies and to undermine the prestige of Russia.

Even the main international conferences and the meetings of the United Nations degenerated in part into propaganda battles carried on under the guise of "open diplomacy." The troubles in Palestine extended the orgy of propaganda. A main item in the propaganda for the Marshall Plan was that it would defend free enterprise in Europe against the onrush of collectivism, though it was evident to informed observers that virtually all the nations to be aided by the Plan were irrevocably committed to some type of collectivist economy.

## How Business and Labor Use Propaganda

**Propaganda methods of business and labor.** Probably wider use is made of propaganda in business than in any other field of modern life. We are familiar with propaganda methods in every type of advertising. The glittering generality, transfer, testimonial, and band-wagon devices are extensively employed. Sometimes, the reverse testimonial device, in the form of whispering campaigns conducted by

---

3 See below, pp. 843–846.

rivals, seeks to discredit some product—for example, by alleging that tubercular laborers are employed in making a certain brand of cigarettes.

In the struggle between capital and labor, there has been frequent use of propaganda, especially the name-calling technique. Labor union leaders never run out of names to call industrial leaders—"plutocrats," for example—while many capitalists frequently call all labor unions "communistic."

**Card-stacking tactics.** Card-stacking is also widely used by both groups. A notable example was the bitter attack on labor early in 1942, charging that defense industries were being paralyzed by strikes. Even reactionary senators who looked into the situation admitted that the production loss from strikes was only the smallest fraction of the loss of output from the previous refusal or reluctance of employers to co-operate with the government in converting to defense production. The extensive series of strikes in 1946 was represented by great business interests as a deliberate conspiracy against the prosperity and integrity of the nation, though most of them were intended, however unwisely, merely to conserve some of labor's wartime gains in the face of rising prices and the increased cost of living. Another method of card-stacking employed by big business is the ever-present propaganda about the virtues of free enterprise, though, through various production agreements and price-fixing arrangements, business itself has limited industrial freedom as much as has all government intervention.

Labor frequently stacks the cards by representing even senseless jurisdictional and other obstructive strikes as a desperate effort to raise standards of living. A further example of card-stacking by labor was the bitter propaganda against the Taft-Hartley Act in 1947–1949, though a poll of representative labor organizations showed approval of most of the crucial individual clauses of the Act.[4]

**Business propaganda programs.** Big business employs propaganda to sell the American people the idea that it gives outstanding and unique encouragement to economic progress, without any drawbacks. A slogan such as "What serves progress, serves America," is an example of the use of both glittering generalities and transfer by big business. Of late, big business has made a vigorous effort, through the transfer device, to identify its policies with the "American Way."

Big business has made good use of the facilities of the press, radio, and the movies in selling itself to the American public. The National Association of Manufacturers syndicated a daily editorial feature in the leading newspapers known as "You and Your Nation's Affairs," and a cartoon known as "Uncle Abner." These stressed the contribution of business to public welfare, the virtues of competition, and the evils of government interference.

---

4 See *Look,* September 30, 1947; and *Reader's Digest,* January, 1948.

# HOW THE PRESSURE GROUPS WORK

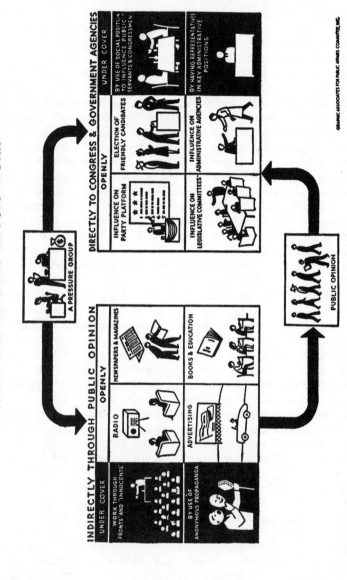

Graphic presentation of methods and operations utilized by the most powerful forces in controlling American life today.

The National Association of Manufacturers also issued a series of films, such as "The Light of a Nation," "Men and Machines," and "The Floodtide." These tried to show that machines do not destroy jobs; they defended free competition; and they extolled the high standards of living enjoyed under the American Way.

The radio is also used. A popular radio program, also sponsored by the National Association of Manufacturers, was the "American Family Robinson," which praised the virtues of free business enterprise and denounced the evils of labor unionism and government interference. Another effective radio program was the "Ford Sunday Evening Hour," which, by employing the transfer device, identified the "Ford way" with the American Way. The plain-folks device was much used, and Mr. Ford's homely ways were stressed. The music of the hour usually ended with a good old hymn, popular in rural areas.

Business has cleverly exploited the recent trends in American foreign policy and political propaganda. The Federal government has justified our interference abroad and the cold war on the ground that it is a struggle of freedom and urbanity against tyranny and terror. Business has adroitly joined up with this line of thought and, on many radio programs, stresses daily the allegation that private business provides the sinews of American freedom and that our free enterprise is more productive than any other economy on earth.

**Subtle foundation propaganda.** Sometimes, a more subtle means of propaganda is used instead of testimonials, card-stacking, and the like. Some business psychologists know that, if a company boasts too much or too openly about its product, people may become prejudiced against it. For this reason, the advertisers adopt an indirect method. So-called institutes or "research" foundations are created, and these serve, by the transfer technique, to give the voice of authority and dignity to the propaganda. "Studies" made by supposedly learned scientists, research chemists, engineers, or labor experts are more effective in breaking down prejudice and instilling confidence than flat statements made in praise of a product or a policy by its manufacturer or promoter. The people do not know that these "experts" may be in the pay of the propagandists and advertisers, or that, if the investigations themselves are honestly conducted, the conclusions are warped, distorted, or exaggerated in the advertising or propaganda. The public relations agencies have done the most to encourage this more subtle approach to influencing public opinion. Nearly all clever propaganda today is deftly handled by public relations agencies.

## Propaganda in Religion and Education

**Devices of religious propaganda.** Propaganda against the Jews and other religious sects or denominations by rival sects and denominations uses all the familiar devices. The Lord's Day Alliance has carried on an extensive propaganda designed to keep "Blue Sundays" and to prevent saloons, recreation places, movie theaters, and other distracting enterprises from doing business on Sunday. A powerful type of religious and moral propaganda was conducted by the Anti-Saloon League and other organizations defending Prohibition, making special use of name-calling and card-stacking. Propagandists for the liquor interests responded in kind by seeking to show that the manufacture of beer, wines, and whiskey was essential to the prosperity of the nation and, by providing employment, reduced misery, crime, and vice.

**Educational propaganda.** In the field of education, much use has been made of the devices of propaganda. One of the best examples of propaganda in education has been super-patriotic teaching, based mainly on glittering generalities. Such instruction gives the impression that the institutions, particularly the political institutions, of one's country, must be superior to the institutions of any other country. It instills the idea that one's nation has always been right in its dealings with other states and has always waged just wars and won them. This super-patriotic instruction has reached its most extreme development in totalitarian countries.

Education has on occasion been directly linked up with the vested economic interests and their propaganda. Private institutions supported by endowments vigorously oppose heavy taxes on the wealthy who contribute to their support. In many instances, spokesmen for these institutions have protested against the taxation and public-spending policies of the government, by asserting that taxation for public welfare will undermine and impoverish all learning, research, and cultural activities. The transfer device is used in this connection by attributing the existence of all culture and education to wealth and to the endowments and foundations established by the wealthy. In Soviet Russia, on the other hand, educational propaganda glorifies Communism.

## How to Prevent Propaganda from Undermining Democracy and Liberalism

**The propaganda threat to democracy.** Propaganda can be dangerous to democracy and liberalism. Even in a country like ours, where there is still much freedom of speech and the press, it is usually the wealthiest group that can carry on the most extensive and successful propaganda, since mass propaganda requires money to command attention. Thus, when the more powerful interests are opposed to democratic ideas, the democratic way of life is in danger.

Propaganda is a menace to democracy in another way. Successful democracy requires intelligent voting by every citizen. But modern propaganda is rarely designed to give people the facts on public issues. Propaganda, with its emotional appeal, either makes still more extreme the previous prejudices of the average voter or so confuses him that he cannot arrive at any clear understanding of the public issues at stake. Today, as never before, accurate knowledge and calm judgment are needed about national and international affairs, but the average person is often so confused by conflicting propaganda that he is badly muddled in his judgments. Or, propaganda may, in other cases, lead to blind rage, as in the case of witch-hunting, rather than to mere confusion. In either case, there is little opportunity for intelligence to assert itself.

Our country is founded on freedom of speech and thought; every class must be able to express itself. If we are to preserve our democracy, propaganda should not be suppressed, but steps must be taken to study and expose propaganda methods.

**Possible means of combating propaganda.** To expose the ways of propaganda is easy, but to get sufficient publicity for such an exposure is very difficult. Propaganda has such a strangle-hold over the press, the radio, and the movies that to find an effective means of discrediting it with the public becomes a serious problem. Those interested in getting the truth before the public are relatively few and lacking in financial resources. Some hold that the main source of relief is for the government, in some way, to see to it that money and political intimidation are not the only, or even the main, way of gaining access to public opinion. The trouble here is that the government is becoming ever more devoted to propaganda rather than truth and is itself a main source of political intimidation and bias. Government intervention may well mean, not less propaganda, but only less propaganda opposing the ideology and policies of the party and administration in power.

Not all propaganda is bad. We can stamp democratic and liberal principles even more firmly on people's minds by sound propaganda measures. Therefore, analysis is needed to determine which propaganda is good and which is bad for democracy. The public policies of the nation can be so shaped by propaganda as to uphold or to overthrow our democracy. We should not try to outlaw bad propaganda, for to do so is contrary to democratic principles. It would set a precedent that might lead to unlimited suppression of all ideas opposed to those of the ruling clique. Everybody should be given the right to express his ideas. But, in case harmful propaganda is given free expression, there must be equal freedom and opportunity to expose it. The proper procedure for a democracy is to keep all channels of communication open to all groups, and to rely on fearless education to expose dangerous propaganda.

**Outlook for dealing with the propaganda menace.** Since prejudice and propaganda are interdependent and inseparably related—prejudice always leading to propaganda as its means of expression—what we said earlier about the grave prospect that prejudice will grow and spread rather than subside in the generation or so to come also applies to the outlook for propaganda. As we go on in a period of sweeping and unsettling social change, of a cold war, of intense ideological struggles both at home and in foreign relations, of purges and witch-hunting, it is inevitable that propaganda will be more voluminous, crude, and ruthless.   And the communication agencies for spreading it are likely to become more efficient with the introduction of television and other innovations.   The popularity of unscrupulous propagandists employing the smear technique well illustrates the increasing emotional tension.

## Summary

Prejudice is a bias, whether a like or a dislike, and propaganda is a means used to build up either favorable or unfavorable prejudices toward persons, groups, ideas, or products.

We find prejudice in all fields of American life.   There is political, economic, legal, religious, moral, racial, and educational prejudice. Democracy is threatened by prejudice, since those who try to force their opinions on groups often suppress liberty.   The totalitarian countries were able, by effective use of propaganda, to suppress all semblance of democracy.

The outlook for the elimination of prejudice is grave.   There are still signs of racial prejudice.   Economic prejudice is growing, and religious and political prejudice is still strong.   But the main reason why it will be difficult to check prejudice is that the present period of social change increases the sense of economic and social insecurity that is at the root of all fears and prejudices.   Another reason for anticipating an increase of prejudice is the cold war between the Anglo-American bloc of nations and Soviet Russia and her satellites. This intensifies nationalism and the clash of ideologies, both of which stimulate fear and hatred.

Propaganda is an effort to control the thought and actions of people by various forms of emotional appeal.   There are seven main devices used by propagandists—name-calling, glittering generalities, transfer, testimonial, plain folks, card-stacking, and the band wagon.   All of these are used by propagandists in politics, foreign affairs, business, religion, and education.   Public opinion polls threaten us with a band wagon civilization.

Propaganda can be a threat to democracy.   Even in a country like ours, where there is still considerable freedom of speech and expression, certain wealthy and powerful groups may spend large sums on propaganda in the effort to make the mass of people believe in un-American or undemocratic ideas.   But the danger is not wholly from the wealthy. Certain warmongering liberals and radicals at times develop attitudes and policies as inimical to democracy and liberty as those of the so-called plutocrats.

Dangerous propaganda can be combated only by revealing the methods used by propagandists and by keeping the channels of communication open to all classes and opinions.

## Selected References

\* Albig, William, *Public Opinion*, McGraw-Hill, 1939. A large and comprehensive work, and one of the best books dealing with the genesis of public opinion.

Baus, H. M., *Public Relations at Work*, Harper, 1949. Highly favorable exposition of the field and operations of the public relations profession.

Beard, C. A., *President Roosevelt and the Coming of the War, 1941*, Yale University Press, 1948. Part I of this book is a masterly presentation of the propaganda which led the United States into the second world war.

Bernays, E. L., *Crystallizing Public Opinion*, Liveright, 1934. Sympathetic account of propaganda and the profession of public relations by the leading public relations counsel of our day.

\* Cantril, Hadley, *Gauging Public Opinion*, Princeton University Press, 1944. Sympathetic account of the public opinion polls.

Clinchy, E. R., *All in the Name of God*, Day, 1934. An able discussion of religious prejudice by a leader in the movement to promote religious unity and toleration.

Doob, Leonard, *Propaganda: Its Psychology and Technique*, Holt, 1935. A pioneer work on the nature, motives, and methods of propaganda.

\* ————, *Public Opinion and Propaganda*, Holt, 1948. Revision and elaboration of the earlier book.

Finot, Jean, *Race Prejudice*, Dutton, 1907. An able work, but written before the rise of recent racial propaganda and the theories of race superiority.

Gallup, George, *A Guide to Public Opinion Polls*, Princeton University Press, 1948. Authoritative defense of polling methods and objectives by the pioneer pollster.

Harral, Stewart, *Patterns of Publicity Copy*, University of Oklahoma Press, 1950. Interesting recent book on methods of publicity agents and publicity directors.

Hays, A. G., *Trial by Prejudice*, Covici, Friede, 1933. A leading liberal lawyer discusses the effect of racial, religious, political, and economic prejudice on the administration of American justice.

Irion, F. C., *Public Opinion and Propaganda*, Crowell, 1950. The most recent and comprehensive book dealing with propaganda and the formation of public opinion. .

Jastrow, Joseph, *The Betrayal of Intelligence*, Greenberg, 1938. Important book suggesting possible ways of combating prejudice and propaganda.

Keith, Arthur, *The Place of Prejudice in Modern Civilization*, Day, 1931. A great English anthropologist argues in a small book that prejudice, especially race prejudice, is a valuable dynamic force in promoting competition and progress.

\* Lavine, Harold, and Wechsler, James, *War Propaganda and the United States,* Yale University Press, 1940. Good preliminary exposure of propaganda methods seeking to involve the United States in the second world war.

Linebarger, P. M. A., *Psychological Warfare,* Infantry Journal Press, 1948. Interesting and informing survey of propaganda techniques, objectives and achievements in the second world war.

Lippmann, Walter, *Public Opinion,* Macmillan, 1927. The classic study of mental sterotypes and their influence on public opinion.

Lumley, F. E., *The Propaganda Menace,* Appleton-Century, 1933. A sociologist expounds at length the dangers of prejudice and propaganda to democracy and liberty.

Meier, N. C., and Saunders, H. W. (Eds.), *The Polls and Public Opinion,* Holt, 1949. Symposium on the methods, effects, and limitations of public opinion polls.

\* Miller, C. R., *The Process of Persuasion,* Crown Publishers, 1946. The best introduction to the meaning and methods of propaganda by the world's chief critical authority on the subject.

Mosteller, F.. *et al. The Pre-Election Polls of 1948,* Social Research Council, 1949. Symposium on the failure of the polls in the 1948 election campaign, including a fine analysis of the polling process.

Munson, Gorham (Ed.), *Twelve Decisive Battles of the Mind,* Greystone Press, 1942. Interesting exposition and analysis of great historic controversies in the past in which propaganda has played a decisive rôle.

\* Peterson, H. C., *Propaganda for War,* University of Oklahoma Press, 1939. A brilliant account of the propaganda that led the United States into the first world war.

Read, J. M., *Atrocity Propaganda,* Yale University Press, 1941. An able presentation of the atrocity lies which so deeply affected American public opinion during the first world war.

Smith, C. W., *Public Opinion in a Democracy,* Prentice-Hall, 1947. Good study of publicity and propaganda methods.

Stouffer, S. A., *et al., Public Opinion and Communication,* American Journal of Sociology, 1950. Able symposium on communication and public opinion formation in contemporary society.

Valentin, Hugo, *Anti-Semitism Historically and Critically Examined,* Viking, 1936. A detailed survey of the basis and nature of anti-Semitism, but with little attention to the Nazi campaign ,against the Jews.

Warburg, J. P., *The Unwritten Treaty,* Harcourt, Brace, 1946. Account of the activities of the Office of War Information and of psychological warfare in the second world war.

# CHAPTER XXII

# The Challenge of Censorship to Democracy and Freedom

## The Nature and Development of Censorship

**Nature and leading forms of censorship.** Censorship is any attempt to place restrictions on free expression. Censorship may be physical, as in the case of a deaf-mute; mental, and by mental censorship we usually mean self-restraint, however motivated; or official, and enforced by law. The official restraints are those with which we are here mainly concerned, though we shall deal also with relevant, related mental restraints.

There are three chief forms of official restraints: (1) libel and slander laws, which restrain written or spoken assertions about persons and private business enterprises; (2) sedition laws, and "contempt of court" practices, which restrict the free expression of ideas concerning government and public officials; and (3) obscenity laws, which forbid the expression of ideas that may offend against decency. In addition to laws, we have both official and informal regulations affecting the giving out of opinions or news in any country. These regulations control both news printed at home and that sent out of the country by the press, cable, or the radio.

Censorship is an ancient institution. In early Roman times, the censor was at first a collector of taxes; later in the Roman period, he passed judgment on morals. In early modern times, following the invention of printing, the censor superintended the licensing of the press. Today, he is an officer who, in one capacity or another, has authority over what can be printed, presented in pictures, produced in the theater, shown in the movies, or broadcast over the air.

**Evolution of censorship.** Primitive peoples were very alert to censor anything which did not accord with traditional thought and usages. Forbidden thoughts and actions were usually covered by taboos. Rulers in the ancient Near East were equally vigorous in censoring novelty in thought and action. In Greek and Roman times, books, which existed only in manuscript form, were rarely censored, and authors freely criticized the government and society. This freedom existed largely because there were few copies of books; and, since these could not be widely circulated, they were not especially injurious to the general public or dangerous to the government. Moreover, the masses were illiterate and could not have read "dangerous" books, even if copies had fallen into their hands. In Greek and Roman days, speeches and orations were more often censored than books, for such rhetorical exercises were more likely to influence public opinion.

In the medieval period, the manufacture and sale of books were mostly in the hands of the monks and were controlled by the Church. In the Middle Ages, when persons not connected with the church tried to write or sell books, the Church often attempted to censor their activities. If a churchman wrote something the church regarded as dangerous, he also was severely censored. Not until the invention of printing in the middle of the fifteenth century, however, was the church able to exercise a systematic censorship over books.

The invention of printing, by enabling thousands of copies of books and pamphlets to be quickly distributed, raised new and more serious problems of censorship. The governments, usually spurred on by the Church, undertook censorship by licensing printing presses; by preparing lists of prohibited books; and by placing heavy penalties on those who printed books without a license, sold forbidden books, or had in their possession illegally printed materials. The famous Catholic Index of Prohibited Books was first published by Pope Paul IV in 1559. In ever expanded form it has continued to our own day.

There was sweeping censorship of books in both Protestant and Catholic countries in early modern times. Its general effect was to retard the spread of information and the progress of enlightenment. Protestant countries, however, relaxed their rigid censorship sooner than did the Catholic nations. Further, with less unity of opinion or authority in Protestant countries, it was difficult for them to enforce a consistent censorship.

In the seventeenth and eighteenth centuries, such writers as John Milton, Montesquieu, Voltaire, Thomas Paine and William Godwin made vigorous attacks on the censorship of pamphlets and books. In the United States, John Peter Zenger and Thomas Jefferson took up the cause of the freedom of the press. Jefferson regarded a free press as one of the most important elements of a real democracy—even more important than government.

While there has never been complete freedom of the press in the United States, there was a great deal of freedom down to 1860. There were, as yet, no obscenity laws imposing restrictions on books offending the public decency, and the right of debate and petition was freely allowed. In fact, until the period of the first world war, there was comparative freedom of the press, despite some annoying and infantile obscenity laws passed in the 1870's and 1880's. During the war, a thoroughgoing, almost universal, system of censorship arose. When the war ended, political censorship was relaxed to a certain extent, but the freedom of the press remained hampered by sedition and obscenity laws.

With the rise of Fascism and Communism in recent years, censorship became one of the most powerful weapons of the dictators in suppressing the freedom of speech and press. The second world war produced a thoroughgoing censorship in all the countries involved. It was not fully removed after the war. Russia and its satellites maintained a so-called Iron Curtain of censorship. The occupation forces thoroughly censored speech and press in central Europe and Japan. More freedom was restored in England and the United States, but witch hunts in the latter country kept alive a spirit of intimidation.

## Types of Censors and Censorship

**Censorship policies and practices.** In the United States, there is little peacetime censorship of books or newspaper material before printing. Some European countries, especially totalitarian states, do not permit the publication of books, pamphlets, and magazine and newspaper articles until they have been censored. There is a general pre-broadcasting censorship of radio manuscripts in the United States. The fear of loss of advertisers and of slander and libel suits has made the broadcasting companies exceedingly careful to prevent any material that might be considered libelous or slanderous from being broadcast. As we shall also see later on, motion pictures are carefully censored before release.

**Informal and unofficial censors.** In the United States, today, there are several kinds of censors—private, semi-official, and official. The unofficial or private censors are persons who have no official capacity but express their opinions informally and voluntarily. They may write to newspapers protesting against a play or movie they do not like; they may go to legislators and propose censorship laws; or they may approach the police and ask for the arrest of a publisher or the closing of a theater. While these censors have no official authority, they exert much influence by frightening authors, producers, and public speakers into censoring or suppressing their own material.

Private censorship also may take the form of refusal by a publisher to publish books that present opinions of which he disapproves. Or, booksellers may refuse to sell books they dislike, whatever their merit or the public demand.

**Semi-official censorship.** The semi-official censors are private individuals or organizations who work closely with those public authorities who have the legal right to suppress books, plays, and movies. Good examples of the semi-official type of censor are the New York Society for the Suppression of Vice, and the Watch and Ward Society of Boston. Such organizations bring to the attention of the authorities materials which they believe should be censored and obtain special privileges in the courts in informing and aiding the prosecutors. They have even censured and tried to intimidate judges who hear censorship cases. The New York Society for the Suppression of Vice has taken the lead in the field of semi-official censorship. It has gained prominence and authority, because most of the important publishing houses and theaters are concentrated in New York City. The Society's activities have been unpopular with publishers and producers because it will give no opinion on a book until it has been published or on a play before production.

Another form of semi-official censorship exists in connection with the central bureaus of publicity set up in the Cabinet departments in Washington during the first world war and still operating. These bureaus control the information given out to the press by the departments.

**Official censors and censorship.** There are several types of official censors. In the states and cities, censorship authority is given to the police, commissioners of licenses, and moving picture censors, who prevent "objectionable" plays and movies from being presented, or close them down speedily. The state courts have power to suppress books. In the Federal government, wide powers of censorship are given to the Post Office Department, whose officials can refuse to let material go through the mail if they regard it as improper. The postal authorities can thus exert a strong restraining influence upon what the public may read in all cases where literature must go through the mail. The Customs officials also have considerable influence on censorship, since they can prevent allegedly objectionable foreign books, pictures, and films from entering the country.

## Censorship of Publications and Entertainment Under Obscenity and Libel Laws

**Comstockery.** Except in wartime, most censorship of publications and entertainment in the United States is carried on at the instigation of unofficial and semi-official censors. The man who started this procedure was Anthony Comstock (1844–1915), who founded the New York Society for the Suppression of Vice in 1873, and obtained financial support from rich New York bankers. He secured the passage of many anti-obscenity statutes, which even included the outlawing of birth-control information. Peacetime censorship outside the political field in the United States has been almost wholly a product of the work of Comstock and his followers. Comstock once boasted that he had brought about 2,500 prosecutions of those who did not share his moral and artistic views and had destroyed 80 tons of indecent literature.

Most suppression of books, plays, and pamphlets has been executed under the obscenity laws, especially the New York statute of 1884, which are designed to protect the public from reading, hearing, or seeing anything which may offend traditional standards of decency, as interpreted by Comstock and his successor. At present, it is often difficult for an author or publisher to know whether a publication will be regarded as obscene by some state authority, local board, or private group. The usual procedure is to print the book or produce the play, await arrest, stand trial, and secure the verdict. If the verdict is favorable, the book is allowed to be circulated or the play produced; otherwise, they are suppressed. Fear of obscenity laws has operated as an effective pre-censorship force in many instances.

**Censorship often gives added popularity.** Sometimes, censorship makes for increased popularity of the work censored. A censored book will often become a best seller if people hear that it has been suppressed in some quarters. John Steinbeck's *Grapes of Wrath* was widely read by many persons after they found it was suppressed by their local library boards. One book, *The Well of Loneliness,* sold only 5,000 copies in England before being censored, but 200,000 copies were sold in the United States after attempts were made to suppress it. James Joyce's *Ulysses* owed some of its vast popularity to censorship. There is little doubt that Kathleen Winsor's *Forever Amber* and Edmund Wilson's *Memoirs of Hecate County* gained much additional publicity and circulation as a result of attempts to suppress them. Stage plays and movies also have occasionally gained great popularity from the demand that they be suppressed.

**Victories over obscenity censorship.** A number of legal victories have been able to check to some degree the inroads upon the freedom of publication made by various state obscenity laws, especially the New York law of 1884. Much of the credit for this can be assigned to the legal work of Morris L. Ernst. One of his latest exploits was the resounding victory won when censors in the state of Massachusetts sought to suppress *Forever Amber.* Notable also was the *Esquire* case, in 1945, in which Federal Judge Thurman W. Arnold rebuked the censorship activities of the United States Post Office in what was one of the great free-press legal opinions of modern times. The greatest victory over the censors was won, however, in March, 1948, when the notorious New York statute of 1884 was set aside by the United States Supreme Court. This law had banned the sale of publications devoted to details of "bloodshed, lust and crime," and had been the cornerstone of the censorship edifice in New York State. More books and other publications had been suppressed under this statute than under any other in the country.

**Libel laws and suits.** Libel laws are in some cases a more effective type of indirect censorship than the obscenity laws. Libel laws are powerful, because they frighten newspaper publishers, who fear unfair verdicts by emotional juries swayed by clever lawyers. It is often a simple matter to secure liberal damages in a libel suit, and unscrupulous persons frequently try to take advantage of this fact by bringing suit over imaginary or trivial libels. Indeed, libel "rackets" have been engineered in many intances by lawyers who bring to the attention of individuals the possibility of libel suits, even though the persons allegedly libeled had not previously thought of seeking redress.

Because of the libel laws, it is often difficult for the public to get the truth about commercial products. Publishers of books and news-

Press Association, Inc.

Leading censors: Anthony Comstock and John S. Sumner.

Outstanding opponents of censorship: Morris L. Ernst and Alexander Lindey.

papers are always in danger of a libel suit if they criticize a commercial product, however honest or true the criticism may be. There is thus, a natural inclination to refrain from unfavorable comment on commercial articles, however fraudulent their claims. Again, the large revenue from advertisements persuades the average newspaper publisher to accept advertising material containing praise of commodities about which he may have grave personal doubts or open contempt. Certain organizations and consumer publications with no advertising interests at stake have challenged libel threats and have done something to remedy the abuses.

## Political Censorship

**Sedition laws.** Political censorship has become a more serious problem in our day. The majority of the American states during and after the first world war passed sedition laws outlawing "revolutionary" views, oral or written. At one time, some 36 states had laws making the expression of the very ideas on which our Declaration of Independence was based a criminal offense. Even stalwart erstwhile libertarians like Justice Oliver Wendell Holmes succumbed to the wartime hysteria. During and after the first world war there were several sedition trials that alarmed friends of civil liberties; the worst miscarriage of justice was the conviction of Eugene Debs, the able Socialist leader, for uttering much the same words as did President Wilson shortly after the war.

There have been many different interpretations of the term "seditions." Sometimes, mild expressions of opinion against obvious economic and political evils have been regarded as seditious. The most sensible idea about seditious doctrines is the "clear and present danger" interpretation offered by the late Justice Holmes.[1] The Supreme Court's recent inclination to accept this view of the matter has not prevented abuses by Congressional committees and administrative officers. The Smith Act of 1940, making it a crime to advocate overthrowing the government by violence, if upheld by the Supreme Court, would open the way to extensive political censorship.

**Recent censorship of news.** Even more effective than sedition laws, however, as a means of suppressing the information needed by citizens to understand both the domestic and foreign problems of our times is the widespread public or official censorship of news on a national scale in large parts of the world. Not since the era of licensing presses in the sixteenth and seventeenth centuries has there been such extensive political censorship in peacetime as now exists throughout most of the civilized world. In January, 1950, the New York *Times* published the results of a competent survey showing that more than a fourth of the populated area of the world is subject to strict censorship of news. This is probably an understatement.

This overwhelming wave of censorship started with the first world war, as part of the general campaign of wartime propaganda. It was natural that each country engaged in the war should seek to have pub-

---

[1] See above, p. 423.

lished only information favorable to its side and attempt to exclude, as completely as possible, any news considered favorable to the enemy. Censored were not only books and newspapers but also all letters sent by soldiers to relatives and friends.

After the war came the rise of Communism in Russia, the development of Fascism in Germany and Italy, and the suppression of democracy in other countries. In the totalitarian states, there was not even any pretense of maintaining civil liberty. Freedom of the press disappeared, and the people were told only what the government wanted them to know. These countries were also extremely careful in censoring the news that was sent abroad. Their leaders wanted the rest of the world to know only what was favorable to the country in question and its policies. As a consequence, the blight of censorship descended upon most of Europe.

There is no doubt that we have more freedom of the press in the United States than in any other large country. The administration of Franklin D. Roosevelt showed marked tolerance toward the newspapers until after our foreign policy changed following the Chicago Bridge speech of October, 1937. Press conferences can, however, provide a type of censorship, because the President, by that method, gives out only the news he wants made public at the time. Much that is discussed in the conference is "off the record." Sometimes, newspapermen can break through the censorship, as when they forced Mr. Roosevelt to disclose the facts about the myth of the Atlantic Charter.

In the United States, there was considerable censorship of material given out by government officials to the newspapers even before we entered the second world war. Cabinet bureaus not only exercised censorship but they also became propaganda agencies by controlling, on matters of policy, the type of information given out. News relating to the foreign policy of the government has been closely censored until such time as the government decides to give out the facts. At the time of our entry into the second world war, a complete censorship of the press, radio, and movies was established. Almost without exception, all these agencies of communication willingly acquiesced in the censorship, and the Washington Office of Censorship decided what news was good for the people to hear during the great conflict. Even today, it is difficult to get full or unbiased news about world events. Sources of foreign news are still extensively censored, and the news received is carefully screened and selected by American newspapers to suit the current bias.

It has been suggested that our correspondents, reporting the news from abroad for American agencies, might escape from the foreign censorship by appealing to the embassy of their own government. This plan has not, however, proved successful. Few ambassadors, ministers, or consuls will risk their position in a foreign country by making any serious protest against existing censorship rules. In many instances, governments have made no official protests even when foreign

The Roosevelt-Churchill press conference in the White House.

correspondents were ousted for attempting to gather the true facts concerning public events. Foreign correspondents are almost helpless in the face of rigid censorship. If they violate the rules, they are likely to be imprisoned or banished.

**Voluntary censorship by newspapers and radio.** While government censorship of the news is to be combated in the name of liberty at all times when the national safety is not involved, it is well to remember that government censorship is not the only reason why we do not get all the news that is available or desirable. There is little doubt that newspapers, periodicals, and the radio voluntarily suppress more information than has ever been banned by any democratic government in time of peace. Newspapers will rarely publish much material which is opposed to the fundamental foreign policy of the country or to the basic program of the party they favor. Nor are they likely to publish information damaging to the existing economic order. As late as 1950, few newspapers and almost no periodicals would publish the facts concerning the reasons for the American entry into the second world war. This kind of censorship is what Harold L. Ickes once cogently described as "voluntary servitude."

**Other forms of government censorship.** Government censorship may take forms other than sedition laws or the suppression of news. The National Labor Relations Act of July, 1935, for example, an excellent law in some respects, struck a real blow at free speech and a free press. It enabled labor unionists to say anything they pleased, short of libel and slander, against employers, but branded and penalized as an "unfair labor practice" any denunciation of labor union practices or tactics by employers. Henry Ford fought this ban in what was, perhaps, the longest and most expensive civil liberties case ever entered in the American courts, but he won only an incomplete and partial victory. The abuse was not terminated until the passage of the Taft-Hartley Act in 1947.

Another type of Federal censorship, designed to counter the efforts of those seeking to improve the government by reforming bureaucracy, is treated in the preceding chapter.[2]

**Witch-hunting and card-stacking.** The Federal witch-hunting procedure since 1946, while helpful in ferreting out a few disloyal, radical Federal employees, has by its very excesses provided a dangerous type of censorship. This can be well illustrated by the case of the eminent atomic physicist, Dr. Edward U. Condon. Dr. Condon was a victim of the most reprehensible card-stacking. The Thomas Committee on Un-American Activities gave out part of a letter from J. Edgar Hoover of the FBI revealing the fact that Dr. Condon had been "investigated" by the FBI, but withheld the portion of the letter in which Mr. Hoover revealed that the investigation had proved that Dr.

---

[2] See pp. 541–542. See also Forest A. Harness, "Federal Thought Control," in the *Human Events Letter* for September 1, 1948.

Condon's loyalty and devotion to his country were above suspicion. Hence, Dr. Condon was subjected to unjust and protracted suspicion and smearing. Eminent scientists would be justified in resigning from national-defense service, rather than risk being subjected to such indignities; some actually have refused to leave their university posts to serve their country because of the prospect that their reputations might be unjustly placed in jeopardy. In this way, the government was deprived of invaluable services of key scientists at a time when the alleged foreign emergency especially demanded their technical aid. In an official report, published in August, 1949, the American Association for the Advancement of Science thus condemned President Truman's witch-hunting loyalty order:

Nobody doubts the importance of faithful discharge of duty by public officials. No one questions the propriety of the government's demanding that its employes be loyal to their jobs and to the democratic institutions they serve.

The loyalty order is, however, basically objectionable because it seeks to determine the employe's loyalty by inquiring into his supposed thoughts and attitudes, which are established in large part by imputing to him the beliefs of his associates.

If the loyalty order is to be retained, a drastic revision is essential. Instead of focusing on an employe's associations, it should focus on his behavior in overt acts. Legislation already on the statute books amply protects the Federal service against retention of employes who advocate overthrow of the government.

**Contempt of court.** Another type of politico-legal censorship that occasionally produces annoying abuses is what is known as the "contempt of court" practice; this taboos the criticism or discussion of a judge's conduct of a case until after a decision has been rendered. This device often shields incredible arrogance and arbitrariness on the part of irresponsible judges. Certain courageous labor leaders and newspaper men have lately defied this taboo and some Federal court decisions have sustained their action to a certain extent, at least by dismissing their cases.

## Censorship of the Radio

**Methods and examples of radio censorship.** Radio censorship is usually accomplished in one of the following ways: by refusing to sell time on the air, or to fulfill the contract made with the speaker; by demanding copies of radio speeches in advance and censoring them as the station authorities think best; by drowning out or cutting off the speaker in the midst of a program, when he makes allegedly indiscreet remarks or departs from his prepared speech; and by placing speakers who might be considered indiscreet or dangerous on early morning hours, when most radio listeners are in bed, or on their way to work.

In the zeal to censor material that might be considered objectionable, radio censorship overstepped the bounds of reason. For instance, a fisherman who wanted to recommend fishing for trout with worms instead of the "sporting" method of fly-fishing was not allowed to broadcast lest he offend listening trout fishermen who used flies. One of the major broadcasting systems canceled a proposed broadcast by a distinguished scholar on the Malthusian law of population because it might have offended certain religious groups. Even so eminent a public figure and clergyman as Harry Emerson Fosdick was denied the right to present a restrained discussion of the birth-control program over the radio.

**Controversial material on the air.** It was long the policy of the radio to exclude "controversial" subjects from the air. Yet, almost any subject one can think of might in one sense or another be considered controversial. Actually, controversial material is usually limited to religious, social,-economic, and political doctrines. The test of what is a controversial subject on the radio is closely related to the social customs of the listening group; anything that is forbidden or tabooed by the folkways and mores of the group is kept off the air. Where realistic discussion of a subject—such as religion, the family, patriotism, or the economic system—might threaten to undermine our social institutions, it is carefully censored. Many programs on the air deal with our social institutions, but they keep closely to conservative and traditional ideas. As a practical matter of fact, what is regarded as "controversial" is almost invariably the progressive attitude towards any public problem. Rarely is a reactionary view of any problem looked upon as controversial.

The problem of controversial issues on the air was brought to a head by the WHKC case in Columbus, Ohio, when the station was accused of censoring the case of labor. When the Federal Communications Commission ruled that this was against public interest, the National Association of Broadcasters revised the taboo against controversial material, but the practical effect was not great. The conservative side still has the advantage, not only in monetary resources but in the favor of the broadcasting companies.

The large radio companies have often permitted far more expression of liberal opinion than the smaller local stations. The "Town Meeting of the Air," a distinctly liberal program, has been delivered under the auspices of the National Broadcasting Company. The Columbia Broadcasting System put on "The People's Forum," and the Mutual Broadcasting Company supported the "American Forum of the Air."

**Alternatives in radio policy.** The radio is one of the most powerful means of educating or misleading the public. The power of the radio in informing the people and guiding public opinion is now regarded by many competent authorities as far greater than that of our newspapers. Great responsibility rests with the executives of the broadcasting chains. They may follow two courses in relation to the public: (1) they can give the people full knowledge of the facts and an opportunity for free discussion from different angles, in the hope of peacefully adjusting and settling public issues; or (2) they may deceive the public and deny them the facts.

The real interests of the broadcasting companies, in the long run, are actually identified with giving out all the facts and encouraging free discussion. The reason for this is clear. If we suppress facts and paralyze discussion over the air, we help on revolution and dictatorship. Dictatorship brings totalitarianism and the termination of private broadcasting, for totalitarian states own and operate the radio. The American Civil Liberties Union has drawn up a program with respect to freedom of the air which merits attention:

1. All radio stations, in return for the free franchise granted to them by the government, should be required to set aside desirable time for the presentation of public issues.

2. Whenever one side of a controversial matter is presented on the air, at least one other side should be given an opportunity to be heard on the same terms.

3. Stations, but not speakers, should be relieved from responsibility for libel and slander on programs given on free time. This will encourage stations to broadcast discussions on controversial topics and will do away with censorship of manuscripts before they are delivered over the air.

4. Stations should keep records of all applications for time which are refused, as well as time granted, so that station policies may be checked and censorship recorded.

**Federal powers in radio censorship.** In addition to censorship of material by the broadcasting companies, there may be government censorship of the broadcasting companies themselves by the Federal Communications Commission (FCC). The Commission may refuse to grant or renew a license to any station, or it may cancel a license altogether. It threatened to revoke station licenses over so trivial a matter as a Mae West-Charlie McCarthy program. In wartime, there is complete government censorship of radio.

**Enlightened policy of the Federal Communications Commission.** In general, however, the Federal Communications Commission has acted in the public interest and, in any event, it is the only powerful public organization that can oppose conventional radio censorship and demand a hearing for both sides of an issue. It cannot directly order a chain or station to put on a particular person or program at any time, but it does have the power to revoke chain or station licenses if, after a review of performances over a sufficient time, it believes that the record of any station has not been in the "public interest, convenience, or necessity." The FCC has very eloquently and effectively stated the principles of desirable freedom of the air:

Under the American system of broadcasting, it is clear that the responsibility for the conduct of a broadast station must rest initially with the broadcaster. It is equally clear that the public interest can never be served by the dedication of any broadcast facility to the support of his own private ends.

Radio can serve as an instrument of democracy only when devoted to the communication of information and the exchange of ideas fairly and objectively presented. . . .

If freedom of speech is to have any meaning, it cannot be predicated on the mere popularity or public acceptance of the ideas sought to be advanced.   It must be extended as readily to ideas which we disapprove or abhor as to ideas which we approve.   Moreover, freedom of speech can be as effectively denied by denying access to the public means of making expression effective—whether public parks, meeting halls, or the radio—as by legal restraints or punishment of the speaker.

The main drawback is that the members of the FCC are political appointees and there is always a temptation to judge "public interest" by the relation of any performance to the policies of the Federal administration then in power.   But, in case the opposition party is at all alert, it possesses the power of protest and this is likely to assure some semblance of fairness.   It is also pertinent to point out that while the FCC has the power to revoke licenses, it has rarely used this authority.

## Motion Picture Censorship

**Rigors of movie censorship.**   The censorship of moving pictures is even more highly developed than radio censorship.   The legality of movie censorship was established by a Supreme Court decision in 1915, which ruled that films fall in the same class with circuses or other amusements, rather than with newspapers, and thus are legally subject to public censorship.

The censorship of films has grown to an almost incredible degree. At present, state censors cut or reject about 40 per cent of the films submitted to them, and their action is taken after the producer and the Hollywood censors have already censored the script and film before releasing the picture.   No producer wants to waste money in making films that are sure to be rejected or fatally mutilated.   The extent of this post-release movie censorship indicates that the actions of official censors are unpredictable.   After years of experience, the most skillful producers are able to guess with only about 60 per cent accuracy what the censors will accept and reject.

**National Board of Review.**   Motion picture censorship in the United States has been in the hands of three different groups.   The first was the National Board of Review, organized in New York State in 1909.   Its original purpose was to protect public morals through advising producers, thus avoiding the need of censorship.   Made up largely of club women of New York suburbs—the type satirized by Helen E. Hokinson in her cartoons in the *New Yorker*—it proposed to censor scripts before production and suggest to producers which items might be left out of completed movies.   The Board also passed on movies when they were released and rated them, for example, as "good," "educational," or "poor moral influence." It exerted a powerful influence over motion picture exhibition. For example, in the state of Florida and the city of Boston, it was even illegal to show a film that did not have the approval of the National Board of Review. The Board, now disbanded, invaded most localities in the United States through local "better films committees," usually made up of people who were eager to protect the moral traditions and tastes of the community.

**"Bishop" Hays and Hollywood censorship at the source.** In Hollywood itself, we have the famous Motion Picture Producers and Distributors of America, organized in 1922 under the direction of Will Hays, who was frequently called "the Bishop of Hollywood." This organization was set up by the movie producers themselves to provide for censorship at the source of production, so that money would not be wasted in producing pictures that would be fatally censored or banned later on.

The Motion Pitcure Producers and Distributors pass on all films produced for commercial purposes in the United States. They examine both scripts and completed films and advise the producers to omit material they regard as likely to be objectionable when viewed from the standpoint of those who see movies, especially those groups who take the initiative in inspecting and suppressing films. Mr. Hays resigned in 1945 and was succeeded by Eric A. Johnston, formerly president of the United States Chamber of Commerce, and the organization name was changed to the Motion Picture Association of America.

**State and local censors.** There are state censorship boards in New York, Pennsylvania, Maryland, Kansas, Virginia, and Ohio.[3] For the most part, these boards are made up of petty politicians and meddlers, although they contain some open-minded and intelligent members. The state boards do most of the overt post-release censoring, and their work is usually incompetent and superficial. In New York State, the board has frequently been so busy that it has had to call in state troopers to help in reviewing the films.

On the whole, state censors tend to remove many scenes dealing with sex and to discourage frankness in regard to war and political graft. The state boards want films invariably to reward virtue and punish sin and crime. The New York board is probably the most liberal of the six, yet it cuts or rejects 20 to 40 per cent of the films that come before it, most of which have already been subjected to elaborate pre-production and pre-release censorship. Frequently, state boards reject films that have been warmly approved by other censoring agencies. The film "High Treason," strongly approved by the National Board of Review, was rejected by the Pennsylvania state board. It was a peace movie, dealing with the problems of war and

---

3 Massachusetts has a state board of moving-picture censors which is limited to examining and censoring pictures to be shown on Sundays.

international organization against world war. The reason for its suppression is not fully known, although it was locally charged that pressure was put upon the Pennsylvania board by the steel industries that were opposed to anything encouraging the cause of peace and disarmament.

In addition to these state censorship boards in 7 states, some 50 American cities maintain urban boards of censorship to examine and supervise the censorship of all pictures shown in these municipalities.

Censorship "without stint or limit." It is amazing that we get even passable entertainment from the movies, when we consider that every feature picture has gone through a system of rigid censorship, from the time that the story is offered to the producer for possible production.

If the movie is to be based on a book, the person who prepares the script keeps in mind censorship rules. When a producer accepts a script, he further edits and censors it. It is then submitted to the Johnston Office, which views the script from the standpoint of its probable reception by censorship organizations and movie audiences throughout the country. Its code, drawn up in 1930 by a Jesuit priest and another Catholic censor and revised in 1934, is well known to producers, who take heed of the extensive stipulations for censorship before submitting their scripts. If any dubious materials have slipped by, they are deleted by the Johnston Office. After the picture script has been scrutinized and edited by this group, it is returned for filming and then the film is reviewed after production by Johnston and his associates. After the recommended cuts are made, the film is finally released for distribution and exhibition, subject to state and local censorship.

Despite all this, there is still a demand for more drastic censorship of motion pictures, especially by the Catholic Legion of Decency. It is no wonder that producers fear censorship; yet, although they may be personally indignant over the censorship regulations, they refuse to make any public protest, for fear it would lead to more thorough and malicious cutting of the films by the censors they had attacked. Exhibitors, in their turn, have no more courage than producers in resisting censorship.

One of the most notable battles against film censorship was that conducted by Howard Hughes in the case of his picture "The Outlaw." Hughes defied Hollywood, state, and local censorship, but for a long time he was not able to get wide distribution for his picture.

Censorship kills social significance in pictures. As a result of all this rigid censorship, there is little prospect that moving pictures will ever be a strong intellectual force for human betterment or the elevation of culture. They are adapted to the mass ideas and social thought of the day, and any items which might suggest desirable social changes are usually deleted. Only occasionally, a film that is important for its social viewpoint, such as "Mr. Deeds Goes to Town," "Lost Horizon," "Citizen Kane," and "State of the Union," slips through the censors. The picture, "I Am a Fugitive from a Georgia Chain Gang," was worth while from a sociological point of view, but this film was drastically cut before being released. Indeed, in the last few years the movie censors have shown as much concern over suppressing progressive social ideas as in eliminating obscenity.

The foreign market for films often exerts a restraining influence on movies shown in this country. The filming of "It Can't Happen Here," a dramatization of Sinclair Lewis's novel, was abandoned by Metro-Goldwyn-Mayer because it criticized Fascism and thus could not be shown in Fascists countries that bought many American films. Sometimes, the process is reversed. Powerful American pressure groups here prevented the exhibition of the English-made film "Oliver Twist" in the United States during 1948.

**The prospect of reducing censorship.** The prospect of reducing censorship, at least political censorship, whether in newspapers, on the air, or in motion pictures, is far from hopeful. With prejudice, propaganda, ideological warfare, and witch-hunting definitely on the gain and likely to increase for an unpredictable period, there is little likelihood that censorship will abate. It will fade away only when the fears and hatreds that support prejudice and propaganda have been rooted out.

## Summary

The problem of censorship deals chiefly with restrictions on the expression of ideas and opinions. Usually, ideas are censored because they challenge the current opinions of the dominant social groups. Ideas considered slanderous or libelous to individuals are, however, also censored.

Until the first world war, there was comparative freedom of the press in the United States. The war, however, brought drastic censorship in the interest of defense. Though this censorship was afterwards relaxed to some degree, freedom of the press was never fully restored. In Europe and other parts of the world, censorship has become one of the most powerful weapons of dictators. Through censorship, they have completely controlled the expression of opinion and established the supremacy of the state over the individual and social groups, especially in Fascist and communistic countries.

There are several types of censors: private, semi-official, and official. The worst type of private censorship today is the smear terror. The worst nuisance in semi-official censorship is obscenity snooping. Few of the official censors are trained experts; most exercise powers of censorship in addition to other duties. The Post-Office Department, Customs officials, and the Federal Communications Commission are examples.

Libel, obscenity, and sedition laws represent the most important types of public censorship over printed material. Frequently, the application of these laws is carried out to further the interests of favored social groups and attitudes. In few cases are the laws enforced with primary consideration for authors, publishers, or the public; usually, the publishers must invest their money in a publication before they learn whether or not the book is objectionable. Censorship of ideas on politics and economics is especially serious in modern society, for only by the frank and open discussion of our social problems can we hope to solve them and preserve democracy.

Two of the most powerful agencies for the spread of information, the radio and the movies, are subjected to extremely severe censorship. As a general rule, this censorship is biased in judging material dealing with political, economic, and social issues. The conservative or reactionary viewpoint on public issues is encouraged both on the air and in the films. Severe censorship reduces the value of the movies and radio as media of public education. The artistic and cultural level of moving pictures is also lowered by censorship.

The very future of civilization in our complicated age depends on the promotion of truth. If prejudices, effectively enforced by propaganda and safeguarded by censorship, are to rule the world, the outlook for civilization is dark. A country in the grip of censorship is in a dangerous situation, for suppression of facts may lead to dictatorship. Freedom of speech and of the press are the foundation of democracy. Censorship curtails these liberties.

A certain amount of censorship may be needed, especially in wartime. There should be libel and slander laws to prevent unfair, untrue, or injurious statements. But every citizen is entitled to know the true facts concerning commercial products and public affairs and to have the right to express himself about them. If we are to preserve our democracy, we must have full information on public affairs, in order to permit citizens to reach intelligent solutions of our political and economic problems.

### Selected References

Barnes, H. E., *The Struggle against the Historical Blackout,* privately printed, 1950. Brief summary of the determined effort to prevent the facts about our entry into the second world war from being known.

* Brock, H. I., *Meddlers—Uplifting Moral Uplifters,* Washburn, 1930. A scathing attack on busybodies, purists, uplifters, and other would-be censors. The best book on unofficial censorship.

Broun, Heywood, and Leech, Margaret, *Anthony Comstock: Roundsman of the Lord,* Boni, 1927. An ironical but reliable study of the life and activities of the high priest of American censorship.

Davis, Jerome, *Character Assassination,* Philosophical Library, 1950. First important book on smear tactics, but ignores many leading smear groups and smear artists.

# CENSORSHIP 571

* Ernst, M. L., and Lindey, Alexander, *The Censor Marches On,* Doubleday, Doran, 1940. The best book on censorship, by the leading American authorities on the subject.

Ernst, M. L., and Lindey, Alexander, *Hold Your Tongue!* Morrow, 1932. A revealing survey of the incredible ramifications of libel and slander responsibility, which has assumed the proportions of a legal racket.

Ernst, M. L., and Lorentz, Pare, *Censored: The Private Life of the Movie,* Cape and Smith, 1930. A pioneer study of motion picture censorship.

Ernst, M. L., and Seagle, William, *To the Pure,* Viking, 1928. The standard treatise on obscenity censorship, revealing the far greater moral turpitude of the unofficial censors.

Flynn, J. T., *The Smear Terror,* privately printed, 1947. Brief but devastating exposure of smear censorship in our time.

Gellerman, William, *Martin Dies,* John Day, 1944. Interesting study of the longtime chairman of the Committee on Un-American Activities and his attempt to censor the political and economic opinions of groups and individuals.

Mock, J. R., *Censorship, 1917,* Princeton University Press, 1941. An authoritative account of censorship in the United States during the first world war.

Riegel, O. W., *Mobilizing for Chaos,* Yale University, 1934. Account of political censorship, especially of the press, in totalitarian and quasi-totalitarian countries.

Seldes, George, *You Can't Print That!* Harcourt, Brace, 1929. A good account of newspaper censorship before the triumph of Hitler in Germany.

Summers, R. E., *Wartime Censorship of Press and Radio,* H. W. Wilson Co., 1948. A thorough collection of materials illustrating the extent and nature of the censorship of the news during the second world war.

Young, E. J., *Looking Behind the Censorships,* Lippincott, 1938. Important examination of the forces responsible for political censorship and their modes of operation.

# PART VII

# Leading Social Problems in an Age of Transition

## CHAPTER XXIII

## Rural Society Enters the Machine Age

### The Rural Heritage of Mankind

**Rural life and society have dominated most of human experience.** Throughout the history of mankind, rural life and an agrarian economy have played an important rôle. In the New Stone Age, long before the dawn of history, groups of men settled down to cultivate the soil and raise food for themselves and their families. The life of the great majority of humanity was rooted in a rural economy until recent times. In fact, it is not inaccurate to say that, until after the Industrial Revolution, which began about 1750, an overwhelming proportion of the population of the world lived within a rural pattern of culture. Although cities have produced the highest achievements of civilization and have been the source of much social progress, the farmers have, until recent times, been the economic, political, and military "backbone" of their nations. Most important of all, since the great majority of the human race have lived in the country until recent years, rural social institutions have created human personality and shaped the social attitudes of mankind. The undermining of rural primary groups by mechanization and urbanization is the source of many of the more serious and pressing social problems of our day.

**Rural basis of ancient and medieval society.** The rulers of ancient Egypt maintained their authority by establishing control over the grain supply, the herds that grazed in the fertile Nile Valley, and the indispensable irrigation projects; by controlling agriculture, they controlled Egypt. The Assyrian armies triumphed over their enemies because their hardy peasant farmers made brave and efficient soldiers. The Greek city-states and the Roman Republic depended on a rural economy. Although the Roman Empire is often regarded as an urban civilization, the majority of the Roman soldiers who, in earlier centuries, conquered the lands which made up the Empire came from the small Roman farms. The rise of great estates and the suppression of the small Roman landholders helped, in great measure, to bring about the decline of the Roman Republic and fatally weakened the Empire.

Medieval culture also was predominantly rural. The great mass of people were bound to the land under a socio-economic arrangement called the manorial system. Great feudal lords each controlled hundreds of acres, and serfs tilled the land for them.[1]

Urbanization gradually challenges the rural pattern of life. Even after the modern commercial and industrial age made its appearance, agriculture long remained the greatest influence in economic life. The majority of people lived in rural communities until well along in the nineteenth century. The agricultural revolutions of the eighteenth and nineteenth centuries increased farm production and made it possible to feed the many workers that flocked into the new industrial cities.[2] The increased efficiency of the new farming methods freed workers from agriculture and thousands left the farms to find employment in the factories of the city. In 1790, 94.9 per cent of our population lived in rural and rural town areas; in 1940, 43.5 per cent; and in 1950, 39.8 per cent. Only about 19 per cent of the population actually dwelt on farms in 1950.

The "empire of machines," which developed after 1750, has created our urban industrial economy. The majority of the populations of the Western world now live in urban centers. New developments in communication and transportation have tended to make the present century urban-minded. Even those who have remained on the farm have changed many of their ways and attitudes to conform to city patterns. The increasing predominance of city life and the decline of the old type of rural community represent a major turning-point in the institutional and cultural history of mankind.

Because the United States has become one of the greatest agricultural nations of the world, we have a special interest in tracing the development of our farm economy.

## Historical Trends in Our American Farm Life

Agriculture and rural life in colonial times. The early settlers in this country soon learned to combine the ideas of agriculture they had brought from Europe with those of the Indians, who had long been cultivating corn and other native products with much success. Colonial agriculture thus combined the best agricultural methods of the Old World with those of the New.

---

[1] See above, pp. 272–275.
[2] See above, pp. 23–24, 275–277.

The size of colonial farms differed according to the sections of the country. In New England and the Middle Atlantic colonies, small farms were the rule, with the exception of the huge estates of the Dutch patroons along the Hudson River. The New England farmer raised a variety of cereal and vegetable crops, although his land was hilly, rocky, and wooded. The southern farm or plantation was usually large, sometimes including as many as 5,000 acres. In the South, the farmers specialized in raising rice, cotton, and tobacco. Southern land was more level and freer from stones and trees. Because of the large amount of free land available for cultivation, colonial agricultural methods were often wasteful, and there was usually only a slight development of intensive agriculture or scientific fertilization.

**Agriculture from the Revolution to the Civil War.** From the Revolutionary War to about 1860, the chief development in American agriculture consisted in the extension of agricultural operations to the West. In this period, also, came the invention of better iron and steel plows, mechanical mowers and reapers, and a crude threshing machine. With these inventions at hand, it was possible to place more land under cultivation and to supply the increased food demands of the rising commercial and industrial cities of the East.

By 1860, there were, from an agricultural viewpoint, three distinct sections of the country. In New England, commerce and manufacturing had come to play a more important rôle than farming. Such farming as continued to exist centered around the production of dairy products, beef, wool, fruit, and some grain. Although more grain was produced in the Middle Atlantic states, the agricultural pattern of small farms and mixed crops in this region was generally similar to that of the New England states. The second major section of the country was the territory between the Allegheny mountains and the Mississippi River and north of the Ohio, which had been opened to settlement by the canals and railroads. Here, farming was the principal occupation, and a large amount of grain, as well as large numbers of livestock, was produced. The South was the third important agricultural section. After the invention of the cotton-gin in 1793, the South turned more and more to the cultivation of cotton, which was grown, for the most part, on great plantations worked by Negro slaves.

**Revolution in farming methods since the Civil War.** After 1860, marked changes occurred in American farming. A greatly increased demand for grain arose during the Civil War, and this encouraged the settlement of Iowa, Minnesota, and the Dakotas. The government aided the development of this region by the passage, in 1862, of the Homestead Act, which granted 160 acres free to bona fide settlers. This size of farm—the quarter section—became characteristic of western farming. The mechanical binder and steam thresher were the two most important inventions of the generation after the war. After 1865, the large southern plantations were widely replaced by small farms, worked by Negro or white laborers. Tenant farmers also appeared in the southern regions, often working land on shares and receiving a part of the crop in return for their labor. In our generation, the poorer of these are known as "sharecroppers."

The older farming methods have gradually disappeared since 1900, along with the moss-covered bucket and the gourd dipper. Farming operations, especially in the West, have become highly mechanized. Gasoline tractors with powerful headlights for night work, gang plows, giant disc harrows, and harvesting combines (the last replacing the old binder, threshing machine, cook wagons, and harvest crew) make it possible to carry on farming operations efficiently on a large scale. Irrigation canals provide water in many arid regions and reduce the crop loss from drought. Farm tenancy and sharecropping have increased in the South; but, in the last thirty years, many of the smaller farms have been combined into large estates owned by farming corporations. Here, the tractor, mechanical cotton-picker, and chemical weed-exterminator have taken the place, in part, of the Negro slaves of 1860. In the Northeast, specialized, small-scale farming is still the rule, but the production of grain has lessened, giving way to dairy farming, market gardening, and fruit raising. In the South and on the Pacific Coast, market gardening and the citrus fruit industry have become increasingly important as refrigerator cars have facilitated the shipping of such products to the great urban districts of the North and East.

Before discussing in more detail the changes in farming methods after 1900, it will be of interest to indicate how farm life shaped and colored the social, political, and economic institutions of an earlier age.

## The Farm and Rural Society in American Life before 1900

Rural society based on "in-groups." The early American farm was virtually self-supporting. Families were large, for children were an economic asset in farm work. At an early age, the boys did the lighter chores, while the girls helped with the household work. The farmer chose a wife in part because he needed her to do the countless tasks around the house. She did not usually question the right of her husband to exert full authority over her and her children. The household fireside was the center of family and neighborhood life in leisure hours. Because neighbors were few and far between, the family was dependent on its own resources, social as well as material. Family loyalty was part of the home teaching. An intense "we-group" or "in-group" was developed. In the family circle, the children also learned the moral ideals of the community.

Much was made of kinship in this early farm home. Not only the immediate family, but other relatives—the cousins, the aunts, and the uncles—were bound by close ties. People were expected to be proud and fond of their relatives. Usually the whole "clan" gathered on holidays, birthdays, or wedding anniversaries, the kinfolk bringing some of the food for the celebration.  Outside the home, the social life of the rural community centered in such interests and activities as the play group, the rural church, co-operative work with neighborhood families, and the lodge.

**Co-operative activities in the earlier rural community.**  There was a "help thy neighbor" spirit in the rural community.  Barn raising, husking-bees, carding contests in a sheep-raising country, and quilting-bees provided opportunities for neighbors to get together, gossip, and help each other to do necessary work.  In threshing time, the men joined forces and did the work, while the women prepared hearty dinners.  Farming emergencies were quickly and pleasantly taken care of by such community effort.

**The rural church and lodges.**  The local church played a large rôle in the social life of most rural communities.  There was in those days less to lure the farmer from church.  Outstanding events, such as births, deaths, and marriages, were celebrated with religious services.  The church was the scene of "sociables"—rural parties—because it was often the only community building large enough to house any considerable gathering.  One reason why people went to church regularly was that it gave them an opportunity to meet and talk with others.  How else would some of the young folk have been able to get acquainted?  Girls often met their future husbands at a church sociable, after a Christian Endeavor meeting, or at a religious revival.

Lodges or fraternal organizations, many with quasi-religious rituals that appealed to church-goers, were popular with the farmers.  They gratified the farmer's love of the mysterious, while the ranks or grades in the lodge ministered to the desire for prestige and social superiority, which was otherwise lacking in the democratic rural communities.  The mystical ceremonial and brilliant dress of the lodge appealed to artistic impulses, which had so little opportunity for expression in the humdrum life on the farm.  The fraternal ideals of the lodge fitted in well with the co-operative and neighborly feelings of the community.  One of the most important rural organizations, the Grange,[3] or the Patrons of Husbandry, was originally a rural lodge.

**Mental outlook of the farmer.**  The farmer has been criticized for being cautious and conservative, suspicious of strangers, and often believing in nature myths, signs, and superstitions.  But his mental attitudes and habits were a natural result of his environment.  The old rural community, without telephone, telegraph, radio, daily newspaper, rural free delivery, good roads, or automobiles naturally made for isolation and the mental attitudes that go with it.  Superstitions connected with nature had come down through the centuries in rural areas.  The seasons of the year, the routine of the crops, and the daily feeding of the stock—the same tasks over and over again—

---

[3] See below, p. 590.

naturally habituated the farmer to routine; repetition bounded his intellectual horizon.

The farmer thus tended to be suspicious of anything new. This mental attitude stands in sharp contrast to the curiosity, the desire for movement, the search for novelty, and the restlessness that characterize city folk. The farmer was at the mercy of nature: his welfare depended on rainfall and temperature; droughts, floods, storms, and insect pests brought ruin. Since he could do little about them, he resigned himself and placed his trust in God and hard work. He thought the Almighty would care for him if he obeyed the ten commandments and worshiped faithfully.

The conditions of rural life made for both personal and cultural isolation. The farmer was often smug and provincial, but he personally faced with confidence a wide variety of problems and learned to depend on his own ingenuity and native intelligence in an emergency. His resourcefulness stands in striking contrast to the behavior patterns of the urban dweller, whose helplessness in the face of even a slight mechanical difficulty is often a standing joke in rural circles. The farmer had to work hard to obtain a mere living, and it is no wonder that he learned the value of a dollar. Farmers did not take kindly to schemes involving financial risk, nor did they favor plans to speculate with their hard-earned money.

Most of the farmer's property was in concrete things, such as land, buildings, and animals. This "real" property created in the farmer a strong sense of individual ownership and property rights. He valiantly resisted attempts to limit his personal property rights. Radical reform parties, even those with sound programs, have gained rural support only when the farmers were suffering grievously from a severe economic depression. Before the New Deal, the Democrats had an old gibe: "Let a farmer have two dollars in his pocket and he becomes a Republican." Republican farmers retorted that only in a Republican administration does a farmer have two dollars.

**Traditional rural education.** Education, like religion, was held in respect by the rural dwellers. The farmer admired an educated man if the latter was not snobbish. He wanted his children to learn, because it was a democratic ideal—a part of the "American Dream"— that every boy could become president of the United States or at least a bank president. But, despite his theoretical appreciation of learning, the farmer could spare his children little time for education. During the few months out of the year when boys and girls could be spared from the farm, they went to school and managed to get the fundamentals of education in the "3 R's" (Reading, 'Riting, and 'Rithmetic), but they were often removed from school at an early age for full-time farm work.

The "little red school house" has been colorfully written up in sentimental song and story, but it did not offer a high type of education. The teachers were generally poorly trained and underpaid. They were usually part-time teachers, with other occupations when the school was closed. The school building was all too often small, unhealthful, dark, and drafty. The school year was too short for much to be accomplished; and children often forgot during the long vacations much of what they had previously learned. Old-time rural education was also inadequate because it ignored instruction in good agricultural methods, domestic science, mechanical trades, and other practical knowledge of special value to farm children.

Although the educational training was poor and the school year short, the country school, as a leading primary group, was an important moral and social force in the community. The school group was also a play group. The children, coming from the same locality, had common interests and traditions, which they kept alive and passed along through the influence of the country school.

**The primary-group pattern of earlier rural life.** In short, rural life, before the coming of the mechanized era, was the more or less complete exemplification of the simple, personal type of social organization and experience. It was the age of primary groups and of small and simple secondary groups. The mechanization of farm life, the coming of new methods of transportation and communication, and the reaction of cities on country areas gave to rural dwellers wider horizons and new attitudes, ideologies, opportunities, and responsibilities. But they also disrupted the rural primary groups which for thousands of years had shaped character and personality and provided community discipline. Community planning, which is the only possible substitute, has not developed as rapidly as rural primary groups have disintegrated and decayed.

## The Farmer, Politics, and Reform

**Partisan alignment of farm vote.** The farmer has exerted a strong influence on American political life. The farm vote provided the main support for Thomas Jefferson and his Republican party of 1800 and thereafter. In 1828, Andrew Jackson owed his election, in large part, to the support of the frontier farmers. The rural voters supported the new and then liberal Republican party in large numbers after its formation in 1856. Since the Civil War the depressed farmers, especially western farmers, have been the main backbone of such reform movements as the Greenback-Labor, the Granger, the Populist, and the Farmer-Labor parties. In almost every case it was the impoverished farmers who supported these reform movements. The farmers who were not suffering deprivation and misery tended to remain conservative and support one of the old parties, usually the Republican outside the South.

**Farmers and third-party movements.** The Greenback movement arose as a protest against the plan to restore specie payment and retire greenbacks (depreciated paper money) after the Civil War. Many of the farmers had borrowed money when its value was low during the Civil War to buy farm implements or more land. They thus became debtors, and the proposed return to specie payment promised to work hardship on the debtor class, because they were compelled to pay their debts in money worth much more in terms of purchasing power than it was when they borrowed it. The Greenback-Labor party became strong enough to cast a million votes and elect 14 congressmen in the congressional election of 1878, but it collapsed in 1879 when specie payment was resumed.

The Granger movement, so called because it was backed by the Patrons of Husbandry or Grange, was the next important political movement sponsored by the impoverished farmers. The Granger movement arose in the Middle West in the 1870's as a protest against the oppressive rates and high-handed methods of the new western railroads in the shipment of grain, cattle, and farm supplies. The Grangers were temporarily successful in passing state laws to subject the railroads to rate control. Although the Supreme Court later declared much of this legislation unconstitutional, the Granger movement helped along the creation of the Interstate Commerce Commission in 1887.

The strongest of all farmer movements of the time was the Populist party, which, beginning in the 1880's, reached its greatest strength in the election of 1892, when it polled over a million popular votes and secured 22 electoral votes. The Populist platform was designed to promote the interests of the farmers. It advocated an income tax; a postal savings bank; government ownership of railroads, telegraphs, and telephones; reduction of the tariff; and readjustment of taxes. Attracted by William Jennings Bryan's radical program in 1896, the Populists joined forces with the Democrats under Bryan's leadership.

**Recent trend toward state intervention.** The more radical farmers supported Bryan in 1896 and 1900, but many of them swung over to the Republicans, and supported Theodore Roosevelt in 1904 and Taft in 1908. Many of Taft's former supporters from the rural districts fell out of sympathy with the policies of his administration and joined Roosevelt and his "Bull Moose" movement in 1912. In 1916, the western farmers were inclined to support Wilson's reform legislation, but they did not line up with either party decisively in 1920.

The great depression in American farm life, which did not cease until the second world war, began in 1921. Many farmers became discontented with the farm policies of the two major political parties and enthusiastically supported Senator Robert M. LaFollette and the Farmer-Labor ticket in 1924. Franklin D. Roosevelt devoted many of his New Deal reforms to agriculture; as a result, many farmers enthusiastically helped to re-elect him in 1936 and 1940. A large number of farmers came to favor the Democratic party, because it was in the best position to aid them.

Observers attributed the 1948 Truman victory in part to the resentment of the farmers at the hesitancy of the Republicans to pass farm-aid legislation during the 80th Congress and to the fear that a Republican Congress might revive the anti-farm policy of the Coolidge administration.

**Rural government.** Rural county government, while not as important as city government in the American political scene, has its own significance. And the political corruption and chicanery, is, in a more modest way, as evident and traditional as that in city machines. The control of county government and its policies is usually in the hands of a board of supervisors, which elects its own chairman. The supervisors legislate in a rudimentary way for the county, appropriate county funds, determine taxes, and allot expenditures. The administrative and police operations of the county are in the hands of an elective sheriff, who also usually administers the county jail. The judicial powers of the county are usually vested in a county court, the judge of which is generally elected by popular vote. County expenditures have reached an impressive total in recent years, partly as a result of the cost of building and maintaining good roads. The total county expenditures in 1946 were $1,967,000,000, very nearly the total expenditures of the Federal government in 1917.

## The Mechanization of Rural Life

**Mechanical inventions revolutionize agriculture.** Earlier, we suggested that the invention of new farm machinery, especially since 1900, has revolutionized farming methods and farm life. It is true that many important inventions occurred before 1900. The early settlers brought the plow, the cultivator, and other simple farm implements to the New World, but there were few striking improvements in farm machinery until the nineteenth century. Then, in the first half of the century, better iron and steel plows and harrows were invented, and a simple seed-drill was devised. A mechanical mowing-machine was produced, and mechanical reapers appeared between 1833 and 1845. About 1860, crude threshing machines, usually run by horsepower, put in their appearance. From that time on, numerous important inventions were placed on the market. The wire self-binder, at first crude and clumsy, was replaced by the twine binder in the 1880's. The mechanical header, which hastened the harvesting process, was soon invented. The steam threshing-machine produced a revolution all its own. The corn harvester and the corn husker were invented about 1900 and transformed the handling of the corn crop. Later, there came the corn picker. It is estimated that all the farming inventions of the nineteenth century brought a saving of about 80 per cent in farm labor and cut farming costs by nearly 50 per cent.

But the most sweeping advances in farm technique were yet to come.

A successful and economical gasoline farm tractor was introduced by Benjamin Holt in 1903. The tractor and the automobile truck soon displaced the horse and mule on most large farms. The gang-plow and the disc-harrow revolutionized the preparation of the soil. Tractor-drawn grain drills speeded up the sowing of crops. Today, even airplanes are sometimes used for sowing rice and wheat and dusting the crops with insecticides. The combines cut, thresh, clean, weigh, and bag grain in one process. Trucks, speeding over good roads, carry the grain to market. In short, the machine has taken over the farm. The effect of farm mechanization in the present century, in the way of increasing farm production, can be seen from the fact that agricultural production in the United States in 1945 was 59 per cent greater than in 1914, even though the number of farm workers was 20 per cent less and the soil has become less fertile.

Chemistry and agriculture. An acre of ground can produce more today than ever before, because chemistry has made possible the scientific analysis and fertilization of the soil. The farmer knows which fertilizers he must use to have a good crop; and, with irrigation and insecticides, he can better protect himself against drought and insects. Better fertilization and mechanical inventions have created almost unlimited possibilities in agricultural production, once the most efficient methods are adopted. Few persons realize what the most efficient known methods of production can do in the way of increasing production per acre. As a result of what is known as hydroponic, or forced, cultivation, making scientific use of water and chemicals, the production of potatoes, for example, can be increased from a high normal yield of 120 bushels per acre to 2,500 bushels.

Not only has farm production of foodstuffs been put on a more efficient basis, but we are on the eve of remarkable developments in synthetic chemistry. The chemist is now able artifically to produce many basic foodstuffs in the laboratory—sugar from sawdust, and the like.

New methods of transportation and communication. The mechanical changes in rural life have by no means been limited to methods of food production on the farm. New means of transportation and communication have revolutionized farm living as well. The automobile and good roads have brought the farmer and his family closer to the city. Parcel post has been a great convenience to the farmer in making varied mail-order purchases from distant points. The improved methods of communication have broken down rural isolation. The daily newspaper is carried promptly to the farmhouse door by rural free delivery, and the telephone, radio, and television place rural areas in contact with both nearby cities and distant regions. The movie newsreels enable the farmer to observe the happenings of the world outside his community and give him a glimpse into the life and customs of other regions.

**Electrification of the farm.**  Most of these revolutions in communication are based on electricity, which has also brought new conveniences in the form of light, power, and heat.  In January, 1949, the Rural Electrification Administration announced that 70 per cent of the nation's farms had electrical service, and in another five years, or less, all accessible farms would be so supplied.  The ever increasing use of electricity on farms was revealed by the assertion of the REA that the farm consumption of electrical current in 1948 was 84 times greater than in 1946, thus causing power shortages in some areas. The Power Age is now established in rural communities.  Machinery and electricity have lightened the work of both the farmer and the rural housewife.

**Substandard farm dwellings.**  Despite all the improvement in farm life brought about by machinery and electricity, and despite the attractive nature of many rural settings, it is well not to overidealize the situation.  Many urban dwellers take it for granted that, while country people may not live lavishly, they are at least comfortably and decently housed.  Any such conception is a gross illusion.  Aside from the fact that country dwellers have more air and sunshine, the rural housing situation is as deplorable as the urban.

It has been estimated that, out of around seven million rural farm homes, at least five million are in need of major repairs.  The Farm Housing Survey of 1934, which sampled some 8 per cent of farm homes in all states except New York and Pennsylvania, found that 70 per cent had no running water; 88 per cent had no bathrooms; and 90 per cent had no indoor toilets.  Few farm homes have gas, and, until the recent work of the Rural Electrification Administration, only about one-third of them had electricity.  Former Secretary of Agriculture Claude Wickard testified in 1945 that two-thirds of our farm houses are definitely substandard and that one-third of them are unfit for human habitation.  Another expert asserted that one-third of them are so bad as to be beyond economical repair and should be demolished. The farm housing situation is especially bad in southern states.  It has been estimated that it would require at least 20 billion dollars to bring all American rural dwellings up to minimum standards.  A related illusion is that farm homes are not crowded, but official surveys have revealed almost incredible overcrowding in poor farm homes— as many as a dozen persons living in one-room shanties, and up to 20 living in houses with two or three rooms.

Little has been done as yet to remedy this deplorable situation. Better facilities for getting government loans were provided by the establishment of the Federal Land Banks in 1917, the Federal Security Administration in 1937, and the Farmers Home Administration in 1946.  But these authorities were primarily interested in lending money to buy or enlarge farms and only indirectly in improving farm housing.  The Resettlement Administration and the Farm Security Administration moved about 15,000 families to better farming sites between 1935 and 1942. The United States Housing Authority, created in 1937, was primarily concerned with urban housing; by 1946 only 515 new rural housing units had been completed under its auspices. As the United States moved into the second half of the twentieth century, only the surface of the rural housing problem had been scratched.

## The Revolution in Rural Culture in the Machine Age

**Impact of city life on rural communities.** The rural population has deeply felt the impact of urban influences and the mechanization of life in the last thirty-five years. As Professor Wirth has well said:

> While he may cherish the illusion of independence, the farmer even in what he plants, how he cultivates the soil, the tools he uses, and the prices he gets for his products, cannot be oblivious to the city. His physical well-being, his housing, his health, the education of his children, his politics, his taxes, his social security, his income and standard of living, his ideas, and his attitudes are shaped as much or possibly even more by what goes on in the cities than by what transpires in his own immediate neighborhood.[4]

**Mechanization and the rural family.** Machinery, to a considerable extent, has made the labor of children on the farm less essential. Therefore, farm families have fewer children, though still more than most city families. Women and girls are less dependent on the male head of the family. They can now leave the country to find work in the city. The farm home, since the coming of the automobile, is no longer the only center of social and recreational life. The telephone, radio, television, the daily paper, up-to-date farm journals, popular magazines, and movies have widened rural interests. Not only has the family ceased to be the sole recreational and social center, but many services once performed by the family have been taken over to an increasing extent by other agencies. Consolidated schools, community or school nurses, clinics, and public playgrounds have come to rural areas, though not as yet to the extent needed.

**Changes in the rural neighborhood.** The older neighborhood social gatherings are fast disappearing. All-day visiting is rare, and sociables and box-suppers are now unusual in the country. Urban amusements, made accessible by the automobile, have taken their place. More efficient machinery has in some areas all but done away with the spirit and need of neighborhood co-operation. The combine, for instance, takes the place of the many hands formerly needed for harvesting and threshing. The city has not, however, entirely supplanted the influence of rural villages, where the farmer still patronizes local stores, makes purchases at the farm co-operatives, consults his family doctor, and attends Grange meetings, community sings, and band concerts.

---

[4] Louis J. Wirth, *Urban and Rural Living*, National Education Association, 1944, p. 9.

**Effect of mechanization on the rural church and ι.hool.** The church has lost much of its former hold on the rural population. The automobile takes them touring or visiting on Sunday. Other more exciting forms of social life have replaced church suppers, revivals, and camp meetings. The young people crowd into the family car and go to town to dance, listen to a concert, or see a movie. Yet the level of rural religion has often been elevated in the present generation. Several rural churches sometimes combine to form a community church, which unites all the religious forces of the section, reduces expenses, provides a better preacher, and produces a church better suited to modern rural needs.

It is in the new rural education that we find, perhaps, the most striking improvements in modern farm life. Improved means of transportation have made it possible to combine school districts, to build a central school, and to hire better-trained teachers. The new, large, consolidated school building is modern and sanitary; teaching methods are more efficient; and supervised play is possible on ample playgrounds. Manual training and domestic science are now taught. The new centralized school is, perhaps, the outstanding cultural feature in rural social progress in our generation.

Nevertheless, the level of rural education is still much below that of urban schools. In 1946, the average urban schoolteacher's salary

*Courtesy of Board of Education, Port Byron, New York.*

**Picture of an attractive centralized rural school, the main triumph in rural education in the twentieth century. Note ample playgrounds at left and rear of school building.**

was $1,995, compared with $959 for the rural teacher; the urban expenditure per pupil was $104.72, the rural $69.66; and the urban school property value per pupil $405, to $185 in the rural areas.

**Medical care for rural areas.** The country has always been rated as a more healthful place than the city because rural dwellers have pure air and sunshine in abundance. Dairy products and green vegetables are cheaper, and the nervous tension of the crowded city is absent. Good hospitals are within reasonable motoring distance of most rural areas; and, because the medical profession has often seemed overcrowded in the city, well-trained young doctors have frequently gone to the villages to "hang out their shingle."

Rural medical treatment and hospital services are, however, still relatively inadequate, despite the great improvements in the last fifty years. Moreover, the recent and rapid growth of cities has increased the demand for doctors in urban areas, and there is now a shortage rather than an excess of physicians and surgeons. The result has been that, in late years, there has been an especially acute shortage of good doctors in rural areas. This has been intensified by the trend toward specialization in medicine, which acts to cut down the number of general practitioners needed in rural medical practice.

**Social problems in the rural community of today.** While the new technology and urban influences have made possible an easier and richer life for the farmer, they have also brought new social problems. The sterner moral discipline of the country districts has been lessened. Modern communication and transportation have led to the weakening of family and neighborhood life, and, along with this, the influence of parents over their children.

As a result, rural crime is increasing, as is rural participation in urban crime. Rural youths, because of the independence and resourcefulness acquired on the farm, make dangerous criminals. Rural crime, while less frequent than urban, long tended to be more violent because of the relative scarcity of movable wealth to make off with. As Professor E. A. Hooton has observed, in the country one must murder, rape, or behave. In the years after the second world war, however, rural crime grew more rapidly than urban crime, and crimes against property increased more than violent crimes against persons. This change was probably due to the effect of war experiences, the increased wealth of farmers, and the impact of city patterns on rural conduct.

Until the defense and war boom following 1940, unemployment was a serious social problem in the country. While the rural birth rate is still far higher than that in the city, there is less and less need for farm laborers because of increasing mechanization of farms. The unemployed rural workers, in normal times, often cannot find jobs in the city. The machine has taken the place of many human hands in the city as well as on the farm. The farmer, who once worried mainly about the weather, has been compelled to face many other economic troubles—unemployment, low farm prices, farm surpluses, difficulties in marketing his products, and the like. It is likely that this situation has only been temporarily improved by the second world war and its aftermath.

**Farmers become more world-minded.** The dependence of the farmer for his prosperity upon shipments of grain abroad in the last two decades has tended to broaden his horizon and to make him conscious of world society. His marketing problem is no longer merely one of disposing of farm products in a local town but one of seeking foreign markets, even by the support of a government subsidy. A main resentment of the farmers against the Republican 80th Congress was its refusal to pass laws designed to assure farmers a fairly large and stable foreign market for grain until 1952. This economic influence, and the constant emphasis on foreign issues, policies, and disputes by the newspaper, radio, and movies have broken down the provincialism and isolation of the farmer and made him to some extent a citizen of the world.

## The Crisis in American Farming after 1920

**Rural economics before the first world war.** Despite the mechanical and cultural advantages of the twentieth century, the average farmer was scarcely able to make more than a bare living between the two world wars—especially between 1920 and 1933. There had been periods of severe depression and hard times in rural areas, especially in the West, in the decades following the Civil War. These had led to the origin of the Greenback, Granger, and Populist movements and to the rise of organizations like the Farmers' Alliance. But, after the turn of the century, farming conditions became better and the decade of the first world war brought unprecedented prosperity to most American farmers.

The relative prosperity of the farmer before 1920 was the result of favorable conditions both at home and abroad. American foodstuffs helped to feed England after 1846 when the English Corn Laws were repealed. The English needed our surplus farm products for their factory laborers. Our farm exports to England and other European countries helped us to pay the interest on the large sums we borrowed abroad and also paid for the raw materials and goods needed by the growing American industrial system. The farmer profited by foreign trade; the capitalists also benefited. Since American industry grew rapidly after the Civil War, the farmer was urged to raise more foodstuffs so that more surplus farm products could be sent abroad.

**Effects of the first world war on the rural economy.** When the first world war sent farm prices skyrocketing, the far western farmer, with government encouragement, plowed up pasture land which was not suitable for permanent cultivation without irrigation and sowed it in wheat. This land, without the buffalo grass to hold down the soil, later became the great dust bowl of the plateau country just east of the Rockies. For a short time, American farmers enjoyed an unusual prosperity, as huge quantities of American foodstuffs were shipped to war-torn Europe. This war-built prosperity disappeared, however, when Europe returned to peace and her own farmers again took up their tasks.

European countries did not buy as many farm products from the United States after the war, in part because they did not have the money. They had also discovered new sources of wheat in the Argentine, Canada, and Australia, where they could pay for wheat by their exported manufactures, which our high tariff wall kept out of the United States. We became almost a self-sufficient nation, and the farmer lost some of his European customers, because we did not need to send farm products abroad to pay debts or pay for imports.

Moreover, the high protective tariff, which the farmers supported because they thought it protected them, actually kept Europeans from buying American wheat, because they could not send their own manufactured goods here in payment. The farmer found a greatly reduced demand abroad for his products, while at home he had to pay high prices for needed manufactured goods that were protected by the tariff from foreign competition.

Other factors reduced the farmers' home market. The chemists, who had once shown him how to raise more crops, now invented substitutes for his farm products. Knowledge of vitamins reduced the American use of wheat, corn, potatoes, beef, and pork. People ate more fruit and vegetables and less bread and oatmeal. The per capita consumption of the traditional staple farm products dropped by about 11 per cent between 1913 and 1940. The popularity of the automobile, truck, and tractor reduced the market for hay, which was formerly fed to farm and city horses. It is estimated that some 15,-000,000 acres were devoted to producing horse feed before the days of mechanization. This amount of land has been released to produce crops, such as wheat, corn, and cotton, of which there is usually a surplus in normal times.

The surplus grain, especially wheat, which piled up in the 1920's as a result of the declining foreign and domestic market, was a main cause of farming distress. If the surplus was sold on the world market at the low world price, it tended to depress the price of wheat on the domestic market in the United States. If it was not offered on the world market, it only helped to increase the unsold surplus at home.

Many farmers in the eastern United States turned from wheat raising to dairy farming. But the dairy farmers have had to cope with the excessive profits of the "middleman"—the great milk-distributing corporations. The farmer has received as little as two cents a quart for milk, which the city consumer bought for twelve to fifteen cents. Somewhere along the line the middleman collected an absurdly large profit. The development of refrigerator cars caused the eastern truck farmers to suffer, since the California, Texas, and Florida farmers could send their grapefruit, oranges, melons, and lettuce and other vegetables, profusely grown in their warm climate, to the city markets of the Northwest and Middle West. These shipped-in cold-storage fruits and vegetables brought good prices, but they reduced the market for local gardeners.

**The lack of mass purchasing power.** All of the above-mentioned causes of the depression of American agriculture after 1920 are important but they are of quite secondary significance compared to inadequacy of mass purchasing power arising from the maldistribution of the national income. If the city factory workers, mechanics, and clerks had been well-paid and steadily employed and thus enabled to buy the food and clothing they needed, American farmers from 1920 to 1940 could have been enjoying a material utopia.[5]

**Collapse of rural prosperity after 1920.** From 1915 to 1920, the farmer rejoiced in his good fortune, but, in less than ten years, he witnessed the collapse of his economic world. Many farmers used up their savings and mortgaged their homes; even if they knew other ways of making a living, they could not often find jobs. Many dispossessed farmers had to rent land, and thus farm tenancy increased markedly all over the country. When the great depression came in 1929, the tenant farmers, notably the southern sharecroppers, were hit still harder, for the price of cotton fell to a new low. In other regions, the harvesting combine took jobs from farmhands. Many of the migratory workers on the road in the 1930's were former sharecroppers from Arkansas, Louisiana, Mississippi, and Texas, displaced farmhands from the wheat belt, and ruined farmers fleeing the dust bowl.

Even the elements seemed to have conspired against the farmer, with serious droughts and dust storms seriously damaging millions of acres. Plans were made to restore some of this land under Federal conservation projects but not in time to avoid serious suffering.

A few representative figures will indicate the seriousness of the economic blows dealt to the farmer. In 1919, the gross farm income was nearly 18 billion dollars, but it had shrunk to less than $6,500,000,000 in 1932. In June, 1932, farm prices were only 52 per cent of their prewar level, while the prices of the commodities farmers had to buy were 10 per cent higher than in 1914. The per capita income of the American farm population, even in the boom year, for business, of 1929, was only $273, as compared with $908 for the non-farming group. The value of farm property in the United States fell from 80 billion dollars in 1920 to 36 billion dollars in 1933. Farm mortgage indebtedness grew impressively, from $3,300,000,000 in 1910 to $9,500,000,000 in 1931. The New Deal assistance to farmers had reduced farm tenancy from over 42 per cent in 1930 to about 39 per cent in 1940, but in the corn belt states more than half of the land is still cultivated by tenants.

---

[5] See above, pp. 308–311.

The revived prosperity of the farmers after 1940 led to a reduction of tenancy to about 29 per cent by 1946.

## Farmers' Organizations and Movements to Improve Rural Conditions

**Farmers organize to better their condition.** Depressed farmers have attempted to improve their lot, first through their own organized efforts, and later by acceptance of Federal plans for farm relief. The interest of farmers in attending meetings to promote organizational activity and acquire the best technological knowledge has been one of the most notable recent trends in rural life. Just before the second world war, it was estimated that the annual attendance at farm meetings was 46,000,000, and that the farmers attending traveled some 500 million miles annually.

**Leading farm organizations.** American farmers created a number of organizations designed to promote their knowledge, well-being, and prosperity. The Grange, or Patrons of Husbandry, founded in 1867, developed, as we have seen, from the farmers' interest in lodges. The Grange is a semi-secret and fraternal order; it devoted its earliest efforts to securing a fair deal for the farmer from the railroads, increasing the political unity and power of the farmers, and promoting co-operative marketing in rural areas. The Grange declined in membership and power for some years after 1890, but was revived after the first world war. It is now considered one of the chief organizations working for the general interest of the farmers and promoting richer community life in rural neighborhoods.

The decline of rural interest in conventional fraternal societies or lodges in recent years, due largely to the greater accessibility of urban amusements, may account not only for the increased popularity of the Grange but also for the growth of farmers' clubs. These extend even to the children, one of the most popular being the 4-H Club, limited to rural youth between 4 and 16 years of age.

The Farmers' Alliance was another important farm organization. It aimed to promote comprehensive rural social reforms, similar to those recommended by the Populist party. In fact, in 1892, the Alliance merged with the Populist party and disappeared as an independent organization. In 1902, two new farm organizations arose, the American Society of Equity, in Indiana, and the National Farmers' Union, in Texas. The American Society sought to promote the farmer's national economic interests and to stimulate fraternal and social activities among farmers. The Union is a fraternal and relatively progressive organization, which advocates extensive changes in our economic system to solve the farm problem; it lays great emphasis on agricultural co-operation. Both the Farmers' Alliance and the Farmers' Union have favored a united front with organized labor.

The American Farm Bureau Federation came into being after the first world war.  Its greatest strength lies in the Middle West.  The Federation devotes much time to promoting large-scale co-operative marketing, and stresses scientific farming and better vocational education for farmers.  Following the growth of the co-operative movement among farmers after the first world war, the National Council of Farmer Coöperatives came into being and is now the central organization promoting co-operative enterprise in rural areas.

**Inadequacy of farm organizations.**  While such of the above-mentioned farmers' organizations as are still extant do good work, they are quite inadequate to the task of promoting the interests of the rural population; over 70 per cent of American farmers are not affiliated with any organization to promote their interests on a national scale.  Membership has declined rather than increased.  The Grange has about 800,000 members, the Farm Bureau Federation 1,325,000, and the Farmers' Union only 425,000, including all members of the farm families.  Away back in 1890, the Farmer's Alliance alone had more than 2,000,000 members, nearly equal to the combined membership today of these three chief farm organizations.  The inadequacy of farmers' organizations can be further emphasized by comparing their membership with the 7,500,000 members of the American Federation of Labor and the 6,000,000 members of the Congress of Industrial Organizations.  Even though there are fewer farmers than laborers in the country, the ratio of farm organization members to labor union members—less than 1 to 4—is disproportionately small.  And the financial budgets of the farm organizations are also small compared with those of the organizations representing labor and business.  Moreover, none of these farm organizations makes any perceptible effort to admit and organize hired farm laborers, of whom there were about 2,317,000 in 1948.

**The farm institute.**  The farm institute has been perhaps the most important type of local farm organization.  Such institutes date from the period following the Civil War.  They have helped to acquaint farmers with new agricultural trends and have offered suggestions for improving rural living conditions.  Farm institutes have become somewhat less popular and influential since 1920.

**The farmers and co-operatives.**  The co-operative movement has made increasing headway among American farmers, though it cannot as yet be compared in scope and membership to the movement in some European countries, particularly in the Scandinavian countries and England.  The most extensive and powerful American co-operatives are marketing organizations.  There are over 8,300 marketing co-operatives, with about 2,500,000 members, doing an annual business of around three billion dollars.  The largest agricultural marketing co-operative is the California Fruit Growers' Association.  Next in order would rank certain large dairy co-operatives, such as the National Cheese Producers' Federation, and the Land O' Lakes Creameries, both of which have their main strength in Minnesota, Iowa, and Wisconsin.

Co-operative marketing of grain has assumed greater importance; the outstanding organization in this field is the Farmer's National Grain Corporation, founded in 1929.

There have been a number of rural experiments with consumers' co-operatives. For a long time, they were mainly local in character and relatively small in size. The movement, however, is gaining headway. The Farm Credit Administration estimates that there are 2,650 farmers' purchasing or consumers' co-operatives, with over 900,000 members. In the season of 1939–40, they purchased about 360 million dollars worth of supplies. Added to the supplies bought by marketing co-operatives, this brought the grand total of purchases through farmers' co-operatives up to about 450 million dollars for the season. The business of the farmers' purchasing co-operatives held up well during the war, and in 1945 it showed a gain of 11 per cent over 1944. The wholesale societies showed a gain of about 15 per cent. It is estimated that today over twelve per cent of all farm purchases are made through co-operatives. But our co-operative movement is far smaller than that of Great Britain, where the co-operative retail societies alone did a business of a billion dollars in 1935.

## Government Efforts in Behalf of the Farmers

**Movements to secure federal aid for farmers.** The various farm organizations worked hard to benefit their members, but the plight of the farmer became so desperate in the 1920's that the private organizations were unable to cope with the situation. Government aid was sought. Under the leadership of Senator Arthur Capper of Kansas, a farm bloc was organized in the Senate in 1921. Like the previous farmers' organizations, it urged the government to undertake a program of farm relief.

Many plans were set forth, most of them seeking to increase and stabilize the price of wheat, of which there was a large surplus produc tion. The most widely discussed plan was that embodied in the McNary-Haugen bills, which were passed by Congress in 1927 and 1928, but were twice vetoed by President Coolidge. They advocated the export of surplus wheat at the world price. The losses sustained on wheat exported at the world price, because of the difference between the world and domestic price, would be made up to the farmers through an equalization payment. The farmers would gain by this plan, since the great bulk of the wheat could be sold at the domestic price, protected by our tariff wall. The losses on the surplus exported at the world price would be relatively slight by comparison.

Another much discussed scheme was the Moline Plan, set forth by George Peek and Hugh S. Johnson. It proposed to create a financial corporation, supported by American farmers, which would buy up all surplus wheat and sell it at the world price plus 40 per cent, the latter being about equal to the tariff on wheat in the Fordney-McCumber

Tariff Act of 1923. The farmers would be assessed through a sales tax to make up this 40 per cent addition to the world price. The advantage to American farmers would be that the domestic price of wheat could not be forced down to the level of the world price. Although these plans were not adopted, they demonstrated the widespread and well-organized interest in solving the farm problem.

In 1929, a Federal Farm Board was established, with Alexander Legge as chairman. This board undertook the task of controlling the farm surplus and stabilizing wheat and cotton prices; but it could not make much headway against the adverse trends of the depression years, and the farm situation went from bad to worse. About 350 million dollars were spent in a fruitless effort to stabilize prices, while farm surpluses piled up still further.

**New Deal farm measures.** The farm problem, one of the most pressing issues confronting President Roosevelt after his inauguration in 1933, was promptly faced by the new administration. On May 12, 1933, the Agricultural Adjustment Act (AAA) was passed. The government, by this act, endeavored to control and reduce excess production of crops and to raise farm prices by agreeing to pay bounties to farmers who retired land from the cultivation of cotton, wheat, and several other crops. The revenue for these bounties was to be obtained chiefly from the manufacturers and the millers in the form of processing taxes. The AAA was declared unconstitutional by the Supreme Court in January, 1936, but government aid had at least temporarily increased farm income. Gross farm income grew from 5,337 million dollars in 1932 to 8,508 million in 1935. It is esti-

*Farm Security Administration, photo by Lee.*

A sharecropper's cabin in southeastern Missouri. This picture strikingly emphasizes the stark poverty, underprivileged existence, and ramshackle habitat of the sharecropper tenant farmer.

mated that, under the AAA, cotton growers benefited by 780 million dollars, wheat farmers by 356 million, and hog producers by 320 million.

The basic policy of the short-lived AAA was revived, without the processing tax, in the Soil Conservation and Domestic Allotment Act of

*Courtesy of J. C. Allen and Son.*

**Typical prosperous Indiana farm in the era of good times following Pearl Harbor. Reveals charming setting of rural life for well-to-do farmers.**

1936, superseded by the second Agricultural Adjustment Act, passed in 1938. The latter act also aimed to keep up farm prices by restricting production. The 1938 law was upheld by the Supreme Court, and many farmers signed contracts with the government whereby they agreed to take certain land out of production and place other sections in soil-building crops. The government payments for crop control helped to provide the farmers with money for taxes and interest on mortgages. Government subsidies to farmers under the new act were actually higher than under the AAA. In 1939, government payments to farmers were 807 million dollars, as compared with 573 million in 1935. In 1946, the government payments were nearly as large as in 1939.

While the New Deal farm legislation helped to solve the immediate farm crisis, it was fundamentally wrongheaded, for it subsidized scarcity at a time when only about 10 per cent of the American families were getting what government experts regarded as a liberal or desirable diet, and over half the population was ill-clothed and ill-shod. What the New Deal should have done was to stimulate urban production and employment sufficiently to produce the mass purchasing power needed to enable the city workers and white-collar groups to buy the farm products needed to insure a high standard of living. This was not done, partly through lack of initiative in the early days of the New Deal, and partly because of the resistance of conservative economic groups as they recovered more power after 1936.

The financial crisis in American agriculture brought forth a number of other acts designed to tide farmers over the emergency. The AAA had provided 2 billion dollars of government bonds for farm loans at 4 per cent interest. The Farm Credit Act (1933) centralized the credit agencies extending loans to farmers and set up banking facilities to handle the loans. The Farm Mortgage Refinancing Act (1934) created the Federal Farm Mortgage Corporation to supervise refinancing of farm mortgages and loans and to forestall foreclosures. The Crop Loan Act (1934) helped farmers to carry on their farming operations during the difficult season of 1934. The Farm Mortgage Foreclosure Act (1934) enabled the Federal Farm Land Bank to extend loans to farmers to redeem the farms they had lost by foreclosure.

**Farmers still depressed at end of New Deal.** While there is little doubt that the New Deal farm measures at least temporarily benefited the farming class, irrespective of whether the program was sound or not, it is also certain that the New Deal failed conspicuously to solve the farm problem in the United States. This may plainly be seen from a few representative facts about the state of farm life and the farm economy in 1940, at the end of the New Deal and before armament and war had worked a temporary revolution in farm production and income for the better class of farms and farmers.

In 1940, there were about 6,100,000 farms, of which at least a million were submarginal and barely able to provide subsistence for their operators. There were about two million small, family farms, not well equipped or very productive, which provided no more than a "living" for the operators. The remaining half of the farms produced 90 per cent of all the farm products to reach a market. Clearly the poorest half of the farms produced only a microscopic income per farm in the form of revenue from products marketed. Nearly 40 per cent of the farms of 1940 were operated by tenants.

The figures for farm income in 1940 are equally instructive and dolorous. The total farm income from one-fourth of the nation's farms was less than $400 each. The income from nearly an additional fourth of the farms was less than $750 each. Farm families received only 7.8 per cent of the total national income, although some 22.9 per cent of the people lived on farms. The farmer's share of the consumer's dollar spent for staple foods in 1940 was only 42 cents, whereas it has been 53 cents in 1913. At least one-third of all the farms in 1940 were so small, poorly equipped, or so lacking in fertility that the operators could not be fully employed throughout the year in their farm work. As we have already noted, over half the farm dwellings were substandard, lacking in conveniences, and in need of major repairs.

## Temporary Effect of the Second World War on American Farming

**Temporary farm gains produced by second world war and relief programs.** The New Deal measures did not bring full employment or prosperity to either American manufacturing industry or American agriculture. It remained for the second world war and postwar conditions to provide such results, at least temporarily. The demand for food for our armies and workers, and for those of our allies, during the war, quickly wiped out the farm surpluses of the previous two decades and provided a market for everything the farmers could raise.

We shall need to cite only a few basic figures to show how the trends in the farm economy from 1940 to 1950 more than reversed the picture between 1920 and 1930 and produced an unprecedented temporary boom in American agriculture. The total cash receipts of farmers, exclusive of government payments, rose from $9,130,000,000 in 1940 to $31,018,000,000 in 1948—the peak year. Of course, farm costs rose during this period—but not quite as spectacularly—from $5,953,000,-000 in 1940 to $15,954,000,000 in 1947. The net cash income of farmers, after all expenditures, rose from $3,177,000,000 in 1940 to over 18 billion dollars in 1948. Even after making allowances for the greatly reduced purchasing power of the dollar, the farming class, at least those above the level of sub-marginal and marginal farmers, gained more from the economic trends of the 1940's than the wage earning and salaried classes.

**Why there was no depression in American farming after the second world war.** We noted earlier that, after the end of the first world war, there was a rapid and serious decline of farming prosperity which lasted for virtually twenty years, though mitigated somewhat from 1933 to 1940. After the second world war a decline did not come at once, mainly because of the great demand for goods to meet current needs, delayed wartime orders, rearmament, foreign rehabilitation, and the like, which kept city workers employed and able to buy food in large quantities, and because of the shipment of large quantities of food abroad for relief. What are the prospects of continuing this set of favorable conditions for the farmers for some time in the future?

The Marshall Plan, or the European Recovery Program, as it is now known, is in operation under the Economic Co-operation Administration, and is expected to continue in one form or another for years. This means that large quantities of American farm products may continue to be sent abroad. The demand for manufactured products is still ahead of the supply, so city workers can be expected to go on buying farm products in large quantities for some time to come. We now have in operation a plan of government support for farm products—the parity system—which guarantees minimum prices each year and will make up the difference to farmers in case actual prices fall below this minimum.   This encourages farmers to keep up a large production, for they do not have to fear any immediate probability that the bottom will fall out of farm prices.

Temporary and precarious nature of present farm prosperity. These conditions and circumstances would appear to assure farm pros-

## FACTS ABOUT THE FARM PROBLEM

| | CASH FARM INCOME FROM CROPS AND LIVESTOCK | GOVERNMENT PAYMENTS |
|---|---|---|
| 1930 | ●●●●●●●●●● $ 8,883,000,000 | NONE |
| 1932 | FARM POPULATION 1930 – 30,169,000 1948 – 27,440,000 ●●●●● $ 4,682,000,000 | NONE |
| 1933 | ●●●●●● $ 5,278,000,000 | ( $131,000,000 |
| 1935 | ●●●●●●●● $ 6,969,000,000 | ( $573,000,000 |
| 1937 | ●●●●●●●●● $ 8,744,000,000 | ( $367,000,000 |
| 1939 | ●●●●●●●● $ 7,733,000,000 | ( $807,000,000 |
| 1948 | ●●●● ●●●●●●●● ●●●●●●●● ●●●●●●●● $31,018,000,000 | ( $256,000,000 |

Each disc equals one billion dollars

Courtesy The New York Times.

This graph reveals amazing increase of gross farm cash income as a result of the second world war and the cold war.

perity for some years, but there are limits and dangers. The more completely the foreign nations recover, the less their demand for American food and the greater their ability to produce their own, as was the case after 1920. The abnormal demand for manufactured goods is likely to fall off in a few years, even if it is not prematurely curtailed by exorbitant prices, and this will reduce the urban demand for farm products. The government may abandon its present lavish support of farm prices, though this is not likely under the second Truman administration, since it was the farmers, in considerable part, who elected Mr. Truman in 1948.

The parity and price support program seemed to be falling apart at the seams as we entered the second half of the century. The government had over 4 billion dollars tied up in its price support program, but cash farm income fell off from $31,332,000,000 in 1948 to $28,100,000,000 in 1949, and net farm income from 18 billion to 15 billion. A drop of another 2 billion was predicted for 1950. The old problem of agricultural surpluses, which had plagued the Coolidge, Hoover, and New Deal administrations, returned once more. For example, early in 1950, the government had on its hands some 25 million bushels of potatoes, purchased at $1.10 a bushel, which it was selling back to the farmers at three-fifths of a cent a bushel for cattle feed or fertilizer—though there were still millions of Americans who could not get enough potatoes to eat. It was reminiscent of New Deal days when wheat and cotton were being plowed under while the country was ill-fed and ill-clothed. The trends and figures for 1949 and 1950 seemed to indicate that the first big break in postwar "prosperity" might come in agriculture.

In the case of an impending recession, it is proposed by farm leaders that the farm economy shall be protected by government subsidy of continued food shipments abroad, even at low prices; by government subsidy of greater food consumption by American citizens; and by the establishment of a new sort of AAA which will pay the farmer for reduced production of crops. It is rather obvious that, even if such measures can be provided, they will be mainly temporizing rather than any permanent solution of our farm problem. In 1949 and 1950 Secretary of Agriculture Charles F. Brannan proposed to substitute for the parity and price support program a plan whereby the prices of farm products would be fixed by demand and supply in the market, and farm income would be sustained by cash subsidies to farmers, but his plan was coolly received by most farm leaders and organizations.

**Basic reforms essential to permanent rural prosperity.** The great problem of the farmer in the postwar period is, therefore, to keep his present larger market and high prices. So long as full industrial employment in cities, large shipments of food abroad for relief, and a great rearmament program continue, it appears likely that the farmer may hold his own. In short, the farmer's prosperity is tied up to the same general abnormal and necessarily temporary conditions that give prosperity to the urban workers and provide a powerful but passing "shot in the arm" to an otherwise wobbly capitalism.

We pointed out in an earlier chapter that fundamental reforms in our economic system will be necessary to sustain capitalism under normal conditions, and the same is true of our agricultural system. The New Deal and succeeding years have not provided these reforms for either industry or agriculture. When the abnormal demand fades out at home and abroad, recession is inevitable. Then, we shall have to institute the needed economic reforms or else face a great depression, unless we once more seek to stave off depression by a foreign war. In short, the current rural prosperity is wholly temporary and abnormal, and nothing connected with it materially lessens the need for sweeping reforms in our economic system.

**A farm program to maintain rural prosperity.** Anticipating the time when the abnormal conditions of the second world war and its aftermath, which have proved a momentary godsend to American farmers, will come to an end, the leading farm organizations have formulated the following policies and objectives, designed to assure some measure of prosperity and security for farmers in the years to come:

1. Maintaining abundant or adequate production of food and fiber products.
2. Securing an equitable share of the national income for farmers.
3. Conserving and building up our soil resources.
4. Improving the co-ordination of the Federal agencies that work with farm people.
5. Improving and modernizing the parity formula.
6. Using price supports and production control.
7. Improving facilities for rural development, including health, education, nutrition, and recreation.
8. Improving marketing, processing, and distribution of farm products.

**Farmers embrace the welfare state.** Amidst all this uncertainty as to the future of farm conditions, one certainty exists, and that is that the former vigorous individualism of the American farmer and his opposition to government interference in business and to government aid to individuals are now dead, apparently forever. As a result of the great farm depression after 1921, of changing living conditions, and of new political and economic ideologies, no group in American society today is more insistent upon government aid than the farmers. This was well demonstrated not only by the ardent farmer support of the New Deal, but also by the fact that it was the farmer vote that helped to defeat Mr. Dewey and elect President Truman in November, 1948.

## Large Farms as a Solution of the Rural Problem

**Large collective farms under government supervision.** Many students of rural economics believe that the only solution of our farm problem, in many areas, is the large collective farm; that is, government ownership or control of lands, buildings, and equipment, and the cultivation of the land by families under a co-operative organization with a government contract. This has worked successfully in some government projects in New Mexico. The advocates of the collective farm contend that, if we hold to the old American tradition of private farm ownership, the improvements in technology will make the agricultural class ever more dependent on the government for mere relief and farm subsidies, without gaining the advantages that the large collective farm promises in the way of greater mechanical efficiency, larger production, a higher standard of living, and greater security for the cultivators of the soil. This collective farm program is a drastic plan, and, if tried, should be sharply scrutinized.

**Trend toward larger farms.** While as yet there has been only a very slight development of large collective farms under government control, there has been a very marked tendency towards much larger farms. Between 1910 and 1945, the farms of 1,000 acres or more increased in number from 50,135 to 112,899, and the acreage in these larger farms increased from 167 million acres to 460 million; by 1945, these farms contained over 40 per cent of all farming land.[6] At the other end of the scale, the number of farms between 20 and 260 acres decreased by 694,781 between 1910 and 1940. The largest one-third of our farms produce about four-fifths of all our farm products for the market. In 1945, the largest 8.7 per cent of the farms produced 45.4 per cent of the gross value of all farm production. These farms have only 12.2 per cent of the total farm population. The concentration of farming units is even more impressive than such statistics suggest, for great farming corporations have leased and united many small farms in actual operation, though they are still listed in the census as separate, small farms.

**Social and cultural disadvantages of large-scale farming.** This tendency toward the growth of very large farms has usually been hailed as a great advance and an important step toward the solution of our farm problem. Such an attitude has been based on the consideration that large farms permit the most complete utilization of advanced types of farm machinery and, hence, are more efficient. But this appraisal leaves aside the matter of the effect of such large-scale, mechanized farming on the personal and social side of the picture. Studies have been made of large-scale and small-scale farming areas, under comparable conditions, and these indicate that personal inde-

---

6 A considerable portion of the 460 million acres in these large farms was ranch and pasture land.

pendence and dignity, public utilities, and social services are far superior in the small-farm districts. The large farms are more efficient in sheer production, in terms of manpower units, but they tend to reduce the social aspects of the process to the status of servility and neglect. There is a danger that these large corporate farms may develop into great mechanized *latifundia*.

The Bureau of Agricultural Economics made a study of a large-scale farming area and a small-farm district in the San Joaquin Valley in California, the former known as Arvin and the latter as Dinuba. General agricultural conditions and population make-up were virtually the same in the two areas. But personal relations, local business, and social services were far superior in Dinuba. The latter had two banks to none in Arvin. It had two newspapers to one in Arvin. Its streets were paved, while those in Arvin were not. Its housing facilities were far superior to those in Arvin. It had a high school and four grammar schools to one grammar school in Arvin. Its service and social clubs were far more numerous and active. There were more recreational facilities and far less juvenile delinquency. There were more retail business establishments, doing an amount of business about double that in Arvin. Only five out of ten of the inhabitants of Dinuba worked for wages, while eight of ten of those who lived in Arvin did so. In short, as Carey McWilliams puts it, "Dinuba was a real farming community while Arvin was more of a camp than a community." Few who lived in Arvin contemplated identifying their lives with any permanent habitation or career in the region.

Such comparisons need not be taken as any blanket condemnation of large-scale farming, which certainly could be so conducted as to combine technical efficiency with a well socialized community life, but they do show that the issue involves something more than merely the matter of expensive mechanical equipment and high crop output. In the light of these facts, it is both instructive and ominous that in January, 1949, the United States Department of Agriculture issued a report indicating that the future economic outlook for the million small farms in the nation that produce only from $500 to $1,000 worth of products annually, even at the high prices of 1949, is highly dubious, even in the current period of temporary rural prosperity.

Probably the best solution of the farm problem is to obtain the increased efficiency which the latest mechanization on large farms makes possible, and then to insure the proper development of community spirit and facilities by systematic community organization service supplied, if necessary, by the Federal government. What such community service could provide is made clear in a later chapter dealing with community organization. Such a solution would be more in harmony with American traditions and temper than collectivized farms under government ownership or control.

The farm laborers displaced by increased mechanization could very properly be employed on the public works and in the service industries which we shall require if a condition of security, abundance, and leisure which would constitute true civilization is ever to be attained in this country.

## The Future of Country Life

**General outlook for American farming.** In the following chapter we shall see that the city has come to a turning-point in its development. Either the city will continue to grow until it collapses as a result of congestion or atom bombing, or there will be a marked trend toward breaking up large cities into suburban areas and small "Greenbelt" communities. The rural community is in fully as critical a stage today as are the urban centers. Farm life, as it existed fifty years ago, is seemingly doomed. The day of the small farm is coming to an end in many areas. There is every reason to believe that more and more cereal and cotton farming will be carried on in the future by large-scale operations, using the newest and most efficient machinery. Outside of cereal and cotton farming, the trend is likely to be toward specialized agriculture, such as fruit raising, vegetable growing, and dairy farming. These cannot be mechanized as completely as cereal farming.

**Rural life takes on a new pattern.** Although the long-range outlook for many farmers is dark, there is little possibility that the rural areas will be abandoned in wholesale fashion. On the contrary, there seems to be a marked trend of population movement from the city to the country. Henry Ford once started a system of small industries— model small plants located in country areas—which he hoped would make possible an ideal combination of manufacturing and rural life. Their success proved the wisdom and practicality of such a program. Improvements in transportation will probably cause an ever greater migration of urban workers to rural regions bordering on urban centers. Even today, many thousands of workers live in the country and daily commute to the city.

**Movement from city to country.** The movement from the city to the country has already begun. The rural farm population declined by about 1,900,000 between 1910 and 1930. But, during that same period, the rural population not engaged in farming increased by 5,900,000. Some of this latter gain came from births within that segment of the former farm population that had abandoned farming but still remained in the country; most of it, however, came from the migration of urban dwellers to the country. After the depression began in 1929, the movement to the country was even more rapid. In 1932, the rural population gained over a million and, in this year, exceeded the city population growth by over 500,000. This was the first time in recent American history that cities had suffered a relative loss in population.

After economic conditions improved in 1933, some of those who had migrated to the country returned to the city. But it is evident that the rural non-farming population is already making steady gains and that this element is likely to increase as time goes on. The census of 1940 amply bears out this view. The rural farm population has virtually ceased to grow; it was 30,157,513 in 1930 and 30,216,188 in 1940. On the other hand, the rural non-farm population increased from 23,-662,710 in 1930 to 27,029,385 in 1940, an increase of 14.5 per cent. Moreover, the counties containing or adjacent to cities increased more rapidly than any other section of the country. As a result of the abnormal conditions during the war, the American farm population shrank by about 3 million between 1940 and 1948, but current tendencies indicate that the non-farming rural population will continue to increase. It even held its own in the period from 1940 to 1948, in contrast to the shrinkage in the rural farm population. By 1948, the rural non-farm population had become larger than the rural farm population; in that year the rural non-farm population constituted 22.4 per cent of the total population, and the rural farm population only 19.2 per cent.

This movement to the country and suburbs by thousands who remain employed in cities, and commute back and forth, may have important social and cultural results for the nation. The urban centralization and the contact of cities with rural conditions may produce a mixed urban-rural type of life and culture, combining the good (or the bad) features of both. The stabilizing trends in rural life may be united with the greater tolerance and breadth of interests characteristic of city life. Of course, there may be unfortunate results, in bringing certain pathological aspects of city life out into the country, but even these are likely to be less flagrant in a rural environment. One ominous symptom indicating that the urbanization of country mores may produce bad results has been the great increase in rural crimes, especially crimes against property, since the second world war.

## The Outlook for Country Youth

**Farm youth and the "American Dream."** For no rural group has the farm crisis been more serious than for youth. The great "American Dream" has usually revolved around the country boy who has made good. The Horatio Alger and Rover Boys stories, which have become part of the folklore of America, often depicted the country boy, born of poor but honest parents, who went to the city and fought his way to the top, ultimately becoming President of the United States, a captain of industry, an urban banker, or something of the sort. Many of the more notable achievements in our national history were actually those of rural youth who went to the cities, bringing with them the energy, ambition, and natural ingenuity taught by rural life, the initiative and independence characteristic of the country, and the strong physique gained by living in healthful surroundings. The youths remaining in the country bought farms; and although, with few exceptions, they did not become wealthy, they acquired economic stability and personal independence. These persons built up and carried on the sturdy farm character that had made our farming population the backbone of the nation.

In former days, and even down through the first world war, young people born on a farm had a fairly promising future in prospect. The more venturesome and alert often went to the city, found positions, and established themselves in business or the professions. Those who did not go to the city could set themselves up in some form of village industry or retail trade, or become owners of farms and able to support themselves and their families on a decent standard of living.

**Bleak outlook for many rural youth.** What are the prospects of farm youth today? The outlook is not too bright, if we are to believe the careful study, *Rural Youth: Their Situation and Prospects,* made by the Division of Social Research of the Works Progress Administration. With rural life losing its distinctive characteristics, the long-range outlook for rural youth is one of economic instability and relative cultural decay in many rural areas. During the decade from 1930 to 1940, farm families received less than 10 per cent of the national income, but had to shoulder the task of educating 30 per cent of the nation's children.

Farms are getting larger and, therefore, are becoming fewer in number. In 1930, the average size of farms was 157 acres; by 1940, it was 174 acres, and concentration has gone on since 1940. All this means that there will be a smaller number of farms available for young men to take over as owners and operators. In the coming generation there will be about three boys born and reared on farms for each farm left open for occupation as a result of the death or retirement of the owner.

The cities, in normal times, have a large number of unemployed persons who must go on relief or work on government projects. It has, therefore, become increasingly difficult for country youth to find work in the city. Small-scale village industry is often unable to compete with efficient large-scale production. The automobile has taken much of the trade from the country store. Rural dwellers now do much of their shopping in city stores, where there is a greater volume and variety of goods and usually lower prices. The mail-order firms, such as Montgomery Ward and Sears, Roebuck, have also helped to undermine the small town and village establishments. These companies also have large local retail stores in many American cities.

The increased volume and efficiency of agricultural machinery may well produce a farm crisis more serious than at any earlier period in our history. As we have seen, it has been estimated that, if our farming were carried on in the most efficient known manner, all the farm products we need could be produced on one-fifth of the land now cultivated, with one-fifth the farm labor now used. Formerly, the chief farm problem was to strain and struggle to produce enough crops to feed the country, most of which could usually be sold at a fair price. Today, the main problem, in normal times, is to dispose of the large amount produced, and at a price that will enable the farmer to live. All too many farmers just about break even or carry on their operations at a loss, except under the abnormal conditions produced by war and foreign relief.

**Attempts to aid rural youth.** The country areas have improved their educational facilities, but they are still backward compared with those in the city. Even the marked improvement in rural education is of little practical use if farm youths cannot secure jobs after they have been trained for them. Although rural facilities for recreation and leisure time have been increased, the provisions are still far less adequate than in urban areas.

The government set up a number of programs designed to help rural youth. The United States Department of Agriculture, working through the state colleges of agriculture, promotes 4-H Clubs designed to teach young people better farming methods, home economics, new ideas of community life, and better types of recreation. Many high schools have received Federal grants for courses in agriculture and home economics, and the Office of Education has contributed radio programs and public forums. The now abandoned National Youth Administration, organized chiefly for youth on relief, aided those who could not attend school without financial assistance, provided special courses in agricultural schools for farm boys and girls, supplied work projects for unemployed youth, and offered some guidance in choosing a job and finding employment. The Farm Credit Administration has provided financial aid to young farmers who want to get a start in agriculture. Whatever farm aid came as a result of the various agricultural acts of the New Deal has, directly or indirectly, helped rural youth. The United States Employment Service helps young people in the country as well as in the city to secure jobs.

Despite these many and varied government programs and agencies to help rural youth, no proposal has yet been launched which in any way copes with the seriousness of the situation. As the above-mentioned WPA report concludes: "A concerted frontal attack has yet to be made on the long-time factors responsible for the widespread destitution and restricted social opportunities of rural youth."

**War temporarily alters the picture.** The coming of war improved the picture to a certain degree. Many farm youths joined the armed services; others found profitable employment in the booming war industries. The great increase in the demand for farm products, coupled with the drafting of farm boys and the migration of many rural youth to war-industry centers, temporarily created an actual shortage of farm labor. This temporary improvement in the prospects of rural youth does not, however, alter the bleak general prospect for the future.

The hardships faced by rural youth during the depression may return, possibly with increased force, as soon as the artificial demand for farm products for relief abroad subsides.

To be sure, the large demand for farm products could be sustained in part if we were to adopt, before foreign relief falls off, such means of assuring steady employment and high wages for urban workers as a large Federal housing program, extensive highway construction and other public-works projects, adequate Federal support for recreational and other service facilities, Federal aid to public education, national health, and the like, but there seems no probability that such steps will be taken, at least to the extent needed to produce substantial results. In President Truman's "welfare" national budget of 1950 only six per cent of Federal expenditures was allotted to such purposes.

## Summary

The farm was the most important factor in the American economy until the end of the nineteenth century. It molded the character of American political, social, and economic institutions and provided a livelihood for the majority of people. The traditional American ideals of family life, democracy, independence, thrift, and industry found their origins on the farm. Rural districts supplied many of the leaders who built up American industry and business and took the lead in political life. The farming community represented the era of the primary society and personal relations in its most complete form.

Agriculture prospered during most years before 1920, especially during the first world war. After that time, however, the position of the American farmer steadily became worse until the agricultural legislation of the New Deal era. Coupled with the shrinkage of markets abroad was the effect of constantly improved methods of production. These resulted in the creation of huge surpluses of unsold farm products and put the small farmer and the farm laborer in a desperate financial situation. Only the second world war and world relief served temporarily to stay the hand of rural depression.

New methods of transportation and communication have undermined the old rural culture and greatly increased the importance of the city in relation to farm life. More than 60 per cent of Americans now live in urban areas and 25 per cent more live in such proximity to cities that their attitudes have been pretty thoroughly urbanized. The old-time farm family and neighborhood, with their distinctive social life, are fast disappearing. Rural life is beginning to feel the full impact of contemporary mechanization and communication.

Efforts were made by the New Deal administration after 1933 to relieve the economic plight of the farmer and to aid rural youth in making a new start in life. These measures, however, did not strike at the roots of the farm problem and accomplished little of a substantial nature. For the most part, they put the farmer on a dole.

The abnormal conditions of huge wartime demands for food, and the great need of food by industrial workers in the United States and starving peoples abroad after the war, brought a temporary revival of rural prosperity, though the spectacular rise in the income from farm products was partly absorbed in increasing costs of farm life and operation.

No adequate reforms have been made in either the national or the rural economy, and when the recession comes in the course of time, the farm problem will have to be tackled about where it was in 1933 —or at least in 1940.   Some experts in rural economics believe that the mechanized collective farm under governmental supervision may be the only solution of the farm problem in many parts of the country. Others believe that the development of large, mechanized farms to assure the greatest efficiency in farm production, along with elaborate community planning to produce good living conditions, constitute a better solution.

While the future of the American farm is today uncertain, there is, nevertheless, a marked movement of people from cities to rural regions, especially of city professional workers and laborers, who wish to live in the country during non-working hours.   These people are seeking to combine the best of two patterns of living—rural and urban —and may create a new and superior type of American culture.

### Selected References

* Baker, O. E.; Borsodi, Ralph; and Wilson, M. L., *Agriculture and Modern Life,* Harper, 1939.   An appreciative discussion of the place of the farm and rural life in modern American civilization.

Cole, W. E., and Crow, H. P., *Recent Trends in Rural Planning,* Prentice-Hall, 1937.   Valuable for impact of New Deal philosophy on rural life.

Gee, Wilson, *Social Economics of Agriculture,* Macmillan, 1942.   Important analysis of economic aspects of American rural life.

Hacker, L. M., *The Farmer Is Doomed,* Day, 1933.   A brief pessimistic analysis of the status of American agriculture on the eve of the New Deal.

Hawthorn, H. B., *The Sociology of Rural Life,* Century, 1926.   A substantial and sane manual on rural social life before the New Deal era.

Hicks, Granville, *The Small Town,* Macmillan, 1946.   Brilliant and very readable analysis of the social and cultural character and problems of the rural town.

Holmes, R. H., *Rural Sociology,* McGraw-Hill, 1932.   Good textbook stressing the primary institutions and personal society of rural life.

* Landis, P. H., *Rural Life in Process,* McGraw-Hill, 1948.   Good textbook, with emphasis on social forces of rural life.

Lindstrom, D. E., *American Rural Life,* Ronald Press, 1948. Valuable for stress laid on the growing complexity of rural society and culture.

Loomis, C. P. and Beegle, J. A., *Rural Social Systems,* Prentice-Hall, 1949. Voluminous and comprehensive description and analysis of the structure and functions of rural society.

McDonald, Angus, *Old McDonald Had a Farm,* Houghton Mifflin, 1942. Inspiring and absorbing account of how toil, intelligence, and persistence turned a run-down Oklahoma farm into a model and profitable homestead.

* McWilliams, Carey, *Ill Fares the Land,* Little, Brown, 1942. Able and thoughtful description of the farm problems created by drought, the mechanical revolution, and marginal farming.

Nelson, Lowry, *Rural Sociology,* American Book Company, 1948. Brings the resources of sociological theory to bear on the analysis of rural society and social problems.

* Sanderson, Dwight, *The Rural Community,* Ginn, 1932. A study of contemporary rural life by a leading rural sociologist, who stresses the continuing importance of the rural village as a social community.

Schafer, Joseph, *Social History of American Agriculture,* Macmillan, 1936. Best general historical account of evolution of American rural society.

Sims, N. L., *Elements of Rural Sociology,* Crowell, 1940. One of the best introductory studies of rural life and institutions.

Smart, C. A., *R.F.D.,* Norton, 1938. An interesting analysis of rural life, laying special stress on the way farm life promotes originality and ingenuity in meeting practical problems.

* Smith, T. L., *The Sociology of Rural Life,* Harper, 1946. One of the ablest presentations of the leading social processes involved in rural life.

Taylor, C. C.; Raper, A. F.; et al., *Rural Life in the United States,* Knopf, 1949. Excellent recent description of rural life in the main farming areas of the United States.

Woofter, T. J., and Winston, Ellen, *Seven Lean Years,* University of North Carolina Press, 1939. An able analysis of the distressed farmers under the New Deal and convincing evidence of the inadequacy of New Deal measures in solving the problems of the marginal farmers.

# CHAPTER XXIV

# American Society Moves Into an Urban Pattern

## Nature and Growth of Modern Cities

Modern cities bring in a new pattern of civilization. Having now surveyed the leading traits and social patterns of rural life, we may now turn to living conditions and social processes in urban life. The latter really represent a new stage and a different pattern of human civilization. This fact has been well described and emphasized by Professor Wirth:

City and country are not merely distinct types of physical entities; they are also contrasting modes of life. Life on the farm or in rural areas is relatively stable and simple compared with life in the city. Rural life is close to nature, relatively isolated, uncomplicated by an advanced technology, and self-sufficient. The rural community involves few people and these few are much alike in their origins, their occupations, and their ways of living. Rural life rests upon intimate associations. It is held together by rumor, gossip, personal controls, and a common culture.

City life on the other hand is carried on remote from nature in a highly complex man-made technological environment. The city is interdependent and in close contact with the outside world. It gives rise to a great division of labor. The urban community consists of great numbers of heterogeneous persons both as to origins, occupations, and ways of living. Although densely crowded together, people in the city do not rely upon intimate associations with all of those who live near them to carry on an orderly life. The inhabitants of a city are held together by news and publicity, by formal laws, and by impersonal controls. In contrast with life in the country, urban life is characterized by complexity, instability, and indirect interrelations.[1]

The great industrial and commercial city of the twentieth century is, therefore, probably the outstanding social innovation of our civilization. No simple definition, such as "a large number of persons living in a relatively small area," is sufficient to characterize the modern city. It provides a highly complicated social, economic, political, legal, and cultural pattern of life, and a striking example of the shifting social scene in the wake of the revolutionary technological and economic changes of recent times.

---

[1] Wirth and Lussenhop, *op. cit.*, p. 7.

The rise and location of early cities. City life is not new; men long ago discovered the advantages of living together in a given locality. The sites of early cities depended, to a great extent, upon favorable natural conditions. Many towns were located along the seacoast or near the mouths of rivers where fishing or harbors were good. Until steam power developed and railroads became common, a waterside location was probably the most important single factor in determining the site of important cities. Locations were also selected for defensive reasons; valleys surrounded by high mountains and islands were often chosen for defensive purposes. Ancient cities owed their growth, not only to geographic location, but to economic and political factors (often related to the geographic) as well; advantageous location frequently offered a favorable opportunity for trade and prosperity and for conquest and increased political power. Cultural prestige also aided in attracting people to such settled locations as Athens, Alexandria, Rome, and Baghdad.

ROTHENBURG-ON-THE-TAUBER

Rothenburg, Germany: A fortified town of the Middle Ages. This picture of one of the best preserved cities of the Middle Ages shows the small and restricted character of most cities prior to the era of industrialization.

Gradual development of the modern urban era. Although there were a number of cities in some of the ancient civilizations, such as those of the Near East, Greece, and Rome, the great majority of the people lived in rural areas throughout both ancient and medieval times. Urban growth was slow until after 1500. Paris, the largest city in western Europe, then had a population of about 300,000; London had only 40,000 persons, and Berlin was an unimportant town of a few thousand.

The expansion of Europe and the Commercial Revolution, following the discovery of new sea routes to America and the Orient, greatly stimulated urban growth. By 1800, London had over 800,000 people, Paris half a million, and Berlin about 172,000. Despite this marked increase of population in some of the larger cities, urbanization was not extensive throughout western Europe until after the industrial and agricultural revolutions which began in the latter part of the eighteenth century. In 1800, there were only 21 cities in the world with a population of over 100,000 each; today, there are over 500 such cities. At the opening of the nineteenth century, only 15 cities in England had a population of over 20,000; ninety years later, 185 cities in England had reached the 20,000 mark. By 1930, more than 80 per cent of the English population lived in urban communities. The following table will indicate the rapid and impressive urbanization of the western world since the Industrial Revolution has thoroughly taken root.[2]

PERCENTAGE OF THE TOTAL POPULATIONS IN URBAN AREAS

| Year | United States | England and Wales | France | Germany |
|---|---|---|---|---|
| 1800 ........... | .... | 20.0 | .... | .... |
| 1850 ........... | .... | 50.2 | 25.5 | .... |
| 1860 ........... | .... | 54.6 | 28.9 | .... |
| 1870 ........... | .... | 61.8 | 31.1 | 36.1 |
| 1880 ........... | 28.6 | 67.9 | 34.8 | 41.4 |
| 1890 ........... | 35.4 | 72.0 | 37.4 | 47.0 |
| 1900 ........... | 40.0 | 77.0 | 40.9 | 54.3 |
| 1910 ........... | 45.8 | 78.1 | 44.2 | 60.0 |
| 1920 ........... | 51.4 | 79.3 | 46.3 | 64.4 |
| 1930 ........... | 56.2 | 80.0 | 49.1 | 67.1 |

The latest available statistics give the urban population of the United States in 1950 as 60.2 per cent; that of England and Wales in 1930 as 80 per cent; that of France in 1936 as 52.4 per cent; and that of Germany in 1939 as 69.9 per cent. It is an impressive fact that, of the 93.5 million increase in population in Europe and the Soviet Union between 1919 and 1939, 80 million went into urban population.

In 1790, the United States did not have one city with 50,000 inhabitants; today, we have over 200 such cities, six of them with over a million inhabitants, though it was not until 1880 that we had even one city with a population of a million. In 1800, less than 4 per cent of our inhabitants lived in cities; in 1948, about 85 per cent lived in cities or so close to cities that their life pattern was primarily urban. We had not one metropolitan district in 1800; by 1948, we had 145 of them, and in them half of the population of the United States. Perhaps the most striking fact about our urbanization is that we have today 375 times as many urban dwellers as in 1800, and less than 15 times as many rural inhabitants. The following table presents the essential facts on the urbanization of the United States since 1790.[3]

---

2 Adapted from W. S. Thompson, *Population Problems*, McGraw-Hill, 1930.
3 *Postwar Problems of Migration*, Milbank Memorial Fund, New York, 1947, p. 162.

| Year | Total Popula- tion | Urban Population | | Increase in Per Cent Urban dur- ing Preceding Period | |
|---|---|---|---|---|---|
| | | Number | Per Cent of Total | Absolute Increase | Percentage Increase |
| 1790 | 3,929,214 | 201,655 | 5.1 | — | — |
| 1800 | 5,308,483 | 322,371 | 6.1 | 1.0 | 19.6 |
| 1810 | 7,239,881 | 525,459 | 7.3 | 1.2 | 19.7 |
| 1820 | 9,638,453 | 693,255 | 7.2 | −0.1 | −1.4 |
| 1830 | 12,866,020 | 1,127,247 | 8.8 | 1.6 | 22.2 |
| 1840 | 17,069,453 | 1,845,055 | 10.8 | 2.0 | 22.7 |
| 1850 | 23,191,876 | 3,543,716 | 15.3 | 4.5 | 41.7 |
| 1860 | 31,443,321 | 6,216,518 | 19.8 | 4.5 | 29.4 |
| 1870 | 38,558,371 | 9,902,361 | 25.7 | 5.9 | 29.8 |
| 1880 | 50,155,783 | 14,129,735 | 28.2 | 2.5 | 9.7 |
| 1890 | 62,947,714 | 22,106,265 | 35.1 | 6.9 | 24.5 |
| 1900 | 75,994,575 | 30,159,921 | 39.7 | 4.6 | 13.1 |
| 1910 | 91,972,266 | 41,998,932 | 45.7 | 6.0 | 15.1 |
| 1920 | 105,710,620 | 54,157,973 | 51.2 | 5.5 | 12.0 |
| 1930 | 122,775,046 | 68,954,823 | 56.2 | 5.0 | 9.8 |
| 1940 | 131,669,275 | 74,423,702 | 56.5 | 0.3 | 0.5 |

**Main causes of urbanization.** The causes of the remarkable urbanization of modern society all revolve around the sweeping economic changes since the eighteenth century. It is generally understood that our rapid urbanization has been closely related to the Industrial Revolution, the rise of machines, and the factory system, but the Agricultural Revolution made an equally important contribution to city growth. Agricultural improvements made it possible to produce a far greater amount of food on less land with fewer farmers; agricultural laborers were thus freed to work in the cities, where the increased farm production could feed them.

The factory system, rendered necessary by the rise of machines, constituted the main stimulus to modern urban growth. Machines could not be set up in the homes of the workers. They were heavy and expensive and had to be placed in buildings built especially to house them. Until steam power was available for machine power and land transportation, suitable water power and waterways were the most vital factor in determining the location of industrial cities. After the development of steam power to run the machines, the factories had to be located around the engines that generated the power. Steam power was probably the most important and vital single factor in creating the modern industrial city. Laborers had to move near the factories, for working hours were long and transportation facilities poor. As factories became more numerous, more laborers were needed and factory towns became larger and more congested.

The new problems of business administration after the first Industrial Revolution also helped to create urban concentration. Before the days of the telephone, offices had to be located at the factory. Subordinate managers, clerks, and white-collar employees all had to live close to their work. Wholesale warehouses and their operating personnel were located around factories, in order to be near the source of goods. Retail merchants also tended to congregate in the same general section as the factory district, with a view to obtaining the workers' trade. The professional classes—doctors, lawyers, dentists— serving both employers and laborers, also flocked to the urban centers. In this way, the modern city grew ever larger as new developments in urban architecture, such as the skyscraper, made possible ever greater concentration of population within a small area.

**Factors determining location of modern urban centers.** The rapid growth of urban areas since 1800 was thus based on the series of changes in the methods of making a living. What factors determined the location of these concentrated settlements? Location at the mouth of a river, a lake harbor, a canal terminal, or at a terminus of railroad routes; proximity to water power or to minerals and oil—these are only a few of the more prominent. For example, Gary, Indiana has become a great iron and steel city because it can draw upon the coal mines to the south and the iron ore of the Lake Superior district. Some cities thrive because they are healthful; high altitudes, dry climate, and medicinal springs have been the making of many a city.

A powerful spur to urban growth is found where there are sufficiently varied natural advantages to make possible the development of several major industries. In short, if an area has good natural resources, a sufficient quantity of cheap power, an adequate labor force, a wide trading region, and natural transportation advantages, cities will tend to develop rapidly within it.

## The Ecological Pattern of the City

**Ecological pattern of modern metropolitan areas.** O. Henry, the American short-story writer, once said that every city has a personality of its own. But, if each city has individuality, all have certain characteristics in common, such as rather definite locations for factories, shops, and dwellings, and a marked separation of the habitations of social classes. The "downtown" business and financial district, the inner industrial area, the slum and tenement area, the middle-class zone, the exclusive district inhabited by the well-to-do, and the suburban or commuter zone—these six zones of activity and population distribution are typical of most large cities. This spatial distribution of the city districts and population is what the sociologists call the ecology of city life.

"Downtown" means the business and financial area, with its skyscraper office buildings, department stores, imposing banks, restaurants, and hotels. Traffic is heaviest in this district during the day, but very few, except the permanent residents of hotels, make their homes here.

If we draw circles out from this downtown hub of the city, we can mark the ring nearest the downtown area as that of "the inner industrial zone." Here we find, for the most part, small businesses, such as leather goods, cigar and clothing manufacturers, furriers, and the like. These small enterprises hover on the fringes of the downtown zone, in part to take advantage of the customers drawn to the center of the city. In this region old mansions are often turned into cheap rooming houses. Owners of such buildings make few repairs, as a rule, because they hope that, sooner or later, somebody will buy the block and erect an office building.

Backing up against this second zone we find the tenement and slum districts and the back street areas. The buildings are usually dilapidated remains of houses and apartments that once served the well-to-do and the middle class. Working people crowd into this zone. Foreigners live in these tenement districts because of the cheaper rents, and here also we usually find the Negroes, who have been barred from better residential regions. Soon a slum area is created. Recreational facilities are limited or totally lacking. Sanitary conditions are often deplorable. Crime and vice breed easily. Here are located what Clifford Shaw and others have called "delinquency areas."

In the zone immediately beyond the tenements, there are usually the middle-class apartments and the stores serving this large element of the population. Except in the largest cities, we also find in this district single houses which are occupied by the middle class.

Further from the downtown section, in the restricted parts of the city, live the rich and well-to-do, either in impressive private houses or in lavish apartments. There are some "class" stores and exclusive specialty shops.

The commuter or suburban district is the farthest removed from the downtown zone. This area is populated by families who do not like to live in the "city square" but still wish to enjoy the advantages of urban life. They go to work each morning by bus, railway, or other fast interurban transportation and come home at night to their suburban apartment or house and garden.

**Louis Wirth's ecological description of the medium-sized city.** Much the same pattern of urban ecology has been submitted by Professor Wirth, but his deserves attention since it is, perhaps, more precisely descriptive of the medium-sized city than the one just summarized. Wirth suggests the following six zones of urban demarcation.

First, there is the central business district containing the business offices and service facilities. Buildings are mainly of the skyscraper type and there are few residences. Next, comes what Wirth calls the "zone of transition." This combines the wholesale establishments, warehouses, storage places, railroad yards, and small business shops. From the standpoint of human habitation it is a place of "deterioration and transition." Here are the slum dwellings of the poorest economic classes, the shabby stores that serve them, and the appropriate service units and entertainments, such as flophouses, saloons, cheap restaurants, burlesque houses, and centers of vice and gambling. The lesser members of the underworld usually hang out in this district, as do some artists and intellectuals, because of the bohemian and exotic atmosphere.

Third in the concentric layout comes the district made up mainly of the homes of workingmen and the stores and shopping facilities that serve them. There are rows of connected houses, small apartments and a few old mansions which have been remodeled as flats. A number of what Walter Rollo Brown calls "short wheelbase churches" will be located here. Fourth, we find the apartment house area in which dwell many of the rich and most of those of the middle-income groups, such as the white-collar contingent of salaried employees and the highly skilled workmen. The more impressive and stylish churches are found here. Fifth is the single residence area, which has some lavish mansions of the rich and many modest cottages, the latter inhabited mainly by those who work in the factories located on the outskirts. Sixth and last, we have the scattered suburban area which fades out into parks, woods, and open fields and is inhabited mainly by the rich and by the professional classes.

The location of particular zones and the distribution of population within this ecological pattern change as time goes on. The wealthy move out of one district, and the less well-to-do move in. If the business district expands and becomes crowded, it pushes out toward the slum area; the poor then have to hunt new quarters in the homes left vacant by those who have moved out into a more exclusive district. Even some of the former suburbs may be swallowed up by the metropolis as it expands outward.

**Psychological and social traits of present-day urban communities.** One of the most striking aspects of the city as a social community is the fact that all types of persons are thrown together in a comparatively small area. But, although they may live only a few blocks apart, as wide a social gulf separates the slum dweller from the penthouse resident as existed between the medieval serf and the feudal baron. This formal gap between urban social classes is known as "social distance."

In the small town, it is possible to become acquainted with everyone. If a man is reputable and self-respecting, he can usually associate with anybody, regardless of the size of his bank account. The barber plays golf or billiards with the banker or shopkeeper, and the baker's daughter may marry the banker's son. A moderate caste system is, however, observed in the city. It is only in fiction that mechanics, clerks, and stenographers have an opportunity to move in the same circles with the executive or professional class, except in an occasional holiday party given for employees. Neighborliness, too, passed away with the coming of congested urban life; today, apartment dwellers rarely know many of those who live on the same floor with them.

Because people seek companionship, even in the large cities, city dwellers join clubs, lodges, secret societies, and recreational groups. City social groupings, aside from industrial and professional associations, are selective rather than natural and spontaneous; city dwellers deliberately choose their friends and associates rather than taking them on the basis of physical propinquity, as in the country.

## City Government

**Corrupt political machines in cities.** Whenever people are massed together, there must be rules to govern them, so that all will have fair treatment and suitable protection. Good city government endeavors to help people secure the necessities of living, and to protect them from unnecessary risk and violence. Water, light, fuel, public sanitation, and garbage removal are necessities. Protection is needed from gangs, thugs, thieves, and racketeers, and against fire. From the fact that all people have some share in these common interests city government arises.

City governments have played an important rôle in the political organization of the United States. Political machines, first developing on a large scale in American cities, became powerful and dominated not only city politics but state politics as well, often also exerting a powerful and corrupt influence over even national politics. Despite the New Deal's intellectual brain trust and its commendable social welfare program, few national administrations ever depended more on corrupt political machines than the Roosevelt régime and none ever welcomed more heartily the support of the political bosses. Graft and corruption have been present in city government for generations. The story was told years ago in Lincoln Steffen's great book, *The Shame of the Cities.* The attempts to reform city government of late have improved the situation somewhat, but the increasing size of cities and the difficulty of securing united action by the diversified urban populations have made it difficult to establish good city government, free from graft or corruption. Three outstanding examples of great cities controlled by corrupt machines for many years are New York, Chicago, and Kansas City.

**Leading city machines.** In New York City, corrupt politics prevailed for decades. Tammany Hall, a club to which most of the Democratic political leaders belonged, became so powerful that it was often able to control the state legislature. Millions voted for city improvements fell into the pockets of the Tammany Hall bosses before the election of Mayor Fiorello La Guardia on a fusion ticket in 1933. The Seabury investigation, two decades ago, revealed the graft and corruption under the affable playboy, Mayor James J. Walker, a typical Tammany administrator. Fee-splitting was common; one

fee-splitting lawyer in the zoning department banked some $5,283,-
000 in six years. A clerk in the marriage license bureau deposited
$384,000 in six years. The city bus system was honeycombed with
graft. Vice and gambling flourished under police protection. La
Guardia's Fusion Administration, however, and La Guardia's successor,
Mayor William O'Dwyer, have given New York honest and relatively
efficient government since 1933.

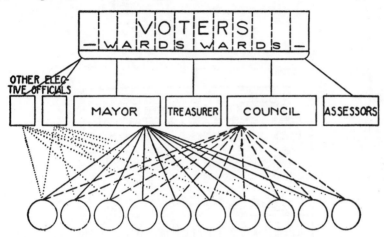

Mayor-council form of city government.

Chicago politicians were even more corrupt than the Tammanyites.
They frightened voters by bombings and shootings, and used any and
all illegal means to attain their ends. During the days of Mayor "Big
Bill" Thompson, who was alleged to be controlled by the grafters and
racketeers, the city lost over 100 million dollars a year in graft. All
kinds of schemes were used to steal money from the city treasury.
False names appeared on the public payrolls, and the salaries were
pocketed by public officials. Special companies were organized to get
the official city business at exorbitant prices. Conditions in Chicago
have improved but little since Thompson's day. The régime of Anton
Cermak, regarded by some as more corrupt than that of Thompson,
was cut short by Cermak's assassination in 1933. The Kelly-Nash
machine was smoother in its operations than the Thompson machine
and, hence, became more firmly entrenched.

The Pendergast machine in Kansas City needed no lessons from
either Tammany Hall or Chicago, and maintained its corrupt system
unchallenged until President Roosevelt, who had earlier warmly welcomed Pendergast's assistance, broke it up in order (critics claimed)
to rival Thomas E. Dewey's record as a "gangbuster."

One of the smoothest-running and most thoroughly "reform-proof"
city machines ever developed in the United States was that in Jersey
City, created and operated by the colorful Mayor Frank Hague.

**The mayor-council plan of city government.** One reason why graft and corruption prevail to such a degree is the complex structure of city government. The mayor-council administration system resembles the three separate departments of the Federal government. The chief

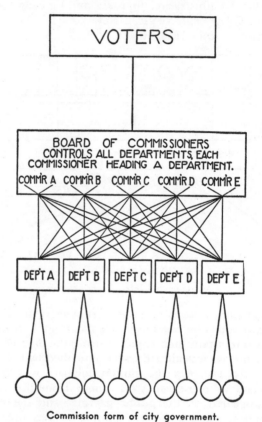

Commission form of city government.

city executive is the mayor, elected by popular vote; the council, also elected, resembles the Federal Senate; and the elective board of aldermen is comparable to the Federal House of Representatives. There is also a city judicial system, usually elective. Nearly three-fifths (59.8 per cent) of United States cities over 5,000 in population still operate under the mayor-council system.

**Formation of National Municipal League.** Periodic attempts to oust the corrupt politicians made but little headway until striking changes occurred in the structure of urban government early in the twentieth century. In 1894, an important national conference was held on city government. This marked the beginning of systematic reform efforts to improve urban administration. Out of this conference grew the National Municipal League, which laid. down certain basic principles on which honest and efficient city government could be founded. The more important of these were:

(1) Urban communities should be granted full rights of self-government by the states.
(2) Democratic practices should prevail.
(3) City property should be protected against grafters.
(4) Municipal government should be placed in the hands of experts, subject to checks by popular control.

As an outgrowth of this reform movement, the commission form of government and the city manager system have been substituted in many cities for the older mayor–council system.

**Commission form of city government.** The commission form of government originated in Galveston, Texas, where, in 1900, a flood almost destroyed the city. A commission of five persons was elected to deal with the emergency and did an excellent job of rebuilding their city. They reorganized the city departments, giving nobody full authority to rule, but placing a person at the head of each department, subject to checking and restraint by the vote of the citizens. These department heads, usually five in number, make up the commission, of which one department head is chosen to act as chairman. This commission form of government became very popular during the next decade. It lost ground after 1918 to the city manager plan. The main defect of the system has been the frequency of quarrels and squabbles within the commission. In 1947, some 308 cities, each with a population of over 5,000 (15.1 percent of the total number of such cities) used the commission form of government.

**The city manager plan.** The city manager plan is a combination of the best in the mayor-council system and the commission form of government. The people elect a small council and a mayor who make and administer the laws and determine general city policy. An expert in urban administration is hired as city manager, and he appoints the lesser city officials. Staunton, Virginia, in 1908, was the first city to set up the city manager plan. It has since been popularized by Dayton and Cincinnati, Ohio, and adopted by many other cities. In 1947, among cities of over 5,000 population, 433, or 21.3 per cent, were making use of the city manager type of municipal government.

Another outstanding reform in the personnel of city government has been the use of the civil service system in selecting officials. The government of the modern city is, however, a gigantic political enterprise, and it has proved difficult to remove inefficiency and corruption from municipal politics and administration. Moreover racial, cultural, and social differences and conflicts make it difficult for reform movements to obtain a united front against political rascals.

**Police and fire protection.** One of the most important city departments, and one often undermined by graft, is the Department of Public Safety, which usually includes the police and fire departments. The police force in our great metropolitan centers constitutes a miniature army. In 1947, New York City had 18,027 men on its police force, Chicago 7,646, Philadelphia 5,205, Los Angeles 4,413, and Detroit 4,260. The per capita cost of the police force in all cities over 10,000 inhabitants stood at $6.17 in 1947.

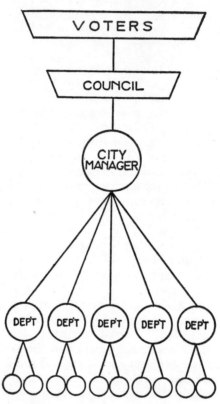

City manager form of government.

Urban police often become tools of corrupt politicians and promise to give protection to, or overlook the crimes committed by, the friends of those who enabled them to get their jobs. By no means all law enforcement officers are dishonest, and, if corruption were removed from the higher offices of the city, there would be more honest policemen and more efficient law enforcement.

Three glaring faults exist in our urban police systems: (1) Policemen are rarely professionally trained for their jobs. In many cities, appointment to the police force is not based on ability, training, or personal integrity but on political pull. Many lawbreakers escape because the police have not been as well schooled in the art of catching criminals as the criminals have been in the ways of committing crime and evading arrest. (2) There is not enough differentiation in assignments in the police service. Policemen are all too often compelled to combine routine inspection, control of traffic, and other minor duties with the complex science of crime detection. (3) Police are frequently poorly paid and poorly equipped. The average policeman receives such low wages that he is an easy prey to bribery by corrupt politicians.

In the very large cities during the last quarter of a century there has been a great improvement in police departments with respect to crime detection—that is, unless the city is graft-ridden. Metropolitan police departments have tended to separate the crime detection functions from routine patrolling, and have followed the Federal Bureau of Investigation in perfecting the science of crime detection. This has led to a marked reduction in many types of crime in the more populous cities of the nation.

One of the outstanding examples of progress in urban administration has been the improvements in fire fighting and fire prevention. Not only have fire departments learned to fight fires more effectively but the number of conflagrations has been decreased by teaching people better methods of fire prevention. Cities have passed ordinances requiring fire escapes for every building of two or more stories and adequate fire extinguishers for every public building. Firemen have learned better how to save the lives of those trapped in burning buildings. All these precautions have lowered the number of fires and of deaths from fires in large cities. The loss from fire is still high, however—about 715 million dollars in 1948—and experts still classify half the annual loss as preventable. The arson racket, while being curbed by the activities of the Fire Underwriters' organization, still continues and is responsible for a considerable number of fires.

**Urban public utilities.** Since the public affairs of a great city constitute a big business enterprise, some urban communities have found that they can furnish indispensable necessities, such as water, light, and gas, to the citizens more cheaply if the utility is owned and operated by the city. Three-fourths of the cities in the United States now own and operate their own water supply systems, and over 60 per cent own their sewage disposal or incinerator plants. Some 21 per cent own light plants, and over 4 per cent have tried to provide their gas supply. Omaha, Nebraska, took over the private gas companies in 1920 and has since served the people more cheaply and efficiently. Over 18 per cent of the cities have a municipal auditorium. Some cities have tried the experiment of municipal ownership of coal, ice, and fuel companies, but private companies continue to fight these enterprises. Coastal towns like New York, Baltimore, Los Angeles, and Seattle own city piers and docks for loading and unloading ships. Many cities are constructing city airports, giving airline companies an advantage over railroads and buses, which have to provide their own terminal facilities. Out of a total of 6,414 airports in the United States in 1948, some 2,050 were municipally owned.

Urban finances and financial crises. Closely related to the problem of city government is the matter of city finances. Most of the better governed cities have put their financial system on a budget basis. But even in such cases municipal finances have often been in a precarious condition, often owing to municipal extravagance in the competitive effort "to keep up with the Joneses"—that is, to match or surpass rival cities in expenditures leading to urban expansion and prestige. This competition was particularly strong between 1919 and 1929; bankers eagerly floated municipal bonds to help along the process. When, after the depression of 1929, the bankers withdrew their support, many cities were left in a condition of near bankruptcy and required Federal relief. City expenditures are still increasing. In 1948, the 397 American cities with a population of over 25,000 spent about 4 billion dollars. Since there were 15,823 cities with a population under 25,000, a total urban expenditure of $4,500,000,000 would be a very restrained estimate. This is about equal to the total Federal budget in 1932 and 1933. As a group, American cities have piled up a tremendous debt burden. In 1948, the gross debt of American municipalities totaled some 10 billion dollars, or over eight times our total national debt in 1916.

But, it is important to point out that this increased urban indebtedness has not all been due to extravagance. It has also been a result of essential expenditures and of the increasing movement of urban populations to the suburbs. This movement has affected urban finance adversely in two ways. In the first place, when metropolitan districts are abandoned by relatively well-to-do dwellers the property value drops and taxes fall correspondingly. Further, when the abandoned homes are occupied by less prosperous groups, tax delinquency increases. Second, inhabitants of many suburbs that are entirely outside urban corporation limits cannot be taxed at all by the city in which they formerly dwelt. But the suburban dwellers come to the city during the day to work and shop, and they enjoy all of the urban facilities tax free. Another cause of urban financial difficulties has been the fact that the lack of housing construction and repair has hastened the deterioration of urban housing and the increase of the slum areas. These are a great financial liability to any city, for slum districts contribute only 6 per cent of urban real estate tax income, while they absorb nearly half of urban expenditures.

One interesting item is the great value of urban property. For example, the taxable real estate and special franchises on Manhattan Island alone in 1947–1948 amounted to $7,754,603,790, or a sum nearly equal to the municipal debt of the larger cities in the United States. The total assessed valuation of all taxable property in greater New York in 1948 was $17,584,492,413. Incidentally, New York City has suffered especially from migration to the suburbs and has been reduced to desperation in the task of raising enough money to support the essential urban services. It can only do so by state aid. The total assessed valuation of all taxable property in Chicago in 1948 was $7,527,708,198; in Detroit, $3,745,817,710; in Philadelphia, $3,417,497,435; in Los Angeles, $2,306,818,400; and in Baltimore, $2,052,954,229. It has been estimated that the total assessed valuation of all urban property in the United States in 1948 was between 125 and 150 billion dollars. The assessed value per capita in 300 cities of over 25,000 population was $1,788; and the average tax per $1,000 of assessed value was $42.66.

## Special Public Problems of the City

Urban transportation problems. The large city has created many special social problems. Among the more important are transportation, health, and housing.

One of the most important urban problems is that of adequate transportation. So long as cities remained small, travel through the narrow streets in horse-drawn carriages and wagons was easy and feasible. There were no street-car tracks, subway entrances, elevated railways, taxicabs, or buses. The width of streets was of little importance, because there was usually plenty of room for the vehicles. But, with thousands coming to the city to work or shop every day, some new means of convenient and rapid transportation had to be provided.

The first street car, invented in 1832, was drawn by horses on a track. These horse-drawn vehicles were gradually replaced, after 1890, by electrically-driven vehicles which ran on tracks with trolley wires above or below ground. After the appearance of automobiles, trucks, and buses, street cars became a traffic hazard. In most cities, they have of late years been abandoned and the tracks removed to provide more space for the buses and other motor vehicles.

Surface railroads were not sufficient, however, to supply the growing demand for more rapid city transportation. In 1870, the first elevated railroad was built in New York City, and this was followed after 1900 by the underground railway—the subway—which city dwellers used extensively because of its great speed.

Automobiles provided a new traffic problem. The honk of the taxicab soon added its clamor to the noise of the city, creating a special problem. Because of increasing competition, earnings of the taxicab drivers were so low that many could not make a decent living. Some cities passed laws to reduce the number of cabs in operation, granting licenses only to one or two companies.

Urban traffic problems are particularly acute today because of the increase in motor vehicles of all types: automobiles, taxicabs, buses, and trucks. Downtown traffic has become more congested because streets cannot be widened without tearing down valuable buildings. It is increasingly difficult to find adequate parking space for automobiles and trucks.

Cities have attempted to solve the automobile and parking problem in numerous ways. Some have routed traffic away from the business

Typical view of traffic-glutted streets of our larger cities. Conditions like these threaten to paralyze urban transportation, and encourage dispersion to suburbs and smaller towns.

districts and have built elevated streets or tunnels for interurban traffic, especially for exits from the city. Better ways of getting in and out of traffic are provided by bridges and tunnels. Robert Moses, Park Commissioner of New York City, has performed the greatest feats of genius in seeking to provide adequate urban transportation facilities, especially in the way of elevated streets and ingenious exits from metropolitan districts. Parking meters, requiring payment on the basis of time parked, have been installed in congested areas to discourage the parking "hogs." Nearly 900 cities have installed such parking meters in congested districts. "No Parking" zones have been marked off in the business districts. Over 425 cities operate municipal parking lots near the business areas where cars may be parked at a minimum charge. In addition to parking lots, both municipally and privately owned, there are indoor parking stations several stories high. But, even with all these improvements, the traffic problem remains unsolved.

**Urban sanitation and public health.** Cities have made remarkable progress in sanitation and public health; but, despite better medical care, improved sanitation, and a pure water supply, the city is still a less healthful place to live than the country. Congestion in slum areas, buildings that shut out fresh air and sunshine, restricted facilities for exercise, noise, smoke and dust, and the general tension of urban life all make the average urban dweller's prospect of remaining healthy, either physically or mentally, less than that of the country resident. City boosters often quote statistics to prove that the mortality rate of the city is lower than that of the country. Such statistics, however, are misleading as a proof of greater urban healthfulness. There are more young persons in the city, and there are more females than males; sickness and death are less frequent among youth, and the female death rate is lower than the male. The preponderance of the healthiest age and sex groups, often drawn from rural areas and brought into the city, thus serves to give the erroneous impression of a relatively low urban sickness and mortality rate. There is also no doubt that deaths from accidents are much more frequent in the city and that nervous and mental diseases occur there far more often, because of the additional stresses and strains of city existence.

**Serious urban housing problems.** There has been an increasingly acute urban housing problem ever since the first factories attracted workers to hastily constructed shacks nearby. Early factory workers had no idea of efficient sanitation; the death rate from disease among them was high. Because the Industrial Revolution began later in the United States than in England, the homes of American factory workers have been somewhat less crude, dirty, and crowded than those in England. Yet, over one-third of our city population today live in houses or apartments not fit for human habitation, and another third live in no better than substandard homes. To prove the inadequacy of too much city housing, Professor Wirth has pointed out that over 5 million city dwellings have no private baths, 3 million no refrigeration equipment, over one million no gas or electricity, and over one million no central heating or stoves.

The earliest alarm expressed in the United States over slums and bad housing conditions came in connection with the fear of epidemics. This was expressed in the famous report of Dr. John H. Griscom on New York City, in 1842. The great increase of immigration after the Civil War added to urban crowding and made housing conditions even more deplorable. The first tenement house law was enacted in New York City in 1867. It forbade cellar apartments unless the ceiling was at least a foot above ground and required one water closet or privy for every 20 persons. There were minor additions to tenement house regulations during the remainder of the century. In 1901, a sweeping Tenement House Act was enacted for New York City, lay-

## WHERE WE STOOD IN 1940

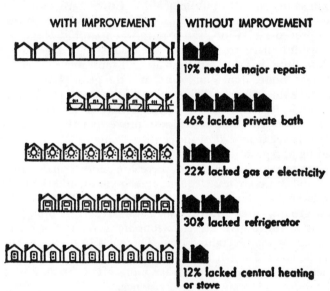

| WITH IMPROVEMENT | WITHOUT IMPROVEMENT |
|---|---|
|  | 19% needed major repairs |
|  | 46% lacked private bath |
|  | 22% lacked gas or electricity |
|  | 30% lacked refrigerator |
|  | 12% lacked central heating or stove |

EACH SYMBOL REPRESENTS 10% OF TOTAL DWELLING UNITS

GRAPHIC ASSOCIATES FOR PUBLIC AFFAIRS COMMITTEE, INC.

Chart showing defective character of urban housing before Pearl Harbor. The conditions have become far worse since 1940, due to rapid population growth, war-time and post-war congestion, cessation of building during the war, and inadequate housing construction since V-J Day.

ing down specifications for future tenements and setting the precedent for tenement control. The famous New York Code of 1901, drawn up by Lawrence Veiller and Robert DeForest, was widely imitated in city planning during the next generation.

Since 1901, and especially since the first world war, many improvements have been made in American housing. Perhaps the first impressive effort to provide better housing for those with moderate incomes grew out of what are known as "limited dividend" housing projects. Under this plan, money has been invested in housing by philanthropists who expect only a small return on their investment. In this manner, funds from the Russell Sage, John D. Rockefeller, Rosenwald, Marshall Field, Ginn, and Buhl estates have provided comfortable apartments for many families who would otherwise have been forced to live in dingy and unsanitary tenements. The Metropolitan Life Insurance Company has constructed some vast apartment developments, such as the Parkchester group in the Bronx and the more recent Peter Cooper Village and Stuyvesant Town in downtown New York. The size of some of these apartment projects may be illustrated by the Parkchester development, which combines 51 apartment units, houses over 40,000 tenants, and cost over 50 million dollars. Stuyvesant Town and Peter Cooper Village, combined, cover some 80 acres and provide living quarters for 31,000 persons. They represent the latest in the combination of skyscraper apartment, inner courts, and small park planning and construction.

Other good examples of better urban housing are co-operative apartments. In 1917, a Finnish co-operative apartment house was built in Brooklyn. It was successful and has been imitated by other Finnish groups. The Amalgamated Clothing Workers in New York City, by pooling their resources, erected two large and attractive co-operative apartment buildings. The James Weldon Johnson Houses, built in Harlem by New York City with state aid, provide decent abodes for some Negroes in that crowded area.

**Government housing projects.** Federal interest in urban housing began during the first world war, when the government built housing facilities to care for some 15,000 families. The Reconstruction Finance Corporation, established in 1932, was empowered to make loans to assist urban housing; it aided in the construction of the famous Knickerbocker Village project in lower Manhattan in New York City. Some attention was given to housing by the New Deal administration after 1933. Housing was part of the emergency economic program and also a practical item in "the more abundant life" ideal of President Roosevelt. New Deal legislation provided money for urban housing construction by the Public Works Administration. A few slums were cleared away, and some model apartments erected. Examples of such Federal slum clearance and housing projects are the Jane Addams Houses in Chicago, the Lake Terrace Apartments of Cleveland, the Williamsburg Houses in Brooklyn, the Harlem River Houses in New York (for Negroes), and the Techwood Project in Atlanta. However, these 49 Federal projects in some 36 cities provided homes for only about 22,441 families, only a small fraction of those urban residents who needed new and better apartments in the areas involved. In 1937, the Wagner-Steagall Housing Act created the United States Housing Authority, and in 1939 the latter took over the PWA housing operations. It was empowered to make liberal loans for new housing, and by 1941 230 projects, with facilities for 73,132 families, had been completed. The United States Housing Authority is now the Federal Public Housing Authority (FHA).

In 1938, President Roosevelt tried to enlist private industry in a "house America" program, rightly contending it would provide a great stimulus to business recovery, but his appeal brought little response. The second world war greatly intensified the urban housing problem, for war workers swarmed to the cities, but there was far less new construction than was needed. Only 850,000 housing units were built and most of these were temporary and substandard. After the war, the Taft-Ellender-Wagner bill was introduced in 1945 to provide a comprehensive Federal housing program, but when it was finally passed in 1949, it provided for less than 5 per cent of the estimated need. President Truman set up an emergency housing program in 1946, under Wilson W. Wyatt as housing expeditor, but the construction which grew out of it hardly more than scratched the surface of the needs. Only about 850,000 units were built in 1947, a year in which there were 900,000 marriages.

Most of the completed Federal housing projects will not be accessible to slum dwellers, since few of the new housing units are really low-cost homes because of the enormous increase in building costs since 1940. It would require from 100 to 150 billion dollars to rehouse those of our urban population now living in substandard homes. As yet, little progress has been made. President Truman was sincerely interested in adequate government support of housing construction, but his cold war crowded out this aspect, as it did most other aspects of his Fair Deal welfare projects. In March, 1950, Congress rejected most of his housing program by an overwhelming majority.

## City Life and Social Problems

**City life undermines primary groups.** Since city life is a relatively new experience for the majority of mankind it is not surprising that it has complicated and intensified some older social problems and created many new ones.

The conditions of city life have tended to have a distintegrating influence upon the primary groups, such as the family, the neighborhood, the play group, and the rural church. Children are less needed and more of an expense in the city. Home life is less integrated and unified. There are many distractions from the former interests of the family hearth. The former functions of the rural family are scattered and divided in urban life among many public agencies—such as educational, health, and welfare organizations, public recreational facilities, social clubs, health clinics, philanthropic groups, and the like.[4] Church life is more formal and impersonal, and its socializing function has all but faded out in the city, with its numerous distractions.

**Loneliness and suicide.** One of the most common personal and social problems of the city is loneliness, especially for those who have come from rural areas, or for immigrants who have no contacts with fellow-countrymen. The newcomer to the city discovers to his dismay that his old patterns of rural life are not to be found in the city. There is little urban community spirit to compensate for this loss; the city dweller meets his professional associates or fellow-workers only during working hours, with little opportunity to build up any intimate friendship or personal communion. He goes home to an apartment or rooming house, where few know their next-door neighbor. Human morale is buoyed up by close association in some intimate group. When city life breaks this group down, or leaves it undeveloped, it also undermines personal confidence and happiness.

The nervous activity, sophistication, bravado, or bohemianism shown by many city dwellers is only a compensatory mask to cover loneliness and a feeling of inadequacy. The desire for some kind of companionship leads to participation either in the artificial café society, if one can afford it, or in other forms of dissipation. It is not infrequent for men to drift into a criminal gang in the sheer quest of companionship. Morbidity and even suicide may grow out of loneliness, but more tragic than the few who commit suicide are the thousands who live in the silent unhappiness of psychic and social isolation.

**Urban crime.** The problems of crime, mental disease, poverty, and old age have increased as more people have come to live in cities. It was to be expected that social problems would multiply with city growth, because urban living conditions call for such sweeping social readjustments. Men and women accustomed to farm life poured into the cities by the thousands. They had no appropriate social standards to guide them, because they had been brought up in rural traditions and had been guided by rural public opinion. The cities had no established communal tradition to provide social control; the altogether different modes of urban life confused and bewildered the newcomers and increased the amount of crime and vice. As Professor Wirth has well said: "Where there are no deep traditional and emotional ties between great masses of people and where there is no common culture to hold them together and to enforce conformity to accepted standards, conflict, disorder, and violence are often rampant. When people are not economically self-sufficient but are dependent

---

[4] See below, Chapter XXVI, *passim.*

upon all the rest of the world for their livelihood in specialized occu-pations, unemployment and economic maladjustment frequently have a ravaging influence." [5]

Cities are especially productive of juvenile crime. Children in the slums have, as a rule, no place to play except in the streets. They often get into mischief because wholesome recreation has not been pro-vided for them. Family scrutiny and discipline have been under-mined by urban conditions; working mothers have less time for safe-guarding their children. City youth do not sit around the hearth fire but frequent poolrooms, night clubs, and bars. Until better control can be exercised over urban youth, juvenile delinquency will continue to be a serious city problem.

Another cause of an excess of crimes by the young in cities lies in the fact that the children of immigrants are concentrated there. It used to be assumed that immigrants are prone to crime; this, of course, is not so. Immigrants may have their peculiar customs, some of which are regarded as criminal or quasi-criminal by American standards, but they are not more given to deliberate commission of crime than native-born Americans. But the first-generation descendants of immigrants are less controlled by the traditions of the immigrant group while they have not been fully assimilated to American ways. Hence, they have no strong stabilizing or restraining influence. This, taken in con-junction with bad living conditions and the unusual urban tempta-tions to crime, has produced a high crime rate among the children of immigrants.

Delinquency among the native-born is also more frequent in urban areas. The city offers many greater opportunities for crime because of its accumulation and display of wealth. The criminal also has a better chance to hide out in the larger cities. The census of 1910 showed that, although farmers made up over 18 per cent of total male population over 10 years of age, they represented only about 3.3 per cent of those committed to penal institutions. Since our population has become predominantly urban, the national crime rate has greatly increased. It has been shown that, up to a certain size, urban crime increases as our cities grow larger. Serious felonies, however, do not increase as rapidly as petty crimes and racketeering. Once the cities reach a population of a half million or more, the crime rate for serious felonies, except for robbery, appears to fall off, since larger cities usually provide a better police department and spend more money on personnel and devices designed to prevent and detect crime. Adverse living conditions make certain slum districts acute delinquency areas.

The leading causes of the high rate of urban delinquency are, in short, the breakdown of family life, greater incentives and opportu-nities for crime, greater facilities for hiding from the police, the preva-

---

[5] Wirth and Lussenhop, op. cit., p. 8.

lence of unassimilated immigrant elements, slums, and bad living conditions in delinquency areas.

**Prevalence of mental disease in cities.** From what we have said about the impersonal character of city life, the breakdown of primary groups, loneliness, the lack of normal outlets for play and physical energy, and the haste, tension, complexity, and confusion of city existence, it would naturally be expected that there would be vastly more mental and nervous disease per capita in cities than in the country districts, and this is indeed the case. The first admissions to hospitals for the insane are twice as great from urban regions as from the rural. Further, the larger the city the higher the rate of admissions, the percentage from cities with a population of over 100,000 being nearly twice as great as that from cities with a population of less than 100,000. It is true that authorities are more alert in detecting and segregating mentally-diseased types in the city than in rural regions, but such qualification does not change the general picture. The city insanity rates differ among the various urban areas; the rate of mental disease in crowded and rundown areas, where social disorganization is greatest, is ten times that in the better residential sections.

**Urban poverty and relief.** Poverty, measured in terms of income in dollars and cents, may not be greater in the city than in the country. In fact, in normal times, the city dweller has earned on the average, about three times as much as the rural dweller. But the expense of living in the city is correspondingly greater. We notice poverty more in the city and it is a more acute problem there. The destitute in a large city have no way to help themselves. When a person loses his job in the city, he soon becomes a public charge. He must have money to pay rent, food, and utility bills. The country poor can usually farm a small piece of land to get food, and they can gather fuel, or they can accept the help often freely given by neighbors. Only droughts, floods, and other "acts of God" are likely to render rural dwellers so helpless and destitute that they have to migrate to avoid starvation.

The problems of old age are acute in urban regions. There is less chance of attaining a ripe old age in the city, so the city has somewhat fewer old persons per capita. But the city deals ruthlessly with its aged. A farmer may be productively engaged until he is 70 or older, but in the city it is often difficult to find new employment, or even keep a job, after 40. Those in the city who have had steady employment are frequently turned out of their jobs after they have reached middle age. Our cities thus accumulate a large proportion of aged persons who become personal or public charges. It is more difficult to take care of the aged in the city, for there is little room in city apartments. It also costs more to support an aged person in cities.

Although delinquency and dependency are more serious problems in the city, the city also has developed better means of coping with them. Public welfare and relief agencies are much better organized.

Social work is more highly developed in urban areas, social settlements exist only in cities, and there is better policing as well as more scientific methods of crime prevention. These improved agencies are able in part to control what would otherwise be a far more dangerous social situation in urban communities.

**Urban conditions and the declining birth rate.** In the chapter on population trends we pointed out that city life seems invariably to reduce the birth rate, owing in part to the expense and other disadvantages of large families in rising in the social scale. Other important items leading to the same result are the distractions of city life, the diversion of interest from the family, and the depletion of physical energy essential to vigorous procreative efforts. This restriction of population growth may be regarded as one of the few beneficial aspects of urban life, though it is tempered by the fact that the falling urban birth rate is to be found mainly among the classes best able to rear children under decent conditions. The great majority of urban children are born in families of unskilled workers and others not able to provide good housing and living conditions.

## Psychic Traits, Social Types, and Cultural Life in Cities

**Psychic traits and attitudes of the city dweller.** Cities have been the birthplace of all high culture. From ancient times to modern days, the chief cultural achievements of mankind have been produced by urban populations. Life in the city exerts a powerful stimulating influence on cultural interests and activities and shapes the personalities of those who live within its boundaries.

Many students of cities point out, however, that city life tends to produce a superficial culture. In order to keep pace with urban life, a man must know a little about everything. He reads the newspaper headlines as he gulps his morning coffee and then races for the bus or subway. All day, the city man must make contacts with others. He assumes a "sophisticated" mask to impress people on short acquaintance, because his contacts with them are necessarily brief and hurried. The city man, to be successful, must be self-assertive, aggressive, and have a good opinion of himself; even though he may actually feel nervous and inadequate, he must try to appear calm, confident, and self-possessed. These facts are significant because the psychology of city life pervades our whole present-day civilization. This superficial and snap-judgment urban state of mind is a severe handicap in an age that requires serious and concentrated intellectual analysis to cope with complex social and economic problems.

**Social types in urban life.** The city has produced special social types. Conspicuous examples are the rich man, who has gained social distinction or public repute because of wealth; the philanthropist, whose reputation rests on giving away his fortune in a conspicuous manner; the "Babbitt" or booster type, who is ostentatiously loyal to his city and loses no opportunity publicly to praise it. There are others, such as the club man, the bohemian, and the rebel. The city also has its special female types, among them the society woman, the feminist, and the club woman. These types are so common in our large cities that certain mannerisms, ways of dress, and activities have come to be associated with them.

The most characteristic social and economic type in the contemporary industrial city is, of course, the factory worker, mechanic, and the like; members of this group are known in the jargon of economic and social history as "the proletariat." The best brief description ever written of the socio-psychological traits of the urban proletariat is the following from the pen of the famous economic historian, Werner Sombart.

First, there appears the important fact that the proletarian is a typical representative of that type of man who is no longer in relation (either internal or external) to Nature. The proletarian does not realize the meaning of the movement of the clouds in the sky; he no longer understands the voice of the storm.

He has no fatherland, rather he has no home in which he takes root. Can he feel at home in the dreary main streets, four stories high? He changes his dwelling often either because he dislikes his landlord or because he changes his place of work. As he moves from room to room, so he goes from city to city, from land to land, wherever opportunity (i.e. capitalism) calls. Homeless, restless, he moves over the earth; he loses the sense of local color; his home is the world. He has lost the call of Nature, and he has assimilated materialism.

It is a phenomenon of today that the great mass of the population has nothing to call its own. In earlier times the poorest had a piece of land, a cottage, a few animals to call his own; a trifle, on which however he could set his whole heart. Today a handcart carries all his possessions when a proletarian moves. A few old scraps are all by which his individual existence is known.

All community feeling is destroyed by the iron foot of capitalism. The village is gone; the proletarian has no social home; the separate family disappears.[6]

**The rôle of cities in modern culture.** The city provides special opportunities for passing on the culture of the past to its inhabitants, through ample libraries, museums, university extension courses, and other facilities for adult education. Many urban communities offer ample opportunity for those who wish to study or practice music, literature, or the arts. However, the flashy, sensational, and superficial character of many urban attitudes prevents a full appreciation of these cultural advantages by any except those few who seek to find the best the city affords. Moreover, city life often so distracts and confuses writers, artists, and musicians that they feel it necessary to retire to the seclusion of the country to do their best creative work.

---

6 Werner Sombart, *Das Proletariat,* cited in Milton Briggs, *Economic History of England,* London, 1914, pp. 213–214.

In the city, one finds excellent public schools. Considerable provision is made, as we have noted, for adult education. There are public libraries with abundant resources, museums of science and art, and public concerts. Public forums are held, so that the city dweller may hear distinguished speakers on topics of world interest. Never in the history of man have the riches of the world's culture been so lavishly and freely offered as in the modern city.

**"Spectatoritis" and urban recreation.** In line with the desire of the urban dweller for distraction and change is his normal use of leisure time. There is great interest in sports and recreation; commercialized spectator sports, in particular, usually draw large crowds in the city. As a result of this desire for vicarious participation, jokingly called "spectatoritis," American cities spend about four billion dollars each year on commercialized sports and amusements, entirely aside from Bowl games, World Series, and other special occasions.

But commercialized spectator sports and amusements do not meet the needs of all urban dwellers. Many cities have provided facilities for supervised recreation, such as tennis courts, outdoor playgrounds, baseball diamonds, skating rinks, bowling alleys, athletic fields, swimming pools, and bathing beaches. In 1946, almost 1750 cities had supervised recreational facilities, and spent about 54 million dollars to support them. Additional facilities are still badly needed; an estimated 6 million urban children are almost entirely without recreational facilities.

## City Planning and the City of the Future

**Reasons for redistributing the urban populations.** The New York World's Fair of 1939 gave sightseers a glimpse of the "World of Tomorrow." What will the cities of that world be like? Some students of urban problems believe that cities have reached a saturation point. Men will either continue to live in these vast, over-congested areas until they destroy civilization, as Spengler insisted they must, or they will find a way to redistribute the now bulging metropolis into saner living units.

Four main reasons have been advanced for the impending breakdown of the great cities: (1) the problem of providing adequate and decent housing; (2) the difficulty of obtaining a sufficient water supply and a good sewage disposal system; (3) the problems of transportation between the suburbs and the city centers; and (4) the generally unfortunate and pathological impact of metropolitan life upon the mental habits and social reactions of most urban dwellers.

**Electricity opens the way.** Just as steam power brought men to the city and created urban congestion, so electricity and the internal-combustion engine, which brought in the automobile, may be the means of taking people away from urban areas. Electricity can be transmitted cheaply over considerable distances, thus making it possible to redistribute factories and offices. Telephones, teletype and deskfax telegraphy enable the executive, for example, to conduct his business in New York from a Palm Beach office.

*Courtesy of Fairchild Aerial Surveys, Inc.*

Stuyvesant Town and Peter Cooper Village: two gigantic housing projects in lower New York City recently completed by Metropolitan Life Insurance Company. They well illustrate the New York City type of city planning.

This proposal to break up our great megalapolitan centers does not involve any sentimental "back to the country" movement, but rather calls attention to the realistic arguments for a greater development of suburban life and the creation of smaller urban communities. In small cities—for example, those under 100,000 population—a saner cultural and social life may be developed, without the noise and confusion of the great congested areas, or the loss of time required in getting to work or to shopping centers.

**Main programs of city planning.** The problem of how to eliminate the disastrous aspects of metropolitan life and yet enjoy its advantages has inspired the city-planning movement. Three types of city plans have been suggested as a means of overcoming the present congestion: (1) the New York City method, developed mainly by Robert Moses, which concentrates the business and apartment skyscrapers and thus gets more room for parks, playgrounds, and the like; (2) the "garden-city" plan of Ebenezer Howard, which spreads the city population over a wide area, allowing only 50 persons per housing acre; and (3) a sort of combination of these two plans, which has been suggested by a French city planner, Le Corbusier (C. E. Jeanneret). This envisages well-scattered skyscraper business buildings and apartments, surrounded by ample park districts. There have been more drastic proposals, such as those of Lewis Mumford and Ralph Borsodi. Mr. Mumford, a disciple of Geddes and Branford in England, warmly supports breaking up great cities into small Greenbelt towns, the nature of which will be described more fully in a later chapter on community planning. Mr. Borsodi urges us to abandon cities altogether, to build up small co-operative groups in country areas, and to establish self-sustaining homesteads.

Growing cities can carry out these proposals in planning new additions, but it is very doubtful if any existing business sections will be speedily torn down to make way for "Cities Beautiful" in the near future. It will require a very serious crisis in city life to bring about a sane redistribution of urban population.

Pending the reconstruction of our cities, some progress in improving urban architecture and ecology is being made through what is known as the "zoning movement," first systematically adopted by New York City in 1916. This is an attempt to plan city building and redistricting so that similar kinds of buildings—residences, apartment houses, skyscrapers, stores, or factories—will predominante in a given section of the city. Building permits are refused for any except certain kinds of structures in a given zone. Supplementary zoning ordinances restrict the height, area, and bulk of buildings by specific districts. This zoning program is designed to end the ugliness and confusion which arise when all kinds of structures and activities are found in a single city district. In 1947, there were 1,072 cities with a population of over 10,000; of these, some 617 had an official city-planning agency, 83 had an unofficial planning agency, 246 had none, and the others did not report. Some 548 of these cities had comprehensive zoning ordinances in operation in 1947.

**Has the limit of urban concentration been reached?** The census of 1940 seemed to indicate that the former trend toward intense urban concentration has been checked, at least temporarily. From 1880 to 1930, the urban population had increased by an amount equal to 5 per cent of the whole population in each decade. But from 1930 to 1940, the urban population increased only from 56.2 per cent of the whole to 56.5 per cent, a gain of only three-tenths of one per cent. Moreover, cities of 25,000 or over grew more slowly than the country as a whole between 1930 and 1940.

During this decade, about one-third of the cities with a population of over 100,000 actually decreased in size, and so did about one-fourth of the cities in the 25,000 to 100,000 population class. The metropolitan districts of the large cities grew by only about 6 per cent in the decade, while the suburban population increased by 17 per cent. About one person out of every five in our country today is a suburban dweller, and there is one suburbanite for every two persons who live in crowded metropolitan cities.

This slowing down in the rate of urban and metropolitan growth has been attributed mainly to reduced employment opportunities in cities, the relative cessation of the northward migration of Negroes from 1930 to 1940, and the movement of many city dwellers to the suburbs and to non-farm rural homes outside city limits.

**The second world war, the atom bomb, and the future of cities.**
The abnormal conditions produced by the second world war once
more stimulated the rate of urban growth. During the war itself, the
civilian urban population barely held its own, relative to 1940 figures,
because of the large number of men drafted from cities for military

*Courtesy of the Institute of*
*Contemporary Art, Boston.*

A Le Corbusier apartment in Marseille, France. Shows the
broad open spaces provided for in this method of city planning to relieve congestion.

service. But, by the time the veterans had returned at the end of
1946, the urban population constituted nearly 60 per cent of the total,
or a growth of 3.5 per cent in six years, as compared with the growth
of only 0.3 per cent from 1930 to 1940. This revived growth of the
urban population took place both in metropolitan centers and in
suburban areas. The further concentration in metropolitan districts
was due mainly to the desire to find housing; it was further stimulated
by the tendency to build large war plants on the outskirts of great
cities. Here the housing was usually inferior and often temporary—
war emergency structures or mere trailer camps.

Fear of the atom bomb may do more to break up great metropolitan
centers than has ever been achieved through common-sense considerations, especially if the cold war continues between Russia and the
United States. In less than a decade atom bombs will be many times
as devastating as those used on Japan in 1945. One or two of them
might destroy the whole metropolitan district of Greater New York.
Indeed, one hydrogen bomb could accomplish just this. If this atomic
threat continues, we may expect a shifting of cities from the seaboard areas to central portions of the country and a scattering of
urban populations in order to make them less vulnerable to the atom
bomb.

## Summary

The twentieth-century city is not only a relatively limited area with a large number of people, it is also a complex social unit. Cities grew rapidly after 1800, as the result of the economic changes which occurred in the wake of the Industrial and Agricultural Revolutions. Today, the Western world is predominantly urban.

All cities have certain characteristics in common; the same general ecological zones and the separation of the population according to social and economic classes. There is a wide social distance in the city between the slum dweller and the penthouse resident, although only a few city blocks may separate them in space.

City government has been pervaded by graft and corruption. Certain necessary reforms have been instituted and new types of government, such as the commission form and the city manager plan, have been fairly successful in bringing democratic practices to city government. Many cities have experimented successfully with municipal ownership of utilities such as traction, light, water, gas, and sewage disposal in order to provide cheaper and more efficient service to their inhabitants.

The city of today has many special and acute problems, brought about by the massing of many persons in limited areas. Traffic and transportation problems are particularly acute because of the increase of motor vehicles on the narrow streets. Some cities have attempted to solve their transit and parking problems in various ways, but much remains to be done. Congestion and other factors create many social problems, such as bad housing, delinquency, poor health, mental and nervous diseases, and increased dependency. Recently some attention has been paid to providing better housing through Federal, state, and municipal aid, but it has been totally inadequate.

The city offers many cultural opportunities to those who seek them although the flashy, superficial character of city life has offset many worth-while elements of city culture. Commercialized spectator sports and recreation occupy much of the leisure time of city dwellers. For those who cannot afford this type of recreation, many cities have set up a Department of Recreation to facilitate the development of sports for underprivileged groups.

It is difficult to forecast the future of the city. The sensible thing to do would be to scatter the great metropolitan populations in well-planned suburban centers, or small, independent towns, admirably equipped with transportation facilities. Man thrives better when he can see the sun, breathe fresh air, and stretch himself psychologically as well as physically. The congested city might have been tolerated when it was indispensable in connection with the steam power of the early Industrial Revolution, but there is little excuse for it in twentieth-century America, with the unlimited potential use of electric power.

Many plans have been suggested for decentralizing the city and moving people and industry into suburban areas. The modern city has grown so rapidly that some workable plan for controlling city growth will have to be developed in the near future, for our cities have already become far too crowded for the efficiency, health, and happiness of their residents. Some relief may be in sight, however; the 1940 census showed that urban concentration was, at least temporarily, slowing down in normal times.

The abnormal conditions of the war decade since 1940 temporarily increased the rate of urban growth, but there is every probability that the trend may be checked once more as peace conditions become better established. Suburban growth is going on much more rapidly than that of the congested metropolitan centers. The fear of the atom bomb may produce revolutionary and rapid trends in the way of breaking up great metropolitan centers and building new and smaller cities in the central, western, and southern portions of the country.

## Selected References

Abercrombie, Patrick, *Town and Country Planning*, Holt, 1933. A brief and authoritative description of the leading types of city planning by a leading English writer on this subject.

* Abrams, Charles, *The Future of Housing*, Harper, 1947. Probably the best of the recent works on American housing problem.

* Anderson, Nels, and Lindeman, E. C., *Urban Sociology*, Crofts, 1928. Perhaps the best introduction to urban social life, its culture and problems.

Anderson, William, *American City Government*, Holt, 1925. A standard manual, clear and comprehensive.

Bogue, D. J., *The Structure of the Metropolitan Community*, University of Michigan Press, 1949. Sociological and statistical analysis of 67 metropolitan communities, illustrating the social position and influence of metropolitan areas.

Borsodi, Ralph, *This Ugly Civilization*, Harper, 1932.

————, *Flight from the City*, Harper, 1933. Two books by the leading American critic of city life, mass production, and the ugliness of the factory town. The first book attacks the ugliness of the industrial city and its ideals, and the second suggests an escape by going to the country and carrying on a subsistence economy. If somewhat idealistic, they are a valuable corrective for current beliefs and practices.

Dickinson, R. E., *City, Region and Regionalism*, Oxford University Press, 1947. The application of regional concepts to urban ecology and city planning programs.

Dobyns, Fletcher, *The Underworld of American Politics*, Dobyns, 1932. A fearless analysis of the incredible Cermak machine in Chicago.

Gist, N. P., and Halpert, L. A., *Urban Society*, Crowell, 1948. A standard and competent manual on urban sociology.

Griffith, E. S., *History of American City Government*, Oxford University Press, 1938. The development of leading types and problems of American municipal government by one of the chief experts in the field.

\* Hart, Smith, *The New Yorkers*, Sheridan House, 1938. An extremely entertaining history of New York City, revealing its seamy side, which is usually glossed over in such accounts. A vivid little book.

\* Lewis, H. M., *City Planning*, Longmans, Green, 1939. Perhaps the best introduction to the whole social and architectural problem of city planning and the redistribution of urban populations.

McKean, D. D., *Boss: the Hague Machine in Action*, Houghton Mifflin, 1940. Good picture of the Hague political machine in Jersey City.

Milligan, M. M., *The Inside Story of the Pendergast Machine*, Scribner, 1948. Spirited exposure of the Pendergast era in Kansas City.

\* Mumford, Lewis, *The Culture of Cities*, Harcourt, Brace, 1938. The most original and stimulating book in the English language on the modern city and human living. Critical of the great city and favorable to the substitution of small communities, like the Greenbelt towns fostered by the New Deal.

Muntz, E. E., *Urban Sociology*, Macmillan, 1938. One of the best sociological texts on the life and social problems of the modern city.

Peterson, E. T. (Ed.), *Cities are Abnormal*, University of Oklahoma Press, 1946. Important symposium by experts, urging the decentralization of our overgrown urban centers of population.

Post, L. W., *The Challenge of Housing*, Farrar and Rinehart, 1938. Expert panorama of American housing needs and costs.

Queen, S. A. and Thomas, L. F., *The City: a Study of Urbanism in the United States*, McGraw-Hill, 1939. Important contribution to urban sociology which skilfully integrates geographical and social factors in urban life.

Saarinen, Eliel, *The City: Its Growth, Its Decay, Its Future*, Reinhold, 1943. A criticism of congested metropolitan areas and a rational planning program, by one of the leading architects of the twentieth century. Makes homes, rather than boulevards and plazas, the core of his plan.

Schnapper, M. B. (Ed.), *Public Housing in America*, Wilson, 1939. A valuable book of readings on city housing problems, including New Deal housing developments.

\* Sinclair, Robert, *The Big City*, Reynal and Hitchcock, 1938. An extremely interesting study of the effect of the city of London, viewed as a typical great metropolis, on human life and culture. A devastating indictment of the contemporary metropolis.

Wood, E. E., *Introduction to Housing*, Government Printing Office, 1940. A survey of the housing problems of the United States and New Deal housing activities, by one of our leading authorities.

# CHAPTER XXV

# Recent Changes in Family Life:
# The Impact of Industrialism,
# Secularism, and War on Domesticity

## The Family Is the Basic Primary Group

**Functions of the family.** The family is the oldest and most fundamental human institution. The basic reasons for its existence have remained the same since primitive times: to bring children into the world and rear them, and to carry on household co-operation for numerous purposes. As the elemental unit of society—the basic primary group—the family has had an importance that can scarcely be overestimated. Not only is the family responsible for the continuation of the human race, but it plays the chief rôle in molding the character of every individual in human society.

The child first knows love and protection in the intimacy of the family circle. There, his personality takes shape; he learns the language of his parents and may be taught the primary ideals or virtues of love, kindness, co-operation, service, truth, justice, and freedom. These fundamental precepts, if acquired in the home at an early age, are carried over by the individual into his later life in the community. The physical heritage, early training, and home environment which the child receives from his parents have more to do with the way he behaves in later years than any other set of conditioning influences.

**Importance of recent changes in the family.** Our realization of the vital rôle of the family as a primary social institution makes the changes that have occurred in the family in the past seventy-five years a subject worthy of serious study. Education, recreation, and training in citizenship, which once centered in the home, have become, in part, the responsibility of the community and the state. Married women now work in offices and factories, and their children are sent to day nurseries or are left in the care of neighbors or servants. Divorce and desertion, once infrequent, have now become increasingly common.

What is responsible for such changes in this important primary institution? Will the family cease to be of fundamental significance in the future? In order to understand more clearly these problems of the modern family, let us look first at the history of the family and its material and social surroundings.

## Origins and Early History of the Family

**Leading theories of the origin of the family.** To many persons a "family" means the immediate members related by blood and marriage—parents and their children—with relationship traced through both father and mother. This type of family may not have existed in the earliest times. In primitive society, family ties were probably more loosely drawn. In fact, writers like Robert Briffault believe that the primitive family consisted of only the mother and her children, and was supported by the mother's male relatives. During this early period, the physiological relation of the father to his offspring was not understood and the mother and her relatives assumed the responsibility for the care and rearing of the children. It is said by these writers that early man was probably promiscuous in his sex relationships and that mating was not permanent. Kinship, therefore, during this period was traced only through the mother, whose position was recognized by reason of the biological tie. This system of family relationships has been known as the matrilineal.

Writers like Edward Westermarck, on the other hand, contend that the natural jealousy of man, the long period of helplessness of the infant, and the need of the father to help with its care early led to permanent mating and the assumption of authority on the part of the husband, even though he did not at first realize his procreative relationship to his child. The family system in which relationships were traced through the father is known as patrilineal, and the societies in which it existed have been called patriarchal. It is hardly likely that either matrilineal or patrilineal relationships exclusively dominated primitive society. But it does seem likely that, in the earliest period of the family, the strongest ties were those between mother and child, and that paternal authority increased with the growth of a stable society.

**Leading forms of the family.** Though monogamy, the marriage of one man to one woman, has been the general rule in human history, plural marriage (polygamy) has been practiced in some areas. The marriage of one man to several women (polygyny) was often the custom in countries where there were wide differences between social classes. It was, however, restricted to a wealthy minority, since only a rich man could afford a number of wives. In countries where it was difficult to make a living and one man could not even support one woman and her children, the family arrangement known as polyandry was sometimes followed. In this system one woman married several men. This form of marriage is still to be found in parts of Tibet and Australia.

**Monogamy the prevailing form of family life.** The monogamous union has been the usual form of the human family. Economic, social, and religious factors have tended to favor the marriage of one man and one woman. The economic extremes of severe poverty, which makes polyandry necessary, and of opulence, which encourages polygyny, have not been usual with most of mankind. In few countries were very many men so wealthy that they could afford several wives, or so poor that one woman had to have several husbands to support her and her children. A more normal economic condition has usually prevailed, in which one man could afford one wife. Moreover, there are usually about an equal number of men and women in any country, and this biological fact, together with the mating tendency, has encouraged monogamy. Social factors have also promoted the monogamous marriage; both parents, for example, can give their undivided attention to the children. This monogamous type of family provides a more closely knit bond and assures the mother and her children more protection and affection than could be found under any plural marriage system.

**Historic development of monogamy.** To the economic and social advantages of monogamy has been added the sanction of religion. The Hebrew religion strengthened the power of the father and the monogamous family. Marriage was later made sacred and brought under the authority of the Christian church. Divorce, which had become common among the upper classes during the period of the later Roman Empire, was forbidden by the church. The authority of the husband over his wife and children was recognized. The home became the undisputed center of religious and social training during the Middle Ages. The fact that life during the medieval period was primarily rural made it easier for the father to control his wife and children. So long as all the necessities of life were produced in the home, women and children were dependent upon the husband and father for security.

## The Rural Patriarchal Family

**Pattern of rural family life.** The early settlers of America brought from England and the Continent these ideals and practices of the monogamous Christian home. In this country, they received their most complete development on the rural frontier.

Courage was needed by both men and women to make homes in the new country. Marriage was almost a necessity and divorce was rare. A man needed a wife to help him and a woman required the support and protection of a husband. Large families were the rule, for each child soon meant another pair of hands to help. The girls were taught to spin, weave, cook, dip candles, and care for the younger children. The boys worked with their fathers in the fields and helped to cut wood for fuel, repair tools, hunt, fish, and trap. Family co-operation made each family almost a self-sufficient unit, producing most of the food and the goods needed to satisfy its wants. Hard work was not only necessary to make a living but the teachings of Calvin, that idleness was a sin and hard work a virtue, were deeply rooted in the pattern of frontier life.

Recreation, although limited because of long working hours, was also centered in the home. Neighbors were scattered and visits were rare. The family gathered around the fireplace in the winter evenings, after the chores were done, to sing, play cards and dominoes, drink cider, shell nuts, or eat apples. Little attempt was made to make many forms of recreation available outside the family group.

Education, for the most part, was the responsibility of the family. To a considerable extent, it was of a practical nature, but the worth of formal education was appreciated; each child was expected to learn to read and write. The nineteenth-century agitation for public education at state expense was due, in large measure, to the individualism, ambition, and democratic ideals of the early settlers.

Much emphasis was placed on religious instruction in the home. Children were taught to fear God and keep his commandments. The ideals of honesty, moral behavior, thrift, and loyalty to country were strengthened by the teachings of the home. America owes much to the family life of the frontier period. The children taught by its precepts became the leaders of a later day.

**Persistence of rural family pattern.** The rural frontier family was, thus, a closely-knit unit, performing important economic, social, and educational functions. The family pattern established in colonial times remained substantially the same as the frontier pushed westward. Each succeeding generation found life a little less difficult, but, as late as the end of the nineteenth century, the typical family was predominantly rural, with the father as head of the household and the mother and children dependent on him for protection and support.

## The Weakening of Family Ties

**Impact of mechanization on the rural family.** Far-reaching changes have occurred in the family in the last 75 years. No longer the chief economic, recreational, educational, and character-building unit, it has lost much of its former stability and prestige.

The frontier family was its own production unit, requiring the effort of all its members. Gradually, however, the making of articles by hand gave way to mass-production manufacturing. Clothing, formerly fashioned by the painstaking efforts of the women in the household, can now be purchased in stores. Less canning and preserving of food is done at home since commercial canning and deep freezing have become safe and efficient. Bakeries have made home baking unnecessary; restaurants have popularized eating away from home.

Lunch may consist of a hasty snack at a drugstore counter; breakfast, often the only meal eaten at home, is a hurried affair. Appliances, such as percolators, toasters, washing machines, electric irons, and the gas or electric stove, have shortened the hours formerly required for housekeeping tasks. Even holiday feasts have lost much of their earlier social significance. Kitchens and dining rooms are smaller, large dinners are expensive, and many families no longer regard Thanksgiving and Christmas as occasions for family reunions, but as opportunities to pursue their own individual recreational interests.

**New agencies take over former family functions.** The state has assumed a large share of the responsibility, formerly the family's, for the education of children. In addition to performing their important educational function, the public schools, to some extent, have gradually become child-caring agencies. The city child is in school a large part of the day and for 9 or 10 months of the year. School cafeterias provide inexpensive, nourishing noon meals. Physical examinations are given regularly in many schools. Parents of children needing dental care, glasses, or medical attention are informed of the need and how it may be filled. Part of the classroom teaching, especially in the elementary grades, is concerned with the training of young children in good health habits.

Psychiatrists and psychologists have recently been added to the staffs of some urban school systems to offer guidance on problems of emotional adjustment. The school playground provides recreational facilities during and after school hours. Supervised play and organized activities are a partial substitute for home training in good sportsmanship, co-operation, loyalty, respect for the rights of others, and citizenship. Some writers contend that physical, mental, and emotional guidance and training in citizenship can be more effectively handled outside the home. They predict that the pre-school (the nursery and the kindergarten) will be included eventually in the public school system. If this expansion should take place, the child will spend only about the first two years of its life wholly within the family.

Religious training is no longer given the same emphasis in the home. Reading the Bible, morning prayers, family church attendance, and strict observance of Sunday as a day of worship have ceased to be characteristic of the urban family, and are losing ground even in the country.

**Effect of industrialization and urbanization on the family.** In the early factory period the employment of women and children at starvation wages threw many men out of work and family life suffered, not only because the mother was taken out of the home, but also because the total family income was not sufficient to maintain a decent standard of living. Not until about the middle of the nineteenth century were laws passed to limit the labor of women and children.

Children, formerly an asset in the rural home, have become an economic liability in the twentieth-century urban family. Homes are smaller, there is less space for play, and a child cannot contribute materially to the family income for a number of years. All states now have laws regulating conditions under which children may be employed and a compulsory school attendance law requiring daily attendance until a certain age. In April, 1948, there were 37,300,000 families in the United States, and the average family was one of 3.6 persons as opposed to 4.76 in 1900. Some 48 per cent of the families had no children under 18 years of age.

**Some American marriage statistics.** According to a Census Bureau report for 1951, some 68.2 per cent of the population over 14 years of age were married, as compared with 60 per cent in 1940, and 53 per cent in 1890. The number of married couples increased from 28,500,-000 in 1940 to 36,000,000 in 1950, and the number of families from 32,200,000 to 39,800,000. According to figures for 1948, about half of the married persons had been married 14 years or more. One out of eight married persons had been married twice or more. The median age of men still married to their first wife was 24.7 years, and that of women still married to their first husband was 21.4. There has been a marked lowering of the age at which marriage takes place. In 1890, the average male married at the age of 26.1; in 1947 at 23.7. The comparable figures for women were 22.0 and 20.5.

## The Changing Status of Women

**Growing independence of women in the machine age.** Many of the outstanding changes in family life have been brought about by the growing independence of women and the altered status of the sexes. As has been noted earlier, the father was head of the rural household; women and children, dependent on him for protection and support, gave him more or less complete obedience. It was then truly a "man's world." Women who took their family responsibilities lightly were criticized by their neighbors. The divorced woman, an outcast condemned by the community, found it difficult to make a living for herself. Since the Industrial Revolution, however, women have become more necessary or useful in industry. Invention of new machinery and the use of mechanical methods in production opened the way, as we have seen, for widespread employment of women in the new factories. Women have proved themselves as efficient as men in many occupations and have overcome the reluctance of employers to hire them for jobs requiring skill and precision. The entry of women into industry has progressed steadily in every industrialized country, and today women are accepted as an integral part of the labor force.

**Increasing number of women in industry.** In the United States, the office and factory have absorbed the activities of a rapidly increasing number of women. From 1900 to 1940, the number of women employed in industry in the United States increased from 5 million to about 13 million; during this period, the percentage of women among those employed in gainful occupations rose to almost one-fourth. This proportion increased greatly during the war years, so that by 1945 one out of every three wage earners was a woman. In 1890, less than five per cent of all married women worked outside the home; by 1940, almost 16 per cent of those married were employed. In 1950, some 50.9 per cent of all women workers were married and another 16 per cent widowed or divorced.

Woman's entrance into industry was not accomplished without opposition from men, who held to the traditional idea that "woman's place is in the home." Although women went to work in the early factories to support their families, men viewed their employment as a threat to the whole wage level. It is true, as was mentioned earlier, that women were hired in preference to men because they were willing to accept the low wages offered to them. For women who had to earn money there were few opportunities except in the textile and clothing industries. Gradually, more occupations were opened to them as increased production demanded an ever-expanding labor force. Today, there are few industries, except foundries and the like, which will not hire women. The employment record made by women in the second world war demonstrated that they can handle almost any kind of job except those for which they are physically unsuited.

Women have invaded not only industry, but the professions as well. Teaching was long regarded as about the only profession suitable for women. Today, women are to be found in medicine, dentistry, law, nursing, social work and many other lines, as well as in such fields of business as real estate, insurance, and banking. In 1940, there were, among professional women in the United States, 4,447 judges and lawyers, 7,708 physicians and surgeons, 20,124 engaged in higher education, and 20,496 authors, editors, and reporters.

**Disabilities of women in industry.** Although occupations once closed to them are now open, discrimination against women, especially married women, still persists. About half our cities discriminate against married schoolteachers. "Equal pay for equal work" is not yet a reality for many women who must work for a living. In the mid-1930's, the median yearly salary of women was $1,548; 88 per cent earned less than $2,500; only 6 per cent earned over $3,000; and only 1.3 per cent over $5,000. The Wage-Hour Law of 1938 has helped to equalize women's wages in industries engaged in interstate commerce, and during the second world war some women in war industries earned very high wages. But women are still at a disadvantage in the wage scale. The wages of both male and female factory workers have doubled in the last decade. However, women still receive an average weekly wage markedly below that of men. The following table shows the weekly wages of men and women workers from 1938 to 1947 as reported by the National Industrial Conference Board, an organization of large manufacturers which reports on wages earned and hours worked in some 25 leading manufacturing industries. It will be noted that women's wages, on the average, are considerably below those of the unskilled male worker.[1]

| YEAR | WOMEN | MEN | |
|---|---|---|---|
| | | All Men | Unskilled |
| 1938 | $15.69 | $26.07 | $20.67 |
| 1940 | 17.43 | 30.64 | 23.88 |
| 1942 | 23.96 | 43.43 | 33.48 |
| 1944 | 31.19 | 54.60 | 41.06 |
| 1946 | 34.13 | 50.65 | 40.81 |
| 1947 | 38.97 | 57.73 | 46.77 |

Most labor organizations, which have been able to bring about higher wages and improved working conditions for men, have had relatively few members among women workers. Some girls plan to work only until they marry and will take a wage even below that of married women rather than ask for higher pay and risk the loss of a job. Although the majority of women work to support a family or to supplement the family income, there are some who have no dependents. These workers can care for themselves on a wage which would be inadequate for a family. Moreover, women, especially wives and mothers, are less likely to be able to move from place to place hunting work, but must take jobs near their homes and families. These are some of the reasons which have placed women at a disadvantage with employers who are eager to make profits and therefore reduce their labor costs as much as possible.

Recently, women have been better protected from serious wage discrimination. The Wage-Hour Law of 1938 now assures a minimum wage to those working in industries engaged in interstate commerce. Some states have passed wages-and-hours laws and a few, notably New York and Massachusetts, have enacted Fair Employment Practices laws which have helped to reduce discrimination. The record made in industry by women in the recent war has also helped considerably to equalize employment opportunities and wages.

The victorious struggle for woman suffrage. Invasion of the previous "man's world" of industry made many women eager to carry their emancipation still further by getting the right to vote and thus be in a position to pass legislation to raise wages and better working conditions. The leaders in the feminist movement, called "suffragettes," spent much of their lives in trying to obtain the vote for women, carrying the battle for suffrage all over the United States. Little success was achieved in the nineteenth century, except in four states—the territory of Wyoming granted suffrage to women in 1869; Colorado in 1893; and Utah and Idaho in 1896. All of the gains in the early twentieth century came in western states: Washington extended the

---

[1] Women's Bureau—United States Department of Labor, *Handbook of Facts on Women Workers*, Bulletin #225 (1948), p. 28.

right of suffrage to women in 1910, California in 1911, Arizona, Kansas and Oregon in 1912, and Montana and Nevada in 1914. In 1920 the United States adopted the Nineteenth Amendment, which gave women over 21 the right to vote.

As soon as women had a direct rôle in elections they began to take an active part in politics and law. In the years since 1920, women have held many important state and national offices. There have been women governors, congresswomen, and senators. From 1933 until her resignation in 1945, Frances Perkins served as Secretary of Labor in the President's Cabinet. Florence Allen has served with distinction as a Federal judge. As noted earlier, there were 4,447 women lawyers and judges in 1940.

**Greater independence of women in marriage.** Formerly, marriage was the only avenue to female security. Today, public opinion has usually ceased to condemn the woman who prefers a job to marriage. If marriage becomes burdensome or a husband unpleasant, a woman may secure a divorce without too much difficulty or loss of status in the community. Since women no longer are forced to regard marriage as the only road to support open to them, they have become more exacting in their choice of mates and less willing to submit to masculine domination. There are large numbers of women who fail to find a husband to meet their desires or standards and remain single.

**Increasing frivolity in marriage.** With marriage no longer a matter of life-and-death with a woman, and with the removal of the fears about the supernatural world and public opinion relative to divorce, there has developed a growing lightheartedness and frivolity about marriage. In an extensively distributed questionnaire, only nine per cent of those answering could give a valid reason why they had married. This frivolous attitude towards marriage and the family has been intensified by modern advertising which contends that all that is needed to obtain and hold a husband or wife is to use the right perfume, soap, hair dressing, toothpaste, automobile, or brand of cigarettes.

## Increasing Prevalence of Divorce

**Early history of divorce and desertion.** In primitive societies, the privilege of divorce was usually accorded only to men and, unless there were good reasons, was not as frequent as might have been supposed. Barrenness, laziness, old age, disease, and invalidism were sufficient causes for a man to cast his wife aside.

There were many centuries of slow development in family relations between primitive society and the ancient civilizations of the Hebrews, Greeks, and early Romans. The power of the male head of the household grew stronger and his absolute authority was firmly established by custom and law. Among the Hebrews, a man for good reasons could write his wife a "bill of divorcement and give it in her hand and send her out of his house." If a wife could secure the approval of her husband, she could get a divorce on such grounds as neglect, desertion, impotence, and disease. In Greece and early Rome, the absolute authority of the husband gave him unquestioned right to divorce his wife at will. Actual cases of divorce were rare, however, and, despite their complete subordination, the women of early Greece and Rome were respected as wives and mothers and exercised considerable influence within their household.

The family pattern changed after Rome became a powerful empire. The wealthy, pleasure-loving groups in the city and on the great landed estates no longer regarded strict marriage with favor. Family life suffered as morals become more corrupt. Divorce was frequent and secured with ease. The early Christians took a firm stand against the moral corruption of the times, but made little attempt to change the customs surrounding marriage and divorce. Marriage remained a private family affair, and divorce, especially for unfaithfulness, was permitted.

**Attitude of Christianity toward divorce.** As the influence of Christianity spread, the Church made marriage a sacrament, refusing to recognize a ceremony as valid unless performed by a priest. Divorce was prohibited, although under certain conditions, such as in the case of a marriage within the degree of blood relationship forbidden by the Church, annulment was permitted. Even today the formal position of the Catholic Church remains the same with respect to divorce. The Protestant churches approve divorce for good and sufficient cause; until recently, however, no person divorced for infidelity might be remarried in the Protestant Episcopal Church. In 1946, the House of Bishops gave each bishop the authority to decide on the remarriage of divorced persons within his diocese.

The divorce capital of the United States: Washoe County court house at Reno.

**Increasing prevalence of divorce in the wake of industrialism and feminism.** Divorce was infrequent in the frontier family. The disapproval of the church and public opinion were sufficiently strong to discourage the use of divorce as a way to solve the problem of unhappiness in marriage. In the past 75 years, the rapid urbanization of society has weakened the influence of the church and rural opinion among many social classes. Laws making divorce easy have been passed in some states. As a result of these new influences, the divorce rate in the United States has been steadily increasing. In 1890, there was one divorce to every 18 marriages; by 1910, one divorce to 11 marriages; by 1920, one divorce to seven marriages. The depression slowed down the rate of increase, but by 1940, the ratio was one divorce to six marriages. An all-time high of 610,000 divorces was reached in 1946; since then the divorce rate has fallen off—only about 385,000 divorces were granted in 1950. The divorce rate is higher in the United States than in most other civilized countries. The rate in England (1947) was 14.2 divorces per hundred marriages; in Scotland (1947) 5.5; in France (1947) 13.6; in Germany (1938) 7.6; in Japan (1947) 8.9; in Sweden (1947) 11.4; and in the United States (1947) 24.4.

The following table gives the marriage and divorce rate in the United States per 1,000 of the population from 1887 to 1950, and the ratio of the number of marriages to the number of divorces. It clearly reveals the remarkable increase in the divorce rate.

| Year | Marriages per 1,000 Population | Divorces per 1,000 Population | Ratio of Marriage to Divorce |
|------|------|------|------|
| 1887 | 8.7 | .5 | 17.4 |
| 1890 | 9.0 | .5 | 18.0 |
| 1895 | 8.9 | .6 | 14.8 |
| 1900 | 9.3 | .7 | 13.2 |
| 1905 | 10.0 | .8 | 12.5 |
| 1910 | 10.3 | .9 | 11.3 |
| 1915 | 10.0 | 1.0 | 10.0 |
| 1920 | 12.0 | 1.6 | 7.5 |
| 1925 | 10.3 | 1.5 | 6.8 |
| 1930 | 9.2 | 1.6 | 5.1 |
| 1935 | 10.4 | 1.7 | 6.1 |
| 1937 | 11.3 | 1.9 | 5.9 |
| 1940 | 12.1 | 2.0 | 6.0 |
| 1941 | 12.7 | 2.2 | 5.7 |
| 1942 | 13.2 | 2.4 | 5.5 |
| 1943 | 11.8 | 2.6 | 4.5 |
| 1944 | 11.0 | 2.9 | 3.8 |
| 1945 | 12.3 | 3.5 | 3.5 |
| 1946 | 16.4 | 4.3 | 3.8 |
| 1947 | 13.9 | 3.4 | 4.0 |
| 1950 | 11.0 | 2.5 | 4.4 |

The divorce rate varies from one section of the country to the other. The Atlantic coastal region and the South have the lowest rates. There is a rapid increase from East to West, and the western and the southwestern areas have the highest rate of all. Laws, customs, and social attitudes explain, in some measure, the differences between various sections of the country. Individual states vary in the grounds on which divorces are granted. New York has only one ground—infidelity—and, until recently, South Carolina granted no divorces for any cause.[2]  Most recent attempts to modify archaic divorce legislation, which leads to numerous and intolerable abuses, have failed.  In some states, such as Nevada and Idaho, only six weeks residence is required and there are several legal grounds on which divorce may be granted. Thousands of divorce seekers go to states that have lax divorce legislation, remain for a brief period, and secure a divorce, usually on the vague and inclusive ground of "cruelty."

Incidentally, in Nevada, which has the most lax divorce laws of any state, the divorce rate among permanent residents is relatively low: lower, in fact, than in many states with stringent divorce laws.  Clearly, ease in obtaining divorce does not necessarily bring about great frequency of divorce, a fact also confirmed by the divorce rate in Sweden and Russia.

**Sex and residence of divorce applicants.**  A study of divorce statistics reveals that over two-thirds of all divorces are granted to the wife. More women than ever before are economically independent of their husbands and able to refuse to continue marriage under unfavorable conditions.  Other factors determining the sex of the person who files the divorce are the greater number of legal grounds on which a wife can secure a divorce and the more tolerant attitude of the community to the woman who divorces her husband.  The fact that the wife sues for divorce and carries through the divorce action may not mean that she was the one who originally proposed the divorce; she may file the suit so that her husband can keep on with his work and thus be better able to finance the cost of the divorce.  The rural divorce rate is still about 50 per cent less than in the urban areas, possibly because rural public opinion, to some extent, still serves as a deterrent against divorce.  Further, there are usually more children; there are not as many opportunities for remarriage or for economic independence; and unhappily married persons often leave the rural community to establish residence elsewhere, and then secure a divorce.

**Divorce most frequent among childless families.**  It is commonly believed that one of the great tragedies of divorce is the effect on children.  It is true that many juvenile delinquents come from broken homes.  As a matter of fact, however, two-thirds of those couples obtaining divorce are childless; one-fifth have only one child.  In fact, there seems to be a definite relationship between childless marriages and divorce.  That there are a relatively small number of children of divorced couples—only about 3.5 per cent of the children in the United States have divorced parents—may be owing, in part, to the fact that

---

[2] As the result of an amendment ratified by the State Legislature on March 17, 1949, four grounds for divorce are now recognized—adultery, cruelty, desertion, and drunkenness.

many couples do not stay married long enough to have a large family. Over 35 per cent of those divorced in 1940 had been married less than four years. The average length of marriages ending in divorce is less than six years.

**WHO gets divorces?**

2/3 of all divorces are granted to women

The divorce rate in the cities is twice that in our country areas

About 2/3 of the people who obtain divorces have no children

The Atlantic coastal region has the Lowest divorce rate; there is a rapid increase as we go west

*Courtesy of Public Affairs Committee, Inc.*

Chart showing effect of some personal and social situations on the divorce picture.

**Family desertion.** The instability of the family is, however, even greater than the divorce rate indicates. Accurate statistics are not available, but it is estimated that about 75,000 to 100,000 homes are broken each year by desertion, mainly by the husband. Sometimes, a divorce follows later, but often the desertion marks the end of the marriage and no legal action is taken. Very often the cost of a divorce prevents the case from ever coming to court. This is why desertion is often known as "the poor man's divorce." While some deserting husbands do not have the money to pay for a divorce, others use desertion as an easy way out of a marriage which has become unhappy, unpleasant, or a financial burden. Welfare agencies report that one-fourth of all their expenditures go to women deserted by their husbands. Studies show that over one-fourth of all juvenile delinquents come from homes deserted by one or the other parent.

**Marriage rate still remains high.** If divorce is undermining the stability of the family, it is not putting an end to marriage. Quite to the contrary, the marriage rate has grown remarkably during the very period of increasing divorce rates. In 1887, the number of marriages per thousand of the population was 8.7; in 1946, it was 16.3. Over 68 per cent of the population over 14 years of age were married in 1950, as compared with 60 per cent in 1940, and only 53 per cent in 1890. The number of married couples between 1940 and 1950 increased even more rapidly than the population during this decade. The population increased by 14.5 per cent, while the number of married couples increased by 23.9 per cent. About 75 per cent of those who obtained divorces between 1943 and 1948 were remarried by 1948.

## Causes of Divorce

**Formal and actual causes of divorce.** The legal grounds for which divorce is granted are ostensibly serious offenses, such as infidelity, cruelty, desertion, drunkenness, neglect to provide, and crime. The actual reasons for divorce, however, are not usually found in the petition presented to the judge, since a couple seeking to have their marriage dissolved must do so on the legal grounds allowed by the state in which they live. The actual causes for divorce and for the increasing divorce rate in recent years are to be found in all those influences, already discussed, which have tended to reduce the importance and cohesiveness of family life and to alter its character.

**Growth of individualism and feminine independence.** With the rise of modern industry and the growth of cities, both men and women have become more determined to "lead their own lives" and less willing to adopt the give-and-take attitude required for a successful marriage. Women, as we have seen, no longer need to depend on husbands for support, but may earn their own living. Commercialized recreation, vocational groups, or social clubs take members of the family outside the home in leisure hours, and the home of today is often little more than a place to sleep. We have already noted in several places that city life invariably tends to reduce the birth rate and the size of the family among the middle and upper classes, who are the groups most likely to seek divorces.

**Waning prestige and authority of father.** Very frequently, today, the father is not the only breadwinner in the family; as a result, he has lost much of his former influence. The distance to and from work, the nervous tension of city life, and extra-family contacts leave many fathers with less time or inclination to be concerned with the problems of their children. Schools and other agencies have taken the child partly away from home and parental guidance and authority. As a result, many fathers and their children are no longer bound together by common interests and duties, and the ties of affection and authority between them have also been weakened.

**Economic causes of divorce.** Studies of marriage difficulties reveal that finances play a much larger rôle in divorce than is commonly realized. The American people suffer from a desire "to keep up with the Joneses." Many families try to live in a more lavish fashion than they can afford and much unhappiness results because husbands and wives, especially the latter, cannot have all they want. When we realize that the majority of families, despite high wages during the war, do not have sufficient income to provide even a decent standard of living, we can understand the seriousness of the situation. A wife whose husband cannot provide her with even the necessities of life is inclined to feel an increasing resentment that she married a man who cannot earn enough to support her. A husband, although he may be at fault in being a poor provider, may become dissatisfied with a wife who is "dowdy," an indifferent housekeeper, or a poor cook. Worries over financial matters fray the nerves of both husband and wife and cause frequent and bitter quarrels. The desperate housing shortage since 1941 has, doubtless, contributed markedly to domestic friction.

**Lack of sexual knowledge.** Probably the most important cause of marital unhappiness and divorce is the fact that few young persons are properly prepared for marriage. Parents fail to teach their children the nature and duties of married life. As a result, they blunder into marriage, with little or no understanding that marriage requires constant effort to adjust to each other's desires and habits. Expecting at the outset that marriage will be constant harmony and bliss, young couples may magnify minor disagreements until they grow into insoluble sources of discontent and unhappiness. Lack of understanding of sexual matters is the outstanding phase of poor preparation for marriage. Those judges and sociologists who have special knowledge and insight in regard to marriage and divorce agree that there are few divorces between couples who have a satisfactory sexual experience in marriage.

These causes of marital discord are, of course, not new, but in earlier days, when divorces were harder to get and carried a greater social stigma, and when women found it difficult to live outside of a family, marriage was entered into with the realization that it was likely to be permanent. Undoubtedly, many marriages in the frontier period, and in rural regions generally, were unhappy, but couples would endure all manner of misery rather than seek a divorce.

**Marriage is too easy.** Another important factor in our high divorce rate is the ease with which a marriage license can be procured and a ceremony performed. This ease of contracting marriage makes possible the large number of hasty and frivolous marriages. In some states, laws make it possible to marry as soon as the decision to wed is made. Knowledge that a mistake can be rectified by divorce without too much difficulty and before too long makes large numbers of couples willing to take a chance that the marriage will be satisfactory. Marriage and the rearing of a family involve serious responsibilities. Those couples who have failed to realize the social implications of marriage are, for the most part, the ones who bolster the increasing number of divorces. This factor became, as we shall now point out, especially important in connection with the flock of hasty wartime marriages after 1940.

## The Effects of the Second World War on the Family

**War stimulates family instability.** War speeds up social change. All the reasons for divorce noted above were given added impetus by the second world war. Divorce rates, already high, rose alarmingly after 1941. Statistics show, however, that, long before the second world war, the traditional patriarchal family pattern of the frontier and rural areas was disintegrating; the war only hastened the break-up. Nearly 15 million men were taken from their home surroundings by enlistments and the draft between 1940 and 1945. Besides this, millions of men and women left their homes to work in defense and war plants. It is estimated that the total industrial migration during the second world war affected over 15 million persons.

Large numbers of families left their homes and migrated hundreds, or thousands, of miles to find employment in war industries. The coming of the war workers to already crowded urban areas made it difficult to find a place to live. Sometimes, only temporary shelters were to be found, often a trailer camp or hastily erected shacks. Overcrowding and poor sanitation were common. Under these conditions, it was inevitable that family relations would suffer. Even where the women and children did not migrate, many men left their homes to work. As a result, husbands and wives drifted apart and found it difficult to resume life together again.

In some instances, changed income brought a weakening of family ties. In many cases, income was lowered as a result of the husband's being drafted, but, in the case of war workers, despite increased living costs and higher taxes, income increased. Women earned high wages in war plants. For many, it was their first employment. Wives became self-reliant and economically independent of their husbands and found it exciting to be free from home responsibilities.

**War marriages.** War conditions greatly stimulated marriages, many of them hasty, ill-considered, and later regretted. By 1942, the marriage rate in 26 states had risen 25 per cent over 1939. Three months after Pearl Harbor, Seattle, Washington, reported a 290 per cent gain in marriages over 1940. Other communities reported similar striking gains. In 1940, about 59 per cent of the female population (14 years of age and over) was married; in 1946, a sample census showed that over 63 per cent of this group was married. The greatest increase in the rate of marriage was among young women between the ages of 20 and 24. In 1940, slightly over 50 per cent were married; in 1946, over 58 per cent.

Some of those who married during the war had previously planned marriage, but for thousands of couples marriage was the result of wartime conditions. Hasty marriages are all too common in peacetime, but in the frenzied haste of war, the glamour of a uniform or the desire to share in the excitement of the moment would draw many girls into marriage after a whirlwind courtship of a few weeks, or even days, with little thought of the future. Sometimes either one or both of the partners had been drinking too much and had no clear recollection of the event or the person they married. Some girls married, not because of the excitement, but for fear they would have no further opportunity; others married for the service allotment, or the possible insurance if the soldier were killed. Some men married with the mistaken idea it would keep them from being drafted; others hoped to have a child to leave if they were killed; some married because they hoped marriage would bring a sense of security in a time of uncertainty. About 1,500,000 soldiers married during wartime at home or abroad. About 100,000 soldiers married women of a race or nationality different from their own. Although service men showed the greatest degree of matrimonial frenzy during the war period, the same tendency to marry hastily was all too common among those at home, many of them encouraged by high wages.

After the parting, in the case of servicemen, thousands who had married in haste decided their marriage had been a mistake, that there was little basis for a happy marriage—no similarity of background, no interests in common, no desire to resume the marriage relationship. It was no wonder that many of these couples decided to be divorced during or after the war. In considering the large number who married in haste, those who delayed marriage are often overlooked. Some marriages were prevented entirely by the death of the serviceman or the subsequent engagement of the girl or the man to another person.

**Wartime separation undermines families.** After V-J Day, demobilization took place rapidly. Veterans returned to take up civilian life. Some of them were changed, maimed, disfigured, or mentally ill and could not successfully resume normal family life. Many returned to find their wives had become so accustomed to financial independence and a feeling of freedom that they were not willing to go back to homemaking. Some veterans, although guilty of extensive infidelity themselves, were outraged to find their wives had been unfaithful; and there were wives who, finding that their husbands had taken advantage of the more liberal sex mores abroad, began suit for divorce. Probably not as many wives sued for divorce on grounds of unfaithfulness as did husbands after the discovery of the infidelity of their wives in their absence.

In some instances, even in a marriage of several years duration, long separation brought about a feeling of strangeness. The husband, in some cases, had seen a life far different from the one he had previously known; he had matured and had developed a new philosophy. Such men returned to find their wives had not changed their point of view and were little matured by the war. In some instances, it was the wife who had matured, had established new values, had found new independence, and who was disillusioned with her returning husband. Many couples had idealized each other during the long absence, had built up an attractive but illusory mental picture of the absent one, and were disappointed when they saw each other again. Sometimes, it was the emotional let-down following worry and suspense, which produced great difficulty in readjustment. There were children who had never seen their fathers and resented the intrusion of a stranger; in like manner, many fathers also resented the fact that their children and their wives had been able to get along without them.

**Housing shortages intensify family crises.** There is no doubt that the desperate housing crisis was a factor in the rising divorce rate and the unstable family situation after the war. Thousands of couples had never had a settled home, for many war brides had lived in hotels, trailers, or tourist camps as near as possible to where their husbands were stationed. After the war, the housing shortage and the exorbitant cost of available homes forced large numbers of veterans and their families to double up with relatives or other couples. Crowding made readjustment even more difficult.

The problem of crowded housing was especially acute for veterans who went to school or college to finish, or to begin, their education under the educational opportunities offered by the Federal government. Over 7 million veterans entered school or college or took on-the-job training under the GI bill. Many lived in trailer camps or Quonset huts, or moved in with other married couples, all trying to manage on the slender stipend allowed veterans and their families to secure an education.

**Postwar economic problems.** Economic problems after the war encouraged GI divorces and broke up marriages of long standing. While most of the returning veterans could get jobs, their wages were, in part, eaten up by high taxes and increased living costs. There was no money left to enjoy the night-club life which had intrigued them in wartime. Moreover, as we have seen, the housing shortage made home living conditions very unattractive, even to couples whose income enabled them to rent pleasant homes under prewar conditions. Many women who had found employment while their husbands were in service announced their intention of continuing to work. A survey in 1945 showed that 40 per cent of the working wives intended to continue working if they could secure a job after the war. In spite of the economic problems faced by returning veterans, many bitterly resented their wives' decision to continue work. In many cases, the friction in the home over money matters led to the divorce court.

**Racial and cultural tensions.** The large number of marriages of American soldiers to foreign women also put a strain on the American family. Cultural, and sometimes racial, differences posed many problems for the new family. Friends and relatives of the man often did not like the foreign wife and, even if they tried to make her welcome in her new country, they resented her presence. The wives, in a new and strange environment far from home, often found American ways unpleasant. This was especially true if the foreign bride discovered, on her arrival in this country, that her husband had exaggerated his wealth or position or had, as was true in some cases, outrageously lied about it. Bitter disillusionment in these cases was inevitable, and divorce virtually certain.

**Increase of divorces in postwar period.** Although the divorce rate increased tremendously after the war for the reasons we have noted, it had been rising even during the war. This was not true of the first world war, but the second world war was so much more disruptive of normal life, took so many more men into the services, put so many more women into war work, and encouraged so many hasty marriages, that it was almost inevitable that the divorce rate would continue to rise over 1940 levels. Although the divorce rate rose during the war, many marriages then almost at the breaking point were temporarily saved until a later time. Some husbands solved their problems by enlisting "for the duration" and many women who otherwise would have sued for divorce waited until the end of the war so that they might receive the allowances given to dependents. There was thus a backlog of already broken marriages which came into the divorce courts with the end of the war.

Another factor was also of some importance. Wives who seek a divorce when their husbands are serving their country are not regarded kindly by their communities. Many wives, to retain the respect of public opinion, waited until after the war to dissolve a marriage which, as a matter of fact, had long before been broken. In 1945, the divorce rate had risen from the 1940 ratio of about one divorce to six marriages to an all-time high of one divorce to 3.5 marriages. By 1950, over half of the marriages contracted during the war had ended in divorce, and many marriages of longer duration had broken under the strain of war.

**High divorce and marriage rates may have reached their peaks.** There is much evidence that the divorce rate has reached its peak and is on the decline. The number of divorces per thousand of the population dropped from 4.3 in 1946 to 3.4 in 1947 and 2.5 in 1950. Presumably, those cases of couples waiting for the end of the war to file for divorce have already been through the courts and the majority of the hasty war marriages have been legally dissolved.

The high marriage rate between 1940 and 1946 has also begun to decline. The marriage rate in 1946 was 16.4 per 1,000; in 1947, 13.9; and in 1950, 11.0. The decline in the marriage rate since 1946 has not been accompanied by a decline in the birth rate. Due to the "cold war," the Korean War, and resulting temporary prosperity, there were 24,000 more children born in 1951 than in 1947.

## How We May Reduce the Divorce Rate

**Attempts to restrain hasty and frivolous marriages.** If it were more difficult to get married, there would be fewer foolish marriages and unstable families, and, therefore, fewer divorces. By 1946, 26 states had passed laws providing that people who want to marry must wait a certain length of time after they get a license, generally three to five days. It is to be hoped that all states will soon pass such laws, since this legislation will accomplish little if persons in a hurry to get married can drive to a state where the law is less strict. The law making provision for a waiting period should not be waived, except for good reason. During the second world war, many cases occurred where the waiting period was waived to allow marriages of servicemen during furloughs.

In recent years, there has been a noticeable trend toward raising the legal age for marriage. There is little uniformity in state laws but legislation in some states has placed the legal age of marriage at 21 for boys and 18 for girls. If young people are prevented from marrying without parental consent until they are old enough to understand the responsibilities of married life, there will be more happy marriages and fewer divorces.

**Improving economic security.** We cannot logically expect married people to be happy without an income sufficient to provide a decent standard of living. Few families can cheerfully endure the suffering and misery that goes with poverty. Children cannot be properly reared in homes where there is constant worry over money matters. We have not yet been able to guarantee everyone a chance to make a good living, but, with our country's vast natural resources and many flourishing industries, it should be possible to provide work at decent wages for all who want it. One of the major problems of this generation is to find a way to bring economic security to the husband, so that he may decently take care of his home and family. The frequency of divorce among the well-to-do proves, however, that economic well-being and security alone will not solve the divorce problem.

**Better education for family responsibilities.** Perhaps the most important of all measures that might be suggested to lessen divorce is the education, preferably premarital, of young people about the facts and responsibilities of sex and marriage. Some 600 colleges and universities now offer courses in family and marriage problems. In some communities, adult education programs are helping young people to understand some of their sex and marriage problems. Even some of the secondary schools are becoming aware of the necessity of preparing students for marriage and helping them build for a happier family life. If young people are taught the principles of sane sex living, there will be fewer divorces granted on the grounds of sexual incompatibility. Even the extension of general education, especially higher education, to a larger number of the population would serve to reduce divorce. Among married couples where both are college graduates there is only about one divorce to 65 marriages in normal times, an enormous increase in stability when compared with the total divorce rate.

**More pleasant family life.** Much more should be accomplished in the way of making married life more attractive. If decent living standards could be secured and maintained, marriage would be less drab. We have already indicated the need for more adequate housing. A survey, in 1948, revealed the fact that two and a half million families were doubling up on living quarters with others or were living in "transient hotels and lodging houses."

A slum apartment, with dingy walls and close quarters, giving no place for privacy, makes for nervous tension and quarrels, which often end in divorce or desertion. More stress should be laid on ways of avoiding extreme and constant intimacy. Homes should be large enough to provide individual members of the family with privacy when they desire to be alone. Husbands and wives should be taught the desirability of occasional separate vacations. Bored wives should be encouraged to develop hobbies and interests outside the home. It has been proposed that domestic relations courts, which usually handle juvenile delinquency cases, could be used to advantage in straightening out marital problems before they come to the divorce courts. Trained social workers might investigate and adjust many family problems which, left unsolved, might result in broken homes and the later delinquency of the children.

**Marriage and family clinics.** Much faith has been placed by some in marriage or family clinics where attempts are made to iron out differences between discontented husbands and wives before they resort to the divorce court. Two notable examples of the family clinic idea are the American Institute of Family Relations of Los Angeles, established in 1930 by Dr. Paul Popenoe, a well-known expert on family problems, and the Marriage Counsel of Philadelphia, founded in 1932. The Family Consultation Service of Cincinnati was a joint enterprise sponsored by the Council of Churches and the Family Welfare Society. In 1938, in response to the growing need for professional guidance in counseling, a National Conference on Family Relations was organized to co-ordinate the efforts of groups interested in the preservation of marriage. Various regional and state conferences have also been held.

**Improved divorce legislation.** There is no doubt that changes should be made in the present divorce legislation. The United States has 48 state divorce laws, which vary from extreme laxity to absolute rigor. Because of the difficulty of securing a divorce in some states, thousands of persons go to states where divorce is easy, secure a divorce, and return to their home state. This has resulted in serious legal problems: for example, a person may have established temporary residence outside his state, may have secured a divorce and returned to his home and remarried, to find that, under his state law, he is not legally married and the children of his second marriage will be considered illegitimate. In recent years, with the rising divorce rate, there has been increasing difficulty because of the lack of uniformity in state laws. Numerous cases involving disputed divorces have been brought before the courts.

On June 7, 1948, the Supreme Court handed down four important decisions that seemed likely to aid the drive for uniform divorce laws. In two similar cases, the Court held by 7–2 decisions that Nevada divorces, although legal to dissolve a marriage, do not cancel the obligations of former husbands to make monthly payments ordered by New York courts in separation proceedings. Since New York has only one ground for divorce, many couples legally separate and, in some cases, the courts order husbands to make monthly payments or alimony. Justice Jackson, disagreeing with the decision, said that the rulings merely added to the existing confusion, for people today do not know, and even a lawyer cannot tell them with confidence, how their out-of-state divorce and later remarriage might be regarded legally by the state in which they make their home. He urged the Court to issue a ruling by which people can live. In the other two cases, also similar, the Supreme Court ruled that the Massachusetts courts could not challenge divorces obtained in Nevada and Florida if both the husband and wife had full opportunity before the divorce to argue the question of legal residence in the courts.

Another ruling regarding Nevada divorces was handed down by the Supreme Court on April 18, 1949. By a decision of 5–4 the Court ruled that "quickie" divorces obtained in Nevada can be overruled by other states under certain circumstances. Justice Jackson, one of the dissenters, protested that this makes the nation's "crazy quilt" divorce laws more confused than ever. The majority held, however, that Connecticut had acted properly in setting aside a Reno divorce and granting the ex-wife a widow's share in the property of her former husband, who died without leaving a will.

There has been increasing agitation for a uniform Federal divorce law. Much opposition has developed from two sources: from commercial interests in states where easy divorce laws bring in large sums of money, and from those persons who believe in the right of states to manage their own problems and who fear infringement by the Federal government. But a Federal law modeled on the legislation of the Scandinavian countries might help to remove some of the divorce evils prevalent today.

**Swedish divorce legislation.** In 1915, Sweden enacted a law based on an extended study of the divorce problem. It provided for divorce by mutual consent in all cases where persistent family discord exists. The parties desiring a divorce must make a written application, to be followed by separation for a year. During that time, under the authority of the court, attempts are made to reconcile the couple and adjust their differences. If these fail, the divorce is granted. A year's separation will generally resolve friction based only on sudden anger, sulking, or nervous tension. If the difficulty cannot be cleared up within a year the couple should not remain married. The law provides, in special cases, that a year need not elapse before the divorce is granted. The example of Sweden was followed in 1918 by Norway, and in 1920 by Denmark. These countries have found this type of divorce law very satisfactory. The divorce rate in Sweden is about one-half that of the United States.

**Curb the alimony racket.** Any reasonable solution of the divorce problem would also involve putting an end to the abuses of the alimony "racket." Alimony is the court-ordered allowance paid by the husband toward the support of his divorced wife, usually a fixed sum of money each week or each month. Most people believe that, if there are children in the family, the divorced father should provide for their support and education, unless the wife is wealthy or remarries. There are, however, numerous cases of women who marry solely in order to get a speedy divorce and collect fat alimony payments. Most students of the divorce problem believe that, if a childless divorced woman is in good health and can earn her own living, she should not expect her former husband to support her. It has been argued by some that, so long as the alimony "racket" prevails, it is logical to require a rich woman who divorces her husband to contribute to the latter's support.

## Future of the Family

**Marriage rate remains high.** Few social problems are more widely discussed than that of the future of the family. We should not, of course, fall into the common error of confusing the future of the family with the future of marriage. No informed student, however pessimistic about the future stability of the family, has any doubt about the continued popularity of marriage. More persons are marrying today than ever before. Even the majority of divorced persons remarry. The problem is not the frequency of marriage but the stability of family relationships.

**Increasing state support of the family.** It is quite likely that the state and other agencies will step in and take over many of the former parental responsibilities in supporting the family. Already the state provides for the education of children. Public health agencies, nursing associations, child guidance clinics, recreational centers, and many other child welfare organizations now give aid to families in matters formerly the responsibility of parents. The Social Security Act recognized the responsibility of the state to mothers and dependent children. The Amendments to the 1935 Act in 1939, 1946, and 1948, increased the contribution of the Federal government to the grants made by the state. More than one million children, representing over 390,000 families, received monthly pensions from the Aid to Dependent Children program in 1947. The old patriarchal family based its cohesiveness in part on the dependence of the mother and children on the father.

**The family can be saved and stabilized.** Some sociologists point to the fact that the marriage and birth rates reached a new high after the war as an indication of stability. There appears to be no evidence, however, that the size of the family is increasing. There have been more marriages and new families with one or two children. Since the majority of divorces occur in the early years of marriage, a temporarily high birth rate is no indication of an increased tendency toward a family stability.

If social reform moves ahead in the United States there is every indication that, although changes will take place in the family, this important social institution will endure. Divorce will probably be made easier and marriage more difficult to contract. Knowledge of the problems of marriage, based upon the education of persons before marriage, will make for more permanent unions. If people can be taught to understand each other's emotions, there will be more tolerance in the family and fewer divorces demanded on grounds of incompatibility or cruelty. If we are able to avoid a third world war, our impressive technology will ultimately bring about better economic conditions and a higher standard of living, either slowly by trial-and-error and the selective process, or rapidly through sound social planning. Greater economic security and abundance will do a great deal to make family life more satisfactory and stable.

## Child Problems and Child Care Outside the Family

**New agencies for child care.** Down to modern times the great majority of child problems and child care fell within the family itself. The child contributed all his labor to the family, and the family gave the child attention in the way of food, clothing and shelter, education, medical care, and the like. The family had well-nigh complete control of the child and received all his services in return. Now that the old authoritarian family is being weakened and the rural economy superseded by an urban industrial age, the family no longer provides complete care for, exerts full authority over, or receives all the services of, children. Indeed, in urban communities there are few services a child can render the family. We may look briefly at some ways in which the community and the state have stepped in to take over many responsibilities that once fell to the family.

**Improved medical care for children.** Great progress has been made in protecting the health of the child since a century ago, when the mother was usually delivered by a midwife and "doctored" her children with various herbs and syrups. The development of aseptic surgical methods in maternity cases and, especially, the recent introduction of the many sulfa drugs and antibiotics have greatly reduced the number of deaths at childbirth. Better control of communicable diseases and of the epidemic diseases of childhood has saved the lives of many thousands of children. Improved knowledge of nutritional science has also greatly reduced the infant death rate.

The community and the state have given special attention to providing public medical care for children. Clinics and socialized medicine in various forms were usually made accessible to children long before they were extended to adults. Gymnasium work and supervised play have also contributed to the improvement of the physical health and resistance of children.

Many communities look after the mental health of children, largely because psychiatrists recognize the critical importance of childhood in the building of the adult mind. Psychological clinics for children appeared in this country as early as 1896. But the movement to create mental health clinics for children, usually called child guidance clinics, did not really get under way until after the National Committee for Mental Hygiene was created in 1909. The movement grew rapidly; by 1914 there were a hundred such clinics, and by 1930 over 500. In 1946, there were 688 mental hygiene clinics in the country, some 285 of which were devoted exclusively to children. These have been of great value in checking mental disease and delinquency and in aiding educators in a more realistic handling of problem children. It has been expertly estimated that at least five per cent of all children in elementary school require psychiatric study and guidance.[3]

**Improved public assistance and care for children.** A century ago orphaned and dependent children were cared for mainly in almshouses and through what is known as indentures, that is, the placing of children in families who agreed to support them in return for their labor. Both were cruel and unsatisfactory; the almshouses made for demoralization, and indenture invited exploitation.

In the middle of the last century, the Children's Aid Society of New York began to take children out of almshouses and put them in foster homes without the abuse of indenture. In 1868, the Massachusetts Board of Charities introduced the practice of boarding out children in foster homes at public expense. In the last fifty years, the care of dependent children in foster homes instead of institutions, wherever possible, has come to be the generally accepted procedure. With the passage of the Social Security Act in 1935, child welfare services at

---

[3] Another problem in the mental and physical development of children is that of child labor. See above, pp. 334–335.

governmental expense were extended to care for children in the home. Although these grants are not yet adequate, the program is based on the principle that the preservation of family life is of fundamental importance, and the care of the dependent child is a necessary item in public expenditure. In 1923, public and private agencies cared for about 400,000 children in free foster homes, boarding homes, and institutions, as well as in their own homes. In 1943, the latest year for which complete figures are available, only 225,000 children were under the care of public and private agencies in foster homes or institutions.[4] In the same year, 676,000 children received help in their own homes through the Social Security programs. By 1947, the Social Security program of Aid to Dependent Children assisted over one million children.

Public care has been extended not only to dependent children but also to neglected children. In 1875, the Society for the Prevention of Cruelty to Children was founded to protect neglected children in New York. Other large cities soon organized similar societies. They brought cases of cruelty and exploitation of juveniles to the courts and helped to punish the guilty. The progress made in protecting children from various abuses can be seen by the fact that, in the early days of these societies, half the cases related directly to physical cruelty, whereas today only about ten per cent of all cases involve cruel treatment.

**Controlling juvenile delinquency.** In earlier days, the rural parents exercised a strong influence on their children, but with the decline in the authority of the family, juvenile courts and guidance clinics for delinquents have been organized for this purpose. The first juvenile court was opened in Chicago in 1899. Ten years later, a juvenile psychiatric institute, under the leadership of Dr. William Healy, was made a part of the court. The work of the institute, in investigating family backgrounds and home environments and giving physical and mental examinations to the children brought before the court, was of great importance. Later, Dr. Healy continued his work in Boston with the Judge Baker Foundation. The juvenile court movement, under psychiatric guidance, has made considerable headway in the last two decades. Today, many communities have become interested in the prevention of delinquency and are trying to cope with the problem of the juvenile gang, especially in the slums, and with the dangers involved in rearing children in areas of the city where social control is too weak to offer protection.

**Educational advances.** Formerly, parents provided much of the education of children. Following the work of Horace Mann in getting a system of free public instruction set up in Massachusetts in 1837, some kind of free public education outside the home was gradually

---

[4] Report of Children's Bureau, "Change in Volume of Foster Care." Supplement to Vol. 9, No. 12 (June 1945), *The Child.*

made available for all children. The rural schools were, however, miserably equipped and offered little opportunity for providing an adequate education. An effort was made by John Dewey and others to free education from the harsh discipline of the traditional schools, through what have come to be known as experimental schools and progressive education. The introduction of mental tests has facilitated the classification of children as superior, average, or retarded. Vocational instruction is now more adequately developed. City schools are far ahead of the rural school in equipment and the type of instruction available, but, recently, the development of consolidated and centralized schools has revolutionized rural educational opportunities in many areas.

**Better facilities for play.** Play, formerly limited to the family group, the neighborhood, and the rural school, is now a major community and national enterprise. Public recreational activities have developed on a large scale and supervised play has grown by leaps and bounds. In 1910, there had been only 1,300 public playgrounds for children; in 1944, there were over 10,000. In 1938, some 1,300 urban communities spent about 30 million dollars on public recreation. About a third of them were aided by Federal funds. During the second world war, recreational facilities of communities, particularly those in the areas of army camps, were greatly expanded. In 1946, expenditures for recreation in 1,488 urban communities amounted to over 54 million dollars.

Although progress has been made, our recreational facilities for children are still woefully limited in some communities. As late as 1948, there were six million urban children who had few or no opportunities for organized and supervised recreation. The rural situation is even worse, although the consolidated schools have begun to enlarge their recreation programs and facilities; there are only about 260 rural community recreation projects in operation today. It is estimated that over ten million rural children have no provision for planned recreation. So far, only a beginning has been made in the rural community, but such youth organizations as the Boy and Girl Scouts, Campfire Girls, Future Farmers of America, and 4-H Clubs have done great service in offering recreational opportunities to their members.

**Increasing recognition of public and community responsibility for children.** Many associations give special attention to child welfare. Some of the most important are the Child Study Association, the National Child Labor Committee, the Child Welfare League of America, the National Commission on Children, and the American Child Health Association. There are also various institutes of child welfare, conducted by leading state universities. The White House Conference on Children in a Democracy, to which are invited representatives of all agencies interested in children, has held four important conferences since 1909 on the problems of the child. Since its establishment in 1912, the Federal Children's Bureau has worked for legislation to limit hours and types of work, particularly for those children not covered by existing legislation, mainly those in the cotton and tobacco areas of the South and in domestic service. Much of its activity has been devoted to investigation of the practices of employers using child labor. Surveys of the work of children in many industries and various agricultural operations have been made.

The growing interest of the community in all aspects of child welfare is of great importance in this period of family instability. As life has become increasingly complex in an urban society, the community has been compelled to share responsibility with the family in meeting the needs of the child to provide "for all children as nearly as possible the equal opportunity in life . . . assumed to be the foundation of this Nation. . . ." [5]

## Summary

The family is the oldest human institution and has been of primary social importance throughout the course of history. Until the Industrial Revolution, the family served as the basic social unit—the fundamental primary group. Around it were centered the economic, educational, recreational, and social activities of its members.

The Industrial Revolution and the growing predominance of urban life brought changes in society that have taken away many of the family's important functions. Today, the necessities of life, such as food and clothing, are no longer produced in the home, but are generally purchased. Recreation and social life are mainly sought outside the family circle, while the state has taken over the education of children and many other family social duties. The increased independence of women has tended to weaken marriage ties and increase divorce.

The reasons for the increase in divorce since 1900 lie in the effect of the new conditions of industrial and city life on the family. Opportunities for employment have increased the independence of women, making them no longer dependent upon their husbands for support. City life has tended to transfer interests outside the home, so that for many people home has become little more than a place to sleep. The family has also lost its unique value as a productive group. The modern desire for more and more luxuries, coupled with the equally widespread inability of husbands to provide incomes sufficient for the necessities of life, have led to much marital unhappiness. Most young people have little knowledge of sexual matters and are unprepared for the duties of marriage, which marriage laws permit them to enter too quickly and easily. Remedies for the breakdown of family life must be directed toward solving these problems.

---

[5] *White House Conference on Children in a Democracy, Final Report,* United States Children's Bureau Publication 272, Washington, 1940, p. 4.

Although family stability was badly shaken as the result of the second world war, it is safe to say that, given normal conditions, there is no probability that the family will disappear from society. The traditional rural family, however, is undergoing radical changes. In its place, will come a family more suited to the needs of modern city life and our industrial society.

The decline of the family as an all-inclusive child-caring institution has been accompanied by the rise of many agencies outside the family devoted to aiding children in the field of physical and mental health, security, education, recreation, prevention of delinquency, and the like. Such agencies are no complete substitute for the family, but their work is a useful supplement to that of the family, and is especially valuable at the present time, when the family is undergoing crucial transformations.

## Selected References

* Apstein, T. E., *The Parting of the Ways*, Dodge, 1935. A clear introduction to the divorce problem by a writer professionally concerned with marriage and divorce situations.

Baber, R. E., *Marriage and the Family*, McGraw-Hill, 1939. A standard and competent text on family problems.

Becker, Howard, and Hill, Reuben, *Marriage and the Family*, Heath, 1942. Able sociological analysis.

Becker, Howard; Hill, Reuben; et al., *Family, Marriage, and Parenthood*, Heath, 1949. Comprehensive and informing symposium.

Bergler, Edmund, *Divorce Won't Help*, Harper, 1948. Excellent psychiatric analysis of the causes of marital discord and possible remedies.

Bowman, H. A., *Marriage for Moderns*, McGraw-Hill, 1942. A clear and lucid introduction to marriage preparation and problems.

Cuber, J. F., *Marriage Counseling Practice*, Appleton-Century-Crofts, 1948. A brief but competent account of the development of marriage clinics and marriage counseling service.

* Das, S. R., *The American Woman in Modern Marriage*, Philosophical Library, 1949. A highly enlightened and stimulating account of the reaction on family life of the emancipation of woman, increased economic opportunities for women, greater tolerance of sex freedom, and divorce.

Duvall, S. M., and Hill, G. W., *When You Marry*, Heath, 1949. Stresses preparation for marriage and family responsibilities.

Folsom, J. K., *The Family and Democratic Society*, Wiley, 1948. A rather reassuring answer to recent alarmist books on current trends in family life.

Frazier, E. F., *The Negro Family in the United States*, University of Chicago Press, 1939. The ablest study of the special problems of the Negro family.

Groves, E. R. and G. H., *Sex in Marriage*, Emerson Books, 1940. A conservative and restrained but important book on the relation of satisfactory sex adjustment to success in marriage. One of the best introductions to the subject for the general reader.

\*—————, *The Contemporary American Family*, Lippincott, 1947. Perhaps the most up-to-date and authoritative presentation of family problems.

—————, *Dynamic Mental Hygiene*, Stackpole, 1949. Comprehensive study of possible applications of mental hygiene to family problems, especially family counselling.

Harper, R. A., *Marriage*, American Book Company, 1949. Readable summary of the more practical problems of marriage and family life.

Hill, Reuben, *et al.*, *Families under Stress*, Harper, 1950. Important case studies of the impact of the second world war on family stability.

Kling, S. G. and E. B. (Eds.), *The Marriage Reader*, Vanguard, 1947. Frank and realistic symposium dealing with sexual, psychological, and social aspects of marriage problems.

Knox, S. T., *The Family and the Law*, University of North Carolina Press, 1941. A useful book on the laws relating to marriage, family usages, and divorce.

Landis, J. T. and M. G., *Building a Successful Marriage*, Prentice-Hall, 1948. Able and up-to-date treatment of marriage and the family in sociological perspective.

Lichtenberger, J. P., *Divorce*, McGraw-Hill, 1931. A standard sociological manual, discussing the extent, causes, and possible remedies for divorce in the United States.

Lindsey, B. B., *Companionate Marriage*, Boni and Liveright, 1927. A much discussed book, advocating early trial unions as the best preventive of mental disease, prostitution, and venereal disease, and as the best preparation for successful permanent unions.

Merrill, F. E., *Courtship and Marriage*, Sloane, 1949. Readable book laying emphasis on preparation for family life and problems.

Neumann, Henry, *Modern Youth and Marriage*, Appleton, 1928. A sane discussion of the marriage problem, based on sound ethical principles divorced from superstition.

Nimkoff, M. F., *Marriage and the Family*, Houghton Mifflin, 1947. One of the best recent manuals on the family in contemporary society.

Rougemont, Denis de, *Love in the Western World*, Harcourt, Brace, 1940. Stimulating historical and psychological account of the social and cultural import of romantic love.

\* Stern, B. J., (Ed.), *The Family, Past and Present*, Appleton-Century, 1938. A good historical and sociological study of the family.

Truxal, A. G., and Merrill, F. E., *The Family in American Culture*, Prentice-Hall, 1947. Comprehensive exposition and analysis of the rôle of the family in American civilization.

* Waller, Willard, *The Family*, Dryden Press, 1938. One of the most complete textbooks on the family, and the best analysis of personal relationships within the family; strong on the psychological side.

Winter, Ella, *Red Virtue*, Harcourt, Brace, 1933. An interesting and competent discussion of the sex and marriage situation in Soviet Russia. Certain restrictions have been imposed since 1933.

Zimmerman, C. C., *Family and Civilization*, Harper, 1947. Valuable for its emphasis on the interrelation between cultural change and family trends. Perhaps a little overpretentious.

# CHAPTER XXVI

# Community Organization to the Rescue

## Need for Community Organization

**Meaning of community.** The trend toward community organization in the twentieth century is one of the more significant movements in modern society. It has developed out of the leading social changes in the last 150 years—the revolution in rural life, the growth of the city, and the breakup of the traditional rural family pattern.

The term "community" is used in various ways and its meaning is often confused. In the broadest sense, community is the mutual awareness among members of a social group of their reciprocal, or interdependent, relationships, and is limited only by the strength of this "consciousness of kind" or "we-feeling." It may be extended to "One World" or limited to the boundaries of a small neighborhood.

In this book, however, we will use the term "community" in a more concise way. A community is a group of people who live in a given area, share a unified set of interests, and have a more or less common culture. The community may be a rural neighborhood, a small town, a whole city, or a section within a city. The economic and social opportunities of the individual as well as his views on politics, religion, and economic and social issues are determined in large part by his social environment. The community is, thus, a vital factor in the life of the individual and the community organization movement may assume great importance. By community organization we mean the promotion of helpful relationships among all groups in the community, the unification and co-ordination of these groups to increase their efficiency and social service, and the adjustment of the local community to the larger social unit of which it comprises an integral part.

**Need for community organization.** Community organization is an attempt to encourage group responsibility and thus compensate in some measure for the breakdown of the earlier types of social control. It represents a definite trend, during the last few decades, toward group responsibility in fields of activity which formerly were considered matters of individual, family, neighborhood, or rural church concern. It seeks, through community organization and activities, to produce substitutes for those relationships and controls which were

672

formerly provided by direct personal association in primary groups but which today are rapidly fading out in an era of increasing mechanization and urbanization. Sociological theory, which was developed chiefly from a study of primary and small secondary groups, must increasingly readjust its perspective and analysis to community and regional activities and problems, as well as to the national and international impact on communities and regions.

**Examples of community activities.** Many phases of life have come to be regarded as matters of community concern. Nowhere is this fact more clearly illustrated than in the provisions made by communities for the prevention and cure of disease and the protection of health. The public health movement arose out of the community's fear of epidemics and the realization that the community must assume responsibility for the maintenance of health to protect the individual within its boundaries from other individuals suffering from contagious diseases. In addition to routine duties, such as inspection of food and milk, provision for a supply of pure water and the like, the public health departments perform a wide variety of functions. Free clinics give examinations and treatment to those unable to pay for them; the large cities maintain hospitals for the sick poor; and the visiting-nurse system is now an integral part of the public health program of many communities. The educational program of the public health movement has helped to reduce the incidence of such diseases as tuberculosis and venereal maladies.

Another example of the group approach in community life is seen in the modern attitude toward education. Once largely centered in the family, the education of the child has become the responsibility of the community. Educational functions have been extended beyond formal education in the classroom. Today, the emphasis is on fitting the child to participate effectively as a member of the group in which he lives. Vocational education and guidance and occupational training are examples of the preparation of youth by the community for adult life. The modern public library supplements the work of the school. Adult education also has received much attention in the last decade. Designed to meet the needs of the adults who wish more specific training, who desire to continue their formal education, or who want to spend leisure time profitably, adult education courses are made available through the high schools, colleges, or state universities.

The group approach to public welfare assistance to the needy, the aged, the blind, the physically and mentally handicapped, the dependent child, and the juvenile delinquent also provides examples of the acceptance of new responsibility on the part of the community. No longer is the individual in need of help blamed personally by the social agencies for his inability to adjust himself to his environment; for the most part, the responsibility is placed on the community. Today, no scientifically-trained social worker would attempt to give financial aid or guidance without obtaining a complete picture of the background of the person involved, his environment, employment, friends, clubs, lodges, use of leisure time, church activities, and the like. In other words, the individual is now studied and aided against the background of his group or community, instead of being regarded as an isolated unit.

So long as men lived under a system of domestic economy, where each family or gild was a separate unit and not so vitally dependent on other units, and so long as the welfare of the whole group was not at stake, group activity in social matters was less necessary. But, with the growth of modern industry and the rise of complex, interdependent social relationships, illness, poverty, and delinquency among group members lessens the efficiency and prosperity of the whole group. If we look briefly at the history of community organization, we can see how group action was made necessary by the sweeping economic and social changes of the last hundred years.

## The History of Community Organization

**Early methods of caring for the poor and distressed.** Our search for the beginnings of the modern community movement might well extend to the earliest days of man's group life, when blood relatives and kinsmen within the tribe helped each other in work and trouble. We find instances of what might be called social work long before the Christian era. In ancient China, refuges for the aged and sickly poor were established, schools for poor children and soup kitchens for laborers were set up, and societies were organized to defray the burial expenses of paupers. But, in early civilizations, there was less need for organized community work than today. There were few neglected persons because economic relationships were relatively simple, and it was easier for people to help each other in the small neighborhood or local groups. Slavery, in its way, took care of many of the lower classes.

The first notable historical situation in which there were any large number of dependent persons was in Rome, from the days of the late Republic onward. They were taken care of by the state, through the classic method of giving them "bread and circuses"—temporary relief and elaborate amusements to distract attention from their plight. In this way the government, for a long time, kept the masses of poor people quiet and loyal.

**Christianity and the poor.** With the rise of Christianity and throughout the Middle Ages, the relief of the poor was gradually taken over, in Christian countries, by the church. With all men theoretically equal before the throne of God, and the poor man's soul, therefore, as worthy as that of a rich archduke, the Christians were inclined to give more attention than the earlier pagans to poverty-stricken fellow-believers. Furthermore, Jesus had specifically recommended the giving of alms and the institution of charity.

In accordance with this doctrine, the medieval church provided institutions for the sick and others in special distress. It had charge of, and responsibility for, hospitals. It was entrusted with safeguarding public health by supervising travel, isolating persons suspected of carrying contagious disease, and protecting people from infected individuals such as lepers. Such orphanages and poorhouses as existed in the Middle Ages were mainly supported by the church. Special religious orders, such as the Knights of St. John and the Knights Hospitalers, arose to devote themselves almost solely to social work.

Christianity also held that poverty might be a great virtue, and, since the rich were taught that they could not take their worldly goods to Heaven, they readily believed that giving to the church was pleasing to God. By the twelfth century, it is estimated that almost half the land in Germany, for example, was owned by the church. It was inevitable, therefore, that the church should become the leading social organization of the time in Christian lands. Not until after the Protestant Reformation, when internal dissension arose within the church and much of its property was confiscated in some countries, did the state assume responsibility for the care of the poor.

The institutional set-up of medieval society naturally provided for the relief of much of the misery of that age. The medieval manor—the village community—held within it the great majority of all the poor, including serfs and a few slaves. They shared their common poverty and solved their problems together. The gilds of the town provided charity for poverty-stricken members. Yet, there were, in both town and the country, many poor and miserable people who could rely neither on the manor nor on the charity of the gilds, and to these the church ministered.

**Origins of public relief of dependents.** Modern times brought in their train new circumstances, both social and economic, that made it necessary to change the medieval methods of caring for the poor. This was particularly true in the Protestant countries, where the power and wealth of the Catholic church were drastically reduced. Feudalism and the manorial system broke up and disappeared. The enclosure of land for sheep-raising led to the ejection of many poor peasants from their tiny holdings and thus wiped out their sole means of support. Monasteries, which had long aided many beggars, were closed down, and the relief system of the church was upset or ended entirely. In the new era, it was logical that the state would try to replace the church in helping the poor.

In 1601, England passed a comprehensive poor law, the harbinger of a long series of laws dealing with public poor relief. At first, these laws were harsh repressive measures, designed to discourage begging, but gradually the attitude of the state toward the poor changed. The English Poor Law of 1834 was based on the recognition of the state's full responsibility for the relief of the poor, but it also introduced more rigorous tests for eligibility for relief. The changes in poor-relief philosophy made in England in the twentieth century illustrate the lengths to which group acceptance of social responsibility has proceeded.[1]

**Rise of the charity organization movement.** The growth of the distressed classes, following the Industrial Revolution, led to the development of numerous charitable organizations and activities in urban centers. But, at first, there was much duplication and chaos in this relief work. Many needy persons did not get the relief they needed, while clever grafters got assistance from several agencies.

Early in the second half of the nineteenth century, these evils were observed by English students of the problem of relief. They proposed a centralized organization of all agencies operating in any given city and a careful investigation of individuals who applied for relief. To bring this about, they founded in London, in 1869, the Society for Organizing Charitable Relief and Repressing Mendicity. The next year, the name was changed to the Charity Organization Society. The charity organization society was not itself a relief-giving agency. Its function was chiefly to investigate, organize, and co-ordinate the existing relief-giving and charitable agencies of the community and to carry on broad educational programs relative to the relief and prevention of dependency.

The situation in nineteenth-century American cities was much the same as in England. The American city had grown rapidly following the Industrial Revolution. Thousands migrated to cities from the rural areas, immigrants came from foreign countries, and the slums grew ever more congested with poorly paid workers. A number of social agencies came into existence to help these victims of urban industry during the fifty years following the Civil War. Working alone, they were, however, only able to care for the most urgent cases. Orphanages of many types, rescue homes for children and wayward girls, hospitals, clinics, nursing associations, and many other groups were established from widely varying motives and with different objectives. Some of them were managed intelligently, while others were ineffectively operated.

The charity organization society had a marked effect upon the administration of relief after 1870. In 1877, Buffalo, New York, was able to co-ordinate the city's relief activities and set up a successful charity organization society. Some other cities quickly followed this example; 10 years later, there were about 25 charity organization societies in the United States. The aim of these societies was to eliminate the defects of earlier urban relief—insufficient grants to those really in need, "chiselers" on the relief rolls, duplication of efforts by many overlapping agencies, and the absence of a central clearing house of information—as well as to co-ordinate relief agencies properly.

The charity organization movement under the particular name

---

[1] See below, pp. 776–778.

chosen by different communities—COS, Associated Charities, United Charities, and the like—continues to function in cities to unite the charitable work of the community under a single agency. In some cities, the Catholic and Jewish welfare groups have not affiliated with the co-ordinating agency but maintain similar organizations to unify their welfare activities. Recently, the COS movement has spread to smaller cities.

The importance of the charity organization movement to the urban community cannot be overemphasized. It utilized and developed the existing resources within the community, in order to help the individuals who most needed relief. Not only did the charity organization movement attempt to co-ordinate the activities of existing agencies, but it also set up principles which are today the backbone of almost every social agency—namely, the investigation of individual cases, registration of cases at a central bureau to avoid duplication, and the co-operation of all agencies to give adequate relief.

**The social settlement.** The charity organization movement is important in all community welfare work, but the social settlement movement has dealt more directly with the problem of cultural adjustment and neighborhood welfare. The social settlement can be regarded as an even more important forerunner of the modern community organization movement than the COS. The approach of the settlement is through the neighborhood, where, with a spirit of friendliness and neighborliness, persons interested in the welfare of the poor may meet to discuss problems and find a solution for them. This is community organization in a richer and more intimate sense.

Beginning with a group of Oxford and Cambridge students who, in the 1870's, found lodging in the London slums to lend a helping hand to the underprivileged, the settlement movement spread to America. Hull House, in Chicago, founded by Jane Addams and Ellen Gates Starr in 1889, served as an inspiration to other cities wishing to help the unfortunate. Much important legislation designed to improve working and living conditions of the low-income groups was initiated by the settlement workers at Hull House. In the 1890's, the Henry Street Settlement was organized by Lillian Wald to improve the health conditions of persons living in an area of the lower East Side of New York. The Henry Street Settlement had great influence on the work in community health. It has been responsible for instituting programs which led to medical inspection of school children, providing of school lunches, the use of visiting teachers, and many other services. Today, there are over 500 settlement houses carrying out programs planned to meet the needs of disorganized and underprivileged urban neighborhoods. Sometimes one need is more acute than another and the settlement house will attempt to meet it, whether it be a day nursery for children of working mothers, an Americanization program for the foreign born, a club for boys and girls, clinics for infants and children, or instruction in arts and crafts. Some of the other better known settlement houses are the University Settlement in New York City, founded in 1886 and the first American social settlement, the South End House in Boston, Hiram House in Cleveland, and Kingsley House in Pittsburgh.

The chief difference between the settlement movement and the charity organization movment is that the former is more directly concerned with the poor and their personal and cultural problems, while the latter represents an attempt to organize the relief work of various agencies. The contribution of the charity organization movement cannot be overlooked, yet the settlement movement has a warm human side. The settlement house attempted to alleviate the misery of the poor by friendly and understanding contact with them. The settlements are supported mainly by volunteer contributions raised by settlement leaders. Some of the more recently established settlement houses are today financed by urban community chests.

**Development of the social survey technique.** Community studies, that is, analysis of a community to throw light on its social problems, are part of the history of community movements because they indicate the growing awareness of the community as a responsible social unit. The social survey technique was first outlined by the French sociologist Frédéric Le Play about a decade before the American Civil War. Many years later, it was brought over to England by Charles Booth, Patrick Geddes, and Victor Branford. As early as 1880, public interest in England had been sufficiently aroused over the squalor and hardships of slum life to warrant a scientific study of the slum areas. The most complete study was the great work of Charles Booth, *The Life and Labour of the People of London,* which appeared in 17 volumes between 1886 and 1902. It was the first monumental example of the social survey method of studying social problems. In America, the miseries of slum life were dramatically exposed in *How the Other Half Lives* by Jacob A. Riis in 1890, followed two years later by his *Children of the Poor.* These two books did not pretend to be statistically complete but they stimulated interest in the problem of the slum dweller as no purely statistical evidence could have done. Other books followed; some were general studies of conditions in cities, such as Lincoln Steffens' great exposure of city corruption, *The Shame of the Cities.* Jane Addams and other well-known social workers gave firsthand impressions of conditions they encountered and urged a constructive program through the treatment of social ills with a background of scientific knowledge. But, on the whole, the growth of a scientific attitude toward the community was slow.

In 1902, the National Conference of Charities and Correction presented, for the first time, a full discussion of "Neighborhood and Civic Improvements," and, about this time, a new interest in housing reform was taken by certain state legislatures. Social conditions were scientifically studied in various American cities. The first to be investigated was Washington, D. C. The evils found almost in the shadow of the

Capitol were so startling that other cities began to investigate their slum neighborhoods. Pittsburgh, Pennsylvania, was studied in 1906 under the direction of Paul V. Kellogg, and the resulting six-volume report was published by *Charities and Commons,* the official magazine of social workers which later became *The Survey.* This report marked the first comprehensive application of the survey technique in the United States.

The social survey is an important technique in the community organization movement. It is impossible to plan for the adequate organization of relief unless a clear-cut picture is obtained of the social set-up and needs of the community, and the interrelationship of all the organizations within it. The survey of a town or city thus furnishes a working basis on which to begin the organization of the community. By 1912, the social survey idea had become so popular that numerous American cities began to study conditions within their limits. Some of the resulting surveys, such as that of Springfield, Illinois, by Shelby M. Harrison, still stand as models. Not only were surveys made of entire cities, but different organizations also began to make special surveys. The churches began to study their rural and urban church communities. The Federal Children's Bureau examined the needs of mothers and children, and the National Child Labor Committee investigated the labor of children in urban textile mills and factories. Both states and cities carried on surveys of crime and its causes, with particular attention to delinquency areas. In 1914, the Cleveland Foundation was established and began to make surveys in the fields of education, recreation, relief, and the administration of justice. The survey method was gradually improved until it was combined with sociological acumen in the classic study of Muncie, Indiana, by Robert and Helen Lynd in *Middletown* (1929) and their later *Middletown in Transition* (1937). It was found that these surveys, by giving publicity to the existing evils, stirred the whole community into action to alleviate them.

It was inevitable that the social survey, based on the desire of social workers to uncover and describe the leading problems of a community, would provide a powerful impetus to community organization and serve as the basis for informed and well-planned activities.

Today, the social survey is an accepted procedure for beginning any kind of community program. Experts in survey methods are, however, expensive, and many communities do not have the funds to employ experts and then carry out the program. Community Surveys, Inc., a foundation established to aid in drawing up plans for health, welfare, and recreation programs, meets this problem. It was organized in 1947 to provide a body of specialists who could appraise and measure the needs of local communities, estimate their resources, plan community organization, and launch essential activities.

The three most important elements in the history of community organization are thus: the charity organization societies, the social settlements, and the survey method of investigating community problems. In each of these trends we see the gradual acceptance of responsibility by the community for its members and a desire to deal with their problems scientifically.

*National Housing Agency, Federal Public Housing Authority.*

The upper picture shows the drab city slum that was the site of the St. Thomas project in New Orleans. The bottom picture shows the project after its completion. This is an example of what has been accomplished in community housing after bad slum conditions have been revealed by social surveys.

## Activities and Agencies Included in Community Organization

**Nature and functions of community organization.** From the preceding history of community organization it is evident that varied activities have been involved in what has been included under the general name of "community organization." Any program with a civic or social aim and sponsored by a coherent group has been called a "community" project. A survey of any maladjustment within the community, regardless of its value, became a community survey. There have been many incomplete ideas about the real meaning of community organization, because the community offers an excellent laboratory to study all types of human relations. The student of economics finds it an ideal place to study the economic régime and the interplay of the factors of production and consumption. The student of sociology tries to prove from a community survey his theories concerning the behavior of the individual, human reactions to environment, and the relations of both primary and secondary social institutions. The student of religion finds the community a fertile field to study religious organizations, their membership, activities, and functions.

The underlying basis for the confusion leading to an inadequate conception of the term "community organization" is the failure to distinguish between those local public activities which are necessary to enable the group to live, such as protection from fire and theft and the establishment of courts of justice, and the well-rounded operations of the community as a whole. These basic and necessary activities of the group are not the essence of community organization. The modern community movement is an intelligent attempt to devise means by which the educational, recreational, social, economic, political, and artistic forces in the community may be correlated, so that all members of the group, so far as possible, will be able to adjust and express themselves satisfactorily.

**Examples of community spirit and activities.** In order to get a more adequate idea of the types of activities sponsored by the community movement, it is well to know the kind of methods that have been found successful in promoting community solidarity. Sometimes the activity of one agency, such as the local housing authority in launching a housing project, will stimulate community interest. Occasionally, a strong leader or small group can be the means of organizing the whole community. For example, the entire community of Holland, Michigan, is engaged in a year-round preparation for the tulip festival it gives each May. Started by a local civic club in 1929, the project has grown to include all groups and social classes.

A crisis, such as war, a depression, flood, or fire can provide a stimulus for co-ordinating and directing the efforts of citizens to desired ends. A threat to health and safety is a potent force in community organization. During the height of the polio epidemic in 1947, one

North Carolina community, roused to action because of its inadequate hospital, built and equipped a modern hospital in a short time. Materials, labor, and all equipment were donated or made available at cost. Committees organized to meet such crises, however, are often responsible for social waste in trying to solve problems in an improvised fashion without an over-all view of the needs and potentialities of the community.

**The council of social agencies.** The council of social agencies, a federation of all or most social agencies within the community to co-ordinate their work, is an illustration of over-all planning. Representatives from the public and private agencies which promote health, welfare, recreation and education make up the council. Meetings are usually held every month. Standing committees on health, housing, delinquency, and family and child welfare survey and evaluate the work done in the appropriate agency and report to the council. Often the work done in one committee stimulates action on the part of other committees. The council of social agencies thus acts as a co-ordinator and clearing house for all agencies and, as a result, the work of each agency is more purposeful and more likely to meet the needs of the group it serves.

**Community councils.** In the last two decades, community councils and co-ordinating councils, made up of interested citizens and local government officials, have been formed. These councils are not to be confused with the council of social agencies. In 1929, a group of citizens in Alexandria, Ohio, formed a community council to discuss common problems. Today, there are over 300 community councils, over one-half of which are in California.

The great value of the community council is the inclusion, wherever possible, of local government officials. Part of the task of community organization is to interest local government officials in community problems; to get organizations such as the Chamber of Commerce, Rotary, Kiwanis, Lions, and Elks clubs interested in community progress; to educate the public concerning the rôle played by public and private agencies; and to show that, although Federal funds are made available for certain programs, the local community must bear the costs of those programs not covered by the Federal funds. It is also necessary for the populace to learn that private agencies are not supported by public appropriations and must depend on the generosity of the community to continue to carry on their work. The community council has minimized conflict and reduced misunderstanding and has been valuable as an interpreter of the welfare program to the whole community.

Any plan to organize a community must take into consideration the fact that the community is always changing. Because a particular approach to a problem has once been successful, there is no reason to assume that it will be equally so in the future. The community consists of individuals who have personal aims, interests, and ambitions that reflect living conditions at any given time. So any well-planned program of community organization must take into account the changing and complex economic and social situation within the community.

## Community Organization in the Field of Recreation

**Need for community recreation programs.** The old neighborhood play group, one of the most important primary groups, has broken down as a result of the growth of the modern city. Community organization offers a substitute for the earlier informal play group in the form of a planned recreation movement, which arose in the twentieth century in response to a definite community need. Without play, some of the benefits of group life are lost. Play aids in building a wholesome, well-balanced personality; and, since a healthy body can do better work, it helps to develop a more efficient type of social life.

There was a time when the social value of play was not recognized. Although children have always played, their play formerly was regarded mainly as a means of amusement and as a body builder. Little emphasis was placed on play as necessary training for group living. Although the modern city has destroyed the older play group, it has also brought about an extension of leisure,[2] and the growing realization that the use of leisure time is important has led to further recognition of the socializing value of play.

The eight-hour day and the five-and-a-half day week, with vacations and time off for holidays, have given workers more spare time than ever before. In the past few decades technological unemployment has increased enforced leisure time. Child labor laws in many states prohibit children from working; and, although compulsory education compels school attendance, many hours are left for recreation. The demands and policies of modern industry have forced the retirement of men from work earlier in life.

**Increased leisure time challenges community action.** As a result of increased leisure time, many of our social problems have become more complicated or acute; juvenile delinquency, for example, often occurs because young people have been led into mischief during their spare time. The increase in adult crime may also be partly due to the increase of leisure time. Some persons believe that many divorces are the result of increased leisure, which gives more time for domestic bickering and dissatisfaction of all sorts. The modern electrical home conveniences have made housekeeping simple and freed women not only for industry but for leisure-time activities. Many women occupy their afternoons playing bridge or going to the movies; for some persons increased leisure has meant time for cultural improvement, but for others it has made for boredom, dissatisfaction, or dissipation.

---

2 See below, pp. 741–751.

The recognition that unwise use of leisure is partly responsible for many problems of the modern age has led to emphasis on supervised recreation. Children must have guidance in recreation, in the same way that they must have guidance in education or in building up their health. In a society where the traditional patterns of living have been altered by the transfer to a larger group of many fundamental activities and services which were formerly individual or family matters, such as making a living, transportation, fire and police protection, and education, we cannot assume that the problem of leisure time can be handled without community aid.

**Development of supervised community recreation.** The organized play movement began in Boston, in 1885. By 1887, ten playgrounds had been opened, and in 1893 a trained supervisor was hired, but it was not until 1899 that the city of Boston contributed even a small sum ($3,000) towards the costs. This is often called the "sand garden" stage of the play movement, because most of the playgrounds had little equipment except sand boxes. Boston opened the first public gymnasium in America in 1889. The social settlements were quick to grasp the possibilities of playgrounds as a means of establishing friendly relationships, teaching good citizenship and sportsmanship, and guarding against the development of antisocial tendencies. Through the interest of the settlements, particularly of Hull House in Chicago, the supervised playground movement entered a new period of expansion and supervision after 1890. The first model playground was opened at Hull House in 1892. It was largely due to the success of the settlements in stimulating interest in play that Massachusetts decided to include supervised play as a part of the school curriculum in 1901. Joseph Lee, a wealthy Boston philanthropist, was the leader in creating and promoting the playground movement in the United States.

By 1900, there was considerable organized recreational activity in many cities, led by Boston. Large cities converted open spaces or vacant lots in congested areas into playgrounds where children might play under the watchful eyes of supervisors, who were there to keep them out of mischief, as well as teach them how to play. Through the influence of Jane Addams, the city of Chicago established excellent municipal playgrounds. Chicago appropriated 5 million dollars for ten playground parks in 1903, and they were opened in 1905. President Theodore Roosevelt declared this to be "the most notable civic achievement of any American city." Philadelphia, St. Louis, Washington, Pittsburgh, and Cleveland followed suit. Usually, the beginnings of the playground movement in each city were fostered by small private organizations that were able to secure municipal support. There were few instances in which a city government itself took the lead in establishing a playground without the prompting of some social agency.

The Playground Association of America was established in Washington, D. C., in 1906 and became the leading force in the play movement.

It was rechristened the Playground and Recreation Association of America in 1911, and in 1930 its name was finally changed to the National Recreation Association. At the time of its organization, only about 40 cities had made even a half-hearted attempt to establish playgrounds. It was difficult to arouse public enthusiasm and to persuade public authorities to turn over elaborately planned parks to "rowdy children" for play; school authorities were loath to allow the use of school property for playgrounds. Thus, it was left to the National Recreation Association to build up enthusiasm for supervised recreation. The Association launched an active educational program. To-day, its national magazine, *Recreation*, still carries on its program of education.

Between 1906 and the outbreak of the first world war in 1914, over 350 cities in the United States established recreational programs; and by 1929, about 950 cities had supervised recreation, at an annual expense of 33 million dollars. The number of paid full- and part-time recreation leaders grew from 10,218 in 1920 to 22,920 in 1929, and to 46,300 in 1946. In the latter year, there were 5,147 full-time paid leaders and, in addition to the part-time leaders, there were no less than 65,992 volunteer leaders.

The number of parks and playgrounds increased markedly as more Federal funds were made available through the WPA and the PWA. The number of municipal parks increased from 11,686 in 1930 to 19,336 in 1940. There were over 10,000 supervised urban playgrounds operating in 1944, as compared with 1,300 in 1910. There were 1,743 fully supervised urban community recreational programs in operation in 1946, and expenditures reported by 1,488 communities totaled 54 million dollars.

In 35 states, the laws permit cities to set up public recreation systems and to appropriate funds for them. Although the municipal playground movement has spread rapidly, there are still about 339 cities, nearly half of which have populations over 5,000, without adequate provision for municipal recreation. Some cities have grown so rapidly that they have little space for playgrounds in congested areas.

Since the end of the second world war, a large number of communities, especially towns and small cities, have developed recreation programs on a year-round basis. Recreation agencies report that participation by all age groups in established recreation programs far exceeds prewar totals. One interesting development has been the increasing emphasis on social and hobby groups for older people. Special activities for older people were reported by 264 cities in 1946.

Another postwar development has been the growth of Federal and state advisory services in recreation to local communities. Advisory service is now furnished by 43 states through such agencies as state recreation commissions, youth authorities, conservation and forest departments, colleges of agriculture, state universities, and departments of commerce. In 14 states, full-time consultant service in recreation was available from some state agency in 1948. This was in addition to those states provided with full- or part-time personnel employed in the Extension Service of the U.S. Department of Agriculture to help with local recreation programs.

Local recreation budgets have increased since the war. In some cases, the increased costs of living have been the cause; in other cases, recreation services have been greatly expanded. Many cities are now planning long-range recreation projects which include plans for the acquisition of new areas and the improvement of existing facilities.

## The Community Center

**Origin of community centers.** Along with the development of the recreation facilities as a municipal function came the establishment of neighborhood social centers for recreation, education, and art. As we have pointed out earlier, the recognition of the importance of recreation as a socializing force in the neighborhood has been due in part to the influence of the social settlements and the direct teaching of Jane Addams at Hull House. Since the settlement houses were located in the more congested areas and emphasized work with the community, there was no better place to organize a recreation, education, and art center than in connection with the social settlement.

The community center movement grew slowly because it was difficult at first to get persons to volunteer for service on some neighborhood program. Settlements could not afford to hire enough trained workers who understood the local situation. The program of a community social center usually included such activities as sports, games, dancing, music, dramatics, art, parties, and educational classes. The Y.M.C.A., the Y.W.C.A., the Y.M.H.A., the Girl Scouts, and the Campfire Girls, have established social centers which conduct programs in health, vocational and general education, recreation, art, and citizenship.

**Use of school buildings as community centers.** The development of recreation on a neighborhood basis and its sponsorship by the social settlement paved the way for the extension of the community movement to the schools. School authorities, for a time, retarded the growth of this program since they did not want the school grounds or building to be used after school hours; many traditional educators believed that the school building should be locked after the day's work was over. But, by 1901, because of successful experiments in using school grounds for community purposes in other cities, a few school buildings in New York City were opened for evening meetings. This was a simple beginning, enabling people to get away from home to read, talk, play games, or listen to music. The following year, Boston opened two schools for evening classes for adults.

It was not, however, until 1907 that the school community center movement formally began. Eleven organizations in Rochester, New

York, formed a school extension committee and persuaded the local board of education to grant $5,000 to develop educational, social, and recreational centers in the public schools. The committee stressed the importance of the school as a meeting-place to discuss questions of public interest and build up community spirit. The first Rochester centers were in the nature of public forums, and the social and recreational side was not heavily stressed; but, as additional funds permitted, more emphasis was placed on recreation.

The philosophy of the Rochester group was that the school is a logical meeting-place for the whole community and that here various needs might be satisfied—recreational, social, educational, and cultural. The school gymnasiums were thrown open to adults, and game rooms were equipped and placed under capable supervision. The entire proceedings were put on a democratic basis; the people planned their own programs. Within three years, the movement had become so popular that an appropriation of $20,000 was made to open 18 public schools as social centers.

The Rochester experiment spread to other parts of the country. Wisconsin passed a law in 1910 giving school boards the right to open school buildings for recreational and educational purposes outside of school hours, and also to allow their use for public forums. In 1911, the National Education Association approved the use of school buildings for community purposes. Although many administrative difficulties have arisen in using the schools and laws have occasionally proved troublesome, the movement has grown steadily and has proved to be a satisfactory method of organizing the cultural and recreational activities of the community.

**Public forums as a community agency.** One of the most important developments in the community center movement, whether located in school buildings or elsewhere, has been the provision of public forums where local and visiting speakers can present important public and local issues and then submit them to discussion and questioning after the formal lecture. In this way, community opinion on local, state, national, and international issues can become better informed. Previously, in small primary groups, such matters were dealt with in face-to-face discussion groups—the family, neighborhood, after-church conversations, and congeniality groups. Today, the forum is the chief substitute for such earlier and informal discussion. Of course, people can now get information on such issues from newspapers and over the air, but they have no way of discussing such information with editors, columnists, and commentators, save through the limited medium of newspaper correspondence columns. The public forum provides not only for the dissemination of information, but also for group discussion of the issues presented. In New Deal days, Federal Commissioner of Education John W. Studebaker provided for the financing of a corps of able forum leaders who traveled over the country addressing local forums. The discontinuance of this service was as regrettable as the ending of the Federal theater, music, art, and writing projects.

**Effect of the first world war on community organization.** Organized community planning rose to a new high level of activity during the first world war. The National Education Association appointed a Co-ordinating Committee on the Development of Community Centers to unify community activities during the war. Where training camps were located, the National Recreation Association undertook to organize all the resources of the community, so that the leisure hours of the soldiers and sailors might be pleasantly and profitably spent.

The request came at a time when all public energies were devoted to war. Community Service, Inc., composed of those who had been most active in the supervised playground movement, was organized to promote recreational activities on a large scale with full community support. The location of training camps in many communities served to focus public attention on the need for a recreational program in peacetime as well as in war. Interest developed on a national scale, large sums of money were raised, special recreational buildings were erected, and all social agencies co-operated to provide adequate recreation for the enlisted men encamped in the community. The united spirit shown in this emergency demonstrated the possibilities of community efforts in a common cause. The wartime interest in recreation had a permanent effect. The emergency activities and successes demonstrated that sufficient funds could be found and that trained leadership and a community spirit could be stimulated if the community banded together.

Although the wartime efforts stimulated organized community recreation, they did not effectively further the school community center movement. The National Education Association had shown interest, but it was not shared by the whole teaching profession. In 1924, a Committee on Community Relations was organized in the N.E.A. to extend the use of school buildings for recreation, but it met with little success and disbanded two years later. Thereupon, an organization known as the Community Center Association, which had been founded in 1915, took over leadership in this field. It owed its beginning to the work of the N.E.A. Since 1924, the *Journal of Social Forces* (now *Social Forces*) has served as the official organ of the Community Center Association.

**Community activities extended during the second world war.** The second world war had even greater influence than the first, again because larger numbers of persons were involved. There were more war workers and more members of the armed services stationed in army and navy camps and bases. Some of the recreation programs were provided at the camps by the Red Cross and the USO (United Services Organization). By 1943, through the efforts of the Recreation Section of the Office of Community War Services, over 1,500 cities and towns had organized Defense Recreation Committees to develop and correlate their community programs and direct them toward serving the needs of wartime recreation. Some communities were able to meet the entire cost of the expanded recreation program, but in other communities professional and financial aid was given by the Federal government.

Buildings were hastily erected to serve as clubhouses for servicemen and women. Athletic programs were organized and trained leaders were in demand. Tennis courts and swimming pools were built. Hobby classes in bridge, dancing, and the like, were formed. Volunteer helpers served at the USO headquarters, which held almost continual "open house" and furnished food and entertainment. Private households were urged to take servicemen and women as guests for dinner and the weekend. Some communities, especially those in the vicinity of the larger camps and bases, had well-organized programs in which a wide variety of recreational facilities were made available. Some camps were located, however, near small towns where the opportunities for recreation were limited to a picture show, an occasional USO show, and infrequent visits to the homes of the townspeople.

Recreation for war workers received considerable attention from many communities because the crowded and substandard living conditions under which many workers lived, the three work shifts daily, and the increased employment of both men and women made it desirable that recreational facilities should be made available for longer periods of time—late at night and over the weekend. Some firms employing war workers expanded their recreational programs. As early as 1942, the Industrial Recreation Association was formed to aid industries in enlarging their recreational facilities. After the war, some firms and some communities continued their programs, partly owing to the demands of the war workers and veterans who returned to their communities. It may be that the impetus given to community and industrial recreation during the war will result in a permanent increase in public recreational facilities.

**Community recreation stimulates other community activities.** The recreation movement, as a whole, offers an excellent example of community organization. Its early leaders had to utilize all available forces in the community to put their program across. This meant placing primary emphasis on recreation and neglecting other phases of public welfare, but such overemphasis on one program was to be expected when there was no co-ordination of activities. When the whole community was ready to support a program of recreation, a step had been taken toward community organization. The school center movement represented a more comprehensive approach to community organization because it recognized that recreation is only one possible community use of a school building. It demonstrated that recreation is only one of the many social problems in a congested area of the city, and thus paved the way for other phases of community action.

## Community Music, Drama, Pageantry, and Art as a Socializing Force

**Community interest in the arts develops after the first world war.** Some of the recent community activities in music, pageantry, festivals, and drama show a definite trend toward community organization of a permanent character. The remarkable development of community interest in the arts after the first world war may be seen from the 1924 report of the Carnegie Corporation on "The Place of the Arts in American Life." Out of 660 community houses, 236 had community singing, 219 theatrical performances, 192 pageants, 168 instruction in crafts, 256 bands and orchestras, and 58 community theaters.[3]

**Growth of community music.** Since the first world war, music has come to be recognized as a valuable recreational, educational, moral, and spiritual force in the community. The emphasis on music springs in part from the fundamental fact that it helps to develop the latent tastes, hopes, and aspirations of the individual. The growing popularity of concerts, the organization of community choruses, pageants, and masques with musical accompaniment, and Christmas tree celebrations also indicate the desire for self-expression through co-operation and association with others. Larger cities, such as New York, Boston, and Rochester, have long had excellent community choruses, but within recent years the movement has spread to smaller towns and rural communities.

A first attempt to create community music in an isolated rural community in Delaware is an example. The first meeting took place in a small schoolhouse. At the end of a hard day's work on the farm, eighteen or twenty persons came in farm wagons and old buggies to see what the "singin' teacher" wanted. None of them had any musical training, and there was no musical instrument of any sort. The teacher had to instruct them in simple songs, and encourage them to join in the singing. The first meeting was not altogether successful but gradually the farmers grew interested because they found they enjoyed singing together. As time went on, the original group increased to forty. A man with a strong tenor voice gradually became courageous enough to take the lead in some of the songs. The exhilaration of singing together created a friendly feeling that lasted after the meeting. The group lingered around the stove to talk over some of their mutual problems. The interest fostered in the singing class carried over into the daily life of the participants. The radio programs they listened to took on more meaning; the simple folk songs of other countries taught them by the leader gave them a certain amount of sympathy for people of other lands. But most important of all were the expressions of neighborliness, loyalty, and co-operation.

---

3 *Recent Social Trends*, McGraw-Hill, 1933, Vol. II, p. 983.

**Community music enriches community life.** From such modest beginnings, many communities have carried their musical activities much further. Participation in local group singing has led to a desire to combine with other communities. Some communities have worked up county festivals. In larger groups community music took on new social significance. It gave new meaning to co-operation, not only along the lines of music but on larger community issues.

Industrial districts have found that, in many instances, music has served a real community need. To workers and their families, the community chorus has meant relaxation and an appreciation of their own efforts. Music has helped to engender community pride and a spirit of fellowship, and has encouraged participation in a common interest.

The formation of music groups has also led to a growth in initiative and leadership for both the individual and the community. One of the leaders in a community music group was so encouraged by the praises of his association that he began seriously to study vocal music, and finally secured a scholarship at a conservatory of music. One community music group, meeting in a dilapidated schoolhouse, raised funds to supply a stove, more light, and a piano for the schoolhouse, and to repaint the walls. This same group decided to form a dramatics group, which also was to meet in the schoolhouse, and later formed a handicraft class to make draperies for the room, and a woodworking unit to remodel the furniture. Community interest was thus focused around the schoolhouse, and community organization and group unity of a permanent and valuable nature were achieved through an initial concern with music.

Schools and colleges have long been aware of community interest in school bands and orchestras. In many communities, the school band and orchestra have become an important unit in every community celebration. In Richmond, Indiana, interest in the school band led to the appointment of the public school music teacher as the paid leader of community singing. Not all communities can achieve as much prominence as has Bethlehem, Pennsylvania, for its Bach festival, or Lindsborg, Kansas, for its yearly presentation of Handel's *Messiah*, but music as a socializing force can become a significant phase of community organization. The famous Berkshire Music Festival, held each summer in western Massachusetts, while performed by outside artists, has developed not only a community, but even a regional, interest in good music.

**The community theater.** The local theater has also helped along the trend toward community organization. In recent years, graduates of universities and schools of dramatic art have gone into communities where there was no theater and have established drama groups backed by some local civic organization or by subscriptions sold in the community. The community theater has come to be an important part of community life in many towns. In some instances, the theater is subsidized by the city; in others, it pays its own way; and in others, it is even built and operated by the city for the benefit of the people.

The growth of the community theater movement was hastened by the Federal Theatre—a project of the Works Progress Administration. The Federal Theatre made it clear that people are interested in attending plays, if they can afford to do so, and that motion pictures have not destroyed all interest in the legitimate stage. The Federal Theatre has also shown that the theater movement, to be successful, must be "sold" to the people of the community, and that, if the people have a chance to help in creating it and carrying it on, they will heartily support it.

One of the most interesting examples of theater-minded communities is found in North Dakota. Alfred G. Arwold of the North Dakota Agricultural College believed that the theater might play an important part in promoting community life in ordinarily drab areas. Although the movement began in Fargo, North Dakota, it has spread throughout the state. Under the leadership of Professor Arwold, hundreds of men and women have dabbed grease paint on their faces and have appeared before lantern footlights in old barns. In many communities, the plays are written by local persons using themes familiar to the people of the plains and are performed by the local farmers. Plays during the Christmas season, on the Fourth of July, or at harvest time, have been most successful, for the festivals give the whole community an opportunity to participate. The community theater experiment in North Dakota illustrates the point that the whole community must be interested to make a project successful.

The St. Louis Little Theatre is a combination of professional and community talents. Many of the actors are residents of the community, but the theater maintains a permanent staff of actors. The St. Louis Little Theatre has been operating successfully for over twenty years. It is supported by the community without any private endowment because it has made the community not only a spectator but a part of the cast. Summer theaters maintained in healthful and scenic communities by professional urban actors have helped to develop community interest in the drama.

**Community pageantry.** Most sections of the country have become pageant-conscious. The pageant is an excellent vehicle for community organization because it requires large casts and usually depicts an event of local community interest. The pageant movement has become nationwide. Between 1925 and 1931, history came alive on the battlefields of the North and the South when many communities celebrated famous battles by portraying them in the form of pageants. In August, 1940, to celebrate the sesquicentennial of the founding of Cooperstown, New York, a pageant was given with a cast of 400. Covered wagon trains left Independence, Missouri, in 1938, to retrace the trails to the West. One of the most interesting of the community pageants was that of the "Lost Colony" staged on Roanoke

Island off the coast of North Carolina. Here, in the sixteenth century, legend has it, the first English colony in America was organized and later disappeared. With the help of Federal Theatre artists and technicians, the "Lost Colony" became not only a community project, but a money-making proposition. It is estimated that in the summers of 1938 and 1939 over 250,000 persons visited Roanoke Island. Colonial Virginia as "the seedbed of democracy" is the theme of the community pageant, "The Common Glory," given each summer since 1947 at Williamsburg, Virginia. So far, the pageant has not been a financial success but has attracted large crowds.

Community pageants and folk festivals have become popular throughout the Southwest. Each year, fiestas are held in various sections to commemorate religious or historical events. For example, in New Mexico, the entrance of Diego de Vargos, who recaptured the village which is now Albuquerque from the Pueblo Indians in 1692, is celebrated with an elaborate community festival. Schoolteachers instruct the children in native dances so that they can participate in the festival. Such folk dramas as "Our Lady of Guadalupe," "The Lost Child," and "The Comanche" are presented, along with religious celebrations, songs, and folk dances.

**Community art and community life.** The teaching of art and appreciation of art is a slow process. Usually, the natural desire of women to beautify the home is a starting point. Most women want attractive homes but many do not know how to go about making the necessary improvements. Farm women, living most of their lives in drab dwellings, and women in small towns living in rented homes derive benefit from a community art project. The methods used by teachers of art groups have been varied. Teaching women how to make hooked rugs, lamps shades, or similar objects, and how to rearrange furniture, set attractive tables, and make the proper use of color in the home are only a few of the effective types of instruction. Working in groups, the women have not only added to their own knowledge and appreciation of art, gained confidence in their own judgment, and lost some of their prejudices, but have gained in friendliness and in appreciation of the ideas of others.

Classes in community art have also led to a desire to beautify the community. In one instance, an adult art class decided to decorate the schoolhouse and worked in co-operation with the parent-teacher organization to decorate the teachers' rest room and the classrooms in an artistic but inexpensive fashion. In one Delaware town, a "clean-up" and "paint-up" campaign was sponsored by the art class, which had become aware of the dingy physical environment in which they lived. A garden club was begun, prizes were given for the neatest lawns and the most beautiful gardens, and a vacant lot was converted into a park. Daily life thus took on a new meaning through community art, which contributed to an enrichment of community life.

Through lecturers brought in by the instructor, the members of an art class learned that a house can be constructed along good architectural lines as cheaply as along poor ones. Several young couples built homes according to the sound architectural ideas learned in class. One adult art class in a community in which a new town hall was being built was able to bring about a change in the plans so that the building would be more pleasing to the eye. In one instance, the interest stimulated by an adult art class in civic architecture led to city planning.

Education in art has meant increased appreciation of general community problems. Some communities have found that interest in adult art classes has led to a serious concern with problems of race, health, sanitation, and education. Appreciation of beauty has created a desire to improve the community.

In many communities, adult art and music classes have thus meant that individuals and groups have found a path to a fuller and richer life. The individual has often found that he can overcome shyness and timidity by participating in community activities, such as singing in the church choir, helping with the cleaning up of the "sore spots" in the town, or aiding in the renovation of an abandoned schoolhouse to provide a community meeting place. The improvement in daily living and the extension of the individual's efforts into those of the group have developed better social values. Learning to appreciate beautiful things is of permanent value. In working together, tolerance, appreciation of others, and co-operation in worth-while enterprises are learned. With an art or music group as an opening wedge, community organization of all activities is made easier.

One of the reasons why music and art are so valuable as a means of community organization is that they appeal to every age group. There is no limit to the possibilities of the growth of this influence in the community. Today, in particular, when primary groups are dissolving, the problems of living are becoming increasingly more complicated, and individual and group needs are greater than ever before, the group must use every means at its command to make community life richer. So far no better means than community music, drama, and art have been discovered.

## Community Organization and Public Health

**Rise of the public health movement.** The public health movement, as we have already noted, is also a vital part of community organization. Laws may be passed and regulations enforced; but, unless the whole community co-operates in carrying out unified health education, the program will not be fully successful.

The public health movement deals with the community rather than the individual. Those who are ill have always been the concern of humanitarian-minded persons, but the organized efforts of the community in promoting better health are relatively new. Any well-organized public health program will be concerned with a safe water supply, the disposal of waste, and the control and isolation of infectious and contagious disease. But there must also be emphasis on health education to acquaint the general public with early symptoms of disease and to enable each citizen to help himself, his children, and his neighbors to keep healthy. In other words, the logical approach to the public health problem is from the community viewpoint and is based on the theory that the welfare of the individual means the welfare of the community. Thus the public health program is an excellent field for stimulating community interest. In many cases, interest in the health of the group leads to well-directed organization in other fields of community activity.

**Development of the city health council.** The health activities of urban communities are under the direction of the state and local boards of health. Many public health activities, such as the maintenance of a safe water supply and the sanitary disposal of sewage and garbage, are maintained by law. Other activities, such as the construction of hospitals and the establishment of clinics, are usually carried on voluntarily. It is to the private or semi-private organizations, such as the American Red Cross, the American Public Health Association, the American Child Health Association, the National Tuberculosis Association, and countless others, that we are indebted for most of the constructive movements in community health. As might be expected, the intervention of these numerous agencies in community affairs at first caused much confusion and wasteful duplication of efforts. As with public welfare, attempts have been made to coordinate the work of the numerous health agencies. The city health council, a federation of all urban health agencies, operates as a clearing house in health matters, as does the charity organization society in welfare work, and serves to unify the efforts. The health council idea has been adopted by many cities, such as Cincinnati, Boston, and Cleveland.

**The community health center.** Although the city health council federates the city health agencies, the health center is a better example of the possibilities of community organization for public health. The health center is to the neighborhood what the city health council is to the entire city. In most cities, the health center represents a step forward in community organization because it unifies the activities of all the welfare and health agencies operating in one neighborhood. So many aspects of the health problem are connected with social work that it is impossible to think of one without the other. The social worker depends to a great extent on the services of the health agency, and the health agency cannot carry on an effective therapeutic program without the welfare agency. The health center operates on the principle that its services will be utilized by the people who need them most.

The first health center in the United States was established in Milwaukee, in 1911, but the movement did not grow rapidly until the first world war, when the American Red Cross adopted it as a project. By 1920, about 900 Red Cross Chapters were engaged in some form of health-center activities, along with first-aid and nursing work.

To illustrate its community emphasis, a notable health center may be cited as an example. The East Harlem Health Center in New York City, which serves a population of about 112,000, was organized in 1930. The enterprise was sponsored by the Red Cross and approved by the city department of health. Twenty-three organizations, composed of nursing agencies, family welfare societies, health officers, and settlements, joined the unified program. Representatives from each agency comprise an advisory council, which tries to prevent duplication of effort. The Health Center is a neighborhood institution, and it is impressed on the people, through its educational program, that the Center belongs to them and is for their use. The program is both therapeutic and preventive. Hospitals and clinics are accessible, nursing facilities are available, and the family welfare societies have cooperated by promoting a boys' club and community work in the Center's school. The local physicians and druggists, once they understood the program, gave the closest co-operation. The East Harlem Health Center has gained the trust and confidence of the entire community.

As a whole, health centers have proved very successful, and one of their most important contributions to community organization is to serve as a demonstration area or laboratory. The idea of using the community as a laboratory, to show what can be done through social organization, gained favor after the first world war. The usual practice is to choose a particular community with a definite problem and then develop and carry out a carefully planned program as a model for other communities. The health demonstration idea has been used to show how diseases may be both cured and prevented and better health promoted.

The health demonstration project carried on in the Bellevue-Yorkville area in New York City is an illustration of the value of health services in a community. With financial assistance from the Milbank Memorial Fund, the project covered a seven-year period from 1927 through 1933. The demonstration was carried on under the direct supervision of the Department of Health and the co-operation of all agencies. The 175,000 persons living in this crowded area received intensive health services during this seven-year period. During the time when the project was in operation, the infant mortality rate decreased notably; the death rate from tuberculosis, diphtheria, and typhoid also declined. The project cost about $900,000 for the entire period—a per capita annual cost of 61 cents, in addition to the regular expenditures of the health department and the private agencies.[4]

---

[4] See C. E. A. Winslow and Savel Zimand, Health under the El, Harper, 1937, for a more detailed discussion of this project.

The survey method has also been used as a phase of community efforts to promote public health. As with all social surveys, health surveys may be limited to one phase of the health problem, or they may cover the entire health situation of a community. By means of the survey, an accurate picture of health conditions may be gained, and, with sufficient publicity, the community is often awakened to its needs and encouraged to solve some of its more pressing public health problems.

**Community safety campaigns.** Closely related to the public health activities of communities are community safety programs. Though sometimes launched by independent community action, they are usually stimulated or guided by the National Safety Council, founded in 1912. Most community safety programs are devoted primarily to reducing traffic accidents. For this, the National Safety Council has a tripartite program built around the so-called Three E's—Engineering, Enforcement, and Education. Engineering covers the problem of safer highways, streets, and motor cars, and better traffic facilities and regulations. Enforcement implies the rigorous execution of the laws covering traffic and its violations—arrest and conviction of as many violators as possible. Education involves complete and accurate instruction concerning the safest and most skillful methods of driving on highways and city streets. In 1943, Lansing, Michigan, launched a community safety program built around the Three E's. After it had been in operation for a year the number of fatal accidents was cut in half.

An interesting case of independent community activity in behalf of safety was conducted by Topeka, Kansas, which in 1945 ranked 57th in traffic safety among 64 American cities with a population of 50,000 to 100,000. In April, 1946, the Chamber of Commerce and various civic groups decided to set up a Safety Council. The Topeka safety campaign made use of all the Three E's, but laid special stress on safety education, in the course of which much use was made of safety forums, radio talks, safety movies, safety pamphlets, warning cards, and the like. The Boy Scouts, Girl Scouts, and other groups were drafted into service to carry on safety propaganda and pageantry. As a result of the community safety activities, Topeka reduced the traffic death toll by 55 per cent in one year and, instead of being near the bottom of the cities of its class with respect to safety, it rose to fourth place.

The most conspicuous example of success in community safety programs, however, is that of Stillwater, Oklahoma, a city of 30,000 inhabitants which had no deaths from traffic accidents during the ten years following January, 1939. Engineers worked with the city authorities in mapping out a good safety plan. Streets were marked off properly and plenty of stop signs installed. Traffic officers were strategically placed. The schools, starting with the kindergartens, stressed safety education. The newspapers and radio stations co-operated heartily in the safety campaign. It worked almost perfectly, despite the fact that the community had to cope with about 80,000 visitors annually. The city was awarded top honors in the country by the National Safety Council.

The examples of Lansing, Topeka, and Stillwater are only representative of what can be done to promote community safety with a program intelligently conceived and earnestly executed.

## Community Organization and Public Welfare

**Co-ordination of private and public agencies in community work.** Brief mention was made earlier of the attempts to co-ordinate the efforts of private charitable agencies in the nineteenth century. Despite the work of charity organization societies, the more constructive efforts in the social welfare field have come only in recent years. In the decades following 1900 there was an awakening of public consciousness and a realization that the community had to take over some of the burden of caring for the needy.

Private and public welfare agencies have long existed side by side. Formerly, a great gulf separated them. Private agencies attempted to deal scientifically with poverty and allied problems, to set up high standards for professional social workers, and to develop the case-work technique. Public agencies, on the other hand, all too often gave funds to those in need without understanding the causes of poverty or how the community was responsible for their plight. Recently, however, the public and the private social agencies have co-ordinated and unified their activities more successfully. One indication of this is the entrance of professional social workers into public agencies. Since 1935, the Social Security Act has caused rapid strides to be made in the professionalization of public relief work. Gradually, the feeling of community responsibility is growing and, with it, the demand for trained workers to administer relief. Today, the majority of persons believe that welfare work has as vital a claim on the community's taxes as education, recreation, or health. Instead of leaving the care of orphans, neglected children, and the handicapped to private charity, public opinion is slowly coming to support the idea that it is the duty of the community to care for its dependents with public funds. Recently, there has been much emphasis on co-ordination and co-operation in the administration of relief, so that efficient care may be given at a minimum cost. In the future, it is likely that every enlightened community will appraise its needs and co-ordinate its program of both private and public social work from the standpoint of the entire community.

**Rise of the community chest movement.** The financial federation is an important step in the direction of co-ordinated social work as well as an excellent example of the substitution of group effort for individual action. The financial federation is now ordinarily known as the community chest. The first financial federation was launched in Denver in 1888. Owing to the endorsement of the Cleveland Chamber of Commerce the movement was developed there between 1900 and

1913, and in the latter year the Cleveland Federation was founded. This was the first real community chest organization, and Cincinnati immediately followed suit. The first world war gave an impetus to the community chest movement. A lump sum of money was contributed to the war chest and was then distributed to member agencies. After the war, the community chest came to be widely used as a means of securing money for civilian welfare activities in peacetime.

The community chest movement rests on sound social and financial principles. The several private agencies determine their monetary needs, based in part on those of the preceding year, and then submit an estimate to the budget committee of the community chest. The combined estimates of all the private agencies sharing in the chest is the gross amount set as the goal to be met in the annual drive. Volunteers canvass the community and the money raised is then divided among the agencies. Today, about 1,250 cities and large towns have a community chest that operates on a year-round basis. Community Chests and Councils of America is the national organization to which the majority of local chest organizations belong. The community chest movement developed remarkably during the 1940's. The number of chests more than doubled and the funds raised grew from 83 million in 1938 to 185 million in 1949. The all-time high was 221 million raised in 1945 as a result of wartime conditions.

A paid director and staff have the responsibility of acquainting the public with the work of the agencies participating in the chest. The success of this educational program carried on throughout the year determines, to a large extent, the outcome of the next year's drive for funds.

With few exceptions, businessmen like the idea of the community chest because they prefer to give a lump sum at one time rather than to be called upon for several smaller donations during the year; they also realize that, in the long run, their single annual donation may cost them less. The community chest is a practical method of raising funds for another reason. To social workers and those interested in the community, it provides a unified and co-ordinated program expressing the will of the community. Another less important result of the establishment of the comunity chest, but one worth noting, is that the record of each agency's work and expenses is carefully considered by the budget committee of the chest. An agency failing to perform its task will not continue indefinitely to receive funds from the community. The community chest thus represents the vital organization of a community working toward a common goal—the well-being of all its members.

## Community Organization in the Small Community

**Relative neglect of the small community.** The community problems of the city have become so engrossing and evident that the needs of the rural areas and the small towns have often been overlooked.

Dr. A. E. Morgan, in his book, *The Small Community*, says that it is "high time that the significance of the small community be recognized." [5] Small communities are the sources of city populations. The birth rate of cities is so low that the population must be renewed from outside sources in order that the city may survive many more generations. The small community is a chief source of local leadership. Within the small community, the sharing of problems and the development of mutual respect and tolerance are principles which must guide anyone who is to be a leader. Dr. Morgan believes that the enduring basis of our civilization is to be found in those traits fostered by the intimate associations of the small community.

**Examples of community organization in small communities.** There are many difficulties inherent in a small area which hinder community organization. Many towns and rural areas are stagnant and devoid of leadership. There is often jealousy and clannishness between families; religious and political factions hamper development; and vested interests prevent co-operation. Often, the lack of qualified persons limits welfare activities because most small towns and rural communities insist on having home or county persons handle the welfare work.

During the last 15 years, however, there have been encouraging developments. To secure Federal funds for Social Security programs, minimum standards of case work must be maintained. The insistence that a social worker must be something more than just a person "who likes people" has helped to bring in better trained welfare workers from outside the narrow limits of the town or county. There are signs of increasing awareness of community problems on the part of persons and groups. Some forward-looking ministers of small-town churches have taken the lead in helping their communities to develop a neighborly spirit. The rôle of the church in leading the small community to organize its resources has been limited, but if the church does take an active part in community organization, its influence is likely to be considerable. Consolidated churches in rural communities have at times exerted considerable influence in the way of promoting community projects.

As evidence that a town or rural community can successfully develop community organization, a few examples can be mentioned. Schools, such as Squaw Point in a rural area of Minnesota, have become the focal point of many a community. In the Squaw Point area, the school is a practical workshop drawing the whole community into its projects. The children plant gardens in the spring as part of their schoolwork. Not only do the children learn how seeds grow, but the garden supplies vegetables for the school lunches prepared by the mothers and the girls at the school. There is a community store located at the school which sells surplus vegetables at cost to the parents of the school children. One year, sufficient profit was made to purchase 300 "baby chicks," which the children raised and sold. The

---

[5] A. E. Morgan, *The Small Community*, Harper, 1942, pp. 3–5.

whole community has become interested in the school project and co-operation in other enterprises has thus been made easier.

In Montpelier, Vermont, a town of about 8,000, the unused basement in the city hall was converted into a recreation center for the young people. Funds were collected to install a juke-box, and equipment for playing pool, table tennis, and basketball was secured. As a result of growing interest, the facilities of the community were studied by a citizens' committee, the municipal park was enlarged, and a recreational supervisor was employed. The numerous small industries that Henry Ford set up in the environs of Detroit represented an effort to provide a sound material basis for a rich small-community life which would combine steady industrial employment with the advantages of rural life.

**Small community finances.** The problem of community finance in the small community often creates difficulties because the county and state officials control the distribution of funds to a large extent. There are a limited number of persons with sufficient personal incomes to make it possible for them to give generously to private agencies or community projects. The small businessman usually cannot afford to contribute large sums. Although finance is a serious problem, many phases of community organization require only knowing how to make the most of the existing community resources and enlisting the aid of the citizens. The organization, Community Services, Inc., sponsored by Dr. A. E. Morgan, meets, in part, this pressing problem of the small community. Community Services offers professional assistance and counsel to small towns and rural neighborhoods who wish to discover their group potentialities and the meaning of "community."

**Community organization a solution of corporate farming life.** In an earlier chapter on the rural community in the machine age we discussed the disadvantages in regard to community spirit and public utilities and services which are to be found in the great mechanized corporate farming communities, which tend to develop into a sort of present-day mechanized *latifundia*. They are far inferior to the small farming areas in comparable surroundings with respect to community spirit, public facilities, health programs, recreational projects, and the like. Yet, economic forces are producing a very definite trend towards large-scale mechanized farming. The solution of this perplexing situation probably lies in the development of systematic community organization in mechanized farming areas. If necessary, Federal and state funds should be provided to support this type of community work, which promises to be the most needed and useful form of organized effort in small rural communities.

## The Region as a Community

**Rise of regionalism.** The idea that a natural geographic region should provide the physical framework for unified community efforts was first suggested by Frédéric Le Play, the founder of the social survey movement. The regional approach was further developed by Le Play's English disciples, Patrick Geddes and Victor Branford, and brought to this country by Lewis Mumford, Professor Howard W. Odum of the University of North Carolina, and some American ecologists.

**Nature of regions.** Although the idea of regionalism is relatively new, regional problems have long existed. City, county, or state lines do not act as fences to enclose social problems within their boundaries. A river, such as the Tennessee, the Colorado, the Missouri, the Columbia, or the Ohio, serves several states. Whole areas, regardless of political boundaries, have common problems arising from similar natural resources, geographic influences, or cultural patterns. To treat social and economic problems from a regional point of view is to recognize a community of interest and to utilize the total resources of a whole region in order to raise the level of living for all.

Socially regarded, the regional concept is sound; politically, there may be difficulty in organizing communities without primary regard for political boundaries. The state, county, and local municipalities are "sovereign" powers in many matters and can prohibit the use of funds outside their boundaries, or prevent the extension of Federal activities into their area of control. There is some confusion whether regionalism should be applied to a unified geographical and economic area or only to areas in which there are already similar interests. Some regions to the United States, according to Professor Odum, have common interests and problems because they have similar geographic conditions. Professor Odum, one of the ablest exponents of regionalism, develops the thesis that, if the Southeast region can transcend state lines and consider its problems on a regional basis, it will improve its economic, social, and political conditions and better develop its potentially great natural and human resources.[6]

**Achievements of community organization in the regional framework.** One of the best examples of the development of the total resources of a region is the Tennessee Valley Authority, which serves the region drained by the Tennessee River and four of its tributaries. As a result of the development of the river for effective navigation, the generation of elctric power, and provision for flood control, an area of over 40,000 square miles, occupied by over two and one-half million persons, has been transformed. Resources have been conserved as well as developed. Erosion has been halted. Demonstrations of the new fertilizers and farming techniques have raised the standard of living of the whole area. Health programs have improved the level of efficiency by reducing illness; recreation centers and social case work have helped to solve many of the former personal and social problems. Some persons regard the TVA as having produced a new high in social democracy; others of a conservative cast of mind fear that the planned community, such as the TVA and the "Greenbelt" communities, under

---

[6] Howard W. Odum, *Southern Regions of the United States*, University of North Carolina Press, 1936.

the supervision of the Farm Security Administration, represent a dangerous trend toward expanded governmental control.[7]

Recently, regionalism has received much emphasis in the long-range plans of the Bureau of Reclamation. The projects are planned around the development of western land and water resources through the building of dams and reservoirs and extended irrigation to create new farms, factories, jobs, and homes. If Reclamation Bureau plans are carried out, the 17 western states will have large regions served by power provided by Federal funds. The concept of the social community developed in the TVA may thus be extended to the areas reclaimed by the reclamation projects, and the basins of the Missouri, Colorado, Columbia, and many other rivers may be the locus for developing human and natural resources far beyond the present limit of achievement.

## The Planned Community as a Way of Promoting Community Organization

**Origin of community planning.** The development of natural and human resources of large areas, such as the Tennessee Valley, the river basins of the West, or a special section of the country, is regional planning on a large scale. However, the rebuilding of a city or a section within the city is also regional planning in miniature.

A community so planned that its physical layout and equipment provide the maximum of comfort and well-being for those groups living within its limits has long engaged the attention of social reformers. The French Utopian Socialist, Charles Fourier, based his scheme for social reorganization on a community limited in size and organized into small groups to promote efficiency and greater enjoyment of life. Robert Owen, the English industrialist and social reformer of the first half of the nineteenth century, put his ideas into practice in New Lanark, Scotland, the site of his cotton factories. Owen regarded the unsanitary, poverty-stricken condition of his workers as a hindrance to their industrial efficiency and contentment. Not only did he organize a large-scale welfare program in his textile mills, but he built better homes and set up stores for his workers.

**The garden city.** At the close of the 19th century, Ebenezer Howard, an office worker in London, appalled by the living conditions in the English slums, planned a model community which he called a "garden city." Howard's idea, inspired by Patrick Geddes, was to decentralize the industrial city by distributing small units over the whole urban area. These small units combined the best features of both urban and rural life—small, one-family dwellings, open spaces for recreation, and an industrial area separate from the residential. In 1903, the garden city of Letchworth, with a population of 15,000, was

---

[7] See above, pp. 136–138.

founded on the Howard plan; it was followed from time to time, by others throughout England.

**Radburn, New Jersey.** A few model communities developed in the United States after the first World War. For example, Radburn, New Jersey, within a short distance of New York City, was developed as a "garden city." It was a limited-dividend project of the City Housing Corporation. Under the limited-dividend plan, philanthropic capital is invested to return only a small dividend. In Radburn, special areas were designed for business, residence, shopping, and recreation, but no agricultural area surrounded the city as in the case of the English "garden city." The automobile hazard received special attention. Underpasses were constructed so that persons might go from one part of the city to the other without crossing the highway; children could go to school and to the parks and playgrounds without danger. Radburn is still a middle-class community with a large number of children and has developed a strong feeling of community responsibility. It is a good example of community organization, made possible, in part, by good physical planning.

**The Federal Greenbelt projects.** During the 1930's several experiments in planned communities were tried. The most notable of these were the Greenbelt projects.[8] Begun in 1935 by the Resettlement Administration, the projects were taken over in 1937 by the Farm Security Administration of the Department of Agriculture. The Greenbelt communities were designed to be rural-industrial communities financed by Federal funds and located near cities of rapid growth. Five communities were planned, but only three were developed to any extent—Greenbelt, Maryland, near Washington, D. C.; Greenhills, Ohio, near Cincinnati; and Greendale, Wisconsin, near Milwaukee. Of these, Greenbelt, Maryland, was the most important because of the size and maturity of development attained. The Greenbelt town differed from the "garden city" program in that it was not expected to be self-sufficient, but was planned to provide homes and community life for the low-salaried worker of the near-by city.

Greenbelt, Maryland, was laid out to give full scope for community life. It was built in the shape of a crescent with pastures for the community dairy, space for athletic fields and playgrounds, and a wooded area surrounding the crescent to give privacy and a rural atmosphere. The residential district was laid out in oversize blocks. Each block formed a natural neighborhood with a small park and playground in its center. A town common and a business center were within easy distance of the residential and recreational areas. The combination community center and school served as the focal point for all types of activities of the members of the community—religious, civic, and recreational. The citizens organized a Greenbelt Citizens' Association,

---

8 Material summarized from G. H. Gray, *Housing and Citizenship*, 1936, pp. 237 ff.

a health association, a credit union, a community dramatic society, and a public forum.

Before the second world war, a considerable degree of solidarity had been reached, although the occupants had lived in the project only for a short time. In 1942, the Greenbelt community was made a part of the defense housing program. The original plan to admit only families with small incomes who could adjust to community life was abandoned as the need for housing increased. The Greenbelt communities are illustrations of a planned development, with the government as landlord, in which community organization took shape in a democratic fashion in a relatively short time.

**Low-cost housing projects in community planning.** The low-cost public-housing project is an example of the way in which solidarity may be reached through the co-operation of local, state, and national agencies. In states that have passed enabling acts, a community decides whether it desires a housing project. Funds may be advanced to the local housing authority on easy terms from the Federal Public Housing Authority, or direct grants, to be matched by community funds, are made to the community to finance the project. The local authority, made up of citizens of the community serving without pay and the paid administrative staff, operates the project on a non-profit basis. The wide representation on local housing authorities from industry, welfare, and the professions is indicative of the community nature of the project and the co-operation of groups on a problem of mutual interest. By 1948, some 41 states had low-rent housing laws and 450 cities and towns had housing programs. Today, over 189,800 projects are completed and in operation. The public low-rent project serves not only to clear the slums and improve the general level of community living, but also to promote community co-operation.

**The unique Baltimore slum clearance program.** While Federal aid has provided or stimulated much desirable slum clearance and housing construction, the city of Baltimore has been the only American urban community to develop a comprehensive and effective plan to enforce slum clearance. In 1941, the city adopted a municipal housing code that embodied minimum housing requirements in specific terms and gave health officials the power to enforce a program of sanitary housing. Owners of slum housing had the choice of losing their property and income through condemnation proceedings or bringing their property up to the designated standards. A housing court was created to hear such cases, and the court was presided over by a magistrate who was an expert on housing and the housing code. The rebuilding program wisely concentrated on the complete reconstruction of one slum block at a time rather than scattering its efforts over a number of sore spots throughout the whole city. The taxpayers have become convinced that the project pays them off handsomely. They learned that 40 per cent of their city budget went to operate and support the downtown slum areas that made up only 10 per cent of the city's residential districts. They were paying 14 million dollars more each year on the slums than they got back in taxes from the slum regions. It was also pointed out that the slum areas are the crime-breeding regions of the city, and that slum clearance is one of the more important items in any sound crime-prevention program. Hence, citizens have been willing to support city bond issues to carry out the slum clearance program. It is to be hoped that other cities will heed and profit by the Baltimore experiment.[9]

Planning in the community may thus be broad and include all levels of the population; it may be the creation of a new community or it may be the rehabilitation of a section of the city. Physical rehabilitation does not necessarily lead to the mobilization of the entire resources of the community and the awakening of social consciousness, but it is a means to this end and one which offers unlimited possibilities for community organization in the future.

The "Yardville" project in Philadelphia. Improved living conditions through community planning may include projects other than new housing. The so-called Yardville program, developed in Philadelphia in 1948, was devoted to transforming the dingy back yards of typical working-class city blocks into a combination of flower-garden, playground, and park. The idea was started by *McCall's Magazine* and was soon sponsored and supported by the Philadelphia City Planning Commission and related organizations. But the program was not forced on the residents. It was explained to them and, after considerable discussion, was accepted with enthusiasm. The residents helped with the reconstruction, which has been summarized as follows:

The high board fences were replaced by trim wire ones. Each back door received a terrace for sitting outside. The cracked, uneven alley was widened and repaired. Garbage cans were recessed out of sight in attractive little alcoves built alongside the gate of each yard. The alley is now a garden path; instead of garbage, you smell fresh-cut grass and flowers.

The greatest effect has been on the children. They are no longer forced to risk their lives playing at dangerous street intersections, or to suffer loneliness indoors. Yardville has become the play center of all the children in the fifteen houses along the alley. . . . Teen-agers and adults now have a place for picnics, sings and dances. Some of the residents prefer to spend their vacations at home. Yardville residents are so enthusiastic about their renovated backyards that they describe the old days as "living in a chest of drawers." Yardville has also paid off in dollars and cents. It has boosted its own property values a good 25 per cent.

Since *McCall's Magazine* has a circulation of about 3,750,000, the Yardville experiment attracted much attention at once. It was also conducted in connection with the advice of one of the country's foremost public relations experts. As a result, the Yardville plan became a national movement almost overnight. Within a month after it had

---

[9] See E. L. Jones and Burke Davis, "Slum Clearance at a Profit," *Atlantic Monthly*, May, 1949.

been described in *McCall's* no less than 300 cities from 46 states, among them 21 of the most important cities in the country, requested full information about the project. Several cities have since instituted their own "Yardville" programs.

*Courtesy of* McCall's Magazine.

**The Yardville project in Philadelphia. These pictures show backyard areas in Philadelphia before and after the completion of the Yardville reconstruction program.**

## Community Organization as a New Mode of Social Control

**Community groups.** Community organization is a means of social control. We have seen how economic changes have caused the breakdown of the primary groups—the family, the neighborhood, and the play group—and how it has been necessary for other agencies to take over some of the functions formerly performed by the primary groups. Among these have been the charity organization society movement, the settlement movement, the playground movement, and the coordination of public health activities. We might add to this the organization of school centers and of community forum programs.

In addition to these modes of socialization and control, there are more specialized forms of community organization. Businessmen form a chamber of commerce; farmers unite in a marketing association; farm women form canning and cooking clubs; farm boys and girls join 4-H clubs; and industrial companies sometimes organize the communities in which their employees live—all these activities represent the modern trend of community organization for welfare purposes. If unity and co-ordination are achieved through organization, then the field of community organization is unlimited. For instance, poverty, crime, juvenile delinquency—all forms of antisocial behavior—might be restricted if the community set about to eliminate them.

**Community organization a substitute for primary group controls.** On the whole, however, the main significance of the community movement as a new means of social control lies in the fact that it is a substitute for the face-to-face activities and controls earlier provided by the primary and small secondary groups of the rural areas. The control of conduct and the services formerly supplied by the family, neighborhood, play group, and rural church through gossip, public opinion, and small-scale rural co-operative endeavors have now tended to be assumed by community organization. The rapidity and success of this substitution will be a determining factor in preserving the stability and functional efficiency of contemporary society.

## Summary

Community organization is an attempt to bridge the gap created by the breakdown of primary groups, the disintegration of traditional patterns of living, and the changes in economic and social life since the Industrial Revolution.

There are many evidences of group action to protect the community as a whole. Fields of activity that were formerly the responsibility of the family, or small groups of individuals, have now become matters of state, county, or municipal concern. For instance, housing, public health, child labor, education, and child and public welfare are now dealt with by public agencies or by governmental legislation.

In earlier civilizations, there was little need for organized community effort because there were fewer needy persons, communities were small, and families and neighborhoods helped each other. In the days of the later Roman Republic and the Empire, the state provided "bread and circuses" for the city poor. Slavery took care of many of the destitute. The ideals of the Christian church altered these practices. The church taught that responsibility for one's fellows is a cardinal virtue. During the first 1,000 years of Christian history, most of the aid to the unfortunate in Christian countries was under the direction of the church. With the breakup of the manorial system and the coming of the Protestant Reformation, the state had to assume increasing responsibility for the care of the distressed and needy.

Three important developments helped to create present-day community organization: (1) the charity organization society movement, originating in London in 1869, to co-ordinate and centralize the work of the numerous charitable organizations in the city; (2) the settlement house movement, based on neighborly contacts with the community; and (3) the survey method, which served to acquaint the community with its social problems.

The modern community movement is an attempt to devise a means by which the educational, recreational, social, economic, and political forces in the community may be co-ordinated, so that all members, so far as possible, can adjust themselves satisfactorily to new ways of life and make the best use of community resources. Any plan to organize the community must take into consideration the fact that society is dynamic, not static. The social setting is constantly changing. One plan of organization may be successful at one period but will not work so well at another time. Furthermore, the community consists of individuals whose interests change from time to time.

The supervised recreation movement is an excellent example of community organization because it offers a substitute for the old neighborhood play group and fills a definite need, that of taking up the increased leisure time of the twentieth century. Although the play movement was first launched to provide recreation for small children, it has grown until it includes recreation for adults as well, and is carried on in parks, community centers, and school buildings. Likewise, the social settlements have stimulated the growth of the play movement because they offered an excellent opportunity to establish cordial relations between the settlement workers and the people of the neighborhood. Today, a supervised recreation program is sponsored and financed by many cities, although there are still many urban communities that have not yet included this item among their social services. Planned and supervised recreation in rural areas is still only in its infancy. The recreation movement was greatly stimulated as a result of recreational needs of the armed services and war workers during the second world war.

The public health movement has aided community organization because it has focused interest on the welfare of individuals in order to promote the welfare of all. The public health program, to succeed, must include an educational program, and it is only through the efforts of the community that such education can be carried on. Through the health center, health demonstrations, and surveys, community interest has been stimulated and the public health movement has thus become one of the outstanding results of community organization.

The public welfare program is closely related to community organization, because the community must take responsibility for its members and co-ordinate its efforts to meet their needs. The financial federation or community chest is an excellent example of the substitution of group effort for individual action and represents a unified and co-ordinated attempt to provide for some of the chief social welfare needs of the community.

Small towns and rural areas have received little attention in the community organization movement. Potentially, the small town offers great possibilities for development of community spirit, and gradually the attention of those interested in community organization is turning toward the small community. The idea of the region as a community transcending political boundaries and solving its common problems is relatively new. Such projects as the TVA and the plans of the Bureau of Reclamation indicate possible trends in the future if regional communities should develop further.

Community organization has provided a new type of social control to replace that which was formerly exerted by such primary groups as the family, the neighborhood, the play group, and the rural church. It has stepped in to act as a substitute for the inadequacies or growing weaknesses of the latter and to soften the impact of the more harsh and formal types of government intervention in local life through the federal and state agencies. While community organization is of great importance in promoting various forms of social welfare, its main functional significance has been to provide a workable program during the transition from local, rural societies to the complex social organization of our urban age, and to create in the latter substitutes for the services once rendered by rural primary groups. As our culture changes, community organization, its work and techniques, will be correspondingly modified and extended.

### Selected References

* Bernard, Jessie, *American Community Behavior*, Dryden Press, 1949. Recent comprehensive description of community life and organization. Probably the best sociological study of the community as a social force and agency.

* Butler, G. D., *Introduction to Community Recreation*, McGraw-Hill, 1949. The standard work on the development of community planning and supervision of recreational activities.

Colcord, Joanna, *Your Community*, Russell Sage Foundation, 1941. Good study of community organization from standpoint of social work.

Elliott, M. A., and Merrill, F. E., *Social Disorganization*, Harper, 1941. Excellent book on the institutional disorganization of our time caused by cultural lag and the disruption of primary institutions. May be supplemented by more recent book of R. E. L. Faris, *Social Disorganization*, Ronald Press, 1948.

Fink, A. E., *The Field of Social Work*, Holt, 1942. A comprehensive work which touches on many areas in which social work contributes to community planning and programs.

Hillman, Arthur, *Community Organization and Planning*, Macmillan, 1949. An up-to-date textbook covering most phases of community organization projects.

* Holden, A. C., *The Settlement Idea*, Macmillan, 1922. A competent account of the social settlement and its rôle in community organization.

Kennedy, A. J., and others, *Social Settlements in New York City*, Columbia University, 1935. A thorough and well-illustrated description of the great social settlements in New York City and their varied community activities.

* Kinneman, J. A., *The Community in American Society*, Crofts, 1947. Excellent survey of the rôle of the community in the American social order.

Lee, Joseph, *Play in Education*, Macmillan, 1915. A thorough discussion of play in health and character building by the founder of the playground movement in the United States.

Meyer, H. D. and Brightbill, C. K., *Community Recreation: A Guide to Its Organization and Administration*, Heath, 1948. Elaborate work on the organization and operation of community recreation projects. Contains valuable source-material.

Mowrer, E. R., *Disorganization, Personal and Social*, Lippincott, 1942. Able analysis of the breakdown of primary groups.

* North, C. C., *The Community and Social Welfare*, McGraw-Hill, 1931. One of the standard treatments of community work by a veteran sociologist.

Odum, Howard and Moore, H. E., *American Regionalism*, University of North Carolina Press, 1938. Pioneer work on regionalism in the United States, stressing its importance in sociology and social geography and as a technique of social planning.

* Osborn, L. D., *Community and Society*, American Book Company, 1933. A standard work on the relation of the community to contemporary social life.

Pettit, W. W., *Case Studies in Community Organization*, Century, 1928. Valuable material on early programs of community work.

Quinn, J. A., *Human Ecology*, Prentice-Hall, 1950. The standard sociological treatise on the subject. Valuable in relation to regional planning.

Rainwater, C. E., *The Play Movement in the United States,* University of Chicago Press, 1922. An authoritative history of the playground movement as a phase of community organization. Should be supplemented by G. D. Butler, *Introduction to Community Recreation,* McGraw-Hill, 1949.

\* Sanderson, Dwight, *The Rural Community,* Ginn, 1932. The most authoritative study of contemporary rural community life.

Steiner, J. F., *The American Community in Action,* Holt, 1928.

————, *Community Organization,* Century, 1930. Two pioneer works by one of the leading authorities on community organization.

Warner, W. L., and Lunt, P. S., *The Social Life of a Modern Community,* Yale University Press, 1941. Good case study and analysis of modern community life.

\* Watson, F. D., *The Charity Organization Movement in the United States,* Macmillan, 1922. The authoritative history and description of the movement for scientific organized charity.

\* Winslow, C. E. A., and Zimand, Savel, *Health under the El,* Harper, 1937. Description of a classic community health project.

Zimmerman, C. C., *The Changing Community,* Harper, 1938. Competent survey of the transformations of community living resulting from cultural and institutional shifts in our era.

# CHAPTER XXVII

# Education in the Machine Age: Anchor or Motor?

## Education and Cultural Lag

**Education an example of cultural lag.** Many persons contend that cultural lag can and must be bridged by education, if we are to escape violence and revolution. Unfortunately, education in our day is still a sadly lagging social institution, itself one of the most conspicuous examples of cultural lag. In social guidance and reconstruction today, conventional education presents a good illustration of the blind trying to lead the blind.

Education did not save us from either world war or from the 1929 depression. The leaders of the countries involved in both wars were educated men; those who were mainly responsible for the depression were educated in our best universities. It would appear that we must revise our educational system if education is to help us bridge the gulf between our technology and our social institutions.

**How education might solve cultural lag.** We must rely on realistic education, not education of the type tried and found wanting. We must eliminate from the courses of study all useless, archaic, and irrelevant subjects and lay more emphasis upon the realities of the twentieth century. The teaching profession must be encouraged to teach facts. Especially should more attention be given to the social studies, those with information directly bearing on cultural lag—history, sociology, psychology, government, and economics. The realistic linking up of the social studies with present-day problems would provide the only basis for destroying cultural lag and promoting an understanding of the social world in which we live. Education is our best safeguard against totalitarianism and violence. It is only through education, courageous and realistic, that we can maintain democracy and liberalism and assure steady and peaceful social progress.

## The Development of Education

**Primitive and ancient education.** In primitive tribes, social customs, beliefs, and daily ways of doing things were taught to children

713

at an early age.  At certain times, there were special ceremonies—initiation rites and the like—devoted to instructing children in moral and religious customs.  The purpose of primitive education was to transmit the "wisdom" of the elders and to instill respect in the young for that wisdom and for the folkways of the group.

In ancient oriental times, the priesthood took over part of the task of teaching the wisdom of the past, but children were still taught many things in the family group.  Instruction in the use of tools was derived chiefly from skilled workmen.  Ancient education was by word of mouth, because the mass of people could neither read nor write.  There were, however, some libraries for those who were literate, as well as educational centers where the learned gathered and taught the favored few who had money and leisure to get an education.  Scribes and clerks were given instruction to fit them for religious and public responsibilities.

**Education in classical times.**  We owe the origin of formal education to the Greeks, although Greek education was limited mainly to the children of citizens.  The children of slaves and foreigners received such education as was given to them in a purely informal manner.  The Spartans introduced rigorous discipline into education and stressed military training and patriotic loyalty.  Spartan education was designed to produce loyal and vigorous soldiers, men who were trained to endure physical hardship and pain.  There was little literary education.

Ancient Athens had a broader conception of education than Sparta.  Music, reading, writing, and physical training were the main subjects taught to Athenian boys.  Literature, logic, rhetoric, and public speaking were considered necessary for those who planned to enter public life.  In fact, it was from the Greeks that we inherited the idea that a flair for rhetorical verbiage and a mastery of literary allusions are the prime traits of an educated man.  Philosophy was regarded as the highest intellectual discipline.

Universities were first established among the Greeks, at Athens, Alexandria, and elsewhere.  Here scholars gathered and discussed philosophy, natural science, and art.  While the training in athletics and rhetoric was relevant to the needs of Greek private and public life, much Greek education was abstract and metaphysical and not designed to be practical.  Groups like the Sophists, who wanted to bring education "down to earth," were not popular.

The Romans, influenced by the Greeks in their educational standards as in all other phases of their intellectual life, stressed rhetorical, oratorical, and legal studies as the best preparation for public life.  Toward the end of the Roman Empire, a formal course of study was created in the "seven liberal arts"—grammar, rhetoric, logic, arithmetic, geometry, astronomy, and music.  Although much of the liberal arts curriculum had been in use a long time, it was not formally outlined until about the fourth century A.D., in a textbook written by

Martianus Capella, entitled *The Marriage of Mercury and Philology*. With minor changes and additions from time to time, especially the introduction of the classics in early modern times, this course of study has remained the basis of formal education from Roman days to our own time. Our bachelor of arts degree is derived from this late Roman curriculum.

**Medieval education and the rise of universities.** Extensive changes in education occurred in the Middle Ages. A great part of the learning of Greece and Rome was lost in the barbarian invasions of the Roman Empire and the cultural decline that followed. Medieval education was far more limited than in the days of the Greeks and Romans, and its content was much less reliable. It was primarily concerned with religion rather than with training for public life. Most of the learned men were churchmen. For a long time, the schools were almost exclusively in the hands of the monks. Even after medieval universities were firmly established, the churchmen exercised control over most of them. The course of study during this period was mainly restricted to grammar, rhetoric, and logic. The brief and extremely dull textbooks were compiled by monks on the basis of the works of earlier Greek and Roman scholars. There were also textbooks in theology written by the church fathers and medieval theologians. Most of the teachers in the universities were learned monks.

The great mass of people during the Middle Ages were illiterate and received no education except some informal instruction in the family, the church, the gilds, and on the manor. Most of this was either simple moral and religious instruction or manual training in farming methods or manufacturing techniques. The young men of the nobility were given instruction in the normal course of castle life, where they were taught how to fight as a knight on horseback and the amenities of courtly conduct, known as chivalry. The formal teaching in the schools was devoted chiefly to training clergymen, doctors, lawyers, and clerks to aid churchmen and officials.

The rise of the universities in the twelfth and thirteenth centuries is associated with the influence of the church. A French monk, Peter Abelard (1074–1142), demonstrated that a knowledge of logic was necessary to the mastery of theology. In order to improve the study of theology, the medieval universities were brought into being and were devoted chiefly to training in logic, grammar, and rhetoric. The corporate organization of the universities was patterned upon the medieval craft gild. The words "college" and "university" came from the titles of these medieval gilds or corporations. The colleges and universities were corporations of faculty and students. The degree of bachelor of arts was given for proficiency in the seven liberal arts, especially grammar, rhetoric, and logic. Contrary to the general impression, the degree was not based upon a mastery of the Greek and Latin languages and literature, as it came to be in later centuries.

Many of the official titles used in education today, such as rector, chancellor, dean and professor, as well as academic ritual, gowns, degrees, and even examinations, have come down to us directly from the medieval university.

The university of the later Middle Ages placed main emphasis on logic and theology, with the latter known as the "queen of the sciences." That the main goal of medieval higher education was the mastery of theology is well illustrated by the medieval formula: "The sword of God's word is fashioned by grammar, sharpened by logic, and burnished by rhetoric, but only theology can use it." While medieval universities gave instruction in law and medicine, even these subjects were taught by the same appeal to logic and authority that governed the teaching of theology. There was little laboratory work in medicine or case work in law. Virtually the only practical education offered in the universities lay in training scribes, clerks, and secretaries for the secular and ecclesiastical bureaucracy, especially the latter. Such persons were taught how to write letters, execute legal forms, draw up proclamations, and make out bills.

**The classics in education.** Classical languages and literature, relatively neglected until about the fifteenth century, gradually came to occupy a large place in the educational system, and the mastery of classical Greek and Latin again became the mark of an educated man. Thus arose the framework of what is known as our "liberal education." The beauty of Greek and Roman culture and the sane, secular classical philosophy of life were soon buried, however, in a maze of grammar and syntax, taught for discipline more than for culture. Harsh mental and physical discipline became educational ideals. The subjects taught and the methods of instruction came to be valued about in proportion to the hatred of students for them.

**Early educational reformers.** In the seventeenth and eighteenth centuries, a number of educational reforms were suggested. A few social thinkers, as early as the seventeenth century, advocated female education, the adaptation of subject-matter to the mental age of the child, and a pleasant and natural manner of instruction. The most notable expositor of such progressive educational ideals was John Amos Comenius (1592–1670), whose book, *The Great Didactic,* is one of the classics in educational history. It was not, however, until the late nineteenth century that these advanced educational notions were put into practice in general education.

The English philosopher, John Locke (1632–1704), laid great emphasis on education as the means of developing a well-trained mind. He also suggested the value of manual training for children of the poor. In the middle of the eighteenth century, the French reformer, Claude Helvétius, anticipated the democratic educators of the nineteenth century by arguing that the masses had a right to education. He was one of the first to believe that the lower classes are just as capable mentally as the upper classes. Jean Jacques Rousseau's book,

*Émile*, published in 1762, was one of most influential treatises in the history of education. Rousseau, a sharp critic of the school system of his day, formulated the theory that sensible education consists in giving wise direction to a child's natural curiosity. He advocated adapting education to human nature instead of making the pupil conform to the dry, lifeless type of formal classical training prevalent in the eighteenth century. Rousseau also believed in universal education. His ideas had tremendous influence on nineteenth-century educational reformers, especially the great apostles of the new pedagogy, Heinrich Pestalozzi, Johann Herbart, and Friedrich Froebel.

**Rise of free public education.** The nineteenth century was a period of remarkable changes in education. The power of the church over education was broken in many countries, and public education under state auspices became more usual. Frederick the Great had created a public school system in Prussia and here, in 1794, free compulsory education was first established by law. France did not adopt free compulsory education until 1882. England lagged behind and did not begin to provide an adequate public school system until 1918.

The leaders of the struggle for free public education in the United States were James Gordon Carter, Horace Mann, and Henry Bernard. They believed in the equality of man, although they saw evidence on all sides of obvious differences in social and economic status. It seemed to them that democracy could not succeed without free public instruction, which would be open to all, without class distinction. In 1837 Mann introduced such a system of free public education in the state of Massachusetts; other states eventually followed suit.

Unfortunately, when free public education was established a century ago, little attention was given to the type of education needed for democratic life. No basic changes were made in the school curriculum, and we proceeded to teach "little democrats" subjects that had been taught the offspring of feudal and urban aristocrats in the later Middle Ages and the period of Humanism. And, a century after Mann's era, we now wonder why our schools have not been more successful in training citizens for a democratic way of life.

**Better pedagogical methods.** After free public instruction was instituted, reforms in the philosophy and procedure of formal instruction followed gradually, unfortunately not accompanied by comparable reforms in the curriculum. Teachers received better training in the normal schools and teachers' colleges. A more intelligent attitude toward the child was advocated by educators like G. Stanley Hall, and scientific child study began. Kindergartens and nursery schools were established. In every grade, teachers began to try to make subjects more interesting. The old grammar school,[1] where students suffered through harsh methods of training and an antique curriculum, began to disappear.

---

[1] About the age level of our high school and not to be confused with our present grammar school grades.

**Improved curriculum and educational structures.** In colleges and universities, during the latter part of the nineteenth century, some headway—but not enough—was made in replacing the old curriculum, which had been worked out in the Middle Ages and by the Italian Humanists of the fifteenth and sixteenth centuries and was hardly suitable for teaching a democratic way of life.

Less emphasis came to be placed on the classics and more on natural science. A little more attention was given to history, political science, and economics. More subjects were offered, and a greater choice was allowed students in selecting their courses of study. This "elective system" was first introduced in the United States at Harvard University by President Charles W. Eliot in 1869. Eliot's action was violently criticized and rigorously fought by the eminent custodians of cultural lag in higher education. Even in our own day, a leading educational historian called Eliot's elective program "the greatest educational crime of the century."

The twentieth century has brought many interesting changes in American education. The public support of education has made it possible to build some splendid school structures. A modern high school building in a small American city or one of the better consolidated rural schools is an impressive structure when compared with the largest of medieval university buildings. Mass education is carried on in a smooth and efficient fashion, even though the subject-matter taught still leaves much to be desired. Twenty-five million children now attend public schools in place of the few thousands who were lucky enough to go to school in earlier centuries.

**Introducing democratic methods into education.** Some modern educational leaders, like Francis Parker and John Dewey, believed that mass education cannot be well adapted to the brighter or slower children. Hence, experimental schools, devoted both to instruction and a study of the mind of the child, have been established. The progressive education movement, a revolt against the drab formality of mass education, is a product of the twentieth century—in part of Dewey's ideas. Progressive education seeks to give sensible and realistic instruction in such a pleasant way that children will like to go to school. One of the most extreme examples of progressive education is the Dalton system, where pupils study what they wish, when and as they desire to do so.

With the rise of the mental hygiene movement and a more scientific understanding of mental defects, better provision has been made for instructing mentally retarded children. It has been found that mentally defective children can sometimes make a great deal of progress in manual arts. Not enough attention, however, has been given to individual instruction for specially talented children.

Some educators have insisted on the introduction of more suitable subjects for instruction, particularly the social sciences, with emphasis on realistic civic education. Further, they have logically contended that not only the material taught but also the mode of instruction and school administration should take on democratic characteristics and help to instill democratic attitudes and practices.

**The revolution in higher education.** A revolution has also taken place in higher education in the last 50 years. In the nineteenth century, few persons attended a college or university. Today, there are about 2,500,000 students in our American colleges and universities. While too much of the older course of study, some of it dating from the days of the Greeks and Romans, remains, there have been important changes in the curriculum. The social sciences have become popular in colleges and universities and are now being introduced into high schools. Too much of our college and university instruction in the social sciences, however, still remains a rationalized defense of antique social ideas and the existing social, economic, and political system. Many of our colleges and universities have a gigantic enrollment— New York University 48,000, University of California 44,000, Columbia University 29,000, and the University of Minnesota and the University of Illinois 25,000 each.

Before we analyze the defects of our modern educational system let us examine our vast public educational structure.

## Mass Education in Operation

**Rise of mass education.** One of the most important influences of democracy on education was to bring about mass education, modeled on the lines of big business. Mann and others taught convincingly that democracy requires education for everyone. Compulsory education laws were passed, and the expenses of school attendance, including, in some places, textbooks, paper, and pencils, were taken over by public authorities. Many schools, especially consolidated rural schools, provide free transportation for students, and free lunches or milk for children.

**Increased enrollment.** Thus, it is not surprising that in 1949 over 30 million students were enrolled in all American educational institutions. In 1949, there were 921,594 teachers. Over one-fifth of the whole population of the United States is engaged in the business of getting or giving an education. The total expenditure of the public schools in 1946–47 was about $3,300,000,000.

The increase in school attendance in recent years, especially in high schools and colleges, has been remarkable. In 1900, there were 14,-481,000 pupils in elementary schools; in 1949, elementary school pupils numbered 20,034,000. In 1900, there were only about 695,000 pupils in secondary schools, while in 1949 there were 5,633,000. In 1900, there were 237,000 students in colleges and universities; in 1949, there were 2,456,000. Enrollment in educational institutions grew far more rapidly than the population at large between 1900 and 1950. From the little red schoolhouse, the village academy, and the rustic college campus of a generation ago to our modern educational plants represents an almost incredible advance in enrollment and facilities.

**Increased value of school property.** School property rose enormously in value between 1900 and 1940. The rate of increase in the value of school property was even greater than the growth of enroll-

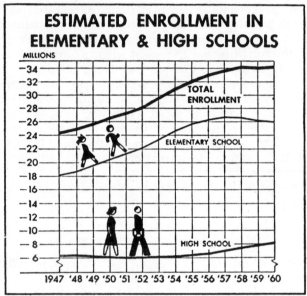

## ESTIMATED ENROLLMENT IN ELEMENTARY & HIGH SCHOOLS

*Courtesy of National Education Association.*

This graph shows predicted increase of children in public schools as a result of the marked spurt of the birth rate in the 1940's.

ment. In 1936, the total value of all educational property, from elementary schools to universities, including endowments, was $12,-353,084,000. The value of all public school property in 1944 was approximately 8 billion dollars. An accompanying change took place in the size and design of school buildings. Many one-room country schools were abandoned, and modernized and consolidated rural structures, accommodating students from several districts, replaced them. The new buildings are scientifically, and often artistically, built; attention is given to lighting, ventilation, heating, sanitation, comfort, and convenience. School grounds are made larger, in order to provide better recreational facilities. The equipment has also been greatly extended. In some of the outstanding school plants there are auditoriums, gymnasiums, libraries, shops of many kinds, art studios, suites for health officers and nurses, cafeterias, and rest rooms.

**The financial basis of higher education.** Our universities, colleges, normal schools, and junior colleges—the institutions of higher learning—while not representing such a huge investment as our public schools, are impressive in size and beauty. There were, in 1950, some 1,808 institutions of higher learning, representing an investment of over 3 billion dollars, with an annual operating cost of nearly one billion dollars. Students in these institutions of higher learning make up nearly 16 per cent of all persons of college age in the United States. The majority of the colleges and universities in the East are private institutions and depend upon voluntary endowment and tuition for their support, while, in the West and South, most of the more impressive institutions are state-owned and operated. The University of North Carolina, chartered in 1789, is the oldest state university. The total endowment and other permanent funds of the private institutions of higher learning amounted to about 2 billion dollars in 1950. This was a growth of over 1,000 per cent since 1900. Registration is about equally divided between state and private institutions of higher learning.

In order to increase their earning power and meet increasing expenditures, some universities and colleges have of late ceased to derive their income exclusively from tuition and from interest and dividends on their securities, and have gone into business on their own account. In 1949, some 455 institutions of higher learning had over a billion dollars invested in business enterprises and derived a tax-exempt income of 150 million dollars therefrom. These businesses varied from real estate investments to the manufacture of leather products and spaghetti. What effect such innovations will have on freedom in instruction in economics remains to be seen.

In any event, it has long since become evident that private institutions of higher learning must take some drastic action to improve their financial situation. Most of their endowment funds are quite naturally invested in fixed-income securities, mainly corporation bonds and the like. As we noted in the chapter on recent economic trends, income from bonds has increased but slightly since 1939. Price rises have virtually cut in half the income from college and university endowments when measured in terms of dollar purchasing power.

## Recent Innovations and Improvements in Education

**Improvement in teaching.** The extension of educational facilities has brought a greater demand for competent teachers. Professional teachers' colleges have been established, and numerous university summer schools have been opened to enable teachers to keep up with their subjects. There were 184,000 students registered in teachers' colleges and normal schools in 1949. There were 536,000 students attending summer schools in 1946.

Many of the better school systems urge teachers to carry on studies along with their teaching and offer as inducements the promise of a raise in salary or rank. After the first world war, a movement for increasing teachers' pay temporarily attracted to the teaching field more men who formerly sought employment in business. The requirements for teaching in the way of training and experience became more rigorous until the great teacher shortage after 1942.

One of the notable features in modern education has been the elimination of corporal punishment and an emphasis on arousing the interest and enthusiasm of the pupil. With the introduction of various extracurricular activities, such as athletics, dramatics, and scientific clubs, the process of education is proceeding more enthusiastically than under the older drab régime, which placed complete emphasis on formal subjects.

**Modernizing the curriculum.** In a secondary school of 1890, the curriculum usually offered only nine subjects: Latin and Greek, French or German, English, algebra, geometry, physics, chemistry, and history. By 1940, the subjects taught had been increased to over fifty. The greatest gains have been made in the social sciences and vocational studies. Many city high schools have made commendable extensions of the amount of time given to technical and vocational subjects. The insistence of school administrators on instruction in the classics is fading out. Less stress is laid on mathematics, except for those preparing for careers in science and engineering. There have, naturally, been fewer changes in the traditional curriculum of the elementary school, but even here the social studies have recently made much headway.

**The junior high school and the junior college.** New types of educational institutions have come into being. The junior high school movement, launched in Berkeley, California, in 1909, has made great progress since the first world war. The junior high school developed a new educational set-up by shifting the seventh and eighth grades from the grammar school and adding the first year of the high school curriculum. One of the outstanding features of the junior high school has been the inclusion of more courses in the social studies and vocational instruction. The ordinary vocational subjects in the junior high school may cover printing, manual training, and metal work for boys, and three years of domestic science for girls.

By taking care of many subjects formerly handled in the senior high school, the junior high school has made it possible to provide for much more advanced work in the senior high school. In fact, in some of the better high schools of today, the quality and level of instruction are far better than in some small present-day colleges. Some educators, such as Dean Louis A. Pechstein, prophesy that, in time, the senior high school may do the work of the colleges, at least of the junior colleges.

Another novelty, in education, mainly introduced since the first world war, is the junior college, of which there are now about 500 with an enrollment of about 225,000. There were only 46 junior colleges with a total enrollment of 4,500 in 1918. The junior college curriculum level is approximately the same as in the first two years of the regular college; but, since the junior college is new, it has eliminated many archaic non-essentials and added practical and semi-professional courses designed to enable the graduate to earn his living. More and more students who might, in earlier times, have gone to a four-year college, are now attending junior colleges, where, in addition to saving two years of college expenses, they graduate with some practical knowledge and are often better able to support themselves upon graduation.

**Extension courses, better professional schools, and the expansion of vocational education.** With our educational opportunities, even the adult who missed out on a good formal education in his youth has a chance to make up for his former deficiencies. University extension courses for adults are offered in many cities, and night schools are filled with men and women who desire to improve themselves through education. There were about 250,000 persons taking extension courses of college rank in 1944.

One of the notable advances in education has been the higher requirements for entrance to the professional schools. Not many years ago, a boy could enter a medical school or an engineering college directly from high school without any formal examination or special previous training, and many law students simply read law in the office of a practicing attorney. Today, no first-class medical school will accept a student unless he is a college graduate and has had special premedical training. Outstanding engineering and law schools take only college graduates.

One important improvement in the way of providing practical educational facilities has been the increasing generosity of the Federal government in matching funds contributed by state and local governments for vocational instruction, especially in agriculture, trade and industry, and home economics. In 1947, some 2,500,000 students were enrolled in such federally-aided vocational classes.

## Some Leading Defects in Modern Education

**Illiteracy persists.** A very serious defect in our educational system is that it has not even yet abolished illiteracy or near-illiteracy, despite the vast registration in our public schools. The census of 1940 showed that the average American citizen had attended school for only nine years. Some 350,000 registrants in the draft in the second world war could only sign their names with a mark. Some 12 per cent of those found unfit for service were rejected solely because of educational deficiency. It is estimated that 10 million Americans are functionally illiterate. In 12 states, one-fifth of the adult population had never gone further than the fourth grade; some 14 per cent of all adult American citizens have had less than five years of education. About a million children of migratory workers get virtually no formal education whatever.

**Gloom and boredom as educational ideals.** The school classroom has often been a place of routine, mental punishment, and gloom. The solemn atmosphere all too frequently attached to learning and teaching dates back to the Middle Ages and early modern times, when it was believed that study must be accompanied by solemnity, misery, and fear. The difficulties of higher mathematics, and the emphasis on grammar instead of culture in foreign languages, especially in the classics, have served to make those subjects unpleasant. Another cause for student disgust or indifference has arisen from the standardization of courses and examinations.

The idea of education as a solemn process was formulated long before the rise of modern educational psychology. We now realize that nothing is more opposed to mental health and stimulating intellectual life than solemnity and gloom, but old punitive ideals die hard. They were never better expressed than only a few years ago by former president George B. Cutten of Colgate University, when he said, in all seriousness: "It doesn't matter what you study, so long as you hate it!"

Until educators recognize that alert student interest is more important than mental punishment in the form of examinations and of drill in unpleasant subject-matter, students will not be eager to learn, nor will they learn as rapidly or easily as they might. A certain amount of routine is necessary to administer our huge educational system, but knowledge forced on one is not remembered as long a time as knowledge acquired from the desire to learn. The purpose of education should not be merely to "get by" in examinations.

**Our present curriculum mainly a museum piece.** Most of our curriculum innovations have consisted in adding a few highly modern notions to the old courses of study. In other words, instead of remodeling our whole educational set-up, we merely add new courses. An ancient oriental ox-cart adorned with fragments from Greek and Roman chariots, armor plate from the coat-of-mail of a medieval knight, the top from an early modern stage coach, an automobile steering gear, an airplane propeller, and a radio—this is our modern educational system. It has added new gadgets but has not given up its old basic parts or chassis.

For instance, the subjects relating to religion have come down from the time when the primary purpose of education was to make clear the will of God. The Greeks and Romans added training in rhetoric and oratory to provide the technique for achieving success in public life. Medieval churchmen stressed the importance of religion in education, and revived logic, grammar, and rhetoric to substantiate and polish theology. The Humanists of early modern times contributed the notion that the classical languages embodied the full flower of literary expression. Mathematics was added in the seventeenth and eighteenth centuries, natural science in the nineteenth century, and social science in the twentieth.

**Archaic education cannot guide social change.** It is hard to justify emphasis on antique subjects in the light of twentieth-century requirements. Statesmen are in much greater need of a knowledge of government and an ability to analyze social problems correctly than of formal rhetorical skill. Statistical tables are more valuable than figures of speech. The classics are not the sum total of learning, nor are the classical languages valuable today in meeting the world crisis. We do not need religious instruction so much as a well-directed secular intelligence in solving our perplexing problems.

We are living in the midst of the greatest social crisis in history and one so complicated that we need, as never before, the counsel and direction of organized intelligence. Education, too often, does not give us guidance but merely distracts or confuses us. We are vaguely aware of our social problems, yet we do not fully investigate them through education because the irrelevance of the curriculum makes us fall back on conservative attitudes. Democracy is in headlong retreat in most countries in the Western world, and yet we still refuse to provide adequate education in the basic principles of citizenship under democratic auspices. We know that one marriage in four ends in a divorce court, but we make little effort to prepare students for marriage and family responsibilities. Above all, we are often opposed to practical subjects. It is no exaggeration to say that half the subjects now taught in our schools and universities have no useful or direct application to living in the twentieth century.

**Difficulties presented by mass education.** For economy's sake, we teach the same courses to all students in the process of mass education, even though we have learned that there are wide differences in intelligence, talents, and interests among pupils. So far, the main attempt at differentiation in instruction has been made in the special treatment of handicapped and defective children. Educators and psychologists have worked out fairly satisfactory tests for vocational abilities and talents, which should be recognized and encouraged, but these tests have not been widely adopted as a basis for arranging classes, selecting and diversifying subject-matter, and distributing students.

In an effort to provide mass education, we have created a smoothly running educational machine, but we have frowned on independence of thought and action. The entire progressive education movement has been, for the most part, a revolt against the complex machinery of our mass educational system, but it has made comparatively little headway, except among the relatively few children of the wealthy classes. The enormous increase in the size of our educational institutions has meant that the individual must be subjected to mass treatment. Teachers often must present their courses in lecture form to large classes, and, so far, the only way they know of testing the student's grasp of the subject-matter imparted is by giving formal examinations on the material presented.

**Emphasis on research undermines good teaching.** Overemphasis on professorial research and esoteric scholarship has done much to hamper good instruction in our colleges and universities. Through the routine technique of procuring the Ph.D. degree, which is the "teacher's certificate" or "union card" for institutions of higher learning, we train college teachers to be research experts and authors of learned treatises rather than to be effective classroom teachers. We pay and promote them all too often on the basis of their research and publications rather than for their enthusiasm and ability in classroom work. While even instructors of undergraduates should have a mastery of the subject-matter they impart, their tenure and rewards should be based on their ability as teachers, not on their facility for research and publication. The latter should be carried on chiefly by those who instruct in graduate schools or in such educational centers as the Institute for Advanced Study at Princeton, New Jersey, where there are virtually no formal instruction duties whatever.

*Courtesy of Fairchild Aerial Surveys, Inc.*

**Picture of gigantic physical plant of Columbia University on Morningside Heights in New York City.**

**The custodial function versus education.** Because children are sent to colleges and boarding-schools for safekeeping, the administrators of these institutions find it necessary to make strict rules of conduct to prevent escapades and scandals. This means that, all too often, the success of an institution is measured, not by its high educational achievements but by its success in preventing unpleasant happenings and unconventional conduct. This overemphasis on the school and college as custodial institutions for safely "jailing" children affects the teachers and professors. A professor is not encouraged to promote independence of thought and action, because it may provoke unconventional thinking or action on the part of students and bring undesirable publicity to the institution.

**Fear of "radical teachers."** Many of the old social traditions have been swept away in recent times, but teachers, because of their fear of being branded as radicals, have failed to offer sound new ideas and practices to replace the old. Human beings long for safety and assurance, and require formulas or patterns of behavior to show them what to do and when to do it. The teacher or professor who has original ideas is looked upon as a "radical" by those who still hold to the old traditional attitudes and his tenure is never secure. Educational institutions that rely on money from conservative business leaders have been slow to recognize the fact that new ideas are needed in our changing world. College trustees and presidents often fear they might lose a large potential monetary gift from a wealthy but reactionary donor if the professors teach modern ideas in the classroom.

**Overemphasis on intercollegiate athletics.** The modern educational system has overemphasized competitive intercollegiate athletics. Too often, when the average American hears the name of a college or university, he associates it with a football team or hero, rather than with the high educational standards of the institution. A third-rate quasi-vocational college with a good football team is often better and more favorably known than a great university which lays primary stress on intellectual life and seeks to promote clear thinking, but does not have a winning football team. Star athletes make better publicity for a college than scholarly professors who have added another honorary degree or brought out another book. Dr. Robert Maynard Hutchins of the University of Chicago has been virtually the only prominent university executive to go "all out" in resolutely placing intellectual attainments and interests above athletic renown in the scale of university values.

One bad aspect of our current intercollegiate athletics is that only a few students benefit from them. Those who do not become members of the football, baseball, basketball, or track teams shy away from unrequired classes in physical education, which are not made pleasant for the "dub" or person who has difficulties in sports. Most required courses in college gymnasiums are dull and drab setting-up exercises, into which the spirit of play and gusto rarely enters.

Athletic abuses have also entered secondary schools. College scouts sign up promising athletes before they finish high school. Teachers in high school, as well as in college, are sometimes urged by the coaches to give their boys a "break" and not let them flunk tests before the "big game." There is little doubt that commercialized college athletics are a serious handicap to a realistic rebuilding of our educational system.

**Disciplinary anarchy.** A number of other defects and handicaps in our educational system demand at least casual comment. In justly repudiating and abandoning the old system of brutal corporal punishments—a traditional European schoolmaster once boasted that in his years of teaching he had given 911,527 strokes with a stick, 124,000 lashes with a whip, 136,715 slaps with the hand, and 1,115,800 boxes on the ear—we have often gone to the other extreme and virtually eliminated any possibility of maintaining discipline in an unruly schoolroom. In some of our metropolitan districts, where students are drawn from all races and economic levels, teachers in high schools are virtually at the mercy of young rowdies and ruffians. Physical assaults on teachers are not uncommon, and even homicidal attacks are not unknown. Such conditions not only demoralize the educational process but help to breed juvenile delinquency.

**Inadequate training of teachers today.** All too many of our teachers are inadequately trained, although the worst of them are worth more than they are paid. Nearly one-sixth of our teachers are giving instruction today on the basis of emergency certificates. The situation is especially bad in rural schools, where some 62 per cent of the teachers have had less than two years of college education. This was true even in 1945, before we lowered standards to obtain the teachers sorely needed at the end of the war. Even in village schools, some 21 per cent of the teachers have had less than two years of college work. And, in all too many instances, the slight amount of college work taken had little bearing on training for teaching. In 1948, 3.2 per cent of teachers had no college preparation; 9.5 per cent had less than two years of college work; and 27.9 per cent had two years but less than four, making over 40 per cent without a bachelor's degree.

**Education at times a football of politics.** In many cities, political corruption hampers or undermines the educational system. Superintendents of education may be political appointees and may use their position for political favoritism and graft in the selection, promotion, and tenure of teachers, in purchasing school equipment, and in letting contracts for school construction. All of this lowers teaching standards and morale and invites pedagogical anarchy and indifference. The educational system of one of our largest cities was recently completely demoralized for some years by such a situation, which was so flagrant as to be all but incredible.

We have suggested only a few of the outstanding defects of our educational system. If our eyes are opened to existing defects, we can better deal with the problems of the present and future. The educational defects we have mentioned can be remedied if educators will work together for the preservation and improvement of democracy through education.

## Some Needed Reforms in Education

**Adjusting education to different intellectual levels.** What changes are necessary in our educational system to enable it to meet the needs of our changing age? The reforms we suggest below may not be accomplished in this generation, but they should be considered by every forward-thinking American.

We should make wider use of intelligence and vocational tests as a means of determining what kind of education will fit a given child for a successful life. Those with a low intelligence quotient should not seek an advanced general education in literature, science, and the arts, but should be placed in institutions where they would learn their native language, arithmetic, and vocational subjects. A frank realization that a considerable group of our children can only profit by education of this kind would go a long way towards solving our social problems and reducing the unnecessary waste in our educational system.

If we started the sorting-out process in the elementary schools, it would make later elimination less difficult and embarrassing. There would be two main classes of pupils: (1) those who, according to tests of mental ability and vocational capacities, belong in manual and industrial courses; and (2) those who are intellectually capable of pursuing the formal and usual courses in high school and colleges. It is far better and fairer actually to train the child of low intelligence to earn his living than to make a vain attempt to teach him to appreciate art and literature. Moreover, if students of this type were removed from senior high school and college preparatory courses, the others, who are capable of receiving higher education in the arts and sciences, could be more effectively taught.

The futility of trying to push through the conventional educational machinery students who are not suited for such a program because of mental defects or emotional maladjustment is shown by the fact that just about half of those who enter high school and nearly half of all college freshmen fail to graduate. This is a waste of time and money all around. If such young persons were properly placed in the educational system through intelligence and vocational tests, they might complete an appropriate educational program and be prepared for a self-sustaining existence.

**A rational revamping of the curriculum.** Instruction in foreign languages should be given in the early grades, so that college students will not need to spend long hours in the study of elementary grammar. Certain basic subjects are necessary for a literary education, but far greater attention should be given to the social studies. Those who have the ability to study them may profit by a prolonged consideration of social problems. Because vocational students will also later have to face the responsibilities of citizenship, they too should know something of the social sciences, but they need not waste their time in studying foreign languages. We have mentioned the junior high school as a place where much of the preparatory work for senior high school and college can be done. Languages and intermediate mathematics should be completed in the junior high school, before the student enters the secondary field. Junior high schools should also teach the social studies and offer more courses in vocational and industrial arts.

The senior high school curriculum should primarily prepare students to live successfully in the middle of the twentieth century. The modern senior high school curriculum, however, still prepares the students mainly for college, and an unrealistic college at that. In the reorganized high school course of study there should be four divisions: (1) natural science, (2) industrial arts, (3) social studies, and (4) aesthetics, including literary subjects. The majority of high school students do not go on to college. Therefore, high school should prepare them for a successful personal and social life. The industrial arts course should be broadened to include commercial studies. High school graduates might not so often turn to criminal pursuits if they were prepared to get jobs after graduation. Likewise, the average high school graduate would be more likely to be an intelligent and law-abiding citizen and less likely to become a delinquent if more complete and realistic instruction in the social studies enabled him to have a better grasp on the facts and responsibilities of public life. This new type of high school curriculum could give graduates a more advanced and realistic education than many of our average colleges now provide.

One gratifying trend toward greater realism and practicality in education has been promoted by defense industry and war, namely, the increase in technical, industrial, and vocational instruction and training-in-industry. As we noted earlier, federal grants have been made to this type of education in the hope of providing more and better skilled workers.

**Need for two different types of college.** Our whole educational procedure should be revamped to handle college students sensibly and intelligently. There should be two kinds of colleges: one for those who desire social polish, excitement, or the prestige of going to college, and another for those vitally concerned with higher learning—that is, those seriously interested in getting an education. The character of these institutions should be very different.

For the first type of college, the institutional facilities should be set up to provide training for modern living, to place emphasis upon intramural athletics, and to assure a sufficient amount of social poise and glamour. Emphasis on grades should be reduced to a minimum, and instruction should be confined mainly to broad orientation courses, designed to equip the students with a general knowledge of man and the world in which he lives. Probably at least 75 per cent of all students who now attend college should go to this type of institution, where they could be taught good manners, sportsmanship, and the essential outlines of knowledge and culture, achievements rarely attained by the majority of college students today at the end of four years. And all this could be brought about in two years of college work, at the end of which a suitable bachelor's degree could be given and two years gained for later professional work or employment in some remunerative occupation.

Colleges of a quite different nature should be provided for students who really desire an education in the true sense of the word. Here, professors should not only "teach" subjects but also stimulate students to study and to do research work. By the time a student graduated from this type of institution, after four years of college work, he would be well informed about the past achievements of mankind and intelligently aware of the problems of present-day civilization.

Educational reforms should be begun promptly. Educators have exerted, and will continue to exert, a great deal of influence on public life. Political leaders know that to achieve permanent success they must create suitable public attitudes. Dictators have laid great stress on education in bringing about changes in the attitudes, prejudices, and loyalties of whole populations; by the same token, a reformed education can strengthen democracy.

## Educational Reform and the Rôle of Education in Social Change

**The three great branches of education.** There are three major divisions or departments of education: (1) the scientific and technological; (2) the social studies; and (3) the broad field of aesthetics, embracing literature, the arts, music, and the like—in short, what Plato once called the "supra-pig" interests of mankind.

The first branch of education has already accomplished wonders, having given us a mechanical heritage which has completely outdistanced the institutional equipment through which we seek to control it and adapt it to the service of society. What we most need right now is far greater emphasis on the second division, namely, the social studies, to make the most effective use of the contributions of scientific and technological education. Unless we succeed in attaining domestic plenty and security and world peace, aesthetics will never have the opportunity to raise mankind, as a whole, above the animal level of absorption in the problems of sheer physical existence.

**False doctrines in educational procedure.** The greatest fallacy of our educational system today is probably the assumption that each of these three main divisions of education is of equal importance at all times. Right now, the social studies are more critically important to us than both of the others combined. To give an equal amount of time and effort to all three in our day is as great folly as it would be to give a middle-aged man suffering from diabetes equal doses of castoria, insulin, and digitalis. Unless the social studies fulfill their current and vital rôle in the educational program, that of reducing or eliminating cultural lag, the contributions of science and engineering will be largely wasted, and aesthetics will not get a chance to create a truly human culture, worthy of "the lords of all creation."

In the Middle Ages, men strove for salvation in the world to come. Hence, it was logical that theology, the science of salvation, should be "the queen of sciences." Today, when we wish to be saved here and now, it is just as logical to contend that the social studies are our only road to social salvation—the temporarily reigning dynasty in the educational realm, the "brain trust" of education. If they accomplish their mission, then permanent ascendency may be conceded to aesthetics, the guide to living in an era of security, peace, and leisure.

Especially must we be on our guard against subtle attempts to drag us back into medievalism through the false fronts and fake shibboleths of "straight-thinking," "intellectual discipline," "mastery of the masters," "how to read books," and other innocent appearing slogans of those who conspire against realistic education for the twentieth century. Such is the essence of the Hutchins-Adler-St. Johns educational program. While this subject-matter might be admirable as the basis of a single college class or course, it is obviously fraudulent and bankrupt as the total curriculum of a modern institution of higher learning in the mid-twentieth century, when we are tottering on the brink of social chaos. Education must teach us not only to think straight on appropriate and vital subjects; but also how to act straight amidst our social perplexities.

Unless the social studies enable us to use our material equipment more wisely and efficiently, the latter may well prove a liability rather than an asset, and be used as an instrument for the destruction of such civilization as we now possess. Hence, greater educational emphasis on the social studies is perhaps all that can even potentially separate and protect us from revolution, violence, totalitarianism, and chaos. For a generation or more, we must devote more than half of all educational effort, from the elementary grades to the graduate school, to the social studies, if we are to have even a gambling chance of moving ahead to peace, security, and a social order that will give the majority of mankind some justifiable reason for living. The arrival of atomic energy and the atom bomb are proof enough that we shall not have too much time to bring our institutions up to date, subdue our technology to human use, and put an end to war.

**Needed reforms in social science education.** Yet little will be accomplished if we simply give more time to the social studies as they are taught today, for they are now mainly a bulwark of a disintegrating social order, not a sure guide to a better social era. There must be more social criticism, clearer vision of the type of society that will give us security and peace, and greater courage in showing how we may realize such a state without the wastes and dangers of revolution. In short, adequate education in the social studies is probably the surest safeguard against revolution and more world wars.

If the social studies do not rise to their responsibility while we still remain a democracy, they may never have an opportunity to do so. Official and brutally enforced political catechisms, rather than social studies, are the favorite devices of the dictators and totalitarians. Timidity in the social studies today may mean their extinction tomorrow.

**Raids on education.** The social studies can never be taught realistically and adequately unless our teachers are protected against the raids on education conducted by short-sighted representatives of the vested interests.

There are two types of raids on education. One is the intellectual raid, through which teachers are intimidated and prevented from teaching the truth, especially in the social studies. Legislation requiring teachers' oaths, insecurity of tenure, the firing of able and progressive teachers, petty moral inquisitions, and the like destroy intellectual independence and prevent educators from directing the processes of social change in an orderly fashion.

The other raid is financial, education always being the first to suffer from economy drives engineered by bankers, businessmen, politicians, and others. Education often is, to them, the least essential phase of modern life, and educators are too poorly organized to defend themselves effectively. The slashing of educational budgets after 1929 was a deplorable scandal. Though we were not spending more than a quarter of what was actually needed for a really adequate system of education in 1929, total public expenditures for education were cut from $2,605,000,000 in 1930 to $1,940,000,000 in 1934. This cut was made despite the fact that the depression came, in large part, because of inadequate education in the generation before 1929. One of the most disastrous aspects of such educational cuts is that they fall most heavily on the socially most valuable activities in education. In times of false economy, the first things to be sacrificed are the so-called "educational frills," namely, the most vital items in educational enterprise, such as experimental schools, vocational schools, school clinics, and the like.

The only effective answer to either type of raid on education is to provide a strong professional organization of teachers. Only in this way can teachers be assured of freedom in teaching, of adequate salaries, and of security in tenure.

**Prospects of adult education.** One of the most encouraging signs of the realization of the importance of realistic education to social change is the growth of the adult education movement. The social crisis now upon us means that we may have to take some decisive action before those now in school or college are old enough to help formulate our public policies. Only by adult education can we bring these problems to the attention of those who are in a position to do something about them at once. Many adults denied the privileges of high school and college instruction have taken advantage of adult education. Persons who work during the day go to night school to continue their education. Others take correspondence courses in the extension departments of universities. There are some outstanding institutions for adult education, for example, the New School for Social Research in New York City, where those who are interested in learning about social, economic, and political problems and the arts have an opportunity to study with outstanding scholars and public figures. Educational experts estimated that in 1950 some 30 million American adults were enrolled in some form of educational program.

## The Second World War and Education

**The second world war produces an educational crisis.** The educational crisis, which had been simmering from the days of the depression following 1929, was brought to a head by the second world war and its aftermath. The pay of teachers was so low that many of those who still taught were disgruntled and lacking in morale. It is estimated that about 350,000 teachers left the profession between 1939 and 1946. About 60,000 of the vacancies have not been filled at all, and most of the replacements have been of an inferior quality, measured by prewar standards.

After the war there was a vast increase in the number of persons who sought educational opportunities. Over 7 million veterans participated in some form of educational enterprise under the "GI Bill of Rights" or some other favoring law. Over 2 million entered colleges and universities, some 2,500,000 returned to high schools, and 2 million took work in various institutions providing vocational training. In 1949–50 there were about 2,500,000 enrolled in American colleges, an increase of over 30 per cent above the highest prewar enrollment. At the present time, however, the greatest increase in pupils is coming in the elementary schools, as a result of the abnormally high birth rate from 1940 to 1948. In 1948, the enrollment of pupils in the first grade increased by 16 per cent over 1947, and in 1949, there were 893,000 more pupils in our elementary schools than in 1948. It is predicted that by 1957 there will be 27 million pupils in elementary schools, as compared with 18 million in 1946. There were in 1950 over 31 million pupils in all our schools and colleges.

**Poor pay and shortage of teachers.** Many teachers, women as well as men, left their teaching posts for war service of one kind or another, while others took better paying jobs in war industries. Those students who might have been trained to teach also often went into war service or war industry. Former teachers who had led exciting lives or obtained high pay during the war were loath to return to the relatively drab life and low pay of the teaching profession. In 1941, the average salary of public school teachers was $1,470, while the average net income of lawyers was $4,794, and of doctors $5,047. The salaried classes, of which the teachers were one of the largest groups, failed to gain in real income as a result of the war.

In 1939, the national average salary of teachers, principals, and supervisors, combined, in public elementary and secondary schools, was $1,440. In 1948–49, it had risen to $2,750. But, after deducting the increased income taxes, this amounted to only $1,458 in terms of 1939 purchasing power (real income). This national average of $2,750 for all teachers was $250 less than the average annual income of all employed workers. It was about one-fourth of the average net income of doctors in 1948. Some slight improvement seemed in store for 1949–50, when the National Education Association experts estimated a national average salary of $2,985. The pay of teachers in many states is grotesquely low. In 1944, the annual salary of public school teachers in Maine averaged $1,158; in Georgia, $923; and in Mississippi, $790. Even in 1949, the Maine salary was only $1,767; the Georgia salary, $1,724; and the Mississippi salary, $1,256.

## PER PUPIL EXPENDITURE FOR PUBLIC SCHOOLS

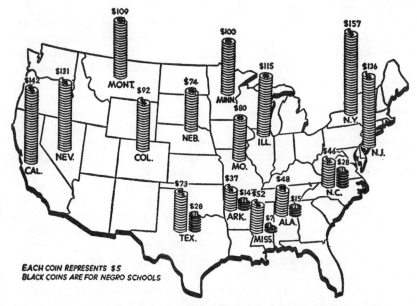

EACH COIN REPRESENTS $5
BLACK COINS ARE FOR NEGRO SCHOOLS

GRAPHIC ASSOCIATES FOR PUBLIC AFFAIRS COMMITTEE, INC.

Graphic map revealing wide variation in expenditures for public education throughout the country. Note also the contrast in expenditures for white and Negro education in the South.

Mainly as a result of this lamentably low pay for teachers, there is a shortage of some 500,000 teachers today, with at least 125,000 being needed to meet bare minimum standards. Further, of those now teaching, some 125,000 are doing so on emergency or substandard licenses; there were only 2,300 such teachers before the second world war. In July, 1949, a group of leading educators declared that at least 260,000 elementary school teachers were not properly prepared to carry on their work.

Despite the willingness to take substandard teachers in order to provide some sort of classroom instruction, it was estimated that, in 1946–1947, over 7,000 classrooms had been closed, over 75,000 children were being deprived of all schooling, and some 2 million children were suffering "major losses in instructional opportunities" as a direct result of the teacher shortage. Indeed, the Census Bureau estimated that in 1947 there were 4 million children between the ages of 5 and 17 who were not attending any school.

That the crisis due to teacher shortage is likely to become more acute is evident from the prediction of educational experts that, by 1955, we shall need 134,000 more elementary school teachers and 36,500 more high school teachers than in 1946. With teachers' salaries what they are today, it is not likely that new personnel will be attracted into the ranks of teachers in any overwhelming numbers. Indeed, the number of those taking professional work to prepare for teaching has declined by nearly one-half since 1941.

The educational plant is becoming even more inadequate than the teaching force, since there was a virtual cessation of all building of schools after Pearl Harbor. Leading educational experts estimate that it would require an expenditure of at least a billion dollars a year for 10 years to bring our educational plant in the public school system up to anything like desirable minimum standards. While there has not been as great a shortage of teachers in high schools and colleges as in the elementary schools, the inadequacy of plant facilities has been very serious. The great increase of college enrollment has meant not only overcrowded classrooms but a desperate shortage of housing facilities, particularly for veterans and their families.

The rapid rise of living costs, especially after 1945, led to alarm on the part of teachers and created many teachers' strikes throughout the country that were not likely to be settled by the harsh legislation proposed. The educational scene is today in a state of flux and crisis as rarely before in the history of American education.

An adequate educational system can be financed. The crisis in the financial basis of public education has been due largely to increased prices and salaries, even though the teachers' salaries have not increased as rapidly as the cost of living. There has been a considerable increase in per-pupil expenditures by school boards since 1940, actually about 66 per cent between 1940 and 1947. But they would have had to rise by 86 per cent to keep pace with increasing costs. Hence, in three-fourths of our states, school board funds had less purchasing power in 1947 than in 1940.

A commission of educational experts estimated in 1948 that at least 5 billion dollars more must be spent each year on American public education than is expended today, if the standards of education are to be maintained on even a reasonably good level. Of this, at least a billion dollars would need to be spent annually on buildings and equipment. This would only bring the total educational outlay up to a little over 8 billion dollars annually, and inasmuch as we spent $9,640,000,000 for alcoholic beverages in 1947, an outlay of 8 billions for all public education would seem a rather moderate figure. A figure of 10 to 12 billions annually to support public education would not be at all excessive, if we wish to achieve and maintain anything like high standards, and to promote and safeguard democracy.

It is important to keep in mind the fact that, though we are now spending slightly more for public education than we did in the "depression decade," a smaller percentage of our total national income is going into public education than at any time in the last quarter of a century. The fact that experts predict that the enrollment of about 25,700,000 pupils in our public schools in 1949 will grow to 33,-500,000 by 1957 underlines the need for rapidly coming to grips with the task of providing a more adequate financial basis for our public school system. The Federal government certainly has not awakened to the need for adequate support of public education. Even the trifling appropriation of 300 million dollars which was proposed to aid public education was shelved by the first session of the 81st Congress.

## Summary

If education is to bridge the gap between the machine age and our out-of-date social institutions, we must bring our educational system up to date. It is now too deeply rooted in the past in attitudes and subject-matter.

A democracy implies an education for everyone. Today, over one-fifth of our population is engaged in the business of getting or giving an education. We have improved buildings, grounds, equipment, and faculties; progressive educators are attempting to remodel school discipline so that the child will learn with enthusiasm. Some desirable changes have been made in the curriculum of the secondary schools. The classics are gradually being replaced by more practical subjects. The junior high school and the junior college are important new developments, while adult education is becoming available to those who missed earlier opportunities to obtain an education or who wish to train for new occupations.

However, despite many improvements in the past century, there are still major defects in our educational system. Our curriculum is sadly out of date in many respects and fails to prepare students for living in the contemporary world. In few places do our educators face current social problems with the frankness necessary to solve them and preserve our democracy. Much of our instruction does not suit the individual student, for, in the attempt to provide mass education, we have turned the schools into educational factories and have neglected the individual pupil. Too often, the schools are used as relatively humane "jails" by parents seeking to avoid the custodial responsibility of caring for their own children. This results in making discipline and regimentation, rather than enlightenment, the main task of many teachers. There is too much emphasis on commercialized athletics, especially in our colleges.

Among needed educational reforms, the two most important are the separation and training of students according to their abilities, and the provision of up-to-date training for modern life, with strong emphasis on vocational instruction and current social problems.

The failure to appropriate enough money to support education on a sound scale and a rapid increase in the number of pupils in our public schools have led to a serious shortage of teachers. As a result, a grave crisis exists today in American public education.

### Selected References

Beale, H. K., *Are Teachers Free?* Scribner, 1936. Comprehensive study of the status of academic freedom in the United States in the 1930's.

Beck, H. P., *The Men Who Control Our Universities,* King's Crown Press, 1947. Competent study of the relation of wealth and business to the control and administration of institutions of higher learning.

Bunting, D. E., *Liberty and Learning,* American Council on Public Affairs, 1947. Important study of academic freedom in America, with special reference to the work of the Academic Freedom Committee of the American Civil Liberties Union.

Cole, S. G., *Liberal Education in a Democracy,* Harper, 1940. Realistic examination of the responsibility of education for democratic citizenship, and a critical answer to the Hutchins-Adler-St. Johns program of evading contemporary knowledge and issues.

Counts, G. S., *The American Road to Culture,* Day, 1930.

————, *The Schools Can Teach Democracy,* Day, 1941. Two thoughtful books by the leading American student of the relation of education to democracy.

Curti, M. E., *The Social Ideals of American Educators,* Scribner, 1935. Best book on the social forces and theories that have shaped American educational doctrine and practice.

Elsbree, W. S., *The American Teacher,* American Book Company, 1939. Probably the best introduction to the history of the American teaching profession.

* Fi■e, Benjamin, *Democratic Education,* Crowell, 1945. Excellent liberal interpretation of American higher education by one of the leading publicists in the educational field.

Gulick, L. H., *Education for American Life,* McGraw-Hill, 1938. A critique of the defects of American public education, drawn from an elaborate study of the educational system of the state of New York.

Hewitt, Dorothy, and Mather, K. F., *Adult Education: a Dynamic for Democracy,* Appleton-Century, 1937. A splendid and spirited statement of the rôle and program of adult education in democratic society.

Judd, C. H., *Education and Social Progress,* Harcourt, Brace, 1934. A famous professor of education describes the defects of our school system as a means of inculcating democratic principles and leading us to a better social order.

Kelley, J. A., *College Life and the Mores,* Teachers College, Columbia University, 1949. One of the few scholarly studies of the social life and moral attitudes of college faculties and students.

* Langford, H. D., *Education and the Social Conflict,* Macmillan, 1936. Perhaps the best book on the rôle of education in guiding social change.

* Lynd, R. S., *Knowledge for What?* Princeton University Press, 1939. A powerful argument for using social science as an instrument for social change.

McConn, C. M., *College or Kindergarten?* New Republic Press, 1928. A noted college dean argues for special types of colleges—one for the general run of college students and another for those who wish to get a college education.

Meiklejohn, Alexander, *Education between Two Worlds,* Harper, 1942. Brilliant analysis of the transition from religious to secular control of education and of the rôle of the latter in social betterment.

Melvin, A. G., *The Technique of Progressive Teaching,* Day, 1932. A thorough and authoritative presentation of the theory and program of progressive education.

* Meyer, A. E., *The Development of Education in the Twentieth Century,* Prentice-Hall, 1949. Excellent study of educational expansion and trends in recent times.

* Newlon, J. H., *Education for Democracy in Our Time,* McGraw-Hill, 1939. A telling argument for the necessity of adapting education to democratic needs if we wish to preserve democracy.

Rugg, Harold, *That Men May Understand,* Doubleday, Doran, 1941. A spirited argument for the ca⁻.did presentation of the social studies in the public schools.

Raup, Bruce, *Education and Organized Interests in America,* Putnam, 1936. Able summary of the various pressures and pressure groups which affect American education.

Scott, Virgil, *The Hickory Stick,* Morrow, 1948. A devastating picture of educational experience in a small-town school by a veteran educator.

Valentine, P. F. (Ed.), *The American College*, Philosophical Library, 1949. Excellent symposium covering the more important problems of American higher education.

Wilson, Logan, *The Academic Man*, Oxford University Press, 1942. Probably the most competent of all sociological studies of academic freedom, academic life, and the psychology of the traditional academician.

# CHAPTER XXVIII

# Life on the Supra-Pig Level:
# Problems of Leisure, Recreation, and Art

## Our New Age of Leisure

**Plato's ideas of life on the supra-pig level.** In one of the great books of all time, *The Republic,* Plato discussed the nature of an ideal society. He cautioned men about being satisfied with mere material comforts, plenty and security, the blessings enjoyed by well-treated pigs. A truly worthy human civilization, he said, must go on to supra-pig heights and provide for the cultivation of those interests we do not share with other animals—art, music, drama, athletics, philosophy, and the like. What Plato called the supra-pig interests of man we now know as the arts and activities of leisure.

Throughout human history, most of man's efforts have been concerned with the struggle to obtain food, shelter, and clothing—the essentials of sheer existence. Only a very small number of people have ever been successful in getting enough material possessions to make life really worth living. And even those fortunate enough to become wealthy have been so busy making money that they have taken little time to enrich their lives with literature and the arts.

Today, for the first time in man's history, tools and machines can speedily produce all that is needed for human comfort; as a result, we are faced with the possibility of a new pattern of living conditions.

**The increase of leisure time a challenge to social planning.** Among the most important of these novel elements in modern life is the ever increasing amount of leisure time. All age groups have benefited from the reduction of working time during the last 150 years. The working day of adults has been virtually cut in half. Children, who formerly went to work in factories and shops at an early age, are now freed from back-breaking labor by compulsory school attendance laws and child-labor legislation. There are many leisure hours for children after school hours are over.

The coming of the Power Age and the introduction of automatic machinery have shortened working hours and given working men and women more leisure each day as well as a longer weekend. Even the housewife, who once was chained to her kitchen, now has more leisure because mechanical appliances have reduced the number of hours she must spend in housework. Much work formerly done at home has been taken over by outside agencies, such as the bakery, the laundry, the canning industry, the textile mill, and the dress manufacturer.

Today, for the first time in human history, leisure for recreation and the arts is available to almost all classes in normal, peacetime life. Instead of regarding leisure as dangerous, we should use it as a means of rounding out our personalities. We must realize that leisure time, properly spent, will make life more worth while and give us an opportunity to indulge in activities beyond those involved in merely making a living. Play and creative activities should occupy more of our attention. Routine work is done for the sake of earning a livelihood and satisfying the sheer needs of physical existence; play and recreation can, on a higher level, satisfy our cultural desires, whether through sports, the arts and crafts, or other activities.

## The History of Leisure

**Leisure and leisure classes prior to modern times.** Down to the invention of recent labor-saving devices, the few who had leisure time secured it mainly by exploiting others. In early societies, the medicine men or priests and the warriors were about the only ones freed by the tribe from the necessity of heavy labor. The medicine men protected the group from evil spirits; the warriors gave protection from earthly enemies, and their services were considered so important they were released from most other onerous responsibilities. Out of the warrior group later arose the rulers and the nobility, who made use of their political power and their landed wealth to avoid physical work. Scribes and scholars later on were also permitted to escape manual labor.

In the ancient Near East, and later in Greece and Rome, the landed nobles were able to escape work by using slaves and serfs. By the time of the Middle Ages, social classes were sharply divided. The nobility had time to enjoy the pleasures of the day—hunting, fishing, tournaments, and entertaining guests—while the serfs worked the land, harvested the crops, and gave the lords a large part of the produce. The landed nobles formed the basis of court society and, along with the rich churchmen, made up the bulk of the leisure class down to the rise of the middle class.

**Rise of the middle class.** After 1500, a new leisure class arose, that of the wealthy merchants and manufacturers. As capitalism developed, the trend toward the separation of ownership from the control and management of business increased. Today, the most complete man of leisure is the capitalist who lives on the income from his investments, that is, by collecting dividends on stocks and clipping coupons on bonds. His money is handled for him by bankers or brokers; he takes little or no part himself in the actual conduct of business. He may have almost unbroken leisure, if his income is adequate.

**Balance sheet of leisure class activities in the past.** If we look at the accomplishments of the leisure classes of the past, we can understand what the extension of leisure time to all classes in modern society may mean. Men of leisure have been responsible for the development of much of human culture. The leisure class first established law and order on a large scale in the ancient Near East. Their needs, interests, and activities led to great engineering and architectural projects, all the way from the pyramids of Egypt to the roads and aqueducts of Rome and the cathedrals of the Middle Ages. The leisure classes also encouraged the arts; palaces, sculpture, painting, and poetry were produced for, and supported by, families of wealth and leisure. Of course, the actual work connected with these engineering, artistic, and literary achievements was carried on by men who had little leisure.

Although the wealthy leisure classes of the past made valuable contributions to culture, millions of persons paid an enormous price for these benefits by being forced to work as slaves, serfs, or "free" men under wretched and cruel conditions. Many did not fare as well as the better treated beasts of burden. The wealthy leisure class, by its control over political life, was also responsible for most war, graft, and incompetence.

**Activities of the leisure class today.** Under the modern capitalist system, the leisure classes have been able to amass fortunes greater than were ever known before and to become economically and socially powerful. Prestige came to be associated with the possession and parade of wealth. The desire of the wealthy to display their possessions, in order to prove that they had money to waste, led to what Thorstein Veblen called "conspicuous waste," and "honorific consumption."

This may take the form of expensive dress, sumptuous penthouses, yachts, motor cars, the wearing of precious stones, or elaborate and expensive entertainment. The height of conspicuous display seems to be the ability to refrain from any type of manual labor. A wide gulf or "social distance" is thus created between the wealthy and the laboring masses, who live a hand-to-mouth existence.

Although men of wealth have made contributions to the cultural heritage of our age, it is doubtful if, with such notable exceptions as Andrew Carnegie, John D. Rockefeller, and Henry Ford, their contributions to culture and social welfare have been at all in proportion to their wealth. They have collected famous paintings and endowed art museums in which to place them; they have established libraries, universities, and scientific foundations; they have encouraged art, scholarship, and research. However, as we pointed out earlier (Chapter XV), many wealthy men become restrained benefactors and patrons of the arts and sciences chiefly to increase their prestige and to justify their possession of great wealth, as well as to create a basis for propaganda against government efforts to tax or limit wealth and its inheritance. For the most part, even those who have contributed most notably to science, education, and the arts have given but a small portion of their fortunes to such causes.

**The problem of leisure in the Machine Age.** The appearance of modern machinery has worked a revolution in the history of leisure by increasing production, throwing thousands of persons out of work, and reducing the working hours of those remaining in industry. And the age of automatic machinery has as yet barely begun. It is probable that even more startling inventions will further increase the efficiency of production and make it unnecessary for any man to work more than fifteen or twenty hours each week to produce everything needed for a high standard of living. Work can be spread out among all the population, giving each a very short working day and assuring a large amount of leisure, at least to the majority of people in the most advanced countries, provided we put an end to devasting world wars.

This new leisure created by modern machine culture is as yet a mixed blessing. The city child, released from school in midafternoon on week days, and with long weekends and a three-month summer vacation, may use his leisure unwisely. He may join the gang that gathers on the street corner and plots petty thefts and other criminal activities. For the adult man and woman, poorly-spent leisure may bring misery and unhappiness. On the other hand, leisure may be a blessing, a chance to rest the mind and body and cultivate hobbies, artistic talents, social life, or sports.

Urban living conditions, especially, demand an increased amount of rest, for modern industry is marked by routine tasks that make for fatigue, and city life produces greater nervous tension. Though the hours of work are not as long as formerly, the work is more monotonous. Large numbers of workers are engaged in indoor occupations, in which they get little opportunity for physical exercise. Even trips to and from work provide no relaxation. Crowded buses, street cars, or subways, and traffic jams make for further nervous strain. In the city, the sensible use of leisure is thus vitally important to mental and physical health and rehabilitation.

## The Philosophy of Leisure

**Leisure, thrift, and craftsmanship.** Few persons criticized the leisure classes, as such, until the end of the Middle Ages, though some ancient Egyptian scribes and the Jewish social prophets did protest against the social injustice involved, and Aristophanes and Juvenal satirized leisure-class excesses. With the rise of Protestantism, however, hard work was glorified and leisure condemned. John Calvin and his followers, particularly, emphasized the virtues of thrift and labor, and considered idleness a leading sin. Calvinistic ideals were especially suitable to the pioneers who settled our country, for they justified the hard work that was required to conquer the land and push the frontier westward.

In the nineteenth century, the notion that hard work is virtuous was emphasized anew by writers like Thomas Carlyle, John Ruskin, William Morris, and others. They stressed the belief that all men should spend part of each day in manual labor and find pleasure in turning out a fine piece of work. But Ruskin and Morris were interested in promoting fine craftsmanship rather than in extolling mere drudgery. In our own age, many writers on leisure have adopted this view as a means of solving the problems of leisure rather than as a continued justification of hard work.

**Leisure for leisure's sake.** By itself, hard work is surely no virtue. Productive labor can furnish us with only the material basis for living. The less time we give to making a living, the more time we have for the things that make life truly worth while. Mr. Lawrence Conrad, in an article, "Leisure for Its Own Sweet Sake," emphasized this point of view. He pointed out that, for thousands of years, people have longed for freedom from toil and a chance to indulge in some idleness. But, just as we are now ready to profit by the toil of our ancestors and enjoy the leisure we have earned, there arise those who say that we shall be "ruined" unless our use of leisure is "worthy." Mr. Conrad believes that this attitude is spoiling the enjoyment of our newly gained freedom from drudgery. His view is at the opposite extreme from that of the Calvinists, namely, that idleness is a sin and hard work a virtue. Mr. Conrad's views illustrate the change of attitude toward leisure which has arisen in the present century. Although we may not follow either Calvin or Conrad, the problem of leisure must be faced intelligently; for, unless we work out plans which bring the uses of leisure into harmony with the nature and needs of man, the collapse of our culture is likely to follow.

**Allport's theory of leisure.** One interesting attitude toward the problem of leisure, called the biological theory, was put forth by Professor Floyd H. Allport, in an article, "This Coming Era of Leisure." Professor Allport believes that work and play cannot be separated. Leisure should not mean freedom from work but rather making work pleasant and easy. If monotony, strain, and fear of accidents and occupational diseases were removed from work, people would enjoy working and would not try to shirk it. In short, according to Allport, any rational use of leisure time must be associated with pleasant and productive work.

**Fairchild's ideas of leisure.** At the opposite extreme from the biological theory is that expounded by Professor Henry Pratt Fairchild, in an article, "Exit the Gospel of Work." According to Professor Fairchild, work is a necessary evil to provide mankind with the means of existence, but it is a social and cultural nuisance that should be removed, so far as possible, by the use of machines. Professor Fairchild calls attention to the tremendous change in our attitude toward work in the last fifty years as a result of mechanical inventions. Formerly, society needed the full output of the productive energy of all its members just to exist. Famine and starvation were never far away. But, today, machines have so increased productivity that, if all our efforts were expended on production, there would be more goods than we could use. Fairchild believes that we must learn how to consume, as well as to produce, and that adequate consumption is the only justification of production.

In other words, work is justifiable only if it enables men to secure the things needed to make life worth while. Leisure time, spent in ways that contribute to the development of the personality and enrich life, is the most worthy goal of man. If Fairchild's philosophy of leisure were adopted, it would mean that all socially unnecessary work would be tabooed by the folkways of the group. Instead of considering hard labor a virtue, man would spend his time creating beautiful and useful things with which to enjoy a truly human civilization.

A compromise between Allport's and Fairchild's extreme viewpoints has been suggested by Dr. L. P. Jacks in an article on "Today's Unemployment and Tomorrow's Leisure." Dr. Jacks contends that man wants to know how to do things well and demands a certain amount of leisure for creative activity to satisfy this yearning. If our solution of the problem of leisure is to be successful, it must fully satisfy the basic human drive for creative activity.

The chief sociological authority on leisure, Professor George A. Lundberg, contends that the study and guidance of leisure-time activities has now become one of the chief problems to be dealt with by sociology and the social sciences.

## Leisure and Recreation

**Theories of the social significance of play.** During the nineteenth century, various writers and educators discussed the theory and function of play. Professor Edward S. Robinson has summarized their theories. The sociologist Herbert Spencer held that play is a form of spontaneous activity necessary to get rid of surplus nervous energy. He also suggested that imitation plays an important rôle in play, a point of view more fully developed by the French writer, Gabriel Tarde. The psychologist Moritz Lazarus suggested a sound theory, since widely accepted, that play provides a means of recovering from overactivity and fatigue and is truly "recreative" because it is more stimulating than inactivity.

Another psychologist, Karl Groos, held that play is a basic preparation for adult life; in play the child's natural instincts are gradually socialized and brought into accord with life in the group in which he lives. Miss Lilla Appleton, who studied play among both savages and civilized men, maintained that play has a definite physical basis and that the stages and types of play are associated with the bodily changes that occur during growth. G. Stanley Hall, the genetic psychologist, looked upon play as a carry-over from primitive types of motor habits and mental traits. In play, we relive our savage ancestral activities.

There have been other theories of play, such as those of Alexander Shand, who held that play is carried on to express the emotion of joy; of William McDougall, who contended that play is produced by the instinct of rivalry, which makes one strive to surpass others; and, finally, of Alfred Adler, the psychiatrist, who held that play is a way of making up for physical and mental inadequacy and of overcoming our inferiority complexes.

Socializing influence of play. Each of these theories makes a valuable contribution to a complete and well-rounded interpretation of the place and function of play in society. Play is socializing. It teaches the individual how to adapt himself to the group. Not only rivalry but the conception of fair play is developed in carrying on games and sports. Educators have laid great stress on play as a means of preparing children for the responsibilities of adult life. Since children show far more enthusiasm for play than for work in the classroom, educators have tried to devise new types of educational procedure to make the child as enthusiastic about learning as he is about play. The progressive education movement has tried to introduce into the classroom the idea that learning can be, to a limited extent, a form of playful activity.

All persons recognize that play is healthful from both a physical and a mental standpoint. Special types of exercise will build up weak physiques and correct physical deficiencies. Students of mental hygiene recognize that play is valuable in treating some mental and nervous disorders. Today, more than ever before, play occupies an important place in educational theory and mental hygiene.

## Recreation in the Twentieth Century

Recent innovations in recreation. The development of recreation since the turn of the twentieth century has been more striking and revolutionary than in any other period. The chief trends have been the tremendous growth of spectator sports and games, the inclusion of recreation as a phase of social planning, the promotion of many games and sports by private enterprise, and the growth of great commercialized public spectacles.

Changes in living conditions, the rise of large cities, the advances in motor transportation, the increasing freedom of women, the relaxation of religious objections to recreation, and many other factors have brought about an expansion of recreational interests, activities, and facilities.

New inventions and games have done much to change recreation in the twentieth century. Sports, which formerly were diversions enjoyed by the few who had money and leisure, have been commercialized on a vast scale, and new forms of amusement, such as the moving-picture, radio, and television, have appeared.

The automobile and trailer have put the nation on wheels. Travel, camping, hunting, and fishing have become increasingly popular. The interest of the public in golf and tennis has increased, although golf, because of the expense attached to it, does not have as much popular appeal as tennis. Bowling and roller-skating have become increasingly popular.

**Increase of public recreation areas.** The increased interest in recreation in the twentieth century is shown by the expansion of public facilities for play, both in the country and city. The automobile made relatively distant recreation facilities accessible. National parks, with facilities for campers and travelers, have been opened up; in 1946, they comprised some 22 million acreas and drew 22 million visitors, one for every acre. Our national forests, which now include about 207 million acres and contain extensive recreational facilities, were visited by about 20 million persons in 1947. There are also many state, county, and municipal parks and forests.

**Travel and camping.** No phase of recreation has been more completely revolutionized than travel, owing to the enormous expansion of the automobile industry, the development of low-priced cars, and the building of good roads. In 1941, the peak year thus far, there were 547 billion passenger miles of automobile travel, as compared with 29 billion passenger miles for all railroad travel. Automobile tours have become universally popular; the American Automobile Association estimated that, even as early as 1929, about 45 million persons took vacation trips by automobile. Even more important than vacation tours from the point of view of leisure are the short automobile rides taken within or near the community on holidays or during the workers' spare time. The automobile has popularized other forms of recreation. A man can get in his car and go to the movies or golf links, hunt, fish, or visit friends or neighbors.

Outdoor camping has become an important form of recreation since the automobile has made it easy to go from one place to another in a short time. The American Camping Association has raised the standards of public camping grounds, and the Federal government, through WPA and CCC projects, has increased camping facilities. One of the most popular means of camping is the trailer; trailer camps have been built in nearly every state, especially in resort areas like Florida and California. Many people rent space for their trailer and automobile, and spend the winter in them.

The progressive railroad genius Robert R. Young predicts that railroads in the future will adapt their equipment and facilities to exploit this increased vacationing tendency; he believes that vacation trains or "traveling hotels" will become common in the future. These trains will take vacationing Americans on tours to the Grand Canyon, Yellowstone Park, and other famous spots. Clean and comfortable, and equipped with all conveniences, they will be a far cry from the old "excursion trains" of the past.

Motoring and camping in our national parks—A scene in the Colorado Rockies.

**Federal aid to recreational projects.** The Federal government has taken an extended interest in public recreation since 1933 and has given much aid to community recreation projects.[1] It is estimated that, by 1938, the emergency relief agencies of the Federal government, including the CCC, the National Youth Administration, the Works Progress Administration, and the Farm Security Administration, had spent one billion dollars for recreational and quasi-recreational pur-

---

[1] For a detailed discussion of community recreation developments and problems, see pp. 683–686.

poses.   Camps, swimming pools, picnic grounds, and trails were among the facilities provided for public comfort and relaxation.

One of the most important Federal agencies promoting recreation is the National Park Service.   In addition to administering the national parks, the Service acquired some 400,000 acres of submarginal land and, in conjunction with the CCC, developed recreation demonstration centers in some 24 states.   Between 1936 and 1941 it conducted a nationwide survey of the recreational facilities and needs of the states and the nation and published the results in 1941 in *A Study of the Park and Recreation Problem of the United States.*   The Forest Service of the Department of Agriculture administers and directs the recreational activities in the national forests; the U.S. Office of Education gives out much information on national recreational facilities; the Fish and Wildlife Service aids sportsmen; and the Bureau of Reclamation plans recreational facilities in its projects.

**Spectator sports: Baseball, boxing, and racing.**   While many men, women, and children enjoy playing their own games, others are content to watch professional or amateur sports.   One of the outstanding developments in American recreation in the twentieth century has been the extensive commercialization of spectator sports.   Millions attend baseball, football, hockey, and basketball games; boxing, wrestling, and professional tennis matches; and horse, auto, and dog races. Many more millions enjoy reading about them in the daily papers, listening to play-by-play accounts over the radio, or following the games on television.   At a conservative estimate, Americans spend between four and five billion dollars a year on various forms of commercialized recreation.

Some 20,972,601 persons attended major league baseball games in 1948, and a record 389,763 persons paid $2,137,549 to see the 1947 World Series.   The largest attendance at a single baseball game was on October 10, 1948, when 86,288 fans saw the World Series' game between Cleveland and Boston at Municipal Stadium, Cleveland.   The gate receipts for the game were $378,778.

Boxing matches, particularly in the heavyweight class, have produced greater attendance and larger receipts than any other commercialized sporting spectacle.   On occasion, boxing fans have spent over a million dollars to see a single fight; the Dempsey-Tunney fight at Chicago in September, 1927, set a record of $2,650,000 that remains the all-time high for boxing receipts.

Despite efforts to curb race-track gambling, horse racing has become an important commercial sport.   Large sums of money running into billions of dollars are won and lost each year in gambling on horse races.   It is estimated that nearly six billion dollars were bet on horse races in 1949.

**Intercollegiate and professional football.**   Football, both intercollegiate and professional, has become a big business since the first world war.   In 1948, there was a total attendance of 13,051,248 at the games played by 99 leading college and university teams. Since there are 1,800 institutions of higher learning, it would be reasonable to assume that the total attendance at intercollegiate football games in 1948 was in excess of 25 million, and that total gate receipts approached 100 million dollars. The Bowl games alone, during the holiday season of

*Thomas Airviews.*

The Yankee Stadium in New York City is one of the great professional baseball grounds of the United States.

1948–1949, were played before 600,000 spectators and drew gate receipts of two million dollars. Professional football has grown by leaps and bounds in the last decade. In the season of 1948, the teams of the National Football League played before 1,639,858 spectators, and the teams of the All-America Football Conference before 1,638,625.

## Leisure and the Arts in the United States

Art as a leisure activity. Leisure-time activities are not limited to recreation; ample attention should be given to the arts as well. The latter include the skilled crafts, architecture, painting, sculpture, music, and the like. The arts make a greater appeal to the creative aspects of man's nature than do play and sports.

Early American art. That the American people are not gifted artistically passes as a truism, and it must be admitted that the masses of our people have remained relatively indifferent to the creation of objects of beauty. The Indian, the Negro, and certain European immigrant groups have probably displayed more spontaneity and originality in art than other elements within the United States.

The fact that art has not flourished among the American masses does not mean that we have not had artists capable of understanding and adapting to our conditions the best that Europe has offered. The achievements of the American colonies, under strong English and

Dutch influence, in the fields of architecture, interior decoration, and painting were of a high order and constitute a just basis for national pride.

The artistic impulses rooted in colonial life and the European background bore some fruit in our early national period. Thomas Jefferson was greatly interested in classical and Renaissance art and did much to introduce it to this country. Notable examples were his plans for the library at the University of Virginia and the state capitol at Richmond. The European city-planning concept was brought over early, when Major Charles Pierre l'Enfant was invited to lay out the new capital city of Washington. Classical architecture was popularized by Benjamin Latrobe, once described as the man who brought the Parthenon to America in his "grip-sack." The Treasury building in Washington is a good example of this tradition. In the next generation, Charles Bulfinch, sometimes called the Sir Christopher Wren of America, adapted Renaissance styles to American tastes in such buildings as the state capitol at Boston.

**Eclipse of American art.** There, however, American art seemed to halt, and during our entire middle period, extending, roughly speaking, from the second war with England (1812) to about 1880, our aesthetic life went through a long eclipse. Not only did the United States fail to contribute to the world stream of the fine arts, but the life of our people on its artistic side was marked by appalling mediocrity. Our cities, generally speaking, were paragons of ugliness, and anything like creative painting, sculpture, and architecture almost ceased to exist. For this blight, the political revulsion against all English and European traditions that accompanied the Revolution and the War of 1812 was unquestionably partly responsible, but it must not be forgotten that during this time Europe itself had less than it once had to offer in the field of the fine arts. Though France is an exception, the earlier part of the nineteenth century was everywhere a period of relative artistic sterility and ugliness.

The social and economic background of the middle period was in this field, as in so many others, the determining factor. This was the time when the new nation, largely cut off from Europe, was wrestling as it never had before with problems of material improvement, when the great westward movement was in full swing, and when our ideals were those of Jacksonian democracy, "the apotheosis of coarseness and vulgarity." Pioneers are often a great folk, but never has a nation dominated by pioneer ideals been creative along aesthetic lines.

It is surprising, however, that this very period, when American art was at so low an ebb, saw the beginnings of a literature upon which many have placed a high value. For this was the time of Emerson, Melville, Lowell, and Longfellow, of Whittier, Hawthorne, and Poe.

During the decades just after the Civil War rapid economic changes altered our whole background. The increasing use of machines in industry, by making possible a reduction in the hours of toil, gave more leisure to the masses for some interest in the arts. The immediate outcome was, however, something of an aesthetic tragedy.

The monstrosities perpetrated in architecture, design, painting, and sculpture have given to the years referred to as the "Era of President Grant" or the "Black Walnut Period" a reputation for ugliness which becomes only a shade more pardonable when considered in comparison with the worst products of the Mid-Victorian artistic collapse in England.

In the field of architecture the decades of the 1860's, 1870's and 1880's of the last century saw the sway in both public and domestic architecture of the Victorian Gothic, often in red brick, and that of forms supposedly based on the French and Italian. Love of profuse ornament prevailed, and jumbling of styles seemed to be regarded as almost a matter of course. The Philadelphia Centennial Exhibition of 1876 greatly stimulated interest in architecture, as in other lines of fine art, but it did not purify taste. This was the time when the ideal of the self-made millionaire was the "house with a cupola," a form which seems to have been taken over with strange variations from the Italian villa. It was the time, too, when New York and other cities saw the rise in their better sections of the long rows of aristocratic "brownstone fronts." In themselves, these were not without a certain dignity, but they condemned the cities to a distressing "sameness." A little later, domestic architecture came under English influence; this was the time of the Eastlake House with its marvelous jigsaw ornamentation, and the curious Queen Anne structures with their shell-covered roofs and useless colored windows.

Such a riot of grotesque architecture could only result from the acquisition of sudden wealth by a people combining aggressive character with an unformed taste. Yet, before we indict ourselves too abjectly for lack of artistic sense, it is fair to recall that, after only about three decades of the worst atrocities, we were at least on our way to better things.

**The artistic revival in the United States.** Though the methods employed in the United States since the "Black Walnut Period" to secure a more worthy art have sometimes suggested business efficiency rather than the upward cravings of the soul, they have certainly been successful in bringing about the creation of objects of artistic value. American art is still, to some extent, deficient in originality, its cult is still limited to the greater cities and the chief routes of transatlantic intercourse; but, if beauty is the end, then contemporary American art need not fear comparison with that of other nations. Though our people are slow to realize the high achievement of their own artists, it is but stating the truth to observe that American architecture, design, painting, and sculpture have now reached a high plane of excellence. America does not lead the world, but it is doubtful whether any people except the French can claim general cultural superiority to us. New

York and Washington are at present among the world's greatest art centers.

It is an interesting fact that the beginnings of the aesthetic movement in America coincide very closely with the arrival of large numbers of immigrants from continental Europe, and there can be little question that their influence has done much to alter the attitude of near suspicion felt by certain Puritan elements among our older population toward creative art. Unquestionably of greater influence, however, has been the closer relationship with Europe into which the United States has gradually been drawn as a result of improved means of communication and transportation. The "thought-mother" of America is no longer England alone, but all the great nations of the continent as well.

## Recent American Architecture

**The Chicago World's Fair.** In the 1890's progress in both artistic interest and achievement was rapid. An enormous influence was unquestionably exerted by the Chicago World's Fair of 1893, which served as a remarkable advertisement of the possibilities of the beautiful. Under the most capable direction of Daniel H. Burnham, a mobilization of gifted architects—Richard M. Hunt, Charles F. McKim, Stanford White, Louis Sullivan, and Charles B. Atwood—and leading interior decorators was effected which eventuated in a "White City," impressing indelibly even materialistic America. Though temporary in character, the buildings with their steel frames and "staff" screens produced the appearance of marble and were designed on a grand scale. A practice school was thus offered to our artists which proved of great utility in developing their genius. The value of order and arrangement in buildings was also so decisively demonstrated that the Fair proved to be the practical beginning in the United States of the movement for city planning. The general architectural lessons of the Chicago World's Fair were worthily continued in our later expositions.

**Main lines of development in recent American architecture.** Since 1900, architectural advances in the United States, in both public and domestic buildings, have been remarkable. The outstanding characteristic has been the successful adaptation of many historic architectural forms to modern situations. This has given to recent American architecture an eclecticism with an element of originality, and has largely freed our cities of the curse of monotony. Efforts worthy of note were made, especially by the talented architect Louis Sullivan, to disregard the past and evolve along purely original lines, combining functional utility with beauty. Though Sullivan achieved very striking and commendable results, he did not succeed in instilling equal daring into many other architects. At least he did not until the appearance of the contemporary movement that seeks to substitute pure efficiency in the form of cages of steel, cement, and glass for the historic architectural forms. It was, however, a disciple of Sullivan, Frank Lloyd Wright, who became the most original architectural genius of the twentieth century, combining in his work a sense of functional utility, the fitness of a building to its general surroundings, and the experimental opportunities in form provided by new building materials. Eliel Saarinen has, perhaps, been even more influential than Wright in promoting modernism in our skyscraper architecture.

Through the achievements of Wright and others, the increase of cosmopolitan influence among our citizens, and the teaching of well-equipped schools of architecture in our universities, a deep impression has at last been made upon the urban public. Though most of our cities, with the exception of Washington, New York, Boston, New Orleans, and San Francisco, still suggest a machine-made sameness, they are no longer without numerous admirable structures and attractive streets.

**The American skyscraper.** The crowning achievement of recent American architecture is, of course, the skyscraper. However much some have tried to belittle skyscrapers for their appeal of mere "giantism" and their suggestions of big business, their purely aesthetic claims cannot be successfully denied. Moreover, these remarkable structures have given to the sky lines of our cities fantastic and wonderful outlines that impress even the most blasé Europeans. The skyscraper is the result of the introduction of steel construction, which enabled engineers and architects to surpass the old limit of six or eight stories and to set up structures of sixty or seventy—102 in the case of the Empire State Building. The skyscrapers, great cages of steel, are both safer and lighter than their more conservative rivals.

The earlier skyscrapers were ugly in the extreme—usually bare, rectangular boxes, but possibilities of improvement existed in the fact that the walls instead of being supports were mere screens. Thus windows could be enlarged to any extent without endangering the structure, and when gifted architects seriously applied themselves to the problem, they saw how ornament of historic form could be adjusted even to this new type of building. The zoning limitations, later imposed by most cities, requiring the tapering of the higher stories. actually aided the artistic result. Such buildings as the Singer and Woolworth Buildings, the Metropolitan Tower, and the Bush Terminal in New York, and the Chicago Tribune Building in Chicago were remarkable early products of improved skyscraper art. Later achievements, even more impressive in the mass, have been the New York Telephone Company Building, the Chrysler Building, the Empire State Building, the Bank of Manhattan Building, and Rockefeller Center. Though various styles are combined in such work, the Gothic and Renaissance have given the most successful results.

**Public buildings, churches, and memorials.** Although the achievement of the skyscraper is unique and largely original, the United States has now produced many admirable public buildings of other types.

The absurd ugliness of our railway stations has now given way before such triumphs as the Pennsylvania Station and the Grand Central Station in New York and the Union Stations in Washington, Kansas City, and Cincinnati. Much successful work has been done in libraries and churches, though it must be admitted that, on the whole, ecclesiastical

*Courtesy of Wide World Photos, Inc.*

New United Nations Building on East River in New York City. A good example of modern urban architecture.

building has not kept pace with that destined for trade. There has been, however, a remarkable revival of ecclesiastical Gothic by Ralph Adams Cram, and the uncompleted Cathedral of St. John the Divine in New York and the National Cathedral in Washington give promise for the future. Wright and Saarinen have designed church structures as modernistic as any public building or art museum. On the other hand, as if by common consent, the form of the Greek temple has been everywhere adopted for bank buildings with excellent results. Among national monuments, perhaps the most notable are the Lincoln Memorial in Washington, designed by Henry Bacon, the National Masonic Memorial at Alexandria, Virginia, and the Jefferson Memorial in Washington. As a result of the enormous sums recently lavished upon educational building, some striking results have been secured, as in the Harkness Dormitory at Yale, the Harvard residence halls, Willard

Straight Hall at Cornell, the buildings of the University of Chicago, and the Law Courts at the University of Michigan and Cornell University. Elsewhere in this field the disposition to copy English examples has been rather slavish.

**Frank Lloyd Wright and domestic architecture.** In domestic architecture, the effects of the American Renaissance are very marked, but our success has still been achieved mainly within the limits of styles approved by historic use. Remarkable results have been attained in apartment houses through the use of Italian Renaissance motifs. In our larger cities, the styles of the Italian Renaissance, of the various French periods, of English and Colonial Georgian, and even of Spanish colonial, have been employed with success, while in country residences American colonial style in numerous variations has returned to its own. Everywhere appears an eclecticism that advertises the cosmopolitan spirit of the new America.

The most revolutionary force in American domestic architecture has been the original genius of Frank Lloyd Wright, who has made much use of glass and steel, has departed from conventional forms, and has sought to fit each house to its peculiar environment and needs. Wright condemned traditional house architecture as no more than a box containing smaller boxes. As he put it: "We can never make the living room large enough, the fireplace important enough, or the sense of the relationship between exterior, interior, and environment close enough." In short, American architecture has emphatically arrived. The forces of ugliness in building have been exposed and their doom is sealed. One question that has been raised, whether the new architecture is indeed "American," is of little moment, so long as the product is beautiful.

## American Painting.

**American painting before the artistic revival.** The story of painting in contemporary America is strikingly similar to that of architecture. After the encouraging beginnings of the Colonial and early National periods, in the work of men like John Singleton Copley, John Trumbull, Benjamin West, Gilbert Stuart, and Charles Wilson Peale, American painting went into the long night of the middle period. In general, cut off from the art traditions of Europe, our painters showed little power. Then, worst of all, as the period of the 1860's and 1870's approached, their work became more and more pretentious, and so more and more ugly, until it reached its climax in those "views" of nature's monstrosities in mountain, volcano, and glacier which make up the product of the "Rocky Mountain School." It was a fit accompaniment to the houses, statues, and interior decoration of the "Black Walnut Era." The best American painting of the middle period was done by the Hudson River School of landscape artists. They established the cult of American landscape painting and, in the work of their best exponent, Asher B. Durand, reached a level of undeniable merit.

**American supremacy in landscape painting.** The new cosmopolitan forces of the 1880's and 1890's helped to retrieve the situation in painting, as in architecture. Indeed, evidences of dawn appear much earlier. Among Americans trained abroad in Paris and Munich, under the influences of the awakening art of continental Europe during the middle decades of the century, were the New Englander William Morris Hunt, brother of the architect, and the Kentuckian, Frank Duveneck. Upon their return, both carried on a notable work of education, though rather by their personal influence and their teaching of technique than by any unusual power in their own painting.

Meanwhile, a group of American artists, possessed of notable talent and influenced, though not formed, by European example, had begun to produce an art far superior to anything this country had seen since the days of Stuart. It was, however, in landscape painting, a field which for some unexplained reason has appealed to American painters beyond all others, that this development took place. Most prominent among these painters were George Inness, Alexander H. Wyant, Ralph A. Blakelock, and Winslow Homer; the last, who devoted himself to the painting of powerfully realistic New England sea scenes, has been called the most distinctly American of all our painters.

Following these really gifted artists, American landscape painting has maintained and does maintain an unusually high level. Since the day of Inness and Homer, literally dozens of Americans have produced admirable paintings that show deep appreciation of nature as we know it. It is doubtful whether any European nation during recent years has produced work in this field which even approaches our own. Yet, as usual, though the general standing is high, the United States has lacked men of towering genius and originality; it is the uniformly high order of the product rather than especial work of inspiration which is remarkable.

**American portrait painting.** In lines other than landscape, American painting was not, until recent decades, particularly commendable —that is, if we except the work of the two great expatriates, J. A. McNeill Whistler (1834–1903) and John Singer Sargent (1856–1925). Whistler, though of native American stock and of American birth, was driven from our shores by the dearth of art tradition and preferred to practice in London. Sargent was probably the most notable portrait painter of the early twentieth century; he too, was of American stock and proud of his American citizenship, but his training was European and nearly all his life was spent abroad. Neither Whistler nor Sargent can in fairness be regarded as a representative of America.

Although modern schools, particularly those headed by Grant Wood and Thomas H. Benton, have done some excellent portrait work, nevertheless American painters have, on the whole, been more successful in interpreting mountain and forest than in depicting human beings.

Outside the field of landscape and portrait painting, perhaps the only American artists to rank with Innes and Homer were Thomas Eakins and Albert P. Ryder, whose realistic pictures were more or less unique in encouraging those who looked at them to ponder their meaning and the emotions of the persons and scenes depicted.

**Modern art and illustration.** In certain more specialized lines there appear names which cannot be omitted from the barest sketch of recent American art. John La Farge, noteworthy as a painter, stands out as artist, designer, and craftsman in stained and painted glass. Great progress has been made in mural decoration, though the most notable work done in this country was probably that of the Frenchman Puvis de Chavannes, and the Mexicans Diego Rivera and Jose Clemente Orozco. The most widely-known frescoes are those in the Library of Congress, in the Boston Public Library, in Rockefeller Center, and in various college buildings. The interest of the public in this form of art has been awakened and much really beautiful work is being done.

The United States, of course, felt the influence of the revolutionary ideas of cubism, post-impressionism, and futurism. To the public much of this new art has seemed to be a hoax, yet by bold experimentation the disciples of the recent cults have forced upon their more conservative contemporaries a reaction which has been highly beneficial in more daring use of color, and greater emphasis in fundamentals, as distinct from details. Nowhere, however, is the increasing conservatism of American thought brought out better than by the fact that futurism has not had the vogue here that its strange gyrations have enjoyed in Europe.

In the field of illustration, so closely related to painting, recent America has done exceptionally well. The American public had been prepared for an interest in illustration on a mass scale by the vastly popular commercialized illustrations in the Currier and Ives prints. Possibly the more recent suggestion of the mechanical craft and advertising power involved have increased public interest. At any rate, John La Farge and Edwin Abbey showed the way to new levels of excellence. Frederic Remington, depictor of the western frontier, and Charles Dana Gibson, blasé interpreter of social life of the *fin de siecle* period, gave us work which will live because of its historic, if not its aesthetic, value. Admirable illustration appeared in the work of such men as Norman Rockwell, Howard Pyle, Maxfield Parrish, Jessie Wilcox Smith, Willy Pogany, and many more. American illustrators are more widely known than contemporary painters because of the circulation given their work by national magazines.

**Interior decoration.** Among the fine arts, that of design, including interior decoration, is, from some points of view, most vital, because it concerns itself most directly with the lives of the people and doubtless makes the deepest impression upon them. Of this very complicated field it is difficult to speak intelligently without much technical knowledge, but even to the layman it is apparent that enormous changes have taken place since 1876. In interior decoration, for example, the "Black Walnut Period" gave us rooms crammed with furniture and *objets d'art,* with what-nots, plaques, festooned tennis nets, and even the ever-present pug dog. This chaos has long since been replaced by simplicity and balance, based upon intelligent study of aesthetics. There has also appeared a strong trend back to our own older and simpler colonial traditions, to old furniture, to old ornamentation—back to the art of Duncan Phyfe. On the other hand, the newer trends of thought toward fuller and more individualistic self-expression have led, over the ruins of Puritanism, to a delight in bright color, modernistic furniture, and other freedom from convention which would have been held in the "immaculate" era of President Grant to be the height of vulgarity.

## American Sculpture

**Drabness of early American sculpture.** There were but three American sculptors of any note before the Civil War, Hiram Powers, Horatio Greenough, and William W. Story. They were influenced by Greek models, in the main; Powers' "Greek Slave" is one of the earliest examples of fine American sculpture.

As might have been expected, however, the period just after the Civil War reached the nadir, and its dip down was the more disastrous because this was the time when the nation was engaged in erecting great numbers of war memorials and monuments. It is impossible to regard the vast majority of these statues as art; only John Q. A. Ward among these sculptors is worthy of wide recognition. This was the time, too, when the much loved "Rogers Group" carried a love of bad art into thousands of middle-class homes.

**The genius of Saint-Gaudens.** Then, expressing himself first in the 1880's, came our great master, Augustus Saint-Gaudens (1848–1907). Saint-Gaudens, though born in Dublin of French-Irish parentage, was brought to America as an infant, passed his youth in New York, and received his first art training in Cooper Union. A product of that newer cosmopolitan America that has been so variously judged, Saint-Gaudens was the pre-eminent genius of recent American sculpture. Some of the greatest products of sculpture in North America, all bronzes, are his—the unequaled "Grief" in Rock Creek Cemetery, Washington, the Shaw Memorial in Boston, the statue of Abraham Lincoln in Lincoln Park, Chicago, and that of General Sherman in Central Park, New York.

**Other leading American sculptors.** To Saint-Gaudens there is among American sculptors indeed no second. Nevertheless, since the arrival of the artistic renaissance in this country, many able artists in stone and bronze have maintained a high standard. The New Eng-

land sculptor, Daniel Chester French, a most prolific artist in spite of
the unevenness of his work, has achieved notable success in some instances. His most famous work is the "Minute Man" at Concord,
Massachusetts. Frederick Mac-
Monnies, pre-eminent for "sheer
dexterity of manipulation," is
remembered for his striking results at the 1893 World's Fair
in Chicago and his remarkable
"Horse Tamers" at the entrance
to Prospect Park, in his native
Brooklyn. Gutzon Borglum has
gained immortality by his execution of the colossal presidential
heads on a mountain face in the
Black Hills. This group combines the most ambitious sculp-
tural project of all history with
execution through modern mechanical facilities, including
blasting with dynamite. George
Grey Barnard introduced into
American sculpture the style and
tradition of Rodin. The Swed-
ish-American sculptor, Carl
Milles, is famed for his strong
and original work with fountain

*Courtesy of Ewing Galloway.*

Augustus St. Gaudens' noted Adams Memorial
statue in Rock Creek Park, Washington, D. C.
(1891). Often referred to as "Grief."

groups, a field in which Lorado Taft also became justly famous. Our
contemporary sculptors, especially Paul Manship and Jacob Epstein,
are particularly adept in the molding of smaller realistic and half-
playful bronze work.

## Latest Trends in American Art

**New economic influences.** The economic and social conditions of
the twentieth century had important reactions on art. The graphic
arts were extended by the remarkable developments of advertising.
Whatever the ethical and economic limitations of advertising, there is
no doubt that it contributed to art, especially in bringing advertising
art before a large public. The growth of parks and the development
of city planning gave a notable impulse to landscaping. Great business structures were more beautifully built and more completely and
artistically decorated. Interior decoration was greatly improved, more
attention being paid to the entire house, even kitchens and bathrooms,
and simplicity and beauty of line were stressed. Modernistic interiors
and furniture enlivened city apartments.

**Art collections and art museums.** Meanwhile, public appreciation of fine arts has been powerfully aided by the development in our larger cities of worthy art collections. It is not to be expected that, for collecting the treasures of the past, our museums will equal those of Europe, but much progress has been made. At the time of the Philadelphia Centennial in 1876 there was hardly a collection of fine art in the United States worthy of mention. At the present time, the Metropolitan Museum and the Museum of Modern Art in New York have grown into noteworthy institutions, even when judged by European standards. The museums of Boston, Brooklyn, Chicago, Philadelphia, and Cincinnati and the Freer Collection in the Corcoran Gallery in Washington contain no small number of treasures. The new National Gallery of Art in Washington, to which the Mellon art treasures were donated, may ultimately dominate the museum scene in this country. A most encouraging feature is the appearance of interesting collections in many cities of smaller size.

The 14 largest art museums have a plant investment of over 40 million dollars, and it has been estimated that the art objects in museums and private collections in this country have a reasonable sale value of over two billion dollars. While art museums may still be a bit stuffy and formal, nevertheless great progress has been made in opening them to public view, in encouraging mass patronage, and in making their treasures more accessible to students of art.

**Better art education.** Much better and more extensive facilities have been provided for art education. Art education in the public schools has become more adequate and comprehensive, and art has been rescued from the stigma of effeminacy. As early as 1928, some 5,000 high schools had an enrollment of over a million pupils in art subjects.

The fine arts in America in the past have not been nourished by a favorable environment. We may safely predict that the future will tell a different story, especially since, because of foreign persecutions, the importation of European art and artists increased rapidly after 1933. In 1948, many of the great masterpieces from German art museums were brought to the United States and exhibited to thousands before being returned to Germany. Not the frontier, but the cultural traditions of the older world, including the Orient, as well as our native industrial civilization, will be the dominating influences in the years to come.

## Music in the United States

**Origins of American music.** While the United States produced no notable composers until around the middle of the nineteenth century, a considerable interest developed in music early in the century. The Handel and Haydn Society was founded in Boston in 1815 and soon became one of the world's great choral societies. The Musical

Fund Society was established in Philadelphia in 1820.  The first grand opera was performed in New York City in 1825 and an opera house was built there in 1833.  The New York Philharmonic Society was created in 1842.  The Boston Academy of Music came into being in 1833, and music instruction was introduced in the Boston Public Schools in 1835.  The German element, which came to the country in large numbers after 1830, stimulated interest in choral singing, opera, and orchestra music.  A hearty welcome was shown to such great foreign artists as the singers Jenny Lind and Adelina Patti and the violinist Ole Bull.  Around the time of the Civil War there appeared the work of our first great American composer, Stephen Collins Foster (1826–1864), known for his immortal Negro and other folk songs.

**Recent trends in American music.**  In the last half of the century there were notable developments in music.  The New York Philharmonic Society engaged its first conductor in 1866, and in 1877 came under the distinguished leadership of Theodore Thomas.  He brought in the best European music.  In 1878, Leopold Damrosch founded the New York Symphony Society, and soon thereafter most of the large American cities established symphony or orchestral societies, one of the most famous being the Boston Symphony Orchestra.  The Metropolitan Opera House was opened in New York City in 1883.  Not only grand opera, but also light and comic opera, especially that of Gilbert and Sullivan, were enthusiastically received in this country.  American composers of note, such as Edward McDowell, John K. Paine, and Horatio Parker, produced works of real merit.  The phonograph, which appeared at the turn of the century, increased popular interest in music, if it did not elevate the level of musical appreciation.  A number of worthy schools of music and musical conservatories were established, among them the New England Conservatory in Boston and the Juilliard school in New York.  The National Federation of Musical Clubs, created in 1898, provided unity and organization for the promotion of musical interest on a national scale.

In the twentieth century both grand and light opera have flourished.  The Chicago Civic Opera, of which the chief financial supporter was Samuel Insull, came to rival the Metropolitan in New York.  Victor Herbert and Reginald DeKoven ranked as the master composers of light opera.  Orchestral music grew in interest and distinction under such conductors as Karl Muck, Walter Damrosch, Sergei Koussevitzky, and Arturo Toscanini.  The great summer Berkshire music festival at Tanglewood in Massachusetts has attracted thousands.  Beginning in the late 'twenties, the best orchestral and operatic music began to be put before the masses through the radio.  Band music was popularized by John Philip Sousa's Marine Band.  Jazz, along with Negro folk songs, the unique American contribution to music, was produced and promoted by George Gershwin, Irving Berlin, Paul Whiteman, and others.  Musical comedy attained lyric distinction in the productions of Cole Porter and Jerome Kern.  The radio became the greatest instrument ever known for the popular dissemination of all kinds of music. Musical instruction became more widespread, especially in the public schools.

Until recently, Americans made few original or distinctive contributions to music, but twentieth-century American composers, musicians, and vocal artists rival or surpass the best in Europe.

## Recent Leisure-Time Projects

**The leisure-time projects of the New Deal.** The new approach to the problem of leisure can best be illustrated by a brief survey of the leisure-time projects sponsored by the Works Progress Administration of the New Deal. We have seen how the government has made possible the extension of many recreational activities by providing parks, playgrounds, swimming pools, good roads, and camping facilities. Under the New Deal, a program for enriching the leisure time of the American people was undertaken through the auspices of various emergency government agencies. We have already referred to the government contributions to recreation through such agencies as the PWA, the WPA, and the CCC.

Four WPA projects were outstanding, not only because they gave considerable employment during the depression, but because they offered many persons a chance to enlarge and develop their own creative abilities. These projects were the Federal Theatre, the Federal Art Project, the Federal Music Project, and the Federal Writers' Project.

**The Federal Theatre Project.** Between February 1, 1936 and July 1, 1939, the Federal Theatre Project played to more than 30 million persons, with an average of 65 per cent free admissions. At the peak of its activity in May, 1936, it employed more than 12,000 persons. From the leisure-time point of view, the enthusiasm and interest of the public were all-important. For example, in Valley, Nebraska, which has a population of only 1,000, over 800 people attended a performance by the Theatre Project. They came from miles around in wagons, old cars, and on foot. The admission fee was 35 cents, but those who could not afford to pay were admitted free. The enthusiasm of rural communities like Valley was matched by many villages, towns, and cities where Federal Theatre performances were given. In New York City, Federal Theatre actors played each week to audiences totaling between 25,000 and 34,000. Over 14,000 children attended a single circus performance.

One of the most interesting of the Project's undertakings was the series of "Living Newspapers" which dramatized vital, timely subjects, interspersing excellent social criticism with lively satire. Such plays as "Power," "Injunction Granted," "Triple A Plowed Under," and "One-Third of a Nation" were instant hits. The last was a highly skillful dramatization of the deplorable housing situation in urban

America; the first an effective indictment of the private utility companies and their efforts to balk the Federal government's power program. The Federal Theatre Project was abandoned by act of Congress on July 1, 1939.

**The Federal Art Project.** The Federal Art Project employed as many as 5,500 persons at one time, mostly men and women of proved ability, and gave tremendous impetus to the appreciation and creation of art in the United States. The works of its artists—murals, prints, easel paintings, and sculpture—were placed in numerous public buildings throughout the country, and attracted much favorable attention. The Project made notable strides in teaching art to children and adults in populous cities as well as isolated communities. In New York City over 30,000 children attended its modeling classes.

*Courtesy N.Y.C. W.P.A., Art Project.*

Government-supported art for the masses: "Normal Pursuits of Man," a mural by W.P.A. artists at Bellevue Hospital.

Through the Federal Art Project, thousands of persons were enabled to participate personally in the arts and crafts. Civic Art Centers were established with the help of the WPA in many communities; the Cleveland Art Center was an excellent example. The building and instructors were furnished by the WPA. Here, people who could not afford to pay for instruction in art might spend their time profitably. Classes were available in landscape painting, wood carving, modeling, raffia work, and portrait painting. Men, women, and children of all nationalities and color were welcome. Those who could paid a nominal sum for materials; the others received materials free.

The possibilities of art in promoting sane living have long been recognized, but the Federal Art Project made them even more apparent. Today, in many hospitals throughout the country, instruction in sculpture and painting has proved useful in the treatment of mental cases.

**The Federal Music Project.** The Federal Music Project gave attention to both performance and teaching. Good orchestras and chamber music groups were developed in many cities, and famous conductors and virtuosi were hired to conduct or accompany them. The Federal Music Project became an important part of the musical life of every community to which its activities were extended. Even opera troupes were formed. The Project also recorded folk music and stimulated creative work, including in its repertoire new music of native composers like Roy Harris, Howard Hanson, and Roger Sessions. Everywhere, the Project stimulated an appreciation of the old and the new music, of folk music as well as sophisticated classics.

The Federal Music Project also carried on extensive instruction in music. At one time, 1,300 teachers taught over 200,000 students between the ages of 6 and 75. Millions heard music performed by WPA groups. School orchestras, group singing, and bands were sponsored by the Federal Music Project in many schools and community centers.

**The Federal Writers' Project.** The Federal Writers' Project, like the music, art, and theater projects, not only gave employment to needy individuals, but performed valuable cultural services; at one time, it gave employment to as many as 6,500 persons. Its most notable work was the collection of historical materials and the writing of state guides. Thanks to the Federal Writers' Project, each of the 48 states now has an excellent guide. The Federal Writers' Project published books covering such diverse fields as local history and folklore, nationality and racial groups, native vernacular, travel, sport, natural history, and labor and industry. The several hundred books produced by the Writers' Project form an important contribution to American culture. All books were prepared by the Project but were published by private companies or by local public organizations. The Writers' Project was hampered by the lack of understanding on the part of state officials of the purpose of the work, and in many cases persons were put in charge who were unequipped to carry on the projects. The Writers' Project, however, gave many persons who wanted to write but could not do so because of lack of money an opportunity to express themselves.

**A great cultural contribution at small cost.** The contribution of the WPA cultural projects can hardly be overestimated. They enriched the lives of millions of people and also rescued thousands of creative men and women from idleness and despair and gave them an opportunity to express themselves fully—all at less than the cost of one quickly outmoded battleship. It was an irreparable blow to American culture when Congress, allegedly in the name of economy, abolished the Federal Theatre Project in 1939 and returned the Music, Art, and Writers' Projects to state and local control. The co-ordinated program was thus interrupted and activities fatally curtailed.

## Summary

Today man has more leisure time than ever before. Tools and machines can now do the work of human hands and quickly produce all that is needed to provide a decent standard of living. The increase of leisure time for all classes is a means by which civilization can reach a higher level. Leisure offers an opportunity for activities that broaden and enlarge the individual's personality.

Before the invention of labor-saving devices, few persons had leisure time. There were special leisure types and leisure classes even in primitive society. The first great leisure class was made up of the kings, nobles, priests, and scribes of oriental and classical antiquity. The feudal system sharply divided social classes, and the nobility and churchmen were the leisure class of the medieval period. After 1500, a leisure class of rich businessmen came into existence. As capitalism developed, the trend toward separation of ownership from the control and management of business increased, and today those capitalists who turn over their money to banks and brokers for investment have a great deal of time on their hands. Although the leisure class made notable contributions to culture, it is doubtful if, with few exceptions, their contributions have been at all in proportion to their wealth. In recent decades, the introduction of more efficient machinery has made possible a tremendous increase in production and has greatly increased the number of leisure hours of the average worker.

Since all leisure time cannot be spent in creative activity the problem of play is important. There have been various attitudes toward play, but today most persons recognize that play is desirable as a socializing activity and is helpful from a physical standpoint. Until about 200 years ago, play and sports were largely the privilege of the upper and middle classes.

Primitive peoples associated sports with religious rites, and this association continued to be important until well into the Middle Ages. The Greeks and the Romans developed sports and games to a high level and were the first partly to separate play from religion. Protestantism exercised a restraining influence on recreation, for the Puritans disapproved of much play. After the Industrial Revolution made more leisure time available, the demand for recreation increased among all classes. Since not everyone had an opportunity to engage in sports, because of the lack of space in the cities, commercialized spectator sports became popular, especially baseball, football, basketball, tennis, hockey, boxing, and wrestling.

In the twentieth century, there have been many striking developments in recreation. Sports have been commercialized on a vast scale. The automobile has put the nation on wheels; travel, camping, hunting, and fishing have become popular; national parks and forests have been opened up. The playground movement, which provides children with places for supervised play, has become widespread. Recreation in rural areas still lags behind that of urban areas, despite the backing of a number of organizations.

Art, meaning craftsmanship, painting, sculpture, architecture, music, the theater, and the like, is as important as recreation and play in the new perspective of leisure-time activity. To be fully significant in this respect, art must become an integral part of the life of all literate persons, as it was in Greek days. It will not be very potent so long as it remains a distant "museum piece" or a plaything for a wealthy minority.

The art projects sponsored by the Works Progress Administration illustrate the new attitude toward leisure time. The Federal Theatre, the Federal Art Projects, the Federal Music Project, and the Federal Writers' Project show that, if given a chance, millions of Americans will spend their leisure time in worth-while artistic activities. These projects met with enthusiastic response and greatly stimulated appreciation of, and participation in, the arts in the United States. Their abandonment was a major blow to American culture.

### Selected References

Brownell, Baker, and Wright, F. L., *Architecture and Modern Life,* Harper, 1938. Clear exposition of the rôle of architecture in American culture as seen by the greatest living architect.

* Burns, C. D., *Leisure in the Modern World,* Century, 1932. One of the better books on the nature and responsibilities of our new age of leisure.

Butcher, Devereux, *Exploring Our National Parks,* Houghton Mifflin, 1950. Best book on our national parks and their recreational facilities. Magnificently illustrated.

* Dulles, F. R., *America Learns to Play,* Appleton-Century, 1940. The play movement and recreation in the United States. May be supplemented by Butler, G. D., *Introduction to Community Recreation,* McGraw-Hill, 1949.

Durant, John, *The Story of Baseball,* Hastings House, 1948. Absorbing and well illustrated popular history of our national pastime.

* Faulkner, Ray; Ziegfield, Edwin; and Hill, Gerald, *Art Today,* Holt, 1941. A very practical and competent account of the relations of art to the various phases of human life in our time.

Flexner, J. T., *American Painting: First Flower of Our Wilderness,* Houghton Mifflin, 1948. Monumental but interesting study of the origins of American art and its social background.

Goldstein, Harriet and Vetta, *Art in Everyday Life,* Macmillan, 1940. A very interesting account of the rôle and activities of art as a social and cultural force in contemporary American society.

Hambidge, Gove, *Time to Live,* McGraw-Hill, 1933. A sane presentation of the philosophy of leisure time.

Jacks, L. P., *The Education of the Whole Man,* Harper, 1931. A program for dealing successfully with the problems of leisure, by a leading English educator.

Keppel, F. P., and Duffus, R. L., *The Arts in American Life,* McGraw-Hill, 1933. A thoughtful brief account of the state of American arts on the eve of the New Deal.

Krout, J. A., *Annals of American Sport,* Yale University Press, 1929. A competent American historian tells the story of American sports, dealing also with commercialized sports in recent times.

Loeb, Harold, *Life in a Technocracy,* Viking Press, 1933. What life might be in a society dominated by production for use, through efficient engineering direction.

Lundberg, G. A., *Leisure: A Suburban Study,* Columbia University Press, 1934. Case study of Westchester County, N. Y. First important study of leisure as a problem of social science.

Meyer, H. D., and Brightbill, C. K., *Community Recreation,* Heath, 1948. The most recent and comprehensive treatment of this field.

Orton, W. A., *America in Search of Culture,* Little, Brown, 1933. An English-born scholar appraises the level of American arts before the Federal art projects.

* Overmyer, Grace, *Government and the Arts,* Norton, 1939. Includes a clear, competent account of the various art projects fathered by the New Deal.

Steiner, J. F., *America at Play,* McGraw-Hill, 1933. A good acount of American recreation before the New Deal developments.

Terry, Walter, *Invitation to Dance,* A. S. Barnes, 1942. Excellent introduction to the dance and the great contemporary dancers. Regards the dance as an important social function of community life and as a significant form of leisure-time expression.

* Van Loon, H. W., *The Arts,* Simon and Schuster, 1937. Brilliant and absorbing introduction to the history of all the arts. Remarkably successful in relating the arts to daily life. The best book for the general reader and the beginning student of art.

* Young, C. V. P., *How Men Have Lived,* Stratford, 1931. An introductory historical survey of the types of play followed by man from early historic times to the present.

# CHAPTER XXIX

# How the Other Half Lives:
# Poverty, New Methods of Relief, and
# Social Insurance

## The Nature of Poverty and Pauperism

**What we mean by poverty.** As far back as the historical record extends, there seem to have been persons who were hungry, cold, sick, and miserable. And, despite all our mechanical inventions and the enormous increase of wealth in the hands of the fortunate few, there is almost as much poverty now as at any previous time in the history of mankind. Indeed, in the wake of the second world war, there is probably more extensive deprivation and suffering than in any earlier period of history. But, today, the problem is different, because we now have the material basis for plenty and security.

Sociologists make a distinction between poverty, the state of being poor or underprivileged, and pauperism, a condition of dependency upon others for the very necessities of life; the difference is one of degree only. Not all poverty-stricken individuals and families become paupers; some manage to stay on the ragged edge of dependency. Others, struggling against odds too great for them, are forced to ask for relief to live at all.

**Rural and urban poverty.** Poverty and pauperism exist in both the country and the city. But the plight of the poverty-stricken is worse in the city than in the rural areas. In the country, there is usually greater personal interest in welfare, and neighbors help unfortunate families. Rural dwellers may also have a small garden or a few animals, as well as wood for fire, sometimes to be had merely for the cutting. In the city, a family must have money to buy food and fuel and to pay rent. If the rent is not paid, the family is evicted by a court order. The impersonal attitude which prevails in the city has made wretched the plight of the unaided poverty-stricken there.

**Social basis of poverty.** Society as a whole has tended to regard both poverty and pauperism as disgraceful. All too often, the unfortunate victims of circumstances have been treated as chronically lazy, stupid, or criminal.   They are blamed for their destitute condition, although their unhappy estate arises often directly from personal or economic misfortunes over which they have little or no control.   Studies of poverty reveal the fact that many needy persons are the victims of the economic system and cannot fairly be blamed because the Machine Age has made their labor unnecessary.   Many others are incapacitated as a result of accidents or of illness due to inadequate medical care, and still others are thrown out of work because they are over forty years of age.   Even actual shiftlessness and laziness are usually the result of insufficient food, or of illness, worry, or mental disease.   In the majority of cases, normal persons want to work and will work if they can find a job.   Society, rather than the individual, is, more often than not, responsible for poverty.

## The Extent of Poverty in the United States

**Early estimates of American poverty.**   How many people are living in a state of poverty in the United States at the present time?   In 1904, Robert Hunter said that 10 million Americans were in dire need.   At the time, his estimate was regarded as exaggerated, but later studies showed it to be extremely conservative.   In 1919, the National Bureau of Economic Research estimated that 86 per cent of all American families earned less than $2,000 a year, the income regarded by the government at that time as the least on which a family of five could maintain itself in decent and healthful surroundings.

**Poverty in the depression years.**   Many persons believed that the 1920's were a uniquely prosperous period for all Americans, and that good times continued until the crash of 1929.   Actually, although the rich made more money after the first world war, the poor failed notably to improve their condition.   In other words, the national income wa: by no means evenly distributed.[1]

In the years of the depression, the situation grew worse.   In 1933, it was estimated that from 12 to 17 million persons were unemployed and over 50 million were living in a state of poverty.   Studies made in 1935 show a striking increase of poverty after 1929.   The National Resources Committee presented a summary of the income of consumer units (mainly families) in 1933–1935.   The poorest third of these units received about 10 per cent of the national income—about equal to that received by the richest .5 per cent.   The poorest half of the consumer units received 21 per cent of the total national income— less than the richest 3 per cent.   The average income of the poorest third of the units was $471; of the middle third, $1,076; of the richest third, $3,000.   It would not be inaccurate to say that, as late as the year 1936, two-thirds of all American families were living at or below the poverty line, and over 10 per cent were in a state of pauperism. Only Federal relief kept many families from starvation.

---

[1] For statistics on the maldistribution of income in 1928–1929, see pp. 308–309.

**Poverty survives the second world war.** As late as 1942, when the depression was supposed to be conquered, millions of Americans were still living far below a decent standard. Labor Department studies of 33 cities, based on the WPA budget of 1935 brought up to date for December, 1941, living costs, showed that $29 a week was the minimum income requirement for a worker's family of four. Yet, at that time, the Treasury Department revealed that 3,324,000 workers were earning only from $5 to $10 a week; 4,975,000 from $10 to $15; and 10,747,000 from $20 to $30. In other words, millions of families had insufficient income for bare subsistence.[2]

In Chapter XIV we made it clear that, despite superficial evidence of greater mass prosperity in the postwar period, there was no great change in the inequitable distribution of income which is responsible for the inadequate mass purchasing-power that is a main cause of poverty and depressions. Taking into consideration the decreased purchasing power of the dollar and the increase in taxation, the situation at the mid-century was not markedly different from what it had been in prewar days. The situation can be summed up by stating that it now costs more to be poor and needy. A congressional sub-committee reported in February, 1950, that 16,000,000 families, or 38,000,000 persons, had an income of less than $2,000 a year, about equal to $1,000 in prewar years, and 4,100,000 families had an income of less than $1,000.

**Main classes of dependent persons.** Dependent persons fall into several classes. First, there are those on direct relief, that is, receiving cash allowances for food, shelter, and clothing from the government. In June, 1938, over 20 million persons were still on the relief rolls. As the Social Security program was extended, the number receiving direct assistance sharply declined; in 1949, there were only 461,000 recipients of cash allowances. The second class of dependents includes those aided by the Social Security Act of 1935. In 1949, about 2,500,-000 persons received monthly benefits under the Old Age and Survivors program, and about 2,600,000 aged were helped by Old Age Assistance payments. In addition, 1,370,360 children and 71,200 blind persons received government pensions in 1949. Persons in public institutions comprise the third class of dependents. In 1946, the Bureau of the Census reported 514,000 insane and 112,000 feeble-minded and epileptic patients in public institutions. There are about 90,000 dependent aged persons in state, city, and county poorhouses, and around 150,000 dependent children cared for in institutions, state and local. There are about 150,000 prisoners in Federal and state institutions. In March, 1949, the Census Bureau stated that there were a total of 1,300,000 persons living in institutions, most of them public institutions.

Not all persons in need of aid are eligible for pensions or institutional care. In 1940, there were 5,700,000 widows reported by the

---

[2] See *In Fact*, March 1942, p. 3.

census.  Some receive pensions under one of the Social Security programs.  Many are not eligible, however, and are dependent on the
community.  We have already pointed out that over 7 million persons
are ill on any given day in the year.  There are 10 million persons

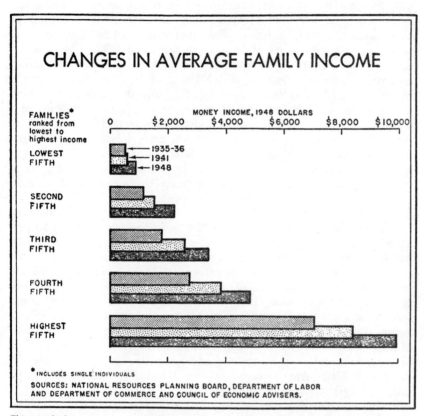

## CHANGES IN AVERAGE FAMILY INCOME

This graph shows increase in monetary income of five income classes in the United States
between 1935 and 1948. This increase was largely offset by increased cost of living and
taxes, and reveals little substantial improvement in the lot of the lower income groups
as a result of the second world war and the cold war.

injured in accidents each year, many of them permanently.  Workmen's compensation laws are not yet adequate and many victims of
industrial accidents, as well as those injured outside of industry, become dependent on public and private agencies.

These are only the major classes of dependents, but their number
and variety make clear the enormous extent of the problem of poverty.

## The Causes of Poverty

**Basic and contributory causes of poverty.**  In general we can divide
the causes of poverty into two categories: (1) those that are basic
and account for the existence of poverty as a social problem, and (2)

those that are contributory to the existence of poverty in any particular case.

As we have suggested elsewhere, the basic causes of poverty are poor or exhausted soil, physical and mental deficiency, the inability of our economic system to manufacture and distribute adequately the vast amount of food, goods, and services that our machine age is capable of producing, and the failure to provide the masses with income enough to purchase such necessities of life as are produced. The contributory causes of poverty are the misfortunes that affect an individual or family and result in the reduction or total loss of income. For example, sickness or a physical handicap, like blindness, deafness, or lameness, may prevent an individual from earning his living. The death of a husband may cause a wife and children to lose their sole means of support. Epidemics may sweep over the land. Natural cataclysms, like floods and tornadoes, may leave families homeless. In any type of economic system, these contributory factors are likely to be present. It is to the basic factors underlying poverty that most attention must be paid, however, if this serious social problem is to be eliminated.

**Economic causes of poverty.** The main cause of poverty, and one that cannot be stressed too often, is the failure of our economy to produce at full capacity and to provide for adequate mass purchasing power. Next would rank the waste of our natural resources.

A less widely recognized cause of poverty is the inability or unwillingness of half or more of the American people to carry insurance against the crises or emergencies of life. In the event of a long illness, serious accident, or death, few families will have saved enough to defray the necessary expenses. Still another factor is the wastefulness of most Americans. The average American family has not learned to be truly economical in using food and goods, as the French have, for example. Many Americans also try to live far beyond their means, thus adding extravagance to waste.

**Political causes of poverty.** Political factors also play a rôle in causing poverty. Waste, inefficiency, and graft in government increase the high taxes that absorb a large share of the national income. These taxes usually fall with special severity on the poor. One of the outstanding political defects underlying poverty has been the failure of our public authorities to provide an adequate system of industrial and vocational education, which would enable the graduates of our schools to obtain employment easily. Too much money has been spent operating an educational system that does not meet the practical needs of the majority of youth. Political responsibility for poverty also includes the failure to assure adequate medical care and to provide a sound conservation program to eliminate the danger of floods, soil erosion, and other losses created by the careless exploitation of our natural resources. Lack of an adequate public-works blueprint for depression periods, and tardy recognition of the dangers of excessive immigration and its possible effects on industry and employment are other political deficiencies that have added to the burden of poverty. The most important political factor, however, in causing poverty has been the failure to eliminate war and thus avoid its tremendous costs. War consumes staggering sums of money which might otherwise provide human beings with necessities and comforts and set up pension plans and public-works programs. Moreover, war kills off or injures permanently millions of family breadwinners. The aftermath of past wars and preparation for future wars leaves little public income to be used for non-military purposes.

## Development of Poor-Relief Legislation: England

**Rise of public poor relief in England.** In England, after the revolt from Catholicism in the reign of Henry VIII, the state slowly took over the relief work handled down to that time by the church. The first important "poor law" was passed in 1536. Other laws were passed in 1547, 1555, 1563, and 1572. This legislation was revised and consolidated in the famous Elizabethan Poor Law of 1601, which divided the poor into three classes: (1) the able-bodied; (2) those who could not work; and (3) children. The able-bodied were sent to workhouses (provided in laws of 1547–1563) where they were put to work on raw materials furnished by the public authorities. Those who could not work were cared for in almshouses, and children were bound out to those willing to care for them in return for their work. The almshouses and workhouses were supported both by taxes levied on the local parish and by gifts from the well-to-do. The officials in charge of poor relief, called overseers, were appointed from each parish by the justice of the peace.

**Development of the English Poor Law System.** The law of 1601 remained the backbone of English poor relief until 1834, although a number of supplementary laws were passed in the meantime. The most important changes were the establishment of more workhouses and the passage, in the latter part of the eighteenth century, of laws which tended to encourage indiscriminate charity by basing relief on the cost of living and the size of the family, regardless of age.

The notable Poor Law of 1834 was based on ideas set forth by English reformers like Jeremy Bentham. It was designed to prevent and discourage poverty and pauperism, as well as to provide public support for the worthy poor. It forbade outdoor relief to all save the aged and the sick and required all others to enter a workhouse to get relief. It also provided better organization and administration of poor relief, transforming it, in part, from a local to a national basis.

**Provision of social insurance in England.** The Poor Law of 1834 endured, with a few minor administrative changes, throughout the rest of the nineteenth century. The minority report of a Poor Law Commission, appointed by the Crown in 1905, recommended in 1909 the abolition of the existing system of poor relief and the creation of a national program of social insurance resembling that which Bismarck had introduced into Germany twenty years before. The report, written by Mrs. Sidney Webb, further recommended that dependents be divided into classes and be handled by the proper authorities, as, for instance, the sick poor by the Health Commission and the mentally defective poor by the Asylum Commission.

Workmen's compensation laws were introduced in 1897 and extended in 1906. Old age pensions on a limited scale were provided for in 1908. The first great National Insurance Act, providing for insurance against sickness and unemployment, was passed in 1911, and went into operation the next year. Social insurance was extended by a series of acts after the first world war. The Ministry of Health was set up in 1919. In 1924, a comprehensive National Health Insurance Act was passed. In 1934, a new law was passed, following which the British unemployment insurance system was reorganized and placed in the hands of a National Unemployment Insurance Board.

**The Beveridge Report.** In June, 1941, Sir William Beveridge was named chairman of a committee, appointed by the Crown, to survey and recommend changes in the British insurance system. The Beveridge Report, made public in November, 1942, recommended the unification and expansion of all existing social insurance into a plan involving complete coverage of all needy citizens, regardless of income. Every person would be expected to contribute. Under this plan, workers would receive increased unemployment, sickness, and disability payments, based on need rather than on previous earnings and to be continued as long as necessary. Maternity benefits were included for women workers and for housewives whose husbands were employed. Funeral benefits were to be provided. Family allowances were suggested for those with two or more children under 16 years of age. Free medical care for all persons was recommended. For those cases not covered by contributions, payments would be judged on the basis of need. In addition to the social insurance proposals, minimum-wage legislation was urged. To facilitate the unification and expansion of social insurance, the establishment of a Ministry of Social Security was recommended.

**The Labour Government program of cradle-to-grave social insurance.** In 1945, a Labour Government replaced the wartime Conservative-Labour Coalition Government. The new Labour Government, soon after its formation, took up the task of extending and applying the security and insurance measures of the Beveridge Report. The National Insurance Act of August, 1947, which went into effect in July, 1948, extended contributory insurance to provide for an improved and more uniform scale of insurance benefits for unemployment, sickness, old age, and death, and for orphans, mothers, and widows.

The insurance plan is financed by contributions from the employer, the employee, and the government. About a dollar a week is deducted from the pay check of an employed man; a working woman contributes about 76 cents weekly. The employer's share amounts to about 83 cents a week for each employee, male or female. To this total weekly contribution of the employer and employee, an additional 50 cents a week is contributed by the government. When the worker has made the required number of payments—they vary with different benefits—he and his family are eligible for sickness, unemployment, and other benefits. In case of illness, for example, the benefits received amount to about $5.25 weekly for the man, plus $3.20 for his wife, and $1.50 for the oldest child. If there are other children in the family, they do not receive benefits because they are covered by the system of family allowances financed by the government entirely out of taxation.

Self-employed persons and those living on private income are required to register and make weekly payments. These payments amount to about $1.23 for the self-employed and about 93 cents for the person who lives on private income. The self-employed and the persons living on income will not be eligible for all benefits of the insurance plan; unemployment benefits, for example. It is expected, however, that few persons from the self-employed or private income groups will wish to apply for the small weekly benefit, but will consider their contributions as additions to their taxes paid to the government. The National Insurance Act covers over 30 million persons; the annual cost of the plan is estimated at 2 billion dollars.

The Health Service Act went into effect at the same time as the National Insurance Act. By this Act free and complete medical, dental, and optical care is provided to every man, woman, or child who desires it. The costs of medical care are financed out of taxation. The plan for free medical care is not to be confused with the sickness benefit provided by the National Insurance Act. The sickness benefit is a small weekly payment made to a worker during such time as illness keeps him away from work. In order that the sickness benefit be conferred, contributions from the employer, the employee, and the government must have been made for a certain number of weeks.

The new English social insurance system, offering "cradle to grave" security, is one of the most comprehensive plans in existence. It has not been put in operation without opposition. This has been particularly true of the Health Service Act—many physicians and dentists objected to "becoming civil servants," that is, receiving their fees from the government, and some of the insurance companies also opposed the socialization of medical services. In spite of these objections, however, the program is operating for over 30 million persons who have signed for free medical service. Over 90 per cent of the doctors and dentists have now joined the service, and the health budget for 1950 is somewhat in excess of a billion dollars. The new medical service plan has met so great a need for medical and dental care that not even the most powerful and reactionary Conservative has dared to assail it in forthright fashion. The English death rate of 10.8 during the first full year of the operation of the new medical plan was the lowest on record, despite Britain's austerity regimen.

## Pre-New Deal and New Deal Relief Policies

**Early forms of American poor relief.** The early American system of poor relief was based directly on the Elizabethan Poor Law of 1601. Many families lived close to poverty in early America, and crop failures and misfortunes often reduced them to actual pauperism. A usual method of providing poor relief in the New England colonies was for each family, if necessary, to care for a destitute person sometime during the year. Widows, orphans, and old men and women were sent around for several weeks at a time to different village homes. Children were bound out to work. In the larger towns, almshouses soon appeared; Boston had one as early as 1660. The New Englanders wasted little sympathy on the able-bodied poor, who were either put into jail, whipped out of town, or bound out as indentured servants. As the number of able-bodied poor increased, it cost a great deal to keep them idle in jail, so workhouses were built. Since each town had to care for its destitute, the New England colonists did not welcome any newcomer who was not able to care for himself and his family.

In the South, poverty was treated somewhat differently. The Virginia colony, for instance, bound out the able-bodied and the orphans as indentured servants. There seem to have been few almshouses, hospitals, or workhouses. The sick poor were put into private homes, and the parish paid for their care.

After the Revolutionary War, almshouses or poorhouses became the usual public institution to care for the poor, the aged, and the very young. Children were later taken out of the almshouses and placed in separate children's institutions or bound out. By the end of the nineteenth century, routine poor relief had been transferred in part to a system of aid given to the poor in their own homes. Almshouses were continued mainly as homes for the indigent aged.

**Two systems of supervised public outdoor relief.** The scientific method of supervising outdoor relief was introduced in this country by enlightened social workers who had observed the methods used in Germany. The scheme developed in Germany was known as the Hamburg-Elberfeld system (it originated in Hamburg, but was perfected in Elberfeld). The city was divided into small units each in the charge of an overseer. District supervisors were appointed to direct the workers in the smaller units. A central committee, or policy-making board, unified the work of the supervisors. Each applicant for aid was investigated on an individual basis.

Indiana was the first state in the United States to apply these principles of investigation and supervision to correct abuses in the granting of relief. Between 1895 and 1899 laws were passed requiring supervision of all cases asking help. Overseers were appointed in each township to see that no one able to work received relief, and district supervisors co-ordinated the work in the townships. The Indiana plan, based in large part on the Hamburg-Elberfeld system, made it possible to reduce the cost of relief and yet give more adequate aid where it was needed most. Its success also encouraged the development of the charity organization movement [3] in this country.

**Private charity.** Public relief under governmental supervision has become increasingly important since the 1930's. Private agencies are still necessary, however, to give temporary or permanent care to those persons not eligible for pensions or grants from the government. Private contributions to welfare amounted to over 3 billion dollars in 1945. Here is the dollar breakdown, according to income-tax returns: individual donations, 2.6 billion; corporations, 266 million; bequests, 202 million; foundations, 72 million; and miscellaneous sources, 37 million. Experts estimated in 1949 that, in the next ten years, there would be a need for at least a billion dollars in gifts from private sources for philanthropic purposes, to be distributed as follows: 500 million for hospitals; 105 million for religious and allied activities; 100 million for social work; 100 million for higher education; 44 million for secondary education; and 4 million for medical education.[4] The enormous cost of social benefits was revealed in a report of the Community Research Associates in 1949, which showed that some 13 billion dollars are being spent annually from public and private sources for such social services as relief, Social Security, health, correction, welfare, and recreation—a sum about equal to all the public expenditures for relief during the entire New Deal period.

**The development of scientific social case work.** The development of scientific social work has been indispensable to the effective and economical relief of the poor. Originating in the days when private relief dominated the picture, it has become even more indispensable with the extensive growth of public relief measures and the vastly larger number of recipients of relief.

Scientific social work was a by-product of the charity organization movement. It first attained a truly effective form in what is known as social case work, a technique devised especially by Edward T. Devine and Mary E. Richmond, and set down in the classic work of the latter, *Social Diagnosis* (1917). It operates on the case-history method of investigating needy cases, seeking to gather all the relevant facts concerning the personal and family history, social background, and economic situation of every person who applies for aid. Only in this way can social workers accurately determine the type and amount of relief, if any, that should be given.

---

3 See above, pp. 676–677.
4 See above, pp. 677–678 for the role of social settlements in poor relief.

**Psychiatric social work.** In the last quarter of a century, the traditional social case work, which was chiefly concerned with the family and economic condition of relief cases, has been expanded to envisage and apply psychiatric social work. It has come to be recognized that mental conditions are often the immediate cause of dependency, though these disturbed or diseased mental states may arise out of domestic and economic tensions. If Mary E. Richmond's *Social Diagnosis* may rightly be called the "bible" of traditional social case work, the same position in psychiatric case work may be accorded to E. E. Southard and M. C. Jarrett's *The Kingdom of Evils,* published in 1922. The first school exclusively devoted to psychiatric social work was established at Smith College right after the first world war, owing mainly to the efforts of Dr. Southard, a distinguished psychiatrist, and Dr. Frankwood E. Williams, Medical Director of the National Committee for Mental Hygiene. It was long directed by Everett Kimball of the Smith College faculty. Most of the good schools of social work now make ample provisions for instruction in psychiatric social work.

**Revolutionary relief policies of the New Deal.** Future historians will undoubtedly mark the depression of 1929 as the turning-point in the attitude of not only the Federal government, but of state and local governments as well, toward relief and unemployment. Prior to that time, most poor relief was handled either by private agencies or by municipal and county authorities. The depression following 1929 led to such an enormous increase in unemployment throughout the nation that private agencies were unable to care for all those in need of relief. Many cities became bankrupt under the increased relief burden, and thousands of persons were without sufficient food and clothing. Breadlines grew longer and longer. There were numerous evictions for failure to pay rent.

Despite the desperate plight of the unemployed and the empty treasuries of the private agencies and the municipalities, President Hoover was reluctant to take steps to make adequate Federal funds available for relief. Toward the end of his administration, he was persuaded to request Congress for a small appropriation for public relief, but the situation became increasingly acute. When President Roosevelt was inaugurated in March, 1933, a new philosophy of public relief was immediately adopted, and the most extensive program in the history of American poor relief was devised and instituted. Between March, 1933, and January, 1940, over 13 billion dollars were spent in various programs for relief purposes by the Federal, state, and local governments.

**Direct relief under the New Deal.** In May, 1933, the Wagner-Lewis Act was passed by Congress appropriating funds for direct relief of the distressed. The Federal Emergency Relief Administration was set up with Harry Hopkins, an experienced social worker, as administrator. Funds were allocated to the states to be distributed through state emergency relief administrations created for that purpose. Local public relief agencies investigated the financial condition of each applicant before granting requests for food, rent, and clothing. Additional supplies were also made available to relief clients through the Federal Surplus Relief Corporation, which bought up surplus food and clothing for distribution through the local offices.

This shantytown, built by jobless on New York City's East River in 1932, shows the desperate straits of the poverty-stricken in urban centers during the depression years. (From *History of Public Welfare in New York, 1867–1940*, by Deutsch and Schneider. University of Chicago Press, 1941.)

There was much public dissatisfaction with the FERA program. Many relief clients objected to investigation of their needs and resented the visits of investigators, calling them "pantry snoopers" and "busybodies." At the same time, there was vigorous opposition to the relief system on the part of those who felt that direct relief was a "waste of the taxpayer's money" and a means of developing a permanent class of parasitical dependents living off the government.

**Public-works projects.** The Roosevelt administration, although making direct relief available to the unemployed, favored the general policy of sponsoring public-works projects that would make some permanent contributions to the community. The Civil Works Administration, which spent over a billion dollars during the winter of 1933–1934 on "made work," was the transitional stage between direct relief and a public-works program. The public-works policy was sound, but the programs were criticized by some who objected to the expenditure of such large sums of money. The Public Works Administration, created early in 1933, was an attempt to create more purchasing power and put money in circulation, but it indirectly aided the unemployed. Over 7 billion dollars was allocated for the construction of public buildings, roads, dams, and sewers. Private contractors, not the relief offices, hired the labor. For the most part, PWA employees were skilled workers, not yet on relief.

The Works Progress (later Projects) Administration was the public-works program that most directly helped relief clients. The WPA was set up in 1935. It gave employment to workers who were taken off relief and paid the prevailing wage in their community. A nominal sum was set as the maximum to be earned each month in order not to interfere with private industry. The local community usually furnished the materials and the government paid the wages. Roads, school buildings, parks, playgrounds, water systems, and dams were constructed by the WPA workers.

One other program associated with public works also was of importance. The Civilian Conservation Corps was created to give employment to young men between the ages of 17 and 24. The majority of the enrollees were from the relief rolls and, of the $30 paid each one monthly, $25 was sent to their families. In addition to aiding the needy, the CCC made a permanent contribution to the conservation program. Much was accomplished in the way of forest and soil conservation. With the entrance of the United States in the second world war, the program was abandoned.

**Other New Deal measures aiding dependents.** Two important pieces of legislation provided for relief or helped to reduce poverty and unemployment. The Soldiers' Bonus Bill had been passed in 1924 over President Coolidge's veto. It provided for the payment of a veterans' bonus in 1945. In 1936, an act was passed, also over the President's veto, to set the date of payment ahead by nine years. This action distributed over two billion dollars to veterans of the first world war—about $800 to every veteran. Another important law established the United States Employment Service, which created a system of labor exchanges, under Department of Labor supervision, in co-operation with the states. Federal funds were made available to every state for maintaining the employment offices, provided the state appropriated a sum equal to the Federal grant. For the first time, a fairly adequate system of public employment offices was provided. Every person on relief was required to register at the nearest employment office so that, if a job were listed, he might be called. Many unemployed persons secured jobs through the United States Employment Service. As workers were needed for defense and war plants after 1940, the Employment Service helped in finding applicants to fill the jobs. In 1946, the administration of the Employment Services was returned to the states. Federal funds, however, were still used to aid in the financing of the program. The main functions of the United States Employment Service today are to co-ordinate the work of the state offices, to provide a system for clearing labor among the states, and to maintain a veterans' employment service.

The Roosevelt administrations thus introduced public relief on a scale hitherto unknown in this country. It is doubtful if the capitalistic system could have weathered the depression as well as it did had the philosophy of President Roosevelt been that of President Hoover. More important than the specific relief measures was the social philosophy introduced by the New Deal, namely, that the government will not allow the poor to starve. Public responsibility for the welfare of all citizens is probably the most important single contribution to American life made by the New Deal relief programs.

**Lack of scientific supervision of New Deal relief.** The emergency created by the depression made it difficult to use the principles of scientific social case work at all times. Case loads were large and

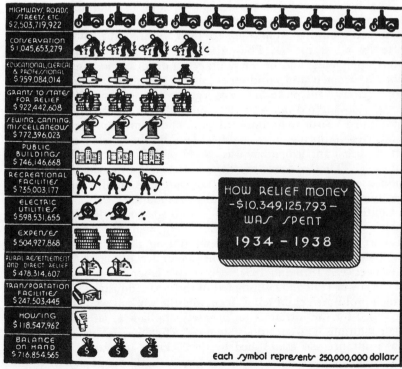

*From* The New York Times, *Jan. 22, 1939.*

This graphic chart indicates the distribution of New Deal pump-priming and relief expenditures.

workers were not always trained in case-work procedures. Since the passage of the Social Security Act in 1935, however, scientific techniques and trained social workers have again been made an essential item in the welfare program. The Social Security Act requires minimum standards of training for workers in all states that receive funds for benefits from the Federal government. Although the scope of private charity has been reduced, the scientific principles and careful supervision procedures introduced by private-agency investigation will remain as an integral part of any public relief program.

## Steps Toward Social Security

**British labor legislation.** If private industry is unable or unwilling to care for its employees, then some form of legislation must be enacted to safeguard them. Legislation to protect labor and social insurance plans designed to eliminate the need for emergency relief are two of the more widely suggested methods of providing security for workers. We have already summarized British social insurance, so we need consider here only the more important stages in British labor legislation.

The first successful labor legislation was inaugurated by Great Britain in the first half of the nineteenth century. Generally speaking, these acts, running from 1802 to 1853, secured the 10-hour day in virtually all factories. They also provided for factory inspection, safety appliances, and better sanitary conditions, and discouraged the labor of women and children in many industries. Labor organizations, strikes, and picketing were legalized by laws of 1871 and 1875. Legislation enacted between 1905 and 1914 by the British Parliament established boards to fix hours of work and minimum wages in certain industries—tailoring, box making, lace finishing, coal mining, and agriculture. In 1920, a law was passed prohibiting child labor in any industry. The Labour Goverment's nationalization since 1945 of key industries such as public utilities, transportation, mining, and shipping, has further extended minimum-wage standards.

**Continental social legislation.** Although social legislation began earlier in England than on the Continent, many European countries also set up social insurance systems during the nineteenth century. Germany's comprehensive plan, begun under Bismarck, was inaugurated between 1878 and 1891. Protective labor legislation was begun in the law of 1878 and culminated in the great Industrial Code of 1891, which prohibited child labor, regulated the work of women and youth, provided for the introduction of safety appliances, safeguarded laboring conditions, and set up a system of factory inspection. German social insurance was established by the Sickness Insurance Act of 1883, the Accident Insurance Act of 1884, and the Old Age and Invalidity Insurance Act of 1889. After 1890, labor unions were given greater freedom to organize and conduct strikes.

French protection of labor began in 1841 with a law prohibiting child labor and regulating the labor of youth. This protection was extended in 1848 by a 12-hour law, and in 1874 by an act that further regulated the labor of youth, provided special protection for the labor of women, and established minimum sanitary and safety measures in factories. Between 1874 and 1914, a further series of laws were passed which covered hours of work, working conditions, labor of minors, Sunday rest, and factory inspection. The law of 1906 created a Ministry of Labor. On the eve of the first world war a new labor code systematized the French legislation protecting labor. Labor unions and strikes had been legalized in 1884. French social insurance began with the Workmen's Compensation Act of 1898 and the Old Age Pensions Act of 1905. A comprehensive Social Insurance Law was passed in 1930.

Italy instituted social insurance by the Accident Insurance Act in 1885, and in 1898 laws were passed providing for compulsory accident, sickness, invalidity, and old age insurance. Austria passed an accident insurance law in 1887 and another providing for sickness insurance in 1888. The Scandinavian countries provided for comprehensive social insurance as a part of their "Middle Way" program of social and economic reform. The Socialist economy of Soviet Russia provides comprehensive "cradle to the grave" social insurance.

**Lag in American social legislation.** Down to 1935, the United States had made less progress than most civilized countries in protective labor legislation and social insurance, principally because the American legislatures and courts, deeply influenced by conservative businessmen, had assumed the attitude that neither the Federal nor state governments had any right to interfere in such private business matters as employment and wages. Because of this "hands off" policy, the Supreme Court was unsympathetic to legislation designed to improve laboring conditions; among the laws it declared unconstitutional during this period were state minimum-wage laws and two Federal child-labor laws.

**Early American labor legislation.** Most labor legislation in the United States down to 1933 had been passed by the states. Massachusetts passed a law in 1842 restricting the labor of children to 10 hours a day. New Hampshire, in 1847, limited the work of women to 10 hours daily. Some other states passed similar laws after 1850. Fifteen states, beginning with Massachusetts in 1912, passed minimum-wage legislation, setting the lowest wage that can legally be paid industrial workers.

For the most part, the Supreme Court, as in the Lochner case in 1905, and in the Adkins case in 1923, took a hostile attitude toward this type of legislation. Not until 1938 was the first satisfactory national labor legislation passed, although an attempt had been made previously, in the National Industrial Recovery Act, to legalize labor unions and to introduce Federal regulation of wages and hours in industries producing goods sold in interstate commerce. We have already referred to the Wagner National Labor Relations Act of 1935 which finally legalized labor unionism, and to the remarkable growth of union membership which followed.

**The Fair Labor Standards Act of 1938.** The first comprehensive Federal effort to regulate hours of work and the wages paid came in the Fair Labor Standards Act of 1938, commonly referred to as the "Wage-Hour Law." It applied to workers engaged in commerce and those who produced goods shipped in interstate commerce. Most directly affected were the communications, transmission and transportation, iron and steel, saw mill, flour milling, textile, automotive, cottonseed oil, and fertilizer industries.

The law was intended not only to set a minimum wage but also to eliminate labor conditions deemed detrimental to the efficiency, health, and well-being of workers. The minimum wage was set at 25 cents an hour with a standard maximum of 44 hours work each week. The employer was required to pay his employees time and a half for all hours worked beyond the 44-hour maximum. Only about one-fourth, or 11 million, of the workers of the country were covered by the law when it went into operation. The minimum wage was gradually raised until it reached 30 cents in 1940, and 40 cents in 1945, where it remained until January, 1950. The standard maximum work week was reduced to 40 hours in 1940, where it still remains.

The increased cost of living made the minimum wage of 40 cents extremely inadequate for postwar times, and President Truman urged Congress to raise the minimum to 75 cents an hour. In October, 1949, the 75-cent minimum was approved by Congress and went into effect in January, 1950, but supplementary legislation nullified some of the gain for labor. Some 1,116,000 workers, mainly in the retail and service trades, logging, and irrigation were removed from coverage under the Wage-Hour Law. But the workers now covered—some 22 million—are about double the number protected in 1938.

There were many problems connected with the enforcement of the law. An extensive body of inspectors and enforcement officers was established to inspect factories and other places of employment and see to it that the law was complied with. At the outset the work was done comprehensively and efficiently. But, later on, decreases in the budget appropriations cut down the number of inspectors and thus hampered enforcement. The law originally gave the U. S. Children's Bureau authority to enforce the child-labor provisions. Later on, this authority was transferred to the Secretary of Labor. The minimum age for general employment was set at 16 years; that for occupations declared hazardous was 18 years. The chief opposition to the child-labor sections of the law came from seasonal industries and those textile mills which employed child labor.

**The Social Security Act of 1935.** The severity of the depression following 1929 pointed up the inadequacy of state and local bodies to cope with the hardships caused by mass unemployment, sickness, and old age. Although by 1930 some 20 states had laws providing aid for the blind, 45 had laws to aid mothers, and 12 had old-age pension laws, many of these laws were inoperative because of lack of funds, and others were so restrictive as to be virtually worthless. No state had a system of unemployment insurance, though bills to provide for it had been introduced in six different states.

In President Roosevelt's message to Congress in June, 1934, he asked that a Federal law be passed to provide safeguards against "misfortunes that cannot be avoided in this man-made world of ours." He mentioned certain definite objectives: old-age pensions for the needy; a long term old-age insurance plan; unemployment insurance; health insurance for industrial workers; and pensions for the blind and for mothers and dependent children.

The Social Security Act, finally passed in 1935, established three separate programs. Two were insurance plans involving payroll taxes: an old-age pension system and unemployment insurance. The third program provided Federal grants-in-aid to the aged, the blind, dependent children, and crippled children; to vocational rehabilitation; to maternal and child health services; and to an extension of public health measures. A Social Security Board was established to supervise the plan.

The old-age pension system was based on the contributory insurance method. Not all workers were included. The self-employed, agricultural laborers, domestic workers, maritime service, employees of nonprofit institutions, and federal employees were excluded. A tax of one per cent levied on each worker and his employer covered by the plan financed the scheme. Pension payments, based not on need but on previous earnings, were to be made to the insured worker after he reached 65 years of age, provided his wages thereafter were less than $15 per month.

The unemployment insurance plan was financed by a payroll tax of 3 per cent on employers of eight or more workers. Against this tax, employers could get a credit offset up to 90 per cent for contributions they paid under a state unemployment compensation law. In other words, if a state passed such a law employers would pay a Federal tax of .3 per cent and a state tax of 2.7 per cent. Benefit payments began in 1938, and workers eligible for compensation received between $15 and $28 per week for a maximum of 26 weeks.

In order to secure Federal grants-in-aid, states were compelled to meet certain minimum general standards set forth in the Federal law. Federal assistance to the needy over 65 was 50 per cent of the first $30 per month paid the aged recipient; if more than $30 was granted, as it rarely was, the state paid the full balance. Federal funds for aid to dependent children, the blind, the disabled, and maternal and child health services ranged from one-third to one-half the amount granted by the state certifying agency.

POVERTY AND RELIEF

**Amendments to the Social Security Act.** In 1939, the Social Security Act was amended. The unemployment insurance plan remained the same, but the old-age pension system was put on a sounder basis and became Old Age and Survivors' Insurance (OASI). The 1939 amendments recognized the family group rather than the individual alone. The amount granted to the worker after age 65 is based on average wages, rather than on the total wages earned. On reaching 65, all properly insured workers (those who have worked at least half the time since the program began, or have a total of ten years employment in a type of work covered by the act) receive a monthly benefit equal to 40 per cent of the first $50, plus 10 per cent of the next $200, monthly wage. Benefits are not paid on wages over $250. In addition to the benefit calculated on the average wage, one per cent is added for each year worked before retirement. If the worker dies before he has become fully insured, but has worked one-half of the three years before his death, his family is eligible for certain benefits. The minimum payment to a single individual or family is $10; the maximum monthly pension is $85. In June, 1949, the average pension received was $26.20. If a worker dies partially or fully insured, his widow at 65 is entitled to three-fourths of his pension. If the worker leaves no widow, his parents become eligible at 65 years of age for pensions. Widows with children under 18 receive a widow's benefit. More protection was thus offered to the family against risk of premature death and the hazards of old age. The oldest and the poorest received the greatest amount of protection.

Further amendments to the Social Security Act were made in 1946 and 1948. Old Age Assistance grants were increased by each amendment. The Federal government now pays $25 of the first $50 granted to the aged recipient. In June, 1949, the average OAA grant was $44, ranging from $19 in one state to $71 in another. The Aid to Dependent Children grants were also increased. The government now pays $27 for one child and $18 for each additional child in the family. In July, 1949, the average ADC grant was $73. Payments to the blind were also increased; in July, 1949, the average pension to a blind person amounted to $46.50.

Despite this liberalization of Federal grants-in-aid, the payments were still insufficient fully to care for those in need. In 1947, Congress amended the Social Security Act to freeze the OASI contributions at 1 per cent each on employers and employees for 1948 and 1949, 1½ per cent each for 1950 and 1951, and 2 per cent each thereafter. The Federal unemployment tax remained unchanged from the 1935 figure. Since 1937, when the system went into full operation, employers and employees have contributed by payroll taxes $14,550,000,000.

In his message to Congress in January, 1948, President Truman asked for a broad expansion of the Social Security program, but the law which Congress passed in June, 1948 was vetoed by the President because he believed that it restricted rather than extended the cover-

age.  Congress passed the law over his veto, and some of the gains have
been described in the preceding paragraph dealing with payments in
1949.  In his message of January, 1949, Mr. Truman again took up the
problem of Social Security expansion and urged that payroll taxes be
raised to 2 per cent and that benefits should be paid on the first $4,800
of income.  In October, 1949, the House of Representatives passed a
bill which added about 11 million persons to the coverage, increased
benefits about 70 per cent, and raised payroll taxes on both employers
and employees, but the Senate did not act.  The President repeated
his recommendations for more extended coverage and increased benefits in his message of January, 1950, and it seemed likely that a
majority of his recommendations would be enacted into law.

Liberalizing action was needed despite the fact that some 35 million
persons were already covered by some phase of Social Security legislation in January, 1950.  Over 6 million persons were then receiving
benefits, and total disbursements were about a billion dollars annually.
More than 20 million workers were not covered by Social Security in
mid-1950, however, and the increased payments made possible by the
amending acts of 1946 and 1948 did not match the increase in living
costs.  Total Federal disbursements for Social Security from 1936
through 1948 amounted to about $5,400,000,000.

**Summary appraisal of the Social Security Act.**  The Social Security
Act, although limited in coverage and inadequate as to size of benefits
and grants to the needy, the blind, and dependent children, is a beginning in the right direction.  It rests on a civilized desire to give a
minimum of economic protection to those unable to help themselves;
it recognizes the responsibility of the community; and it serves, to
some degree, as a means of maintaining the purchasing power of the
masses.  The extension of old age and survivors insurance to the
family unit protects society as well as the individual against dependency resulting from old age and death.  So far, the Social Security Act
offers one of the few rays of hope to millions of persons who are unemployed, aged, sick or disabled, or fear the time when they are no
longer able to work.

One limitation is certain: the unemployment insurance provisions
can only serve to cushion the shock of a mild business recession; they
would not carry the country through a serious depression.  As Albert
L. Warner well states the situation: "Everyone is agreed on one thing:
Unemployment insurance would not rescue us in a real depression.
It would be like a couple of leaky lifeboats for a sinking *Queen Mary*.
In a business slump or a mild recession, however, unemployment in-
surance can cushion the shock."

**Union social welfare projects.**  The labor unions have set up additional coverage for nearly five million workers in health, welfare, and
retirement plans.  The best known of these is the one developed for
the United Mine Workers by the aggressive policy of John L. Lewis.
The UMW collects about $135,000,000 a year in mining royalties and

devotes this sum to welfare activities for the miners. The International Ladies Garment Workers and the Amalgamated Clothing Workers have collected about $110,000,000 in their welfare funds. Enlightened employers often contribute to these union welfare funds. In the Philadelphia garment industry they contribute about 8 per cent; a more usual figure is 2 to 5 per cent. The retirement funds are the most important of these union welfare activities. They run from a dollar-for-dollar matching of the Federal payment of $26 per month to the $100 per month paid to retired members of the UMW.

In May, 1949, Mr. Lewis announced that his miners had received $106,000,000 in benefit payments down to that time. At that time the UMW welfare program provided the following benefits and services: death benefit of $1,000; disability payments up to a maximum of $60 a month to each disabled miner, $20 for his wife, and $10 for each child; widow's assistance grants up to a maximum of $60 a month, and $10 for each child; medical, health, and hospital care; and pensions of $100 monthly for miners over 60 years of age who retired after May 29, 1946.

**Non-contributory industrial pensions.** John L. Lewis's program of collecting royalties from the coal industry and using the proceeds to provide social benefits for his miners was an opening wedge to what is likely to prove one of the most epoch-making developments in the history of security for the working classes, namely, pensions to workers provided by industrial employers without contribution from the workers.

A steel strike was called in 1949 mainly to secure non-contributory pensions for members of the CIO steel workers' union. After a bitter struggle, the employers' front was broken when the Bethlehem Steel Company agreed on October 31, 1949, to pay a monthly pension of $100 and some other benefits from company assets. Other steel companies followed suit, as did the Ford Motor Company. It is too early to predict the extent or success of such plans, but they seem likely to dominate the industrial and labor scene and to constitute a great gain in behalf of workers' security. Probably there will have to be some adjustment in Social Security payments.

## The Prevention of Dependency

If we are to solve the problem of poverty, we must abandon the idea that poverty is permanent and necessary for large numbers of the population. This was the basic frame of reference in the famous Beveridge Report of 1942. There must be a clear understanding of the causes of dependency and a determined effort to root them out.

Poverty arising from defects in the physical environment may be conquered. Conservation will check waste; irrigation will eliminate drought; veterinary science and bacteriology will help wage war against animal diseases and insect pests. Biological causes of poverty can also, in some measure, be controlled. A better health program may be assured. Free clinics are already available, and socialized medicine or compulsory health insurance would reduce illness, one of the important causes of poverty. Accidents can be reduced by safety education. Defectives can be prevented from having children.

In the social field, better relief administration will alleviate misery, and the extension of social settlements will do much to overcome the impersonal relationships of the city and make for a genuine spirit of neighborliness. An improved vocational-education system could train young men and women to earn a living, and adequate instruction in civics and other social sciences would enable them to take an intelligent interest in government policies and practices.

Much more can be done in the field of social security. Coverage should be extended so that all workers will be protected by Old Age and Survivors' Insurance. Benefits for workers and their families should be substantially increased and the age at which old-age benefits are received should be lowered. Both Federal and state grants-in-aid are still too low to assure a decent standard of living for recipients. Unemployment compensation is in need of drastic upward revision to meet present-day conditions.

We must wipe out political inefficiency. In the future, the government will be forced to provide more extensive programs of public works to absorb those temporarily unemployed or not insured under the Social Security program. Some method must be found for averting the losses and wastes of wars and promoting world peace.

All other efforts to eliminate poverty are, however, secondary to the reform of our economic society. Only by making the most efficient use of our machines and assuring high wages and steady employment for all able-bodied citizens can we supply the mass of the people with the necessities of life under the capitalistic system.

## Summary

Poverty is one of the oldest social problems. Its causes are complex, but may be reduced to four main classes: geographical, biological, economic, and political. Poor or exhausted natural resources, natural cataclysms, sickness, accidents, unemployment, low wages, social and industrial waste, political graft and inefficiency, inadequate and impractical education, the costs of war—all these factors contribute to the creation of a poverty-stricken class. Historically, the church, and later the state, took over the care of the needy. Poor relief laws date from 1536 in England. The comprehensive Elizabethan Poor Law of 1601 was carried over into the American colonies. Through the years, the emphasis in legislation has changed from the relief to the prevention of poverty.

A scientific approach to the problem of understanding and treating poverty was introduced by social case work, which attempts to investigate and analyze the background of all individuals requiring relief, and to help them make their adjustments successfully.

In the crisis resulting from the depression of 1929, emergency programs were found necessary to help the millions of unemployed. The government stepped into the breach and organized direct-relief and public-works agencies calling for the expenditure of billions of dollars. More comprehensive and epoch-making than any of these agencies was the Social Security Act of 1935, amended in 1939, 1946, 1947, and 1948, which provided some measure of security for millions of workers, mothers and dependent children, the aged, the sick, and the disabled. In postwar days labor unions have launched a movement to provide insurance and other benefits for members, and to secure non-contributory pensions paid for exclusively by employers.

Poverty is one of our most important social problems. It can be effectively reduced only if a concerted effort is made to eliminate its causes. Most important of all, we must reorganize our economic system so that it will produce goods efficiently, provide high wages, guarantee steady employment, and thus assure an abundance for all. Such a program has little prospect of success unless we find some way of curbing international wars.

## Selected References

Abbott, Edith, *Public Assistance*, 2 Vols., University of Chicago Press, 1940–1941. The most complete account of the entry of the state into the relief of the needy, with special reference to New Deal measures.

Beveridge, Sir William, *Social Insurance and Allied Services*, Macmillan, 1943. The famous Beveridge Report on the "cradle-to-the-grave" program of social protection of the needy.

——————, *Voluntary Action*, Macmillan, 1948. Up-to-date supplement to the author's famous report on social insurance.

Bruno, F. J., *The Theory of Social Work*, Heath, 1936. Authoritative exposition of the field and methods of social work from the sociological standpoint.

* Burns, E. M., *The American Social Security System*, Houghton Mifflin, 1949. The most adequate survey of our existing plans and systems of social insurance and relief in the United States.

* Calcott, M. S., and Waterman, W. C., *Principles of Social Legislation*, Macmillan, 1932. A good introductory survey of the nature of modern legislation for the relief and protection of workers and the needy classes.

Clarke, H. I., *Principles and Practice of Social Work*, Appleton-Century, 1947. Valuable survey of the problems and techniques involved in social welfare work, interpreted from the sociological and psychiatric viewpoint.

Douglas, P. H., *Social Security in the United States*, McGraw-Hill, 1939. History and appraisal of security legislation in the United States, including the Social Security Act of 1935.

* Fink, A. E., *The Field of Social Work,* Holt, 1948. The most complete manual on the methods and all major fields of social work. An invaluable survey and summary.

Ford, James and K. M., *The Abolition of Poverty,* Macmillan, 1937. The most competent survey of the measures and programs needed to abolish poverty and prevent dependency.

* Hamilton, Gordon, *Theory and Practice of Social Case Work,* Columbia University Press, 1941. Supplements Miss Richmond's classic book by assembling and appraising the knowledge and experience gained in the quarter of a century since Miss Richmond's volume was published.

* Kelso, R. W., *Poverty,* Longmans, Green, 1929. Probably the best single volume on the causes and extent of poverty and the pre-New Deal methods of relief.

————, *The Science of Public Welfare,* Holt, 1928. Excellent historical survey of public welfare legislation and agencies prior to the New Deal.

Lane, M. S., and Steegmuller, Francis, *America on Relief,* Harcourt, Brace, 1938. A brief but reliable introduction to the revolution in relief methods after 1933.

Lindeman, E. C., *Wealth and Culture,* Harcourt, Brace, 1935. Gives a negative reply to the allegation that the benefactions of the rich justify the present concentration of wealth.

Lowry, Fern, (Ed.), *Readings in Social Case Work,* Columbia University Press, 1939. Valuable collection of case material.

McMahon, Arthur, Millett, J. D., and Ogden, Gladys, *The Administration of Federal Work Relief,* Chicago Public Administration Service, 1941. The standard history of the Works Progress Administration and its accomplishments.

Miles, A. P., *An Introduction to Public Welfare,* Macmillan, 1949. A good up-to-date textbook, providing a historical survey as well as a full treatment of contemporary public welfare techniques and programs.

Richmond, M. E., *Social Diagnosis,* Russell Sage, 1917. The classic formulation of the principles of social case work. On psychiatric social work, see the book by L. M. French in the bibliography for the next chapter.

* Riis, J. A., *How the Other Half Lives,* Scribner, 1892. The pioneer work in arousing Americans to the sorry plight of the poverty-stricken in great cities.

* Scheu, F. J., *British Labor and the Beveridge Plan,* Island Press, 1943. Good presentation of the background and provisions of the famous Beveridge plan of social security from the cradle to the grave, which has been applied and extended by the British Labour Government.

Stroup, H. H., *Social Work,* American Book Company, 1948. Able discussion of the field and the techniques employed.

# PART VIII

# Social Pathology: Human Wreckage, Its Nature, Extent, and Solution

## CHAPTER XXX

# Toward the Normal Mind: Mental Disease, Feeble-Mindedness, and the Rise of Mental Hygiene

### The Tempo of Modern Life and Mental Disorders

**The increase in mental and nervous diseases.** The increase of mental and nervous disease in the last fifty years is one of the most serious problems of modern society; like the other problems, it can be laid, in considerable part, to the speed, haste, and complications of modern life. In New York State, which is quite thoroughly urbanized, about one person out of every 20 now spends some part of his life in an institution for mental and nervous diseases. Indeed, on the basis of careful statistical studies, it was estimated in 1940 that about one out of twelve new-born infants in New York State would develop some form of serious mental disease at some time during his life.

The number of feeble-minded has also grown as the population has increased. And the presence of a large number of mentally defective persons in an urbanized industrial age is a far more serious problem than it was in a rural economy.

**Number of mentally afflicted in our population.** It has been estimated that nearly ten million persons in the United States are temporarily or permanently disabled by mental diseases and serious mental defect at any given time. Those actually disabled have millions of dependents, who are thus deprived of their support. In August, 1948, Professor Esther Lloyd-Jones of Columbia University, using United States Public Health Service statistics, summarized the situation as follows: About 5,000,000 suffered from psychoneuroses and allied mental diseases; 2,500,000 had serious character and behavior disorders; 1,500,000 were mental defectives of such a low order as to need institutional treatment or segregation; and 500,000 were epileptics. It has been estimated by leading psychiatric experts that, even on the basis of prewar conditions, one person out of every twenty now at the age of fifteen, will at some time during his life enter a hospital for the treatment of mental illness, and that one person out of ten will need medical treatment of some kind for a disabling mental disorder. Professor Lloyd-Jones estimates that 20 to 30 million Americans require, or would definitely benefit by, psychiatric treatment.

From 1880 to 1945, the number of insane confined in psychiatric hospitals increased from 63.5 to 371.1 per 100,000 of the population. At the beginning of the year 1946 an official government census stated that there were 527,000 patients in mental hospitals. Nearly 150,000 new cases are admitted to hospitals each year, and the net hospital population increases annually by over 10,000. It would increase much more strikingly if there were room for more new patients. More than half the beds in the public hospitals of the country are occupied by those suffering from mental and nervous diseases. Not only are these beds always full, but there is a long waiting list of patients seeking admission. State hospitals are now overcrowded to an extent of 15 to 75 per cent of their normal capacity. It is estimated that institutions cannot now receive much more than half of the really serious cases which should have hospital segregation and treatment. No less than 1,850,000 men were rejected by the selective service boards during the second world war as bad psychiatric risks. Some 700,000 later discharged from the army for psychiatric reasons made up over half of those receiving medical discharges from the army.

The cost of maintaining public hospitals for the mentally diseased is enormous—over 200 million dollars annually—and this figure is trivial compared to the loss of wages and productive power on the part of the afflicted. Albert Deutsch estimates that the minimum figure for the annual cost of mental diseases to the United States is a billion dollars.

**Why life today aggravates mental disorders.** Modern industrialized urban life has produced many disturbing circumstances which have a direct bearing on nervous and mental disorders. Nearly all city dwellers carry on their daily activities indoors—in homes, factories, offices, and stores. Living in artificial, man-made surroundings, they are out of contact with nature. The cities are filled with a thousand and one types of noise, day and night. The sound of taxis, sirens, motor cars, trucks, and so on tends to wear upon the human nervous system and make the city dweller nervous and "jumpy." Walking or driving on the streets is dangerous and nerve-wracking. Overcrowded tenements and small apartments offer little place for healthful rest, while cities still afford all too few facilities for play and recreation.

Factory and office jobs are monotonous. The speed-up system in industry may keep workers going at top speed with few rest periods during the working day. The work itself is usually uninteresting. Constant fear of losing a job and worry over how to pay the rent and buy food on a small income, especially in a period of rising prices, obsess the average working man and his family. The traditional close-knit family life, neighborhood friendliness and interest, and dependence on the assurances of the religious teachings of the past have been broken down and, as yet, no adequate substitutes have been provided. Large numbers of persons find the traditional standards of conduct and morals disappearing, with nothing comparable to take their place. All this has also contributed to nervous and mental instability.

**Mental disorders most numerous in cities.** Statistics confirm the conviction that modern city life is far more conducive to mental and nervous disorders than rural life. Twice as many admissions to hospitals for the insane, in proportion to population, come from urban as from rural areas. Even the greater laxity of rural authorities in discovering and segregating mental patients cannot wholly account for the great difference in urban and rural rates of admission to state hospitals. Furthermore, the rate of first admissions in cities of over 100,000 population is nearly twice as high as the rate in those with a population of 10,000 to 100,000. Robert E. L. Faris and H. W. Dunham found that the insanity rate in the crowded central district of Chicago and in the hobo, rooming-house, and bohemian areas nearby was about ten times as high as in the outlying residential and suburban areas inhabited by the relatively well-to-do elements of the urban population.

The number of insane from rural communities has, however, shown a tendency to increase in the past twenty years. This trend will probably become more marked as urban industrial life extends its influence into rural areas. An increasing alertness and determination about detecting and committing the mentally diseased in rural areas also, naturally, increases the number of the insane recorded as coming from rural regions.

**Other reasons for increase of admissions to mental hospitals.** Other factors besides the tempo of modern urban life have contributed to the increase in the number of mentally diseased in public hospitals. To-day, we are far more alert in detecting those who are suffering from mental afflictions because we have a more scientific knowledge of the nature of mental diseases. There are more and better public mental hospitals, and the more sympathetic understanding of the public has made relatives of mentally diseased persons more willing to have them committed. Hospitals have been enlarged, so that persons may be kept under treatment for a longer period, thus increasing the total hospital population. Dementia-praecox patients, one of the largest groups of the insane, live out their normal life span as relatively incurable patients and pile up the total hospital population, since many are committed and very few released each year. The general life expectancy has increased by over 20 years since 1880, so that the number of persons in the older age groups suffering from those mental diseases common to senility has risen.

**Causes of increase in mental disorders not the cause of individual cases of mental disease.** It should be understood that these factors mentioned in the previous pages which have led to an increase in the total number of mental and nervous patients are not the specific causes of any particular mental disease in a given individual. The immediate causes of a mental breakdown, as we shall explain later on, are mainly personal—organic diseases or mental conflicts in the individual mind—and can only be understood after a careful study of each patient by a neurologist or a psychiatrist. What modern life does is to augment susceptibility to mental and nervous disease and to increase the pressure of the tensions, conflicts, worries, and frustrations that help to cause individual breakdowns.

## Some Important Facts about Mental Disease

**Neuroses and psychoses.** Mental and nervous diseases are classified according to their type and seriousness. It was not until 1896 that a great European psychiatrist, Emil Kraeplin, gave us our first scientific and systematical classification of these disorders. Mild mental and nervous diseases that do not require institutional segregation of patients are called neuroses. The serious mental disorders, which render the patient dangerous or incompetent and in need of institutional segregation, are called psychoses. Almost invariably, mental and nervous diseases start as neuroses. If they are not recognized and treated in the early stage, they may become psychoses, which are much more dangerous and far harder to cure.

**Organic and functional mental diseases.** These diseases are also classified as organic and functional. An organic mental or nervous disease is one caused by some impairment of, or physical injury to, the brain and nervous system. These organic cases may be caused by brain tumors, diseases of the brain tissues or the central nervous system, physical accidents, toxic poisoning, chemical poisoning (as by alcohol and other drugs), or the physical changes accompanying old age.

In a functional mental or nervous disease, there is nothing discernibly wrong with the physical aspects of the brain and nervous system; emotional disturbances simply prevent the brain and nervous system from functioning normally. In most cases, functional nervous and mental diseases grow out of difficult living conditions which make individual existence painful, unhappy, and repulsive. Worries, disappointments, frustrations, sex problems, and the like produce such intolerable conditions of life that a person may seek refuge and comfort by building up an imaginary, happier world through fantasy. In time, this imaginary world may occupy the major attention of the individual, and reality may be forgotten. Often, however, this imaginary world in which the psychotic person dwells is not pleasant. Mental conflicts and frustrations may produce painful and terrifying delusions and hallucinations.

Among the more common organic mental diseases are brain tumor, inflammation of the brain, cerebral arteriosclerosis (or hardening of the brain arteries, most common among older persons), paresis (a disorder caused by syphilis), and senile dementia, namely, mental disintegration caused by old age. The more usual functional mental disorders are dementia praecox or schizophrenia, manic-depressive insanity, involutional melancholia, and paranoia.

While there are many cases of senile dementia and paresis committed to state hospitals, there are relatively few of these types in hospitals at any time. The senile dementia types are always old people and they soon die. The paretics either die quickly or are cured by new and revolutionary methods of treatment. The largest number in any patient group in state hospitals are those suffering from dementia praecox, a sad and hitherto all but incurable form of mental breakdown which occurs mainly in young people. Since most of those suffering from this disorder are committed early in life and usually live out in state hospitals the full life span of a normal person, they accumulate and constitute the bulk of the patients in any institution for mental diseases. At the present time, about half of the patients confined in mental hospitals are suffering from dementia praecox. There are many who suffer from manic-depressive insanity, but they are "in and out" of hospitals, since it is often not necessary to keep them in an institution except when their cases are most serious, usually in periods of severe depression. The number of those suffering from involutional melancholia is limited since it affects chiefly persons between 45 and 60 years of age. Many psychoneurotics are committed to state hospitals but their stay is usually relatively short. There are relatively few true paranoid patients.

**Relative curability of mental diseases.** It is obvious that the more rapidly mental disorders are treated, the greater the prospect that they will be cured. Neuroses are far easier to cure than psychoses, but they are all too often ignored until they become serious psychoses. Senile dementia is, quite naturally, incurable, since there is no way of rejuvenating old people. Paresis was formerly incurable, but new discoveries, especially penicillin and fever treatment, now make it possible to cure or arrest this disease unless its treatment has been too long delayed. Dementia praecox was also regarded as incurable in all except rare instances, but new experiments with drugs such as insulin, with psychosurgery, and with electric shock give some hope that this type of patients may be helped in many cases. Manic-depressive patients have frequently been cured through expensive private treatment by skilled psychiatrists but can only rarely be cured by the mass treatment necessary in state hospitals. Paranoia is generally regarded as the most difficult of all the functional mental diseases to cure. Involutional melancholia frequently yields to psychoanalytical treatment, and it has been reported that improvement has been shown as a result of electric shock treatment. Psychoneuroses, the most easily relieved or cured, are handled mainly in private medical practice.

In general, one may say that state hospitals are more successful in relieving and arresting mental disorders than in curing them. Indeed, because they are so meagerly staffed, such institutions can often do little more than segregate dangerous cases from public circulation and keep them alive. In some state hospitals there is only one doctor to a thousand patients, and this doctor may be only a master of "horse-and-buggy" psychiatry. It would require at least 2,000 well-trained psychiatrists, in addition to those now in service, to bring the institutional treatment of mental patients up to even minimum standards, along with probably 10,000 additional psychiatric nurses, clinical psychologists, and other trained technicians.

**Epilepsy.** Epilepsy is a not uncommon mental disorder. It was formerly regarded as an incurable and hereditary organic mental disease. More careful study by very able psychiatrists, such as L. Pierce Clark, John T. MacCurdy, and others, has made it seem more likely that epilepsy is a functional disorder, characterized by exaggerated egocentricity, impatience, selfishness, and the like, which can be arrested by skillful treatment and occasionally cured, even in its advanced stages.

Mainly as a result of investigation through the relatively new technique of electroencephalography there has recently been a swing back towards the idea of epilepsy as an organic brain disorder, and certain drugs, such as paradione and phenurone, have been found helpful in its treatment, especially in the reduction of seizures. But little has been discovered to alter Clark's conception of the epileptic personality.

There are two types of epilepsy—*grand mal* and *petit mal.* The former leads to serious convulsions and prolonged lapses into unconsciousness, while the latter manifests itself chiefly in brief and temporary lapses of consciousness and orientation. But the main mark of the epileptic personality, in both types, is extreme egocentricity and excessive impatience with any frustration of, or opposition to, personal wishes or action. It has been estimated that there are at least a half million epileptics in the whole population, and over 21,000 are now segregated in special colonies for epileptics.

**Inheritance of mental diseases.** It is popularly believed that mental and nervous diseases are hereditary. But psychiatrists and geneticists have shown that this is rarely true in any literal and precise sense. An eminent Boston psychiatrist, Abraham Myerson, in his book *The Inheritance of Mental Diseases,* has shown that there are few, if any, mental and nervous diseases that are directly inheritable. What can be inherited is a predisposition to mental and nervous disease in the form of a weak, nervous constitution. Hence, more than usual caution should be observed in the rearing of children in families where mental and nervous disease has been frequent.

## Hospitals for the Mentally Diseased

**Early treatment of mentally diseased.** Although the number of those suffering from mental and nervous diseases has notably increased, it is gratifying to find that there has been a great deal of improvement in treating these unfortunates. Down to the opening of the nineteenth century, the insane were treated with incredible brutality. They were put in jails and dungeons or shut up in poor houses, often to freeze or starve. If placed in hospitals they were usually chained to the walls and treated like animals.

**Reforms of Pinel, Esquirol, and Tuke.** A French physician, Philippe Pinel (1745–1826), is usually associated with the beginnings of some insight into the nature of insanity. About 1790, Pinel was appointed physician to an insane asylum in Paris. Here, he found the inmates bound with chains and irons and regarded by their keepers as savage and dangerous beasts. Against the advice of both physicians and public authorities, Pinel took the chains off most of the inmates and introduced humane methods of treatment. The predicted violence and other disasters did not follow and Pinel's methods were extended to other Paris asylums. Unfortunately, it was a long time before Pinel's methods were generally adopted, although in the generation following Pinel another French physician, Jean Esquirol, was able to establish some model "asylums" in which to treat the mentally diseased.

In England, Pinel's methods were adopted with many improvements at the Quaker sanitarium known as the York Retreat, under the direction of Samuel Tuke. The York Retreat exerted a great influence on the humane treatment of the insane, in both England and America. Johann Reil took up the cause of the insane in Germany.

**Early treatment of insane in the United States.** In the United States, the insane were long treated in the same brutal manner as they were in Europe. While Boston had earlier considered building an insane asylum, the first state hospital for the insane in the United States was opened at Williamsburg, Virginia, in 1773. The number of hospitals for the insane grew slowly. As late as 1843, there were only 14 hospitals, both public and private, for patients suffering from mental disease. By and large, as late as the second third of the nineteenth century, the majority of the insane in this country were still confined in prisons, jails, and almshouses. They were brutally treated, chained fast or locked in miserable cells, poorly fed, and half clothed.

**The reform work of Dorothea Dix.** Dorothea Lynde Dix (1802–1887), one of America's greatest humanitarians, was chiefly responsible for arousing public interest in the shameful treatment of the insane. After visits to the jails and almshouses of Massachusetts, where she was shocked at the wretched condition of mental cases, Miss Dix waged a campaign throughout the country, beginning in 1841, urging legislatures to establish separate institutions for the insane and to give them humane treatment. Her campaign was directly responsible for the state hospital for the insane opened in Trenton, New Jersey, in 1848. Altogether, twenty states answered her appeals by either building new institutions for the insane or enlarging those already in operation. Pinel, Esquirol, Tuke, Reil, Dorothea Dix, and later Clifford Beers were the leaders in bringing about a better understanding of mental diseases and encouraging more humane methods of treating the insane.

*Courtesy National Committee for Mental Hygiene.*

**The dawn of humane treatment of the insane. Dr. Pinel orders the chains removed from inmates of the Salpêtrière, Paris insane asylum for women. (*From a painting by Robert Fleury.*)**

**Advances in treatment of mental diseases.**  Since Miss Dix's day, there have been many improvements in the better institutions designed for the mentally diseased.   More state hospitals were built; today there are some 190 of them, along with 33 Federal neuro-psychiatric hospitals, mainly built after the first world war.  Separate institutions, with specialized treatment for the different forms of mental disease, have been erected.   In the early state hospitals, all insane types were herded together, along with mental defectives.  There was little or no special treatment for the epileptic, the feeble-minded, and those suffering from psychoses.

Scientific treatment has now been introduced for most psychotic cases.   Physical restraint by strait jacket or chains has been reduced to a minimum in the better hospitals.   Hydrotherapy and electrotherapy are widely used.  Electric shock and fever treatment have improved many mental patients.   Drugs such as insulin have become part of the treatment in the more modern hospitals. Insulin is used in what is known as "shock" therapy. The new fever therapy, inducing a high fever artificially, has been particularly useful in treating paresis, hitherto an incurable form of insanity. Occupational therapy, based on the belief that mental balance may sometimes be restored by creative work—knitting, hooking rugs, weaving, or wood carving, for example—has proved valuable.

The psychiatric approach has been responsible for curing many patients suffering from mental and nervous disorders. The progress of psychiatry has been mainly due to the advances in our knowledge of the unconscious, for it has been shown that many psychoses are disorders of the unconscious.

It was once believed that man is fully conscious of all his motives and actions. It is now known that the great majority of human responses result from impulses deep in the unconscious mind. Only a small proportion of our mental reactions are fully understood by us.

Just a small part of the iceberg is visible; a great submerged mass lies below the surface. So with the mind of man: the conscious mind is the smallest and most superficial part of it. It is believed by psychiatrists that the so-called functional mental and nervous diseases, which are the most numerous of all, are diseases of the unconscious, caused by conflicts and delusions in the unconscious mind. Therefore, if such forms of mental disease are to be cured, the unconscious, over which the individual has little conscious control, must be understood and redirected.

**The present crisis in mental hospital care and treatment.** Psychiatric knowledge, despite its impressive development, has been applied to only a limited extent in actual practice in state mental hospitals. It would require a medical staff ten times as large as that in the average state hospital to apply any such individualized treatment as a patient can get from a competent private psychiatrist. Hence, there has remained a great and lamentable gulf between our knowledge of psychotherapy and its application to the treatment of patients in public institutions.

Even the segregation and humane physical care of patients, which was about all many hospitals could provide, has suffered a serious deterioration since 1939. The war period was accompanied by a marked increase in the number of those who suffered from mental and nervous diseases and needed hospital segregation, but there was virtually no expansion of hospital plant owing to shortages of materials and labor. The conditions in some state hospitals became almost incredibly bad. A number of intelligent and well-educated conscientious objectors were assigned to duty as orderlies in these state institutions. They were shocked by the conditions they found and gave the facts to newspapers. Their stories produced publicity and further investigation, and mental hygiene experts joined in the movement of protest against the abominable conditions. Mary Jane Ward's book *The Snake Pit* brilliantly portrayed on the screen by Olivia De Haviland, probably did more than anything else to give the public some idea of the nature of the average present-day state hospital.

**Postwar conditions in mental hospitals.** It was found that in some hospitals the daily expenditure for total maintenance per patient was as low as 45¢, while even in the best it was only $1.46, though the American Psychiatric Association had estimated the minimum daily expenditure that would assure decent physical care as $2.50. The food provided was generally inadequate, poorly cooked, and badly served. Patients often lived in indescribable filth. Many were compelled to sleep on the floor. The quality of the hospital attendants dropped seriously, for the institutions could not meet the high wages paid in the war industries. The situation revealed constituted a veritable national scandal. It almost seemed as though we had reverted to the period and conditions at the turn of the century which prompted Clifford Beers to write his immortal book on the cruelties and stupidities of hospital treatment of insane patients.[1] The publicity given to such conditions led to some improvements, but no action at all commensurate with the needs has yet been undertaken by the majority of the states. In an excellent article in the New York *Times* of July 27, 1947, Dr. George S. Stevenson thus describes the general physical condition and operation of the average state hospital for the mentally diseased in one of the better state systems:

Some miles outside almost any major American city, on a two-lane macadam road off the main highway, there is a group of large buildings, quite a few of them, probably of red brick. They sit on broad sweeps of beautiful greensward; a little network of small roads, all studded with signs that read "Speed Limit 15 M.P.H." threads among them. This is the State mental hospital. Externally the setting is attractive, the buildings of good architecture. Inside, the impression a visitor gets is something else again.

There is the pervading, indescribable, institutional odor. There is the barrenness of the interior—little furniture, no pictures on the walls, nothing loose anywhere. Everything is colorless. Patients wear loose hospital clothing that has faded with years of laundering. They have no belts, no shoelaces, nothing with which they might harm themselves.

In one of the wards patients sit on benches or on the floor. They seem absorbed in their own private worlds. Some are weeping or groaning miserably; others are staring abstractedly through the barred windows at the grounds, which apparently are kept better than the patients are. In the small rooms where "disturbed" patients are confined individually there are no furnishings, no bed, just a soiled mattress. Perhaps in the next room there is a patient in a strait jacket. In the large bathroom at the end of the hall a violent case reclines in a tub, his chin held above the water by a canvas harness; the swirling water soothes him. On a near-by table another patient lies swathed in a wet sheet; this is also a sedative device, one that tends to make him drowsy.

What goes on inside the hospital provides a vivid contrast with the orderly external appearance of the institution. And that contrast, to a great extent, symbolizes the status of public psychiatric treatment today. Throughout the

---

[1] See below, p. 816.

United States we are confronted with a seriously ailing system of public psychiatry. The disturbing newspaper and magazine articles of the past few years which have described mental hospitals as "modern Bedlams" have been unpleasant because they couldn't be anything else and still tell the truth.

Dr. Stevenson is describing one of the better state hospitals. Albert Deutsch has this to say of another, the Byberry State Hospital, near Philadelphia, which was at the time housing 80 per cent more patients than its planned capacity: "I was reminded of the pictures of the Nazi concentration camps at Belsen and Buchenwald. . . . I entered buildings swarming with naked humans herded like cattle and treated with less concern. . . . I saw hundreds of patients living under leaking roofs, surrounded by mouldy, decaying walls, and sprawling on rotting floors for want of seats or benches."

Needed extension and improvement of facilities still lags. One good effect of this exposure of scandalous deficiencies in our mental hospitals is that it may shock us out of our complacency and lead to adequate remedial steps. While there was little actual ground for such a misapprehension, it was rather taken for granted in the 1930's that our public mental hospitals were in very satisfactory shape and were doing substantial work in curing patients. The recent publicity demonstrating that the opposite is true today may serve to set in motion another era of reform comparable to that which followed the publication of Mr. Beers' book and the formation of the National Committee for Mental Hygiene in 1908. The National Mental Health Act of 1946 may ultimately assure an adequate staff of trained psychiatrists for our hospitals, provided the states appropriate sufficient funds to hire them.

Much could be done to lessen the acute shortage of psychiatrists if the medical profession would abandon its shortsighted attempt to monopolize the field of psychotherapy. Clinical psychologists have a far more complete training in understanding the operations of the human mind than the average physician, even after two years of general interneship following graduation from a medical school. In treating the functional nervous and mental diseases clinical psychology provides a far more thorough preparation than any general medical training. Likewise, clinical psychologists are better prepared to master psychoanalysis and other recent therapeutic techniques than are persons with a straight medical training.

## The Development of Psychotherapy

Psychiatric knowledge has outdistanced the facilities for its use. While, as we have seen, there is a great gap between medical psychology or psychiatry and actual therapeutic practices in most public hospitals, various phases of psychotherapy have been so well developed that most forms of mental and nervous disease have yielded to them in greater or less degree, provided treatment is begun in time. These resources of medical science are available to hospitals to the extent that they are willing to provide the necessary funds to build up a good medical staff. Hence, in any discussion of the problems of mental hygiene, it is desirable to review at least briefly the main types of progress in the medical treatment of mental diseases.

**Neurological treatment of organic mental diseases.** It has been pointed out that mental diseases have been divided into two main types: organic and functional. The former are treated mainly by what is known as organic neurology, and the latter by psychiatry, though there is some overlapping. Neurology relies mainly on drugs and neurosurgery. Drugs, especially salvarsan and bismuth, have been used to treat disorders arising from syphilis, especially paresis and locomotor-ataxia. About 1917 an Austrian pathologist, Julius Wagner von Juaregg, introduced a revolutionary treatment for paresis by inoculating his patients with malaria, letting them run a high fever, which was believed to kill the germs, and then treating the malaria cases with quinine. More recently, the fever treatment has been applied by means of fever machines, usually controlled by electricity. Electrotherapy is used in a variety of other ways by neurologists in treating mental disorders. The recent development of electroencephalography, which deals with the recording and interpreting of brain waves, has been of great value in diagnosing epilepsy, localizing cortical brain tumors, and helping to distinguish organic from functional mental disorders. Narcotic drugs were used widely during the second world war to assist shell-shocked soldiers to recover their mental poise. We have already referred to the wide use of hydrotherapy in mental hospitals, mainly for its sedative effect. Brain surgery, developed to a high level of technique by Harvey Cushing of Boston and Charles H. Frazier of Philadelphia, has been used effectively in removing brain tumors, and thyroid surgery, improved by Theodore Kocher and George Crile, is often useful in dealing with other types of organic mental and nervous troubles.

**Early developments in psychiatry: Hypnotism and suggestion.** The functional mental and nervous diseases have been attacked most successfully by psychiatry, the approach through mental analysis and treatment. The first step in creating psychiatry was taken by Franz Mesmer in Paris, about 1800. He developed what was known as mesmerism, or the control of mental states by the use of various physical stimuli, such as bottles, mirrors, lights, music, and the like. More scientific was the development of hypnotism by James Braid, a famous English surgeon, about 1850. He was able to dissociate the minds of patients from normal channels of thought solely by the use of mental suggestion. Hypnotism was further developed and utilized as a method of therapy by two French physicians, Jean Martin Charcot and Hippolite Bernheim, in the generation following the work of Braid; they used it to treat various forms of hysteria. The subject was further pursued around the turn of the century by Pierre Janet in France and Morton

Prince in the United States. They developed the idea that functional mental diseases are caused chiefly by the dissociation of personality and the splitting of consciousness into several disunited streams; Prince gave special attention to the double or split personality. While Janet and Prince carried psychiatry along notably toward a broader conception of mental tangles and improved our curative therapy, they were not able to explain the causes of dissociation and the splitting of personality, nor could they probe very deeply into the unconscious with their therapeutic methods.

*Press Association, Inc.*

Sigmund Freud, pioneer in modern scientific psychiatry, contributed more than any other person to our understanding and treatment of mental diseases. He is shown here with his eldest daughter and the famous English psychoanalyst Dr. Ernest Jones in Paris in 1938.

**Sigmund Freud and psychoanalysis.** The problems which puzzled Janet and Prince were largely solved by a Viennese psychiatrist, Sigmund Freud (1856–1939), who had been a student under Charcot in his youth. Freud contended that dissociation arises when our libido, or the focus of our emotional drives, gets out of conscious control, regresses, and becomes fixated on an infantile level of experience, the causes and results thereof being hidden from our conscious comprehension. So long as they remain hidden, compulsions, phobias, and delusions, which make up the core of the functional mental diseases, are likely to develop. Conflicts arise between the ego and the repressed libido. Freud laid great stress upon sex, broadly conceived, and upon sexual frustration as the usual cause of such regressions of the libido. He worked out a technique known as psychoanalysis to probe the unconscious through dream analysis, word association, and the like, to reveal the cause of his troubles to the patient, to free the libido, and thus to effect a cure. Psychoanalysis is a relatively long and intimate process, usually very expensive, but it has revolutionized the treatment of the functional mental disorders. It has been elaborated and extended by other psychiatrists, such as Karl Jung, Alfred Adler, Otto Rank, and others, with results variously appraised by experts. Most functional mental diseases, except for dementia praecox, have yielded to the patient application of psychoanalysis. The most important recent advance in psychoanalytical therapy has been associated with the work of Franz Alexander and his colleagues at the Chicago Institute for Psychoanalysis. They have been able to speed up treatment without losing its curative value, thus making it more economical and accessible to a greater number of patients.

The eminent American psychiatrist, Adolf Meyer, of the Phipps Clinic of the Johns Hopkins Medical School, has been noted for his endeavor to balance and synthesize the organic and mental approaches to the interpretation of mental diseases, and to utilize the best curative techniques of both neurology and psychiatry. Meyer described his approach as that of "psycho-biology." More recent efforts to synthesize the organic and mental viewpoints have been made by E. J. Kempf and J. H. Masserman.

**The Rorschach Personality Test.** A sensational contribution to psychiatry and clinical psychology has been the belated application of the Rorschach Test to patients suffering from mental and nervous disorders. This test, developed by a Swiss clinical psychologist, Hermann Rorschach (1884–1922) in 1921 was long ignored not only by educational psychologists but also by psychiatrists. Introduced into psychiatry in recent years, the Rorschach Test appears to have had revolutionary results in speeding up the insight of psychiatrists into the personality patterns and emotional difficulties of patients. It utilizes mainly verbal responses to ink blots, which are shown to patients in various ingenious arrangements on different colored cards, and evoke numerous symbolic responses, depending upon the subconscious situation of the patients.

While the methods and results may seem fantastic to the uninitiated at first sight, extensive use and comparison with the results of prolonged psychiatric examination and psychoanalysis of the same patients have both increased confidence in the Rorschach Test and demonstrated the vastly greater rapidity with which psychiatrists and clinical psychologists can gain insight into the personality make-up and mental problems of the patient. In a few hours of careful testing by experts much the same insight can be gained by the psychiatrist as could be obtained in weeks or months of psychoanalysis. Of course, the therapeutic results of Rorschach exploration are not at all comparable to the benefits of psychoanalysis. But the Rorschach Test will afford much greater possibility of examining individually the personality problems of the mass of patients in mental hospitals, with their perennial shortage of psychiatrists and clinical psychologists, than could ever have been feasible with the older methods.

**Shock treatment for mental disorders.** Dementia praecox which, as we noted, accounts for about half the patients in most mental hospitals, has recently been attacked by drugs and psychosurgery with some success. About 1933, Manfred Sakel, a Viennese doctor, revealed a method of giving large doses of insulin to produce a severe mental shock, resulting in a temporary coma. Many patients have shown marked improvement, though some need several shocks to produce gratifying results. Other less toxic drugs, such as metrazol, have been substituted for insulin. But, at present, in the better hospitals, electric shock has been substituted for all forms of drug shock treatment because it is easier to administer and less likely to have serious aftereffects. This shock treatment has also been found helpful in treating involutional melancholia. In 1949, a group of psychiatrists at the New York State Hospital at Creedmore on Long Island reported that the effects of electric shock treatment were much more therapeutic when combined with the use of the drug called histamine, which also often produced good results when used without the shock treatment. A remarkable discovery was made in the New York State Psychiatric Institute in 1949 which may alter the whole future of shock therapy. It was found that intravenous injections of ether seemed to be as effective as any form of shock treatment, while avoiding the convulsive seizures and unpleasant after-effects of the shock treatment.

**Revolutionary new developments in psychosurgery.** While shock treatment has given us some hope for the hitherto almost hopeless dementia-praecox cases, psychosurgery has of late proved more effective, not only for dementia praecox, but also for other functional mental disorders, such as involutional melancholia, severe psychoneuroses, and the like. The most common of these psychosurgical operations is what is called prefrontal lobotomy, introduced by a Portuguese surgeon, Almeida Lima, about 1935. Over 2,000 such operations had been performed in the United States by 1948. Other variations are topectomy and temporal lobotomy. The latest technique is to drill through the skull and then, with an electric needle, scar the thalamus tissues. This is known as thalamatomy.

The aim and result of all these operations is essentially the same, namely, to destroy or reduce the activity of the thalamus, which is a sort of emotional center or relay station that transmits impulses to and from the frontal lobes, or thought centers, of the brain. The operations seem to reduce nervous tension and inhibitions, obsession with personal troubles and phobias, morbid introspection, pathological anxiety states, and the like. The record of cures and improvements has been striking—in one large series of cases recovery was claimed in 35 per cent and marked improvement in an equal number. The mortality, surprisingly enough, is very low—around one per cent. While it is too early to give any dogmatic verdict about the ultimate significance of this newer psychosurgical technique, there is some ground for believing that it may work as great and beneficial a revolution as Freudian psychoanalysis; it may also reach types of patients with whom psychoanalysis has not been very effective.

## Feeble-Mindedness as a Social Problem

**Distinction between mental disease and mental defect.** Less than a century ago, there was no clear distinction between feeble-mindedness and insanity. This was partly due to the fact that some types of insane persons—especially advanced dementia-praecox and senile patients— resemble in their behavior the attitudes and conduct of feeble-minded persons. Progress in medical science has, however, enabled us to recognize that feeble-mindedness is quite a different problem from insanity. Insanity implies defective mental reactions, especially defective emotional adjustment; feeble-mindedness is a matter of defective intelligence. Some cases of mental defect are the result of injuries suffered at birth or of illness at a very early age, but at least half the feeble-minded are born without normal mental capacity. All this makes the problem of the mentally defective (those with subnormal intelligence) different from that of the insane (those suffering from mental diseases). The feeble-minded rarely suffer from any mental disease. Theirs is a state of defective mental capacity, frequently hereditary and almost invariably chronic.

**Number of mentally defective in the population.** Estimates of the number of feeble-minded vary from 5 to 20 per cent of the population. If the high-grade morons are included among the feeble-minded, the total number would be close to 25,000,000. About 1,500,000 are classified as low-grade feeble-minded who need institutional treatment, but only about 110,000 are confined in institutions today.

There are over 500,000 seriously retarded children in our public schools who need special educational facilities to prepare them to be self-supporting. There are surely several million persons whose mental limitations disqualify them for professional life of any kind or for intelligent comprehension of, and participation in, public affairs. During the second world war some 582,000 were discharged by the draft boards or the army because of mental deficiency.

**Rise of mental testing.** It has been realized for centuries that people differ in mental capacity, but until the twentieth century this belief was based mainly on guesswork and general observation. In the decade following 1890, various psychologists and educators worked out ways to test the mental capacity of individuals, but the first adequate mental tests were devised by two French psychologists, Albert Binet and Thomas Simon, about 1905. Binet and Simon attempted to find the sort of questions an average child could be expected to answer at any given age. A child who can answer correctly the majority of questions which the average individual of his age answers is regarded as of normal intelligence. For example, a normal child of six is able to answer most of the questions which the majority of six-year-olds can answer. If the child falls behind the average, he is regarded as below normal. If he can answer the majority of questions usually handled successfully by older children—for instance, if a six-year-old child can answer the questions given to eight-year-olds, he is rated as above normal or superior, and would be regarded as having a mental age of eight years. The mental age of a child is, thus, determined by the age level of the questions he can answer satisfactorily.

The Binet-Simon tests were brought to the United States in 1908 by Dr. Henry H. Goddard, of the famous school for the feeble-minded in Vineland, New Jersey. Dr. Goddard improved upon the French tests by using questions more suitable to children brought up in an American environment. He was also the first to use these tests to divide the feeble-minded into three levels of intelligence—idiots, imbeciles, and morons. An improvement on the Goddard tests was provided by Professor Robert M. Yerkes of Yale University, who introduced the "point scale" system. This made allowances for the difficulties of foreign-born children in taking the tests. The next important advance was made by Professor Lewis M. Terman of Stanford University, who worked out a system that provided better methods of testing mental capacity and greater uniformity in the questions asked. Terman's Stanford Revision Test could be answered with about equal ease by any child, regardless of his cultural background. Better tests for superior children were also devised.

**The Intelligent Quotient and the grades of feeble-minded.** Professor Terman also made the idea of the Intelligent Quotient (I.Q.) popular. The I.Q. is the ratio of the mental age to the chronological or actual age of the child. For example, if an eight-year-old child can answer the test questions as successfully as the average child of eight years, his I.Q. is determined by dividing the mental age (8) by the actual age (8). In this case, the I.Q. would be 100 (the actual quotient, 1, is given as a percentage). If the eight-year-old can answer the questions usually answerable by a normal child of ten, his I.Q. would be 125, which is above the average I.Q. If the person tested is over 16, then 16 is taken as the chronological age in all cases.

Since the three levels of mental defect suggested by Dr. Goddard are in general use today, a brief explanation of them will be helpful. The term *idiot* is applied to the lowest type of the feeble-minded. Idiots usually have a mental age of under two years, and their I.Q. runs from 0 to 24. Low-grade idiots are far less intelligent than the higher apes. They are unable to care for their physical needs and require constant attention. The idiot group is a total loss to society. The *imbecile* has a mental age of from two to seven years. He will probably never get beyond the second grade in school, nor be able to support himself without aid and guidance. Although not as helpless as the idiot, he is often a complete burden on society. The I.Q. of an imbecile usually runs from 25 to 49.

The *moron* has a mental age of from seven to ten years. Even the low-grade moron can learn how to perform simple useful tasks, if he is supervised carefully. With painstaking training, he may be taught to act so that he need not be kept permanently in an institution. But neither the idiot, the imbecile, nor the low-grade moron can ever improve in mental capacity, because their brains are defective. The I.Q. of the moron is from about 50 to 75. There is a very large group lying between the morons and those of normal intelligence; this group, known as the "dull normals," has an I.Q. of around 75 to 90. It includes persons whose mental age is between ten and thirteen years. They are dull and slow-witted and find it difficult to keep up with the normal person, whose mental age is thirteen years or more. The bottom I.Q. for a person of what is regarded as fully normal intelligence is 100. Those who have I.Q.'s above 120 are superior mental types.

Some psychiatrists and sociologists estimate that there are about 40–50 million persons in the population who fall in the group of "dull normals," about 10 million who are ordinary morons, and, as we have noted, about 1,500,000 who have such low intelligence as to need constant care, even though, at the present time, there are only about 110,000 of them in institutions.

**Special pathological types of feeble-minded.** In addition to the idiots, imbeciles, and morons, there are special types of pathological feeble-minded persons. Some idiots and low-grade imbeciles have very large heads, owing to the pressure of watery fluid on the inside of the skull; we call these hydrocephalic types. Others having very small heads, often of a pineapple shape, are known as microcephalic cases. Another type of feeble-minded person is known as a cretin—cretins, no matter what their ages, never appear older than a baby of several months, nor do they usually gain enough control of their limbs to walk without assistance. Cretinism is caused by defects of the thyroid gland and can frequently be relieved by feeding the cretin thyroid extract. Another type of feeble-mindedness known as Mongoloidism because of a fancied facial similarity of those thus afflicted to members of the Mongolian race. The causes of this freak are not known at present, but there is a relationship between Mongoloid birth and the age of the mother, and glandular defects may be involved.

**Pseudo-feeble-mindedness.** While carefully administered mental tests will usually show the mental age and degree of mental defect, there are, as William H. Burnham has shown, many instances of pseudo-feeble-mindedness. The true mental defective has a definite and incurable lack of normal mental capacity; his innate mental capacity cannot be changed to any marked degree. He may be taught to adjust himself to his environment, but his I.Q. can never be notably raised. In the case of pseudo-feeble-mindedness, however, the individual is innately of normal mental capacity, but emotional difficulties, morbid fears, physical disease, or shock prevent his mind from functioning normally. The apparent mental defect is due to some form of emotional frustration. The behavior of the pseudo-feeble-minded person may resemble that of the true mental defective in every way. For this reason, a psychiatric examination should be made of any doubtful case, so that the pseudo-feeble-minded child may be given special training and treatment to restore his normal mental faculties.

A classic case of a pseudo-feeble-minded child was that of the boy Don, a patient of Dr. Lightner Witmer. When he came to the doctor's attention he seemed to be a hopeless idiot or low-grade imbecile. He was found to be a victim of infantile fears. He was successfully treated, and in a few years was in school along with normal pupils and was rated as among the best 20 per cent of all the pupils attending the school.

**Heredity and sterilization in relation to feeble-mindedness.** Twenty-five years ago it was generally believed that feeble-mindedness is always inherited and that the feeble-minded are a vicious group, invariably more prone to crime, vice, and acts of degeneracy than normal persons. More complete investigation, however, has shown that only around half the cases of even true feeble-mindedness are the result of heredity. The remainder are caused by injuries at birth, physical disease in early life, accidents to the brain, or malnutrition. Scientific study has also made it evident that the feeble-minded are not naturally criminal or vicious. But, since they are lacking in sufficient mental power to exert full self-control, they are more easily influenced by their surroundings, for either good or bad conduct, than are normal persons.

Better understanding of the problems of mental defectives, brought about in part by the work of Walter E. Fernald of Massachusetts, has made two points clear. The first is that feeble-mindedness cannot be wholly eliminated from the population by sterilization or segregation. Even if all feeble-minded persons today were prevented from reproducing, there would still be some feeble-mindedness resulting from delayed heredity reactions, accidents, and disease. Nevertheless, prevention of breeding by the mentally unfit is advisable, for it would greatly lessen the number of feeble-minded, even though it would not eliminate the problem. Fernald's second point is that if the feeble-minded are properly protected and directed, it is easy to keep them law-abiding. If, however, they are exposed to conditions leading to evil ways, they constitute a real menace to society. All above the level of the imbecile can be made self-supporting, even if some of the low-grade morons will need to be kept in institutions.

## Scientific Care of the Feeble-Minded

**Development of special institutions for the segregation and care of the feeble-minded.**Differentiation of the mentally defective from the mentally diseased, and a clear knowledge of the nature of mental defects, have led to the development of special institutions for the care of the feeble-minded.   Dr. Edouard Seguin of Paris, in the middle of the nineteenth century, first recognized the importance of special institutional care and treatment for the feeble-minded; his work with the feeble-minded may be compared to that of Pinel and Esquirol with the insane.   The first state school for the feeble-minded in the United States was the Massachusetts State School for Idiotic and Feeble-minded Youth, opened in Boston in 1848.   This school, later moved to Waverly and directed by Dr. Fernald, has exercised an important influence on recent developments in treating mental defectives.   In 1855, New York State opened a special institution for the care of the feeble-minded at Syracuse.   There are now about 180 institutions for the feeble-minded and epileptics, of which 87 are state institutions.

**Cottage and colony institutions.**   The first institutions for the feeble-minded were large, gloomy, prison-like structures.   In the twentieth century, there has been a trend toward the more humane cottage and colony system.   Dr. Charles Bernstein, of the Rome (New York) Institution for the Feeble-minded, introduced the idea of the cottage and colony system in 1906.   He believed that a farm colony provides the best method of caring for the higher level of imbeciles and the morons, who can be trained in simple skills and later released, under supervision, to work on farms or perform other tasks involving manual labor.   Dr. Bernstein maintained that the colony would serve as a halfway station between full institutional care and release to the outside world.   The colony system has been widely adopted, and through it many mental defectives have become self-supporting.   Since 1907, many colonies for the feeble-minded have been constructed, a notable one being Letchworth Village, at Thiells, New York, opened in 1911. This is a village community, which attempts to adjust the feeble-minded to normal social life.   Laboratories for the study of feeble-mindedness have been set up in connection with state institutions. Among the most important of these has been the Vineland, New Jersey, laboratory opened in 1906 and conducted by Dr. H. H. Goddard.

**Feeble-mindedness as a social problem in our day.**   Our public schools have long realized that some students are incapable of learning as much or as quickly as others.   Better provisions are now being made to help these mentally retarded pupils.   As was noted earlier, there are over 500,000 defective children who need special instruction.   Manual training has proved very effective in instructing the mentally retarded pupils, who cannot acquire much knowledge or skill except with their hands.

We have already mentioned the need of preventing the feeble-minded from reproducing. Some thirty of the states have laws that permit the sterilization of the mentally defective, but these laws have been applied with great restraint except in a few states like California, Virginia, Delaware, Oregon, and Kansas, and even here their enforcement has been lax. California and Virginia have the best record. The ineffectiveness of such laws to date may be seen by the fact that while the birth rate of the hereditary feeble-minded per 100,000 of the population is about 45, the average number of operations, even in states that take the law with some seriousness, is about 2 per 100,000 population.

The feeble-minded are a serious social problem today because of the complicated nature of modern society. Even the normal person finds it difficult enough to think and act intelligently in the confusion of present-day living. A large group of mentally defective persons in our urban industrialized society tends to retard social progress and increase our social problems. Even if feeble-minded persons do not happen to be of the hereditary type, they should not be allowed to have children, though their children might possess normal mentality. Feeble-minded parents are not fit to rear children, and there are surely plenty of normal persons in the population to produce all the needed children in any generation.

It has been frequently argued that we need a large number of feeble-minded in the population to do the "dirty work" of society, such as digging ditches, collecting garbage, and the like. This contention was never sound, and it has even less validity in our mechanical age, when machines can do most of our "dirty work" quickly and economically. And machines, when their work is done, can be stored away, in no danger of falling into crime or vice, breeding more defectives, or voting unintelligently.

## The Rise of the Mental Hygiene Movement

**Nature of mental hygiene.** Mental hygiene combines all the efforts to deal with mental disease and mental defects through reducing, so far as possible, the prevalence of mental and nervous disorders and mental defects, and by providing humane and scientific treatment for those who are mentally afflicted. The mental hygiene movement is also doing much to suggest more sane and healthful ways of living to those who are still relatively normal. While mental hygiene has had a large and beneficial influence on methods of curing mental and nervous diseases, its main aim and program are directed toward preventing mental breakdowns or checking them in the early stages of their manifestation.

**Place of Clifford W. Beers in the mental hygiene movement.** The movement had a dramatic beginning in the efforts of Clifford W. Beers to arouse public concern over the inhuman treatment of the mentally ill in state hospitals early in the present century. Beers suffered a mental breakdown a short time after graduating from Yale University and for three years was confined in various hospitals for the insane. In 1903, he regained his mental health. He came through his experience with an accurate memory of nearly everything that had happened to him while in the institutions.

Beers was one of the few mentally diseased persons of that time who completely recovered his sanity. To enter an "insane asylum" for treatment fifty years ago meant almost a living death. The few persons who ever came out of an "asylum" tried to forget their sufferings and the abuse they had endured in the way of discipline and "treatment." Fortunately for the progress of mental hygiene, Beers was an exception. Upon recovery, he determined to devote himself to the elimination of the mistaken medical and social ideas that were responsible for the unintelligent and inhumane handling of mentally diseased persons. In a remarkable book, *A Mind That Found Itself*,[2] Beers related his experience calmly and clearly. His book attracted wide attention.

**The National Committee for Mental Hygiene.** Beers conceived the idea of organizing state and national committees to promote the study and practice of mental hygiene. In May, 1908, he organized the first state society for mental hygiene, in Connecticut. A National Committee for Mental Hygiene was established a year later. Prominent leaders in many walks of life became interested in the movement. Among the more notable were William James, the famous psychologist, and Adolf Meyer and William Russell, leading psychiatrists. The philanthropist, Henry Phipps, gave indispensable financial assistance at the outset. The Committee was put on a permanent basis in 1909. Its program consisted of: (1) securing money to carry on effective work; (2) taking up "after care" of the insane to prevent relapses; (3) carrying on a program of education to acquaint the public with the salient facts concerning insanity, mental balance, mental hygiene, and healthy mental habits; and (4) attempting to revise the laws and procedure relating to insanity, so that they would be in accordance with scientific conceptions of mental instability.

At first, it proved difficult to make much headway because financial aid was not prompt or adequate. But, by 1912, sufficient funds had been secured to enable the Committee to commence active work. Progress was still slow, however, because of the prejudice and misinformation concerning mental disorders. Although the treatment of physical illness had been revolutionized in the previous 100 years, even many

---

2 Published in 1908. See Selected References for more recent edition.

educated people in the era immediately preceding the first world war regarded mental disease as beyond the reach of medical science.

**Achievements of the National Committee.** In 1912, a mental hygiene exhibit was prepared for the International Congress on Hygiene and Demography held in Washington. This exhibit graphically revealed the extent, cost, and social significance of mental disease and feeble-mindedness and the value of preventive work in the field. At this meeting, a section on mental hygiene appeared on the program for the first time, and mental hygiene thus received formal recognition as a vital movement in the field of public health. After 1916, new developments in mental hygiene came rapidly. In 1917, a splendid quarterly magazine, *Mental Hygiene,* was launched. During the first world war mental hygiene, under the leadership of eminent psychiatrists like Thomas W. Salmon, proved its real worth, not only in the treatment of the mental and nervous disorders usually called "shell-shock," but in keeping up the spirits and morale of the men in service. In the period following the war, mental hygiene proved invaluable in aiding discharged soldiers, sailors, and marines suffering from mental and nervous disorders. Leaders in mental hygiene, like the psychiatrist William Menninger, were able to accomplish even more during the second world war, for public and military authorities were more willing to listen to psychiatric experts in 1942 than in 1917. The National Committee for Mental Hygiene worked vigorously to improve the lamentable condition of state hospitals for the insane during and after the second world war and to secure the passage of the Mental Hygiene Act of 1946.

**The National Mental Hygiene Act of 1946.** The greatest single victory in the history of the mental hygiene movement was the passage on June 3, 1946, of the National Mental Hygiene Act. This provided for the building and equipment of a great National Mental Health Institute at Bethesda, Maryland, in connection with the vast Naval Hospital there. This Institute is to be an impressive research center on all problems connected with psychiatry and mental hygiene, covering the "nature, causes, treatment and prevention of mental diseases." The Act provides for grants for local research in the field. It also makes possible liberal grants to approved training centers for young psychiatrists. This will help to provide many more competent psychiatrists and thus partly remedy the scandalous present situation where one doctor has to deal with as many as a thousand patients in the poorer state hospitals. But the states will have to increase their budgets for psychiatric staffs if they are to take advantage of the new opportunity to secure adequate medical assistance.

**What mental hygiene has accomplished.** The mental hygiene movement has accomplished work of great significance in promoting better mental health. Forty years ago, there was a discouraging lack of public interest in nervous and mental diseases. Even students who graduated from good medical colleges knew little about psychiatry. The significant early manifestations of nervous diseases were all but ignored. In order to be admitted to a hospital for the insane, a person had to be regarded as dangerous and homicidal. The relationship between mental disease and dependency, delinquency, and general inefficiency was not understood even by social workers and other persons dealing with those problems.

Today, we can note a different situation. "Asylums" have become hospitals, and people are beginning to understand that it is no disgrace to be sent to them for treatment. Several states are adding mental hygiene divisions to their health departments. Changes in laws are being made, so that persons may be admitted to a hospital for the insane at their own request and receive temporary care. The care and treatment of patients in hospitals have improved, and the proportion of persons who recover is increasing, though the overcrowding of mental hospitals since 1940 has greatly handicapped the work of such institutions. More attention is being paid to the early symptoms of mental disorders, and the frequent relationship between mental and nervous disorders and dependency and crime is now recognized.

Social workers have come to realize that family, poverty, and delinquency problems may often be approached most effectively through mental hygiene. Psychiatric clinics have been established in both juvenile and adult courts, and in prisons and reformatories. Special institutions have been set up for the various types of feeble-minded. Universities and colleges now give courses in mental hygiene, and colleges of education train prospective teachers to promote healthy mental attitudes in their pupils. Books and pamphlets on mental hygiene have been published in large numbers, and statistics on mental disease have been systematically collected and distributed. With the increasing recognition of the place of mental hygiene and psychiatry in general medical practice, a whole new field of medicine, known as psychosomatic medicine, has recently been developed. Psychosomatic medicine stresses the interrelation between mental and bodily states and emphasizes the importance of psychiatric techniques and attitudes in treating physical disorders.

**The prevention of mental disease.** Beers and his associates wanted to do more than cure those already afflicted with mental or nervous disorders. They visioned a pattern of living that would keep people mentally fit and prevent or check mental disease. For this reason, they began with the problems of childhood. Problem children, who are antisocial and refuse to act like normal children, furnish the recruits from whom adult neurotics and psychotics are drawn. By linking up the mental hygiene clinic with the public school system, we may be able to discover and treat problem children before their warped personalities have caused them to establish dangerous and incurable habits of thought. These children can often be saved from mental disorders that might later take them to institutions for the insane or lead them to commit criminal acts. There are nearly 700 mental hygiene clinics in the country today, and about 300 of them are devoted entirely to child patients.

**Mental hygiene as a new technique of social work.** The mental hygiene movement recognizes the importance of mental and nervous factors in every phase of life and has extended its work to such fields as crime, industry, sex, the family, and education. Scientific criminology is virtually a department of mental hygiene. The use of mental hygiene in industry has been of importance in aiding the worker to adjust himself to new, complex patterns of living. Family life may be given a sound foundation as a result of mental hygiene's effort to create better family understanding and adjustment. A new and sound body of social ethics may be created through the combination of mental hygiene, biology, medicine, sociology, and psychology.

**A rational program of mental hygiene principles and activities.** Mental hygiene has suggested definite ways in which the mental health of the individual may be strengthened, so that he will be better equipped to cope with the complex problems of our ever-changing machine age. A few of these suggestions follow:

1. Everything should be done to develop physically strong and healthy bodies. Mental health means a strong mind in a strong body.
2. Children should be provided with a healthy, happy environment. The old idea of driving knowledge in with a club has been outmoded. School should be made interesting, so that the child will desire to learn. The promotion system in schools needs to be altered to take account of the wide variations in mental ability. Mental hygiene clinics for child guidance should be linked with the public school system in order to detect all problem children before their lives have been permanently warped and twisted.
3. We must do everything possible to eliminate the influence of fear on children, because the timid and nervous child is often mentally and emotionally retarded.
4. Much better provision must be made for organized play and recreation, in order to train the individual to get along with others, to learn to live in the world of today, and to keep in good physical trim.
5. The subject of sex should be taught in a scientific manner. Wrong attitudes toward living and family troubles have often been traced to lack of sex knowledge and to the unwholesome and inaccurate ways through which many children learn the biological "facts of life."
6. We must provide every normal person with an opportunity for employment that will give him security. Nothing promotes mental tension more surely than worrying over the loss of a job, or trying to discover where the money to pay rent and buy food and clothes is to come from.
7. Employers, through trained personnel workers and industrial psy-

chologists, must provide better working conditions in order to reduce nervous tension and lessen fatigue among workers.

8. Planned community work must be provided in various fields— education, health, character building, recreation, forums, club life, aesthetics, and the like, to supply the conditioning and guidance formerly provided by the rural primary groups, which have been disrupted by mechanization, urbanization, and the rise of contemporary modes of transportation and communication.

## Summary

Among the most serious of our social problems is the marked increase in the frequency of mental diseases. It has been estimated that there are around ten million persons in the United States temporarily or permanently disabled by mental diseases and mental defects at any given time. Within the past fifty years, the number of those confined to hospitals for mental diseases has increased six-fold.

Mental diseases seem to have increased principally as a result of the strains and stresses of modern urban and industrial life—the noise and confusion of cities, the worry and strain produced by the uncertainties of modern economic life, the monotony of work in factories and offices, the lack of adequate housing and facilities for recreation, and other similar factors.

Until well into the nineteenth century, the insane were treated with even less consideration than criminals. Neither the general public nor the medical profession understood the nature of insanity. Philippe Pinel, Jean Esquirol, Dorothea Lynde Dix, Samuel Tuke, and Clifford Beers were among the pioneers in bringing about the creation of special hospitals to care for the mentally unbalanced. Prior to the second world war, in most states, efforts were being made to provide adequate care for the insane, and medical science is now bending every effort to discover cures for the various types of mental diseases. Overcrowding of state hospitals and shortages in their medical staffs have become a national scandal since 1940.

While the insane are persons of normal intelligence who are suffering from mental diseases, the feeble-minded are persons who, as a result of heredity, disease, accidents, and the like, lack normal mental capacity. Estimates of the number of feeble-minded in the United States range from 5 to 20 per cent of the population according to the classification used. There are three principal levels of feeble-mindedness: idiots, imbeciles, and morons. It is estimated that there are about 1,500,000 idiots, imbeciles, and very low-grade morons in the population, most of whom need care in institutions; only about 110,000 of these are receiving such care.

Since the introduction of intelligence tests by Binet and Simon about 1905, progress has been made in understanding and caring for the mentally defective. Special institutions have been erected for their segregation and treatment, the cottage and colony system proving especially suitable. Some provisions have also been made in the public schools to aid the education of the 500,000 pupils of low mental capacity needing special guidance.

The mental hygiene movement, inaugurated by Clifford W. Beers in 1908, seeks to co-ordinate and promote all scientific efforts to care for the mentally diseased and the mentally defective, and to encourage healthy mental habits in the general public. The guiding agency in the movement is the National Committee for Mental Hygiene, founded by Beers in 1909. The mental hygiene movement has many accomplishments to its credit in the improved management of institutions for the insane and feeble-minded; the introduction of psychiatric clinics into schools, courts, prisons, and reformatories; the setting up of courses in mental hygiene in schools and colleges; the co-ordination of psychiatric clinics with social agencies; and the publication of helpful books and pamphlets dealing with the problems of mental health.

## Selected References

Barker, Elsa, *Fielding Sargent,* Dutton, 1922. An excellent introduction to the methods of psychoanalysis presented in the form of a novel.

* Beers, C. W., *A Mind That Found Itself,* Doubleday, Doran, 1923. The absorbing autobiography of the founder of the mental hygiene movement. Gives much insight into methods of dealing with the insane early in the present century.

Benedek, Therese, *Insight and Personality Adjustment,* Ronald Press, 1945. Valuable for its concentration on problems of mental health in the period of postwar readjustment, international tension, and social upheaval.

Bisch, L. E., *Be Glad You're Neurotic,* McGraw-Hill, 1936. A popular medical presentation of the frequency of neurotic traits in normal persons and of the constructive functions of mild neuroses. A somewhat reassuring book.

* Bond, E. D., *Thomas W. Salmon, Psychiatrist,* Norton, 1950. A biography of one of the world's greatest practical psychiatrists and the one most active in the mental hygiene movement in the United States. An invaluable source of information on the growth of a more scientific and humane treatment of mental disorders in this country.

* Bromberg, Walter, *The Mind of Man,* Harper, 1937. Readable and authoritative history of psychiatry and mental hygiene.

Brown, H. C., *A Mind Mislaid,* Dutton, 1937. Another autobiography revealing the symptoms and experiences of mental disease.

Davies, S. P., *The Social Control of the Mentally Deficient,* Crowell, 1930. The standard work on the feeble-minded in the United States and the methods of dealing with them.

* Deutsch, Albert, *The Mentally Ill in America*, Columbia University Press, 1949. An admirable book dealing with the treatment of those afflicted with mental and nervous disease. It gives a good history of the stages in the evolution of concepts of mental disease, the improvements in medical treatment, and the evolution of institutions for treating the mentally ill.

————, *The Shame of the States*, Harcourt, Brace, 1948. Shocking but authoritative revelation of conditions in state hospitals for the mentally diseased during and after the second world war.

Faris, R. E. L., and Dunham, H. W., *Mental Disorders in Urban Areas*, University of Chicago Press, 1939. Detailed study of mental disease in the city of Chicago, showing variation of disease rates in different residential areas.

French, L. M., *Psychiatric Social Work*, Commonwealth Fund, 1940. Pioneer work on the entry of mental hygiene concepts and practices into social work.

Freud, Sigmund, *The Question of Lay Analysis*, Norton, 1950. Authoritative criticism of the monopolistic pretensions of the medical profession in the psychoanalytical field. Calls for broad and well-rounded training, in which routine medical education plays a very small rôle.

Hall, J. K. (Ed.), *One Hundred Years of American Psychiatry*, Columbia University Press, 1945. Symposium by experts on history of American psychiatric concepts and practice.

Hart, Bernard, *The Psychology of Insanity*, Cambridge University Press, 1922. A leading psychiatrist presents a clear primer of the mental traits which characterize those suffering from mental disorders.

Hoskins, R. G., *Endocrinology: The Glands and Their Functions*, Norton, 1941. Authoritative work on the psychiatric significance of the glands of internal secretion.

Lemkau, P. V., *Mental Hygiene in Public Health*, McGraw-Hill, 1949. Valuable and thoughtful book, stressing the preventive function and responsibilities of psychiatry and indicating the important rôle that mental hygiene should play in public health work.

Lewis, N. D. C., *A Short History of Psychiatric Achievement*, Norton, 1941. A clear and untechnical review of the history of psychotherapy.

Lichtenstein, P. M., and Small, S. M., *A Handbook of Psychiatry*, Norton, 1943. A professional but non-technical description of the main mental disorders.

Marshall, H. E., *Dorothea Dix*, University of North Carolina Press, 1937. A good biography of the first great crusader for the humane treatment of the insane in the United States.

Masserman, J. H., *Principles of Dynamic Psychiatry*, Saunders, 1946. Best recent summary and synthesis of psychiatric knowledge. Written from a broad and well-balanced point of view.

* Menninger, Karl, *The Human Mind*, Knopf, 1930. Perhaps the best single book to serve as an introduction to mental disease and mental hygiene. Sane and interesting.

Menninger, W. C., *You and Psychiatry*, Scribner, 1948. A good introduction to psychiatry for the layman by one of America's leading psychiatrists.

Nicole, J. E., *Normal and Abnormal Psychology*, Macmillan, 1948. Excellent introduction to clinical psychology and psychiatry for nurses and social workers.

* Rennie, T. A. C., and Woodward, L. E., *Mental Health in Modern Society*, Commonwealth Fund, 1948. The best up-to-date survey of the field of mental hygiene.

* Roberts, Harry, *The Troubled Mind*, Dutton, 1939. An admirable elementary introduction to the nature, symptoms, and treatment of mental disorders.

* Terhune, W. B. (Ed.), *Living Wisely and Well*, Dutton, 1949. Excellent, popular symposium on mental hygiene by leading American psychiatrists.

Thompson, Clara, *Psychoanalysis: Its Evolution and Development*, Hermitage House, 1950. Clear and up-to-date account of the development of psychoanalytical concepts and techniques from Freud to the present time.

# CHAPTER XXXI

# Streamlined Crime in the Twentieth Century

## The Meaning of Crime

**Our rising crime wave.** The crime problem is another social issue that has been brought to a head by the strains and stresses of our era of war and rapid social change. The crime rate in the year 1947 was the highest since national crime statistics were first tabulated by the Federal Bureau of Investigation in 1930. According to *Uniform Crime Reports,* 1,665,110 serious felonies were committed in 1947, while crimes of all types averaged one every 18.9 seconds. Compared with the figures for the prewar years of 1938–1941, murder showed an increase of 15.4 per cent for 1947; burglary, 15.3 per cent; robbery, 14.6 per cent; and larceny, 2.6 per cent. Crime continued its upward trend in 1948 and 1949, and the most notable and alarming trend, aside from juvenile deliquency, was the great increase of crime in the once relatively law-abiding rural areas—the increase in 1949 was 2.7 per cent for cities and 7.6 per cent for rural areas.

**Nature of crime.** Crime is a word that often conjures up a vivid picture of masked bandits fleeing from police officers, of a ruthless kidnapper seizing a small child, and of chain gangs working at hard labor in prison camps. Many newspapers daily carry such headlines as "Five New Holdups in Crime Wave." The neighboring movie house shows a picture in which the moral is "Crime does not pay," and the radio blares forth with the staccato of machine-gun fire in the latest "G-man" serial.

With so much emphasis on the subject of crime in our country, we need a clear understanding of the term. Crime means any type of behavior—any act—which is forbidden by law. The offense may be as serious as murder or as petty as chicken stealing. The lesser crimes are formally classified as misdemeanors, the more serious offenses as felonies.

**Crime concepts often archaic and inconsistent.** Many acts today are called criminal only because, at an earlier time, laws were passed forbidding them. In some instances, the ideas and customs of the group have changed to such an extent that what was once considered a serious crime is no longer regarded as even a minor offense. But the offense may remain on the statute books.    There are still laws on the books against the practice of witchcraft, failure to attend church, Sunday baseball, blasphemy, and the like.    As examples of petty crimes, a southern law forbids persons to put salt on a railroad track (lest salt-loving cattle be lured to their death); it is illegal to make personal remarks about a passer-by in a midwestern state; a law in an eastern state makes it a crime to shoot a rabbit or a bird in a cemetery; another in a western state requires hotels to take in horses as well as men; and a West Virginia law declares it to be a felony for a doctor or dentist to give an anaesthetic to a woman without a third person being present.

At the same time, many acts, really disastrous to the well-being of the group, are not considered criminal or immoral, because they are approved by men in power, who see to it that no legislation is passed to hinder their type of activity.    For instance, the man who speculates recklessly on the commodity market with the funds of his customers may lose the hard-earned savings of honest men and women, but he usually keeps out of prison, for there is no law to cover his irresponsible handling of other people's money.    Until recently, we had almost no protection against great losses through the chicanery of holding-companies, which John T. Flynn once described as "the machine guns of the corporate racketeers."    As Bernard Shaw once put it, "If a man steals a loaf of bread he is run into jail, but if he steals a railroad he is run into Parliament."

**Economic causes of crime.**    Although there are many ways of classifying and explaining crime, the great majority of serious crimes today have an economic motive; they are usually crimes against property instead of persons.    Very few criminals, except gangster gunmen, deliberately intend to murder their victims, since the penalties for taking human life are severe.    If murder takes place during a holdup, it usually occurs because of the haste, fear, or excitement of the criminal.

If need is the main reason for most petty crimes, greed is the basis of most modern large-scale crime.    Those who break the law because they need food, clothing, and small sums of money are not the most important criminals today.    The most dangerous lawbreakers are those who, moved by the desire to become rich and powerful without working for success, will adopt almost any means to realize their ambition for "easy money."

**Crime waves may be exaggerated.**    Crime causes a large number of deaths, but "crime waves" are often exaggerated in the public mind through the newspapers, which increase their circulation by playing up sensational murder cases.    The homicide (murder) rate, though far too high, is small compared with the death rate from suicide, accidents, and preventable disease.    Although the total deaths from homicide average around 10,000 a year, almost 20,000 persons commit suicide annually, and 100,000 die from accidents, while over 300,000 lose their lives from preventable disease and lack of medical care.

Before we take up the various phases of modern crime, let us pause for a moment to see why there is more crime in some parts of the country than in others, and why certain types of crime seem to be most prevalent in particular sections of the United States.

## The Social Background of Crime

**Centers of racketeering and organized crime.** Racketeering and large-scale organized crime, which is the most important crime of our day, is centered mainly in the great cities of the urban North and East, including also such midwestern cities as Chicago, Minneapolis, and St. Louis, and in the few large cities on the Pacific coast. The urban location of big time criminal activity is no accident; it results from the greater opportunities for racketeering in the city and from direct contact with the "something-for-nothing" psychology of the urban leisure class and corrupt machine politicians.

**Crimes of violence.** Violent crimes, such as murder and assault, are most frequently found in the southern states and are the natural outgrowth of the wide gap between social classes in the Old South. It formerly was necessary for the whites to use strong discipline to keep the Negroes and poor whites under control. Lynching was a fairly common type of punishment.[1]

**Crimes against property.** We find that the West has more violent crimes against property; over half the bank robberies in the United States, in one recent year, were committed in six western states, California, Missouri, Illinois, Kansas, Texas, and Oklahoma. These crimes may be attributed, in part, to the tradition of robbery and lawlessness on the early frontier.

**Delinquency areas in cities.** Just as special types of crime predominate in different sections of the country, so there are certain areas, usually slums, in large cities in which crime seems to center. The more dangerous types of crime, however, are organized crime and racketeering. Those who engage in this form of crime, except for the gangsters who handle the dirty work, do not live in the slum areas. They dwell in the more aristocratic parts of the city—on Park Avenue, New York, for example—and often own mansions in Miami and other resort towns. They have their headquarters in the business and financial districts of our great cities and in the hangouts of the politicians with whom they connive.

**Rural crimes.** If cities produce their special crime trends, notably organized crime, racketeering, and gambling syndicates, rural criminality has long exhibited its peculiar patterns, chiefly that of crimes of physical violence against persons—murder, manslaughter, and assault. This was due to the lesser amount of money and movable

---

[1] Crimes of violence have predominated in rural areas, at least until very recent times, whereas crimes against property have formed the majority of urban crimes. See above, pp. 586–587.

property in the country which thieves and robbers could make away with, and also to the smaller and more scattered population of the country and its greater inaccessibility. This special phase of rural crime before the second world war was well portrayed by Stewart H. Holbrook in his book *Murder Out Yonder*. Moreover, the crime rate per capita was far lower in rural regions before 1945.

Since the second world war there has been a marked change in rural crime. This ranks along with the shift of much "big crime" from more violent and desperate acts to "fixed," syndicated gambling as one of the two most notable trends in crime at the mid-century. The increase of criminality since 1945 has been far greater in the country than in cities, and the largest growth of postwar rural crime has been in the field of crimes against property. For example, in 1946 rural robbery increased by 48.4 per cent over 1945; and rural auto thefts by 34.3 per cent, as against a 23.9 per cent increase in rural assault cases. This trend is still continuing. In 1949, crime increased by 2.7 per cent in cities, and by 7.6 per cent in rural areas. Burglaries and larcenies increased in cities by only 4.4 and 3.3 per cent, respectively, over 1948, but they increased by 13.1 per cent and 8.8 per cent, respectively, in rural districts. On the other hand, assault cases rose by 4.4 per cent in cities, while they gained only 3.8 per cent in the rural regions.

There has been no definitive study of the reasons for this remarkable transformation in the nature and extent of rural crime since 1945. It is, probably, the result of a complex combination of circumstances— the increasing impact of urban influences on rural life, the experiences of rural youth in wartime, the disruption of rural living conditions and social controls by the war, and the relatively defective character of rural crime control and repression.

Let us now look at the spirit of modern crime, born mainly of the something-for-nothing philosophy that is a part of American culture.

## The Something-for-Nothing Philosophy and Crime

**Origins of the something-for-nothing attitude.** Many Americans have always been attracted by the idea of securing vast wealth without any appreciable mental or physical effort. Visions of limitless gold and silver, to be had for the taking, drew large numbers to our shores in the days of exploration and settlement. Many colonists soon turned, however, from searching for gold to swindling the Indians. They swapped beads and trifles for valuable furs and then sold the pelts at a good price.

**Land speculation and the Gold Rush.** Another early example of the something-for-nothing philosophy in American life was the land speculation that lasted from 1789 down to the time of the Civil War and was revived with the building of the western railroads after 1865. The desire for easy money also took thousands to the gold fields of California after 1849. Thousands of prospectors died and thousands more endured all sorts of hardships in their search for a "rich strike." When some of the successful prospectors started back East with their golden treasure, they were waylaid and robbed by bands of outlaws who wanted quick riches without hard work. The western frontier also added its bit to the American tradition of lawlessness through the romance attached to its "two-gun" outlaws, like the James brothers and Billy the Kid.

**Stock speculation.** The Civil War was followed by a period of wild gambling in the securities of American railroads, many of whose owners and directors were far more interested in using the railroads as a substitute for poker chips in a huge stock-market gambling game than in furnishing cheap and efficient transportation to the public. Later, the securities of other corporations also became the prize in a series of wars between groups of financiers, interested less in producing goods than in making huge profits through dubious financial operations.

The ease of making money through gambling in securities attracted even the man on the street during the 1920's. Bootblacks, stenographers, taxi drivers, and housewives rubbed elbows with millionaire financiers in brokerage offices, all trying to make fortunes overnight by buying and selling stocks.

The something-for-nothing, or easy money, motivation of conduct has, of course, been greatly stimulated by our competitive economic society, which asks "Have you got it?" rather than "How did you get it?" As Morris Ploscowe puts it: "Our competitive system places a premium on success. Success has been translated into monetary terms. It is not what a man is that matters, but what he has."

**Genesis of racketeering and organized crime.** It was inevitable that this something-for-nothing philosophy would seep down from the upper levels of the financial world into the lives and thoughts of the lower classes. The "small fry," too, adopted the motto that "only saps work." The "small fry" were, in part, the children of immigrants. Their parents had earned an honest living by hard work as unskilled laborers, pushcart peddlers, clothes cleaners, or shoe shiners. But the younger generation had little taste for the back-breaking labor their parents had done. So, for example, instead of pushing carts of bananas and oranges, they organized "rackets" that gave them control of the sale of fresh fruit in entire cities, or a "rake-off" on the proceeds from the sale.

Large numbers of rural youths joined the city racketeers and gangsters. As we have seen, the introduction of machinery and improved methods of transportation have tended to break up the old rural cultural and social standards. Moreover, many rural youths were out of work. The movies, sensational newspapers, magazines, and other agencies for the dissemination of information brought to rural youths lurid and alluring accounts of the easy money city gangsters were making. It is from these two groups, urban loafers and rural youth, that the army of organized criminals, racketeers, and gangsters has been mainly recruited. The city element supplies most of the racketeers, and the country youth the majority of the daring and intrepid bank robbers, truck robbers, and the like.

It is highly important to keep in mind the altered character of the crime picture since the first world war. It has been estimated that the total annual cost of crime in the United States today, including the damage done by criminals, and the expense of catching, convicting, and confining them, is at least 12 billion dollars. Of this, the cost of organized crime, racketeering, and white-collar crime is at least five billion while the cost of traditional crimes, such as robbery, burglary, larceny, forgery, theft, and the like, does not exceed 500 million.

**Main patterns and trends in twentieth-century crime.** In the evolution of the crime picture in the United States in the twentieth century, there have been three main stages or patterns: (1) the period before the first world war, when the crime scene was dominated by the traditional crimes, such as robbery, burglary, larceny, forgery, assault, and the like; (2) the spectacular rise of "big crime" between the first world war and the termination of Prohibition in the form of organized crime and racketeering; and (3) the remarkable growth of organized and "fixed" gambling since about 1940, and the shifting of more and more of the big criminal and underworld operators into the gambling field to obtain the advantages of its greater gains and reduced risks.

## White-Collar Crime and Gambling

**Corporate chicanery.** Dishonest financial and business operations—what Professor E. H. Sutherland calls "white-collar crimes"—constitute perhaps the most widespread method of getting something for nothing. If a petty criminal breaks open the safe of a company and takes out a few hundred dollars, he renders himself liable to a long prison sentence. If, however, ambitious promoters organize a holding company that takes millions of dollars of the earnings of a corporation out of the pockets of the stockholders, they may not be punished at all. Indeed, they may be praised for their cleverness, held in high esteem by the community, and even rewarded with important public offices.

**Unnecessary bank failures.** Inefficient and dishonest management of banks has also brought tremendous financial losses to the American public. Between 1921 and 1932, some 11,800 American banks closed their doors, with losses of around 5 billion dollars to depositors. This avalanche of unjustified bank failures led one of our more famous economic historians to observe that the burglar alarm is often misplaced in banks; instead of being placed on the vault, it should be attached to the executive room of the officers and directors. Banking should be safer and more profitable in the United States than anywhere else in the world. Yet, our banking record is far worse than that of most other important nations. Canada has had but one bank failure since 1914, and there has not been a bank failure in England in recent times.

**Stock gambling.** Likewise, reckless and crooked operations on the stock exchanges have brought financial ruin and personal disaster to hundreds of thousands of ordinary men and women who invested their savings in securities. The shrinkage of stock values between 1929 and 1933 amounted to over 100 billion dollars on the New York Stock Exchange alone. This huge sum far exceeded the total cost of crime and racketeering during these years.

**War profiteering.** The second world war brought us face to face once more with a particularly reprehensible type of crime, and one which usually goes unpunished, namely, profiteering on war contracts. Billions were stolen from the government and from the American people in this way during the first world war, and almost no one was punished. Indeed, high government officials, including the then Vice-President of the United States, were able to prevent a real investigation of the profiteering. Similar scandals in the second world war have been revealed, with black-market criminal operations especially prevalent.

**Frauds, swindles, and embezzlements.** Less impressive in volume, but still serious in the amount of injury they cause innocent persons, are the more overt forms of financial crookedness, known as fraud and swindling. It would be difficult to estimate the total amount of money filched from the public by fake enterprises each year. Before the great stock market crash of 1929, the sale of worthless stocks and bonds brought swindlers over a half-billion dollars every year. Investors in one large investment trust lost 580 million dollars between 1929 and 1935. Swindles involving worthless merchandise have at times reached an annual volume of 500 million dollars. A single fake real estate enterprise took in over 100 million dollars from the "suckers" of Washington, D. C., in one year. Embezzlement is a common form of white-collar crime. In only four cases, in 1931, the losses amounted to 9 million dollars. Virgil W. Peterson, an expert on the subject, estimates the annual losses from embezzlement in the United States to be about $400,000,000. The public loses far more each year through swindles and embezzlement than all the robbers, burglars, and pickpockets are able to collect. Ironically enough, these frauds and swindles result in part from the investors' desire to get something for nothing.[2]

**Fraud and extortion in union labor circles.** It is well to make it clear that not all swindling is done by crooked business. We have already pointed out, in dealing with labor unions, that there are plenty of crooks and racketeers in the unions. They fleece the poor workers, frequently confiscate union funds, betray the union workers, blackmail and cajole employers, and the like. William Bioff and George E. Browne were accused and convicted of extorting $500,000 from four large moving picture companies by threatening to call a strike and tie

---

[2] See the Ponzi swindle, below, pp. 834–835.

up production. George Scalise was convicted of stealing $60,000 from the International Building Service Union, of which he was president. It is not unknown for union crooks both to call unwise strikes, thus injuring the workers, and also to furnish strike breakers to employers to help break these strikes.

**Sundry other forms of white-collar crime.** There are various other types of white-collar criminals, among them the loan sharks, who defy the laws against usury and filch large sums from the poor and others in desperate need of funds by charging outrageous interest rates. Others defraud reckless or needy persons through profiteering excessively on installment sales. Fraudulent advertising and the sale of worthless nostrums are other types of white-collar crime; worthless patent medicines and the services of quacks cost the country over $600,000,000 a year, not counting the cost of the unnecessary deaths which result. Fee collectors, both public and private, often gouge their victims severely. With the increase of taxes, a popular type of crime or quasi-criminality is tax evasion, aided and abetted by tax evasion services. The enormous increase of taxes during and since the second world war will probably increase this type of borderline criminality.

Political graft constitutes a large sector of white-collar crime, but since we have covered this in detail in the chapters dealing with politics and city government, the description of this form of crime need not be repeated here.

**Nature and extent of gambling.** Gambling, which ranks as a great American pastime, is another enterprise based upon the something-for-nothing philosophy. Gambling may be as mild as a bingo game at a charity church supper or a bank night at the local theatre, or as simple as risking a dime on a patchwork quilt or putting a nickel in a slot machine. But the gambling mania also extends into the realm of high finance and organized crime.

Gambling dates back to the very beginning of civilization. It usually was approved, or at least permitted, by society until the rise of Protestantism in the early sixteenth century, when bitter opposition arose to games of chance in any form. The Protestant disapproval of gambling was carried over to the United States, where gambling has usually been declared illegal. Nevertheless, gambling has continued to flourish under the protection of venal and crooked politicians and the control of criminal gangs and syndicates.

There are, naturally, no definitive figures on the nation's annual gambling bill, but the best recent studies by experts place it between 15 and 21 billion dollars. One study estimates that 3 billion dollars are gambled on the some 75,000 slot machines in the country; 3 billion on the policy racket or numbers game, in which people bet on a three-figure number, the winning combination being determined by the final three figures in the daily United States Treasury balance, the scores of baseball games, or the outcome of horse races; 7 billion on horse races; and 2 billion on other forms of gambling, making a total of 15 billion dollars. Another estimate lists 1.5 billion bet on horses through pari-mutuel betting and 4.5 billion through "bookies," making a 6 billion total on horse racing; 6 billion on baseball games; 1 billion each on football and basketball games; .33 billion on boxing; and .67 billion on hockey. If the 6 billion bet on slot machines and the policy game is included, it would give a total gambling bill of 21 billion.

**Underworld control and "fixing" of gambling.** Strong opposition to any legal prohibition of gambling is voiced by many persons, who argue that an individual should be free to spend his money as he wishes. Such an argument might have some merit, were it not for the fact that the average "sucker" has little or no chance of winning, and, therefore, is throwing his money away. The underworld controls nearly all gambling activity in the United States and "fixes" the results so that the ordinary person almost always loses. Only enough winning is permitted to keep the "suckers" interested. Not even the pari-mutuel racetrack gambling, in which the system is supervised by the state, has been able to eliminate underworld control of gambling. The gamblers and syndicates have usually joined forces with the politicians who control the pari-mutuel operations. Moreover the system always prevents the small bettor from getting an even break.

Since the opportunities for gain in gambling are so much greater than in most forms of organized criminality, and the risks of life, severe legal penalities, and conviction are so much less, the operators in "big crime" are now tending to shift more and more into gambling. It is said on good authority that the most powerful group controlling racetrack gambling is a remnant of the old Capone gang. This trend of big crime towards gambling is, along with increasing rural criminality, the main recent development in the American crime picture at the mid-century.

## Organized Crime

**Criminal gangs dominate large-scale crime operations.** In the United States today the "lone wolf" or independent criminal plays but a slight rôle in the complex pattern of crime. The major portion of serious criminal activity is directed by criminal gangs. During the Prohibition period, criminal gangs were able to develop a large-scale and highly profitable business in bootlegging liquor, since many American citizens were not in sympathy with Prohibition and demanded their liquor. The huge profits from bootlegging enabled the illicit liquor moguls to organize their operations on a comprehensive and efficient basis.

**The rôle of Al Capone in organized crime and racketeering.** "Scarface" Al Capone was the first important criminal leader to raise organized crime to the level of "big business." He developed a reputation in the Brooklyn and New York underworld at an early age, and, in 1925, became the leader of a bootleg ring in Chicago. In the next five years there were numerous dramatic and bloody battles between Capone's henchmen and other gangs for the control of the Chicago liquor trade. Capone finally achieved supreme power by a particularly bloody massacre of his opponents on St. Valentine's Day, 1929. It is estimated that, at the height of his power, Capone controlled bootlegging in four states and that his gross income from the liquor racket was six million dollars a week. He and his associates also branched out into the vice and gambling fields.

Capone maintained his power by two means: (1) through the use of a private army of mobsters and killers, and (2) through his association with, and control over, politicians. His killers gave him power over the underworld, while his influence with politicians kept him safe from the law. His career did not come to an end until the Federal government put him in prison—for not paying income taxes on his huge revenue from crime. Amusingly enough, Capone's prosecution actually grew out of the fact that his carousals in his Miami "palace" had annoyed President-elect Hoover while visiting a friend in Florida in the winter of 1928–1929.

**Later crime leaders develop a smoother technique.** While Al Capone was the first important well-known American to put crime on a business basis, he must be looked upon as only a crude beginner, in the light of the developments of the last thirty years. Later gang leaders have gone into numerous other fields of more vital and immediate concern to the average American citizen than the liquor and vice business. Their methods have become more "refined" and every attempt is made to see to it that the game is worked as smoothly as possible and with little violence. The more sophisticated racketeers have come to realize that the crude and impolite methods of Capone stir up an unnecessary amount of public excitement and may lead to annoying demands for the investigation and suppression of their activities.

When the repeal of Prohibition put an end to the bootlegging of liquor, the big criminals turned their efficient organization to other uses. They entered such forms of organized crime as well-planned bank robberies and thefts from warehouses and railroads. Kidnapping was another field to which the gangsters turned, but the "G-Men" soon made this form of criminal enterprise risky and unprofitable. At the present time, the organized criminal groups devote themselves to safer and more lucrative forms of activity; of late, more and more to gambling syndicates.

**Operations of criminal gangs.** Outside the realm of racketeering, which we shall describe shortly, organized crime falls chiefly into two fields: the operations of criminal gangs, and criminal syndicates. Criminal gangs today usually specialize in the theft of merchandise and automobiles, and in bank robberies. Rings of automobile thieves frequently steal and dispose of hundreds of cars before they are caught. One of the largest single items in organized robbery is the wholesale stealing of merchandise from trains, trucks, and warehouses. Losses from this source are estimated at over 100 million dollars a year. Bank robbers, whose annual "take" has reached 250 million dollars, have become more daring and active, since they can now dispose of stolen stocks and bonds to well-organized syndicates that make a business of selling stolen securities. Formerly, bank robbers had no means of safely and profitably getting rid of stocks or bonds. They had to sell them to a semi-criminal "fence" at "cut prices."

**Activities of criminal syndicates.** There are numerous activities in which criminal syndicates indulge. Arnold Rothstein, one of the founders of the criminal syndicate, and his associated gamblers "rigged" the infamous World Series of 1919. Criminal syndicates usually "rig" and operate the crooked gambling activities of a city or region. They usually manage the black market when conditions are favorable to such activity. After the second world war, the shortage of automobiles and the frenzied demand for them encouraged black-market activities in the purchase and sale of both new and second-hand cars. In 1946, a single black-market car syndicate in South Carolina was discovered to have done 100 million dollars worth of business in this field.

One of the favorite types of syndicate operation is the "confidence game," into which are lured the greedy who may possess considerable wealth and hope to make vast profits quickly out of what seem to be quasi-legitimate business enterprises. As much as a quarter of a million dollars has been taken from a single victim. Embezzlements are also often engineered by criminal syndicates.

**The Ponzi swindle of 1930.** Interestingly enough, the most dramatic example of the confidence game in all American history was the work of a lone wolf, Charles Ponzi of Boston, rather than of a criminal syndicate.[3] Ponzi had a previous criminal record and, six months before his great swindle, had been a $16-a-week clerk. He organized a confidence concern, The Ponzi Securities Exchange Co., and promised investors 50 per cent interest on their investments within 90 days and agreed to double their money in six months. Within eight months he had induced some 40,000 persons to hand over to him no less than $15,000,000. He took in as much as two million dollars in a single day before he was exposed by the Boston *Post* as an ex-convict and a confidence man. His procedure, according to him, was to buy depreciated foreign currencies with American dollars, convert the depreciated foreign currency into International Postal Union reply coupons at par, and then convert the latter into dollars, at a profit of 400 per cent. Actually, he took part of the money paid by one group of "investors" to pay off another group and thus keep the game operating. Most of

---

[3] See *Time*, January 31, 1949, p. 21.

the money "invested" was lost, and Ponzi was sent to prison by the Federal courts for fraudulent use of the mails.

**COST OF CRIME
AND GAMBLING**
*(IN BILLIONS OF DOLLARS)*

CONVENTIONAL
CRIMES
½ BILLION

ORGANIZED
CRIME AND
RACKETEERING
5 BILLION

GAMBLING
15 BILLION

Graph indicating extent of organized crime, racketeering, and gambling in recent years.

## Racketeering

**Nature of racketeering.** Racketeering is actually a form of organized crime and is usually lumped in with it in most descriptions of modern "streamlined" crime. But, while racketeering is organized and is criminal, it is of a specialized type, the essence of which is extortion through threats of violence and, if threats are not sufficient, any and all kinds of violence, including murder. Rackets are nothing new in human history. The great fortune of Crassus in ancient Rome was built up in part by means of a flourishing arson and real estate racket. The early Stuart kings of England and the French Bourbons developed the taxation and confiscation racket into a fine art. The English forced the Opium War on China to continue the dope racket.

**How a racket is set up.** Let us take a typical racket of our day, the restaurant racket, and see how it is operated. A criminal gang decides that the restaurants of a certain city offer a good field for setting up a racket. A member of the gang visits the owner of a profitable restaurant. The racketeer suggests to the proprietor that he is in need of "protection" and that, if he will pay the gang $100 a week, he will be safe from danger. The restaurant owner is amazed and protests that he does not need protection; no one has ever harmed him or his business, and he cannot afford to pay for protection against an imaginary danger. The racketeer departs, having warned the puzzled proprietor that, if he has not needed protection in the past, he will need it in the future.

Next day, the restaurant owner enters his place of business to find the plate-glass window smashed and the food in the kitchen spoiled. A day or so later, his cook and head waiter are set upon while going home from work and seriously beaten up. Worst of all, reports begin to circulate through the city that the food in this restaurant is inferior and dangerous. Customers begin to fall off, cooks and waiters leave, and the desperate restaurant owner faces ruin. When the racketeer next calls to inquire if he needs protection, the owner may be only too glad to hand over the money demanded. One by one, the other restaurant owners in the city find that they too need "protection" and soon the restaurant racket in that city is forthwith "sewed up." In every case, the principle is the same; honest businessmen are forced to pay tribute to organized gangsters or face the dangers of physical violence and financial ruin.

**Types of rackets.** Among the principal fields into which racketeering has entered at one time or another are: the cleaning, dyeing, and laundry industries; the sale of meat, milk, baked goods, vegetables, fruits, and other necessities; warehouse and dock operations; building construction; night clubs, gambling, horse racing, and commercialized sports; garages and the taxi business; and union labor and strike-breaking. It has been estimated that there were, and probably still are, around 170 industrial rackets operating in Chicago, in addition to many other types.

The building trades unions have been notoriously permeated by racketeers. Their activities have delayed building operations and increased building costs. In a notable case, Joseph S. Fay, international vice-president of the Union of Operating Engineers, and James Bove, vice-president of the Hod Carriers Union, were convicted of extorting a huge sum from contractors who built the Delaware Aqueduct for New York City. For years, these men and their associates had tyrannized construction work in the metropolitan area.

**How rackets affect the daily life of the citizen.** In nearly every instance, it is the ordinary man and his family who, in the long run, pay for these rackets, in the form of higher prices for goods and services. Yet, few persons realize that they are paying this tribute to gangsters. For example, when the price of meat, vegetables, or fruit rises in their town, Mr. and Mrs. John J. Jones may have to cut out the pleasure of a weekly movie in order to pay their higher grocery bills. They complain that the "cost of living has gone up," but they think the rise due to poor crops, food shortages, failure to balance the Federal budget, and the like. Little do they realize that one of the reasons why they are giving up their weekly movie is that storekeepers, directly or indirectly, pay protection money to racketeers. This is why the mass of the people are chiefly annoyed and agitated by the traditional crimes, such as robbery, burglary, thievery, forgery, and the like, which are played up in the papers.    They have little knowledge of the nature or ravages of organized crime and racketeering.

**Cost of organized crime and racketeering.**    There is, of course, no way of computing exactly the total annual cost to the nation of organized crime and racketeering.    The New York State Crime Commission has estimated that the annual cost of all crime and law enforcement in the United States runs between 12 and 18 billion dollars. Estimates of the cost of organized crime and racketeering put the figure at around five to seven billion dollars.    In any case, the annual "take" of the racketeers represents a huge cost to the United States.    It would, doubtless, be enough to provide all communities in the country with well-equipped schools and hospitals, to pay for a large-scale conservation program, or to finance public-works projects that would furnish jobs to most of the unemployed in the country.    Certainly, the vast gambling bill of 15 to 21 billion a year would provide all these things, and more.

## Difficulty of Eliminating Organized Crime and Racketeering

**How organized crime is directed.**    Organized crime and racketeering have become "big business" not only in size and importance, but in their organization and management as well.    The leaders who direct organized crime are not ignorant or desperate thugs, but intelligent and clever executives.    In many cases, the crime groups are organized along the lines of modern business corporations, operating with highly paid legal advice.    The real leaders of the criminal syndicates and rackets act as boards of directors, carefully planning and supervising the activities of the criminal gangs.    Rarely do they carry out any of the actual violent work themselves, or even associate closely with their underlings.    Rather, the real leaders of modern organized crime remain hidden in the background, posing as ordinary respectable citizens.    They may live in expensive homes, belong to exclusive clubs, and travel in the best social circles.    Frequently they conduct some ostensibly honest business enterprise as a "front" to cover up their criminal activities.

Consequently, the real leaders of organized crime are seldom, if ever, in danger of being arrested.    The gunmen so luridly pictured in the movies and in detective magazines are only the small fry of the organized underworld who do the dirty work under orders from their chiefs.

In an article in *The New York Times*, January 2, 1942, on "Exploded Big Shots," Meyer Berger argued that the racketeers, particularly in New York City, have been squelched.    The truth is that the crude boys of the earlier days have been wiped out.    In their place, we have smoother crooks who conduct the rackets with greater finesse and shrewdness.    Indeed, it is said on good authority that one single "big-shot" operator in New York City today has more power than all the

New York racketeers combined had when Thomas Dewey began his "crime-busting" career. Prominent politicians, even judges, do his bidding. And his power extends to many other states throughout the nation. Not only is the technique of racketeers and big-shot criminals smoother than in the days of Al Capone and "Bugs" Moran, but their fields of activities are less violent and desperate. Instead of going in for bootlegging, kidnapping, gang murders, and the like, they operate criminal syndicates for big swindling enterprises, control illicit gambling, or "fix" legal forms of gambling.

**Alliance of crime with crooked politics.** How is it possible for such a network of well-organized crime to exist in modern America? The answer lies in the fact that organized crime in the United States is closely allied with party politics. Many public officials know the real leaders of organized crime, but they are unwilling or powerless to move against them. In many cases, the racketeers make large payments to dishonest public officials to buy their friendship and protection. Especially is this true in cities and states where dishonest political machines are in control of the government. The generous contributions of racketeers to political campaign funds are secretly welcomed by the political machine, and gangster underlings can be used handily to frighten reformers and honest voters, to stuff ballot boxes, and to perform other necessary chores for the political machine.

At the funeral of one prominent Chicago racketeer, there were among the honorary pallbearers some 21 judges, 9 attorneys, a special state prosecutor, several city officials, and a number of union officials. The most prominent gambler in New York City held a quasi-charitable conference early in 1948 at which there were in attendance at his command a large number of prominent public officials, judges, and political leaders. The story of the collaboration between racketeers and politicians has been told in detail by Dennis T. Lynch, in his *Criminals and Politicians,* and by Fletcher Dobyns, in his *Underworld of American Politics.* Lynch deals mainly with New York City and Dobyns with Chicago.

Many of our public officials who are honest and refuse to have anything to do with crime are nevertheless powerless to bring racketeers to justice. In the first place, so clever and slippery are the real leaders of organized crime that the police are often unable to get adequate legal evidence of their misdoings. Even if this is secured, the criminal leaders are able to hire clever lawyers to defend them; they also resort to the bribing of judges and juries to keep their freedom. Even more important, however, is the fact that organized crime maintains an efficient "secret service bureau," which has fairly complete records of the private and public lives of all public officials and others who might act against the racketeers. Few are the prominent public figures who have not "slipped" in some way or other once during their lives and would not fear to have their past mistakes publicly exposed. Even should a public official possess a spotless public and private career, it is easy, through trick photography and other means, to "frame" him and damage his reputation. Or physical violence, even death, may be threatened against the wife and children of an honest public official determined to battle the "big-shot" criminals. Such threats are often carried out if all else fails to restrain would-be reformers.

## Convicts in the Crime Picture

**The conventional or traditional criminals.** What the average citizen thinks of as crime—robbery, burglary, pocket-picking, theft, forgery, and so forth, are carried on by the small fry of the criminal world and bring in only "chicken feed" compared to the huge booty seized by the organized criminal groups.

**Convicts and criminals.** When we hear the word "criminal" used we usually think of the inmates of prisons, namely the convicts. But the convicts represent only a very small group of lawbreakers who have been stupid or unlucky enough to get caught. Our penitentiaries and prisons confine only about 150,000 prisoners, while there are probably at least two million more criminals who should be behind the bars. The prison population is mainly made up of those who have been convicted of ordinary crimes, such as forgery, larceny, robbery, burglary, theft, and murder. In the county jails and city workhouses we find those imprisoned for such offenses as drunkenness, disorderly conduct, violation of liquor laws, and vagrancy—over half a million of them on the average. The group of criminals who are conspicuous by their relative absence from penal institutions are the big operators in organized crime, racketeering, and gambling.

**Make-up of the convict population of a typical prison.** Though the convicts who are confined today are chiefly the small criminals, and only the more stupid or unlucky of these, still it will be illuminating for us to consider briefly the character of those found in our prisons. Most of our information about criminals has to be based on what we know about convicts, for they are the only offenders who can be studied. Our information and generalizations about criminals are therefore limited and imperfect, since we can rarely study the more clever and serious criminals.

Among any representative group of convicts we would find some who are feeble-minded. These persons have the intelligence of normal children four to ten years old and are easily influenced by suggestion. Brought up in evil surroundings, they have easily drifted into a life of crime. There is little hope of reforming them.

Others have glands that are too active or too sluggish in their operation. This condition has made them vicious, abnormal, or insane. Without proper medical attention or decent surroundings, they turn to crime. Many are psychopathic, that is, mentally and nervously unbalanced. They may have superior minds, but lack stability and self-control. Extreme nervousness may have prevented them from getting and holding a job. Their lack of control leads them to succumb easily to temptation. Some are driven by strong compulsions to commit crimes of violence.

Some are physically sick. Their diseases reduce their capacity for labor and their resistance to the strains of life. They may lapse into crime from sheer despair or desperation. A great many more have healthy bodies but have been compelled to live in an unhealthy environment. They have dwelt in slums which swarmed with criminal gangs. They have been denied healthy recreation. Crime has been all around them and, usually beginning in their youth, they have climbed on the criminal band wagon. Others have started out with good bodies and decent surroundings but have been the victims of bad habits. They were not trained for profitable employment, but were permitted to loaf, and drifted from loafing into petty crimes, and from these into more serious offenses. Extreme poverty or hard luck may have driven some into crime as the only way to escape starvation or extreme privation.

Our jury trial system is such that in a prison population of five thousand we might well expect to find at least five hundred entirely innocent men who have been sacrificed by the savagery of prosecutors or the incompetence of defense attorneys.

**Mental traits of criminals.** Many popular ideas about criminals have little basis in fact. Studies of our prison populations have shown that the once common idea that all criminals are feeble-minded is false. Mental tests given convict groups show a spread very similar to that of the general population. The notion that criminals are all mentally unbalanced or insane is equally untrue. Even more silly is the popular belief that there are born criminals. Though some people are more easily influenced towards crime than are others, criminal conduct is, in almost every case, the result of mental disease or defect, ill health, bad habits, social training, or surroundings.

Altogether, about one-quarter of those in our prisons are feeble-minded, another quarter are mentally unbalanced, and about half are victims of a "crime area" environment, bad habits, evil associates, and poverty. Some expert authorities put the number of mentally diseased and defective prisoners higher than the above estimates. The first extensive study of criminals from the psychiatric point of view was that conducted of 608 prisoners in Sing Sing Prison, New York, by Dr. Bernard Glueck in 1916. He found that 59 per cent of those whom he studied were feeble-minded, mentally diseased, or mentally abnormal. Drs. Frankwood Williams and V. V. Anderson concluded that 77 per cent of the inmates of the New York County jail and prison were psychopathic or feeble-minded. The medical director of the Federal Bureau of Prisons estimates that only about 15 per cent of the convicts in any Federal or state prison are completely normal mentally. The other 85 per cent are psychopaths, psychoneurotics, and mental defectives. This expert freely admits that much of this mental abnormality is due to the effects of prison life. Many of those who are psychoneurotics were not such when first admitted to prison.

Foolish laws, court injustices, and prison experience may also help to make criminals. A normally law-abiding person, in ignorance of the law, may commit a crime and be thrown into prison because he cannot get a competent lawyer. Here, he is forced to associate with hardened criminals and may come out a full-fledged graduate of the school of crime. He went to prison for breaking a minor law; he may return to prison later for a serious offense.

**Warped mental attitude of the criminal.** After a man has been launched on a criminal career, his attitude toward life changes. The ordinary person keeps his self-respect and position in society by obeying laws. The criminal finds that he can hold the respect of the underworld only as long as he breaks laws successfully and avoids conviction. The bigger and better his crimes, and the greater his success in evading the officers of the law, the greater the respect in which a criminal is held by the underworld. The "public opinion" of his associates, therefore, favors committing crime and dodging the police. If a criminal attempts to reform, the underworld scorns him; and he is not welcome in the society of honest men after he has been in prison, whatever his efforts to reform.

## The Juvenile Offender and the Growing Challenge of Juvenile Crime

**Youth predominates in our crime picture today.** Case histories of criminals show that many of them began their criminal careers early in life. The Wickersham Commission, appointed by President Hoover in 1929 to study the problem of law enforcement in the United States, found that 54.8 per cent of convicts were under 21 at the time of their first conviction. The rate of juvenile crime increased during the second world war. The number of boys under 18 arrested for delinquency increased 18.8 per cent between 1941 and 1944, and the number of girls by 117.8 per cent. Arrests for drunkenness doubled for boys and trebled for girls. In 1944, 40.1 per cent of all persons arrested for robbery, burglary, larceny, auto thefts, embezzlement, fraud, forgery, counterfeiting, receiving stolen property, and arson were under 21 years of age. In the year 1945, the largest number of crimes in any one-year age group were committed by persons 17 years of age. Over 80 per cent of the automobile thefts, 65 per cent of the burglaries, 58 per cent of the robberies, 40 per cent of the larcenies, and 48 per cent of the rapes were committed by persons under 25 years of age.

**Some explanations of the prevalence of juvenile crime.** There are several reasons for the alarming amount of juvenile delinquency: (1) With the growth of the large city, family discipline has broken down, and, even in the rural districts, the restraining influence of family life is not so strong as it was in former days. The importance of the family situation is further pointed up by the fact that over one-fourth of all juvenile delinquents come from families in which the father or the mother or both have deserted their children. A number of students of juvenile delinquency, such as Professor Charles W. Coulter, believe that disorganized families and those with defective

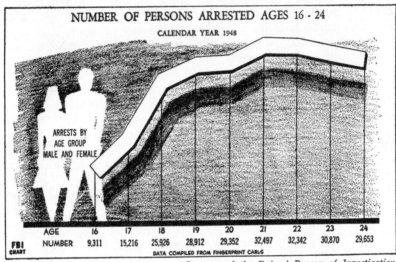

NUMBER OF PERSONS ARRESTED AGES 16 - 24

CALENDAR YEAR 1948

ARRESTS BY
AGE GROUP
MALE AND FEMALE

| AGE | 16 | 17 | 18 | 19 | 20 | 21 | 22 | 23 | 24 |
|-----|-----|-----|-----|-----|-----|-----|-----|-----|-----|
| NUMBER | 9,311 | 15,216 | 25,926 | 28,912 | 29,352 | 32,497 | 32,342 | 30,870 | 29,653 |

FBI CHART

DATA COMPILED FROM FINGERPRINT CARDS

*Courtesy of the Federal Bureau of Investigation.*

**Graph indicating the incidence of arrests in the 16–24 year age-group.**

discipline and training habits do even more to increase juvenile delinquency than broken homes. Cyril Burt, in England, found that these family defects were seven times as numerous in the homes of delinquents as in those of non-delinquents, and Sheldon Glueck found such defects of discipline in 70 per cent of delinquent homes. (2) At the same time that the influence of parents is becoming less potent there is more opportunity for young folks to get into mischief. The city is a place of excitement and temptation. With no restraining background of sound family discipline, it is small wonder that many boys have trouble with the law. (3) A large percentage of boys from 16 to 21 cannot find work; others, who do not want jobs, hunt for schemes that will bring in money without involving work. Both types are often persuaded to take jobs of a crooked nature offered to them by criminals and racketeers.

Many juvenile offenders take the first step toward a life of crime because they need money for recreation or to entertain a girl friend. Once the first downward steps are taken the juvenile delinquent finds it easier to follow the criminal pattern than to take up a life of hard work and discipline.

In addition to these generally accepted socio-economic causes of juvenile crime, Sheldon Glueck, a leading student of youthful criminals, has reminded us that the very energy, vitality, restlessness, and adventurous spirit of youth are always likely to produce a relatively greater amount of delinquency in the 16–25 year age-group than in any other one of comparable span.

Professor Frederic M. Thrasher, in his study of over 1,300 juvenile gangs in the city of Chicago, came to the conclusion that juvenile delinquency centers in the slum areas of large cities, and that the juvenile delinquent's career usually begins with truancy from school and membership in some youthful gang. The children of the slums often have no place to play except in the streets. Here they form bad associations. They raid the corner fruit store, break store windows, and soon are arrested by the patrolman on the beat. They are then on the high road to professional criminality.

The problems created by wayward youths have received serious attention in the last few years because of the enormous increase of juvenile delinquency that accompanied and followed the second world war. Frequently suggested measures to deal with the growing menace of juvenile delinquency have included better civic and vocational education, family counseling, better recreational facilities, linking up psychiatric clinics with the public school system, and wider use of juvenile courts and probation.

## International Crimes and War-Guilt Trials

**New concepts of international crime.** Following the second world war, there was an effort to set up the concept of international crime as an individual offense punishable by death or imprisonment. "War criminals" were those guilty of starting and waging an "aggressive war" or carrying out cruel and barbarous acts ("atrocities") in the course of wars.

**The postwar trials.** Accordingly, leading German and Japanese officials and military figures were brought to trial in the Nuremberg, Tokyo, and lesser trials, which began in 1946 and lasted for several years. Most of the leading Nazis, except for Hitler, Goering, Himmler, and Goebbels, who committed suicide, and leading Japanese, including Premier Tojo, were executed. Many breathed a sigh of satisfaction and seemed to believe that all wrong had been avenged and that peace and humanity had once more been restored to reign indefinitely and unchallenged.

**Reason returns and observers are shocked in retrospect.** In retrospect, however, most discerning and rational observers came to regard the whole procedure as having set a most unfortunate precedent, and one likely to make future wars far more ruthless than the second world war. Moreover, it was perceived that the trials had delivered a rude shock to many of our foremost principles of legal procedure and equity. As an affront to established principles of law and equity, these trials were based on *ex post facto* law, which is contrary to our most sacred principles, and, even worse, they introduced the practice of having the accusers also serve as judges.   The latter practice was a repudiation of every basic concept of equity established over the centuries.   Such trials were bound to be travesties from the outset.   Only neutral nations could fairly try the accused in such cases, but it was

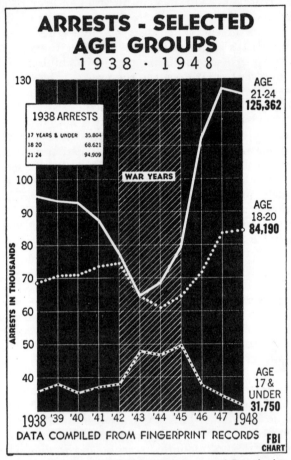

*Courtesy of the Federal Bureau of Investigation.*

Graph showing increase in delinquency of 18–24 year age-group since 1943. Also shows marked decline of delinquency in age-group under 17. This may have been due to higher family income and better living conditions.

argued that weak neutral nations would be open to intimidation by the powerful accuser nations and might not be able to enforce their verdicts, especially if they acquitted the accused.

**Who are the aggressors?**   There are a number of other logical and factual objections to such trials.   The facts about who was actually the aggressor nation or nations may not be known for many years after the war.   The accepted facts about the leading aggressor nations in regard to the first world war underwent an almost complete change between 1918 and 1928, and it is already likely that there will be an equally great alteration of opinion about the aggressors in the second world war. The same is true with respect to war crimes and atrocities. The alleged Germany atrocities in Belgium in 1914 were vouched for by no less an authority than Lord Bryce, but a little over a decade later they were completely exposed as lies and repudiated by an Englishman of equal probity and better information, Lord Ponsonby.

**The pot tries and punishes the kettle.** By the time of the Nuremberg and Tokyo trials it was evident that many of the accusers were as guilty of war crimes and atrocities as the Germans or the Japanese. This has been amply proved by two able English writers in restrained and amply documented books: F. J. C. Veale, in his *Advance to Barbarism;* and Montgomery Belgion, in his *Victor's Justice.* No single act of the Nazis was more brutal or inexcusable than the Anglo-American bombing of Dresden, neither a military nor an industrial center, on the night of February 13, 1945, in which about 200,000, mainly women and children, were killed. Few of Hitler's acts in wartime were more brutal than the conduct of the Russians in Poland and the Baltic States, Germany, and Austria, as they drove the Nazis back. The Russian labor camps were as bad as the worst Nazi concentration camps, and many more were confined therein. The deportation of Germans from East Germany, Hungary, Czechoslovakia, and Transylvania was carried out with greater brutality than Hitler's movement of conquered people during the war. American judges and publicists reluctantly revealed the fact that American officials, in trying to get Germans to confess or to produce damaging evidence, were guilty of all manner of brutalities. Our dropping of atom bombs on Hiroshima and Nagasaki months after the Japanese had earnestly been seeking peace equaled any Japanese barbarities. In the case of the Tokyo trials, the travesty was too much even for some of the leading participants among the accusers. The distinguished Indian jurist, Judge Pal, presented a devastating indictment of the procedure, as also did Justices Murphy and Rutledge in their dissenting opinions.

**Wars will be made more brutal in the future.** But the most unfortunate aspect of these trials is the fact that, instead of assuring more humane procedure in the third world war, they will inevitably make it the most brutal and ruthless war ever fought. In future wars, no one can afford to lose, for the leaders of the losing side will be shot or hanged, whether they were aggressors or not. The effect of this psychology of desperation on the conduct of war was well revealed by the increase in Nazi ruthlessness after the Casablanca unconditional surrender announcement of January, 1943, which made it clear that Hitler would be executed if he lost the war and was captured.

**Elimination of war the only remedy.** All reasonable persons regard war as a crime and hold in horror all brutal atrocities; but the way to end such international crimes, great and petty, is to put an end to war rather than to attack the more or less inevitable traits and accompaniments of warfare.  And it would be doubly unfortunate if our established national tenets and ideals of justice and equity in peacetime were to be undermined and discredited by any perverted and hypocritical procedure in respect to international criminal concepts and postwar trials.

## Summary

Based upon the twin drives of need and greed, modern crime extends from crooked business operations, political graft, and highly-organized crime and racketeering to petty thievery and juvenile delinquency.

Crime is based primarily on the something-for-nothing philosophy, which has always had a strong influence in American life.  The most important expression of this philosophy of greed is found in the ever growing amount of white-collar crime, such as dishonesty in business and finance.  Crooked bankers and corporation directors may use their power virtually to steal from gullible or ignorant depositors and investors.  Dishonest businessmen may resort to numerous kinds of frauds.  Gambling on the stock exchanges represents a form of antisocial behavior not forbidden by law and approved by a large group in our society.  Embezzlement, fraud, swindling, and "fixed" gambling also represent a huge financial cost to society; there is insufficient legal or educational protection against their ravages.

By far the most important forms of crime today are organized crime and racketeering, which arose with the establishment of bootlegging gangs during Prohibition.  Today, racketeering affects a large part of American life.  Businessmen are forced by racketeers to pay tribute in order to carry on their activities.  Racketeers often control labor union operations.  Organized crime finds expression in wholesale automobile thefts, bank robberies, thefts from warehouses, confidence games, crooked gambling, and the like.  The directors of organized crime and racketeering are clever men who usually remain unknown to the general public.  Through their influence with public officials, the organized criminals and racketeers are usually able to escape arrest and conviction.  Especially since the second world war there has been a marked trend among organized criminals to shift into "fixed" gambling because of its greater revenue and reduced risks.

The average person regards robbery, burglary, forgery, and the like, as the most serious crimes.  Actually, these types of unlawful activity, although annoying to the public, are financially unimportant compared with the ravages of large-scale organized crime and racketeering.  Such petty crimes are carried out by the "small fry" of the underworld, those who fill our prisons and make up our convict class.  The racketeers and organized criminals are seldom caught or convicted.

The factors tending to produce petty or conventional criminals are many and varied.  Briefly, they may be summed up mainly as economic need, mental disease, feeble-mindedness, poor health, bad associations, slum habitats, and inadequate education. Then, too, our present-day prisons are training schools for crime. Many who were petty offenders when convicted come out of prison hardened and skillful criminals. Especially alarming is the proportion of young people among our criminals. Over half of those now in prisons were first sentenced to prison before they were 21 years of age.

The attempt to set up concepts of international crime in postwar trials after 1945 proved shortsighted and disastrous. The accusers were guilty of the same crimes as the accused. Basic concepts of equity were destroyed by introducing *ex post facto* law and letting the accusers also act as judges. The net result of these trials will be to make future world wars more brutal than ever before, because it will be known in advance that the losers will be tried and executed.

## Selected References

Adams, S. H., *The World Goes Smash,* Houghton Mifflin, 1938. A fictional analysis of racketeering in New York City, from the extreme developments of which the war may temporarily have delivered us.

Barnes, H. E., and Teeters, N. K., *New Horizons in Criminology,* Prentice-Hall, 1945. The most comprehensive manual on criminology and penology.

* Belgion, Montgomery, *Victor's Justice,* Regnery, 1949. The best analysis and critique of the Nuremberg trials.

Cantor, N. F., *Crime and Society,* Holt, 1939. A learned sociological study of the crime problem.

* Cavan, R. S., *Criminology,* Crowell, 1948. A recent, brief, and clear survey of the whole field of criminology.

Cooper, C. R., *Here's to Crime,* Little, Brown, 1937. A graphic account of organized crime by one of the leading journalistic students of crime.'

Holbrook, S. H., *Murder Out Yonder,* Macmillan, 1941. A valuable study of rural crime and violence, a subject usually overlooked in dealing with criminality.

* Kirchbaum, Louis, *America's Labor Dictators,* Industrial Forum, 1940. Good review of racketeering in labor unions.

Lever, Harry, and Young, Joseph, *Wartime Racketeers,* Putnam, 1945. Preliminary study of wartime profiteering, black-market activities, and the like.

McDougall, E. D. (Ed.), *Crime for Profit,* Stratford, 1933.

————, *Speculation and Gambling,* Stratford, 1936. Two pioneer books on white-collar crime.

* Merrill, M. A., *Problems of Child Delinquency,* Houghton Mifflin, 1947. Penetrating discussion of the leading causes of juvenile delinquency and its solution.

\* Mooney, Martin, *Crime Incorporated*, McGraw-Hill, 1935. Probably the best single book on streamlined, organized crime and racketeering prior to the extensive shift of big criminal operators to gambling syndicates.

Neumeyer, M. H., *Juvenile Delinquency in Modern Society*, Van Nostrand, 1948. Excellent recent survey of the field.

Pasley, F. D., *Al Capone*, Garden City Publishing Company, 1930. An interesting biography of the first nationally famous "big shot" criminal.

Raine, W. M., *Guns of the Frontier*, Houghton Mifflin, 1940. A popular account of lawlessness, outlaws, and gunmen in the West.

Reckless, Walter, *The Crime Problem*, Appleton-Century-Crofts, 1950. Recent basic text, especially notable for its treatment of the reformation of criminals and rehabilitative techniques.

Reel, A. F., *The Case of General Yamashita*, University of Chicago Press, 1949. Competent and fair, but critical account of the trial and execution of the Japanese commander. The first good book on the post-war trials of Japanese leaders.

Reeve, A. B., *The Golden Age of Crime*, Mohawk, 1931. Interesting attempt to estimate the financial losses through organized crime and racketeering.

Sheldon, W. H., *Varieties of Delinquent Youth*, Harper, 1950. Massive case-study approach to juvenile delinquency from the bio-psychic viewpoint.

Sullivan, E. D., *Rattling the Cup on Chicago Crime*, Vanguard, 1929. Vivid exposure of rackets and organized crime in Chicago.

Sutherland, E. H., *The Principles of Criminology*, Lippincott, 1947. Long the standard textbook in the field of criminology.

\* ————, *White Collar Crime*, Dryden, 1949. The long awaited book by a pioneer student of the subject.

Taft, D. R., *Criminology*, Macmillan, 1950. A sane and balanced coverage of the field.

\* Tannenbaum, Frank, *Crime and the Community*, Ginn, 1938. A valuable book, strong on the social causes of crime, and one which takes into consideration recent streamlined crime.

Tappan, P. W., *Juvenile Delinquency*, McGraw-Hill, 1949. Comprehensive recent study of all aspects of juvenile delinquency, including the operations of the juvenile court.

Teeters, N. K., and Reinemann, J. O., *The Challenge of Delinquency*, Prentice-Hall, 1950. Thorough treatment of juvenile delinquency, its causes, extent, and prevention.

Terrett, Courtenay, *Only Saps Work*, Vanguard, 1930. A good study of rackets in New York City, stressing the ignorance of the public on the matter.

# CHAPTER XXXII

# The Treatment of Criminals:
# Punishment vs. Rehabilitation

## Difficulty of Repressing Organized Crime and Racketeering

**Realistic attitude toward crime repression today.** In the preceding chapter we made it clear that the most serious and dangerous criminals of today are the overlords of organized crime and racketeering and the white-collar criminals. The fact that these major criminals are rarely arrested and even more rarely convicted should be the focal point of any realistic discussion of the repression and prevention of crime.

A generation ago most discussions of crime problems were directed toward improving the police system, capturing more criminals, convicting the guilty, and improving the construction and administration of our prisons. We still discuss such topics, but we must recognize that most of them have little bearing upon the repression of the more important forms of crime or the reformation of our major criminals. Even if we had better police systems, able to arrest the criminal "big shots," and honest courts, willing to convict them if guilty, there would be little accomplished while the moguls of organized crime remain shielded by political machines. Therefore, most of what we can write about better police systems, courts, and prisons has little direct bearing on the problem of preventing the more challenging types of criminal operations today. This is a sad fact, but the more quickly we realize its truth, the sooner we may do something effective about our present scandalous crime situation.

**Reorganization necessary to repress organized crime.** There is little prospect of our being able to check organized crime and racketeering unless we bring about far-reaching changes in the economic and political system that produces this form of antisocial behavior and permits it to flourish. It will be necessary to suppress the something-for-nothing attitude and widespread poverty, and wipe out the corrupt political machines that dominate party politics and protect racketeers. Such changes and reforms will take a long time to bring about, if they can be accomplished at all.

**Education as a technique of crime prevention.** If we cannot get our more dangerous criminals into courts and prisons, it would seem that perhaps education represents the only practical approach to crime prevention in respect to this group of offenders. We cannot restrain or reform the present generation of "big shot" criminals through education, but we might possibly reduce the future supply of gangsters, racketeers, swindlers, and crooked businessmen. Such an educational policy would have to provide adequate training for jobs, so that youth can earn a living by law-abiding methods. It would have to be backed up by realistic character education, in order that we might destroy the prevalent belief that "only saps work." Moreover, education as a defense against crime would have to include better civic training of our citizens, so that they would act to eliminate graft and corrupt political machines. We must recognize, however, that at present the best police systems, courts, and prisons cannot crush organized crime and racketeering, and that all practical discussion of crime repression today must be limited to the repression of conventional crimes.

## A Rational Program for the Apprehension and Conviction of Small Criminals

**Needed reform of criminal codes.** The first step in improving our methods of repressing and preventing crime must be a thorough overhauling of our criminal law. In few things do we lag so far behind reality as in our legal code. Many serious forms of antisocial behavior are not forbidden by law. On the other hand, our statute books are cluttered up with thousands of outworn, unnecessary, and ridiculous laws that penalize trivialities.

The absurdity of many of our laws is shown by the fact that the average law-abiding citizen of a modern city unwittingly commits enough crimes in a single day to warrant a sentence of several years in prison and heavy fines. One expert has estimated that an average "law-abiding" citizen of Philadelphia commits in one day enough crimes to call for five years' imprisonment and fines of $2,895.67. His unintended criminals acts in a single year would call for 1,825 years in prison and $1,055,019.55 in fines.[1] Many unfortunate persons are caught in these unintentional crimes, arrested, convicted because of incompetent defense counsel, and sent to prisons, where they get competent instruction in serious crime.

Many laws still in force reflect the ideas and conditions of long ago. For instance, in one southern state, failure to attend church on Sunday three times in a row is still legally punishable by death. Most persons suppose that we had long since ceased to imprison persons for debt in the United States. But the imprisonment in Vermont of three veterans

---

[1] L. M. Hussey, "Twenty-four Hours of a Law Breaker," *Harper's Magazine,* March, 1930.

of the second world war for debt started an investigation that revealed
a scandalous situation.    Some 12 states—Connecticut, Illinois, Maine,
Massachusetts, Michigan, New Hampshire, New Jersey, New York,
North Carolina, Rhode Island, Vermont, and Wisconsin—still permit
imprisonment for debt.    The law in Rhode Island is about as bad as
that of England in the eighteenth century.

In addition to these numerous old laws, several hundred thousand
new laws have been passed by our Federal and state governments since
1900.    Many of these cannot be readily enforced, because they are not
supported by public opinion.    It may be argued that, if the silly laws
are not enforced, no harm is done.    This, however, is incorrect, for
such an attitude would leave it up to the individual to decide
what laws to obey.    It is an easy step from disregarding trivial and
archaic laws to contemplating the violation of sound and important
ones.

**Improvement of police personnel and procedure.**    An indispensible
item in a successful program of crime prevention is a competent, well-
trained police force, equal to any emergency.    We can make little
headway with either the punishment or the treatment of criminals
unless we catch them.    Greater certainty of arrest has a more powerful
influence in restraining criminals than do occasional punishments.
In a careful study, in 1942, of 610,000 reported offences, Dr. C. C.
Van Vechten found that there were arrests for only 25 per cent of the
crimes reported, convictions for only 5.5 per cent, and prison sentences
for only 3.5 per cent.    In *Uniform Crime Reports,* 1949, the Federal
Bureau of Investigation claimed some improvement in the postwar
period.    It stated that, in 1948, the police made arrests in 28.9 per cent
of all known offenses.    In the majority of crimes against property there
were arrests for only 25.6 per cent of the reported cases.    There were
convictions for about 22 per cent of all reported crimes, and for about
15 per cent of serious crimes.    Some European countries have milder
forms of punishments than ours, but less crime because they catch their
criminals.    We probably get fully as much out of our police as we pay
for, but no reasonable price is too great to pay for a competent and independent police force.    The most immediately urgent improvement is
a sharp differentiation between routine patrolmen and traffic supervisors, on the one hand, and the detective or crime detection personnel,
on the other.    The latter should be given rigorous professional training, and, they should be provided with the very latest knowledge and
equipment.

**Third degree should be eliminated.**    The policeman's job should
end, however, when he has arrested his man and given his reasons for
doing so to the proper authorities.    The police may gather evidence,
but it is not their responsibility to determine guilt.    At the present
time, the police all too often do their job of arresting in a miserably
inefficient fashion.    They also attempt to determine the guilt of suspects by use of the third degree, a perpetuation of the ancient practice

of torture that has no defensible place in American justice. According to our laws, an accused person is considered innocent until he is found guilty in a court of law. Under the third degree, innocent persons may be beaten, tortured, starved, and kept without sleep until they confess crimes they did not commit. Occasionally, men die, so harsh are third degree methods. The police do not, however, give the third degree to all suspects. For the most part, it is only the unfortunate, the friendless, and those without "political pull" who must face this relic of barbarism. The "big-shot" criminals are hardly ever treated in this fashion if they happen to be arrested.

**Jury trial of today an archaic travesty.** After his arrest, the person accused of crime must await trial. Often, he must spend months in jail before his case comes to court, because our legal system is inexcusably slow in handling cases. The accused man is tried before a jury of twelve persons, chosen by lot. This jury decides upon his innocence or guilt after what is supposed to be a fair trial, in which all the facts of the case have been honestly presented.

But, what we usually have in a modern jury trial is a battle of wits and words between the prosecuting attorney, who wants more convictions so he may be re-elected or promoted, and the defense attorney, who desires to see his client freed so that he may earn his fee and secure more clients. Relevant facts are often not seriously considered, except as they may be used to sway the emotions of the jury. Violent verbiage, a blood-stained knife, a sobbing black-robed widow, or a tearful plea to save a mother's only child often has more to do with the jury's decision than the actual facts of the case. Clarence Darrow, one of the greatest criminal lawyers in American history, used to say that his strategy was to get the jury to identify themselves with the accused—to put themselves in his or her place—on the assumption that no man will vote to hang himself.

Why are modern juries unable to arrive at fair, unbiased verdicts in many trials? Part of the answer is that it is hard to get intelligent persons to serve on a jury. Professional people, such as engineers, doctors, lawyers, and schoolteachers, are all excused from jury duty. Anyone who has read and formed an opinion of the case is not allowed to serve. Most intelligent persons read the crime news and form opinions on what they have read. This means then that our average jury is made up of twelve men and women who are either dishonest enough to say that they have not read about the case, in order to collect the fees paid for jury service, or those who are too ignorant, stupid, or indifferent to read and form an opinion of the case.

Even if the jury were serious, honest, and intelligent, it would be difficult for such amateurs in the study of evidence to render an accurate verdict in any but the simplest cases. It requires professional training and a high degree of concentration to be able to follow, interpret, and evaluate evidence given in a courtroom. There is a great deal of perjury and faked testimony. Even honest witnesses may exaggerate.  Only a trained person can well judge the credibility of witnesses and testimony.  Further, the highly technical rules of legal evidence in the courtroom often prevent the jury from getting many of the more relevant facts.  The attention of the jury is often distracted from even those facts which are available by the highly emotional appeals and the horseplay antics of the lawyers in the case.  At the other extreme, in the dull moments of a trial, the judge may possibly lapse into thoughts about his poker losings the night before or his desire to slake his thirst during recess or after adjournment for the day, while the minds of the jury wander off into their various personal interests, distractions, and problems.  All in all, one may safely say that, in any complicated case, we are no more likely to get an accurate verdict from the average jury than ancient peoples were from the ordeal or trial by battle.

The judge can also exert a strong influence over trial by jury.  He can refuse to allow evidence to be presented.  He can favor the prosecution or defense in his rulings.  His charge to the jury may influence the verdict more than the testimony given or the arguments of the attorneys in the case.  A fair judge can do a great deal for justice and equity, while a biased judge can make it almost impossible to decide a case on the facts at issue.

As soon as the admissible evidence has been presented, the jury retires behind closed doors to arrive at its verdict.  Decisions must be unanimous.  There is an old story of the judge who was disgusted at a jury that could not arrive at a verdict.  When lunch came, and the jury members were still arguing among themselves, this judge ordered eleven lunches to be brought from a nearby restaurant; he also ordered a twelfth lunch, a bale of hay.  Sometimes, the stubborn, "mule-like" juror has been bribed to hold out for one verdict or another.  Dominating or persuasive personalities on a jury may have more influence on the verdict rendered than all the evidence presented in the courtroom.

**Paid boards of experts should decide guilt or innocence.**  What would happen if we should do away with the jury?  We might have, instead of jurors, permanent boards of high-grade paid experts to decide criminal cases.  These men and women would be thoroughly trained in criminal law, criminology, and the psychology of testimony.  They would not be under political influence.  They would decide cases on the facts and not on prejudice and emotion.

No sensible person would claim that such a board of trained experts would invariably decide cases with complete accuracy.  All that is claimed, and that may be asserted with complete assurance, is that their verdicts would be infinitely more in accord with the facts than those rendered by the haphazard collection of untrained and inexperienced laymen who serve on juries.  Expert boards would also do away with the delays and the legal horseplay which now characterize our jury trials.

**Indeterminate sentence indispensable to correctional procedure.**
If our police and courts were honest and competent, our criminals
could be quickly caught, tried, and convicted. Once the guilty were
in prison, we could proceed with plans for treatment and reform.

The task of running our prisons efficiently is made difficult by the
methods employed by the courts in sentencing criminals. A jury renders a verdict of guilty; the judge pronounces sentence. Unless the
crime is murder in the first degree and the judge has no choice in his
sentence, the law usually states only the shortest and the longest periods
that can be served in prison for the given crime. Within these limits,
the judge has the power to decide how long a sentence a man shall
serve. For example, in some states, burglary carries a maximum
penalty of ten years. This may be given to one convicted criminal.
Another person convicted of the same offense may draw two years from
the same judge. No judge can possibly know, merely by listening to a
trial, what kind of person any criminal really is. The judge is in no
position to know whether he can be reformed during a year or two in
prison or whether he should be given the full penalty of the law.

If judges were compelled to impose indeterminate sentences and
leave it to the prison authorities and the parole boards to decide when
a prisoner has proved his right to be free, sentences would be fairer
to the criminal and a better protection for society. This plan would
do away with at least one type of unfair law, the habitual criminal acts
such as the Baumes Law in New York. Under the Baumes Law, any
man who is convicted of a felony for the fourth time gets a life sentence. A stupid crook, caught four times for crimes like house-break-
ing or stealing an automobile, goes up for life, while a clever criminal
may commit a hundred more serious crimes and escape conviction
entirely. Warden Lewis E. Lawes of Sing Sing said that less than two
per cent of the lifers who were sentenced under the Baumes Law were
really serious criminals. They are stupid, unlucky, or too poor to hire
a clever lawyer to keep them out of prison.

These unfortunate lifers, placed in prison by the habitual criminal
acts, become desperate; they know they will never be paroled. They
often try to break out or start riots. As a result, wardens and guards
have to be stern and sometimes brutal to keep order. We blame our
prisons for harsh methods of treatment, yet part of this responsibility
should be placed on the shoulders of the police departments, juries,
lawyers, and judges for encouraging the passage of such acts as the
Baumes Law. If we had efficient police departments, a criminal would
be fairly certain of arrest early in his lawless career. After a fair trial by
experts to determine his guilt, he would, if found guilty, be imprisoned
for the length of time needed to reform him, or be placed on probation
under suspended sentence. Only by such methods can the American
public secure protection from the small criminal.

## Punishment and the Rise of the Modern Prison System

**Leading stages in society's attitude toward the convicted criminal.**
The development of society's attitude toward persons convicted of
crime has undergone an interesting evolution. From the dawn of history down to about the time of the American Civil War, criminals
were punished harshly; until about 1800, this punishment was usually
some form of brutal corporal punishment. Then came the establishment of prisons, and imprisonment became the most popular form of
punishment. Next, with the rise of the Elmira Reformatory system
between 1850 and 1876, the more enlightened penologists argued that
our institutions for delinquents should be used to reform inmates.
With the development of probation, parole, conditional release under
close supervision, and the Youth Correction Authority program, the
next great stage in our thinking along this line contended that,
if we wish to reform criminals, we must do so outside of institutions
and in the environment to which the reformed men are to be adjusted
if the experiment is to prove a success. In short, American penological
thought has passed through three chief periods: (1) that in which we
concentrated on punishment in institutions; (2) that in which main
stress was placed on using institutions for rehabilitative purposes; and
(3) the stage into which we are now entering, which embraces rehabilitation exclusively, but holds that it must be accomplished, for the
most part, outside of institutions.

**Primitive punishments.** In primitive society, crimes against the
public welfare were punished by summary execution of the culprit, by
exile, or by corporal punishment. Private crimes, such as murder,
were avenged by the relatives of the victim. As time passed, punishment gradually came under the supervision of the elders of the group
and formal procedure against crime was established. The criminal
was often forced to endure the same injuries that he had inflicted on
the victim. This is the "eye-for-an-eye" doctrine, well-known in Old
Testament times. It meant just what it said. If the victim had been
killed, the offender was killed; if a man gouged out another's eye, he
also had to lose an eye.

**Cruel and barbarous forms of corporal punishment.** When the
state took over the repression of crime, it adopted the earlier forms of
corporal punishment as the usual method of punishing criminals. Corporal punishment for crime was the rule from primitive times until the
opening of the nineteenth century. Most early punishment, both on
the continent of Europe and in our country, was corporal punishment,
marked by cruelty and brutality. Some of the favored methods were
pouring hot lead in the eyes; slitting or piercing the tongue; branding
with a red-hot iron, sometimes with a letter signifying the nature of
the crime; or lashing at the whipping post. Brutal mutilation continued, even in England, until the beginning of the sixteenth century,

with the cutting off of ears and hands persisting, in some places, until the eighteenth century.

The pillory and stocks were instruments of punishment used to place a disgraced culprit in public view. The pillory was a platform on which the offender stood with his head and hands thrust through holes in a board. His punishment was thus an object lesson to the whole community. The stocks were similar to the pillory, except that both the hands and feet of the seated offender were firmly fixed between two boards. An offender might be pelted with rotten eggs and vegetables while in the pillory or stocks. There were variations of punishment on the pillory. Sometimes the culprit was forced to stand with his ears nailed to the board, and after a time, the ears were cut off. This custom of cutting off the ears was practiced extensively on runaway slaves in the colonial South. The mutilation furnished a means of identification, and it also served as a warning to other would-be runaways. The ducking stool, milder than other punishments, was usually reserved for women gossips and scolds. The stool was attached to the end of a long pole, and the chattering offender was ducked into the water a number of times.

**Late origins of prisons.** Strangely enough, prisons in early times were not used as places of punishment for criminals, but as a dumping ground for debtors, vagrants, heretics, and those accused, but not yet convicted, of crime. Convicted criminals, instead of being placed in confinement, were usually executed, deported, subjected to various forms of corporal punishment, or fined. Banishment from the country was much favored by England after she had established the American and Australasian colonies.

During the seventeenth and eighteenth centuries, reformers in both Europe and America became interested in the idea of substituting imprisonment for corporal punishment. In 1704, the Pope built the Hospital of Saint Michael, a small prison mainly for juvenile delinquents, at Rome; it was visited by reformers and helped to arouse interest in the idea of imprisonment. American Quakers, by their penal code of 1681, established a system of workhouses in New Jersey and shortly afterwards in Pennsylvania, but it required over 100 years for their humane methods to be accepted generally in this country.

John Howard and Elizabeth Fry, in England, were among the early prison reformers. Between 1773 and 1791, John Howard not only did much to improve the condition of the debtors imprisoned in English prisons, but also made a very thorough study of prison conditions on the continent of Europe. He urged the substitution of imprisonment for brutal corporal punishments, and some new jails were built as a result of his agitation. Twenty years after Howard's death a Quaker, Elizabeth Fry, began her work among the women prisoners in London. Although the influence of reformers like John Howard and Elizabeth Fry was important, the credit for substituting imprisonment for corporal punishment must go mainly to the Quakers of New Jersey and

Pennsylvania, who had struggled since 1681 to uphold their humane theories. The Revolutionary War removed British control and enabled the Quakers to put their theories into practice. To these Quaker reforms we may also trace the idea of solitary confinement.

**Rise of the Pennsylvania system.** Horrified at the filth of the eighteenth-century prisons, and the association of both sexes and all ages in one room, the Philadelphia Quakers, aided by other reform leaders, hit upon the idea that solitary confinement would both remove the prisoner from evil associations and give him plenty of time to think about his sins and repent. Between 1790 and 1829, a cell block in the Walnut Street Jail in Philadelphia and two state penitentiaries were opened in Pennsylvania on this principle of one person to a cell. The solitary confinement plan was known as the Pennsylvania system. According to its sponsors, the Pennsylvania system possessed these advantages: (1) it was impossible for first offenders to associate with habitual criminals; (2) there was plenty of time in the solitary cell for sober reflection and penitent thoughts; (3) it was easy to administer the system; and (4) the horrors of loneliness made the prisoner eager to work in prison and thus learn to lead a useful life after release.

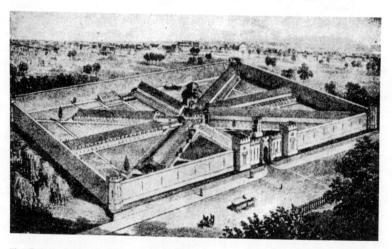

The Eastern State Penitentiary, 1829, original home of the Pennsylvania system of prison discipline. This picture reveals the radial-wing and outside-cell construction typical of the architecture of the Pennsylvania system.

**Growing popularity of the Auburn system.** The Pennsylvania system, although used in some of the new American prisons, soon lost popularity in the United States, because a new idea of prison administration arose in the state prison at Auburn, New York, in 1824. This plan, known as the Auburn system, modified the solitary confinement of the Pennsylvania system. The prisoners worked together in shops by day and were placed alone in their cells only at night. Prisoners at Auburn were not allowed to converse at any time or under any circumstances.  Hence, the Auburn system was also known as "the silent system" of prison discipline, in distinction from the "solitary system" of Pennsylvania.  Auburn prisoners also had to march in lockstep. They had closely cropped hair and wore striped suits.  Sing Sing Prison, also in New York State, and the prisons of Massachusetts and Connecticut soon adopted this system.

The Auburn plan was thought by many to be far better than the Pennsylvania system, because it was more humane and economical. The prisoners could be put to work in shops and thus help to pay for their keep.  The advocates of this system also said that solitary confinement by night provided enough time for moral reflection.  In addition to these alleged advantages of the Auburn system, another reason for its wide adoption was that Louis Dwight, the energetic secretary of the Boston Prison Discipline Society, traveled all over the country, praising the virtues of the Auburn system and working for its adoption whenever any state seemed likely to build a new prison.  Though the Auburn plan was much more popular than the Pennsylvania system in the United States, the Pennsylvania system was far more widely copied in Europe; many European prisons are still run on this solitary-confinement plan.

Although both the Pennsylvania and Auburn systems must be regarded as important forerunners of our present prison system, neither applied scientific measures to reform prisoners.  Both were based mainly on the principle of punishment.  But, some good features came out of the two systems: the accused, thereafter, were separated from the convicted, and male from female prisoners; and prisoners were put in separate rooms or cells at night and made to work during the daytime.

The Pennsylvania and Auburn prison systems not only provided the two main types of prison discipline but also furnished the basic design of prisons for a century after 1825.  Pennsylvania prisons were built with spoke-like wings containing outside cells—that is, cells located off a central corridor running the length of each wing.  Auburn prisons were constructed with rectangular cell houses which flanked the entrance of the prison.  These cell houses contained inside-cell blocks, with a corridor around the cell block.  The Auburn-style prison most widely imitated was Sing Sing, New York, which was opened in 1828.

## Rehabilitation Challenges Punishment and Revenge

**Basic items in the reform program.**  For the idea that the rehabilitation of the prisoner should be the aim of a prison program, we must look to the series of progressive reforms that finally produced the Elmira Reformatory system in New York State in 1876.  The contention that reformation should be the main purpose of imprisonment was set forth by a French penologist, Charles Lucas, about 1830.

The first practical step in this reform program was taken by Captain Alexander Maconochie who, in 1840, assumed control of the prison colony at Norfolk Island, far off the coast of Australia. His ideas of prison discipline must have seemed quite rash at the time. Maconochie was able to control and encourage his convicts by slashing time off their sentences for good behavior and hard work. Every convict, on his arrival at the prison, had a number of "marks" put against him. The number depended on the seriousness of the crime for which he had been convicted. In other words, instead of receiving ten years for stealing, the prisoner would receive a given number of "marks," which could be erased by good behavior and hard work. The better the prisoner's behavior and the harder he worked, the sooner he would be released.

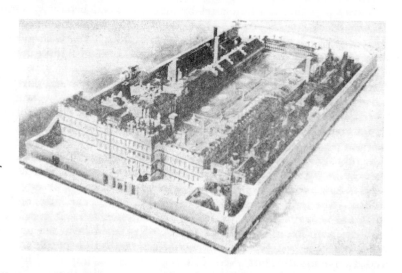

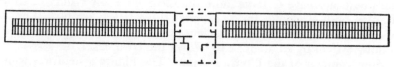

Pictured above is the State Prison at Auburn, New York. Opened in 1825, it is the parent institution of the Auburn system of prison discipline. Diagrammed below are the rectangular flanking cell houses and the inside cell blocks typical of Auburn-Sing Sing prison design. This type of construction dominated American prison architecture during the hundred-year period that followed 1825.

At about the same time, European reformers introduced the indeterminate sentence and parole. Archbishop Whatley of Dublin, George Combe in Scotland, and Frederick and Matthew Hill in England argued convincingly in favor of the indeterminate sentence, while a French reformer, Bonneville de Marsangy, urged the adoption of parole in conjunction with the indeterminate sentence. Under the indeterminate sentence a man may be sent to prison for an indefinite length of time, to be released whenever the prison authorities think it is safe to release him. The indeterminate sentence is usually employed in connection with parole, a plan whereby the convict, when selectively released from prison on an indeterminate sentence, is placed under the supervision and protection of parole officers. In this case, it is usually the parole board that determines when the convict shall be released from prison and put on parole.

Maconochie's plan of basing the length of the prison term on the convict's behavior was combined with the indeterminate sentence, parole, and industrial training in the famous Irish prison system, set up chiefly by Sir Walter Crofton and Sir Joshua Jebb during the 1850's. They introduced the practice of graded groups or classes. Each convict had to pass through all classes by means of good behavior before obtaining his release on parole. The conduct of a prisoner determined the rapidity of his advancement through the classes. The Irish prison system was utilized with adult convicts, whereas its Elmira imitation in the United States was restricted to youthful offenders.

**Creation of the Elmira Reformatory system.** These enlightened methods attracted the attention of leading American prison reformers between 1860 and 1875, who were able, at first, to adopt these policies only for younger first offenders, usually between the ages of 18 and 25. A law was passed in New York, in 1869, embodying these new theories, and a reformatory was opened at Elmira in 1876, with Zebulon R. Brockway as superintendent. The inmates were divided into three classes, through which they might advance to parole by virtue of good conduct. The term of confinement depended, within the limits of the law, on the behavior of the criminal. For instance, a youth convicted of robbery with firearms might be sentenced to serve from one to five years. With the best behavior he would be released on parole at the end of twelve months, but, even if he failed to try to improve himself, he would not have to serve more than five years. A system of education in both academic and vocational subjects was set up. The old idea of punishment to avenge society was thus partially replaced in the Elmira system by an attempt to reform the lawbreaker.

**Shortcomings of the Elmira system.** The Elmira system was widely copied in both the United States and Europe in the treatment of juvenile delinquents, and was undoubtedly a great advance over the earlier practice of throwing young persons into the more or less brutally administered state prisons for adults. It did much to popularize the idea, if not the practice, of reform in the place of revenge and punishment. It was especially notable for laying more stress on the value of education, especially vocational education, in the reformation of inmates.

But the system also had a number of defects. The Elmira plant had been originally built as an ordinary state prison for adults, and contained the usual high wall, the gloomy prison architecture, and the conventional brick and steel cage construction in cells. The institutional atmosphere was, thus, that of an ordinary prison. The next two reformatories set up, at Huntington, Pennsylvania and Concord, Massachusetts, had also been built as state prisons for adults, and when New Jersey built a new reformatory for younger inmates, at Rahway, it also erected a conventional prison structure. It was difficult to develop a real spirit of reform in such unfavorable physical surroundings. Not until the reformatory at Annandale, New Jersey, was opened in 1929, some 53 years after the first inmates were received at Elmira, was a plant built that conformed to the ideals of reformatory treatment.

Moreover, the Elmira principles were limited to a fraction of the convict population, namely, a small group of youthful offenders. The great improvements, such as the indeterminate sentence, grading and promotion of inmates, speedy release on parole for good behavior, and a reformative educational system, were only very slowly and incompletely introduced into the conventional prisons for adults. Indeed, the original ideals of the Elmira system were very imperfectly applied in the reformatories themselves, so that many have termed the reformatory program a failure. The real failure, however, has been the inability or disinclination to work out the system thoroughly in practice. Wherever the reformatory system has been given a fair trial, it has succeeded as well as most experiments with difficult human materials. On the whole, the Elmira system was an outstanding landmark in the development of a more enlightened attitude towards convicted delinquents.

**The New Penology.** The extension of Elmira principles to prisons for adults during the 75 years since the opening of the Elmira Reformatory constitutes what is commonly known as the New Penology—more humane treatment and more emphasis on rehabilitation and classification. Since the Irish system was built around adult convicts, it is not an exaggeration to say that, so far as basic ideals are concerned, the best American prisons are today about where the Irish system was 100 years ago. About all that have been added are useful innovations, such as psychiatric treatment, classification clinics, and the like.

## Separation and Classification of Convict Types

**Demoralizing conditions in early congregate prisons.** An important aspect of the progress of penology during the past century has been the separation of convicts into various classes. In the early congregate prisons, which existed before the introduction of the Pennsylvania and Auburn systems, all prisoners were herded together in one large room or group of rooms. Here mingled accused and convicted; debtors and criminals; men and women; young and old; insane, defectives, and those of normal mentality; first offenders and hardened criminals. Reform, under such conditions, was rendered impossible at the outset.

**Auburn and Pennsylvania systems introduce segregation.** The Auburn and Pennsylvania systems marked the first step in classifying and separating criminal classes. Here the accused were segregated from the convicted, and the males from the females. Accused persons were put in jails and kept there until convicted or discharged as innocent. Women prisoners were put in separate institutions or quarters.

**Institutions for juvenile offenders.** The next step was to provide separate institutions for juvenile offenders. In 1825, a semi-public institution was created in New York City for young offenders, but it was not until 1847 that the first state institution for juvenile delinquents was opened, in Massachusetts. Such institutions were, however, little more than prisons for convicted youthful delinquents.

The more modern and humane method of handling juvenile delinquents is the "cottage" or family system, imported from France, where it had been introduced by Frédéric Auguste Demetz in 1840. It was first put into use in the United States in the state reform school at Lancaster, Ohio, in 1855. The cottage system is based on the assumption that providing normal family life is a better method for reforming a young criminal than putting him, along with scores of other juvenile delinquents, in a single large building. Under the cottage system, several juvenile offenders, usually 8 to 20 of them, live in a cottage with a housemother and a housefather. The inmates are taught self-control, and are expected to do the domestic work of the cottage—in some institutions, they make their own rules and govern themselves. This plan emphasizes rational discipline, self-reliance, self-respect, reform, and training for future freedom, instead of punishment for past crimes.

**Special institutions for insane and defective criminals.** The movement to transfer the insane and feeble-minded to special institutions originated, as we have seen, about 1840. Dorothea Lynde Dix (1802–1887) worked unceasingly for a generation after 1840 to place the insane in separate institutions.[2] Miss Dix was able, after a long effort, to induce various state legislatures in the East to pass laws establishing hospitals for the insane. She also succeeded, in some measure, in getting the insane out of the jails and prisons. In the present century, chiefly as the result of the efforts of men like H. H. Goddard, Walter E. Fernald, and Walter N. Thayer, there has also been a growing recognition of the necessity of creating separate institutions for treating those lawbreakers who are feeble-minded.

**Classification essential to any program of rehabilitation.** Considerable progress has been made in studying and classifying convicts in order to meet the particular needs of each convict and to individualize his treatment. In the better prison systems, like the Federal system and that of New Jersey, the classification of prisoners has made great headway and has notably assisted in the process of reformation. Con-

---

2 See above, pp. 801–802.

victs are carefully examined and classified according to their records, personalities, and prospects of reformation. They are then distributed among specialized institutions, which are fitted to deal with each type of prisoner according to his needs. In this way, administrative problems are simplified and the possibility of reformation greatly enhanced.

*Courtesy Federal Bureau of Prisons.*

**The famous but archaic Federal super-security prison on Alcatraz Island in San Francisco Bay.**

**Adapting prison design to prisoner needs.** An important phase of the differentiation, classification, and treatment of prisoners according to the seriousness of their crimes and their prospect of reformation has been the tendency to construct prisons better adapted to special types of convicts. For the most part, even to our own day, there has been only one type of grim institution—the fortress prison—to house both hardened criminals and trivial first offenders.

Nothing in the whole archaic prison picture is more absurd than the traditional practice of building all the cells in a prison of equally secure construction. It is like a zoo in which equally heavy bars were used for the cage of the lion and of the gazelle. The Federal Bureau of Prisons has repudiated this preposterous procedure, and even when it builds a peniteniary today it provides maximum-security inside cells for only about 15 per cent of the inmates. The facilities for others a.re about equally divided between outside cells and dormitories.

For the minority of "hard-boiled" and dangerous criminals we may still need the old-style fortress prison with its thick cell-house walls, tool-resisting steel cages, and high wall around the prison yard. This is called a "maximum-security" prison; the most extreme example is the Federal prison at Alcatraz in San Francisco Bay.

Undoubtedly, far too much money is expended on maximum-security prisons. Only a few are needed. Not only are they very expensive to build, but they create a mental atmosphere highly unfavorable to the application of rehabilitative programs. New York State provides a good example of excessive investment in maximum-security prisons.

It has six large and expensive prisons of this sort, and only one small medium-security plant, accommodating about 500 inmates.

For less dangerous convicts medium-security prisons, of much less expensive construction, are more economical, humane, and effective. The walls of the cell houses are not as thick, there is less steel-cage cell equipment, and either a lower wall or an electrified wire fence is used

*Courtesy of Federal Bureau of Prisons.*

**The most nearly perfect maximum-security prison ever conceived. Designed to replace Alcatraz when Federal funds become available, it substitutes skylights for the old-fashioned barred windows, thus insuring better-lighted cell blocks and increased security.**

to enclose the institution. Single rooms, squad-rooms, and dormitories are used to supplement maximum-security inside cells. In a good medium-security prison not over 15 per cent of the inmates are confined in the most secure inside cells. Most sensible penologists believe that medium-security prisons would be adequate to confine safely almost any type of criminal. A good reform program, one that can interest the inmates in self-improvement, has been found more effective in reducing escapes than high walls and steel cages.

For the first offenders, the more easily reformable types, and those nearing release, there are "minimum-security" prisons, in which the fortress aspect, the steel cages, and the high walls are almost entirely replaced by cottages or dormitories. These are usually securely locked at night, but inmates have considerable freedom to work out-of-doors in the daytime under general supervision of guards. Minimum-security institutions never have walls, but it is regarded as good sense to enclose them by a high woven wire fence, topped with barbed wire. This procedure eliminates what would otherwise be an overt and constant temptation to inmates to stray from the institution.

Such institutions usually have a good rehabilitative program, including interesting work, vocational education, and ample recreation. As a result, inmates lose the ordinary obsession of convicts with escape or release and begin to take an interest in trying to prepare for a law-abiding life.

While states still go on building their large and expensive "white elephants" in the form of fortress prisons, the best scientific opinion would limit most new prison construction to medium-security and minimum-security prisons.  The tendency now among enlightened penologists is to believe that several small and inexpensive prisons, each housing about 500 inmates, are preferable to one large and costly fortress, housing thousands of convicts.   According to them, no prison should be built to house more than 1,200 to 1,500 inmates.

**Introduction of the French "telephone-pole" prison.**  In all improved recent trends in prison architecture, whether of maximum-, medium-, or minimum-security construction, the chief advance in the twentieth century has been the introduction of the so-called telephone-pole layout, first used in the great French prison at Fresnes, opened in 1898.   It is so called because the housing and service units of the institution are located at right angles to a covered central corridor, with the whole structure resembling the cross-bars on a telephone pole.

Previously, most prisons had been built on the wheel-spoke plan of the Eastern Penitentiary of Pennsylvania, or with long, flanking cell houses, opening off a central entrance.   This latter design was inherited chiefly from the famous long cell house of the Sing Sing prison in New York State, opened in 1828.   Both the spoke and the flanking cell house designs made for long and dark cell corridors and increased the distance over which convicts had to move to the dining room, shops, or chapel.

**American adaptations and improvements.**  The telephone-pole design made possible shorter corridors, lessened the distance in routine convict circulation throughout the plant, facilitated supervision with a minimum of guards, and made possible better natural lighting in the cell corridors.   Alfred Hopkins was mainly responsible for introducing the telephone-pole plan into the United States; the first struc-

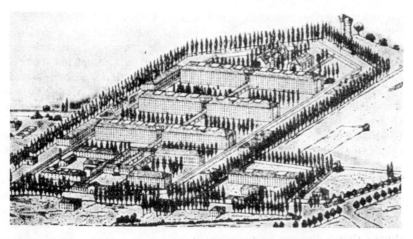

*From Alfred Hopkins,* Prisons and Prison Building.

Layout of the prison in Fresnes, near Paris, France. Opened in 1898, it is the parent institution of the telephone-pole type of prison design now adopted in up-to-date prison building in the United States.

ture fully designed along this line was his medium-security prison at Wallkill, New York. He greatly improved this design in the famous Federal mixed-custody penitentiary at Lewisburg, Pennsylvania, opened in 1932.

The Federal prison system has most thoroughly adopted the telephone-pole design for its new institutional construction, and the most perfect examples are the Federal penitentiary at Terre Haute, Indiana, the Federal medium-security institution at Texarkana, Texas, and the new U.S. Military Prison at Camp Cooke, near Santa Barbara, California.

The most important American improvement over the French telephone-pole prison has been the work of Robert D. Barnes, senior architect of the Federal Bureau of Prisons. He has devised an ingenious system of consolidating prison cell houses and skylighting and air conditioning prison corridors. These innovations give greater economy in construction, shorten the distance of convict movements, do away with long, narrow, bar-darkened windows in cell house walls, greatly reduce the possibility of escape from cell corridors, and provide more comfortable and healthy living quarters.

## Treatment versus Punishment for Criminals

**Fictitious basis of the theory of revenge and punishment.** Our criminal law is still based on the theory of making a punishment fit a crime. The hope is that, if we punish the criminal harshly and long enough, we shall avenge the wrong he has done to society, and, at the same time, issue an effective warning to other would-be lawbreakers.

Underlying this theory is the notion that a man is a free moral agent, completely free to choose the line of conduct he will follow. He alone, according to this theory, is responsible for his behavior, whether he is born in a tenement or palace, is educated or ignorant, rich or poor, healthy or diseased. At any time, he may freely decide whether he will go into a church to worship reverently or will stay outside and cast stones through the stained-glass windows. The theory of willful choice, still basic in our criminal law, explains the two traditional reasons for punishment: to avenge society, and to make an example of the criminal, so that others will not try to follow in his footsteps.

**Punishments cannot arbitrarily be made to fit crimes.** But can a man freely choose his way of life? The whole idea of willful choice has been destroyed by scientific studies of how men actually behave in the surroundings in which they live. No longer can we accept the theory that a human being is invariably a free moral agent. Most conventional criminals are so warped by inherited defects, so weakened by poverty and poor health, so undermined morally by bad habits formed in adverse surroundings, that it is more natural to them to commit criminal acts than to live honestly and uprightly. Even the leaders of organized crime and racketeering are the victims of perverted social and economic ideals, such as the "only saps work" formula. If a criminal does what is natural in the light of his background, it is senseless to punish him. We would not think of punishing a man for contracting tuberculosis, yet we punish the criminal for having absorbed the "germs of crime."

Moreover, history shows that severe punishments have never effectively restrained people from committing crime. For example, England, in 1800, imposed capital punishment for more than 200 crimes. Yet England, today, with a far milder criminal code, has a much lower crime rate than in 1800. About 1800, England held public hangings of pickpockets, in hopes of turning other pickpockets from the ways of crime; unfortunately, there was so much pickpocketing at these hangings that the practice had to be abandoned.

Moreover, there is a basic logical inconsistency in the free-will doctrine in relation to punishment. If a man is always free to will his actions, irrespective of all external influences, then he is fully free to

*Courtesy of Federal Bureau of Prisons.*

This Federal Penitentiary at Terre Haute, Indiana, was opened in 1940. Designed on the telephone-pole pattern, it has radial cell houses at each end to prevent overextension of plant. It is the finest American penitentiary, and the first to be built without a wall.

will to disregard the awful example of punishment for crime, no matter how hideous.

**Individualized treatment for each criminal.** We are at last beginning to realize that we cannot devise a punishment to fit a crime. Crimes are committed by criminals, and when we speak of criminals, we are dealing with individual men and women like ourselves, instead of general theories in a textbook. Many different types of men—some feeble-minded, others insane, many merely stupid, and others who regard a life of crime as the means of getting something for nothing— may commit the same kind of crime. It is impossible for any trial judge to impose a punishment that will fit the crime in every case, because a sentence that is just for one man might be too mild for another and too severe for a third.

Our aim in all scientific penology should be to protect society from criminals and to prevent crimes from being committed. We have failed to accomplish this result in the past merely by punishing criminals; we shall also fail in the future, if we continue to use the same unsuccessful methods. The records of ex-convicts show that most of them continue their criminal activities after their release from prison. The only way to decrease crime is to replace the old doctrine of finding a punishment to fit a crime by the new ideal of providing scientific treatment to fit a particular criminal.

All convicted men and women should have a thorough physical and mental examination. A case history should also be prepared by experts at the time of the examination. After such thorough study, the authorities will be better able to know why a particular individual became a criminal, to estimate the chances of his reformation, and to provide the desirable program of treatment. Examination and diagnosis are as important in treating crime as in treating disease.

The scientific examination of criminals reveals three large classes: (1) those for whom there is little hope of reformation, like the feeble-minded and the hardened criminals, who should be segregated from society and permanently kept in prison; (2) an intermediate group for whom there is hope of reformation, but who need treatment and training within an institution; and (3) another large group, chiefly younger first offenders, who do not require imprisonment at all, but can best be handled by means of probation on suspended sentence.

**The Youth Correction Authority Plan.** The most completely scientific application of the newer ideas about treating criminals is that embodied in the Youth Correction Authority Plan, worked out by the American Law Institute under the inspiration and guidance of Professor John B. Waite. Here, for the first time, there is provided an opportunity to carry out in unhampered practice the ideals that motivated the reformers who introduced the Elmira system over eighty years ago. The program is designed for juvenile delinquents from 16 to 21 years of age. Under this system of procedure, the judge does not impose any sentence unless the boy is fined or is remanded to a prison for a capital offense. The judge simply hands the convicted youth over to the Youth Correction Authority. Its trained staff studies the youth carefully and plans treatment according to his individual needs. The treatment may be probation, occupational training and therapy in a camp or on a farm, or temporary confinement in a conventional reformatory. The youth is not released until the authorities are convinced that reformation has been accomplished and the person is suitable for release on parole. Nothing save an inadequate staff can prevent such a program from being as good a mode of handling juvenile delinquents as our present knowledge in the field permits.

The state of California adopted the plan in 1941. Wisconsin and Minnesota adopted it in 1948, and Massachusetts in 1949. New York and New Jersey have adopted it in less complete form. It has worked out with all the success that could be reasonably expected in the nine years of California experience. What is now needed is its adoption by all states that have the ability to supply a suitable staff to administer it, and the extension of such a plan to a large number of adult offenders. This latter advance has also been introduced to a limited extent in California, in the Prison Reorganization Act of 1944, which created an Adult Correction Authority and gave it considerable power over adult prisoners and institutions.

**No scientific basis for capital punishment.** The considerations set forth above about crime and punishment naturally undermine all basis for the barbarous practice of capital punishment. The only arguments for it are the ancient doctrine of an eye for an eye and the notion that capital punishment reduces the homicide rate.

The eye-for-an-eye doctrine is a vestige of savagery and has no support in twentieth-century thought. Careful studies of the homicide rates in states that have capital punishment and in those that have abolished it prove conclusively that the death penalty does not reduce the homicide rate. Further, a study of murderers and of the motives of murder shows that there is little probability that many persons who commit a murder would be deterred by fear of the death penalty. Most murders are committed by otherwise normal persons in a moment of passion, by robbers and the like who become panicky, by cold-blooded professional gunmen, and by persons with disordered minds. The fact that murder is a capital crime on the statute books would not be likely to stay the homicidal hand in many such cases. The abolition of capital punishment is a fundamental tenet of the new criminology.

## Leading Problems of Prison Administration

**Prisons usually make inmates more hardened and confirmed criminals.** The problem of prison administration is not a mere academic question. It not only touches the lives of all American citizens, who desire protection from criminals, but also very directly affects about 150,000 men and women who are confined annually in our Federal and state prisons. The following official table, based on information supplied by the Bureau of the Census, gives a general picture of our convict population in 1947, as well as a good idea of the nature and extent of the changes in this population in any normal year:

MOVEMENT OF PRISON POPULATION: 1947

| ITEMS | ALL INSTITUTIONS: FEDERAL AND STATE | | |
|---|---|---|---|
| | Total | Male | Female |
| Prisoners present January 1 | 141,340 | 135,114 | 6,226 |
| Admitted during year | 84,568 | 79,165 | 5,403 |
| Received from court | 68,281 | 64,060 | 4,221 |
| Returned as a conditional release violator. | 8,263 | 7,720 | 543 |
| Returned from escape | 2,254 | 2,135 | 119 |
| Returned by court order | 460 | 457 | 3 |
| Other admissions | 5,310 | 4,793 | 517 |
| Transferred from other institutions | 20,106 | 19,761 | 345 |
| Discharged during year | 73,216 | 68,415 | 4,801 |
| All releases | 61,752 | 57,768 | 3,984 |
| Unconditional release | 24,963 | 23,309 | 1,654 |
| Expiration of sentence | 24,086 | 22,606 | 1,480 |
| Pardon | 49 | 45 | 4 |
| Commutation | 828 | 658 | 170 |
| Conditional release | 36,789 | 34,459 | 2,330 |
| Parole | 29,129 | 27,187 | 1,942 |
| Conditional pardon | 238 | 228 | 10 |
| Other conditional release | 7,422 | 7,044 | 378 |
| Death, except execution | 825 | 804 | 21 |
| Execution | 88 | 88 | – |
| All other discharges | 10,551 | 9,755 | 796 |
| Escape | 2,361 | 2,243 | 118 |
| Court order | 1,921 | 1,842 | 79 |
| Other discharges | 6,269 | 5,670 | 599 |
| Transferred to other institutions | 20,234 | 19,649 | 585 |
| Prisoners present December 31 | 152,564 | 145,976 | 6,588 |

It has long been the belief of many persons that imprisonment will reform convicts. So powerful is this belief that many persons still cannot face the fact that prisons usually make men worse instead of better. The very nature of prison life only further demoralizes the personality of inmates. The whole scheme of life is unnatural and in no way adapted to prepare convicts for a normal social life when released. The swift and arbitrary termination of all normal sex life encourages homosexuality and many associated forms of degeneracy. Tough and hardened convicts instruct the amateurs in better ways of committing crime and escaping conviction. The best that most prisons can do is to produce a good convict, which is something entirely different from turning out a good citizen. Most convicts emerge from prison even more hardened and embittered against society than they were when admitted. They find that the world does not accept them as free men. People are suspicious of a man with a prison record, no matter how earnestly he wishes to reform. He has a hard time finding a job, and his old companions in crime are generally waiting for him to join them.

Because it was observed that many convicts cease their criminal careers in mid-life, it was assumed that prisons do reform some minority of inmates.   But Sheldon Glueck showed rather convincingly that such cases are primarily a product of the stabilizing influence of physical and mental maturity rather than the result of any rehabilitative effects of prison life.  This is Glueck's famous "maturation theory" of criminality.

*Courtesy of Federal Bureau of Prisons.*

**Federal medium-security prison at Texarkana, Texas. Model institution built on telephone-pole plan. Note substitution of fence for traditional prison wall.**

Society cannot be forced overnight to change its attitude toward the ex-convict, but the prison should prepare the criminal to adjust himself to normal conditions upon release.  He should be built up mentally and physically while he is confined; he should be educated for a trade and enabled to earn money while working in prison; above all, he should be trained in responsible citizenship.  On the whole, American prison systems, so far, have failed adequately to provide good health and hygiene programs, sufficient prison labor, vocational education, and training for citizenship.

**How the rehabilitative treatment of prisoners is prevented.**   Although all progressive penologists have for nearly a hundred years accepted in theory the concept of reformation, rather than punishment, as the ideal to be sought in treating convicted criminals, there has been lamentably little progress in putting this ideal into operation, except in certain Federal institutions and in the systems of a few enlightened states. The main obstacle to extending rehabilitative treatment from theory and rhetoric into practice has been what we call the convict bogey.

Curiously and illogically enough, the populace does not seem to fear criminals until they have been pronounced guilty by a jury. Indeed, if the criminal is sufficiently dangerous and glamorous and has been well publicized, those financially able to do so are frequently willing to pay a stiff cover charge at a fashionable night club to get a look at him at a nearby table. But let a man be convicted of even a minor felony and put safely behind prison bars and he becomes a menace to society and is regarded with fear and horror.

This convict bogey leads directly to the so-called jailing psychosis, which continues to dominate the actual operation of our penal institutions, however much we may give lip service to the nobility of rehabilitative treatment. It is believed to be the fundamental function of a penal and correctional institution to prevent convicts from escaping, at whatever cost. The good warden or superintendent is the one who keeps his convict charges safely jailed, even though he never reforms a single one of them—indeed, even though the vast majority are turned out more desperate characters than they were upon entrance.

*Courtesy of Federal Bureau of Prisons.*

Federal minimum-security prison at Seagoville, near Dallas, Texas. America's finest minimum-security prison plant. Note open, campus-like construction. Despite its apparent lack of secure construction, dangerous criminals have been safely confined here because of excellent rehabilitation program which eliminates most of the incentive to escape.

Because most institutional officials desire to hold their jobs, they have to be extremely solicitous and apprehensive in executing this jailing function. Therefore, rehabilitative treatment, however dominant in theory, tends to be subordinated or discarded altogether in practice. The jailing psychosis demands major emphasis upon high walls, steel cages, machine guns, arbitrary inmate routine, and a rigorous punitive discipline. Treatment, on the other hand, stresses the primacy of a flexible program that can be tempered to the needs of the different types of inmates, and inevitably carries with it some custodial risks.

The best answer to the convict bogey and the jailing psychosis is to emphasize the all-important fact that the main danger from convicts is not that they may escape from prison but that we may fail to reform them before they are released in lawful fashion. The average time served by all inmates of our penal and correctional institutions is only about two years and three months. Even those sentenced for life serve on an average only about ten years.

The average convict, then, will be released every two and a quarter years to resume his antisocial depredations unless he is reformed while in prison. This is a far more alarming fact than the possibility that a negligible fraction may escape to resume their criminal activities a few months before they would have been released in the ordinary course of events. These facts make it obvious that our only real protection against convicts is to reform them; making them more bitter, determined, and skillful criminals by locking them in steel cages for a couple of years provides slight protection indeed.

**Better medical care and hygiene needed.** The bad health of a convicted man may have had something to do with his criminal activities. In all too many instances, too little attention is paid to the convict who is physically diseased or is suffering from mental and nervous disorders. To have health and efficiency, men must eat wholesome food; yet, even in some of our better prisons, meals are poorly balanced, poorly prepared, and inferior in quality. Sanitation is often bad; the cells may be cold and dark or hot and stuffy. With little work to do, the prisoner may sit in his cell all day, idle and shiftless, brooding over his treatment. If the estimate of the medical director of the Federal system that 85 per cent of prisoners are mentally disturbed, unbalanced, or defective is true, then a model prison is in about as great need of a good staff of psychiatrists and clinical psychologists as a state hospital for the insane.

**The curse of convict idleness.** Reformation can rarely be accomplished in idleness. "Idle hands are the Devil's workshop" is an old adage that has great truth when applied to prison life. Laws restricting prison labor, especially those passed between 1929 and 1940, introduced wholesale idleness into state prisons. These laws did not affect the prisons in the Federal system. The industrial and labor system in state prisons became so bad by the eve of the second world war that only a small portion of the inmates could be employed at anything save the chores and drudgery connected with the routine maintenance of the prisons. The whole system of discipline was threatened with demoralization.

**Types of prison labor.** There have been several ways of handling convict labor. Formerly, some states allowed contractors to *lease* the labor of convicts and work them as they pleased. In many cases, the men were taken out of prison, and put to work on private projects, a system most popular in the South. The leasing of convict labor has been abandoned, Alabama being the last state to give it up, in 1928. More popular has been the practice of *contracting* for the labor of convicts who remain in prison, supervised by the agents of contractors. Nine states still used this system when it was outlawed by Federal legislation two decades ago.

Another scheme was the *piece-price* system, under which the prison was paid by contractors for making, by convict labor, various types of goods at a certain price per piece. In 1932, this system furnished employment for some 9,000 prisoners, who produced goods valued at 10 million dollars. It has been abandoned because of adverse Federal legislation. A fourth plan was the *public-account* system, according to which the prison authorities took complete charge of prison labor and sold the products in the open market. About 15,000 convicts, or 20 per cent of all gainfully-employed prisoners, were operating under this system in 1932, and they produced 12 million dollars worth of goods. This, also, was wiped out by the Federal laws passed between 1929 and 1940.

Finally, prisons have developed the *state-use* system, whereby convicts manufacture automobile license plates, institutional furniture, bedding, towels, clothing, shoes, and all sorts of goods for use in prisons and other state institutions. Some states employ convicts on state roads and public buildings. Prison farms have become more numerous and productive. Where states now provide for any extensive prison labor, the state-use plan is invariably adopted. Some 42 per cent of all productively employed prisoners were on the state-use system as early as 1932. The main defect of the state-use system is that the laws establishing it have been notoriously one-sided. While prisons are restricted to manufacturing only for state agencies and institutions, the latter are rarely restricted to buying prison-made goods.

In no plan was primary stress laid on helping the prisoner to learn a trade or acquire a desire to work. With the exception of the Federal prison system and a few of the better state systems, prison labor, today, is rarely profitable to either the convict or the prison. Before the paralyzing Federal legislation went into operation in the 1930's and 1940's, West Virginia, Minnesota, Wisconsin, Michigan, Missouri, Texas, and California had a large income from prison industries, even though most prisons were rarely self-supporting.

**Unwise legislation paralyzes prison labor.** Beginning about 1875, there arose strong objections to contract prison labor on the part of unions and industries that feared the competition of cheap, prison-made products. Many laws were, therefore, passed limiting contract prison industries to coarse products. Hence, we find that the chief prison-made products manufactured under contract between about 1885 and the second world war were cocoa mats, burlap bags, coarse brushes and brooms, cheap clothing and hosiery, shoes, bricks, and heavy hardware, products that were not highly profitable in the market and offered no industrial training.    About all that can be said is that such work kept the convicts from sheer idleness.

The various influences that opposed prison labor got the upper hand in Congress and passed the Hawes-Cooper Act in 1929, and the Ashurst-Sumners Act in 1935.   These laws, giving the states full power to regulate both intra- and interstate shipment of prison-made goods, threw thousands of convicts into idleness.   The final step came in the act of October 14, 1940, which forbade the shipment of most prison-made products in interstate commerce, thus ending all except state-use prison industry.   This restrictive legislation did not apply to prisons in the Federal system.

**Opposition to prison-made products is foolish.**   Even when the contract system was going full blast, seventy-five years ago, prison-made products did not constitute more than a small fraction of one per cent of the total industrial production of the country.   In 1929, they did not make up one-fourth of one per cent of national production.

Through the Prison Industries Reorganization Administration, set up in 1935, the Roosevelt administration offered aid and counsel to states that wished to reorganize their prison industries on the state-use plan.   Only a few states took advantage of the opportunity, but the PIRA made some valuable reports on prison labor conditions.

**Second world war revives prison industry.**   The second world war proved a godsend to prison industry in state prisons.   The frantic demand for war materials led to the mobilization of all available manpower, including the thousands of idle and able-bodied men in our state prisons.   Maury Maverick organized a Prison War Industries Branch of the War Production Board to enlist and direct the work of prisoners on war contracts.   Restrictive legislation was waived temporarily, and by 1944 most of the able-bodied prisoners not employed in maintenance operations were at work producing war materials—clothing, shoes, metal products, and the like.

Altogether, state and Federal prisons produced some $138,000,000 worth of manufactured products for the war effort, together with some $75,000,000 worth of farm products, and prisoner morale was raised to an all-time high.   An effort was made to perpetuate the wartime gains and keep prisoners employed, and the great demand for goods after 1945 made this effort temporarily successful.   By the end of 1947, however, the return of millions of service men to normal industrial pursuits ended the need for convict labor in most fields of industrial activity.   With the failure to compel state institutions and agencies to buy prison-made products holding back prison industry in peacetime production, our state prisons seem headed once more toward demoralizing idleness.   The Federal prison system, which is not hampered by restrictive legislation, has the most complete and thriving system of prison industry in our country.

**Wages for prisoners.** It has been suggested that convicts should be paid real wages; not just a few cents a day, but enough to make them feel that they are really earning money. In this way, they could help their families and save some money for use after their release from prison. Earning power will do a great deal to restore the convict's self-respect, teach him work habits, and help in his reformation. Warden Lewis E. Lawes once made the sensible suggestion that prisons should pay all employed inmates a wage equal to that paid for comparable work in the outside world. Then, from this wage payment, the cost of maintaining a prisoner could be deducted and the balance paid to his account, to be used to support his dependents and help the inmate get a law-abiding start in life after release. No such rational plan has ever been put into operation. The Federal system pays inmates a maximum of $50 a month. Many states pay no wages whatever and those that do pay wages rarely pay more than around 30 cents a day.

**Prison education.** Educational opportunities are also necessary if prisoners are to be reformed; it is difficult for a man without any education to get a job. Thirteen states have no prison schools, while in many penitentiaries the school is taught by the chaplain, with the aid of a few convict teachers. Only in an occasional prison and in a few of the better reformatories do we find an extensive system of inmate education conducted by trained teachers. Even the excellent Federal system fails to provide proper educational facilities.

Vocational education of prisoners has also been sadly neglected. No released convict has much chance to go straight if he does not know a trade. No penitentiary in the United States has a thoroughly adequate program of vocational training. Some slight progress has been made along vocational lines in those institutions which employ the state-use system—prisoners are taught how to manufacture articles like furniture, clothing, and metal products.

**Prison recreation.** Recreational facilities are among the most indispensable items in an effective program of convict treatment, but they have been pretty generally ignored except in the better juvenile institutions. Adequate convict recreation improves convict health, teaches inmates the essentials of good sportsmanship, and makes them more generally responsive to treatment methods. Most important of all, recreational interests tend more powerfully than anything else to distract the minds of convicts from their otherwise constant obsession with release or escape.

We should begin to spend less for steel cages and high walls and more for gymnasiums, athletic fields, and smaller playgrounds. Moreover, no system of convict recreation will be adequate where the majority remain mere spectators. Provision must be made to allow all able-bodied convicts who wish to do so to participate in inmate sports and games.

**Self-government for prisoners.** Not only have our prisons failed to make convicts healthy and to teach them a useful trade, but, even more important, they have given little time to training convicts to become good citizens. Many convicts have healthy bodies and know a trade, but their ideas about society and government are warped and biased by past criminal experiences. These men did not learn to conform to the best standards of society or to obey the law before they entered prison; they have had little encouragement or opportunity in the past to change their attitude toward life while serving their prison terms. It is the prison's duty, however, to teach them good citizenship. To become an asset to society, the convict must be taught how to control himself and be given some responsibilities in self-government. If a man cannot control himself in a prison democracy, how can he be expected to control himself in a larger democracy outside the prison?

The idea of convict self-government is not new. It existed in the Boston House of Refuge over a century ago. But its effective introduction into prison administration and discipline was mainly the work of the distinguished publicist and philanthropist, Thomas Mott Osborne, who first observed the system at work in the George Junior Republic, a private institution for juveniles at Freeville, New York. In the decade after 1913, Osborne introduced the famous "Mutual Welfare League" in the prisons at Auburn and Sing Sing, New York, and in the United States Naval Prison at Portsmouth.

Osborne grasped the fundamental truism, neglected by even enlightened prison administrators, that the best an efficient system of repressive prison discipline can do is to turn out a good convict. Osborne believed that an inmate should have a chance to learn how to govern himself while still in prison. He also thought that, if a convict has a part in carrying out prison discipline, he will be more likely to obey prison rules. While Osborne, by keeping guards on hand, took no chances on a riot or prison break, he put most of the discipline under convict control. The prisoners controlled prison discipline by means of an elected governing council and had their own court. The warden kept a general veto power over their decisions.

The Mutual Welfare League, despite criticisms by conservative wardens and the outside world, operated remarkably well as long as Osborne could personally supervise it. It is, however, unlikely that such a scheme would work perfectly in every prison or for all prisoners. Prisoners who cannot conform should be ruled by guards. But for those who could benefit from the plan, the Mutual Welfare League proved an excellent way to teach good citizenship. A convict should earn his right to self-government by going through a period of supervision and instruction by prison authorities; he should not be allowed to govern himself or others on entering prison.

Systems of self-government are not to be recommended unless the warden has the personality and enthusiasm needed to make the experiment a success. Where self-government has been introduced and then neglected, it has degenerated into a system of inmate tyranny, favoritism, corruption and extortion, and, as in the case of the great riots in the Auburn prison in 1929, a means of plotting and executing wholesale escape.

**Release and supervision on parole.** The problems related to the release of prisoners are almost as important as those connected with prison administration and discipline. In the past, prisoners were released under conditions that meant for most a return to crime and eventually to prison.

In any scientific system of prison administration and convict treatment, an employment department would be an indispensable unit in the prison staff. No convict should be released until a job is found for him, since an unemployed ex-convict is almost inevitably forced into a resumption of his criminal career.

The system of parole, which was recommended by reformers as early as the 1830's, has gradually been introduced to help discharged convicts to get adjusted to freedom when they leave prison. Parole officers are supposed to help the discharged convict to get a job, to give him sympathetic and intelligent aid and counsel, to keep him from vicious associations, and otherwise to check on and guide his conduct. When there are enough well-trained and earnest parole officers to take care of all the discharged convicts, the parole system is of the utmost value in the guidance and reformation of criminals and has worked well.

Unfortunately, only the Federal government and some ten or twelve states have an efficient parole system. Many parole systems are no more than "paper parole" systems, which operate in a purely perfunctory fashion and exercise little actual supervision of discharged prisoners. These inadequate parole systems, obviously, cannot perform the tasks expected of them. They thus bring discredit on all parole, and do great damage to the reputation of an admirable idea and administrative practice. Reorganization and improvement of the parole system are as imperative as reforms in the conventional system of prison administration.

**Illogical premises and practices of parole systems.** Even the better parole systems are operated upon a completely illogical principle, namely, that of letting out the less risky prisoners on parole quickly and keeping the more dubious cases incarcerated until near the end of their maximum sentence before admitting them to parole. There is no objection to letting good risks out speedily on parole—the sooner the better, within reason. But it is a great mistake to keep the possibly more dangerous types in prison until about the time their sentences will expire.

If parole is any aid to rehabilitation, and all good parole is surely just this, then it is the more risky type of prisoners who most need parole aid and guidance. The longer they can have it the better.

But, under the present system, these more risky types get only a few months of parole supervision before their sentences expire and they are turned completely free. Moreover, the chances are that the extra years spent in prison will have made them worse risks for parole than they would have been if released on parole after one or two years of imprisonment. It is likely that, given our present prison system, any average inmate is a better parole risk after two years of imprisonment than after ten years.

Another mistaken procedure that characterizes even the better parole systems is the practice of allowing parole boards, the members of which rarely have any previous contact with inmates, to decide which prisoners should be admitted to parole and when they should be admitted. There is no sound basis for such an arrangement. The only group qualified to recommend a convict for parole is the trained, professional treatment staff of prisons and reformatories, just as the physicians in a state mental hospital have the sole authority to decide when a patient is safe to discharge.

**Conditional release under close supervision.** Thus far, the boldest proposal with respect to convict release has been one already used with success in several European countries, namely, limited conditional release under much closer supervision than is provided by either traditional probation or parole.

The type of inmate to be released under this plan would be one who presumably could not, for the time being, be safely let out under probation or parole, but does not require complete segregation, even in a minimum-security institution. Perhaps one-third or more of the inmates of our penal and correctional institutions today would fall within this group. They would require closer inspection and a larger supervisory force than are necessary for probationers or parolees, but, even so, such released convicts could be supervised at far less expense than the cost of their care in an institution. It should, of course, be stipulated that employment be provided for those admitted to supervision.

In countries where this plan has been tried successfully a start is usually made by letting inmates go home under close supervision during weekends. Then, the period of supervised release may be extended to include working in emergency periods, such as harvest time. If the prisoner's behavior is satisfactory in these short test periods, he may be released indefinitely under supervision, so long as he keeps at work and does not violate the law. In due time, those who have behaved well under close supervision may be admitted to routine parole, where the extent of supervision would be greatly reduced. This supervised release would also help to solve the degrading and demoralizing prison sex problem, which remains virtually untouched in even the most advanced treatment programs.

As a general proposition, this conditional release has most of the advantages of probation, except for the fact that the released prisoners have taken on the stigma of a prison sentence.   It is more economical than institutional care, can make use of community facilities for rehabilitation, and brings about the readjustment of the released men to the environment in which we hope they will live as law-abiding citizens.   The whole plan is in harmony with the growing conviction that most of the successful rehabilitation of convicts must take place outside of institutions.   Indeed, the eminent penologist, Howard B. Gill, who is the leading American exponent of the conditional release program, would limit the rôle of prisons, save in the case of desperate and non-reformable offenders, mainly to studying and diagnosing inmates prior to their release under various forms of supervision.

## Probation and the Juvenile Court

**Nature and advantages of probation.**  Some persons have felt that, since prisons usually make men and women worse criminals, the only sensible procedure is to treat outside prison walls such convicted persons as may be safely handled in this manner.  Probation, the suspended sentence, and the juvenile courts (for those accused delinquents under 18 years of age) are outgrowths of this idea.

Probation means that, instead of sentencing a man to prison, the judge permits him to go free, on condition that he conform to certain regulations.   He must report to the probation officer at stated times, live a law-abiding life, avoid establishments where liquor is served, and not be seen with criminals or evil companions while his probationary period lasts.   To illustrate, if probation is resorted to for an offense carrying a specific time sentence, the sentence will be suspended (held up) and the person placed under probationary supervision during the term of his sentence.   Probation and the suspended sentence are now being employed in many states for adults, but they are still most frequently used in handling juvenile delinquents.   New York State has placed about 25 per cent of its convicts on probation.   In almost three-fourths of all probation cases definite improvement has been noted.

The great advantages of probation over the conventional treatment of convicts in a prison institution are the following: (1) probation is much more economical because the probationer has to support himself; (2) a person on probation avoids the stigma of a prison sentence and the demoralizing association with hardened criminals; (3) probationary treatment gives a person a strong incentive to attempt to reform and keep out of prison; (4) if a man is on probation, the authorities can make use of many reform facilities not available to a prisoner, such as guidance clinics, health clinics, night schools, social settlements, and the like; and (5) under the probation procedure, a convicted person is able to make his adjustment to society on a law-abiding basis in the environment in which he must live after discharge rather than in the highly artificial and specialized social environment of a prison.

**Rise of the juvenile court movement.** One of the most important advances in providing a more scientific and humane handling of delinquents has been the juvenile court. Public attention was first directed to the juvenile court through the pioneer work of Judge Ben B. Lindsey in Denver, Colorado. Judge Lindsey, a kindly man, instead of putting children behind bars, tried to get to the bottom of their troubles and to help them straighten out their problems by fatherly advice and encouragement. He also understood the necessity of providing work, play, and proper home surroundings. Lindsey served as juvenile court judge from 1900 to 1927.

More scientific study of juvenile delinquents was provided when Dr. William Healy, one of our greatest criminologists, instituted a psychological laboratory in the Chicago Juvenile Court in 1909. Dr. Healy did much to increase our knowledge of the mental and nervous problems of delinquent children, as well as to recommend humane treatment of them in the place of the old brutalities. It was in such laboratories as those started by Dr. Healy that some of the first really scientific studies were made of the criminal personality and of criminal behavior. These studies were possible because public opinion will permit a more humane approach to the problems of delinquent children than it will tolerate in dealing with adult criminals. This pioneer work by Lindsey and Healy aroused widespread interest, and the juvenile court movement grew rapidly. Today all states except Wyoming and Maine have some form of juvenile court.

The juvenile court movement has been mainly responsible for encouraging the wider use of probation and the suspended sentence. A sensible juvenile court judge is not eager to send boys and girls who get into trouble to prisons or reformatories. He wants to give them a chance to become useful citizens. The majority of juvenile offenders come from families broken up by divorce or desertion, or have not had good home training. Others have lived in wretched slums, with no place for recreation except the streets, where they associated with evil companions. It is the juvenile court's task to handle each case individually and attempt to devise for each offender some plan that will convert him into a law-abiding citizen.

The "Big Brother" movement in some large cities offers another way to help juvenile delinquents. Interested professional men and businessmen agree to look after a boy or girl for a period of time if he or she has no responsible relatives. This plan is based on the theory that, if a youth can receive advice and help from somebody he respects, he will be less likely to get into trouble.

## The Jail Problem

**Jails in the crime repression picture.** Our prisons, according to some critics, are "universities of crime." In them, offenders receive further instruction in burglary, safe-cracking, pickpocketing, and other phases of the criminal's trade. We might likewise call our county and city jails, workhouses, and detention houses "grammar schools of crime." Jails do not supply as much drama as the prison; we seldom hear of exciting jail riots, fires, or escapes. Yet the jail problem is fully as important as the prison challenge. Many more persons are confined in jails and detention houses than in the prisons of the United States, and living conditions in them are usually far worse.

There are about three thousand county jails, workhouses, and city police lockups. From the standpoints of construction, cleanliness, food, segregation, and discipline, many of them are not fit for human habitation. Around three million persons go through them every year, awaiting examination or trial or serving out petty sentences. Perhaps half of these, including many held on suspicion, or as witnesses for trials, are not guilty of any crime or misdemeanor. There is also the most unfortunate mixture of types, from the innocent, held on suspicion, to the hardened criminal and the vicious sex offender. Young people are headed toward crime every year as a result of degrading associations in jails.

*Courtesy of Federal Bureau of Prisons.*

Model jail designed to house 250 inmates. Ideal structure for large urban counties or for regional jail used by a number of counties, no one of which is able to construct a suitable jail. This structure may be fruitfully compared with the jail structures in the home counties of students.

**Inferior character of most jails.** For the most part, our jails are managed inefficiently and corruptly. The average sheriff is far inferior to the general run of prison wardens in his understanding of the problems of crime and criminals. He usually holds his post too briefly to acquire any professional competence; he is usually a politician, without training for his work, and interested in his position only for the money he can get out of it. One way in which sheriffs add to their income is to underfeed prisoners and pocket the difference between what they are allowed and what they actually spend for food.

Most of our jails are dirty, disorderly, and reeking with filth and vermin. Not only are they degrading and demoralizing, but they are not even safe places in which to keep prisoners. The number of escapes from jails amounts to about 3,000 annually.

**How to deal with the jail problem.** The only solution of the jail problem is to get rid of all jails, as they exist today. We should provide decent and suitable detention institutions to house those held as witnesses or awaiting trial. Since, under the Constitution, a person must be considered innocent until he is proved guilty by a fair trial, those awaiting trial should not be treated like ordinary criminals, as they are in our jails. They should be held in clean and comfortable houses of detention, entirely separate from jails which house sentenced persons. The great mass of drunkards, vagrants, and petty offenders, who make up the bulk of the inmates in our jails, should be placed on probation or in scientifically-planned institutions for degenerates, vagrants, and incurables. Those who are convicted of petty crimes and need temporary segregation should be placed in clean and well-administered jails.

Since many counties in rural districts cannot afford such institutions, several counties should join in creating suitable regional jails. It is the more progressive opinion that such regional jails should be located in rural areas where the jail can operate a large farm and thus keep the inmates employed. The running of simple industries, such as laundries, has also been suggested for county and regional jails.

## Crime Prevention

**Essentials of a program of crime prevention.** Inasmuch as we do not even arrest the majority of criminals, especially the more dangerous ones, and those who are convicted and sent to prisons, reformatories and reform schools are in most cases made more serious criminals as a result of their incarceration, it is obvious that the best protection from criminals is to prevent crimes from being committed.

Crime prevention is a complex problem and we do not have space here to go into the matter in detail. But we can briefly itemize what must be accomplished if we are greatly to reduce crime in this country.

In essence, the problem of crime prevention is one of eliminating the causes of crime. Education is probably the basic technique involved. An adequate system of education would discredit the "something-for-nothing" motivation of economic life, teach civic responsibilities and respect for law, provide the vocational training needed to prepare persons for a self-supporting and law-abiding existence, and give enough sex education to make family life more successful and permanent. Economic reconstruction is needed to provide jobs for all with adequate salaries and wages. This would eliminate the incitement to steal or kill in order to live. Family problems should be solved by marriage counselling and other techniques, so that there may be fewer broken and disorganized families to head offspring towards juvenile deliquency. Child guidance clinics should be provided in sufficient number to detect and reorient problem children before they fall into serious delinquency. Community programs should be instituted to check the social disorganization produced by the decay of primary groups. Cities should be replanned and better housing provided to wipe out the slums and delinquency areas. Urban youth should be supplied with healthy recreation facilities. Law enforcement agencies should become more efficient so that they can demonstrate that, actually, "crime does not pay."

One could proceed with many other secondary, but important, items in a crime prevention program, but the foregoing will indicate the complexity of this problem and underline the fact that it will take many years to bring about conditions which promise to reduce crime to the minimum which may reasonably be expected in any human community.

## Summary

In dealing rationally with crime we should overhaul our criminal law, in order to remove from it trivial offenses and outmoded crimes and bring into it all serious forms of antisocial behavior. Then when a man breaks the law he will be committing a serious crime. Further, if we had a criminal law worthy of respect, we might teach people to respect it.

There is little prospect of dealing effectively with our more serious criminals, the racketeers and organized criminals, until we have made fundamental economic, political, and legal reforms. Until then, we can only hope to reduce this form of crime slightly through education.

At present, we must deal chiefly with traditional or conventional criminals—the usual run of burglars, robbers, pickpockets, thieves, forgers, "con" men, and the like. However efficient our prisons, we cannot get very far with such criminals, unless we catch them and convict the guilty. To this end our police system should be more honest and efficient, more highly paid, and divorced from all crooked politics. The police should not be allowed to use the third degree on suspects; their function is to arrest. The courts alone should ascertain guilt.

Our present courtroom procedure and jury trial are very poorly adapted to get at the facts in any criminal case. We should supplant the jury by a paid body of experts, interested solely in the facts and determined to get at the facts. If a man is found guilty, the judge should impose an indeterminate sentence and leave it the prison and parole authorities to decide when the convict's conduct justifies his release on parole. A judge can never know this at the conclusion of the trial.

So far, society has been mainly interested in punishing criminals, though it has been vainly hoped that punishment will also reform them. Until the opening of the nineteenth century, most punishment was corporal. Beginning in Pennsylvania, about 1790, the Quakers

and other reform leaders substituted imprisonment for corporal punishment, believing that it was both more humane and more likely to
bring about reformation. The Pennsylvania prison system advocated
continuous solitary confinement to encourage meditation and a
desire to reform. The Auburn prison system locked prisoners in their
cells at night, but permitted them to work together in silence in shops
during the day. The Pennsylvania system was most widely copied in
Europe, the Auburn system in the United States. A great improvement came in the Elmira Reformatory system, introduced in 1876 for
youthful first offenders. This combined a classification system with
an indeterminate sentence, so that the better an inmate's behavior the
sooner he would be released. Unfortunately, the Elmira system was
imperfectly applied, and was not extended to the mass of adult convicts.

Our present prison system is a deplorable failure, though some of
the former brutalities have been eliminated. Most convicts are more
hardened and cleverer criminals on release than on admission. We
must individualize treatment by making a careful case-study of each
convict. Such convicts as are non-reformable should be humanely
segregated for life. Others do not need any institutional treatment
and should be released on probation. A third class may be reformed
if given sane institutional treatment.

These last should be given the medical attention they need to insure
good physical and mental health. Those who are illiterate should be
given an elementary education. Those who have no trade should be
taught one. Productive work should be provided and reasonable
wages paid, from which the prisoners' living expenses might well be
deducted. Prisons could be made self-supporting under efficient management, providing they are not paralyzed by hostile legislation.
Training in self-government through a prison democracy should be
provided, for no man can be a good citizen when released from a prison
if he is not trained to be such within prison walls. Before any convict
is released, a job should be found for him, and parole officers should
do all possible to help him make a successful adjustment to a normal,
law-abiding life. Such a rational system of prison administration
would not reform all convicts, but it would reform many more than
we do under our present archaic system.

We need to make much greater use of probation, especially with
adult convicts. Probation is cheaper and more efficient than imprisonment, and should be used on all convicts to whom it may be safely
applied. The juvenile court has done much to encourage the use
of probation and to introduce a scientific and humane approach to
delinquency. We are more tolerant of sense and science when applied
to children.

Our jails are a deplorable heritage from antiquity and should be
completely wiped out. Many of the present jail population should be
sent to homes for degenerates or to institutions for the feeble-minded

and insane; others should be put on probation. Those merely accused of crime or held as witnesses should be decently housed in detention stations and treated like innocent persons until they are found guilty. Those who require temporary incarceration should be sent to large, well-built, and well-administered regional jails, preferably located in open country where prisoners can operate jail farms.

More important than anything else in a campaign to control and reduce crime are measures to prevent crime. These would involve preventing, so far as possible, the breeding of inferior types, and providing decent medical treatment, good housing, adequate recreation, vocational training, good civic instruction, mental hygiene clinics, and other economic, political, and social reforms for the entire United States population. We cannot hope to bring about all these changes at once, but the harder we work for them the quicker we shall reduce the scandalous crime rate of today.

### Selected References

* Barnes, H. E., *The Story of Punishment,* Stratford, 1930. An introductory survey of the history of the treatment of crime from primitive days to modern psychiatric clinics.

————————, *Prisons in Wartime,* Washington, War Production Board, 1944. Survey of the remarkable transformation of state prison industry and morale during the second world war.

Beard, B. B., *Juvenile Probation,* American Book Company, 1934. A description of the principles and techniques of probation as applied to juvenile delinquents.

Bennett, J. V., et al., *Handbook of Correctional Design and Construction,* Federal Bureau of Prisons, 1950. The most complete work in any language on the history and present nature of prison architecture, from super-security prisons to juvenile detention homes.

Borchard, E. M., *Convicting the Innocent,* Yale University Press, 1932. A startling book by an eminent legal scholar revealing many representative cases in which innocent men were convicted on what seemed to be absolutely convincing evidence.

Branham, V. C., and Kutash, S. B. (Eds.), *Encyclopedia of Criminology,* Philosophical Library, 1949. Elaborate and up-to-date compilation covering nearly every phase of criminology and penology.

* Clemmer, Donald, *The Prison Community,* Christopher, 1940. Probably the best treatment of convict life, routine, social attitudes, and mental traits.

Ellingston, J. R., *Protecting Our Children from Criminal Careers,* Prentice-Hall, 1948. Able and interesting discussion of juvenile delinquency built around the theory and development of the Youth Correction Authority program.

Fishman, J. F., *Sex in Prison,* National Library Press, 1934. The first good book in English on the most serious problem of prison life.

——————, *Crucibles of Crime,* Cosmopolis Press, 1923. The best description and criticism of American jails.

Gillin, J. L., *Taming the Criminal,* Macmillan, 1931. An interesting account of some of the typical foreign prisons and prison methods.

Glueck, Sheldon and Eleanor (Eds.), *Preventing Crime,* McGraw-Hill, 1935. Valuable symposium on crime prevention measures, including case studies of crime prevention centers.

Haynes, F. E., *The American Prison System,* McGraw-Hill, 1939. A valuable factual survey of institutions and penal methods.

Hopkins, E. J., *Our Lawless Police,* Viking, 1931. The most complete and authoritative account of the third degree and other lawless practices of our police, justifying the assertion of the Wickersham Commission that the lawlessness of our law-enforcing officers is greater than that of the criminals.

Kirby, J. P. (Ed.), *Criminal Justice,* Wilson, 1926. A collection of readings covering every phase of the processes and agencies used in convicting criminals. A very convenient collection.

La Roe, Wilbur, *Parole with Honor,* Princeton University Press, 1939. The best book on the parole system.

Lawes, L. E., *20,000 Years in Sing Sing,* Long and Smith, 1932. Interesting discussion of prison problems by the best known warden of the twentieth century.

* McKelvey, Blake, *American Prisons,* University of Chicago Press, 1936. The best history of American prisons and prison systems.

* Nelson, V. F., *Prison Days and Nights,* Little, Brown, 1933. A vivid and appalling account of life in an average prison by an intelligent former convict. It is invaluable as a source of information on the abnormal life of prisoners.

Robinson, L. N., *Penology in the United States,* Winston, 1921. Substantial survey of main problems of prison life and administration.

——————, *Should Prisoners Work?* Winston, 1931. Probably the best book on prison labor prior to the restrictive legislation passed in the period from 1929 to 1940.

Tannenbaum, Frank, *Osborne of Sing Sing,* University of North Carolina Press, 1935. Good account of the personality and ideas of the leading prison reformer of the twentieth century—the founder of the convict self-government idea.

Teeters, N. K., *World Prison Systems,* Pennsylvania Prison Society, 1944. Best brief survey of the main prison systems of the world.

——————, *Penology from Panama to Cape Horn,* University of Pennsylvania Press, 1946. Interesting portrayal of some of the novel elements in Latin American penal theory and practice.

* Wilson, Margaret, *The Crime of Punishment*, Harcourt, Brace, 1931.   Good picture of rise and nature of modern prisons, supporting the author's thesis that our prisons are a worse crime than the acts of criminals.

Winning, J. R., *Behind these Walls*, Macmillan, 1933.   Another staggering revelation of the horrors of prison life in the average prison.   Perhaps even more shocking than Nelson's book.

Note: For references on the jury trial and court procedure, see Chapter XIX, above.

# CHAPTER XXXIII

# Personal Maladjustment and Inadequacy:
# Venereal Disease, Drug Addiction,
# Alcoholism, and Suicide

## The Challenge of Venereal Disease

**Prudery frustrates a scientific approach to venereal disease.** The problem of understanding, treating, controlling, and preventing venereal disease, particularly syphilis and gonorrhea, has been complicated by the prudish and evasive attitude that society has maintained for generations toward such topics. Until recent years, to suffer from a venereal disease was considered so disgraceful that the victim attempted to conceal the fact from his physician as well as from those who knew him. The words "syphilis" and "gonorrhea" were uttered only in a hushed, secretive manner, and public speakers, physicians, or ministers did not dare to discuss the problem of venereal disease publicly. A generation ago, no magazine or newspaper dared to risk the loss of subscribers by even mentioning the names of the leading venereal diseases. In fact, until a few years ago, the mention of syphilis was forbidden in radio broadcasts. So long as the problem was not openly discussed, the public refused to admit—indeed, did not know—its seriousness.

**Sound educational and medical attitude indispensable.** To quote the words of former Surgeon-General Thomas Parran, who conducted a courageous campaign against venereal disease for several years, these disorders are a "shadow on the land." They cannot be eradicated unless the American people are made aware of their extent and danger. Only through education can victims of venereal disease be taught that consulting quacks and paying large sums for fake "cures" may bring them much mental and physical anguish later on. The sore or chancre in the first stage of syphilis disappears within a few weeks or months, and the discomfort and local manifestations of gonorrhea also usually subside within a relatively short time. Quacks take advantage of these favorable incipient aspects of both diseases to charge the patients who seek them out, under cover of secrecy, large sums for useless pills, ointments, and salves. The sufferer may remain uncured, a menace to society; moreover, his future health and sanity may be seriously endangered.

Unless the symptoms of venereal diseases, particularly of syphilis, are understood, the disease cannot be checked by early treatment, so necessary to effect an easy cure. Syphilis has been known as "the great deceiver" because its symptoms are similar to those of many other diseases.

Medical science can now readily conquer all venereal disease, if given the opportunity. Completely effective remedies are well known and easily procured. The problem is one of public education, to direct attention to the seriousness of the situation, and to urge patients to obtain scientific treatment. The cost of treatment is fairly reasonable. In public clinics a complete cure of syphilis, if begun in an early stage, may be secured for less than fifty dollars. Most cases of gonorrhea can be cured with less than five dollars' worth of sulfa drugs or penicillin, but both should be administered by a competent physician.

**Amount of venereal disease in the United States.** It is difficult to estimate the extent of venereal disease because of the secrecy surrounding it. There is no other field of disease where the statistics vary or conflict so widely. In 1934, the United States Public Health Service made a conscientious effort to ascertain the extent of syphilis and gonorrhea. So far as could be estimated from all available sources, 1,037,000 new cases of gonorrhea and 518,000 new cases of syphilis were reported in 1934. Many new cases were probably not brought to the attention of physicians. In the same year, there were 131,000 new cases of tuberculosis, 7,517 cases of infantile paralysis, and 220,050 cases of scarlet fever. The United States Public Health Service estimated in 1946 that there are about 400,000 new cases of syphilis each year, and about 1,200,000 new cases of gonorrhea. In 1945, there were reported 104,967 new cases of tuberculosis, 13,614 cases of infantile paralysis, 175,398 cases of scarlet fever, and 87,241 cases of pneumonia. Some 60 per cent of the new cases of venereal disease today are persons in the 15–25 year age group. Clearly the problem of the contraction and spread of venereal disease remains extensive and menacing. Estimates of the number of persons suffering from venereal disease in the United States vary, but the minimum figures would still show the problem to be a serious one.

Competent students of venereal disease estimate that about 20 million Americans are suffering from syphilis and gonorrhea. Of this number, 6 to 7 million have syphilis, and the remainder gonorrhea. The American Social Hygiene Association estimates that about 5 per cent of the population is infected with syphilis and from 10 to 15 per cent with gonorrhea. In 1947, Dr. Walter Clarke estimated that about 13,000,000 Americans were suffering from venereal diseases.

On the other hand, the Committee on the Costs of Medical Care estimated two decades ago that only about one case of venereal disease is under care per 100 of the population. Whether the number suffering from venereal disease is 1, 10, or 15 per cent of the population, the situation is appalling, because even a mere handful of cases are unnecessary from a medical point of view. Moreover, and amazingly enough, venereal disease increased rapidly in the United States after 1940, at the very time when methods of prophylaxis and treatment were being perfected.

Venereal diseases appear to be more prevalent, per capita, in rural areas and small cities than in larger urban communities. For example, while the venereal disease rate in New York City rose by some 29 per cent in 1946 over 1945, the rise was 50 per cent in the rest of the state. This is to be explained by the greater difficulty in getting treatment in rural districts, fear of public knowledge, and ignorance of methods of protection (prophylaxis) against contracting the diseases.

**Economic cost of venereal disease.** The economic cost of venereal disease is impressive. It has been estimated that 150 million dollars in wages are lost each year by men and women suffering from these diseases. If to this and the cost of medical care is added the expense of supporting those blinded, crippled, or made insane by venereal disease, the amount is staggering; an estimate of half a billion dollars annually would be moderate. Dr. Donald Pillsbury of the Veterans Administration has estimated that the ultimate cost of caring for the syphilitic veterans of the second world war alone will run to a billion dollars. At the end of the war there were over 400,000 syphilitic soldiers. The situation is the more pathetic and lamentable, because there is, medically speaking, almost no excuse for it.

**Late appearance of syphilis in Western society.** Although there are several types of venereal disease, syphilis and gonorrhea are the most important. Gonorrhea is a far older disease than syphilis, so far as we can judge from records. It was known more than 5,000 years ago in China, and is frequently mentioned in the Old Testament. It was well known to physicians of the ancient world, and was at times a scourge of the Middle Ages. Syphilis may be as ancient as gonorrhea, but we have no historical proof of its origins. At the close of the fifteenth century syphilis reached almost epidemic proportions in western Europe, and attracted the attention of many writers who believed that the disease had been brought from the New World to the Old by sailors who accompanied Columbus. Columbus himself is said by some to have died from syphilis.

It is quite possible that syphilis did originate in America, since prior to the fifteenth century no Greek, Christian, or Moslem physician had mentioned it, while after 1500 it was frequently described. Regardless of where the disease originated, the first great epidemic of syphilis in western Europe seems to have been spread by the soldiers who dispersed widely following the siege of Naples by King Charles VIII of France in 1494. The disease spread among royalty as well as soldiers,

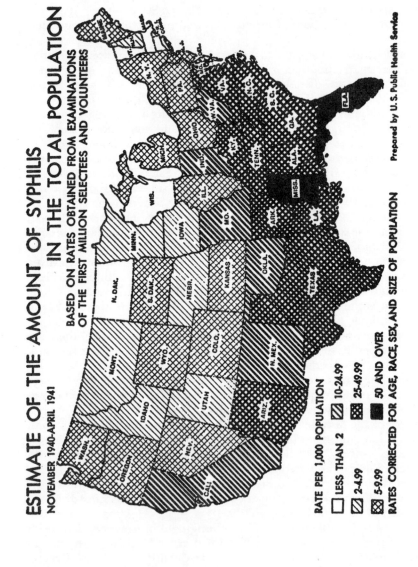

ESTIMATE OF THE AMOUNT OF SYPHILIS
IN THE TOTAL POPULATION

NOVEMBER 1940-APRIL 1941

BASED ON RATES OBTAINED FROM EXAMINATIONS
OF THE FIRST MILLION SELECTEES AND VOLUNTEERS

RATE PER 1,000 POPULATION

LESS THAN 2    10-24.99
2-4.99         25-49.99
5-9.99         50 AND OVER

RATES CORRECTED FOR AGE, RACE, SEX, AND SIZE OF POPULATION

Prepared by U. S. Public Health Service

workers, and the peasantry. Monarchs like Henry VIII of England, Charles VIII and Francis I of France, and Ivan the Terrible of Russia, are known to have contracted syphilis. Syphilis was carried from Europe to Asia, and was brought back from Europe to America by white settlers. An epidemic of syphilis is recorded as having occurred in Boston in 1646.

**Nature and pathology of syphilis.** Before the microscope was discovered and improved, there were many, such as Dr. John Hunter, a leading eighteenth-century English physician, who believed gonorrhea to be a mild form of syphilis, with both diseases coming from the same germ. It was not until 1812 that a French physician, Jean Hernandez, proved that gonorrhea and syphilis are distinct. All doubt that they are distinct was removed when Dr. Albert Neisser isolated the germ of gonorrhea (the *gonococcus*) in 1879. In 1905, the syphilis germ, *spirochete pallida*, was isolated by Fritz Schaudinn, a German pathologist. Two years later, August von Wassermann devised a blood test whereby it is fairly easy to determine whether or not a person is suffering from syphilis. In the past thirty years, the tests for syphilis have been extended and simplified by such men as Drs. Kolmer, Kahn, Klein, and others.

Although gonorrhea is rarely contracted except by sexual intercourse, syphilis germs can enter the blood stream through a break in the skin anywhere on the body. Formerly, it was believed that syphilis was contracted only through sexual intercourse, but today we know that it may also be spread by kissing or by using drinking cups, towels, or silverware that have been used by a syphilitic. Fortunately, the germ of syphilis quickly perishes when exposed to dry surfaces, and heat and light. Medical experts incline to the belief that, whatever the theoretical possibility of other sources of infection, most syphilitic infections are contracted and spread through sexual relations.

After the spirochete of syphilis enters the body, a syphilitic sore or chancre forms at the point of infection within 12 to 40 days. This is the primary stage. Since the chancre is not acutely painful and disappears within a month or two, treatment is often neglected. In the secondary stage there is physical discomfort, such as rashes, headaches, indigestion, and fever. Again, the secondary symptoms also disappear in a few months; and, if allowed to go untreated, the disease enters the third stage, which may not be apparent until years after the original infection. This final stage has numerous symptoms, such as the caving in of the nose or the roof of the mouth, serious heart disorders, paralysis of the limbs, and syphilis of the brain (paresis). Until recently, when fever treatment was introduced, paresis always meant a fairly speedy death.

**Revolutionary success in treatment of syphilis.** As earlier stated, medicine has, apparently, completely conquered the syphilis germ. In the first quarter of the sixteenth century, physicians, more or less by accident, discovered that calomel or mercury is useful in combating syphilis, if the patient is strong enough to stand the violent effects of the mercury. Improvements were made in administering mercury and, together with iodide of potassium (introduced in 1834 by Dr. William Wallace of Dublin), this chemical formed the basis of the medical battle against syphilis until 1910. In that year, Dr. Paul Ehrlich of Germany produced the arsenic preparation known as salvarsan or "606" (the number of experiments required to produce the proper chemical combination). At first, "606" was hailed as a miraculous cure, but it was soon found that, unless treatment was continued over a long period, relapses would occur. In 1922, a Paris doctor, Constantin Levaditi, discovered that a bismuth preparation was a valuable aid in fighting syphilis. Bismuth injections could be given without serious after-effects to persons whose systems could not stand repeated doses of mercury or salvarsan.

After the first world war, the attack on syphilis was revolutionized by the introduction of a new type of treatment, known as the fever treatment. An Austrian doctor, Julius Wagner von Jauregg, discovered that syphilitic patients were greatly improved after they had contracted malarial fever. It was first believed that the malaria germ killed the spirochete of syphilis, but it was soon discovered that any type of high fever killed or retarded the syphilis germ. An electric fever-producing machine, perfected by two doctors in Dayton, Ohio (Drs. Fred K. Kislig and Walter M. Simpson), has now been substituted for malarial fever and has proved especially useful in the treatment of brain syphilis, where it is impossible to use chemicals effectively.

More recently, a revolutionary treatment for syphilis was announced—the so-called "drip treatment." By this method, a weak solution of salvarsan is allowed to drip steadily into the patient's system for several days. This permits a persistent attack on the germs without too much toxic effect on the patient. It is said that many cases of primary syphilis are cured in from 5 to 7 days by this treatment. Another method of rapid cure was found in combining the standard arsenical drugs and bismuth with the fever treatment. Of late, penicillin has been used more widely than any other drug to check and cure syphilis. Permanent cure of primary syphilis with penicillin appears to be accomplished in about nine days of hospital treatment. Despite the increase in the number of new cases until 1947, the more effective remedies have notably reduced the number of deaths from syphilis—from 15 per 100,000 of the population in 1939 to 10.7 in 1945. Early in 1949, the United States Public Health Service announced that the annual deaths from syphilis had dropped from 21,000 in 1938 to 13,000 in 1948. It was also announced that the number of new civilian cases had, at long last, begun to decline, from 480,140 in 1947 to 338,141 in 1948.

Syphilis can thus be quickly and permanently cured, if treatment is begun in the primary stage. If it is delayed until the secondary stage, the disease can usually be cured, although the cure will take longer.

And even in the third stage, a combination of chemicals, antibiotics and the fever treatment may work wonders in arresting the disease, if the germ has not yet damaged the brain or nerve tissues too severely.

What may prove the most effective of all medical attacks on syphilis was announced late in 1949 by Dr. Lee J. Alexander of Dallas, Texas, who for three years had been testing the efficacy of injections of penicillin and bismuth during the incubation period following known exposure to syphilitic infection.  By the time the primary chancre of syphilis has appeared the disease has become firmly implanted in the system.  Dr. Alexander based his procedure on that followed in giving serum to those bitten by rabid dogs immediately after possible infection. It was shown that treatment by penicillin and bismuth as soon as possible after exposure was almost completely effective in preventing the development of syphilis, while in a comparable "control group" not treated after exposure, some two-thirds developed primary syphilis. If this promising new technique is to be effective, patients must be educated to the necessity of presenting themselves for prophylactic treatment as soon as possible after infection.

**Nature of gonorrhea.**  Gonorrhea is much less complicated than syphilis, especially in males.  Within 4 to 12 days after the infection, the first or acute stage appears, bringing much local discomfort.  The acute stage seldom lasts long, disappearing within a week to a month, and often those persons suffering from the disease believe they are cured when the acute stage ends.  Unless treated promptly and effectively, however, the disease may become chronic and cause serious disorders.  Gonorrhea frequently results in sterility of both males and females.  The disease often brings about chronic ailments, such as gonorrheal arthritis, long regarded as an innocent form of rheumatism, prostatic troubles, and the like.  Some of the serious pelvic disorders of females are frequently a result of a gonorrheal infection that has not been treated effectively.  Until recently, at least 30 per cent of all blindness was due to infection of children at birth by mothers suffering from gonorrhea.  This type of blindness has been greatly reduced by the routine use of a weak silver nitrate solution in the eyes of newborn babies.

**Gonorrhea now quickly cured by sulfa drugs and antibiotics.**  Until recently, the treatment of gonorrhea was mainly limited to lessening pain in the acute stages and keeping the patient quiet, so that his natural resistance might aid in fighting off the disease.  Unless treatment was started early, there was little hope of a speedy and complete cure.

After 1936, a new drug, sulfanilamide, revolutionized the methods of treatment.  Sulfanilamide, taken through the mouth in pill form, cures many cases of gonorrhea in from 4 to 10 days.  Those cases which cannot be cured by pills alone are cured by the use of pills and the fever treatment.  Sulfanilamide apparently does not kill the gonorrhea germs but paralyzes them, preventing their rapid increase and giving time for the white corpuscles of the blood to destroy them. The drug is inexpensive and the average case of gonorrhea can be cured at a very small cost. Sulfanilamide should be given under medical supervision, for in some cases it produces serious after-effects; but, administered by a skilled physician, the drug seems to be relatively safe and very effective for most cases.

The newer sulfa drugs, such as sulfadiazine, sulfathiazole, and sulfapyridine, have also been used effectively in the treatment of gonorrhea. Their action on the gonococcus is far more decisive and they seem to cause fewer bad after-effects. Since penicillin has become readily available, it has pretty generally superseded the sulfa drugs in treating gonorrhea, mainly because there are no toxic results or serious after-effects. Permanent cure can be achieved by three large injections given at intervals of four hours. A new penicillin preparation, known as duracillin, will cure most cases with only one injection. It is possible that the technique of Dr. Alexander in preventing the development of syphilis by giving penicillin injections during the incubation period may also prove effective in preventing the development of gonorrhea after exposure.

**Venereal disease increases despite medical victories.** Despite the effectiveness of the new remedies for venereal disease and the provision of cheap and almost certain methods of prophylaxis, the rate of venereal disease rose alarmingly after the onset of the second world war. First cases of civilian gonorrhea (no second exposures were reported in these statistics) increased from 191,000 per annum in 1941 to 367,000 in 1946. One reason for this increase is that a great number of cases apparently go without good medical treatment. Though the United States Public Health Service estimates that there are 1,200,000 new cases of gonorrhea each year, private physicians and public clinics report only some 315,000, leaving some 885,000 cases unaccounted for. Many of them are doubtless uncured and spread infection. Further, the publicity given to easy cures has made persons more careless about prophylaxis and more ready to rely on self-medication.

**Rational program for eliminating venereal disease.** There is no reason why syphilis and gonorrhea cannot be completely wiped out if prompt and efficient treatment, at public cost if necessary, is made easily available. Full information should be given about the very effective means now known for preventing venereal infection. Prostitution, which is responsible for the spread of much venereal disease, should be controlled by public authorities, and frequent and rigorous medical inspection should be made of all prostitutes.

The only way in which we can conquer venereal disease is by thorough educational methods that will make the public conscious of the seriousness of the problem and of the effective ways of preventing and curing such disorders. Where such steps have been taken, as in Sweden, venereal disease has all but disappeared. During the second world war, the Army and Navy used extensive educational and publicity campaigns to instruct the servicemen about venereal diseases, and after their demobilization, these men carried this information back to civilian life. Concentrated campaigns for the detection and cure of venereal disease have been instituted in a number of American cities, but most campaigns against venereal disease in the United States have been weakened through mixing up antique moralistic conceptions with sound medical principles. This weakness characterized even the campaign waged by Dr. Parran. At any rate, the rise of the venereal disease rate after 1941 emphasizes the need for a rational and determined program of public education and medical treatment.

## PUBLIC AGENCIES WORKING TO CONTROL VENEREAL DISEASES

From Prostitution and the War, by Philip S. Broughton, published by the Public Affairs Committee, Inc., 30 Rockefeller Plaza, New York City. Chart by Pictograph Corporation.

Chart indicating co-operative activities and agencies essential to an effective campaign against venereal disease.

**Morals versus medical science.** The venereal disease problem is unique; there is no other type of major malady in which medicine has so complete a mastery of the methods of preventing and curing the disorder, yet there is still an appalling amount of venereal disease. The number of victims grew steadily during the very period when the revolutionary new medical methods of prevention and therapy have been applied. Smallpox, diphtheria, typhoid fever, whooping cough, and other once prevalent epidemic or contagious diseases have been virtually wiped out, although medical science has not as efficient means of preventing and curing these diseases as it does for handling venereal disease. This amazing state of affairs can only be explained as being a result of the frustration of medical insight and therapy by the interjection of religious and moral biases and controls into what should be a purely medical situation.

## The Problem of Narcotic Drug Addiction

**Origin of narcotics.** The use of narcotic drugs as a means of achieving an escape from unpleasant reality into a dream world of narcotic euphoria is apparently as old as the practice of using drugs in the treatment of disease. Among the writings of the Sumerians, who lived over five thousand years ago in the Tigris-Euphrates Valley of ancient Mesopotamia, we find reference to the "sleep poppy" and the "joy plant." The original home of the opium poppy may have been in Mesopotamia. Babylonian and Assyrian literature frequently mention the poppy, and the Egyptians and Persians were also acquainted with the use of opium. By classical times, narcotic drugs derived from opium had become very common and were used both in medical practice and for personal indulgence. The Moslems of the Middle Ages are believed to have carried knowledge of the opium poppy to India and China, for the first mention we have of the poppy in Chinese literature is in the year 973 A.D. Apparently, however, the poppy was not widely cultivated as a narcotic in China until about 1700. Until that time, much of the opium used by the Chinese was imported from India. In 1800, the importation of opium was forbidden by the Chinese government, but the British, who reaped great profits from the opium trade between India and China, fought the notorious "Opium War" in 1840–1842 to undermine the Chinese embargo, which was not enforced until 1838. The English and the Dutch made large profits out of importing opium from India into western Europe.

**Main narcotic drugs.** A number of narcotic drugs have been compounded from opium. Among the most important are laudanum, which first appeared in the early sixteenth century, and morphine, which was first produced early in the nineteenth century. The use of morphine was fostered by the discovery of the hypodermic needle in the middle of the nineteenth century. At first, it was believed that the use of the hypodermic needle to inject morphine under the skin would eliminate the habit-forming quality of the drug, but it was soon found that needle injections only served to supply drug addicts with a more effective means of taking their "dope."

Some of the present-day narcotics have been developed as the result of efforts to find a drug that would be non-habit-forming and furnish a controllable substitute for morphine. Heroin, one of the most popular modern narcotic drugs, was hailed on its discovery, in 1898, as a non-habit-forming substitute for morphine. Unfortunately, this claim proved to be far from correct; heroin is about as habit-forming as morphine.

**Cocaine and its effects.** Cocaine, although commonly supposed to be a form of opiate, is actually derived from the coca shrub grown in Peru and Bolivia. It was used by the Indians of these countries for centuries but did not become commercialized until after the middle of the nineteenth century, when it was widely used by physicians and dentists as a local anaesthetic. Cocaine is a habit-forming drug; therefore novocaine has been substituted as an anaesthetic. It is of vital importance to note that the effects of cocaine are quite different from those of opium. Opium produces a calm, peaceful flight from reality, while the use of cocaine stimulates and excites the user. Hence, it is not, properly speaking, a sedative narcotic drug. The treatment of opium and cocaine addicts differs considerably.

**Origin and extent of drug addiction in the United States.** Drug addiction in the United States did not become common until the time of the Civil War, when it became so widespread and well known that drug addiction was often referred to as "the army disease." Between 1865 and 1914, drug addiction grew steadily, although it probably did not grow as rapidly as the population.

Estimates vary concerning the number of drug addicts in our generation. Investigators estimated that, in 1919, there were 200,000 drug addicts in New York City alone. In 1918, a special committee of the U.S. Treasury Department estimated that there were about 1,500,000 addicts in the United States as a whole. We have no way of learning the exact number. There are probably at least 100,000 chronic addicts; and, if we take into consideration the mild and occasional addicts, there may be over 500,000, perhaps several million. There are surely more at present than there were in 1914, when the Harrison Narcotic Act, outlawing the sale of narcotics, was passed; but they are harder to locate and count, since the purchase and taking of narcotic drugs has been made illegal, except for very restricted medical use.

There are many chronic users of narcotic drugs who are not true addicts. The true drug addict is of a definitely psychoneurotic type, and the addiction is a form of mental disease. The occasional users of drugs, thus, cannot accurately be called addicts, nor can some chronic users who "watch their step." Most of the serious cases of drug addiction are the result of mental and nervous disorders that have grown out of mental conflicts. As Dr. J. D. Reichard has written: "The more abnormal the individual, the more desirous he is of escape from his own painful realm of reality and the more he tends to use any or all narcotic substances to excess." The use of a narcotic drug produces a sense of well-being (euphoria), which temporarily permits the sufferer to forget his mental conflicts and fears. Depriving a true addict of the drug thus does not cure him. It merely forces his psychoneurotic symptoms to take on other and usually more serious and dangerous manifestations. He cannot be cured unless a psychiatrist can determine the cause of his mental conflicts and release the sufferer from his mental torment.

**How and why people become drug addicts.** Some persons acquire the drug habit from medical treatment; opiates are often given, for example, to relieve pain or sleeplessness. In the days before narcotics became difficult to obtain, some persons acquired the drug habit as a result of doctoring themselves with patent medicines containing narcotic drugs. Today, the drug laws restrict the sale of patent medicines containing opiates, but there are still some medicines of that kind on the market.

The normal person, even if he uses powerful narcotic drugs occasionally, will probably not become addicted to them. As pointed out above, true drug addiction is the result of deep-seated mental conflicts, from which the individual seeks an escape. Most chronic narcotic addicts are psychoneurotics. Many degenerates, prostitutes, and petty criminals also resort to the use of drugs to give them a sense of well being and courage or to make them forget the sordid or dangerous conditions under which they live. Some drug addiction results from the desire of addicts to convert others to the habit. Many distinguished medical authorities claim that more drug addiction is caused by the laws that have been passed to suppress it than by any other single factor. The addicts wish to secure companions in vice and misery, and thus they work to spread the habit through the underworld, in prison, and among innocent persons. Moreover, the fact that drug addiction is banned by law makes it difficult to seek treatment or advice from reputable physicians.

**Effect of narcotic drug addiction on physical health.** Contrary to the popular belief, narcotic drug addiction seldom leads to serious physical disability or to death. Studies have been made of prison populations, and of the New York City prison on Welfare Island, in particular. Many of the 1,166 drug addicts studied by Joseph F. Fishman at Welfare Island had been chronic users of drugs for years. Even those who had taken narcotics for twenty-five years or more were in relatively good physical condition. It does not seem, then, that the use of narcotics, such as opiates and heroin, causes physical disability. Any physical damage grows out of the slovenly ways of living often associated with the drug habit. With cocaine addicts, the situation is much different. Cocaine is much more likely to impair the physica' constitution, and those seriously addicted to cocaine usually die within a few years or are forced to give up the drug. Fortunately, it is easier to break the cocaine than the opiate habit.

**Behavior patterns of addicts.** Addicts to narcotic drugs seldom commit serious crimes, though cocaine addicts occasionally do. While there are many petty offenders among them, narcotic drug addicts are almost never found among organized criminals, racketeers, and gamblers. These professional criminals refuse to have anything to do with a drug addict because he may easily be persuaded to confess his participation in a crime after arrest if sharply deprived of his supply of "dope." Almost any drug addict will tell all he knows to the police in order to get another supply. Besides, an addict does not have the steady nerves required of a modern gunman. Dr. Michael J. Pescor investigated 1,000 consecutive admissions to the Federal Narcotic Hospital at Lexington, Kentucky, and found no record of delinquency in 75 per cent of these cases. Much of the delinquency in connection with the other 25 per cent was due, directly or indirectly, to efforts to get drugs.

The average addict is thus inclined to be peaceful and law-abiding when supplied with drugs. He usually commits crime only in the effort to get drugs. Even cocaine addicts, who are likely to be more active and aggressive when stimulated by the drug, are not often guilty of serious offenses. The chief evils of the drug habit are found in the fact that the addict may be a complete or partial economic loss to himself and his family. In the case of narcotic drug addiction (which excludes cocaine addiction) the usual behavior pattern is an increase of lethargy and shiftlessness, often going so far as indifference to personal hygiene.

**Treatment of drug addicts.** There is no scientific cure for true drug addiction except long and expensive psychiatric treatment to remove the underlying mental conflict. Unfortunately, treatment of this sort is rare, except among wealthy addicts. The most common type of treatment is to deprive the patients of their narcotic drugs. One harsh type consists in suddenly taking the drug away from the patient —the "cold turkey" treatment. Frequently, some less habit-forming drug is substituted until the addict learns to adjust himself to living without any drug. Mathadon, or dolphine, produced by the Germans during the second world war, is the most widely used of such drugs at the present time. While habit-forming, it can be withdrawn from addicts with less suffering than morphine.

These types of treatment are not real cures for any except cases of mild or pseudo-addiction. Sometimes, withdrawing the drug actually serves the purpose of the addict. If he has taken opiates over a long period of time, he needs an ever larger dose to get the needed effect, because his system has gradually become accustomed to the drug and does not respond to a small amount. If the drug is withdrawn for a period of time, a small dose will once again give the desired effect. Many addicts deliberately take a withdrawal treatment in order to be able to resume the use of drugs with less expense to themselves. With chronic addicts, sudden withdrawals of the opiate sometimes leads to serious physical consequences. There have been instances in which death has resulted from a sudden deprivation. In fact, in many cases withdrawal has a more serious effect on the physical and mental health of the addict than prolonged use of the drug.

There should be specialized institutions or hospital wards for drug addicts only. In 1928, the Federal government created two Federal narcotic hospital farms, one at Lexington, Kentucky, and the other at Fort Worth, Texas. Most of those convicted for using drugs have to be reached through state laws, and the states have been backward in providing specialized institutions for treating addicts. Of course, if we dealt with addicts in a sensible fashion, we would treat them as patients rather than convicts. As in the case of alcoholic addiction, there must be adequate and inexpensive clinical psychiatric and social work facilities, if we hope to make many lasting cures among the mass of chronic drug addicts. Recently, there has been an attempt to organize a voluntary movement among addicts for self-cure called "Addicts Anonymous," modeled after "Alcoholics Anonymous," which we shall describe shortly.

**The Harrison Act as misguided as the Volstead Act?** The basis of Federal procedure to suppress the drug trade as illegal and criminal is the Harrison Narcotic Act, which was first passed on December 17, 1914, and amended in 1918, 1922, 1924, 1927, and 1928. It was also strengthened by a Supreme Court decision of 1919. The Harrison Act, originally more of a revenue than a police measure, was designed to prosecute manufacturers and large-scale smugglers of narcotics, leaving the prosecution of street vendors and addicts to the states. The Harrison Act provided that all persons who dispose of narcotic drugs must register with the Bureau of Internal Revenue and all narcotic goods sold must bear a revenue stamp. Druggists have to keep records of all narcotic drugs sold, together with the name of the purchaser. Physicians, dentists, and veterinarians were allowed, in connection with the duties of their professions, to dispense narcotic drugs. This latter provision leaves a large margin of freedom in interpreting the needs of patients, and, occasionally, physicians have been guilty of dispensing drugs to addicts. A Narcotic Division was created in the Bureau of Internal Revenue to enforce the Harrison Act. Numerous amendments to the original act have extended the scope of Federal control over narcotics, and a special effort has been made to shut off the source of supply by restricting the importation of opiates and cocaine.

Many states have passed drastic laws limiting the possession and use of narcotics. Some have even made the possession of small quantities of the drugs a crime. Other states have failed to pass stringent legislation. In such states, the dope ring may not only sell its products but also concentrate its activities relating to the underground shipment and distribution of drugs into states with restrictive legislation. Gigantic dope rings have been able to operate successfully because there has been only enough legislation to drive the traffic under cover but not enough to wipe it out. It is estimated that the total revenue from the dope racket in some years has amounted to a billion dollars.

Students of the narcotic problem claim that the anti-narcotic laws send to prison many persons who are not real criminals. In prison, the drug addicts come into association with real criminals and may become criminals themselves. While in prison, they may convert nonaddicts to the use of the drug. There is a large expense involved in caring for addicts who are committed to prisons. Many addicts deprived of narcotics become serious mental and nervous cases, expensive and dangerous to society. Again, anti-narcotic legislation has encouraged the formation of dope rings and rackets and has put the dispensing of drugs partly in the hands of the racketeers instead of physicians and druggists.

It seems safe to conclude that, so far, the Harrison Narcotic Act and restrictive state laws have increased rather than lessened the problem of drug addiction. Some of the foremost authorities on narcotics believe that the Harrison Act has been as wrongheaded and disastrous in its way as the Eighteenth Amendment and the Volstead Act were as a means of suppressing the use of alcoholic liquor. Whatever the unwisdom of such drastic control of opiates as that set up by the Harrison Act and its amendments, there is little doubt that the importation and use of cocaine should be rigorously restrained. But restrictive drug legislation has now gone to ludicrous extremes, even to requiring a physician's prescription to procure such innocent sedatives as luminol and seconal. This is partly the result of the work of extremists and meddlers, and partly a combined medical and drugstore "racket." The physicians get an office fee for virtually no work, and druggists can sell such drugs on a prescription at many times their cost in unrestricted sale. If the present trend continues, it may not be long before a physician's prescription will be required to obtain such a drug as aspirin. We have made nothing like the same progress in treating the drug addiction problem from a medical and sociological point of view as we have in the general area of mental hygiene and psychiatry, or even in approaching chronic alcoholism. Drug addiction remains enmeshed in the same moralistic fog that has hampered progress in dealing with venereal disease.

**Dangerous effects of marijuana.** A far more serious form of drug addiction than the taking of opiates or cocaine is the smoking of marijuana, the American substitute for the Asiatic hashish. Marijuana is dangerous because it may destroy all sense of self-control and restraint. It dulls the moral sense: girl addicts may be headed toward prostitution and boy addicts toward gangs and rackets. A large number of loathsome and degenerate crimes have been committed by young people of both sexes while under the influence of marijuana. For a number of years, we had little legislative protection from the use of marijuana, but many laws outlawing its use have recently been enacted. It is a field to which public attention should be turned because the largest consumption of this drug is by young people.

**Smuggling narcotic drugs.** Some international efforts have been made to shut off the sources of the narcotic drug supply. In 1912, a treaty providing for the gradual suppression of traffic in drugs was signed at The Hague by several nations. After the first world war, the supervision of the suppression of the drug trade was turned over to the League of Nations.

Most of our opium comes from China, and is smuggled in by way of Mexico, Central America, and the ports along the Gulf of Mexico. One reason why it is difficult for Federal authorities to control the opium traffic is that profitable shipments can be made in packages small enough to be carried by airplanes. And the inducement to smuggle is great, since the value of the amount which can be carried in a single valise may run into hundreds of thousands of dollars.

**Health and hygiene aspects of the tobacco habit.** Since nicotine is a mild form of narcotic, there has been much discussion of the physical and mental effects of smoking tobacco. Many writers claim that smoking raises the blood pressure, causes serious heart trouble, has a bad effect on digestion, increases infant mortality, and is one of the main causes of tuberculosis.

These charges have been investigated by eminent medical experts, many of them non-smokers. They find that there seems to be little difference between the blood pressure of those who smoke and those who do not. There seems to be no proof that moderate smoking produces heart ailments, that it seriously affects digestion, or that the children of smoking mothers die as a result of prenatal nicotine poisoning. Some specialists have recently demonstrated that nicotine contracts the blood vessels of the heart, and have advised heavy smokers to drink moderately, since alcohol dilates the blood vessels. Scientists have shown that smoking has no effect on babies nursed by mothers who smoke. If infants of such mothers die more frequently than others, bad habits often associated with cigarette smoking are responsible, rather than the nicotine itself. Psychiatrists believe that persons often smoke to excess because they are nervous and physically run down. Thus, heavy smoking seems to be the result rather than the cause of nervous or physical disorders. From all available evidence there seems to be no proof that smoking causes tuberculosis. The greatest increase in smoking has occurred within the past twenty-five years, but during this same period tuberculosis has decreased.

**Economic wastes in tobacco habit.** The tobacco habit is, however, expensive. The tobacco bill of the nation runs to about 3 billion dollars annually, a large expenditure for a product that cannot be classed as a necessity of life. We spend about as much for tobacco as we do for all public education. In addition to the amount spent for tobacco itself, smokers spend a great deal of money each year for accessories, like pipes, smoking stands, cigarette holders, and ash trays. Clothes, cushions, and car seats are often burned, a. d sometimes even houses are burned down as a result of the careless habits of smokers While the bad physical effects of moderate smoking are trivial, much of the money spent on smoking, even though it does furnish work and income for thousands engaged in raising tobacco and in making tobacco products, might possibly be used to better advantage.

## Chronic Alcoholism as a Social Problem

**The heavy drinker and the addict.** To treat the problem of alcoholism intelligently, a distinction must be drawn between a person who drinks for sociability, whether occasionally or heavily, and the unfortunate individual who is a true alcoholic addict. A person who drinks intoxicating beverages in large amounts is often called an addict, but true alcoholic addiction is one of the manifestations of more deep-seated mental or nervous disorders; it is as much a psychoneurosis as drug addiction. Heavy social drinking, on the other hand, is more directly related to group customs. Many persons who generalize loosely on the evil effects of alcohol inaccurately assume that all who drink become addicts.

**Some facts about alcoholism and alcoholic consumption.** Prohibition propaganda has exaggerated the amount of serious alcoholism in the United States. Professors Haggard and Jellinek, in their book *Alcohol Explored,* estimated that there were in 1942 only about 600,000 chronic alcoholics in the United States, and about 1,800,000 who use alcoholic liquor to excess. Around 50 million drink in moderation with few evil effects, whereas some 40 million Americans do not drink alcoholic liquor at all. Thus, not over 6 per cent of those adults who use alcoholic liquor do so to excess, while 94 per cent use it in moderation or not at all. There has been a great increase in the amount of liquor consumed in the last hundred years; but this increase is largely in the consumption of beer and wine, rather than of "hard" liquor. In 1850, the per capita consumption of liquor was 7.33 gallons and, in 1945, 29.05 gallons. Yet, the actual per capita consumption of "absolute alcohol" was 2.07 gallons in 1850 and 2.09 in 1945. Likewise, though there was an increase of 35.8 per cent in the number of drinkers from 1940 to 1945, there was an increase of only 4.5 per cent in the total per capita consumption of absolute alcohol. But the expense of indulgence in alcoholic liquor is great, indeed, especially since the skyrocketing of prices and liquor taxes. The liquor bill of the country in 1947 was $9,640,000,000, or nearly three times what was spent on public education.

**Chronic heavy drinking a menace to society.** Although the true alcoholic addict is a pathological type, and is not directly the product of overindulgence in alcohol, no sensible person can approve of chronic heavy drinking. Liquor takes vast sums of money that might be spent on more worth-while things. Consumed in large quantities, liquor impairs health and vitality and clouds the mental processes. Drunken motorists endanger their own lives and those of others. Family difficulties are increased, and broken homes often result from heavy drinking. Alcohol sometimes leads to the commission of serious crimes and is often an indirect factor in juvenile delinquency. It has been estimated that the economic cost of chronic alcoholism today in the United States is close to a billion dollars a year.

**Moderate drinking has few serious effects.**   Although numerous evils are thus associated with excessive consumption of liquor, moderate drinking is a widespread social custom.   For every heavy drinker, there are about twenty-five who drink in moderation as a means of relaxation in leisure hours and suffer no bad physical or mental effects.   A survey of several thousand Baltimore workers and autopsy records of 7,500 cases on file in the Johns Hopkins University Hospital show that life expectancy is not shortened by moderate drinking.   Heavy drinkers, however, have a shorter life expectancy than either the moderate drinkers or those who are total abstainers.

**Two types of alcoholic addicts.**   There are two types of alcoholic addicts.   The first is commonly known as a pseudo-addict or a "misery drinker"; the other is the true or psychoneurotic alcoholic addict. Found most frequently among the lower classes, the misery drinker tries to forget his bad living conditions, poor wages, fear of losing his job, or other troubles, by clouding his mind with alcohol.   Intoxication, to the misery drinker, makes possible a temporary, but pleasant and exciting, flight from the harsh realities of his existence.   Eliminating this form of alcoholic indulgence will be possible only when the social and economic system provides greater opportunity for the lower classes to have a better standard of living and some sense of economic security.

The real alcoholic addict usually suffers, like the true drug addict, either from mental defect or from severe conflicts, which produce nervous or mental disorders.   Out of a hundred excessive drinkers, it has been estimated that there may be 40 chronic alcoholics (real addicts), of whom 30 will be psychoneurotic, 5 psychotic, and 5 suffering from mental defect.   The other 60 will be mainly misery drinkers and convivial drinkers who indulge to excess.   Often, the mental conflict that afflicts the chronic alcoholic lies deep in the unconscious mind and is a result of conditions in early childhood—frequently resentment against one or both parents—which have been forgotten but affect the personality of the individual and make it difficult for him to adjust to normal adult life.   The conflict may be intensified by especially unhappy, unsuccessful, uncertain, or complicated aspects of life for the alcoholic at any given time.

Cutting off the supply of liquor will not cure a true addict.   Prolonged psychiatric treatment, usually psychoanalysis, offers the best prospect for permanent cure, but unless both patient and physician are persistent, a cure will be unlikely.   Thus, the nature of alcoholic addiction makes it apparent that no mass treatment is likely to be very successful.   Specialized institutions or wards for segregating addicts are inadequate substitutes for individual treatment, but, in some measure, they protect society from the occasionally dangerous actions of the true alcoholic addict.

**Methods of treating alcoholic addiction.**   While, as we have pointed out above, prolonged, personal psychiatric treatment is the surest cure for chronic alcoholic addiction, such treatment is available, for the most part, only to the well-to-do addict. Other more direct, briefer, and less expensive treatments have been tried. The oldest of these, "aversion therapy," attempts to build up a conditioned-reflex that will produce an aversion to alcoholic liquor. Along with his drink the patient is given a drug that will cause violent nausea. When this is repeated many times, the patient may find drinking repulsive. One defect of this treatment is that it is likely to have to be repeated at frequent intervals, but improvement has been claimed for from 50 to 75 per cent of the cases treated. At times, complete cure seems to have been effected, but in such cases we may doubt whether the patient was a true addict.

An interesting recent development has been the work of a society known as "Alcoholics Anonymous," which came into being in 1934 and now has over 25,000 members. They are almost exclusively chronic alcoholics. A strong moral and religious atmosphere dominates their activities and association. They frankly and fully discuss their problems together, and seek mutual understanding, insight, and tolerance. Through this voluntary discussion and group therapy they seek to achieve personal catharsis and an elimination of the drink habit. The claim is made that around 75 per cent are cured or notably helped.

Perhaps even more promising is the Yale Clinic Plan. This is a public clinic where treatment costs from $60 to $100 a patient. It is conducted by psychiatrists, social workers, and nurses. As much psychiatric advice and social case-work investigation as possible are provided, though not as much can be done in such a clinic as through private psychiatric practice. Improvement has been noted in over 50 per cent of all cases treated, and in 90 per cent of all cases in which the patient co-operated faithfully. This method would appear to have more promise than any other that can be made available to the majority of addicts. These clinics could be made nationally accessible to addicts for far less than the two and a half billion dollars paid annually in government liquor taxes. At present, only about $500,000 dollars is available annually from all funds to study and treat chronic alcoholism, compared with over 150 million dollars to help cure tuberculosis and a far larger sum to deal with polio.

**Education and temperance the solution of the problem of alcoholism.** Any sensible solution of the alcohol problem in its broader economic and social aspects must revolve around the campaign for reasonable temperance. Sane education with respect to the nature and consequences of alcoholic consumption will do more to bring about a reasonable attitude toward the problem than endless and violent ranting against the "evils of drink." Education will do more than laws to discourage exhibitions of vulgarity and bad taste in connection with drinking.

Our experience with Prohibition, from 1919 to 1933, showed that it is useless to attempt to solve the alcohol problem by forbidding the manufacture and sale of liquor. There seems little doubt that Prohibition both increased the prevalence of heavy drinking and made it more respectable. It became the "smart" thing to drink great quantities of more or less vile liquor and to flaunt defiance of the law. Prohibition distracted attention from drinking as a pleasant social pastime and made it a matter of principle to secure "bootleg" liquor and "swill" it, regardless of disastrous and often fatal effects. Selling "bootleg" liquor became a big business, provided the basis for racketeering and organized crime, both in the liquor field and beyond, and led to extensive political and legal corruption. There seems to be no doubt that it would have been wiser and cheaper to have instituted a sane educational program in behalf of temperance and civilized drinking.

More progress has been made in introducing a scientific and medical approach to the alcohol problem in the last ten years than in all previous history. In this field, we are now about where we were in the general mental hygiene movement around 1915.

## Suicide as a Social Problem

**Prevalence of suicide in the United States.** For some people drugs and alcohol provide a temporary flight from a bitter and unendurable reality; others, for whom a temporary escape from existence is not enough, commit suicide.

Suicides are often given a prominent place in the headlines, but we seldom analyze the causes of, and possible remedies for, suicide. We hear much of our high homicide rate, but our suicide rate is usually far greater. About 10,000 persons meet their death annually through homicides, but the annual number of reported suicides is usually about double that figure. Moreover, there is no way of knowing how many deaths reported as accidental are actually suicides—possibly as many as the reported suicides—or how many persons try to commit suicide but do not succeed. Known suicides account for more violent deaths than any other single cause except automobile accidents. If we include unreported suicides and deaths listed as accidental but really suicides, we might find that our suicide rate is not far below our death rate from automobile accidents, which now reaches between 30,000 and 40,000 yearly.

**Social attitudes toward suicide.** Social attitudes toward suicide have varied greatly. In the Orient, there are ceremonial forms of suicide, which carry great honor with them, such as the Japanese hara-kiri. In Christian and Moslem lands, however, there has always been much hostility to suicide. Although suicide was not specifically forbidden by the Old and New Testaments, the Christians denounced suicide as a sin, and the church has held suicide to be almost on a par with murder. Those committing suicide have been treated with contempt and indignity in Christian lands and in some cases they have been refused decent burial.

**Who commits suicide?**   Certain significant facts may be noted in the relation between suicide and race, age groups, sex, economic status, and religion.   Negroes are much less prone to commit suicides than whites; in 1930, their suicide rate was one-third that of the white race. More than half of all suicides take place after the age of forty-five. Male suicides exceed females by more than three to one, except in the case of young females (15–20 years of age) where the sex ratio is about equal.   Suicide is more common in cities than in rural areas, owing probably to the more stable and conventional habits of living in rural communities, to the deeper influence of rural religion, and to the lonely, unstable, and complex conditions of urban life.   Among economic classes, it appears that suicide is most common either among the wealthy or those near or just below the poverty line.   Catholics commit suicide less frequently than Protestants, Jews, and freethinkers.

**The causes of suicide.**   It is difficult to determine the true causes of suicide.   Although many persons who commit suicide leave notes of explanation, these explanations usually fail to give the true reasons. The real causes of suicide are complex, the result of many social and psychological factors.   Expert studies of this phase of the subject indicate that between 25 and 35 per cent of persons who commit suicide are mentally or nervously deranged.   A few suicides are the result of sudden compulsive acts under inciting conditions, like looking out of a high open window or off a high cliff.

Suicide usually occurs, however, when unusual and harsh events strike a person already overburdened with mental conflicts and suffering from mental distress.   Persons of normal mental and emotional make-up are able to bear heavy shocks, disappointments, and economic blows, but individuals whose life patterns are already distorted cannot adjust so readily to additional troubles.   Hence, they take what seems the only way out.   Some psychoanalysts believe that suicide is the great regression to an infantile level, to the protection of the mother— in this case, Mother Earth.

While such distressing mental troubles as lead to suicide are in large part individual problems, their origins may lie, in part, in general social disorganization.   Social disturbances produced by the rapid change from rural to urban life, the growing instability of the family, the lack of economic security, and the like tend to destroy stabilizing social habits and customs and make adjustment to life more difficult for many individuals.   The great French sociologist Émile Durkheim held that anything tending to break down the intimate contact between an individual and his primary social groups is favorable to suicidal tendencies.   Urban life produces just such conditions. All studies of suicide indicate a close correlation between a high suicide rate and social disorganization.

One interesting fact about suicide, most thoroughly expounded by the French sociologist, Maurice Halbwachs, is that the suicide rate falls off markedly in periods of war and other great social crises, provided the latter are not also economic crises.   The explanation appears to be that the group excitement seems to absorb the attention of persons who might commit suicide in normal times and to distract them from their personal frustrations and distress.   In other words, the crisis gives them a temporary socio-psychic lift.

**How to reduce the suicide rate.**   Any effective attack on the suicide problem must begin with its causes.   Mental hygiene, economic reconstruction, and community organization appear to be among the possibly effective general approaches.   Mental hygiene, working through psychiatry, may relieve the mental conflicts that place a person in a position to want to commit suicide under any conditions, and help discover the subconscious compulsion to suicidal acts.   Then, external reality and the social environment must be made more endurable.   Greater economic security must be brought about through economic reforms that will provide either more stable employment or public support through relief and social insurance.   Community organization must supply new social contacts, group interests, and social agencies to replace those which are being destroyed by the transition from a rural to an urban area.

**Outlook for checking suicide.**   The outlook for checking suicide is not good.   The progress of mental hygiene is the only favorable element in the picture.   Economic disorganization and insecurity appear to be increasing as humanity moves along in an era of unprecedentedly rapid and extensive social change.   It is increasingly difficult to find work after middle age, and community organization and social reconstruction may be slowed down as the funds and energies of the public are turned toward the making of munitions for a third world war.

The effect of the second world war in the United States, in the way of providing full employment at very high wages, both during and after the war, served to lessen the suicide rate somewhat—from 14.3 (per 100,000) in 1940 to less than 12 in 1947.   Following the general rule mentioned earlier, the suicide rate during the war was very low—10.2 in 1943, 10 in 1944, and 11.2 in 1945.   In especially devastated countries like Germany, however, in which millions were reduced to starvation, the suicide rate reached epidemic proportions after 1944.   If we enter a third world war, the resulting physical and personal devastation will be far greater.   Suicide promises to be a major social problem of the future.

## Summary

The chief venereal diseases, syphilis and gonorrhea, have been completely conquered scientifically by medicine, but the prudish attitude of society has hindered their prevention and cure.   Today, venereal disease could be almost completely eradicated if the public were educated to its dangers and to the need of getting proper and efficient treatment in an early stage. Until the venereal disorders are considered diseases, not disgraces, syphilis and gonorrhea will remain prevalent. They must be handled on the basis of sound medical principles, unmixed with prudish scruples.

Drug and alcoholic addiction are forms of flight from reality. The true addict is not one who takes drugs occasionally or drinks moderately, but an individual who resorts to drugs and liquor to secure relief from deep-seated mental stress. Complete and permanent cures for true drug and alcoholic addiction are rare. Psychiatric treatment to get at the underlying mental causes, probably the only means of assuring a complete cure, is expensive and requires long individual treatment. As a result, the prospect of successful mass treatment of addicts by psychiatric methods is limited.

Most laws restricting liquor and drugs have served only to complicate the problem. Our experience in the Prohibition era showed not only that the evils of drinking were increased by drastic legal prohibition, but that new and more serious social problems arose. The Harrison Narcotic Act, likewise, has intensified and complicated the problem of drug addiction and has created new social problems, such as underground traffic in dope, the formation of huge smuggling rings, and the consigning of many addicts to prisons instead of hospitals.

There has been much public excitement over automobile accidents and homicides, but few persons realize that suicides are, perhaps, almost as numerous as deaths from automobile accidents. The breakdown of the primary groups of rural society and the growing predominance of urban life seem to have stimulated suicide. Suicide is the supreme flight from reality. As with drug and liquor addiction, unless one knows the underlying mental conflicts that make existence intolerable for the individual, there is no effective way of coping with the suicide problem. Mental hygiene, economic and social reconstruction, and community organization appear to be means by which the life pattern of individuals can be more successfully adjusted to changing social and economic conditions. In the present crisis of rapid urbanization, economic disintegration, wars, and rumors of wars, there seems to be little hope that the suicide rate can be notably reduced.

### Selected References

*Barnes, H. E., *Prohibition versus Civilization*, Viking, 1932. A brief attack on all aspects of Prohibition and an argument for temperance and civilized drinking.

Binkley, R. C., *Responsible Drinking*, Vanguard, 1930. A sane and telling argument for temperance versus prohibition.

* Cavan, R. S., *Suicide*, University of Chicago Press, 1928. The best treatment of suicide in English; a clear and sensible book.

Dublin, L. I., and Bunzel, Bessie, *To Be or Not to Be,* Smith and Haas, 1933. Important for extensive statistical data on suicide.

Haggard, H. W., and Jellinek, E. M., *Alcohol Explored,* Doubleday, Doran, 1942. Pioneer treatise on the use and effects of alcohol.

* Hirsch, Joseph, *The Problem Drinker,* Duell, Sioan and Pearce, 1949. Excellent and reliable analysis of the problem drinker and chronic alcoholic.

Jellinek, E. M., *Alcohol and Chronic Alcoholism,* Yale University Press, 1942. Survey of the extent and nature of chronic alcoholism by the leading American authority on the subject.

——————, *Recent Trends in Alcoholism and Alcohol Consumption,* Hillhouse Press, 1947. Authoritative information on drinking and the consumption of alcohol.

Lindesmith, A. R., *Opiate Addiction,* Principia Press, 1947. A recent treatment of drug addiction and its causes.

Mangold, G. B., *Social Pathology,* Macmillan, 1932. A standard sociological treatise.

Menninger, K. A., *Man Against Himself,* Harcourt, Brace, 1938. An invaluable book dealing with chronic alcoholism and other types of personal psychopathology and maladjustment.

Mowrer, E. R., *Disorganization: Personal and Social,* Lippincott, 1942. Competent study of personal disorganization in modern urban life. Describes the social basis of personality disintegration.

Parran, Thomas, *Shadow on the Land,* Reynal and Hitchcock, 1937.

——————, and Vonderlehr, R. A., *Plain Words About Venereal Disease,* Reynal and Hitchcock, 1942. Two earnest books about the ravages of venereal disease. The second deals also with venereal disease as a military problem. Both books are weakened somewhat by intruding moralistic attitudes into a strictly medical issue.

Queen, S. A., and Gruener, J. R., *Social Pathology,* Crowell, 1940. A leading textbook in this field.

* Robinson, W. J., *The Oldest Profession in the World,* Eugenics Publishing Company, 1929. Probably the best brief introduction to the nature of the prostitute and prostitution. A sane little book, debunking most of the common illusions about the prostitute.

Seabrook, William, *Asylum,* Harcourt, Brace, 1935. A revealing account of the chronic alcoholic and his efforts to get effective treatment.

* Warren, Carl, *On Your Guard,* Emerson Books, 1937. A good introductory book on venereal disease. Sane in attitude, but a trifle alarmist and exaggerates the extent of venereal disease.

Williams, H. S., *Drugs against Men,* McBride, 1933.

* ——————, *Drug Addicts Are Human Beings,* Shaw, 1938. An introduction to the problem of drug addiction by a famous doctor, wisely advocating a medical rather than a police approach to the drug problem.

Index

# Index

## A

915

DATE